Brazil

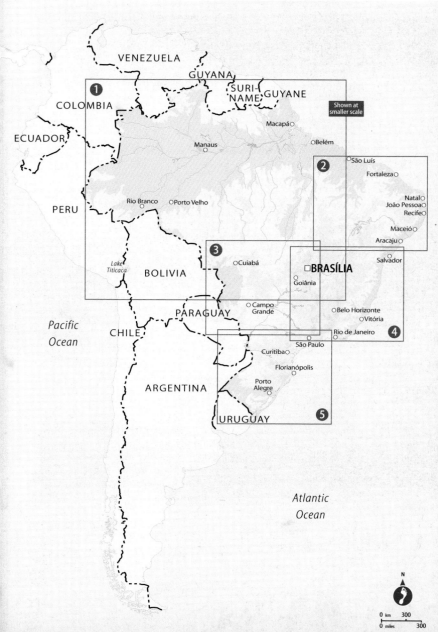

Altitude in metres	
1000	
500	
200	
0	
Neighbouring Country	

	Primary Routes
	Main Roads
	Minor Roads
BR285	Route Number
◆	National Park
	International Border
	State Border

See back of book for colour maps 1-5

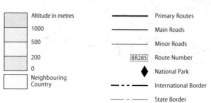

Shown at smaller scale

VENEZUELA

GUYANA

SURI-NAME GUYANE

COLOMBIA

ECUADOR

PERU

Manaus

Macapá

Belém

São Luís

Fortaleza

Natal
João Pessoa
Recife

Maceió

Aracaju

Rio Branco   Porto Velho

Lake Titicaca

BOLIVIA

Cuiabá

BRASÍLIA

Goiânia

Salvador

PARAGUAY

Campo Grande

Belo Horizonte
Vitória

Rio de Janeiro

Pacific Ocean

CHILE

ARGENTINA

Curitiba   São Paulo

Florianópolis

Porto Alegre

URUGUAY

Atlantic Ocean

N

0 km   300
0 miles   300

Brazil Handbook
Second edition
© Footprint Handbooks Ltd 2000

Published by Footprint Handbooks
6 Riverside Court
Lower Bristol Road
Bath BA2 3DZ. England
T +44 (0)1225 469141
F +44 (0)1225 469461
Email discover@footprintbooks.com
Web www.footprintbooks.com

ISBN 1 900949 50 4
ISSN 1363-7401
CIP DATA: A catalogue record for this
book is available from the British Library

Distributed in the USA by
Publishers Group West

Neither the black and white nor coloured
maps are intended to have any political
significance.

Credits

Series editors
Patrick Dawson
Rachel Fielding

Editorial
Editor: Jo Williams
Maps: Sarah Sorensen

Production
Pre-press Manager: Jo Morgan
Typesetting: Richard Ponsford and
Emma Bryers
Maps: Kevin Feeney, Robert Lunn
and Claire Benison
Proof reading: Tim Heybyrne and
Howard David

Design
Mytton Williams

Photography & drawings
Front cover: South American Pictures
Back cover: Tony Stone Images
Inside colour section: Michael Mirecki,
Impact Photos; Trip Photographic
Library; South American Pictures;
Eye Ubiquitous; Robert Harding Picture
Library; Pictor International

Print
Manufactured in Italy by LEGOPRINT

Every effort has been made to ensure
that the facts in this Handbook are
accurate. However, travellers should still
obtain advice from consulates, airlines
etc about current travel and visa
requirements before travelling. The
authors and publishers cannot accept
responsibility for any loss, injury or
inconvenience however caused.

Footprint Brazil Handbook

The travel guide

Ben Box and Mick Day

*Oh, the pleasure of being anonymous, - a tourist
for a few hours, for a few days,
eyes wide open for everything and every joy,
finding new enchantment in every street, at every
turn, in every face that passes and moves on,
in every strange and vibrant word, whose
unknown meaning we can barely guess*

J G Araujo Jorge, *Poema ao turista e à Kodak*

Contents

Left: brightly painted houses in the colonial city of Ouro Preto, Minas Gerais.

Right: a walk beside Rio de Janeiro's famous Copacabana beach towards the Sugar Loaf peak is a popular evening activity.

A foot in the door

Highlights

Brazil, the fifth largest country in the world, dominates the sub-continent of South America geographically. While colonization by the Portuguese left it separated by language from its neighbours, Brazil also has great differences within itself, in its landscapes, people and culture, which allows even Brazilians to become tourists in their own country.

A modern capital Located in the country's empty centre is Brasília, the radically designed city built to become the new federal capital in 1960. The city is rich in sculptures and impressive architecture such as the cathedral, which is in the shape of the crown of thorns.

The marvellous city Brazil's tourist capital, however, is Rio de Janeiro, beautifully situated between the mountains and the sea. It is home to the Cariocas, whose lives revolve around the beach, as well as probably the world's most famous carnival. The views over the city from Pão de Açúcar and the Christ on Corvocado peak are not to be missed.

Racial mix The Northeast was the heart of the slave trade and this African legacy is still apparent today in the region's music, dance, cuisine, religion and festivals. In the North some of the land's original inhabitants such as the Yanomami Indians still manage to cling precariously to their way of life in demarcated reserves. The South, however, has a distinct European and Oriental flavour because of the large numbers of immigrants who arrived during the nineteenth century.

Economic powerhouse With mineral riches and a strong industrial base Brazil is also a giant among the developing economies, although it has one of the most uneven distributions of this wealth. In the modern city of São Paulo, faced with the volume of traffic and office workers with their mobile phones, you might think you were in a tropical New York. This is where Brazilians and foreign investors come to work although there are also plenty of leisure and cultural options.

Colonial heritage Some of the world's finest examples of colonial architecture are to be found in Brazil with several sites such as the Jesuit Missions in Rio Grande do Sul being part of Unesco's world heritage list. The sense of the past is easily conjured up amongst these monuments to past glories and riches.

Coastal ports As the Portuguese attempted to assert control over their colony in the face of rival claims, they began to build fortifications along the northeastern coast. This resulted in churches and towns being built on the highest points, such as Salvador on the cliff overlooking its harbour and bay. The Dutch and the French also left their mark in Olinda, Recife and São Luis. There are many other fine examples all along this coastline.

Mining towns At the beginning of the 18th century prospectors began to push inland, searching for precious metals and gemstones. Some of the wealth that flowed to the Portuguese Crown remained in the form of imposing churches lavishly decorated in Ouro Preto, Tiradentes, and Diamantina in Minas Gerais, as well as Pirenópolis in Goiás. Ports such as Paraty, through which these riches were shipped, also benefited from this trade.

Baroque sculpture The genius of one man defines the Golden Age of Brazilian sculpture. Aleijadinho, although later crippled by a wasting disease, continued to work until his death leaving behind some of the most detailed and animated statues yet seen. His finest piece is the Twelve Prophets in the Basilica at Congonhas do Campo, but there are many other superb examples throughout the region.

Left: the lights of Avenida Paulista at dusk illuminate the skyline of São Paulo, the largest city in South America. **Below**: the riches of its gold mining past are reflected in the colonial architecture and lavishly decorated churches of Ouro Preto in Minas.

Above: at the bottom of Largo do Pelourinho, in Salvador is the Igreja do Rosário dos Pretos, built by slaves brought from Africa. *Left*: angels hang from the stained glass ceiling of the modern cathedral in Brasília. **Overleaf**: rainbows form in the spray of the Iguaçu Falls, near the triple border between Argentina, Brazil and Paraguay.

Right: a beach hat vendor passes Cariocas, sunbathing on Copacabana beach. *Below*: fanatical supporters of Flamengo cheer on their team at the Maracanã Stadium in Rio de Janeiro.

Above: the drummers of the afro blocos regularly practice in the Pelourinho district of Salvador. *Right*: the energy of a samba school during the Rio carnival must be maintained for the 1 ½ hours it takes to parade the entire length of the Sambódromo.

Pursuit of leisure

To Brazilians work, while obviously necessary, is very much secondary to leisure, whether it be watching a football match, chatting with friends over an ice-cold beer in the neighbourhood bar, or in an improvised samba session that can occur anytime and anywhere.

Carnival

Brazilians know how to hold a party and the biggest party of them all is Carnival, which is held in either February or March. In fact the year doesn't really begin until after this outbreak of hedonism in which the populace can indulge their fantasies and forget the reality of their daily lives.

Origins of carnival

Although the pre-lenten festivities have a long history, the present-day carnival tradition was brought to Brazil in the 18th century by settlers from the Azores. Mock battles were fought in the streets with revellers throwing water, ashes and even perfume over each other. Masked balls became popular in the 19th century but it wasn't until the 1920s that the colourful parades with imaginative costumes and floats became established.

Samba schools

Community groups from the poorest neighbourhoods of Rio de Janeiro began to compete against each other for the honour of becoming carnival champion. The parades grew in sophistication and creativity, finally being moved from the main avenues to a purpose-built stadium. Every year the peoples' hard work and the designer's riotous imagination are displayed to the cheers of the crowd for one night only.

Street carnival

Carnival in the streets still exists with *Blocos* accompanied by bands playing popular music from the top of trucks. In Bahia and Pernambuco processions of *Afoxes* and *Maracatus* have maintained traditions brought from Africa. Costumed *Bandas* often formed by transvestites can be found everywhere and represent defiance of authority and the overthrow of society's rules during the carnival period.

Music & dance

These permeate the rhythm of daily life throughout the country. Although Bossa Nova became famous abroad in 1960s, the country really is a musical treasure chest with widely different styles mainly unknown to foreign ears. The sensual Lambada is still danced in Porto Seguro whilst Forró accompanies the São João festivities of the northeast.

Beach culture

Brazilians have a strong affinity with water and the beach, which could be a river bank in the deep interior or one of the many city beaches of Rio de Janeiro, packed with families, lovers and sports players at weekends. All levels of society become briefly equal in this most democratic of forums, which serves as park, gymnasium and dancehall, among many other things.

Sporting nation

Brazil has produced some outstanding sporting figures in disciplines as diverse as motorsport and volleyball, often from some of its most disadvantaged citizens. One of the heroes of the team that won the World Cup several times, Pelé graduated from the football field to become minister of sport and is one of Brazil's most popular celebrities both at home and abroad.

14

Right: one of Brazil's most beautiful birds is the Scarlet Macaw. *Below*: the distinctive Victoria Regia water lilies are to be found throughout the Amazon region.

Above: the dense rainforest is divided into channels, or igarapés, by the River Amazon and its many tributaries. *Right*: indigenous tribes are still to be found practising their rituals away from the encroachment of modern civilisation. *Overleaf*: the Baianas of a Rio samba school are a kaleidoscope of colour as they twirl in unison.

Natural beauty

The rainforests of the Amazon and the wetlands of the Pantanal are home to a wide variety of plants, animals and birds. National parks in the rugged interior offer breathtaking views from mountain peaks as well as many opportunities for adventure sports. Deserted beaches and dunes on the extensive coastline can still be enjoyed in all the tranquillity of their natural state.

Rainbows & waterfalls

The Iguaçu Falls are among the biggest and most spectacular in the world. Located on the Rio Iguaçu, dividing Brazil and Argentina, walkways lead to a viewpoint looking into the Devil's Throat. The subtropical rainforest around the falls is rich in flora and fauna such as coatis, often found near the visitors' centre, and many colourful butterflies.

Pantanal wildlife

This vast wetland on Brazil's borders with Bolivia and Paraguay is one of best places to see wildlife in the world. The fishing here is exceptional especially during the dry season from May to October. This is also the nesting and breeding season and the best time to view the animals and birds such as the jabiru stork and maned wolf.

The Great River

Fed by many smaller rivers originating in the Andes, the mighty Amazon flows through northern Brazil to the Atlantic Ocean, passing many river communities - such as Santarém - on its way. At its mouth the force of the river meeting the sea causes a distinctive roar called Pororoca. River boats leave from Belém in the delta and are the main form of transport in the region.

Amazon rainforest

Sometimes described as the 'World's Lungs', this is the largest expanse of rainforest still existing and is one of the last great wildernesses. Largely unaffected by human settlement, there is much to be explored in the depths of the tree canopy and along the many tributaries of the River Amazon.

Ecotourism

The main centre for jungle tours is the river city of Manaus, once prosperous during the rubber boom. Easily accessible by air, from here a variety of wildlife can be seen on boat trips or stays in nearby jungle lodges. For the more adventurous, longer journeys to explore the region are also possible.

Biodiversity

Despite recent exploitation much of Amazônia remains unspoilt and is home to a wide variety of flora and fauna, such as the giant water lily and the jaguar. There are still many unknown species to be discovered and medicine is finding new remedies for many illnesses from research carried out in the rainforest.

Indian tribes

Some of the continent's original inhabitants continue to live by hunting and gathering in forest reserves. Although it is very difficult to get permission to visit these areas the Indian heritage is expressed in the region's cuisine, handicrafts and festivals, such as the Festa do Boi of Parintins.

Essentials

2

18

Essentials

Planning your trip

Where to go

If you are thinking of going to Brazil on holiday, or to do some serious travelling around it, you should already have realized that it is a big place. This section makes the assumption that you are aware of this and gives a survey of some of the things which may attract your attention as you are planning your trip. On this basis you can then make choices about where you would like to go and how to make the most of your time in the country. This is not meant to exclude people who are confined to one place in Brazil because of business, or for whatever other reason. The Handbook gives plenty of options for short and long excursions.

Brazil is usually divided into five regions which can be briefly summarized as: the Southeast, the industrial, mineral and agricultural heartland, but with a strong tourist tradition; the subtropical South, where European immigration has had a strong influence; the Northeast, where Portuguese Brazil began, with a beautiful coast and an arid interior; the North, islands of development in the Amazon forest, itself under threat; the Centre West, frontier lands where the Amazon meets the central plateau, also the great wildlife reserve of the Pantanal wetlands. On this region's eastern edge is Brasília, the symbol of the nation's commitment to its empty centre.

The Southeast The first port of call in this overview of Brazil is **Rio de Janeiro**. So many journeys begin and end here. In recent years the city has had a poor reputation regarding its tourist facilities, but concerted efforts are being made now to improve the situation. Being also one of Brazil's gateway cities, it is one of the logical places to start, but this does not mean that it is compulsory to begin a Brazilian vacation here.

Rio de Janeiro, the state capital and the state itself, offers a good mix of history and hedonism. The city's colonial history has largely been built over by successive regimes, but there are remnants of all the periods of Rio's time as a capital city. In the state there is an exceptionally fine example of a colonial Portuguese town, Paraty, and there are others. Later periods are represented by the Imperial cities of Petrópolis and Teresópolis and the *fazendas* and towns which date from the coffee era. The 20th century has seen some fine modernizations in Rio, but also some questionable 'improvements'.

You will probably find that anywhere you go on Brazil's Atlantic coast, reference is made to the Mata Atlântica, the coastal forest which covered the mountains of the seaboard, and especially to how little of it is left. In Rio de Janeiro a few tiny pockets remain, such as the reserve at Poço das Antas, where experts are trying to save the golden lion tamarin from extinction. Outsiders are not encouraged to visit, but there are other national parks which offer good opportunities to see natural habitats. The Serra da Bocaina contains Mata Atlântica, while the national parks of Serra dos Órgãos and Itatiaia preserve fine mountain landscapes. Within the city itself is the Tijuca Forest, one of the biggest urban forest parks anywhere.

As for having fun, Rio is one of the world's capitals of entertainment, with its famous annual carnival, its spirited and varied nightlife and the beach, with all the sports that go on there. In fact, the beach can be found the length of the Rio de Janeiro coast. Culturally, Rio is also rich, and a recent development has been the movement to integrate *favelas* (shanties) into city life, including tourism.

In the city of Rio one could easily spend a week and not get bored. At one of the beach resorts like Búzios or Angra dos Reis you can spend a weekend (or the equivalent in midweek to avoid the crowds), while Paraty deserves a couple of days. Petrópolis and Teresópolis can just about be done together in a day trip, but an overnight stop is recommended, especially if you want to explore the Serra dos Órgãos. The same would apply to the former coffee zone of the Rio Paraíba do Sul and Itatiaia.

Essentials

São Paulo From the tourism point of view, a visit to the city may just be long enough to know that you want to move on, or you can spend as long as you like trying to fathom the megalopolis. There are good museums, such as the Museu de Arte de São Paulo and the Butantã Institute. Cultural life and restaurants are very good. All the São Paulo coast is worth visiting; the resorts are quite varied so find one which suits you and your purse best. In comparison with the Linha Verde which goes from Santos to Rio de Janeiro, the southern part of the coast is less developed and has more in the way of protected environments. Inland, the usual excursions are to hill resorts or colonial towns, either for a day or a weekend. If you want to explore the far west of the state, where tourism is just beginning to open up, you will need a few more days.

Minas Gerais This state has everything except beaches. The capital, Belo Horizonte, is modern, especially the planned suburb of Pampulha, so you need not stop here for more than a couple of days. But it is a good starting point for the colonial cities which surround it and deserve some thorough exploration. If Portuguese colonial architecture, sculpture and painting is your thing, you can spend a good week in this area: Ouro Preto, Mariana, Sabará, São João del Rei, Tiradentes and Congonhas do Campo are all within a relatively short distance of each other, so touring around is not difficult. Further afield are Diamantina and Serro, which may be included on a route from Belo Horizonte to Bahia. If you decide to limit your exposure to the colonial, Ouro Preto is the one to choose for the concentration of so much fine work in a single place.

Other options in Minas include hydrothermal resorts, and it might be a nice way to relax to visit one of these, especially if *en route* between São Paulo and Belo Horizonte. Nature reserves like Caraça, Caparaó, Serra do Cipó and Ibitipoca offer good opportunities for seeing different types of hill scenery and for birdwatching. For those seeking gemstones to buy, Minas Gerais is a good place to look because so many are mined in the state. This is not to say that they cannot be bought elsewhere; the major Brazilian cities all have shops which specialize in precious stones and jewellery. One could easily spend two weeks in Minas Gerais alone and, even though the state has no beaches, it is not far to the sea in **Espírito Santo**, or Rio de Janeiro.

Southeast

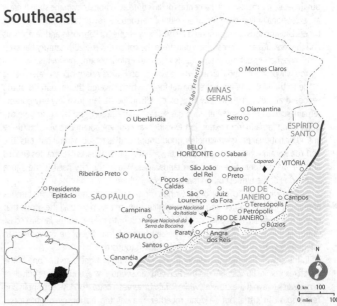

The Name

All the guide books will tell you that the name Brazil (in English) – Brasil (in Portuguese) – is derived from the tree, pau do brasil, which Europeans prized in the Middle Ages for its red dye. Since, in the early days of European awareness of the east coast of South America, pau do brasil was its only useful commodity (except perhaps the Indians who logged and transported it), the place became known as A Terra do Brasil (the Land of Brazil wood), instead of A Terra da Santa Cruz (Land of the Holy Cross). Pedro Alvares Cabral first named the land A Ilha da Vera Cruz (the Island of the Holy Cross) before the realization that this was no island.

Pau do brasil was called by the local Indians ibira-pitanga (red wood). Its scientific name is Caesalpina echinata. It grows up to 30 metres high, the trunk and boughs are covered in thorns, and it has yellow, aromatic flowers. The wood is hard, heavy and reddish-orange, turning darker as it ages. In the Middle Ages it was used in cabinet-making, musical instruments and the naval industry, but mainly as a dye. Brasilina is the colourant which dissolves in water; on extraction it oxidizes, becoming brasileína, which was used for colouring fabrics and ink. In the 19th century, artificial dyes replaced pau do brasil and its main use now is in violin bows and as an ornamental tree. Its heyday was before the introduction of sugar to Brazil. Not only the Portuguese, but also the Spanish and French, shipped large quantities of the wood out of Brazil.

The name brasil was not new in the 16th century. Brazil wood was known as a source of dye since at least the 10th century AD and the term was often applied to any tree that produced red dye. A Persian Geography of the World, dated 982, lists islands where brazil wood could be found. Marco Polo talks of the brazil crops in Sumatra. The island of Terceira in the Azores used to be called Insola de Braçil because the dyewood grew there (one of its volcanic peaks is still called Monte Brazil). Even though JH Parry calls it "a somewhat inferior red dye", its use had a long history before the Portuguese began to colonize their new territory.

Inferior or not, brazil wood lent its name to one of the more potent legends of the Middle Ages. It was believed that Brazil, or Hy-Brazil, was a perfectly circular island, divided in two by a channel, close to the west coast of Ireland. It was shrouded in fog and only appeared every seven years. Those who managed to reach its shores found it to be a pleasant, but enchanted place. Several documented reports of sightings and landings exist and the last sighting was in 1872. It remained on maps from 1325 until 1865 (by then no more than a rock). Its fame was such that mariners of the calibre of John Cabot set out to find it. To some it was the Promised Land, to others just a mirage. In the age of Geosat and global positioning, Brazil's whereabouts are known to be a long way west and south of Ireland, but when you get there, who knows ...

For more information on Hy-Brazil, and other mythical islands, see Donald S Johnson, Phantom Islands of the Atlantic. The Legends of Seven Islands that Never Were (London: Souvenir, 1997).

If confining yourself to the Southeast for a holiday, allow a minimum of two weeks, but in four weeks you will have no difficulty in finding different things to do and see. A possible route might be to start in Rio de Janeiro, go down the coast to Paraty, then to São Paulo. Head inland to Belo Horizonte via a hydrothermal resort. From Belo Horizonte explore the colonial cities of Minas Gerais. Return to Rio de Janeiro via Petrópolis and Teresópolis. At any point on this journey you will be able to visit at least one national park.

The South Making the most of this region depends a bit on the time of year that you are visiting because the winters are more pronounced than further north. In addition, Santa Catarina's beaches can become very crowded in summer as they are popular with Argentine holidaymakers. This is a part of Brazil that has been heavily influenced by European immigration. The Oktoberfest in Blumenau (Santa Catarina) is evidence of this.

Paraná The main attraction in this state is Iguaçu, the magnificent series of waterfalls in the far west. This is also a frontier with Argentina and Paraguay so, together with its worldwide fame, it has an international feel. The state capital, Curitiba, is in the east. Its railway to the sea at Paranaguá is one of the best on the continent. Paraná's coastline is short, but there are beaches to enjoy.

Santa Catarina The fact that Argentines flock to the Ilha Santa Catarina each summer suggests that the beaches here are worth a visit. Indeed they are, but if you do not like crowds, April and May are ideal months. Other resorts include Camboriú, Porto Belo and other smaller places. It is in this state that the coastal range is high enough and far enough south to receive snow in winter, around the town of São Joaquim. This is also the state where German immigration was mostly concentrated, hence the Oktoberfest referred to above.

Rio Grande do Sul Also an immigrant area, the strongest influence being Italian; this can be seen in the wine-growing area around Caxias do Sul. Having said that, there is also a Bavarian feel to the towns of the Serra Gaúcha. The state capital, Porto Alegre, is an important industrial city, but gives access to yet more coastal areas, the beaches and the Lagoa dos Patos. Rio Grande do Sul shares its southern border with Uruguay and the west with Argentina. In the far west (strange how little of interest seems to happen in the middle of these states) are the Sete Missões, all that remains of the Jesuit missions which flourished in this region in the 17th and 18th centuries. Rio Grande do Sul is the land of the Brazilian cowboy, the gaúcho, and there are many items associated with this way of life that can be bought.

South

If just going to the South alone, the chances are that you would spend a few days on the coast and you would definitely visit Iguaçu (two days minimum). In fact, it is likely that you would go to Iguaçu whatever part of Brazil you intend to visit; it is easy to fly there. Even though the South has enough for a satisfying one or two week holiday, it is probably fair to say that it is usually combined with another part of the country: Rio de Janeiro and São Paulo are within easy reach by air and not too far by road, while the North and Northeast provide greater contrast.

This part of Brazil is mainly known for colonial history, African influence and beaches. As elsewhere, though, a little delving yields rich rewards, eg in national parks, the *sertão* (see box, page 754) and culture.   **The Northeast**

Bahia This state has as its capital one of Brazil's most famous cities, Salvador. Commonly referred to as Africa in Brazil because of the ever-present black culture (notably in music, customs and food), Salvador is also one of Brazil's best known colonial centres. Huge sums of money have been lavished on its restoration. The city also has a famous carnival, which has its own unique character. Not surprisingly, Salvador and the coast of Bahia are lined with beaches so here, too, the visitor can mix culture and leisure without having to journey very far.

The coast south of Salvador leads through cocoa plantations to Porto Seguro, a very popular holiday destination, which is close to the point where the Portuguese made their first landfall in Brazil. Further south, offshore, is an accessible marine national park, Abrolhos. North of Salvador the coast road is known as the Estrada do Coco because

Northeast

the beaches fulfil the picture-postcard image of palm trees and golden sands. At Praia do Forte, however, there is serious work attached to the beach, for here is one of the sites where the marine turtle is studied, with a view to saving it from extinction.

The interior of Bahia is mostly a harsh land, where success in making a living is determined by the amount of rain that falls. Through this region runs one of Brazil's most famous rivers, the Rio São Francisco. One town that attracts a great many visitors is Lençóis, a historical monument in an area where diamonds are found. The nearby national park of the Chapada Diamantina is a great place for trekking, exploring caves and swimming in the rivers.

Sergipe and **Alagoas** are two small states which do not usually figure as major stops on itineraries. However, being in the zone which was first colonized by the Portuguese and which was intensively cultivated for sugar, they have historical associations which are worth a look if you are in the area and, needless to say, they have good beaches.

Pernambuco The capital of the state, Recife, and the neighbouring former capital, Olinda, once again provide the colonial/beach combination, but unlike Salvador, where the two are combined in one place, Recife is basically a modern city (although not without historic buildings), while colonial Olinda boasts one of the greatest concentrations of Portuguese architecture in the country. Situated 345 km off the coast is Fernando de Noronha, a small archipelago which is strictly protected, quite unspoilt and which is becoming particularly well known for its diving.

Inland from Recife is one of Brazil's best known handicraft centres, Caruaru, which has a famous market and a strong tradition in ceramics. This is one aspect that this survey has so far overlooked, not deliberately, because handicrafts can be found in every region, but because the Northeast is where more traditional arts can be found. This is partly a result of the strong African presence, which can be seen in musical instrument making, costume and wood carving, but also because the societies themselves are perhaps more traditional, not having the cosmopolitan, commercial drive of the larger cities further south.

From Pernambuco, the main attraction as you travel onto the north-facing coast of Brazil's 'bulge' is the sea: for the visitor, it means bathing and surfing, zooming up and down dunes in buggies, staying in resorts that are either sophisticated and thoroughly developed, or fishing villages for whom tourists are just becoming a source of income. The beaches of Ceará, such as Jericoacoara, are a prime example and the state capital, Fortaleza, is a good base for exploring the coast. But the sea is also a way of life and one of the typical sights here is the *jangada*, a fishing vessel that is a cross between a sailing boat and a surf board. **Rio Grande do Norte, Ceará, Piauí** and **Maranhão**, despite being maritime states, all have distinct features, including national parks such as the caves of Ubajara, the strange rock formations of Sete Cidades and the beaches, lakes and dunes of Lençóis Maranhenses. The last city before the great Amazon delta is São Luís, in whose centre the old houses are mostly covered in colonial tiles.

Salvador, like Iguaçu, is one of the 'musts' of Brazil and more than likely will be included on any itinerary. It also deserves a visit of several days (one or two for the colonial centre, one for the beach, one for an excursion – minimum). If you add in trips to Porto Seguro and Lençóis, you already have over a week in Bahia. If you are travelling extensively in the Northeast, the main decision to be made is how many stops you are going to make. This will depend largely on the time available, but remember that if you are going by road the distances involved are very large.

This section is dominated by the Amazon River and its tributaries. Although some **The North** roads have penetrated the vast forest, eg Belém to Brasília, the Transamazonian highway, Manaus to Boa Vista and the BR-364 in the far west, it is the great waterways which visitors like to experience. Besides, river traffic can be more reliable, especially in the wet season.

Pará Starting at the mouth of the Amazon, Belém is the major port, associated with much of Brazil's history. The Ilha de Marajó, opposite Belém, is a huge river island, whose links with Brazil's earliest inhabitants and present culture make it a special place. It also is home to large numbers of water buffalo. Upriver is Santarém, a good place to stop to see life on the Amazon. As an aside, **Amapá** is a bit off the beaten track, but is on the overland route to Guyane.

Amazonas The next major stop upriver is Manaus, the city most people visit in the Amazon. It can, of course, be reached by air, so could easily be included in any itinerary in Brazil (similarly Belém). Manaus, its centre shaped largely by the rubber boom in the early 20th century and its life determined by its position as the largest port on the river, is also geared up for jungle tours, but you have to go some distance and spend a couple of extra days to reach parts of the rainforest that are beyond the city's influence.

To go on from Manaus, the options are north to Boa Vista in **Roraima** and into Venezuela or Guyana, west on the river to Colombia and/or Peru, or south to Porto Velho in Rondônia. A road covers this route, but it is in such bad condition that boat or plane are the only realistic alternatives.

Rondônia and **Acre** Porto Velho and, further west, Rio Branco, are at the political frontier of Brazil and at the frontier between the jungle and the land invaders. Either city would provide an insight into the way of life of the cattle rancher, or the rubber tapper, but you would need time to get there and then to explore.

If just going to Belém or Manaus, two to three days as an excursion to either on a trip including other parts of the country would probably suffice. Add two to three days at least for a trip into the jungle. Boating up the Amazon requires a lot more time: Belém-Santarém two days; Santarém-Manaus two days (allow a day or two in Santarém to see the city and its surroundings and to make connections); Belém-Manaus five days. Remember that journey times are shorter going downstream. To continue from Manaus to the Colombia/Peru border is another eight days. Manaus to Porto Velho by boat takes four days. Manaus to Boa Vista by road takes 18 hours.

North

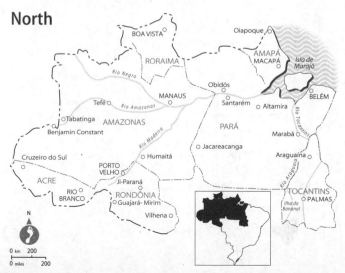

Tocantins In Tocantins is the Ilha do Bananal, which disputes with Marajó the title of largest river island in the world. At certain times of the year, Brazilian and foreign fishers come here to make the most of the fish-filled rivers. Tocantins is the country's newest state; the Brasília-Belém highway cuts through it, passing areas which previously were home to many Indian tribes whose contact with the modern world is now speeding up.

The Centre West Being right in the middle of the country, **Brasília** is a long way from anywhere by road, but not by air. The politicians fly in and out so it is well served. If you want to see this remarkable 20th century construction, it warrants a couple of days as an excursion from elsewhere.

Goiás Goiânia is another 20th-century, planned city, like Brasília, but in the vicinity are old gold mining centres and colonial towns such as Goiás Velho and Pirenópolis. There are some wonderful national parks such as Emas and Chapada dos Veadeiros, with impressive waterfalls and wildlife.

Mato Grosso and **Mato Grosso do Sul** The principal reason why most people go to the far western states is to see the wildlife in the Pantanal. The wetlands provide the opportunity to view a remarkable array of animal and birdlife at close quarters, which is making this an increasingly popular tour. You can either visit from the north (Cuiabá, in Mato Grosso) or the south (Corumbá or Campo Grande, in Mato Grosso do Sul). In the former case, you can also go to the Chapada dos Guimarães, an immense geological formation with many interesting natural sites. In the south, from Campo Grande, a worthwhile excursion is to the delightful area around Bonito, different in what it has to offer and in its approach to tourism. Corumbá is on the border with Bolivia, so trips to the Pantanal from here are usually made by those coming into, or leaving, Brazil by this route. Day trips into the Pantanal are not much good: the further you go, the more wildlife you are likely to see, so allow three to four days.

Centre West

If you compare this brief run-down of suggested trips and places to visit in Brazil with a map, it does not take more than a swift glance to realize that there are large areas of the country that have not figured. This does not mean that the gaps are uninteresting. What it does mean, though, is that the areas not mentioned have different characteristics in different regions. In the Southeast and South you don't have to go far to find cities, towns and villages. They may well be industrial or agricultural (or a combination of the two), with little of what is normally considered 'tourist interest'. But there will be a hospitable welcome and the chances are that there will be scope for one or more of the Brazilian forms of entertainment.

The further north you go, the emptier the gaps become, but there is no pattern to this. There is the barren *sertão* in the Northeast, which is not without its fascination, but don't expect any luxury. The other big hole, perhaps the biggest of the lot, is the Amazon basin. Where the jungle remains it is still largely unexplored, containing all the potential benefits for mankind if it is given the chance to survive. The cleared areas – for mining, resettlement of urban overpopulation, or agriculture – are pioneer lands, hard to get to know. But there are also parts which are under the protection of the national parks service and there are reserves for indigenous peoples.

Whether you venture into the heart of the forest, or stay outside in other parts of Brazil, it is hard to avoid its presence as a significant geographical, sociological and anthropological entity. You may find that the opinions you bring with you from abroad will differ greatly from Brazilian opinions, but you probably will find that the concern for the future of the rainforest has spread to many other pockets of Brazilian flora and fauna. The recognition that so many types of habitat in the country need defending goes hand-in-hand with a shift in perception. The forest was seen as a mysterious and distant world, but modern concerns, expressed in the relationship to it of household names like the Body Shop or Ben and Jerry's, have personalized it. And as the rainforest is now a part of our schools' curriculum, so its impact makes the Mata Atlântica, the dunes, the *cerrado*, the wetlands as much a part of our consciousness of Brazil as the colonial churches, the samba and the concrete jungles of the large cities.

If you have the time, it is worth going off the beaten track, but be aware of what you may be heading into. Do not assume that the countryside of Santa Catarina will require the same equipment, preparation or attitudes as the backlands of Bahia or the forests of Amazonas. Brazil, as this Handbook will never tire of pointing out, is full of differences and the further you get from the main centres, the more marked those differences become. Exploring those differences is one of the delights for the traveller.

When to go

The best time for a visit is from April to June, and August to October, inclusive. Business visitors should avoid from mid-December to the end of February, when it is hot and people are on holiday. In these months hotels, beaches and means of transport tend to be crowded. July is a school holiday month. If visiting tourist centres like Salvador, Rio and the colonial cities in Minas Gerais in the low season, be aware that some tourist sights may be closed for restoration.

Climate Conditions during the winter (May to September) are like those of a North European summer in Rio de Janeiro (including periods of rain and overcast skies), temperatures vary at this season from 14°C to the high 20s. It is more like a North European autumn in São Paulo and the southern states. It can get very cold in the far south. In São Paulo, which is in the Highlands, light-weight clothing is only required in the summer; the climate can be treacherous, however, with large temperature changes in a brief space of time. It can get surprisingly cold south and west of Rio, and on high ground anywhere in Brazil, at night; warm clothes are needed. The season of heavy rains is from November to March in Rio and São Paulo, January to April in the north, and from

April to August around Recife. In the Amazon the heaviest rain falls between December and May and the least in October. Rain can be expected, however, throughout the whole year and humidity is high.

Summer conditions all over the country are tropical, but temperatures of 40°C are comparatively rare. On the coast there is a high degree of humidity. The luminosity is also very high; sunglasses are advisable.

Festivals The most famous festival in Brazil is Carnival, particularly that of Rio de Janeiro although there are other cities that have traditions just as interesting. Carnival dates vary between February and early March. New Year's Eve is another popular party with beaches all over the country becoming packed with revellers. June is a busy month with São João festivities, especially in the Northeast, as well as the bull festival of Bumba-meu-Boi held in the North and Maranhão. Brazilians need little excuse to hold a party and there are plenty of other options throughout the year.

What to take

A good principle is to take half the clothes, and twice the money, that you think you will need

Everybody has his/her own list. Those most often mentioned include **air cushions** for slatted seats, inflatable **travel pillow** for neck support, **strong shoes**, a small **first-aid kit** and handbook, fully **waterproof top clothing**, **waterproof treatment** for leather footwear, **wax earplugs** (which are almost impossible to find outside large cities) and an airline-type **eye mask** to help you sleep in noisy and poorly curtained hotel rooms, **sandals** (rubber-thong Japanese-type or other – can be worn in showers to avoid athlete's foot), a **polyethylene sheet** 2 x 1m to cover possibly infested beds and shelter your luggage, **polyethylene bags** of varying sizes (up to heavy duty rubbish bag size) with ties, a **toilet bag** you can tie round your waist (if you use an **electric shaver**, take a rechargeable type), a **sheet sleeping bag** and pillowcase or separate pillowcase (a 1½-2m piece of 100% cotton can be used as a towel, a bedsheet, beach towel, makeshift curtain and wrap), a **mosquito net** (or a hammock with a fitted net), a **straw hat** which can be rolled or flattened and reconstituted after 15 minutes soaking in water, a **clothes line**, a **nailbrush** (useful for scrubbing dirt off clothes as well as off oneself), a **vacuum flask**, a **water bottle**, a **small dual-voltage immersion heater**, a small dual-voltage (or battery-driven) **electric fan**, a light nylon waterproof **shopping bag**, a universal bath- and basin-**plug** of the flanged type that will fit any waste-pipe (or improvise one from a sheet of thick rubber), **string**, **velcro**, **electrical insulating tape**, large **penknife** preferably with tin and bottle openers, scissors and corkscrew – the famous Swiss Army range has been repeatedly recommended (for knife sharpening, go to a butcher's shop), **alarm clock** or watch, **candle**, **torch** (flashlight) – especially one that will clip on to a pocket or belt, **pocket mirror**, **pocket calculator**, an **adaptor and flex** to enable you to take power from an electric light socket (the Edison screw type is the most commonly used), a **padlock** (combination lock is best) for the doors of the cheapest and most casual hotels, spare **chain-lengths** and padlock for securing luggage to bed or bus/train seat. Remember not to throw away spent batteries containing mercury or cadmium; take them home to be disposed of, or recycled properly.

Useful medicaments are given in **Health** (see page 76); to these might be added some lip salve with sun protection, and pre-moistened wipes (such as 'Wet Ones'). Always carry **toilet paper**. Natural fabric sticking plasters, as well as being long lasting, are much appreciated as gifts. Dental floss can be used for backpack repairs, in addition to its original purpose.

NB contact lens: major cities have a wide selection of products for the care of lenses, so you don't need to take kilos of lotions. Ask for products in a chemist/pharmacy, rather than an optician's.

Tours and tour operators

See page 68 for an explanation of phone codes in Brazil

Cox & Kings Travel St James Court, 45 Buckingham Gate, London, T020-78735001. **Encounter Overland** 267 Old Brompton Rd, London, SW5 9JA, T020-73706845. **Explore Worldwide** 1 Frederick St, Aldershot, Hants, GU11 1LQ, T01252-344161, F343170. **Field Guides** 9433 Bee Cave Rd, Building 1, Suite 150, Austin, Texas 78733, T1-800-7284953, F1-512-2630117, fgileader@aol.com, www.fieldguides.com. Specialists in birdwatching with regular tours to Brazil. **Focus Tours** 103 Moya Road, Santa Fe, NM87505, USA, T505-4664688, F505-4664689, FocusTours@aol.com, www.focustours.com. Specialists in birdwatching and environmentally responsible travel. **Hayes & Jarvis** 152 King St, London, W6 0QU, T020-82227844. **Journey Latin America** 12 & 13 Heathfield Terrace, Chiswick, London, W4 4JE, T020-87478315, F87421312, sales@journeylatinamerica.co.uk and Suites 28-30 Barton Arcade (2nd floor), Deansgate, Manchester, M3 2BH, T0161-8321441, F8321551, man@journeylatinamerica.co.uk, www.journeylatinamerica.co.uk. Long established company running escorted tours throughout the region. They also offer a wide range of flight options. **Ladatco Tours** 2220 Coral Way, Miami, Florida 33145, USA, T800-3276162, F2850504, tailor@ladatco.com, www.ladatco.com. **Last Frontiers** Fleet Marston Farm, Aylesbury, Buckinghamshire, HP18 0PZ, T01296-658650, F658651; info@lastfrontiers.co.uk; www.lastfrontiers.co.uk. **Passage to South America** Fovant Mews, 12 Noyna Rd, London, SW17 7PH, T020-87678989. **South American Experience** 47 Causton St, Pimlico, London, SW1P 4AT, T020-79765511, F79766908; sax@mcmail.com; www.sax.mcmail.com. **STA Travel** Priory House, 6 Wrights Lane, London, W8 6TA, T020-73616161, F73616262; www.statravel.co.uk. **Tatur Turismo**, Av Tancredo Neves 274, Centro Empresarial Iguatemi, Sala 228, Bloco B, Salvador, 41820-020, Bahia, Brazil, T0XX71-4507216, F4507215, tatur@svn.com.br. **Trailfinders** 194 Kensington High St, London, W8 7RG, T020-79383939.

Special interest travel

To some extent there is a mingling of ecotourism and adventure tourism in Brazil. This is partly because the adventurous activities nearly always take place in unspoilt parts of the country, but also because the term 'ecotourism' is applied to almost any outdoor activity. This section will deal specifically with participation sports, but that should not rule out the awareness of keeping the impact of one's activities to a minimum. This applies as much on land as in the sea or on rivers. The three main sports are **trekking**, **mountain biking** and **horse riding**.

Adventure sports **Climbing** As Brazil has no mountain ranges of Alpine or Andean proportions, the most popular form of climbing (*escalada*) is rock-face climbing. In the heart of Rio, you can see, or join, climbers scaling the rocks at the base of Pão de Açúcar and on the Sugar Loaf itself. Not too far away, the Serra dos Órgãos provides plenty of challenges, not least

the Dedo de Deus (God's Finger – see page 168). In the state of São Paulo a good location for climbing is Pedra do Báu near São Bento do Sapucaí, and Brotas is popular for abseiling (*rappel*). Pedra Branca and the Serra do Cipó are recommended locations in Minas Gerais. Mato Grosso has the Serra do Roncador and there are other good areas in Paraná and Rio Grande do Sul.

Trekking This sport is becoming very popular, especially in Rio de Janeiro, São Paulo, Minas Gerais, Paraná and Rio Grande do Sul. There are plenty of hiking shops and agencies which handle hiking tours. Trails are frequently graded according to difficulty; this is noticeably so in areas where *trilhas ecológicas* have been laid out in forests or other sites close to busy tourist areas. Many national parks and other protected areas provide good opportunities for trekking (eg the Chapada Diamantina in Bahia) and local information can easily be found to get you on the right track.

Horse riding Some of the best trails for horse riding are the routes that used to be taken by the mule trains that transported goods between the coast and the interior. A company like *Tropa Serrana* in Belo Horizonte (T0XX31-3448986/9832356) is an excellent place to start because their tours, including overnight horse treks, explore many aspects of the Minas Gerais countryside that visitors do not normally see.

Rafting Whitewater rafting started in Brazil in 1992. There are companies offering trips in São Paulo state (eg on the Rios Juquiá, Jaguarí, do Peixe, Paraibuna), in Rio de Janeiro (also on the Paraibuna, at Três Rios in the Serra dos Órgãos), Paraná (Rio Ribeira), Santa Catarina (Rio Itajaí) and Rio Grande do Sul (Três Coroas). Serra da Canastra in Minas Gerais is also popular for the local sport of *Bóia-cross* (rafting with rubber tubes).

Canoeing Canoeing is supervised by the Confederação Brasileira de Canoagem (CBCa – Brazilian Canoeing Federation), founded in 1989. It covers all aspects of the sport, speed racing, slalom, downriver, surfing and ocean kayaking. For downriver canoeing, go to **Visconde de Mauá** (Rio de Janeiro state – see page 175 where the Rio Preto is famous for the sport); also the Rio Formoso at **Bonito** (Mato Grosso do Sul – see page 705). A recommended river for slalom is the Paranhana, **Três Coroas**, Rio Grande do Sul. For kayak surfing the best places are Rio, the Ilha de Santa Catarina and Ubatuba, while ocean kayaking is popular in Rio, Búzios and Santos (São Paulo).

Information *Confederação Brasileira de Canoagem*, R Fernando Abott 582/703, Estrela, CEP 95880-000, Rio Grande do Sul, T0XX51-7122600.

Mountain biking Brazil is well-suited to cycling, both on and off-road. On main roads it is important to obey the general advice of being on the look out for motor vehicles as cyclists are very much second-class citizens. Also note that when cycling on the coast you may encounter strong winds which will hamper your progress. There are endless roads and tracks suitable for mountain biking, and there are many clubs in major cities which organize group rides, activities and competitions. Serra da Canastra in Minas Gerais is a popular area. *Tamanduá* in São Roque de Minas offer personalized tours and equipment hire.

Parapenting and hang gliding Hang gliding and paragliding are both covered by the Associação Brasileira de Vôo Livre (ABVL – Brazilian Hanggliding Association, Rio de Janeiro, T0XX21-3220266). There are state associations affiliated with ABVL and there are a number of operators who offer tandem flights for those without experience. Launch sites (called *rampas*) are growing in number. Among the best-known are: Pedra Bonita at Gávea in **Rio**; Parque da Cidade in **Niterói**; in **São Paulo**, Pico do Urubu (Mogi das Cruzes), Serra de São Pedro, Pedra do Baú (Campos do Jordão), Pico Agudo (Santo Antônio do Pinhal), Pedra Grande (Atibaia); in **Espírito Santo**, Morro de Filette,

Essentials

Venda Nova do Imigrante; in **Minas Gerais**, Pico do Ibitiruna (Governador Valadares), Pico do Gavião (Andradas) and Serra de Santa Helena (Sete Lagoas); in **Paraná**, Morro do Picouto and Morro da Queixada at Foz do Iguaçu; **Santa Catarina**, Careca – Praia Brava (Itajaí), Pelado (Gaspar), Morro Azul, Morro da Turquia and Intermediário (all at Pomerode), Pico das Antenas (Jaraguá do Sul); in **Rio Grande do Sul**, Morro do Farrabraz (Sapiranga) and Ninho das Águias (Nova Petrópolis); in **Ceará**, Aratuba, Urucu (Meruoca) and Urucu (Queixada); Morro do Urucum, Corumbá, **Mato Grosso do Sul** (which offers views of the Pantanal); and the Vale do Paranã in **Brasília**. For more details, contact names and addresses for most of the these *rampas*, see www.iis.com.br/~afett for *Brazil Paragliding Hang-Gliding*.

Surfing This can be enjoyed in just about every coastal state. It does not require permits; all you need is a board and the right type of wave. **Surfers Associations** *Associação Brasileira de Surfe Profissional*, T0XX48-2231226; *Associação Brasileira de Bodyboard*, T0XX21-2590669.

Brazilians took up surfing in the 1930s and have been practising ever since: in this beach-obsessed country, with 8,000 km of coastline, all shore and watersports are taken seriously. A favourite locale is **Fernando de Noronha**, a cluster of idyllic islands belonging to Pernambuco state, 345 km out in the Atlantic, but the best waves are found in the south, where long stretches of the Atlantic, often facing the swell head-on, give some excellent and varied breaks. The season is November to March in the archipelago, but it is an expensive palce to surf. Many Brazilian surf spots are firmly on the international championship circuit: best known is **Saquarema**, in Rio de Janeiro state.

There are many other good surf spots in Rio de Janeiro state. Most of the coastline faces south, head-on to the powerful swell, and is freshened by an early morning north-northeast offshore wind blowing off the mountains which run parallel to the coast. It receives a consistent winter swell, although in summer it stays flat for long periods. The urban beaches have good surf, and are friendly, but beware of thieves. Don't leave your board unattended: get straight in the water.

The beautiful, mountainous coast along the BR-101 between Ubatuba and Rio de Janeiro, with its many beaches and forested coves, is well worth a visit for its scenery, its historic villages and peaceful resorts. Scattered with small islands, it is great for sailing and diving, but there is no surf except to the ocean side of Ilha Grande, which protects the mainland coast.

In the state of São Paulo, on the coast between Santos and Rio de Janeiro (Linha Verde) the best-known and the busiest beach near the city is **Pitangueiras**, complete with shopping centre and a plethora of bars and restaurants; good surfing. Professional and amateur championships are held at the spot known as Maluf, where the waves consistently break at 8 ft. São Sebastião has 21 good beaches and an adequate, but not over-developed tourist infrastructure. The many small islands offshore are very good for scuba diving; these include sailing, fishing and canoeing. **Beaches**: During high season, lively watersports events are held at **Marésias**, truly excellent surfing.

One of the best states for surfing, **Santa Catarina** has a straight coastline with several islands offshore. Heavily frequented during the summer holidays, its beaches have evidently attracted creative types for more than 8,000 years, when 'Sambaqui Man' (see page 736) is thought to have inscribed the varied, abstract patterns that have now been found in rocks at 32 sites along the coast. Surfing is prohibited at some beaches from 15 May-15 July, because of the *tainha* fish harvest. Ilha de Sta Catarina has more than 40 beaches, all different and all highly sought-after during the holiday season. The minute Carnival has ended, the smaller villages to the south of the island are deserted by holidaymaking city-dwellers, leaving the beaches relatively uncrowded and cheap accommodation available for surfers and the many young travellers from Argentina, Paraguay and Uruguay who come to spend time here.

Considered one of Brazil's finest surfing spots, **Silveira** is 3 km east of Garopaba, 96 km south of Florianópolis: follow the SC-434 for about 1 km and take a left turn. Swimming can be risky here because of the surf and sudden drops in the ocean floor; there is excellent fishing, with *tainha* in season (see above), lobsters, anchovies and a host of other varieties to be caught.

Surfing in the northeast: in Salvador: the majority of the city beaches are polluted, but south of the city there is surfing near Itaparica, Itacaré and Ilhéus. **North of Bahia**: protected by the reef which runs off the northeast shore up the coast to Recife, waves tend to be smaller and much less powerful than on the southern coasts. There are some interesting reef breaks, however, and a chain of palm-fringed, white sand beaches that beg to be visited even without your board. For other advantages of this coast, see under **Diving** below.

At **Recife** surf is weak in the urban area, but despite this it was popular at Boa Viagem until a ban was imposed owing to shark attacks. Porto de Galinhas has pretty beaches and a variety of surf spots to choose from.

Rio Grande do Norte and Ceará also have surfing beaches, but not of the quality or quantity of further south.

Diving The Atlantic coast offers many possibilities for scuba diving (*mergulho*). The best site is the archipelago of **Fernando de Noronha** (Pernambuco). Being 345 km off the northeast coast, the islands are in the open Atlantic. The underwater landscape is volcanic, with cliffs, caverns and some corals, but the marine life that shelters here is magnificent. There are sharks, a protected breeding ground for hawksbill and green turtles and, the greatest draw for divers, a bay which is the home for a pod of several hundred spinner dolphin (diving with the dolphins is not allowed). In the archipelago there are a number of dive sites including the wreck of the corvette *Ipiringa* at a depth of 53m (*Atlantis* is an operator that specializes in deepwater diving). Average visibility is 30m with an average depth of 22m. The best time of year is January-February and July-October. Also in Pernambuco, **Recife** (from where planes leave for Fernando de Noronha) is a diving centre, particularly for wrecks. The reef that protects the shore up to Recife provides sheltered swimming, natural pools and many, very rewarding diving spots. Full of marine life, with warm, clear, greenish-blue sea. Visiting sea anglers are, however, urged to respect local traditions: many species are in danger of extinction, as is the coral, which is threatened by any disturbance and all forms of pollution.

Moving south, Bahia's most popular dive sites are the marine park of **Abrolhos** and **Porto Seguro**. The best time to visit Abrolhos is July-November, when whales come from the Antarctic to breed, and January-February. Other attractions are Moray eels, Barracudas, a wide variety of corals and the wreck of the cargo ship *Rosalina* that sank in 1939. Visibility varies between 8m and 20m, with an average depth of 10m in the archipelago.

In the Southeast, **Búzios**, **Arraial do Cabo**, visibility of 8m to 15m, depths of 7m to 70m, grottoes, ridges and the greatest number of wrecks in the country, and **Cabo Frio** are sites to the north of Rio. South of the state capital, the island filled bay of **Angra dos Reis**, together with **Ilha Grande**, and **Paraty**, best from December-April with calm seas, visibility from 5m to 20m and an average depth of 15m, are all recommended sites. **Ilhabela/São Sebastião** in São Paulo state, best visited January-May, offers good opportunities for wreck diving. Visibility is up to 12m with depths from 6m to 85m. Other places in the state include **Ubatuba, Laje de Santos**, 22 km from the mainland with an anchor graveyard and rays has visibility up to 20m and depths between 18m to 40m, and **Ilha de Alcatrazes**.

At Fernando de Noronha and Recife you can dive all year, although Recife (like anywhere on the coast) may be subject to strong currents. The further south you go, the lower the water temperatures become in winter (15-20°C). Visibility can also be affected by currents and weather. Many resorts have dive shops, some of which are listed in the Handbook. Whether you are already a qualified diver or a beginner seeking tuition, get local advice on which companies provide the level of expertise and knowledge of local waters that you need.

The First US Brazilian Dive Club, 704 SE 2nd Ave No 438, Deerfield Bch, FL 33441, USA, T/F954-7255094; the club can be accessed through www.brasilia.com.br/underwater, which belongs to *UnderWater Brasilia*, which also contains information about diving in Brazil, including dive sites around Brasília – in lakes, rivers and caves. There is a diving magazine called *Mergulho*. *Océan* is a dive shop and tour operator based in Rio de Janeiro state (Rio, Angra dos Reis, Ilha Grande, Arraial do Cabo) which has a *Diving in Brasil* website, www.ocean.com.br.

Fishing Brazil has enormous potential for angling given the number and variety of its rivers, lakes and reservoirs. Add to this the scope for sea-angling along the Atlantic coast and it is not difficult to see why the sport is gaining in popularity (but see under **Diving** above). Officially, the country's fish stocks are under the control of Ibama (see **National Parks**, page 761) and a license is required for fishing in any waters. The states of Mato Grosso and Mato Grosso do Sul require people fishing in their rivers to get the states' own fishing permit, which is not the same as an Ibama license. All details on prices, duration and regulations concerning catches can be obtained from Ibama; the paperwork can be found at Ibama offices, some branches of the Banco do Brasil and some agencies which specialize in fishing. In Mato Grosso and Mato Grosso do Sul information is provided by Sema, the Special Environment Secretariat, and documents may be obtained at fishing agencies or Bamerindus in Mato Grosso do Sul.

Freshwater fishing can be practised in so many places that the best bet is to make local enquiries in the part of Brazil that you are visiting. You can then find out about the rivers, lakes and reservoirs, which fish you are likely to find and what types of angling are most suited to the conditions. Favoured rivers include tributaries of the Amazon, those in the Pantanal and the Rio Araguaia, but there are many others. Many agencies can arrange fishing trips and there are several local magazines on the subject. As an example, the best time to go fishing in the Araguaia and around the Ilha de Bananal is the dry season, May to October. In Aruanã, one of the towns which gives access to the river, the Associação dos Barqueiros de Aruanã (ABA), Praça Couto Magalhães, gives information about boat rentals and fishing tours. Lages in Santa Catarina is good for trout fishing, as is Campos do Jordão in São Paulo which also has good opportunities for salmon.

Information: two agencies that can be contacted are: *Pura Pesca Tour*, which operates tours in the Pantanal, Rio Araguaia and elsewhere, in São Paulo T0XX11-5355880/5435901, F0XX11-55616447, or Cuiabá T0XX65-6241660, F0XX65-6249966; *Eldorado Pantaneiro*, which operates tours in fishing boats with a/c apartments, bar and all equipment, T0XX11-4340283, or Corumbá T067-2316369. The fishing magazine *Aruanã* has a website with lots of information in English or Portuguese, www.wfc.com.br/aruana/index1.htm, while *Fishing World's* website, http://wfc.com.br/fishing, is in Portuguese, but is also informative. The latter is not exclusively about Brazil and also includes diving.

Other sports **Swimming** With an extensive coastline and the beach being an integral part of Brazilian culture, there are plenty of opportunities for good bathing. Do, however, observe local warnings as strong undertows and currents can make it extremely dangerous to swim in places. A number of people are drowned every year from recklessness on Rio de Janeiro's beaches. Triathlon has become a popular sport in the south and southeast of Brazil with many organized competitions.

Caving There are some wonderful cave systems in Brazil and Ibama (see **National Parks**, page 761) has a programme for the protection of the national speleological heritage. National parks such as Ubajara (see page 574) and Chapada Diamantina (page 444) and the state park of PETAR (page 244) have easy access for the casual visitor, but there are also many options for the keen potholer in the states of São Paulo, Paraná, Minas Gerais and the federal district of Brasília. The Sociedade Brasileira de Espeleologia, R Minas Gerais 221, Caixa Postal 56, Monte Sião, CEP 37580-000 Minas Gerais, T/F035-4652041, is the sport's controlling body and can provide information.

Cave diving Cave diving can be practised in many of the 200 underwater grottoes such as Bonito, Mato Grosso do Sul, Lapa de São Jorge, 280 km from Brasília, in Chapada Diamantina and Vale do Ribeira located between São Paulo and Paraná. Gabriel Ganme, Diving College, R Dr Mello Alves 700, São Paulo, T011-8814723, and Rafael de Nicola, Divers University, are instructors in this specialized sport.

Yachting A popular sport along Brazil's Atlantic coastline. Angra dos Reis and Paraty in Rio de Janeiro state as well as Bahia are good locations among many others.

Ecotourism

This is becoming very important as a form of sustainable development in the parts of Brazil most threatened by deforestation and as a way of alleviating local unemployment in a way that doesn't harm the environment. Many opportunities for visiting the rainforest are to be found in the North and efforts are being made to save what is left of the Atlantic forest cover in the Southeast.

There is a Brazilian institute of ecotourism, *Instituo Brasileiro de Ecoturismo* (IEB), R Wanderley 750, CEP 05011-001, São Paulo, T011-2622069, F8648691. In Minas Gerais, *Amo-Te*, the Associação Mineira dos Organizadores do Turismo Ecológico, Caixa Postal 3059, CEP 31130-140, Belo Horizonte, T031-3448986/2854030, is helpful. *Terra Virgem* is a publishing house in São Paulo, R Galeno de Almeida 179, CEP 05410-030, T/F8837823, terravirgem@originet.com.br, which publishes guides in Portuguese and English for adventure tourism, accompanied by books of photographs.

Cultural tourism

Several of the tour operators listed above offer customized packages for special interest groups. Local operators offering these more specialized tours are listed in the text under the relevant location.

Archaeology

There are many sites where remains can be found of the continent's original inhabitants, whether human or other species such as dinosaurs. The best areas are probably in the central west and the northeast. Cave paintings are to be found in Serra do Roncador in Mato Grosso, Serra da Capivara in Piauí and near Xique-Xique in Bahia. Dinosaur tracks can be seen at Souza in the interior of Paraíba, whilst eggs have been found at Peirópolis in western Minas Gerais.

Mystical tourism

There are many locations in Brazil that have been claimed by seekers of hidden knowledge, or those interested in unusual sciences. Some of the best sites are to be found in the central west such as Alto Paraíso de Goiás, north of Brasília, and Barra do Garças in Mato Grosso. In these places 'new age' communities have formed dedicated to natural healing, alternative religions, or the search for UFOs and alien life-forms. In the south of Minas Gerais, a similar ambience is found at São Tomé das Letras, but there are many other examples across the country.

Birdwatching

There are many good opportunities for birdwatching in Brazil due to the availability of large areas of unspoilt wilderness which are still little visited. There are also popular and accessible tourist destinations such as Iguaçu Falls that are excellent for viewing many species. Some of the specialist tour agencies listed above such as *Focus Tours* and *Field Guides* offer packages to many good areas in all parts of Brazil.

Birds A good field guide for light travelling is *South American Land Birds: A Photographic Aid to Identification* by John S Dunning (Harrowood Books 1987). Other comprehensive (but heavier) guides are *Birds of South America Volumes 1 & 2* by Robert S Ridgely and Guy Tudor (University of Texas Press 1989 and 1994), or *Birds in Brazil* by Helmut Sick (Princeton University Press 1993). Also recommended is *Where to Watch Birds in South America* by Nigel Wheatley (London: Christopher Helm/A & C Black 1994, pages 101-154 on Brazil).

Key sites Details of the following sites are given in the main travelling text. More information on the birds of Brazil is given in **Flora and Fauna**, page 757.

The Amazon Although probably not as good for viewing as the Pantanal, there are many interesting species such as the horned sungem which has the fastest wing beat yet discovered. Toucans and macaws are often seen, although probably the most common birds are vultures. Some birds can be seen in the Lago de Januari reserve only a short distance from Manaus and there are plenty of jungle lodges further away from the city. The Rio Negro with its many islands is a good area, as are the Rio Tapajós near Santarém and the Rio Xingu which extends as far as Mato Grosso.

Minas Gerais This state is host to a large number of accessible national and state parks which are excellent for viewing a variety of different bird species. Recommended are the Parque Natural de Caraça, Parque Nacional da Serra do Cipó, Parque Florestal de Ibitipoca, Parque Florestal do Rio Doce and the Parque Nacional da Serra Canastra, among many other lesser known areas.

The Northeast The interior of Bahia, Pernambuco and Ceará is an excellent area for spotting many species such as blue macaws and cactus parakeets which make their homes in the arid *caatinga*. Many new species have recently been found in the Atlantic forests of Alagoas. The south of Bahia is also a good area for parrots and antbirds, as well as many other varieties of birds.

The Pantanal This large area of swampland on the Bolivian and Brazilian borders is home to more than 600 species of birds including the Rhea, a tall ostrich-like bird. The best time to visit is probably between late June to early October which is the nesting and breeding season for many species such as cormorants, wood ibises and jabiru storks. Parakeets are a common sight especially at dusk and dawn. Other residents are egrets, kingfishers, spoonbills, as well as birds of prey such as the caracara. Nearby are the national parks of Chapada dos Guimarães in Mato Grosso and Emas in Goiás, which are both good areas with more undulating terrain.

The Serra do Mar This mountain range runs parallel to the coast from Rio Grande do Sul to Espírito Santo and still has some remains of the once mighty Atlantic rainforest. It is an excellent site for birds of prey including three types of eagles and the *acuuã* or laughing falcon. Turkey-like *Guans* are frequently seen, as are hummingbirds and parrots. Other common species are the pigeon-like *araponga* and the colourful varieties of *tanager*. Itatiaia National Park is a good starting point for this range but there are many others.

Finding out more

Tourist information

See page 68 for an explanation of phone codes in Brazil

This is handled by the Brazilian Tourist Board, *Embratur*, Setor Comercial Norte, Quadra 02, Bloco G, Brasília, DF, CEP 70710-500, Brazil, T0XX61-3289100, F0XX61-3283517, webm@embratur.gov.br, http://embratur.gov.br/. *Embratur* also has an office in Rio de Janeiro at R Uruguaiana 174, 8 andar, Rio de Janeiro, RJ, CEP 20050-090, T0XX21-5096017, F0XX21-5097381, rio@embratur.gov.br.

Details of state and municipal tourist offices are given in the Essentials section of the respective towns and cities. They are not usually too helpful regarding information on cheap hotels. It is also difficult to get information on neighbouring states.

Outside Brazil, tourist information can be obtained from Brazilian embassies and consulates (see box on page 40). Other sources of information are:

South American Explorers, formerly the *South American Explorers Club*, is a non-profit educational organization functioning primarily as an information network for South America. It is a useful organization for travellers to Brazil and the rest of the continent. They can be contacted in the USA at 126 Indina Creek Rd, Ithaca, NY 14850, T607-2770488, F2776122, explorer@samexplo.org, www.samexplo.org.

The *Latin American Travel Advisor* is a complete travel information service offering the most up-to-date detailed and reliable information about Brazil and countries throughout South and Central America. Public safety, health, weather and natural phenomena, travel costs, economics and politics are highlighted for each nation. You can subscribe to this comprehensive quarterly newsletter (a free sample is available), obtain country reports by email or fax and choose from a wide selection of Latin American maps. Orders may be placed by mail, fax, or through the Web; credit cards accepted. Individual travel planning assistance is available for all customers. Contact PO Box 17-17-908, Quito, Ecuador, F593-2562566, USA and Canada toll free F1-800-3273573, LATA@pi.pro.ec, www.amerispan.com/lata/.

Before you travel

Getting in

Consular **visas** are not required for stays of up to 90 days by tourists from Andorra, Argentina, Austria, Bahamas, Barbados, Belgium, Bermuda, Bolivia, Chile, Colombia, Costa Rica, Denmark, Ecuador, Finland, France, Germany, Greece, Iceland, Ireland, Italy, Liechtenstein, Luxembourg, Monaco, Morocco, Namibia, the Netherlands, Norway, Paraguay, Peru, Philippines, Portugal, San Marino, South Africa, Spain, Suriname, Sweden, Switzerland, Trinidad and Tobago, the United Kingdom, Uruguay, the Vatican and Venezuela. For them, only the following documents are required at the port of disembarkation: a passport valid for at least six months (or *cédula de identidad* for nationals of Argentina, Chile, Paraguay and Uruguay); and a return or onward ticket, or adequate proof that you can purchase your return fare, subject to no remuneration being received in Brazil and no legally binding or contractual documents being signed. Venezuelan passport holders can stay in Brazil for 60 days on filling in a form at the border.

Documents
See box on page 40 for a list of Brazilian embassies and consulates worldwide

Extensions Foreign tourists may stay a maximum of 180 days in any one year. Ninety day renewals are easily obtainable, but only at least 15 days before the expiry of your 90-day permit, from the Polícia Federal. The procedure varies, but generally you have to do the following: fill out three copies of the tax form at the Polícia Federal, take them to a branch of Banco do Brasil, pay US$15 and bring two copies back. You will then be given the extension form to fill in and be asked for your passport to stamp in the extension. According to regulations (which should be on display) you should be able to show a return ticket, cash, cheques or a credit card, a personal reference and proof of an address of a person living in the same city as the office (in practice you simply write this in the space on the form). Some offices will only give you an extension within 10 days of the expiry of your permit.

Some points of entry such as the Colombian border refuse entry for longer than 30 days, renewals are then for the same period, insist if you want 90 days. For longer stays you must leave the country and return (not the same day) to get a new 90-day permit. If you overstay your visa, or extension, you will be fined US$7 per day, with no upper limit. After paying the fine to Polícia Federal, you will be issued with an exit visa and must leave within eight days. If you cannot pay the fine you must pay when you next return to Brazil.

Essentials

Insurance tips

Insurance companies have tightened up considerably over recent years and it is now almost impossible to claim successfully if you have not followed procedures closely. The problem is that these often involve dealing with the country's red tape which can lead to some inconvenience at best and to some quite long delays at worst. There is no substitute for suitable precautions against petty crime.

The level of insurance that you carry is often dictated by the sums of medical insurance which you carry. It is inevitably the highest if you go through the USA. Also don't forget to obtain sports extensions if you are going to go diving, rafting, climbing etc. Most policies do not cover very high levels of baggage/cash. Don't forget to check whether you can claim on your household insurance. They often have worldwide all risks extensions. Most policies exclude manual work whilst away, although working in bars or restaurants is usually alright.

Here are our tips: they apply to most types of policies but always check the details of your own policy before you leave.

1. Take the policy with you (a photocopy will do but make sure it is a complete one).

2. Do not travel against medical advice. It will invalidate the medical insurance part of the cover.

3. There is a 24 hour medical emergency service helpline associated with your insurance. You need to contact them if you require in-patient hospital treatment or you need to return home early. The telephone number is printed on the policy. Make sure you note the time of the call, the person you were talking to and get a reference number. Even better, get a receipt from the telephone company showing the number you called. Should you need to be airlifted home, this is always arranged through the insurance company's representative and the hospital authorities. Ironically, this can lead to quite intense discussions which you will not be aware of: the local hospital is often quite keen to keep you!

4. If you have to cancel your trip for whatever reason, contact your travel agent, tour operator or airline without delay.

5. If your property is damaged by an airline, report it immediately and always within three days, and get a 'property irregularity report' from them.

6. Claims for baggage left unattended are very rarely settled unless they were left in a securely locked hotel room, apartment etc; locked in the boot of a car and there is evidence of a forced entry; cash is carried on your person or is in a locked safe or security box.

7. All loss must be reported to the police and/or hotel authorities within 24 hours of discovery and a written report obtained.

8. If medical attention is received for injury or sickness, a medical certificate showing its nature must be obtained, although some companies waive this if only out-patient treatment is required. Keep all receipts in a safe place as they will be needed to substantiate the claim.

9. Check your policy carefully to see if there is a date before which claims must be submitted. This is often within 30 days of returning home. It is now usual for companies to want your policy document, proof that you actually travelled (airline ticket or travel agent's confirmation of booking), receipts and written reports (in the event of loss).

NB photocopies are not accepted.

NB Officially, if you leave Brazil within the 90-day permission to stay and then re-enter the country, you should only be allowed to stay until the 90-day permit expires. If, however, you are given another 90-day permit, this may lead to charges of overstaying if you apply for an extension. For UK citizens a joint agreement signed in 1998 allows visits for business or tourism of up to six months a year from the date of first entry into Brazil. Don't, however, expect many immigration officials to be aware of this yet and you will more than likely have to follow the same procedure as detailed above.

Identification You must always carry identification when in Brazil. It is a good idea to take a photocopy of the personal details in your passport, plus your Brazilian immigration stamp, and leave your passport in the hotel safe deposit. This photocopy, when authorized in a *Cartório*, US$1, is then a legitimate copy of your documents. Be prepared, however, to present the originals when travelling in sensitive areas such as near the frontiers. Always keep an independent record of your passport details. It is a good idea to register with your consulate to expedite document replacement if yours gets lost or stolen.

Visas US and Canadian citizens, Australians and New Zealanders and people of other nationalities, and those who cannot meet the requirements above such as those requiring to stay longer than 180 days, *must* get a visa before arrival, which may, if you ask, be granted for multiple entry. Visa fees vary from country to country, so apply to the Brazilian consulate in the home country of the applicant. The consular fee in the USA is US$55. Students planning to study in Brazil or employees of foreign companies can apply for a one or two year visa. Two copies of the application form, two photos, a letter from the sponsoring company or educational institution in Brazil, a police form showing no criminal convictions and a fee of around US$80 is required.

Warning Do not lose the emigration permit they give you when you enter Brazil. Leaving the country without it, you may have to pay up to US$100 per person. It is suggested that you photocopy this form and have it authenticated at a *cartório*, US$1, in case of loss or theft.

Duty free allowance Clothing and personal articles are free of import duty. Such **Customs** articles as cameras, movie cameras, portable radios, tape recorders, typewriters and binoculars are also admitted free if there is not more than one of each. Tourists may also bring in, duty-free, 24 alcoholic drinks (no more than 12 of any one type), 400 cigarettes, 25 cigars, 280 grams of perfume, up to 10 units of cosmetics, up to three each of any electronic item or watch, up to a total value of US$500 monthly. There is a limit of US$150 at land borders and a written declaration must be made to this effect. Duty free goods may only be purchased in foreign currency.

You should be protected by immunization against typhoid, polio, tetanus and **Vaccinations** hepatitis A. Vaccination against smallpox is no longer required for visitors. *See also page 77* Poliomyelitis vaccination is required for children from three months to six years.

Proof of vaccination against **yellow fever** is necessary if you are visiting Amazônia and the Centre West, or are coming from countries with Amazonian territories, eg Bolivia, Colombia, Ecuador, or Peru. It is strongly recommended to have a yellow fever inoculation before visiting northern Brazil since those without a certificate will be inoculated on entering any of the northern and centre-western states. Although yellow fever vaccination is free it might be administered in unsanitary conditions.

Yellow fever and some other vaccinations can be obtained from the *Ministério da Saúde*, R Cais de Pharoux, Rio de Janeiro. Less common vaccinations can be obtained at *Saúde de Portos*, Praça 15 de Novembro, Rio de Janeiro.

Money

The unit of currency is the *real*, R$ (plural *reais*) introduced on 1 July 1994 on a par with **Currency** the US dollar. In December 1999, however, the official rate for the *real* had fallen to R$1.88 = US$1. Any amount of foreign currency and 'a reasonable sum' in *reais* can be taken in, but sums over US$10,000 must be declared. Residents may only take out the equivalent of US$4,000. Notes in circulation are: 100, 50, 10, 5 and 1 *real*; coins: 1 *real*, 50, 25, 10, 5 and 1 centavo.

Brazilian embassies and consulates

Argentina C Cerrito 1350, 1010 Buenos Aires, T005411- 48158737, F48144689.

Australia 19 Forster Crescent, Yarralumla, Canberra ACT 2600, T00612-62732372. Consulate: St Martins Tower L 17, 31 Market St, Sydney NSW 2000, T00612-92674414/4415, F92674419.

Austria Am Lugeck 1/5/15, A-1010 Wien, T00431-5120631, F5138374.

Belgium 350 Ave Louise, 6eme Étage, Boite 5-1050 Bruxelles, T00322-6402015/6402111, F6408134.

Bolivia C Capitán Ravelo 2334, Ed Metrobol, Sopocachi, La Paz, Casilla 429, T005912-8112233, F8112733.

Canada 450 Wilbrod St, Sandyhill, Ottawa, ON K1N 6M8, T001613-2371090, F2376144. Consulates: 2000 Mansfield, Suite 1700, Montreal, Quebec, H3A 3A5, T001514-4990968/4990969, F4993963. 77 Bloor St West, Suite 1109, Toronto, Ontario, M5S 1M2 T001416-9221058/9222503, F9221832. 1140 West Pender St, Suite 1300, Vancouver, BC V6E 4G1, T001604-6874589, F6816534.

Chile C Alonso Ovalle 1665, Santiago, T00562-6982347, F6715961.

Colombia C 93, No 14-20, 8th floor, Bogota 8, Aptdo Aéreo 90540, T00571-2180800, F2188393.

Denmark Ryvangs Alle, 24-2100 Kobenhavn, T00453-9206478, F9273607.

Finland Itainen Puisotie 4B 1/2-00140 Helsinki, Suomi, T003589-177922, F650084.

France 34 Cours Albert I, 75008 Paris, T00331-45616300, F42890345. Consulates: 11 Bis, Rue Saint-Ferreul, 4eme Étage, 13001 Marseille, T003391-543391/338837, F555176. 34 bis de Cour Albert, 1er Étage, 75008 Paris, T00331-44139030, F43590326.

French Guiana Consulate: 23 Chemin Saint Antoine (Troubiran), BP793, 97337 Cayenne Cedex, T00594-296010, F303885.

Germany Kennedyallee 74-53175 Bonn, T0049228-959230, F373696. Consulates: Esplanade 11, Berlin Pankow, 13187 Berlin, T004930-4459121/4459185, F4459184. Stephanstrasse 3, 4 Stock 60313 Frankfurt Am Main, T004969-9207420, F9207430. Grosse Theaterstrasse, 42-7 Stock 20354, Hamburg, T004940-351827, F351929. Widenmayerstrasse 47, 80538 Munchen, T004989-2103760, F29160768.

Guyana 308 Church St, Queenstown, Georgetown, PO Box 10.489, T005922-57970/57977, F69063.

Ireland Harcourt Centre, Europa House, 5th Floor, 41-54 Harcourt St, Dublin 2, T003531-4756000/4751338, F4751341.

Israel Beit Yachin, 2 Kaplin St, 8th Floor, Tel Aviv, T009723-6963934, F6916060.

Italy 14 Piazza Navona, 00186 Roma, T003906-683981, F6867858. Consulate: Via Santa Maria Dell'Anima 32, 00186 Roma, T003906-6889661/6877891, F68802883.

Japan 11-12 Kita-Aoyama 2-Chome, Minato-Ku, Tokyo 107, T00813-34045211,

---

Exchange Banks in major cities will change cash and travellers' cheques. If you keep the exchange slips, you may convert back into foreign currency up to 50% of the amount you exchanged. This applies to the official markets only; there is no right of reconversion unless you have an official exchange slip. The parallel market, found in travel agencies, exchange houses and among hotel staff, was of marginal benefit compared with bank rates in 1999. Many banks may only change US$300 minimum in cash, US$500 in travellers' cheques. Dollars cash are becoming more frequently used for tourist transactions and are also useful for those places where travellers' cheques cannot be changed and for when the banks go on strike. Damaged dollar notes may be rejected. Parallel market and official rates are quoted in the papers and on TV news programmes.

Travellers' cheques Travellers' cheques are a safer way to carry your money, but rates for cheques are usually lower than for cash and they are less easy to change, commission may be charged.
Tourists cannot change US dollars travellers' cheques into dollar notes, but US dollar travellers' cheques can be obtained on an American Express card (against official policy).

F34055846. Consulate: Gotanda Fuji
Building, 2nd floor, 13-12 Higashi
Gotanda, 1 Chome Shinagawa-Ku, Tokyo
141, T00813-54885451/54885452,
F54885458.
Netherlands Mauritskade 19-2514 HD,
The Hague, T003170-3023959, F3023950.
Consulate: Stationsplein 45-3013 AK
Rotterdam, T003110-4119656/4119657,
F4110088.
New Zealand 19 Brandon St, level 9,
Wellington 1, T00644-4733516, F4733517.
Norway Sigurd Syrs Gate 4, 1st floor,
0273 Oslo, T0047-22552029/22552070,
F22443964.
Paraguay C Coronel Irrazabal esq Eligio
Ayala, Casilla de Correo 22, 1521 Asunción,
T0059521-214466/213450, F212693.
Consulate: C Gen Díaz esq 14 de Mayo, N
521 Ed Faro Internacional, 3rd floor,
Asunción, T0059521-448069/448084,
F441719.
Peru Av José Pardo 850, Miraflores, Lima
100, T00511-4212759/4216102,
F4452421.
Portugal Estrada das Laranjeiras,
144-1600 Lisboa, T003511-7267777,
F7267623.
South Africa 201 Leyds St, Arcadia,
Pretoria, Code 0007,
T002712-3411712/3411720, F3417547.
Spain C Fernando El Santo, 6 DP 28010
Madrid, T00341-7004650, F7004660.
Consulate: Carrer Consell de Cent, 357/1a
Ed Brasilia, 08007 Barcelona,

T0034-934-882288, F934-872645.
Sweden Sturgegatan 11, 2 Tr 114 36
Stockholm, T00468-234010, F234018.
Switzerland Monbijouster 68-3007
Berne, T004131-3718515, F3710525.
UK 32 Green St, London W1Y 4AT,
T004420-74990877, F74935105.
Consulate: 6 St Albans St, London SW1Y
4SQ, T004420-79309055, F78398958.
USA 3006 Massachusetts Ave NW,
Washington DC 20008-3699,
T001202-2382700/2805, F2382827.
   Consulates: 401 North Michigan Ave,
Suite 3050, Chicago, Illinois 60611,
T001312-4640245, F4640299. 1700 West
Loop South, Suite 1450, Houston, Texas
77027, T001713-9613063/9613064,
F9613070. 8484 Wilshire Blvd, Suite
711/730 Beverley Hills, California
90211-3216, T001213-6512664,
F6511274. 2601 South Bay Shore Drive,
Suite 800, Miami, Florida 33133,
T001305-2856200, F2856232. 630 Fifth
Ave, 20th floor, New York 10020,
T001212-4897930/9570624, F9563465.
300 Montgomery St, Suite 900, San
Francisco, CA 94104-1913,
T001415-9818170, F9813628.
Uruguay Blvd Artigas, 1328, Montevideo,
Aptdo Postal 16022, T005982-7072119/
7072115, F7072086.
Venezuela Centro Gerencial Mohedano,
6th floor, C Los Chaguaramos con Av
Mohedano, La Castellana, 1060 Caracas,
T00582-2616529/2615505, F2619601.

Essentials

Credit cards are widely used; Diners Club, Mastercard, Visa and American Express are useful. Mastercard/Access is accepted by Banco Real. Overseas credit cards need authorization from São Paulo, this can take up to two hours, allow plenty of time if buying air tickets. Mastercard and Diners are equivalent to Credicard, and Eurocheques can be cashed at Banco Alemão (major cities only). Banco Bradesco and Banestado handle the international Visa automatic teller machine (ATM) network, Visa cash advances up to US$600 also at Banco do Brasil. Some of Banco Itaú's. ATMs give cash withdrawals on Mastercard/Cirrus, but not as common as Visa ATMs. Both Bradesco and Itaú have machines at airports, shopping centres and major thoroughfares; Banco 24 Horas machines, at similar locations, operate with Amex, Diners, Boston and Citibank among others. Credit card transactions are charged at the tourist official rate.

   Cash advances on credit cards will only be paid in *reais* at the tourist rate, incurring a 1½% commission. Banks in small remote places may still refuse to give a cash advance: if you have run out of cash and travellers' cheques, try asking for the manager

Credit cards
See box on page 42 for a
list of emergency
telephone numbers to
report card loss or theft

Essentials

 Emergency numbers

Credicard: T0800-784411	*American Express:* T011-2470966
Diners Club: T0800-784444	*Thomas Cook Visa:* T000811-7840553
Mastercard: T000811-8870533	*Thomas Cook refund service:*
Visa: T000811-9335589	F+44-1733-502370.

('gerente'). Automatic cash dispensers are common in Brazil, but machines which accept foreign cards are harder to find than in some other South American countries. Mastercard is generally difficult to use outside large cities. It's worth remembering your PIN number since queues can be extremely long. In some instances, especially Visa, the card is swiped down a slot, not inserted into the machine, thus avoiding the possibility of the card not being returned.

There are two international ATM (automatic telling machine) acceptance systems, Plus and Cirrus. Many issuers of debit and credit cards are linked to one, or both (eg Visa is Plus, Mastercard is Cirrus). Look for the relevant symbol on an ATM and draw cash using your PIN. Frequently, the rates of exchange on ATM withdrawals are the best available. Find out before you leave what ATM coverage there is in Brazil and what international 'functionality' your card has. Check if your bank or credit card company imposes handling charges. Obviously you must ensure that the account to which your debit card refers contains sufficient funds. With a credit card, obtain a credit limit sufficient for your needs, or pay money in to put the account in credit. If travelling for a long time, consider a direct debit to clear your account regularly. Do not rely on one card, in case of loss. If you do lose a card, immediately contact the 24-hour helpline of the issuer in your home country (keep this number in a safe place).

Money transfers Money can be transferred between banks. Money sent to Brazil is normally paid out in Brazilian currency, so do not have more money sent to Brazil than you need for your stay. A recommended method is, before leaving, to find out which local bank is correspondent to your bank at home, then when you need funds, telex your own bank and ask them to telex the money to the local bank (confirming by fax). Give exact information to your bank of the routing number of the receiving bank. Funds can be received within 48 banking hours.

In most large cities Citibank will hold US personal cheques for collection, paying the day's tourist dollar rate in *reais* with no charge. Banco do Brasil offers the same service with a small charge. From the UK the quickest method of having money sent is Swift Air.

To open a bank account in Brazil, you need to have a visa valid for more than one year.

Money matters Low-value US dollar bills should be carried for changing into local currency if arriving in Brazil or a neighbouring country when banks or *casas de câmbio* are closed (US$5 or US$10 bills). Take plenty of local currency, in small denominations, when making trips away from large cities.

It is a good idea to take two kinds of cheque: if large numbers of one kind have recently been forged or stolen, making people suspicious, it is unlikely to have happened simultaneously with the other kind.

Cost of living Since the devaluation of the *real* in January 1999, prices for visitors have decreased. Eating in smart restaurants is still costly but hotel accommodation is much more affordable. Budget hotels have responded by cutting extras, cramming more beds into rooms etc. A cheap room will cost about US$10. Shopping prices are equivalent to Europe. Hotel price categories and transport fares in this book reflect the depreciation of the *real*, but travellers may find some variations as the *real* fluctuates against the dollar. Prices are higher in Amazônia than elsewhere in Brazil.

Travelling with children

Travel with children can bring you into closer contact with Latin American families and, generally, presents no special problems – in fact the path is often smoother for family groups. Officials tend to be more amenable where children are concerned and they are pleased if your child knows a little Spanish or Portuguese. Moreover, even thieves and pickpockets seem to have some of the traditional respect for families, and may leave you alone because of it!

People contemplating overland travel in South America with children should remember that a lot of time can be spent waiting for buses, trains, and especially for aeroplanes. On bus journeys, if the children are good at amusing themselves, or can readily sleep while travelling, the problems can be considerably lessened. If your child is of an early reading age, take reading material with you as it is difficult and expensive to find. A bag, say 30 pieces, of Duplo or Lego can keep young children occupied for hours. Travel on trains, while not as fast or at times as comfortable as buses, allows more scope for moving about. Some trains provide tables between seats, so that games can be played. Beware of doors left open for ventilation, especially if air-conditioning is not working.

Food This can be a problem if the children are not adaptable. It is easier to take biscuits, drinks, bread etc with you on longer trips than to rely on meal stops where the food may not be to their taste. Avocados are safe, easy to eat and nutritious; they can be fed to babies as young as six months and most older children like them. A small immersion heater and jug for making hot drinks is invaluable, but remember that electric current varies. Try and get a dual-voltage one (110v and 220v).

Fares On all long distance buses you pay for each seat, and there are no half-fares if the children occupy a seat each. For shorter trips it is cheaper, if less comfortable, to seat small children on your knee. Often there are spare seats which children can occupy after tickets have been collected. In city and local excursion buses, small children generally do not pay a fare, but are not entitled to a seat when paying customers are standing. On sightseeing tours you should *always* bargain for a family rate – often children can go free. (In trains, reductions for children are general, but not universal.)

All civil airlines charge half for children under 12, but some military services don't have half-fares, or have younger age limits. Note that a child travelling free on a long excursion is not always covered by the operator's travel insurance; it is advisable to pay a small premium to arrange cover.

Hotels Try to negotiate family rates. If charges are per person, always insist that two children will occupy one bed only, therefore counting as one tariff. If rates are per bed, the same applies. In either case you can almost always get a reduced rate at cheaper hotels. Occasionally when travelling with a child you will be refused a room in a hotel that is 'unsuitable'. On river boat trips, unless you have very large hammocks, it may be more comfortable and cost effective to hire a two-berth cabin for two adults and a child. (In restaurants, you can normally buy children's helpings, or divide one full-size helping between two children.)

Getting there

Air

Regulations state that you cannot buy an air ticket in Brazil for use abroad unless you first have a ticket out of Brazil

International flights into Brazil generally land at both Rio de Janeiro and São Paulo. São Paulo has better flight connections, both domestic and international. Both of these are good points to enter Brazil, although tourists tend to choose Rio de Janeiro as their point of disembarkation. There are, however, excellent transport connections between the two cities. Check all flight details with the agencies concerned. Prices are more competitive during the low season but cheap flights can be very difficult to find during the high season (generally between 15 December and 15 January, the Thursday before Carnival to the Saturday after Carnival and 15 June to 15 August). Flight frequency changes regularly and you are advised to check current timetables.

If buying a ticket to another country but with a stopover in Brazil, check whether two tickets are cheaper than one. Airline tickets are expensive in Brazil, buy internal tickets with *reais* (you can pay by credit card). External tickets must be paid for in dollars.

Varig also has an extensive 'Stopover' programme which gives reduced rates on transfers and hotel rooms in many cities in Brazil and throughout South America (plus San José, Costa Rica).

From Europe Rio de Janeiro and São Paulo are connected to the principal European cities direct by *Aerolíneas Argentinas* (Amsterdam and Madrid), *Air France* (Paris), *Alitalia* (Rome), *British Airways* (London), *Iberia* (Barcelona and Madrid), *KLM* (Amsterdam), *LanChile* (Frankfurt and Madrid), *Lufthansa* (Frankfurt), *Pluna* (Madrid), *Swissair* (Zurich), *TAM* (Paris), *TAP Air Portugal* (Lisbon), *Transbrasil* (Amsterdam, London and Vienna), *Varig* (Copenhagen, Frankfurt, London, Lisbon, Paris and Milan) and *Vasp* (Athens, Barcelona, Brussels, Frankfurt and Zurich).

Varig flies to Recife and Fortaleza from Milan; Salvador from Rome. *TAP Air Portugal* flies to Fortaleza, Natal, Recife and Salvador from Lisbon. *Transbrasil* flies from Amsterdam and London to Recife and Salvador.

From the USA & Canada Rio de Janeiro and São Paulo are connected to the USA direct by *American Airlines* (Chicago, Dallas, Miami), *Continental* (New York), *Delta* (Atlanta), *TAM* (Miami), *Transbrasil* (Miami, New York, Orlando and Washington), *United Airlines* (Chicago, Miami), *Varig* (Los Angeles, Miami and New York) and *Vasp*. Other US gateways are Boston, Cincinnati, Denver, Detroit and San Francisco. The cheapest routes are probably from Miami.

American Airlines fly from Miami to Belo Horizonte. *LAB* fly from Miami to Manaus. *Transbrasil* fly from New York, Orlando and Washington to Brasília. *Varig* fly from Miami to Belém, Fortaleza, Manaus and Recife. *Canadian Airlines* fly direct to São Paulo from Toronto.

From Latin America Most Latin American cities are connected by air to São Paulo and Rio de Janeiro. There are flights from Asunción with *American Airlines*, *TAM* and *Varig*; Bogotá with *Varig* and *Avianca*; Buenos Aires with *Aerolíneas Argentinas*, *TAM* and *Varig*; Caracas with *Varig*; Córdoba with *Varig*; Guayaquil with *Ecuatoriana* and *Vasp*; La Paz with *Varig*; Lima with *Aero México*, *TAM* and *Varig*; Mexico City with *Aero México* and *Varig*; Montevideo with *TAM*, *Pluna* and *Varig*; Santa Cruz with *LAB*, *TAM*, *Varig* and *Vasp*; San José, Costa Rica with *Lacsa*; Santiago with *LanChile*, *TAM* and *Varig*; Quito with *Ecuatoriana* and *Vasp*.

Penta fly from Cayenne to Belém and Macapá. *Pluna* fly from Montevideo to Porto Alegre. *Surinam Airways* fly from Paramaribo to Belém. *Varig* fly from Asunción to Curitiba, Florianópolis and Foz do Iguaçu; Buenos Aires to Porto Alegre; Mexico City to Manaus; Montevideo to Porto Alegre; Santiago to Porto Alegre.

There are flights to São Paulo from Abidjan and Beirut with *Middle East Airlines*; **From elsewhere**
Johannesburg with *South African Airways*; Nagoya, Japan with *Varig*; Osaka with *Vasp*;
Seoul with *Korean Airlines*; Tokyo with *JAL* and *Varig*.

Aerolíneas Argentinas, Austral, Lan Chile, Lapa, Líneas Aéreas Paraguayas, Pluna, **Air passes**
Transbrasil, Varig and *Vasp* operate the **Mercosur Airpass**. Valid for a minimum of
seven and a maximum of 30 days, the pass is for a maximum of eight flight coupons
with no more than two stops allowed per country. At least two Mercosur member
countries must be included; rerouting is not permitted. The air pass is available to all
international return ticket holders travelling by air into the participating countries.
Passes are price-banded according to mileage flown and fares range from US$225 to
US$870. Children pay 67% whilst infants pay 10% of the adult fare and some of the
carriers operate a blackout period between 17 December and 10 January.

LAB, Ecuatoriana and *Vasp* operate a **South American Airpass** valid for 90 days,
available to non-residents of Brazil arriving in South America on longhaul flights. There
is no child discount and infants pay 10% of the price which varies between US$560 for
up to four flights and US$1,100 for the maximum of nine flights. Up to two transfers of
less than five hours are permitted and coverage is from northern Argentina, Chile,
Bolivia, Peru, Ecuador and Brazil.

Airlines will only allow a certain weight of luggage without a surcharge; this is **Baggage**
normally 30 kilos for first class and 20 kilos for business and economy classes, but **allowance**
these limits are often not strictly enforced when it is known that the plane is not going
to be full. On some flights from the UK, special outbound concessions are offered (by
Iberia, Air France) of a two-piece allowance up to 32 kilos, but you may need to request
this. Passengers seeking a larger baggage allowance can route via the USA, but with

Essentials

certain exceptions, the fares are slightly higher using this route. On the other hand, weight limits for internal flights are often lower; best to enquire beforehand.

Prices & discounts

1 Fares from Europe to Brazilian destinations vary from airline to airline, destination to destination and according to time of year. Check with an agency for the best deal for when you wish to travel. There is a wide range of offers to choose from in a highly competitive environment in the UK.

2 Most airlines offer discounted fares of one sort or another on scheduled flights. These are not offered by the airlines direct to the public, but through agencies who specialize in this type of fare.

The very busy seasons are 7 December-15 January and 1 July-10 September. If you intend travelling during those times, book as far ahead as possible. Between February-May and September-November special offers may be available.

3 Other fares fall into three groups, and are all on scheduled services:

Excursion (return) fares (A) With restricted validity, eg 5-90 days. Carriers are introducing flexibility to these tickets, permitting a change of dates on payment of a fee.

Yearly fares (B) These may be bought on a one-way or return basis. Some airlines require a specified return date, changeable upon payment of a fee. To leave the return completely open is possible for an extra fee. You must fix the route (some of the cheapest flexible fares now have six months validity).

Student (or under 26) fares Some airlines are flexible on the age limit, others strict. One-way and returns available, or 'Open Jaws' (see below). Do not assume that student tickets are the cheapest; though they are often very flexible, they are usually more expensive than A or B above. On the other hand, there is a wider range of cheap one-way student fares originating in Latin America than can be bought outside the continent.

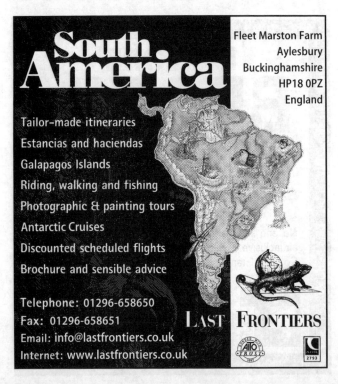

4 For people intending to travel a linear route and return from a different point from that which they entered, there are 'Open Jaws' fares, which are available on student, yearly, or excursion fares.

5 Many of these fares require a change of plane at an intermediate point, and a stopover may be permitted, or even obligatory, depending on schedules. Simply because a flight stops at a given airport does not mean you can break your journey there – the airline must have traffic rights to pick up or set down passengers between points A and B before it will be permitted. This is where dealing with a specialized agency will really pay dividends. There are dozens of agencies that offer the simple returns to Rio at roughly the same (discounted) fare. On multi-stop itineraries, the specialized agencies can often save clients hundreds of pounds.

6 Although it's a little more complicated, it's possible to sell tickets in London for travel originating in Latin America at substantially cheaper fares than those available locally. This is useful for the traveller who doesn't know where he/she will end up, or who plans to travel for more than a year. Because of high local taxes (see paragraph 7), a one-way ticket from Latin America is more expensive than a one-way in the other direction, so it's always best to buy a return (but see **Student fares**, above). Taxes are calculated as a percentage of the full IATA fare; on a discounted fare the tax can therefore make up as much as 30-50% of the price.

7 Certain Latin American countries impose local tax on flights originating there. Among these are Ecuador, Peru, Bolivia, Argentina and Uruguay. This often applies if you happen to have bought a ticket, say, London-Rio-Santiago-Lima-Los Angeles and then on to Australia.

8 Travellers starting their journey in continental Europe should make local enquiries about charters and agencies offering the best deals.

9 If you buy discounted air tickets *always* check the reservation with the airline concerned to make sure the flight still exists. Also remember the IATA airlines' schedules change in March and October each year, so if you're going to be away a long time it's best to leave return flight coupons open (but see **NB** under **Student fares**, above).

In addition, check whether you are entitled to any refund or re-issued ticket if you lose, or have stolen, a discounted air ticket. Some airlines require the repurchase of a ticket before you can apply for a refund, which will not be given until after the validity of the original ticket has expired. The Iberia group and Air France, eg, operate this costly system. Travel insurance in some cases covers lost tickets.

10 Note that some South American carriers change departure times of short-haul or domestic flights at short notice and, in some instances, schedules shown in the computers of transatlantic carriers differ from those actually flown by smaller, local carriers. If you book, and reconfirm, both your transatlantic and onward sectors through your transatlantic carrier, you may find that your travel plans have been based on out of date information. The surest solution is to reconfirm your outward flight in an office of the onward carrier itself.

Road

International buses There are good road connections between Argentina, Paraguay, Uruguay and the south of Brazil. Rio de Janeiro and São Paulo can easily be reached by international buses from Asunción, Buenos Aires, Santiago and Montevideo. Transport is not so easy in the north and west of the country, although a reasonable road now exists between Caracas and Manaus. Entry from Bolivia at Corumbá is fairly straightforward. Buses from here connect with the main Brazilian road system at Campo Grande. Other border crossings from French Guiana at Oiapoque and from Guyana at Bonfim require some effort to actually get to the Brazilian border. Once there bus services are frequent, although heavy rains may make for slow going or cause cancellations.

Driving According to Detran, the state transport department, foreign tourists driving in Brazil need an international driving licence and a passport, which must be presented to the police if requested. A national driving licence is acceptable as long as your home country is a signatory to the Vienna and Geneva conventions. If it is not a signatory, your home driving licence will only be accepted if it is translated into Portuguese by a public notary. Car hire companies say they will accept national driving licences, but this may not be acceptable to the traffic police. Detran in Rio de Janeiro is at Av Presidente Vargas 817, 2nd floor, T5509744.

There are agreements between Brazil and all South American countries (but check in the case of Bolivia) whereby a car can be taken into Brazil (or a Brazilian car out of Brazil) for a period of 90 days without any special documents; an extension of up to 90 days is granted by the customs authorities on presentation of the paper received at the border, which must be retained; this may be done at most customs posts and at the Serviço de Controle Aduaneiro, Ministério da Fazenda, Av Presidente Antônio Carlos, Sala 1129, Rio de Janeiro.

For cars registered in other countries, the requirements are proof of ownership and/or registration in the home country and valid driving licence (see above). A 90-day permit is given by customs and procedure is very straightforward. Nevertheless, it is better to cross the border into Brazil when it is officially open because an official who knows all about the entry of cars is then present. You must specify which border station you intend to leave by, but application can be made to the Customs to change this.

Boat

There is an 8% tax on international shipping line tickets bought in Brazil

Voyages on passenger-carrying cargo vessels between Brazilian ports and Europe, the USA, or elsewhere, are listed here: the Grimaldi Line sails from Tilbury to Brazil (Vitória, Santos, Paranaguá, Rio) and Buenos Aires via Hamburg, Amsterdam and Antwerp, Le Havre, Southampton and Bilbao, round trip about 51 days, US$3,040-5,400, also from Genoa to Paranaguá, Santos and Rio for US$1,100-1,400 (round trip or southbound only, no northbound only passages). A number of German container ships sail the year round to the east coast of South America: Felixstowe, Hamburg, Antwerp, Bilbao or Algeciras, Santos, Buenos Aires, Montevideo, Rio Grande do Sul, Itajaí, Santos, Rio de Janeiro, Rotterdam, Felixstowe (about 45 days, £3,100-3,500 per person round trip). Four German vessels make a 49-day round trip: Tilbury, Hamburg, Antwerp, Le Havre, Suape, Rio de Janeiro, Santos, Buenos Aires, Montevideo, São Francisco do Sul, Paranaguá, Santos, Suape, Rotterdam, Tilbury. There are also German sailings from Genoa or Livorno (Italy), or Spain to the east coast of South America.

A cheaper option is Polish Ocean Line's services to the east coast, Gdynia to Buenos Aires, Montevideo and Santos (2-2½ months).

From the USA, Maritime Reederei of Germany sails to Charleston, Miami, Puerto Cabello, Santos, Buenos Aires, Montevideo, Rio Grande do Sul, Santos, Puerto Cabello, Freeport, New York, from £3,540 per person on a 42-day round trip. A German consortium has a 48-day round trip to New York, Savannah, Miami, Rio, Santos, Buenos Aires, Montevideo, Rio Grande do Sul, Santos, Salvador, Fortaleza, Norfolk, Philadelphia, New York, £4,020 per person (one-way to Rio, 15 days £1,395).

Enquiries regarding passages should be made through agencies in your own country, or through John Alton of *Strand Voyages*, Charing Cross Shopping Concourse, The Strand, London WC2N 4HZ, T020-78366363, F74970078. *Strand Voyages* are booking agents for all the above. Advice can also be obtained from *Cargo Ship Voyages Ltd*, Hemley, Woodbridge, Suffolk, IP12 4QF, T/F01473-736265. Also in London: *The Cruise People*, 88 York St, W1H 1DP, T020-77232450 (reservations 0800-526313). In Europe, contact *Wagner Frachtschiffreisen*, Stadlerstrasse 48, CH-8404, Winterthur, Switzerland, T052-2421442, F2421487. In the USA, contact *Freighter World Cruises*, 180 South Lake Ave, Pasadena, CA 91101, T818-4493106, *Travltips Cruise and Freighter Travel*

Association, 163-07 Depot Rd, PO Box 188, Flushing, NY 11358, T800-8728584, or *Maris Freighter Travel Inc*, 215 Main St, Westport, CT06880-3210, T1-800-9962747. Do not try to get a passage on a non-passenger carrying cargo ship to South America from a European port; it is not possible.

A popular entry point to the Amazon region is along the Rio Amazonas from Iquitos in   **River**
Peru to Tabatinga in Brazil. Onward travel is then by river boat or air to Manaus. This border can also be crossed by land from Leticia in Colombia. Security is particularly tight on this triple border and there have been reports that Brazilian immigration often refuse to allow entry to Brazil for more than 30 days.

Touching down

Airport information

For most visitors the point of arrival will either be Tom Jobim international airport (also   *See also pages 146 and*
known as Galeão) on the Ilha do Governador, some 16 km from the centre of Rio de   *220 for detailed airport*
Janeiro, or Cumbica international airport at Guarulhos in São Paulo. Details of other entry   *information in Rio de*
airports are given in their respective sections. **NB** Arrive two hours before international   *Janeiro and São Paulo*
flights and it is wise to reconfirm your flight as departure times may have changed.   *respectively*

The amount of tax depends on the class of airport. All airports charge R$69.50 (US$36)   **Airport**
international departure tax. First class airports charge R$9.50 domestic tax; second   **departure tax**
class airports R$7; domestic rates are lower still in third and fourth class airports. Tax must be paid on checking in, in *reais* or US dollars. Tax is waived if you stay in Brazil less than 24 hours.

Tourist information

For full details of the Brazilian Tourist Board, *Embratur*, and for on-line information see under **Finding out more** (page 36). The addresses of tourist offices are given in the main travelling text. See **Tours and tour operators** (page 30) for a list of specialist tour operators operating from both inside and outside of Brazil.

Many of the more expensive hotels provide locally produced tourist information   **Guide books**
magazines for their guests. Travel information can be very unreliable though and it is wise to recheck details thoroughly.

The following are recommended guidebooks and relevant reading:

Ana Augusta Rocha, Roberto Linsker, *Brasil Aventura Guia/Guide*. Ilhas/Islands (São Paulo: Terra Virgem, 1996); one of a series of excellent books on adventure tourism. Each is accompanied by a volume of photographs. *Brazil*, edited by Edwin Taylor, updated Patrick Cunningham. *Insight Guides* (London: Apa, 1996). Richard Dawood, *Travellers' Health. How to Stay Healthy Abroad* (Oxford: Oxford University Press, 1992). John Hatt, *The Tropical Traveller: The Essential Guide to Travel in Hot Countries* (London: Penguin, 1993). *Rio de Janeiro, Cidade e Estado* (Rio de Janeiro: Michelin, 1990, 2nd edition 1999). Miranda Haines, *The Traveller's Handbook 7th edition* (London: Wexas International, 1997). Miranda Haines and Sarah Thorowgood, *The Traveller's Healthbook* (London: Wexas International, 1998). For practical information on South American motoring conditions and requirements, see *Driving to Heaven* by Derek Stansfield (available from the author, Ropley, Broad Oak, Sturminster Newton, Dorset DT10 2HG, T/F01258-472534, £4.95 plus postage, if outside the UK). For information on Bradt Publications' Backpacking Guide Series, other titles and imported maps and guides, contact 41 Nortoft Rd, Chalfont St Peter, Bucks, SL9 0LA, UK, T/F01494-873478.

Essentials

Touching down

Official time Brazil has 4 time zones: Brazilian standard time is 3 hours behind GMT; the Amazon time zone (Pará west of the Rio Xingu, Amazonas, Roraima, Rondônia, Mato Grosso and Mato Grosso do Sul) is 4 hours behind GMT, the State of Acre is 5 hours behind GMT; the Fernando de Noronha archipelago is 2 hours behind GMT. Clocks move forward 1 hour in summer for approximately 5 months (usually between October and February or March), but times of change vary. This does not apply to Acre.
IDD code 55. Equal tones with long pauses means the phone is ringing; equal tones with equal pauses indicates engaged.
Business hours Generally 0900-1800 Monday to Friday; closed for lunch some time between 1130 and 1400. **Shops** are open on Saturday till 1230 or 1300.
Government offices: 1100-1800 Monday to Friday. **Banks:** 1000-1600 or 1630, closed on Saturday.
Voltage Generally 110V 60 cycles AC, but in some cities and areas 220V 60 cycles AC is used.
Weights and measures The metric system is used by all.

Maps

Telephone yellow pages in most cities (but not Rio) contain good street maps which, together with the Quatro Rodas maps, are a great help for getting around

A recommended series of general maps is that published by International Travel Maps (ITM), 345 West Broadway, Vancouver BC, V5Y 1P8, Canada, T604-8793621, F8794521, compiled with historical notes, by the late Kevin Healey. Available are South America South, North East and North West (1:4M), Rio de Janeiro (1:20,000). Another map series that has been mentioned is that of New World Edition, Bertelsmann, Neumarkter Strasse 18, 81673 München, Germany, *Mittelamerika, Südamerika Nord, Südamerika Sud, Brasilien* (all 1:4M).

Quatro Rodas, a motoring magazine, publishes an excellent series of maps and guides in Portuguese and English from about US$10. Its annual *Guia Brasil* is a type of Michelin Guide to hotels, restaurants (not the cheapest), sights, facilities and general information on hundreds of cities and towns in the country, including good country and street maps. These guides can be purchased at street newspaper vendors throughout the country. Address: Av das Nações Unidas 7221, 14 andar, Pinheiros, CEP 05425-902, T0XX11-30376004, F0XX11-30376270, www.publiabril.com.br. Quatro Rodas Guides may be bought in Europe from: 33, rue de Miromesnil, 75008 Paris, T00331-42663118, F00331-42661399, abrilparis@wanadoo.fr; and *Deltapress-Sociedade Distribuidora de Publicaçõ*es, Capa Rota, Tapada Nova, Linhó, 2710 Sintra, Portugal, T003511-9249940, F9240429. In the USA: Lincoln Building, 60 East 42nd St, Suite 3403, New York, NY 10165/3403, T001212-5575990/3, F9830972, abril@walrus.com.

Information for business travellers

A useful guide is 'Hints to exporters visiting Brazil', available from DTI Publications Orderline, Admail 528, London, SW1W 8YT, T0870-1502500, F1502333. Furthermore, specific information for UK exporters can be obtained from the Department of Trade and Industry's Brazil Desk, Bay 826, Kingsgate House, 66-74 Victoria St, London, SW1E 6SW, T020-72154262, F72158247, exportinfo.brazil@xpdv.dti.gov.uk, www.dti.gov.uk/ots/brazil/.

Brazil Report, published by Latin American Newsletters, has well written articles on recent political and economic news. They can be contacted at 61 Old St, London, EC1V 9HW, T020-72510012, F72538193, www.latinnews.com.

The American Chamber of Commerce in São Paulo is another good source of information on local markets (see page 223), www.amcham.com.br.

Special interest groups

If you are in full time education you will be entitled to an International Student **Student** Identity Card, which is distributed by student travel offices and travel agencies in 77 **travellers** countries. The ISIC card gives you special prices on all forms of transport (air, sea, rail etc), and access to a variety of other concessions and services. If you need to find the location of your nearest ISIC office contact: The ISIC Association, Box 15857, 1001 NJ Amsterdam, Holland, T+45-33939303. ISIC cards can be obtained in Brazil from STB agencies throughout the country such as Av Brig Faria Lima 1713, São Paulo, T0XX11-8700555. Remember to take photographs when having a card issued.

In practice, however, the ISIC card is rarely recognized or accepted for discounts outside of the south and southeast of Brazil. It is nonetheless useful for obtaining half price entry to the cinema. Youth hostels will often accept it in lieu of a IYHA card or at least give a discount, and some university accommodation (and subsidized canteens) will allow very cheap short term stays to holders.

As in most Latin American countries, facilities for disabled travellers are severely **Disabled** lacking. Wheelchair ramps are a rare luxury and getting a wheelchair into a bathroom **travellers** or toilet is practically impossible, except for some of the more modern hotels. Pavements are often in a poor state of repair or crowded with street vendors requiring passers-by to brave the passing traffic. Disabled Brazilians obviously have to cope with these problems mainly by relying on the help of others to get on and off public transport and generally move around.

Brazil is a good country for gay and lesbian travellers as attitudes are fairly liberal, **Gay & lesbian** especially in the big cities. Opinions in the interior and rural areas are far more **travellers** conservative and it is wise to adapt to this. There is a well developed scene in Rio de Janeiro and São Paulo while Salvador is also a popular destination. More specific information can be obtained from the Rio Gay Guide, www.ipanema.com/rio/gay/.

Rules, customs and etiquette

In general, clothing requirements in Brazil are less formal than in the Hispanic countries. **Clothing** It is, however, advisable for men visiting restaurants to wear long trousers (women in shorts may also be refused entry), trousers and jackets or pullovers in São Paulo (also for cinemas). As a general rule, it is better not to wear shorts in official buildings, cinemas, interstate buses and on flights. Female fashions are provocative, and while women are advised to dress in the local style, this can have unnerving effects.

Men should avoid arguments or insults (care is needed even when overtaking on the **Conduct** road); pride may be defended with a gun. Gay men, while still enjoying greater freedom than in many countries, should exercise reasonable discretion. It is normal to stare and comment on a woman's appearance, and if you happen to look different or to be travelling alone, you will undoubtedly attract attention. You are very unlikely to be groped or otherwise molested: this is disrespectful, and merits a suitable reaction. Be aware that Brazilian men can be extraordinarily persistent, and very easily encouraged; it is safest to err on the side of caution until you are accustomed.

The people of Brazil represent a unique racial mix: it is not uncommon for the children **Colour** of one family to be of several different colours. Individuals are often described by the colour of their skin (ranging through several shades of brown), and 'white' can refer to people who would not necessarily be thought white in Europe or North America. Generally speaking, the emphasis is on colour rather than racial origins.

Essentials

Racial discrimination is illegal in Brazil. There is, however, a complex class system which is informed both by heritage and by economic status. This effectively discriminates against the poor, who are chiefly (but by no means exclusively) black due to the lack of inherited wealth among those whose ancestors were servants and slaves. Some Brazilians might assume that a black person is poor, therefore of low status. Black visitors to the country may encounter racial prejudice. We have also received a report from a black North American woman who was the subject of sexual advances by non-Brazilian, white tourists. Black women travelling with a white man may experience some problems, which should disappear with the realization that your partnership is not a commercial arrangement. A surprising number of Brazilians are unaware that black Europeans exist, so you could become the focus of some curiosity.

Time-keeping Brazilians have a very 'relaxed' attitude towards time. It is quite normal for them to arrive an hour or so late even for business appointments. If you expect to meet someone more or less at an exact time, you can add 'em punto' or 'a hora inglesa' (English time) but be prepared to wait anyway.

Tipping Tipping is usual, but less costly than in most other countries, except for porters. In restaurants, tip 10% of bill if no service charge is added, but give a small tip if there is. Taxi drivers are not tipped. To cloakroom attendants give a small tip; cinema usherettes, none; hairdressers, 10-15%; porters, fixed charges but tips as well; airport porters, about US$0.50 per item.

Prohibitions Despite the wide distribution and use of drugs such as marijuana and cocaine, they are still illegal and you will face a heavy sentence if you are caught with them. Be especially aware when crossing borders and on no account bring coca leaves from Bolivia. A campaign against the exploitation of minors for sexual purposes gained wide publicity in 1997 (in Brazilian law a minor is considered to be under the age of 18). Although the local bikinis leave little to the imagination you will be prosecuted for nude bathing except on an official nudist beach of which there are very few. **Never** carry firearms. Their possession could land you in serious trouble.

Responsible tourism
See also ecotourism, page 35

Travel to the furthest corners of the globe is now commonplace and the mass movement of people for leisure and business is a major source of foreign exchange and economic development in many parts of South America. In some regions (eg the Galapagos Islands and Machu Picchu) it is probably the most significant economic activity.

The benefits of international travel are self-evident for both hosts and travellers – employment, increased understanding of different cultures, business and leisure opportunities. At the same time there is clearly a downside to the industry. Where visitor pressure is high and/or poorly regulated, adverse impacts to society and the natural environment may be apparent. Paradoxically, this is as true in undeveloped and pristine areas (where culture and the natural environment are less 'prepared' for even small numbers of visitors) as in major resort destinations.

The travel industry is growing rapidly and increasingly the impacts of this supposedly 'smokeless' industry are becoming apparent. These impacts can seem remote and unrelated to an individual trip or holiday (eg air travel is clearly implicated in global warming and damage to the ozone layer, resort location and construction can destroy natural habitats and restrict traditional rights and activities), but individual choice and awareness can make a difference in many instances (see box), and collectively, travellers are having a significant effect in shaping a more responsible and sustainable industry.

In an attempt to promote awareness of and credibility for responsible tourism, organizations such as Green Globe (greenglobe@compuserve.com, T020-79308333)

A few ideas

Where possible choose a destination, tour operator or hotel with a proven ethical and environmental commitment – if in doubt ask;

Spend money on locally produced (rather than imported) goods and services and use common sense when bargaining – your few dollars saved may be a week's salary to others;

Use water and electricity carefully – travellers may receive preferential supply while the needs of local communities are overlooked;

Learn about local etiquette and culture – consider local norms and behaviour and dress appropriately for local cultures and situations;

Protect wildlife and other natural resources – don't buy souvenirs or goods made from wildlife unless they are clearly sustainably produced and are not protected under CITES legislation (CITES controls trade in endangered species);

Don't give money or sweets to children – it encourages begging – instead give to a recognized project, charity or school;

Always ask before taking photographs or videos of people;

Consider staying in local accommodation rather than foreign owned hotels – the economic benefits for host communities are far greater – and there are far greater opportunities to learn about local culture.

and the Center for Environmentally Sustainable Tourism (CERT) (T01268-795772) in the UK now offer advice on destinations and sites that have achieved certain commitments to conservation and sustainable development. Generally these are larger mainstream destinations and resorts, but they are still a useful guide and increasingly aim to provide information on smaller operations.

Of course travel can have beneficial impacts and this is something to which every traveller can contribute – many national parks are part funded by receipts from visitors. Similarly, travellers can promote patronage and protection of important archaeological sites and heritage through their interest and contributions via entrance and performance fees. They can also support small-scale enterprises by staying in locally run hotels and hostels, eating in local restaurants and by purchasing local goods, supplies and arts and crafts.

In fact, since the Responsible Travel section was first introduced in the *South American Handbook* in 1992 there has been a phenomenal growth in *tourism that promotes and supports the conservation of natural environments and is also fair and equitable to local communities*. This ecotourism segment is probably the fastest growing sector of the travel industry and provides a vast and growing range of destinations and activities in South America. For example, the Una Ecopark in Bahia offers visits and experiences in Brazil's Atlantic forest (one of the most endangered ecosystems in the world). A visit to the Park provides opportunities to undertake walks in the forest canopy walkway suspended high above the forest floor (T/F0XX73-6341118, Vrisea@bitsnet.com.br). Other initiatives can be found in São Paulo state (amazonadv@aol.com).

While the authenticity of some ecotourism operators' claims need to be interpreted with care, there is clearly both a huge demand for this type of activity and also significant opportunities to support worthwhile conservation and social development initiatives.

Organizations such as Conservation International (T202-4295660, www.ecotour. org), the Eco-Tourism society (T802-4472121, http://ecotourism.org), Planeta (www2.planeta.com/mader) and the UK-based Tourism Concern (T020-77533330, www.gn.apc.org/tourismconcern) have begun to develop and/or promote ecotourism projects and destinations and their web sites are an excellent source of information and details for sites and initiatives throughout South America.

Essentials

Additionally, UK organizations such as Earthwatch (T01865-311601, www.earth watch.org) and Discovery International (T020-72299881, www.discoveryinitiatives. com) offer opportunities to participate directly in scientific research and development projects throughout the region.

South America offers unique and unforgettable experiences – often based on the natural environment, cultural heritage and local society. These are the reasons many of us choose to travel and why many more will want to do so in the future. Shouldn't we provide an opportunity for future travellers and hosts to enjoy the quality of experience and interaction that we take for granted?

Safety

Personal safety in Brazil has deteriorated of recent years, largely because of economic hardship, and crime is increasing. Some recommend avoiding all large cities, but efforts are being made to improve the situation in major tourist centres like Rio de Janeiro and Salvador. The situation is far less insecure in smaller towns and in the country. Where you need to take most care is in crowded places, eg bus stations, markets, because this is where opportunistic crime occurs. If you are aware of the dangers, act confidently and use your common sense, you will lessen many of the risks.

Protecting money & valuables Apart from the obvious precautions of not wearing jewellery (wear a cheap, plastic *digital* watch), do not camp or sleep out in isolated places and if you are hitchhiking, never accept a lift in a car with two people in it.

Consider buying clothing locally to avoid looking like a gringo. Take only your towel and lotion to the beach, tuck enough money for cold drinks into your trunks/bikini bottom. A few belongings can safely be left at a bar. If you are held up and robbed, it is worth asking for the fare back to where you are staying. It is not uncommon for thieves to oblige. Do carry some cash, to hand over if you are held up. Never trust anyone telling 'sob stories' or offering 'safe rooms', when looking for a hotel, always choose the room yourself. Ted Stroll of San Francisco advises, "remember that economic privation has many Brazilians close to the edge, and that they are probably as ashamed of exploiting you as you are angry at being exploited". The corollary is be generous to those who give you a good deal.

Always photocopy your passport, air ticket and other documents, make a record of travellers' cheque and credit card numbers and keep them separately from the originals. Leave another set of records at home. Keep all documents secure; hide your main cash supply in different places or under your clothes: extra pockets sewn inside shirts and trousers, pockets closed with a zip or safety pin, moneybelts (best worn below the waist rather than outside or at it or around the neck), neck or leg pouches, a thin chain for attaching a purse to your bag or under your clothes and elasticated support bandages for keeping money and cheques above the elbow or below the knee have been repeatedly recommended (the last by John Hatt in *The Tropical Traveller*). Keep cameras in bags or briefcases; take spare spectacles (eyeglasses). If you wear a shoulder bag in a market, carry it in front of you.

If someone follows you when you're in the street, let him catch up with you and 'give him the eye'. While you should take local advice about being out at night, do not assume that daytime is safer than night-time. If walking after dark, walk in the road, not on the pavement/sidewalk.

Avoiding con tricks Be wary of 'plainclothes policemen'; insist on seeing identification and on going to the police station by main roads. Do not hand over your identification (or money – which he should not need to see anyway) until you are at the station. On no account take them directly back to your lodgings. Be even more suspicious if he seeks confirmation of his status from a passer-by. If someone tries to obtain a bribe from you, insist on a receipt.

Do not leave valuables in hotel rooms, except where a safe is provided. Hotel safe deposits are generally (but not always) secure. If you cannot get a receipt for valuables in a hotel safe, seal the contents in a plastic bag and sign across the seal. Always keep an inventory of what you have deposited. If you can trust your hotel, leave any valuables you don't need in safe-deposit when sightseeing locally. If you don't trust the hotel, lock everything in your pack and secure that in your room (some people take eyelet-screws for padlocking cupboards or drawers). If you lose valuables, always report to the police and note details of the report – for insurance purposes. **Hotel security**

Visitors should not enter favelas except when accompanied by workers for NGOs, tour groups or other people who know the local residents well and are accepted by the community. Certain parts of the country are areas of drug cultivation and should be avoided. These are mentioned where appropriate in the travelling text. All border areas should be regarded with some caution because of smuggling activities. Violence over land ownership in parts of the interior have resulted in a 'Wild West' atmosphere in some towns which should therefore be passed through quickly. **Dangerous places**

When you have all your luggage with you at a bus or railway station, be especially careful. Take a taxi between airport/bus station/railway station and hotel, if you can possibly afford it. Keep your bags with you in the taxi and pay only when you and your luggage are safely out of the vehicle. Make sure the taxi has inner door handles, in case a quick exit is needed. Avoid night buses; never arrive at your destination at night. Major bus lines often issue a luggage ticket when bags are stored in the bus' hold. When getting on a bus, keep your ticket handy; someone sitting in your seat may be a distraction for an accomplice to rob you while you are sorting out the problem. If travelling alone, first-class *frescão* buses are a safe option as they always have an attendant who screens people who get on. **Public transport**

As mentioned above under **Prohibitions**, illegal drugs should be avoided. Not only will you be entering the criminal underground with all the associated risks, but you are also opening yourself up to extortion. **Drugs**

Red-light districts should also be given a wide berth as there are reports of drinks being drugged with a substance popularly known as 'Good night Cinderella'. This leaves the victim easily amenable to having their possessions stolen, or worse.

This can happen anywhere in the world. If you are the victim of a sexual assault, you are advised in the first instance to contact a doctor (this can be your home doctor if you prefer). You will need tests to determine whether you have contracted any sexually transmitted diseases; you may also need advice on post-coital contraception. You should also contact your embassy, where consular staff are very willing to help in cases of assault. **Rape**

The main areas where violent crime occurs are places that no visitor should go anyway. If the worst does happen and you are threatened with a firearm, don't panic, hand over your valuables and the incident should pass quickly. Do not resist, but report the crime to the local tourist police later. It is extremely rare for a tourist to be hurt during a robbery in Brazil. **Violent crime**

Many points of security, dress and language have been covered already. First-time exposure to countries where sections of the population live in extreme poverty or squalor and may even be starving can cause odd psychological reactions in visitors. So can the exceptional curiosity extended to visitors, especially women. Simply be prepared for this and try not to over-react. These additional hints have mainly been supplied by women, but most apply to any single traveller. When you set out, err on **Women travellers** the side of caution until your instincts have adjusted to the customs of a new culture. If, as a single woman, you can befriend a local woman, you will learn much more about the country you are visiting. Unless actively avoiding foreigners like yourself, don't go too far from the beaten track; there is a very definite 'gringo trail' which you can join, or follow, if seeking company. This can be helpful when looking for safe accommodation, especially if arriving after dark (which is best avoided). Remember that for a single woman a taxi at night can be as dangerous as wandering around on her own. At borders dress as smartly as possible. It is easier for men to take the friendliness of locals at face value; women may be subject to much unwanted attention. To help minimize this, do not wear suggestive clothing and, advises Alex Rossi of Jawa Timur, Indonesia, do not flirt. By wearing a wedding ring, carrying a photograph of your 'husband' and 'children', and saying that your 'husband' is close at hand, you may dissuade an aspiring suitor. If politeness fails, do not feel bad about showing offence and departing. When accepting a social invitation, make sure that someone knows the address and the time you left. Ask if you can bring a friend (even if you do not intend to do so). A good rule is always to act with confidence, as though you know where you are going, even if you do not. Someone who looks lost is more likely to attract unwanted attention. Do not disclose to strangers where you are staying. (Much of this information was supplied by Alex Rossi, and by Deirdre Mortell of Carrigaline, Co Cork.)

Police There are several types of police: Polícia Federal, civilian dressed, who handle all federal law duties, including immigration. A subdivision is the Polícia Federal Rodoviária, uniformed, who are the traffic police on federal highways. Polícia Militar are the uniformed, street police force, under the control of the state governor, handling all state laws. They are not the same as the Armed Forces' internal police. Polícia Civil, also state-controlled, handle local laws and investigations. They are usually in civilian dress, unless in the traffic division. Polícia Civil are to merge with Polícia Militar in the near future. In cities, the Prefeitura controls the Guarda Municipal, who handle security. Tourist police operate in places with a strong tourist presence. In case of difficulty, visitors should seek them out in the first instance.

Where to stay

Hotels The best guide to hotels in Brazil is the *Guia Brasil Quatro Rodas*, with good maps of
For a quick reference towns. Motels are specifically intended for very short-stay couples: there is no stigma
price guide to our hotel attached and they usually offer good value (the rate for a full night is called the
categories, see inside the *pernoite*), though the decor can be a little unsettling. The type known as *hotel familiar*,
front cover to be found in the interior – large meals, communal washing, hammocks for children –
is much cheaper, but only for the enterprising. *Pousadas* are the equivalent of bed-and-breakfast, often small and family run, although some are very sophisticated and correspondingly priced. Usually hotel prices include breakfast; there is no reduction if you don't eat it. In the better hotels (our category A and upwards), the breakfast is well worth eating: rolls, ham, eggs, cheese, cakes, fruit. Normally the *apartamento* is a room with a bath; a *quarto* is a room without a bath. Leave rooms in good time so frigobar bills can be checked.

The star rating system for hotels (five-star hotels are not price-controlled) is not the standard used in North America or Europe.

Business visitors are strongly recommended to book accommodation in advance, and this can be easily done for Rio or São Paulo hotels with representation abroad. Varig has a good hotel reservation service, with discounts of up to 50% for its passengers.

It's a good idea to book accommodation in advance in small towns which are popular at weekends with city dwellers eg near São Paulo and Rio de Janeiro.

Hotel prices and facilities

*Prices include taxes and service charges, but are without meals unless otherwise stated. They are based on a double room, except in the **E** and **F** ranges, where prices are almost always per person.*

***LL** (over US$150) to **AL** (US$66-99) Hotels in these categories can be found in most of the large cities in Brazil, but especially so in areas with a strong concentration of tourists or business travellers. They should offer pool, sauna, gym, jacuzzi, all business facilities (including email), several restaurants and bars. A safe box is usually provided in each room. In cities such as São Paulo and Rio de Janeiro the top hotels compare with the highest standards in the world, although service can sometimes still be very Brazilian.*

***A** (US$46-65) and **B** (US$31-45) Hotels in these categories should provide more than the standard facilities and a fair degree of comfort. Most include a good breakfast and many offer extras such as colour TV, minibar, a/c and a swimming pool. They may also provide tourist information and their own transport for airport pickups. Service is generally good and most accept credit cards, although a lower rate for cash is often offered.*

***C** (US$21-30) and **D** (US$12-20) Hotels in these categories range from very comfortable to functional and there are some real bargains to be had. You should expect your own bathroom, constant hot water, a towel, soap and toilet paper. There is sometimes a restaurant and a communal sitting area. In tropical regions rooms are usually equipped with a/c, although this may be rather old. Hotels used to catering for foreign tourists and backpackers often have luggage storage, money exchange and kitchen facilities.*

***E** (US$7-11) and **F** (US$6 and under) Hotels in these categories are often extremely simple with bedside or ceiling fans, shared bathrooms and little in the way of furniture. Breakfast when included is very simple, usually no more than a bread roll and coffee. The best accommodation and facilities for under US$10 per night is generally found in the Youth Hostels (see below), although tourist areas with high quantities of bed spaces such as Porto Seguro often have good quality rooms at this price during low season.*

Roteiros de Charme In some 30 locations in the Southeast and Northeast, this is an association of hotels and *pousadas* which aims to give a high standard of accommodation in establishments which represent the town they are in. It is a private initiative. If you are travelling in the appropriate budget range (our A price range upwards), you can plan an itinerary which takes in these high class hotels, with a reputation for comfort and good food, and some fine places of historical and leisure interest. Roteiros de Charme hotels are listed in the text and any one of them can provide information on the group. Alternatively, contact the office in the *Caesar Park Hotel* in Rio de Janeiro (Av Vieira Souto 460, Ipanema, F021-2871592, or www.roteirosdecharme.com.br).

The service stations (*postos*) and hostels (*dormitórios*) along the main roads provide excellent value in room and food, akin to truck-driver type accommodation in Europe, for those on a tight budget.

Advice & suggestions

Most sizeable towns have laundromats with self service machines. *Lavanderias* do the washing for you but are very expensive.

The electric showers used in innumerable hotels should be checked for obvious flaws in the wiring; try not to touch the rose while it is producing hot water.

Some taxi drivers will try to take you to the expensive hotels, who pay them commission for bringing in custom. Beware!

Essentials

Cockroaches are ubiquitous and unpleasant, but not dangerous. Take some insecticide powder if staying in cheap hotels; Baygon (Bayer) has been recommended. Stuff toilet paper in any holes in walls that you may suspect of being parts of cockroach runs.

Away from the main commercial centres, many hotels, restaurants and bars have inadequate water supplies. Almost without exception, used toilet paper should not be flushed down the pan, but placed in the receptacle provided. This applies even in quite expensive hotels. Failing to observe this custom will block the pan or drain, a considerable health risk. Some people stand on the toilet seat (facing the wall – easier to balance).

Youth hostels For information about Youth Hostels contact Federação Brasileira dos Albergues da Juventude, R dos Andradas 1137, conj 214, Porto Alegre, Rio Grande do Sul, CEP 90.020-007, www.albergues.com.br; its annual book provides a full list of good value accommodation, with the addresses of the regional representatives. Also see the Internet Guide to Hostelling which has a list of Brazilian youth hostels: www.hostels. com/br.html; a list of hostels can also be found on www.skynet.com.br/albergue/ telbras.html.

Low-budget travellers with student cards (photograph needed) can often use the Casa dos Estudantes (CEU) network.

Camping Members of the Camping Clube do Brasil or those with an international campers' card pay only half the rate of a non-member, which is US$10-15 per person. The Clube has 43 sites in 13 states and 80,000 members. For enquiries, Camping Clube do Brasil, Divisão de Campings, R Senador Dantas 75, 29th floor, Centro, Rio de Janeiro, CEP 20037-900, T0XX21-2103171. It may be difficult to get into some Camping Clube campsites during the high season (January-February). Private campsites charge about US$8 per person. For those on a very low budget and in isolated areas where there is no campsite, service stations can be used as camping sites (Shell stations recommended); they have shower facilities, watchmen and food; some have dormitories; truck drivers are a mine of information. There are also various municipal sites. Campsites often tend to be some distance from public transport routes and are better suited to those with their own transport. Never camp at the side of a road; wild camping is generally not possible.

Good camping equipment may be purchased in Brazil and there are several rental companies. Camping gas cartridges are easy to buy in sizeable towns in the south, eg in HM shops. *Guia de Camping* is produced by Artpress, R Araçatuba 487, São Paulo 05058; it lists most sites and is available in bookshops in most cities. Quatro Rodas' *Guia Brasil* lists main campsites.

Homestays Experiment in International Living Ltd, 287 Worcester Rd, Malvern, Worcestershire, WR14 1AB, T01684-562577, F562212, or Friesdorferstrasse 194A, 53175 Bonn 9, T0228-957220, F358282, can arrange stays with families from one to four weeks in Brazil; EIL has offices in 38 countries. This has been recommended as an excellent way to meet people and learn the language.

Getting around

Air

Because of the great distances, flying is often the most practical option. Internal air services are highly developed, but expensive. The larger cities are linked with each other several times a day. A monthly magazine, *Panrotas*, gives all the timetables and fares. All national airlines offer excellent service on their internal flights. The largest airlines are *TAM*, *Transbrasil*, *Varig* and *Vasp*. Two other airlines, *Rio-Sul* and *Nordeste* (both allied to Varig), have extensive networks. Smaller airlines include *Penta*, who have recently built up a wide and cheap network throughout the Amazon region, and *Pantanal*, mainly operating flights between São Paulo state and Mato Grosso do Sul.

For addresses and telephone numbers of airline offices, see Directory of individual towns

Between 2200 and 0600, internal flights cost 30% less than daytime flights. (Ask for the *vôo coruja*.) On some flights couples can fly for the price of 1½. A 30% discount is offered on flights booked seven days or more in advance. Discounts on flights are available at airports a few hours before a domestic flight. It is well worth enquiring in detail. Double check all bookings (reconfirm frequently) and information given by ground staff as economic cutbacks have led to pressure on ground service (but not to flight service). Toll free numbers for the major airlines are given under domestic airlines.

Nordeste Av Tancredo Neves 1672, 1o andar, Pituba, Salvador, BA 41820-020, T0800-992004, www.nordeste.com. *Pantanal* Av Nações Unidas, São Paulo, SP 04578-000, T0800-125833, www.pantanal-airlines.com.br. *Penta* Travessa 15 de Novembro 183, Santarém, PA 68005-290, T091-5221014, F5226025. *Rio-Sul* Av Rio Branco 85, 10° andar, Rio de Janeiro, RJ 20040-004, T0800-992004, www.rio-sul.com. *TAM* R Gen Pantaleão Teles 210, São Paulo, SP 04355-900, T0800-123100, www.tam.com.br. *Transbrasil* R Gen Pantaleão Teles 40, São Paulo, SP 04355-900, T0800-151151, www.transbrasil.com.br. *Varig* Av Almte Silvio de Noronha 365, Rio de Janeiro, RJ 20021-010, T0800-997000, www.varig.com.br. *Vasp* Edif VASP, Aeroporto Congonhas, Praça Comandante Lineu Gomes, São Paulo, SP 04626-910, T0800-998277, www.vasp.com.br.

Domestic airlines

TAM, Transbrasil, Varig and *Vasp* offer good value 21-day air passes for people resident outside of Brazil. There are no discounts for children and infants pay 10% of the price. The **Varig airpass** covers three zones: All Brazil US$540 high season (490 low) for five flights (six if Santarém is included), with a maximum of four extra coupons available for US$100 each; Central and South Brazil US$400 (350 low season) with a maximum of four coupons; and North East Brazil US$340 (290 low season) with a maximum of four coupons (Varig sells 'linking' flights from São Paulo or Rio to the North East for US$150 return). Routes must be specified before arrival. High season is 10 December-29 February, 25 June-25 July. Amendments may be made once prior to commencement of travel at US$30 per change. The Varig pass is only available to travellers arriving in Brazil from the UK with Varig or British Airways. A new Airpass 500 (1999), costing US$450, is valid for 21 days with unlimited coupons.

Airpasses

The **Transbrasil airpass**, also divided into three zones, is available to individuals arriving on the services of other carriers as well as their own. Unlike the *Varig* pass, it does not have the facility to start the North East pass in São Paulo or Rio and it has no Santarém connection. Both *Varig* and *Transbrasil* require an itinerary to be specified and reserved at time of purchase. It is essential to check all arrangements very carefully.

The All Brazil **Vasp airpass** costs US$440 for five flights with a maximum of four extra coupons available for US$100 each (must be purchased with the air pass). A maximum of two connections can be made, but there is no high or low season and it is only available to non-residents of Brazil arriving in Brazil on a *Vasp* flight.

Essentials

The **TAM airpass** is similar to the *Varig* airpass except that you can arrive in Brazil on any airline; two connections are permitted at specified hubs, but these must not exceed four hours and re-routing is permitted for US$50.

Nordeste have an **Air Pass Bahia**, three stops around Bahia for approximately US$170.

All airpasses must be purchased outside Brazil, no journey may be repeated and none may be used on the Rio-São Paulo shuttle. Make sure you have two copies of the airpass invoice when you arrive in Brazil; otherwise you will have to select all your flights when you book the first one. Remember that domestic airport tax has to be paid at each departure. Hotels in the Tropical and Othon chains, and others, offer discounts of 10% to Varig airpass travellers; check with *Varig*, who have a hotel reservation service (Av Paulista 1765, first floor, São Paulo, SP 01311-200, T0XX11-2532003, F2533510). Promotions on certain destinations offer a free flight, hotel room etc; enquire when buying the airpass. We have been told that it is advisable for users of the airpasses to book all their intended flights in advance or on arrival in Brazil, especially around summer holiday and Carnival time. Converting the voucher can take some hours, do not plan an onward flight immediately, check at terminals that the airpass is still registered, faulty cancellations have been reported. Cost and restrictions on the airpass are subject to change. An alternative is to buy an internal flight ticket which includes several stops.

Small scheduled domestic airlines operate Brazilian-built *Bandeirante* 16-seater prop-jets into virtually every city and town with any semblance of an airstrip. **NB** Internal flights often have many stops and are therefore quite slow. Most airports have left-luggage lockers (US$2 for 24 hours). Seats are often unallocated on internal flights; board in good time.

Domestic air routes

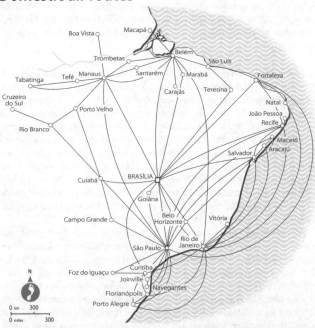

Boat

The main areas where travel by boat is practical (and often necessary) are the Amazon region, along the São Francisco River and along the Atlantic coast. There are also some limited transport services through the Pantanal. *Clipper Voyages*, Albany House, Suite 404, 324/326 Regent St, London, W1R 5AA, T020-74362931, has a 122-passenger expedition cruise ship which sails the Amazon and parts of the Brazilian coast.

See also page 598 for details of river transport in the Amazon

Train

There are 30,379 km of railways which are not combined into a unified system. Brazil has two gauges and there is little transfer between them. Two more gauges exist for the isolated Amapá Railway and the tourist-only São João del Rei line. There are passenger services in the states of Rio de Janeiro and São Paulo. More and more services are being withdrawn. Full details are given in the text.

Road network

Though the best paved highways are heavily concentrated in the southeast, those serving the interior are being improved to all-weather status and many are paved. Brazil has over 1,650 000 km of highways, of which 150,000 km are paved, and several thousand more all-weather. Most main roads between principal cities are paved. Some are narrow and therefore dangerous. Many are in poor condition.

Bus

There is no lack of road transport between the principal cities of Brazil. There are three standards of bus: *comum*, or *convencional* (conventional), which are quite slow, not very comfortable and fill up quickly; *executivo* (executive), which are a few reais more expensive, comfortable (many have reclining seats), but don't stop to pick up passengers *en route* and are therefore safer; and *leito* (literally, bed), which run at night between the main centres, offering reclining seats with foot and leg rests, toilets, and sometimes refreshments, at double the normal fare. For journeys over 100 km, most buses have chemical toilets. Air conditioning can make *leito* buses cold at night, so take a blanket or sweater (and plenty of toilet paper); on some services blankets are supplied. Some companies have hostess service. Ask for window seats (*janela*), or odd numbers if you want the view.

Brazilian bus services have a top speed limit of 80 kph (buses are supposed to have governors fitted). They stop fairly frequently (every 2-4 hours) for snacks. The cleanliness of these *postos* is generally good, though may be less so in the poorer regions. Standards of comfort on buses and in *postos* vary from line to line, which can be important on long journeys. Take something to drink on buses in the north.

Bus stations for interstate services and other long distance routes are usually called *rodoviárias*. They are frequently outside the city centres and offer fair facilities in the way of snack bars, lavatories, left-luggage stores ('guarda volume'), local bus services and information centres. Buy bus tickets at rodoviárias (most now take credit cards), not from travel agents who add on surcharges. Reliable bus information is hard to come by, other than from companies themselves. It is not easy to sell back unused bus tickets. Some bus companies have introduced a system enabling passengers to purchase return tickets at the point of departure, rather than individual tickets for each leg. Buses usually arrive and depart in very good time; you cannot assume departure will be delayed.

Many town buses have turnstiles which can be inconvenient if you are carrying a large pack. Urban buses normally serve local airports.

Travel in the back of trucks used to be common in the North and Northeast but is now being replaced by frequent bus and minibus services between smaller towns.

Taxi

Rates vary from city to city, but are consistent within each city. At the outset, make sure the meter is cleared and shows tariff 1, except 2300-0600, Sunday, and in December when 2 is permitted. Check that the meter is working; if not, fix the price in advance. The radio taxi service costs about 50% more but cheating is less likely. Taxi services offered by smartly dressed individuals outside larger hotels usually cost twice as much as ordinary taxis. If you are seriously cheated note the number of the taxi and insist on a signed bill, threatening to go to the police; it can work.

A new service in the last year or so is the Moto-Taxi, which is much more economical for the majority of the population. This is not a recommended form of travel because, apart from the unreliability of Brazilian roads, many Moto-Taxis are unlicensed and there have been a number of robberies of passengers.

Car

Any foreigner with a passport can purchase a Brazilian car and travel outside Brazil if it is fully paid for, or if permission is obtained from the financing body in Brazil. Foreigners do not need the CPF tax document (needed by Brazilians – you only have to say you are a tourist) to purchase a car, and the official purchase receipt is accepted as proof of ownership. Sunday papers carry car advertisements and there are second-hand car markets on Sunday mornings in most cities – but don't buy an alcohol-driven car if you propose to drive outside Brazil. It is essential to have an external intake filter fitted, or dust can rapidly destroy an engine. VW Combi vans are cheapest in Brazil where they are made, they are equivalent to the pre-1979 model in Europe. Be sure to travel with a car manual and good quality tools, a VW dealer will advise. There are VW garages throughout the continent, but parts (German or Latin American) are not always interchangeable. In the main, though, there should be no problems with large components (eg gears). If a lot of time is to be spent on dirt roads, the Ford Chevrolet pickup is more robust. A letter in Spanish from your consul explaining your aims and that you will return the vehicle to Brazil can make life much easier at borders and check points. Brazilian cars may not meet safety regulations in North America and Europe, but they can be easily resold in Brazil.

In 1998 new driving laws were introduced which impose severe fines for many infringements of traffic regulations. Driving licences will be endorsed with points for infringements; 20 points = loss of licence.

Fuel It is virtually impossible to buy premium grades of petrol/gasoline anywhere. With alcohol fuel you need about 50% more alcohol than regular gasoline. Larger cars have a small extra tank for 'gasolina' to get the engine started; remember to keep this topped up. Fuel is only 85 octane (owing to high methanol content), so be prepared for bad consumption and poor performance and starting difficulties in non-Brazilian cars in winter. Diesel fuel is cheap and a diesel engine may provide fewer maintenance problems. Service stations are free to open when they like. Very few open during Carnival week. **Fuel prices vary from week to week and region to region**: *alcool comun* US$0.35-0.45 per litre; *gasolina comun* US$0.65-0.73 per litre; *gasolina maxi* US$0.68-0.75 per litre; *maxigold* US$0.75 per litre. There is no unleaded fuel. Diesel is sold for commercial and public service vehicles and costs US$0.32 per litre, the same price as oil.

Essentials

What kind of motoring you do will depend on what kind of car you set out with. While **The machine** a normal car will reach most places of interest, high ground clearance is useful for badly surfaced or unsurfaced roads and for fording rivers. Four-wheel drive vehicles are recommended for greater flexibility in mountain and jungle territory, although you may not get far in Amazonas, where roads are frequently impassable. Wherever you travel you should expect from time to time to find roads that are badly maintained, damaged or closed during the wet season, and delays because of floods, landslides and huge potholes. There is also the possibility of hold-ups from major roadworks. Do not plan your schedules too tightly.

Preparing your own car for the journey is largely a matter of common sense: obviously **Preparation** any part that is not in first class condition should be replaced. It's well worth installing extra heavy-duty shock-absorbers (such as Spax or Koni) before starting out, because a long trip on rough roads in a heavily laden car will give heavy wear. Fit tubes on 'tubeless' tyres, since air plugs for tubeless tyres are hard to find, and if you bend the rim on a pothole, the tyre will not hold air. Take spare tubes, and an extra spare tyre. Also take spare plugs, fan-belts, radiator hoses and headlamp bulbs; even though local equivalents can easily be found in cities, it is wise to take spares for those occasions late at night or in remote areas when you might need them. You can also change the fanbelt after a stretch of long, hot driving to prevent wear (eg after 15,000 km/10,000 miles). If your vehicle has more than one fanbelt, always replace them all at the same time (make sure you have the necessary tools if doing it yourself). Find out about your car's electrics and filters and what spares may be required. Similarly, know how to handle problems arising from dirty fuel. It is wise to carry a spade, jump leads, tow rope and an air pump. Fit tow hooks to both sides of the vehicle frame. A 12 volt neon light for camping and repairs will be invaluable. Spare fuel containers should be steel and not plastic, and a siphon pipe is essential for those places where fuel is sold out of the drum. Take a 10 litre water container for self and vehicle. Note that in some areas gas stations are few and far between. Fill up when you see one: the next one may be out of fuel.

Spare no ingenuity in making your car secure. Your model should be the Brink's **Security** armoured van: anything less secure can be broken into by the determined and skilled thief. Use heavy chain and padlocks to chain doors shut, fit security catches on windows, remove interior window winders (so that a hand reaching in from a forced vent cannot open the window). All these will help, but none is foolproof. Anything on the outside – wing mirrors, spot lamps, motifs etc – is likely to be stolen too. So are wheels if not secured by locking nuts. Try never to leave the car unattended except in a locked garage or guarded parking space. Remove all belongings and leave the empty glove compartment open when the car is unattended. Also lock the clutch or accelerator to the steering wheel with a heavy, obvious chain or lock. Adult minders or street children will generally protect your car fiercely in exchange for a tip. Be sure to note down key numbers and carry spares of the most important ones (but don't keep all spares inside the vehicle).

Be very careful to keep **all** the papers you are given when you enter, to produce when **Documents** you leave. Bringing a car in by sea or air is much more complicated and expensive: *See Driving, page 48, for* generally you will have to hire an agent to clear it through customs, expensive and slow. *required documents*

Insurance for the vehicle against accident, damage or theft is best arranged in the country of origin, but it is getting increasingly difficult to find agencies who offer this service. In Latin American countries it is very expensive to insure against accident and theft, especially as you should take into account the value of the car increased by duties calculated in real (ie non devaluing) terms. If the car is stolen or written off you will be required to pay very high import duty on its value. Get the legally required minimum cover for third party insurance, not expensive, as soon as you can, because if you should be involved in an accident and are uninsured, your car could be confiscated. If anyone is hurt, do not pick them up (you may become liable). Seek assistance from the nearest police station or hospital if you are able to do so.

Car hire

It is essential to have a credit card in order to hire in Brazil; very few agencies accept travellers' cheques, dollars cash may not be accepted, but *reais* cash may qualify for a discount. Renting a car in Brazil is expensive: the cheapest rate for unlimited mileage for a small car is about US$50 per day. Minimum age for renting a car is 21. Companies operate under the names *aluguel de automóveis* or *autolocadores*. *Avis* is found only in the major cities and has only a time-and-mileage tariff. *National* (or *Localiza*) is represented in many places, often through licencees; it is connected with *InterRent/Europcar* in Europe, will accept credit cards from *InterRent/Europcar* and offers unlimited mileage if booked in advance from Europe on a fixed US$ rate. Compare prices of renting from abroad and in Brazil. If you intend to hire a car for a long time, buying and reselling a vehicle within Brazil may be a reasonable alternative. Toll free numbers for nationwide firms are *Avis*, T0800-558066 and *Localiza*, T0800-992000 (www.localiza.com.br).

Car hire insurance Check exactly what the hirer's insurance policy covers. In many cases it will only protect you against minor bumps and scrapes, not major accidents, nor 'natural' damage (eg flooding). Ask if extra cover is available. Also find out, if using a credit card, whether the card automatically includes insurance. Beware of being billed for scratches which were on the vehicle before you hired it.

Motorcycling

People are generally very amicable to motorcyclists and you can make many friends by returning friendship to those who show an interest in you.

The machine It should be off road capable, eg the BMW R80/100/GS for its rugged and simple design and reliable shaft drive, but a Kawasaki KLR 650s, Honda Transalp, XR600, or XR250, or the ubiquitous Yamaha XT600 Tenere would also be suitable. A road bike can go most places an off-road bike can go at the cost of greater effort.

Preparations Many roads are rough. Fit heavy duty front fork springs and the best quality rebuildable shock absorber you can afford (Ohlins, White Power). Fit lockable luggage such as Krausers (reinforce luggage frames) or make some detachable aluminium panniers. Fit a tank bag and tank panniers for better weight distribution. A large capacity fuel tank (Acerbis), +300 mile/480 km range is essential if going off the beaten track. A washable air filter is a good idea (K&N), also fuel filters and fueltap rubber seals. A good set of trails-type tyres, as well as a high mudguard, are useful. Get to know the bike before you go, ask the dealers in your country what goes wrong with it and arrange a link whereby you can get parts flown out to you. If using a fully enclosed chaincase on a chain driven bike, an automatic chain oiler, to stop it getting it, is a good idea. The Scott-Oiler (106 Clober Road, Milngavie, Glasgow G62 7SS, Scotland) has been recommended. Fill it with Sae 90 oil. A hefty bash plate/sump guard is invaluable.

Spares Reduce service intervals by half if driving in severe conditions. A spare rear tyre is useful but you can buy modern tyres in most capital cities. Take oil filters, fork and shock seals, tubes, a good manual, spare cables (taped into position), a plug cap and spare plug lead. A spare electronic ignition is a good idea, try and buy a second-hand one and make arrangements to have parts sent out to you. A first-class tool kit is a must and if riding a bike with a chain then a spare set of sprockets and an 'o' ring chain should be carried. Spare brake and clutch levers should also be taken as these break easily in a fall. Parts are few and far between, but mechanics are skilled at making do and can usually repair things.

Take a puncture repair kit and tyre levers. Find out about any weak spots on the bike and improve them. Get the book for international dealer coverage from your manufacturer, but don't rely on it. They frequently have few or no parts for modern, large machinery.

A tough waterproof jacket, comfortable strong boots, gloves and a helmet with which you can use glass goggles (Halycon) which will not scratch and wear out like a plastic visor. The best quality tent and camping gear that you can afford and a petrol stove which runs on bike fuel is helpful. | **Clothes & equipment**

This is not a problem in most parts of the country. Try not to leave a fully laden bike on its own. An Abus D or chain will keep the bike secure. A cheap alarm gives you peace of mind if you leave the bike outside a hotel at night. Most hotels will allow you to bring the bike inside. Look for hotels that have a courtyard or more secure parking and never leave luggage on the bike overnight or whilst unattended. | **Security**

Passport, International Driving Licence, bike registration document are necessary. Temporary import papers are given on entry, to be surrendered on leaving the country. | **Documents**

You must drain the fuel, oil and battery acid, or remove the battery, but it is easier to disconnect and seal the overflow tube. Tape cardboard over fragile bits and insist on loading the bike yourself. | **Shipping**

Cycling

A bicycle may not appear to be the most obvious vehicle for a major journey, but if you have time and reasonable energy it is probably one of the best. It can be ridden, carried by almost every form of transport from an aeroplane to a canoe, and can even be carried for short distances. Cyclists have many advantages over travellers using other forms of transport, since they can travel at their own pace, explore more remote regions and often meet people who are not normally in contact with tourists.

Unless you are planning a journey almost exclusively on paved roads – when a high quality touring bike such as a Dawes Super Galaxy would probably suffice – a mountain bike is strongly recommended. The good quality ones (and the cast iron rule is **never** to skimp on quality) are incredibly tough and rugged, with low gear ratios for difficult terrain, wide tyres with plenty of tread for good road-holding, cantilever brakes, and a low centre of gravity for improved stability. Although touring bikes – and to a lesser extent mountain bikes – and spares are available in the larger cities, remember that most locally manufactured goods are shoddy and rarely last. Buy everything you possibly can before you leave home. | **Choosing a bicycle**

A small but comprehensive tool kit (to include chain rivet and crank removers, a spoke key and possibly a block remover), a spare tyre and inner tubes, a puncture repair kit with plenty of extra patches and glue, a set of brake blocks, brake and gear cables and all types of nuts and bolts, at least 12 spokes (best taped to the chain stay), a light oil for the chain (eg Finish-Line Teflon Dry-Lube), tube of waterproof grease, a pump secured by a pump lock, a Blackburn parking block (a most invaluable accessory, cheap and virtually weightless), a cyclometer, a loud bell, and a secure lock and chain. *Richard's Bicycle Book* makes useful reading for even the most mechanically minded. | **Bicycle equipment**

Luggage and equipment Strong and waterproof front and back panniers are a must. When packed these are likely to be heavy and should be carried on the strongest racks available. Poor quality racks have ruined many a journey for they take incredible strain on unpaved roads. A top bag cum rucksack (eg Carradice) makes a good addition for use on and off the bike. A Cannondale front bag is good for maps, camera, compass etc. (Other recommended panniers are Ortlieb – front and back – which is waterpoof and almost 'sandproof', Mac-Pac, Madden and Karimoor.) 'Gaffa' tape is excellent for protecting vulnerable parts of panniers and for carrying out all manner of repairs.

All equipment and clothes should be packed in plastic bags to give extra protection against dust and rain. (Also protect all documents etc, carried close to the body, from sweat.) Always take the minimum clothing. It's better to buy extra items *en route* when you find you need them. Naturally the choice will depend on the terrain you are planning to cover, and whether rain is to be expected.

Useful tips Wind, not hills, is the enemy of the cyclist. Try to make the best use of the times of day when there is little; mornings tend to be best but there is no steadfast rule. Take care to avoid dehydration, by drinking regularly. In hot, dry areas with limited supplies of water, be sure to carry an ample supply. For food, carry the staples (sugar, salt, dried milk, tea, coffee, porridge oats, raisins, dried soups etc) and supplement these with whatever local foods can be found in the markets. Give your bicycle a thorough daily check for loose nuts or bolts or bearings. See that all parts run smoothly. A good chain should last 3,200 km or more but be sure to keep it as clean as possible – an old toothbrush is good for this – and to oil it lightly from time to time. Remember that thieves are attracted to towns and cities, so when sight-seeing, try to leave your bicycle with someone such as a café owner or a priest. Country people tend to be more honest and are usually friendly and very inquisitive. However, don't take unnecessary risks; always see that your bicycle is secure (most hotels will allow bikes to be kept in rooms). In more remote regions dogs can be vicious; carry a stick or some small stones to frighten them off. Traffic on main roads can be a nightmare; it is usually far more rewarding to keep to the smaller roads or to paths if they exist. Most cyclists agree that the main danger comes from other traffic. A rearview mirror has been frequently recommended to forewarn you of vehicles which are too close behind. You also need to watch out for oncoming, overtaking vehicles, unstable loads on trucks, protruding loads etc. Make yourself conspicuous by wearing bright clothing and a helmet. Most towns have a bicycle shop of some description, but it is best to do your own repairs and adjustments whenever possible. In an emergency it is amazing how one can improvise with wire, string, dental floss, nuts and bolts, odd pieces of tin or electrical 'Gaffa' tape!

The Expedition Advisory Centre, administered by the Royal Geographical Society, 1, Kensington Gore, London, SW7 2AR, has published a useful monograph entitled *Bicycle Expeditions*, by Paul Vickers. Published in March 1990, it is available direct from the Centre, price £6.50 (postage extra if outside the UK). (In the UK there is also the Cyclist's Touring Club, CTC, Cotterell House, 69 Meadrow, Godalming, Surrey, GU7 3HS, T01483-417217, cycling@ctc.org.uk, for touring and technical information.)

Hitchhiking

Information on hitchhiking (*carona* in Portuguese) suggests that it is difficult everywhere; drivers are reluctant to give lifts because passengers are their responsibility. Try at the highway police check points on the main roads (but make sure your documents are in order) or at the service stations (*postos*).

Keeping in touch

Points of contact

Details of organizations which can help sort out problems or give advice, such as embassies, consulates or cultural centres like the British Council and Alliance Française, can be found in the Directory of individual towns and cities.

Essentials

Language

No amount of dictionaries, phrase books or word lists will provide the same enjoyment of being able to converse directly with the people of Brazil. Learning Portuguese is an important part of the preparation for any trip there and you are encouraged to make the effort to grasp the basics before you go. As you travel you will pick up more of the language and the more you know, the more you will benefit from your stay. Efforts to speak Portuguese are greatly appreciated and for the low-budget traveller, Portuguese is essential. If you cannot lay your tongue to Portuguese, apologize for not being able to speak it and try Spanish, but note that the differences in the spoken languages are very much greater than appears likely from the printed page and you may not be understood: you will certainly have difficulty in understanding the answers.

See inside back cover for a list of useful words & phrases

There are Brazilian tutors in most cities (in London, see *Time Out* and *Leros*, the Brazilian magazine, for advertisements).

There is no standard Portuguese and there are many differences between the Portuguese of Portugal and Brazil. If learning Portuguese before you go to Brazil, get lessons with a Brazilian, or from a language course which teaches Brazilian Portuguese. Within Brazil itself, there are variations in pronunciation, intonation, phraseology and slang. This makes for great richness and for the possibility of great enjoyment in the language. Describing the complex Portuguese vocalic system is best left to the experts; it would take up too much space here. A couple of points which the newcomer to the language will spot immediately however are the use of the til (~) over a and o. This makes the vowel a nasal vowel; vowels also become nasal when a word ends in m or ns, when a vowel is followed by m + consonant, or by n + consonant. Another important point of spelling is that words ending in `i' and `u' are accented on the last syllable, though (unlike Spanish) no accent is used there. This is especially important in place names: Buriti, Guarapari, Caxambu, Iguaçu. Note also the use of ç, which changes the pronunciation of c from hard [k] to soft [s].

General pronunciation

Postal services

To send a standard letter or postcard to the USA costs US$0.45, to Europe US$0.53, to Australia or South Africa US$0.60. Air mail takes four to seven days to or from Britain or the US, whilst surface mail takes some four weeks. 'Caixa Postal' addresses should be used when possible. All places and streets in Brazil have a post code, *CEP*; these can be obtained from a book displayed in most post offices. You can buy charge collected stamps, Compraventa de Francamento (CF), for letters only, to be paid on delivery.

Letters & postcards

Franked and registered (insured) letters are normally secure, but check that the amount franked is what you have paid, or the item will not arrive. Aerogrammes are most reliable. It may be easier to avoid queues and obtain higher denomination stamps by buying at the philatelic desk at the main post office.

Parcels   The Post Office sells cardboard boxes for sending packages internally and abroad (they must be submitted open); pay by the kilo; you must fill in a list of contents; string and official sellotape are provided in all post offices. Courier services such as DHL, Federal Express and UPS (recommended) are useful, but note that they may not necessarily operate under those names.

Receiving mail   Postes restantes usually only hold letters for 30 days. Identification is required and it's a good idea to write your name on a piece of paper to help the attendant find your letters. Charge is usually minimal but often involves queuing at another counter to buy stamps which are attached to your letter and franked before it is given to you. Poste Restante for Amex customers is efficiently dealt with by the Amex agents in most large towns.

Telephone services

For the area codes see under individual towns, the inside front cover, or look in the telephone directory   There is a trunk dialling system (DDD) linking all parts of Brazil. Recent privatization of the telephone system has led to increased competition. The consumer must now choose a telephone company for long distance and international calls by inserting a two-digit code between the zero and the area code. Phone numbers are now printed thus: 0xx21 (0 for a national call, xx for the code of the phone company chosen, 21 for Rio de Janeiro, for example), followed by the seven-digit number of the subscriber.

Nationwide and international telephone operators and their codes are: *Embratel*, 21 (nationwide); *Telefônica*, 15 (state of São Paulo); *Telemar*, 31 (Alagoas, Amazonas, Amapá, Bahia, Ceará, Espírito Santo, Maranhão, most of Minas Gerais, Pará, Paraíba, Pernambuco, Piauí, Rio de Janeiro, Rio Grande do Norte, Roraima, Sergipe); *Tele Centro-Sul*, 14 (Acre, Goiás, Mato Grosso, Mato Grosso do Sul, Paraná, Rondônia, Santa Catarina, Tocantins and the cities of Brasília and Pelotas); *CTBC-Telecom*, 12 (some parts of Minas Gerais, Goiás, Mato Grosso do Sul and São Paulo state); *Intelig*, 23.

National calls   There are telephone boxes at airports, post offices, railway stations, hotels, most bars, restaurants and cafés, and in the main cities there are telephone kiosks, for local calls only, in the shape of large orange shells, for which fichas can be bought from bars, cafés and newsvendors; in Rio they are known as *orelhões* (big ears). Local phone calls and telegrams are quite cheap.

Phone cards are available from telephone offices, newstands, post offices and some chemists. They cost US$0.75 for 10 local calls up to US$3 for 90. Public boxes for intercity calls are blue. To use the telephone office, tell the operator which city or country you wish to call, go to the booth whose number you are given; make your call and you will be billed on exit. Not all offices accept credit cards. Collect calls within Brazil can be made from any telephone – dial 9, followed by the number, and announce your name and city. Local calls from a private phone are normally free.

If you need to find a telephone number, you can dial 102 in any city (*auxílio à lista*) and the operator will connect you to a prerecorded voice which will give the number. To find the number in a different city, dial the DDD code, followed by 121 (so, if you are in Salvador and want to know a Rio number, dial 021 121). If your Portuguese is not up to deciphering spoken numbers, ask a hotel receptionist, for example, to assist you.

International calls   At the moment it is possible to call abroad from public telephones only in areas with large numbers of foreign tourists such as Rio de Janeiro or Salvador. There are, however, boxes within most telephone offices for international calls. Make sure you buy at least one 90-unit card or pay at the desk after making your call from a booth. Calls are priced on normal and cheaper rates, depending on time of day. Check with the local phone company. Peak rate to Europe is US$4 per minute, to USA US$3. There is a 40% tax added to the cost of all telephonic and telegraphic communications, which makes international service extremely expensive.

NB Brazil is now linked to North America, Japan and most of Europe by trunk dialling (DDI). Codes are listed in the telephone directories. Home Country Direct is available from hotels, private phones or blue public phones to the following countries (prefix all numbers with 00080); Argentina 54, Australia 61, Belgium 03211, Bolivia 13, Canada 14, Chile 56 (Entel), 36 (Chile Sat), 37 (CTC Mundo), Colombia 57, Costa Rica 50, Denmark 45, France 33, Germany 49, Holland 31, Hong Kong 85212, Israel 97, Italy 39, Japan 81 (KDD), 83 (ITJ), 89 (Super Japan), Norway 47, Paraguay 18, Peru 51, Portugal 35, Singapore 65, Spain 34, Sweden 46, Switzerland 04112, UK 44 (BT Direct), USA 10 (AT&T), 12 (MCI), 16 (Sprint), 11 (Worldcom), Uruguay 59, Venezuela 58. For collect calls from phone boxes (in Portuguese: 'a cobrar'), dial 107 and ask for the *telefonista internacional*. No collect calls are available to New Zealand.

See also the inside front cover for international phone codes

Essentials

These have made a big impact in Brazil owing to past difficulties in getting fixed lines, especially outside the main towns. When using a *celular* telephone you do not drop the zero from the area code as you now have to when dialling from a fixed line. In Rio de Janeiro and São Paulo, mobile phones, or even a line for your own phone, can be hired. Pay-as-you-go phones are now available, which is another option for travellers. **NB** The systems in Brazil are mainly AMPS analog or TDMA digital. There are a few CDMA systems but no GSM.

Mobile phones

These operate in main post offices in major cities, at telephone offices, or from private lines. In the last case the international fax rates are as for phone calls; from the post office the rates are US$3-4 per page within Brazil, US$10.50 to Europe and US$9 to the USA. To receive a fax costs US$1.40.

Fax services

Internet and email

It is estimated that some three million people in Brazil are now on-line. Email is becoming more common and public access to the Internet is growing, with cybercafés opening in most large towns. There is usually an hourly charge and you can use partial hours. A website http://netcafeguide.com gives a regularly updated list of locations around the world.

For cybercafé locations and other places offering internet access see Communications, in the Directory under individual towns

Media

Nationwide TV channels are Globo based in Rio de Janeiro and SBT, Record, Bandeirantes based in São Paulo. Rede Amazônica operates in the northern region. TVE is an educational channel showing documentaries and original language films. Programming revolves around light entertainment, soap operas, foreign films dubbed in Portuguese and football.

Television

There is no national newspaper although the news magazines (see below) are distributed nationally. The main **Rio** papers are *Jornal do Brasil* (www.jb.com.br), *O Globo* (www.oglobo.com.br), *O Dia* (www.uol.com.br/odia) and *Jornal do Commércio* (www.jornaldocommercio.com.br). In **São Paulo** Morning: *O Estado de São Paulo* (www. estado.com.br), *Folha de São Paulo* (www.uol.com.br/fsp), *Gazeta Mercantil* (www.gazeta.com.br/) and *Diário de São Paulo*. Evening: *Jornal da Tarde*, *A Gazeta*, *Diário da Noite* and *Ultima Hora*. Around the country, the major cities have their own local press. Of particular note are *A Tarde* in Salvador (www.atarde.com.br), the *Diário de Pernambuco* in Recife (www.dpnet.com.br) and the *Estado de Minas* in Belo Horizonte (www.estaminas.com.br).

Newspapers

Foreign language newspapers include *The Brazilian Post* and *Sunday News* in English, and *Deutsche Zeitung* in German. In Europe, the *Euro-Brasil Press* is available in most capitals; it prints Brazilian and some international news in Portuguese. London office 23 Kings Exchange, Tileyard Rd, London N7 9AH, T020-77004033, F77003540, eurobrasilpress@compuserve.com.

Magazines   There are a number of good, informative weekly news magazines which are widely read: *Veja* (www.uol.com.br/veja), *Istoé* (www.uol.com.br/istoe), *Epoca* and *Exame*.

Radio   South America has more local and community radio stations than practically anywhere else in the world; a shortwave (world band) radio offers a practical means to brush up on the language, sample popular culture and absorb some of the richly varied regional music. International broadcasters such as the BBC World Service, the Voice of America and Boston (Mass)-based Monitor Radio International (operated by *Christian Science Monitor*) keep the traveller abreast of news and events, in English, Portuguese and Spanish.

Compact or miniature portables are recommended, with digital tuning and a full range of shortwave bands, as well as FM, long and medium wave. Detailed advice on radio models (around US$240 for a decent one) and wavelengths can be found in the annual publication, *Passport to World Band Radio* (Box 300, Penn's Park, PA 18943, USA), £14.99. Details of local stations is listed in *World TV and Radio Handbook* (WTRH), PO Box 9027, 1006 AA Amsterdam, The Netherlands, £19.99. Both of these, free wavelength guides and selected radio sets are available from the BBC World Service Bookshop, Bush House Arcade, Bush House, Strand, London WC2B 4PH, UK, T020-75572576.

English-language radio broadcasts daily at 15290 kHz, 19m Short Wave (Rádio Bras, Caixa Postal 04/0340, DF-70 323 Brasília).

Food and drink

Eating out
See also Useful words &
phrases on the inside
back cover

Meals are extremely large by European standards; if your appetites are small, you can order, say, one portion and one empty plate, and divide the portion. However, if you are in a position to do so tactfully, you may choose to offer the rest to a person with no food (many Brazilians do – observe the correct etiquette), alternatively you could ask for an *embalagem* (doggy bag) or get a takeaway called a *marmita* or *quentinha*. Most restaurants have this service but it is not always on the menu. Many restaurants now serve *comida por kilo* where you serve yourself and pay for the weight of food on your plate. Unless you specify to the contrary many restaurants will lay a *couvert* (*coberto opcional)*, olives, carrots etc, costing US$0.50-0.75.

The main meal is usually taken in the middle of the day; cheap restaurants tend not to be open in the evening. In a restaurant, always ask the price of a dish before ordering.

If travelling on a tight budget, remember to ask in restaurants for the *prato feito* or *sortido*, a money saving, excellent value *table-d'hôte* meal. The *prato comercial* is similar but rather better and a bit more expensive. *Lanchonetes* are cheap eating places where you generally pay before eating. *Salgados* (savoury pastries), *coxinha* (a pyramid of manioc filled with meat or fish and deep fried), *esfiha* (spicey hamburger inside an onion bread envelope), *empadão* (a filling – eg chicken – in sauce in a pastry case), *empadas* and *empadinhas* (smaller fritters of the same type), are the usual fare. *Pão de queijo* is a hot roll made with cheese. A *bauru* is a toasted sandwich which, in Porto Alegre, is filled with steak, while further north has tomato, ham and cheese filling. *Cocada* is a coconut and sugar biscuit.

Warning   Avoid mussels, marsh crabs and other shellfish caught near large cities: they are likely to have lived in a highly polluted environment.

Tap water in Brazil is not suitable to drink unless it has been passed through a filter. Bottled mineral water is the safest option.

Food and drink

Drinks *Bebidas*	**pineapple** *abacaxi*
beer *cerveja*	**strawberry** *morango*
coffee *café*	**watermelon** *melancia*
fruit juice *suco*	
hot chocolate *chocolate quente*	**Meat** *Carne*
milk *leite*	**beef** *bife*
mineral water *água mineral*	**chicken** *frango/galinha*
soft drink *refrigerante*	**fish** *peixe*
tea *chá*	**ham** *presunto*
tonic water *água tónica*	**hot dog** *cachorro quente*
whisky *uísque*	**kid** *cabrito*
wine *vinho*	**pork** *porco*
	toasted cheese and ham
Fruit *Frutas*	**sandwich** *misto quente*
apple *maçã*	**sausages** *salsichas*
banana *banana*	**steak** *filé*
coconut *coco*	**turkey** *peru*
grape *uva*	
lime *limão*	**Vegetables** *Legumes*
mango *manga*	**carrot** *cenoura*
orange *laranja*	**lettuce** *alface*
papaya *mamão*	**onion** *cebola*
passion fruit *maracujá*	**potato** *batata*

Essentials

Vegetarians For vegetarians, there is a growing network of restaurants in the main cities. In smaller places where food may be monotonous, try vegetarian for greater variety. We list several. Most also serve fish. Alternatives in smaller towns are the Arab and Chinese restaurants.

Bars These can vary from basic neighbourhood bars open to the street, often known as *pé sujos* or *botequins*, to sophisticated places with waiter service. Food and snacks are often served and there is usually some form of music, whether a live band or the customers providing their own in an improvised samba session with guitars and drums.

Different cuisines The most common dish is *bife (ou frango) com arroz e feijão*, steak (or chicken) with rice and the excellent Brazilian black beans. However, due to Brazil's rich cultural mix many other influences are found in the various regions. São Paulo is by far the best place for international and foreign cuisines. See also recipes for *sonhos* (small, sweet dumplings served in the south) page 400; *moqueca de peixe* (marinaded fish), page 427; coconut rice with shellfish, page 522; and *xinxim de galinha* (chicken in shrimp and peanut sauce served in the northeast), page 523.

Feijoada The most famous dish with beans is the *feijoada completa*: several meat ingredients (jerked beef, smoked sausage, smoked tongue, salt pork, along with spices, herbs and vegetables) are cooked with the beans. Manioc flour is sprinkled over it, and it is eaten with kale (*couve*) and slices of orange, and accompanied by glasses of *aguardente* (unmatured rum), usually known as *cachaça* (booze), though *pinga* (drop) is a politer term. Most restaurants serve the *feijoada completa* for Saturday lunch (up to about 1630). *See recipe in box, page 72*

Minas Gerais has two splendid special dishes involving pork, black beans, *farofa* and kale; they are *tutu á mineira* and *feijão tropeiro*. A white hard cheese (*queijo prata*) or a slightly softer one (*queijo Minas*) is often served for dessert with bananas, or guava or quince paste. *Comida mineira* is quite distinctive and very wholesome and you can often find restaurants serving this type of food in other parts of Brazil.

Traditional recipes

Feijoada Completa

Brazil's national meal requires lengthy preparation, usually a social activity with several family members milling around the kitchen. A satisfying casserole of meat and beans, which benefits from slow cooking and/or reheating, it may be prepared ahead of time (feijoada is traditionally eaten on Saturdays).

Substitute any unavailable meats with suitable alternatives: cheap cuts work best. A meal of 7 dishes, the casserole should be served with farofa, arroz Brasileiro (Brazilian rice), hot pepper and lime sauce, couve (kale greens) and slices of fresh orange.

Quantities

This quantity makes 8 generous portions.

Casserole ingredients

225g lean, unsliced smoked bacon
450g piece of salt or corned beef
450g piece of lean beef (eg chuck or braising)
450g fresh pork sausages
225g smoked spicy pork sausage (eg chorizo)
1 split pig's foot
1.4 kg smoked ox tongue
700g (4 cups) black beans, canned or dried
2 tbsp vegetable oil
2 chopped, medium onions
2 chopped cloves of garlic
2 large tomatoes, chopped and seeded
1 small hot chilli, seeded and chopped
salt and freshly ground pepper

Method

Cover the pig's foot in cold water and simmer in a covered pan until the meat falls off the bone (90 minutes). Allow it to cool, separate the meat from the bone and put the whole lot, with the liquid, in the fridge overnight. Cover any salted meats – tongue, bacon, salt beef – with cold water and soak overnight, with a cloth over the pan. If you are using dried beans, rinse and soak them overnight.

Next day, drain the beans and put them into a large casserole. Add the pig's foot and its liquid, plus enough cold water to fill the pan 5 cm above the beans, then simmer gently for 90 minutes with the lid on. While the beans are cooking, put the salted meats in fresh cold water to cover and simmer, covered, over a low heat for 1 hour.

After 90 minutes, add the bacon, salt beef and fresh beef to the beans, but leave the tongue cooking separately (it will take longer to become tender). Simmer both pans for two hours more. During this time, stir the beans regularly to keep them from sticking. The beans should become very soft and mushy: add hot water whenever they look dry. When the tongue is cooked, remove it from the heat, throw out the water and, when the meat is cool enough to handle, peel it and remove any bones or gristle. Add it to the beans. Prick the fresh sausages, cut up the smoked sausage and add them both to the casserole. Simmer for 15 minutes, adding enough hot water to keep the whole dish moist. Take the pan off the heat and leave to stand.

In a frying pan, heat the oil and sauté the onions, on a low heat, until they are soft (about 10 minutes). Add the garlic halfway through. Add the tomatoes and chilli; cook for a further 5 minutes or until the mixture is thick. Add salt and pepper, then mash a cupful of beans into the frying pan. Stir this mixture back into the casserole and return to a low heat for 10 minutes before serving.

Serving

Lift out all the meats and serve them on a large platter. The tongue should be sliced, heaped in the centre, with the slices overlapping. Slice the other meats and arrange them round the tongue in separate piles, with the sausages

Bahia has some excellent fish dishes (see the note on page 426); some restaurants in most of the big cities specialize in them. *Vatapá* is a good dish in the north; it contains shrimp or fish sauced with palm oil, or coconut milk. *Empadinhas de camarão* are worth trying; they are shrimp patties, with olives and heart of palm.

scattered in between. The bean mixture is served in a soup tureen. Overlapping orange slices go on another plate, and the other accompaniments are also served separately.

Farofa de Azeite Dendê

Toasted cassava meal accompanies nearly all Brazilian main courses. The basic flour is available from Portuguese grocers as farinha de mandioca, from African shops as cassava meal or manioc flour, and Asian suppliers call it gari. Dendê, or palm oil, is sold by African, Caribbean or Portuguese grocers. As an alternative, use soft butter.

To make 125g (1 cup) of farofa, stir it, dry, in a heavy frying pan over a low heat until it is pale brown: it's better to undercook than to let it burn. Add 2 tablespoons of palm oil, stirring constantly, until the farofa is well blended and a bright golden colour. Serve it in a bowl: farofa does not need to be hot.

Arroz Brasileiro

The only compulsory ingredients of this dish are the rice, onions and oil. This recipe, which serves 8, is fairly simple. Popular extras, added towards the end of the simmering time, are small shellfish, such as mussels, or pre-cooked chopped peppers.

Ingredients

450g (2 cups) long-grain rice
5 ml dendê or corn oil
1 small onion, finely chopped
1 clove garlic, crushed
700 ml (3 cups) water
salt

Method

Wash the rice in cold running water, drain it and put it into a bowl or pan. Cover it with hot water and leave to stand for 15 minutes. Pour it into a sieve and leave to drain for at least 10 minutes. Heat the oil in a large pan, then add the rice, onion and garlic. Keeping the heat very low, stir the mixture constantly with a wooden spoon until all the oil is absorbed and the rice is golden. Add the water and some salt, bring to a fast boil and then reduce the heat as low as possible. Cover the pan and leave to simmer gently for about 25 minutes, until the rice is tender and all the water has gone.

Molho de Pimenta e Limão

This fiery pepper and lime sauce forms the basis of Brazilian salsa, served with many dishes. As an accompaniment to feijoada completa, put it in a small separate bowl. Use tiny, hot chillis.

Ingredients

6 hot red or green chilli peppers, seeded and chopped
1 small onion, finely chopped
1 crushed garlic clove
125 ml lime (or lemon) juice
salt

Method

Either purée very briefly in a blender or crush the ingredients in a mortar, adding the lime juice a little at a time.

Couve

Kale, collard, winter greens, or any leafy green cabbage variety may be used. Brazilian markets sell machine-shredded kale: if this is unavailable, trim the leaves and cut them into fine strips using scissors.

For 8 people, you need 1.5 kg kale, 50g bacon fat and some salt. Bring a large pan of water to a fast boil. At the same time, melt the fat in a large, heavy pan (if bacon fat is unavailable, use chopped streaky bacon or offcuts). Drop the kale in the water and boil vigorously for 3 minutes. Drain thoroughly, by pressing down on the leaves in a colander. Add them to the melted bacon fat with some salt and stir, with a wooden spoon, over a medium heat until the greens are tender (about 5 minutes).

Churrasco Throughout Brazil, a mixed grill, including excellent steak, served with roasted manioc flour (farofa; raw manioc flour is known as farinha), goes under the name of churrasco (it came originally from the cattlemen of Rio Grande do Sul), normally served in specialized restaurants known as churrascarias or rodízios (or espeto corrido). In the latter, waiters ask you in advance what types of meat you want and then bring them round to you until you tell them to stop. Each *rodízio* has its own variation on the red light/green light system for communicating to the staff that you are full. *Churrascarias* usually have a self-service salad bar; they are good places for large appetites.

Desserts & fruits There is fruit all the year round, ranging from banana and orange to mango, pawpaw, custard-apple (*fruta do conde*) and guava. One should try the *manga de Ubá*, a non-fibrous small mango. Also good are *amora* (a raspberry that looks like a strawberry), *jaboticaba*, a small black damson-like fruit, and *jaca* (jackfruit), a large yellow/green fruit.

The exotic flavours of Brazilian ice creams should be experienced. Try *açaí, bacuri, biribá, buruti, cupuaçu* (not eveyone's favourite), *mari-mari, mucajá, murici, pajurá, pariri, patuá, piquiá, pupunha, sorva, tucumá, uxi* and others mentioned below under 'drinks'.

Drinks Imported drinks are expensive, but there are some fair local wines. Among the better ones are Château d'Argent, Château Duvalier, Almadén, Dreher, Preciosa and Bernard Taillan. The red Marjolet from Cabernet grapes, and the Moselle-type white Zahringer, have been well spoken of. Also reckoned to be good is Anticuário from Caxias do Sul; its Vinho Velho do Museu and Vinho Fino Branco do Museu sell for about US$12.50 a bottle and its Reserva Especial red at US$10. It has often been noticed that a new *adega* starts off well, but the quality gradually deteriorates with time; many vintners have switched to American Concorde grapes, producing a rougher wine. Greville Brut champagne-type wine is inexpensive and very drinkable. A white wine *Sangria*, containing tropical fruits such as pineapple and papaya, is worth looking out for. Chilean and Portuguese wines are sometimes available at little more than the cost of local wines.

Some genuine Scotch whisky brands are bottled in Brazil; they are very popular because of the high price of Scotch imported in the bottle; Teacher's is the most highly regarded brand. Locally made gin, vermouth and campari are very good. The local firewater, *aguardente* (known as *cachaça* or *pinga*), made from sugar-cane, is cheap and wholesome, but visitors should seek local advice on the best brands; São Francisco, Praianinha, Nega Fulô, '51' and Pitu are recommended makes. Mixed with fruit juices of various sorts, sugar and crushed ice, *cachaça* becomes the principal element in a *batida*, a delicious and powerful drink; the commonest is a lime batida or *batida de limão*; a variant of this is the *caipirinha*, a *cachaça* with several slices of lime in it, a *caipiroska* is made with vodka. *Cachaça* with Coca-Cola is a *cuba*, while rum with Coca-Cola is a *cuba libre*.

The beers are good and there are plenty of brands: *Antarctica, Brahma, Bohemia, Cerpa, Skol* and *Xingu* black beer. Beers are cheaper by the bottle than on draught. The best known of many local soft drinks is *Guaraná*, which is a very popular carbonated fruit drink (see box, page 458). Buying bottled drinks in supermarkets, you may be asked for empties in return.

There is an excellent range of non-alcoholic fruit juices, known as *sucos: açai, acerola, caju* (cashew), *pitanga, goiaba* (guava), *genipapo, graviola* (= *chirimoya*), *maracujá* (passion fruit), *sapoti* and *tamarindo* are recommended. *Vitaminas* are thick fruit or vegetable drinks with milk. *Caldo de cana* is sugar-cane juice, sometimes mixed with ice. *Água de côco* or *côco verde* (coconut water from chilled, fresh green coconut) cannot be missed. Remember that *água mineral*, available in many varieties at bars and restaurants, is a cheap, safe thirst-quencher (cheaper still in supermarkets). Apart from the ubiquitous coffee, good tea is grown and sold. **NB** If you don't want sugar in your coffee or *suco*, you must ask when you order it.

Shopping

Gold, diamonds and gemstones are good buys throughout Brazil. Innovative designs in jewellery: buy 'real' at reputable dealers (the best value is in Minas Gerais); cheap, fun pieces can be bought from street traders. There are interesting furnishings made with gemstones, and marble. Clay figurines from the Northeast, lace from Ceará, leatherwork, strange pottery from Amazônia, carvings in soapstone and in bone, tiles and other ceramic work, African-type pottery and basketwork from Bahia, are all worth seeking out. Many large hotel gift shops stock a good selection of handicrafts at reasonable prices. Brazilian cigars are excellent for those who like the mild flavours popular in Germany, the Netherlands and Switzerland. Recommended purchases are musical instruments, eg guitars, other stringed, and percussion instruments.

What to buy

There are excellent textiles: good hammocks from the Northeast (ironmongers sell hooks – ganchos pararede – for hanging your hammock at home); other fabrics; design in clothing is impressive, though unfortunately not equalled by manufacturing quality. Buy your beachwear in Brazil: it is matchless.

For those who know how to use them, medicinal herbs, barks and spices can be bought from street markets; coconut oil and local skin and haircare products (fantastic conditioners) are better and cheaper than in Europe, but known brands of toiletries are exorbitant. Other bad buys are film (including processing), cameras and any electrical goods (including batteries). Sunscreen, sold in all department stores and large supermarkets, is expensive.

As a rule, shopping is easier, quality more reliable and prices higher in the shopping centres (mostly excellent) and in the wealthier suburbs. Better prices are posted at the small shops and street traders. Shopping is most entertaining at markets and on the beach. Bargaining (with good humour) is expected in the latter.

Prices & bargaining

Holidays and festivals

The major festival is *Carnaval*, which is held three days up to and including Ash Wednesday and is celebrated all over Brazil. See boxes under Rio de Janeiro page 138, São Paulo page 219, Salvador page 432 and Pernambuco page 500. *Semana Santa*, which ends on Easter Sunday, is celebrated with parades in many cities and towns. The *Festas Juninhas* throughout the country and *Bumba-meu-boi* in Maranhão are held throughout June, while the *Festa do Boi* is held in Parantins at the end of the month.

Festivals

Bahia has many festivals throughout the year but some of the most interesting are the *Lavagem do Bomfim* in January, the *Presente para Iemanjá* in February and the *Festa da Boa Morte* in August.

In the south the *Festa Nacional da Uva*, a grape and wine festival, is held in Caxias do Sul during February. São Paulo has the Brazilian Grand Prix at the end of March or beginning of April and the *Festa do Peão Boiadeiro in Barretos* during August.

In May the *Festa do Divino Espírito Santo* is celebrated throughout Brazil, but the parades in Pirenópolis are especially interesting.

Towards the end of the year in October the *Oktoberfest* is held in Blumenau, whilst the Círio de Nazaré festival takes place in Belém.

The festival year ends on 31 December with the hugely popular *Reveillon* festivities being held particularly on beaches.

Aside from the festivals listed above, the main holidays are: 1 January, New Year; 21 April, Tiradentes; 1 May, Labour Day; June Corpus Christi; 7 September, Independence Day; 12 October, *Nossa Senhora Aparecida*; 2 November, All Souls' Day; 15 November,

National holidays

Essentials

Proclamation of the Republic; and 25 December, Christmas. The local holidays in the main cities are given in the text. Four religious or traditional holidays (Good Friday must be one; other usual days: 1 November, All Saints Day; 24 December, Christmas Eve) must be fixed by the municipalities. Other holidays are usually celebrated on the Monday prior to the date.

Health

With the following advice and precautions you should keep as healthy as you do at home. Most visitors return home having experienced no problems at all apart from some travellers' diarrhoea. In Latin America the health risks, especially in the lowland tropical areas, are different from those encountered in Europe or the USA. It also depends on where and how you travel. There are clear health differences between the countries of Latin America and in risks for the business traveller, who stays in international class hotels in large cities, the backpacker trekking from country to country and the tourist who heads for the beach. There is huge variation in climate, vegetation and wildlife, from the rain forests of Amazonia to the teeming cities. There are no hard and fast rules to follow; you will often have to make your own judgement on the healthiness or otherwise of your surroundings. There are English (or other foreign language) speaking doctors in most major cities who have particular experience in dealing with locally occurring diseases. Your embassy representative will often be able to give you the name of local reputable doctors and most of the better hotels have a doctor on standby. If you do fall ill and cannot find a recommended doctor, try the Outpatient Department of a hospital – private hospitals are usually less crowded and offer a more acceptable standard of care to foreigners.

Before travelling

Take out medical insurance. Make sure it covers all eventualities, especially evacuation to your home country by a medically equipped plane, if necessary. You should have a dental check up, obtain a spare glasses prescription, a spare oral contraceptive prescription (or enough pills to last) and, if you suffer from a chronic illness (such as diabetes, high blood pressure, ear or sinus troubles, cardio-pulmonary disease or nervous disorder), arrange for a check up with your doctor, who can at the same time provide you with a letter explaining the details of your condition in English and if possible Spanish and/or Portuguese. Check the current practice in countries you are visiting for malaria prophylaxis (prevention). If you are on regular medication, make sure you have enough to cover the period of your travel.

Children   More preparation is probably necessary for babies and children than for an adult, and perhaps a little more care should be taken when travelling to remote areas where health services are primitive. This is because children can become more rapidly ill than adults (on the other hand they often recover more quickly). Diarrhoea and vomiting are the most common problems, so take the usual precautions, but more intensively. Breastfeeding is best and most convenient for babies, but powdered milk is generally available and so are baby foods in most countries. Papaya, bananas and avocados are all nutritious and can be cleanly prepared. The treatment of diarrhoea is the same for adults, except that it should start earlier and be continued with more persistence. Children get dehydrated very quickly in hot countries and can become drowsy and unco-operative unless cajoled to drink water or juice plus salts. Upper respiratory infections, such as colds, catarrh and middle ear infections are also common, and if your child suffers from these normally take some antibiotics against the possibility. Outer ear infections after swimming are also common and antibiotic eardrops will help. Wet wipes are always useful and sometimes difficult to find in South America, as, in some places, are disposable nappies.

There is very little control on the sale of drugs and medicines in South America. You can **Medical** buy any and every drug in pharmacies without a prescription. Be wary of this because **facilities** pharmacists can be poorly trained and might sell you drugs that are unsuitable, dangerous or old. Many drugs and medicines are manufactured under license from American or European companies, so the trade names may be familiar to you. This means you do not have to carry a whole chest of medicines with you, but remember that the shelflife of some items, especially vaccines and antibiotics, is markedly reduced in hot conditions. Buy your supplies at the better outlets where there are refrigerators, even though they are more expensive and check the expiry date of all preparations you buy. Immigration officials occasionally confiscate scheduled drugs (Lomotil is an example) if they are not accompanied by a doctor's prescription.

Self-medication may be forced on you by circumstances, so make sure you carry a **What to take** **first aid kit**, a small pack containing a few sterile syringes and needles and disposable gloves. The risk of catching hepatitis etc from a dirty needle used for injection is now negligible in Brazil, but some may be reassured by carrying their own supplies – available from camping shops and airport shops. The following is a list of further items which you may also find useful in an emergency or in out-of-the-way places:

   Sunglasses ones designed for intense sunlight; **earplugs** for sleeping on aeroplanes and in noisy hotels; **suntan cream** with a high protection factor; **insect repellent** containing DET for preference; **mosquito net** lightweight, permethrin-impregnated for choice; **travel sickness tablets**; **tampons** can be expensive; **condoms**; **contraceptives**; **water sterilizing tablets**; **antimalarial tablets**; **anti-infective ointment** eg Cetrimide; **dusting powder** for feet etc containing fungicide; **antacid tablets** for indigestion; **sachets of rehydration salts** plus anti-diarrhoea preparations; **painkillers** such as Paracetamol or Aspirin; **antibiotics** for diarrhoea etc; **hydrocare contact lens products** are available, but are expensive.

Smallpox vaccination is no longer required anywhere in the world. Neither is cholera **Vaccination &** vaccination recognized as necessary for international travel by the World Health **immunization** Organisation – it is not very effective either. Nevertheless, some immigration officials are demanding proof of vaccination against cholera in Brazil and in some countries outside Latin America, following the outbreak of the disease which originated in Peru in 1990-91 and subsequently affected most surrounding countries. Although very unlikely to affect visitors to Brazil, the cholera epidemic continues making its greatest impact in poor areas where water supplies are polluted and food hygiene practices are insanitary.

   Vaccination against the following diseases are recommended:

   Yellow Fever This is a live vaccination not to be given to children under nine months of age or persons allergic to eggs. Immunity lasts for 10 years, an International Certificate of Yellow Fever Vaccination will be given and should be kept because it is sometimes asked for. Yellow fever is very rare in Brazil, but the vaccination is practically without side effects and almost totally protective.

   Typhoid A disease spread by the insanitary preparation of food. A number of new vaccines against this condition are now available; the older TAB and monovalent typhoid vaccines are being phased out. The newer, eg Typhim Vi, cause fewer side effects, but are more expensive. For those who do not like injections, there are now oral vaccines.

   Poliomyelitis Despite its decline in the world this remains a serious disease if caught and is easy to protect against. There are live oral vaccines and in some countries injected vaccines. Whichever one you choose it is a good idea to have a booster every 3-5 years if visiting developing countries regularly.

Tetanus One dose should be given with a booster at six weeks and another at six months, and 10 yearly boosters thereafter are recommended. Children should already be properly protected against diphtheria, poliomyelitis and pertussis (whooping cough), measles and HIB, all of which can be more serious infections in Brazil than at home. Measles, mumps and rubella vaccine is also given to children throughout the world, but those teenage girls who have not had rubella (German measles) should be tested and vaccinated. Hepatitis B vaccination for babies is now routine in some countries. Consult your doctor for advice on tuberculosis inoculation: the disease is still widespread in Brazil.

Infectious Hepatitis is less of a problem for travellers than it used to be because of the development of two extremely effective vaccines against the A and B form of the disease. It remains common, however, in Brazil. A combined hepatitis A & B vaccine is now licensed and available – one jab covers both diseases.

Other vaccinations might be considered in the case of epidemics, eg meningitis. There is an effective vaccination against rabies which should be considered by all travellers, especially those going through remote areas or if there is a particular occupational risk, eg for zoologists or veterinarians.

Further information Further information on health risks abroad, vaccinations etc may be available from a local travel clinic. If you wish to take specific drugs with you such as antibiotics these are best prescribed by your own doctor. Beware, however, that not all doctors can be experts on the health problems of remote countries. More detailed or more up-to-date information than local doctors can provide are available from various sources. In the UK there are hospital departments specializing in tropical diseases in London, Liverpool, Birmingham and Glasgow, and the Malaria Reference Laboratory at the London School of Hygiene and Tropical Medicine provides free advice about malaria, T0891-600350. In the USA the local Public Health Services can give such information and information is available centrally from the Centre for Disease Control (CDC) in Atlanta, T404-3324559.

There are additional computerized databases which can be accessed for destination-specific up-to-the-minute information. In the UK there is MASTA (Medical Advisory Service to Travellers Abroad), T0020-76314408, F020-74365389, Tx8953473 and Travax (Glasgow, T0141-9467120, ext 247). Other information on medical problems overseas can be obtained from the book by Dawood, Richard (Editor) (1992) *Travellers' Health: How to stay healthy abroad*, Oxford University Press 1992, £7.99. We strongly recommend this revised and updated edition, especially to the intrepid traveller heading for the more out of the way places. General advice is also available in the UK in *Health Information for Overseas Travel* published by the Department of Health and available from HMSO, and *International Travel and Health* published by WHO, Geneva.

Staying healthy

Intestinal upsets The thought of catching a stomach bug worries visitors to Brazil but there have been great improvements in food hygiene and most such infections are preventable. Travellers' diarrhoea and vomiting is due, most of the time, to food poisoning, usually passed on by the insanitary habits of food handlers. As a general rule the cleaner your surroundings and the smarter the restaurant, the less likely you are to suffer.

Foods to avoid: uncooked, undercooked, partially cooked or reheated meat, fish, eggs, raw vegetables and salads, especially when they have been left out exposed to flies. Stick to fresh food that has been cooked from raw just before eating and make sure you peel fruit yourself. Wash and dry your hands before eating – disposable wet-wipe tissues are useful for this.

Shellfish eaten raw are risky and at certain times of the year some fish and shellfish concentrate toxins from their environment and cause various kinds of food poisoning. The local authorities notify the public not to eat these foods. Do not ignore the warning.

Water purification

There are a number of ways of purifying water in order to make it safe to drink. Dirty water should first be strained through a filter bag, which is available from camping shops, and then boiled or treated. Bringing water to a rolling boil at sea level is sufficient to make the water safe for drinking, but at higher altitudes you have to boil the water for longer to ensure that all the microbes are killed.

There are sterilizing methods that can be used and there are proprietary preparations containing chlorine (eg Puritabs) or iodine (eg Pota Aqua) compounds. Chlorine compounds generally do not kill protozoa (eg giardia).

There are a number of water filters now on the market available in personal and expedition size. They work either on mechanical or chemical principles, or may do both. Make sure you take the spare parts or spare chemicals with you and do not believe everything the manufacturers say.

Heat treated milk (UHT), pasteurized or sterilized, is becoming more available in Brazil as is pasteurized cheese. On the whole, matured or processed cheeses are safer than the fresh varieties and fresh unpasteurized milk from whatever animal can be a source of food poisoning germs, tuberculosis and brucellosis. This applies equally to ice cream, yoghurt and cheese made from unpasteurized milk, so avoid these homemade products – the factory made ones are probably safer.

Tap water is rarely safe outside the major cities, especially in the rainy season. Streamwater, if you are in the countryside, is often contaminated by communities living surprisingly high in the mountains. Filtered or bottled water is usually available and safe, although you must make sure that somebody is not filling bottles from the tap and hammering on a new crown cap. If your hotel has a central hot water supply, this water is safe to drink after cooling. Ice for drinks should be made from boiled water, but rarely is so stand your glass on the ice cubes, rather than putting them in the drink. The better hotels have water purifying systems.

Travellers' diarrhoea This is usually caused by eating food which has been contaminated by food poisoning germs. Drinking water is rarely the culprit. Sea water or river water is more likely to be contaminated by sewage and so swimming in such dilute effluent can also be a cause.

Infection with various organisms can give rise to travellers' diarrhoea. They may be viruses, bacteria, eg Escherichia coli (probably the most common cause worldwide), protozoal (such as amoebas and giardia), salmonella and cholera. The diarrhoea may come on suddenly or rather slowly. It may or may not be accompanied by vomiting or by severe abdominal pain and the passage of blood or mucus when it is called dysentery. How do you know which type you have caught and how to treat it?

If you can time the onset of the diarrhoea to the minute ('acute') then it is probably due to a virus or a bacterium and/or the onset of dysentery. The treatment in addition to rehydration is Ciprofloxacin 500 mg every 12 hours; the drug is now widely available and there are many similar ones.

If the diarrhoea comes on slowly or intermittently ('sub-acute') then it is more likely to be protozoal, ie caused by an amoeba or giardia. Antibiotics such a Ciprofloxacin will have little effect. These cases are best treated by a doctor, as is any outbreak of diarrhoea continuing for more than three days. Sometimes blood is passed in amoebic dysentery and for this you should certainly seek medical help. If this is not available then the best treatment is probably Tinidazole (Fasigyn), one tablet four times a day for three days. If there are severe stomach cramps, the following drugs may help but are not very useful in the management of acute diarrhoea: Loperamide (Imodium) and Diphenoxylate with Atropine (Lomotil). They should not be given to children.

Essentials

Any kind of diarrhoea, whether or not accompanied by vomiting, responds well to the replacement of water and salts, taken as frequent small sips, of some kind of rehydration solution. There are proprietary preparations consisting of sachets of powder which you dissolve in boiled water, or you can make your own by adding half a teaspoonful of salt (3.5 gms) and 4 tablespoonfuls of sugar (40 gms) to a litre of boiled water.

Thus the linchpins of treatment for diarrhoea are rest, fluid and salt replacement, antibiotics such as Ciprofloxacin for the bacterial types and special diagnostic tests and medical treatment for the amoeba and giardia infections. Salmonella infections and cholera, although rare, can be devastating diseases and it would be wise to get to a hospital as soon as possible if these were suspected.

Fasting, peculiar diets and the consumption of large quantities of yoghurt have not been found useful in calming travellers' diarrhoea or in rehabilitating inflamed bowels. Oral rehydration has on the other hand, especially in children, been a lifesaving technique and should always be practised, whatever other treatment you use. As there is some evidence that alcohol and milk might prolong diarrhoea they should be avoided during and immediately after an attack.

Diarrhoea occurring day after day for long periods of time (chronic diarrhoea) is notoriously resistent to amateur attempts at treatment and again warrants proper diagnostic tests (most towns with reasonable sized hospitals have laboratories for stool samples). There are ways of preventing travellers' diarrhoea for short periods of time by taking antibiotics, but this is not a foolproof technique and should not be used other than in exceptional circumstances. Doxycycline is possibly the best drug. Some preventatives such as Enterovioform can have serious side effects if taken for long periods. Paradoxically **constipation** is also common, probably induced by dietary change, inadequate fluid intake in hot places and long bus journeys. Simple laxatives are useful in the short term and bulky foods such as maize, beans and plenty of fruit are also useful.

Heat & cold   Full acclimatization to high temperatures takes about two weeks. During this period it is normal to feel a bit apathetic, especially if the relative humidity is high. Drink plenty of water (up to 15 litres a day are required when working physically hard in the tropics), use salt on your food and avoid extreme exertion. Tepid showers are more cooling than hot or cold ones. Large hats do not cool you down, but do prevent sunburn. Remember that, especially in the highlands, there can be a large and sudden drop in temperature between sun and shade and between night and day, so dress accordingly. Warm jackets or woollens are essential after dark at high altitude. Loose cotton is still the best material when the weather is hot.

Insects   These are mostly more of a nuisance than a serious hazard and if you try, you can prevent yourself entirely from being bitten. Some, such as mosquitoes are, of course, carriers of potentially serious diseases, so it is sensible to avoid being bitten as much as possible.

Sleep off the ground and use a mosquito net or some kind of insecticide. Preparations containing Pyrethrum or synthetic pyrethroids are safe. They are available as aerosols or pumps and the best way to use these is to spray the room thoroughly in all areas (follow the instructions rather than the insects) and then shut the door for a while, re-entering when the smell has dispersed. Mosquito coils release insecticide as they burn slowly. They are widely available and useful out of doors. Tablets of insecticide which are placed on a heated mat plugged into a wall socket are probably the most effective. They fill the room with insecticidal fumes in the same way as aerosols or coils.

You can also use insect repellents, most of which are effective against a wide range of pests. The most common and effective is diethyl metatoluamide (DET). DET liquid is best for arms and face (care around eyes and with spectacles – DET dissolves plastic). Aerosol spray is good for clothes and ankles and liquid DET can be dissolved in water and used to impregnate cotton clothes and mosquito nets. Some repellents now contain DET and Permethrin, insecticide. Impregnated wrist and ankle bands can also be useful.

If you are bitten or stung, itching may be relieved by cool baths, antihistamine tablets (care with alcohol or driving) or mild corticosteroid creams, eg hydrocortisone (great care: never use if any hint of infection). Careful scratching of all your bites once a day can be surprisingly effective. Calamine lotion and cream have limited effectiveness and antihistamine creams are not recommended – they can cause allergies themselves. Bites which become infected should be treated with a local antiseptic or antibiotic cream such as Cetrimide, as should any infected sores or scratches.

When living rough, skin infestations with body lice (crabs) and scabies are easy to pick up. Use whatever local commercial preparation is recommended for lice and scabies. Crotamiton cream (Eurax) alleviates itching and also kills a number of skin parasites. Malathion lotion 5% (Prioderm) kills lice effectively, but avoid the use of the toxic agricultural preparation of Malathion, more often used to commit suicide.

Be very careful about bathing in lakes or slow rivers anywhere in Brazil: harmful parasites abound (including the snails that carry schistosomiasis – this disease is rampant in Minas Gerais and most of central Brazil). Dengue fever (see below) is now endemic in Brazil, and Rio is one of the worst places: protect yourself against mosquitoes. In the Amazon basin, sandflies abound; take a good repellent. South of the Amazon beware of *borrachudos*, small flies with a sharp bite that attack ankles and calves; coconut oil deters them.

Ticks

They attach themselves usually to the lower parts of the body often after walking in areas where cattle have grazed. They take a while to attach themselves strongly, but swell up as they start to suck blood. The important thing is to remove them gently, so that they do not leave their head parts in your skin because this can cause a nasty allergic reaction some days later. Do not use petrol, vaseline, lighted cigarettes etc to remove the tick, but, with a pair of tweezers remove the beast gently by gripping it at the attached (head) end and rock it out in very much the same way that a tooth is extracted.

Certain tropical flies which lay their eggs under the skin of sheep and cattle also occasionally do the same thing to humans with the unpleasant result that a maggot grows under the skin and pops up as a boil or pimple. The best way to remove these is to cover the boil with oil, vaseline or nail varnish so as to stop the maggot breathing, then to squeeze it out gently the next day.

Sunburn

The burning power of the tropical sun, especially at high altitude, is phenomenal.

Always wear a wide brimmed hat and use some form of suncream lotion on untanned skin. Normal temperate zone suntan lotions (protection factor up to 7) are not much good; you need to use the types designed specifically for the tropics or for mountaineers or skiers with protection factors up to 15 or above. These are often not available in Brazil. Glare from the sun can cause conjunctivitis, so wear sunglasses especially on tropical beaches, where high protection factor sunscreen should also be used.

Prickly heat

A very common intensely itchy rash is avoided by frequent washing and by wearing loose clothing. Cured by allowing skin to dry off through use of powder and spending two nights in an a/c hotel!

Athletes foot

This and other fungal skin infections are best treated with Tolnaftate or Clotrimazole.

Other risks and more serious diseases

Rabies Remember that rabies is endemic throughout Brazil, so avoid dogs that are behaving strangely and cover your toes at night from the vampire bats, which also carry the disease. If you are bitten by a domestic or wild animal, do not leave things to chance: scrub the wound with soap and water and/or disinfectant, try to have the animal captured (within limits) or at least determine its ownership, where possible, and seek medical assistance at once.

    The course of treatment depends on whether you have already been satisfactorily vaccinated against rabies. If you have (this is worthwile if you are spending lengths of time in developing countries) then some further doses of vaccine are all that is required. Human diploid vaccine is the best, but expensive: other, older kinds of vaccine, such as that derived from duck embryos may be the only types available. These are effective, much cheaper and interchangeable generally with the human derived types. If not already vaccinated, then anti rabies serum (immunoglobulin) may be required in addition. It is important to finish the course of treatment whether the animal survives or not.

AIDS In South America, AIDS is increasing but is not wholly confined to the well known high risk sections of the population, ie homosexual men, intravenous drug abusers and children of infected mothers. Heterosexual transmission is now the dominant mode and so the main risk to travellers is from casual sex. The same precautions should be taken as with any sexually transmitted disease. The AIDS virus (HIV) can be passed by unsterilized needles which have been previously used to inject an HIV positive patient, but the risk of this is negligible. It would, however, be sensible to check that needles have been properly sterilized or disposable needles have been used. If you wish to take your own disposable needles, be prepared to explain what they are for. The risk of receiving a blood transfusion with blood infected with the HIV virus is greater than from dirty needles because of the amount of fluid exchanged. Supplies of blood for transfusion should now be screened for HIV in all reputable hospitals, so again the risk is very small indeed. Catching the AIDS virus does not always produce an illness in itself (although it may do). The only way to be sure if you feel you have been put at risk is to have a blood test for HIV antibodies on your return to a place where there are reliable laboratory facilities. The test does not become positive for some weeks.

Sexual infections Brazilians are famous for their open sexuality: appearances can be deceptive, however, and attitudes vary widely. To generalize, the coastal cities are very easy-going, while in smaller towns and the interior, traditional morals are strictly enforced. AIDS is widespread, commonly transmitted by heterosexual sex, and tolerance of male homosexuality is diminishing. You should take reliable condoms with you, even if you are sure you won't be needing them. The primary means of HIV infection in Brazil is now heterosexual sex. Local condoms are reported not to be reliable.

Malaria In South America, malaria is theoretically confined to coastal and jungle zones, but is now on the increase again. Mosquitoes do not thrive above 2,500m, so you are safe at altitude. There are different varieties of malaria, some resistant to the normal drugs. Make local enquiries if you intend to visit possibly infected zones and use a prophylactic regime.

    Start taking the tablets a few days before exposure and continue to take them for six weeks after leaving the malarial zone. Remember to give the drugs to babies and children also. Opinion varies on the precise drugs and dosage to be used for protection. All the drugs may have some side effects and it is important to balance the risk of catching the disease against the albeit rare side effects.

The increasing complexity of the subject is such that as the malarial parasite becomes immune to the new generation of drugs, it has made concentration on the physical prevention from being bitten by mosquitoes more important. This involves the use of long sleeved shirts or blouses and long trousers, repellents and nets. Clothes are now available impregnated with the insecticide Permethrin or Deltamethrin, or it is possible to impregnate the clothes yourself. Wide meshed nets impregnated with Permethrin are also available, are lighter to carry and less claustrophobic to sleep in.

Prophylaxis and treatment If your itinerary takes you into a malarial area, seek expert advice before you go on a suitable prophylactic regime. This is especially true for pregnant women who are particularly prone to catch malaria. You can still catch the disease even when sticking to a proper regime, although it is unlikely. If you do develop symptoms (high fever, shivering, headache, sometimes diarrhoea), seek medical advice immediately. If this is not possible and there is a great likelihood of malaria, the treatment is:

Chloroquine, a single dose of four tablets (600 mg), followed by two tablets (300 mg) in six hours and 300 mg each day following.

Falciparum type of malaria or type in doubt: take local advice. Various combinations of drugs are being used such as Quinine, Tetracycline or Halofantrine. If falciparum type malaria is definitely diagnosed, it is wise to get to a good hospital as treatment can be complex and the illness very serious.

Infectious hepatitis (jaundice) The main symptoms are pains in the stomach, lack of appetite, lassitude and yellowness of the eyes and skin. Medically speaking there are two main types. The less serious, but more common is Hepatitis A for which the best protection is the careful preparation of food, the avoidance of contaminated drinking water and scrupulous attention to toilet hygiene. The other, more serious, version is Hepatitis B which is acquired usually as a sexually transmitted disease or by blood transfusions. It can less commonly be transmitted by injections with unclean needles and possibly by insect bites. The symptoms are the same as for Hepatitis A. The incubation period is much longer (up to six months compared with six weeks) and there are more likely to be complications.

Hepatitis A can be protected against with gamma globulin. It should be obtained from a reputable source and is certainly useful for travellers who intend to live rough. You should have a shot before leaving and have it repeated every six months. The dose of gamma globulin depends on the concentration of the particular preparation used, so the manufacturer's advice should be taken. The injection should be given as close as possible to your departure and as the dose depends on the likely time you are to spend in potentially affected areas, the manufacturer's instructions should be followed.

Gamma globulin has really been superseded now by a proper vaccination against Hepatitis A (Havrix), which gives immunity lasting up to 10 years. After that boosters are required. Havrix monodose is now widely available as is Junior Havrix. The vaccination has negligible side effects and is extremely effective. Gamma globulin injections can be a bit painful, but it is much cheaper than Havrix and may be more available in some places.

Hepatitis B can be effectively prevented by a specific vaccine (Engerix) – three shots over six months before travelling. If you have had jaundice in the past it would be worthwhile having a blood test to see if you are immune to either of these two types, because this might avoid the necessity and costs of vaccination or gamma globulin. There are other kinds of viral hepatitis (C, E etc) which are fairly similar to A and B, but vaccines are not available as yet.

Typhus This can still occur and is carried by ticks. There is usually a reaction at the site of the bite and a fever. Seek medical advice.

Intestinal worms	These are common and the more serious ones such as hookworm can be contracted from walking barefoot on infested earth or beaches.

Various other tropical diseases can be caught in jungle areas, usually transmitted by biting insects. They are often related to African diseases and were probably introduced by the slave labour trade. Leishmaniasis (Espundia) is carried by sandflies and causes a sore that will not heal or a severe nasal infection. Wearing long trousers and a long sleeved shirt in infected areas protects against these flies. DET is also effective. Epidemics of meningitis occur from time-to-time. Be careful about swimming in piranha or caribe infested rivers. It is a good idea not to swim naked: the Candiru fish can follow urine currents and become lodged in body orifices. Swimwear offers some protection.

Leptospirosis Various forms of leptospirosis occur throughout Brazil, transmitted by a bacterium which is excreted in rodent urine. Freshwater and moist soil harbour the organisms which enter the body through cuts and scratches. If you suffer from any form of prolonged fever consult a doctor.

Snake bites This is a very rare event indeed for travellers. If you are unlucky (or careless) enough to be bitten by a venomous snake, spider, scorpion or sea creature, try to identify the creature, but do not put yourself in further danger. Snake bites in particular are very frightening, but in fact rarely poisonous – even venomous snakes bite without injecting venom.

What you might expect if bitten are: fright, swelling, pain and bruising around the bite and soreness of the regional lymph glands, perhaps nausea, vomiting and a fever. Signs of serious poisoning would be the following symptoms: numbness and tingling of the face, muscular spasms, convulsions, shortness of breath and bleeding. Victims should be got to a hospital or a doctor without delay.

Commercial snake bite and scorpion kits are available, but usually only useful for the specific type of snake or scorpion for which they are designed. Most serum has to be given intravenously so it is not much good equipping yourself with it unless you are used to making injections into veins. It is best to rely on local practice in these cases, because the particular creatures will be known about locally and appropriate treatment can be given.

Treatment Reassure and comfort the victim frequently. Immobilize the limb by a bandage or a splint or by getting the person to lie still. Do not slash the bite area and try to suck out the poison because this sort of heroism does more harm than good. If you know how to use a tourniquet in these circumstances, you will not need this advice. If you are not experienced do not apply a tourniquet.

Precautions Avoid walking in snake territory in bare feet or sandals – wear proper shoes or boots. If you encounter a snake, stay put until it slithers away, and do not investigate a wounded snake. Spiders and scorpions may be found in the more basic hotels, especially in the Andean countries. If stung, rest and take plenty of fluids and call a doctor. The best precaution is to keep beds away from the walls and look inside your shoes and under the toilet seat every morning.

Certain tropical sea fish when trodden upon inject venom into bathers' feet. This can be exceptionally painful. Wear plastic shoes when you go bathing if such creatures are reported. The pain can be relieved by immersing the foot in extremely hot water for as long as the pain persists.

Dengue fever This is increasing worldwide including in South American countries. It can be completely prevented by avoiding mosquito bites in the same way as malaria. No vaccine is available. Dengue is an unpleasant and painful disease, presenting with a high temperature and body pains, but at least visitors are spared the more serious forms (haemorrhagic types), which are more of a problem for local people who have been exposed to the disease more than once. There is no specific treatment for dengue – just pain killers and rest.

This is a chronic disease and difficult to treat. It is, however, very rarely caught by travellers. It is transmitted by the simultaneous biting and excreting of the Reduvid bug, also known as the Vinchuca or Barbeiro. Somewhat resembling a small cockroach, this nocturnal bug lives in poor adobe houses with dirt floors often frequented by opossums. If you cannot avoid such accommodation, sleep off the floor with a candle lit, use a mosquito net, keep as much of your skin covered as possible, use DET repellent or a spray insecticide. If you are bitten overnight (the bites are painless) do not scratch them, but wash thoroughly with soap and water.

Chagas' disease (South American Trypano-somiasis)

Apart from mosquitoes the most dangerous animals are men, be they bandits or behind steering wheels. Think carefully about violent confrontations and wear a seat belt if you are lucky enough to have one available to you.

Dangerous animals

Remember to take your antimalarial tablets for six weeks after leaving the malarial area. If you have had attacks of diarrhoea it is worth having a stool specimen tested in case you have picked up amoebas. If you have been living rough, blood tests may be worthwhile to detect worms and other parasites. If you have been exposed to bilharzia (schistosomiasis) by swimming in lakes etc, check by means of a blood test when you get home, but leave it for six weeks because the test is slow to become positive. Report any untoward symptoms to your doctor and tell the doctor exactly where you have been and, if you know, what the likelihood of disease is to which you were exposed.

When you get home

Further reading

A number of books are referred to in the text; see especially **Literature**, page 777 where a list of Brazilian works in English translation is given. What follows is a selection of books by topic which may be of interest to travellers. All have been consulted at some stage in the preparation of this Handbook.

For information on maps and guidebooks, see page 49

Louis and Elizabeth Agassiz, *A Journey in Brazil* (New York: Praeger, 1969), describes a journey in 1868 through Rio de Janeiro, Juiz da Fora, up the coast to Pará, to Manaus, the Amazon, then back to Rio; illustrated. Frederick Alcock, *Trade and Travel in South America* (London: George Philip, 1907). Captain Richard F Burton, *Explorations of the Highlands of Brazil*, with a full account of the Gold and Diamond Mines, 2 volumes (New York: Greenwood, 1969), first published in 1869. Jean Baptiste Debret, *Viagem Pitoresca e Histórica ao Brasil* (São Paulo: Livraria Martins, 1954), translated by Sérgio Milliet, 2 volumes; text and black and white reproductions of Debret's wonderful illustrations. CR Enock, *Spanish America. Its Romance, Reality and Future*, Vol II (London: T Fisher Unwin, 1920), Chapters XI & XII. Lt-Col PH Fawcett, *Exploration Fawcett*, arranged from his manuscripts, letters, logbooks and records by Brian Fawcett (London: Hutchinson, 1953). See also Kevin Healey, 'The Road less Travelled', *South American Explorer*, 24 (January 1990), pages 4-11, and Peter Fleming, *Brazilian Adventure* (London: Pimlico, first published in 1933). Jean de Léry, *History of a Voyage to the Land of Brazil. Otherwise called America*, translated by Janet Whatley (Berkeley, Los Angeles, Oxford: University of California Press, 1990). Theodore Roosevelt, *Through the Brazilian Wilderness* (London: John Murray, 1914), contains photographs of the expedition. See also *Missão Rondon*, notes on the work on the Mato Grosso ao Amazonas telegraph by Coronel Cândido Mariano da Silva Rondon, 1907-15, with photos; includes an account of Rondon's exploration of the Rio da Dúvida with Roosevelt. Auguste de Sainte-Hilaire, *Viagem pelo Distrito dos Diamantes e Litoral do Brasil*, translated by Leonam de Azeredo Penna (São Paulo: Livraria Itatiaia, 1974), from the original *Voyage dans le District de Diamants et sur le Littoral du Brésil*, 2 volumes (Paris 1833); *Segunda Viagem do Rio de Janeiro a Minas Gerais e a São Paulo*, translated by Vivaldi Moreira

Historical travellers

Essentials

(same publisher and date as above), from the original *Livre du Voyage que j'ai entrepris de faire de Rio de Janeiro a Villa-Rica et de Villa-Rica a Saint-Paul pour aller chercher les 20 caisses que j'ai laissées dans cette dernière ville* (Orléans, 1887). Johann Spix and Carl Friedrich von Martius, *Travels in Brazil in the Years 1817-1820* (London, 1824). Hans Staden, *The True History of his Captivity. 1557*, translation and introduction by Malcolm Letts (London: Routledge, 1928), contains the fabulous woodcuts and maps. See also Alan D Eames, 'Autobiography of Hans Staden', *South American Explorer*, 26 (August 1990), 5-15; 27 (November 1990), 18-24; 28 (February 1991), 16-21. Charles Waterton, *Wanderings in South America*, introduction by David Bellamy (London: Century, 1983). Annabel Williams-Ellis, *H.M.S. 'Beagle' in South America*, adapted from the narratives of Charles Darwin and Captain Fitz Roy (London: Watts 1930).

Modern travellers *Brasil*, 217 photographs by A Bon, M Gantherot and P Verger (Paris: Hartmann, 1950). Richard Gott, *Land without Evil. Utopian Journeys across the South American Watershed* (London/New York: Verso, 1993). Joe Kane, *Running the Amazon*, describes adventures kayaking the length of the river. Brian McPhee, *Down the Nowhere River. A Brazilian Journey* (Lewes: The Book Guild, 1992). *Margaret Mee's Amazon*, paintings of plants from Brazilian Amazonia by Margaret Mee, text by Simon Mayo (Royal Botanical Gardens, Kew, 1988). Redmond O'Hanlon, *In Trouble Again* (London: Penguin). Alex Shoumatoff, *The Rivers Amazon* (London: Hutchinson, 1987); one of many books by Shoumatoff on Brazilian and South American topics. *Travelers' Tales, Brazil*, collected and edited by Annette Haddad and Scott Doggett (San Francisco, CA: Traveler's Tales, 1997); not simply about travelling, but contains many interesting pieces on a wide variety of topics.

Literature Elizabeth Bishop, *Complete Poems* (London: Chatto & Windus, 1991). Jason Wilson, *Traveller's Literary Companion, South & Central America* (Brighton: In Print, 1993, pages 287-335 on Brazil).

Culture Oriana Baddely and Valerie Fraser, *Drawing the Line. Art and Cultural Identity in Contemporary Latin America* (London, New York: Verso, 1989). Yves Bottineau, Henry Stierlin (ed), *Iberian-American Baroque* (Lausanne: Benedikt Taschen, u/d), translated by Kenneth Martin Leake. Alma Guillermoprieto, *Samba* (London: Bloomsbury, 1991). Ed David J Hess & Roberto A Damatta, *The Brazilian Puzzle. Culture on the Borderlands of the Western World* (New York: Columbia University Press, 1995). Edward Lucie-Smith, *Latin American Art of the 20th century* (London: Thames and Hudson, 1993). Roberto Schwartz, *Misplaced Ideas* (London: Verso, 1992). *Essays on Brazilian Culture*, introduction by John Gledson.

History & politics Leslie Bethel, editor, *Colonial Brazil* (Cambridge: Cambridge University Press, 1987); *Brazil, Empire and Republic, 1822-1930* (Cambridge: Cambridge University Press, 1989), both in the Cambridge History of Latin America series. Also, *On Democracy in Brazil Past and Present* (University of London Institute of Latin American Studies Occasional Papers No 7, 1994). CR Boxer, *The Dutch in Brazil, 1624-1654* (Oxford: Clarendon Press, 1957). CR Boxer, *The Golden Age of Brazil, 1695-1750* (Berkeley & Los Angeles: University of California Press, 1962). Ed Michael L Coniff & Frank D McCann, *Modern Brazil. Elites and Masses in Historical Perspective* (Lincoln & London: University of Nebraska Press, 1991). Bailey W Diffie, *A History of Colonial Brazil, 1500-1792* (Malabar, FL: Krieger, 1987). Gilberto Freyre, *New World in the Tropics. The Culture of Modern Brazil* (New York: Alfred A Knopf, 1959); see also Freyre's major work, *Casa-Grande e Senzala (The Masters & The Slaves)*. These are just two of Freyre's many books. Fernando Gabeira, *O que é isso, companheiro?* (Rio de Janeiro: Codecri, 1979); by one of the guerrillas who kidnapped the US ambassador in 1969 (see the 1998 Oscar-nominated film, 'Four Days in September'). Paulino Jacques, *A Guerra dos Farrapos (1835-1845)* (Rio de Janeiro: Reper, 1969). Donald S Johnson, *Phantom*

Islands of the Atlantic. The Legends of Seven Lands that Never Were (London: Souvenir, 1997). Regina Johnson Tomlinson, *The Struggle for Brazil. Portugal and 'The French Interlopers' (1500-1550)* (New York: Las Americas, 1970). Robert M Levine and John J Crocitti (eds), *The Brazil Reader* (Durham: Duke University Press, 1999). Marcio Moreira Alves, *A Grain of Mustard Seed. The Awakening of the Brazilian Revolution* (New York: Doubleday, 1973); also on the Marxist guerrillas' campaign in the 1960s. Ed Richard M Morse, *The Bandeirantes. The Historical Role of the Brazilian Pathfinders* (New York: Alfred A Knopf, 1965). Ronald M Schneider, *Brazil, Culture and Politics in a New Industrial Powerhouse* (Boulder, Oxford: Westview, 1996). Anna Curtenius Roosevelt, *Moundbuilders of The Amazon. Geophysical Archaeology on Marajó Island, Brazil* (San Diego/New York/London etc: Academic Press, 1991). León Tenenbaum, *Tiradentes* (Buenos Aires: Eudeba, 1965). Ed José Toribio Medina, *The Discovery of the Amazon*, translated by Bertram T Lee, edited by HC Heaton (New York: Dover, 1988). Edwin Williams, *The Penguin History of Latin America* (London: Penguin, 1992).

Sarah de Carvalho, *The Street Children of Brazil* (London: Hodder & Stoughton, 1996). Ed Helen Collinson, *Green Guerrillas: Environmental Conflicts and Initiatives in Latin America and the Caribbean. A Reader.* (London: Latin America Bureau, 1996). Adrian Cowell, *The Decade of Destruction* (Sevenoaks: Headway/Hodder & Stoughton, 1990); on the Amazon. Ralph Della Cava, *Miracle at Joaseiro* (New York & London: Columbia University Press, 1970); on Padre Cícero. Alain Gheerbrant, *The Amazon, Past and Present* (Thames & Hudson: London & New York, 1992 – originally Gallimard, 1988). John Hemming, *Amazon Frontier. The Defeat of the Brazilian Indians* (London: Papermac, 1987/1995); *Red Gold. The Conquest of the Brazilian Indians* (London: Papermac, 1995); *Roraima: Brazil's Northernmost Frontier* (University of London Institute of Latin American Studies Research Papers, 20, 1990). Claude Lévi-Strauss, *Tristes tropiques* (Paris: Plon, 1955). Jan Rocha, *Brazil in Focus* (London: Latin America Bureau, New York: Interlink 1997). Nancy Scheper-Hughes, *Death Without Weeping. The Violence of Everyday Life in Brazil* (Berkeley and Los Angeles: University of California Press, 1993). Candace Slater, *Trail of Miracles, Stories from a Pilgrimage in Northeast Brazil* (Berkeley/Los Angeles/London: University of California Press, 1986); on Padre Cícero and his following. Phillip Wearne, *The Return of the Indian. Conquest and Revival in the Americas* (London: Cassell/Latin America Bureau, 1996).

Social & environmental issues

Celso Antunes, *Geografia e Participação 2. Regiões do Brasil* (São Paulo: Scipione, 1996). **Geography**

Compañeras: Latina Lesbians, edited by Juanita Ramos (Routledge, 1994). João Trevisan, *Perverts in Paradise* (CMP, 1986). See also the *Spartacus Guide*. **Gay studies**

Brazil A/Z. Larousse Cultural (São Paulo: Editora Universo, 1988). James L Taylor, *A Portuguese-English Dictionary* (London: Harrap, 1970). **Reference**

Useful websites

Some useful websites with good links in English include: **Brazilian embassies** Canberra: http://brazil.org.au/ London: www.brazil.org.uk/. Washington: www.brasil emb.org/. **Brazilian Foreign Ministry** www.mre.gov.br. **BrazilInfo** www.brazilinfo.com/.
   Destinations Bahia: http://members.xoom.com/sorria/. Rio de Janeiro: www.ipanema.com. **São Paulo**: www.spguia.com.br. **Various cities**: www.guiado executivo.com.br
   Other information News and culture: www.brazil-brasil.com
   For newspaper and magazine websites, see page 69.

See also under individual sections in this chapter for more websites

Essentials

Rio de Janeiro

3

Rio de Janeiro

MINAS GERAIS

Parque Nacional do Itatiaia

Vassouras

Teresópolis

Petrópolis

SÃO PAULO

Búzios

Niterói

Cabo Frio

RIO DE JANEIRO

Paraty

Atlantic Ocean

Rio, the 'Marvellous City' as its inhabitants, the Cariocas, call it, is beautifully situated between the mountains and the sea. Although best known for the famous Copacabana beach and its spectacular Carnival, there are also many fine buildings and museums from its time as capital of both Imperial and Republican Brazil. There are wonderful views over the city and the bay from the statue of Christ, the Pão de Açúcar (Sugar Loaf) and other vantage points. Sport and music are the main activities of this city dedicated to leisure, where a day spent hang gliding or surfing could easily be followed by an evening of jazz or samba. Should you wish to venture out from the city there are many beach and mountain resorts within easy reach. On the coast, historic Paraty, fashionable Búzios or the pirate lair of Ilha Grande could be visited. Inland you will find the imperial palace at Petrópolis and national parks near Teresópolis and at Itatiaia.

Background

History Evidence from *sambaquis* (see page 736) indicates settled coastal communities the length of the Rio de Janeiro seaboard about 5,000 years ago. When the Europeans arrived in the region, the indigenous inhabitants belonged to the Tupi or Tupi-Guarani, Puri, Botocudos and Maxacali linguistic groups. No Indian people in what is now Rio de Janeiro state survived the European incursions.

In the early years of colonization, the Baía de Guanabara was the focus of attention, as described below under the city's history. The bay and then Rio de Janeiro itself were initially part of the Capitania de São Vicente (São Paulo) and São Tomé. As in the rest of the Portuguese colony, great efforts were put into enslaving the Indians to work plantations and converting them to Christianity. Gradually, routes up and down the coast were made to connect the far-flung outposts. Similarly, trails followed Indian tracks into the interior, as pioneers explored for wealth and mule drivers transported goods over the Serra do Mar. The history of the state was associated with the development of and settlement along the roads. In the 16th century, the first established road became that which linked Paraty (see page 181) with the valley of the Rio Paraíba, continuing into southern Minas Gerais. This became a route for exporting gold in the 18th century and it was followed by the Caminho Novo, also from Minas Gerais, which ended on the shores of the Baía de Guanabara. Other gold routes were created, including one between Rio and São Paulo. The demise of the Minas Gerais gold fields and the expansion of coffee growing in the Paraíba valley at the beginning of the 19th century opened up new routes between the interior and the coast. The crop was taken by mule train to new ports on the Baías de Guanabara, Sepetiba and Ilha Grande, and these roads were the main means of communication until the coming of the railways after 1855. At this point, Rio de Janeiro added to its political importance the trading dominance that came with the rail terminus, first from Petrópolis (see page 162), then from São Paulo and Minas Gerais. Industrialization soon followed.

In comparison with Rio de Janeiro city's steady growth, other centres rose and fell with the changing economic climate: Paraty was a major port while gold and, later, coffee were flowing through it, but fell almost into obscurity after the railways were built. Towns in the coffee zone, such as Vassouras (see page 171) and Valença, lost their importance as the coffee frontier moved.

Until 1960, the state in which the city of Rio de Janeiro stood was called the Estado de Guanabara, with its capital at Niterói. The city of Rio, as capital of Brazil, was a federal district in its own right. After Brasília had been made the capital of the country, the states of Guanabara and Rio de Janeiro were amalgamated into the new Estado do Rio de Janeiro, with its capital at Rio.

Geography One of the main attractions of Rio de Janeiro state is its varied geography. The coast has three large bays, intricately carved with inlets and dotted with islands. Where erosion has deposited soils at the foot of the coastal mountains, lowlands (*baixadas*) have formed a wide belt between the mountains and the sea. In these lowlands there are sand banks, salt marshes (*restingas*) and lakes. Another feature of the coast is the number of fine beaches, some on the open sea and others, which are calmer, in the bays or on the lakes behind the sand bars. Just inland from the Atlantic litoral is the Serra do Mar, a range of mountains which includes, among other features, the weird shapes of the Serra dos Órgãos. Further inland again is the Serra da Mantiqueira, which has the highest mountain in the state, Pico das Agulhas Negras (2,787 metres). Between the two ranges runs the Rio Paraíba do Sul, the main valley of many in the state. Before the conquest of Brazil by the Portuguese, the entire region was covered in tropical forest, hardly any of which now remains.

In general terms the climate of the state is characterized by a dry season, usu- **Climate** ally between June and August, with the rest of the year rainy to a greater or lesser degree. Being a tropical zone, temperatures should be high, but the influence of the Serra do Mar affects all aspects of climate, giving the state a wider variation in temperature and rainfall than would otherwise be expected. On the highest parts of the Serra, facing the Atlantic, rainfall is the heaviest and temperatures the lowest in the state; there is no dry season to speak of. A little lower on these slopes, for instance at Petrópolis and Teresópolis, the climate falls somewhere between the extremes of the hot, humid coast and the cool, wet summits, which is why this amenable area was favoured by the Imperial court. In the rain shadow of the Serra do Mar, in the Rio Paraíba valley, temperatures are higher and the dry season lasts longer. The heat and humidity of the central coast is modified in the west (for example at Paraty) by the closeness of the mountains to the shore, almost eliminating the dry season. In the other direction, north of Rio, the dry season is more prolonged as the region suffers less from the prevailing winds off the sea.

Covering 43,653.3 square kilometres and with a population of 14.4 million **Economy** (1998), 94.3 percent of whom lived in metropolitan areas, the state is Brazil's second-largest industrial producer. Due to the presence of the influential Globo network Rio de Janeiro remains an important media centre in both news and entertainment, with its soap operas being exported to many parts of the world. As a world-famous tourist destination, Rio de Janeiro attracts many holidaymakers and is also developing this infrastructure for the hosting of conferences and events.

Rio de Janeiro

Population: 6 million
Phone code: 021
Colour map 4, grid C3

Rio de Janeiro is on the southwestern shore of the Baía de Guanabara, whose perimeter is 143 kilometres and area 412 square kilometres. The setting is magnificent. The city sweeps 20 kilometres along a narrow alluvial strip between the mountains and the sea. The combination of a dark blue sea, studded with rocky islands, with the tumbling wooded mountains and expanses of bare grey rock which surround the city, is very impressive. Brazilians say: God made the world in six days; the seventh he devoted to Rio (pronounced Heeoo by locals).

The best known of these rocky masses are the Pão de Açúcar (Sugar Loaf), the highest peak of a low chain of mountains on the fringe of the harbour and the Corcovado (Hunchback), a jagged peak rising behind the city. There are other peaks, including Tijuca, the tallest point in the foreground, and 50 kilometres away rise the strangely shaped Serra dos Órgãos.

Ins and outs

Getting there
See also Transport,
page 144

Air Most international flights stop at the Aeroporto Internacional Tom Jobim (formerly Galeaeão) on the Ilha do Governador. The air bridge from São Paulo ends at Santos Dumont airport in the town centre. Taxis from here are much cheaper than from the international airport. There are also frequent buses.

Bus International and buses from other parts of Brazil arrive at the Rodoviária Novo Rio near the docks.

Rio de Janeiro orientation

Related maps
A Barra da Tijuca &
National Park,
page 126
B Rio west of centre,
page 110
C Rio de Janeiro centre,
page 100
D Glória, Santa Teresa,
Catete, Flamengo,
page 116
E Urca, Botafoga,
Cosme Velho,
page 118
F Copacabana,
page 122
G Ipanema, Leblon,
page 124

To São Paulo
To Petrópolis
Ilha de Paquetá
Galeão/ Tom Jobim
Ilha do Governador
Baía de Guanabara
To Cabo Frio
To Paraty
Ilha do Fundão
Rio-Niterói bridge
NITERÓI
Santos Dumont
B
C
D
E
F
G
A
Recreio dos Bandeirantes
Atlantic Ocean
N
Not to scale

Safety in Rio

The following are risky places: the tunnels are not safe to walk through; the city centre on Sunday when it is deserted; quiet alleyways; jostling crowds; dark corners. Locals don't walk on the beaches at night: if you must, do not go out of sight of the pavement. The Tijuca forest is best explored with a group of six or more, except the stretch between Afonso Vizeu square and Cascatinha which is well policed during the day; the tram to Santa Teresa (see page) attracts pickpockets, but a note on security in this area is given below; robberies sometimes happen in city buses: don't use them if guarding your property is essential (private frescão buses are more secure). The main bus station is patrolled inside, but uncomfortable outside. If you go to the Zona Norte at night, use a taxi; wandering around favelas alone at any time of day is both ill-advised and in questionable taste. Street vendors and children working the tables at your bar or restaurant will have been permitted by the management and there is little risk, though children can be light-fingered, so watch your wallet. It seems that far too many crimes against tourists are the result of thoughtlessness:

remember that you are in a busy city and that the beaches are a pivot of daily life; leaving things unattended on the sand is equivalent to leaving them on Times Square while you go for a walk. We have been asked to advise male readers that all the usual risks apply if hiring prostitutes of either sex (police may well take your companion's side in a dispute over prices – don't argue). The 'red light' districts of the Zona Sul are unlikely to offend anyone walking about at night, even children or unaccompanied women. Do, however, be suspicious of any club that you are invited into by a stranger (have your drink opened in front of you) and of anyone offering drugs. When ordering drinks in red-light bars, check prices first. Some girls may ask for a bottle of imported champagne, a little extravagance that may set you back US$300. You have the most to lose when carrying all your belongings and as you go in and out of banks, exchange houses and expensive shops, so take extra care then. At other times, put your passport, travellers' cheques etc in the hotel safe. Don't take too much out with you, have some sense and relax.

Getting around

In four days you can see a lot of Rio, but you should build into your itinerary time for finding your bearings and time for relaxing. Because the city is a series of separate districts connected by urban highways and tunnels heavy with traffic, you will need to take some form of public transport to get around. Walking is only an option once you are in the district you want to explore (for example, the Centre, Copacabana). An underground railway, the Metrô, runs under some of the centre and the south and is being extended. Buses run to all parts, but should be treated with caution at night when taxis are a better bet. There is a also a tram that runs from the Largo da Carioca to Dois Irmãos or Paula Mattos in Santa Teresa. For newcomers the advice in the box on page 96 will be helpful.

Orientation & safety
See also box

The city is usually divided into north and south zones, Zona Norte and Zona Sul, with the historical and business centre, O Centro, in between. The Zona Norte is the part of the city which stretches through São Cristóvão and Penha, passing Ilha do Governador on which is the international airport. Through this part runs the main entry/exit routes to São Paulo, Petrópolis, Belo Horizonte and the north of the country. The parts that most interest visitors are the centre itself and the Zona Sul, which has the famous districts of Flamengo, Botafogo, Urca, Copacabana, Ipanema, Leblon and then out to the newer suburb of Barra de Tijuca. Also in the southern zone is the Lagoa Rodrigo de Freitas and the Jardim Botânico. The Pão de Açúcar is right on the coast, above Urca. Besides Corcovado, other peaks rise behind the city, forming the Parque Nacional de Tijuca. (All these places will be described in more detail below.)

Rio de Janeiro

Chill out, you're in Rio

When I first flew into Rio de Janeiro, I was not an inexperienced traveller, but the city's reputation preceded it: I was scared. A few weeks after that nervous landing at Galeão airport, Brazil got the better of me. I've been back countless times, and it's still not enough. I know Rio as well as I know my home town (London), and I feel a sense of elation arriving there that, as much as I love London, I've never felt at Heathrow.

Nobody can tell you how to enjoy Rio: each person is different, and this marvellous city has plenty to satisfy everyone. What I can do is to share with first-time visitors my arrival routine in the belief that, if you're a little more confident than I was seven years ago, you'll get the best out of the place sooner than I did.

Head for the Zona Sul. Copacabana and Ipanema are tourist traps for the good reason that they are breathtakingly beautiful beaches, in the city's social centre, with many shops and hotels.

If you are arriving from another South American country, remember that Brazilians speak Portuguese, not Spanish. The bus station (Rodoviária) is in a rough district. Do not use the taxis waiting outside; Cariocas don't, for good reason. Use the regulated taxi service (pre-paid, see page 145), or catch the blue air-conditioned bus which waits in front of the bus station. If you tell the conductor/conductress where you want to get off, the bus will stop near your required street.

Arriving by plane, you will walk down a short corridor which has the tropical, damp-concrete smell that you are going to get used to during your stay here. You will have to queue for an entry visa. Apply for the maximum, 90 days. Keep your visa in your passport and make a mental note to photocopy both as soon as you can (leaving the country without your paperwork can be a nightmare). The airport is a pleasant three-storey building with one of everything: not at all primitive, but neither confusingly big. There is a duty free shop in arrivals: useful if you need presents for Brazilian friends because it sells fashionable brands at discount prices. Otherwise, don't bother. Customs operate a push-button system. Each passenger gets either a red or green light; red-light passengers are automatically searched.

The restaurant at Galeão's expensive hotel stays open 24 hours a day, but there is only one hour, early in the morning, when no other refreshments are available in the building. The airport chapel is next to the hotel. A bit further on, in the main area, is a lanchonete (pay first, ordering from the cashier, collect a ticket which you give to the server) and a smart restaurant which does an enormous tropical breakfast for US$10. Don't pay for any tourist information at Galeão: you can get basic maps free if Riotur is open, otherwise wait until you get into town.

The most expensive, and safest, way to get to the Zona Sul is by the pre-paid radio taxis. Most will drive you around for a while, if you haven't booked a hotel, without extra charge, but they are not chauffeurs. If you are in this situation try to have a list of addresses ready, so the driver can plan a sensible route around Copacabana's intricate one-way system - and smile! He's doing you a favour. The Real bus (see page 146) will drop you on the nearest corner to your hotel and your luggage is secured. The taxis outside Galeão are fairly reliable, but probably best kept for your next visit.

The 16-kilometre drive into town cuts past some of the city's least attractive areas, through Rio's smelly industrialized Zona Norte. The six-lane highway that makes up most of the route then curves alongside the bay, giving a fabulous impression both of a glittering ocean framed by mountains and of Brazilian driving techniques: if you had been in any doubt, you will see why motor racing is a national passion. A whole range of Brazilian housing nestles among the forested hills to your right, from favelas to ordinary middle-class estates, and several impressively ornate colonial buildings. You are now approaching the Rio you will be getting to know during your stay.

Cherry Austin

The majority of visitors enjoy Rio's glamour and the rich variety of experience it has to offer without any problems. It is worth remembering that, despite its beach culture, carefree atmosphere and friendly people, Rio is one of the world's most densely populated cities. If you live in London, Paris, New York or Los Angeles and behave with the same caution in Rio that you do at home, you will be unlucky to encounter any crime. There is extreme poverty in Rio: most robberies that occur are committed out of desperation. Overseas visitors are an obvious target: simply by having been able to afford the ticket, you are comparatively wealthy. Brazilians can usually tell you are foreign just by the way you carry yourself, but there is no sense in looking as if you have something worth stealing by wearing expensive clothes, valuable jewellery, a large daypack, or your camera – put it in your shoulder bag, worn in front of you, or buy disposable cameras as often as you need them. If you are unfortunate enough to be threatened, try to remember that the assailant is probably as scared as you are and will not hurt you if you give him what he's asking for (keep some money easily accessible, just in case). If you see someone having trouble, don't interfere, but try making a lot of noise to frighten the attacker away; if you think you are being followed, go up to a policeman. The streets are not excessively dangerous at night, but if you're going out in your best clothes, don't know the way, or are drunk, it's wisest to get a taxi. All the above advice comes from the **Tourist Police**, Avenida Afrânio de Melo Franco, Leblon (in front of the Casa Grande theatre), T5115112, who publish a sensible advice leaflet (available from hotels and consulates: consulates also issue safety guidelines). Tourist police officers are helpful, efficient and multilingual. All the main tourist areas are patrolled. If you have any problems, **contact the tourist police first**.

Climate

Rio has one of the healthiest climates in the tropics. Trade winds cool the air. June, July and August are the coolest months with temperatures ranging from 22°C (18° in a cold spell) to 32°C on a sunny day at noon. December to March is hotter, from 32°C to 42°C. Humidity is high. It is important, especially for children, to guard against dehydration in summer by drinking as much liquid as possible. October to March is the rainy season and the annual rainfall is about 1,120 mm.

History

The Portuguese navigator, Gonçalo Coelho, arrived at what is now Rio de Janeiro on 1 January 1502. Thinking that the Baía de Guanabara (the name the local Indians used) was the mouth of a great river, they called the place the January River. Although the bay was almost as large and as safe a harbour as the Baía de Todos Os Santos to the north, the Portuguese did not take of advantage of it. In fact, it was first settled by the French, who, under the Huguenot Admiral Nicholas Durand de Villegagnon, occupied Lage Island on 10 November 1555, but later transferred to Seregipe Island (now Villegagnon), where they built the fort of Coligny. The fort has been demolished to make way for the Naval College (Escola Naval) and the island itself, since the narrow channel was filled up, has become a part of the mainland. Villegagnon set up a colony as the starting point for what he called Antarctic France. Although it was not a peaceful place, it was reinforced by 300 colonists led by Villegagnon's nephew, Bois-le-Comte. Among them was the chronicler Jean de Léry.

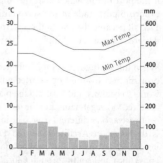

Climate:
Rio de Janeiro

A British view of Rio

This view of Rio de Janeiro by Frederick Alcock FRGS was published in 1907, but must have been written before the construction of the Avenida Central/Rio Branco: "Rio de Janeiro, although the streets are, with one or two exceptions, narrow and maladorous, is an extremely fine city. The Rua do Ouvidor is no doubt the most attractive street for the traveller, as it contains the finest shops, and in some of these are sold most beautiful humming and other birds, and imitation flowers made from bird feathers. We had determined, as a matter of precaution, to stay outside the city, and we therefore took up our quarters at the International Hotel, which is situated about half-way up the Corcovado (Hunchback) Mountain. [From the funicular railway] views of the harbour and mountains beyond, bathed in soft atmospheric blue, are presented, which cannot but perpetually live in the memory, amongst the choicest of scenes ever witnessed. And then the sunsets, as seen from 'Corcovado's' heights, beggar all description, and vie with the finest Turner ever painted. A critic once said to Turner, 'I never saw such sunsets as those you paint,' and he at once replied, 'No! don't you wish you could'. Well, you can if you go to Rio."

Trade and Travel in South America, pages 165-66.

In early 1559-60, Mem de Sá, third governor of Brazil, mounted an expedition from Salvador to attack the French, who were supported by Tamoio Indians. The Portuguese succeeded in capturing the French fort and putting an end to Antarctic France, but did not colonize the area. The French were thus able to continue to trade and maintain relations with the Tamoio, which offended the Portuguese not only territorially, but also on religious grounds, since most of the French were protestants or non-conformists. Battles on land and sea culminated in Mem de Sá sending his son Estácio, with Temiminó allies, to destroy the French in 1565. The Portuguese finally took control in 1567 when they transferred their settlement to the Morro de São Januário. It was also called the Morro do Castelo – the Esplanada do Castelo covers the site today. 1567 is generally considered the date of the founding of the city of São Sebastião do Rio de Janeiro, so called in honour of the Portuguese prince who would soon assume the throne. Though constantly attacked by Indians, the new city grew rapidly and when King Sebastião divided Brazil into two provinces, Rio was chosen capital of the southern captaincies. Salvador became sole capital again in 1576, but Rio again became the southern capital in 1608 and the seat of a bishopric. There was a further French incursion in 1710-11 as a result of the tension between France and Portugal during the war of Spanish Succession, and because of the flow of gold out of Minas Gerais through Rio.

Rio de Janeiro was by now becoming the leading city in Brazil. Not only was it the port out of which gold was shipped, but it was also the focus of the export/import trade of the surrounding agricultural lands. On 27 January 1763, it became the seat of the Viceroy. After independence, in 1834, it was declared capital of the Empire and remained the capital for 125 years.

Town planning When the Portuguese royal family fled to Brazil in 1808, the ideas that were brought over from Europe started a major transformation of the city. True, works to beautify and clean up the place had been undertaken when the city acquired viceregal status, but the remodelling which occurred in the early 19th century was on a different scale. The introduction of neoclassicism at this time is discussed in **Architecture** and **Fine Art**, page 788, but the city also expanded beyond its historical boundaries. It grew north into São Cristóvão and Tijuca and south through Glória, Catete, Flamengo and Botafogo. The prosperous coffee barons and business class built their mansions and the Imperial court was the centre of the nation's attention. The decline of the coffee trade in Rio de Janeiro state and the proclamation of the Republic did not affect the city's dominance as political, economic and cultural heart of Brazil.

Growth continued into the 20th century and one of the most significant acts was the construction of a monumental new boulevard through the middle of the commercial district. The 33 metres wide Avenida Central was driven through the old city's narrow streets in 1904-05 as the principal means of access in Rio; in 1912 it was renamed Avenida Rio Branco. Other 20th century modernization schemes included the levelling of the Morro do Castelo in the 1920s, with the earth being used to reclaim land in the bay (known as the *aterro*) for the Santos Dumont airport. Between 1941-44, the Avenida Presidente Vargas became another main access when two streets became one as the buildings in between were knocked down. While these great projects were progressing, the city was continuing to expand outwards: north into industrial zones; south around the coast; and inland, up the hills, mainly in the form of the slums known as *favelas*.

When, in 1960, the nation's capital was moved from Rio de Janeiro to Brasília, the city went into decline, especially in the commercial centre. The work that God is supposed to have devoted to Rio began to suffer badly from poor urban planning decisions, too many high-rise buildings and a failure to maintain or clean the city adequately. However, in the late 1990s, the mayor of the city, Luiz Paulo Conde, has embarked on a massive programme of regenerating the centre through remodelling and attracting residents to neglected districts. As an architect and urbanist he has brought a social vision which encompasses the improvement of *favelas* and a plan to clean up the south of the city as far as Leblon.

In December 1997 a new expressway, the Linha Amarela, was opened from the Ilha do Fundão, near the international airport, to Barra de Tijuca. It is designed, like the Linha Vermelha which runs around the bay, to speed traffic across the city, avoiding the horrendous traffic jams on the older access roads. The Linha Amarela is 25 kilometres long, cost US$400m (almost twice the original estimate) and cuts by more than half the journey time to Barra. It goes through the neighbourhoods of Bonsucesso, Meier, Água Santa and Jacarepaguá and includes four tunnels, the longest, Covanca, being 2,180 metres. There are tolls of US$1.50 and buses run along it.

While it was realized that Rio's physical and social infrastructure needed an overhaul, the authorities also recognized that the tourism sector was suffering from the negative image that the city had gained. Hence the *Plano Maravilha*, a strategic plan for tourism, which was drawn up in 1997 with Spanish assistance. The plan not only identifies the strong and weak points of the city for tourism, but also aims to contribute to the improvement of life for the citizens of Rio by including them in the sector's development. Obviously there are a great number of elements within the plan which will be accompanied by a strong campaign to sell the city in the United States and Europe and there is a lot of coordinated work to be done.

Tourism

Sights

Our description of the city's places of interest will be divided into the following areas: central Rio; south of the centre (from Lapa to the Pão de Açúcar); Copacabana, Ipanema and Leblon; Leblon to Barra de Tijuca. **Viewpoints** not mentioned under Tijuca, Corcovado and Pão de Açúcar (see below) include the Vista Chinesa (420 metres), where from a Chinese-style pavilion one can see the Lagoa Rodrigo de Freitas, Ipanema and Leblon; and the Mirante da Dona Marta (340 metres) off the Corcovado road, with the same direction of view as the Corcovado, but as it is lower the details can be seen more clearly. There is no public transport to these places.

NB Check the opening times in advance of all churches, museums and other public buildings; they change frequently. All museums and the Jardim Botânico are closed over Carnival.

Rio de Janeiro centre

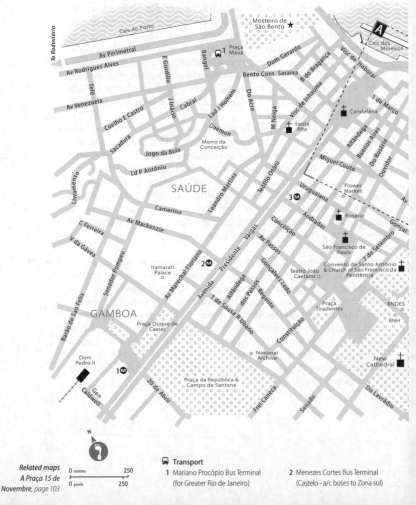

Related maps
A Praça 15 de
Novembre, page 103

0 metres 250
0 yards 250

🚌 **Transport**
1 Mariano Procópio Bus Terminal (for Greater Rio de Janeiro)

2 Menezes Cortes Bus Terminal (Castelo - a/c buses to Zona sul)

Central Rio

This is the historical part of the city, which dates from 1567 when the Portuguese moved their settlement from the area now known as Urca to the Morro de São Januário. Today the centre stretches from the Mosteiro de São Bento to the Santos Dumont airport and inland as far as the Campo de Santana park.

The hill on which the original city was located was removed in the 1920s, so the historical centre effectively ends at the São José church. The 400 years following the founding of the city saw so many changes in architectural design and fashion that, today, the centre appears to be an incoherent collection of buildings, with the ultra-modern towering over the neoclassical, which in turn sits uneasily beside the colonial. Add to this the crowded streets and the constant traffic and it may seem a daunting place to explore. Don't give up! There is much to discover and it will repay your perseverance.

An example of the juxtaposition of so many elements in close surroundings is the **Travessa do Comércio**, which runs between the Praça 15 de Novembro

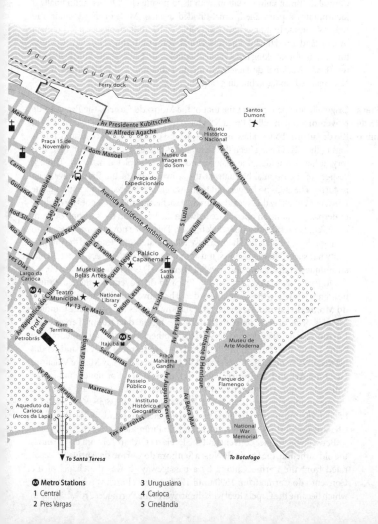

Rio de Janeiro

Ⓜ Metro Stations

1 Central
2 Pres Vargas
3 Uruguaiana
4 Carioca
5 Cinelândia

and the Rua do Ouvidor. On the northwest side of Praça 15 de Novembro (renovated in 1997, see below) is the Arco do Teles, all that remains of an 18th century construction, now incorporated into a modern building. Through the arch is the Travessa do Comércio, a narrow, twisting street with neoclassical houses and wrought iron arches over the street lamps. This is how the whole city was in the 19th century. The Travessa, now dwarfed by 20th century office blocks, leads to the church of Nossa Senhora da Lapa dos Mercadores, another 18th century construction sandwiched between the concrete and glass. On Friday nights the Travessa is very lively; along it are several restaurants, including the *Arco Imperial*, where Carmen Miranda lived between 1925-30 (her mother kept a boarding house).

Two of the main streets are particularly impressive. The Avenida Rio Branco, nearly two kilometres long, is intersected by the city's main artery, the Avenida Presidente Vargas, four and a half kilometres long and over 90 metres wide, which starts at the waterfront, divides to embrace the famous Candelária church, then crosses the Avenida Rio Branco in a magnificent straight stretch past the Central do Brasil railway station, with its imposing clock tower, until finally it incorporates a palm-lined, canal-divided avenue. Most of the Avenida Rio Branco's ornate buildings have been replaced by modern blocks; a few remain by Cinelândia and the Biblioteca Nacional. Some of the finest modern architecture is to be found along the Avenida República do Chile, such as the Petrobrás, the Banco Nacional de Desenvolvimento Econômico and the former Banco Nacional de Habitação buildings and the new Cathedral.

Around Praça 15 de Novembro Originally an open space at the foot of the Morro do Castelo, the **Praça 15 de Novembro** (often called Praça XV) has always been one of the focal points in Rio de Janeiro. Today it has one of the greatest concentrations of historic buildings in the city. Having been through various phases of development in its history, it has just undergone major remodelling (completed in 1997). The last vestiges of the original harbour, at the seaward end of the Praça, have been restored. The steps no longer lead to the water, but whereas in recent years the Praça was cut off by the Avenida Alfredo Agache, this road now goes through an underpass, creating an open space between the Praça and the seafront, beneath the Avenida Presidente Kubitschek flyover. This space now gives easy access to the ferry dock for Niterói. The area is well illuminated and clean and the municipality has started to stage shows, music and dancing in the Praça. At weekends an antiques, crafts, stamp and coin fair (Feirarte II) is held from 0900-1900.

On Rua 1 de Março, across from Praça 15 de Novembro, there are three buildings related to the Carmelite order. The convent of the **Ordem Terceira do Monte do Carmo**, started in 1611, is now used as the Faculdade Cândido Mendes. The order's present church, the **Igreja da Ordem Terceira do Carmo**, also in Rua Primeiro de Março, the other side of the old cathedral (see below) from the convent, was built in 1754, consecrated in 1770 and rebuilt between 1797 and 1826. It has strikingly beautiful portals by Mestre Valentim (see **Fine Art and Sculpture**, page 784), the son of a Portuguese nobleman and a slave girl. He also created the main altar of fine moulded silver, the throne and its chair and much else. ■ *Monday-Friday 0800-1400, Saturday 0800-1200.* A fountain designed by Mestre Valentim stands in the Praça: the Chafariz do Mestre Valentim, or Chafariz do Pirâmide.

Between the former convent and the Igreja da Ordem Terceira do Carmo is the old cathedral, the **Igreja de Nossa Senhora do Carmo da Antiga Sé**, separated from the Carmo Church by a passageway. It was the chapel of the Convento do Carmo from 1590 until 1754. A new church was built in 1761, which became the Capela Real with the arrival of the Portuguese royal family in

1808 and subsequently the city's cathedral. In the crypt are the alleged remains of Pedro Alvares Cabral, the Portuguese explorer (though Santarém, Portugal, also claims to be his last resting place). Another change instigated by the royal family was the appropriation of the Carmo convent as a residence for the queen, Dona Maria I (nicknamed A Louca because of her mental illness). Such buildings were called PR, that is, taken over by the Príncipe Regente (or, in popular terminology, *prédio roubado* – stolen building). To prevent the members of the Imperial family sullying their feet on streets used by all and sundry, a covered bridge was built between the ex-Convento and the Cathedral when the Rua 7 de Setembro was driven between them in 1857. At the rear of the old cathedral and the Carmo Church, on Rua do Carmo, is the **Oratório de Nossa Senhora do Cabo da Boa Esperança**, one of the few remaining public oratory from the colonial period in Rio.

The **Paço Imperial** (former Royal Palace) is on the southeast corner of the Praça 15 de Novembro. This beautiful colonial building was built in 1743 as the residence of the governor of the Capitania. It later became the king's storehouse and armoury (Armazens), then the Casa da Moeda, before being made into the Paço Real when the Portuguese court moved to Brazil. After Independence it became the Imperial Palace. During the Republic it was used as the post and telegraph office and fell into decline. In the 1980s it was completely restored as a cultural centre. It has several exhibition spaces, one theatre, one cinema for art films, a library, a section showing the original construction, a superb model of the city and the *Bistro* and the *Atrium* restaurants; recommended. ■ *T2328333, Tuesday to Sunday 1100-1830.*

Beside the Paço Imperial, across Rua da Assembléia, is the **Palácio Tiradentes**, built between 1922 and 1926. It is now the legislative assembly of the State of Rio de Janeiro, but the building was closed twice in the 1930s as

Praça 15 de Novembro

different administrations did not feel the need for a Chamber of Federal Deputies. The palace is in eclectic style (see **Architecture**, page 786), with a façade displaying heavy Greek influence. In front stands a statue of the Independence fighter, Tiradentes (see page 295), by Francisco de Andrade; the palace was given his name because it was on this spot, the site of the old prison, that the national hero was held prisoner while awaiting execution. ■ *Monday-Friday 1300-1900 by prior appointment, T5881000.*

In the next block southeast is the **Igreja de São José** (Rua São José e Avenida Presidente Antônio Carlos), considerably altered since its construction in the 17th century. The current building dates from 1824; it was remodelled in 1969. ■ *Monday-Friday 0900-1200, 1400-1700, Sunday 0900-1100.*

One block further southeast again, at Rua Dom Manoel 15, is the **Museu Naval e Oceanográfico**. It had a collection of paintings and prints, as well as a display of weapons and figureheads, but most of the exhibits have been moved to the Espaço Cultural da Marinha.

Turning to the northwest side of Praça 15 de Novembro, you go through the Arco do Teles and the Travessa do Comércio (see above) to Rua do Ouvidor. The **Igreja Nossa Senhora da Lapa dos Mercadores** (Rua do Ouvidor 35) was consecrated in 1750 and remodelled in 1869-72. Restoration has been completed and it is worth visiting. ■ *Monday-Friday 0800-1400.* Across the street, with its entrance at Rua 1 de Março 36, is the church of **Santa Cruz dos Militares**, built 1780-1811. It is large, stately and beautiful and has inside been well renovated in a 'light' baroque style.

The Church of **Nossa Senhora da Candelária** (1775-1810), on Praça Pio X (Dez), at the city end of Avenida Presidente Vargas where it meets Rua 1 de Março, has beautiful ceiling decorations and romantic paintings. It is on the site of a chapel founded in 1610 by Antônio da Palma after he had survived a shipwreck, an event depicted by paintings inside the present dome. ■ *Monday-Friday 0730-1200, 1300-1630, Saturday 0800-1200, Sunday 0900-1300.*

In this part of the city a number of cultural centres have opened in recent years. The **Espaço Cultural dos Correios**, Rua Visconde de Itaboraí 20, holds temporary exhibitions and a postage stamp fair on Saturdays. ■ *1000-1600, T2636566.* Opposite, with entrances on Avenida Presidente Vargas and Rua 1 de Março 66, is the **Centro Cultural Banco do Brasil (CCBB)**, which is highly recommended for good exhibitions and has a library, multimedia facilities, a cinema, concerts (US$6 at lunchtime) and a restaurant (T2160600/0626; open Tuesday-Sunday 1000-2200). At the corner of Rua Visconde de Itaboraí (No 253) and Avenida Presidente Vargas is the **Casa França-Brasil**. This building holds temporary exhibitions and is dedicated to cultural exchanges between the two countries, but is much more important for its history. Its construction dates from the first French Artistic Mission to Brazil (see **Architecture** and **Fine Art and Sculpture**, pages 786 and 783 respectively) and it was the first neoclassical building in Rio. The interior is entirely neoclassical, although the pillars and mouldings are made of wood. The roof, though, is a hybrid between the colonial Brazilian style and the newly-introduced European fashion. It was built as a customs house and the strong-room can still be seen. ■ *Tuesday-Sunday 1200-2000, T2535366.* The newest cultural centre here is the **Espaço Cultural da Marinha**, on Avenida Alfredo Agache at Avenida Presidente Kubitschek. This former naval establishment now contains museums of underwater archaeology and navigation and the *Galeota*, the boat used by the Portuguese royal family for sailing around the Baía de Guanabara. Moored outside is the warship, *Bauru*. ■ *The building is open 1200-1630, the* Bauru *Tuesday-Friday 1200-1630, Saturday-Sunday 1000-1600, T2166025.*

Offshore, but connected to the mainland by a causeway to Ilha das Cobras,

Favelas, a numberless existence

Rio de Janeiro's favelas, the slums which creep up the city's hillsides and spread out across the flat lands, have been the source of much of the city's bad press for many years. They have been represented in the press as no-go areas, where drug lords rule and fight for dominance, and out of which the city's criminals came. No sensible visitor would venture within their radius until favela tours were started in the mid-1990s. One such tour is to Vila Canoas, see page 125. The tours have the same motivation as a major scheme, Favela-Bairro, designed to rehabilitate the favelas, to show that the favelados are hardworking, simple people, and that their communities deserve the same facilities and rights as elsewhere in the city.

The name favela was first used at the end of the 19th century after soldiers on the Canudos campaign in Bahia set up their guns on a hill called the Morro das Favelas. The hill was so-called because of a type of nettle that grew there. The soldiers became known as favelados. When they returned to Rio after the campaign (see page 468), the soldiers built their homes on the Morro da Providência, but the favela nickname stuck. In time, any temporary settlement acquired the name favela and, as urban and rural poor alike strove to make it in the city, many people stayed initially in the shanties before moving to better accommodation. Many, of course, were unable to better themselves. In the 1970s and 1980s, there were some attempts to improve conditions in the favelas and residents, given assurances that they would not be forcibly removed, began to make their dwellings more permanent. Electricity and water supplies can be tapped into, usually illegally, but waste disposal and other basic facilities are rare. One of Rio's problems is that the favelas are in the middle of the city, not on the outskirts

as in other metropolises. Almost a million people live in these conditions. The huge number of entries and exits make them difficult to police. Because the shanties rub shoulders with wealthier districts, it is easy for the young favelados to see the lifestyle of the young rich, even mix with them on the beach. This can lead to envy which, for some, leads to criminality. Most of the leading criminals are in their late teens, and they die young. Their motto is: live life to the maximum as fast as possible.

Since 1993, an ambitious project has been underway to upgrade the majority of the city's favelas by 2004. A US$350m programme, aided by the Inter-American Development Bank, is providing the shanties with streets in place of alleys, sewerage, lighting, day-care centres, recreational areas, rubbish collection and transport. The favelas will be integrated with the surrounding neighbourhoods. The work also includes reforestation and the prevention of hill slides. Residents are given a say in how their district should be improved and no family will be rehoused in a part of the city which is alien to it. Having accepted that the favelas are permanent, not transitory, the city's authorities' task is to incorporate them into the whole, not leave them marginalized. An IADB special report on the project quoted O Globo: "Every citizen ought to have the right to live on a street in a house with a number".

The Secretaria Municipal da Habitação and IplanRio, the Empresa Municipal de Informática e Planejamento, produce a magazine on Favela-Bairro, available from Avenida Afonso Cavalcanti 455, bloco B, 4 andar, CEP 20.211-110, Rio de Janeiro, T2732345, or R Gago Coutinho 52, Largo do Machado, CEP 22.221-070, Rio de Janeiro, T5563399.

With thanks to Marcelo N Armstrong

is the **Ilha Fiscal**. It was built as a customs house at the emperor's request, but he deemed it too beautiful, so he said that it should be used only for official parties. Only one was ever held, five days before the Republic began. It is now a museum, linked with the Naval Cultural Centre. Boats leave Wednesday, Friday and Sunday at 1300, 1430 and 1600 (30 minutes later October to March). T2339165. The island is passed by the ferry to Niterói.

Rio de Janeiro

Wild Jock of Skelater

The crypt of Convento de Santo Antônio contains the tomb of a Scottish soldier of fortune known as 'Wild Jock of Skelater'. He was in the service of the Portuguese Government during the Napoleonic War, and had the distinction of being appointed the first Commander-in-Chief of the Army in Brazil. The statue of Santo Antônio was made a captain in the Portuguese army after his help had been sought to drive out the French in 1710, and his salary paid to the monastery. In 1810 the statue became a major, in 1814 a lieutenant-colonel, and was granted the Grand Cross of the Order of Christ. He was retired without pay in 1914. The church and convent are open Monday-Friday 1400-1700.

Just north of Candelária, on a promontory overlooking the bay, is the **Mosteiro** (monastery) **de São Bento**. The monastery's church, dedicated to Nossa Senhora de Monserrate (but usually referred to as the Igreja do Mosteiro de São Bento) contains much of what is best in the 17th and 18th century art of Brazil. Monks of the Benedictine order arrived in Rio de Janeiro in 1586, five years after their installation in Salvador.

São Bento is reached either by a narrow road from Rua Dom Gerardo 68, or by a lift whose entrance is at Rua Dom Gerardo 40 (taxi to the monastery from centre US$5). Both routes lead to a praça with tall trees, but stepping out of the lift into this oasis increases the sense of escape from the city below. The church's façade is in the mannerist style, plain and undecorated. You go throught the *galilé*, the antechamber for the unbaptized with its fine tiles, and enter the main body of the church. *Corta ventos*, doors which keep out the draughts so that the candles inside are not extinguished, are the last obstacle to the sight of the interior. Not an inch is unadorned in gold and red. The carving and gilding is remartable, much of it by Frei Domingos da Conceição (see **Fine Art and Sculpture**, page 783). The paintings, too, should be seen; 'O Salvador', the masterpiece of Brazil's first painter, Frei Ricardo do Pilar, hangs in the sacristy. The lamps (*lampadarios* – two of which are attributed to Mestre Valentim) are of solid silver which, coming from Peru and Bolivia, was of greater value than Brazil's own gold. See also the two *anjos tocheiros*, angels carrying torches, common in many baroque churches. On top of the main altar is a statue of Nossa Senhora de Monserrate, made by Frei Domingos da Conceição; the eyes of both the Virgin and her Child are made from painted birds eggs. The Chapels of the Immaculate Conception (Nossa Senhora da Conceição) and of the Most Holy Sacrament (Santíssimo Sacramento) are masterpieces of colonial art. The organ, dating from the end of the 18th century, is very interesting.

Every Sunday at 1000, mass is sung with Gregorian chant and music, which is free, but you should arrive an hour early to get a seat. On other days, mass is at 0715. At other times you may be lucky enough to hear the monks singing. There is a bookshop. The monastery is a few minutes' walk from Praça Mauá, turning left off Avenida Rio Branco; Rua Dom Gerardo 68 is behind the massive, new RBI building. ■ *Daily 0800-1230, 1400-1730, shorts not allowed.*

Also easily reached from Praça Mauá and requiring a climb is the **Morro da Conceição**, another hill from which the early Portuguese settlers could survey the bay. The first constructions on the hill were religious and a bishop's palace was built in 1702, the Palácio da Conceição. This and the subsequently built Fortaleza da Conceição are currently in the hands of the military. The Palácio has a small museum and the area is perfectly safe to visit as another remnant of colonial Rio. Above the door of the Fortaleza is another of the few remaining public oratories; it is lit at night.

The **Largo da Carioca**, a remarkable ensemble of old and new plus the muddle of the street vendors who have occupied the praça beween Rua da Carioca and the Metrô station, is another good location for seeing a variety of sites within a small area.

The second oldest convent in the city is the 17th century **Convento de Santo Antônio**, on a hill off the Largo da Carioca, built between 1608 and 1615. Its church has a marvellous sacristy adorned with blue tiles and paintings illustrating the life of St Anthony. In the church itself, the baroque decoration is concentrated in the chancel, the main altar and the two lateral altars. Santo Antônio is a particular object of devotion for women who want to find husbands and many will be seen in the precincts.

Separated from this church only by some iron railings is the charming church of the Ordem Terceira de **São Francisco da Penitência**, built in 1773. Currently closed for renovation, it contains much more carving and gilding of walls and altar than its neighbour. The workmanship is superb. In the ceiling over the nave is a fine panel painted by José de Oliveira. There is a museum attached to the church. The church is due to reopen in 2000 when a new Museu de Arte Sacra will be inaugurated. This group of buildings is called officially the Conjunto Arquetetônico do Morro de Santo Antônio.

Across Ruas da Carioca and 7 de Setembro is the Church of **São Francisco de Paula**, at the upper end of the Rua do Ouvidor. The first stone was laid in 1759 and construction was completed in 1801. It contains some of Mestre Valentim's work – the carvings in the main chapel and the lovely Capela da Nossa Senhora da Vitória (Our Lady of Victory). The beautiful fountain at the back of the church plays only at night. ■ *Monday-Friday 0900-1300.*

One long block behind the Largo da Carioca and São Francisco de Paula is the **Praça Tiradentes**, old and shady, with a statue to Dom Pedro I. Erected in 1862, it is the work of Luís Rochet and shows the Emperor on horseback, declaring Independence. At the northeast corner of the praça is the **Teatro João Caetano**, named after a famous 19th century actor. It was most recently restored in 1979 (T2211223). Shops in nearby streets specialize in selling goods for *umbanda*, the Afro-Brazilian religion.

South of the Largo da Carioca are the modern buildings on Avenida República do Chile mentioned above. The **New Cathedral**, the **Catedral Metropolitana**, was dedicated in November 1976. It is a cone-shaped building with an internal height of 68 metres, diameter 104 metres and external height 83 metres; its capacity is 5,000 seated, 20,000 standing. The most striking feature is four enormous 60 metre-high stained-glass windows. It is still incomplete. ■ *0800-1800.*

Crossing Avenida República do Paraguai from the east side of the Catedral Metropolitana, you come to an open area with the Petrobrás building and the station, with museum, for the tram to Santa Teresa (entrance on Rua Senador Dantas – see below). Soon after leaving the station the tram traverses the **Arcos da Lapa**, which were built as an aqueduct to take water from the Rio Carioca to the Largo da Carioca.

We are concerned here only with the southeastern end of the avenue, after it has crossed Avenida República do Chile/Avenida Almirante Barroso. Here are the last vestiges of the early 20th century project of the grand Avenida Central.

Facing Praça Marechal Floriano is the **Teatro Municipal**, one of the most magnificent buildings in Brazil in the Eclectic style (see **Architecture**, page 786). It was built in 1905-09, in imitation of the Opéra in Paris. On either side of the colonnaded façade are rotundas, surmounted by cupolas. Above the columns are statues of two women, Poetry and Music. The decorative features

Around Largo da Carioca

See also box, page 106

Avenida Rio Branco

Rio de Janeiro

inside and out represent many styles, all lavishly executed. Opera and orchestral performances are given here (T2974411). To book a tour of the theatre, ask for extension – *ramal* – 236 in advance, Monday-Friday 0900-1600, US$2 per person; the tour is worth it to see front and back stage, the decorations and the machine rooms. The box office is at the back of the building and is hard to find; ticket prices start at about US$15. The small museum that used to be below the theatre is now at Rua São João Batista 103/105, Botafogo, **Museu dos Teatros**. ■ *1100-1700 Monday-Friday*.

Across the avenue is the **Biblioteca Nacional**, at Avenida Rio Branco 219. This building also dates from the first decade of the 20th century. The monumental staircase leads to a hall, off which lead the fine internal staircases of Carrara marble. The first national library was brought to Brazil by the Prince Regent, Dom João, in 1808, the collection coming from the Ajuda Palace in Lisbon. Today it houses over three million volumes and documents, among which are many rare manuscripts. ■ *Monday-Friday 0900-2000, Saturday 0900-1500; T2628255.*

The third major building in this group, opposite the Teatro Municipal, is the **Museu Nacional de Belas Artes**, Avenida Rio Branco 199. It was built between 1906 and 1908, also in Eclectic style. It has about 800 original paintings and sculptures and some thousand direct reproductions. There is a gallery dedicated to works by Brazilian artists from the 17th century onwards, including paintings by Frans Janszoon Post (Dutch 1612-80), who painted Brazilian landscapes in classical Dutch style (see **The Dutch in Brazil**, page 492) and the Frenchmen Debret and Taunay (see **Fine Art and Sculpture**, page 783, for these and other painters represented). Another gallery charts the development of Brazilian art in 20th century, including works by Cândido Portinari, Alberto da Veiga Guignard and others. A third gallery contains work by foreign artists. There is also a hall for temporary exhibitions. ■ *Tuesday-Friday 1000-1800; Saturday, Sunday and holidays 1400-1800; US$1, T2409869.*

Those interested in contemporary art will also visit the **Palácio Capanema**, the former Ministry of Education and Health building, then the Palácio da Cultura. It is on the Esplanada do Castelo, at the junction of Avenida Graça Aranha and Rua Araújo Porto Alegre, and dates from 1937-45 (Unesco has declared it an International Monument). A team of architects led by Lúcio Costa and under the guidance of Le Corbusier designed it; Oscar Niemeyer and Affonso Reidy were in the group (see **Architecture**, page 786). Inside are the great murals of Cândido Portinari, paintings and tiles, as well as other works by renowned artists. The gardens were laid out by Roberto Burle Marx (see page 128).

In the Rua de Santa Luzia, close by the Palácio Capanema and overwhelmed by tall office buildings, is the attractive little church of **Santa Luzia**. When built in 1752 it had only one tower; the other was added late in the 19th century. Feast day is 13 December, when devotees bathe their eyes with holy water, which is considered miraculous.

Praça Mahatma Gandhi, at the end of Avenida Rio Branco, is flanked on one side by the old cinema and amusement centre of the city, known as Cinelândia. The cast iron fountain in the ornamental garden was moved here from Praça 15 de Novembro.

Next to the praça is the **Passeio Público**, a garden planted in 1779-83 by the artist Mestre Valentim, whose bust is near the old former gateway. A coin and stamp market is held here on Sunday mornings. ■ *Daily 0730-1900.*

Museu do Instituto Histórico e Geográfico, Avenida Augusto Severo 8 (10th floor), just off Avenida Beira Mar, is across the street from the Passeio Público. It has an interesting collection of historical objects, Brazilian products and the artefacts of its peoples. ■ *Monday-Friday 1200-1700.*

In the corner of the centre bounded by Praça 15 de Novembro and the Esplanada do Castelo is an area which has changed significantly since colonial times. Most alterations were made in the 20th century, first with the removal of the old municipal fish market, for health reasons, then with the levelling of the Morro do Castelo in the 1920s. There are two squares here, Praça Marechal Âncora, or Praça Rui Barbosa and Praça do Expedicionário. The only remnant of the Morro do Castelo is a short stretch of the Ladeira da Misericórdia, at the foot of which is the church of Nossa Senhora de Bonsucesso, also known as the church of the Santa Casa da Misericórdia. The Santa Casa itself is behind the church. The colonial hospital made way for a neoclassical building in the mid-19th century. The main focus here is the **Museu Histórico Nacional**, which contains a collection of historical treasures, colonial sculpture and furniture, maps, paintings, arms and armour, silver and porcelain. The building was once the old War Arsenal of the Empire, part of which was built in 1762 (this part is called the Casa do Trem). Two years later the Pátio de Minerva was added and significant expansion was done in 1808. Further changes were made in 1922 when the museum was inaugurated. ■ *Tuesday-Friday, 1000-1730; Saturday, Sunday and holidays 1400-1800; admission US$1, T2409529.*

Praça Marechal Âncora/Praça Rui Barbosa

Museu da Imagem e do Som, also on Praça Rui Barbosa, has many photographs of Brazil and modern Brazilian paintings; also collections and recordings of Brazilian classical and popular music and a non-commercial cinema Friday-Sunday. ■ *Monday-Friday, 1300-1800.*

Praça da República and **Campo de Santana** is an extensive and picturesque public garden close to the Pedro II, or Central Railway station. The Parque Júlio Furtado in the middle of the square is populated by agoutis (or gophers), best seen at dusk; there is also an artificial grotto, with swans. At Praça da República 197 lived Marechal Deodoro da Fonseca, who proclaimed Brazil a republic in 1889 (plaque). On the same side of the Praça is the Arquivo Nacional in the neoclassical former Casa da Moeda (Praça da República e Rua Azeredo Coutinho; closed for repairs) and the Faculdade de Direito, Rua Moncorvo Filho 8, in the Solar do Conde dos Arcos. On the opposite side of Avenida Presidente Vargas from the Praça are the Palácio and Panteão do Duque de Caxias.

West of the centre: to São Cristóvão

Palácio do Itamaraty (**Museu Histórico e Diplomático**, Historical and Diplomatic Museum), Avenida Marechal Floriano 196, is in the next block east from the Palácio do Duque de Caxias. Built in neoclassical style in the 1850s for the coffee baron Francisco José da Rocha, it became the president's residence between 1889 and 1897 and then the Ministry of Foreign Affairs until the opening of Brasília. ■ *Guided tours on Monday, Wednesday and Friday hourly between 1315 and 1615, T2532828, recommended.*

Over the Morro da Providência, which is between the Estação Dom Pedro II and the bay, is the **Cemitério dos Ingleses**, Rua da Gamboa 181. The cemetery was granted to the British community by Dom João, Regent of Portugal, in 1810. It is the oldest cemetery in Rio. Catholics who could afford a burial were laid to rest inside their churches (see the numbers on the church floors, marking the graves), but the British in Rio, being non-Catholic, were not allowed to be buried in the religious establishments.

About three kilometres west of the Praça da República (beyond the Sambódromo – see box on **Carnival**, page) is the **Quinta da Boa Vista**, formerly the Emperor's private park, from 1809 to 1889. The Palace in which the Imperial family lived now houses the Museu Nacional. In recent years the Quinta da Boa Vista has had the problem of thieves operating by the park entrance and in the park itself. The safest way to reach the museum is by taking a taxi to the main door. Having said that, it can be reached by Metrô to São Cristóvão, then cross the railway line and walk a few metres to the park. This is safer than taking a bus. If you are comfortable in crowds, perhaps the best time to visit the Quinta da Boa Vista is Saturday or better still Sunday afternoon. There are more people and therefore more police because it is full of Cariocas looking for fun and relaxation. It is a good time for people watching (but don't take an expensive camera to do so). The park becomes a noisy mixture of colours, smells of hot dogs and corn, people playing football, preachers warning of the end of the world, street sellers and so on.

The **Museu Nacional** in the Quinta da Boa Vista has important collections which are poorly displayed. The building was the principal palace of the Emperors of Brazil, but only the unfurnished Throne Room and ambassadorial reception room on the second floor reflect past glories. In the entrance hall is the famous Bendegó meteorite, found in the State of Bahia in 1888; its original weight, before some of it was chipped, was 5,360 kilograms. Besides several foreign collections of note (for example, of Peruvian and Mexican archaeology, graeco-roman ceramics, Egyptian mummies), the Museum contains collections of Brazilian Indian weapons, dresses, utensils etc, of minerals and of historical documents. There are also collections of birds, beasts, fishes and

Rio west of centre

butterflies. Despite the need for conservation work, the museum is still worth visiting. ■ *1000-1600, closed Monday; entrance US$2; T5676316. Some of the collections are open to qualified research students only.*

Museu de Fauna, also in the Quinta da Boa Vista, contains a most interesting collection of Brazilian fauna. ■ *Tuesday-Sunday 1200-1700.*

The **Jardim Zoológico** in the Quinta da Boa Vista contains Brazilian and imported wild animals and a comprehensive collection of tropical birds. Many 'visitors' come to the gardens, so it is a good place for birdwatchers. The gateway is a replica of Robert Adam's famous gateway to Syon House, near London. The zoo is maintained by a special foundation, the Fundação Rio Zoo, which is making efforts to provide the animals with good conditions. ■ *Daily 0900-1630, except Monday (best in the morning), US$2; T5692024.*

Transport As said above, the nearest Metrô is São Cristóvão on Linha 2. If you want to go by bus, take 472 or 474 from the centre; 472 from Glória, Flamengo, Botafogo or Leme; and 474 from Copacabana, Ipanema or Leblon.

Maracanã Stadium, officially called Estádio Mário Filho, is one of the largest sports centres in the world. The football ground has seating capacity for 200,000 spectators. Matches are worth going to if only for the spectators' samba bands. There are three types of ticket: *cadeiras* (individual chairs), the most expensive; *arquibancadas* (terraces), good for watching the game, but don't sit at the edge of two rival groups of fans; *geral* (standing), the cheapest, not recommended, not safe. Prices vary according to the game, but note that agencies charge much more for tickets than at the gate. It is cheaper to buy tickets from club sites on the day before the match.

Maracanã is now used only for major games; Rio teams play most matches at their home grounds (still a memorable experience). Hotels can arrange visits to football matches: a good idea on Sunday when the metrô is closed and buses are very full. ■ *A guided tour of the stadium (in Portuguese) from Gate 16 costs US$2 and of the museum, US$0.50, T5689962, highly recommended to football fans.*

Useful information Don't take valuables or wear a watch; take special care when entering and leaving the stadium. The rivalry between the local clubs Flamengo and Vasco da Gama is intense, often leading to violence, so it is advisable to avoid their encounters. Don't be tempted to buy a club shirt or favour on match day: if you find yourself in the wrong place, you could be in trouble.

Transport Metrô station Maracanã is on Linha 2, one stop beyond São Cristóvão.

Buses: 238 and 239 from the centre; 434 and 464 from Glória, Flamengo and Botafogo; 455 from Copacabana; 433 and 464 from Ipanema and Leblon.

The **Museu de Astronomia/ National Observatory**, founded 1827, is on São Januário hill, Rua General Bruce 586, São Cristóvão. The building housing the National Observatory was inspired by castles on the river Loire in France. The museum contains scientific instruments, a model of the solar system and an exhibition called The Four Corners of the Universe (*Quatro Cantos de Origem*). ■ *Tuesday-Friday 0930-1700, guided tours 1000-1200; 1400-1600. T5807010 after 1700 to arrange a night viewing.*

The church of **Nossa Senhora da Penha**, in the northern suburb of Penha, is on a bare rock in which 365 steps are cut. This staircase is ascended by pilgrims on their knees during the festival month of October; there is a funicular for those unable to do this. The church in its present form dates from the early 20th century, based on an early 18th century chapel. The first religious building, a hermitage, was built in 1632. Its prominent position makes Nossa Senhora da Penha a major landmark and its balustrade provides fine views. ■ *Buses 497 from Copacabana, 340 and 346 from centre go there.*

South of the centre: Lapa to the Pão de Açúcar

The commercial district ends where the Avenida Rio Branco meets the Avenida Beira Mar. This avenue, with its royal palms, bougainvilleas and handsome buildings, coasting the Botafogo and Flamengo beaches (too polluted for bathing), makes a splendid drive; its scenery is shared by the urban motorway, Avenida Infante Dom Henrique, along the beach over reclaimed land (the *Aterro*), which leads to Botafogo and through two tunnels to Copacabana. To your left as you head south is the bay, ahead of you the Pão de Açúcar (Sugar Loaf) and inland the districts of Lapa, Glória, Catete and Flamengo. In this section we shall also deal with Santa Teresa, the district west of Glória reached by tram from beside the Catedral Metropolitana (see above).

On the Glória and Flamengo waterfront, with a view of the Pão de Açúcar and Corcovado, is the **Parque do Flamengo**, designed by Burle Marx (see page 128), opened in 1965 during the 400th anniversary of the city's founding and landscaped on 100 hectares reclaimed from the Bay. The park (officially called Parque Brigadeiro Eduardo Gomes) runs from the *aterro* on which Santos Dumont airport stands to the Morro da Viúva and Botafogo beach. The area was reclaimed from the sea using 1.2 million metric tonnes of earth. Behind the War Memorial (see below) is the public yacht marina. In the park are many sports fields; there are a sailboat basin and model plane flying field; for children, a marionette theatre, a miniature village and a staffed nursery. There are night amusements, such as bandstands and areas for dancing. Security in the park is in the hands of vigilante policemen and it is a popular recreation area. On Sunday and holidays between 0700 and 1800 the avenues through the park are closed to traffic.

At the city end of the Parque Flamengo is the **Museu de Arte Moderna**, a spectacular building at Avenida Infante Dom Henrique 85, near the National War Memorial. It suffered a disastrous fire in 1978; the collection is now being rebuilt and several countries have donated works of art. There is also a non-commercial cinema. The collection of contemporary Brazilian art includes very expressive drawings by Cândido Portinari from the 1940s and 50s and drawings and etchings of everyday work scenes by Gregório Gruber, made in the 1970s. ■ *Tuesday-Sunday 1200-1800, US$2, T2102188.*

The **Monumento aos Mortos da Segunda Guerra Mundial/National War Memorial** to Brazil's dead in the Second World War is at Avenida Infante Dom Henrique 75, opposite Praça Paris. The Memorial takes the form of two slender columns supporting a slightly curved slab, representing two palms uplifted to heaven. In the crypt are the remains of the Brazilian soldiers killed in Italy in 1944-45. ■ *Crypt and museum are open Tuesday-Sunday 1000-1700, but beach clothes and rubber-thonged sandals are not permitted.*

Praça Paris, built on reclaimed ground near the Largo da Glória, is much admired for the beauty of its formal gardens and illuminated fountains.

The beautiful little church on the Glória Hill, overlooking the Parque do Flamengo, is **Nossa Senhora da Glória do Outeiro**. It was the favourite church of the imperial family; Dom Pedro II was baptized here. The building is polygonal, with a single tower. Construction began in 1735 and was completed in 1791. It contains some excellent examples of blue-faced Brazilian tiling. Its main altar, of wood, was carved by Mestre Valentim. ■ *The church, 0800-1200 (only Saturday-Sunday) and 1300-1700 weekdays, is reached by bus 119 from the centre and 571 from Copacabana. The adjacent museum of religious art keeps the same hours, but is closed on Monday, T2252869/5574600.*

Another main route runs behind Glória Hill from the centre to Botafogo. Avenida Augusto Severo starts at the Passeio Público, passes Praça Paris, then becomes Rua do Catete as it runs through Catete to the Largo do Machado.

Parque do Catete is a charming small park between the Palácio do Catete (Museu da República) and Praia do Flamengo; it has many birds and monkeys.

Museu da República, on Rua do Catete 153, is the former palace of a coffee baron, the Barão de Nova Friburgo. The palace was built in 1858-66. In 1887 it was converted into the presidential seat, until the move to Brasília. The ground floor of this museum consists of the sumptuous rooms of the coffee baron's mansion. The first floor is devoted to the history of the Brazilian republic. You can also see the room where Getúlio Vargas shot himself. The museum is highly recommended. Behind the museum is the Parque do Catete. ■ *Tuesday-Sunday, 1200-1700, US$2.50, T5573150, take bus 571 from Copacabana, or the Metrô to Catete station.*

Museu do Folclore Edison Carneiro, on Rua do Catete 181, houses a collection which should not be missed. The very interesting objects have been well selected and arranged, but there are no explanations other than in a book in Portuguese which costs US$2.50. There is a collection of small ceramic figures representing everyday life in Brazil, some very funny, some scenes animated by electric motors. Many artists are represented and displays show the way of life in different parts of the country. There are fine Candomblé and Umbanda costumes, religious objects, ex-votos and sections on many of Brazil's festivals. It has a small, but excellent library, with helpful, friendly staff for finding books on Brazilian culture, history and anthropology. ■ *Tuesday-Friday 1100-1800, Saturday-Sunday 1500-1800, free, T2850441. Photography is allowed, but without flash. Take bus 571 from Copacabana, or the Metrô to Catete station.*

Museu do Telefone, on Rua 2 de Dezembro 63, exhibits old telephones. On the top floor there is a semi-mechanical telephone exchange from the 1940s plus Getúlio Vargas' golden telephone and a replica of the telephone of Dom Pedro II. Recommended. ■ *Tuesday-Sunday 0900-1900, T5563189.*

Museu Carmen Miranda, in Parque do Flamengo in front of Rui Barbosa 560 (beneath the Morro da Viúva), displays over 3,000 items, including the famous singer's gowns, jewellery, reviews, recordings etc. A video compilation is shown, a treat for cinema buffs. ■ *Tuesday-Friday 1100-1700, Saturday, Sunday and holidays 1000-1600, US$0.30, Sunday free, but not always open Sunday; T5512597.*

Santa Teresa

This hilly inner suburb southwest of the centre is well known as the coolest part of Rio. It boasts many colonial and 19th century buildings, set in narrow, curving, tree-lined streets.

History   In 1624, Antônio Gomes do Desterro erected a hermitage dedicated to Nossa Senhora do Desterro on the hill which was to become Santa Teresa. The name was changed from Morro do Desterro to Santa Teresa after the construction in 1750 of a convent in honour of two Carmelite sisters, Jacinta and Francisca. The Convento da Santa Teresa, at Joaquim Murtinho e Ladeira de Santa Teresa, can only be seen from the outside; the Carmelite nuns do not admit visitors. From the 17th to the mid-18th century, work was done in various stages to bring water from the Rio Carioca to the city. The final project was the Aqueduto dos Arcos (**Arcos da Lapa**), which carried water from Santa Teresa to the Chafariz da Carioca, with its 16 fountains, in the centre of the city. The aqueduct's use was changed at the end of the 19th century with the introduction of electric trams in Rio. The inaugural run along the tracks laid on top of the arches was on 1 September 1896. It has been a major task to preserve the Santa Teresa tram, called the *bondinho*, the last such service in Rio.

Santa Teresa attracted well-to-do and foreign inhabitants not only because of its cooler climate, but also because it was free of the yellow fever which infested the lower parts of the city. Some of the fine historical residences that can be seen include a castle-like house in Vista Alegre (the Casa de Valentim), the tiled Chácara dos Viegas in Rua Monte Alegre, the Casa de Benjamin Constant at Rua Monte Alegre 255 (open Thursday to Sunday 1300-1700), the Chácara do Céu Museum and the Chalé Murtinho, Rua Murtinho Nobre 41. This was the house in which Dona Laurinda Santos Lobo held her famous artistic, political and intellectual salons at the turn of the 20th century. The house was in ruins until it was partially restored and turned into a cultural centre called **Parque das Ruínas** in 1998. It has superb views of the city, an exhibition space, an open-air stage (live music Thursday) and a snack bar. It is open 1000-1700 daily and a bridge connects it to the Chácara do Céu (see below). Also in the district is the old hotel known as the *Hotel das Paineiras*. See also the Rua Aprazível and Largo de Guimarães.

Today, Santa Teresa's old houses are lived in by artists, intellectuals and makers of handicrafts. Twice a year artists open their houses to visitors, called *Arte de Portas Abertas*. Many buildings between Largo do Guimarães and Largo das Neves are being restored.

Most visitors in the daytime will arrive on the tram (see **Transport**, page 144). If you stay to the end of the line, Largo das Neves, you will be able to appreciate the small-town feel of the place. There are several bars here, including *Goiabeira*, simple and charming with a nice view of the praça. Either on the way back, or on the way up from the centre, the essential stop is the Largo do Guimarães, which has some excellent eating places (see **Eating**, page 133) and a great atmosphere.

The 'bond'

The tram which runs to and from Santa Teresa is the last example of a form of public transport which used to run in many Brazilian cities. Before electrification, street cars were pulled by mules. The first street car lines were financed by securities, or share bonds, but when one of the first tramway companies failed, its shares became worthless. The term 'bonds', though, stuck, first as a form of rebuke, then as the name for all trolleys and trams. Hence bonde and, in Rio, the even more familiar bondinho.

The **Chácara do Céu**, or Fundação Raymundo Ottoni de Castro Maia, Rua Murtinho Nobre 93, has a wide range of art objects and modern painters, including Brazilian; exhibitions change through the year. ■ *Daily except Tuesday 1200-1700, US$1, T2321386, take the Santa Teresa tram to Curvelo station, walk along Rua Dias de Barros, following the signposts to Parque das Ruínas.* Castro Maia's former residence, **Museu Açude**, Estrada do Açude 764, Alto da Boa Vista, Floresta da Tijuca, is also a museum. Every Sunday it has a 'brunch' with music, 1230-1700. ■ *T2380368.*

Security

In recent years, visitors have been put off going to Santa Teresa because of a reputation for crime which has spilled over from neighbouring *favelas*. It would, however, be a great shame to miss this unique town-within-a-city. The crime rate has been reduced and normally a policeman rides each *bondinho*, but you are advised not to take valuables or look 'wealthy'. A T-shirt, shorts and enough money for a meal should be sufficient. Avoid long walks on streets that are far from the main centres of Largo das Neves and Largo do Guimarães. The area around the Hotel das Paineiras is well-patrolled.

Transport

Santa Teresa is best visited on the traditional open-sided **tram**, the *bondinho* (see **Arcos da Lapa** above). To get to the *bondinho* station, take the Metrô to Cinelândia, go to R Senador Dantas then walk along to R Profesor Lélio Gama (look for *Banco do Brasil* on the corner). The station is up this street. Take the line called Paula Mattos (a second line is Dois Irmãos) and enjoy the trip as it passes over the aqueduct, winding its way up to the district's historic streets. The journey ends at the round praça called Largo das Neves; here the tram turns round for the journey back to R Prof L Gama. The trams are open-sided; do not carry valuables. Fare US$0.50 one way. **Buses**: Nos 206 and 214 run from Avenida Rio Branco in the centre to Santa Teresa. At night, only take a **taxi**.

Pão de Açúcar and Corcovado

The district of Botafogo sits roughly mid-way between the Pão de Açúcar and Corcovado, as the crow flies. On the ground, access to either peak from this part of the city is quite straightforward, but involves many more twists and turns than a bird would take. There are also plenty of other attractions at ground level.

Pão de Açúcar

At 396 metres, the Pão de Açúcar, or Sugar Loaf, is a massive granite cone at the entrance to Guanabara Bay. The bird's eye view of the city and beaches is very beautiful. There is a restaurant (excellent location, mixed reports on food, closes 1900) and a playground for children on the Morro da Urca, half way up, where there are also shows at night (consult the cultural sections in the newspapers). You can get refreshments at the top.

The sea level cable car station is in a military area, so it is safe to visit. At Praia Vermelha, the beach to the south of the rock, is the *Círculo Militar da Praia*

Rio de Janeiro

Vermelha restaurant, which is open to the public (no sign). It has wonderful views, but is not so good for food or service; stop there for a drink anyway. From Praia Vermelha, the Pista Cláudio Coutinho runs around the foot of the rock. It is a paved path for walking, jogging and access to various climbing places. It is open until 1800, but you can stay on the path after that. Here you have mountain, forest and sea side-by-side, right in the heart of the city. You can also use the Pista Coutinho as a way of getting up the Pão de Açúcar more cheaply than the US$12.50 cable-car ride. About 350 metres from the path entrance is a track to the left which leads though the forest to Morro de Urca,

Glória, Santa Teresa, Catete, Flamengo

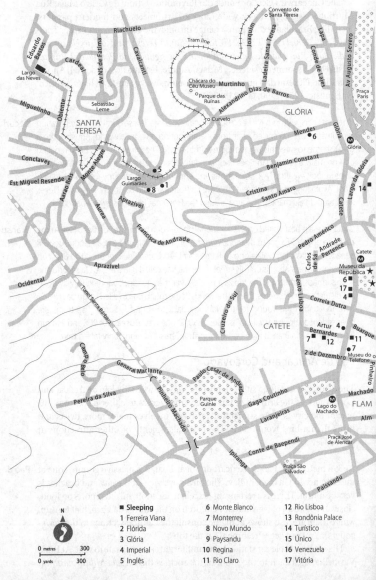

■ Sleeping	6 Monte Blanco	12 Rio Lisboa
1 Ferreira Viana	7 Monterrey	13 Rondônia Palace
2 Flórida	8 Novo Mundo	14 Turístico
3 Glória	9 Paysandu	15 Único
4 Imperial	10 Regina	16 Venezuela
5 Inglês	11 Rio Claro	17 Vitória

from where the cable car can be taken for US$10 (you can come down this way, too, but if you take the cable car from sea level you must pay full fare). You can save even more money, but use more energy, by climbing the Caminho da Costa, a path to the summit of the Pão de Açúcar. Only one stretch, of 10 metres, requires climbing gear (even then, some say it is not necessary), but if you wait at the bottom of the path for a group going up, they will let you tag along. This way you can descend to Morro de Urca by cable car for free and walk down from there.

There are 35 rock routes up the mountain, with various degrees of difficulty. The best months for climbing are April to August. See **Sports**, page 142, for climbing clubs; there is also a book on climbing routes.

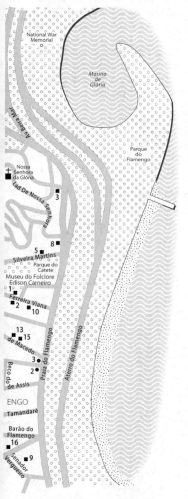

Transport Buses: Bus 107 (from the centre, Catete or Flamengo) and 511 from Copacabana (512 to return) take you to the cable-car station, Avenida Pasteur 520, at the foot. **Cable car**: Praia Vermelha to Morro de Urca: first car goes up at 0800, then every 30 minutes (or when full), until the last comes down at 2200. From Urca to Sugar Loaf, the first connecting cable car goes up at 0815 then every 30 minutes (or when full), until the last leaves the summit at 2200; the return trip costs US$8 (US$6 to Morro da Urca, half-way up). The old cableway has been completely rebuilt. Termini are ample and efficient and the present Italian cable cars carry 75 passengers. Even on the most crowded days there is little queuing.

Urca The suburb of Urca was built in 1922 when an *aterro* was made at the base ot the Pão de Açúcar on its north side. It is mostly residential. Note the small statue of São Pedro holding the keys to heaven on a rock in the sea in front of the church. From the esplanade there are lovely views of the sunset behind Corcovado.

Botafogo For a long time, Botafogo was the terminus of Linha 1 of the Metrô, but an extension to Arcoverde in Copacabana is now under construction. It is a major road junction for routes from the centre to Urca, Copacabana and Jardim Botânico. In the district is the Morro do Pasmado, which has fine views of the bay. Also in Botafogo is one of the city's main shopping malls, Rio Sul, a good place to go for

Rio de Janeiro

● **Eating**
1 Adega do Pimenta
2 Alcaparra
3 Alho e Oleo
4 Amazônia
5 Bar do Arnaudo
6 Casa da Suiça
7 Galicia Grill
8 Sobrenatural

entertainment, services, eating and, of course, shopping. It has been totally refurbished and is completely safe (more details are given under **Shopping**, page 140). As well as the Theatre Museum mentioned above (see **Teatro Municipal**, page 107), there are three important museums in Botafogo.

The **Casa de Rui Barbosa**, Rua São Clemente 134, T5370036, former home of the Brazilian jurist and statesman, contains his library and other possessions and a public library specializing in law and literature. ■ *Tuesday-Friday 0900-1615, Saturday, Sunday and holidays 1400-1715. The large garden is also open to the public. Buses 106, 176, 178 from the centre; 571 from Flamengo; 591 from Copacabana.*

The **Museu do Índio**, Rua das Palmeiras 55, is being partly renovated so there is only a small exhibition. It houses 12,000 objects from many Brazilian Indian groups, including basketry, ceramics, masks and weapons. There is also a small, well-displayed handicraft shop (shop closes for lunch 1200-1400). It belongs to the Fundação Nacional do Índio (Funai) and was set up by Marechal Rondon. ■ *Monday-Friday 1000-1730, Saturday-Sunday 1300-1700, T2868799, from Botafogo Metrô it's a 10-minute walk; from Catete, bus 571 (Glória-Leblon) passes Ruas Bento Lisboa and São Clemente. There is also a library of ethnology at the same location, which has friendly and helpful staff. ■ Weekdays.*

Museu Villa-Lobos, Rua Sorocaba 200, houses a collection of personal objects belonging to the great composer, with instruments, scores, books and recordings. ■ *Monday-Friday 1000-1700, T2663845.*

Urca, Botafogo, Cosme Velho

To reach the statue of the Cristo Redentor at the summit of Corcovado, you have to go through Laranjeiras and Cosme Velho. The road through these districts heads west out of Catete. Near the station for the cog railway which climbs to the statue are two important cultural sites.

Corcovado

The **Museu Internacional de Arte Naif do Brasil** (MIAN), Rua Cosme Velho 561, T2058612, F2058884, is one of the most comprehensive museums of Naive and folk paintings in the world. It is only 30 metres uphill, on the same street as the station for Corcovado. There is a permanent collection of some 8,000 works by Naive artists from about 130 countries. The museum also hosts several thematic and temporary exhibitions through the year. Parts of its collection travel to other museums and exhibitions around the world. There is a coffee shop and a souvenir shop where you can buy small paintings by some of the artists on display, books, postcards and T-shirts. Courses and workshops on painting and related subjects are offered. ■ *Tuesday-Friday 1000-1800, Saturday, Sunday and holidays 1200-1800; closed on Monday. The entry ticket costs US$2.50, but there are are special prices for groups, students and senior citizens.*

See also box on page 120

Those who want to see what Rio was like early in the 19th century should go to the **Largo do Boticário**, Rua Cosme Velho 822, a charming small square in neo-colonial style. Much of the material used in creating the effect of the square came from old buildings demolished in the city centre. The four houses that front the square are painted different colours (white, pale blue, caramel, pink), each with different features picked out in decorative tiles, woodwork and stone. The square is close to the terminus for the Corcovado cog railway.

Corcovado is a hunch-backed peak, 710 metres high, is surmounted by a 38 metres high statue of Christ the Redeemer, O Cristo Redentor, which was completed on 12 October 1931. There is a superb view from the top (sometimes obscured by mist), to which there are a cog railway and a road; both car and train put down their passengers behind the statue. The 3.8 kilometre railway itself offers fine views. The railway was opened on 9 October 1884 by Emperor Dom Pedro II. Steam trains were used to begin with, but electric trains replaced them in 1910. The current rolling stock is Swiss and dates from 1979. Average speed is 15 kph on the way up and 12 kph on the way down. From the upper terminus there is a climb of 220 steps to the top, near which there is a café. To see the city by day and night ascend at 1500 or 1600 and descend on the last train, approximately 1815. Mass is held on Sunday in a small chapel in the statue pedestal. The floodlighting was designed in 1931 by Marconi and came into operation in the following year.

Rio de Janeiro

Brazil's International Museum of Naive Art

MIAN, the Museu Internacional de Arte Naif do Brasil, grew out of the private collection of Lucien Finkelstein, a French jewellery designer who lives in Brazil and who, about 40 years ago, started to buy Naive paintings all over Brazil and abroad, on his frequent international trips. As the collection grew so large, he decided to create a foundation and in October 1995 the museum opened its doors to the public. The current director is Jaqueline Finkelstein. The museum is located in a huge, spacious old house surrounded by gardens and trees.

Naive painters have no formal academic training. For this reason, each develops his or her own personal style, using pure, bright colours, as well as peculiar uses of perspective, composition and materials. The subject matter varies from scenes of daily life, to folk festivals, religion and lively landscapes. The international section gathers together works from several countries, from the 17th century to today, including the world-famous paintings on glass from former Yugoslavia (The Hlebine school) and impressive campesino paintings on leather from Ecuador.

The Brazilian section is remarkable for the vibrant tropical colours and the diversity of subjects. Among the most representative Brazilian Naive painters, the museum has several works by Antônio Poteiro, José Antônio da Silva, Rosina Becker do Vale, Lia Mittarakis and others (including our own Fábio Sombra). One of the most interesting works is an enormous painting (four metres by seven metres) by Lia Mittarakis, in the main hall, showing the city of Rio de Janeiro. This colourful work, full of funny details, is considered the biggest Naive painting in the world and took five years to complete.

Transport Take a Cosme Velho bus to the cog railway station at Rua Cosme Velho 513: from the centre or Glória/Flamengo No 180, 184; from Copacabana take No 583, from Botafogo or Ipanema/Leblon No 583 or 584; from Santa Teresa Microônibus Santa Teresa. The train runs every 20-30 minutes according to demand between 0800 and 1830, journey time 10 minutes (cost: US$9 return; single tickets available). Also, a 206 bus does the very attractive run from Praça Tiradentes (or a 407 from Largo do Machado) to Silvestre (the railway has no stop here now). An active walk of 9 km will bring one to the top and the road is shady. Take the narrow street to the right of the station, go through the gate used by people who live beside the tracks and continue to the national park entrance. Walkers are not usually charged entrance fees. Allow a minimum of 2 hours (up to 4 depending on fitness) for the climb. For safety reasons go in company, or at weekends when more people are about. If going by car to Corcovado, the entrance fee is US$4 for the vehicle, plus US$4 for each passenger. Coach trips tend to be rather brief and taxis which wait in front of the station offering tours of Corcovado and Mirante Dona Marta are expensive and offer no information.

Copacabana, Ipanema and Leblon

As our survey of the city has progressed south from the centre, a couple of beaches have been passed, but it is at Copacabana and beyond, facing the open Atlantic Ocean, that Rio de Janeiro's true *praia* culture comes to the fore. As Priscilla Ann Goslin puts it in *How to be a Carioca* (see under Tourist information, page 150), a Carioca is someone who goes to the beach before, after or instead of work. The beach is divided into numbered *postos*, where the lifeguards are based. Different sections attract different types of people, for example young people, artists and gays. "Where do you go on the beach?" is the defining question for Cariocas. The safest places are in front of the major hotels which have their own security, for instance the *Meridien* on Copacabana beach

or the *Caesar Park* on Ipanema. The *Caesar Park* also has 24-hour video sur-
veillance during the summer season, which makes it probably the safest patch
of sand in Rio. Also outside this hotel, Brazil's Olympic beach volley ball players practise. Sports of all types, however, can be seen or played all along the
beaches: volley ball, football, aerobics, jogging and so on.

Built on a narrow strip of land (only a little over four square kilometres)
between mountain and sea, Copacabana has one of the highest population
densities in the world: 62,000 per square kilometre, or 250,000 in all.

Copacabana
This celebrated curved beach backed by skyscraper apartments is a must for visitors

Copacabana began to develop when the Túnel Velho (Old Tunnel) was built
in 1891 and an electric tram service reached it. Weekend villas and bungalows
sprang up; all have now gone. In the 1930s the Copacabana Palace Hotel was the
only tall building; it is now one of the lowest on the beach. The opening of the
Túnel Novo (New Tunnel) in the 1940s led to an explosion of population which
shows no sign of having spent its force. Unspoilt Art Deco blocks towards the
Leme (city) end of Copacabana are now under preservation order.

There is almost everything in this 'city within a city'. The shops, mostly in
Avenida Nossa Senhora de Copacabana and the Rua Barata Ribeiro, are excellent. Even more stylish shops are to be found in Ipanema, Leblon and in the
various large shopping centres in the city (see **Shopping**, page 140). This is the
area in which to watch, or participate in, the city's glamorous nightlife. A fort at
the far end of the beach, Forte de Copacabana, was an important part of Rio's
defences and prevents a seashore connection with the Ipanema and Leblon
beaches. Parts of the military area are now being handed over to civilian use,
the first being the Parque Garota de Ipanema at Arpoador, the fashionable
Copacabana end of the Ipanema beach. Tourist police patrol Copacabana
beach until 1700.

Transport Buses to and from the city centre are plentiful and cost US$0.40. The
buses to take are Nos 119, 154, 413, 415, 455, 474 from Avenida Nossa Senhora de
Copacabana. If you are going to the centre from Copacabana, look for 'Castelo', 'Praça
15', 'E Ferro' or 'Praça Mauá' on the sign by the front door. 'Aterro' means the expressway between Botafogo and downtown Rio (not open on Sunday). From the centre to
Copacabana is easier as all buses in that direction are clearly marked. The 'Aterro' bus
does the journey in 15 minutes.

Beyond Copacabana are the beautiful seaside suburbs of Ipanema (a good place
from which to watch the sunset) and Leblon. The two districts are divided by a
canal from the Lagoa Rodrigo de Freitas to the sea, beside which is the Jardim de
Alá. Ipanema and Leblon are a little less built-up than Copacabana and their
beaches tend to be cleaner. Praia de Arpoador at the Copacabana end of
Ipanema is a peaceful spot to watch surfers, with the beautiful backdrop of
Morro Dois Irmãos; excellent for photography, walk on the rocks. There is now
night-time illumination on these beaches. The seaward lane of the road running
beside the beach is closed to traffic until 1800 on Sundays and holidays; this
makes it popular for rollerskating and cycling (bicycles can be hired).

Ipanema & Leblon

Backing Ipanema and Leblon is the middle-class residential area of **Lagoa
Rodrigo de Freitas**, by a saltwater lagoon on which Rio's rowing and
small-boat sailing clubs are active. The lake is too polluted for bathing, but the
road which runs around its shores has pleasant views. The avenue on the eastern shore, Avenida Epitácio Pessoa, leads to the Túnel Rebouças which runs
beneath Corcovado and Cosme Velho. Once out of the tunnel, the urban
motorway meets up with the Linha Vermelha for the north, or continues to
Avenida Presidente Vargas and the Rodoviária.

Rio de Janeiro

On the western side of the lake is the Hipódromo de Gávea, the city's horse-racing track. By the track and the lake is the residential area known as Jardim Botânico, so called because of its proximity to the Botanical Gardens.

Well worth a visit are the **Jardim Botânico/Botanical Gardens** (Jardim Botânico). These were founded in 1808 by the king, Dom João VI, as a garden for acclimatizing plants on land in the Real Fazenda. When the electric tram line arrived in this part of the city, housing and industries soon followed, but the gardens, then as now, remained a haven of peace. The Jardim Botânico covers 137 hectares. The most striking features are the transverse avenues of 30 metres high royal palms. Among the more than 7,000 varieties of plants from around the world are examples of the *pau-brasil* tree (see page 761), now endangered, and many other threatened species. Look for monkeys in the trees. There is a herbarium, an aquarium and a library (some labels are unclear). A new pavilion contains sculptures by Mestre Valentim transferred from the centre. Many improvements were carried out before the 1992 Earth Summit, including a new Orquidário, an enlarged bookshop, an expensive *lanchonete*, replanting and cleaning up. Visitors needing information in English should ask for Beatriz Heloisa Guimarães, of the Society of Friends of the Garden.

Birdwatchers should visit the Botanical Gardens, preferably early in the morning; 140 species of birds have been recorded here: flycatchers are very prominent (the social flycatcher, great and boat-billed kiskadees, cattle tyrant); also tanagers (the sayaca and palm tanagers and the colourful

Copacabana

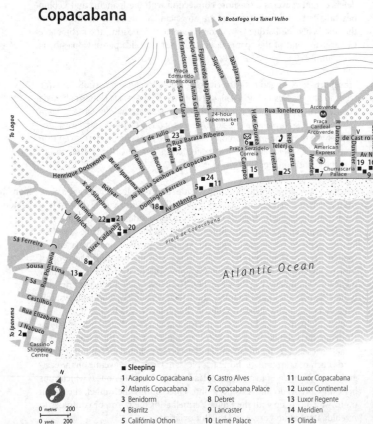

■ Sleeping

1 Acapulco Copacabana	6 Castro Alves	11 Luxor Copacabana
2 Atlantis Copacabana	7 Copacabana Palace	12 Luxor Continental
3 Benidorm	8 Debret	13 Luxor Regente
4 Biarritz	9 Lancaster	14 Meridien
5 Califórnia Othon	10 Leme Palace	15 Olinda

green-headed tanager) and over 20 different kinds of hummingbird. Birds of prey include the roadside hawk, the laughing falcon and the American kestrel, and there are doves, cuckoos, parakeets, thrushes and woodpeckers and occasional flocks of toucans (John and George Newmark, Eastbourne, UK).

Essentials The gardens are open 0800-1700 (US$2). They are 8 km from the centre; take bus No 170 from the centre, or any bus to Leblon, Gávea or São Conrado marked 'via Jóquei'; from Glória, Flamengo or Botafogo take No 571, or 172 from Flamengo; from Copacabana, Ipanema or Leblon take No 572 (584 back to Copacabana).

Parque Laje, near the Jardim Botânico at Rua Jardim Botânico 414, almost jungle-like, has small grottoes, an old tower and lakes, as well as the Escola de Artes Visuais (Visual Arts School) housed in the mansion. ■ *Daily, 0900-1700, free.*

In Ipanema are the headquarters of two stores which have successfully adapted the Brazilian gemstone industry to the modern world: Amsterdam Sauer and H Stern. Both have exhibitions which you can visit without any pressurized selling attached. (See **Brazilian Gems**, page 769.)

Amsterdam Sauer Museum, Garcia d'Ávila 105 e Visconde de Pirajá, has reproductions of two Brazilian mines and a large exhibition of gemstones in both their rough state and cut into precious stones. ■ *Monday-Friday 1000-1700, Saturday 0930-1300; T5121132.*

To Botafogo

To Urca & Praia Vermelha

Tunel Novo

Cable car to Pão de Açúcar

Lad do Leme

Princesa Isabel

Roxo

Prado

Praça Demétrio Ribeiro

Villa Lobos Theatre

Cervantes

Lopes

LEME

■ 17

de Copacabana

1 ■

Praça Lido (weekend fair)

■ 14

Gustavo Sampaio

Anchieta

■ 12

■ 10

Leal

M Afonso

Av Atlântica

Praça Júlio de Noronha

Praia do Leme

MORRO DO LEME

Rio de Janeiro

H Stern, Garcia D'Ávila 113, has a self-guided exhibition which shows the complete process of turning an uncut stone into a piece of jewellery. As you walk around the display, you can see the experts at work in front of you. There is also a permanent exhibition of jewellery, including items which have won international prizes. ■ *Monday-Friday 0830-1800, Saturday 0830-1230; T2597442.*

The **Planetário** (Planetarium), on Padre Leonel Franco 240, Gávea, was inaugurated in 1979, with a sculpture of the Earth and Moon by Mario Agostinelli. On Wednesday evenings at dusk, in clear weather, astronomers give guided observations of the stars that are visible (entry free); on Saturday and Sunday there are shows for children at 1630 and for adults and children over 12 at 1800 and 1830; also on Sunday at 1800 there are observations. There are occasional *chorinho* concerts on Thursday or Friday; check the press for details. ■ *T2740096, buses 176 and 178 from the centre and Flamengo; 591 and 592 from Copacabana.*

16 Ouro Verde	**21** Rio Roiss
17 Plaza Copacabana	**22** Savoy Othon
18 Rio Atlântica	**23** Sol
19 Rio Internacional	**24** Toledo
20 Rio Othon Palace	**25** Trocadero

Transport Buses run from Botafogo Metrô terminal to Ipanema: some take integrated Metrô-Bus tickets; look for the blue signs on the windscreen. Many buses from Copacabana run to Ipanema and Leblon.

Leblon to Barra da Tijuca

The Pedra Dois Irmãos overlooks Leblon. On the slopes is Vidigal *favela*. From Leblon, two inland roads take traffic west to the outer seaside suburb of Barra da Tijuca: the Auto Estrada Lagoa-Barra, which tunnels under Dois Irmãos, and the Estrada da Gávea, which goes through Gávea.

Parque da Cidade, a pleasant park a short walk beyond the Gávea bus terminus, has a great many trees and lawns, with views over the ocean. The proximity of the Rocinha favela (see below) means that the park is not very safe. It is advisable to carry a copy of your passport here because of frequent police checks. ■ *Daily 0700-1700, free. Buses, Nos 593, 592, 174, 170, 546, leave you just short of the entrance, but it should be OK to walk the last part if in a group. Similarly, do not walk the trails in the park alone.* In the park is the **Museu Histórico da Cidade**, a former coffee *fazenda* with historical exhibits. Every third Sunday in the month it holds a gastronomic event with music from 1400. See the Capela de São João Bautista whose murals by Carlos Bastos so scandalized the patrons for their inclusion of famous people into the life of Christ that they were never finished (only open weekends). ■ *Tuesday-Sunday 1100-1700, US$1.*

Ipanema, Leblon

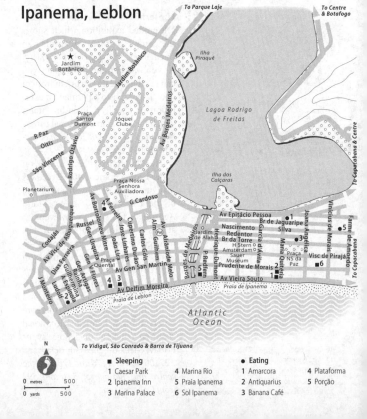

To Parque Laje

To Centre & Botafogo

To Vidigal, São Conrado & Barra de Tijuana

■ Sleeping		● Eating	
1 Caesar Park	4 Marina Rio	1 Amarcora	4 Plataforma
2 Ipanema Inn	5 Praia Ipanema	2 Antiquarius	5 Porção
3 Marina Palace	6 Sol Ipanema	3 Banana Café	

Beyond Leblon the coast is rocky. A third route to Barra da Tijuca is the Avenida Niemeyer, which skirts the cliffs on the journey past Vidigal, a small beach where the *Sheraton* is situated. Avenida Niemeyer carries on round the coast to São Conrado, with its Fashion Mall and the Gávea golf club ; a very exclusive neighbourhood, few tourists stop here. On the slopes of the Pedra da Gávea, through which the Avenida Niemeyer has two tunnels, is the Rocinha *favela*.

Favela Tour It is possible to visit Vila Canoas and Rocinha *favelas* close to São Conrado. This is very interesting and leads to a greater appreciation of Rio and its people. It is best to visit on an organized tour. ■ *See Tour agencies, page 149, for guides who can offer a safe, different and interesting experience.*

The flat-topped **Pedra da Gávea** can be climbed or scrambled up for magnificent views, but beware of snakes. Some say that the rock is sphinx-like and from the Tijuca Forest side there is clearly a conformation similar to a face with a beard. Claims have been made that Phoenician inscriptions have been found and many other legends surround the rock.

Behind the Pedra da Gávea is the Pedra Bonita. A road, the Estrada das Canoas, climbs up past these two rocks on its way to the Tijuca National Park. There is a spot on this road which is one of the chief hang-glider launch sites in the area (see **Sports**, page 142).

This rapidly developing residential area is also one of the principal recreation areas of Rio, with its 20-kilometre sandy beach and good waves for surfing. At the westernmost end is the small beach of Recreio dos Bandeirantes, where the ocean can be very rough. The channels behind the Barra are popular with jetskiers. It gets very busy on Sundays. There are innumerable bars and restaurants, clustered at both ends, campsites (see page 132), motels and hotels: budget accommodation tends to be self-catering. The facilities include Riocentro, a 600,000-square metre convention complex, and the huge Barra Shopping and Carrefour shopping centres.

Barra da Tijuca
Although buses do run as far as Barra, getting to and around here is best by car. A cycle way links Barra da Tijuca with the centre of the city

The **Bosque da Barra/Parque Arruda Câmara**, at the junction of Avenida das Américas and Avenida Ayrton Senna, preserves the vegetation of the sandbanks which existed on this part of the coast before the city took over. ■ *Daily 0700-1700.*

The **Autódromo** (motor racing track) is behind Barra and the Lagoa de Jacarepaguá, in the district of the same name. The Brazilian Grand Prix was held here during the 1980s before returning to Interlagos, São Paulo.

Terra Encantada, Avenida Ayrton Senna 2800, T4309800, is a 300,000 square metre theme park in Barra whose attractions are based on the different cultural heritages of Brazil: the indigenous, African and European. Among the attractions are roller coasters, river rapids, a cinema and shows. After 2200 on the main street restaurants, bars and nightspots open. Check it out first on the internet, http://www.terra-encantada.com.br.

A bit further out is the **Museu Casa do Pontal**, Estrada do Pontal 3295, Recreio dos Bandeirantes. This is another collection of Brazilian folk art, put together by the French designer Jacques van de Beuque. Recommended. ■ *Saturday and Sunday only, 1400-1800, T4376278.*

Transport Buses from the city centre to Barra are Nos 175, 176; from Botafogo, Glória or Flamengo take No 179; Nos 591 or 592 from Leme; and from Copacabana via Leblon No 523. A taxi to Zona Sul costs US$15 (US$22.50 after midnight). A comfortable bus,

Pegasus, goes along the coast from the Castelo bus terminal to Barra da Tijuca and continues to Campo Grande or Santa Cruz, or take the free 'Barra Shopping' bus. Bus 700 from Praça São Conrado (terminal of bus 553 from Copacabana) goes the full length of the beach to Recreio dos Bandeirantes.

Tijuca National Park

History The vegetation in the Parque Nacional da Tijuca, for all its abundance, is not primeval. Most of what is now the largest urban, forested national park in the world is reforested. The first Europeans in the area cut down trees for use in construction and as firewood. The lower areas were cleared to make way for sugar plantations. When coffee was introduced to Rio de Janeiro in 1760, the logical place to start cultivating it was on the hillsides surrounding the city. Huge tracts of the forest were cut down and coffee estates created. Conditions for the bushes were ideal, but for the city itself, it did not prove ideal. Although many people made lots of money, deforesting the hills disrupted the rainfall pattern and the water supply for the expanding city became insufficient. In 1861, therefore, the Imperial government decided that the whole area should be reforested. The job was given to Major Manuel Gomes Archer who, with just six slaves, completed the task in 13 years. They used saplings taken from neighbouring areas, but added to the native species many exotic varieties. The work was continued by Tomás de Gama. A national park of 3,300 hectares, which united various different forests, was set up in 1961.

Exploring the park The Pico da Tijuca (1,022 metres) gives a good idea of the tropical vegetation of the interior and a fine view of the bay and its shipping. A two to three hour

Barra da Tijuca & National Park

walk leads to the summit: on entering the park at Alto da Boa Vista (open 0600-2100), follow the signposts (maps are displayed) to Bom Retiro, a good picnic place (1½ hours' walk). At Bom Retiro the road ends and there is another hour's walk up a fair footpath to the summit (take the path from the right of the Bom Retiro drinking fountain; not the more obvious steps from the left). The last part consists of steps carved out of the solid rock; look after children at the summit as there are several sheer drops, invisible because of bushes. The route is shady for almost its entire length. The main path to Bom Retiro passes the Cascatinha Taunay (a 30 metre waterfall) and the Mayrink Chapel (built 1860). Panels painted in the Chapel by Cândido Portinari have been replaced by copies and the originals will probably be installed in the Museu de Arte Moderna. Beyond the Chapel is the restaurant *A Floresta* and Major Archer's house, now in ruins.

Other places of interest not passed on the walk to the peak are the Paulo e Virginia Grotto, the Vista do Almirante and the Mesa do Imperador (viewpoints). Allow at least five to six hours for the excursion. Maps of the park are available. If hiking in the national park other than on the main paths, a guide may be useful if you do not want to get lost: Sindicato de Guías, T2674582.

Buses Take bus No 221 from Praça 15 de Novembro, No 233 (which continues to Barra da Tijuca) or 234 from the rodoviária or from Praça Sáens Pena, Tijuca (the city suburb, not Barra – reached by Metrô), or No 454 from Copacabana to Alto da Boa Vista, for the park entrance.

Jeep tours are run by *Rio Jeep Tour, Atlantic Forest Operadora de Turismo*, daily; T5112220, F2740875, Mobile 99827986/99740218, or contact through travel agencies.

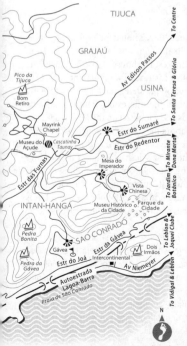

Western Rio

Almost 50 percent of the municipal area of Rio de Janeiro is in what is referred to as the Zona Oeste (the West Zone). On the coast, this stretches from Barra de Tijuca past the beaches at Prainha (a little cove, good for surfing) and Grumari (very attractive, rustic beach bars), neither accessible by public transport, but attracting heavy traffic at weekends. Further west still are the Barra de Guaratiba and Pedra de Guaratiba beaches and, finally, those at Sepetiba (on the bay, with calm sea, medicinal mud). This stunning coastal road (the start of the Costa Verde highway) is becoming obliterated by executive housing developments – visit soon, if you can.

Inland are suburbs such as Campo Grande and Santa Cruz, the Parque Estadual da Pedra Branca (T4453387) and sites such as the 19th century Capela Magdalena (T4107183). The authorities are planning to develop the

Zona Oeste. A Centro Cultural (NOPH), Praça Dom Romualdo 11, Santa Cruz, in the Igreja Matriz, can supply information, T3950260.

Two museums in the northwest of the city are well-established. **Capão do Bispo Estate**, Avenida Suburbana 4616, Del Castilho, is an 18th century estate house with an archaeological exhibition. ■ *Monday-Friday 1400-1700.* **Museu Aeroespacial**, Avenida Marechal Fontenele 2000, Campo dos Afonsos, has displays of early Brazilian civil and military aircraft, historic weapons and documents. ■ *Tuesday-Friday 0930-1500, Saturday, Sunday and holidays 0930-1600.*

Of more than passing interest is the **Sítio Roberto Burle Marx**, Estrada da Barra de Guaratiba 2019, Barra de Guaratiba. This was the home of the great landscape designer from 1949 to 1994. Roberto Burle Marx (1909-94) was world-famous as a landscape designer and artist. His projects achieved a rare harmony between nature, architecture and man-made landscapes. He created many schemes in Brazil and abroad; in Rio alone his work includes the Parque do Flamengo, the pavements of the Avenida Atlântica in Copacabana, Praça Júlio de Noronha in Leme, the remodelling of the Largo da Carioca, the gardens of the Museu Nacional de Belas Artes and of the Biblioteca Nacional and the complex at the Santa Teresa tram station near the Catedral Metropolitana.

Covering 350,000 square metres, the estate contains an estimated 3,500 species of plants, mostly Brazilian. It is run now by the Instituto do Patrimônio Histórico e Artístico Nacional and one of its main aims is to produce seedlings of the plants in its collection. Also on view are Burle Marx's collection of paintings, ceramics, sculptures and other objets d'art, plus examples of his own designs and paintings. The library houses 2,500 volumes on botany, architecture and landscape design. ■ *Monday-Friday 0930-1330 by prior appointment only, T4101171/1412.*

Ilha de Paquetá/Paquetá Island

The island, the second largest in Guanabara Bay, is noted for its gigantic pebble shaped rocks, butterflies and orchids. Its name means 'many shells' in Tupi, but it has also been called the Ilha dos Amores. The house of José Bonifácio, the opponent of slavery, may be seen. Another historical building is the Solar D'El Rei, which today houses the Biblioteca Popular de Paquetá and has recently been refurbished. At the southwest tip is the interesting Parque Darke de Mattos, with beautiful trees, lots of birds and a lookout on the Morro da Cruz. The island has several beaches, but ask about the state of the water before bathing. The only means of transport are bicycles and horse-drawn carriages (many have harnesses which cut into the horse's flesh). Neither is allowed into the Parque Darke de Mattos. A tour by *trenzinho*, a tractor pulling trailers, costs US$1.25, or just wander around on foot, quieter and free. Bicycles can be hired. The island is very crowded at weekends and on public holidays, but is usually quiet during the week. The prices of food and drink are reasonable.

Transport Paquetá Island can be visited by ferry services that leave more or less every two hours from Praça 15 de Novembro, where there is a general boat terminal; there are boats from 0515 (0710 on Sunday and holidays) to 2300, T5336661, or hydrofoils between 1000 and 1600, Saturday and Sunday 0800-1630 hourly, T3970656 (fare US$1 by boat, one hour, US$4 by hydrofoil, 20 minutes' journey, which more than doubles its price Saturday, Sunday and holidays). Buses to Praça 15 de Novembro: No 119 from Glória, Flamengo or Botafogo; Nos 154, 413, 455, 474 from Copacabana, or No 415 passing from Leblon via Ipanema.

Other boat trips: *Aquatur* (T2309273), *Brazilian Marina Turismo*, Camargo (T2750643), *Passamar*, Siqueira Campos 7 (T2364136), *Greyline* (T2747146), *Soletur* (Bay trips Saturday and Sunday only) and *American Sightseeing*, Avenida Nossa Senhora de Copacabana 605, Sala 1204 (T2363551). The last three offer a day cruise, including lunch, to Jaguanum Island (see page 177, under Itacuruçá) and a sundown cruise around Guanabara Bay, also deep-sea fishing expeditions and private charters. *Saveiros Tour*, Rua Conde de Lages 44, Glória, T2246990, F2522227, saveiros@skydome.com.br, offers tours in sailing schooners around the bay and down the coast, also 'Baía da Guanabara Histórica' historical tours, plus yacht charters.

Essentials

Rio de Janeiro

Sleeping

All hotels of 2-stars and above in the following list are a/c. A 10% service charge is usually added to the bill and tax of 5% or 10% may be added (if not already included). Note that not all higher-class hotels include breakfast in their room rates. Economy hotels are found mainly in 3 districts of Rio: Flamengo/Botafogo (best), Lapa/Fátima and Saúde/Mauá. The city is noisy. An inside room is cheaper and much quieter.

Price codes: see inside front cover

The only 5-star hotels according to a new system introduced in 1997 are the Sheraton, **Caesar Park** and **Intercontinental**. Others previously rated as 5-star were expected to upgrade their services to meet the new standards.

The following list begins with expensive hotels and then gives economy establishments, by area.

L *Novo Mundo*, Praia Flamengo 20, T5574355, F2652369. Well recommended but noisy. **L** *Glória*, R do Russel 632, T5557272, F5557282. Stylish and elegant old building, 2 swimming pools. Highly recommended.

Flamengo
■ *on map, page 116*

5-star hotels (old and new classification) **LL** to **L**: *Copacabana Palace*, Av Atlântica 1702, T5487070, F2357330. Swimming pool, good. *Le Meridien*, Av Atlântica 1020, T5460866, F5416447. Air France hotel, world-renowned, very expensive, pool, rooms quite small, breakfast (US$15 if not included in room rate) is huge. *Rio Othon Palace*, Av Atlântica 3264, T5221522, F5221697, www.hoteis-othon.com.br. Pool, very good, as is *Sofitel Rio Palace*, Av Atlântica 4240, T5221232, F5220570. Frequented by the likes of Michael Jackson and Madonna, all rooms locked by central system at 0130. There are 2 excellent suites: **L** *Rio Atlântica*, Av Atlântica 2964, T5486332, F2556410, pool, 2 restaurants and other facilities (Swiss management, very high standards), recommended; and *Rio Internacional*, Av Atlântica 1500, T5431555, F5425443, pool.
4-star hotels L-**A**: There are 6 Othon hotels in this category, some rooms are more expensive (www.hoteis-othon.com.br): *Califórnia Othon*, Av Atlântica 2616, T/F2571900, good. *Savoy Othon*, Av Copacabana 995, T/F5220282. Very central, popular, commercial, quite noisy. *Olinda*, Av Atlântica 2230, T/F2551890. Also good. *Lancaster*, Av Atlântica 1470, T/F5411887. Recommended, easy to change travellers' cheques, non-smoking rooms, balconies overlook the beach, helpful management, airline discount can cut price. *Trocadero Othon*, Av Atlântica 2064, T/F2571834. *Leme Othon Palace*, Av Atlântica 656, T/F2758080. Also good, but poorer location, popular with tour groups. Next door to the *Lancaster* is *Ouro Verde*, Av Atlântica 1456, T5421887, F5424597. Good value, excellent all round, expensive restaurant. Three Luxor hotels: *Luxor Continental*, Gustavo Sampaio 320, T5411946, F5411946; *Luxor Copacabana*, Av Atlântica 2554, T5482245, F2551858; and *Luxor Regente*, Av Atlântica 3716, T2677693, F2677693. All good hotels in this range, well-placed. *Benidorm Palace*, R Barata Ribeiro 547, T5488880, F2566396. Suites and double

Copacabana
■ *on map, page 122*
The famous seaside residential and commercial area: many hotels on Av Atlântica charge about 30% more for a room with a seaview, but some town-side upper rooms have equally fine views of the mountains

rooms, sauna. Recommended. *Rio Roiss*, R Aires Saldanha 48, T5221142, F5227719. Very good, restaurant. *South American Copacabana*, R Francisco de Sá 90, T5216040, F2670748. Good location 2 blocks from the beach, safe area, front rooms noisy, helpful front desk staff, highly rated. **3-star hotels A**: *Castro Alves Othon*, Av Nossa Senhora de Copacabana 552, T/F5488815. Central. Very comfortable and elegant. Recommended. *Debret*, Av Atlântica 3564, T5220132, F5210899. Good, helpful staff, some inner rooms dark. *Parthenon Real Residence*, Av Princesa Isabel 500, T5466565, F5466581. Rooms and long-stay lets, well-equipped and well-run, studios and rooms with sitting room and kitchen, good. *Rio Copa*, Av Princesa Isabel 370, T2756644, F2755545. Good value, English spoken. Recommended. **2-star hotels A-B**: *Atlantis Copacabana*, Av Bulhões de Carvalho 61, T5211142, F2878896. Very good, swimming pool, turkish bath, good breakfast, close to Ipanema and Copacabana beaches. *Biarritz*, R Aires Saldanha 54, T5220542, F2877640. Good, accepts American Express. *Sol*, R Santa Clara 141, T2571840, F2550744, www.hpm.com.br/copacabanasol.html. A/c, modern, safe, quiet, good breakfast, helpful. *Toledo*, R Domingos Ferreira 71, 1 block from beach, T2571991, F2571931. Good breakfast, single rooms are gloomy, but excellent value. *Acapulco Copacabana*, R Gustavo Sampaio 854, T2750022, F2753396. TV, simple. Recommended.

Ipanema &
Leblon
■ *on map, page 124*
Outer seaside residential
and commercial area

All the following are good, starting with the most luxurious. **LL** *Caesar Park*, Av Vieira Souto 460, T5252525, F5216000. Five-star, pool, beach patrol. **L** *Mar Ipanema*, R Visconde de Pirajá 539, Ipanema, 1 block from the beach, T2749922. Helpful, good buffet breakfast. **L** *Marina Palace*, Av Delfim Moreira 630, T2595212, F2941644. **L** *Marina Rio*, Av Delfim Moreira 696, T2398844, F2590941. **L** *Praia Ipanema*, Av Vieira Souto 706, T2399932, F2396889. Pool, helpful. **A** *Sol Ipanema*, Av Vieira Souto, 320, T5230095, F5216464. Recommended. **A** *Ipanema Inn*, Maria Quitéria 27, behind *Caesar Park*, T5233092, F5115094. Good location. **A** *Arpoador Inn*, Francisco Otaviano 177, T5230060, F5115094. Recommended. *San Marco*, R Visconde de Pirajá 524, T2395032. Two-star. Recommended.

São Conrado &
further out
Spectacular settings,
but isolated and far
from centre

The first 2 are luxury hotels with pools: **LL** *Sheraton*, Av Niemeyer 121 (Vidigal), T2741122, F2395643. Several pricey restaurants located directly on beach front, 3 pools and full sports facilities, Gray Line travel agency and other services associated with 5-star hotel; **LL** *Intercontinental*, Av Prefeito Mendes de Moraes 222 (São Conrado), T3222200, F3225500. Five-star. In Barra da Tijuca: **AL** *Barra Sol*, Av Sernambetiba 690, T/F4942658; **AL** *Praia Linda*, Av Sernambetiba 1430, T4942186, F4942198; **A** *Atlântico Sul*, Av Sernambetiba 18000 (Recreio), T4378411, F4378777.

T Jobim airport **L** *Luxor Hotel do Aeroporto*, T3985960, F3983983. Three-star.

Flamengo &
Catete
■ *on map, page 116*
Residential area
between centre and
Copacabana, with good
bus and Metrô
connections

From the centre, you will come across the hotels in this order: **D** *Opera*, Santa Amaro 75, T2423585. On the hillside is Ladeira da Glória: **B** *Turístico*, Ladeira da Glória 30, T5577698. With breakfast, a/c, tourist information provided, mixed reports, some highly favourable. **B** *Imperial*, R do Catete 186, T5565212, F5585815. A/c, TV, phone, pool, garage, smart. Also on R do Catete: **D** *Vitória*, No 172, T2055397. With breakfast, hot water, a/c, friendly, mixed reports. Also on R do Catete: **D** *Rio Claro*, No 233, T5585180. Small rooms, breakfast, a/c, safe. Recommended. **D** *Monte Blanco*, No 160, T2250121. Breakfast, a/c, radio, refurbished in 1999. To the left is R Silveira Martins: **C** *Inglês*, No 20, T5583052, F5583447. A/c, TV, phone, reasonable breakfast. Walking down Praia de Flamengo you will come across the next streets: Ferreira Viana: **AL** *Flórida*, No 71/81, T5565242, F2855777. Sauna, pool, safe, quiet. Good views, great breakfast. Highly recommended. **A** *Regina*, No 29, T5561647, F2852999, hotelregina@hotelregina.com.br. Very safe, good breakfast. **D** *Ferreira Viana*, No 58, T2057396. No reservations, not of the same quality as others on this street. On Correia

Dutra: **C** *Caxambu*, No 22, T2659496. With bath, TV, popular cheap hotel. On Buarque de Macedo, **AL** *Rondônia Palace*, No 60, T5560616, F5584133, www.ism.com.br/ ~comsut/hotelrondonia. A/c, sauna, TV, safe, bar and restaurant. **C** *Unico*, No 54, T2059932, F2058149. TV, a/c, fridge. Recommended. Also near Largo do Machado Metrô: **D** *Monterrey*, R Artur Bernardes 39-B, T2659899. Fan, TV, some rooms small and poorly lit. At No 29, **D** *Rio Lisboa*, T2659599. A/c (but staff will not always turn it on), a few cheaper single rooms **E**, safe, breakfast is just coffee, a roll and some crackers; both hotels in this quiet street are family hotels (luck and patience are needed to get a room, no reservations either by phone or in person). R Paissandu: No 34, **D** *Venezuela*, T5577098. Very clean, a/c, TV, but rooms small and breakfast poor. **B** *Paysandu*, opposite *Venezuela* at No 23, T2257270. Very clean, comfortable and good value, helpful staff, good location, organized tours available. Beyond Largo de Machado: R Gago Coutinho: No 22, **D** *Serrano*, T2853233. Pleasant, helpful. **B** *Argentina*, Cruz Lima 30, T5587233, F5574447. Best rooms on fifth floor, cheapest on first. Recommended.

Near Cinelândia Metrô station are a lot of cheap hotels, but many are short stay. This is not an area really recommended for tourists to stay as it is not very safe and the nearby sites of interest should only be visited in daylight. In Cinelândia is **A** *Itajubá*, R Álvaro Alvim 23, T2103163, F2407461, in need of refurbishment so not very clean, no English spoken but the staff are friendly, no credit cards accepted, convenient for the centre, museums etc, but the area is not for the faint-hearted. In Lapa itself, near the Arches just beyond Passeio Público, is R Joaquim Silva: No 99, **D** *Marajó*, T2244134. With breakfast, varied rooms; also **E** *Love's House*, R Joaquim Silva, ask for room with window, safe, respectable. Good value. Passing under the Arches you come to Av Mem de Sá (bus 127 from bus terminal): No 85, **E** *Mundo Novo*, T2343805. A/c. Turning towards Praça Tiradentes is R Resende: No 31, **D** *Estadual*, T2521481. Good; No 35, **D** *Pouso Real*, T2242757. Good, gay area. Recommended; **D** *Marialva*, Gomes Freire 430 (near New Cathedral, convenient for Av Rio Branco, buses etc), 2-star, a/c, breakfast in room. Recommended. Praça Tiradentes: **D** *Rio Hotel*, R Silva Jardim 3, T2821213. Noisy rooms on Praça, quieter overlooking São Sebastião cathedral, with breakfast (only served in rooms).

Lapa & Fátima

Between Lapa and Praça Tiradentes is an inner residential area, less desirable than Flamengo. Parts of this area are deserted from 2200 onwards

D *Chave do Rio de Janeiro*, R Gen Dionísio 63, Botafogo, T2860303, F2865652. IYHA, cheaper for members, clean, laundry and cooking facilities. Superb breakfast. Noisy but frequently recommended. **E** pp *Copacabana Praia*, R Tte Marones de Gusmão 85, Bairro Peixoto, T2353817, F2375422. Dormitory. Apartments also available. **D** *Copacabana Chalet*, R Pompeu Louveiro 99, T2360047, F5312234. Recommended, very friendly. **E** *Saint Roman*, R Saint Roman 48, Copacabana, T5527685, F5312234. Convenient, but dirty and not a safe area. Associations: ALBERJ (for Rio), R da Assembleia 10, room 1616, T5312234, F5311943. Federação Brasileira (Brazil), at *Chave do Rio de Janeiro* hostel, T5274365. Youth hostels are fully booked between Christmas and Carnival; if intending to stay at this time reserve well in advance.

Youth hostels

A popular form of accommodation in Rio, available at all price levels: eg furnished apartments for short-term let, accommodating up to 6, cost US$300 per month in Maracanã, about US$400 per month in Saúde, Cinelândia, Flamengo. Copacabana, Ipanema and Leblon prices range from about US$25 a day for a simple studio, starting at US$500-600 a month up to US$2,000 a month for a luxurious residence sleeping 4-6. Heading south past Barra da Tijuca, virtually all the accommodation available is self-catering. Renting a small flat, or sharing a larger one, can be much better value than a hotel room. Blocks consisting entirely of short-let apartments can attract thieves, so check the (usually excellent) security arrangements; residential buildings are called *prédio familial*. Higher floors (*alto andar*) are considered quieter.

Self-catering apartments

Rio de Janeiro

'Apart-Hotels' are listed in the *Guia 4 Rodas* and Riotur's booklet. Agents and private owners advertise in *Balcão* (like *Exchange and Mart*), twice weekly, *O Globo* or *Jornal do Brasil* (daily); under 'Apartamentos – Temporada'; advertisements are classified by district and size of apartment: 'vagas e quartos' means shared accommodation; 'conjugado' (or 'conj') is a studio with limited cooking facilities; '3 Quartos' is a 3-bedroom flat. There should always be a written agreement when renting.

The following rent apartments in residential blocks: **Hamburg Imobiliária**, Av Copacabana 195, loja 104, T5421446, F2364541. German run, specialize in flats. Very reasonable, helpful. Highly recommended. Also offer tours at good rates, flights and exchange. **Yvonne Reimann**, Av Atlântica 4066, Apto 605, T5130281/2670054. Rents apartments, all with phone, near beach, a/c, maid service, English, French, German spoken, all apartments owned by the agency, prices from US$60 per flat. **Yolanda Thiémard**, Av Prado Junior 165 CO2, T2952088. Multilingual, good value. Recommended. **Dona Lígia**, R Ministro Viveiros de Castro 141 apto 101, T5416367. Speaks English, lower-price apartments. **Fantastic Rio**, Av Atlântica 974, Suite 501, Copacabana, BR-22020-000, T/F5432667, hpcorr@hotmail.com, all types of furnished accommodation from US$20 per day. Owned by Peter Corr. Recommended. **Copacabana Holiday** at R Barata Ribeiro 90A, Copacabana, T5421525/5416580, F5421597. Recommended, well-equipped small apartments from US$500 per month, minumum 30 days let. **Rio Residences**, Av Prado Júnior 44, apto 508, T5414568, F5416462. Swiss run, includes airport transfer. **Marly** and **Olympia**, R Paula Freitas 45/1101, T2565061. These have a room to let in their apartment at US$400 per month.

Camping *Camping Clube do Brasil*, Av Sen Dantas 75, 29th floor, Centro, CEP 20037-900, T2103171, has 2 beach sites at Barra da Tijuca: Av Sernambetiba 3200, T4930628 (bus 233 from centre, 702 or 703 from the airport via Zona Sul, US$5 – a long way from the centre), sauna, pool, bar, café, US$12 (half price for members), during January and February this site is often full and sometimes restricted to members of the Camping Clube do Brasil; a simpler site at Estrada do Pontal 5900, T4378400, lighting, café, good surfing, US$6. Both have trailer plots. *Ostal*, Av Sernambetiba 18790, T4378350; and **Novo Rio**, at Km 17 on the Rio-Santos road, T4376518. If travelling by trailer, you can park at the Marina Glória car park, where there are showers and toilets, a small shop and snack bar. Pay the guards to look after your vehicle.

Eating

Cariocas usually have dinner at 1900 or 2000, occasionally later at weekends after going out to the cinema, theatre or a concert or show

With the devaluation of the *real*, the cost of eating out in Rio has come down, but you can still expect to pay US$20-40 per person in the first-class places, more in the very best restaurants. You can, however, eat well for an average US$10-20 per person, less if you choose the *prato feito* at lunchtime (US$1.50-6), or eat in a place that serves food by weight (starting at about US$0.65 per gram). While many of Rio's quality hotels offer world-class food and service, they may lack atmosphere and close at midnight. There are much livelier and cheaper places to eat if going out for an evening meal. In Rio, avoid mussels! There are many juice bars in Rio with a wide selection (eg the *Rei dos Sucos* chain). Most restaurants are closed on 24 and 25 December.

The guide *Restaurantes do Rio*, by Danusia Bárbara, published annually by Record (in Portuguese only), is worth looking at for ideas on where to eat; also on the Internet http://www.brazilweb.com/rio/contents.htm. For the best traditional bars and eating places, see *Rio Botequim*, published annually by the Prefeitura da Cidade do Rio de Janeiro.

Centre *Republique*, Praça da República 63 (2nd floor), T5324000. Chic, designed by the architect Chicô Gouveia, good food, expensive (US$50 without wine). *Café do Teatro*, Rio Branco, Teatro Municipal. Good food in the grand manner, shorts and scruffy gear not admitted. *Bistro do Paço*, Praça 15 de Novembro 48 (Paço Imperial), Centro, T2526353. Excellent food, good value, cosy surroundings, fancy place, Swiss run. Recommended. *Albamar*, Praça Marechal Âncora 184-6. Fish, very good and reasonable. *Rio Minho*, R do Ouvidor 10. For seafood, expensive, old-fashioned, very good. For *comida mineira*, *Mala e Cuia*, R Candelária 92, T2534032. Recommended. On Trav do Comércio (see page 101) are several restaurants, eg *Santa Fé*, No 20. Good. *Dito e Feito*, *Arco Imperial* and *Guilhermina*. R Miguel Couto (opposite Santa Rita church) is called the *Beco das Sardinhas* because on Wednesday and Friday especially it is full of people eating sardines and drinking beer. There are several Arab restaurants on Av Senhor dos Passos, also open Saturday and Sunday.

Pensão Nutricentro, R 7 de Setembro 235, near Praça Tiradentes. Cheap *prato feito*, 2nd floor with balcony, open 1100-1500 week days, good value, pleasant surroundings. *Luciano*, R das Marrecas 44. All you can eat buffet and others on this street. *Salad Market*, Av 13 de Maio 33C. Sobreloja, weekday lunches only, US$16 per kg; many *lanchonetes* for good, cheap meals in the business sector. In Cinelândia: *Oxalá*, R Álvaro Alvim 36. Bahian food, reasonable. *Simpatia de Cinelândia*, Praça Floriana, small, popular, huge portions (about US$30 for 2 including beers). *Fiorino*, Av Heitor Beltrão 126, Tijuca, T5674476/5679189, very good and cheap. Recommended.

One of the best restaurants in Rio is the *Bar do Arnaudo*, in the Largo do Guimarães, R Almte Alexandrino 316, T2527246. Open Tuesday-Saturday 1200-2200, Sunday 1200-1600, it is simple inside, decorated with handicrafts; the cuisine is northeastern, prices are reasonable and portions huge; try the *caipirinhas*, the *carne do sol* (sun-dried beef, or jerky) with *feijão de corda* (brown beans and herbs), or the *queijo coalho* (a country cheese, grilled). Also in the Largo do Guimarães is *Adega do Pimenta*, R Almte Alexandrino 296. Open Monday, Wednesday-Friday 1130-2200, Sunday 1100-1800. Good. Nearby is a very small German restaurant with excellent sausages, sauerkraut and cold beer. Not expensive. Highly recommended. At night, on the same praça, the best bet is *Sobrenatural*, where musicians play samba from about 2300, informal but of a high standard; it's hard to find a table after 2230, but you can sit outside, which is still fun. Best nights are Wednesday, Thursday and Friday; closed Sunday. Two Italian restaurants are *Cantina Guzzo*, R Almte Alexandrino 256-A, and *Sobrada das Massas* at Curvelo. *Sansuchi*, R Almte Alexandrino 382, Japanese.

Santa Teresa
● *on map, page 116*

Adega Flor de Coimbra, R Teotônio Regadas 34, Lapa. Founded 1938, serving Portuguese food and wines, speciality *bacalhau*. Very good. *Semente*, R Joaquim Silva 138, vegetarian. *Casa da Suíça*, R Cândido Mendes 157, T2525182, bar/restaurant, good atmosphere; several others on this street. *Café Glória*, R do Russel 734, T2059647. Open Tuesday-Sunday for lunch and dinner, beautiful Art Nouveau building, helpful staff, excellent food, main dishes cost about US$20-25, varied wine list.

Lapa & Glória
● *on map, page 116*

There are a lot of eating places on R do Catete: *Catete Grill*, No 239, good. *Amazônia*, No 234B, downstairs, 1-price counter service, upstairs for good, reasonably priced evening meals. Recommended. *Catelandia*, No 204, excellent and cheap, pay by weight. *Restaurante e Pizzaria Guanabara*, No 150, excellent value and selection. *Galícia Grill*, No 265, very good pizza, good service. At Largo do Machado, *O Bom Galeto*, R do Catete 282, for chicken and meats. Next door is *Trattoria Gambino*, recommended for pasta, pleasant on summer evenings. In the gallery at Largo de Machado 29 is *Rotisseria Sirio Libaneza*, ljs 32 e 33, very good value Arabic food. *Parmê*, R do Catete 311, chain restaurant, pizzas, pastas and cakes. *Alcaparra*, Praia do Flamengo 144, elegant Italian, reasonable. *Alho E Óleo*, R Buarque de Macedo 13, T5578541. Fashionable, pleasant. Recommended. *Lamas*, Marquês de Abrantes 18A, excellent value, good food, great atmosphere, opens late, popular with Brazilian arts/media people. Recommended. *Churrascaria Gaúcha*, R das Laranjeiras 114, good.

Flamengo & Catete
● *on map, page 116*

Botafogo *Manolo*, Bambina and M de Olinda, very good value. *Raajmahal*, R Gen Polidoro 29, Indian, reasonable. *Zen Japanese Restaurant*, Praia de Botafogo 228. Highly recommended. In Baixo Botafogo R Visconde de Caravelas has several interesting bars and restaurants, eg *Aurora*, corner of R Capitão Salomão 43, and *Botequim*, No 184, varied menu, good food and value. Also in this area is *Cobal Humaitá*, a fruit market with many popular restaurants (Mexican *tacos*, pizzería, etc). Rio Sul Shopping has a lot of choice for food: *Viena* (pay by weight), *Chez Michou* (crêpes and chopp, 4th floor), *Habib's* (fast Arabic food); there is a small delicatessen, *Normandia*, on 4th floor.

Copacabana The main hotels (see above); most expensive is *Le Saint Honoré* at the *Meridien*, Leme, **& Leme** good food and wonderful view. Near the *Meridien* is *Shirley*, R Gustavo Sampaio 610, T2751398. Spanish, small, seafood, book in advance. *Churrascaria Marius*, at Leme end of Av Atlântica, 290B. All you can eat US$20 with drinks. Excellent, another branch at R Francisco Otaviano 96, Arpoador (reported to be not quite so good). *Churrascaria Palace*, R Rodolfo Dantas 16B, 20 different kinds of meat, very good food and value. *Nino*, Domingos Ferreira 242. Italian cuisine, Argentine beef. Excellent dinner with wine for US$25 pp. *Mala e Cuia*, *comida mineira* at another of the restaurants in this recommended chain (see **Centre**, above and throughout Minas Gerais). *Arataca*, Figueiredo de Magalhães 28, try *carne-de-sol* and *lagosta ao molho*, excellent duck, expensive. *Cervantes*, Barata Ribeiro 07-B e Prado Júnior 335B, stand-up bar or sit-down, a/c restaurant, open all night, queues after 2200, specializes in meats and sandwiches (all with a slice of pineapple). Recommended. *A Marisquera*, Barata Ribeiro 232, good seafood. *Ponto de Encontro* at No 750. Portuguese, try baked *bacalhau*. *Marakesh*, Av NS de Copacabana 599. Good quality and value, pay by weight. *Rian*, Santa Clara 8. International, reasonable, very popular. *Maximix*, R Siqueira Campos 12, loja A. Buffet by weight, opens late, very popular, cheap. Recommended. *Arosa*, No 110. *lanchonete*, very good and cheap. *Siri Mole & Cia*, R Francisco Otaviano 90. Brazilian cuisine, don't miss coffee after the meal from an old-fashioned coffee machine. *La Tratoria*, Av Atlântica, opposite *Hotel Excelsior*. Italian. Good food and service very reasonable. Recommended. *Manuel e Joaquim*, Av Atlântica e República de Peru, good *botequim* with good appetizers, better than most on Av Atlântica where international food is the norm.

Ipanema *Il Capo*, Visconde de Pirajá 276. Recommended. *Alho e Óleo*, next door. Fashionable,
● *on map, page 124* friendly. Recommended. *Bistro 1800*, Av Vieira Souto 110, T2870085, good, reasonably priced, Brazilian menu, fish and meat. *Porcão*, Barão de Torre 218, a very good *churrascaria*, US$25 pp. *Pax Delícia*, Praça Nossa Senhora de Paz, good food, lively crowd. *Amarcord*, R Maria Quitéria 136, T2870335. Recommended. *La Mashera de Pulcinela*, R Farme de Amoedo 102, Italian. *Arlechino*, R Prudente de Morais 1387. Italian. *Satyricon*, R Barão da Torre 192. Italian. *Yemenjá*, R Visconde de Pirajá 128. Brazilian. *Mostarda*, Av Epitácio Pessoa 980. Not cheap but food excellent (often seasoned with mustard sauce), nightclub upstairs, entry fee can be avoided if you eat in the 1st floor restaurant before 2200-2300. Recommended. *La Frasca*, R Garcia d'Ávila 129. Good Italian, pleasant atmosphere. Ipanema is quieter than Copacabana, many nice places round Praça Gen Osório. *Del Mare*, at corner of Prudente de Morais and Vinícius de Morais. Recommended. *Grottamare*, R Gomes Carneiro 132. Good seafood. *Amarelinho*, R Farme de Amoedo 62. Great corner lanchonete with tables outside, fresh food, good value, friendly, open until 0300. Recommended. *Casa da Feijoada*, Prudente de Morais 10. Serves an excellent *feijoada* all week. *Delicats*, Av Henrique Dumont 68. Good Jewish deli.

Leblon *Un, Deux, Trois*, R Bartolomeu Mitre 123. Very fashionable, restaurant, nightclub.
● *on map, page 124* *Ettore*, Av Ataulfo de Paiva 1321, loja A, T2595899. Excellent Italian, moderate prices. *Antiquarius*, R Aristides Espínola 19. Restaurant-cum-antique shop, seafood and

international cuisine. *Mediterráneo*, R Prudente de Morais 1810. Excellent fish, reasonable prices. *Bel Beef*, Av Afrânio Melo Franco 131. *Churrascaria rodízio*; *Celeiro*, R Dias Ferreira 199. Salads and light food.

Claude Troisgros, R Custódio Serrão 62, T5378582. Elegant French restaurant. Recommended. *Enotria*, R Frei Leandro 20, T5279003. Excellent Italian food, service, atmosphere and prices. Recommended. *Mistura Fina*, Av Borges de Medeiros 3207, T2665844/5372844. Classy, popular, friendly nightclub upstairs (US$25).

Jardim Botânico & Lagoa

Amarelinho, Av Ayrton Senna 3000. Warmly recommended lanchonete, see Ipanema above. *Caffe Milano*, R Rodolfo Amoedo 360, T4944671. Good Italian, US$35 (no credit cards).

Barra

Grill or barbecue houses (*churrascarias*) are relatively cheap, especially by European standards. There are many at São Conrado and Joá, on the road out to Barra da Tijuca (see page 125). Look for the 'Churrascaria Rodízio', where you are served as much as you can eat. *McDonalds* and *Bob's* (similar) can be found at about 20 locations each (Big Mac US$3). *Galetos* are lunch counters specializing in chicken and grilled meat, very reasonable. In the shopping centres there is usually a variety of restaurants and snack bars grouped around a central plaza where you can shop around for a good meal. Most less-expensive restaurants in Rio have basically the same type of food (based on steak, fried potatoes and rice) and serve large portions; those with small appetites, especially families with children, can ask for a spare plate and split helpings. *La Mole*, at 11 locations, serves good, cheap Italian food, very popular.

Fast food
There are plentiful hamburger stands (literally 'stands' as you stand and eat the hamburger) and lunch counters all over the city

For those who like their teas served English style, the sedate *Confeitaria Colombo*, R Gonçalves Dias 32, near Carioca Metrô station, is highly recommended for atmosphere, being the only one of its kind in Rio. Over 100 years old, it has the the original Belle Epoque décor, open 0900-1800, lunch available, no service charge so tip the excellent waiters. More modern but similar establishments in some of the main hotels, eg *Pergula*, *Copacabana Palace Hotel*, Av Atlântica 1702, Monday to Friday 1400-1700. Recommended. Also *Casarão*, Souza Lima 37A, Copacabana. *Traiteurs de France*, Av NS de Copacabana 386. Delicious tarts and pastries, not expensive. *La Bonne Table*, Visconde de Pirajá 580 sala 407, Ipanema. *Café de la Paix*, Av Atlântica 1020. *Chá e Simpatia*, Av Atlântica 4240; *Concorde*, Av Prudente de Morais 129.

Cafés

Bars and nightclubs

Rio nightlife is rich and infinitely varied, one of the main attractions for most visitors. If you are not in Rio for Carnival, it's worth seeing a samba show; entry is cheaper if you pay at the door. *Plataforma I*, R Adalberto Ferreira 32, Leblon, T2744022, has a lavish show, arrive by 2100, show starts at 2200 and ends at 2350, US$32, expensive drinks.

See the book *O Guia dos Botequins do Rio de Janeiro*, which describes Rio's best, most traditional bars and their history, US$20.

A beer costs around US$1.50, but up to US$5 in expensive hotel bars. A cover charge of US$3-7 may be made for live music. Snack food is always available. Single drinkers/diners are usually welcome, though you may not remain alone for long unless you stick your nose in a book. Copacabana, Ipanema and Leblon have many beach *barracas*, several open all night. The seafront bars on Av Atlântica are great for people-watching. The big hotels have good cocktail bars (*Copacabana Palace*, poolside, recommended). *Alla Zingara*, corner of Ministro Viveiros de Castro and Belfort Roxo, is friendly. There are only 4 seafront bars in Ipanema: *Barril 1800*, Av Vieira Souto 110. Highly recommended, nice place to watch the sunset. *A Garota de Ipanema*, R

Bars
Wherever you are, there's one near you

Rio de Janeiro

Rio de Janeiro

Samba across the globe

The samba, an utterly Brazilian art form, has, in recent years, become an irrepressible musical force across the world. Samba percussion is now regarded as the community art form par excellence. From Sweden to Japan, from France to Israel, professionals and aficionados have joined forces to recreate the collective abandon of the blocos and escolas.

In the UK alone there are more than 100 groups playing some form of samba, meeting regularly to beat out their rhythms on the surdo and tamborim, practise their dance steps and prepare for the local carnival parade.

Some are small percussion workshops, others form huge parades modelled on the classical forms of Rio, with 200-strong baterias and dancers of all types, Bahianas and Passistas all moving to the sound of a specially composed story-samba. In Helsinki, there is a carnival devoted entirely to samba where a select few of the hundreds of Scandinavian bands take to the streets. Street parades across the US are set alight by the American escolas; San Francisco alone boasts 10 or more samba groups. Mexicans, Italians, Austrians, Germans, Danes, all have fallen under the spell of the samba, getting together at regular encontros to share techniques, learn from Brazilian mestres and celebrate

their particular brand of samba.

Many groups are striving to produce their own sound by incorporating such influences as jazz, Jamaican ragga and even Punjabi bhangra. The development of samba-jungle rhythms in London and beyond demonstrates that groups are often committed to innovation as well as celebration.

It's not hard to see why the samba school idea has proved so popular. Providing a focus for collective activity, the samba carnival is open to all who want to participate, a non-stop creative party. Whether struggling with the complex batucada rhythms, building carros alegóricos, sewing bahiana skirts or cooking a feijoada, making a parade involves a group effort where for one day in a year the streets of Tokyo, Brighton and Berlin ring to the irresistible rhythms of the samba.

You can find out about samba worldwide through the internet and email. The UK samba website is at http://www.farrie.demon.co.uk/samba/b ands/htm. To subscribe to the UK samba email address, contact tardis.ed.ac.uk and send on sambistas@tardis.ed.ac.uk. The worldwide samba home page is at www.worldsamba.org/.

Dave Willetts

Vinícius de Morais 49, is where the song 'Girl from Ipanema' was written, very lively; on the same street, No 39, 2nd floor, is **Vinícius**, live music and international cuisine from 1900. In Leblon is the **Academia da Cachaça**, R Conde de Bernadotte 26-G, with another branch at Av Armando Lombardi 800, Barra da Tijuca; **Pepe** at Posto 2, Barra da Tijuca beach, is very popular with young people (1997). Lots more bars are opening in districts to the south. **Bar Lagoa**, Av Epitácio Pessoa 1674, Lagoa. Recommended ('arty crowd', evenings only). On weekday evenings, Cariocas congregate at the bars around Praça Santos Dumont, Gávea. British ex-pats meet at **Porão**, under the Anglican church hall, R Real Grandeza 99, Botafogo, Friday only.

Nightclubs The usual system in nightclubs is to pay an entrance fee (about US$10) and then you are given a card onto which your drinks are entered. There is often a minimum consumption of US$10-15 on top of the entry charge. Do not lose your card or they may charge you more than you could possibly drink, sometimes US$200-300. Most places will serve reasonable snack food.

Trendiest clubs (contemporary dance music) are *El Turf* (aka *Jockey Club*) , opposite the Jardim Botânico, Praça Santos Dumont 31, T2741444, opens at 2200, gets going at 2300, you may have to wait to get in at the weekend if you arrive after midnight, no T-shirts allowed, very much a singles and birthday party place; another branch in Rio Sul Shopping Centre. *Fun Club*, also in Shopping Centre Rio Sul, 4th floor, T5411478. *Le Maxim's Club*, R Lauro Müller 119, Cobertura, T5419342, at the top of the Rio Sul tower. With a superb night view of Rio (single women and couples only). *Le Boy*, Raul Pompéia 94, Copacabana, T5210367, gay. *Papillon*, Av Prefeito Mendes de Moraes 222, São Conrado, T3222200. *The Basement*, Av Nossa Senhora de Copacabana 1241, alternative. In Barra da Tijuca, *Rock 'n' Rio Café*, Barra Shopping. Good food, young crowd, a long way from the centre (taxis hard to find in the early morning). *Ilha dos Pescadores*, on an island in the lagoon. Often has live samba and Bahian music. *Greenwich Village*, at Posto 6 on the beach front. Good reputation. There are dozens of other good clubs, most open Wednesday-Sunday, action starts around midnight, lone women and male-only groups may have trouble getting in.

Gafieiras, for Samba dancing, including *Elite Club*, R Frei Caneca 4, 1st floor, Centro, T2323217, also reggae. *Estudantina*, Praça Tiradentes 79, T2321149, Thursday-Sunday: there are many cheaper *gafieiras*: one, enthusiastically recommended, under the beach highway at Botafogo. All types of music and entertainment are represented: *Copa Show*, Av Nossa Senhora de Copacabana 435, has been recommended for forró and disco music (safe). *Reggae Rock Cafe*, Largo de São Conrado 20, T3224197. *Raizes*, Av Sernambetiba 1120, T3896240, for Afro-Brazilian beats.

Discoteca Fundição do Progresso, downtown, near Lapa/Centro. Very trendy disco. Copacabana is full of discos where the girls are for hire: biggest and most entertaining is *Help* on Av Atlântica; it opens about 2400. Entry charge (US$9) does not include drink. Music is usually good, trade is low-pressure, women with female friends and a sense of humour can have a lot of fun (but not recommended for couples). Sleazier shows are concentrated around Leme, as are gay clubs; many gay clubs also around Lapa (Cinelândia), but good ones exist all over the city. *Stop-Night*, a disco bar at Av Atlântica (near *Copacabana Palace* hotel) is a popular gay pick-up joint: be careful.

Entertainment

See also **Useful local publications**, page 151, for guides to what's on.

New American releases (with original soundtrack), plus Brazilian and worldwide films **Cinemas** and classics are all shown. See the local press. The normal seat price is US$4, discounts on Wednesday and Thursday (students pay half price any day of the week).

Tango is very popular at the moment. *Escola de Dança de Salão Maria Antonieta*, R **Dance classes** do Catete 112, 2nd floor, next to Catete Metrô, T2258589.

Many young Cariocas congregate in Botafogo for live music. There are free concerts **Music** throughout the summer, along the Copacabana and Ipanema beaches, in Botafogo and at the parks: mostly samba, reggae, rock and MPB (Brazilian pop): there is no advance schedule, information is given in the local press (see below). *Canecão* is a big, inexpensive venue for live concerts, most nights, see press for listings: R Venceslau Brás 215, Botafogo, T2953044. Rio's famous jazz, in all its forms, is performed in lots of enjoyable venues, see the press.

There are about 40 theatres in Rio, presenting a variety of classical and modern perfor- **Theatre** mances in Portuguese. Seat prices start at about US$15; some children's theatre is free.

Rio de Janeiro

Rio de Janeiro

Carnival

Carnival in Rio is spectacular. On the Friday before Shrove Tuesday, the mayor of Rio hands the keys of the city to Rei Momo, the Lord of Misrule, signifying the start of a five-day party. Imagination runs riot, social barriers are broken and the main avenues, full of people and children wearing fancy dress, are colourfully lit. Areas throughout the city such as the Terreirão de Samba in Praça Onze are used for shows, music and dancing. Bandas and blocos (organized carnival groups) seem to be everywhere, dancing, drumming and singing.

There are numerous samba schools in Rio divided into two leagues both of which parade in the Sambódromo. The 14 schools of the Grupo Especial parade on Sunday and Monday whilst the Grupos de Acesso A and B parade on Saturday and Friday respectively. There is also a mirins parade (younger members of the established schools) on Tuesday. The judging takes place on Wednesday afternoon and the winners of the various groups parade again on the following Saturday.

Every school presents 2500-6000 participants divided into alas (wings) each with a different costume and 5-9 carros alegóricos, beautifully designed floats. Each school chooses an enredo (theme) and composes a samba (song) that is a poetic, rhythmic and catchy expression of the theme. The enredo is further developed through the design of the floats and costumes. A bateria (percussion wing) maintains a reverberating beat that must keep the entire school, and the audience, dancing throughout the parade. Each procession follows a set order with the first to appear being the comissão de frente, a choreographed group that presents the school and the theme to the public. Next comes the abre alas, a magnificent float usually bearing the name or symbol of the school. The alas and other floats follow as well as porta bandeiras and mestre salas, couples dressed in 18th century costumes bearing the school's flag, and passistas, groups traditionally of mulata dancers. An ala of bahianas, elderly women with circular skirts that swirl as they dance is always included as is the velha guarda, distinguished members of the school who close the parade. Schools are given between 65 and 80 minutes and lose points for failing to keep within this time. Judges award points to each school for

Festivals

Carnival
See also box

Tickets The Sambódromo parades start at 1900 and last about 12 hours. Gates (which are not clearly marked) open at 1800. There are cadeiras (seats) at ground level, arquibancadas (terraces) and camarotes (boxes). The best boxes are reserved for tourists and VIPs and are very expensive or by invitation only. Seats are closest to the parade, but you may have to fight your way to the front. Seats and boxes reserved for tourists have the best view, sectors 4, 7 and 11 are preferred (they house the judging points); 6 and 13 are least favoured, being at the end when dancers might be tired, but have more space. The terraces, while uncomfortable, house the most fervent fans, tightly packed; this is where to soak up the atmosphere but not take pictures (too crowded). Tickets start at US$40 for arquibancadas and are sold at travel agencies as well as the Maracanã Stadium box office. Tickets are usually sold out before Carnaval weekend but touts outside can generally sell you tickets at inflated prices. Samba schools have an allocation of tickets which members sometimes sell, if you are offered one of these check its date. Tickets for the champions' parade on the Saturday following Carnival are much cheaper. Taxis to the Sambódromo are negotiable and will find your gate, the nearest metrô is Praça Onze and this can be an enjoyable ride in the company of costumed samba school members. You can follow the participants to the concentração, the assembly and

components of their procession, such as costume, music and design, and make deductions for lack of energy, enthusiasm or discipline. The winners of the Grupos de Acesso are promoted to the next higher group while the losers, including those of the Grupo Especial, are relegated to the next lowest group. Competition is intense and the winners gain a monetary prize funded by the entrance fees.

The Carnival parades are the culmination of months of intense activity by community groups, mostly in the city's poorest districts. To understand the traditions of the schools, the meanings of the different parts of the parade, and carnival as a whole, visit the **Museu do Carnaval** in the Sambódromo; although small, it has lots of photographs and the English-speaking staff are very informative (entrance in R Frei Caneca, T5026996. Monday-Friday 1100-1700, free). The **Sambódromo**, a permanent site at R Marquês de Sapucai, Cidade Nova, is 600 metres long with seating for 43,000 people. Designed by Oscar Niemeyer and built in 1983-84, it handles sporting events, conferences and concerts during the rest of the year.

Rio´s bailes (fancy-dress balls) range from the sophisticated to the wild. The majority of clubs and hotels host at least one. The Copacabana Palace hotel´s is elegant and expensive whilst the Scala club has licentious parties. It is not necessary to wear fancy dress; just join in, although you will feel more comfortable if you wear a minimum of clothing to the clubs (crowded, hot and rowdy). The most famous are the Red & Black Ball (Friday) and the Gay Ball (Tuesday) which are both televised.

Bandas and blocos can be found in all neighbourhoods and some of the most popular and entertaining are Cordão do Bola Preta (meets at 0900 on Saturday in Rua 13 de Maio 13, Centro), Simpatia é Quase Amor (meets at 1600 Sunday in Praça General Osório, Ipanema)and the transvestite Banda da Ipanema (meets at 1600 on Saturday and Tuesday in Praça General Osorio, Ipanema). It is necessary to join a bloco in advance to receive their distinctive t-shirts, but anyone can join in with the bandas.

The expensive hotels offer special Carnival breakfasts from 0530. Caesar Park is highly recommended for a wonderful meal and a top-floor view of the sunrise over the beach.

formation on Avenida Presidente Vargas, and mingle with them while the queue to enter the Sambódromo. Ask if you can take photos.

Sleeping and security Visitors wishing to attend the Carnival are advised to reserve accommodation well in advance. Virtually all hotels raise their prices during Carnival, although it is usually possible to find a room. Your property should be safe inside the Sambódromo, but the crowds outside can attract pickpockets; as ever, don't brandish your camera, and only take the money you need for fares and refreshments (food and drink are sold in the Sambódromo.) It gets hot! Wear as little as possible (shorts and a t-shirt).

Taking part Most samba schools will accept a number of foreigners and you will be charged upwards of US$125 for your costume as your money helps to fund poorer members of the school. You should be in Rio for at least two weeks before carnival. It is essential to attend fittings and rehersals on time, to show respect for your section leaders and to enter into the competitive spirit of the event. For those with the energy and the dedication, it will be an unforgettable experience.

Rehersals Ensaios are held at the schools' quadras from October onwards and are well worth seeing. It is wise to go by taxi, as most schools are based in poorer districts. Tour agents sell tickets for glitzy samba shows, which are nothing like the real thing. When buying a Carnival video, make sure the format is compatible (Brazilian format matches the USA; VHS PAL for most of Europe).

Rio de Janeiro

Samba Schools *Acadêmicos de Salgueiro*, R Silva Teles 104, Andaraí, T2385564, www.salgueiro.com.br; *Beija Flor de Nilópolis*, Pracinha Wallace Paes Leme 1025, Nilópolis, T7912866, www.beija-flor.com.br; *Imperatriz Leopoldinense*, R Prof. Lacê 235, Ramos, T2708037, www.love-rio.com/imperatriz/; *Mocidade Independente de Padre Miguel*, R Coronel Tamarindo 38, Padre Miguel, T3325823, www.mocidade. com; *Portela*, R Clara Nunes 81, Madureira, T3900471, www.gresportela.com.br; *Primeira Estação de Mangueira*, R Visconde de Niterói 1072, Mangueira, T5674637, www.mangueira.com.br; *Unidos da Viradouro*, Av do Contorno 16, Niterói, T7177540, www.databrasil.com/viradouro/.

Useful information Carnival week comprises an enormous range of official and unofficial contests and events which reach a peak on the Tuesday. Riotur's guide booklet gives concise information on these in English. The entertainment sections of newspapers and magazines such as *O Globo*, *Jornal do Brasil*, *Manchete* and *Veja Rio* are worth checking. *Liga Independente das Escolas de Samba do Rio de Janeiro*, www.liesa.com.br. The book, *Rio Carnival Guide*, by Felipe Ferreira, has good explanations of the competition, rules, the schools, a map and other practical details.

Other festivals   Less hectic than Carnival, but very atmospheric, is the festival of Iemanjá (see **Religion**, page 767) on the night of **31 December**, when devotees of the *orixá* of the sea dress in white and gather on Copacabana, Ipanema and Leblon beaches, singing and dancing around open fires and making offerings. The elected Queen of the Sea is rowed along the seashore. At midnight small boats are launched as offerings to Iemanjá. The religious event is dwarfed, however, by a massive New Year's Eve party, called *Reveillon* at Copacabana. The beach is packed as thousands of revellers enjoy free outdoor concerts by big-name pop stars, topped with a lavish midnight firework display. It is most crowded in front of *Copacabana Palace Hotel*. Another good place to see the fireworks is in front of *Le Meridien*, famous for its fireworks waterfall at about 10 minutes past midnight.

NB Many followers of Iemanjá are now making their offerings on 29 or 30 December and at Barra da Tijuca or Recreio dos Bandeirantes to avoid the crowds and noise of Reveillon.

The festival of São Sebastião, patron saint of Rio, is celebrated by an evening procession on **20 January**, leaving Capuchinhos Church, Tijuca and arriving at the cathedral of São Sebastião. On the same evening, an *umbanda festival* is celebrated at the Caboclo Monument in Santa Teresa.

Throughout Brazil, **June** is a month of festivals, the Festas Juninas. In Rio they start with the festival of *Santo Antônio* on **13 June**, whose main event is a mass, followed by celebrations at the Convento do Santo Antônio and the Largo da Carioca. Throughout the state, the festival of *São João* is a major event, marked by huge bonfires on the night of **23-24 June**. It is traditional to dance the *quadrilha* and drink *quentão*, cachaça and sugar, spiced with ginger and cinnamon, served hot. The Festas Juninas close with the festival of *São Pedro* on **29 June**. Being the patron saint of fishermen, his feast is normally accompanied by processions of boats.

October is the month of the feast of *Nossa Senhora da Penha* (see page 112).

Shopping

Jewellery   Buy precious and semi-precious stones from reputable dealers. *H Stern*, R Visconde de Pirajá 490/R Garcia D'vila 113, Ipanema, have 10 outlets, plus branches in major hotels throughout the city (as well as branches elsewhere in Brazil and worldwide); see page 123. *Amsterdam Sauer*, R Garcia D'Ávila 105, have 10 shops in Rio and others throughout Brazil, plus St Thomas (US Virgin Islands) and New York; they offer free taxi rides to their main shop; see page 123. The headquarters of these 2 establishments are next door to each other. *H Stern* is much the bigger of the 2 in terms of premises, shop space, tours etc. There are several good jewellery shops at the Leme end of Av NS de Copacabana: *Lido*, R Rodolfo Dantas 26B, T5418098. Recommended. For mineral specimens as against cut stones, try *Mineraux*, Av NS de Copacabana 195, Belgian owner. *Saara* is a multitude of little shops along R Alfândega and R Senhor dos Passos (between city centre and Campo Santana), where clothes bargains can be found (especially jeans and bikinis); it is known popularly as 'Shopping a Céu Aberto'. Little shops on Aires Saldanha, Copacabana (1 block back from beach), are good for bikinis and cheaper than in shopping centres.

Bookshops

For international stock, *Livraria Kosmos*, R do Rosário 155, good shop (in the centre and Av Atlântica 1702, loja 5), and there are many others, eg *Livros Técnicos*, R Miguel Couto 35, wide selection; *Nova Livraria Da Vinci*, Av Rio Branco 185 lojas 2, 3 and 9, all types of foreign books, *South American Handbook* available; *Livraria Argumento*, R Dias Ferreira 417, Leblon, sells imported English books; also branches of *Sodiler* at both airports and Barra Shopping, Rio Sul (2 branches), Via Parque, Iguatemi and Tijuca shopping centres and at R São José 35, loja V. *Livrarias Siciliano*, Av Rio Branco 156, loja 26, European books, also at Nossa Senhora de Copacabana 830 and branches; French books at No 298. *Saraiva* has a megastore at R do Ouvidor 98, T5079500, a massive bookshop which also includes a music and video shop and a café; other branches in Shopping Iguatemi and Shopping Tijuca. *Unilivros*, Largo do Machado 29C, French and English bestsellers (7 branches); *Livraria Nova Galeria de Arte*, Av Copacabana 291D, international stock. *Eldorado*, Av das Américas 4666, loja 207. Second-hand books also at *Livraria São José*, R Carmo 61 (only a few in English); *Livraria Brasileira*, Av Rio Branco 156, sobreloja 229; Aimée Gilbert, R da Carioca 38 (some in English); *Livraria Antiquário*, 7 de Setembro 207 and in R Pedro I, all in centre. Also on Av Marechal Floriano, near Av Rio Branco, especially at No 63. On the south side of Praça Tiradentes, *Casa dos Artistas* trades in second-hand paperbacks. Second-hand English books at the Anglican church, R Real Grandeza 99, Botafogo. Also at Av NS de Copacabana 400, small selection, US$1 per book.

Camping equipment

On R 1 de Março, north of Av Pres Vargas, are military shops which sell jungle equipment, such as hammocks, mosquito nets and clothing, eg *Casa do Militar*, No 145 and *London*, No 155; you can also buy the Brazilian flag in any size you want here. *Malamada*, R da Carioca 13, recommended for rucksacks.

Markets

Northeastern market at Campo de São Cristóvão, with music and magic, on Sunday 0800-2200 (bus 472 or 474 from Copacabana or centre). Saturday antiques market on the waterfront near Praça 15 de Novembro, 1000-1700. Also in Praça 15 de Novembro is *Feirarte II*, Thursday-Friday 0800-1800. *Feirarte I* is a Sunday open-air handicrafts market (everyone calls it the *Feira Hippy*) at Praça Gen Osório, Ipanema, 0800-1800, touristy but fun: items from all over Brazil. A Sunday stamp and coin market is held in the Passeio Público. Markets on Wednesday 0700-1300 on R Domingos Ferreira and on Thursday, same hours, on Praça do Lido, both Copacabana (Praça do Lido also has a *Feirarte* on Saturday-Sunday 0800-1800). There is an *artesania* market nightly near the *Othon* hotel, near R Miguel Lemos: one part for paintings, one part for everything else. Sunday market on R da Glória, colourful, cheap fruit, vegetables and flowers; early-morning food market, 0600-1100, R Min Viveiros de Castro, Ipanema. Excellent food and household-goods markets at various places in the city and suburbs (see newspapers for times and places). *Feira do Livro* is a book market that moves around various locations (Largo do Machado, Cinelândia, Nossa Senhora da Paz – Ipanema), selling books at 20% discount.

Music

For a large selection of Brazilian music, jazz and classical, try *Modern Sound Música Equipamentos*, R Barata Ribeiro 502D, Copacabana.

Photography
Kodachrome slide film is difficult to get in Rio

For processing, *Flash Studio*, R Visconde de Pirajá 156, expensive; *One Hour Foto*, in the Rio Sul and Barra shopping centres, is recommended; *Honório*, R Vinícius de Moraes 146E. Stocks lithium batteries. Nikon camera repairs, *T Tanaka Cia Ltda*, Av Franklin Roosevelt 39, of 516, T2201127. Also *Mecánica de Precisão*, R da Conceição 31, shop 202, good.

Shopping centres

The *Rio Sul*, at the Botafogo end of Túnel Novo, has almost everything the visitor may need. As mentioned above, it has been refurbished and is convenient and very safe. Some of the services in Rio Sul are: *Telemar* (phone office) for international calls at A10-A, Monday-Saturday 1000-2200; next door is *Belle Tours Câmbio*, A10. There is a post office at G2. A good branch of *Livraria Sodiler* is at A03. Entertainment includes the *Fun Club* nightclub on the fourth floor, open all night, very young crowd (see under **Entertainment** above); live music at the *Terraço*; the *Ibeas Top Club* gym; and a cinema. Eating places include fast food restaurants, 2 branches of *Kotobuki* sushi bar (another branch on the road to Praia Vermelha, recommended) and *Chaika* for milkshakes, ice creams and sandwiches (fourth floor, original branch on Praça Nossa Senhora da Paz, Ipanema). A US$5 bus service runs as far as the *Sheraton* passing the main hotels, every 2 hours between 1000 and 1800, then 2130.

Other shopping centres, which include a wide variety of shops and services, include: *Cassino* (Copacabana), *Norte Shopping* (Todos os Santos), *Plaza Shopping* (Niterói), *Barra* in Barra da Tijuca (see page 125). At São Conrado, *The Fashion Mall* is smaller and more stylish.

Sports

There are hundreds of excellent gyms and sports clubs; most will not grant temporary (less than 1 month) membership: big hotels may allow use of their facilities for a small deposit. *Paissandu Athletic Club*, Av Afrânio de Melo Franco 330, Leblon – tennis, bowls, swimming, Scottish dancing, Tuesday, April-October, 2000-2230, may admit non-members.

Horse racing and riding *Jockey Club Racecourse*, by Jardím Botânico and Gávea, meetings on Monday and Thursday evenings and Saturday and Sunday 1400, entrance US$1-2, long trousers required, a table may be booked. Take any bus marked 'via Jóquei'. Betting is by totalizator only. *Sociedade Hípico Brasileiro*, Av Borges de Medeiros 2448, T5278090, Jardim Botânico – riding.

Sailing *late Clube do Rio de Janeiro*, Av Pasteur, Urca, T2954482 – yachting. Information: Federação Brasileira de Vela e Motor, R Alcindo Guanabara 15, sl 801, Centro, T2203738; Federação de Vela, Praça Mahatma Gandhi 2, 12th floor, T2208785.

Cycling Tours (hire available) with *Rio Bikers*, R Domingos Ferreira 81, room 201, T2745872.

Diving *Squalo*, Av Armando Lombardi 949-D, Barra de Tijuca, T/F4933022, squalo1@hotmail.com offers courses at all levels, NAUI and PDIC training facilities, also snorkelling and equipment rental.

Golf clubs There are both 18-hole and 9-hole courses at the Itanhangá Golf Club, Jacarepaguá, visiting cards from Av Rio Branco 26, 16th floor. The Gávea club, São Conrado, T3994141, and the Teresópolis Golf Club, Estr Imbuí (Várzea), both have 18 holes; 9 holes at Petrópolis Country Club, Nogueira.

Hang-gliding *Just Fly*, T/F2680565, Cell99857540, flycelani@ax.apc.org, US$80 for tandem flights with Paulo Celani (licensed by Brazilian Hang Gliding Association), pick-up and drop-off at hotel included, in-flight pictures US$15 extra, flights all year, best time of day 1000-1500 (5% discount for *South American* and *Brazil Handbook* readers on presentation of book at time of reservation), *Ultra Força Ltda*, Av Sernambetiba 8100, Barra da Tijuca, T3993114; 15 minutes. Rejane Reis, *Exotic Tours*, (see **Tour**

Brazilian football – a beautiful game

It has been more than 100 years since Charles Miller, an English expatriat, returned to São Paulo from a trip to the UK and brought with him a couple of leather footballs and arranged a kickabout with some other Englishmen employed at the local banks, railway and gas companies.

For the first decades of the 20th century Brazilian football was still a middle-class game. For example, Flamengo and Fluminense, two of Rio's most popular clubs, were originally both sports clubs frequented by the wealthy and the white. Then in 1923 Vasco da Gama, with a team of black and poor white players, won the Rio championship in the first year of their promotion to the first division. Other local clubs responded by forming their own league and barring Vasco from joining.

Brazilian soccer has come a long way since then. Players now come from all walks of life, colours and creeds, and they become national heroes. When Garrincha, one of the heroes of the 1962 World Cup finals, died in 1983, millions of Brazilians mourned; the funeral cortège took two hours to travel 56 kilometres through Rio.

The most famous Brazilian footballer remains Edson Arantes do Nascimento, better known as Pelé. He played for Brazil for the first time when he was 17 in 1958 when Brazil won its first World Cup and was still playing for the national squad when it claimed the Jules Rimet trophy in Mexico 1970. Pelé is still very popular and became Minister of Sport.

Some critics argue that Brazilian football has lost its way in recent years. Brazilians relish their national team playing elaborate stylish 'samba' football that they played in the 1970s and early 1980s. The 1994 World Cup winning squad were criticized for not playing the jogo bonito, or 'beautiful game'. But there were a new set of stars, two of whom, Denilson and Ronaldo, were at the time the most expensive in the world. And in Mario Lobo Zagalo, Brazil had a highly experienced manager. He played in two of the World Cup winning squads and was coach in the other two finals. He liked his team to play with flair and laid down strict rules on their conduct in the run-up to France 1998. Despite some setbacks, not least losing 1-0 to the US in the Gold Cup in February 1998, Brazil were still firm favourites.

Unfortunately the campaign for the Penta didn't go quite as planned. The standard of play was not brilliant and marked by disagreements between the captain Dunga and some of his players. After a heroic defence by keeper Taffarel Brazil managed to win the semi-final on penalties and the country celebrated as if they had won already. In the final, however, there were team changes as Zagallo made the weighty decision of whether to play Ronaldo who had suffered a surprise fit hours before. France triumphed easily over a dispirited and disorganised Brazilian squad.

Even if you really hate football, attending a match between some of the bigger clubs in Rio or São Paulo is a must. They are a riot of colour – each teams' supporters bring flares and flags to match the teams' strip – noise and live samba music. And the football's not bad either!

The story has in some ways gone full circle. Early last year Simon Clifford, a British school teacher returned from Brazil with a few smaller heavier balls preferred by Brazilian kids when they play futebol do salo, a type of five-a-side game suited to the limited space available in Brazil's crowded cities and their favelas. He is convinced that the British could learn a thing or two from the inventors of the jogo bonito.

Steve Collins and Mick Day

agencies, below) also arranges hang-gliding, as well as paragliding, ultra light flights, walks and other activities.

Parachuting Tandem jumping (*Vôo duplo*); *Barra Jumping*, Aeroporto de Jacarepaguá, Av Ayrton Senna 2541, T3252494/9881566. Several other people offer tandem jumping; check that they are accredited with the Associação Brasileira de Vôo Livre.

Paragliding   From Leblon beach with Sr Ruy Marra, Brazilian paragliding champion (US$75), T3222286, or find him at the beach: "Just fantastic!"

Rock climbing and hill walking   *ECA*, Av Erasmo Braga 217, room 305, T2426857/5710484, personal guide US$100 per day, owner Ralph speaks English; *Clube Excursionista Carioca*, also recommended for enthusiasts, R Hilário Gouveia 71, room 206, T2551348, meets Wednesday and Friday. *Paulo Miranda*, R Campos Sales 64/801, RJ20.270-210, T/F2644501.

Surfing   For the state of the waves on the beaches in Rio de Janeiro and its environs, see Surfing, page 32. Various organizations you may wish to contact are: Organização dos Surfistas Profissionais do Rio de Janeiro, T4932472; Federação de Surf do Estado do Rio de Janeiro, T2872385; Associação Brasileira de Bodyboard, T2743614; and Federação de Bodyboard do Estado do Rio de Janeiro, T2565653.

Transport

Local
See also Ins & outs, page 94
Car hire   *Avis*, Galeão international airport T3983361, Santos Dumont airport T2200171, Av Princesa Isabel 150A and B, Copacabana, T2958197; *Golden Car*, R Ronald de Carvalho 154C, Copacabana, T2754748; *Hertz*, international airport T3984338, Av Princesa Isabel 273-A, Copacabana, T2757440; *Interlocadora*, international airport T3983181; *Localiza*, international airport T3985989, Santos Dumont airport T2205455, Av Princesa Isabel 214, Copacabana, T2753340; *Nobre*, Av Princesa Isabel 7, Copacabana, T5414646; *Telecar*, R Figueiredo Magalhães 701, Copacabana, T2356778. Many agencies on Av Princesa Isabel, Copacabana. A credit card is virtually essential for hiring a car. Recent reports suggest it is cheaper to hire outside Brazil, you may also obtain fuller insurance this way.

Motoring   Remember service stations are closed in many places on Saturday and Sunday. Road signs are notoriously misleading in Rio and you can end up in a *favela*. Take care if driving along the Estr da Gávea to São Conrado as it is possible to unwittingly enter Rocinha, Rio's biggest slum.

Car repairs   *Kyoso Team Mecânico Siqueira Campos*, at the entrance to the old tunnel, T2550506. A good mechanic who enjoys the challenge of an unusual car. Recommended.

Buses   There are good services to all parts, but buses are very crowded and not for the aged and infirm during rush hours; buses have turnstiles which are awkward if you are carrying luggage. Hang on tight, drivers live out Grand Prix fantasies. At busy times allow about 45 minutes to get from Copacabana to the centre by bus. The fare on standard buses is US$0.40 and suburban bus fares are US$0.75. Bus stops are often not marked. The route is written on the side of the bus, which is hard to see until the bus has actually pulled up at the stop.

Private companies operate air-conditioned *frescão* buses which can be flagged down practically anywhere: Real, Pegaso, Anatur. They run from all points in Rio Sul to the city centre, Rodoviária and the airports. Fares are US$2 (US$3.50 to the international airport).

City Rio is a tourist bus service which runs between all the major parts of the city. You can buy tickets valid for 24, 48 or 72 hours and use the bus as often as you want within that period. Good maps show what sites of interest are close to each bus stop. There are security guards on the buses.

Trams   The last remaining tram runs from near the Largo da Carioca (there is a museum, open only Friday 0830-1700) across the old aqueduct (Arcos) to Dois Irmãos or Paula Mattos in Santa Teresa – historical and interesting, US$0.60. For more details see above under **Santa Teresa**.

Metro The Metrô provides good service, clean, air conditioned and fast. Line 1 operates between the inner suburb of Tijuca (station Saens Peña) and Arcoverde (Copacabana), via the railway station (Central), Glória and Botafogo. Line 2 runs from Pavuna, passing Engenho da Rainha and the Maracanã stadium, to Estácio. It operates 0600-2300, Sunday 1400-2000; closed holidays. The fare is R$1 (US$0.50) single; multi-tickets and integrated bus/Metrô tickets are available. Substantial changes in bus operations are taking place because of the extended Metrô system; buses connecting with the Metrô have a blue-and-white symbol in the windscreen.

Trains There are suburban trains to Nova Iguaçu, Nilópolis, Campo Grande and elsewhere. Buses marked 'E Ferro' go to the railway station.

Taxis The fare between Copacabana and the centre is US$7. Between 2300 and 0600 and on Sunday and holidays, 'tariff 2' is used. Taxis have red number plates with white digits (yellow for private cars, with black digits) and have meters. Smaller ones (mostly Volkswagen) are marked TAXI on the windscreen or roof. Make sure meters are cleared and on tariff 1, except at those times mentioned above. Only use taxis with an official identification sticker on the windscreen. Don't hesitate to argue if the route is too long or the fare too much. Radio Taxis are safer but more expensive, eg *Cootramo*, T5605442, *Coopertramo*, T2602022, *Centro de Táxi*, T5932598, *Transcoopass*, T5604888. Luxury cabs are allowed to charge higher rates. Inácio de Oliveira, T2254110, is a reliable taxi driver for excursions, he only speaks Portuguese. Recommended. Grimalde, T2679812, has been recommended for talkative daytime and evening tours, English and Italian spoken, negotiate a price.

Rio de Janeiro Metrô

Long distance
See also Ins & outs, page 94

Air   Rio has 2 airports: Jobim international airport, previously called Galeão, and the Santos Dumont airport on Guanabara Bay for domestic flights. **Tom Jobim international airport** is situated on Governador Island some 16 km from the centre of Rio. It is in 2 sections: international and domestic. It is possible to book seats on international flights destined for São Paulo which stopover in Rio for as little as US$100 one-way, but you must balance against this the extra cost of the higher taxi fares to and from the international airports.

There are a/c taxis; *Cootramo* and *Transcopass* have fixed rates (US$40 Copacabana), buy a ticket at the counter near the arrivals gate before getting into the car. The hire is for the taxi, irrespective of the number of passengers. Make sure you keep the ticket, which carries the number to phone in case of difficulty. Ordinary taxis also operate with the normal meter reading (about US$30, but some may offer cheaper rates from Copacabana to the airport, US$15-20). Do not negotiate with a driver on arrival, unless you are a frequent visitor. Beware pirate taxis which are unlicensed. It is better to pay extra for an official vehicle than run the risk of robbery.

The a/c 'Real' bus runs very frequently from the first floor of the airport to Recreio dos Bandeirantes via the municipal rodoviária and city centre, Santos Dumont Airport, Flamengo, Copacabana, Ipanema and Leblon. Luggage is secured in the hold (receipted), passengers are given a ticket and fares are collected during the journey; to anywhere in Rio it costs US$3.50. The driver will stop at requested points (the bus runs along the seafront from Leme to Leblon), so it's worth checking a map beforehand so that you can specify your required junction. The bus returns by the same route. Town buses M94 and M95, *Bancários/Castelo*, take a circular route passing through the centre and the interstate bus station. They leave from the second floor of the airport.

There are *câmbios* in the departure hall of the airport. There is also a *câmbio* on the first floor of the international arrivals area, but it gives worse rates than the Banco do Brasil, 24-hour bank, third floor, which has Visa ATMs and will give cash advances against Visa card (beware 'officials' who say there are no *câmbios* or banks).

Duty-free shops are well-stocked, but not especially cheap. Duty free is open to arrivals as well as departures. Only US dollars or credit cards are accepted on the air-side of the departure lounge. There is a wider choice of restaurants outside passport control.

Check at the *Riotur* counter before leaving, for folders, maps and advice, T3984073. They will give help in booking hotels if required. **NB** Tourist packs are sold at the International Airport – they are completely unnecessary.

The **Santos Dumont airport** on Guanabara Bay, right in the city, is used for Rio-São Paulo shuttle flights (US$150 single, US$300 return), other domestic routes, air taxis and private planes. The shuttle services operate every 30 minutes throughout the day from 0630 to 2230. Sit on the right-hand side for views to São Paulo, the other side coming back, book in advance for particular flights. The main airport, on Governador Island, some 16 km from the centre of Rio, is in 2 sections, international and domestic (including Vasp and Transbrasil's jet shuttle from Rio to São Paulo). It is possible to book seats on international flights destined for São Paulo which stopover in Rio for as little as US$100 1-way, but you must balance against this the extra cost of the higher taxi fares to and from the international airports.

Details of journey times and fares are given under destinations throughout the chapter

Buses   Rodoviária Novo Rio, Av Rodrigues Alves, corner with Av Francisco Bicalho, just past the docks, T2915151. Some travel agents sell interstate tickets, or will direct you to a bus ticket office in the centre. Agencies include *Dantur Passagens e Turismo*, Av Rio Branco 156, subsolo loja 134, T2623424/3624; *Itapemirim Turismo*, R Uruguaiana 10, loja 24, T5098543, both in the centre; *Guanatur*, R Dias da Rocha 16A, Copacabana; and an agency at R Visconde de Pirajá 303, loja 114, Ipanema. They charge about US$1 for bookings. Buses run from Rio to all parts of the country; it is advisable to book tickets in advance. For latest bus prices from Rio, check *O Globo's* website, www.oglobo.com.br, click 'Boa Viagem', then 'Guia de Viagem'.

The rodoviária has a Riotur information centre, which is very helpful. Left luggage costs US$3. There are *câmbios* for cash only. The local bus terminal is just outside the rodoviária: turn right as you leave and run the gauntlet of taxi drivers – best ignored. The rodoviária attracts thieves; exercise caution. The air conditioned *Real* bus (opposite the exit) goes along the beach to São Conrado and will secure luggage. If you need a taxi collect a ticket, which ensures against overcharging, from the office inside the entrance (to Flamengo US$7.50). On no account give the ticket to the taxi driver.

International buses Asunción, 1,511 km via Foz do Iguaçu, 30 hours (Pluma), US$70; Buenos Aires (Pluma), via Porto Alegre and Santa Fe, 48 hours, US$100 (book 2 days in advance); to Uruguaiana, US$90, cheaper and quicker to get a through ticket; Santiago de Chile, with Pluma US$135, or Gen Urquiza, about 70 hours.

The main bus station is reached by buses M94 and M95, Bancários/Castelo, from the centre and the airport; 136, 172, Rodoviária/Glória/Flamengo/Botafogo; 127, 128, 136, Rodoviária/Copacabana; 170, Rodoviária/Gávea/São Conrado; 128, 172, Rodoviária/Ipanema/Leblon.

Hitchhiking To hitch to **Belo Horizonte** or **Brasília**, take a C-3 bus from Av Pres Antônio Carlos to the railway station, cross through the station to a bus station and catch the Nova Iguaçu bus. Ask to be let off at the Belo Horizonte turn off. For the motorway entrance north and south, take bus 392 or 393 from Praça São Francisco.

Routes Distances in km to some major cities with approximate journey time in brackets: Juiz de Fora, 184 (2¾ hours); Belo Horizonte, 434 (7 hours); São Paulo, 429 (6 hours); Vitória, 521 (8 hours); Curitiba, 852 (12 hours); Brasília, 1,148 (20 hours); Florianópolis, 1,144 (20 hours); Foz do Iguaçu, 1,500 (21 hours); Porto Alegre, 1,553 (26 hours); Salvador, 1,649 (28 hours); Recife, 2,338 (38 hours); Fortaleza, 2,805 (48 hours); São Luís, 3,015 (50 hours); Belém, 3,250 (52 hours).

Directory

Airline offices

Aerolíneas Argentinas, R da Assembléia 100, 29th floor, T2103121, airport T3983539. *Air France*, Av Pres Antônio Carlos 58, 9th and 10th floors, T5323642, airport 3983698. *Alitalia*, Av Pres Wilson 231, 21st floor, T2622544, airport T3983663. *American*, Av Pres Wilson 165, 5th floor, T2103126, airport T3984053, also at *Hotel Intercontinental*, T3221960. *Avianca*, Av Pres Wilson 165, offices 801-08, T2404413, airport T3983778. *British Airways*, Av Rio Branco 108, 21st floor, T2210922, airport T3983888. *Canadian Airlines International*, R da Ajuda 35, 29th floor, T2205343, airport T3983604. *Iberia*, Av Pres Antônio Carlos 51, 8th and 9th floors, T2102415, airport T3983168. *Japan Airlines*, Av Rio Branco 156, office 2014, T2206414, airport T3983023. *KLM*, Av Rio Branco 311A, T2103242, airport T3983700. *LanChile*, R 7 de Setembro 111, office 701, T2209722, airport T3983797. *LAB*, Av Calógeras 30A, T2209548, airport T3983738. *Lufthansa*, Av Rio Branco 156D, T2176111, airport T3983855. *Nordeste*, T2204366/2213131. *Pluma*, Av Rio Branco 147, 11th floor, T2624466, airport 3983851. *RioSul*, Av Rio Branco 85, 11th floor, T2636171 information, 2213131 bookings (has an advance check-in desk in Rio Sul Shopping). *South African*, Av Rio Branco 245, 4th floor, T2626252, airport T39833665. *Swissair*, Av Rio Branco 108, 10th floor, T2975177. *TAP*, Av Rio Branco 311-B, T2101277/8, airport, T3983455. *Transbrasil*, R Santa Luzia 651, T2974422; Av Atlântica 1998, Copacabana, T2367475. *United*, Av Pres Antônio Carlos 51, 5th and 6th floors, T5321212. *Varig*, Av Rio Branco 277G, T2821319 information, T2926600 bookings; R Rodolfo Dantas 16A, Copacabana, T5416343; R Visconde de Pirajá 351C/D, T2879440; airport T3983420/3410. Most staff speak English in Varig offices. *Vasp*, R Santa Luzia 735, T0800-998277, or 2922112. R Visconde de Pirajá 444, Ipanema, T2922112 ext 356.

Rio de Janeiro

Banks *Lloyds Bank*, R da Alfândega 332, 7th floor. *Banco Internacional* (Bank of America and Royal Bank of Canada), R do Ouvidor 90. *Banco Holandês Unido*, R do Ouvidor 101. *Citibank*, R Assembléia 100, changes large US$ TCs into smaller ones, no commission. *The First National Bank of Boston*, Av Rio Branco 110. Many others. *Banco do Brasil*, there are only 2 branches in Rio which will change US$ TCs, Praia de Botafogo, 384A, 3rd floor (minimium US$200) and the central branch at R Sen Dantas 105, 4th floor (minimum US$500 – good rates, also changes Argentine pesos, US$20 per transaction). *Banco do Brasil* at the International Airport is open 24 hrs a day. The international airport is probably the only place to change TCs at weekends. Visa cash withdrawals at *Banco do Brasil* (many ATMs at the R Sen Dantas branch, no queues) and *Bradesco* (personal service or machines). *Citibank* advances cash on Eurocard/Mastercard. Mastercard and Cirrus cash machines at *Itaú*, on Av Atlântica (next to *Copacabana Palace*), R Visconde de Pirajá, close to Praça Gen Osório (Ipanema) and other locations. Also at Santos Dumont airport. Mastercard hotline, 0800-784422 24 hrs a day.

Money changers *American Express*, Av Atlântica 1702, loja 1, T2552148/2677 Mon-Fri 0900-1800, Av Pres Wilson 231, 18th floor, Centro, T2921212/2963131 and at Galeão airport, T3984251 (VIP room 1st floor), good rates (toll-free number 0800-785050). Most large hotels and reputable travel agencies will change currency and TCs. Copacabana (where rates are generally worse than in the centre) abounds with *câmbios* and there are many also on Av Rio Branco. *Câmbio Belle Tours*, Rio Sul Shopping, ground floor, loja 101, parte A-10, Mon-Fri 1000-1800, Sat 1000-1700, changes cash. In the gallery at Largo do Machado 29 are *Câmbio Nick* at loja 22 and, next door but one, *Casa Franca*. Eurocheques, TCs and currency can be changed at *Hamburg Imobiliária*, see **Apartments** above. **NB** Some *câmbios* will change US$ cheques for US$ cash with a 4% commission. These transactions are not strictly legal, so you will have to look around for the *câmbios* that do them.

Communications **Post Office:** The central Post Office is on R 1 de Março 64, at the corner of R do Rosário. Av Nossa Senhora de Copacabana 540 and many other locations. All handle international post. There is a post office at Galeão airport. Poste Restante: American Express, Av Atlântica 1702 loja 1, Copacabana (for customers). Correios, Av Nossa Senhora de Copacabana 540 and all large post offices (letters held for a month, recommended, US$0.10 per letter). Federal Express, Av Calógeras 23 (near Santa Luzia church) T2628565, is reliable.

Telecommunications: International calls can be made at Av NS de Copacabana 540, 2nd floor. Galeão international airport. Santos Dumont airport, mezzanine (0530-2300). Novo Rio rodoviária. R Dias da Cruz 192, Méier-4, 24 hrs, 7 days a week. Urca, near the Pão de Açúcar cable car. Praça Tiradentes 41, a few mins' walk from Metrô Carioca. R Visconde de Pirajá 111, Ipanema. R do Ouvidor 60, Centro. International telephone booths are blue. Larger Embratel offices have telex and fax, as do many larger Correios, eg Av NS de Copacabana 540, fax number for receiving messages F5474774.

Internet: *@cafe*, Shop 125, Barra Shopping, Av das Americas 4666. *Bell Sul*, Posto Telefônico, loja 101, Rio Sul Shopping, Botafogo, T2759048, bellsul@openlink.com.br, US$2.50 for 30 mins. *Clube Israelita Brasileira* (CIB), Av Barata Ribeiro 489, T2571963, ext 247, US$3 per hr. *CompRio*, R da Assembléia 10, SS114. *CopaCyberCafé*, R Siqueira Campos 43/901, Centro Comercial de Copacabana, T5491366/5487953, spinola@az.apc.org, 0830-2200 Mon-Sat, also has tourist information and tour guides speaking several languages. *Estacão*, R Visconde de Pirajá 572, Ipanema, T2944233, US$2 per hr, good food, live music Thur. *Image Link*, R Visconde de Pirajá 207, suite 216, T5225850, US$6 per hr. *Internet House*, Av NS de Copacabana 195, Shop 106, T5423348, cybercafe@internethouse.com.br, US$5 per hr. Internet access also at *El Turf* in Rio Sul shopping centre.

Cultural centres *British Council*, R Elmano Cardim 10, Urca, T2957782, F5413693. *British School of Rio de Janeiro*, R Real Grandeza 99. *Sociedade Brasileira de Cultura Inglesa*, Av Graça Aranha 327 and in Copacabana, T2674048 (central information). *American Chamber of Commerce for Brazil*, Praça Pio X 15, 5th floor. *American Society and American Club*, Av Rio Branco 123, 21st floor. *USICA Reference Library*, US Consulate General, Av Pres Wilson 147. *American School of Rio de Janeiro*, Estr da Gávea 132. *Marc Apoio Cultural* Contact Center, Av Pres Vargas 446, 1101, T/F2758605. *German Cultur-Institut* (Goethe), Av Graça Aranha 416, 9th floor. Open Mon-Thu 1200-1900, Wed-Thu 1000-1100. *Australian Trade Commission*, R Voluntários da Pátria 45, 2°, Botafogo, T2867922 (for visas etc you must go to Brasília).

Argentine, Praia de Botafogo 228, T5531646. Very helpful over visas, 1130-1600. *Austria*, Av **Embassies &**
Atlântica 3804, T2670048. *British*, Praia do Flamengo 284, 2nd floor. T5535507 (consular section **consulates**
direct line)/3223, F5536850, consular section is open Mon-Fri 0900-1245 (the consulate's hrs are
0830-1700), Metrô Flamengo, or bus 170, the consulate issues a useful 'Guidance for Tourists'
pamphlet. *Canada*, R Lauro Müller 116, T5427393. *Denmark*, Av das Américas 3333, Apt 805, Barra
da Tijuca, T3254711/4312080. *France*, Av Pres Antônio Carlos, 58, T2101272. *German*, R Pres
Carlos de Campos 417, T5536777. *Greece*, Praia do Flamengo 344/201, T5526849. Israel, Av NS de
Copacabana 680C, T5482388. *Netherlands*, Praia de Botafogo 242, 7th floor, T5529028. (Dutch
newspapers here and at KLM office on Av Rio Branco.) *Paraguay*, same address, 2nd floor,
T5532512. Visas US$5. *Sweden*, *Finland* and *Norway*, Praia do Flamengo 344, 9th floor,
T5535540/5535505. *Switzerland*, *R Cândido Mendes 157, 11° andar, T2211867*. *Uruguay*, Praia de
Botafogo 242, 6°, T5536030. *USA*, Av Pres Wilson 147, T2927117. *Venezuela*, same address, 5th
floor, T5515248. Will not issue visas, see under Manaus and Boa Vista.

Vaccinations at *Saúde de Portos*, Praça Mcal Âncora, T2408628/8678, Mon-Fri 1000-1100, **Hospitals &**
1500-1800 (international vaccination book and ID required). *Policlínica*, Av Nilo Peçanha 38. **medical services**
Recommended for diagnosis and investigation. *Policlínica de Botafogo*, Av Pasteur 72, Botafogo,
T5431804. A good public hospital for minor injuries and ailments is *Hospital Municipal Rocha Maia*,
R Gen Severiano 91, Botafogo, T2952295/2121, near Rio Sul Shopping Centre. Free, but there may be
queues. *Hospital Miguel Couto*, Mário Ribeiro 117, Gávea, T274-6050. Has a free casualty ward. Eye
doctors can be found at *Hospital Souza Aguiar*, Praça da República 111, T2964114. Free casualty
ward. **Health:** Take note of local advice on water pollution. Air pollution also occurs. Dentist:
English-speaking, Amílcar Werneck de Carvalho Vianna, Av Pres Wilson 165, suite 811. Dr Mauro
Suartz, R Visconde de Pirajá 414, room 509, T2876745. Speaks English and Hebrew, helpful.

Instituto Brasil-Estados Unidos, Av Copacabana 690, 5th floor, T5488332, 8-week course, 3 **Language**
classes a week, US$200, 5-week intensive course US$260. Good English library at same address. **courses**
IVM Português Prático, R do Catete 310, sala 302, T2857842, F2854979, US$18 per hr for individual
lessons, cheaper for groups. Helpful staff. Recommended. *Cursos da UNE* (União Nacional de
Estudantes), R Catete 243, include cultural studies and Portuguese classes for foreigners. *Curso
Feedback*, branches in Botafogo, Centre, Barra and Ipanema, T2211863.

Fénix, R do Catete 214, loja 20. Praça Gen Osório, Ipanema. *Laundromat* at Av NS de Copacabana **Laundry**
1216. R Barata Ribeiro 662, Copacabana, self-service. In Rio Sul are self-service laundrettes such as
Lavelev, about US$7 for a machine, including detergent and drying, 1 hr. Also at R Buarque de
Macedo 43B, Catete, R Voluntários da Patria 248, Botafogo, Av Prado Junior 63B, Copacabana.
Lavlev Flamengo, RC de Baependi 78, or R das Laranjeiras 43, L28.

Services other than in Portuguese: Christ Church, R Real Grandeza 99, Botafogo, T2262978 (Church **Places of**
of England/American Episcopalian). The proceeds of books sold here go to help the Boys' Town **worship**
Charity for street kids. The British School, for children of 5-16, is nearby. Chapel of Our Lady of
Mercy, R Visconde de Caravelas 48, Botafogo, T2465664 (Roman Catholic, with primary school).
Union Church (Protestant nondenominational), services held at R Parque da Lagoa de Marapendi,
CP 37154, Barra da Tijuca. *International Baptist Church*, R Desembargador Alfredo Russel 146,
Leblon, T2460900. *First Church of Christ Scientist*, Av Mcal Câmara 271, room 301. *Masonic
Temple*, in the British School at R da Matriz 76, Botafogo. **Synagogues:** *Israelita Bethel*, R Barata
Ribeiro 469, Copacabana, includes kosher bakery. *Associação Religiosa Israelita*, R Gen Severiano
170, Botafogo, T2956444. *Beit Yaacov*, R Capelão Alvares da Silva 15, Copacabana, T2550191.
Swedish Church, Igreja Escandinava, Carlos Sampaio 251, Centro, T5091992, open 1300-2200,
Sun 1700-2100, will store luggage.

American Express, see **Banks** above. *Thomas Cook* is associated with *Stella Barros*, *Copacabana* **Tour agencies**
Palace Hotel, Av Atlântica, loja 01, T5473050, F5474994, R Visconde de Pirajá 647, Sl 701/726,
Ipanema, T2946740, T2747392, Av das Américas 4485, loja 111, Barra da Tijuca, T4311607, F3258730
and Av Roberto Silveira 196, loja 01, Icaral, Niterói, T/F6116669. *Turismo Clássico*, Av NS de
Copacabana 1059/805, CEP 22060-000, T5233390, F5214636. Warmly recommended. *Roxy*,
established 1948, Av Franklin Roosevelt, 71/601, Centro, CEP 20021-120, T5320141, F5323165. Ask
for Michael or Ricardo Werwie who speak English. Recommended. *Manhattan Turismo Ltda*, R da
Assembléia 10, GR 3503, Centro, T2423779/3064. Very helpful, English spoken. *Metropol*, R São José

Rio de Janeiro

46, T5335010, F5337160, metropol@arras.com.br. Eco, adventure and culture tours to all parts of Brazil. *Tour Brazil*, R Farme de Amoedo 75/605, near Ipanema, T5214461, F5211056. Very good English spoken. *Victor Hummel*, Av Pres Vargas 290/4, T2231262, Swiss-run. Recommended, T2311800. *Marlin Tours*, Av NS de Copacabana 605/1204, CEP 22050-000, T5484433, F2352081, bbm.robin@openlink.com.br. Recommended for hotel, flights and tours, Robin and Audrey speak English. *Quality Travel*, Av NS de Copacabana 387, T2356888, F2366985. Helpful with hotel bookings. *Hamburg Imobiliária*, see **Apartments** above. Recommended. *Hanseatic*, R 7 de Setembro 111/20, T2246672. German-run (English, French, Portuguese spoken). Recommended. *Blumar Turismo*, R Visconde de Pirjajá 550, Subsolo 108/109, Ipanema, T5113636, F5113739, blumar@blumar.com.br, run extensive tours throughout Brazil as well as reservations for Rio.

Organized trips to Samba shows cost US$50 including dinner, good, but it's cheaper to go independently. *Fenician Tours*, Av NS de Copacabana 335, offers a cheaper tour than some at US$33 including transport from/to hotel. Regular sightseeing tours are operated by *Gray Line*, T2941196. *American Sightseeing*, T2363551, *Sul América*, T2574235), *Canbitur* (of Copacabana), *Passamar Turismo*, Av Rio Branco 25, T2338883/2334833/2531125, also at *Hotel Nacional*. *Adrianotour*, T2085103. For guided tours, reservations and commercial services (English, French, German and Spanish spoken). *Atlantic Forest Operadora de Turismo*, T5112220, F2740875, mobile 9827986/9740218. As well as running jeep tours to the Tijuca National Park (see above), run tours to coffee *fazendas* in the Paraíba Valley, trips to Angra dos Reis and offshore islands and the Serra dos Órgãos. *Sangetur*, Largo do Machado 29 (Galeria Condor), loja 39, T5560993. Credit cards only accepted for airplane tickets. *Dantur*, Largo do Machado 29 (Galeria Condor) loja 47, T5577144. Helena speaks English and is friendly and helpful. *Guanatur Turismo*, R Dias da Rocha 16A, Copacabana, T2353275, F2353664. Sells long distance bus tickets.

Marcelo Niemeyer Armstrong, Estr das Canoas 722, Bl 2, apt 125, CEP 22610-210, T3222727/9890074, F3225958. The 1st in Rio to offer guided tours of Rio's favelas, safe, different and interesting, US$25, 3 hrs. Also ask Marcelo about eco tours, river rafting and other excursions. He speaks English, French, Spanish, Italian and can provide guides in German and Swedish. For the best attention and price call Marcelo direct rather than through a hotel desk. See box on page 105. Rejane Reis, *Exotic Tours*, also has favela tours, 2½ hrs, US$30 (transport included) – tours are combined with a guide-training programme. English spoken. *Cultural Rio*, tours escorted personally by Professor Carlos Roquette, R Santa Clara 110/904, Copacabana, T3224872 or 99113829, F5474774, English and French spoken, almost 200 options available. *Fábio Sombra* offers private and tailor-made guided tours focusing on the cultural aspects of Rio and Brazil, T2959220, answering machine 2758605, Cell97295455, fasombra@altavista.net.

Helicopter sightseeing tours: *Helisight*, R Visconde de Pirajá 580, loja 107, Térreo, Ipanema, T5112141, F2945292, infohsgt@helisight.com.br, www. helisight.com.br. Prices from US$43 pp for 6-7 mins from Morro de Urca over Sugar Loaf and Corcovado, to US$148 pp for 30 mins over the city. *Leizer Air*, Av Luiz Carlos Prestes 431, Barra da Tijuca, T4319494, F4319343, prices start at US$20.

Tourist information
Tourist offices do not normally provide lists of cheap accommodation for travellers; some initiative is required

There are several information centres. *Embratur*, R Uruguaiana 174, 8th floor, Centro, T5096017/6185/6292, webmaster@embratur.gov.br, http://embratur.gov.br. Gives information on the whole country. Also at R Mariz e Barros 13, 20270 Rio de Janeiro, T2732212/2931313, F2739290. *Riotur*, R da Assembléia 10, 9th floor, T2177575, F5311872, riotur@rio.rj.gov.br, http://www. rio.rj.gov.br/riotur. Information on the city of Rio de Janeiro, small, helpful information desk and English spoken by some staff, has good city maps and a very useful free brochure *RIO*, written in both

Portuguese and English. More information stands can be found at Pão de Açúcar cablecar station (0800-2000). Marina da Glória, Flamengo. Rodoviária Novo Rio (the bus station – 0600-2400, very friendly and helpful in finding accommodation but has no printed information) and at Copacabana, Av Princesa Isabel 183, T5417522/5428004 or 8080, German spoken. Riotur also has a multilingual telephone service operating 24 hrs, T5808000. English information service, T2428000. *TurisRio*, R da Assembléia 10, 8th floor, T5311922, F5312506. For the state of Rio de Janeiro. Very helpful. *Touring Clube do Brasil*, Pres Antônio Carlos 130 and Ave Brasil 4294 (out of town) no English spoken. *Centro Cultural* Banco do Brasil (see above), R 1 de Março 66, has a free, computerized information service. The best guide to Rio, with excellent maps, is *Guia Quatro Rodas do Rio* in Portuguese and English (the *Guia Quatro Rodas do Brasil*, published annually in Nov, also has a good Rio section). Also, *The Insider's Guide to Rio de Janeiro*, a guide book by Christopher Pickard, available from Rio bookshops, or enquire at Marlin Tours (T5484433). In 1990, Michelin published a *Guia de Turismo Rio de Janeiro, Cidade e Estado*, which is full of detailed historical and cultural information, maps and illustrations. If you are lucky you may be able to find a copy in a bookshop. *Trilhas do Rio*, by Pedro da Cunha e Meneses (Editora Salamandra, 2nd edition), US$22.50, describes walking trips around Rio. For a light-hearted approach to living in Rio, see *How to be a Carioca* by Priscilla Ann Goslin. Many hotels provide guests with the weekly *Itinerário* (*Rio This Month*).

Useful local publications Maps: *Guia Rex* street guide. *Guia Schaeffer Rio de Janeiro* is a good map. Maps are also available from Touring Clube do Brasil, news stands, touring agencies and hotels. The Geomapas tourist map is clear. Cia de Comunicação publishes a map of the city in perspective, which is good for orientation (US$2). Paulini, R Lélio Gama 75 (outside the entrance of the downtown tram station) sells topographical and other maps of Brazil and of South America.

Newspapers & magazines *Balcão*, an advertising newspaper, US$2, twice weekly, offers apartments in and around Rio, language lessons, discounted tickets, items for sale and advertises shops; similar advertisements in the classified sections of *O Globo* and *Jornal do Brasil*, daily. Both dailies have entertainments pages. *O Globo* has a travel section on Thurs; the *Jornal do Brasil's Programa* on Fri is an essential 'what's-on' magazine, as is the *Rio* supplement to *Veja*, a weekly news magazine (*Veja* publishes similar supplements in other major cities). Riotur's fortnightly booklet listing main attractions; *Rio This Month* (less reliable), free from hotels. *TurisRio's* free magazine about the State of Rio de Janeiro is interesting; if your hotel does not have these publications, just ask at the reception of one of the larger establishments.

FAVELA TOUR

A tour to the Favelas is an illuminating experience if you are looking for a new perspective of Rio and its people. The Tour integrates visitors with local people revealing a whole new vision of the Favelas, changing their reputation of violence and poverty forever.

You will go to the Favela of Vila Canoas, near the rich São Conrado district, and Rocinha, the largest Favela in Brazil. There you will visit the school, handicraft centre (also supported by the Tour) and other community works. You can bring your camera, and don't be shy; local people will greet you in a friendly manner and enjoy your visit.

Despite their bad reputation, Favelas are safer than most Cariocas believe. However, no matter how brave and adventurous you are, go to a Favela with an organized Tour; Marcelo Armstrong is the pioneer of Favela Tours, you can call him (322-2727, 9989-0074 mobile), or contact your Travel Agent.

If you really want to understand this city, don't leave Rio without visiting a Favela.

Useful addresses Immigration: Federal Police, Praça Mauá (passport section), entrance in Av Venezuela. To renew a 90-day visa, US$12.50. The web site www.addresses.com. br/ is a comprehensive guide to addresses in the city. *Student Travel Bureau*, Av Nilo Peçanha 50, SL 2417, Centro, T/F5442627, and R Visconde de Pirajá 550, lj 201, Ipanema, T5128577, F511437, www.stb.com.br (with offices throughout the country) has details of travel, discounts and cultural exchanges for ISIC holders.

Useful information On all Rio's beaches you should take a towel or mat to protect you against sandflies. In the water stay near groups of other swimmers. There is a strong undertow. There are very few public toilets in Rio de Janeiro, but many bars and restaurants (eg Macdonalds) offer facilities. Just ask for the 'banheiro' (banyairoo). Good toilets are to be found in the Shopping Centres. Many people look for *umbanda* religious ceremonies. Those offered on the night tours sold at hotels are not genuine and a disappointment. You need a local contact to see the real ones, which are usually held in *favelas* and are none too safe for unaccompanied tourists.

Telephone numbers often change in Rio de Janeiro and other Brazilian cities. If in doubt, phone 102, *Auxílio à Lista*, which is the current daily updated directory of telephone numbers. This number can be used all over the country, but if you want to find out a Rio phone number from outside Rio, dial the city code 021, then 121. If you do not understand Portuguese, you should seek assistence from a hotel receptionist or similar because the numbers are only spoken in Portuguese. **Voltage** 110-220 volts, 60 cycles, AC.

Niterói

Population: 450,500
Phone code: 021
Colour map 4, grid C3

Just across Guanabara Bay is Niterói, the old capital of Rio de Janeiro state. It is a pleasant excursion and has some good beaches nearby.

When the French under Villegagnon, with their Tamoio allies, established their colony on the western side of the mouth of the Baía de Guanabara, the Portuguese and the Temiminós set up camp on the eastern shore. The formal founding of a settlement here was in 1573 and once the Portuguese had established sovereignty, the area became a centre for sugar growing in the 17th century. It only really became important after Dom João VI's visit in 1816, when it was given the name of Vila Real da Praia Grande. In 1834 it was renamed Niterói ('hidden waters' in Tupi-Guarani) and was made capital of the province (later state) of Rio de Janeiro until the founding of Brasília and Rio de Janeiro's reintegration into the state.

Sights
The centre of Niterói is easily explored on foot

Many buildings associated with the city's period as state capital are grouped around the Praça da República (none is open to the public). The main avenue is Av Ernâni do Amaral Peixoto, with buildings similar to Av Presidente Vargas in Rio. At the end of the avenue is the dock for Rio, a statue of the Indian chief Araribóia and *Bay Market* shopping centre. The main green area in the centre is Campo de São Bento, which has many trees and handicraft stalls at weekends.

Colonial churches include São Lourenço dos Índios, Praça General Rondon, which dates from at least 1627 and the Capela da Boa Viagem (1663), which stands on a fortified island, attached by a causeway to the mainland (open one day a month for mass). By Gragoatá beach in the city is the Capela São Domingos (1662) and the Forte de Gragoatá, from the same period (closed to the public). The most important historical monument, however, is the 16th century **Fortaleza Santa Cruz**, which is still a military establishment. It is situated on a promontory which commands a fine view of the entrance to the bay. Tours show the Capela de Santa Bárbara, whose statue was destined for Santa Cruz dos Militares in Rio. All attempts to move the saint were accompanied by great storms, which was taken as a sign to leave her at the fortress. Also shown are the dungeons, fortifications, execution sites and gun batteries. It is about 13 kilometres from the centre of Niterói, on the Estrada General Eurico Gaspar Dutra, by Adão e Eva beach. ■ *Daily 0900-1600; US$1.50, tours have a compulsory guide, Portuguese only, T7149297.*

An early 20th century church is the Basílica de Nossa Senhora Auxiliadora, Rua Santa Rosa 207. Its famous organ, made in Italy, was bought by the Salesian order during the Second World War and is one of the largest pipe organs in the world, certainly the largest in Latin America. ■ *Daily 0600-1100, 1500-2000.*

Museums **Museu Antônio Parreira**, Rua Tiradentes 47, Ingá, is in the house of the eponymous artist (1860-1937). It houses a collection of 19th and 20th century art. ■ *Saturday-Sunday and holidays 1400-1700, T7198728.*

The **Museu de Arqueologia de Itaipu** is in the ruins of the 18th century Santa Teresa Convent and also covers the archaeological site of Duna Grande on Itaipu beach. It is 20 kilometres from the city. ■ *Wednesday-Sunday 1300-1800, T7094079.*

Museu de Arte Contemporânea, Mirante da Praia da Boa Viagem, is an Oscar Niemeyer project and worth visiting. It is best seen at night, expecially when the pond beneath the spaceship design is full of water. The exhibition inside changes. ■ *Tuesday-Sunday 1100-1900, US$1, Saturday 1300-1900, free, T6202400.*

The beaches closest to the city centre are unsuitable for bathing (Gragoatá, Vermelha, Boa Viagem, das Flechas). The next ones, also in the city with polluted water (Icaraí – the smartest district, good nightlife, São Francisco – even better nightlife, eg Rua das Pedras, and Charitas), have more in the way of restaurants, bars and nightlife. The road continues round the bay, past Preventório and Samanguaiá to Jurujuba, a fishing village at the end of the bus line, beautiful ride (take Bus No 33 from the boat dock; sit on the right-hand side). About two kilometres from Jurujuba along a narrow road are the attractive twin beaches of Adão and Eva beneath the Fortaleza da Santa Cruz, with lovely views of Rio across the bay.

Beaches
To get to the ocean beaches, take a 38 or 52 bus from Praça Gen Gomes Carneiro

Piratininga, Camboinhas, Itaipu (note the archaeology museum, above) and Itacoatiara are fabulous stretches of sand and the best in the area, about 40 minutes' ride through picturesque countryside (buses leave from the street directly ahead of the ferry entrance, at right angles to the coast street). The undertow at Itacoatiara is dangerous, but the waves are popular with surfers and the beach itself is safe. Itaipu is also used by surfers.

A *Icaraí Praia*, R Belisário Augusto 21, T7102323, F7106142. A *Niterói Palace*, R Andrade Neves 134, T6202155, F7192800. **Camping** *Piratininga*, Estr Frei Orlando Km 2, T6094581.

Sleeping & eating

Three good value restaurants opposite the Ruínas de Estação da Cantareira (which has occasional shows and handicraft market): *Tio Cotó*, *Vila Real* and *Zia Amélia*. *Cantina Buonasera*, Estr Leopoldo Fróes 34, Icaraí, T6102762. Italian. *Bicho Papão*, Jurujuba, good seafood, neither fancy, nor cheap.

March/April and **May**, *Festa do Divino*, a festival which traditionally begins on Easter Sunday and continues for the next 40 days, in which the Bandeira (standard) do Divino is taken around the local municipalities. The festival ends at Pentecost with sacred and secular celebrations. **24 June**: *São João*. **22 November**: founding of the city.

Festivals

Clubs *Rio Cricket Associação Atlética* (RCA), R Fagundes Varela 637, T7175333. Bus 57 from ferry. *Rio Sailing Club* (late Clube de Niterói), Estr Leopoldo Fróes 418, lote 338, T6105810. Bus 33 marked 'via Fróes'.

Sports

Boats Niterói, across Guanabara bay, is reached by ferry boats and launches crossing every 10 minutes (15-20 minutes, US$0.50) from the 'Barcas' at Praça 15 de Novembro (ferry museum at the terminal). There are also catamarans ('aerobarcas') every 10 minutes (about 3 minutes, US$2.45; the fare is US$1.25 between 0700 and 1000 Rio-Niterói and after 1700 Niterói-Rio). The slow, cheaper ferry gives the best views. Ferries and catamarans to Rio de Janeiro leave from the terminal at Praça Araribóia.

Transport

Buses Buses 996 Gávea-Jurujuba, 998 Galeão-Charitas, 740-D and 741 Copacabana-Charitas, 730-D Castelo-Jurujuba, US$0.60-0.75.

Road The toll on the 14 km Rio-Niterói bridge for cars is US$0.65 (paid only when entering Niterói). If you are crossing the bridge frequently, there is a phone number and website available for checking traffic conditions. High winds can close the bridge. (The approach to the bridge is on the elevated motorway Av Rio de Janeiro in the Caju district, take Av Rodrigues Alves past the docks.) Bus 999 from the corner of R Sen

Rio de Janeiro

Dantas and Av Beira Mar, crosses the bridge to Niterói and Icaraí (US$0.85); also 996 and 998 from the Jardim Botânico and the Rodoviária.

Directory **Banks** *Banco 24 Horas*, Niterói Shopping, R da Conceição 188. *Bradesco*, R Gavião Peixoto 108. **Communications** Internet: *O Lido Cyber C@fé*, Av Rui Barbosa 29, lj 124, São Francisco, T6119641, Mon-Wed 1000-2000, Thu-Sat 1100-2200. **Hospitals & medical services** *Universitário Antônio Pedro*, Av Marques do Paraná, T6202828. **Laundry** *Lavlev*, R Pres Backer 138. **Tourist information** *Neltur*, Estr Leopoldo Fróes 773, São Francisco, T7102727, open daily. *Centro de informações*, R XV de Novembro 8, 2nd floor, Plaza Shopping, Mon-Sat 1000-2200, Sun 1500-2200. A monthly newspaper, *Niterói, Esporte, Lazer, Turismo e Cultura*, is free. **Voltage** 110 volts, AC, 60 cycles.

The Costa do Sol

To the east of Niterói lie a series of saltwater lagoons, the Lagos Fluminenses. Two small lakes lie behind the beaches of Piratininga, Itaipu and Itacoatiara, but they are polluted and ringed by mud. The next lakes, Maricá and Saquarema (with other lagoons between), are much larger. Although they are still muddy, the waters are relatively unpolluted and wildlife abounds in the scrub and bush around the lagoons. This is a prime example of the restinga *environment. The RJ-106 road runs behind the lakes en route to Cabo Frio and Búzios, but an unmade road goes along the coast between Itacoatiara and Cabo Frio, giving access to the many long, open beaches of Brazil's Costa do Sol. The whole area is perfect for camping.*

Maricá
Population: 60,500
Phone code: 024

The 36 kilometre Itaipu-Açu, with many wild, lonely stretches, leads to Maricá, a small fishing village on its own lagoon. There is good walking in the Serra do Silvado, 14 kilometres away on the road to Itaboraí. Between Maricá and Saquarema are Ponta Negra and Jaconé, both surfing beaches.

Sleeping and eating At Ponta Negra are **B** *Pousada Colonial*, T/F6481707. Suites and bungalows with breakfast and **B** *Solar Tabaúna*, T6481626. Pool. Both highly recommended. *Caranguejo e Cia*, Estr do Boqueirão. Seafood.

Directory **Banks**: *Bradesco*, R Sen Macedo Soares 44. **Tourist information** *Casa do Turismo*, Av Ver Francisco Sabino da Costa 477, T6371999.

Saquarema

Population: 44,000
Phone code: 024
Colour map 4, grid C3

At the outlet to the lake of Saquarema (turn right off the RJ-106 at Bacaxá) is the holiday village of Saquarema. The little white church of Nossa Senhora de Nazaré (1675) is on a green promontory jutting into the ocean. The local legend has it that on 8 September 1630, fishermen, saved from a terrible storm, found an image of the Virgem de Nazaré in the rocks. A chapel was founded on the spot and subsequent attempts to relocate the Virgin (as when the chapel was falling into disrepair) resulted in her miraculously returning to the original site. Today Saquarema is still a fishing town, but is much better known as the centre for surfing in Brazil. Its cold, open seas provide consistent, crashing waves of up to three metres. Frequent national and international championships take place here. Beware of strong currents, though.

Sleeping & eating **B** *Pousada Pedra d'Água Maasai*, Trav de Itaúna 17, T/F6511092. Seafood restaurant. **C** *Pousada do Holandês*, Av Vilamar 377, Itaúna beach. Highly recommended, many languages spoken by Dutch owner and his Brazilian wife. Good meals – follow the signs, or take a taxi, from Saquarema. **D** *Itaúna Surf*, R dos Robalos 17, Itaúna. Recommended. **Youth hostel** *Ilhas Gregas*, R do Prado 671, Itaúna, T6511008. With pool, sauna, bar, restaurant. **Camping** *Itaúna's*, R dos Tatuís 999, access from Av Oceânica, T6511711. *Le Bistrô*, Av São Rafael 1134, Itaúna. Portuguese. *Tem Uma Né Chama Teré*, on the main square. Very good.

Festa do Divino, as above under Niterói; **8 May**, founding of the town; **29 June**, festi- **Festivals** val of São Pedro, at the end of the Festas Juninas; **7 September**, *Nossa Senhora de Nazaré*, the town's patron saint's day.

Buses To **Rio de Janeiro**, *Mil e Um (1001)*, every 2 hours 0730-1800, 2 hours, US$3.40. **Transport**

Banks *Bradesco*, Rod Amaral Peixoto 83. **Directory**

Araruama

The largest lake is Araruama (220 square kilometres), famous for its medicinal *Population: 66,500* mud. The salinity is high, the waters calm and almost the entire lake is surrounded *Phone code: 024* by sandy beaches, making it popular with families looking for unpolluted bathing. *Colour map 4, grid C4* The constant breeze makes the lake perfect for windsurfing and sailing. The major industry of the area is salt, and all around one can see the saltpans and the wind pumps used to carry the water into the pans. The town of Araruama is at the western end of the lake on the inland shore, 116 kilometres from Rio, 101 from Niterói.

At the eastern end of the lake, also inland, is **São Pedro de Aldeia** (*population*: 55,500) which, despite intensive development, still retains much of its colonial charm and has a lovely Jesuit church built in 1723.

Araruma: **A** *Ver a Vista*, R São Sebastião 400, T/F6654721. **C** *Pousada do Peu*, RJ-132, **Sleeping** Km 12, T6653614. **Camping** *Camping Clube do Brasil*, R República da Argentina 286. *Veneza*, Estr de Praia Seca Km 13, T6652667.

São Pedro de Aldeia **A** *Enseada das Garças*, R José Costa 1088, Ponta da Areia, about 5 km from town, T/F6211924. A member of the Roteiros de Charme group. **B** *Pousada Pontal da Praia*, Praia do Sudoeste, T/F6212441. **Youth hostel** *Praia do Sudoeste*, R Pedro Américo, Lt 27, T6212763. Open high season only. **Camping** *da Colina*, RJ-106, Km 108, Praia da Teresa, T6211919.

Araruma *Gigi*, RJ-106, Km 87. Seafood. **São Pedro de Aldeia** *Don Roberto*, Av **Eating** Getúlio Vargas 272. Pizzas.

Like Saquarema, São Pedro celebrates the feast of São Pedro (the town's patron saint) **Festivals** on 29 June, but also its founding on 16 May.

São Pedro de Aldeia **Banks**: *Bradesco*, Av São Pedro 120. **Tourist information**: Av São Pedro, **Directory** T6211559.

The lake and the ocean are divided by the Restinga de Massambaba, mostly **Arraial do Cabo** deserted except for the beaches of Massambaba and Seca at the western end *Population: 21,500* and Grande in the east. The latter is the main beach for Arraial do Cabo, the *Phone code: 024* town at the end of the Restinga de Massambaba, on the southern side of Cabo Frio. Arraial has lots of other small beaches on the bays and islands which form the cape, round which the line of the coast turns north. Excursions can be made by boat around the islets and by jeep or buggy over the sand dunes.

Praia do Farol, on Ilha do Cabo Frio, is considered one of Brazil's best beaches. It has dunes and crystal clear water. To get there you must obtain a free permit from the Navy (Marinha) office in Arraial do Cabo, then go to Praia dos Anjos from where fishermen will take you to Farol, about US$60 for nine people. You must arrange a pick-up time, take your own food and water and leave no rubbish behind. Included in the price can be a stop at the Gruta Azul, a cave carved in the rocks by the ocean. Festivals include 13 May, founding of the town and *Corpus Christi* in May/June.

Sleeping and eating **A** *Pousada Nautilus*, R Marcílio Dias 100, T6221611. Recommended. **B** *Orlamar*, Av Beiramar 111, Recanto da Prainha, T/F6222410. **B** *Pousada dos Atobás*, R José Pinto Macedo 270, T6222461. **Camping** *Camping Clube do Brasil*, Praia dos Anjos, T6221023. Crowded beach. For eating, try *Todos os Prazeres*, R José Pinto Macedo, T6222365.

Transport A very steep road connects the beaches of Itaipu and Itacoatiara with RJ-106 (and on to Bacaxá and Araruama) via the village of Itaipu-Açu. Most maps do not show a road beyond Itaipu-Açu; it is certainly too steep for buses. An alternative to the route from Niterói to Araruama through the lagoons is further inland than the RJ-106, via Manilha, Itaboraí and Rio Bonito on the BR-101 and RJ-124; this is a fruit-growing region. Bus Rio de Janeiro to Arraial do Cabo US$6.

Directory **Tourist information** Praça da Bandeira, T6205039.

Cabo Frio

Population: 101,500
Phone code: 024
Colour map 4, grid C4

Situated 168 kilometres from Rio, the town is a popular holiday and weekend haunt of Cariocas because of its cool weather, white sand beaches and dunes, scenery, sailing and good underwater swimming (but mosquitoes are a problem). A new nautical theme park, *Reino de Netuno*, has recently opened.

History The navigator Americo Vespucci landed at Cabo Frio in 1503 and returned to Portugal with a boatload of *pau-brasil*. Since the wood in these parts was of better quality than that further north, the area became the target for loggers from France, the Netherlands and England. The Portuguese failed to capitalize on their colony here and it was the French who established the first defended settlement; their presence was strengthened after the Portuguese had driven the French from Guanabara Bay. By 1575, the Portuguese had had enough of the corsairs operating into and out of Cabo Frio, so they took it by force, but it was not until the second decade of the 17th century that they planned their own fortification, Forte São Mateus, which was started in 1616 on the foundations of the French fort. It is now a ruin at the mouth of the Canal de Itajuru.

Beaches The canal, which connects the Lagoa Araruama and the ocean, has a small headland at its mouth, which protects the nearest beach to the town, Praia do Forte. Backed by hotels, restaurants and bars, the water is calm and clear, the sand fine. The beach stretches south for about seven and a half kilometres to Arraial do Cabo, its name changing to Praia das Dunas and Praia do Foguete. These waters are much more suited to surfing. North of the canal entrance are the small, surfing Praia Brava (not too easy to get to, naturist beach) and the small, calm Praia das Conchas, which is ideal for watersports. Next is Praia do Peró, seven kilometres of sand on the open sea; it is used by surfers, fishermen and by sandboarders, who slide down the dunes on wooden boards.

Sleeping & eating
Reservations are necessary in Dec-Feb

L *La Plage*, R dos Badejos 40, Praia do Peró, T/F6435690. **A** *Pousada Portoveleiro*, Av dos Espadartes 129, T/F6473081. **B** *Pousada Suzy*, Av Júlia Kubitschek 48, 100m from the rodoviária, T6431742. **C** *Jangada*, Granaola 220, near the canal. Good breakfast. Recommended. **D** *Praia das Palmeiras*, Praia das Palmeiras 1, T/F6432866. **Youth**

hostel **E** pp *São Lucas*, R Goiás 266, Jardim Excelsior, 3 minutes from the rodoviária, T6453037. IYHA. **Camping** *Camping Clube do Brasil*, Estr dos Passageiros 700, 2 km from town, T6433124; on the same road, at No 600, is *Bosqu Clube*, T6450008, and No 370 *Camping da Estação*, T6431786. On Praia do Peró, *Dunas do Peró*, Estr do Guriri 1001, T6292323. *Picolino*, R Mcal Floriano 319, T6432436. Seafood.

29 June: *São Pedro* (as above); **13 November**: founding of the town; **25 December**: patron saint's day, *Nossa Senhora da Assunção*.

Festivals

Air A new airport has opened linking the area with Belo Horizonte, Brasília, Rio de Janeiro, São Paulo. **Buses** The rodoviária is 2 km from the centre. Bus from Rio every 30 minutes, 2½ hours, US$5.50. To Búzios, from the local bus terminus in the town centre, every hour, US$1.

Transport

Banks *Banco 24 Horas*, Av Assunção 925. *Bradesco*, Av Assunção 904. **Tourist information** Av Américo Vespúcio 200, T6471689.

Directory

Rio de Janeiro

Búzios

From Cabo Frio the RJ-102 heads 25 kilometres northeast to the next resort up the coast, the sophisticated yet informal Búzios. This charming seaside town (full name Armação de Búzios) is well-spread out with low-rise, but attractive development. It is situated on a peninsula and is the perfect choice for those who want to enjoy the sun and the sea by day and, after dark, its internationally famous nightlife and gastronomy. Its climate is sunny and windy all year round.

Population: 10,000
Phone code: 024
192 km to Rio
37 km to Arraial do Cabo
Colour map 4, grid C4

Originally a small fishing community, founded in 1740 when a trader called Braz de Pina started a whale fishery, Búzios remained virtually unknown until the 1950s when its natural beauty started to attract the Brazilian jet-set who turned the village into a fashionable summer resort. In 1964, Brigite Bardot visited Búzios and the photos of her, walking barefoot along the beach, brought the focus of the world's press to this 'lost paradise in the tropics'. Soon many wealthy families, foreign tourists and the travel and leisure industry started to move to Búzios, building over 150 *pousadas*, around 50 restaurants as well as open-air cafés, bars, clubs, art galleries and fashion shops. As many of these businesses are foreign-owned, English, French, German and Spanish are widely spoken. A local joke says that, in population, Buenos Aires is the second city in the world in summer; Búzios is the first.

Unless it is absolutely necessary, avoid visiting Búzios at Carnival, New Year's Eve and other main holidays. The city gets crowded, the price of food, accommodation and other services rises substantially and the long, stressful traffic jams on the roads will be an experience to be remembered forever.

During the daytime, the best option is to head for the beaches, of which there are 25. The most visited are Geribá (many bars and restaurants; popular with surfers), Ferradura (deep blue sea and calm waters), Ossos (the most famous and close to the centre), Tartaruga and João Fernandes. To help you to decide which beach suits you best, a good idea is to join one of the local two to three hour schooner trips which pass many of the beaches. These trips cost around US$10-15 and can be arranged with through: *Escuna Buziana*, T6236760/6232157, and *Escuna Queen Lory*, T6231179/6232286.

Sleeping

Even though there are more than 150 pousadas, prior reservations are needed in summer, at holidays such as Carnival and the New Year's Eve, and weekends

AL *Galápagos Inn*, Praia de João Fernandinho, T6236161, F6232297. Right on the beach. **AL** *Colonna Park*, Praia de João Fernandes, T6232245, colonna@colonna. com.br. Fantastic view of the sea. **AL** *La Mandrágora*, Av J B Ribeiro Dantas, Portal da Ferradura, T6231348. One of the most famous in Búzios. **A** *Fazendinha Blancpain*, Estr Velha da Raza, T6236490, F6236420, a member of Roteiro de Charme group, see page 57. **A** *Pousada Casa de Pedra*, Trav Lúcio Antônio Quintanilha 57, T6231499, F6232410. Safe. **A** *Pousada Hibiscus Beach*, R 1, No 22, Quadra C, Praia de João Fernandes, T6236221. Run by its British owners, 15 pleasant bungalows, garden, pool, light meals available, help with car/buggy rentals and local excursions. **B** *Pousada dos Tangarás*, R dos Namorados 6, lote 4, Geribá, T6231275. Good. **B** *Pousada La Coloniale*, R das Pedras 52. Ideally located for nightlife, but you will hear all the noise of Rua das Pedras until the early hours. **D** *Casa da Ruth*, R dos Gravatás, Geribá, T6232242. **D** *Brigitta's Guest House*, Rua das Pedras 131. Beautifully decorated little pousada with a nice restaurant, bar and tea house, worth a visit. **Youth hostel E** *Praia dos Amores*, Av José Bento Ribeiro Dantas 92, T6232422. IYHA, not far from the bus station. Recommended. Several private houses rent rooms, especially in summer and holidays. Look for the signs: 'Alugo Quartos'. **Camping** *Country Camping Club*, R Maria Joaquina 895, Praia Rasa, T6291122, 12 km from Búzios.

Eating

Búzios has plenty of restaurants for all tastes and budgets. International cuisine can be found mostly in the R das Pedras and the streets surrounding it, in the centre

El Lorenzo, Travessa dos Arcos, Loja 6, Rua das Pedras 100. Good for Italian food. *La Tropezienne*, Av José Bento Ribeiro Dantas 712, Armação. French, with a nice view of the sea. *Muqueca Capixaba*, R Manoel de Carvalho 116, Centro. Brazilian seafood. *Estância Don Juan*, R das Pedras, 178, Centro. Grill and restaurant. *Kassai*, R das Pedras 275. Japanese. **Cheaper options**: *Chez Michou*, R das Pedras, 90, Centro. An open-air bar with videos and music, dozens of choices of pancakes accompanied by ice cold beer. Always crowded. *Pastello*, in front of the *Shopping One*, at the entrance to R das Pedras. A stand serving pastéis, thin, fried pastries filled with cheese, meat, chicken or preserve. *Skipper*, Av J B Ribeiro Dantas 392, Praia do Canto. Pizza House.

Nightlife

A must in Búzios. All you have to do is walk along the R das Pedras (Stone Street, as it is paved with irregular, huge blocks of stone). Here is the best choice of restaurants, cafés, art galleries and bars. Crowded at weekends and holidays, especially after 2300. Good options are: *Zapata Mexican Bar*, R das Pedras. One of the hottest spots at night. *Number One*, R das Pedras 1. A 2-storey shopping centre just at the entrance to the street. Here are some good bars with live pop music at night. *Ta-ka-ta ka-ta*, R das Pedras 256. One of the craziest bars in Búzios: weird decoration, owned by a foreigner who obstinately refuses to tell where he came from, but who can speak fluent Portuguese, Spanish, English, German, Dutch, worth a visit.

Sport

Diving *Casamar*, T6232441 (located in Rio de Janeiro). A highly professional dive operation offers 1-day diving trips costing US$25 pp if you bring your own equipment, US$50 pp if you rent equipment, both prices include 2 bottles of air. Casamar is closed in May and on Tuesdays during low season. Recommended.

Road By car via BR-106 takes about 2½ hours from Rio. **Buses**: from Rio's Rodoviária **Transport**
Novo Rio, go to the 1001 counter T00XX21-5161001. Rio-Búzios US$ 7, 2 hours 40
minutes (be at the bus terminal 20 minutes before departure). Five departures daily
0815 from Rio a/c, 1300 from Búzios a/c. You can also take any bus to Cabo Frio (many
more during the day), from where it's 30 minutes to Búzios and vice versa. Buying the
ticket in advance is only recommended on major holidays. The Búzios rodoviária is a
few blocks' walk from the centre. Some pousadas are within 10 minutes on foot, eg La
Coloniale, Brigitta's, while others need a local bus (US$0.50) or taxi. The buses from
Cabo Frio run the length of the peninsula and pass several pousadas.

Banks *Banco do Brasil*, R Manuel de Carvalho 70, Centro, T5232302. *Malizia*, R das Pedras, **Directory**
T6232022/6231226. **Hospitals** Public: *Posto Municipal de Saúde de Manguinhos*, Av J B Ribeiro
Dantas, Manguinhos, T192. Private: *Clínica Búzios*, Av J B Ribeiro Dantas 3000, Manguinhos,
T6232465. **Tour companies & travel agencies** *Malizia*, see **Banks** above. *Mister Tours*, R das
Pedras 168, Centro, T6232100. *Webtur*, Av J B Ribeiro Dantas 1144, Armação, T6236661. Guided
tours in English: Adriana Rainho, T6232146, arainho@mar.com.br.

Macaé

Continuing to the north, one comes to Barra de São João, **Rio das Ostras** (*pop-*   *Population: 113,500*
ulation: 28,500) and Macaé. These beaches are at the northern end of the Costa   *Phone code: 024*
do Sol, all containing sheltered coves with good swimming and scuba diving.   *Colour map 4, grid C4*
    Macaé is the supply centre for the offshore oil industry but is attempting to
develop tourism as well. There are good views from the **Igreja de Santana** on
Morro de Santana, two kilometres away. Cavaleiros beach is good for surfing
and has many bars and restaurants.

Macaé **A** *Colonial*, Av Elias Agostinho 140, Praia de Imbetiba, T/F7225155. Helpful, **Sleeping**
comfortable. **A** *Ouro Negro*, Av Pres Sodré 466, Praia do Forte, T7723305, F7723205.
A *Panorama*, Av Elias Agostinho 290, T/F7724455. **C** *Central*, R Rui Barbosa. Nice,
good breakfast, secure parking. **Rio das Ostras** **A** *Pousada do Wagner*, R Nova
Iguaçu 1199, Costa Azul, T7641889, F7641973. **B** *Hotel Mirante do Poeta*, T641910.
Camping *Costazul*, Av Heleno Nunes, Costa Azul, T7641389.

Macaé *Albatroz*, Av Atlântica 2374, Praia dos Cavaleiros. Seafood. *Xandoca's Bar*, R **Eating**
Col José de Lima 365. Seafood. **Rio das Ostras** *Bar da Boca*, R Teresópolis 69, Praia
Boca da Barra. Seafood.

Macaé **Air**: airtaxis with *Líder*, T7723202, and *Aeróleo*, T7725995. **Bus**: Bus station, **Transport**
Av Ver Abreu Lima, T7724500. To Rio de Janeiro 2½-3 hours, every 30 minutes, *Mil e*
Um or *Rápido Macaense*. To Campos, 1¾ hours, US$4.

Banks *Bradesco*, Av Rui Barbosa 614, Macaé. **Hospitals & medical services** *Casa de Caridade*, **Directory**
Praça Veríssimo de Melo 391, Macaé T7721005.

Rio de Janeiro

North to Espírito Santo

From Rio and Niterói, the BR-101 runs northeast past to Campos and the border with Espírito Santo. There are many *fazenda* hotels in the area of **Rio Bonito**, 64 kilometres from Niterói. These include *Fazenda Pedras Negras* (**AL**), BR-101 Km 257, T/F7340425 and *Fazenda Serra dos Cambê* (**B**), BR101 Km 265, T7340027.

See also box opposite   At Km 222 is the **Biological Reserve of Poço das Antas**, the only natural habitat of the *mico-leão*, Golden Lion Tamarin (two hours' drive from Rio); it is not open to the general public). ■ *Contact Ibama, Av Pres Antônio Carlos 607-12°, CEP 20000, Rio de Janeiro.*

Campos

Population: 385,500
Phone code: 024
Colour map 4, grid C4

Campos (dos Goitacazes – after the Indian tribe which used to inhabit the area) is a busy industrial city, some 276 kilometres from Rio de Janeiro and 70 kilometres from Macaé. It stands 56 kilometres from the mouth of the Rio Paraíba, up which coffee planting originally spread to São Paulo state. Coffee is still grown near Campos, but the region has always been one of the largest sugar-producing zones in Brazil.

In the 1970s Brazil's answer to rocketing oil prices was the conversion of sugar into alcohol fuel for cars, where Campos became one of the major centres for this industry. Subsequently, important offshore oil and gas discoveries have been made nearby. On a historical note, this was the first Brazilian city to install electric lighting, inaugurated in 1883.

Beaches The sea can be reached by road to São João da Barra (41 kilometres), then a further four kilometres to Atafona, at the mouth of the Rio Paraíba do Sul. The outflow of the river here pollutes the beach, but if you go further south to Grussaí or Açu, the sea is mostly OK. Further south still are beaches around Farol de São Tomé, Barra do Furrado and Quissamã. North of the Rio Paraíba are several beaches in the vicinity of São Francisco and Itabapoana.

Sleeping & eating **A** *Antares*, R Vig João Carlos 19, T7334055, F7220011. **B** *Palace*, Av 15 de Novembro 143, T7332277, F7223661. **B** *Terrazo Tourist*, Joaquim Távora 22, T7331405, F7221605. Two-star. **C** *Planície*, R 13 de Maio 56, T7234455, F7223377. For eating, try *Kantão do Líbano*, Av Pelinca 101. Arabic. *Picanha Grill*, in Shopping Estrada, Av Nilo Peçanha 614. Churrasco.

Festivals **28 March**: founding of the city; **May/June**: *Corpus Christi*; **29 June**: *São Pedro* (as above); **6 August**: patron saint's day, *Santíssimo Salvador*.

Transport **Air** Airport, BR-101, Km 5, T7330144. Flights to **Rio de Janeiro**. **Buses** Bus station, BR 101, T7331001. To **Rio de Janeiro**, Mil e Um (1001), hourly, 4½ hours.

Directory **Banks** *Banco 24 Horas*, Parque Centro Shopping, Av Pelinca 116. *Bradesco*, Blvd Francisco P. Carneiro 28. **Hospitals & medical services** *Beneficência Portuguesa*, R Barão de Miracema 142, T7330055.

Santo Antônio de Pádua
Population: 34,000
Phone code: 024

As an alternative to taking the BR-101 to Vitória, one can take a detour inland, going through São Fidélis, Cambiasca, Itoacara and on to Santo Antônio de Pádua, 106 kilometres from Campos, a pleasant town on the Rio Pomba. Canoeing is popular in this area due to the large number of rapids. The hydromineral spring at Avenida Dr Themístocles de Almeida is unique for the chemical composition of its waters. ■ *Monday-Friday 0700-1100, 1300-1600,*

The golden lion tamarin

The tamarin, or mico-leão in Portuguese, is a primate of the genus Leontopithecus. It is a small mammal, about the size of a squirrel, which lives off fruit, flowers, tender vegetation and insects. In Brazil there are three species of tamarin, all under threat of extinction: L rosalia, the mico-leão-dourado or golden lion tamarin; L chrysopygus, the mico-leão-preto or black lion tamarin; and L chrysomela, the mico-leão-de-cara-dourada or golden-headed lion tamarin. The main problem for the tamarins is that their habitat, the mata atlântica of São Paulo, Rio de Janeiro, Espírito Santo and Bahia, has all but been destroyed and there has been further threat from predation by man.

These engaging creatures are quite beautiful, so much so that they were popular pets with European royalty in the 17th and 18th centuries. The golden lion tamarin, with its face surrounded by a bright, silky mane, was considered the most beautiful. It has been described as having a coat that "shines like gold dust in the light." And thereby hangs another of the animal's problems; its attractiveness made it a prize pet for non-royal collectors and demand in the trade soon contributed to the golden lion tamarin's dwindling numbers. By the 1970s it seemed a foregone conclusion that the golden lion tamarin and its Brazilian relatives were doomed to extinction.

Fortunately, the Golden Lion Tamarin Conservation Project, set up in 1983 at the Poço das Antas Biological Reserve (which was created in 1974), has been successful in breeding tamarins in captivity and returning them to the wild. Around the world, zoos have been helping with the breeding programme. In 1997, a WWF estimate for the number of golden lion tamarins living in the wild in Poço das Antas was put at 800, but other figures suggest 550 (some even as low as 150). Whatever the number, the severest test for the survival of the species is the creation of more forest in which the tamarins can live. Corridors of suitable vegetation have to be set up so that the tamarins can move about safely and breed freely in their natural surroundings. This goal was undermined during the drought of 1997 which led to an increase in forest fires in Brazil (the majority started by man), posing a renewed threat to the tamarin's habitat. So the mico-leão-dourado's future is by no means secured; despite this, the animal has become a symbol of hope for forest conservation throughout Brazil. Many Brazilian and international agencies and specialist centres have contributed to its survival, but as with all such projects, the work never stops.

Besides the mico-leão-dourado population at Poço das Antas, there is a conservation project for the mico-leão-da-cara-dourada at Una in Bahia, and the mico-leão-preto can be seen near Praia do Forte, north of Salvador.

Sources WWF Update (World Wide Fund for Nature), Summer 1997, website http://www.wwf-uk.org; in the UK T01483-426444, F01483-426-409, or contact your local office. Marya Rowan, 'Breeds Apart', South American Explorer (25 May 1990), pages 32-3. Wildlife Fact File, International Masters Publishers Ltd (London), #120.

Saturday 0700-1100. A short walk from the centre of Santo Antônio de Pádua is *Hotel das Águas* (**C**), Rua Luís da Silva Magacho 170, T8510805. It is set in a park and associated with the health centre and bottling plant for the local mineral water. The bus station is at Rua José de Alencar Leite, T8510823.

Take road No 393 to Itaperuna, Bom Jesus do Itabapoana and into Espírito Santo, then road No 484 to **Guaçuí** (with hotels and restaurants), one of the starting points for the Parque Nacional do Caparaó (see page 304). Then take the road 482 to Cachoeira do Itapemirim and the BR-101 (see page 275).

Inland resorts

There are three main resorts in the Serra do Mar close to Rio de Janeiro: Petrópolis, Teresópolis and Nova Friburgo. Among the principal reasons for their existence are their altitude, which gives cooler temperatures than Rio, the lack of yellow fever and other diseases which festered in the unhealthy port on the bay in the 19th century, and the access provided by the routes which brought first gold, then coffee to the coast. The mountains at first sight appear to be a rugged barrier between the coast and the interior, but once mule trains had established permanent roads through to the Rio Paraíba and Minas Gerais, it became obvious to early travellers that the highlands have many benefits. Nowadays weekenders from Rio and other tourists tend to agree. One such visitor was Dom Pedro I, the emperor, who in 1822 stopped at a *fazenda* belonging to Padre Correia on his way to Minas Gerais. He was so taken with the place that he subsequently made frequent visits. At the prompting of his wife, Dona Amélia, he purchased a nearby estate, Córrego Seco, in 1830, setting in motion the process which led to the building of Petrópolis.

Petrópolis

Population: 270,000
Phone code: 024
Colour map 4, grid C3

A summer hill resort and industrial city, 68 kilometres north of Rio, Petrópolis is reached by bus along a steep, scenic mountain road. It stands at 809 metres in the Serra da Estrela range of mountains in the Serra do Mar.

The city is referred to as *A Cidade Imperial*, a name given to it in 1981. It is also nicknamed *Cidade das Hortênsias* (hydrangeas) because of the abundance of these flowers there. For some 80 years Petrópolis was the 'summer capital' of Brazil. Now it combines manufacturing industry (particularly textiles) and tourism with floral beauty and hill scenery.

Climate The pleasant climate which attracted the imperial family has an average high temperature of 23°C and a low of 14°C. The warmest months are September to December. The wettest months are January to March, although it can start getting wet in November and rain can be expected at any time. It can get chilly at night all year round, but especially in winter. A unique climatic feature of the area is a dense fog, called *o ruço*, which usually forms in the late afternoon. While this can be atmospheric, it can also be dangerous for drivers as the fog can descend very quickly.

History Because the emperor Pedro I abdicated in 1831, he never realized his dream of building a summer palace in the Serra. Córrego Seco was rented out, lastly to Júlio Frederico Koeler, a German engineer who worked on the construction of a road to Minas Gerais. Koeler proposed the colonization of Córrego Seco by Germans. When the new emperor, Dom Pedro II, approved this plan in 1843, he stipulated that a summer palace should be built in addition to a town and the settlement scheme. Petrópolis dates its founding from 1843 and in little over a decade had become an important place. Once the imperial palace was built, the emperor and his family began to spend six months of each year there (November to April). His court had to accompany him, so other fine residences sprang up in the city that Koeler had designed. In April 1854, Brazil's first railway line was opened, from Porto Mauá on Guanabara Bay to Raiz da Serra, which greatly shortened the journey time between Rio and Petrópolis. By the 1880s the railway had crossed the mountains to Petrópolis itself. So by the time the Republic was proclaimed in 1889, Petrópolis was administrative capital of the country for half the year, an intellectual centre for the same months, had its own commercial importance and was directly connected to Brazil's rapidly growing transport links.

In the early 20th century, it became the official summer seat of the president of the republic (the residence being the Palácio Rio Negro). In the 1940s it had a brief flirtation with gambling, when the Hotel e Cassino Quitandinha attracted Hollywood stars and other members of the international jet set until the banning of gaming in 1946. Since then, the city has thrived industrially and, most recently, in tourism.

Sights

Three rivers are dominant features in the design of Petrópolis: the Piabanha, Quitandinha and Palatino. In the historic centre (Centro Histórico), where most of the sites of tourist interest are to be found, the rivers have been channelled to run down the middle of the main avenues. Their banks, especially the Quitandinha, are planted with fine trees and flowers and the overall aspect is completely different from elsewhere in Brazil. You quickly get a sense that this was a city built with a specific purpose and at a specific time in Brazil's history.

The main commercial streets are Rua do Imperador, which runs southwest from the Praça da Inconfidência by the Rodoviária and Rua 16 de Março. At right angles to Rua do Imperador is the stately Rua da Imperatriz, which passes the Imperial Museum, bends round to the cathedral as Avenida Tiradentes, then turns again, as Avenida Koeler, towards Praça Rui Barbosa. The view from Praça Rui Barbosa, up the canal and Avenida Koeler to the cathedral, gives a fine impression of Petrópolis' design. These three avenues straddle the

Rio de Janeiro

Petrópolis

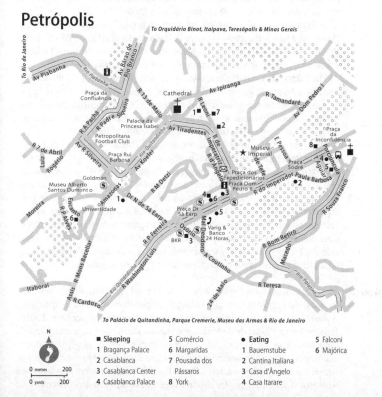

To Orquidário Binot, Itaipava, Teresópolis & Minas Gerais

To Palácio de Quitandinha, Parque Cremerie, Museu das Armas & Rio de Janeiro

N		
0 metres 200		
0 yards 200		

■ Sleeping	5 Comércio	● Eating	5 Falconi
1 Bragança Palace	6 Margaridas	1 Bauernstube	6 Majórica
2 Casablanca	7 Pousada dos	2 Cantina Italiana	
3 Casablanca Center	Pássaros	3 Casa d'Ângelo	
4 Casablanca Palace	8 York	4 Casa Itarare	

Rio Quitandinha, which now turns northwest, then northeast, until it meets the Rio Piabanha by the Palácio de Cristal.

The **Museu Imperial** (Imperial Palace), which seems to express very faithfully what we know of Dom Pedro II's character, is a modest but elegant building, neoclassical in style, fully furnished and equipped. It contains the Crown Jewels of both Pedro I and Pedro II and other imperial possessions. It is assiduously well-kept: one might think the imperial family had left the day before one's visit, rather than in 1889. Many of the rooms and salons are open to visitors. In a separate building is the Salão das Viaturas (vehicles), which houses coaches, litters, the *Leopoldina* locomotive which worked the Rio-Petrópolis line from 1883-1964 and a Merryweather of London fire engine (entry free). The gardens in front of the palace are pleasant. Horse-drawn carriages wait to be hired outside the gate (not all the horses are in good shape). ■ *Tuesday-Sunday, 1200-1700, US$3, you pay at a small kiosk outside the entrance, then queue to deposit any bags and be admitted. On Sunday, expect long queues. Rua da Imperatriz 220, T2427012.*

The Gothic-style **Catedral de São Pedro de Alcântara**, completed in 1925, contains the tombs of the Emperor and Empress. The Imperial Chapel is to the right of the entrance. ■ *Tuesday-Saturday 0800-1200, 1400-1800.*

The summer home of air pioneer **Alberto Santos Dumont**, known as 'A Encantada', is at Rua do Encanto 22. The small house was built in 1918 as a mock Alpine-chalet. Downstairs is an exhibition devoted to his flying career. His first flight was on 23 October 1906: the plane *14 Bis* flew 60 metres in seven seconds; on 12 November 1906 it flew 220 metres in 21.5 seconds. Upstairs is Santos Dumont's office/bedroom, with information on other aspects of his life, including his celibacy. ■ *Tuesday-Sunday 0900-1700, US$1.*

'A Encantada' stands on a bluff, below which is the Universidade Católica de Petrópolis. Outside the university is the **Relógio das Flores** (Flower Clock), built in 1972. Above the university, on the hill of Quinta do Sol, is the **Trono de Fátima**, a shrine to Nossa Senhora de Fátima, with good views. ■ *Daily 0700-1830.*

The **Palácio de Cristal** in Praça da Confluência (where the Rios Quitandinha and Piabanha meet), was designed in the same style as several similar crystal palaces in Europe. This one was built in France in 1879, with the original intention of being an exhibition hall for local products. However, it became the imperial ballroom, but has now reverted to being an exhibition centre.

Opposite the Palácio de Cristal, across Rua A Pachá, is the Bohemia brewery. The **Bohemia Beer Festival** is held in June.

Fine mansions built by the aristocracy of both the imperial and republican eras can be seen on Avenida Koeler and Avenida Ipiranga. Among them are the neoclassical Palácio Rio Negro and the Palácio da Princesa Isabel at Avenida Koeler 255 and 42 respectively and the Casa de Rui Barbosa, in the eclectic style, at Avenida Ipiranga 405. Another palace is the mid-19th century Casa do Barão do Rio Branco, Avenida Barão do Rio Branco 279. It was here that the Treaty of Petrópolis was signed, settling with Bolivia the issue of the annexation of Acre (1903). The house is not open to the public.

Parks & praças The twin praças of dos Expedicionários and Dom Pedro II (in which there is a tourist kiosk) are at the junction of Rua do Imperador and Rua da Imperatriz. A short distance up Rua da Imperatriz, on the same side as Praça Dom Pedro II, is the **Praça Visconde de Mauá**, in which is a statue of an eagle and a snake. On one side of the praça is the Palácio Amarelo (1850), now the Câmara Municipal, and on another the modern Palácio da Cultura. On Sundays in the square is a small antiques market. **Praça Rui Barbosa** is very busy on Sunday, with goat-drawn carriages for children and occasional open-air concerts.

Southwest of the centre is the **Museu Casa do Colono**, Rua Cristóvão Colombo 1034, Castelânea, with exhibits on the way of life of the early German colonists. ■ *Tuesday-Sunday 0900-1700*. Also southwest is the **Parque Cremerie**; and the **Palácio Quitandinha**, Avenida Estados Unidos 2, T421012. This vast, grandiose palace, built in 1944 as a casino and hotel, is now a tourist centre (open Tuesday-Sunday 0900-1700) that holds events. The lake in front of the building is in the shape of South America.

Museu das Armas Ferreira da Cunha, Km 40 on the BR-040 (on the old road to Rio), shows a large collection of arms. ■ *By appointment only, T420373*.

The Avenida Barão do Rio Branco, which heads north out of the city, passes the turning to the **Orquidário Binot**, Rua Fernandes Vieira 390. This has a huge collection of orchids from all over Brazil (plants may be purchased). ■ *Monday-Friday 0800-1100, 1315-1630, Saturday 0700-1100, T420833, take bus to Vila Isabel*. Continuing north, the road becomes the Estrada União-Indústria, going through Corrêas, the district in which is the Casa of Padre Correia (see **History**, above); it is not open to the public. Further out is **Itaipava**, about 20 kilometres from Petrópolis, near where this road joins the BR-040 highway to Belo Horizonte and at the junction of the road to Teresópolis. This district is rapidly becoming a popular centre for eating, shopping and staying the weekend for Cariocas. There are outlets and boutiques for the local textile industry, a *feira* every Wednesday and Friday night and at weekends, a wide variety of good restaurants and several good *pousadas* (for example, *Pousada Capim Santo*, a Roteiro de Charme hotel, two kilometres on the road to Teresópolis, T/F221395; *Pousada Tambo Los Incas*, Estrada Ministro Salgado Filho 2761, T221313; *Pousada das Araras*, in nearby Araras, T251143).

In the Roteiros de Charme group (see page 57) is **AL** *Locanda della Mimosa*, Al das Mimosas 30, Vale Florido, T/F2425405. **A** *Margaridas*, R Bispo Dom José Pereira Alves 235, Trono de Fátima, T2424686, F2435422. A chalet-type hotel set in lovely gardens with a swimming pool, charming proprietors. There are 3 *Casablanca* hotels: **A** *Casablanca*, R da Imperatriz 286, T2426662, F2425946, good atmosphere in the older part, pool, very clean; **A** *Casablanca Center*, Gen Osório 28, T2422612, F2426298; and **A** *Casablanca Palace*, R 16 de Março 123, T2420162, F2425946. **A** *Riverside Parque*, R Hermogéneo Silva 522, Retiro, 5 minutes from the centre, T2310730, F2432312. **B** *York*, R do Imperador 78, a short walk from the Rodoviária, T2432662, F2428220. Convenient, helpful, the fruit and milk at breakfast come from the owners' own farm. Recommended.

On R Raul de Leoni (the continuation of R da Imperatriz) are: **A** *Pousada dos Pássaros*, whose prices are in the **C** range Monday-Friday; and almost opposite, at No 109, *Bragança Palace*, T2420434, F2435276.

B *Comércio*, R Dr Porciúncula 55, opposite Rodoviária, T2423500. Shared bath, basic.

Camping *Associação Brasileira de Camping and YMCA*, Araras district. Space can be reserved through Rio YMCA, T021-2319860.

Bauernstube, Dr Nelson de Sá Earp 297. German, closed Monday. *Cantina Italiana*, R Paulo Barbosa, just by Praça Sodré. Upstairs, popular, cheap, Italian, pizzas, Brazilian daily specialities. *Locanda della Mimosa*, Al dos Mimosas 30, T2425405. Italian. Best to reserve at weekends. *Majórica*, R do Imperador 754. Churrasco; *Falconi*, R do Imperador 757. Italian. Recommended.

There are several bars and cafés in the centre, eg *Casa d'Ángelo*, R do Imperador 700, by Praça Dom Pedro II and *Casa Itarare*, at the corner of R do Imperador and R Dr Porciúnculo.

Excursions

Rio de Janeiro

Sleeping
■ *on map, page 163*
Price codes: see inside front cover

Eating
● *on map, page 163*

Sports   **Whitewater rafting** At Três Rios, on the junction of rivers Paraibuna, Piabanha and Paraíba do Sul, arranged by **Klemperer Turismo**, T2434052, also from Rio, T021-2528170. Highly recommended.

There are also possibilities for hiking, climbing, riding and cycling in the vicinity.

Festivals Petrópolis celebrates its foundation on **16 March**. Its patron saint's day, *São Pedro de Alcântara*, is **29 June**. See also the Bohemia beer festival, page 164.

Shopping R Teresa, southeast of the centre, is where the textile industry exhibits its wares. In common with Itaipava (see above), it draws buyers from all over the country and is a good place to find good quality knitwear and other goods.

Transport **Buses** From **Rio** every 15 minutes throughout the day (US$3) with *Única Fácil*, Sunday every hour, 1½ hours, sit on the left hand side for best views. Return tickets are not available, so buy tickets for the return on arrival in Petrópolis. The ordinary buses leave from the rodoviária in Rio; a/c buses, hourly from 1100, from Av Nilo Peçanha, US$4. Bus to **Niterói**, US$4.50; to **Cabo Frio**, US$10. To **Teresópolis**, *Viação Teresópolis*, 8 a day, US$3. *Salutário* to **São Paulo**, twice daily Monday-Friday, 1 at 2300; the night bus only runs Saturday-Sunday.

Directory **Banks** *Banco do Brasil*, R Paulo Barbosa 81. There are several banks on R do Imperador and R Marechal Deodoro. A *Banco 24 Horas* ATM is located by the Varig office at R Mcal Deodoro 98. The following travel agencies change money: *BKR*, R Gen Osório 12, *Goldman*, R Barão de Amazonas 46 (between Praça Rui Barbosa and the Universidade) and *Vert Tur*, R 16 de Março 244, from 1000-1630. **Communications** Post Office: R do Imperador 350 in the Palácio dos Correios (built 1922) at the corner of Av Epitácio Pessoa. **Telecommunications**: R Mcal Deodoro, just above Praça Dr Nelson de Sá Earp, no fax. **Tourist information** *Petrotur*, in the Prefeitura de Petrópolis, at the rear of the Casa do Barão de Mauá, address: Praça da Confluência 03, T2433561, F2420639. It has a list of tourist sites and of hotels and a good, free coloured map of the city. Petrotur is open Mon-Thu 0830-2000, Fri 0830-2100, Sat 0900-2100, Sun 0900-1500. The tourist kiosk on Praça Dom Pedro II is open Tue-Sat 0900-1700, Sun 0900-1500, closed for lunch 1300-1400. News stands sell a *Guia de Petrópolis* (Guia Castor) for US$9, which has a full description of the city's attractions, hotels, restaurants and services. The map, though artistic, is not too helpful.

Teresópolis

Population: 125,500
Phone code: 021
Colour map 4, grid C3

Near the Serra dos Órgãos, 91 kilometres northeast of Rio, at 910 metres this is the highest city in the state of Rio de Janeiro. Its name is a homage to the Empress Teresa Cristina, of whom it was the favourite summer residence.

History Because of its height above sea level and the relatively low temperatures, the area was not exploited by the early colonists since they could not grow the tropical crops which were in demand in Europe. The Michelin guide points out that the existence of *fazendas* in the region was first documented in the early-19th century, the best known being that belonging to an Englishman, George March. To accommodate a constant stream of visitors, March added lodgings to his farm and, not long after, other landowners followed suit. Before taking the name of the Empress, the parish was called Santo Antônio de Paquequer. Building in recent years has destroyed some of the city's character, but most visitors do not go only to see the town. Its location, at the foot of the Serra dos Órgãos, with the associated outdoor activities, is an essential part of the charm.

Sights See the **Colina dos Mirantes** hill, a 30-minute steep climb from Rua Jaguaribe (two kilometres from the centre), which has sweeping views of the city and surroundings (a taxi up is not expensive). Around the town are various attractions, such as the Sloper and Iaci lakes, the Imbui and Amores waterfalls and the Fonte Judith, which has mineral-rich water, access from Avenida Oliveira Botelho, four kilometres southwest. Just off the road to Petrópolis is the **Orquidário Aranda**, Alameda Francisco Smolka, T7420628, five kilometres from the centre.

The road to Nova Friburgo (see below) is known as the Vale das Hortaliças because it passes through a zone where vegetables and some flowers are cultivated. There is a rock formation called A Mulher de Pedra, 12 kilometres out of Teresópolis on this road.

In the Roteiros de Charme group (see page 57): **L** *Fazenda Rosa dos Ventos*, Km 22 on the road to Nova Friburgo, T7428833, F7428174. **AL** *São Moritz*, outside on the Nova Friburgo Rd, Km 36, T/F6411115. Swiss-style with meals. **A** *Alpina*, Av Pres Roosevelt 2500, Parque Imbui, on Petrópolis Rd, T/F7425252. **A** *Fazenda Montebello*, at Km 17 on the same road, T/F6446313. A modern hotel with pool, price includes 3 meals. Recommended. **C** *Várzea Palace*, R Sebastião Teixeira 41, T7420878. Highly recommended. Many cheap hotels in R Delfim Moreira, near the Praça.

    Youth hostel *Retiro da Inglesa*, 20 km on road to Nova Friburgo, Fazenda Boa Esperança, in the beautiful Vale dos Frades, T7423109, F5312234. Book in advance in January-February, dormitory accommodation and family rooms, camping beside the hostel. **Camping** *Quinta de Barra*, R Antônio Maria 100, Km 3 on Petrópolis Rd, T6431050.

Da Irene, R Tte Luís Meireles 1800, T7422901. Russian. Reservations necessary. *Taberna Alpina*, Duque de Caxias 131, German cuisine. *Bar Gota d'Água*, Praça Baltasar da Silveira 16, for trout or *feijoada* (small but recommended) and for *batidas*. Cafetería in the ABC supermarket. Clean and cheap. Recommended.

13 June, patron saint's day, *Santo Antônio*; *São Pedro*, **29 June**, is celebrated with fireworks. **7 July** is the anniversary of the city's foundation. A 2nd saint's day is *Santa Terezinha*, **15 October**. In **May** there is *Festa das Colônias*.

Buses Rio-Teresópolis: buses leave every 30 minutes from the Novo Rio rodoviária. Book the return journey as soon as you arrive at Teresópolis; rodoviária at R 1 de Maio 100. Fare US$3.60. From Teresópolis to Petrópolis, 8 a day, US$3. **A suggested day trip**: leave Rio 0800 or before (Viação Teresópolis) for the 1¾-hour ride into the mountains to Teresópolis (sit on the right side). Upon arrival, buy a ticket right away for Petrópolis (Viação Teresópolis) for the 1200 bus. This gives you 2¾ hours to wander around. The 90-minute drive from Teresópolis to Petrópolis is beautiful. (Sit on the left side.) The views on either side are spectacular. Again, upon arrival in Petrópolis, buy your ticket to Rio (Única Fácil). Take the 1715 bus 'via Quitandinha' and you might catch the sunset over the mountains (in May, June, July, take the 1615 bus). This gives you time to visit most of the attractions listed above.

Banks Cash or TCs at *Teretur*, Trav Portugal 46. English spoken. **Communications** Internet: *Cott@ge Cybercafe*, R Alfredo Rebello Filho 996, 2nd floor. US$5 per hr. **Tourist offices** in the bus station, T7420999; *Secretaria de Turismo*, Praça Olímpica, T7423352 extension 284; *Terminal Turístico Tancredo Neves*, Av Rotariana at the entrance to town from Rio, T7423352, extension 2106.

Sleeping

Eating

Festivals

Transport

Directory

Rio de Janeiro

Rio de Janeiro

Serra dos Órgãos

Eleven thousand hectares of the Serra dos Órgãos, so called because their strange shapes are said to recall organ-pipes, are a national park (created in 1939, the second oldest in the country). The main attraction is the precipitous Dedo de Deus ('God's Finger') Peak (1,692 metres). The highest point is the 2,263 metres Pedra do Sino ('Bell Rock'), up which winds a 14-kilometre path, a climb of three to four hours. The west face of this mountain is one of the hardest climbing pitches in Brazil. Another well-known peak is the Pedra do Açu (2,245 metres – the name is a Tupi word meaning 'large'). Many others have names evocative of their shape: for example, O Escalavrado ('The Scarred One'), O Dedo de Nossa Senhora ('Our Lady's Finger'), A Cabeça de Peixe ('Fish Head'), A Agulha do Diabo ('The Devil's Needle') and A Verruga do Frade ('The Friar's Wart'). Near the Sub-Sede (see below) is the **Von Martius** natural history museum, named after a German naturalist, Karl Friedrich Philipp Von Martius (1794-1868), who visited Brazil in 1817-20. ■ *0800-1700.*

Flora & fauna The park belongs to the Mata Atlântica ecosystem which, as frequently mentioned, is seriously threatened. There are 20-30 metre high trees, such as paineiras (floss-silk tree), ipês and cedros, rising above palms, bamboos and other smaller trees. Flowers include begonias, bromeliads, orchids and quaresmeiras (glorybushes). The park is the home of the very rare and endemic grey-winged cotinga, as well as a number of other cotingas, berryeaters and other rare endemic birds. Less rare birds include hummingbirds, guans, araçaris and tinamous. Mammals include some species of monkey, wild cat, deer, armadillo, agouti and peccary. There are also a number of frogs and toads, including the *sapo-pulga* (the flea-toad, at 10 millimetres claimed by local literature to be the smallest amphibian in the world; although other sources say that the Cuban pygmy frog is the smallest).

Serra dos Órgãos

The park has 2 dependencies, both accessible from the BR-116: the Sede (headquarters, T/F6421070) is closer to Teresópolis (from town take Avenida Rotariana), while the Sub-Sede is just outside the Park proper, off the BR-116. By the Sede entrance is the Mirante do Soberbo, with views to the Baía de Guanabara. Anyone can enter the Park and hike the trails from the Teresópolis gate, but if you intend to climb the Pedra do Sino, you must sign a register (those under 18 must be accompanied by an adult and have authorization from the park authorities). Entrance to the park is US$1, with an extra charge for the path to the top of the Pedra do Sino. For information from **Ibama** for the state of Rio de Janeiro, T021-2311772.

Park essentials
A good way to see the park is to do the Rio-Teresópolis-Petrópolis-Rio circuit; a scenic day trip by car. It can also be hiked in 2-3 days (take a tent)

Ibama has some hostels, US$5 full board, or US$3 1st night, US$2 thereafter, a bit rough. At the Petrópolis side of the Park, **A** *Campo de Aventuras Paraíso Açu*, Estr do Bonfim 3511, T024-1426275, or T021-9733618. Has various types of accommodation, from rooms to chalet, and specializes in adventure sports (credit cards not accepted); on the same road, at Km 3.5 and in the same price range, is *Cabanas Açu*, T021-9835041, inside the Park, cabins, restaurant, sports include riding, canoeing and fishing (credit cards accepted). **Camping** Two sites in the Sub-Sede part, 1 close to the Museum, the other not far from the natural swimming pool at Poço da Ponte Velha; 1 site in the Sede part. The Sede has a restaurant and the Sub-Sede a *lanchonete*.

Sleeping & eating

Activities: at both the Sede and Sub-Sede there are natural swimming pools, although between May and October the temperature may be a little too chilly for bathing. In the Sub-Sede they are called Poços Verde, da Preguiça and Ponte Velha. It is possible to trek right through the park, from Teresópolis to Petrópolis, a distance of 42 km, but it is essential to take a guide; contact *Campo de Aventuras Paraíso Açu* (see **Sleeping** above).

Sports
The Serra dos Órgãos is considered Brazil's climbing capital and the park is also good for trekking

Tour companies & travel agents Tours of the park are offered by Francisco of *Lazer Tours*, recommended; T7427616, or find him at the grocery shop on R Sloper 1. *Focus Tours* (see page 30) offers birdwatching tours.

Directory

Nova Friburgo

At 846 metres, in a beautiful valley with excellent walking and riding, the town is a popular resort during the summer months. It was founded by Swiss settlers from Fribourg, the first families arriving in 1820. Apart from the holiday business, Nova Friburgo has an important textile industry, specializing in lingerie, and also produces cheeses, preserves, sweets and liqueurs.

Population: 169,500
Phone code: 024
Colour map 4, grid C3

A cable car from Praça dos Suspiros goes 650 metres up the **Morro da Cruz**, for a magnificent view of the rugged country (US$5). Most of the interesting sites are in the surrounding countryside, so a car may be necessary to see everything. Ten kilometres northeast are the **Furnas do Catete**, an area of forest, caves, waterfalls and rock formations, one of which is called the Pedra do Cão Sentado ('The Seated Dog'); there is a small entry fee. Other natural attractions are the Pico da Caledônia (2,310 metres) 15 kilometres southwest, and the Véu de Noiva waterfall, nine kilometres north. The district of **Lumiar**, 34 kilometres southeast, has beautiful scenery, waterfalls, natural swimming pools and good canoeing in the Rios Macaé and Bonito. These two rivers meet at a point called Poço do Alemão, or Poço Verde, 4½ kilometres south of Lumiar.

Sights

AL *Bucsky*, 5 km out on the Niterói Rd, T5225052, F5229769. With meals. **AL** *Pousada do Riacho*, Estr Nova Friburgo Km 8, Cardinot, T5222823, riacho@openlink.com.br. A Roteiro de Charme hotel (see page 57). **A** *Garlipp*, at Muri, 8 km south, Km 70.5 from

Sleeping

Rio de Janeiro

Rio, T/F5421330. German-run, in chalets, with meals. **A** *Fazenda São João*, 11 km from *Garlipp* (under the same ownership) up a side road, T5421304. Riding, swimming, sauna, tennis, hummingbirds and orchids. The owner will meet guests in Nova Friburgo or even in Rio. **B** *Everest*, R Manuel Ventura 75, T5227350. Comfortable, good breakfast. **B** *Fabris*, Av Alberto Browne 148, T5222852. Central, TV, hot showers, plentiful breakfast buffet. **C** *Maringá*, R Monsenhor Miranda 110, T5222309. **D** without bath. Good breakfast. Recommended. **Camping**: *Camping Clube do Brasil* has sites on the Niterói Rd, at Caledônia (7 km out, T5220169) and Muri (10 km out, T5422275). There is a private site at Fazenda Sanandu, 20 km out on the same road.

Eating   There are many options to choose from, several in European styles which reflect the background of the people who settled in the area. You can also find Brazilian food, pizzas and *confeitarias*. *Auberge Suisse*, R 10 de Outubro, T5411270. Swiss; *Chez Gigi*, Av Euterpe Friburguense 21, T5230107. French.

Festivals   In **May**, Nova Friburgo celebrates its founding (on the 16th) and throughout the month holds a festival (*Maifest*). **24 June**, *São João Batista*, patron saint's day.

Transport   **Buses**   Bus station, Ponte da Suadade, T5220400. To **Rio** (every hour), 2 hours, US$4.

Directory   **Banks** *Bradesco*, Praça Demerval Barbosa Moreira. **Tourist information** *Centro de Turismo*, Praça Demerval Barbosa Moreira, T5238000, extension 236.

Towns in the Coffee Zone

Although coffee no longer dominates this part of Brazil, as it did in the 19th century, there are still many reminders of the wealth of this trade. It can be seen in the towns and especially in the fazendas which were the homes and production headquarters of the coffee barons.

The coffee zone was the valley of the Rio Paraíba do Sul and neighbouring hills and valleys. Before the coming of the railways in the second half of the 19th century, mule trains carried the coffee from the interior to the coast on roads such as the Estrada do Comércio, which ran from Minas Gerais, through Valença and Vassouras, to the town of Iguaçu on the river of the same name. At the end of the 19th century, the abolition of slavery, the exhaustion of the land and lower international prices for coffee caused the collapse of the coffee trade. The towns had to adapt to new economic activities or die, but many of the fazendas remain. Although not easy to get to, a visit is worth the effort. *Fazendas: As Casas Grandes Rurais do Brasil*, by Fernando Tasso Frajoso Pires (Abbeville Press), is a beautiful book showing these magnificent houses.

Miguel Pereira   This town, 113 kilometres north of Rio de Janeiro, has an excellent mountain climate. In the mid-19th century the area was entirely given over to coffee. Other industries were introduced when a railway branch line reached here in the late 19th century. The town was named after a doctor who, in the 1930s, promoted the region for holidays away from the coast. Three kilometres from town on the road to Rio is the Javari lake, a popular recreational spot. Mountain roads through the Serra do Mar head east to Petrópolis (see above) and Vassouras (see below), but ask about their condition before using either of them.

Population: 20,500
Phone code: 024

The **Miguel Pereira-Conrado** railway: a tourist train, also known as the *Trem Azul*, started operations in 1993 and affords beautiful views of mountains, rivers and waterfalls. The round trip of 56 kilometres takes 4½ hours, costs US$25 and leaves Miguel Pereira at 0930 on Saturday, Sunday and public holidays. The diesel train follows a meter gauge line constructed to take coffee to the port of Rio. Among the attractions of the journey is the Paulo de Frontin iron bridge, built in 1889 and said to be the only railway bridge built in a curve. The line is operated by *Montmar Turismo* of Angra dos Reis (see page 179). There is a museum at the railway station. ■ *Thursday-Sunday 0900-1200, 1300-1700, T4844342.*

Sleeping AL *Fazenda Javary*, Praça Frutuoso da Fonseca Fernandes 35, near town, T/F4843611 (or Rio T2409335), restaurant, pool, sports courts. **B** *Pousada Caçarola*, R Luís Marques 1204, 5 km from town, T4841499.

Directory Tourist Information: *Setur*, Av Manuel Guilherme Barbosa 375, T4841616.

Vassouras

Northwest of Miguel Periera are the old coffee towns of Vassouras, Valença and Conservatória, all in the mountains.

Population: 29,000
Phone code: 024
Colour map 4, grid C3

It is hard to believe that the small town of Vassouras was once considered one of the most important cities of the Brazilian Empire. During the coffee boom in the 19th century, Vassouras was surrounded by coffee farms whose owners became immensely rich. These coffee barons acquired noble titles and, as their power increased, they built enormous, opulent town houses in Vassouras. The majority of these buildings are still there, surrounding the beautiful main Praça Barão de Campo Belo. The emperor Pedro II visited the city several times.

In 1875 the railway station was opened in Vassouras, allowing the local farmers to send their produce directly to Rio de Janeiro. But the town went into decline when the coffee boom ended. For many years it had almost no economic activity, except for some cattle ranching and small-scale agriculture. Nowadays, it has a university and is being rediscovered by the tourism industry. It still retains its small-town calm, but the reminders of its golden past mix with the student nightlife in the bars along a street called, unofficially, 'The Broadway'.

The **climate** is much cooler than Rio, as it is in the hills. It rains a lot in January and February.

The best way to explore Vassouras is on foot. Starting at the rodoviária, walk as far as the **Estação Ferroviária**, the former railway station. Recently restored, it is now the headquarters of the Universidade de Vassouras. Carry straight on to the **Praça Barão de Campo Belo**, where you will find the most important old houses and public buildings, all dating from the 19th century. Note the neoclassical influence. One of these old 'baronial' houses, at Rua Custódio Guimarães 65, on the lefthand side of the square as you enter, houses the **Casa da Cultura**, a municipal cultural centre which also provides tourist information. At the Casa da Cultura, there are temporary exhibitions of local art and folklore. Ask if you can go upstairs and on the second floor, at the top of some of the internal walls, look for where the paint has peeled. You can see the 19th century method of house construction, using clay over a frame of interwoven wood and bamboo.

At the top end of the praça is the church of **Nossa Senhora da Conceição**, the most important in the city, finished in 1853 in neoclassical style. Behind the church is the small Praça Sebastião Lacerda, surrounded by huge fig trees. Locals believe there is one fig tree for each of the rich coffee barons who lived in Vassouras in the last century. Keep on walking until you come to the cemetery.

Sights

Rio de Janeiro

A visit is recommended. Most of the wealthiest men of Brazil's second empire are buried there. Rich mausoleums decorated with Italian and Portuguese marble sculptures show the competition among the families. Two of the most important clans are represented: the Teixeira Leite family and the Correa e Castro family. In the cemetery is one of the most curious legends of Vassouras: the 'flesh flower'. Growing on the grave of a catholic priest who died in 1866, Monsenhor Rios, a strange purple flower blooms every year in November on the 'Day of the Dead'. Its intense smell is reminiscent of rotting flesh. Scientists have studied it, but no conclusion has been reached on its nature. The flower vanishes in a few days and the small bush lives on until January or February. It is now protected by a small iron fence and miracles are reported to have occurred there.

Back at Praça Barão de Campo Belo, on Rua Barão de Vassouras, is the **Palacete do Barão do Ribeirão**, the former residence of a coffee baron, later converted into the town's court. Nowadays it is closed for restoration as it has been badly attacked by termites. Turn right and at the end of Rua Dr Fernandes Junior (No 89) you will find the fascinating **Casa da Hera** museum, an old country house covered with ivy, which belonged in the 19th century to one of the richest men in the town, Joaquim Teixeira Leite. After his death the house was inherited by his daughter, Eufrásia Teixeira Leite, who lost interest in the coffee business. She went to Paris, living there for many years a life of parties and luxury. After her death in 1930, the house was made into a museum, according to her will. All the furniture, decoration and architecture is original, from the golden years of coffee. The wide variety of imported tapestries, pianos and porcelain contrasts with very rough building materials: a fantastic portrait of how life was in the 1850s. On some Sundays, depending on the number of visitors, they serve tea in a style that recreates the atmosphere of the old coffee *fazendas*. ■ *Wednesday to Sunday 1100-1700, T4712342.*

The nightlife of Vassouras has more variety than in other towns of a similar size. Being a university centre, many students go out at night for a drink, especially on Friday and Saturday. The action is concentrated in Rua Expedicionário Oswaldo de Almeida Ramos, but you won't need to pronounce that: simply ask for the 'Broadway' and everybody will direct you to the right place. There are many bars and open-air restaurants to suit all tastes and budgets.

Another possibility is a guided visit to the food technology centre at the **Senai**, close to the main praça. Here students learn how to process fruit, vegetables, meat and also how to work in a brewery. Most of the hotels can arrange a guided visit at weekends.

Excursions As yet, Vassouras lacks a well-developed tourist infrastructure. There is a lot to see around the city, especially the old *fazendas*, but they are only just starting to open to the public. The majority of them are privately owned and can only be visited with a prior appointment. The bigger hotels can arrange guided tours with transport at weekends. During the week, the only option is to go by car, as some of the *fazendas* are a long way away, down dirt roads. The best *fazendas* in the vicinity are: Fazenda Santa Mônica, Fazenda São Fernando, Fazenda Paraíso and Fazenda Oriente. More information can be obtained from the Casa da Cultura or from the Tourism Secretary, in the Municipalidade, Praça Barão de Campo Belo.

Sleeping **AL** *Santa Amália*, Av Sebastião Manoel Furtado 526, close to the rodoviária, T/F4711897. Located in a very pleasant and quiet park, swimming pool, sauna, volleyball and soccer pitches, 1 of the best in town, try to negotiate in the low season (March to June and August to November) and during the week. **B** *Gramado da Serra*, R Aldo Cavalcanti 7, T/F4712314. **B** *Mara Palace*, R Chanceler Dr Raul Fernandes 121,

T4711993, F471252. House built in 1870, fully and tastefully preserved, swimming pool, bar, sauna, sports, nice atmosphere and good service, owner (Gerson) can arrange visits to *fazendas*; also **Pousada Bougainville**, T4712451, and **Pousada Veredas**, T4712728.

The best restaurants are located in the centre, on R Expedicionário Oswaldo de Almeida **Eating** Ramos/'The Broadway'. There are many to choose from, but the 2 best known are **Sput-nik** and **Mafioso**; they are close neighbours and have similar layouts and prices, with dishes varying from pasta (around US$8 for 1), steak (around US$13 for 1) and pizzas in different sizes and toppings (pizzas at *Sputnik* are good value). During the week they both offer meals 'by weight' at lunch time, with a buffet of salads, cold and hot dishes. On warm nights you can sit outside, but be sure to arrive before 2000 to avoid the crowds, especially at weekends. Try the *chopp* (beer) and ask for one of the interesting appetizers, such as *mandioca frita* (fried manioc), similar to French fries.

Nightlife is found mostly in the bars and restaurants. University students often orga- **Bars &** nize parties at weekends; look for the advertisements posted on the walls or in other **nightclubs** public places. For people watching, stroll along 'The Broadway' on a Friday night.

Carnival (**February** or **March**) is one of the best in the region, with its own Samba **Festivals** schools and balls. In June, the days of **Santo Antônio**, **São Pedro** and **São João** are cel-ebrated with traditional parties. **8 December**: the feast of **Nossa Senhora da Conceição**, the city's patron saint, with a mass and procession.

Vassouras doesn't have any speciality handicrafts or souvenirs, other than the country **Shopping** cheese and the preserves made with local fruits.

Buses There are several buses every day to Vassouras from Rio de Janeiro's Rodoviária **Transport** Novo Rio. Try to buy your ticket at least 30 minutes before departure; the bus company is Normandy. The average time between departures is 1½ hours: the first bus leaves at 0615 and the last at 2030. Returning to Rio, the 1st bus is at 0430, then 0645, 0815 and others with an average time of 1½ hours between them; the last 1 departs at 1900. The journey takes more or less 2 hours; the fare is US$6.50. These schedules may alter on hol-idays and during the summer, when more buses are added.

Banks The city is definitely not prepared for international tourism and foreign currencies are **Directory** unlikely to be accepted. Change all the money you will need in Rio before departing. As a last resort, try the local *Banco do Brasil* at R Caetano Furquim, in the centre. **Communications** Post Office: R Irmã Maria Agostinha. **Telecommunications:** Long distance and international calls at the office between R Caetano Furquim and R Expedicionário Oswaldo de Almeida Ramos(there are entrances in each street). **Hospital & medical services** *Hospital Eufrásia Teixeira Leite*, Praça Provedor Félix Machado 110, T4711796. **Tourist offices** *Casa da Cultura*, R Custódio Guimarães 65, Praça Barão de Campo Belo. English is not normally spoken, but the staff will try to help you.

Valença and Conservatória

Like Vassouras, **Valença** is a historical monument. Its history follows much the same pattern as Vassouras, with wealth from the coffee trade followed by some small-scale industry and agriculture. There are a number of *fazendas* nearby and in the town a Faculty of Medicine. The best road there from Vassouras follows the Rio Paraíba as far as **Barra do Piraí** (20 kilometres), then doubles back for 30 kilometres to Valença. Barra do Piraí was a major dis-tribution centre for coffee and other goods in the mid-19th century. It was a big rail junction and has retained its importance as a commercial centre.

Rio de Janeiro

Thirty five kilometres from Valença, 15 kilometres from Barra do Piraí, is **Conservatória**, another town in the coffee zone. Although it did not become as wealthy as Vassouras or Valença, it still has some fine 19th century houses. Moreover, today, it is quieter than the other two. In Conservatória, local farm produce can be bought, as well as blankets, macrame and crochet work. A local custom is the serenade through the streets; serenaders meet at the Museu da Seresta on Rua Osvaldo Fonseca on Friday and Saturday. This region can also be reached via the Japeri turn-off on the BR-116 (a beautiful mountain drive).

Sleeping   In and around Valença, Barra do Piraí and Conservatória, there are a number of *fazenda* hotels whose prices start in most cases in our **L** range. Besides lodging and food, most offer riding and other outdoor activities. Others offer day visits, usually guided tours only. Details should be obtained locally; phone Preservale T021-2407539 (*Quatro Rodas* publications list many of these establishments). **Youth hostel** At Barra do Piraí, *Na Toca*, Estr Mun Rui Pio Davi Gomes 1876, Dorândia, T0XX24-4425323.

West of Rio de Janeiro

Volta Redonda
Population: 226,500
Phone code: 024

On a broad bend of the Rio Paraíba, 113 kilometres west of Rio along the railway to São Paulo, Volta Redonda has one of the largest steel works in Latin America. The mills are on the river bank and the town spreads up the surrounding wooded and gardened slopes. To visit, apply for a permit from the Companhia Siderúrgica Nacional, Avenida Treze de Maio 13, Rio de Janeiro (10 days in advance), or locally from the *Bela Vista* hotel. Visits of 2½ to three hours start at 0900. On a hill overlooking town is *Bela Vista* (**A**), Alto de Boa Vista, T3482022, F3482066. On Avenida Alberto Pasqualini is *Sider Palace* (**A**), T/F3481032. Buses or minibuses from Rio de Janeiro take 2½ hours, US$5.

Resende
Population: 94,000
Phone code: 024

Some 30 kilometres west of Volta Redonda, in the town of Resende, is the Military Academy of Agulhas Negras at Km 306 Rodovia Presidente Dutra. The grounds, with captured German guns of the Second World War, are open to the public. There is a military museum. ■ *0800-1700.*

Sleeping **A** *Castel Plaza*, Av Mcal Castelo Branco 301, T3551091, F3544025. **A** *River Park*, Av Nova Resende 262, T3353344, F3547314.

Transport Buses: from Aparecida do Norte (see page 248), several daily, US$2.50; from Rio, frequent, 1¾ hours, US$6, also from São Paulo and Volta Redonda. From Resende buses go to Barra Mansa (*Resendense*, 40 minutes, US$2.50), where you can change for Belo Horizonte (*Útil* 1230, 8-9 hours).

Penedo
Population: 8,000
Phone code: 024
Altitude: 600m

In the same region, 175 kilometres from Rio, is the small town of Penedo which in the 1930s attracted Finnish settlers who brought the first saunas to Brazil. There is a Finnish museum, a cultural centre and Finnish dancing on Saturdays. This popular weekend resort also provides horse riding and swimming in the Portinho River. There are five buses a day from Resende. Tourist information is at Avenida Casa das Pedras, T3511876.

Sleeping and eating **A** *da Cachoeira*, Estr das Três Cachoeiras, T3511262, F3511180. **B** *Bertell*, R Harry Bertell 47, T/F3511288. **B** *Pousada Penedo*, Av Finlândia, T3511309, F3511255. Safe, pool. Recommended. **Camping** *Bandeirante*, Av Brasil 440, T3511071. For eating, try *Pequena Suécia*, R Toivo Suni, T3511275. Swedish.

Visconde de Mauá

Phone code: 024
Altitude: 1,200m
Colour map 4, grid C3

Some 33 kilometres beyond Penedo (part of the road unpaved) is the small village of Visconde de Mauá in the **Serra da Mantiqueira**. Swiss and German immigrants came to this area in the early 20th century. The surrounding scenery is fine, with valleys, cold rivers and lots of flowers. Temperatures range from under 10°C to highs of around 30°C. There are opportunities for good walks and other outdoor activities. Lots of holidaymakers visit the town and the atmosphere is very pleasant. Many places offer acupuncture, shiatsu massage, macrobiotic food etc, and there is a hippy feel to the crafts on sale. Horses can be rented in Visconde de Mauá from Berto (almost opposite *Vendinha da Serra*), or Pedro (Lote 10). Many places in Maringá arrange riding. The Rio Preto is good for canoeing and there is an annual national event (dates change; check in advance). The tourist office, T3543222, is closed out of season.

There are roads to three other small hill towns: to **Mirantão**, at about 1,700 metres, with semitropical vegetation; to **Maringá**, which is just across the state border in Minas Gerais and is a delightful two hours' walk; and to **Maromba**. On the way to Maromba is the Mirante do Posto da Montanha, a lookout with a view of the Rio Preto, which runs through the region and is the border between Rio de Janeiro and Minas Gerais states. Also in Minas Gerais, six kilometres up river from Maringá but on a different road, are the Santa Clara falls (turn off before Maromba). Between Visconde de Mauá and Maringá is a natural pool in the river (turn left before crossing the bridge). After Maromba follow the signs to Cachoeira e Escorrega, a small fall and waterslide with a cold natural swimming pool, a two-kilometre walk. A turning off this road leads to another waterfall, the Cachoeira Véu da Noiva.

Sleeping LL *Fronteira*, Estr Visconde de Mauá-Campo Lindo, Km 4, T3871219, F3871388. A Roteiro de Charme hotel (see page 57). There are many other *fazendas*, *pousadas* and *chalés* in the vicinity. A *Beira Rio*, T3541801; A *Pousada Vale das Hortênsias*, T3543030. Both in Maringá, both provide all meals, recommended; ½ km on road to Maringá is *Hotel Turístico*, with handicrafts and homemade food. Italian owner, Nino, and his Brazilian wife run excursions. Cheap lodgings are limited: enquire at *Vendinha da Serra*, an excellent natural food restaurant and store; next door is *Dona Mariana*, a recommended budget place to stay. **Camping** There are several sites, including *Barragen's*, in Maringá, T3871354.

Eating *Gosto com Gosto*, R Wenceslau Brás. Mineiro. *Bar do Jorge*, café. Everywhere in town shuts at about 2200.

Bars & nightclubs *Adega Bar*, open till midnight, live music and dancing (Saturday only). *Forró da Marieta* for forró dancing.

Transport **Buses** To Visconde de Mauá from Resende, 1500 and 1630, 2 hours, return 0900-0830, US$5. Direct bus Rio-Visconde de Mauá, Cidade de Aço, 0900 daily, plus 1 in evening, 3½ hours, US$7.

Rio de Janeiro

Itatiaia National Park

The park is one of the most popular excursions in the state of Rio de Janeiro and is a good area for climbing, trekking and birdwatching
Founded 1937 on the Serra de Itatiaia in the Mantiqueira chain of mountains, the park was the first to be created in Brazil. Its entrance is a few kilometres north of the Via Dutra (Rio-São Paulo highway). The road to it is paved. The town of Itatiaia is surrounded by picturesque mountain peaks and lovely waterfalls. Worth seeing are the curious rock formations of Pedra de Taruga and Pedra de Maçã and the waterfalls Poranga and Véu de Noiva (many birds). Climbing is good, for instance on the Pico das Agulhas Negras (2,787 metres) and the peaks in the Serra das Prateleiras (up to 2,540 metres). The average temperature is 11°C.

Flora & fauna
The vegetation is determined by altitude, so that the plateau at 800-1,100 metres is covered by forest, ferns and flowering plants (such as orchids, bromeliads, begonias), giving way on the higher escarpments to pines and bushes. Higher still, over 1,900 metres, the distinctive rocky landscape has low bushes and grasses, isolated trees and many unique plants adapted to the high winds and strong sun. There is also a great variety of lichens.

The southern masked titi monkey is common, recognizable by its loud hee-haw-like call. There are also agoutis, sloths, peccaries and other rarer mammals. Sources vary on the number of bird species in the park, from 270 to 300 to 400, but there are many endemics making it a top birding destination. Specialities include swallow-tailed, shrike-like and black-and-gold cotingas, white-bearded ant shrike, black-capped manakin, gilt-edged, brassy-breasted, brown and olive-green tanagers, and a number of hummingbirds. Needless to say, insects are plentiful, including some of the largest flies in the world, and there is a wide range of amphibians. There is a **Museu de História Natural** near the headquarters. ■ *1000-1600, closed Monday.* Also nearby is a wildlife trail, **Três Picos**, which starts near the *Hotel Simon* (see below).

Park essentials
Information and maps can be obtained at the park office. The Administração do Parque Nacional de Itatiaia operates a refuge in the park which acts as a starting point for climbs and treks. Information can be obtained from **Ibama**, T024-3521461, for the local headquarters, or T021-2246463 for the Rio de Janeiro state department. Information on treks can be obtained from Clube Excursionista Brasileira, Avenida Almirante Barroso 2, 8th floor, Rio de Janeiro, T021-2203695. It is very difficult to visit the park without a car and some parts are only possible in a four-wheel drive vehicle (it is 70 km from the *Hotel Simon* to the other side). For tourist information in the town of Itatiaia, T024-3521660.

Sleeping
Basic accommodation in cabins and dormitories is available in the park; you will need to book in season, say 30 days in advance, by writing to Administração do Parque Nacional de Itatiaia, Caixa Postal 83657, Itatiaia 27580-000, RJ, telephone as above. **A** *Simon*, Km 13 on the road in the park, T3521122. With meals, lovely views, beautifully set, helpful with advice on getting around the park. Recommended. **A** *Hotel do Ypê*, on the road in the park, Km 14, T3521453. With meals. Recommended. **A** *Repouso Itatiaia*, Km 11 on the park road, T3521110, F3521509. With meals. **A** *Fazenda da Serra*, Via Dutra Km 151, T3521611. With meals. **B** *Pousada do Elefante*, 15 minutes walk back down hill from *Hotel Simon*. Good food, swimming pool, lovely views, may allow camping; cheap lodging at R Maricá 255, T3521699. Possibility of pitching a tent on the premises, located close to the National Park. **D** *Hotel Alsene*, at 2,100m, 2 km from the side entrance to the Park, take a bus to São Lourenço and Caxambu, get off at Registro, walk or hitchhike from there (12 km). Very popular with climbing and trekking clubs, dormitory or camping, chalets available, hot

showers, fireplace, evening meal after everyone returns, drinks but no snacks. **Youth hostel** *Ipê Amarelo*, R João Maurício Macedo Costa 352, Campo Alegre, T/F0XX24-3521232. IYHA. **Camping** *Camping* Clube do Brasil site is entered at Km 148 on the Via Dutra.

Buses A bus from Itatiaia, marked *Hotel Simon*, goes to the Park, 1200, returns 1700; coming from Resende this may be caught at the crossroads before Itatiaia. Through tickets to São Paulo are sold at a booth in the large bar in the middle of Itatiaia main street.

Transport

Further along the Dutra Highway (186 kilometres from Rio) is the small town of Engenheiro Passos, from which a road (BR-354) leads to São Lourenço and Caxambu in Minas Gerais (see page312). By turning off this road at the Registro pass (1,670 metres) on the Rio-Minas border, you can reach the **Pico das Agulhas Negras**. The mountain can be climbed from this side from the Abrigo Rebouças refuge at 2,350 metres which is manned all year round. Take your own food, US$2.50 to stay. Around Engenheiro Passos there are many *fazenda* hotels: *Fazenda Villa Forte* (**L**), one kilometre from town, T/F3571122, with meals, bar, sauna, massage, gym and other sports and *Fazenda Palmital* (**A**), Km 11 BR-354 towards Caxambu, T/F3571108. The local cuisine is strongly influenced by the *mineira* food of Minas Gerais. *Cachaça* is made in the area and there is a festival.

Engenheiro Passos
Population: 3,500
Phone code: 024

Rio de Janeiro

The Costa Verde

The Rio de Janeiro-Santos section of the BR101 is one of the world's most beautiful highways, hugging the forested and hilly Costa Verde southwest of Rio. The coast is littered with islands, beaches, colonial settlements and mountain fazendas.

The BR101 is now complete through to Bertioga (see page 231), which has good links with Santos and São Paulo. Buses run from Rio to Angra dos Reis, Paraty, Ubatuba, Caraguatatuba and São Sebastião, where it may be necessary to change for Santos or São Paulo. Hotels and *pousadas* have sprung up all along the road, as have expensive housing developments, though these have not spoiled the views. The drive should take seven hours, but it would be better to break the journey and enjoy some of the attractions. The coast road has lots of twists and turns so, if prone to motion sickness, get a seat at the front of the bus to make the most of the views.

The BR-101 does not take the coastal route through Barra da Tijuca out of the city, but goes around the north side, eventually hitting the coast at Coroa Grande. This fishing village with summer houses and beach (the sea is polluted), together with Itacuruçá and Mangaratiba, are all on the shore of the Baía de Sepetiba, which is protected from the open sea by a long sand spit, the Restinga da Marambaia. At the spit's western end is the Ilha da Marambaia. The mouth of the bay is protected by Ilha Grande.

Itacuruçá
Population: 3,500
Phone code: 021

    Itacuruçá, 91 kilometres from Rio, is a delightful place to visit: there is fine scenery, peace and quiet, with islands off the coast. The sea in the town is too polluted for bathing, but you can walk along the railway to Castelo where the beach is cleaner. Separated from the town by a channel is the Ilha de Itacuruçá, the largest of a string of islands stretching into the bay. Further offshore is Ilha de Jaguanum, around which there are lovely walks. Both islands have beaches from which bathing is possible. *Saveiros* (schooners) sail around the bay and to the islands from Itacuruçá; T7801776 for details. Ilha de Itacuruçá can also be reached from **Muriqui**, a popular beach resort nine kilometres from Itacuruçá; bathing is also possible in the Véu de Noiva waterfall. The next beach along the coast is Praia Grande, then **Praia do Saí** which has the ruins of an old port.

Sleeping On Ilha de Itacuruçá are **AL** *Elias C*, Praia Cabeça do Boi, T2537444. Chalets, pool, restaurant, sports courts. **AL** *Hotel Pierre*, Praia da Bica, reached by boat from Coroa Grande on the mainland, 5 minutes (boats also go from Itacuruçá), T/F6881560. Restaurant, bar, sports courts. For bookings in Rio, T2534102. **A** *Pousada Praia Grande*, Praia Grande, T99794882.

Mangaratiba
Population: 20,000
Phone code: 021

Twenty two kilometres down the coast, this fishing village halfway from Rio to Angra dos Reis. It stands on a little bay within the Baia de Sepetiba and in the 18th century was a port for the export first of gold, later coffee and for the import of slaves. During the coffee era, it was the terminus for the Estrada São João Marcos from the Rio Paraíba do Sul. Mangaratiba's beaches are muddy, but the surroundings are pleasant and better beaches can be found outside town, for example Ibicuí (two kilometres) and Brava (between Ibicuí and Saí – see above) to the east, at the head of the bay Saco, Guiti and Cação, and further west São Brás.

Sleeping **D** *Sítio Santo Antônio 12*, T7892192. Family-run, owner Carlito is proud of his shell collection. Recommended. At Rio das Pedras is **LL** *Club Mediterranée*, BR-101 Km 445, T6885050, F6883333, with all the facilities associated with this French chain; in July and December-March, stays of 7 days minimum are required.

Transport Buses: from Rio Rodoviária with *Costa Verde*, several daily, US$4.25. **Ferries**: daily boats to Ilha Grande island (see below) charge US$30 return. This is a highly recommended trip. You can enquire in advance what *Conerj* sailings are operating. Ferry departures and destinations can be checked at the ferry station at Praça 15 de Novembro, Rio de Janeiro (see page 128).

Angra dos Reis

Population: 90,000
Phone code: 024
Colour map 4, grid C3

Said to have been founded on 6 January 1502 (O Dia dos Reis – The Day of Kings), Angra dos Reis is 151 kilometres southwest of Rio by road. A small port with an important fishing and shipbuilding industry, it has several small coves with good bathing within easy reach and is situated on an enormous bay full of islands. It is one of the most sophisticated resorts on the Rio de Janeiro coast.

History Angra's past and present are bound to the sea, in earlier times through its importance as a port, nowadays through tourism. Once a harbour had been established here, Angra became a stop on the sea route to São Vicente (Santos). In the 18th century it was used by the gold traders making their way to and from Minas Gerais. When coffee replaced gold as the boom product, it became the harbour for the exports carried down the Estrada do Caramujo. It was one of the most important ports in the country until the railway shifted the transport emphasis away from the old roads onto the direct route into Rio.

Sights Several buildings remain from Angra's heyday. Of particular note are the church and convent of **Nossa Senhora do Carmo**, built in 1593 (Praça General Osório), the Igreja Matriz de **Nossa Senhora da Conceição** (1626) in the centre of town and the church and convent of **São Bernardino de Sena**

(1758-63) on the Morro do Santo Antônio. On the Largo da Lapa is the church of **Nossa Senhora da Lapa da Boa Morte** (1752) and a museum of sacred art.
■ *Thursday-Sunday 1000-1200, 1400-1800.*

On the Península de Angra, just west of the town, is the **Praia do Bonfim**, a popular beach and a little way offshore the island of the same name, on which is the hermitage of Senhor do Bonfim (1780). Fifteen kilometres east are the ruins of the **Jacuecanga** seminary (1797). **Excursions**

Boat trips around the bay are available, some with a stop for lunch on the island of Gipóia (five hours). Several boats run tours from the Cais de Santa Luzia and there are agencies for *saveiros* in town.

Train The historic *Trem da Mata Atlântica* or *Trem Verde* has been reopened, making the coastal trip to Lidice. A steam locomotive and six carriages were renovated for the line, but the train may be pulled by a diesel engine. The six-hour round trip runs through beautiful countryside (hence the name 'Green Train'). It leaves Angra railway station at 1030 on Saturday, Sunday and public holidays and has a restaurant car; the fare is US$44. The operator is *Montmar Turismo*, Rua do Comércio 11.

L *do Frade*, on the road to Ubatuba, Km 123 BR-101, 33 km from Angra, T3692244, F3692254. Luxury hotel on the Praia do Frade with restaurants, bar, sauna, sports facilities on land and sea. **AL** *Porto Aquarius*, Saco de Itapirapuã, out of town access from Km 101 BR-101, 13 km, T3651642, F3651766. Lots of facilities, pleasant, helpful staff. **A** *Pousada Porto Marina Bracuhy*, Km 115 BR-101, 23 km from Angra dos Reis, T3651153, F3631122. Lots of facilities for watersports, nightly shows and dancing, restaurant. **Sleeping**
There are many hotels around Angra

In town are A *Londres*, Av Raul Pompéia 75, T3650044, F3650511. **A** *Angra Palace*, same avenue No 90, T3653207, F3652656. **A** *Caribe*, R de Conceição 255, T3650033, F3653450. Central. Recommended.

Youth hostel *Rio Bracuí*, Estr Santa Rita 4, Bracuí, on the road to Santos at Km 115 (take any bus going beyond Angra to the bridge over the Rio Bracuí), T3631234, ajriobracui@quick.com.br. Open all year.

Taberna 33, R Raul Pompéia 110. Italian, good, popular, moderate prices. *Tropicalitá*, Largo do Convento do Carmo. **Eating**

In **January** there are several festivals: at New Year there is a *Festa do Mar*, with boat processions; on the 5th is the *Folia dos Reis*, the culmination of a religious festival that begins at Christmas; the 6th is the anniversary of the founding of the city. In **May** is the *Festa do Divino* and, on the 2nd Sunday, the *Senhor do Bonfim* maritime procession. As elsewhere in the state, the *Festas Juninas* are celebrated in June. **8 December**: the festival of *Nossa Senhora da Conceição*. **Festivals**

Diving: *Aquamaster*, Praia da Enseada, take bus marked 'Retiro' from the port in Angra, T3652416. US$60 for 2 dives with drinks and food. **Sports**

Buses At least hourly from Rio's rodoviária with *Costa Verde*, several direct, T2901484, accepts credit cards, new comfortable buses, several go through Copacabana, Ipanema and Barra then take the 'via litoral', sit on the left, US$5.75, 2½ hours (you can flag the bus down in Flamengo, Copacabana, Ipanema, Barra de Tijuca, but it may well be full at weekends). **Transport**

Ferries 1½ hours by boat to Ilha Grande, US$1.50 during the week, US$8 at weekends, one-way (Monday to Friday at 1500, return 1000, so you have to stay overnight; Saturday, Sunday and holidays leaving Angra at 1000, returning from

Abraão at 1600; for day trips, go from Mangaratiba). Fishing boats also take passengers from Angra for about US$5, or there is the *Santa Isabel* schooner, T9828287, which costs about US$10 1-way.

Routes A road runs inland (about 18 km beyond Angra), through Getulândia, to join the BR-116 either just south of Piraí or near Volta Redonda, through nice mountain scenery.

Directory **Banks** *Banco 24 Horas*, R do Comércio 250, *Bradesco*, R do Comércio 196. **Hospitals & medical services** *Santa Casa*, R Dr Coutinho 84, T3650131. **Tourist information** Largo da Lapa, opposite the bus station, T3651175, ext 2186. Very good.

Ilha Grande

Phone code: 021
Colour map 4, grid C3

A two-hour ferry makes a most attractive trip through the bay to **Vila do Abraão**, the main village on Ilha Grande. If you have a couple of days to spare, the island is definitely worth a visit because it encapsulates most of what the name 'Emerald Coast' suggests. It is mountainous, covered in Atlantic forest, surrounded by transparent green waters and largely unspoiled. The weather is best from March to June; it is best to avoid the peak summer months. In fact, visit the island soon, before it becomes overdeveloped.

History Ilha Grande remained relatively untouched by the pressures of development because of what has been called "a strange protection afforded by the forces of evil". It was once an infamous lair for European pirates, then a landing stage for slaves. In the 19th century, it was the site of a leper colony (which we should call unfortunate, rather than evil now). In the 20th century one of Brazil's larger high security prisons deterred visitors. A famous inmate was the writer Graciliano Ramos (see **Literature**, page 779), whose *Memórias do cárcere* relate his experiences. The prison was closed in 1994 and is now overgrown rubble.

In the past, sugar cane and coffee were cultivated on parts of the island, but now most of it is a state park, including the **Reserva Biológica da Praia do Sul**. The main industry is fishing. Cars are not allowed on the island, so transport is either by boat, or on foot.

Beaches & There are about 100 beaches around the island, about three dozen of which are
excursions regular tourist spots. Those on the landward side are good for watersports, diving is good around most of the coast, there is fishing and some surfing. From Vila do Abraão there are trails to most of the beaches, but it is much less effort to go by boat. Even so, some parts of the island are a long journey.

Popular excursions include: the 20-minute walk from Abraão to the peaceful and clean beach at Abraãozinho. Another two hours in the same direction will take you to Palmas beach, which is also calm, and another 20 minutes to Lopes Mendes, good for surfing. This beach can be reached by boat, too, as can other lovely beaches: Lagoa Azul, with crystal clear water and excellent snorkelling, Freguesia de Santana and Saco do Céu.

To Provetá, at the eastern end, for instance, it takes 6½ hours by boat. You can ask in the port at Angra dos Reis for a fishing boat going to Provetá, where you can stay in boat sheds or, if lucky, with a fisherman. It is a beautiful village, from which you can walk through tropical forest over the mountain to Praia do Aventureiro (a day's leisurely walk each way), or go by boat. Take mosquito precautions when walking in the forest.

A couple of good treks are over the mountains to Dois Rios, where the old jail was situated. There is still a settlement of former prison guards here who have nowhere to go. The walk is about 13 kilometres one way and takes about three hours; beautiful scenery and superb views. You can also hike to Pico do Papagaio (980 metres) through forest; a stiff, three hours climb for which a guide is essential. The view from the top is breathtaking. Pico da Pedra d'Água (1,031 metres) can also be climbed.

A *Fazenda Paraíso do Sol*, Praia Saco das Palmas (full board), 2 hours' walk from Abraão, or 40 minutes by boat, for reservations in Rio T2621226. Hotel reservations are necessary. Many new *pousadas* have been opened, most in Abraão: eg, in our **A** range on R da Praia: *Água Viva*, No 26, T/F9862519, *Solar da Praia*, No 32, T9863396 and *Tropicana*, No 28, T99896609, T024-3522073 for reservations. French run. Recommended, good but expensive open-air restaurant. **B** *Pousada da Vanda*, R Antônio Moreira 95, T2852429. In green surroundings. **B** *Pousada do Canto*, 2 blocks from centre, T5950940/97747871. Quiet location, good value. **B** *Beto's*, T7801202, central. Recommended. **B** *Hotel Ori*, R Prof Lima. Recommended. **B** *Sonia/Tuti*, R Antônio Moreira 80, 5 minutes from the beach, T654512. A small house with 2 rooms to let. Recommended. **B** *Albatroz*, R das Flores 108, T6271730. Recommended. **C** *Pousada Canto Verde*, near cemetery, T5940225. English spoken, 5 rooms with fan and bath, welcoming, good breakfast. **C** *Pousada Cachoeira*, at the end of the village. Friendly, run by German-Brazilian couple, English spoken, bungalows in green surroundings, pleasant. **C** *Estalagem Costa Verde*, T0XX11-31047940. Pleasant surroundings near beach, ask for Márcia or Marly. **Youth hostel F** pp *Ilha Grande*, R Pres Vargas, T2646147. Alternatively, you can rent a room in Abraão.

Sleeping

Casa da Sogra, Trav do Beto. Recommended. *Minha Deusa*, R Prof Alice Coury 7, next to church. Brazilian, excellent food, reasonable prices.

Eating

Ferries For boats to Ilha Grande, see above under Angra dos Reis and Mangaratiba. There are 5 ferries called *Isabel*, check which is going to the mainland destination you want. **Boats** Boat trips cost US$10 without food or drinks, but includes fruit. Recommended boats are *Anna Paula*, *Jeremias* (owned by Mario, an Argentine) or *Nina* (owned by 'Baiano'). There is some good scuba diving around the coast but the bottom is becoming littered in places with picnic rubbish. **Bicycles** can be hired and tours arranged; ask at *pousadas*.

Transport

Banks Only open at weekends. **Tourist offices** As you get off the boat. Very helpful. It is run by Angela, who speaks some English and will act as a trekking guide.

Directory

Paraty

Beyond Angra dos Reis the road continues 98 kilometres along the coast. Inland is the **Parque Nacional da Serra da Bocaína** (see page 240). The BR-101 goes past the nuclear-power plant at Itaorna and an array of beaches on the shore of the Baía da Ilha Grande to Paraty, a charming colonial town. The centre has been declared a national historic monument in its entirety. The streets, which are paved with large, irregular stone slabs, have curves to provide ambush points should the town (in colonial times) be attacked by pirates. In the colonial buildings are a great many art galleries, tourist shops and eating places, but none is allowed to impose its presence or disrupt the tranquility of the streets. The hills that surround the town are covered in tropical forest and the coastline has hundreds of beaches within easy reach. Paraty is normally cooler than Rio de Janeiro. The wettest times of year are January-February and June-July.

Population: 27,500
Phone code: 024
Colour map 4, grid C2

Rio de Janeiro

History Paraty was officially founded in the first half of the 17th century. Its name derives from the indigenous word for a small fish common in these waters, called *paratii*. Having a good harbour and a well-worn trail into the interior (used by the Guianas Indians before the Portuguese colonizers), Paraty was a natural choice for a port. Some parts of the old trail can still be walked; ask tour operators (see below). It became the chief port for the export of gold in the 17th century and thus grew rich. Most of its colonial churches date from this period, as do the fortresses which were built to prevent pirates and foreign ships stealing the valuable cargo (see the Forte do Defensor Perpétuo). Walls protected the landward side and the ruins of an old gate can be seen close to the football field at the entrance to town. Commerce prospered and farms around the city produced sugar and fine brands of *cachaça* (the name Paraty is still synonymous with *cachaça*). When a road was built to Rio de Janeiro from the mining regions at the beginning of the 18th century, shortening the journey by some 15 days, Paraty's importance declined.

It recovered in the 19th century as a coffee-exporting port for the *fazendas* of the valley of the Paraíba do Sul. At the same time, through its wharf came the imported European luxuries which furnished the barons' houses. It is now hard to imagine that slaves had to carry French furniture, pianos and fine porcelain over the hills through dense forest.

In the second half of the 19th century, the opening of the railway from the Paraíba Valley to Rio led to Paraty being effectively isolated again. The port being redundant, almost all its inhabitants left. Those that remained grew bananas, but the old sugar plantations were for the most part abandoned. Because so few people stayed in the town, there was no urge to modernize the buildings. In this way, Paraty has become an open air museum.

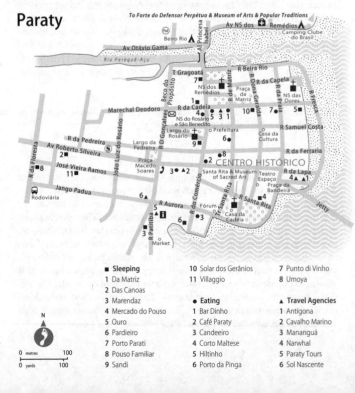

Paraty

■ Sleeping	10 Solar dos Gerânios	7 Punto di Vinho
1 Da Matriz	11 Villaggio	8 Umoya
2 Das Canoas		
3 Marendaz	● Eating	▲ Travel Agencies
4 Mercado do Pouso	1 Bar Dinho	1 Antígona
5 Ouro	2 Café Paraty	2 Cavalho Marino
6 Pardieiro	3 Candeeiro	3 Mananguá
7 Porto Parati	4 Corto Maltese	4 Narwhal
8 Pouso Familiar	5 Hiltinho	5 Paraty Tours
9 Sandi	6 Porto da Pinga	6 Sol Nascente

Only in the 1950s was the town 'rediscovered' as a tourism and cultural centre. It was declared a national historic monument in 1966. Whereas in colonial times Paraty was dependent for its livelihood on the roads across the mountains, in the late 20th century the Rio-Santos road has brought a new prosperity. And even though Paraty is easily accessible to tourists, they only come in great numbers at weekends and on holidays, so the rest of the time it keeps its small-town atmosphere.

In keeping with all Brazilian colonial towns, Paraty's churches were built **Sights** according to social status and race. There are four churches in the town, one for the 'freed coloured men', one for the blacks and two for the whites. **Santa Rita** (1722), built by the 'freed coloured men' in elegant Brazilian baroque, faces the bay and the port. It is probably the most famous 'picture postcard' image of Paraty. It houses an interesting **Museum of Sacred Art**. ■ *Wednesday-Sunday 0900-1200, 1300-1800, entry US$1.* **Nossa Senhora do Rosário e São Benedito** (1725, rebuilt 1757), Rua do Comércio, built by black slaves, is small and simple; the slaves were unable to raise the funds to construct an elaborate building. ■ *Tuesday 0900-1200.* **Nossa Senhora dos Remédios** is the town's parish church, the biggest in Paraty. In fact, the church was never completely finished. Started in 1787, but finished only in 1873, it was built on unstable ground, so the architects decided not to add weight to the structure by putting up the towers. The façade is leaning to the left, which is clear from the three doors: only the one on the right has a step. The church was built with donations from the whites and it is rumoured that a certain Dona Geralda Maria da Silva contributed with gold from a pirate's hoard found buried on the beach. ■ *Monday, Wednesday, Friday, Saturday 0900-1200, Sunday 0900-1500.* **Capela de Nossa Senhora das Dores** (1800) is a small chapel facing the sea. It was used mainly by the wealthy whites in the 19th century. ■ *Thursday 0900-1200.*

There is a great deal of distinguished Portuguese colonial architecture in delightful settings. **Rua do Comércio** is the main street in the historical centre. It was here that the prominent traders lived, the two-storey houses having the commercial establishments on the ground floor and the residences above. Nowadays the houses are occupied by restaurants, *pousadas* and curio shops.

The **Casa da Cadeia**, close to Santa Rita church, is the former jail. It belongs to the Secretaria da Cultura e Turismo and is being converted into a historical museum. Note the iron grilles in the windows and doors.

On the northern headland is a small fort, **Forte do Defensor Perpétuo**, built in 1822. The cannons and the ruins of the thick walls can be seen. From the fort there are good views of the sea and the roofs of the town. To get there, cross the Rio Perequê Açu by the bridge at the end of the Rua do Comércio; climb the small hill, which has some nice *pousadas* and a cemetery, and follow the signs to 'Forte'. It's about 15 minutes' walk from the centre. Also here is the **Museum of Arts and Popular Traditions** in a colonial-style building. It contains carved wooden canoes, musical instruments, fishing gear and other handmade items from local communities. In 1997 it was closed for repairs to the damage done by termites. Also on the headland is the gunpowder store and, set in the grass, enormous hemispherical iron pans which were used for extracting whale oil to use in lamps and to mix with sand and cement for building.

The town centre is out of bounds for motor vehicles; heavy chains are strung across the entrance to the streets. In spring the roads are flooded, while the houses are above the water level.

Rio de Janeiro

Excursions **Beaches** **Praia do Pontal**, 10 minutes' walk, is not very clean; **Praia do Forte** and **Praia do Jabaquara** are worth visiting. There are other beaches further from town, many of which make worthwhile excursions. **Paraty Mirim**, a small town 27 kilometres away with old buildings and nice beaches, is reached by four buses a day (three on Sunday).

There are several waterfalls (*cachoeiras*) in the area, such as the **Cachoeira da Penha**, near the church of the same name. It is 10 kilometres from town on the road to Cunha; take a local bus from the rodoviária, US$1. There are good mountain views on the way. The tourist office and travel agencies (see below) can give details on trips to waterfalls and other hikes, plus information on boat trips around the bays and islands (good value, US$10 per day, lunch extra).

Fazenda Murycana, an old sugar estate and 17th century *cachaça* distillery, is a recommended excursion. You can taste and buy the different types of *cachaça*; some are aged in oak barrels for 12 years (try the *cachaça com cravo e canela*, with clove and cinnamon). The original house and water-wheel are still there. There is an excellent restaurant and horse riding is available. English is not spoken by the employees. Mosquitoes can be a problem at the *fazenda*, take repellent and don't wear shorts. Take a Penha/Ponte Branca bus from the rodoviária, four a day; alight where it crosses a small white bridge and then walk 10 minutes along a signed, unpaved road. Returning to Paraty, there is a good chance of hitching a lift.

Sleeping

■ on map, page 182
Price codes: see inside
front cover
There are a great many
pousadas, more than
we can mention here. If
you have time and you
are here midweek when
hotels are not at a
premium, look around
and find a place that
suits you best

AL *Pousada do Sandi*, Largo do Rosário 1, T3712100, F3711236. 18th century building, charming, spacious rooms. **AL** *Pousada do Ouro*, R Dr Pereira (or da Praia) 145, in the historical centre, T/F3712221, ouro@contracthor.com.br. **A** *Pousada Pardieiro*, R do Comércio 74, T3711370, F3711139. Attractive colonial building with lovely gardens, delightful rooms facing internal patios, extremely pleasant, swimming pool, calm, sophisticated atmosphere, but always full at weekends, does not take children under 15. **A** *Pousada Porto Parati*, R do Comércio, T3711205, F3712111. Good value. Highly recommended. **A** *Pousada do Príncipe*, Roberto Silveira 289, T3712266, F3712120. Belongs to descendents of the former imperial family, lovely atmosphere with genuine works of art from the Brazilian Empire, all facilities, pool. Highly recommended. **A** *das Canoas*, R Silveira 279, T3711133, F3712005. Pool. Recommended. **A** *Morro do Forte*, R Orlando Carpinelli, T/F3711211. Lovely garden, good breakfast, pool, German owner Peter Kallert offers trips on his yacht. Recommended. **A** *Pousada do Portal*, Av Beira-Rio 100, T3712221. Charming, but some distance from the centre, relaxing. **A** *Pousada do Forte*, Al Princesa Isabel 33, Pontal, on the way to the fort, T/F3711462. **B** *Pousada Capitão*, R Luiz do Rosário 18, T3711416, www.paraty. com.br/capitao.htm. Charming, close to historical centre, swimming pool, English and Japanese spoken. **B** *Pousada Mercado do Pouso*, Largo de Santa Rita 43, close to the port and Santa Rita, T/F3711114. Recommended. **B** *Pousada do Corsário*, Beco do Lapeiro 26, T3711866, F3711319. A/c, TV, fridge, pool. Recommended. **B** *Pousada Villaggio*, R José Vieira Ramos 280, between historical centre and rodoviária, T3711870. Pleasant, pool, garden, good. **C** *Pouso Familiar*, R José Vieira Ramos 262, near bus station, T3711475. Run by Belgian (Joseph Yserbyt) and his Brazilian wife (Lucia), laundry facilities, English, French, German and Flemish spoken. Recommended. **C** *Solar dos Gerânios*, Praça da Matriz, T/F3711550. Beautiful colonial building, hard beds, but recommended.

D *Marendaz*, R Patitiba 9, close to the historical centre, T3711369. Family-run, simple, charming. **D** *Pousada da Matriz*, R da Cadeia, close to corner of R do Comércio, in historic centre. Basic but clean rooms, with bath, without breakfast, friendly if a little noisy. **D** *Pousada Miramar*, Abel de Oliveira 19, T3712132. One room has its own kitchen, good value. Recommended. **D** *Tia Palminas Lua Nova*, R Mcal Deodoro. Cheap, pleasant, central.

Outside Paraty If arriving by car, there are 2 good options for staying outside the town: *Refúgio das Caravelas*, Praia da Boa Vista, T/F3711270, 5 km south, on seafront with its own harbour and scuba diving facilities; **B** *Le Gite d'Indaiatiba*, access from Km 172 BR-101, 20 km away. Country *pousada* with chalets, waterfalls and forest, French owner, superb cuisine. Both places can be reached by taxi from the rodoviária.

Camping *Camping Club do Brasil*, Av Orlando Carpinelli, Praia do Pontal. Small, good, very crowded in January and February, US$8 pp, T3711877. Also at Praia Jabaquara, T3712180. *Camping Beira-Rio*, just across the bridge, before the road to the fort.

The best dishes to try in Paraty are those with seafood, eg *peixe à Parati* (local fish cooked with herbs, green bananas and served with *pirão*, a mixture of manioc flour and the sauce that the fish was cooked in); also popular is the *filé de peixe ao molho de camarão* (fried fish filet with a shrimp and tomato sauce). A recommended appetizer is *aipim frito*, fried pieces of manioc, which look like French fries. The *caipirinhas* in Paraty are among the best in Brazil because they include the excellent local *cachaça*. *do Hiltinho*, R Mcal Deodoro 233, historical centre, T/F3711432. Local dishes. Excellent seafood, good service, expensive but worth it. *Corto Maltese*, R do Comércio 130. Italian, pasta. *Punto Divino*, R Mcal Deodoro 129. Excellent Italian. *Dona Ondina*, R do Comércio 2, by the river. Family restaurant, well-prepared simple food, good value (closed on Monday between March and November). *Café Parati*, R da Lapa and Comércio. Sandwiches, appetizers, light meals, also bar at weekends with live music. *Candeeiro*, R da Lapa 335. Good local food. The less expensive restaurants, those offering *comida a quilo* (pay by weight) and the fast food outlets are outside the historical centre, mainly on Av Roberto Silveira. *Bar do Turquinho*, on the side street off Av Roberto Silveira opposite the petrol station. Tasty and cheap *prato do dia*.

Kontiki, Ilha Duas Irmãs, an island 5 minutes from the harbour where a stand offers trips for US$2.50 return, T9999599, www.paraty.com.br/kontiki.htm. Wonderful view, seafood, main courses US$13.50-25, bar, private beach. Recommended.

Eating
● *on map, page 182*

Umoya, R Comendador José Luiz. Video bar and café, live music at weekends. *Bar Dinho*, Praça da Matriz at R da Matriz. Good bar with live music at weekends, sometimes mid-week. *Clube Bandeirantes*, for dancing (Friday Brazilian, Saturday funk, Sunday dance and disco music), an interesting place to meet local people, popular, entry US$3-5.

Bars & nightclubs

Theatre *Teatro Espaço*, *The Puppet Show*, R Dona Geralda 327, T3711575, F3711161, ecparati@ax.apc.org. Wednesday, Saturday 2100, US$8.50. This world-famous puppet show should not be missed. The puppets tell stories, without words, which are funny, sad, even shocking, with incredible realism. It is high quality theatre of an unusual kind.

Entertainment

February/March: *Carnival*, hundreds of people cover their bodies in black mud and run through the streets yelling like prehistoric creatures (anyone can join in). **March/April:** *Semana Santa*, with religious processions and folk songs. **Mid-July:** *Semana de Santa Rita*, traditional foods, shows, exhibitions and dances. **August:** *Festival da Pinga*, the *cachaça* fair at which local distilleries display their products and there are plenty of opportunities to over-indulge. **September (around the 8th):** *Semana da Nossa Senhora dos Remédios*, processions and religious events. **September/October:** *Spring Festival of Music*, concerts in front of Santa Rita church. The city is decorated with lights for Christmas. **31 December:** *Reveillon*, a huge party with open-air concerts and fireworks (reserve accommodation in advance). As well as the Dança dos Velhos (see **Music and dance**, page 771), another common dance in these parts is the *ciranda*, in which everyone, young and old, dances in a circle to songs accompanied by guitars.

Festivals

Shopping The town has plenty of handicraft and souvenir shops. The most interesting items are the small, wooden canoes and boats, oars carved in wood with peculiar designs and colourful T-shirts. You can find paintings and painted wall tiles. Don't forget to buy a bottle of *cachaça*; there are shops such as **Porto da Pinga**, R da Matriz. All the local brands are good, but if you are visiting the distilleries, don't hesitate to buy there (see *Fazenda Murycana* above).

Transport **Buses** Paraty has a new rodoviária at the corner of R Jango Padua and R da Floresta.
On holidays and in high Nine buses a day go to **Rio** (241 km, 3¾ hours, US$8.10, *Costa Verde* – see under Angra
season, the frequency of dos Reis for details – only the 0630 from Rio and the 1730 from Paraty go through
bus services usually Barra da Tijuca); to **Angra dos Reis** (98 km, 1½ hours, every 1 hour 40 minutes, US$4);
increases 3 a day to **Ubatuba** (75 km, just over 1 hour, *São José* company, US$4), **Taubaté** (170 km) and **Guaratinguetá** (210 km); 2 a day to **São Paulo**, 1100 and 2335 (304 km via São José dos Campos, 5½ hours, US$8.50, *Reunidas*, booked up quickly, very busy at weekends), and **São Sebastião**.

Directory **Banks** *Banco do Brasil*, Av Roberto Silveira, not too far from the bus station. Exchange 1100-1430, ask for the manager. **Communications** **Post Office:** R da Cadeia and Beco do Propósito, 0800-1700, Sun 0800-1200. **Telecommunications:** International calls, Praça Macedo Soares, opposite the tourist office. Local and long distance calls can be made from public phones; buy phone cards from the newspaper stand by the tourist information centre. **Hospital & medical services** *Hospital Municipal São Pedro de Alcântara* (Santa Casa), Av Dom Pedro de Alcântara, T3711623. **Tour companies & travel agents** *Antígona*, Praça da Bandeira 2, Centro Histórico, T/F3711165. Daily schooner tours, 5 hrs, bar and lunch on board. Recommended. *Paraty Tours*, Av Roberto Silveira 11, T/F711327. English and Spanish spoken. *Sol Nascente*, Av Roberto Silveira 58, T/F711536. *Manangud*, R Domingos Gonçalves de Abreu 3, T712188. All can arrange schooner trips, city tours, trekking in the rain forest and on the old gold trail, visits to Trindade beach, mountain biking, sugar estate visits and transfers. *Narwhal*, T3711399, and *Cavalho Marinho*, R da Lapa, T/F3712148, offer diving. *Soberana da Costa*, T3711114, and others offer schooner trips in the bay, US$15-US$20, 6 hrs, meals sometimes included. Recommended. *Fausto Goyos*, T99145506, offers off-road tours in an ex-US military jeep to rainforest, waterfalls, historical sites, also photo safaris, He also has highly professional horse riding tours and offers lodging in youth-hostel style rooms for US$5, or US$7.50 with 2 meals. **Tourist offices** *Centro de Informações Turísticas*, Av Roberto Silveira, near the entrance to the historical centre, T371266 ext 218. The website www.paraty.com.br has lots of information. **Voltage** 110 volts.

The coast road continues from Paraty into the State of São Paulo through the Serra do Mar. At the state border, the sea becomes visible again and the route is as attractive as before. The road passes the **Parque Estadual Serra do Mar**. Another road, rough but scenic, climbs the Serra do Mar to Cunha and Guaratinguetá, also in São Paulo.

São Paulo

4

São Paulo

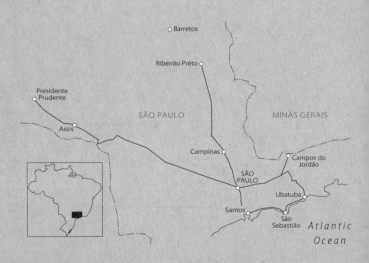

The State of São Paulo is the industrial heart of Brazil as well as being strong in agricultural products. Its capital São Paulo is one of the largest cities in the world and Brazil's undisputed business and finance centre. It is also one of the most cosmopolitan, in both its large immigrant communities and in the varied cuisine of its fine restaurants. Sometimes described as a tropical New York it has excellent art collections and much else of cultural interest. All types of music from heavy metal to rave as well as more local rhythms can be found in its fervent nightlife. It is also home to the famous Butantã Snake Farm and the Brazilian Grand Prix.

Nearby Santos is the largest port in Latin America and a popular destination for cruise liners. There are many fine beaches along the coast especially around São Sebastião and Ilhabela. Inland there are hill resorts such as Campos do Jordão and an important area of caves in the Vale do Ribeiro on the border with Paraná. In the interior of the State, the town of Barretos plays host to the largest rodeo in the world.

Background

History

The history of São Paulo state and São Paulo city were very much one and the same from the arrival of the Europeans until the coffee boom transformed the region's economic and political landscape. According to Hemming (*Red Gold*, see page 762), there were approximately 196,000 indigenous Indians living in what is now São Paulo state. The most numerous were the various groups of Tupi-speaking Indians, such as the Tupinikin, who lived on the coast, on the plateau and in the Paraíba valley. Also on the coast were the Tamoio. The Guarani-speaking Indians of the region were known by the colonizers as the Carijó. In all, Hemming lists eight different groups. Today there are none.

The first official settlement was São Vicente on the coast, near today's port of Santos. It was founded in 1532 by Martim Afonso de Sousa, who had been sent by King João III to drive the French from Brazilian waters, explore the coast and lay claim to all the lands apportioned to Portugal under the Treaty of Tordesillas. Martim Afonso decided to base himself here, rather than near the Portuguese settlement at Bahia, because of favourable geographical and climatic conditions. He was also attracted by the presence of a Portugese man, João Ramalho, who was living with the Indians on the plateau behind the Serra do Mar. Ramalho had been rescued from the beach by the Indians in 1510; it is not documented how he got there. His relationship with the Indians was so strong (son-in-law of Chief Tibiriçá, respected fighter) that he did not fully cooperate with Martim Afonso, but he was extremely useful as an ally and interpreter. Ramalho's village was called Piratininga, which became incorporated into the captaincy of São Vicente. Its name was later changed to Santo André.

In 1554 two Jesuit priests from São Vicente, Blessed José Anchieta and Padre Manuel Nóbrega, founded São Paulo as a *colégio*, a combined mission and school. It was just 15 kilometres from Piratininga, with which it merged in 1562, largely as protection against Indian attack. The Jesuits chose to settle inland because they wished to distance themselves from the civil authority, which was based in Bahia, but was extending up and down the coast to form a defendable colony. Moreover, on the plateau there was much easier access to Indians to convert to Catholicism. Since the São Vicente captaincy was constantly at war with the Tamoio to the north and the São Paulo/Piratininga settlement had eliminated most of the Indians in its immediate vicinity, the need to look further into the continent for Indians was pressing.

This was one factor which led to São Paulo becoming a centre for exploration of the Brazilian hinterland. Another was that the settlers were a resilient breed who shared a vision of wealth which inspired them to penetrate the vast lands around them. So, in parallel with the Jesuit urge to win souls for the faith ran a drive to capture Indians to work on the Paulistas' own farms. The settlers also intermarried with the Indians. Subsequently, Indians were taken to sell as slaves to other parts of Brazil. In due course, the prime target for these enslaving expeditions became the Jesuit missions in Spanish-controlled territory and the Portuguese Jesuits' opposition to this trade carried little weight. The second main stimulus for the Paulistas' journeys into the interior was the search for precious metals and gemstones. This long period of expeditions which pushed the frontiers of Portuguese territory further and further into Brazil was the era of the *bandeira* (see box, page 192).

In a sense, the *bandeirantes'* success in discovering gold led to a demise of São Paulo in the 18th century. Like everywhere else, the inhabitants rushed to the gold fields in the *sertão*, causing ruin at home and allowing São Paulo to fall under the influence of Rio de Janeiro. After the *bandeira* movement the inhabitants of the Paulista plateau concentrated on trade with their neighbours. The relative backwardness of the region lasted until the second half of the 19th century when coffee spread west from Rio de Janeiro. Landowners became immensely rich. São Paulo changed from a little town into a financial and residential centre. Exports and imports flowed through Santos and the industrial powerhouse of the country was born. As the city boomed, industries and agriculture fanned outwards to the far reaches of the state.

Between 1885 and the end of the century the boom in coffee and the arrival of large numbers of Europeans transformed the state out of all recognition. By the end of the 1930s there had arrived in São Paulo state a million Italians, 500,000 each of Portuguese and immigrants from the rest of Brazil, nearly 400,000 Spaniards and nearly 200,000 Japanese. It is the world's largest Japanese community outside Japan.

The first Japanese arrived in 1908, under contract to grow coffee, but it was not a successful immigration. After World War I families began to arrive in greater numbers and they adapted to the living and working conditions of Brazil. Their main contribution to the economy of São Paulo is in horticulture, raising poultry and in cotton farming, especially around cities such as Marília.

In the early 20th century, significant numbers of Syrian-Lebanese came to São Paulo, adding an extra dimension to the cultural diversity of the city. At the time, their homeland was part of the Turkish Empire, so they were called *turcos*. They are associated mostly with retail activities such as the dry goods business.

These immigrants added new cultural aspects to a society with a strong sense of identity. Whereas São Paulo started life as a community whose members sought their livelihood by moving outwards, it grew in the 20th century into a giant which sucked in everything.

Geography

The state of São Paulo, with an area of 247,898 square kilometres, is larger than the states of New York and Pennsylvania together and about the same size as Great Britain and Northern Ireland. Its population is over 35 million.

A narrow zone of wet tropical lowland along the coast rises in an unbroken slope to the ridge of the Great Escarpment – the Serra do Mar – at from 800 to 900 metres above sea level. The upland beyond the Great Escarpment is drained westwards by the tributaries of the Rio Paraná. The broad valleys of the uplands are surmounted by ranges of low mountains; one such range lies between the São Paulo basin and the hinterland of the state. West of the low mountains between the basin and the rest of the state lie the uplands of the Paraná Plateau, at about 600 metres above the sea. One of the soils in this area is the *terra roxa*, the red earth in which coffee flourishes. When dry it gives off a red dust which colours everything; when wet it is sticky and slippery.

The predominant vegetation of the state was originally tropical forest, with a belt of Mata Atlântica on the slopes of the Serra do Mar which receive higher rainfall than the interior. The Atlantic forest has been destroyed in all but the most

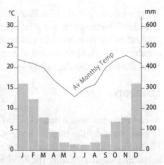

Climate:
São Paulo State

São Paulo

The Bandeirantes

Reviled in some quarters for their appalling treatment of Indians, revered in others for their determination and willingness to withstand extreme hardship in the pursuit of their goals, the bandeirantes are an indispensible element in the formation of Brazil.

The Portuguese knew that South America held great riches; their Spanish rivals were shipping vast quantities back to Europe from Peru. They also knew soon after setting up their colonies on the Atlantic side of the continent that Brazil was not readily yielding up equivalent wealth. Legends proliferated of mountains of precious stones, golden lakes and other marvels, also of terrifying places, all in the mysterious interior. Regardless of the number of expeditions sent into the sertão which returned empty-handed, or failed to return at all, there was always the promise of silver, emeralds or other jewels to lure the adventurous beyond the coast.

The one thing that Brazil had in abundance was Indians. Throughout the colony there was a demand for slaves to work the plantations and farms and the indigenous population satisfied the need for labour. This was especially true in the early 17th century when Portugal temporarily lost its African possession of Angola, from which it sent many slaves to Brazil.

The men who settled in São Paulo, both

the Europeans and those of mixed parentage, the mamelucos, proved themselves expert at enslaving Indians. Without official sanction, and certainly not blessed by the Jesuits, these adventurers formed themselves into expeditions which would leave São Paulo, often for years at a time, to capture slaves for the internal market. The Guaraní Indians who had been organized into reducciones by the Jesuits around the Río Paraguay were the top prize and there developed an intense rivalry between the bandeirantes and the Jesuits. The priests regarded the Paulistas as murderous and inhumane; the slavers felt they had some justification in attacking the missions because they were in Spanish territory and, in the 17th century, the entire western boundary of Brazil was in dispute.

This was one side of the coin. The other was that the bandeirantes were incredibly resourceful, trekking for thousands of kilometres, withstanding great hardships, travelling light, inspired not just by the desire to get rich, but also by a fierce patriotism. They certainly did show barbaric treatment to the Indians, but the enthusiasm that inspired the slave drives combined well with the desire to demystify the sertão, to uncover its riches. It was this which fuelled the prospecting expeditions after Angola had been recaptured in 1648. The bandeirantes trekked into Minas

inaccessible places and the tropical forest has mostly given way to agriculture. In the south of the state, adjoining Paraná, is a zone of pine (araucaria) forest. A small part of the interior is a transitional zone between the tropical forest and the *cerrado* (see page 753) which covers most of central Minas Gerais.

Climate
Tropical climate at an altitude of around 850m above sea level

There is ample rainfall in São Paulo state; indeed, the highest rainfall in Brazil (3,810 millimetres) is over a small area between Santos and São Paulo; at São Paulo itself it is no more than 1,194 millimetres. Temperatures on the plateau are about 5°C lower than on the coast, but it is only south of the latitude of Sorocaba that frosts occur and then not frequently.

Economy

As elsewhere in colonial Brazil, the first agricultural efforts were the cultivation of sugar cane on the tropical lowlands of the coast at São Vicente. On the Piratininga plateau, the settlers were farmers, growing cotton, sugar, wheat and fruit, and raising cattle. The *bandeirantes* opened up the interior, but it was

Gerais, Goiás and Mato Grosso looking for precious metals. Through their efforts, the Minas Gerais gold rush began. They were also enlisted by governors in the northeast to wage war on Indians and they were involved in the destruction of the quilombo *at Palmares (see page 488).*

The principal effect of the expansionist spirit of the *bandeira* movement was that the interior of Brazil was explored. In the bandeirantes' *footsteps came settlers and cattle herders who took over the lands that had been emptied of their Indian population. Although Indians were exploited as labour and became a source of income for the Paulistas, they also intermarried with the Europeans. The mixed-race mamelucos and even Indians themselves took part in the bandeiras, hastening the miscegenation process which became so evident throughout Brazil. Portuguese control of territory was extended by the* bandeirantes' *journeys. In their later phase, these journeys also filled Portugal's coffers because much of the wealth derived from the discovery of gold was sent back to Europe.*

Terminology *There are several explanations of the meaning the name* bandeira. *The Paulistas' expeditions into the interior were not called* bandeiras *until the 1630s (the term* bandeirante *was not used until the mid-18th century). Originally they were called* entradas *(entries),* viagens *or* jornadas *(journeys),* companhias *(companies),* descobrimentos *(discoveries),* occasionally *frotas (fleets). When given official sanction they were called* guerras *(wars). It should be noted that the treks did not only set out from São Paulo, they also entered the* sertão *from Bahia, Pernambuco, Maranhão and along the Amazon. Some historians attribute different names to the expeditions according to their departure point. But what exactly was a* bandeira? *Some say that the name comes from the flag or insignia carried by the adventurers. Others claim that the name has its origins in one of a variety of types of military troop: a band of men raised by a captain or caudillo; a small assault group or raiding party detached from a larger force; a form of medieval municipal militia. For another aspect of the* bandeira, *see the box on the Monsoons, page .*

Further reading *There is a great deal of literature about the* bandeiras. *Easily accessible are chapters 12 and 13 of John Hemming,* Red Gold, *and Richard M Morse (editor),* The Bandeirantes, *which collects together essays and documents by a number of authors on the subject. For full references, see page 87.*

the arrival of coffee after 1850 which really thrust the agricultural frontiers west and north. In the second half of the 19th century, the coffee *fazendas* were concentrated in the valley of the Rio Paraíba and north of São Paulo through Campinas and Riberão Preto. From 1900 to 1950 coffee spread almost to the far west of the state, reaching the far southwest after 1950. Temperatures are too low for coffee in the São Paulo basin itself, but the state produces, on average, about seven million bags a year. Today the state's agriculture is extremely diversified. Coffee either shares the land with other crops or has been entirely substituted by cereals and especially soya. Also of great importance are sugar, rice, cotton, oranges (for juice) and other fruit. Beef cattle, pigs and poultry are the main livestock. In all, the state produces some 20 percent of Brazil's agricultural output.

São Paulo state accounts for 65 percent (40 percent in São Paulo city alone) of Brazil's industrial production. It is one of the principal industrial complexes of the continent with the main activities being textiles, pharmaceuticals, chemical products, automobiles, metallurgical and mechanical industries and foodstuffs. Campinas, 99 kilometres from São Paulo, is the third largest industrial centre in the country (after the state capital itself and Rio de Janeiro). Cities in the centre-west of the state, such as Ribeirão Preto and São José do Rio Preto, are dedicated to the industrialization of the area's agricultural production. The state of São Paulo provides 33 percent of the total exports of Brazil and takes 40 percent of the total imports.

São Paulo

Ins and outs

Getting there

Air Almost all international flights stop at Cumbica international airport at Guarulhos 30 km from the city. Some internal flights from Belo Horizonte and Vitória as well as the shuttle from Rio de Janeiro land at Congonhas airport a short taxi ride from the city centre.

From Guarulhos there are airport taxis which charge US$30 on a ticket system (go to the second booth on leaving the terminal and book a Co-op taxi at the Taxi Comum counter, the best value). *Emtu* bus service every 30 minutes to Praça da República, US$6.50, 30-45 minutes, 0500-0200, very comfortable (buy ticket at the booth in Domestic Arrivals); the same company runs services from Guarulhos to Tietê (every 45 minutes, 0500-0200), Congonhas airport (hourly 0500-0200) and Avenida Paulista (0645-2315 every 45 minutes, passing in front of, or near many major hotels on its route to the city: *Brasilton, Cá d'Oro, Caesar Park, Della Volpe, Crowne Plaza, Sheraton, Maksoud Plaza*). Inter-airport bus US$6.50.

Buses Most buses arrive at the Tietê rodoviária. There is a Metrô and buses to the centre. US$0.60. Buses cost US$0.80. Taxis to Praça da República cost US$5, US$9 at weekends. Buses from southern São Paulo state and many destinations in Paraná arrive at Barra Funda while buses from Minas Gerais arrive at Bresser bus terminals. Buses from Santos and the coast arrive at Jabaquara bus station. All are connected to the centre by Metrô.

Getting around

See also Transport, page 219

The centre is easily visited on foot but other areas of interest are often some way from here. To visit them the best and cheapest way is to use the excellent Metrô system, which is clean, safe, cheap and efficient, as bus routes can be confusing for visitors and slow due to frequent traffic jams. Buses are normally crowded and rather slow, but clean. City bus fare is R$1.15 (or US$0.60). Maps of the bus and metrô system are available at depots, eg Anhangabaú. Some city bus routes are run by trolley buses.

Orientation & safety São Paulo is so vast that it would be foolish to try to tell the visitor how to get to know the whole place. Besides, for most visitors there are only a few parts of the city that he or she will need to be familiar with. These are not that close to each other, so taking some form of public transport will be essential. The areas in question are the centre, Avenida Paulista and the Jardins district, the Cidade Universitária and Butantã, possibly Morumbi and then one or two individual places like the bus stations and airports. Business visitors may also need to know other parts of the city outside the main tourist areas. In addition, there are various excursions that can be made.

Districts The shopping, hotel and restaurant centre embraces the districts of Avenida São Luís, the Praça da República, and Rua Barão de Itapetininga. The central commercial district, containing banks, offices and shops, is known as the Triângulo, bounded by Ruas Direita, 15 (Quinze) de Novembro, São Bento and Praça Antônio Prado, but it is rapidly spreading towards the Praça da República. A large part of the Triângulo and the area between it and Praça da República is mostly closed to cars.

Rua Augusta begins close to Avenida São Luís, extends as far as Avenida Paulista, and continues beyond into one of the most affluent areas, Jardins. Both sides of Rua Augusta have a variety of shops, snackbars and restaurants, but the Jardins side contains the more exclusive boutiques and fashion houses, while the part which leads to the centre is a rather curious but colourful mix of seedy bars, saunas and five-star hotels. Some businesses have moved away from Rua Augusta, possibly because of the growth of shopping centres, which has detracted from the area. Avenida Paulista, once the home of coffee barons and São Paulo's wealthy citizens, is now Brazil's largest financial centre housing most banking head offices (most consulates as well), and the Museu de Arte de São Paulo (see below). It has become a new downtown area, more dynamic, but considerably less colourful than the old centre. Set to replace

Orientation

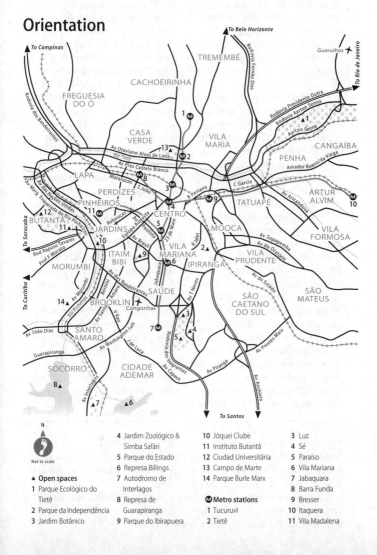

	4 Jardim Zoológico &	10 Jóquei Clube	3 Luz
	Simba Safári	11 Instituto Butantã	4 Sé
N	5 Parque do Estado	12 Ciudad Universitária	5 Paraíso
Not to scale	6 Represa Billings	13 Campo de Marte	6 Vila Mariana
	7 Autodromo de	14 Parque Burle Marx	7 Jabaquara
▲ **Open spaces**	Interlagos		8 Barra Funda
1 Parque Ecológico do	8 Represa de	Ⓜ **Metro stations**	9 Bresser
Tietê	Guarapiranga	1 Tucuruvi	10 Itaquera
2 Parque da Independência	9 Parque do Ibirapuera	2 Tietê	11 Vila Madalena
3 Jardim Botânico			

Getting around São Paulo

The story goes that Ayrton Senna was such a great Formula One driver because he learned to drive on the streets of São Paulo. I can believe it. Indeed it is difficult to decide who is most at risk, pedestrians, car drivers or bus passengers; accidents are all too frequent and can reduce a city already stretched to the limit to total gridlock in a matter of minutes. Returning to São Paulo for the first time in six years I was dismayed to find that, despite the introduction of the rodízio system (literally meaning 'taking turns', where only cars with specific number plates are allowed into the city on certain days), the situation has worsened. The cloud of smog hangs heavy in the sky and it is impossible to escape the roar of the traffic anywhere in the city.

If your Portuguese is poor or you lack confidence, it is best to avoid travelling by bus. I have only ever used buses with Brazilian friends and still managed to feel uncomfortable. Back in 1989, São Paulo's Metrô system was a far more pleasant alternative. Clean, efficient and empty, it was the ideal way to travel, provided you only wanted to go north-south, or east-west. It is on the Metr" that you notice the obvious impact of the rodízio; it is still clean and quite efficient, but bursting at the seams. Even away from rush hour it is difficult to find a seat. The Metrô is, however, a form of transport every visitor to São Paulo should experience. Some of the stations resemble cathedrals with polished marble floors and high ceilings and the trains themselves are spotlessly clean and shiny inside and out. Perhaps the most impressive Metrô station is Sé. It is here that the north-south and east-west lines intersect. Hidden deep underneath Praça da Sé in the heart of the old centre, a huge entrance hall throngs with business people, students, tourists and the like. Escalators whisk you down to two different levels to catch your train, passengers alighting on the opposite side to those embarking to avoid the worst of the crush.

The best way to see São Paulo, however, is on foot. Caetano Veloso, the great Brazilian singer-songwriter sang in "Sampa", his homage to the city: "Something happens to my heart every time I cross Ipiranga and Avenida São João". And there can be little doubt that something will happen to a pedestrian's heart: how can you walk on these streets throbbing with life, dwarfed by tower blocs, homes to millionaires and multinationals, without being affected? Much advice is given on how unsafe it is to walk in São Paulo alone and, like any major city, there are dangers, but with a little common sense and forward planning many dangers can be avoided. But you should remember that in São Paulo unpredictable events are a frequent occurrence.

Some parts of the city are undoubtedly more dangerous than others. Resist the temptation to take photographs in Praça da Sé and the area around the Praça da República. If you are going to risk photos, make it very quick. On Friday afternoons there is often live music outside the Catedral Metropolitana on Praça da Sé. This makes the downtown area even more crowded than normal and, since the crowd is predominantly male, can make female visitors feel distinctly uncomfortable. Avoid Parque Ibirapuera early in the morning or evening (during the rest of the day it's fine); hire a bike to see the park at its best. Avenida Paulista is becoming increasingly unsafe late at night.

Naomi Peirce

Avenida Paulista as the main centre, is Avenida Faria Lima, at the southwest edge of Jardins eight kilometres from Praça da República. Newer still is the movement of offices to Avenida Luis Carlos Berrini, which is yet further southwest, parallel to the Avenida das Naçeõs Unidas and the Rio Pinheiros.

Other popular residential areas are Vila Madalena and Pinheiros, both west of the centre. In the latter is Espaço Paulista on Departamento La Cerda Franco 87, with entertainers on Friday and Saturday evenings.

All the rodoviárias (bus stations) are on the Metrô (underground railway), but if travelling with luggage, take a taxi. Both airports can be reached by taxi and by the good bus service run by Emtu (full details are given in **Transport**, page 219).

The box **Getting around São Paulo** gives a personal view of how to approach the city. A couple of further points to bear in mind are: 1) at night you really need to know where you are going. It is best to go by taxi, but if you find yourself on foot be extra careful. For example, the area under and around the Minhocão (the elevated expressway in the centre), west and south of Praça da República, is used as a pick-up zone for sex. One section is used by female prostitutes, another by transvestite prostitutes and another by male prostitutes. The areas are stricly demarcated and all three are best avoided.

2) The simplest way to proceed in São Paulo is with money, for taxis, hotels, good restaurants and nightlife. The Metrô is good, but not extensive. The buses are advocated by some, but not others. You can eat comparatively cheaply for lunchces and snacks and you can buy supplies in supermarkets. There are good restaurants with reasonable prices for sensible portions, but you may have to research this and travel some distance from the main restaurant areas to find them.

3) If you want to drive in São Paulo, good luck! The traffic pattern is extremely exasperating: you may have to drive around ten blocks to reach a point half a block away. It is very easy to get disoriented (even as a passenger). Buy a street plan from a newsstand if you plan to stay any length of time (eg Quatro Roads' São Paulo, Mapograf or Cartoplam – like an A-Z guide). Some street guides give bus routes, which are equally confusing.

Armed mugging unfortunately occurs in the city. To avoid this use taxis late at night and stay out of deserted areas and streets. If you are unlucky and it happens, do not resist. Hand over your valuables without delay and report the theft afterwards. Beware also of pickpocketing. Thieves may use the mustard-on-the-back or similar trick to distract your attention while someone else robs you. The areas around Luz station, Praça da República and Centro are not safe at night, and visitors should not enter *favelas*. The Jardins area below Alameda Lorena is also best avoided on foot at night.

Tourist Police *Deatur*, Av São Luis 91, T2140209 and R 15 de Novembro 347, T3107564/2. Radio Patrol, T190.

Visitors find the characteristic sharp changes of temperature troublesome and even **Climate** Paulistanos seem to catch cold often. The amount of air pollution can be exasperating and thermal inversions, in which a blanket of warm air prevents the dispersal of the industrial and automobile pollutants, are common. In dry weather eyes and nose are continually troubled.

History

Founded in 1554, the original settlement was at the Pátio do Colégio in the centre of the city, where a copy of Anchieta's original church has been built, using one of the surviving mud-packed walls of the original 16th century structure (see below).

Until the 1870s it was a sleepy, shabby little town known as 'a cidade de barro' (the mud city), as most of its buildings were made of clay and packed mud. The city was transformed architecturally at the end of the 19th century when wealthy landowners began to invest in São Paulo. Not only the coffee barons, but also the merchants of Santos, built their *chácaras* in São Paulo and as the houses of the rich and the finance companies grew in number, the city became well-situated, healthy and prosperous. In the early 20th century, outsiders at least regarded São Paulo as the most progressive state in Brazil, in part because its immigration policy welcomed new arrivals, providing for them until work had been found.

São Paulo

One of the main reasons for the city's development lay in its position at the focus of so much agricultural wealth. But the immigrant labour which flooded in during the early years of the 20th century was not only destined for the coffee *fazendas* and farms. The foreigners also went to work in the industries which were opening up in the city. In the main, the urban working classes enjoyed neither good living standards, nor fair working conditions. Bosses exploited the ethnic differences of the immigrant groups to divide the workforce and therefore rule it. Out of this grew a labour movement which, throughout the century, struggled to improve its members' position in the face of frequent brutal repression and widely-differing government attitudes towards labour. Industry continued to expand, helped by the availability of plentiful hydro-electric power, and workers were needed to operate it. Between 1934 and 1938 alone, São Paulo's industrial base grew by 60 percent; by 1941 there were 14,000 factories. To many, this city, like others in Brazil, acted as a magnet for the rural poor who migrated to the urban area in search of work. And so it grew, until nowadays, it covers more than 1,500 square kilometres – three times the size of Paris.

The overall aspect of the place is one of skyscrapers, long avenues, traffic and crowds. Away from the heart of the city, there is a general sense of red earth, brick, rust and blackening concrete; also graffiti. How did they get to some of those places to write their runes? Nevertheless, most of its citizens are proud of São Paulo's high-rise architecture, of its well-lit streets and of the Metrô, but they also mourn the loss of innumerable historical buildings and green areas through short-sighted planning policies in the 1980s. One such is the Minhocão, an elevated expressway which runs around the centre. While it may speed the flow of traffic, those streets which now lie in its shadow have been totally ruined. The inhabitants of the city are called Paulistanos, to differentiate them from the inhabitants of the state, who are called Paulistas.

Sights

Since much of the centre of São Paulo is pedestrianized, there is no option other than to walk if you wish to explore it. This may seem a daunting prospect with the streets permanently crowded and the buildings towering above, but it is a challenge worth taking. (If in doubt about it, ask your hotel reception how best to proceed and where to go.)

There are several places reached by Metrô where one can start a tour of the centre: Praça da Sé, São Bento, Anhangabaú (for the Teatro Municipal) and Praça da República. There is also traffic access to all these places, and to the Pátio do Colégio (another good starting point), so all can be reached by taxi.

A focal point in the centre is the **Parque Anhangabaú**, an open space between the Triângulo (see **Orientation** above) and the streets which lead to Praça da República (Metrô Anhangabaú is at its southern end). Beneath Anhangabaú, north-south traffic is carried by tunnel. Crossing it are two viaducts: **Viaduto do Chá**, which is open to traffic and links Rua Direita and Rua Barão de Itapetininga. Along its length sellers of potions, cures, fortunes and trinkets set up their booths, an incongruous sight in the middle of a district so dedicated to modern commerce. The **Viaduto Santa Ifigênia**, an iron bridge for pedestrians only, connects Largo de São Bento with Largo de Santa Ifigênia. This viaduct was constructed of 1,100 tonnes of Belgian iron between 1910 and 1913. In 1978 it was completely refurbished, including the instalation of 22 traditional ornamental lampposts. As a backdrop to the viaduct and its thousands of pedestrians is the massive frontage of the Sharp building. The Parque Anhangabaú is roughly on the level of a river bed, so it is

Tietê to Liberdade

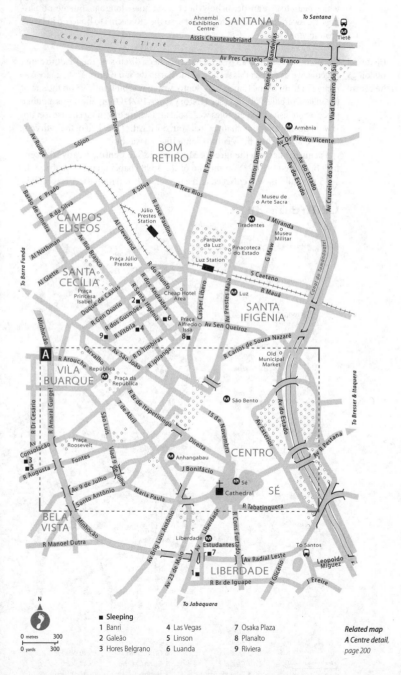

São Paulo

Sleeping

1 Banri	4 Las Vegas	7 Osaka Plaza
2 Galeão	5 Linson	8 Planalto
3 Hores Belgrano	6 Luanda	9 Riviera

Related map
A Centre detail,
page 200

lower than the surrounding streets. This exaggerates the height of the tower blocs, but at the same time it gives a perspective to the skyscrapers themselves. Some of the older high-rise buildings are painted comparatively brightly, which helps to give an idea of how the area was not so long ago. But these buildings are dwarfed by the modern blocks, so the city seems to build up in layers around you.

Historical buildings in the centre For no other reason than that we have just been discussing the Viaduto Santa Ifigênia, we shall start this section at the **Largo de São Bento**. This square was placed in front of the Capela São Bento, which was built in 1598 on the site of the village of chief Tibiriça (see **History**, page 197). Originally it was a public place where fish and vegetables were sold and where travelling circuses set up. It went through various changes in layout during the latter half of the 19th century and again when the Viaduto Santa Ifigênia was built.

Facing the Largo is the **Igreja e Mosteiro de São Bento**, an early 20th-century building (1910-22) on the site of the 1598 chapel mentioned above. In 1635 the building was enlarged and a new church and monastery was built in

Centre detail

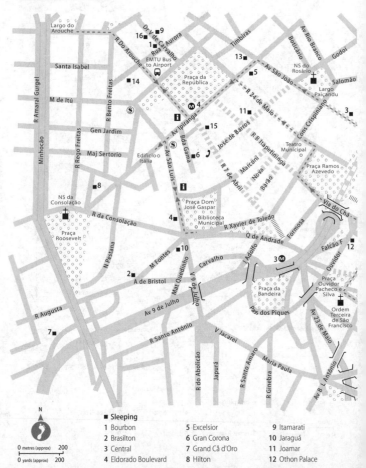

▪ **Sleeping**
1 Bourbon
2 Brasilton
3 Central
4 Eldorado Boulevard
5 Excelsior
6 Gran Corona
7 Grand Cã d'Oro
8 Hilton
9 Itamarati
10 Jaraguá
11 Joamar
12 Othon Palace

1650, financed by the *bandeirante* Fernão Dias Paes Leme. It was reformed on various occasions before being demolished in 1907 to make way for the new church and college. The present church is painted predominantly fawn and maroon inside; the ceilings of the side chapels are blue, with stars. On the main nave's ceiling are religious portraits. The choir stalls are of wood and carved wooden pillars support the organ, which has 6,000 pipes. When the São Bento Metrô station was built, the church had to be reinforced and the Largo was remodelled; the station itself has an exhibition and concert space.

Head due south of São Bento on Rua Líbero Badaró to Avenida São João. At this junction is the **Martinelli building**, the city's first skyscraper. It was built in 1929 by Comendador Giuseppe Martinelli, a businessman, and was restored in 1979. ■ *Monday-Saturday, 0900-1600, entry to 26th floor, free.* If you turn right (west) here, Avenida São João crosses Parque Anhangabaú. It passes the central post office and continues, pedestrianized, to Largo do Paissandu, in which is the chapel of Nossa Senhora do Rosário, which has a completely painted interior. A block beyond Largo do Paissandu is Avenida Ipiranga, which leads to Praça da República.

São Paulo

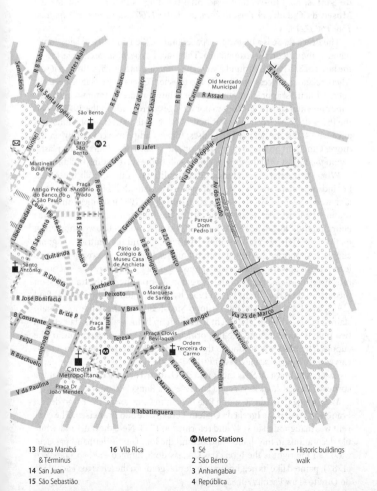

13 Plaza Marabá & Términus	**16** Vila Rica	**M Metro Stations**
14 San Juan		**1** Sé
15 São Sebastião		**2** São Bento
		3 Anhangabau
		4 República

- ▶ - - Historic buildings walk

Back at the Martinelli building, a left turn takes you to Praça Antônio Prado, on which stands the **Antigo Prédio do Banco do São Paulo**. This building, which is two interlinked office blocks, has some art nouveau elements and was constructed in the 1930s. The ground floor is now used for fairs and exhibitions. On the sixth floor is the Secretaria de Esportes e Turismo (see **Tourist offices**, page 224). ■ The building is open Monday-Friday 0900-1800. From Praça Antônio Prado go down Rua 15 de Novembro to Praça Padre Manuel da Nóbrega.

The **Pátio do Colégio** is just east of Praça Padre Manuel da Nóbrega. This is the site of the founding of São Paulo and, as has already been said, the present building is a reconstruction. It houses the **Capela de Anchieta** and the **Museu Casa de Anchieta**. The original chapel collapsed in 1896; it is some of this building that has been preserved in the new complex. ■ *Monday-Friday 0730-1700, US$0.50*. The **Museu Casa de Anchieta**, houses items from the Jesuit era, including paintings and relics. It also has a model of Piratininga/São Paulo in the 16th century museum. ■ *Tuesday-Sunday 1300-1630, US$1*.

A short distance southeast of the Pátio do Colégio is the **Solar da Marquesa de Santos**, an 18th-century residential building, which now contains the **Museu da Cidade**. ■ *Tuesday-Sunday, 0900-1700, Rua Roberto Simonsen 136, T6062218*.

The **Praça da Sé** is a huge open space south of the Pátio do Colégio, dominated by the Catedral Metropolitana. The Praça has been, since colonial times, the heart of São Paulo. Around it were the cathedral and other churches; it was where religious processions started and finished. Over the years its aspect was altered, but most appreciably in 1911 when the whole area was remodelled into a monumental square. Further major changes were made in the 1970s when the Praça da Sé Metrô station was built. Today, with its avenue of palms, it is alive with stalls, music, hawkers, buses, fumes and people constantly on the move. Others sit on the steps or sleep on the grass. The colours of the plastic awnings contrast with the grey, seeping walls of the surrounding buildings.

When you enter the **Catedral Metropolitana**, you leave all the racket behind and enter a massive, peaceful space. The cathedral's foundations were laid over 40 years before its inauguration during the 1954 festivities commemorating the fourth centenary of the city. It was fully completed in 1970. This enormous building in neo-Gothic style has a capacity for 8,000 worshippers in its five naves. Its twin towers are 97 metres high and the central, octagonal cupola is supported by 12 columns 30 metres high. The imposing columns lead the eye upwards, but they are almost too high to follow. The interior is mostly unadorned, except for the two gilt mosaic pictures in the trancepts: on the north side is the Virgin Mary (1952, by Gigotti) and on the south St Paul (1953, by M Avenali, Ravenna Gruppo Mosaicisti). All the windows contain stained glass, letting in a rich light from high up in the walls. The stairs to the two pulpits curve around the two principal pillars at the eastern end of the cupola. The marble surround to the steps which lead up to the main altar is carved with biblical scenes. ■ *Daily 0700-1830*.

East of the Praça da Sé is the **Igreja da Ordem Terceira do Carmo**, at the corner of Praça Clóvis Bevilácqua and Avenida Rangel Pestanha.

West of the Praça da Sé, along Rua Benjamin Constant, is the Largo de São Francisco. Here is the **Igreja da Ordem Terceira de São Francisco**. The convent was inaugurated in 1647 and reformed in 1744. Note the blue-and-white tile decorations in the chancel and behind the font (up the lefthand passageway). To the right is the Igreja das Chagas do Seráphico Pai São Francisco (1787), painted like its neighbour in blue and gold. To the left is the Faculdade do Direito (Law Faculty) of São Paulo.

If you go north up either Rua São Bento or Rua Líbero Badaró you come to Praça do Patriarca, on which stands the church of **Santo Antônio**, next to the *Hotel Othon*. Dating from 1717, the church has a beautifully painted wooden ceiling. ■ *Monday-Friday 0600-1830.* A left turn brings you to the Viaduto do Chá, across which is the **Teatro Municipal**, one of the few distinguished early 20th-century survivals that São Paulo can boast. It is on Praça Ramos de Azevedo. Construction began in 1903 and the theatre was inaugurated in 1911. Many famous international and national stars have played here. Viewing the interior may only be possible during a performance; as well as the full evening performances, look out for midday, string quartet and 'vesperais líricas' concerts (all free, usually once a week). ■ *T2233022.*

It is easy to walk from Parque Anhangabaú to the Praça da República. Either go along Avenida São João (which is rather seedy in this part, with cinemas and shops – including sex shops), or, preferably, take the pedestrian streets from Viaduto do Chá. These streets tend to be crowded, but they have a wide variety of shops, places to eat and some hotels.

Praça da República

Praça da República is always busy. The trees in the praça are tall and shady and there are birds. There are also lots of police. Near the Praça is the city's tallest building, the **Edifício Itália** on the corner of Avenida Ipiranga and Avenida São Luís. There is a restaurant on top, *Terraço Itália*, and a sightseeing balcony (see **Eating**, page 216). Also here is the curving Edifício Copan. Two blocks northwest of the Praça is the **Largo do Arouche**, by which is a large flower market, which is worth seeing.

If you walk up Avenida São Luís, which has many airline offices and travel agencies (especially in the Galeria Metrópole), you come to Praça Dom José Gaspar, in which is the **Biblioteca Municipal Mário de Andrade**, surrounded by a pleasant shady garden. There are tourist information kiosks in both the Praça da República and Praça Dom José Gaspar.

About 10 minutes' walk from the centre of the city is the old **Mercado Municipal** covering 27,000 sqare metres at Rua Cantareira 306. ■ *Monday-Saturday 0400-1600.* A new Mercado Municipal has been built in the outskirts.

North of the centre

Worth a visit is the **Parque da Luz** on Avenida Tiradentes (110,000 square metres). It was formerly a botanical garden. It is next to the Luz railway station. There are two museums on Avenida Tiradentes, near the Parque da Luz: the **Museu de Arte Sacra** in the Convento da Luz, No 676, T2277694 (Tuesday-Sunday 1300-1800) and the **State Art Collection** (**Pinacoteca do Estado**) at No 141, T2276329 (Tuesday-Sunday 1000-1800, free). The **Igreja e Convento Nossa Senhora da Luz** was built in 1774, one of the few colonial buildings left in São Paulo, although the chapel dates from 1579 and is an example of *taipa de pilão* construction (see **Architecture**, page 786). It houses the Sacred Art Museum, which has a large collection of sacred objects from the 17th to the 20th century; not all are on show at one time.

Directly south of the Praça da Sé, and only one stop on the Metrô, is **Liberdade**, the central Japanese district. The Metrô station is in Praça da Liberdade, in which there is an oriental market every Sunday (see **Shopping**, page 218). Here you can buy traditional arts and crafts and sample all types of oriental foods, not just Japanese. On the streets of the quarter are Japanese stores, plenty of places to eat and some hotels. The street lights are designed like oriental lanterns.

Liberdade

Museu da Imigração Japonesa, Rua São Joaquim 381, Liberdade, is excellent, with a nice roof garden; ask at the desk for an English translation of the exhibits. ■ *Tuesday-Sunday 1330-1730, T2795465, US$1.50.*

The next stop south on the Metrô is Vergueiro, near which is the **Centro Cultural São Paulo**, Rua Vergueiro 1000, which has art and photographic exhibitions, a library, music and dance shows (often regional) and films. ■ *Daily until 2200, T2773611.*

Avenida Paulista & the Jardins District Either Metrô station Vergueiro or Paraíso is convenient for the southeastern end of **Avenida Paulista**. This famous avenue was inaugurated in 1891 by the Uruguayan engineer Joaquim Eugênio de Lima, who wanted to construct an avenue similar to those found in European capitals. In no time, the wealthy built their elegant houses, many in the fashionable eclectic style (see **Architecture**, page 786), and transformed this into the grandest part of the city. The industrial explosion in the 1930s and 1940s brought a new role to the avenue as offices for commercial houses and service industries were put up. Land prices rose; residents relocated to other districts. In the 1970s the avenue was widened to cope with the ever increasing flow of traffic and in the 1980s the international finance companies, the banks and the multinationals erected the latest architectural towers that rise up on either side today.

The Avenida Paulista is not entirely given over to finance. Some of the sites of interest along it are: the Shopping Paulista mall at the southeast end; the Centro Cultural Itaú at No 149; the huge Conjunto Nacional (opened in 1956 – between Ruas João Manoel and Augusta), Latin America's first shopping

Jardins & Avenida Paulista

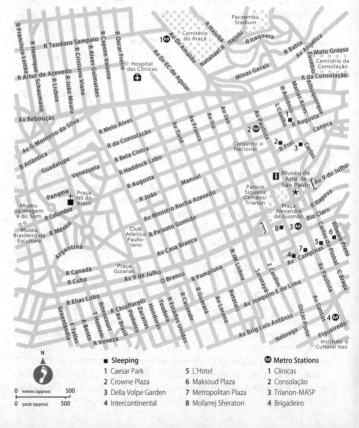

■ Sleeping		Ⓜ Metro Stations
1 Caesar Park	5 L'Hotel	1 Clínicas
2 Crowne Plaza	6 Maksoud Plaza	2 Consolação
3 Della Volpe Garden	7 Metropolitan Plaza	3 Trianon-MASP
4 Intercontinental	8 Mofarrej Sheraton	4 Brigadeiro

N

0 metres (approx) 500
0 yards (approx) 500

centre; and the monumental architecture of the Fiesp/Ciesp (Federation of Industries of the State of São Paulo) building at No 1313. Because Avenida Paulista is the highest point in the city, its buildings include about a dozen radio and television transmission towers.

The highlight of Avenida Paulista is **MASP**. This is the common name for The **Museu de Arte de São Paulo**. The museum was founded by the media magnate Francisco de Assis Chateaubriand in 1947. The present building was designed in 1957 and opened in 1968 by Queen Elizabeth II. It is at Avenida Paulista 1578 (immediately above the 9 de Julho tunnel) and the nearest Metrô is Trianon-MASP (T2515644). The building is a simple parallelepiped, but instead of resting on the ground it is suspended from two red, concrete arches so that the lowest floor spans a 74 metres open space.

The museum has major collections of European painters and sculptors, and some interesting work by Brazilian artists, including Portinari. Particularly interesting are the pictures of northeastern Brazil done by Dutch artists during the Dutch occupation (1630-54): the exotic tropical landscapes have been made to look incredibly temperate. Exhibitions vary, not all the artists above may be on view. Temporary exhibitions are also held and when a popular show is on, it can take up to an hour to get in. In this case, the later you go the better. On Sunday, an antiques fair is held in the open space beneath the museum, see **Shopping**, page 218. ■ *Tuesday-Sunday 1100-1800, US$8; first you must buy a ticket from the booth, then enter the building, bus 805A from Praça da República goes by MASP.*

Opposite MASP is **Parque Tenente Siqueira Campos**, which covers two blocks on either side of Alameda Santos; a bridge links the two parts of the park. Parque Trianon is an alternative name, after the Belvedere Trianon which used to be a popular meeting place for Paulistanos. The Trianon was part of the Parque Villon, as the original Parque Siqueira Campos was called. It is at Rua Peixoto Gomide 949 and Avenida Paulista (■ daily 0700-1830), and is a welcome, luxuriant, green area in the busiest part of the city. The vegetation includes native plants typical of the Mata Atlântica. Neighbouring it is the smaller Praça Alexandre de Gusmão.

At right angles to the Avenida Paulista is Rua Augusta (Metrô Consolação is at the junction), which runs through the *jardins* Paulista, América, Europa and Paulistano to meet the Rio Pinheiros just south of the Jóquei Clube. These suburbs still contain some mansions of beauty and interest and are on the 702U Cidade Universitária bus route to the Butantã Institute (see below). Rua Augusta runs southwest, changing its name to Rua Colômbia as it crosses Praça Nossa Senhora do Brasil, on which is a church with a tiled façade. The street then becomes Avenida Europa.

The **Museu da Imagem e do Som** (MIS) is at Avenida Europa 158. It has photographic exhibitions, archives of Brazilian cinema, video and music, and a nice café on ground floor. ■ *Tuesday-Friday 1400-1800, T8529197.*

At Avenida Europa 218 and Rua Alemanha 221, next door to MIS, is the **Museu Brasiliero da Escultura** (MuBE). As well as holding temporary exhibitions, the museum offers courses in sculpture, painting, engraving and art history. ■ *Free to various temporary exhibitions and to recitals in the afternoons, T8818611.*

Avenida Europa continues to Avenida Brigadeiro Faria Lima, on which is the **Casa Brasileira**, Avenida Faria Lima 774, a museum of Brazilian furniture. It also holds temporary exhibitions. ■ *Tuesday-Sunday, 1300-1800. T2102564.* A little further up the avenue is Shopping Iguatemi.

São Paulo

Searching for the 'real' São Paulo

Arriving at Guarulhos international airport after a 12 hour flight is something of a disappointment. International airports rarely reflect the character of the city they serve, but Guarulhos is worse than most being so dark inside that it feels subterranean. So you finally get through immigration and customs and leave the airport thinking you're finally going to see São Paulo . The first thing you will notice is that it's a very long drive from Guarulhos to the city. The road and scenery is unremarkable (although one route passes the Parque Ecológico do Tietê) and you strain your neck to see if you can spot in the distance the skyscrapers that you saw from the plane (smog permitting).

Eventually you begin to see the adverts for the large multinationals, Shell, Pirelli, McDonalds, and the traffic is certainly what you'd expect to find in one of the world's megacities. But if you are expecting São Paulo to be representative of South American, or even Brazilian, cities then you will be disappointed. São Paulo has grown at such a phenomenal rate that most remains of its colonial past have long since disappeared. Visit the Pátio do Colégio in the old downtown part of the city, where the Jesuits founded the original settlement, and you may be dismayed to discover that it is only a reconstruction. The Anchieta museum here has some furniture from the first house built in São Paulo, but does this represent the real city? If you are searching for some kind of historical framework to help understand the city, then it is perhaps a start, but São Paulo has moved so far from its colonial roots that it doesn't help to make sense of the modern city.

Take a stroll along the three-kilometre Avenida Paulista, a cross between Oxford Street and Wall Street, home to designer boutiques and multinationals today, but once lined with the huge colonial mansions of the coffee barons. Few of these homes survive; some have been turned into offices and one has become perhaps the most beautiful McDonalds in the world. Stand on the balcony and gaze down on the hustle and bustle below and try to imagine the view the barons would have had.

The proliferation of huge shopping centres, such as Shopping Ibirapuera (one of the oldest and one of the biggest) and El Dorado, might make you think that multinationals and designer labels are a symbol of the 'real' city. It certainly provides the opportunity to exercise credit cards and 'shop till you drop'. The marble floored malls are not accessible, however, to the vast majority of the city's population, so is the 'real' São Paulo to be found in the favelas?

Favelas have changed a lot in the last six years, reflecting to some extent a more stable economy. Most houses are now built of brick and there are many state and city government housing schemes currently under way (eg the Projeto Cingapuro). The lives of many of the urban poor are changing, although it remains to be seen if this is for the better. So no common thread here to pin the character of the city on.

Can one actually get to grips with this city and start to make sense of it? Perhaps the obvious key is not to look for characteristics which bind it together, but to look at the diversity which stops it falling apart. Rich and poor live, not in alliance, but beside each other. The citizens have a reputation for working hard and not knowing how to enjoy themselves, at least not by Carioca standards. The city does work incredibly hard, there is an eternal sense of optimism, about the economy, about finding a new job, buying a new car, whatever. There is a real buoyancy which is contagious. There are too many different São Paulos to claim ever to understand the city, but that does not prevent visitors from enjoying the diversity and learning from Brazil's 'Supercap'.

Naomi Peirce

Back at **Avenida Paulista** the avenue ends at the junction of Rua da Consolação and Avenida Rebouças. A little way down the latter avenue is the medical complex served by the Clínicas Metrô station. Just north of here is the large municipal stadium in the **Pacaembu** valley, a residential district. It is built on Olympic lines in an area of 75,500 square metres. It holds nearly 70,000 spectators. Besides the floodlit football ground including athletics field and basketball court, there are also a covered gymnasium, open-air and covered tennis courts, an illuminated 50 metre-long swimming pool, and a great hall for receptions and rallies. Between Pacaembu and Praça da República, bounded on its south side by Rua da Consolação, is **Higienópolis**, a central residential district, which was one of the wealthiest areas at the end of the 19th century.

The **Museu de Arte Brasileira** is at Rua Alagoas 903, Pacaembu. It houses collections of Brazilian artists such as Portinari, Anita Malfatti and Brecheret. Here also there are copies of Brazilian sculptures, including those of Aleijadinho. ■ *Tuesday-Friday 1000-2000, Saturday-Sunday 1300-1800, free, T8240233.*

The **Museu de Lasar Segall**, Rua Alfonso Celso 388/Rua Berta 111, Vila Mariana (near Santa Cruz Metrô station), shows the works of a German expressionist painter who emigrated to Brazil, with a cinema and library. It holds free courses and seminars. ■ *Tuesday-Sunday 1400-1830, T5747322.*

Other museums & sights in the central area

Museu do Telefone, Avenida Ipiranga 200, 2nd floor, is quite good. ■ *Monday-Friday 0900-1700, free, T2145919.*

Museu do Relógio (clocks and watches), Avenida Diógenes Rua de Lima 2333, Alto de Pinheiros, is recommended for enthusiasts as it contains over 800 pieces, including the pocket watch of Alberto Santos Dumont. ■ *Monday-Friday 0800-1100, 1400-1700, T2607922.*

Memorial da América Latina, designed by Oscar Niemeyer, built in March 1989, at Avenida Mário de Andrade 664, next to Barra Funda Metrô station, has a relief map of Central and South America under a glass floor in the section which houses a permanent exhibition of handicrafts from all over Latin America; there is a photo library, books, magazines, newspapers and films shown on video. Very impressive. There is also a restaurant and free concerts at weekends. ■ *Tuesday-Friday 0900-2100, Saturday 0900-1800, Sunday 1000-1800, free.*

Parque Água Branca, Avenida Francisco Matarazzo 455, not far west of Barra Funda, has beautiful gardens with specimens of tropical plants, Brazilian birds and wildlife. Pavilions house a well stocked aquarium, a zoo, and exhibitions of food produce. It is also popular with children. ■ *Daily 0700-1800.*

Anhembi, Avenida Assis Chateaubriand and Rua Olavo Fontoura, Santana, is the largest exhibition hall in the world. It was inaugurated in 1970 and all São Paulo's industrial fairs are held there. It has a meeting hall seating 3,500 people, three *auditórios*, 24 conference rooms (*salas de reunião*) and two restaurants. It's a short walk from Tietê Metrô station.

Ibirapuera

The Parque do Ibirapuera was designed by architect Oscar Niemeyer and landscape artist Roberto Burle Marx for the city's fourth centenary in 1954. The park is open daily 0600-1730 and the entrance is on Avenida Pedro Álvares Cabral. Bicycles can be hired. Within its 1.6 million square metres is the architecturally impressive new **Assembléia Legislativa/Legislative Assembly**. There is also a **planetarium** (shows at 1530 and 1730 at weekends and on holidays, T5755206, entry US$5, half price for those under 18); a Japanese pavilion; a velodrome for cycle and motorcycle racing; an all-aluminium covered stadium for indoor sports which seats 20,000 people; outdoor sports fields; children's play areas; weekend concerts in the Praça da Paz.

The **Museu de Arte Contemporâneo** (MAC), founded in 1963, has an important collection of Western and South American modern art. The collection is divided between the Bienal building, third floor, in Parque Ibirapuera, MAC Ibirapuera, which specializes in temporary exhibitions and courses, (entrance at the back of the building) and two buildings at Rua da Reitoria 109 and 160, Cidade Universitária, which house the main collections. ■ *MAC Ibirapuera: Tuesday, Wednesday, Friday, 1200-1730, Thursday 1200-2200, Saturday, Sunday 1000-1730, closed holidays, free, T5735255; Buses to Ibirapuera, 675-C (Monções) from Ana Rosa Metrô station. Cidade Universitária: Monday-Friday 1200-2000, Saturday 0900-1300, closed Sunday and holidays, students free, T8183327/3539; 6414 (Gatusa) from Praça da Bandeira; to Cidade Universitária 702U or 7181 from Praça da República.*

In this park, too, are the museums of **Arte Moderna** (Modern Art – MAM), with a collection of paintings, sculptures and photographs, a library specializing in Brazilian and international art and a sculpture garden. ■ *Tuesday-Friday 1300-1900, Saturday-Sunday 1100-1800, US$5, T5499688*; **Aeronáutica** (showing the Santos Dumont plane; closed since 1995), and **Folclore/Folklore** (■ *Monday-Friday 1400-1700, Saturday-Sunday 1000-1700, T5758045*). There is also a unique display of nativity scenes and scenes of the life of Christ. (Concerts held at Christmas time.) At the entrance is a majestic monument to the *bandeirantes*.

Every even-numbered year the **Bienal Internacional de São Paulo** (São Paulo Biennial) at Ibirapuera has the most important show of modern art in Latin America, open from the beginning of September till November. The 25th biennial is in 2000, the 26th in 2002.

Cidade
Universitária &
Morumbi
The **Cidade Universitária** (university city) is the campus for the faculties of the Universidade de São Paulo (USP). It is on the west bank of the Rio Pinheiros, opposite the district of Pinheiros, and covers four million square metres. As well as the modern faculty buildings, parks and monuments, the campus also contains the famous Instituto Butantã (see below) and two parts of the Museu de Arte Contemporâneo (see Ibirapuera, above). The **Instituto de Estudos Brasileiros**, in Bloco D, second floor, Avenida Profesor Mello Morias 140, has a collection of art which belonged to the writer Mário de Andrade. ■ *Monday-Friday 1400-1700, T8183199.* Two other museums are the **Museu de Arqueologia e Etnologia**, on the fourth and fifth floors of Bloco D in the students resident blocks (knows as Crusp) in the main Arts Complex of the USP, and the **Museu de Anatomia Veterinária**, in the Veterinary Faculty, block 7. ■ *Monday-Friday 0800-1200, 1300-1600, T8184234.*

Instituto Butantã/The Butantã Snake Farm and Museum, Avenida Dr Vital Brasil 1500, T8137222, is on the university campus. It is one of the most popular tourist attractions in São Paulo. The snakes are milked for their poison six times a day but you may not witness this; the antidotes made from the venom have greatly reduced deaths from snakebite in Brazil. It also deals with spider and scorpion venom, has a small hospital and is a biomedical research institute. What visitors see is the museum of poisonous animals and public health, which is well-organized and educational, with explanations in Portuguese and English. ■ *Daily from 0900-1700 (except Monday), US$1 (children and students half price – take an ISIC). From Praça da República take bus marked 'Butantã' or 'Cidade Universitária' (Nos 701U or 792U) along Avenida Paulista, and ask to be let out at Instituto Butantã.*

Not far from the Butantã Institute, just inside the Cidade Universitária is the **Casa do Bandeirante** at Praça Monteiro Lobato, the reconstructed home of a pioneer of 400 years ago. ■ *T2110920*.

On the west bank of the Rio Pinheiros, just southeast of the Cidade Universitária, is the palatial **Jóquei Clube/Jockey Club** racecourse in the Cidade Jardim area on Avenida Lineu de Paula Machado 1263. Race meetings are held on Monday and Thursday at 1930 and Saturday and Sunday at 1430. ■ *T8164011. It is easily accessible by bus (Butantã from República, among others)*. It has a **Museu do Turfe** on Avenida Lineu de Paula Machado 1263. ■ *Daily except Monday, also closed Saturday and Sunday mornings, T8164011.*

Morumbi is a smart residential district with some very imposing houses due south of the Cidade Universitária. In the area are the state government building, **Palácio dos Bandeirantes** (Avenida Morumbi 4500), the small, simple **Capela de Morumbi** (Avenida Morumbi 5387), and the **Parque Alfredo Volpi** (Rua Oscar Americano 480, ■ *0600-2000*). This small park has native plants which are the last vestiges of the time when this was a farm, paths and a playground (no public transport goes there). Morumbi is most famous for the stadium of São Paulo Football Club, holding 100,000 people (it is known as Morumbi). Motor racing fans might like to visit the Morumbi cemetery, last resting place of Ayrton Senna; take 6291 bus to Rua Profesor Benedito Montenegro.

Museu da Fundação Maria Luisa e Oscar Americano, Avenida Morumbi 3700, Morumbi, close to the Palácio dos Bandeirantes, is a well-displayed, private collection of Brazilian and Portuguese art and furniture. ■ *Tuesday-Friday 1100-1830, Saturday-Sunday 1000-1830.*

In the suburb of Ipiranga (a Tupi-Guarani word meaning 'red clay'), 5½ kilometres southeast of the city centre, the **Parque da Independência** contains the famous **Monumento à Independência** to commemorate the declaration of Brazilian independence; beneath the monument is the Imperial Chapel, with the tomb of the first emperor, Dom Pedro I, and Empress Leopoldina ■ *Tuesday-Sunday, 1300-1700*. The monument is the second to be built, in time for the centenary of independence in 1922. The **Casa do Grito**, the little house in which Dom Pedro I spent the night before his famous cry of Ipiranga – 'Independence or Death' – is preserved in the park. ■ *Tuesday-Sunday 0930-1700*. When independence was declared, Ipiranga was outside the city's boundaries, in an area where bricks were made, on the main trade route between Santos and São Paulo.

The **Museu Paulista** is housed in a huge palace at the top of the park. The original building, later altered, was the first Monument to Independence. The museum contains old maps, traditional furniture, collections of old coins and of religious art and rare documents, and a department of Indian ethnology. ■ *Tuesday to Sunday 0900-1645, US$1, T2154588*. Behind the museum is the **Horto Botânico/Ipiranga Botanical Garden**, designed as a garden for plant study, now a recreational area. ■ *Tuesday-Sunday and holidays, 0900-1700*. There is also a **Museu de Zoologia**, Avenida Nazareth 481, which belongs to the Universidade de São Paulo (Tuesday-Sunday 1000-1700, T2743455) and the **Jardim Francês**. There is a *son et lumière* show on Brazilian history in the park on Wednesday, Friday and Saturday evenings at 2030. Take bus 478-P (Ipiranga-Pompéia for return) from Ana Rosa, or take bus 4612 from Praça da República.

Parque da Independência

São Paulo

Parque do Estado (Jardim Botânico) This large park is a long way south of the centre, at Água Funda (Avenida Miguel Estefano 3031-3687). It contains both the Botanical and Zoological Gardens and a game reserve called Simba Safári. The **Jardim Botânico** has a vast garden esplanade surrounded by magnificent stone porches, with lakes and trees and places for picnics, and a very fine orchid farm worth seeing during the flowering season, November-December. Over 19,000 different kinds of orchids are cultivated. There are orchid exhibitions in April and November. ■ *Wednesday-Sunday 0900-1700; T5846300.* The astronomical observatory nearby is open to the public on Thursday afternoons. Take Metrô to São Judas on the Jabaquara line, then take a bus.

Jardim Zoológico/Zoological Gardens, Avenida Miguel Estefano 4241, near the Jardim Botânico, have a large variety of specimens in an almost natural setting of about 35 hectares of forest. The collection, which is not exclusively Brazilian, numbers over 2,500 animals. Many birds can be seen in the gardens. ■ *0900-1700 (closed Monday), US$5, T2760811, bus 4742, 'Jardim Celeste', from São Judas.*

Burle Marx Park, Avenida Dona Helena Pereira de Moraes 200, was designed by famous landscape designer Burle Marx. It is the only place in the city where you can walk in trails in the Mata Atlântica (Atlantic rain forest). ■ *Daily 0700-1900.*

The wildlife park, **Simba Safári**, nearby (Avenida do Cursino 6338), has over 200 animals roaming free. ■ *Tuesday-Friday 1000-1630, Saturday-Sunday 0900-1630, T9466249. Entry is by car only and price of admission depends on the number of people in the vehicle (eg US$25 for a car with two adults); children under 12 free.*

Excursions

Horto Florestal In Tremembé, a little beyond Cantareira, 30 minutes north from the downtown area, is the Horto Florestal on Rua do Horto 931, in Parque Estadual Alberto Löfgren. The park contains examples of nearly every species of Brazilian woodland flora, 15 kilometres of natural trails, museum with exhibits of regional flora and fauna and a view of São Paulo from Pedra Grande on the right of the entrance to the park. ■ *Daily, 0600-1800, T9528555.*

Pico de Jaraguá *1,135m* This is highest peak in the neighbourhood and has good views of Greater São Paulo on a fine day. Lots of hang gliders fly here at weekends. It is reached from Km 18 on the Campinas highway (Via Anhangüera) by a good road through Taipas and Pirituba.

Miraporanga Botanical & Wildlife Sanctuary Situated in the foothills of the Serra do Mar, this is one hour's drive from São Paulo city centre. It has a vast collection of orchids, carnivorous and aquatic plants, waterlily pools, a lake and 20 glasshouses. It also contains armadilloes, deer and other mammals, monitor lizards and a variety of hummingbirds. ■ *Contact Sr Samuel Jorge de Mello, T8160817, weekends T4766716 for information and prices.*

Santo Amaro Dam (Old Lake) Three kilometres from the centre of Santo Amaro suburb is this popular boating resort with several sailing clubs and many attractive cottages along the shore. There is a bus (30 minutes) from São Paulo to Santo Amaro.

The Brazilian Grand Prix

Motor racing has had a long and distinguished history in Brazil and the first race day for cars and motorcycles at Interlagos was held on May 12 1940 realising founder Louis Romero Sanson's dreams of a high speed circuit. The first victor there was Arthur Nascimento Júnior who won the São Paulo Grand Prix driving an Alfa Romeo 3500 in a time of 46 minutes and 44 seconds for the 25 laps. Second place went to Francisco Landi in a Maserati 3000. The first Brazilian Grand Prix was held there in 1972 and Emerson Fittipaldi won in 1973 driving a Lotus in a time of one hour 43 minutes at an average speed of 183 km/h. He repeated this with an even faster time of one hour 24 minutes the following year in a McLaren and in 1975 another Brazilian José Carlos Pace (after whom the track is named) won in a Brabham. During the eighties the race was held at the Jacarepaguá racetrack in Rio de Janeiro and the outspoken Nelson Piquet won here twice in 1983 and 1986 with some of the fastest lap times seen on this track.

The race returned to the reformed Interlagos during the nineties and the legendary Aryton Senna was the last Brazilian driver to win here in 1991 and 1993. He monopolised the pole position and his laps of honour with the national flag flying from the cockpit won the hearts of his fans. His death in 1994 due to a mechanical failure at Imola racetrack, San Marino, consolidated his position as the country's number one sportsman of all time. With their triple-champion now dead Brazilian viewing figures for motor racing fell drastically afterwards. Today however there are still many very capable Brazilians driving for the Formula One teams such as Pedro Paulo Diniz (Sauber), Ricardo Zonta (BAR) and Rubens Barrichello (Ferrari) who is probably only waiting for the right car to be up there with his fellow countrymen.

The Brazilian Grand Prix is usually the second of the year being held over a weekend at the end of March or the beginning of April. The race consists of 72 laps of the 4.292 km circuit for a total distance of 309.024 kilometres. Approximately 55,000 people attend the race in addition to the millions watching around the world. The training session takes place on Friday morning; the time trial on Saturday morning and the race itself on Sunday afternoon with warm ups and the drivers' parade in the morning. Tickets can be bought from the racetrack during the whole week or by contacting ABN Amro Bank on T011-55072500 from abroad and T0800-170200 inside Brazil. Minimum ticket price is US$75 rising to US$350 depending on the viewing sector. Sectors A and G are uncovered and the cheapest, whilst sector D (S do Senna) is covered, provides a better view and is more expensive. Tickets for the training sessions are cheaper and can be bought from 0700 on the day from the box office at the circuit. VIP hospitality is readily available but at a high price.

Private cars are banned from the racetrack but park and ride facilities (US$5) are available on Saturday from Shopping SP Market, Avenida das Nações Unidas 22540, and on Sunday from Hipermercado, Avenida das Nações Unidas 4403 and Shopping Interlagos, Avenida Interlagos 2255. There are also buses (Saturday-Sunday) from Praça da República, between Rua do Arouche and Rua Marquês de Itu (295), from Praça Com Linneu Gomes at Congonhas airport and from Rua dos Jequitibás in front of the Jabaquara bus station (189). All buses have different coloured stickers to indicate which drop off point they serve. Further general information about the Grand Prix in English can be obtained from www.gpbrasil.org.

São Paulo

Interlagos
See box, page 211, for more on the Brazilian Grand Prix

São Paulo's lake resort on the Santo Amaro dam, Avenida Interlagos, has an 18-kilometres motor-racing circuit. ■ *T5770522*. It can be reached from Santo Amaro by bus. Close to the track, where the Brazilian Grand Prix takes place, is the 32 kilometre long **Guarapiranga** artificial lake with good restaurants and several luxurious sailing and sports clubs (Avenida Guarapiranga 575, ■ *0600-1700 daily*). There is a Camping Clube do Brasil site. Guarapiranga is less polluted than the other artificial lake, Billings, which also has restaurants.

Embu
Population 196,000
28 km to São Paulo

This colonial town has become a centre for artists and craftsmen. The town itself, on a hill, is surrounded by industry and modern developments and the colonial centre is quite small. Many of the old houses are painted in bright colours and most contain arts, furniture, souvenir or antiques shops, or restaurants. The central Passeio das Artes, including the town's Museu da Arte Sacra has been refurbished. Signposts with maps have been erected, but these can be a bit confusing at times. On Sunday there is a large and popular arts and crafts fair (0900-1800), which is highly recommended for a visit. On Monday almost everything is closed.

The Jesuits founded the original settlement of Bohi, later M'Boy, then Embu, in 1554. In 1690, they transferred Embu to its present location, building the church of **Nossa Senhora do Rosário** and their residence in what is now known as the Largo dos Jesuítas. In this complex is the **Museu de Arte Sacra**. ■ *Saturday-Sunday 1200-1700*. The Jesuits and their Indian disciples are said to have inspired Embu's artistic tradition, particularly in the carving of saints, in painting and engraving. In the 20th century, this tradition gained full recognition after the first Arts Exhibition of 1964. Also in the 1960s, the Embu fair became popular, first as a hippy fair, then as a regular event in 1969. There is another chapel in the town centre, **São Lázaro**, which was built in the 1930s by local artists; it is on Rua da Matriz.

There is a tourist office on Rua Capelinha, which is on the Largo 21 de Abril, the praça at which buses from São Paulo stop. The *Festa de Santa Cruz* is held during the second half of May and *Folklore Week* is in August.

Transport **Buses**: from São Paulo, *Soamin* bus no 179 leaves from Avenida Cruzeiro do Sul between Tietê rodoviária and Metrô station (it is marked 'Embu-Engenho Velho'); departures between 0610 and 2310, US$2, 1 hour 45 minutes. The route passes Clínicas Metrô, goes down Avenida Francisco Morato, then through Taboão da Serra: you see a lot of southwest São Paulo, but it is a long ride. A quicker alternative is to take a SP-Pinheiros bus from Clínicas, which takes the main highway to Embu; 40 minutes, it costs US$0.80. Get out at Largo 21 de Abril in Embu. To return to São Paulo, walk up R da Matriz from Lg 21 de Abril, turn left down Al Junior, then left again on R Solano Trindade to a junction where the buses stop.

Essentials

Sleeping
■ on maps, pages 199, 200 and 204
Price codes: see inside front cover

Hotels in our **LL** range have prices in excess of US$200 a night, in some cases approaching (if not pushing through) the US$500 barrier. These are of the highest quality and visitors will probably choose according to the style of hotel they prefer (eg international chain, independent, etc). Most of the top hotels offer discounts during the weekend. The most luxurious (corporate rates available), all with swimming pools, nightclubs and convention halls, are between Av Paulista and Praça Dom José Gaspar.

Near Praça da República there are some slightly cheaper, but very good hotels and cheaper hotels still can be found on the pedestrian streets between Praça da República and Anhangabaú. In the daytime, this area is OK, but at night you should be careful. Ask your hotel which streets should be avoided. The Japanese district of Liberdade, south of Praça da Sé, has some pleasant hotels and is quite a good place to stay.

Good, safe accommodation below our **D** range is very hard to find. Most of the cheaper hotels are in Santa Ifigênia between Av São João and Estação Luz. The area can be approached either from Metrô República or Luz. The red light district is in the blocks bounded by R Santa Ifigênia, R dos Andradas, R dos Gusmões and Av Ipiranga, and is definitely not recommended for women travelling alone. The whole area around Av Rio Branco is rather seedy and not entirely safe late at night.

Around Avenida Paulista **LL** *Caesar Park*, R Augusta 1508, T2536622, F2871123. **LL** *Della Volpe Garden*, R Frei Caneca 1199, T2855388, F2888710. Recommended. **LL** *Holiday Inn Crowne Plaza*, R Frei Caneca 1360, T2532244, F2841144. Small pool, very comfortable. **LL** *Intercontinental São Paulo*, Al Santos 1123, T31792600, F31792666. **LL** *L'Hotel*, Al Campinas 266, T/F2830500, all suites. Part of the Roteiros de Charme group, see page 57. Recommended. **LL** *Maksoud Plaza*, Al Campinas 150, downtown side of Av Paulista, but southeast, rather than northwest of MASP, T2534411, F2534544. **LL** *Metropolitan Plaza*, Al Campinas 474, T2874855, F2853158. **LL** *Mofarrej Sheraton*, Al Santos 1437, on the south side of Av Paulista, T2535544, F2898670. Recommended. **LL** *Renaissance*, Al Santos 2233, T30692233, F30692045. Very good. Good apartment hotels for longer stays are **LL** *George V*, R José Maria Lisboa 1000, T2809822, F2827431. Very comfortable. **L** *Paulista Wall Street*, R Itapeva 636, T2534311, F2535585, reservas@wallstreet.com.br. Good. **A** *Parthenon Crillon Plaza*, R Haddock Lobo 807, T8818511, F30642155. Restaurant, pool, exercise room, one of a chain. **A** *Monterey*, Al Itu 265, T2856111, F2833247. Safe parking, comfortable accommodation. Very few cheaper hotels in this area: try **A** *Pousada Dona Zilha*, Al Franca 1621, Jardim Paulista, T8521444, F8532483. With shower, nice patio, lounge. **B** *Pamplona Palace*, R Pamplona 851, T/F855301. Parking.

Consolação **L** *Brasilton*, R Martins Fontes 330, T2585811, F2585812. **L** *Grand Hotel Cà d'Oro*, R Augusta 129, T2364300, F2364311. **AL** *Linson*, R Augusta 440, Consolação, T2566700, F2585371. Suites, TV security system, restaurant, pool. **B** *Hores Belgrano*, R Marquês de Paranaguá 88, T2580255, F2577803, central. English spoken, gives special rates for long stays.

Near Praça da República **L** *Hilton*, Av Ipiranga 165, T2560033, F2573033. **AL** *Bourbon*, Av Dr Vieira de Carvalho 99, T2500244, F2214076, hbnsao@xpnet.com.br. Very smart, pleasant, one of a local chain (others in Curitiba, Londrina and Foz do Iguaçu). **AL** *Eldorado Boulevard*, Av São Luís 234, T2141833, F2568061. Excellent. **AL** *Excelsior*, Av Ipiranga 770, T2200377, F2216653. **AL** *Othon Palace*, R Líbero Badaró 190, T2393277, F31077203. Only high class hotel in the Triângulo, good. **A** *Gran Corona*, Basílio da Gama 101, T2140043, F2144503, in a small street. Comfortable, good services, good restaurant. Warmly recommended. **A** *Jaraguá*, R Maj Quedinho 44, near Praça Dom José Gaspar T2566633, F2561377. **A** *San Juan*, R Aurora 909, just behind Emtu airport bus terminal, T/F2509100. Recommended. **B** *Itamarati*, Av Dr Vieira de Carvalho 150, T2224133, F2221878. Good location, safe. Highly recommended and very popular. **B** *Plaza Marabá*, Av Ipiranga 757, T2207811, F2207227. Recommended. **B** *Términus*, Av Ipiranga 741, T2222266, F2206162. **B** *Vila Rica*, Av Dr Vieira de Carvalho 167, T/F2207111. **C** *São Sebastião*, R 7 de Abril 364, T2574988. TV, fridge, phone, laundry service. Recommended.

Liberdade **AL** *Nikkey Palace*, R Galvão Bueno 425, T2708511, F2706614. High class, with male only traditional sauna. **A** *Osaka Plaza*, Praça da Liberdade 149, T2701311, F2701788. **B** *Banri*, R Galvão Bueno 209, T2708877, F2789225. Good. *All 3 are near the metrô station*

Santa Ifigênia AL *Planalto*, Av Cásper Líbero 117, T2307311, F2277916. Varig-Tropical chain, secure, helpful, good service, good restaurant. **A** *Best Western São Paulo Center*, Lg de Santa Ifigênia 40, T2286033, F2290959, very central. **B** *Cineasta*, Av São João 613, T2225533. A/c. **B** *Continental*, R Vitória 223, T2211574. Safe. Highly recommended. **B** *Lincoln*, Av Rio Branco 47, T2225466. Excellent breakfast, safe. Recommended. **B** *Natal*, R Guaianazes 41, T2206722. Very well recommended. **B** *Ofir*, R dos Timbiras 258, T2238822. Stores valuables but not money, big rooms, TV, well equipped, good value. **B** *Riviera*, Av Barão de Limeira 117, T2218077. Excellent value. Highly recommended. **B** *Uai*, R Gen Osório 58, T2231370. Pleasant, rooms on street are good. Recommended. **C** *Central*, Av São João 288, T2223044, **D** without shower. Good, helpful, central. **C** *Galeão*, R dos Gusmões 394, T2208211. Safe, helpful, hot showers. **C** *Las Vegas*, R Vitória 390, corner of Av Rio Branco, T2218144. Recommended. **D** *Aliança*, R Gen Osório 235, corner of R Santa Ifigênia, T2204244. Nice, with breakfast, good value.

Brooklin LL *Gran Meliá São Paulo*, Av das Nações Unidas 12559, T30438000, F30438001.

Guarulhos L *Deville*, Av Monteiro Lobato, near the international airport, T64680400, F64640594. Comfortable, excellent food.

Youth hostels *Associação Paulista de Albergues da Juventude*, R 7 de Abril 386, Conj 22, T/F2580388, info@alberguesp.com.br. Membership is US$15 per year. **E** *Praça da Árvore*, R Pageú 266, Saúde, T50715148, spalberg@internetcom.com.br. IYHA (**D** for non-members), kitchen, laundry, includes breakfast, internet service. *Magdalena Tagliaferro*, Estr Turística do Jaguará 651, Km 18, Via Anhangüera. IYHA, open all year, reservations necessary (T2580388), take a Jaguará 8696 bus from Anhangabaú Metrô station to the Parque Estadual Jaguará, the hostel is 100 metres from the entrance. An unaffiliated hostel is *Primavera*, R Mariz e Barros 346, Vila Santa Eulália (bus 4491 from Parque Dom Pedro in the centre), T2153144, cooking and laundry facilities.

Camping A list of sites can be obtained from *Camping Clube do Brasil*, R Minerva 156, Perdizes, T8647133.

Eating

The main restaurant areas are Jardins, Pinheiros/Vila Madalena, Bixiga for Italian food, Liberdade and Pinheiros for Japanese. For fast food, go to the shopping centres

Apart from the international cuisine in the first-class hotels, here are a few recommendations out of many. The average price of a meal in 1999 was US$15-25 in trattorias, US$30-50 in first-class places rising to US$75 in the very best restaurants; remember that costs can be cut by sharing the large portions served. Many restaurants now serve food by weight, even some of the better class places (but these are naturally more expensive per kilo). You should compare prices carefully because an expensive per kilo restaurant can work out more expensive than a normal one.

You can find restaurants catering for every taste and, given the huge influx of immigrants, a wide variety of nationalities. In addition to Brazilian churrasco, seafood and regional food and the more obvious choices such as French, German, Italian, Spanish, Japanese, Chinese, fast food and vegetarian, there are Arabic, Argentine, Greek, Hungarian, Indian, Korean, Mexican and Thai restaurants, to name but a few. Among the publications which give selections of restaurants in the city are the Quatro Rodas guides, the bi-monthly *Go Where?* (US$3), the monthlies *São Paulo Este Mês* and *Magazine Turismo e Hotelaria*. We suggest that if the following list contains nothing that takes your fancy, you should consult any one of the above for ideas.

Arabic *Almanara*, a chain of reasonably priced restaurants serving Middle Eastern/Lebanese food, Oscar Freire 523 (Cerqueiro César), R Basilio da Gama 70 and Av

Vieira de Carvalho 109/123 (either side of Praça da República) and in Shoppings Iguatemi, Morumbi amd Paulista. *Bambi*, Al Santos 59, Paraíso, T2844944. Mostly Arabic food, about US$20. *Rubayat*, Al Santos 86 and Av Faria Lima 583. Excellent meat, fixed price meals. *Mama Leila*, R João Moura 1167, Jardim Paulista, T2827018, Lebanese. Recommended.

Brazilian *Bassi*, R 13 de Maio 334, T6042375, Bela Vista, for meat. *Paulista Grill*, João Moura 257, Pinheiros, T8535426. Top quality meat, popular. *Vento Haragano*, Av Rebouças 1001, Jardim Paulista, T8536039. *Churrascaria rodizio*, very good. *Moraes*, Al Santos 1105, Cerqueira César, T2893347, and Praça Júlio de Mesquita 175, Vila Buarque (Centro), T2218066. Traditional meat dishes. *Sujinho*, R da Consolação 2078, T2315207. Very popular *churrascaria*, with other branches on the same street. *Boi na Brasa*, R Bento Freitas by Praça da República. Very good, reasonable prices. *Churrascaria Eduardo's*, R Nestor Pestana 80, near *Hotel Eldorado Boulevard*, T2570500. Food, service and value are good. *Dinho's Place*, Al Santos 45, Paraíso, T2845333. Friday seafood buffet, also meat, US$45, has daily bargains, also Av Morumbi 7976, T5364299. *Paddock*, R da Consolação 222, sobreloja, T2574768, and R Campo Verde 88, Jardim Paulistano, T8143582. Traditional fare, excellent *feijoada*. *Novo Olido*, Largo do Arouche 193, closed Saturday, regional dishes from interior of São Paulo. *Bolinha*, Av Cidade Jardim 53, Jardim Paulistano, T30612010. For *feijoadas* daily, and other dishes. *Oxalá*, Trav Maria Antônia 72, just off Consolação. Bahian specialities at modest prices.

French *Le Bistingo*, Al Franca 580, Cerqueira César, T2893010. French. *La Tambouille*, Av 9 de Julho 5925, Jardim Europa, T8836276. French and Italian, closed Monday, reserve in advance. *L'Affiche*, R Campos Bicudo 141, Itaim, T2825867. Small, intimate, décor includes the owner's collection of antique French posters. *La Casserole*, Largo do Arouche 346, Centro, T2206283. Best known bistro in São Paulo, closed Monday (US$30-50 pp). *Marcel*, R da Consolação 3555, T30643089. Sensational soufflés.

German *Arnold's Naschbar*, R Pereira Leite 98, Sumarezinho, T2625648. *Eisbein peruruca*. Recommended. *Bismarck*, Av Ibirapuera 3178, T2400313. Good food and excellent draught beer.

Indian *Govinda*, R Princesa Isabel 379, Brooklin Paulista, T5310269. Tandoori specialities, expensive. *Tandoor*, R Dr Rafael de Barros 408, Paraíso, T8859470.

Italian *Massimo*, Al Santos 1826, Cerqueira César, T2840311. Italian and international cuisine. *Il Sogno di Anarello*, R Il Sogno di Anarello 58, Vila Mariana, T5754266. Open Monday-Friday 1900-0100 only, excellent, typical *cantina paulistana*. *Lellis*, R Bela Cintra 1849. Very reasonable, *salada Lellis* is a must, and fresh squid in batter. *L'Osteria do Piero*, Al Franca 1509, Cerqueira César, T8531082. Excellent. *Famiglia Mancini*, R Avanhandava 81, Bela Vista, T2564320. Excellent, salads and cold dishes, always queues between 2000-2400. *Gero*, R Haddock Lobo 1629, Jardins, T30640005. Good pasta. *Cantina Taberna do Julio*, R Conselheiro Carrão 392, Bela Vista. Inexpensive. *Gigetto*, Avanhandava 63, T2566530. For pasta, reasonable prices. *Da Fiorella*, R Bernardino de Campos 294, Brooklin, T55611546. Closed Monday and Sunday evening, top quality vegetarian pasta. *Don Cicillio*, Praça Tomás Morus 185. Perdizes, homecooking in traditional surroundings. *La Trattoria*, R Antônio Bicudo 50, Pinheiros, T2803572. Closed Monday, midweek until 1900, Friday, Saturday till 0100, reasonably priced food, *strozzapreti* a must. There are many Italian restaurants in the Bela Vista/Bixiga area, especially on R 13 de Maio. Recommended pizzerias are *Torre do Bixiga*, 13 de Maio 848, T2897364. Lunchtime only, *Capuano*, R Conselheiro Carrão 416, T2881460. *Margherita*, Al Tietê 255, T8520046.

São Paulo

Oriental *Iti Fuji*, Al Jaú 487, Cerquera César, T2851286. Typical Japanese. *Shian-San*, R Pamplona 1115, Jardins, T2876667. Inexpensive Chinese. *Sushi-Guen*, Av Brig Luis Antônio 2367, Lojas 13 and 14, Cerqueira César, T2895566. For *sushi* and *sashimi* but a bit overpriced, closed Sunday. *Komazushi*, R São Carlos do Pinhal 241, loja 5, Bela Vista, T2871820. Renowned for its *sushi*, closed weekends. *Korea House*, R Galvão Bueno 43, Liberdade, T2783052. *Kar Wua*, R Mourato Coelho 30, Vila Beatriz, T8811581. Chinese, highly praised. Many other Chinese and Japanese restaurants in Liberdade, the Japanese quarter, where there is a Japanese food market in the square by the Metrô station.

Japanese tends to be expensive

Seafood *Antiquarius*, Al Lorena 1884, Cerqueira César, T2823015. Portuguese. *Don Curro*, R Alves Guimarães 230, Pinheiros, T8524712. Closed Monday, for seafood, especially paella. *Mexilhão*, R 13 de Maio 618, Bela Vista, T8662310.

Swiss *Chamonix*, R Pamplona 1446, T8533621. Nice atmosphere, and *Le Jardin Suisse*, Al Franca 1467, T8527566. Both in Jardim Paulista, expensive, very good.

General *Terraço Itália*, on top of Edif Itália (Ipiranga 344 e São Luis), 41 floors up. Open 1130-0100, fixed price lunch and other meals, dancing with excellent band and superb view (minimum consumption charge of US$10 to be allowed to see the view), US$85 pp including wine in dancing part, US$65-70 otherwise, dress smartly. *Charlô*, R Barã de Capanema 440, Jardim Paulista. Mostly French but also Brazilian. *Restaurante do MASP*, Av Paulista 1578. In the basement of the museum, reasonably priced, often has live music.

Vegetarian *Sattva*, R da Consolação 3140, Cerqueira César, T8836237. *O Arroz de Ouro*, Largo do Arouche 88, T2230219. Shop as well, central. *Cheiro Verde*, Peixoto Gomilde 1413, Cerqueira César, T2896853. More expensive than most. *Intergrão*, R Joaquim Antunes 377, Jardins, T8533707. macrobiotic. *Delícia Natural*, Av Rio Branco 211 (4th floor), corner of Av Ipiranga. Lunch only. *Sabor Natural*, same building, 1st floor. Lunch only. *Folhas e Raizes*, Líbero Bádaro 370, Centro. Good value buffet lunch. *Saúde Sabor*, São Bento 500, Centro. Lunch only.

Almost always the cheapest option in São Paulo 'Vida Integral' monthly newspaper has details of health food restaurants & stores

Fast food Comida por kilo restaurants can be found all over the city; there are many on R Augusta, eg *Estoril*, No 2969, Jardim América, T30645458, charging US$1.25 per 100 grams. Such places are very popular at lunchtime.

McDonalds and other chains can be found all over the city as well as many other not quite so fast, but infinitely more interesting alternatives. One recommended local chain is *Viena*. In most Shopping Centers there is a *Praça da Alimentação*, where various food counters are gathered together, fast and simple. The *Arabesco* chain found in Shoppings is good. *Frevinho Lanches*, R Augusta 1563. Famous for its *beirute* (speciality of São Paulo), as well as many other toasted sandwiches with pitta bread. *Baguette*, Consolação 2418, near Av Paulista, opposite Belas Artes cinema. For sandwiches, especially lively around midnight, also at R 13 de Maio 68. *Absolute*, Al Santos 843. Among the best hamburgers in town. *Rock Dreams*, Av Brigadeiro Faria Lima 743. For hamburgers and sandwiches. *Casa da Fogazza*, R Xavier de Toledo 328 and R 7 de Abril 60 (both close to Praça da República). *Calzone*, with different fillings, juices, recommended.

Cafés *Fran's Café*, open 24 hours, Av Paulista 358, R Heitor Penteado 1326 (Sumaré), R Haddock Lobo 586, Al Lorena 1271 (Jardim Paulista), R Tamandaré 744 (Liberdade) and others. A recommended chain for a meal, day or night. *Café Paris*, Av Waldemar Ferreira 55, Butantã. Open every day of the year. There are several chains of bars selling *mate* and other teas and beverages, plus snacks and sandwiches, eg *Rei do Mate*, *Mister Mate*, *Uno e Due*.

Bars *Café do Bexiga*, R 13 de Maio 76. Nice atmosphere, and lots of others in Bixiga/Bela Vista area with live music, eg *Café Piu Piu* (closed Monday) and *Café Pedaço*, at 13 de Maio 134 and 140. Bixiga is traditionally known as the 'Bohemian' area and bars here are usually cheaper than Jardins and Pinheiros areas. *Finnegan's Pub*, R Cristiano Viana 358, Pinheiros. Irish theme, specializes in hamburgers and whisky (not necessarily together). *Pé pra Fora*, Av Pompéia 2517, Sumarezinho. Closed Sunday, open air. Recommended. *Choperia Opçaõ*, R Carlos Comenale 97, behind MASP. Popular open air bar. In **Itaim Bibi** *Hard Rock Café*, R Brig Haroldo Veloso 707. Fake but still sells the T-shirts. *Blue Night Jazz Bar*, Av São Gabriel 558, T8849356, as the name describes.

Bars & nightclubs

Disco bars *Banana-Banana Café*, Av 9 de Júlio 5872, Jardim Paulista. Closed Monday. *DaDo Bier*, Av Juscelino Kubitschek 1203, Itaim, T8662310. Beer made on the premises, live music or disco. *HB Club*, R Cardeal Arcoverde 2958, Pinheiros. Closed Sunday, bar, snooker, and informal dance lessons. Test your new skills at *Blen-Blen*, same address at weekends, live Latin bands. *Cervejaria Continental*, packed, mixed music, Av Pres JK 373, Itaim Bibi, R dos Pinheiros 1275 and R Haddock Lobo 1573.

Entrance/cover charges US$10-20

Nightclubs *B.A.S.E.*, Av Brig Luís Antônio 1137, Bela Vista, techno and dance music. *Love Club & Lounge*, R Pequetita 189, Vila Olímpia. Trance, house, drum 'n' bass. *Columbia* upstairs, R Estados Unidos 1570. Lively. *Hell's Club* downstairs. Opens 0400, techno, wild. *Cha-Cha-Cha*, R Tabapuã 1236. Closed Monday, no Brazilian music, art on walls, candles, gay and straight. *Balafon*, R Sergipe 160. Wednesday-Sunday, small, Afro-Brazilian. *Reggae Night*, Av Robert Kennedy 3914, Interlagos. Thursday-Sunday, outdoors on lakeside. *Limelight Industry*, R Franz Schubert 93. Pop hits, Japanese restaurant upstairs. 5 other nightspots on this street. *Plataforma 1*, Av Paulista 424. Dinner and folkloric show, very touristy but extremely popular.

São Paulo is teeming with clubs catering to most preferences, entrance US$5-20 which may include a drink. We list a small section

See the *Guia da Folha* section of *Folha de São Paulo* and *Veja São Paulo* section of the weekly news magazine *Veja* for listings of concerts, theatre, museums, galleries, cinema, bars and restaurants.

Entertainment

Art galleries *Casa da Fazenda*, Morumbi, exhibits in 19th century house. *Espaço Cultural Ena Beçak*, R Oscar Freire 440. *Galeria São Paulo*, R Estados Unidos 1456.

Cinema The biggest cinema is reckoned to be the *Marabá*, Av Ipiranga 757, which has 1,438 seats. *Belas Artes*, R da Consolação 2423. Multiscreen. In cinemas entrance is usually half price on Wednesday; normal seat price is US$3 in the centre, US$5-6 in R Augusta, Av Paulista and Jardins. There is no shortage of cinemas in the city. As well as those places showing the latest releases there are cine clubs, eg *Cine SESC*, R Augusta 2075; *Espaço Unibanco*, R Augusta 1470/1475 and cinemas at the Museu da Imagem e do Som, Centro Cultural Itaú and Centro Cultural São Paulo.

Theatre The Teatro Municipal (see **Sights**, page 203) is used by visiting theatrical and operatic groups, as well as the City Ballet Company and the Municipal Symphony Orchestra who give regular performances. There are several first-class theatres: *Aliança Francesa*, R Gen Jardim 182, Vila Buarque, T2590086. *Itália*, Av Ipiranga 344, T2573138. *Cacilda Becker*, R Tito 295, Lapa, T8644513. *Paiol*, R Amaral Gurgel 164, Santa Cecília, T2212462. *Ruth Escobar*, R dos Ingleses 209, Bela Vista, T2892358, among others. Free concerts at *Teatro Popular do Sesi*, Av Paulista 1313, T2849787, at midday, under MASP (Monday-Saturday). See also **Museums** above.

São Paulo

Festivals *Foundation of the City*: 25 January. *Carnival* in **February**: Escolas de samba parade in
See also box on Carnival the Anhembi Sambódromo, note that during carnival most museums and attractions
are closed. In **June** there are the *Festas Juninas* and the *Festa de São Vito*, the patron
saint of the Italian immigrants. There is a *Festa da Primavera* in **September**. In
December there are various *Christmas* and *New Year* festivities. Throughout the
year, though, there are countless anniversaries, religious feasts, international fairs and
exhibitions, so it would be wise to look in the press or the monthly tourist magazines
to see what is on while you are in town. See above for the São Paulo Biennial.

Shopping **Handicrafts** Souvenirs from *Casa dos Amazonas*, Al Jurupis 460. *Galeria Arte
Brasileira*, Al Lorena 2163, T8529452, galeria@dialdata.com.br. Good value. *Ceará
Meu Amor*, R Pamplona 1551, loja 7. Good quality lace from the Northeast. There is a
Sutaco handicrafts shop at República Metrô station; this promotes items from the
State of São Paulo, open Tuesday-Friday 1000-1900, Saturday 1000-1500; there is a
showroom at R Augusta 435, 6th floor.

Jewellery Precious stones may be purchased at *H Stern*, jewellers, at Praça da
República 242, R Augusta 2340, R Oscar Freire 652 and at Iguatemi, Ibirapuera,
Morumbi, Paulista and other shopping centres, hotels *Hilton*, *Sheraton* and *Maksoud
Plaza*, and at the international airport. *Amsterdam Sauer* has outlets at Av São Luís 29,
hotels *Maksoud Plaza* and *Sheraton*, shopping centres Iguatemi, Morumbi, and at the
international airport. There are many other shops selling Brazilian stones.

Shopping centres Typical of modern development are the huge Iguatemi,
Ibirapuera and Morumbi shopping centres. They include luxurious cinemas, snack
bars and most of the best shops in São Paulo. Other malls include Paulista and
Butantã. On a humbler level are the big supermarkets of *El Dorado* (Av Pamplona
1704) and *Pão de Açúcar* (Praça Roosevelt, near the *Hilton*); the latter is open 24 hours
a day (except Sunday).

Markets The *'hippy fair'* that used to take place in Praça da República was moved to
Tiradentes Metrô station but is not nearly as lively or colourful. *Oriental fair*, Praça de
Liberdade Sunday 1000-1900, good for Japanese snacks, plants and some handicrafts,
very picturesque, with remedies on sale, tightrope walking, gypsy fortune tellers, etc.
Below the Museu de Arte de São Paulo, an **antiques** market takes place on Sunday,
1000-1700. **Arts and handicrafts** are also sold in Parque Tte Siqueira Campos/Trianon
on Sunday from 0900-1700. Al Lorena, which is one of the upmarket shopping streets
off R Augusta in Jardins, has an open-air market on Sunday selling fruits and juices.
There are **flea markets** Sunday in the main square of the Bixiga district (Praça Don
Orione) and in Praça Benedito Calixto in Pinheiros. São Paulo is relatively cheap for film
and clothes (especially shoes). The *Ceasa flower market* should not be missed, Av
Doutor Gastão Vidigal 1946, Jaguaré, Tuesday and Friday 0700-1200.

Bookshops *Livraria Cultura*, Av Paulista 2073, loja 153, Conjunto Nacional. New
books in English. *Livraria Freebook*, R da Consolação 1924, T2591120. Ring bell for
entry, wide collection of art books and imported books in English. *Livraria Triângulo*,
R Barão de Itapetininga 255, loja 23, Centro. Sells books in English. *Livraria Kosmos*,
Av São Luís 258, loja 6. International stock. In various shopping malls *Livrarias Saraiva*
and *Laselva* (also at airports) sell books in English. *Sodiler*, Shopping Market Place, Av
Nações Unidas 13947, Brooklin, loja 121A, floor T. *Librairie Française*, R Barão de
Itapetininga 275, ground floor. Wide selection, also at R Prof Atilio Innocenti 920,
Jardins. *Letraviva*, Av Rebouças 1986. Monday-Friday 0900-1830, Saturday
0900-1400, specializes in books and music in Spanish. *Book Centre*, R Gabus Mendes
29, between Basílio da Gama and 7 de Abril (Praça da Republica). Has books in English

Carnival

Carnival in São Paulo follows the lead of Rio de Janeiro and is improving in quality every year. The Samba Schools' parades take place in the Sambódromo, Avenida Olavo Fontoura 1209, Anhembi, T69715000. The Grupo 1 (Saturday), Grupo Especial (Sunday and Monday) and the Parade of the Champions on the following Saturday are the ones to watch. Tickets can be obtained from the Sambódromo, from the Saraiva chain of bookshops or by telephone on T8294559. To take part or to visit a practice session at a quadra contact the

Samba Schools directly: Gaviões da Fiel Torcida, Rua Cristina Tomás 183, Bom Retiro, T2212066 (Friday 2200); Mocidade Alegre, Avenida Casa Verde 3498, Bairro do Limão, T8577525 (Wednesday and Friday 2000); Rosas de Ouro, Avenida Coronel Euclides Machado 1066, near Ponte da Freguesia do Ó, T8574555 (Wednesday, Friday and Sunday 2030); Vai-Vai, Rua São Vicente 276, Bela Vista, T31058725 (Sunday 2100); X-9 Paulistana, Av Luiz Dumont Villares 324, Carandiru, T2677081 (Wednesday and Sunday 2000).

and German. **Duas Cidades**, R Bento Freitas 158, near República. Good selection of Brazilian and Spanish American literature. **Cinema Elétrico**, R Augusta 973, Centro, and **Sola Cinemateca**, R Fradique Coutinho 361. Sell postcards and books on cinema and art. A shop selling art books and CDs is **Gusto, Gôsto, Gusta**, R Augusta 2161.

Photography For repairs to Canon and other makes: **Cine Camera Service**, R Conselheiro Crispiniano 97, 2nd floor.

Sports

Football The most popular local teams are Corinthians, Palmeiras and São Paulo who generally play in the Morumbi and Pacaembu stadiums. **Horse racing** (Jockey Club) and **motor racing** (see **Excursions**, Interlagos) are mentioned above. **Yachting, sailing** and **rowing** take place on Santo Amaro reservoir (also see above). For **nature trails**, etc, **Free Way**, R Leôncio de Carvalho 267, Paraíso, T2854767/2835983. **Golf courses** (including outside the metropolitan area) about half an hour's drive from the centre there are 18-hole golf courses at the **São Paulo Golf Club**, Praça Dom Francisco Souza 635, in Santo Amaro, in beautiful surroundings. **Clube de Golf de Campinas**, Via Anhangüera, Km 108, Campinas. **Clube de Campo São Paulo** and **Guarapiranga Golf e Country**, both at Reprêsa Guarapiranga, Estr Paralheiros, Km 34. **São Fernando Golf Club**, Estr de Cotia, Km 29. There is a lakeside club at Km 50 on the Santos road. 9-hole courses at **São Francisco club**, Estr de Osasco, Km 15. **Anglo Sports Center**, Barretos. **International golf club**, Via Dutra Km 232, Guaratinguetá.

Transport

See also Ins and outs, page 194

Local Car hire: **Avis**, Araújo 232 and at the airports, T0800-118066; **Budget**, R da Consolação 328, loja 1, and at Guarulhos, T2564355. **Hertz**, Araújo 216, 1st floor, and at the airports, T8837300 or T0800-147300. **Interlocadora**, several branches, São Luís T2555604, M Fontes T2573544, Guarulhos T64453838, Congonhas T2409287. **Localiza**, T0800-992000, or www.localiza.com.br for all reservations, 8 branches in the city.

Motoring: the rodízio which curbs traffic pollution by restricting car use according to number plate may be extended beyond the winter months. Check.

Motorcycle repairs: BMW São Paulo, Av L Calle Berrini 901, T5354567. Also **Officer Motorcycles** for BMW, Av Paecaembu 1047, T/F36620296, good knowledgeable service. Imported spares and tyres at **Edgar Soares & Cia**, R Gen Osório 663.

São Paulo

Metrô: the first in Brazil, began operating in 1975. It has 2 main lines intersecting at Praça de Sé: north-south from Tucuruvi to Jabaquara; east-west from Corinthians Itaquera to Barra Funda (the interchange with Fepasa and RFFSA railways and site of the São Paulo and Paraná rodoviária); an extension east to Guaianases is to open soon. A third line runs from Vila Madalena in the west, along Avenida Paulista, to Ana Rosa in the south, joining the Jabaquara line at Paraíso and Ana Rosa. A fourth line, Vila Sônia to Luz, is projected. The 2 main lines operate from 0500-2400, Vila Madalena to Ana Rosa 0600-2200. Stations are well-policed and safe. Fare US$0.75, US$6 for a book of 10 tickets; backpacks are allowed. Combined bus and Metrô ticket are available, US$1, eg to Congonhas airport.

Taxis: these display cards of actual tariffs in the window (starting price US$3). There are ordinary taxis, which are hailed on the street, or at taxi stations such as Praça da República, radio taxis and deluxe taxis. For Radio Taxis, which are more expensive but involve fewer hassles, T9740182 (*Central de Táxi*), T69146630 (*Central Rádio Táxi*), T2511733 (*Vermelho e Branco*),T2331977 (*TeleTáxi*), or look in the phone book for others; calls are not accepted from public phones.

Long distance   Air: **Cumbica international airport**: there are air services to all parts of the world from the international airport at Guarulhos, also known as Cumbica, Av Monteiro Lobato 1985, T64452945. *Varig* has its own, new terminal for international flights, adjoining the old terminal which all other airlines use. *Emtu* bus service every 30 minutes to Guarulhos from Praça da República 343 (northwest side, corner of R Arouche) 0530-2300, and from Tietê rodoviária, US$6.50, 30-45 minutes. Buses also run from Bresser bus station to Guarulhos and there are other buses from Jabaquara bus terminal to Guarulhos, without luggage space, usually crowded. Taxi fares from the city to the airport are between US$35-US$40 and vary from cab to cab. Rush hour traffic can easily turn this 30 minute journey into an hour. There are plenty of banks and money changers in the arrivals hall open 0800-2200 daily. There is a post office on the third floor

Metrô

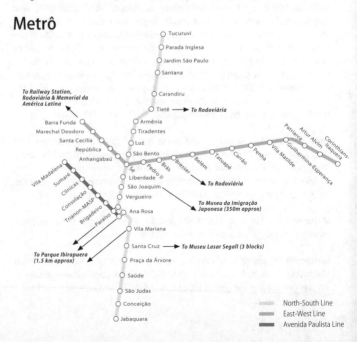

of Asa A and tourist information is also available from the airport branch of *Secretaria de Esportes e Turismo* open 0800-2200, Saturday-Sunday and holidays 0900-2100.

The domestic airport of Congonhas, 14 km from the city centre on Av Washington Luis, T50909000, is used for the Rio-São Paulo shuttle (about 400 flights a week US$100 one-way), some flights to Belo Horizonte and Vitória and private flights only. The airport at Campo de Marte, Av Santos Dumont 1979, T2902699 is used for charter flights and helicopters.

Trains: railways are being privatized and as a result many long distance passenger services have been withdrawn including services to Campo Grande, Corumbá and Brasília via Campinas. São Paulo has four stations: **Estação da Luz**, T2250040, for commuter trains between the northwest and southeast of São Paulo state, on the former Santos a Jundiaí Railway. There is also a Metrô stop here. **Barra Funda**, T7021400, handles commuter destinations on the former Sorocabana and former Santos a Jundiaí railway lines. Services go to **São José do Rio Preto** (overnight), **Barretos**, **Ourinhos**, **Londrina**, **Maringá**, **Sorocaba** and **Ponta Grossa**. There is also a Metrô station and a rodoviária at Barra Funda. **Júlio Prestes** station, T2208862, for commuter services to the west on the former Sorocabana metre gauge railway. **Roosevelt**, T9421132, for commuter trains to east on former Central do Brasil and Santos a Jundiaí railways.

Buses: there is a convenient Metrô connection to the main rodoviária at **Tietê**, T2350322, but the terminal is very badly designed in that it has to cope with millions of people but the only way to the platforms is by stairs. This is very difficult for people with heavy luggage and, for the disabled, almost impossible. Tietê handles buses to the interior of São Paulo state, all state capitals (but see also under Barra Funda and Bresser below) and international buses (see next paragraph). The left luggage charges US$0.80 per day per item. You can sleep in the bus station after 2200 when the guards have gone; tepid showers cost US$2.

Buses from Tietê: To **Rio**, 6 hours, every 30 minutes, US$12.50 (*leito*, 25), special section for this route in the rodoviária, request the coastal route via Santos ('via litoral') unless you wish to go the direct route. To **Florianópolis**, 11 hours (US$23.75, *leito* 36.25). To **Porto Alegre**, 18 hours, US$36.50 (*leito*, 60). To **Curitiba**, 6 hours, US$10.25-12.50. To **Salvador**, 30 hours, US$51 (executive, 64). To **Recife**, 40 hours, US$60-70. To **Campo Grande**, 14 hours, US$33. To **Cuiabá**, 24 hours, US$42. To **Porto Velho**, 60 hours (or more), US$75. To **Brasília**, 16 hours, US$30 (*leito*, 60). To **Foz do Iguaçu**, 16 hours, US$30. To **São Sebastião**, 4 hours US$8.85 (say 'via Bertioga' if you want to go by the coast road, beautiful journey but few buses take this route).

International buses To Montevideo, via Porto Alegre, with *TTL*, departs Monday, Thursday, Saturday 2200, 31 hours, US$100, cold a/c at night, plenty of meal stops, bus stops for border formalities, passengers disembark only to collect passport and tourist card on the Uruguayan side (also *EGA*, same price, US$67 to **Chuy**, Tuesday, Friday, Sunday). To **Buenos Aires**, *Pluma*, 36 hours, US$145. To **Santiago**, *Pluma* or *Chilebus*, 56 hours, US$130, *Chile Bus*, T2676239, poor meals, but otherwise good, beware overbooking. To **Asunción** (1,044 kilometres), 18 hours with *Pluma* (US$57, *leito* 112), *Brújula* (US$64) or *RYSA* (US$110), all stop at Ciudad del Este (US$43, 50 and 84 respectively, *Pluma leito* US$84). *Cometa del Amambay* runs to Pedro Juan Caballero and Concepción.

There are 3 other bus terminals, **Barra Funda**, T664682 (as described above), to cities in southern São Paulo state and many destinations in Paraná, including Foz do Iguaçu (check for special prices on buses to Ciudad del Este, which can be cheaper than buses to Foz). **Bresser** (Metrô Bresser), T8925191, for *Cometa* (T6085625) or *Transul* (T6938061) serving destinations in Minas Gerais. **Belo Horizonte**, 10 hours,

US$15.60, 11 a day (*leito* 31.20), 9 a day with *Gontijo*. *Translavras*, *Cristo Rei* and *Util* also operate out of this station. Prices are given under destinations. **Jabaquara**, T5810856, at the southern end of the Metrô line. Buses from here for **Santos**, US$3.60, leave every 15 minutes, taking about 50 minutes, last bus at 0100. Also serves destinations on the southern coast of São Paulo state.

Roads The following major roads leave the city: Rodovia Presidente Dutra (the Dutra Highway – BR-116) to Rio de Janeiro; Rodovia Ayrton Senna (SP-070), which parallels the Dutra leaving the city, as an alternative route to Rio via Moji das Cruzes, and also going to the Litoral Norte. The Rodovia Fernão Dias (BR-381) branches off the Dutra for Belo Horizonte; this road is in the process of being made into a dual carriageway. Rodovia dos Bandeirantes (BR-348) and Via Anhangüera (SP-330) go northwest to Campinas. Rodovia Presidente Castelo Branco (SP-280) and Via Raposo Tavares (SP-270) go to Sorocaba and the west of the state. Rodovia Régis Bittencourt (BR-116) goes southwest to Curitiba. Rodovia dos Imigrantes (SP-160) and Via Anchieta (SP-150) go to Santos and the Litoral Sul. To take the beautiful coast road to Rio, take the Via Anchieta to the Guarujá turn, before Guarujá take the Bertioga turn and you're on the Santos-Rio highway.

Hitchhiking To hitch to Rio, take the Metrô to Armênia, then a bus to Guarulhos, alighting where the bus turns off the Rio road for Guarulhos.

Directory **Airline offices** *Aeroflot*, Av São Luís 112, loja 201, T2314074. *Aerolíneas Argentinas*, Araújo 216, 6th floor, T2590319 (Guarulhos airport 64453806). *Alitalia*, Av São Luís 50, cj 291, T2571022 (64452005). *American Airlines*, Araújo 216, 1st floor, T2144000, also in *Mofarrej Sheraton*, T0800-124000 (64453234). *Avianca*, R da Consolação 293, 10th floor T2576511, (64453798). *British Airways*, Av São Luís 50, 32nd floor, T2596144 (64452142). *Continental*, Av São Luís 50, 11th floor, T2594500. *Delta*, R da Consolação 348, T2587355/5866. *Iberia*, Araújo 216, 3rd floor, T2576711 (64452726). *JAL*, Av Paulista 542, 3rd floor, T2515222 (64452340). *KLM*, Av São Luís 86, T2574433 (Guarulhos 64453111). *LanChile*, Praça Dom José Gaspar 30, T2592900 (64452824). *LAB*, Av São Luís 72, T2588111 (64452837). *Lufthansa*, Av São Luís 59, T2555172/2367700 (64452220). *Rio-Sul/Nordeste*, Av Wasington Luiz, Congonhas, T2403023/5340572/5310533. *TAM*, Av P Bueno 1400, T55851800. *TAN*, Av P Bueno 1400, T55815537. *TAP*, Av São Luís 187, T2555366. *Transbrasil*, many offices including Av São Luís 258, T2315897. *Varig*, R da Consolação 362/372, Av Paulista 1765, T55611161 (Guarulhos 64452825, Congonhas 5350216). *Vasp*, Praça L Gomes/Aurora 974, T2203540, Av São Luís 72, T2591533, or T0800-998277.

Banking hours are 1000-1600, some banks open at different times, and all have different times for foreign exchange transactions (check at individual branches)

Banks There are many national and international banks; most can be found either in the Triângulo, downtown, or on Av Paulista, or Av Brig Faria Lima. In general, banks change cash and TCs at the bank rate, while travel agencies and *câmbios* use the parallel rate, which is more favourable. Obtaining money with a credit card is usually time-consuming and may involve some investigation to find which branch or machine will accept your card. The simplest way to get cash is by using a Visa credit or debit card in ATMs found in *Banco do Brasil* and *Bradesco* branches. There are *Banco 24 Horas* kiosks all over the city, which advertise that they take a long list of credit cards in their ATMs. In fact, the likelihood of being able to use an international credit card is remote *Banco do Brasil* will change cash and TCs and will advance cash against Visa. All transactions are done in the foreign exchange department of any main branch (eg Av São João 32, Centro), but queues are long. Its branch on R 7 de Abril, near Praça da República, will accept payment orders from overseas but with a US$30 charge and payment in reais. *Citibank*, Av Ipiranga 855, or Av Paulista 1111 (T5761000, 1100-1500) will receive money from abroad (US$20 charge, takes 5 days). *Banespa*, eg at R Duque de Caxias 200, Centro, or Praça da República 295, accepts Visa, TCs and cash. *Itaú* only changes money for its account holders, except in its branch at the international airport. *Bradesco*, Av Ipiranga 200, is the branch for exchange. *Mastercard*, cash against card, R Campo Verde 61, 4th floor, Jardim Paulistano. *Thomas Cook*, Visa TCs refund assistance numbers are given in **Essentials** section, page 42. *American Express*, Al Santos 1437 (Hotel Mofarrej Sheraton) T2513383, Av Maria Coelho Aguiar 215, Bloco F, 8th floor, T37418474 and Guarulhos international airport, terminal 1, 1st floor of Asa A, T64123515. *Western Union* at Banco Itamarati, T0800-119837.

Money changers There are many *câmbios* on or near Praça da República. Most travel agents on Av São Luís change TCs and cash at good rates, but very few are open on Saturday. *Amoretur*, Praça da República 203, will change cheques. *Avencatur*, Av Nações Unidas 1394, Morumbi, changes TCs, Deutschmarks, good rates. *BarcelonaTour*, Barão de Itapetininga 243. *Coraltur*, Praça da República 95. *Interpax*, Praça da República 177, loja 13, changes cash (many currencies) and cheques, 0930-1800, Sat 0930-1300.

Communications Post Office: Correio Central, Praça do Correio, corner Av São João and Prestes Máia, T8315222. Booth adjoining tourist office on Praça da República, weekdays only 1000-1200, 1300-1600, for letters and small packages only. *UPS*, Brasinco, Alameda Jaú 1, 1725, 01420 São Paulo, T8528233, F8538563. *Federal Express*, Av São Luís 187, Galeria Metropole, loja 45, is reliable, also at Av das Nações Unidas 17891, T5247788. *DHL*, Av Vereador José Diniz 2421, T5422744. **Telephone:** *Telefônica*, R 7 de Abril 295, near Praça da República and R Cincinato Braga 144, Paraíso, many other offices. *Embratel*, Av São Luís 50, and Av Ipiranga 344. For the international operator dial 000111, for international collect calls dial 000107. Red phone boxes are for national calls, blue ones for international phone calls. **Internet:** *Banca Henrique Schaumann*, Av Henrique Schaumann 159, Pinheiros, US$3 per ½ hr. *Saraiva Megastore*, Shopping Eldorado, US$3 per ½ hr.

Cultural centres *British Chamber of Commerce of São Paulo*, R Barão de Itapetininga 275, 7th floor, Caixa Postal 1621, T2554286. *British Council*, R Maranhão 416, Higienópolis, Caixa Postal 1604, T8264455, F663765, *Sociedade Brasileira de Cultura Inglesa*, and library at R Deputado Lacerda Franco 333, Pinheiros, T8144155/0100. *American Chamber of Commerce for Brazil*, R Formosa 367, 29th floor, T2469199, www.amcham.com.br. *American Library*, União Cultural Brasil-Estados Unidos, R Col Oscar Porto 208, T2871022. *Goethe-Instituto*, R Lisboa 974, T2804288 (open Mon-Thu 1400-2030). *Instituto Hans Staden*, R Conselheiro Crispiniano 53, 12th floor. *Centro Cultural Fiesp*, Av Paulista, 1313. 0900-1900 Tue-Sun, foreign newspapers, magazines and internet access for research only (email and chat channels not allowed). See under **Entertainment** for *Alliance Française* Theatre.

Embassies & consulates *Argentina*, Av Paulista 1106, T2872949 (open 0900-1300, very easy to get a visa here). *Australia*, R Tte Negrão 140, T8296281. *Austria*, R Augusta 2516, 10th floor, T2826223, Mon-Thu 0930-1130. *Bolivia*, R da Consolação 37, 3rd floor (open 0900-1300), T2553555. *Canada*, Av Paulista 1106, T2855099, open 0900-1200, 1400-1700. *Chile*, Av Paulista 1009, T2842044; *Denmark*, Oscar Freire 379, T30613625, F30689867, open 0900-1700, Fri until 1400 only. *France*, Av Paulista 1842, 14th floor, T2879522, open 0830-1200. *Germany*, Av Brig Faria Lima 1383, 12th floor, T8146644, open 0800-1130. *Greece*, Av Paulista 2073, 23rd floor, T2510675, open 0900-1300. *Ireland*, Av Paulista 2006, 5th floor, T2876362, open 1400-1700. *Netherlands*, Av Brig Faria Lima 1698, T8130522, open 0900-1200. *New Zealand*, R Hungria 888, T2122288. *Paraguay*, Av São Luis 50, T2557818, open 0830-1600. *Peru*, R Votuverava 350, T8701793, open 0900-1300. *South Africa*, Av Paulista 1754, T2835130. *Sweden and Norway*, R Oscar Freire 379, 3rd floor, T8833322 (Caixa Postal 51626), 0900-1130-1400-1600. *Switzerland*, Av Paulista 1754, 4th floor, Caixa Postal 30588, T2880370. *UK*, Av Paulista 37, 17th floor, Caixa Postal 846, T2877722. *Uruguay*, R Teixeira da Silva 660, T8848474, open 1000-1600. *US*, R Padre João Manuel 933, T8816511, open 0800-1700. *Venezuela*, R Veneza 878, T8872318, open 0900-1300.

Hospitals & medical services *Hospital Samaritano*, R Cons Brotero 1468, Higienópolis, T8240022, recommended. *Hospital das Clínicas*, Av Dr Enéias de Carvalho Aguiar 255, Jardins, T30696000. Both have *pronto-socorro* (emergency services). Contact your consulate for names of doctors and dentists who speak your language. **Emergency and ambulance:** T192. **Fire:** T193.

Language courses The official *Universidade de São Paulo (USP)* is situated in the Cidade Universitária (buses from main bus station), beyond Pinheiros. There are a number of architecturally interesting buildings plus the museums mentioned above. They have courses available to foreigners, including a popular Portuguese course, registry is through the Comissão de Cooperação Internacional, R do Anfiteatro 181, Bloco das Colméias 05508, Cidade Universitária, São Paulo. Other universities include the Pontifical Catholic University, and the Mackenzie University.

Laundry *Chuá Self Service*, R Augusta 728, T2584953, limited self-service, not cheap. *Di-Lelles*, R Atenas 409, T72983928, pricey. *Prestomatic*, R Peixoto Gomide 410, near Av Paulista, self service, wash and dry US$5.

Places of worship *St Paul's Episcopal Church*, R Comendador Elias Zarzur 1239, Santo Amaro, T2460383, English services 1000 Sun. *Igreja Metodista*, Av Liberdade 659, T2785895. *Mormon Church*, Av Prof Francisco Morato 2430, T8180344. *Synagogue Israelita Paulista*, R Antonio Carlos 653, T2567811. *Templo Budista*, Av Paula Ferreira 1133, T8765771. *Lutheran church*, Av Rio Branco 34. *Swedish Church*, *Igreja Evangelica Luterana Escandinava*, R Job Lane 1030, T2478829.

Tour companies & travel agents *Lema Turismo*, Av Marquês de Itú 837, T2315199, personalized excursions, Marta Schneider speaks 8 languages, including Hungarian. *AmEx* office in *Hotel Sheraton Mofarrej*, Al Santos 1437, T2843515 (see **Banks** above). *Kontik-Franstur* (American Express representative), R Marconi 71, T2597566/7021. *Stella Barros* (Thomas Cook) has branches throughout the city. *Ambiental Viagens e Expedições*, Av Prudente Morais 344, conj 5, T8148809. English and Spanish spoken, helpful, recommended for trips to less well known places; *Terra Expedições*, Osmar e Valdir, R Silva Jardim 429, Santa Terezinha, Santo André, T4463381/4473535, recommended for motocycle tours and information, Spanish and Italian spoken (English improving). *STB*, Av Brig Faria Lima 1713, T8700555, ISIC cards and student discounts. Visits to coffee fazendas (May-Jun) and round trips into the surrounding country are organized by the travel agencies.

Tourist offices Tourist information for the city is provided at 4 kiosks in the city: **Praça da República** (very helpful, open 0900-1800 daily, T2312922), **Praça Dom José Gaspar** (corner Av São Luís, open Mon-Fri 0900-1800, T2573422), **Av Paulista** at Parque Trianon (open 0900-1800 except Sat, T2510970), and on **Av Brig Faria Lima** opposite the Iguatemi Shopping Center (open Mon-Fri 0900-1800, T2111277); an excellent free map is given at all these offices (on newsstands it sells for US$4). These kiosks are operated by *Anhembi Turismo*, Av Olavo Fontoura 1209, Parque Anhembi, T69715000. Tourist information for the state of São Paulo is given at the *Secretaria de Esportes e Turismo*, in the Antigo Prédio do Banco de São Paulo (see **Sights**, above), entrances on Praça Antônio Prado 9, and R São Bento 380, 6th floor, T2390892/0094, or T2395822, F2393604 or 6056255. There is not much literature available, but the office is helpful. **Tours of the city:** costing US$15 (US$10 for children under 7) leave the kiosk at Praça da República every Sun. There are 5 different itineraries, 2 visiting places of cultural interest (4 hrs each – 1 in the morning, 1 in the afternoon), and 3 visiting places of 'green' interest (5 hrs each – only 1 runs each Sun). Tourist offices have free magazines in Portuguese and English: *Where* and *São Paulo This Month* (also available from most travel agencies and better hotels). Also recommended is Quatro Rodas' *Guia de São Paulo*. Newsstands sell a wide range of magazines and books which deal with tourism in the city and the state.

   Information on the web: *SPGUIA: O Guia Interativo Oficial da Cidade de São Paulo*, has a lot of information, www.spguia.com.br/indexb.html. *Instituto Cultural Itaú* for those interested in cultural articles related to the city and Brazil, www.ici.org.br. For details on *estâncias* in the state, see *Sherwood Informática* site, www.sherwood.com.br and select the Viver São Paulo item. **Maps:** in addition to those already mentioned (Quatro Rodas, Mapograf, Cartoplam, and the map given out by the tourist kiosks), *RGN Public* produces a map which is given out free in various places and which is adapted to show its sponsors' locations (eg Mappin, Pirelli, McDonalds). A variety of maps and timetables are sold in newsstands. **Map shops:** *Mapolândia*, 7 de Abril 125, shop 40. There are 2 private map publishers: *Geo Mapas*, R Gen Jardim 645, 3rd floor, Consolação, T2592166 (40% discount for volume purchases, excellent 1988 1:5,000,000 map of Brazil, town maps), and *Editorial Abril*, R do Cartume 585, Bl C, 3rd floor, Lapa, T8716004, F8716270.

Useful numbers Immigration: Federal Police, Av Prestes Maia 700, open 1000-1600 for visa extensions.

Voltage 110-220 volts AC, 60 cycles.

The Coast

The coast of São Paulo state, referred to as the Litoral Norte or Costa Linha Verde (North of Santos) and the Litoral or Costa Sul (South of Santos) is very popular with Paulistanos for weekends away from the city. In either direction there are many resorts to choose from. The central point is the port of Santos, but even here, the beach is close at hand and it is a good place from which to start exploring, especially if you don't want to waste time with the traffic in the state capital.

History

The coast around Santos is one of the sites which has yielded evidence of the *sambaqui* culture of c 5000 BC (see page 736). The Tupinikin were the people who lived in this region when the Portuguese arrived, but the first European settlements at São Vicente and Santos were under constant attack from the Tamoio (allies of the French), who lived further north. For a long time, it was touch-and-go whether the Portuguese settlements would survive. The colony on São Vicente island was founded in 1532 by Martim Afonso de Sousa and the port of Santos was founded soon after. By the 1580s it was reported that there were 400 houses in São Vicente and Santos.

The French and the Tamoio did not succeed in driving the Portuguese out of their captaincy of São Vicente and Santos became one of the most important ports on the Atlantic coast. The ascent of the Serra do Mar to the Paulista plateau, so treacherous in the early days because of both its steepness and Indian attacks, did not deter the harbour's growth. Sugar was grown on the levels at the foot of the mountains and on the plateau. This was the port's main commodity for shipping, but there was also the trade with São Paulo and, when coffee was introduced to the region, Santos was its outlet.

Up to the end of the 19th century, Santos had an evil reputation for its proneness to yellow fever. "Formerly whole ships' crews were stricken down with fever and died, and the ships being left without the slightest protection, ran ashore, and their skeletons are in evidence at the port at the present day". So wrote Frederick Alcock in 1907, who visited Santos "not without some slight feelings of fear". He was, in fact, pleasantly surprised by the place and, once measures been taken to eradicate the fever, Santos soon became a pleasure resort, in addition to its commercial activities.

The hinterland between the sea and mountains gained another reputation for horrors in the 20th century. A few kilometres inland from the city of Santos an important industrial area, including many chemical plants, built up round the steelworks, oil refinery and hydroelectric plant at Cubatão. At one time the pollution was so appalling that it was called 'The Valley of Death'. In the mid-1980s, it was claimed to be the most contaminated part of the planet, with so much toxic waste undermining the hills that the whole lot threatened to slip down into the sea. Such a tragedy has been averted and cleaning-up operations have taken place.

Santos

Population: 412,500
Phone code: 013
Colour map 5, grid A6

Although better known for its busy commercial port and football team (a museum dedicated to Pelé will be opened soon), the island has a long seafront with popular beaches especially during the weekend and holidays when Paulistanos escape the city and flock to the coast. Gonzaga is the centre of the city's leisure industry with cinemas, bars and restaurants. The centre has some interesting churches and other sights such as the imposing Bolsa Official de Café as well as good views from the summit of Monte Serrat.

Situated 72 kilometres southeast of São Paulo and five kilometres from the open sea, Santos is the most important Brazilian port. Over 40 percent by value of all Brazilian imports and about half the total exports pass through it. The scenery on the routes crossing the Serra do Mar is superb and the roadway includes many bridges and tunnels. From Rio the direct highway, the Linha Verde (see pages 177 and 230) is also wonderful for scenery.

Although best known for its commerce, Santos is also a holiday resort, with magnificent beaches and views. The port is approached by the winding Santos Channel; at its mouth is an old fort (1709). A free-port zone for Paraguay, 1,930 kilometres by rail or road, has been established. The island upon which the city stands can be circumnavigated by small boats.

The centre of the city is on the north side of the island. Due south, on the Baía de Santos, is **Gonzaga**, where hotels line the beachfront and the city's entertainment takes place. Between these two areas, the eastern end of the island curves round within the Santos Channel. At the eastern tip, a ferry crosses the estuary to give access to the beaches of Guarujá. The city has impressive modern buildings, wide, tree-lined avenues, and wealthy suburbs.

Sights The streets around **Praça Mauá** are very busy in the daytime, with plenty of cheap shops. In the centre, an interesting building is the **Bolsa Oficial de Café**, the coffee exchange, at Rua 15 de Novembro 95. There is a coffee museum inside. Two restored churches in the centre are the 17th-century **Santo Antônio do Valongo**, which is by the railway station on Largo Monte Alegre, and the **Capela da Ordem Terceira de Nossa Senhora do Carmo** (1760), on Praça Barão do Rio Branco.

São Paulo coast

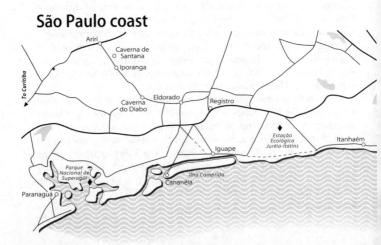

São Paulo

The railway up the hill

The British-built Santos a Jundiaí up the hill to São Paulo is one of the railway wonders of the world; beyond São Paulo it carries on 60 km to Jundiaí. Having passed through Cubatão on the coastal plain, it runs on toothed tracks up the escarpment, going through interesting hill scenery. Today, RFFSA, the national railway company, runs a tourist train at weekends between São Paulo and Santos (see the text for the schedule). Its timetable now bears no relation to how the system operated in the line's heyday. Trains left São Paulo at 0600 in order to get the passengers to their businesses by 0800. At the top of the Serra, the engine was detached from the carriages which were then attached to a wire rope. They then were allowed to go down the slope to the port by force of gravity, with a train coming up acting as a counterweight.

Along the line, which ran through the tropical forest of the Serra do Mar, the steamship companies which sailed into Santos built 'sanitary stations'. These were the places to which the lines sent their crews to avoid the pestilent port in the days before yellow fever had been brought under control.

Monte Serrat, just south of the city centre, has at its summit a semaphore station and look-out post which reports the arrival of all ships in Santos harbour. There is also a quaint old church, dedicated to Nossa Senhora da Monte Serrat, said to have performed many miracles. The top can be reached on foot or by funicular, which leaves every 30 minutes, US$6. Seven shrines have been built on the way up; annual pilgrimages are made by the local people. There are fine views.

There are many monuments: in Avenida Ana Costa to commemorate the brothers Andradas, who took a leading part in the movement for independence; in the Praça Rui Barbosa to Bartolomeu de Gusmão, who has a claim to the world's first historically recorded airborne ascent in 1709; in the Praça da República to Brás Cubas, who founded the city in 1534; and in the Praça José Bonifácio to the soldiers of Santos who died in the Revolution of 1932.

Museu do Mar, Rua República do Equador 81, in the eastern part of the city, has a collection that includes several thousand shells. In the western district of José Menino are the **Orquidário Municipal**, municipal orchid gardens, in the

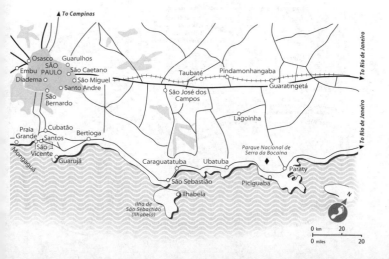

São Paulo

Praça Washington (flowering October-February, orchid show in November). There is the opportunity here to wander among giant subtropical and tropical trees, amazing orchids and, when the aviary is open, to meet macaws, toucans and parrots. The open-air cage also contains hummingbirds of 20 different species and the park is a sanctuary for other birds. ■ *Orquidário, daily 0800-1745; the bird enclosure 0800-1100, 1400-1700. US$1 (children and senior citizens free).*

Beaches Santos' eight kilometres of beaches stretch round the Baía de Santos and lead into those of São Vicente at the western end. From east to west they are Ponta da Praia, below the sea wall and on the estuary, no good for bathing, but fine for watching the movements of the ships. Next come Aparecida, Embaré, Boqueirão, Gonzaga and José Menino (the original seaside resort for the merchants of Santos). São Vicente's beaches of Itararé and Ilha Porchat are on the island, while Gonzaguinha is on the mainland. The last beach is Itaquitanduva, which is in a military area, but may be visited with authorization. In all cases, check the cleanliness of the water before venturing in (a red flag means it is too polluted for bathing). See page 230 for Guarujá.

Excursions **Ilha Porchat** This small island is reached by a bridge at the far end of Santos/São Vicente bay has beautiful views over rocky precipices, of the high seas on one side and of the city and bay on the other. At the summit is *Terraço Chopp*, a restaurant which has live music most evenings; the views from here are wonderful. On summer evenings the queues to get in can last up to four hours,

Santos

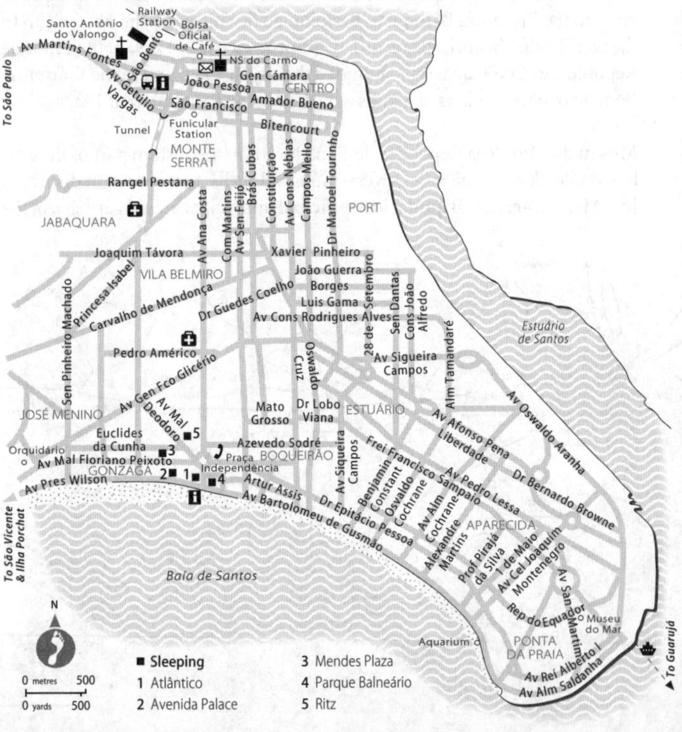

■ **Sleeping**		3 Mendes Plaza
1 Atlântico		4 Parque Balneário
2 Avenida Palace		5 Ritz

0 metres 500
0 yards 500

but in winter, even if it may be a little chilly at night, the queues are non-existent. It is situated at Al Ary Barroso 274, Ilha Porchat, São Vicente, T4687527.

Itatinga This village, 30 kilometres from Santos in the Serra do Mar, offers the chance to see what is left of the Atlantic forest at close quarters and to trek through mangrove, sandbanks and hillside forest. The area is full of wildlife (lizards, toucans, butterflies), and thick with vegetation (bromeliads, orchids, eucalyptus). Each trail is graded according to difficulty. You travel to the village of Itatinga by boat on a three-hour trip down the Estuário and the Rio Itapanhaú and then by street car. Or take the BR-101 (Santos-Rio) road, a three-minute crossing by boat and then 7½ kilometres by street car. Access is with one of the travel agencies officially permitted to lead groups: contact *Sictur* (the tourism department), Praça dos Expedicionários 10, 8th floor, T2224166.

Alto da Serra From here, the summit of the forest-clad mountain range, there are magnificent views. The return journey can be done in under two hours by road.

São Paulo

AL *Mendes Plaza*, Av Floriano Peixoto 42, T2894243, F2848253. A/c, safe, TV, restaurant, sauna, massage, sports facilities. **AL** *Parque Balneário*, Av Ana Costa 555, T2895700, F2840475. Restaurant, rooftop pool, convention centre. **A** *Atlântico*, Av Pres Wilson 1, T2894500, F2895861, www.atlantico-hotel.com.br. A/c, TV, sauna, bar, restaurant. **A** *Avenida Palace*, Av Pres Wilson 10, T2893555, F2895961, www. avenidapalace.com.br. A/c, TV, bar, restaurant. **B** *Indaiá*, Av Ana Costa 431, T/F2895559. **B** *Ritz*, Av Mcal Deodoro 24, T2841171, F2841173. **C** *Independência*, Av Mcal Floriano Peixoto 206, T2376224. A/c. **C** *Pousada do Marquês*, Av Floriano Peixoto 204, T2371951. **D** *Natal*, Av Mcal Floriano Peixoto 104, T2842732. Clean and friendly with good breakfast, recommended. There are many cheap hotels near the Orquidário Municipal a few blocks from the beach.

Sleeping
50% discounts often available in hotels during low season

Hong Kong Palace, Av Conselheiro Nébias 288. Good Chinese. *Tertúlia*, Av Bartolomeu de Gusmão 187, T2361641. Excellent churrasco. *Zi Tereza*, Av Ana Costa 449, T2844382. Good pizzeria. *A Balnearia*, Av Pres Wilson. Recommended for prawns. *Bar Heinz*, R Dr Lincoln Feliciano 104. German food, popular. *Zum Fass*, Av Mcal Deodoro 31. German food, nice place. *Brunella*, Av Pres Wilson 11, Gonzaga. Excellent ice cream.

Eating

Bar do Torto, Av Siquiera Campos 800, Boqueirão, Reggae, MPB. Rock Thursday-Sunday. *Bar do Três*, Av Washington Luis 422. Live music. *Internetbar*, Av Mcal Floriano Peixoto 302. Popular, internet access R$5 per hour when eating or drinking.

Bars & nightclubs

Art galleries *Galeria de Arte Nélson Penteado de Andrade*, Praça dos Expedicionários 10, Gonzaga, T2354245. **Cinemas** Mainstream films at cinemas in Av Ana Costa, Gonzaga. *Cine Arte*, Posto 4, Av Vicente de Carvalho. Brazilian and foreign films. **Theatre** *Teatro Municipal Brás Cubas*, Av Sen Pinheiro Machado 48, Vila Mathias, T2336086.

Entertainment

26 January, *Foundation of Santos; Good Friday; Corpus Christi; Festejos Juninos.* Throughout the summer there are many cultural, educational and sporting events. 8 September, *Nossa Senhora de Monte Serrat.*

Festivals

Golf courses Two 9-hole courses: *Santos Golf Club*, Av Pérsio de Queiroz Filho, São Vicente. *Guarujá Golf Club* (see below).

Sports

Transport   **Local**   It is easy to visit the centre on foot and the only real need to use buses or taxis is to connect between there and Gonzaga or to visit nearby beaches. **Buses**: in Santos, US$.60. To São Vicente, US$0.90. **Taxis**: all taxis have meters. The fare from Gonzaga to the bus station is about US$5. Cooper Rádio táxi, T2327177.

Long distance   Plans for an airport have been put forward but for now the only access is by the Anchieta and Imigrantes highways from São Paulo and the coastal roads running north and south. Buses arrive from São Paulo at the main bus station in the centre as well as stops at Ponta da Praia and José Menino which are both nearer to the main hotel district in Gonzaga. Trains from São Paulo arrive at the station in the centre. Cruise liners anchor at the tourist terminal in the port close to the centre and are met by tour buses.

   Buses: rodoviaria, Praça dos Andrades, T2192194. For most suburbs buses start from Praça Mauá, in the centre of the city. There are buses to **São Paulo** (50 minutes, US$3.60) at intervals of approximately 15 minutes, from the rodoviária near the city centre, José Menino or Ponta da Praia (opposite the ferry to Guarujá). (The 2 highways between São Paulo and Santos are sometimes seriously crowded, especially at rush hours and weekends.) To **Guarulhos/Cumbica airport**, *Expresso Brasileiro* at 0600, 1330, 1830, return 0550, 0930, 1240, 1810, US$5, allow plenty of time as the bus goes through Guarulhos, 3 hours, T2192004. *TransLitoral* from Santos to **Congonhas airport** then to Guarulhos/Cumbica, 4 daily, US$7.25, 2 hours, T2895656. To **Rio** (*Normandy* company), several daily, 7½ hours, US$22.50, to Rio along the coast road is via São Sebastião (US$7.25, change buses if necessary), Caraguatatuba and Ubatuba.

Directory   **Banks**   Open 1000-1730. It is very difficult to get cash against Mastercard in Santos. Visa ATMs at *Banco do Brasil*, R 15 de Novembro 195, Centro and Av Ana Costa, Gonzaga. *Casa Branco*, Praça da Republica 29, Centro and R Galeão Carvalhal 52/54, Gonzaga, changes US$ cash. Many others. **Communications**   **Post office**: R Cidade de Toledo 41, Centro and at R Tolentino Filgueiras 70, Gonzaga. **Telephone**: R Galeão Carvalhal 45, Gonzaga. **Internet**: *Viva Shop*, Shopping Parque Balneário. US$3 per hr. **Embassies & consulates**   *British*, R Tuiuti 58, 2nd floor, T2224622. *Danish*, R Frei Gaspar 22, 10th floor, 106, T2196455, F2328752, open 1000-1100, 1500-1700. *French*, R 15 de Novembro 20, 3rd floor, 41, T2195768. *German*, R Frei Gaspar 22, 10th floor, 104, T2195092. **Hospitals & medical services**   *Ana Costa*, R Pedro Américo 42, Campo Grande, T2229000. *Santa Casa de Misericórdia*, Av Dr Cláudio Luiz da Costa 50, Jabaquara, T2347575. **Laundry**   Av Mcal Floriano Peixoto 120, self service, wash and dry US$5. **Places of worship**   *All Saints Church*, Praça Washington 92, José Menino. Services in English held every Sunday. **Security**   Although poverty is apparent the city is generally safe but it is wise to exercise caution at night and near the port. **Tourist offices**   At rodoviária, Praça da Bandeira and Orquidário Municipal. *Sictur*, Praça dos Expedicionários 10, 8th floor, T2224166. **Useful addresses**   **Immigration**: Polícia Federal, Praça da República. For visa extensions. **Voltage**   220 Ac, 60 cycles.

The Litoral Norte

Guarujá

Population: 226,500
Phone code: 013
Colour map 5, grid A6

This sophisticated resort becomes very crowded in summer as holidaymakers come to take advantage of its fine beaches, hotels, restaurants and spas. There is a strong undertow on nearly all the Guarujá beaches; the Praia de Pernambuco (also called Jequiti-Mar) is the safest. The beaches in town are mostly built-up and can be polluted, while several of those further away have condominium developments which make public access difficult. If you have a car, try São Pedro beach, passing Praia de Pernambuco and Praia do Perequê with a fishing village beside it, where excellent seafood restaurants line the seafront. It was formerly a private beach, now open to the public, but be there as early as possible because only 150 cars are allowed: a beautiful spot.

L *Casa Grande*, Av Miguel Stéfano 1087, T/F3552300. Luxury, in colonial style, with **Sleeping &** clean beach. L *Jequiti-Mar*, 8 km beyond Guarujá on the road to Bertioga, T/F3533111. **eating** Extremely attractive holiday complex with private beaches (excellent swimming and boating), fine fishing grounds, and chalet accommodation, excellent restaurant, 2 nightclubs open each weekend and every night from December to March. **AL** *Delphin*, Av Miguel Stéfano 1295, turn left in the centre of Guarujá and drive less than 1 km to the beginning of the long Praia da Enseada, T3862112, F3866844, delphin@tribuna.com.br, *La Popote* restaurant. **AL** *Ferraretto Hotel*, R Mário Ribeiro 564, T3861112, F3875616. Facing sea, luxurious, nightclub, swimming pool. **B** *Canto da Enseada*, R São Paulo 132, Enseada, T/F3514819. Pool. **B** *Pousada Mira Mar*, R Antônio Marques 328, Tombo, T/F3541453. **Youth hostel E** pp *Guarujá*, R das Carmélias 10, Praia da Enseada, T3517779, IYHA. For eating, try *do Joca*, on the road to Bertioga, Km 12, T3051188. Seafood. There is a good *churrascaria* opposite the rodoviária.

In **August** there is the *Procissão Marítima de Nossa Senhora dos Navegantes* and a **Festivals** *Festival de Folclore*.

The route from the centre of Santos to the resort of Guarujá is along Av Conselheiro **Transport** Nébias to the seafront avenue, Av Vicente de Carvalho (the continuation from Av Pres Wilson, Gonzaga), continuing along the promenade to the Guarujá ferry (every 10 minutes, free for pedestrians) at Ponta da Praia. The ferry is free from Santos, but back to Santos from Guarujá is US$2.80 on weekdays, US$4.20 Saturday-Sunday. On the other side proceed as far as Enseada das Tartarugas (Turtle Bay). During the season and weekends there is a long delay at the Ponta da Praia vehicle ferry; to avoid this take the ferry on foot and get the bus on the Guarujá side; motor boats also cross for US$0.50. A trolleybus runs from Praça Mauá in Santos to the ferry, then take one of the buses.

Banks *Banco 24 Horas*, in Pão de Açúcar supermarket, Av Dom Pedro I 195, Enseada. *Bradesco*, **Directory** Av Dom Pedro I 1015, Praia da Enseada. **Hospitals and medical services** Ana Costa, Via Santos Dumont 3651, T3868787. **Tourist offices** R Quintino Bocaiúva 248, T3877199.

Bertioga

There are good seafood restaurants on the road (SP-061) between Guarujá *Population: 17,000* and Bertioga, the next major beach centre up the coast (one hour by bus). It, *Phone code: 013* too, can be an overcrowded place in the summer. A ferry crosses the mouth of *Colour map 5, grid A6* the Canal de Bertioga. The town is on the north bank of the canal and beyond is a long sweeping bay with seven beaches divided by a promontory, the Ponta da Selada. Going northeast, the beaches are Praias de Bertioga (Enseada, Vista Linda and Indaía), Praia São Lourenço (which has been developed as the Riviera de São Lourenço, with condos, hotels, green areas and sports facilities), Praia Itaguaré, Praia Guaratuba and Praia Boracéia (campsite, meals served). The hills behind Bertioga are covered in forest which is now being used for walking and appreciation of the Mata Atlântica by local agencies.

Two forts were built to protect the coast from attack by the Tamoio Indians in the 16th century, São Felipe and São João. The latter, in Bertioga, can be visited and part of it houses the João Ramalho museum, which contains a variety of historical objects. There is a *Festa da Primavera* in October. The coastal road beyond Bertioga is paved, and the Rio-Santos highway, a few kilometres inland, provides a good link to São Sebastião.

B *Marazul 27*, Av Tomé de Souza 825, Enseada, T3171109, F3171561. Good seafood **Sleeping &** restaurant. **B** *Balsa*, Av Tomé de Souza 3268, T/F3171226. Restaurant. *Zezé e Duarte*, **eating** Av Tomé de Souza 10.

São Paulo

Directory **Banks** *Bradesco*, in Shopping Riviera, Av da Riviera 1256. **Hospitals & medical services** *Unidade Hospitalar Mista*, Praça Vicente Molinari, T3171593. **Tour companies & travel agents** *Suinã Turismo*, T3173945, offers 'eco-tours', including to Itatinga (see above, under Santos). **Tourist offices** *Departamento de Esportes e Turismo Municipal*, R Luiz Pereira de Campos 901, Vila Itapanhaú, T3171213, extension 2075.

Camburi & Beyond Boracéia are a number of beaches, including Barra do Una, Praia da
Maresias Baleia and **Camburi**. The latter is surrounded by the Mata Atlântica. The sea is
Phone code: 012 clean and good for bathing and watersports, including surfing (see **Surfing**, page 32, for this and other recommendations). There are a number of good hotels and restaurants in Camburi. You can walk on the Estrada do Piavu into the Mata Atlântica to see streams, vegetation and wildlife (bathing in the streams is permitted, but use of shampoo and other chemicals is forbidden). Five kilometres from Camburi is Praia Brava, 45 minutes' walk through the forest, camping is possible. The surf here is very heavy (hence the name).

The road carries on from Camburi, past beaches such as Boiçucanga to **Maresias**, a fashionable place for surfers. Its nickname is 'Copacabana without the buildings', although it is well supplied with bars, restaurants and accommodation.

Sleeping & eating **Camburi**: **A** *Canto da Praia*, R Amaragi 85, Praia de Juqueí, T/F4631294. Dinner. Recommended. **B** *Pousada da Rosa*, R das Rosas 139, T/F4651412, **C** in low season. Breakfast, pool. *Manacá*, R do Manacá 102, Camburizinho, T4651566. Fish. **Maresias**: **A** *Piccolo Albergue*, R Nova Iguaçu 1979, T4656227, F4656747. Chalets and natural pool. *Ke Pantai*, Av Dr Francisco Loup 1555, T4656252, Thai cuisine. *Mr Harris Jazz Bar*. Recommended bar.

Transport Three daily buses from **São Paulo** to Camburi, 160 km, *en route* to São Sebastiâo/Ilhabela, US$3.60.

São Sebastião

Population: 44,000 From Maresias it is 21 kilometres to São Sebastião In all there are 21 good
Phone code: 012 beaches and an adequate, but not overdeveloped tourist infrastructure. The
Colour map 5, grid A6 many small islands offshore are very good for scuba-diving. There is also sailing, fishing and canoeing.

São Sebastião is on a narrow strait which separates the mainland from the Ilha de São Sebastião, popularly called Ilhabela, Brazil's largest marine (as opposed to riverine) island. Since colonial times, this has been an important area. The island, which was called Ciribaí, island of peace, by the Indians, was reported by Amerigo Vespucci in 1502, who renamed it after the saint of the day of his discovery. São Sebastião was settled at the end of the 16th century. With good sugar-growing land on the mainland and the island it was both a port for sending the sugar back to Europe and another point of defence against the Tamoio. Gold was discovered in the vicinity in 1722 so this, too, and later coffee were shipped out. Slaves were also brought through here. The oil industry has subsequently taken advantage of the harbour by building a terminal here.

Sights The natural attractions of the area include a large portion of the **Parque**
For tourist information, **Estadual da Serra do Mar** on the mainland, with other areas under protection
contact Sectur, Av Dr for their different ecosystems. Trails can be walked through the forests. There
Altino Arantes 174, are also old sugar plantations. The Centro de Biologia Marinha da
T4521808, who are Univesidade de São Paulo is located here and, for divers, as well as the marine
friendly and helpful fauna, there are a large number of wrecks in the strait that can be explored.
except regarding
Ilhabela

In São Sebastião the colonial centre is under the aegis of the Patrimônio Histórico e Artístico. A **Museu de Arte Sacra** is in the 17th century chapel of São Gonçalo in the town centre (R Sebastião Neves 90 – closed for restoration in 1997). The town's parish church on Praça Major João Fernandes was built in the early 17th-century and rebuilt in 1819. There is a **Museu do Naufrágio** near the church exhibiting shipwrecks and natural history of the local area. ■ *Free*. Other colonial constructions are the Cadeia Pública (the prison), now the military police HQ, on Praça Tobias de Aguiar, and the Casa Esperança at Avenida Altino Arantes 154. There is an internet café on the beachfront.

The beaches within two or three kilometres of São Sebastião harbour are polluted; others to the south and north are clean and inviting. Ilhabela tends to be expensive in season, when it is cheaper to stay in São Sebastião.

Sleeping **A** *Arrastão*, Av Manoel Hipólito do Rego 2097, direction Caraguatatuba, T/F4620099. Restaurant, pool. **A** *Recanto dos Pássaros*, Porto Grande, T4522046. **B** *Roma*, on the main Praça, T4521016. Excellent. Warmly recommended. **C** *Bariloche*, R Três Bandeirantes 133. Basic but clean. South of São Sebastião by 6 km is *Camping do Barraquéçaba Bar de Mar de Lucas*. Hot showers, English spoken, cabins available. Recommended.

Festivals **20 January**, festival of the patron saint, featuring *congadas*, a song and dance derived from slaves from the Congo; *Carnival* in **February**; *Festas Juninas*; folklore festival in **August**; *Mostrart*, a demonstration of arts and crafts, in **December**.

Transport **Buses** Two buses a day from **Rio** with *Normandy*, 0830 and 2300 (plus 1630 on Friday and Sunday), to Rio 0600 and 2330, heavily booked in advance, US$12.50 (US$5 from Paraty); 4 a day from **Santos**, 4 hours, US$7.60; 4 Litorânea buses a day also from **São Paulo**, US$8.85, which run inland via São José dos Campos, unless you ask for the service via Bertioga, only 2 a day. Free **ferry** to **Ilhabela** for foot passengers, see below.

Ilha de São Sebastião

The island of São Sebastião, known popularly as Ilhabela since the 1940s, is of volcanic origin, roughly 390 square kilometres in area. The four highest peaks are Morro de São Sebastião, 1,379 metres above sea-level, Morro do Papagaio, 1,309 metres, Ramalho, 1,285 metres, and Pico Baepi, 1,025 metres. All are often obscured by mist. Rainfall on the island is heavy, about 3,000 millimetres a year. The slopes are densely wooded and 80 percent of the forest is protected by the Parque Estadual de Ilhabela. This state park also encompasses the eight other islands in the archipelago, of which Ilhabela is the largest; only two other islands are inhabited, Vitória and Búzios.

Most of the flatter ground on Ilhabela is given over to sugar-cane. In the 19th century illegal slave traders used the island. The only settled district lies on the coastal strip facing the mainland, the Atlantic side being practically uninhabited except by a few fisherfolk. The place abounds in tropical plants and flowers, and many fruits grow wild, whose juice mixed with *cachaça* and sugar makes as delicious a cocktail as can be imagined.

A 50-kilometre return journey on foot over the hump of the island down towards the Atlantic, sometimes through dense tropical forest following the old slave trail, requires a local guide. There is a rough road to the Atlantic side, but it is very difficult to drive. The terraced **Cachoeira da Toca** waterfalls amid dense jungle close to the foot of the Baepi peak give cool freshwater bathing;

São Paulo

lots of butterflies (entry, US$4, includes insect repellent). You can walk on a signed path, or go by car; it's a few kilometres from the ferry dock. The locals claim that there are over 300 waterfalls on the island, but only a few of them can be reached on foot. Those that can are worth the effort.

In all shady places, especially away from the sea, there thrives a species of midge known locally as *borrachudo*. A locally sold repellant (Autan) keeps them off for some time, but those allergic to insect bites should remain on the inhabited coastal strip. There is a small helpful hospital by the church in town.

Ilhabela

Population: 13,100 (100,000 high season) Phone code: 012 Colour map 5, grid A6

This town is very popular during summer weekends; at such times it is very difficult to find space for a car on the ferry. It is, however, a nice place to relax on the beach, with good food and some good value accommodation. No alterations are allowed to the frontage of the main township, Ilhabela.

Sights The town's parish church, **Nossa Senhora da Ajuda e Bom Sucesso**, dates from the 17th century, but has been restored. Visit the old **Feiticeira** plantation, with underground dungeons. The road is along the coast, sometimes high above the sea, towards the south of the island (11 kilometres from the town). You can go by bus, taxi, or horse and buggy. A trail leads down from the *fazenda* to the beautiful beach of the same name. Another old *fazenda* is **Engenho d'Água**, which is nearer to the town, which gives its name to one of the busiest beaches (the *fazenda* is not open to the public).

Pedras do Sino (Bell Rocks) These curious seashore boulders, when struck with a piece of iron or stone, emit a loud bell-like note. There is a beach here, too, four kilometres north of town. A campsite is nearby.

Beaches & watersports On the mainland side it is not recommended to bathe from the beaches three or four kilometres either side of the town because of pollution. On this side of the island you should also look out for oil, sandflies and jellyfish on the sand and in the water. There are some three dozen beaches around Ilhabela, only about 12 of them away from the coast facing the mainland. **Praia dos Castelhanos**, reached by the rough road over the island to the Atlantic side (no buses), is recommended. Several of the ocean beaches can only be reached by boat. At **Saco do Sombrio**, a cove on the Atlantic coast, English, Dutch and French pirates sheltered in the 16th and 17th centuries. Needless to say, this has led to legends of hidden treasure, but the most potent story about the place is that of the Englishman, Thomas Cavendish. In 1592 he sacked Santos and set it on fire. He then sailed to Saco do Sombrio where his crew mutinied, hanged Cavendish, sank their boats and settled on the island.

On the south coast is the fishing village of **Bonete**, which has 500 metres of beach and can be reached either by boat (1½ hours), or by driving to Borrifos at the end of the road, then walking along a trail for three hours.

The island is considered the **Capital da Vela** (capital of sailing) because its 150 kilometres of coastline offers all types of conditions. The sheltered waters of the strait are where many sailors learn their skills and the bays around the coast provide safe anchorages. There are, however, numerous tales of shipwrecks because of the unpredictable winds, sudden mists and strange forces playing havoc with compasses, but these provide plenty of adventure for divers. There are over 30 wrecks that can be dived, the most notable being the *Príncipe de Asturias*, a transatlantic liner that went down off the Ponta de Pirabura in 1916.

AL *Itapemar*, No 341, T4721329, F4722409. Windsurfing equipment rented. **AL** *Porto* **Sleeping**
Pousada Saco da Capela, R Itapema 167, T4722255, F4721052. **A** *Ilhabela*, Av Pedro
Paulo de Morais 151, T/F4721083, hoibela@mandic.com.br. Good breakfast. Recom-
mended. **A** *Maison Joly*, R Antônio Lisboa Alves 272, Morro do Cantagalo, T4722364,
F4721201. Good restaurant. **B** *Pousada dos Hibiscos*, Av Pedro Paulo de Morais 714,
T4721375. Pool, good atmosphere, recommended. Some less expensive hotels are
found on the road to the left of the ferry.

Youth hostel E pp *Ilhabela*, Av Col José Vicente Faria Lima 1243, Perequê,
T4728468, hostelling@iconet.com.br, IYHA. **Camping** In addition to Pedra do Sino,
mentioned above, there are campsites at Perequê, near the ferry dock, and at Praia
Grande, a further 11 km south.

São Sebastião & Ilhabela

Beaches

1 Ponta das Canas	16 Perequê	31 Saco Grande	46 Cigarras
2 Armação	17 Cabras	32 Figueira	47 Olaria
3 Pinto	18 Pedra Miúda	33 Baía dos Castelhanos	48 Arrastão
4 Ponta Azeda	19 Portinho	34 Ponta da Cabeçuda	49 Pontal da Cruz
5 Pedra do Sino	20 Feiticeira	35 Eustáquio	50 Deserta
6 Arrozal	21 Julião	36 Guanxuma	51 Porto Grande
7 Siriúba	22 Grande	37 Caveira	52 Centro
8 Viana	23 Curral	38 Serraria	53 Preta
9 Mercedes	24 Veloso	39 Ponta Grossa	54 Grande
10 Saco do Indaiá	25 Ponta da Sela	40 Poço	55 Pitangueiras
11 Saco Grande	26 Ponta da Sepetiba	41 Ponta do Lobo	56 Timbó
12 Pequeá	27 Enchovas	42 Fome	57 Barraqueçaba
13 Engenho d'Água	28 Ponta do Diogo	43 Jabaquara	58 Guaecá
14 Itaguaçu	29 Ponta do Boi	44 Pacuíba	
15 Itaquanduba	30 Ponta da Pirabura	45 Enseada	

Eating *Viana*, Av Leonardo Reale 1560, Praia da Viana, T4721089. Fish, best to make reservations. *Perequê*, Av Princesa Isabel 337, reasonable. *Farol*, Av Princesa Isabel 1634, Perequê. Good, especially seafood. Recommended.

Festivals Ilhabela is rich in folklore and legends. Its version of the *congada* (see above and **Music**, page 771) is famous, particularly at the festival of *São Benedito* in **May**. Other saints' days are *São Pedro*, **28 June**, with a maritime procession, and *Santa Verônica*, first week of **July** in Bonete. *Carnival* is held in **February**. The town's anniversary is in **September**. There are sailing weeks and fishing tournaments throughout the year; dates change annually.

Transport **Buses** A bus runs along the coastal strip facing the mainland. *Litorânea* buses from **São Paulo** connect with a service right through to Ilhabela town; office in Ilhabela at R Dr Carvalho 136.

Ferries At weekends and on holidays the 15-20 minute ferry between São Sebastião and Perequê runs non-stop day and night. During the week it does not sail between 0130 and 0430 in the morning. Passengers pay nothing; the fare for cars is US$7 weekdays, US$10 at weekends. Reservations for cars can be made in advance at *Dersa*, R Iaiá 126, Itaim-Bibi, São Paulo, T011-8206655 (this service costs extra); office in São Sebastião, Av São Sebastião, T4521576.

Directory **Banks** *Bradesco*, Praça Col Julião M Negrão 29. **Tourist offices** *Secretaria de Turismo*, R Bartolomeu de Gusmão 140, Pequeá, T4721091.

Caraguatatuba
Population: 67,500
Phone code: 012

On the Santos-Rio road is São Francisco da Praia, opposite the northern end of Ilhabela, beyond which begin the beaches of Caraguatatuba. In all there are 17 good beaches to the northeast and southwest, most divided between two sweeping bays. As well as watersports, Caraguatatuba is known for hang-gliding and, like so many places that are denominated 'capital' of something, is called the **Capital do Vôo Livre** (capital of hang gliding). It is a popular place at weekends and in the summer, with good hotels, restaurants, bars and campsites. For tourist information, contact the *Secretaria Municipal de Turismo*, Praça Diógenes Ribeiro de Lima 140, T4225700.

In common with other places on this coast, there are opportunities for walking in the forest behind the coastal strip. The road which goes inland, called the Rodovia dos Tamoios, climbs steeply into the densely wooded hills, with lots of hairpins. There are striking views of Caraguatatuba and the coast; one viewpoint is called O Mirante da Chegada, at Km 70. It takes about 25 minutes before the road levels out in the district of Paraibuna and crosses the high agricultural lands, running beside the bays of a huge artificial lake, the Represa de Paraibuna. The road joins the Dutra highway at São José dos Campos.

Sleeping **AL** *Pousada Tabatinga*, SP-55 Km 84, Praia da Tabatinga, T4241411, F4241544. Restaurant, pool. **C** *Guanabara*, R Santo Antônio 75, T4222533, F4226399. Pool. **Youth hostels** **E** pp *Recanto das Andorinhas*, R Eng João Fonseca 112, one street from the central bus terminal, 50 metres from the beach, T4221862, F4226181. **Sampa Praia**, R Tourinhos 521, T4242785, open 24 hours.

Transport Direct buses to Caraguatatuba from **Rio** (US$12, same schedule as for São Sebastião), **São Paulo** and **Santos**; direct buses from São Paulo do not use the coast road, but go via São José dos Campos.

Further northeast from Caraguatatuba is **Lagoinha**, 34 kilometres west of Ubatuba, with chalets and sailing boats for hire. There is exotic birdlife in the nearby forest and the ruins of an 18th-century *fazenda*, Engenho Bom Retiro. Boat trips can be made to beaches and islands.

Ubatuba

The Tropic of Capricorn runs through Ubatuba (through the beach of Itaguá to be precise). It is one of the most beautiful stretches of the São Paulo coast and has been recognized as such by the local tourist industry for many years. Surfing is the pastime of which it is said to be capital, but a whole range of watersports is on offer, including sailing to and around the offshore islands. In all, there are 72 beautiful beaches, some large, some small, some in coves, some on islands.

Population: 55,033
Phone code: 012
Colour map 5, grid A6

The beaches are spread out over a wide area, so if you are staying in Ubatuba town, you need to use the buses which go to most of them. Either that, or hire a car. The area gets very crowded at carnival time as people from Rio come to escape the crowds in their city. Ubatuba, though, does celebrate carnival itself.

The commercial centre of Ubatuba is at the northern end of the bay, by the estuary which the fishing boats enter and leave. A bridge crosses the estuary, giving access to the coast north of town. A small jetty with a lighthouse at the end protects the river mouth and this is a nice place to watch the boats come and go. The seafront, stretching south from the jetty, is built up along its length, but there are hardly any high-rise blocks. In the commercial centre are shops, banks, services, lots of restaurants (most serving pizza and fish), but few hotels. These are on the beaches north and south and can be reached from the Costamar bus terminal.

São Paulo

History

This part of the coast was a hotly contested area between the local Indians and the Portuguese. The Jesuits José Anchieta and Manuel Nóbrega came to the village of Iperoig, as it was called in 1563, to put a stop to the fighting; the former was even taken hostage by the Indians during the negotiations. A cross on the Praia do Cruzeiro (or Iperoig) in the centre commemorates the peace which the town proudly claims to be the first peace treaty on the American continent. The colonists eventually prevailed and the town of Vila Nova da Exaltação da Santa Cruz do Salvador de Ubatuba (its next name) became an important port until Santos overtook it in the late 18th century. In the 20th century its development as a holiday resort was rapid, especially after 1948 when it became an Estância Balneária. The shortened name of Ubatuba derives from the Tupi-Guarani, meaning 'place of *ubas*', a type of tree used for making bows and canoes.

Sights

Ubatuba has a few historic buildings, such as the **Igreja da Matriz** (Praça da Matriz), which is 18th-19th century and has only one tower, the old 19th-century prison, **Cadeia Velha** on Praça Nóbrega, the 18th-century **Câmara Municipal** on Avenida Iperoig, which now houses the historical museum, and the **Sobrado do Porto**, the 19th-century customs house (Praça Anchieta 38), which contains **Fundart**, the Art and Culture Foundation. Mostly, though, it is a modern, functional town. In the surrounding countryside there are *fazendas* which are often incorporated into the *trilhas ecológicas* (nature trails) which are proliferating along the coast.

The **Projeto Tamar**, Rua Guarani 835, Itaguá, T4326202, is a branch of the national project which studies and preserves marine turtles. On the same street, at No 859, is the **Aquário de Ubatuba**. ■ *Daily 1000-2200, except Thursday, T4321382.*

There is a small airport from which stunt fliers take off to wheel and dive over the bay. They advertise 10-minute panoramic flights over Ubatuba, but whether these include aerial acrobatics is not stated.

Beaches

The only beach where swimming is definitely not recommended is that part of the beach near the town's outflow between *praias* do Cruzeiro and Itaguá. The sand and water close to the jetty doesn't look too inviting either. The most popular are *praias* Tenório, Grande and Toninhas (4½, six and eight kilometres south respectively). Condominiums, apartments, hotels and *pousadas* line these beaches, on both sides of the coast road. There is no point in listing here all 72 of the municipality's beaches; those to the south are the more developed although the further you go from town in either direction, the less built up the beaches are.

Saco da Ribeira, 13 kilometres south, is a natural harbour which has been made into a yacht marina. Schooners leave from here for excursions to **Ilha Anchieta** (or dos Porcos), a popular four-hour trip (for agencies, see below). On the island are beaches, trails and a prison, which was in commission from 1908-1952. The Costamar bus from Ubatuba to Saco da Ribeira (every 20 minutes, 30 minutes, US$0.85) drops you at the turn-off by the *Restaurante Pizzaria Malibu*. It's a short walk to the docks and boat yards where an unmade road leads right, through the boatyards, to a track along the shore. It reaches the Praia da Ribeira which you can walk along to another track going round a

Ubatuba coast

Beaches	10 Grande	20 Flamengo	30 Fortaleza
1 Vermelho do Norte	11 Toninhas	21 Flamenguinho	31 Cedro
2 Saco da Mãe	12 Fora	22 Sete	32 Deserta
3 Barra Seca	13 Presídio	23 Sununga	33 Grande do Bonete
4 Perequê-Açu	14 Leste	24 Lázaro	34 Bonete
5 Cruzeiro	15 Sul	25 Domingo Dias	35 Lagoínha
6 Itaguá	16 Enseada	26 Barra & Dura	36 Maranduba
7 Cedro	17 Santa Rita	27 Vermelha do Sul	37 Pulso
8 Vermelho do Centro	18 Lamberto	28 Costa	38 Cassandoca
9 Tenório	19 Ribeira	29 Brava	39 Cassandoquinha

headland. This leads to the beaches of Flamengo, Flamenguinho and Sete Fontes. It's a pleasant stroll (about one hour to Flamengo), but there is no shade and you need to take water. Note the sign before Flamengo on one of the private properties: "Propriedade particular. Cuidado c/o elefante!"

Essentials

Sleeping
■ *on map, page 240*
Price codes: see inside front cover
At all holiday times it is expensive, with no hotel less than US$30. On many of the beaches there are hotels and pousadas, ranging from luxury resorts to more humble establishments

Beach hotels L *Recanto das Toninhas*, Praia das Toninhas, T4421410, F4420042, or São Paulo T2882022, F2882260, part of *Roteiros de Charme* group (see page 57). **AL** *Saveiros*, R Lucian Strass 227, Praia do Lázaro, 14 km from town, T4420172, F4421327. Pool, restaurant, English spoken. **A** *Solar das Águas Cantantes*, Estr Saco da Ribeira 253, Praia do Lázaro, 14 km, T4420178, F4420288. Reached by local bus, swimming pool, restaurant. At Baia Fortaleza, 25 km south of Ubatuba is **AL** *Refúgio do Corsário*, T4439148, F4439158. Full board, a clean quiet hotel on the waterfront, sailing and swimming, a good place to relax.

In town A *São Charbel*, Praça Nóbrega 280, T4321090, F4321080. Very helpful and comfortable, TV, restaurant, bar, swimming pool, etc. **A** *Parque Atlântico*, R Conceição 175, T4321336. **A** *São Nicolau*, R Conceição 213, T4325007, F4323310. Good, TV, fridge, good breakfast. **A** *Xaréu*, R Jordão Homem da Costa 413, T4321525, F4323060. Pleasant, quiet, good value, excellent breakfast. Recommended. The latter 3 are all convenient for the town beach, restaurants and services, and their prices fall to **B** in the low season.

North of town B *Jangadeiro*, Av Abreu Sodre (15 minutes' walk from centre, cross bridge, next to beach). Good value. *Maurício*, Av Abreu Sodré 607, near Praia do Perequê-Açu. Has cheap rooms, clothes washing possible.

Youth hostels E pp *Cora Coralina*, Rod Oswaldo Cruz Km 89, near the Horto Florestal, T011-2580388. IYHA, open 0800-2300. **E** pp *JS Brandão*, R Nestor Fonseca 173, Jardim Sumaré, near the Tropic of Capricorn sign south of town, T4322337. IYHA, open 0700-2300.

Camping Two *Camping Clube do Brasil* sites at Lagoinha (25 km from town), T4431536, and Praia Perequê-Açu, 2 km north, T4321682. There are about 8 other sites in the vicinity.

Eating
There are plenty of restaurants to choose from. This is just a brief selection

On Av Iperoig, starting from the roundabout by the airport, many restaurants *Querência*, *La Bonna Pasta*, No 600, *Lulas e Mexilhão*, *O Marinheiro*, No 574, *Via Virão*, *Tio Sam*, No 470, *Império*, No 404. At Galhardo e Corrêa is *Sérgio*, serving ice creams, pizzas and, at weekends, *feijoada*. *Tradição Mineira*, Galhardo e Jordão Homem da Costa. Serves *comida mineira*. There are lots of *sorveterias*.

Festivals

Ubatuba is known for its handicrafts (carved wood, basketware) and it holds a *Festa da Cultura Popular* in **September**. Other festivals include *São Pedro* at the end of **June** and the *Festa do Divino Espírito Santo* in **July**. The town's anniversary is **28 October**. Surfing championships are also held.

Transport

Taxis In town are a rip-off, eg US$6 from the centre to the main bus terminal.

Buses There are 3 bus terminals: 1) Rodoviária Costamar, at R Hans Staden and R Conceição, which serves all local destinations; 2) Rodoviária at R Prof Thomaz Galhardo 513 for São José buses to **Paraty**, US$2.25, some Normandy services to **Rio de Janeiro**, US$9 and some Itapemirim buses; 3) Rodoviária Litorânea, the main bus station: go up Conceição for 8 blocks from Praça 13 de Maio, turn right on R Rio Grande do Sul, then left into R Dra Maria V Jean. Buses from here go to **São Paulo**, 3½ hours, frequent, US$8, **São José dos Campos**, US$6, **Paraibuna**, US$5, **Caraguatatuba**, US$2.

Directory **Communications** Post Office: R Dona Maria Alves between Hans Staden and R Col Dominicano. **Telephone:** On Galhardo, close to *Sérgio* restaurant. **Internet:** *Due Punti Café*, R Tamoios 05. **Tour companies & travel agents** Agencies which run schooner trips to Ilha Anchieta and elsewhere: *Central de Passeios de Escuna*, Saco da Ribeira, T4411338. *Corsário*, Saco da Ribeira. *Mykonos*, Av Leovigildo Dias Vieira 1052, Itaguá, T4322042, office also in Saco da Ribeira. *Oceano Azul*, R Flamenguinho 277, Saco da Ribeira, T4420564. Trips leave Saco da Ribeira at 1000, returning at 1500, 4-hr journey, US$20 pp. A 6-hr trip can be made from Praia Itaguá, but in winter there is a cold wind off the sea in the afternoon, same price. Companies which offer trekking: *Guaynumby*, T4322832, and *Terra Brasil*, T4351275. Trails are graded according to difficulty and last from 2 hrs to 2 days (to Pico do Corcovado). **Tourist information** *Comtur*, Praça 13 de Maio and on Av Iperoig opposite R Prof Thomaz Galhardo, very helpful.

The road from São Sebastião is paved, so a journey from São Paulo along the coast is possible, five buses daily. Ubatuba is 70 kilometres from Paraty (see page 181).

Parque Nacional Serra da Bocaina

Straddling the border of São Paulo and Rio de Janeiro states is the Parque Nacional Serra da Bocaina, which rises from the coast to its highest point at Pico do Tira (or Chapéu) at 2,200 metres, encompassing three strata of vegetation. Up to 1,000 metres the forest is mainly made up of large trees such as *maçaranduba* (milk, or cow trees), *jatobá* (courbaril), cedar and *angelim* (angely). Between 1,000 and 2,000 metres the predominant varieties are pines and myrtles. Higher than this, the landscape is more grassy and open, with bromeliads, orchids and lichens. The main river flowing through it is the Mambucaba, which cascades down the mountainsides in a series of waterfalls. Trails lead to some of the falls and an old gold trail leads through the park (a three to four day hike).

Ubatuba

São Paulo

Permission to visit must be obtained in advance from Ibama, T0XX21-2246489 in Rio **Park essentials**
de Janeiro, or T0XX12-5771225 in São José do Barreiro, the nearest town; there are
hotels and trekking agencies here, including *Vale dos Veados*, Estr da Bocaina, Km 42,
T0XX12-5771194, F0XX12-5771303, part of the Roteiros de Charme hotel group, see
page 57.

All the remaining patches of Mata Atlântica along the Linha Verde provide
habitat for some of Brazil's rarer endemic birds. A book such as Nigel
Wheatley's *Where to watch birds in South America* can give far greater detail
than this guide has space for. Otherwise, contact specialists locally and, where
necessary, ask permission to birdwatch on private land.

The Litoral Sul

The Litoral Sul between Santos and Cananéia is not continuously developed,
unlike the Linha Verde. From São Vicente to Itanhaém, the whole coast is com-
pletely built up with holiday developments. Beyond Itanhaém, though, the road
does not hug the shore, so that a large area has been untouched.

This is the Estação Ecológica Juréia-Itatins, described below. This zone and several others on the southern São Paulo coast add up to almost 80 percent the
region being under some form of environmental protection. An organization
called *SOS Mata Atlântica* aims to help preserve what is left of the coastal vegetation, Rua Manoel da Nóbrega 456, São Paulo, CEP 04001-001, T011-88701195,
F011-8851680, smata@ax.apc.org.

São Vicente (*population*: 279,500) was the first town founded in Brazil but **São Vicente &**
there are few remains of this historic past. See the **Matriz São Vicente Mártir** **Praia Grande**
(1542, rebuilt in 1757) in Praça do Mercado, João Pessoa and the Ponte Pênsil *Phone code: 013*
bridge (1914) on the road to Praia Grande. The beaches here have calmer
waters and are good for watersports although not for bathing.

It is eight kilometres from São Vicente to **Praia Grande** (*population*:
150,500), 22½ kilometres of crowded beach. This is the beach most used by
Paulistanos. The water is polluted but it is used by surfers. There are plenty of
hotels, apartments, restaurants and lively nightlife, especially at Boqueirão in
the middle.

Sleeping and eating São Vicente: **A** *Ilha Porchat*, Al Paulo Gonçalves 264, Ilha
Porchat, T4683437, F4683735. Restaurant, pool. *Beni-Hama*, Av Newton Prado 271,
near Ponte Pênsil, T4698039. Japanese. **Praia Grande B** *Ibérica's Praia*, R Pernambuco
177, Boqueirão, T/F4731178. *Nostra Casa*, R Guarapari 95, T4917245. Italian.

Directory Banks: *Banco 24 Horas*, in Carrefour supermarket, Av Pref Jose Monteiro 1045, São
Vicente. *Bradesco*, Av Antônio Emmerich 772, São Vicente.

Next comes Mongaguá then, 61 kilometres from Santos, Itanhaém. Its pretty **Itanhaém**
colonial church of Sant'Ana (1761), Praça Narciso de Andrade, and the *Population: 58,500*
Convento da Nossa Senhora da Conceição (1699-1713, originally founded *Phone code: 013*
1554), on the small hill of Morro de Itaguaçu, are reminders that all along this
coast the Portuguese had settlements dedicated to the conversion of Indians to
Catholicism. In the town also is the Casa de Câmara e Cadeia, but the historic
buildings are quite lost amid the modern development. The beaches here are
attractive, but like those at Mongaguá and Praia Grande, several stretches are

prone to pollution. Excursions can be made by boat up the Rio Itanhaém. Frequent buses run from Santos, one hour. There are several good seafood restaurants along the beach, hotels and camping.

Sleeping and eating B *Pollastrini*, Praça 22 de Abril 38, T/F4223222. *Taberna Baska*, Av Vicente de Carvalho 776, Praia do Sonho, T4224890. Spanish. *do Maneco*, Av Brasil 800, Praia de Cibratel II, T4251468. Seafood.

Peruíbe

Population: 41,500
Phone code: 013
Colour map 5, grid A5

There are more beaches 31 kilometres south of Itanhaém at **Peruíbe**, but some fall within the jurisdiction of the Estação Ecológica Juréia-Itatins. While the beach culture has been well developed here, with surfing, windsurfing, fishing and so on, a number of 'alternative' options have recently flourished. The climate is said to be unusually healthy owing to a high concentration of ozone in the air; this helps to filter out harmful ultraviolet rays from the sun. UFO watchers and other esoterics claim that it is a very mystical place. Local rivers have water and black mud which has been proven to contain medicinal properties. And the neighbouring ecological station is a major draw now that ecotourism has become big business in São Paulo state.

For **tourist information**, contact the *Secretaria de Turismo*, R Nilo Soares Ferreira 50, T4552070. You may have to ask permission in the *Departamento da Cultura*, Centro de Convenções, Av Sã João 545, T4552232 to visit Abarebebê and other sites. Also at this address is the *Secretaria Estadual do Meio Ambiente*, T4579243, for information on the Estação Ecológico Juréia-Itatins. There is a Feira do Artesanato on Saturday and Sunday on Av São João, 1400-0100 (2300 in winter).

Peruíbe's history dates back to 1530 when the village of Abarebebê was founded. Nine kilometres northeast, the ruins can be visited, with its church built of stone and shells.

Sleeping & eating **A** *Piero Al Mare*, R Indianópolis 20, Praia Orla dos Coqueiros, T4582603. Restaurant. **B** *Waldhaus*, R Gaviotas 1201, Praia do Guaraú, T4579170. Restaurant. **C** *Vila Real*, Av Anchieta 6625, T4582797. *Beira-Mar*, Av Beira-Mar 869, T4551701. Seafood.

Festivals **18 February**: founding of the town; June, *Festival do Inverno*; October, *Mês das Missões*.

Estação Ecológico Juréia-Itatins Peruíbe marks the northernmost point of the **Estação Ecológico Juréia-Itatins**, 820 square kilometres of protected Mata Atlântica, "as it was when the Portuguese arrived in Brazil". The station was founded in 1986. The four main ecosystems are *restinga*, mangrove forest, Mata Atlântica and the vegetation at about 900 metres on the Juréia range of mountains. Its wildlife includes many endangered species, including rare flowers and other plants. There are deer, jaguar, monkeys, dolphins, alligators and birds, including the yellow-headed woodpecker and toucans. Human occupation of the area has included *sambaqui*, builders, *fazendeiros* and present-day fishing communities who preserve an isolated way of life.

Tourism in the ecological station is very carefully monitored and only certain areas are open to the public. These are: the *Núcleo Itinguçu*, 18 kilometres from Peruíbe, which contains the Cachoeira do Paraíso (Paradise Falls) and other pools and waterfalls; *Vila Barra do Una*, a fishing village with a two-kilometre beach, camping and places to eat, 25 kilometres from Peruíbe; and *Canto da Praia da Juréia* at the extreme southern end, 38 kilometres from

Iguape, with seven kilometres of beach and all the coastal ecosystems. Hikers can walk the four kilometre Trilha do Arpoador and the five kilometre Trilha do Imperador, but both need prior reservation and numbers are limited; similarly the Despraiado mountain bike trail. Trips can de made, again with authorization, up the Rio Guaraú (eight kilometres from Peruíbe) and the Rio Una do Prelado (25 kilometres from Peruíbe). Two other places of interest are Vila do Prelado, which used to be an overnight stop on the Imperial São Vicente-Iguape post route (electric light was only installed in 1995), and the Casa da Farinha, where manioc flour is made, 28 kilometres from Iguape.

Park essentials Contact the Secretaria Estadual do Meio Ambiente, address above, or the Instituto Florestal (DRPE), Rua do Horto 931, CEP 02377, São Paulo, T011-9528555, for permission to visit the ecological station.

Iguape and Ilha Comprida

At the southern end of the ecological station is the town of **Iguape** founded in 1538. In the early days of its existence, ownership of the town was disputed between Spain and Portugal because it was close to the line drawn by the Pope marking Spanish and Portuguese territory in the 'New World'. Typical of Portuguese architecture, the small **Museu Histórico e Arqueológico** is housed in the 17th-century Casa da Oficina Real de Fundição, Rua das Neves 45. ■ *Tuesday-Sunday 0900-1730*. There is also a **Museu de Arte Sacra** in the former Igreja do Rosário, Praça Rotary. ■ *Saturday-Sunday 0900-1200, 1330-1700*. The main church, the **Basílica de Bom Jesus**, is a mid-19th century construction. It has a market, hotels and restaurants. For tourist information, contact the *Prefeitura Municipal*, R 15 de Novembro 272, T8411626, F8411620.

Half a dozen beaches, but particularly yachting and fishing, bring tourists to the town. Excursions include the ruined *fazenda* of Itaguá. Handicraft specialities are items in wood and clay, basketware and musical instruments.

Population: 26,000
Phone code: 013
Colour map 5, grid A5

São Paulo

Estação Ecológica Juréia-Itatins

Opposite Iguape is the northern end of the **Ilha Comprida** with 86 kilometres of beaches (some disappointing). This Área de Proteção Ambiental is not much higher than sea level and is divided from the mainland by the Canal do Mar Pequeno. The northern end is the busiest and on the island there are good restaurants, hotels, supermarket – fresh fish is excellent. There is also accommodation.

Sleeping & eating
B *Silvi*, R Ana Cândida Sandoval Trigo 515, T/F8411421, silvihotel@virtualway.com.br. Good. **C** *Solar Colonial Pousada*, Praça da Basilica 30, T8411591, 19th century house. *Veleiro*, Av Beira Mar 579, T8952407. Recommended. Others of varying quality. **Camping** There is a campsite at Praia da Barra da Ribeira, 20 km north, and wild camping is possible at Praia de Juréia, the gateway to the ecological station. Panela Velha, R 15 de Novembro 190, T8411869. Seafood restaurant.

Festivals
In **January** and **February** there is a summer festival in Iguape, while Ilha Comprida celebrates *Carnival* in **February**. *Semana Santa* and *Corpus Cristi*. **August** is the month of the pilgrimage of *Senhor Bom Jesus de Iguape*. **3 December** is Iguape's anniversary. Throughout the year there are other sporting and cultural events.

Transport
Buses To Iguape: from São Paulo, Santos, or Curitiba, changing at Registro (see below). **Ferries** A continuous ferry service runs from Iguape to Ilha Comprida (free but small charge for cars); buses run until 1900 from the ferry stop to the beaches. From Iguape it is possible to take a boat trip down the coast to Cananéia and Ariri (see below). Tickets and information from dpto Hidroviário do Estado, R Major Moutinho 198, Iguape, T8411122. It is a beautiful trip, passing between the island and the mainland.

Caverns of the Vale do Ribeiro

The caves are southwest of the state capital, west of the BR-116, in one of the largest concentrations of caverns in the world. Among the best known is the eight kilometre **Caverna do Diabo** (Devil's Cave), or **Gruta da Tapagem**. It has been described as huge 'as a cathedral' with well-lit formations in the 600 metres open to the public. It is 40 kilometres from **Eldorado Paulista**. ■ *Monday-Friday 0800-1100, 1200-1700, Saturday, Sunday and holidays 0800-1700, US$2; bar and toilets.*

Forty three kilometres from Caverna do Diabo is **Petar**, the Parque Estadual Turístico do Alto Ribeira. Here are three groups of caves: the Núcleo Santana, with the **Cavernas de Santana** (with 5.6 kilometres of subterranean passages and three levels of galleries), Morro Preto and Água Suja, plus a 3.6 kilometre ecological trail to the waterfalls in the Rio Bethary; and the Núcleo Ouro Grosso. This section of the park is four kilometres from the town of **Iporanga**. Iporanga is the most convenient town for visiting all the caves; it is 64 kilometres west of Eldorado Paulista, 42 kilometres east of Apiaí, on the SP-165, 257 kilometres southwest of São Paulo. The third Núcleo is Caboclos, near the town of Apiaí. Guided tours of Petar cost US$50 a day from the Associação Serrana Ambientalista, T015-5561188.

Sleeping
There are hotels in Iporanga, such as the **C** *Pousada das Cavernas*, T015-5561168 (or TXX011-5433082) and the **D** pp *Pousada Rancho da Serra*, T015-5561168 (or TXX011-5882011). **Camping** in Petar costs US$3 pp, 3 sites. There is a **youth hostel** near the Caverna do Diabo, *Província de Tokushima*, Parque Estadual da Caverna do Diabo, Km 43, SP-165, Eldorado Paulista, T0XX11-353077, open 0800-1800.

Transport
Bus São Paulo-Apiaí, from Barra Funda rodoviária, US$22. If coming from Curitiba, change buses at Jacupiranga on the BR-116 for Eldorado Paulista.

A suitable stopping place for visiting the caves area is Registro on the BR-116, in the heart of the tea-growing region, populated mainly by Japanese Brazilians. *Lito Palace* (**B**) is at Av Pref Jonas Banks Leite 615, T8211055, F8214470. Around the corner from the rodoviária is *Brasília* (**D**), R Brasília, with shower, clean, airy. For eating, try *Itatins*, BR-116 Km 444, for churrasco. There is a good *churrascaria* next to the bus station. The bus station is at R Neraldo Previb 835, T8211379.

Registro
Population: 49,000
Phone code: 013

Directory Banks: *Bradesco*, Av Pref Jonas Banks Leite 520. **Communications** International calls can be made in the town centre. **Hospitals and medical services** *São José*, Av Clara Gianotti de Sousa 420, T8216188.

Cananéia and Ilha do Cardoso

At the southern end of Ilha Comprida, across the channel, is Cananéia 270 kilometres from São Paulo. Another town with a long colonial history, it was one of Martim Afonso de Souza's landfalls, it is now a peaceful place of gently decaying colonial charm. The colonial centre, around Praça Martim Afonso de Souza and neighbouring streets, contains the 17th-century church of **São João Batista** and the **Museu Municipal**. On 15 August, there is the Festa de Nossa Senhora dos Navegantes, with a procession of boats. To the south are a number of good beaches and the waterways are popular with fisherfolk.

Population: 9,500
Phone code: 013
Colour map 5, grid A5

For tourist information, contact the *Departamento de Esportes e Turismo*, Av Beira Mar 247, Cananéia, T8511473, extension 342. Guides Manoel Barroso, Av Independencia 65, T8511273, Portuguese only, recommended or try the *Secretaria do Parque Estadual da Ilha do Cardoso*, Av Prof Besnard, near the port.

To reach the densely wooded **Ilha do Cardoso**, which is a Reserva Florestal e Biológica, take a ferry from the dock at Cananéia, four hours, three services daily (Rua Princesa Isabel, T8411122). Alternatively, drive 70 kilometres along an unpaved road, impassable when wet, to **Ariri**, from where the island is 10 minutes by boat. The tiny village of Marujá, which has no electricity, has some very rustic *pousadas* and restaurants. Otherwise, the island is uninhabited. Camping is allowed at designated places. There are lots of idyllic beaches; best for surfing is Moretinho.

A *Cananéia Glória*, Av Luís Wilson Barbosa, T8511377, F8511378. Some chalets **B**, good views. **C** *Villa São João Batista*, R Tristão Lobo 287, T8511587. Colonial-style 18th century house, clean. *Naguissa do Silêncio*, Av Luís Wilson Barbosa 401, T8511341. Seafood.

Sleeping & eating

São Paulo

The Interior

The interior of São Paulo is diverse: there are hill resorts and spa towns, which are good for a break if you don't want to go to the beach. There are also towns with historical associations, industrial and agricultural centres.

About 13 percent of Brazil's population lives within 200 kilometres of São Paulo city, a circle which includes 88 municipalities. Four of them – the big ABCD towns – sharing a population of over a million, are Santo André, São Bernardo, São Caetano and Diadema; they have many of the largest industrial plants. There are some 70 cities in the State with populations of over 50,000 and São Paulo is linked with all of them by road, and several of them by railway.

The Northeast

To Rio de Janeiro There are two major routes from São Paulo heading northeast towards Rio de Janeiro state. The older of the two is the Dutra Highway (BR-116); the more recent is the Ayrton Senna tollway (SP-070), which becomes after 50 kilometres the Carvalho Pinto tollway (SP-075). The newer road bypasses São José dos Campos, where roads branch off to the coast (the Rodovia dos Tamoios – SP-088/099 – see above under **Caraguatatuba**) and to **Campos do Jordão** (see below). The two highways meet at Quirim, near **Taubaté**, a city of 213,370 people. Taubaté was hit by the coffee boom in the 1820s, but in this regard its importance had begun to decline by the 1880s. Now it is a centre for heavy industry. From Taubaté also there are roads to the coast (SP-125 to Ubatuba) and to Campos do Jordão.

Campos do Jordão

Population: 36,000
Phone code: 012
Colour map 5, grid A6

This mountain resort between Rio de Janeiro and São Paulo 1,628 metres high in the Serra da Mantiqueira is prettily set in a long valley. The climate is cold and dry in winter and cool in summer, a great relief from the coastal heat and humidity.

Campos do Jordão, named after a 19th-century landowner, is made up of three districts: Jaguaribe, the original nucleus, Abernéssia, founded by Scotsman Robert John Reid (the name he chose is a mixture of Aberdeen and Inverness), and Capivari, dating from the early 20th century. It was originally a *fazenda*, built in the 18th century by Inácio Caetano Vieira de Carvalho, on the gold route from Itajubá (Minas Gerais) across the Serra da Mantiqueira to the coast.

In April, there is the *Festa do Pinhão*; look out for classical music and dance festivals in June and July. There are plenty of chocolate shops, also jams and cheese for sale. Stalls on the main praça Thursday-Sunday sell local produce. 'Minalba' mineral water is produced here.

Palácio Boa Vista, four kilometres from the centre of Abernéssia, was built in
1964 as a summer residence for the state governor. It was converted into a
museum in 1970 and now houses works of art, furniture, sculpture and other
items. ■ *Wednesday and Thursday, Saturday and Sunday, 1000-1200,
1400-1700, T2621122*. Other collections of art will be found in the **Museu
Felícia Leirner**, an open-air museum with 85 sculptures in a park beside the
Auditório Cláudio Santoro (Felícia Leirner herself was a sculptress); about two
kilometres from the Palácio Boa Vista. ■ *Tuesday-Sunday 0900-1800,
T2622324*. Also the **Casa da Xilogravura**, a museum specializing in woodcuts, founded by Antônio Fernando Costello, Avenida Eduardo Moreira da
Cruz 295, Jaguaribe. ■ *Daily 1400-1700, Sunday 1000-1300, T2621832*.

Sights

Mineral springs within the town include the Fontes da Amizade, Renato
and Simão. In Capivari is the **Morro do Elefante**, which has a road, path and
chairlift to the belvedere at the top. Twelve kilometres from Abernéssia is the
Pedra do Baú (1,950 metres), which has fine views from the summit. To get
there take a bus to São Bento do Sapucaí at 0800 or 1500, then walk to Paiol
Grande and then on an unmarked path to the Pedra. Return buses from São
Bento at 0915 and 1615. Near Paiol Grande is the small waterfall of **Cachoeira
dos Amores**. Also worth seeing is the **Gruta dos Crioulos**, 7½ kilometres
from Capivari. **Pico do Itapeva** (2,030 metres, 14 kilometres southeast from
Capivari) commands a beautiful view of the Paraíba valley. Also good for views
is **Imbiri** (1,950 metres). The nature reserve at **Horto Florestal** (15 kilometres
from Capivari) contains mostly pine forest in a 8,300 hectare Parque Estadual.
It ranges from 1,330 to 2,007 metres above sea level and is very pretty – go in
the morning to avoid crowds. There are lots of streams with bridges, waterfalls
and lakes. Ornamental plants can be bought and various trails are laid out.

Campos do Jordão is a popular place for hikers; most of the roads leading
off the main avenue lead to quiet areas with good views, for example up
Avenida Dr Antônio Nicola Padula, turn left 500 metres past *Refúgio na Serra*
for waterfalls and Pico do Itapeva.

Estrada de Ferro Campos de Jordão Railcars make round trips between
Emílio Ribas station in Capivari (Campos do Jordão) and **Santo Antônio do
Pinhal**, 16 kilometres southwest. In season, the trains run six times a day, out
of season (October-November, March-April) at 1310 only, a bit bumpy, but
beautiful views (sit on the right on the way there, left coming back): hills, valleys, tight corners. The train is very crowded even though you are assigned a
seat (buy your ticket in advance, and get a return immediately on arrival in San
Antônio; watch your belongings on board). The whole trip takes about three
hours: one hour each way on the train, 30 minutes-1 hour in Santo Antônio.
There is not much on offer in Santo Antônio: a few snack bars, handicraft
shops, nice views, the viewpoint of Nossa Senhora Auxiliadora.

The **Emílio Ribas** station and **Recanto de São Cristóvão** are connected by
a tram which runs every 40 minutes from 0630. The journey, which like the
train runs the length of Campos do Jordão, takes one hour 10 minutes.

LL *Toriba*, Av Ernesto Diederichsen 2962, T2621566, F2624211. Part of the Roteiros de
Charme group, see page 57. **AL** *Refúgio Alpino*, Av Sen Roberto Simonsen 1461,
T/F2631332, hralpino@iconet.com.br. Full board. **B** *Refugio na Serra*, Av Dr Antônio
Nicola Padula 275, T2631330. Comfortable, good breakfast, very helpful owners
(some English spoken). Recommended. **Youth hostels E** pp *Recanto Tropical*, Estr
Pindamonhangaba/Campos do Jordão 1650, T2422737, F2428312. IYHA. *Elis Regina
II*, R Benigno Ribeiro 320, Recanto Feliz, T0XX11-353077. Open 0800-2300.
Camping *Camping Clube do Brasil*, T2631130.

**Sleeping &
eating**
*Book accommodation
in advance for June-July*

São Paulo

Sole Mio, Av Dr Emilio Lang 440. *Capivari*, Av Dr Emílio Ribas 814, on road to Horto Florestal, T2631429. Italian. *Baden Baden*, R Djalma Forjaz 93, Capivari, T2633610. German, good.

Transport **Road** The road from Taubaté is 45 km, while that from São José dos Campos is 85 km. By car it takes about 3 hours from São Paulo, 6 to 7 from Rio. **Buses** Bus station, Av Dr Januário Miraglia, T2621996. From **São Paulo**, US$3.60, 3 hours. From **Rio**, changing at São José dos Campos, US$5.75.

Directory **Banks** *Bradesco*, Av Frei Orestes Girardi 1037. **Hospitals and medical services** *São Paulo*, R Agripino Lopes de Morais 1100, T2621722. **Tourist information** The tourist office is in the alpine-looking gateway to the city, the Portal da Cidade, T2622755, F2624100.

The short road down to **Pindamonhangaba**, starting from the paved road 24 kilometres southwest of Campos do Jordão, is paved (five buses daily, 50 minutes). A railcar runs to **'Pinda'** out of season, leaving 1705 Monday-Thursday and weekends, from Pinda 0600 Tuesday-Friday, 0930 weekends (no service during the high season, when all cars are used on the Campos do Jordão-San Antônio route). There is a local railcar service within 'Pinda' (very crowded but cheap). From 'Pinda' buses run to **São Paulo** and to **Aparecida do Norte**, 1030, US$2.

Aparecida do Norte
Population: 34,000

Nearer to Rio than the Pindamonhangaba turn, just off the BR-116, is Brazil's chief place of pilgrimage and the seat of its patron saint, Nossa Senhora Aparecida. This small black image of the Virgin is said to have been taken by a fisherman from the nearby Río Paraíba, and quickly acquired a miraculous reputation. It is now housed in a huge modern basilica (1939) in Romanesque style on top of a hill, with the clean white-walled, red-roofed town below.

To Minas Gerais

The BR-381, Rodovia Fernão Dias eventually leaves São Paulo, passing factories and motels. The motels get more stylish the further they are from the city. The highway is being made into a dual carriageway and as the road climbs into the forested hills it is paralleled by the orange gash that will become the new carriageway. The land is intensively worked; industries such as rustic furniture and swimming pool manufacturers line the highway.

Atibaia
Population: 95,500
Phone code: 011

This spa town in the Serra da Mantiqueira, 69 kilometres from São Paulo, makes several grand claims for itself: the Brazilian Switzerland, with the second best climate in the world (after Switzerland itself). In the top climate stakes it is obviously competing with Peruíbe and Campos do Jordão; the 'Cidade das Flores' (city of flowers); the South American capital of strawberries – there is usually a flower and strawberry festival in September and a festival for strawberries alone in June. The Day of the Kings (*Reis Magos*), 6 January, is celebrated with *congadas* (see **Music**, page 771). Atibaia was founded in 1665 by the *bandeirante* Jerônimo de Camargo, on one of the roads to Minas Gerais.

There is a **Museu Ferroviário** on Avenida Jerónimo de Camargo, which preserves steam engines and rolling stock from the 19th century. It is in a park with a U-shaped railway line around a lake, with a station and turntable at each end. Latest reports indicate that no trains are running. ■ *T78710354*. Fourteen kilometres from town is *Recanto de Paz*, Av Jerônimo de Camargo (**L**), T78751369. It has chalets, restaurant, pool and horse riding. There are many other places to stay.

The Northwest

An important broad-gauge railway (formerly Santos a Jundiaí, now CPTM), runs from Santos to São Paulo and across the low mountains which separate São Paulo city from the interior to its terminus at Jundiaí. This city, 60 kilometres from São Paulo, has textile factories and other industries. The district grows coffee and grain and there is an annual Grape Festival.

Jundiaí
Population: 293,500
Phone code: 011

Sleeping & eating AL *Vale das Vinhas*, access from Km 67 Rod Anhangüera (towards Campinas), T73922436, F73921553. Chalets, pool, sports courts. **B** *Serra Verde*, Av Gumercindo Barranqueiras 80, T73924113, F73929517. *Concert* R Barão de Jundiaí 314, T73965685. *Pontinho Grill*, Av 9 de Julho 2031, T4346045. Churrasco.

Directory Banks *Banco 24 Horas*, Av Antônio Frederico Ozanan 6000. *Banco do Brasil*, R Vig J.J. Rodrigues 233.

Campinas

The city is an industrial centre 88 kilometres from São Paulo by the fine Via Anhangüera highway and important as a clearing point for coffee. Its university has an excellent reputation and there are many students in the town.

Population: 879,000
Phone code: 019
Colour map 4, grid C2

See the fine **Catedral Metropolitana Nossa Senhora da Conceição**, built in 1883 in neoclassical style with baroque elements (Praça José Bonifácio), and the **Mercado Municipal** (old market, 1908) on Avenida Benjamin Constant. There are several museums. **Museu Carlos Gomes**, Rua Bernardino de Campos 989, T2312567, has displays on art, literature and science; the city is the birthplace of the 19th century Brazilian composer Carlos Gomes, his tomb is in Praça Bento Quirino. In the Bosque de Jequitibás are the **Museus de História Natural** and **do Folclore**. The arts centre in the **Centro de Convivência Cultural**, Praça Tom Jobim, T2525857, has a noted symphony orchestra. The modern Universidade Estadual de São Paulo, called Unicamp, is outside the city. Visits can be made to the **Instituto Agronômico** on Avenida Barão de Itapura 1481, Guanabara, to see all the aspects of coffee. ■ *Moday-Friday 0800-1100, 1300-1700, T2315330.*

Sights

Campinas

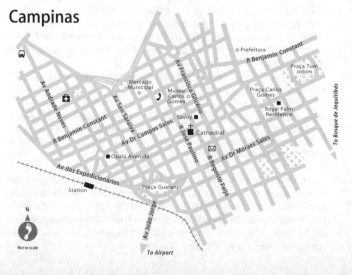

São Paulo

Tourist trains Twenty five kilometres from Campinas, at **Jaguariúna**, is a railway preservation group with steam engines and wagons. Every weekend and public holiday two trains (three on Sunday) run between Jaguariúna and Campinas on a two-hour trip. The route is along the old Mogiana Estrada de Ferro and is part of a tourism project based in Jaguariúna and the historic coffee-growing region. There are plans to restore the stations of Carlos Gomes, Tanquinho and Anhumas. You can either take an hourly bus from Campinas to Jaguariúna, or take the steam train itself from Campinas (station behind Carrefour, Anhumas, reached by town bus). ■ *For schedules and information, T2536067. The second tourist train runs one Saturday a month to Peruíbe, 0700, six hours, run by Pettená-Tur. A tourist tram operates in Parque Taquaral.*

Sleeping **LL** with meals *Solar das Andorinhas*, 20 km outside city on the Mogi-Mirim road, T2571411, F2571299. A health farm with pool, sauna, horses, sports courts. **L** *Royal Palm Plaza*, R Com Dr José Cesar Gazi 200, outside town at the Trevo de Anhangüera, T7388000, F7388001. **A** *Royal Palm Residence*, R Conceicão 450, T2344766, F2326109. Apartment hotel. **B** *Opala Avenida*, Av Dr Campos Salles 161, T2344115, F2316983. Central. **B** *Savoy*, R Regente Feijó 1064, T2329444, F2369207. **C** *Parati Palácio*, R Bernardino de Campos 426, T2320395. German spoken. Recommended. **C** *Hotel IPE*, R Bernardino de Campos 1050, T2317746. Recommended.

Eating *Bar Restaurante Barão*, Barão de Jaguará 1381 and *Churrascaria Gaúcha*, Av Dr Campos Salles 515, T2317449. Excellent for Brazilian food. *Nutrir*, R Dr Quirino 1620. Vegetarian, very good value. *Sucão*, R Benjamin Constant 1108. Good variety of juices. *Pastelaria do Sr Júlio*, R de 13 Maio 143. Friendly, helpful, cheap. Recommended.

Entertainment Weekend nightlife is busy around the Centro de Convivência (see above), in the city centre. There are cinemas in the city centre and the Iguatemi and Galleria shopping centres.

Shopping **Bookshops** *Pontes Editores*, R Dr Quirino 1223, has English books. Second-hand at *Sebo Comércio*, R Bareto Leme 1265, and *O Livrão*, R Barão de Jaguará 936, Loja 11.

Transport **Air** Viracopos international airport, Rod Santos Dumont Km 66, 7255000 is 11 km from Campinas, which also has its own airport. Flights to Belo Horizonte, Brasília, Curitiba, Joinville, Goiânia, Recife, Rio de Janeiro and São Paulo.

Taxis *Central Geral de Taxi*, T2728313; *Disk Taxi*, T2420600.

Trains A metre-gauge line, connecting with the broad-gauge former Paulista at Campinas, serves the northeastern part of the state. It goes through Ribeirão Preto to Uberlândia and Araguari in the Triângulo of Minas Gerais. Latest information suggests that no passenger services run on these lines.

Buses Bus station, R Barão de Parnaíba 690, T2321355. To **São Paulo**, US$3, **Ribeirão Preto** and **Araguari**; to **Rio**, 7 hours, US$12.

Directory **Airline offices** *TAM*, T2369022. *Varig*, T2316000. *Vasp*, T2322566. **Banks** *American Express*, R Irmã Serafina 863, 1st floor, conj 16, T2336797. **Hospitals & medical services** *das Clínicas*, Cidade Universitária, T7887766. **Places of worship** Community church services in English at *School of Language and Orientation*, R Eduardo Lane 270.

Americana
Population: 168,000
Phone code: 019

This town, 42 kilometres from Campinas, is situated in an area settled by Confederate refugees from the south of the US after the Civil War (see box). The town is now a centre for the textile industry and there are various factory outlets. In nearby **Santa Barbara d'Oeste** there is a **Museu de Imigração** explaining the history of the Confederates and other immigrants to this area. The bus station is on Rua Orlando Dei Santi, T4618077.

Confederados

At the end of the American Civil War, some 20,000 former Confederates were tempted to leave the United States and try their luck in Brazil. The emperor, Dom Pedro II, offered some very attractive incentives to the exiles, including subsidized passage, freedom of religion and land at 22 cents an acre. He was hoping that the Southerners would bring their expertise in cotton-growing to Brazil. They would certainly have been aware that slavery had not been banned in Brazil in the 1860s. First attempts at settlement were in the Amazon basin, but conditions there were too unhealthy and many of the original settlers soon returned to the States. Others settled further south and the only community which was successful was Villa Americana in São Paulo state. The confederados, as they were known, cultivated cotton, watermelons, peaches and pecans. A few families still speak English at home.

There is a museum at Santa Bárbara d'Oeste, 12 kilometres west, and a visit to the confederados' cemetery nearby reveals an unusual number of English surnames.

Further reading 'Finding Uncle Will', by Downs Matthews, pages 270-77 of Travellers' Tales: Brazil, is an interesting tale of how Matthews sought out a relative who emigrated to Brazil. An article in The Guardian (UK), on 26 November 1997 by Candace Piette, describes how some confederados are making efforts to strengthen links between Americana and the southern US.

Sleeping **A** *Americana*, Av Cillos 1796, T4613579, F4612635. Restaurant. **A** *Florença Palace*, Av Cillos 820, T4616393, F4618575. Restaurant, pool. *Brüder*, Av Campos Sales 447. *Prima Pizza*, R 12 de Novembro 613.

Directory **Banks** *Banco 24 Horas*, Praça Com Müller 77, *Bradesco*, Av Campos Sales 720.

Spa towns

Four towns some 80 to 100 kilometres northeast of Campinas are well-known for the quality of their mineral waters. Hotels and parks have been established around the springs and the spas have become popular for conferences and conventions.

The region and its medicinal waters began to be settled after the *bandeirantes* and mule trains passed this way on their expeditions and trade routes into Minas Gerais and Goiás. The towns themselves were not created until the 19th century, the latest being Lindóia in 1898.

Serra Negra (*population*: 22,000) is a very pleasant spa town and summer holi- *Phone code: 019* day resort in the mountains, 78 kilometres northeast of Campinas and 152 kilometres from São Paulo. There are several springs, a *Balneário Municipal* with a convention centre and the longest chairlift in Brazil, to the Cristo Redentor on Pico do Fonseca. Tourist information is at Praça John F Kennedy, T8922131.

Thirteen kilometres from Serra Negra is the even better-known spa town of **Lindóia** (*population*: 5,000) whose still waters are bottled and sent all over Brazil. The municipality is the largest producer of mineral water in Latin America. For tourist information, T8681211.

Seven kilometres away is a separate spa, **Águas de Lindóia** (*population*: 13,500), with a *Balneário Municipal*, hotels and a wide range of conference facilities. The bus station is at Av das Nações Unidas 1179, T8241128. Nearby is tourist information, at Av das Nações Unidas 196, T8941126.

Twenty two kilometres southeast of Lindóia is **Socorro** (*population*: 31,000) also with a *Balneário Municipal*. For tourist information, T8953000.

São Paulo

Sleeping & eating **Serra Negra**: **AL** *Rádio*, R Col Pedro Penteado 387, T8923311, F8921992, radiohotel@circuitodasaguas.com.br. Restaurant, pool, sports courts, very nice indeed. **A** *Cordilheira*, Praça João Zelante 53, T8921552, F8921627. Pool. **Youth hostel D** pp *Estância Clube Veraneio*, Km 156 on the road to Águas de Lindóia, T8922155, F8322096. *Carlinhos*, Av Romeu de Campos Vergal 23. Churrasco restaurant. **Lindóia**: **B** *Flamingo's Chalés*, Av 31 de Março, T8981356. Pool, sports courts. **Águas de Lindóia**: **AL** *Vacance*, Av das Nações Unidas 1374, T/F8241191. Restaurant, pool, sports courts. **A** *das Fontes*, R Rio de Janeiro 267, T8241511, F8241872. Pool. *Spaghetti e Cia*, R Rio de Janeiro 403. Italian restaurant. **Socorro**: **A** *Best Western Grinberg's Village*, Estr da Pompéia 210, T/F8952909. **Youth hostel** *Paschoalino Sigolo*, R Antônio Leopoldino 215, in the centre. Restaurant *Marchetti*, R 13 de Maio 43.

Directory **Banks** *Bradesco*, R Col Pedro Penteado 337, Serra Negra; Av Brasil 22, Águas de Lindóia; and R 13 de Maio 100, Socorro.

The North

Ribeirão Preto

Population: 456,500
Phone code: 016
Colour map 4, grid C1

The centre of a rich coffee-growing district, the town also has a steel industry. It is 319 kilometres from São Paulo by the Via Anhangüera (four hours by bus). It also has an airport.

The **Museu do Café**, in the former Fazenda Monte Alegre on the campus of the Universidade de São Paulo, on the road to Sertãozinho, tells the history of coffee in the area. ■ *T6331986*. In the same location is a historical museum. The cathedral, **São Sebastião**, Praça da Bandeira, was built in gothic style and contains stained glass and frescos by Benedito Calixto. On the Morro de São Bento is the **Sete Capelas** sanctuary. *Feapam*, Feira Agropecuária da Alta Mogiana, agricultural show is held early August.

Excursions **The Roteiro Portinari** The artist Cândido Portinari was born in **Brodowski**, 30 kilometres north of Ribeirão Preto. There is a museum at his house at Praça Cândido Portinari 298. In the garden of the house is the Capela da Nona, which Portinari built for his grandmother in 1941 when she was too ill to go to church. The walls are covered with beautiful murals of biblical figures. ■ *Tuesday-Sunday 0900-1700, T6641284*.

Sleeping & eating **AL** *Holiday Inn*, R Alvares Cabral 1120, T6250186, F6351279. **A** *Stream Palace*, R Gen Osório 850, T6100660, F6101007. **B** *Umuarama Recreio*, Praça dos Cafeeiros 140, T6373790, 6 km from centre, very pleasant, pool, gardens. *La Pyramide,* R Marcondes Salgado 1525, T6109121.

Transport **Air** Airport, T6263376. Flights to Brasília, São José do Rio Preto and São Paulo. **Buses** Bus station, Av Jerônimo Gonçalves, T6257386. *Rápido Ribeirão Preto* to **São Paulo**, 4-5 hours, US$20.

Directory **Airline offices** *Interbrasil*, T6280909. *Passaredo*, T6281319. *Rio-Sul*, T6266848. *TAM*, T6282500. **Banks** *Banco 24 Horas*, R Gen Osório 432. *Banco do Brasil*, R Duque de Caxias 725. **Tourist offices** For more details on the Roteiro Portinari, contact the *Departamanto de Cultura e Turismo* in Brodowski, Praça Martim Moreira, T6641666, or the *Secretaria da Cultura* in Ribeirão Preto, Praça Barão do Rio Branco, T6352424.

The biggest rodeo in the world

Some 115 kilometres northwest of Ribeirão Preto is **Barretos** where, in the third week in August, the **Festa do Peão Boiadeiro** is held. This is the biggest annual rodeo in the world. The town (population 100,000) is completely taken over as up to a million fans come to watch the horsemanship, enjoy the concerts, eat, drink and shop in what has become the epitome of Brazilian cowboy culture. There are over 1,000 rodeos a year in Brazil, but this is the ultimate. The stadium, which has a capacity for 35,000 people, was designed by Oscar Niemeyer so that the wind funnels through the middle, cooling the competitors and the spectators. Since the 1950s, when Barretos' rodeo began, the event grew slowly until the mid-1980s when it really took off.

Tours from the UK are run by **Last Frontiers**, Fleet Marston Farm, Aylesbury, Bucks, HP18 0PZ, T01296-658650, F01296-658651, www.lastfrontiers.co.uk.

The West

The Rio Tietê was one of the principal routes used by the early explorers of the interior, either along its banks in the case of the bandeirantes, or as a waterway in the case of the Monsoons (see page). Nowadays, good paved highways travel in the same direction. The Caminho dos Bandeirantes, also called the Estrada dos Romeiros (the pilgrims' way), is the name given to about 130 kilometres of road passing through a number of towns with historical associations.

The SP-300 is a picturesque paved road along the Tietê valley from São Paulo to Bauru. The first colonial town reached is **Santana do Parnaíba**, 41 kilometres from the state capital; it was founded in 1580 and is known for its *cachaça*.. **Pirapora de Bom Jesus** (*Population* 7,935) is a popular place of pilgrimage, in a most attractive setting on both sides of the river. The image of Bom Jesus, found in the river in 1725, is believed to be miraculous. A particularly important festival here is Corpus Christi. Next is **Cabreúva**, another producer of *cachaça*, and then **Itu** (*Population* 122,528), 102 kilometres from São Paulo. Itu was founded by the Bandeirantes in the early 17th century and then became an important centre of sugar cultivation. Today, it contains a number of 18th and 19th century churches, a museum of the Convenção Republicana da Provincia, one of the meetings which prompted the move towards the Brazilian Republic (Rua Barão do Itaim 67) and, in the surrounding countryside, colonial houses, old sugar estates and fine scenery. The beautiful falls of Salto de Itu, eight kilometres north, are flanked by a park and a textile mill. In and around the town are hotels; there are also nine campsites in the vicinity.

West of São Paulo by 87 kilometres is this important centre for industrial and agricultural products. Communications with São Paulo are better by road than by rail; the Castello Branco highway (SP-280) passes nearby.

Sorocaba
Population: 431,500
Phone code: 015

Sleeping and eating **A** *Sorocaba Park*, R Prof Joaquim Silva 205, T/F2282822, restaurant, pool. **B** *Terminus*, Av Gen Carneiro 474, T2216970, F2216983. **C** *Manchester*, R 15 de Novembro 21, basic, friendly. *São Pedro SPA Médico*, Av São Paulo 3333, T2271717, F2271797, part of the *Roteiros de Charme* hotel group see page 57. *Casa do Lago*, part of the same group, T/F2561229, is further west at Campina do Monte Alegre. *Casa Floresta Negra*, Av Washington Luís 1513, T2212549, German restaurant.

Bauru
Population: 292,500
Phone code: 014

This busy commercial town was founded at the end of the last century and is popular with Paulistanos as a weekend resort. There is a large student population due to its five universities and specialist mouth hospital. There is a railway museum in Rua 1 de Agosto, Qd 1 and a zoo at the end of Avenida das Nações Unidas. Águas Quentes de Piratininga at Km 1 of Rodovia Elias Miguel Maluf is the only thermal spa in Brazil with saltwater.

Sleeping and eating A *Obeid Plaza*, Av Nacões Unidas 1950, T2345300, F2344184, large convention centre. B *St Martin*, R Eng St Martin 1326, T/F2343951. Cheaper hotels near the rodoviária and the railway station. *Cantina Tutti Fratelli*, R Arajo Leite 2088, Italian. *Baby Buffalo*, R Ezequiel Ramos 752, churrasco.

The Hidrovia Tietê-Paraná

The main rivers in the west of the state, the Tietê, the Grande, the Paranapanema and the Paraná are an enormous hydrological resource. Dams have formed great lakes, used for power, irrigation and, increasingly, tourism. The Tietê-Paraná system alone links 85 municipalities, accounting for just over 2½ million people. Within the Mercosul Common Market, these two rivers were seen as a possible transportation route uniting São Paulo with the Río de la Plata. The plan involved major engineering works to change river levels and provide access to the waterway for countries involved. Brazil was not completely sold on the idea and in March 1998 vetoed the scheme mainly because altering the water levels in the Paraná would have a disastrous effect on the Pantanal.

Marília
Population: 178,000
Phone code: 014

Ninety six kilometres west of Bauru, Marília is a pleasant, clean town in the middle of the agricultural lands between the Tietê and the Paranapanema. The *Sun Valley Park* (A), R Aimorés 501, T/F4335944, is friendly. *Mamma Mia*, R José Alfredo Almeida 45, serves Italian food.

Ourinhos
Population: 87,000
Phone code: 014

Founded in 1924, Ourinhos is 99 kilometres south of Marília by the Rio Paranapanema, near the border with Paraná state. It is surrounded by sugar cane plantations. A possible stop-over on the road from São Paulo to Foz do Iguaçu or Campo Grande, it is on the railway which runs to Presidente Epitácio (see below) on the Paraná river. *Pousada Ourinhos* (B), R Monsenhor Córdova 333, T3225898, F3226718, is good value. *Comercial* (C), R Amornio Prado 38, is friendly.

Presidente Prudente
Population: 177,500
Phone code: 018

Further west is another useful place to make bus connections for Campo Grande, Porto Alegre, São Paulo, or Ribeirão Preto. *Aruá* (A), Av Col José Soares Marcondes 1111, T2224666, F2220765, is central. *Alves* (C) is opposite the rodoviária and is clean but noisy.

Presidente Epitácio
Population: 37,000
Phone code: 018

The SP-270 continues for 95 kilometres from Presidente Prudente to Presidente Epitácio on the Rio Paraná. A bridge takes traffic into Mato Grosso do Sul. The far southwest corner of São Paulo state is intensely farmed, but the authorities are trying to encourage 'ecoturismo' in the agricultural zone, with camping and hostelling, and on the Paraná and Paranapanema rivers, with marinas, resorts, watersports, fishing and condominiums.

Sleeping and eating A *Hotel Thermas e Fazenda de Presidente Epitácio*, 2½ km from Presidente Epitácio on the road to Campinal, T/F281253. Tourist complex on the Rio Paraná, with swimming pools, sauna, sporting facilities, shopping centre etc. In town are hotels in our **A** range and a variety of restaurants, including some serving fish.

Minas Gerais and Espírito Santo

5

Minas Gerais and Espírito Santo

*Diamonds, gold and other mineral riches were the
driving force behind the settlement of this mountainous
state. This abundant wealth has left behind a legacy of
colonial architecture and sculpture decorating its mining
towns. The modern state capital Belo Horizonte is a
good base for visiting Ouro Preto and the other historic
cities as well as having much of cultural interest itself.
The Mineiros were the first to rebel against exploitation
by Portugal and are still regarded today as independent
and somewhat reserved. They are nonetheless very
hospitable and have one of the best cuisines in Brazil.
The rugged terrain of its national parks such as Serra do
Cipó and Caparaó holds much of interest for trekkers
and birdwatchers. There are some caves, the Rio São
Francisco and a number of spas and hill resorts. Due to
the lack of beaches in Minas Gerais the nearby state of
Espírito Santo is popular during the summer season. The
capital is the port of Vitória.*

Minas Gerais

Background

History As the name implies, Minas Gerais (General Mines) was founded on what the Portuguese took from the ground. Until the first alluvial deposits of gold were discovered in 1693, the region was a wilderness. The *bandeirantes* had pioneered trails in their search for slaves, but few others had penetrated Brazil's interior beyond the coastal mountains. According to the estimates given by Hemming in *Red Gold*, 97,000 indigenous Indians lived in what is now Minas Gerais before the Portuguese came. Hardly 1,000 survive today. Not only did mining affect the land, it also caused the death or displacement of the original communities, huge population shifts of colonists and black slaves, changes in agricultural patterns elsewhere in Brazil and the emergence of an élite to rival the power bases of Rio de Janeiro and São Paulo.

No one is quite sure who actually discovered the gold near what today is the town of Ouro Preto (Black Gold), but it certainly was a member of a *bandeirante* mission sent out from São Paulo. The reaction to the find was immediate. A gold rush of such proportions ensued at the turn of the 18th century that there was a danger that the rest of Brazil would grind to a halt. People of all strata of society hurried to the gold fields, slaves were taken from the sugar plantations and imported from Africa to pan for and wash the gold and immigrants from Portugal poured in to seek their fortune (see box, page 741). Not surprisingly, the Paulistas were infuriated by the newcomers muscling in on what they regarded as their property. Tension quickly led to a brief, bloody war, the **Guerra dos Emboabas** (1708-09) which ended in defeat for the Paulistas, who had failed to win support from the crown. In 1720, Minas Gerais was made a captaincy, which helped to bring the mines under royal control. From 1735 until the middle of the century gold, and the diamonds found further north at what is now Diamantina, transformed Minas Gerais into an area of prosperity and opulence.

Some of the related effects of the gold rush were the eventual relocation of the capital of Brazil from Salvador in Bahia to Rio de Janeiro, which was one of the main gold exporting ports. Sugar was still being planted and exported from the northeast, but it was facing competition from the English and French Caribbean colonies. Because the miners were so intent on working the gold fields and because the land had not been cultivated at all before their arrival there was a shortage of food in Minas. Cattle ranchers in the north and northeast and new ranchers in the south took advantage of this market and drove their herds into the heartland to feed the miners. Farmers were also encouraged by this wealthy market and, once the gold boom began to tail off in the latter part of the 18th century, it was found that much of Minas Gerais had excellent soil for agriculture. Consequently, settlers moved deeper and deeper into the interior. Another factor in the creation of Minas Gerais was the barrier imposed by the coastal escarpment. The mining area remained isolated, other than for the mule trails over the mountains, until the building of roads in the 19th and 20th centuries.

Politically, Minas Gerais was the scene of one of the earliest attempts by Brazilians to end the influence of the Portuguese crown. The **Inconfidência Mineira** of 1788-89 was an attempt to break the royal stranglehold on trade and government, but it failed (see box, page 281). After Independence and into the Republic, the wealth of the state created a powerful élite which, together with that of São Paulo came to dominate Brazilian politics (hence the 'Café com Leite'/Coffee and Milk rule of the early 20th century, see page 744).

Although other parts of Latin America have fine examples of European colonial building, the cities of Minas Gerais have a character which is not found elsewhere, even in Brazil. Because Minas has many other attractions, it is easy to intersperse the colonial with the natural, and all the cities can easily be visited from Rio or Belo Horizonte. Many companies provide tours.

The chief glory of the colonial cities is the architecture and, even more, the sculpture of one of the world's great creative artists, 'O Aleijadinho' (see box, page 281). What makes Minas' colonial art special is the fact that the baroque had to be reinvented in the Brazilian interior because of the difficulty of finding, or bringing in the materials used in coastal Brazilian or European baroque. Also scarce were experienced artists and artisans. The main characteristics in Minas architecture are exuberant decoration, the use of curving forms, the creation of illusions of mass, movement and depth, and spatially complex compositions. The adaptation of the baroque to local conditions saw an even greater degree of ornamentation than elsewhere and an iconography which was decidedly realistic. The Minas artists were expert in combining design, mass and colour and although gold was used extensively, it was not the sole adornment. White and other colours had an equally important part to play in their scheme of colour harmony. Since the baroque was accompanied by a high level of religious mysticism, most effort was put into not only the churches and associated buildings, but also the interior decoration and the sculptures which graced them.

The paintings by Mestre Athayde (1732-1827) are of particular interest: the pigments were obtained from local iron ore and from forest fruits. They are also very fine artistically. He decorated the walls and ceilings of many of the important churches in the mining region. Since rich Portuguese women found it unacceptable to pose for an artist, the majority of the Madonnas he painted were represented as coloured or black women, inspired by the maids or slaves he used as models.

The main religious orders, such as the Jesuits, were prohibited from establishing foundations in Minas Gerais, so it was up to the lay Brotherhoods and Third Orders to commission and finance the religious monuments. These organizations guarded fiercely their identity, hence the individuality in the churches. The wealth of the lay orders determined the style and ornamentation. Less rich were the blacks, who also built churches; these are usually those of Nossa Senhora do Rosário and Nossa Senhora das Mercês.

The inland State of Minas Gerais, with a population of 16 million in an area somewhat larger than France, is mountainous in the south, rising to the 2,787 metres peak of Agulhas Negras in the Mantiqueira range (the peak itself is in Rio de Janeiro state), and in the east, where there is the Caparaó National Park containing the Pico da Bandeira (2,890 metres). Both these areas of highland are part of the continuous chain of mountains which form the escarpment which cuts the state off from the coastal lowlands of the states of Rio de Janeiro and Espírito Santo. Behind this range the valley of the Rio Doce is a depression between it and the Serra do Espinhaço, beyond which there is a larger depression, the valley of the Rio São Francisco, before the Espigão Mestre range. These highlands, in the northwest, are made up of ancient rocks and are heavily eroded. From Belo Horizonte north are undulating grazing lands, the richest of which are in the extreme west: a broad wedge of country between Goiás in the north and São Paulo in the south, known as the Triângulo Mineiro. Being frost-free (except for the very highest altitudes), Minas Gerais is also a major producer of coffee.

The **Rio São Francisco**, which rises in the Serra da Canastra, is one of the major rivers of Brazil, playing a part in the country's history, inland exploration and navigation and economy. Because of its importance it is sometimes called the "river of national unity". Its source is at about 1,000 metres above sea level and its length is some 3,000 kilometres. It runs north through Minas Gerais into Bahia before becoming the border between that state and Pernambuco, then Alagoas and Sergipe. Its hydroelectric potential has been harnessed at Três Marias (Minas Gerais) and Paulo Afonso (Bahia/Pernambuco).

While the coastal range of mountains was predominantly covered in tropical forest, the Mata Atlântica which has mostly been destroyed, much of the interior of Minas Gerais is typical of the *cerrado* (see box, page 753). This zone is hot the year round, with heavy rains in the summer. The far north of the state is hotter and drier, the semi-arid *caatinga*, characterized by spiny bushes and rivers which lack water for much of the year.

Climate Summers are hot and rainy, winters dry. The average annual temperature in Belo Horizonte is 21°C. The main variations are caused by altitude in the south and east, where some places are high enough for winter frosts. As in the neighbouring states of São Paulo and Rio de Janeiro, mountain resorts have been developed in the cooler heights. As said above, the far north of the state where it borders Bahia is semi-arid.

Economy Minas Gerais was once described as having a heart of gold and a breast of iron. Half the mineral production of Brazil comes from the state, including most of the iron ore. Diamonds and gold are still found. Minas Gerais also produces 95 percent of all Brazil's gemstones. The 19th century coffee boom was the first stage in Minas' diversification into large-scale agricultural production. The easy availability of power and the local agricultural and mineral production has created a large number of metal-working, textile, mineral water, food processing and timber industries. Multinational motor manufacturers have located in the state, for example Fiat at Betim (west of Belo Horizonte) and Mercedes Benz at Juiz da Fora.

Today Minas Gerais exports, in order of importance, iron and steel, coffee, automobiles and tractors, wood pulp, heavy machinery, inorganic chemicals, electrical machinery, oilseeds and grains, stone, gypsum and cement, and aluminium and aluminium products. Industry accounts for almost 40 percent of the state's gdp and agriculture almost 15 percent.

Belo Horizonte

The capital of Minas Gerais is the fourth largest city in Brazil. It is surrounded by mountains, and enjoys an excellent climate (16°-30°C) except for the rainy season (December-March). Together with Curitiba (Paraná), it enjoys one of the best standards of living in the country.

Population: 2 million
Phone code: 031
Colour map 4, grid B3

It was founded 12 December 1897 and much was made of the city's centenary. In the late 20th century it is one of Brazil's fastest growing cities, now suffering from atmospheric pollution. It is in the process of introducing an integrated public transport system, like Curitiba's, to improve what is already a good bus network. The industrial area, apart from being the traditional centre of mining and agricultural industries (as well as diamond cutting and precious stones), has steelworks and an automobile industry.

Ins and outs

International flights land at Confins airport, 39 km from Belo Horizonte. Shuttle services from several cities including Rio and São Paulo arrive at Pampulha airport closer to the city. Interstate buses arrive at the rodoviária next to Praça Rio Branco at the northwest end of Av Afonso Pena.

Getting there
See also Transport, page 269

The city has a good public transport system and some buses integrate with the regional, overground Metrô. Belo Horizonte is a hilly city with streets that rise and fall and trees lining many of the central avenues. The large Parque Municipal is in the heart of downtown. High-rise buildings dominate the centre, but they are not quite as imposing as, for instance, São Paulo. Nor is the atmosphere as frantic as São Paulo, but that is not to say that the centre is quiet. The main avenue, Afonso Pena, is broad and constantly full of pedestrians and traffic, except on Sunday morning when cars are banned from part of it which becomes a huge open-air market. The main commercial district is on Av Afonso Pena and the streets which run off it. This is where activity is concentrated during the day (and is the best area to eat in at lunch time); at night the *movimento* shifts to Savassi, southwest of the centre, which is the best area for eating, drinking and entertainment. Av Afonso Pena (and its continuation) cuts right through the city, from the Rodoviária in the northwest to Mangabeiras in the southeast. The Rodoviária is by the Riberão Arrudas and the Av Contorno, a peripheral road around the central area.

Getting around & orientation

As in any large city, watch out for sneak thieves in the centre and at the bus station. The Parque Municipal is not too safe, so it is best not to enter alone.

Safety

Sights

The **Parque Municipal** is an oasis of green, right in the centre of the city. It has a small amusement park and playground and is closed at night and on Monday, except for a small section in the southwest corner (where a tourist office is located). The principal building in the park is the **Palácio das Artes**, Afonso Pena 1567, which contains the **Centro de Artesanato Mineiro**(with craft shop), (Monday 1300-1800, Tuesday-Friday 0900-2100, Saturday 0900-1300, Sunday 1000-1400, T2222400), an exhibition of the development of painting in Minas Gerais (all fairly derivative), a cinema, three theatres and temporary exhibitions. On the stretch of Avenida Afonso Pena outside the Parque Municipal an open-air market operates each Sunday morning (0800-1400). The avenue is transformed by thousands of coloured awnings covering stalls selling every conceivable type of local handicraft. It attracts thousands of shoppers.

Praça Sete de Setembro (usually called Praça Sete) is at the busy junction of Avenida Afonso Pena and Avenida Amazonas, midway between the Parque Municipal and the Rodoviária. An obelisk commemorating Independence is the centre for political protests.

Six blocks up Avenida João Pinheiro from Avenida Afonso Pena is the **Praça da Liberdade**, which is surrounded by fine public buildings, some in eclectic, *fin-de-siècle*-style, others more recent. These include the Secretaria da Fazenda, the Secretaria da Educação and the Casa Falci/Secretaria de Obras Públicas. At the end of the Praça is the **Palácio da Liberdade**. ■ *0900-1800 Sunday only.* Among the new buildings are the Centro de Apoio Turístico Tancredo Neves (1991), which contains the offices of Turminas (see **Tourist offices**, below) and, not actually on the square, but visible from it, the Biblioteca Pública. The Praça itself is very attractive, with trees, flowers, fountains which are lit at night and joggers and walkers making the most of the paths.

On the **Praça da Assembléia** are three fine modern buildings: the Legislative Assembly, a church and Banco Central do Brasil. **Minascentro** is a convention centre for exhibitions and congresses in the city centre. It is near the Praça Raul

Belo Horizonte orientation & Pampulha

Related map
A Belo Horizonte
centre, page 264

Soares. At Rua da Bahia 1149, is a Gothic building near the Parque Municipal, which used to be the Museu da Mineralogia Professor Djalma Guimarães; it is currently being remodelled as the **Centro Cultural de Belo Horizonte**.

Being a modern city, Belo Horizonte has no **churches** to equal those of the colonial towns. In the centre are the **Catedral da Boa Viagem** (completed 1932), Rua Sergipe 175; **São José** (1906), the first church of the new city, Rua Tupis 164; and **Nossa Senhora de Lourdes** (begun 1923, consecrated 1958), Rua da Bahia 1596.

The **railway station**, with a museum on the second floor showing a model railway, is part of a complex which includes a number of buildings dating from the 1920s around the **Praça da Estação** (also called Praça Rui Barbosa). One of the earliest buildings on the Praça is now the Centro Cultural da Universidade Federal de Minas Gerais.

Museu Mineiro, Avenida João Pinheiro 342, houses religious and other art in **Museums** the old Senate building, close to the centre. There is a section dedicated specifically to religious art, six pictures attributed to Mestre Athayde (see under Ouro Preto), exhibitions of modern art, photographs and Naive painters. See also the wood carvings by Geraldo Teles de Oliveira (GTO). ■ *Tuesday-Friday 1230-1830, Saturday-Sunday 1000-1600, T2711354.*

Museu Histórico Abílio Barreto, Rua Bernardo Mascarenhas, Cidade Jardim, in an old *fazenda* which is the last reminder of Belo Horizonte's predecessor, the village of **Arraial do Curral d'el Rey**, built by João Leite da Silva Ortiz in the 18th century, houses most interesting historical exhibits. ■ *T2963896, take bus 2902 from Avenida Afonso Pena.*

Museu do Telefone, Avenida Afonso Pena 4001, Mangabeiras. ■ *Monday-Friday, 0800-1730, T2292873.*

Museu de História Natural, in the Instituto Agronómico, Rua Gustavo da Silveira 1035, Santa Inês, has a local geological and palaeontological display and good archaeological exhibits. ■ *Monday-Thursday 0800-1130, 1300-1630, Saturday-Sunday 0900-1600, T4677723, take bus 8001.* Also here is the **Jardim Botânico**, which is to be combined with the Jardim Zoológico (see below). In the garden is the **Presépio do Pipiripau**, the Nativity of Pipiripau, a huge depiction of the life of Christ. It was made by Raimundo Machado de Azevedo, who began building it in 1906; it was transferred from his house to its present site in 1976.

Suburbs

Eight kilometres northwest from the centre is this picturesque suburb, famous **Pampulha** for its modern buildings and the artificial lake, created in the 1930s. The road around the lake, Avenida Otacílio Negrão de Lima, is 18 kilometres long and affords good views from one side to the other. The water is very polluted, but a clean-up operation is under way with Japanese assistance. The four main buildings on the lake shore, designed by Oscar Niemeyer and landscaped by Roberto Burle Marx, are part of a unified concept. The **Igreja São Francisco de Assis**, Avenida Otacílio Negrão de Lima Km 12, T4912319, was inaugurated in 1943. Its shape, one elongated arch interlocking with the largest of four similar arches, and its separate belltower, have become one of the most common symbols of Belo Horizonte. Its exterior is blue, with sinuous decorations along the side. On the exterior wall of the group of four arches, the painter Cândido Portinari installed beautiful blue and white tiles depicting St Francis' life. On the wall behind the altar is a powerful composition also by Portinari. The interior contains bronze panels by the sculptor Ceschiatti.

On the opposite shore is the glass and marble **Museu de Arte de Pampulha** (MAP), at Avenida Octacílio Negrão de Lima 16585. It exhibits principally a fine collection of modern art from Minas Gerais. It was originally a casino, set up by Juscelino Kubitschek, and was the first project in the complex to be designed and landscaped by the Niemeyer/Burle Marx team. People would dance in the **Casa do Baile**, take a boat across the lake for some gambling, and then dance again in what is now the Auditório in MAP (stand in the centre of the floor to hear the echo). The Casa do Baile is a perfect example of Niemeyer's fascination with the curved line, with its snaking canopy leading up to the main dance hall, which has windows all around to allow full views of the Burle Marx landscaping and the lake. ■ *0800-1800 Tuesday-Sunday, entrance free; T2777946, F4434533, http://www.comartevirtual.com.br, deals with art in general in Belo Horizonte and will have a section on MAP when it is in full operation.* The fourth building in the Pampulha architectural complex is the **Iate Tênis Clube**, the Yacht and Tennis Club. Take bus 2004 from Avenida Afonso Pena to the Lagoa da Pampulha.

Just south of the lake is the **Mineirão** stadium, about 700 metres away. This is the second largest stadium in Brazil after the Maracanã stadium in Rio; it seats 92,000 people, reduced from 130,000 for safety reasons. Seats cost

Belo Horizonte centre

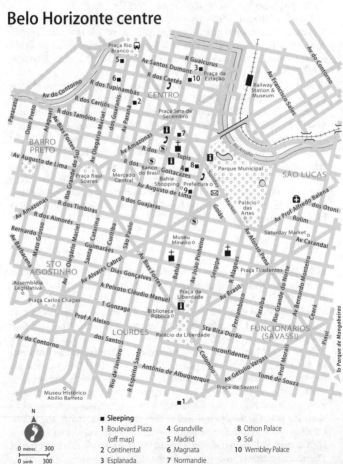

■ **Sleeping**
1 Boulevard Plaza (off map)
2 Continental
3 Esplanada
4 Grandville
5 Madrid
6 Magnata
7 Normandie
8 Othon Palace
9 Sol
10 Wembley Palace

0 metres 300
0 yards 300

between US$5 and US$10. Near it is the smaller, 25,000-seater Mineirinho stadium and multi-sport facility.

The **Jardim Zoológico** is at the western end of the lake. It is administered by the Fundação Zoo-Botânico (Avenida Otacílio Negrão de Lima 8000, CEP 31365-450, T2777968, F2777974), which is moving the Jardim Botânico to the same site as the zoo. Big efforts are being made to improve the educational and recreational facilities of the gardens, in conjunction with a a project of Educação Ambiental (environmental education) for the whole city. The zoo has Brazil's first butterfly house, a house dedicated to brightly-coloured birds (including some rarities), reptiles and animals, well kept for the most part, in sizeable enclosures. The animals are not exclusively Brazilian. ■ *Tuesday-Sunday 0900-1600 (gates close at 1700), US$4 per car. The Jardim Zoológico has two entrances: Pampulha, reached by buses 3302, Nova Pampulha-Zoológico, and 0207A, AABB-Zoológico; Serrano, reached by buses 4403A, Serrano-Zoológico, and 4408, São Mateus, or Tijuca. Special buses run on Sunday and holidays.*

CEPEL, Centro de Preparação Equestre da Lagoa (The Lake Riding School), Avenida Antônio Francisco Lisboa 481, is the largest equestrian centre in South America and is a member of the International Equestrian Federation. ■ *Tuesday to Sunday, 0800-1700, T4410812.*

Mangabeiras

In the southern zone of the city, just three kilometres from the central area, the **Parque de Mangabeiras** is on the Serra do Curral at between 1,000 metres and 1,400 metres above sea level. At its lower altitudes it preserves a small zone of Mata Atlântica, rising to higher altitude vegetation. The recreation areas and public spaces were landscaped by Burle Marx in 1982. Where the bus route ends and where cars park is by the Praça das Águas, in the main building of which is a café. There are good views of the city, especially from the Mirante da Mata. Three forest trails have been laid out: the Roteiros do Sol (Sun Route), da Mata (Woods Route) and das Águas (Water Route). There are picnic spots on the routes and sports facilities at the tourist complex. ■ *Thursday-Sunday, 0800-1800, take bus 2001 from Avenida Afonso Pena between Avenida Amazonas and Rua Tamóios.)*

The natural amphitheatre where the Pope spoke in 1980 is on the way up to Parque Mangabeiras; there is an iron monument marking the occasion. The square, now called **Praça do Papa**, used to be called Praça Israel Pinheiro. Just below the Praça do Papa is a street known officially as Rua Professor Otávio Magalhães but nicknamed the **Rua do Amendoim** (Peanut Street). Its fame rests in an optical illusion that makes it appear that cars in neutral run up the slope, rather than down. The same appears to happen with Coke cans, water in bottles, and so on. If you want to try this out, be patient because it is difficult to find the exact spot without local knowledge.

Excursions

The **Gruta de Lapinha** is only 36 kilometres north of the city. ■ *0900-1700, closed on Monday, to enter the caves and small archaeological museum costs US$2.*

Ten kilometres before Lapinha is the town of **Lagoa Santa** (*Population* 24,890), a weekend resort for Belo Horizonte. The sandy beach on the lake (close to the town centre and bus station) is used for fishing, sun bathing and boating (do not swim, the water is infected with schistosomiasis). Along the beach are bars and restaurants, with more in the nearby main Praça, which also has two small hotels and an interesting modernistic church. The road between Belo Horizonte and Lagoa Santa passes Belo Horizonte's international airport.

Within easy motoring distance from Belo Horizonte are several of the 400 caves and grottoes for which Minas Gerais is famous

Minas Gerais & Espírito Santo

Minas Gerais & Espírito Santo

Peter Lund and Lagoa Santa Man

Born in Copenhagen in 1801, Peter Wilhelm Lund came to be known as the father of Brazilian palaeontology. At the age of 24 he moved to Brazil for health reasons and settled in Nova Friburgo (now in Rio de Janeiro state). He collected material for the Danish Museum of Natural History, before sailing back to Hamburg in 1829. In 1833 he returned to Brazil and began to research the flora of Rio de Janeiro, São Paulo, Goiás and Mato Grosso, the results of which were published in Observações respeito da vegetação dos campos do interior do Brasil, especialmente fito históricas *(1835). His explorations then led him to Lagoa Santa, Minas Gerais, where he lived from 1840 to 1880, the year he died. He turned his attention to palaeontology and the caves in the area; the discoveries he made there were of enormous importance, if not some confusion, in the understanding of early peoples in Brazil.*

Lund found the fossils of humans who were dubbed Lagoa Santa Man. In the caves were also the bones of mammals which, elsewhere on earth, had died out in the Pleistocene age (the first period of the quaternary era, before the Neolithic age). Until it was surmised that these mammals lived longer in South America than in other regions and until carbon dating confirmed that Lagoa Santa Man was not more than about 10,000 years old, Lund's discoveries predated by a long way any other humans found in Brazil. Regardless of the date of the human remains, the significance of Lagoa Santa Man lay in the fact that evidence of these people could be seen in a lasting form. Much of Brazilian palaeontology and archaeology was, and still is, hampered by the reliance of most early peoples on perishable materials (eg wood and natural fibres) for their houses and artefacts. Lagoa Santa Man also figured in the debate that raged after the publication of Charles Darwin's theories of evolution.

Near the town of Pedro Leopoldo, which is between Belo Horizonte and Sete Lagoas, is a village called Dr Lund. Beyond this village is a fazenda *which offers accommodation, riding, fishing, swimming and other country pursuits:* Hotel Fazenda Tarumã, *T031-3375379 Belo Horizonte, or T031-6611965, Pedro Leopoldo. For more details, contact* Ametur *in Belo Horizonte (address under* **Tour companies & travel agents***).*

Transport Buses (*Útil*) to the Gruta de Lapinha leave at 1015 and 1130 daily, returning 1600, also 1830 Monday only; 1¼ hours, US$3.25 one-way. Half-hourly bus service Belo Horizonte-Lagoa Santa, US$2. Bus Lagoa Santa-Lapinha every 30 minutes. The local bus stop for Lagoa Santa is 2 km downhill from the Lapinha caves.

About 80 kilometres northwest of Belo Horizonte is the town of **Sete Lagoas**, near where is the **Gruta Rei do Mato**. In this cave prehistoric inscriptions and cave paintings have been found. ■ *0800-1700, T7730888*. Sete Lagoas, which has hotels, can be reached by Expresso Setelagoano bus from Belo Horizonte in 1½ hours.

The best and most famous of the caves is the **Gruta de Maquiné** with six chambers open to visitors. The caves are well lit, but hot, 26°C; entry is US$5. The restaurants nearby greet potential customers with a combined history and menu leaflet. Maquiné is 114 kilometres northwest of Belo Horizonte. The road is well signposted. In the nearby town of **Cordisburgo** is a museum to the writer João Guimarães Rosa (see page 779), Avenida Padre João 744, ■ *Tuesday-Sunday 0800-1700*.

Transport Buses (*Irmãos Teixeira*) leave Belo Horizonte at 0830, 1115 and 1230, except Monday, 0830 and 1200, returning at 1220, 1445 and 1620 (Monday 1445 and 1620), 2¼ hours, US$8 one-way.

To the northeast of the city, a few kilometres off the BR-262, is the **Serra de Piedade**, a high peak giving spectacular views over the surrounding countryside, only accessible by car or special bus service. On the hill is a telescope belonging to the Universidade Federal de Minas Gerais. ■ *T4995679*. There is a small chapel and a *churrascaria*. From the peak can be seen the small town of Caeté, which is 25 kilometres from Sabará (see page 273).

If you are looking for something different, try *Fazenda Boa Esperança*, which is set in natural surroundings at about 900 metres in the hills to the west of Belo Horizonte. Take the BR-381 south and branch west to Pará de Minas at Trevo Triângulo Mineiro. It is just off the road at Florestal. It is part of the Roteiro de Charme group, see page 57 for likely facilties.

Essentials

LL *Ouro Minas Palace*, Av Cristiano Machado 4001, T4294001 (toll free 0800-314000), F4294002, omhmkt@br.homeshopping.com.br. The most luxurious hotel in the city, palatial suites on the top floors, excellent service, not central but within easy reach of the centre and airports. **L** *Grandville*, R Espírito Santo 901, T2481000 (toll free 0800-311188), F2481100. Well appointed, convenient for the city centre. **L** *Othon Palace*, Av Afonso Pena 1050, T2733844, F2122318. Deluxe, modern, glass-fronted, excellent, safe deposit boxes, good restaurant, pool on roof, helpful staff, right in the centre, opposite the Parque Municipal, rooms on lower floors can be noisy.

AL *Boulevard Plaza*, Av Getúlio Vargas 1640, Savassi district (chic shopping area), T2697000, F2697111. Very nice. **AL** *Sol Meliá*, R da Bahia 1040, T/F2741344. Also in the heart of the city, comfortable, all facilities including pool and sauna.

A *Metrópole*, R da Bahia 1023, T2731544, F2225673. Central, convenient location. **A** *Normandy*, R dos Tamóios 212, T2016166, F2226133. Excellent grill. **A** *Wembley Palace*, R Espírito Santo 201, T2736866, F2249946. Excellent, central.

B *Ambassy*, R dos Caetés 633, near rodoviária, T2795000, F2712286. Helpful, English spoken, hot shower, TV, good restaurant. **B** *Esplanada*, Av Santos Dumont 304, T2735311. **D** without bath, good restaurant, own garage, good value. **B** *Estoril*, R dos Carijós 454, T/F2019322. Comfortable, pleasant.

C *Itatiaia*, Praça Rui Barbosa 187, near railway station, T2740003, F2744576. Central, a/c, good breakfast. **C** *Continental*, Av Paraná 241, T2017944. Central, quieter interior rooms recommended. **C** *Magnata*, R Guarani 124, T2015368. With breakfast, near rodoviária, good hot shower, safe deposit. Recommended. **C** *São Salvador*, R Espírito Santo 227, T2227731. Recommended.

D *Liz*, Av Olegário Maciel 95, T2011757. Basic. **D** *Madrid*, R Guarani 12, opposite the rodoviária, T2011088/6330. Recommended, but in a noisy location. **D** *Minas Bahia*, R Guarani 173, T2014648. **D** *São Cristovão*, Av Oiapoque 284, T2014860. Quiet, breakfast. Near the rodoviária and in R Curitiba many hotels are for very-short-stay couples.

Youth hostels **E** pp *Chalé Mineiro*, R Santa Luzia 288, Santa Efigênia, T4671576. IYHA, splash pool, attractive. Recommended. *Pousadinha Mineira*, R Araxá 514, Floresta, 15 minutes from the rodoviária, T4462911, F4424448, pipe@gold.com.br. IYHA, cheaper for members, popular with Brazilians. Bedding and towels can be hired, breakfast extra on request, very helpful. Recommended.

Local food *Comida mineira* is the local speciality; it is good, wholesome food, served in big black pots and earthenware dishes from which you help yourself. The hot dishes stand on a shelf above a wood-fired oven. There are a number of chicken recipes (such as *frango ao molho pardo*, chicken in a black sauce containing the bird's blood – delicious despite what it sounds like), dishes containing sausage, plenty of vegetables, beans, potatoes, rice and manioc. The other important local ingredient is cheese. In restaurants you usually pay after you have made your selection. Among

Sleeping
■ *on map, page 264*
Price codes: see inside front cover
You may spend the night in the rodoviária only if you have an onward ticket (police check at midnight)

Eating
In all restaurants in the centre, look for lunchtime promotions

Minas Gerais & Espírito Santo

those that serve *comida mineira* are *Chico Mineiro*, R Alagoas 626, corner of Av Brasil, T2613237. Good local chicken specialities; *Dona Lucinha*, R Sergipe 811, Savassi, T2615930. Recommended (also at R Padre Odorico 38, T2270562); *Emporium*, Av Afonso Pena 4034, Mangabeiras, T2811277; *Interior de Minas*, R Rio de Janeiro 1191, T2245549. Central, good for lunch, good value (also at Av Olegário Maciel 1781, Lourdes, T2925835); *Mala e Cuia*, a chain of restaurants serving good *comida mineira* at R Gonçalves Dias 874, Savassi, T2613059, Av Antônio Carlos 8305, Pampulha, T4412993, Av Raja Gabaglia 1617, São Bento, T3421421; *Xapuri*, R Mandacaru 260, Pampulha, T4966198. *Fazenda*, atmosphere, live music, Very good food, expensive and a bit out of the way but recommended.

Other Brazilian *La Greppia*, R da Bahia 1204, Centro. Lunch only, good. Cheap local food is served in the restaurants around the rodoviária, *prato feito* US$1. There are many bars and restaurants around Praça Raúl Soares; more on R Rio de Janeiro. *Flor de Líbano*, R Espírito Santo 234. Cheap and good.

International *Santa Felicidade*, R Prof Morais 659, Savassi, T2215299. Pastas, fish, grill, buffet, open for lunch and in the evening.

Italian *Buona Távola*, R Santa Rita Durão 309, Savassi, T2276155. Excellent. *Dona Derna*, R Tomé de Souza 1380, Savassi, T2236954. Highly recommended. *Pizzarela*, Av Olegário Maciel 2280, Lourdes, T2223000. Good for pizzas. *Vecchio Sogno*, R Martim de Carvalho 75 and R Dias Adorno, Santo Agostinho, under the Assembléia Legislativo, T2925251. Good food, top wine list, closed Sunday evening.

French *Taste Vin*, R Curitiba 2105, Lourdes, T2925423. Recommended.

German *Alpino*, Av Contorno 5761, Savassi, T2219015. Good value and popular.

Oriental *Yun Ton*, R Santa Catarina 946, T3372171, Chinese. Recommended. *Kyoto*, R Montes Claros 323, Anchieta. Japanese. Recommended.

Vegetarian *Mandala*, R Inconfidentes 1006, T2617056.

Cafés *Blue Mountain*, Av Cristóvão Colombo 536, Savassi, T2612296. *Café Belas Artes*, R Gonçalves Dias 1581, Lourdes, in the cinema foyer at Unibanco Belas Artes Liberdade. Popular. *Café Belas Artes Nazaré*, R Guajajaras 37, near Av Afonso Pena, in the foyer of the Unibanco Nazaré Liberdade cinema. *Café Três Corações*, Praça Diego de Vasconcelos, Savassi. Coffees and snacks. *Casa Bonomi*, R Cláudio Manoel 460, Funcionários, T2613460. *Koyote Street Bar*, R Tomé de Souza 912, street café. *Sabor e Saúde*, Av João Pinheiro 232. Vegetarian and meat snacks and meals, also sells *pão integral*. *Tia Clara*, R Antônio de Albuquerque 617. Tea room.

Bars & nightclubs **Bars** Recommended are *Alambique*, Av Raja Gabaglia 3200, Chalé 1D. Specializes in *cachaça*, with *mineira* appetizers, designed like a country house; *Amoricana*, R Pernambuco 1025; *Bar Nacional*, Av Contorno 1076, Barro Preto. Good value; *Heaven*, Av Getúlio Vargas 809.

Nightclubs Recommended are *L'Apogée*, R Antônio de Albuquerque 729, T2275133; *Partenon*, Rio Grande do Norte 1470, T2219856; *Máscaras*, R Santa Rita Durão 667, T2616050; *Ao Bar*, R Cláudio Manoel 572, Funcionários, T2617443.

Entertainment **Cinema** Belo Horizonte is a good place to watch good Brazilians and foreign films beside the usual Hollywood fare. There are many art cinemas and cine clubs in the centre such as the Espaço Unibanco at R Guajajaras 37.

Theatre Belo Horizonte has at least a dozen theatres, eg the *Teatro da Cidade*, R da Bahia 1341, T2731050, *Teatro Alterosa*, Av Assis Chateaubriand 499, Floresta, T2376610, and *Teatro Marília*, Av Alfredo Balena 586, Centro, T2244445. The city prides itself on its theatre and dance companies (look out for the *Grupo Galpão*); don't expect to find many shows in any language other than Portuguese. The local press and tourist literature give details of shows and events.

Minas Gerais & Espírito Santo

Maundy Thursday; Corpus Christi; **15 August,** *Assunção* (Assumption); **8 December,** **Festivals**
Conceição (Immaculate Conception).

Mercado Central, Av Augusto de Lima 744, is large and clean, open every day until **Shopping**
1800. It sells produce, dry goods and crafts. See above for the Sunday handicraft fair
on Av Afonso Pena; hippies still sell their wares on R Rio de Janeiro, 600 block, each
evening. A flower market is held at Av Bernardo Monteiro, near Av Brasil, every Friday
from 1200 to 2000. Also here on Saturday is a drinks and food market.

Shopping centres include *Bahia Shopping,* R da Bahia 1000 block, with a crashed
helicopter built into its structure, and *Shopping Cidade,* R Tupis 337, both in the centre; *Minas Shopping,* Av Cristiano Machado 4000, near the *Hotel Ouro Minas;*
Shopping del Rey, Av Pres Carlos Luz, Pampulha; and others. There are huge hyper-
markets just outside the city on the highways to Rio and to São Paulo.

Gemstones *Manoel Bernardes,* Av Contorno 5417, Savassi, T2254200. Very
reasonable.

Music *Cogumelo,* Av Augusto de Lima 399, T2749915.

Bookshops *Daniel Vaitsman,* R Espírito Santo 466, 17th floor, T2229071. For
English language books. Foreign language books at *Livraria Van Damme,* R das
Guajajaras 505, T2266492. Also good local and Portuguese selection; *Acaiaca,* R
Tamóios 72. Good for dictionaries. Used foreign language books at *Livraria
Alfarrábio,* R Tamóios 320, T2713603.

Ecotourism and adventure sports *Amo-Te,* Associação Mineira dos Organizadores **Sports**
do Turismo Ecológico, R da Bahia 1340, Centro, CEP 30160-011, T/F2241930 or Caixa
Postal 3059, Belo Horizonte, CEP 30130-140, T2854030, oversees ecotourism in the state
of Minas Gerais. This includes trekking, riding, cycling, rafting, jeep tours, canyoning, visiting national parks, or *fazendas.* For companies which arrange these special interest
tours, speak to *Amo-Te* first. **Horse riding** *Tropa Serrana,* Tullio Marques Lopes Filho,
T3448986, Mobile 9832356. Recommended. **Caving** *Grupo Speleo* at the
Universidade Federal de Minas Gerais; this group has the most experience in visiting
out-of-the-way caves. **Guides** A recommended nature guide is Regina Caldeira
Ribeiro, R Herculano de Freitas 1246/202, CEP 30430-120, Belo Horizonte,
T/FXX031-3342901, FocusTours@aol.com; she is a representative for *Focus Tours* (see
page 30). Tours in rural Minas and throughout Brazil can be arranged.

Local **Car hire:** *Interlocadora,* R dos Timbiras 2229, T2754090; *Localiza,* Av Bernardo **Transport**
Monteiro 1567, Pampulha and Confins airports, T2477957, or 0800-992000.
*See also Ins and outs,
page 261*

Buses: red buses run on express routes and charge US$0.75; yellow buses have circu-
lar routes around the Contorno, US$0.50; blue buses run on diagonal routes charging
US$0.65. Some buses link up with the regional, overground Metrô.

A new system is to be introduced, along the same lines as the Curtiba bus system,
in which all routes will feed into an *estação,* or route station; passengers will purchase
tickets before boarding the bus. Only 1 route, the Diamante, has been built so far.

Taxis: plentiful but hard to find at peak hours. BH Táxi, T2158081, Coopertáxi,
T4212424.

Long distance **Air:** Tancredo Neves international airport is at Confins, near Lagoa
Santa, 39 km from Belo Horizonte. From Confins airport, a taxi to the centre costs
US$50, co-operative taxis have fixed rates to different parts of the city. Airport bus,
either *executivo* from the exit, US$11, or comfortable normal bus (Unir) from the far
end of the car park hourly, US$2.20, both go to the rodoviária. Getting to the airport,
buses from the rodoviária, *executivo,* US$10. Closer to the city, the domestic airport at

Minas Gerais & Espírito Santo

Pampulha, has shuttle services to several cities including Rio and São Paulo. Transport from Pampulha airport is cheaper than from Confins. Blue bus 1202 to town leaves across the street from the aiport, 25 minutes, US$0.65, passing the rodoviária and the cheaper hotel district.

Trains: to **Vitória**, daily 0700, tickets sold at 0530, US$17.50 *executivo*, US$11.50 first class, US$7.80 second, 14 hours.

Buses: the rodoviária is by Praça Rio Branco at the northwest end of Av Afonso Pena. Buses leave from the rather gloomy platforms beneath the ticket hall. Do not leave any of your belongings unattended. The bus station has toilets, post office, phones, left-luggage lockers (US$2.50, attended service 0700-2200), shops and is clean and well-organized.

To **Rio** with *Cometa*, T2015611 and *Util*, T2017744, 6½ hours, US$12.75 (ordinary), *leito*, US$25.50. To **Vitória** with *São Geraldo*, T2711911, US$14.50 and *leito* US$29. To **Brasília** with *Itapemirim*, T2919991 and *Penha*, T2711027, 10 hours, 6 a day including 2 *leitos*, only 1 leaves in daylight (0800), US$19.25, *leito* US$38.50. To **São Paulo** with *Cometa* and *Gontijo*, T2016130, 10 hours, US$15.60. To **Foz do Iguaçu**, US$42, 22 hours. To **Salvador** with *Gontijo*, US$40, 24 hours, at 1900 daily, and *São Geraldo* at 1800. *São Geraldo* also goes to **Porto Seguro**, 17 hours, direct, via Nanuque and Eunápolis, US$33. To **Recife** with *Gontijo*, 2000, US$41. To **Fortaleza**, US$63. To **Natal**, US$66. To **Belém** with *Itapemirim* at 2030, US$72. To **Campo Grande** with *Gontijo* (at 1930) and *Motta* (3 a day, T4640480), US$31-36, a good route to Bolivia, avoiding São Paulo. All major destinations served. For buses within Minas Gerais, see under each destination.

Hitchhiking to **Rio** or **Ouro Preto**, take a bus marked 'Shopping', to the *BH* shopping centre above Belo Horizonte on the Rio road.

Directory **Airline offices** *American*, R Guajajaras 557, T2733622, Confins T6892670. *TAM*, Pampulha T4435500. *Transbrasil*, R Tamóios 86, T2743533, Confins T6892475. *United*, R Paraíba 1000, 10th floor, Funcionários, T2617777, Confins T6892736. *Varig/RioSul/Nordeste*, Av Olegário Maciel 2251, Lourdes, T2916444, Confins airport T6892305, Pampulha airport T4912466. *Vasp*, Av Olegário Maciel 2221, T0800-998277, Confins T6892411.

Banks *Banco do Brasil*, R Rio de Janeiro 750, Av Amazonas 303. Cash is given against credit cards at *Banco Itaú*, Av João Pinheiro 195. *Lloyds Bank*, R Paraíba 1000, 8th floor. *Citibank*, R Espírito Santo 871. Visa ATM at *Bradesco*, R da Bahia 947. *Master Turismo*, Av Afonso Pena 1967, T3303603. American Express representative. *Nascente Turismo*, Rio de Janeiro 1314, no commission. Changing TCs is difficult, but hotels will change them for guests at a poor rate.

Communications Post Office: Av Afonso Pena 1270. With fax, philatelic department and small museum, service is slow (unless the quick counter is open), closes 1800. Poste restante is behind the main office at R de Goiás 77. The branch office on R da Bahia is less slow. **Telephones:** Av Afonso Pena 1180, by the Correios, open daily 0700-2200. Also at the rodoviária, Confins airport, R Caetés 487 and R Tamóios 311 in the centre. R Paraíba 1441, Savassi.

Embassies & consulates *Austria*, R José Américo Cançado Bahia 199, T3331046/3621128. *Denmark*, R Paraíba 1122, 5th floor, T2398805, F2398785. *Finland*, Av Contorno 6283, salas 602/4, T2819514. *France*, R Pernambuco 712A, T2617805. *Germany*, R Timbiras 1200, 5th floor, T2131568. *Italy*, Av Afonso Pena 3130, 12th floor, T2814211. *Netherlands*, R Sergipe 1167, loja 5, T2275275. *UK*, Av Afonso Pena 952, sala 500, T2226318. *USA*, R Timbiras 1200, 7th floor, T2131571.

Hospitals & medical services *Mater Dei*, R Gonçalves Dias 2700, T3399000. Recommended.

Laundry *5 à Sec*, Av Prudente de Moraes 421, Cidade Jardim, T2967376. Dry cleaning.

Places of worship *Synagoga Beth Yacov*, R Pernambuco 326, T2246013. *Presbyterian Church*, Av Afonso Pena 2655, T2737044. *Baptist Church*, Praça Raul Soares 203, T2752387. *Mormon Church*, R Levindo Lopes 214, T2237883. *Adventist Church*, R Timbiras 683, T2266144.

Tour companies & travel agents *Master Turismo* (American Express representative), R da Bahia 2140, T3303655, F3303644, at Sala VIP, Aeroporto de Confins, T6892044 and Av Afonso Pena 1967, T3303603. Very helpful. *Stella Barros*, Av Paulo Afonso 304, sl 3/4/5, T2967161, F2967381. Thomas Cook network. **For receptive tourism:** *Ouro Preto Turismo*, Av Afonso Pena 4133, Grupo 109, Serra, T2215005, and *Revetur*, R Espírito Santo 1892, 1st floor, Lourdes, T3372500. Both have been recommended. *Ametur*, R Alvarengo Peixoto 295, loja 102, Lourdes, T/F2921976. Open 0900-1200, 1400-1900, has information on *fazendas* which welcome visitors and overnight guests.

Tourist information *Belotur*, the municipal information office, is at R Tupis 149, 10th floor, T2777669. Very helpful, with lots of useful information and maps. The monthly *Guia Turístico* for events, opening times etc, is freely available. Belotur has offices also at the southwest corner of Parque Municipal, at Confins and Pampulha airports, and at the rodoviária (particularly polyglot). *Turminas*, Av Bias Fortes 50, Praça da Liberdade, T2122134, F2013942, is the tourism authority for the state of Minas Gerais. It, too, is very helpful and its *Gerais Common Ways* booklet has a useful facts section. **Other organizations:** *Ibama*, Av do Contorno 8121, Cidade Jardim, CEP 30110-120, Belo Horizonte, T2916588. *Instituto Estadual de Florestas*, for information on state parks, etc, Maurício Luciano, T3307017. *Touring Club do Brasil*, Av Brasil 1505, T2616868.

Useful addresses Immigration: Polícia Federal, R Nascimento Gurgel 30, T2910005, for visa extensions. To get there take bus 7902 from the corner of R Curitiba and Av Amazonas and get off at the *Hospital Madre Teresa*.

Useful information The daily newspaper, *Estado de Minas*, www.estaminas.com.br, has interesting articles and information on the city and the state.

Voltage 120-220 AC 60 cycles.

Nature reserves near Belo Horizonte

This is a remarkable reserve about 120 kilometres east of Belo Horizonte. It can be visited in a day trip, but you will gain much more if you stay overnight.

Parque Natural de Caraça

Caraça has been preserved so well because the land belongs to a seminary. The seminary buildings and the church with its tall spire stand at about 1,220 metres above sea level, surrounded on three sides by mountains which rise to 2,070 metres at their highest (Pico do Sol). The name means 'big face', so called because of a hill which is said to resemble the face of a giant who is looking at the sky. To appreciate the setting, climb up to the Cruzeiro, a cross which is close to the seminary.

The church was built in gothic style between 1775 and 1880. It has a museum. ■ *Saturday, Sunday and holidays 1300-1500 (or for hotel guests on request)*. In the church is a painting of the Last Supper attributed to Mestre Athayde (see below); Judas Iscariot's eyes follow you wherever you are in the church (he is the one holding the purse). Also in the church is an effigy of São Pio Martir, in the altar. The stained glass windows at the east end were a gift from France. The college which trained young men for the priesthood burnt down in 1968 but has been partly restored. Part of the seminary has been converted into a hotel, which is the only place to stay.

Habitat and wildlife The park extends from 720 metres to 2,070 metres. Its lower altitudes are covered in rich Atlantic forest while the heights are grassland and other mountain habitats. There are lakes, waterfalls and rivers. The rarest mammal is the maned wolf (the only wolf found in Brazil and endangered, partly because of loss of habitat, but also because of its insatiable appetite for chickens).

Since the early 1980s, the monks have been leaving food for the wolves on the seminary steps in the evening. At first one wolf would come, but now up to four may be seen. This is a popular tourist attraction, and the animals do not object to being photographed. Another endangered mammal in the park is the southern masked titi monkey, of which family groups may be seen. Other primates include the black tufted-eared marmoset and the brown capuchin monkey.

Birdlife includes toucans, guans and hummingbirds (such as the Brazilian ruby and the white-throated), various tanagers, cotingas, antbirds, woodpeckers and the long-trained and scissor-tailed nightjars. Some of the bird species are endemic, others rare and endangered.

The trails for viewing the different landscapes and the wildlife are marked at their beginning and are quite easy to follow. A guide is a good idea for seeing the birds and animals.

Park essentials Park entrance US$5 per vehicle. The park is open 0700-2100; if staying overnight you cannot leave after 2100. The part of the seminary which has been converted into a hotel has pleasant rooms; room rates vary, US$40-80 double, full board. For reservations write to Santuário do Caraça, Caixa Postal 12, 35960-000 – Santa Bárbara, MG, T8372698. There is a restaurant serving good food which comes from farms within the seminary's lands. Lunch is served 1200-1330.

Transport Turn off the BR-262 (towards Vitória) at Km 73 and go via Barão de Cocais to Caraça (120 kilometres). There is no public transport to the seminary. Buses go as far as Barão de Cocais, from where you have to take a taxi, US$12 one way. You must book the taxi to return for you, or else hitch (which may not be easy). The park entrance is 10 kilometres before the seminary. The alternatives are either to hire a car, or take a guide from Belo Horizonte, which will cost about US$75 (including guiding, transport and meals).

It is possible to stay in **Santa Bárbara** (**D** *Hotel Karaibe*; **D** *Santa Inés*), 25 kilometres away on the road to Mariana and hitchhike to Caraça. Santa Bárbara is served by 11 buses a day from Belo Horizonte (fewer on Saturday and Sunday). There is also a bus service to Mariana, a beautiful route which is being paved, via Catas Altas, which has an interesting church and a *pousada* belonging to the municipality of Santa Bárbara.

Parque Nacional da Serra do Cipó About 105 kilometres northeast of Belo Horizonte, **Serra do Cipó**, 33,400 square kilometres of the Serra do Espinhaço, has scenic beauty and several endemic plants, insects and birds. In the last category, the Cipó Canestero is only found in one small area in the south of the park. There are also several carnivorous plants, many flowers, frogs, and black and orange grasshoppers. The predominant habitat is high mountain grassland, with rocky outcroppings; there are waterfalls, too. ■ *Full details from Ibama in Belo Horizonte T2916588.*

Park essentials The national park can be reached via road MG-010. This road continues unpaved to Serro (see **Colonial cities**, below); buses run on this route. Agencies offer excursions from the city to the park. It is recommended to take a guide because the trails are unmarked; ask locally. The nearest accommodation is in the municipalities of Santana do Riacho, a town northwest of the park, for example *Pousada Sempre Viva*, Km 99, MG-010, T6811327; *Fazenda Monjolos Pousada*, Km 100, MG-010, T2214253; *Camping Véu da Noiva*, Km 101, T2011166, or Jaboticatubas, *Cipó Veraneio*, Km 95, MG-010, T6511000. Further from the park, but in the municipality of Jaboticatubas, 50 kilometres from Belo Horizonte, is a *Hotel Fazenda, O Canto da Siriema*, with full board, recreation, etc, T4636955, or contact *Ametur* in Belo Horizonte (address under **Tour companies & travel agents**).

Colonial cities

The picturesque colonial cities described below fall roughly into four groups: east of Belo Horizonte (Sabará and Caeté); southeast (Ouro Preto and Mariana); south/southwest (Congonhas do Campo, São João del Rei and Tiradentes); north (Diamantina and Serro). This is the order in which we shall deal with them.

The most visited is without a doubt Ouro Preto; it can be done in a day trip from Belo Horizonte, but if you have decided to see the place, a day trip is nothing like enough. Mariana makes a good day trip from Ouro Preto. Sabará is an easy day trip from Belo Horizonte. The colonial monument in Congonhas do Campo requires only a few hours to visit and a couple of changes of bus to get there, but most regard it as well worth the effort. São João del Rei and Tiradentes make a logical combination and are perhaps best visited as an excursion from the Rio de Janeiro/Belo Horizonte route. Diamantina and Serro are in completely the other direction, on one of the routes to Bahia from Belo Horizonte; either stop off on that journey, or make an excursion from Belo Horizonte.

Sabará

East of the state capital by 23 kilometres is the colonial gold-mining (and steel-making) town of Sabará. The town is strung along the narrow steep valleys of the Rio das Velhas and Rio Sabará. Since the late 17th century the Rio das Velhas was known as a gold-bearing river and a community soon grew up there. By 1702 it was the most populous in Minas Gerais. In 1711 the name Villa Real de Nossa Senhora da Conceição de Sabará was given to the parish and in 1838 it became the city of Sabará.

Population: 100,500
Phone code: 031
Colour map 4, grid B3

Its old churches and fountains, its rambling cobbled streets and its simple houses with their carved doors are of great interest. The main road is beside the river, below the town, and this is the road (Avenida Prefeito Victor Fantini) where buses into town stop. From the terminus, walk up Rua Clemente Faria to Praça Santa Rita, in which is a large *chafariz* (fountain). The square adjoins Rua Dom Pedro II, which used to be called Rua Direita (all colonial cities have a Rua Direita – some have been renamed, as here). Rua Dom Pedro II is lined with beautiful 18th century buildings, among them the **Solar do Padre Correa** (1773) at No 200, now the **Prefeitura**, a mansion with a rococo chapel and main reception room (*salão nobre*); the **Casa Azul** (also 1773), now the INSS building, No 215, with a chapel and a fine portal; and the **Teatro Municipal**, former Opera House, built in 1770 and the second oldest in Brazil. It has a superb interior, with three balconies, a carved wooden rail before the orchestra pit, wooden floors and *esteiro* ceilings (*esteiro* is flattened bamboo woven together).

Sights

At the top of Rua Dom Pedro II is the Praça Melo Viana, in the middle of which is **Nossa Senhora do Rosário dos Pretos** (left unfinished at the time of the slaves' emancipation). Behind the façade of the unfinished building are the chancel, sacristy (both 1780) and the first chapel (1713) which were completed. There is a museum of religious art in the church. ■ *Both church and museum are open Tuesday-Sunday 0800-1100, 1300-1700*. To the right of the church as you face it is the **Chafariz do Rosário**. Also on the Praça are the ornate Fórum Ministro Orozimbo Nonato and two schools. From the Praça Melo Viana, take Rua São Pedro to the church of **São Francisco** (1781); beyond the church is the **Chafariz Kaquende**.

In Rua da Intendência is the museum of 18th century gold mining in the **Museu do Ouro**. It contains exhibits from all the stages of gold extraction, plus religious items and colonial furniture. The building itself is a fine example of colonial architecture. Sources disagree as to its date of construction, but the general concensus is that it was before 1730. Originally the foundry, it became the Casa da Intendência in 1735. For most of the 19th century it was abandoned. It became the gold museum in 1945. ■ *Tuesday-Sunday 1200-1730, US$1.*

Another fine example of civil colonial architecture is the **Casa Borba Gato**, Rua Borba Gato 71, so called because tradition has it that it belonged to the famous *bandeirante*, Manoel de Borba Gato, one of the first to settle on the Rio das Velhas, but exiled from the region after the murder of the king's representative, Rodrigo de Castel Blanco in 1682. The building currently belongs to the Museu do Ouro.

The church of **Nossa Senhora do Carmo** (1763-74), with doorway, pulpits and choirloft by Aleijadinho and paintings by Athayde, is on Rua do Carmo. From the ceilings, painted blue and grey and gold, religious figures look down surrounding the Virgin and Child and the Chariot of Fire. In the chancel, the Ten Commandments in blue work have a distinctly Moorish air, what with the tents and the night-time scenes. ■ *US$1; a leaflet about the town is given out.*

Similar in style externally to NS do Carmo is the **Capela de Nossa Senhora do Pilar**, which is beside the municipal cemetery and in front of a large building with blue gates and doors.

Nossa Senhora da Conceição (begun 1701, construction lasting until 1720), on Praça Getúlio Vargas, has much visible woodwork and a beautiful floor. The carvings have much gilding, there are painted panels and paintings by 23 Chinese artists brought from Macau. The clearest Chinese work is on the two red doors to the right and left of the chancel. ■ *Entry free.*

Nossa Senhora do Ó, built in 1717 and showing unmistakable Chinese influence (paintings much in need of restoration), is two kilometres from the centre of the town at the Largo Nossa Senhora do Ó. ■ *Take local bus marked Esplanada or Boca Grande.*

If you walk up the Morra da Cruz hill from the *Hotel do Ouro* to a small chapel, the Capela da Cruz, or Senhor Bom Jesus, you can get a wonderful view of the whole region. Look for beautiful quartz crystals while you are up there.

Passeio a Sabará, by Lúcia Machado de Almeida, with splendid illustrations by Guignard, is an excellent guide to the place.

Sleeping & eating **A** *Del Rio*, R São Francisco 345, T6713040. **B** *Solar das Sepúlvedas*, R da Intendência 371, behind the Museu do Ouro, T6712705. Grand, pool. **D** *Hotel do Ouro*, R Santa Cruz 237, Morro da Cruz, T6715622. With bath, hot water, clean, with breakfast, marvellous view, best value. For eating, try *314*, Comendador Viana 314, near Praça Santa Rita. *Cê Qui Sabe*, R Mestre Caetano 56. Recommended.

Festivals There are many festivals throughout the year. The most significant are the *Folia de Reis*, 25 December to 6 January; *Festas Juninas* and, also in June, a *Festival da Cachaça*; *Nossa Senhora do Rosário*, 2nd Sunday in October.

The patron saint of Sabará is Nossa Senhora da Conceição

Transport **Buses** *Viação Cisne*, from Belo Horizonte, US$0.75, 30 minutes, from separate part of Belo Horizonte rodoviária from main departure hall. **Routes** There is a road, mostly unpaved, that runs from Sabará to Ravena on the BR-381 Belo Horizonte-Vitória highway which crosses the hills and is a pleasant drive.

Minas Gerais & Espírito Santo

Tourist information *Secretaria de Turismo*, R Pedro II 200, T6711522.

Caeté

Population: 34,000
Phone code: 031

Twenty five kilometres from Sabará and 60 from Belo Horizonte is Caeté. It can also be reached by turning off the BR-262 onto the MG-435, rather than going through Sabará. The town was originally called Vila Nova da Rainha; the nearby district of Morro Vermelho was associated with the Guerra dos Emboabas (see **History**, above). Caeté now has several historical buildings and churches. On the Praça João Pinheiro are the **Prefeitura** and **Pelourinho** (both 1722), the **Igreja Matriz Nossa Senhora do Bom Sucesso** (1756 rebuilt 1790 – ■ *daily 1300-1800*) and the **Chafariz da Matriz**. Also on the Praça is the tourist information office in the Casa da Cultura (T6511855). Other churches are **Nossa Senhora do Rosário** (1750-68), with a ceiling attributed to Mestre Athayde, and **São Francisco de Assis**. The **Museu Regional**, in the house of the Barão de Catas Altas, or Casa Setecentista, Rua Israel Pinheiro 176, contains 18th and 19th century religious art and furniture. The house itself is a fine example of 18th century civic architecture, with two floors and an interior patio. ■ *Tuesday-Sunday 1200-1700*.

From Caeté you can go to the **Serra da Piedade**; see 267.

Nova Lima

Population: 52,500

Situated about 27 kilometres southeast of Belo by a good road which branches off the BR-040, set in eucalyptus forests, Nova Lima's houses are grouped round the gold mine of Morro Velho, the deepest mine in the Americas. The shaft has followed a rich vein of gold down to 2,591 metres (not open to tourists). There are interesting carvings by Aleijadinho, recovered from elsewhere, in the modern parish church.

At 27 kilometres south along the BR-040 Belo Horizonte-Rio de Janeiro highway a 68 kilometres road, the Rodovia dos Inconfidentes, branches off to Ouro Preto. On the way (48 kilometres) it passes **Cachoeira do Campo**, which was the centre of the regional mining administration in colonial times: now a sleepy, unspoilt village. The road through the village is lined with shops selling soapstone objects and traditional cookware.

Ouro Preto

Population: 62,000
Phone code: 031
Altitude: 1,000m
Colour map 4, grid C3

The famous former state capital was founded in 1711. The city, built on rocky ground, was declared a national monument in 1933. Its cobbled streets wind up and down steep hills crowned with 13 churches. Mansions, fountains, churches, vistas of terraced gardens, ruins, towers shining with coloured tiles, all blend together to maintain a delightful 18th century atmosphere. On 24 June of each year, Ouro Preto again becomes, for that day only, the capital of the state of Minas Gerais. From October-February the climate is wet, but the warmest month of the year is February (30°C on average). The coldest months are June, July and August, with lowest temperatures being in July (10°C).

History

The gold that was found in the streams and rivers was covered in a thin black layer of iron oxide, hence the name Ouro Preto: black gold. The first encampments of prospectors were set up in the final years of the 17th century (the date given for the city's foundation is 24 June 1698) and by 1711 a number had become well established. In that year, on 8 July, they were united under the name of Vila Rica de Albuquerque. The town had two parishes: Nossa Senhora da Conceição and Nossa Senhora do Pilar. As the town's wealth increased, so the lay brotherhoods within those parishes were able to lavish more and more money on their temples, creating the baroque and rococo splendours that are still visible in stone, gold, wood and painting.

👉 *Tiradentes and the Inconfidência Mineira*

Minas Gerais & Espírito Santo

In the last quarter of the 18th century, Vila Rica de Nossa Senhora do Pilar do Ouro Preto was a dynamic place. Gold had brought great wealth to the city and this was translated into fine religious and secular buildings. Much of the artistry that went into these constructions and their decoration was home-grown, such as the genius of O Aleijadinho. In conjunction with this flowering of the arts an intellectual society developed. And yet all this went on under the heavy hand of the Portuguese crown, which demanded its fifth share (the quinto), imposed punitive taxes and forbade local industries to operate. While the artists and artisans could not travel and had to seek inspiration in what was around them, the intellectuals were often from families who sent their young to Europe to further their education. So, when the gold yields began to decline and the Portuguese demands became even more exorbitant, some members of society began to look to Europe and North America for ways to free Minas Gerais from the crown.

One side of the argument was the view of the governor, the Visconde de Barbacena, who refused to admit that the mines were exhausted and that poverty was beginning to affect the community. As far as he was

concerned, there was no gold because it was being smuggled out of the captaincy and there was no economic problem, just a large unpaid debt to the Portuguese crown. On the other side was the idea, as expressed by the French poet Parny, that Brazil was a paradise on earth, with everything except liberty. The Jesuit Antônio Vieira, who lived in the previous century, put it thus: 'the cloud swells in Brazil and it rains on Portugal; the water is not picked up from the sea, but from the tears of the unfortunate and the sweat of the poor, and I do not know how their faith and constancy has lasted so long.'

In the late 1780s a group of people began to have secret discussions on how to resolve the intolerable situation. It included the poets Cláudio Manuel da Costa, Tomás Gonzaga and Ignacio de Alvarenga, the doctors Domingos Vidal Barbosa and José Alvares Maciel, Padres Toledo and Rolim and the military officers Domingos de Abreu Vieira, Francisco de Paula Freire de Andrade and José de Resende Costa. Into this group came Joaquim José da Silva Xavier, a junior officer (alferes), who was born at the Fazenda de Pombal near São João del Rei in about 1748. He was also a dentist and

It is hardly surprising that the production of gold created tensions between the miners and the Portuguese crown which demanded its share. From the founding of the Capitania of Minas Gerais in 1720, the citizens of Vila Rica were immediately up in arms. A revolt took place in that very year in protest against the *quinto*, the royal tax. Discontent and opulence continued side-by-side until the conspirators of the Inconfidência Mineira of 1789 attempted to find a way of resisting the demands from Portugal. Before any of their ideas could be put into practice, the leaders were betrayed and arrested. One, Joaquim José da Silva Xavier (Tiradentes), was hanged, the others exiled (see box, page 276). The exhaustion of the gold mines forced the Portuguese to lower their levy and, not long afterwards, the colony gave way to the empire when the Portuguese royal family fled from Europe. A year after their arrival in 1822, Vila Rica de Albuquerque became a city and was renamed A Cidade Imperial de Ouro Preto, capital of the province of Minas Gerais. It lost that title in 1897 when Belo Horizonte was created. After that, the city's fame rested principally on its artistic merit, first gaining the accolade of national monument (1933), then Unesco Cultural Heritage site in 1980.

became known by the nickname Tiradentes – tooth-puller. Already dissatisfied with the way the army had treated him, by failing to promote him among other things, in 1788 he was suspended from active duty because of illness. The subsequent loss of pay roused him further. In trying to get reinstated he met Freire de Andrade and Alvares Maciel and later conversations prompted him to tell them of his idea of an uprising against the Portuguese. The Inconfidência grew out of these types of meeting, some planning action, others the future political and economic organization of a new, independent state.

The conspirators worked to gain support for their cause, but one soldier they approached, Coronel Joaquim Silverio dos Reis, used the information he had been given to betray the cause. The governor received reports from other sources and began to build up a picture of what was going on. Tiradentes was the first to be arrested, at the beginning of May 1789, in Rio de Janeiro. It seems that the plotters at this time still had no clear idea of what their ultimate aim was, nor of the importance of their attitudes. They never got the chance anyway because all were arrested soon after Tiradentes. They were imprisoned and kept incommunicado for two years while the case against them was prepared. Tiradentes was singled out as the most important member of the group and, under questioning, he did not disabuse his captors, taking full responsibility for everything. A defence for the Inconfidentes was prepared, but it almost totally ignored Tiradentes, as if he were being made a scapegoat. It made no difference, though, because the defence lost; 11 Inconfidentes were sentenced to death in November 1791. Soon afterwards the authorities in Brazil read out a surprising letter from the queen, Dona Maria I, commuting the death sentence for 10 of the conspirators to exile in Portugal or Africa. The eleventh, Tiradentes, was not spared. On 21 April 1792 he was hanged and his body was quartered and his head cut off, the parts to de displayed as a warning against any similar attempts to undermine the crown. Even though Tiradentes would never have been freed, one of the astonishing things about the queen's letter was that it was dated 18 months before it was brought to light.

The tourist office on Praça Tiradentes and some hotels and restaurants offer leaflets showing the opening times, which change frequently. Most of the churches now charge for admission (conservation tax), between US$1.50 and US$5. **NB** In most churches and museums, tourists' handbags and cameras are taken at the entrance and guarded in lockers (visitors keep their own key).

Sights
At least 2 days are needed to see everything Photography is prohibited in all the churches and museums

The best place to start exploring the city is the central **Praça Tiradentes**, in which is a statue of the leader of the **Inconfidentes**. Another Inconfidente, the poet Tomás Antônio Gonzaga (whose house at Rua Cláudio Manoel 61 is close to São Francisco de Assis church), was exiled to Africa. Most Brazilians know his poem based on his forbidden love affair with the girl he called Marília de Dirceu – real name Maria Dorotéia Joaquina de Seixas; visitors are shown the bridge and decorative fountain where the lovers held their trysts (the house where she lived, on the Largo Marília de Dirceu, is now a school of that name). Rua Cláudio Manoel runs east off the Praça, while Rua Conde de Bobadela runs west; this was the old Rua Direita.

On the north side of the Praça Tiradentes (at No 20) is a famous **Escola de Minas** (School of Mining), founded in 1876, in the fortress-like **Palácio dos Governadores** (1741-48); it has the interesting **Museu de Mineralogia e das**

Minas Gerais & Espírito Santo

Pedras, a must. ■ *Monday, Wednesday-Friday 1200-1645, Saturday-Sunday 0900-1300, US$1.50.* On the south side of the Praça, No 139 next to Carmo Church, is the **Museu da Inconfidência**, a fine historical and art museum in the former **Casa de Câmara e Cadeia**, which has some drawings by Aleijadinho and the Sala Manoel da Costa Athayde, in an annex. ■ *Monday-Friday 0800-1800, US$1.50.* In the Casa Capitular of NS do Carmo is **Museu do Oratório**, with many fascinating examples of oratories. ■ *Daily 0930-1220, 1330-1730, T5515369, www.oratorio.com.br.*

Ouro Preto

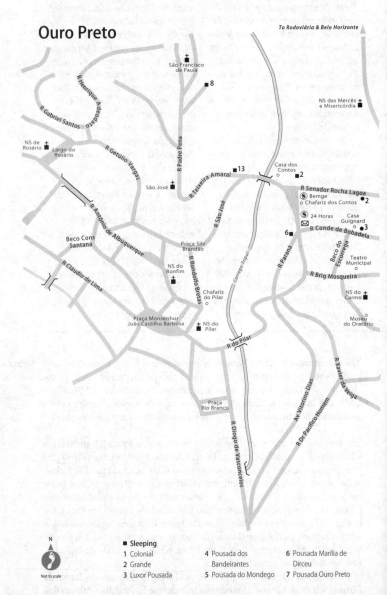

Minas Gerais & Espírito Santo

■ Sleeping
1 Colonial
2 Grande
3 Luxor Pousada
4 Pousada dos Bandeirantes
5 Pousada do Mondego
6 Pousada Marília de Dirceu
7 Pousada Ouro Preto

N
Not to scale

Casa das Contas, Rua São José 12, built between 1782-87, is the Centro de Estudos do Ciclo de Ouro (Centre for Gold Cycle Studies) and a museum of money and finance, with manuscripts and coins; it also has a library. ■ *Tuesday-Saturday 1230-1730, Sunday and holidays 0830-1330, US$0.50.* The **Casa Guignard**, Rua Conde de Bobadela 110, displays the paintings of Alberto da Veiga Guignard. ■ *Tuesday-Saturday 1230-1730, Sunday and holidays 0830-1330, free.* The **Teatro Municipal** in Rua Brigadeiro Musqueiro, is the oldest functioning theatre in Latin America. It was built in 1769. ■ *Daily 1230-1800.*

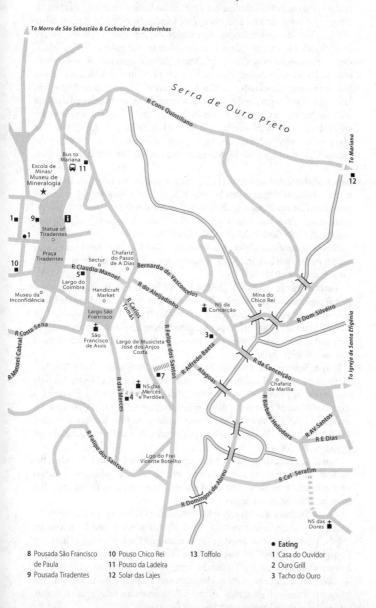

Minas Gerais & Espírito Santo

To Morro de São Sebastião & Cachoeira das Andorinhas

8	Pousada São Francisco de Paula	10	Pouso Chico Rei	13	Toffolo	●	Eating
9	Pousada Tiradentes	11	Pouso da Ladeira			1	Casa do Ouvidor
		12	Solar das Lajes			2	Ouro Grill
						3	Tacho do Ouro

The **Mina do Chico Rei**, Rua Dom Silvério is not as impressive as some other mines in the area, but is 'fun to crawl about in'; restaurant attached. The Chico Rei is supposed to have been an African king, called Francisco, who was enslaved but bought his freedom working in the mine. ■ *0800-1700, entrance US$1.50.*

Close to Padre Faria church is **Mina Bem Querer**, a small mine through which clean water runs, filling a small swimming pool. ■ *US$0.50.*

Churches
The following churches are all closed Mon, but are open at the times given on other days

São Francisco de Assis (1766-96), Largo de Coimbra, is considered to be one of the masterpieces of Brazilian baroque. Aleijadinho (see below) worked on the general design and the sculpture of the façade, the pulpits and many other features. The harmonious lines of the exterior and the beauty of the interior are exceptional. Mestre Athayde was responsible for the painted ceiling which depicts the Assumption of the Virgin Mary. She is in the centre of heaven, surrounded by cherubs and musicians. Pillars support the sky which is a celeste blue with realistic clouds. At the four corners, stand saints Augustine, Hieronymous, Gregory and Ambrosius. Compare the brightness of the ceiling with the brown habits of the statues in the side altars. The blue scenes in the chancel show the life of Abraham. ■ *0830-1145, 1330-1640, US$1; the ticket also permits entry to NS da Conceição (keep your ticket for admission to the museum).* In the Largo outside São Francisco is a handicraft market.

See also box, page 281 **Nossa Senhora da Conceição** (1722), the parish church of Antônio Dias (one of the original settlements that became Vila Rica de Albuquerque), is heavily gilded and contains Aleijadinho's tomb. It has a museum devoted to him, Aleijadinho Paróquia, which also exhibits work by others and religious objects. ■ *0830-1130, 1330-1645, Sunday 1200-1645.*

Nossa Senhora das Mercês e Perdões (1740-72), Rua das Mercês, was rebuilt in the 19th century. Some sculpture by Aleijadinho can be seen in the main chapel. ■ *1000-1400.*

Santa Efigênia (1720-85), Ladeira Santa Efigênia e Padre Faria, has wonderful panoramic views of the city. Some say the church was decorated with gold dust washed out of slaves' hair, others that it was built by Chico Rei (see above). Manuel Francisco Lisboa (Aleijadinho's father) oversaw the construction and much of the carving is by Francisco Xavier de Brito (Aleijadinho's mentor). ■ *0800-1200.*

Nossa Senhora do Carmo, Rua Brigadeiro Mosqueira (1766-72), was planned by Manuel Francisco Lisboa and both his son and Mestre Athayde worked on the project. It was the favourite church of the aristocracy. There is a museum of sacred art with Aleijadinho sculptures. ■ *1300-1700, entry is shared with NS do Pilar.* (1733). Nossa Senhora do Pilar has heavily gilded work by Francisco Xavier de Brito. This church also contains a religious art museum. ■ *1200-1700.*

Nossa Senhora do Rosário, Largo do Rosário, dates from 1785, when the present church replaced a chapel on the site. It has a curved façade, which is rare in Brazilian baroque. The interior is much simpler than the exterior, but there are interesting side altars.

Nossa Senhora das Mercês e Misericórdia (1773-93) is just north of the Praça Tiradentes; further west, on a neighbouring hill, is **São Francisco de Paula**, work on which started in 1804, making it the last colonial church in Ouro Preto. ■ *0900-1700.* **São José**, Rua Teixeira Amaral, was begun in 1752, but not completed until 1811; some carving is by Aleijadinho.

There are a number of other churches and chapels. Also throughout the town are excellent examples of the public fountain (*chafariz*), oratories (*passos*) and stone bridges over the creeks and rivers.

O Aleijadinho

Antônio Francisco Lisboa (1738-1814), the son of a Portuguese architect and a black slave woman, was known as O Aleijadinho (the little cripple) because in later life he developed a maiming disease (possibly leprosy) which compelled him to work in a kneeling (and ultimately a recumbent) position with his hammer and chisel strapped to his wrists. His finest work, which shows a strength not usually associated with the plastic arts in the 18th century, is probably the set of statues in the gardens and sanctuary of the great Bom Jesus church in Congonhas do Campo, but the main body of his work is in Ouro Preto, with some important pieces in Sabará, São João del Rei and Mariana.

Excursions The **Cachoeira das Andorinhas**, a nearby waterfall, is reached by taking a bus to Morro de Santana and then walking 25 minutes. To walk all the way (north of town) takes 1½ hours. It is possible to visit the Zen Buddhist monastery near the waterfall, apply in advance: Mosteiro Zen Pico de Rajos, Morro de São Sebastião, CP 101, 35400-000, Ouro Preto, T0XX31-9612484. Excursions of 2½ hours are arranged at 0830 and 1430 visiting many cultural and ecological sites of interest.

The town is dominated by a huge cross, easily reached from the road to Mariana. It affords lovely views of the sunset, but don't go alone as it's in a poor district.

Parque Estadual de Itacolomi and the **Estação Ecológica do Tripuí** are protected areas close to the city. The former includes the peak of Itacolomi, which the first gold prospectors used for as a landmark for getting their bearings in the area, and the source of the Rio Doce. It also contains some wildlife threatened with extinction. It is a three-hour walk from the centre, splendid views, cars prohibited. Tripuí is in the valley where the first gold was found; it protects a rare invertebrate, the Peripatus Acacioi. It can also be reached on foot, or the bus to Belo Horizonte will drop you near the entrance.

Sleeping Ask at the tourist office for accommodation in *casas de família*, reasonably priced.

Avoid touts who greet you off buses and charge higher prices than those advertised in hotels; it is difficult to get hotel rooms at weekends and holiday periods.

AL *Pousada do Mondego*, Largo de Coimbra 38, T5512040, F5513094. Beautifully kept colonial house in a fine location by São Francisco church, room rates vary according to view, small restaurant, Scotch bar, popular with groups. Recommended (a Roteiro de Charme hotel, see page 57), the hotel runs a *jardineira* bus tour of the city, 2 hours, minimum 10 passengers, US$10 for non-guests. **AL** *Pousada Solar de NS do Rosário*, Av Getúlio Vargas 270, T5514200, F5514288. Fully restored historic building with a highly recommended restaurant, bar, sauna, all facilities in rooms.

A *Grande*, R Sen Rocha Lagoa 164, T/F5511488. Largest hotel in town and the only modern structure, designed by Oscar Niemeyer, the feel of the place is somehow more dated than the colonial buildings that surround it, but that is no reflection on the service. **A** *Luxor Pousada*, R Dr Alfredo Baeta 16, Praça Antônio Dias, T5512244. Converted colonial mansion, no twin beds, comfortable and clean but spartan, good views, restaurant good but service slow. **A** *Pousada Casa Grande*, R Conselheiro Quintiliano, 96, T/F5514314. Including breakfast, safe, good views. Recommended. **A** *Pouso Chico Rei*, R Brig Musqueira 90, T5511274. A fascinating old house with Portuguese colonial furnishings, very small and utterly delightful, book in advance (room No 6 has been described as a 'dream'). **A** *Solar das Lajes*, R Conselheiro Quintiliano 604, T/F5513388. A little way from centre, excellent view, pool, well run.

■ *on map, page 278*

Price codes: see inside front cover
Prices indicated below are for high season; many hotels offer, or will negotiate lower prices outside holiday times or when things are quiet

Minas Gerais & Espírito Santo

B *Colonial*, Trav Cônego Camilo Veloso 26, close to Praça Tiradentes, T5513133, F5513361. With new rooms and older rooms refurbished, pleasant. **B** *Pousada dos Bandeirantes*, R das Mercês 167, T5511996, F5511962, behind São Francisco de Assis. Beautiful views, TV, fridge, very pleasant. **B** *Pousada Itacolomi*, R Antônio Pereira 167, T5512891. Small. Recommended. **B** *Pousada Nello Nuno*, R Camilo de Brito 59, T5513375. Cheaper without bath, charming owner Annamélia speaks some French. Highly recommended. **B** *Pousada Ouro Preto*, Largo Musicista José dos Anjos Costa 72, T5513081. Small, laundry facilities, English spoken by owner, Gérson Luís Cotta (most helpful), noisy, good views. Recommended. **B** *Pousada Tiradentes*, Praça Tiradentes 70, T5512619. Comfortable, clean, TV, fridge, rooms a bit spartan and small, very convenient. **B** *Priskar da Barra*, R Antônio Martins 98, T/F5512666. Good facilities. **B** *Toffolo*, R São José 76, T5511322. Cheaper without breakfast, pleasant if simple rooms, oldest hotel in town.

C *Hospedária de Ouro Preto*, R Xavier da Veiga 1, T552203. Restored colonial house. Recommended. **C** *Pousada Marília de Dirceu*, R Conde de Bobadela 179/R Paraná 12, T5514327. **C** *Pousada São Francisco de Paula*, Padre JM Penna 202, next to the São Francisco de Paula church, T5513456. In a garden, panoramic view, veranda with hammock, free use of kitchen, multilingual staff, trips organized to nearby villages, mountains, mines, waterfalls, 8 rooms including a dormitory, with or without a simple breakfast, private or communal bathroom, full breakfast and snacks available, 100m from rodoviária. Recommended.

D *Pouso da Ladeira*, R Camilo de Brito 50, T5513654. 100m from Praça Tiradentes, colonial style, garden, views, owner speaks English and Spanish. **D** *Pousada Flávia Helena*, Padre Rolim 1273B, T5512069, 500m from rodoviária.

Students may be able to stay, during holidays and weekends, at the self-governing student hostels, known as *repúblicas* (very welcoming, 'best if you like heavy metal music' and 'are prepared to enter into the spirit of the places'). The Prefeitura has a list of over 50 *repúblicas* with phone numbers, available at the *Secretaria de Turismo*. Many are closed between Christmas and Carnival.

Camping *Camping Clube do Brasil*, Rodovia dos Inconfidentes Km 91, 2 km north, T5511799. Quite expensive but very nice.

Eating
● *on map, page 278*
Try the local licor de jaboticaba

Regional food *Casa Grande* and *Forno de Barro*, both on Praça Tiradentes (Nos 84 and 54 respectively). Good local dishes. *Restaurante e Chopparia Ouro Preto*, Praça Tiradentes 68. *Pasteleria Lampião*, Praça Tiradentes. Good views at the back (better at lunchtime than in the evening). *Tacho de Ouro*, Conde de Bobadela 76. Good lunch buffet, popular. *Casa do Ouvidor*, Conde de Bobadela 42, above Manoel Bernardis jewellery shop, good. *Satélite*, R Conde de Bobadela 97. Restaurant and pizzeria, bar next door, good value. *Pizzaria Zebão*, R Paraná 43. *Ouro Grill*, R Sen Rocha Lagoa 61. Self-service at lunchtime, US$5, good value restaurant after 1600. *Vide Gula*, R Sen Rocha Lagoa 79A. Food by weight, good, friendly atmosphere. Recommended. *Taverna do Chafariz*, R São José 167. Good local food. *Café & Cia*, R São José 187. Closes 2300, very popular, *comida por kilo* at lunchtime, good salads, juices. Recommended. Also on R São José, *Deguste*, next to Banco Itaú. Good value. *Adega*, R Teixeira Amaral 24. 1130-1530, vegetarian smorgasbord, US$5, all you can eat. Highly recommended. *Beijinho Doce*, R Direita 134A. Delicious pastries and cakes, try the truffles.

Festivals
Many shops close during Holy Week and on winter weekends

Ouro Preto is famous for its *Holy Week* processions, which in fact begin on the Thursday before Palm Sunday and continue (but not every day) until Easter Sunday. The most famous is that commemorating Christ's removal from the Cross, late on Good Friday. Attracting many Brazilians, Carnival here is also memorable. In **June**, *Corpus Christi* and the *Festas Juninas* are celebrated.

Every **July** the city holds the *Festival do Inverno da Universidade Federal de Minas Gerais (UFMG)*, the Winter Festival, about 3 weeks of arts, courses, shows, concerts and exhibitions. On **8 July**, is the anniversary of the city. **15 August**: *Nossa Senhora do Pilar*, patron saint of Ouro Preto. **12-18 November**, *Semana de Aleijadinho*, a week-long arts festival.

Yoga centre, Shiatsu and Kerala massage, down an alley between Nos 31 and 47 (Cine Teatro Vila Rica), Praça Alves de Brito, T5513337. **Sports**

Gems are not much cheaper from freelance sellers in Praça Tiradentes than from the shops, and in the shops themselves, the same quality of stone is offered at the same price – *Gemas de Minas* and *Manoel Bernardis*, Conde de Bobadela 63 and 48 respectively, are recommended. If buying gems on the street, ask for the seller's credentials. *Videmaju*, owned by Vincente Júlio de Paula, a professor at the School of Mines, sells stones at very good prices from his house at R Conselheiro Santana 175. **Shopping**

Buy soapstone carvings at roadside stalls and bus stops rather than in the cities; they are much cheaper. Many artisans sell soapstone carvings, jewellery and semi-precious stones in the Largo de Coimbra in front of São Francisco de Assis church. Also worth buying is traditional cookware in stone, copper or enamelled metal.

Buses The rodoviária is at R Padre Rolim 661, T5511081. A 'Circular' bus runs from the rodoviária to Praça Tiradentes, US$0.40; it is a long walk to the centre. Taxis charge exorbitant rates. **Transport**

Eleven buses a day from **Belo Horizonte** (2 hours, *Pássaro Verde*), US$3.75, taxi US$30. Day trips are run. Book your return journey to Belo Horizonte early if returning in the evening; buses get crowded. Bus from **Rio**, *Útil* at 0830 or 2300 (US$15, 7½ hours), return bus to Rio at 2330 (book in advance). There are also *Útil* buses to **Conselheiro Lafaiete**, 3-4 a day via Itabirito and Ouro Branco (see below), US$3.75, 2¾ hours, for connections to **Congonhas do Campo**. Other *Útil* services to **Rio**, **Barbacena**, **Conselheiro Lafaiete** and **Congonhas** go via Belo Horizonte. Direct buses to **São Paulo**, 3 a day with *Cristo Rei*, 11 hours, US$19.25. *Gontijo* go to Salvador via Belo Horizonte.

Banks *Banco do Brasil*, R São José 189, good rates, also for TCs. *Bemge*, Praça Alves de Brito. *Bradesco*, on the corner of Sen Rocha Lagoa and Padre Rolim, opposite the Escola de Minas. *Banco 24 Horas*, Praça Alves de Brito, next to Correios. **Communications** **Post Office:** Praça Alves de Brito. **Internet:** *Point* (language school and cultural centre), R Xavier da Veiga 501A, T/F5514427. **Tourist information** Praça Tiradentes 41, T5512655. Opens 0800, very helpful but Portuguese only spoken. Enquire here for details of accommodation in *casas de família, repúblicas* and other places. The *Secretaria de Turismo* is in the Casa de Gonzaga, R Cláudio Manoel 61, T5593282, F5593251. It produces information including hotel and restaurant lists, a map and lists of local sites. **Guides:** Bandeira's *Guia de Ouro Preto* in Portuguese and English (US$3.50 with coloured map, US$1 with black and white one), normally available at tourist office. Also available is Lucia Machado de Almeida's *Passeio a Ouro Preto*, US$6 (in Portuguese, English and French). The tourist office sells a guide with maps to Ouro Preto and Mariana, *Guia Prático*, for US$5. Most churches and historic buildings open to the public have a selection of books for sale. A local guide for a day, *Associação de Guias de Turismo* (AGTOP), can be obtained through the tourist office (a recommended guide is Cássio Antunes), T5512655 at the tourist office, or 5511544 ext 269. Opposite the rodoviária is an office of the Guiding Association (T5512504, or 5511544 ext 205), which offers group tours of US$30 for 1 to 10 people, US$45 for more than 10. The guides also give advice to new arrivals. If taking a guide, check their accreditation. The map sold at either the tourist or the Guiding Association office costs US$2.50. **Voltage** 110 volts AC. **Directory**

Between Ouro Preto and Mariana is the Minas de Passagem gold mine, dating from 1719. A 20-minute guided tour visits the old mine workings and underground lake (take bathing suit), entrance US$7.50, visiting hours 0900-1800, **Minas de Passagem**

Minas Gerais & Espírito Santo

Ouro Preto T5511068, Mariana T5571340/1255. There is a waterfall, Cachoeira Serrinha, where swimming is possible, 30 minutes' walk from the bus stop to the mine. Initially you have to walk 100 metres towards Mariana then ask for directions. Note that some signs say Mina de Ouro, omitting 'da Passagem'.

The nearest town to the Minas de Passagem is **Passagem de Mariana**. Where the bus stops at the edge of town is the *Pousada Solar dos Dois Sinos*, with a church behind it.

Mariana

Population: 40,500
Phone code: 031
Altitude: 697m
Colour map 4, grid C3

Mariana is 12 kilometres east of Ouro Preto on a road which goes on to join the Rio-Salvador highway. Another old mining city, it is much less hilly than Ouro Preto.

Mariana is the oldest town in Minas Gerais. It was first called Arraial de Nossa Senhora do Carmo, a settlement founded by the *bandeirantes* on 16 July 1696. In 1711 it became a town, Vila de Nossa Senhora do Carmo, and became the most important town, bishopric and administrative centre in the newly created Capitania de São Paulo e Minas do Ouro. In the mid-18th century, it was the only city in Minas Gerais, with the first town planning in the province. Its name was changed to Mariana in honour of the wife of Dom João V, Dona Maria Ana of Austria. Most of the fine colonial building was done in the second half of the 18th century. The artist Mestre Athayde was born here, as was the Inconfidente Cláudio Manuel da Costa.

Mariana was declared a national monument in 1945. Unlike Ouro Preto, in whose shadow the town tends to sit, it has remained a working mining centre. For many years the Companhia do Vale do Rio Doce (CVRD), the state mining company, had major operations here and provided a great deal of assistance for the restoration of the colonial heritage. Since CVRD's concentration on its new investments at Carajás and subsequent privatization, there have been doubts about its commitment to mining in Mariana and consequently to the town.

Sights

The historical centre of the town slopes gently uphill from the river and the Praça Tancredo Neves, where buses from Ouro Preto stop. The first street parallel with the Praça Tancredo Neves is Rua Direita, which is lined with beautiful, two-storey 18th century houses. The aspect of the street, with its tall colonial windows and balconies, is very fine. At No 54 is the **Casa do Barão de Pontal** whose balconies are carved from soapstone, unique in Minas Gerais. The ground floor of the building is a museum of furniture. ■ *Tuesday 1400-1700*. At No 35 is the **Museu-Casa Afonso Guimarães** (or Alphonsus de Guimaraens) , the former home of a symbolist poet: photographs and letters. ■ *Entrance free*. No 31 is the office of *Mariana Turismo*. No 7 is the **Casa Setecentista**, another excellent example of 18th century secular architecture which now belongs to the Patrimônio Histórico e Artístico Nacional. It has an enormous archive of documents from the colonial period, an exhibition hall and a multimedia centre.

Rua Direita leads to the Praça da Sé, on which stands the **Cathedral**, Basílica de Nossa Senhora da Assunção. Before Vila de Nossa Senhora do Carmo became a town, a chapel, started in 1703, stood on this spot. In various stages it was expanded and remodelled, mainly 1712-45, until its completion in 1760. The portal and the lavabo in the sacristy are by Aleijadinho. The painting in the beautiful interior and side altars is by Manoel Rabello de Sousa (the cathedral was being restored in 1997). Also in the cathedral is a wooden German organ (1701), made by Arp Schnitger, which was a gift to the first diocese of the Capitania de Minas do Ouro in 1747, installed in 1753. It was restored in 1984 after some 50 years of silence. Organ concerts are given on Friday at 1100 and Sunday at 1200 (US$7.50). Other concerts are held; see the local press for details.

Turning up Rua Frei Durão, on the right is the **Museu Arquidiocesano**, which has fine church furniture, a gold and silver collection, Aleijadinho statues and an ivory cross. ■ *Rua Frei Durão 49, 0900-1200, 1300-1700, closed Monday, US$1.50*. On the opposite side of the street is the **Casa da Intendência/Casa de Cultura** , No 84, which holds exhibitions and has a museum of music. The ceilings in the exhibition rooms are very fine; in other rooms there are *esteiro* (flattened bamboo) ceilings. ■ *0800-1130, 1330-1700*. At No 22 of the same street is the **Centro Cultural SESI Mariana**, with a theatre and occasional cinema presentations.

Praça Gomes Freire used to be where horses were tied up and also the space in which religious and other festivals were held. There is an old drinking trough on one side. Now it has pleasant gardens. On the south side is the **Palácio Arquiepiscopal**, while on the north side is the **Casa do Conde de Assumar**, who was governor of the Capitania from 1717 to 1720; it later became the bishop's palace.

Minas Gerais & Espírito Santo

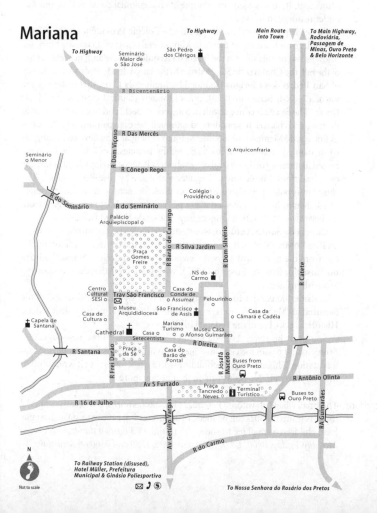

Mariana

From Praça Gomes Freire, Travessa São Francisco leads to Praça Minas Gerais and one of the finest groups of colonial buildings in Brazil. In the middle of the Praça is the **Pelourinho**, the stone monument to Justice, at which slaves used to be beaten. On one side of the square is the fine **São Francisco** church (1762-94), with pulpits designed by Aleijadinho, paintings by Mestre Athayde, who is buried in tomb No 94, a fine sacristy and one side-altar by Aleijadinho. The statue of São Roque is most important as he is the patron saint of the city (his day is 16 August). Among Athayde's paintings are the panels showing the life of St Francis on the ceiling of the right-hand chapel. The church is one of the most simple in Mariana, but in terms of art, one of the richest. There is a small exhibition of the restoration work funded by CVRD. ■ *Daily 0800-1700.*

At right angles to São Francisco is **Nossa Senhora do Carmo** (1784), with steatite carvings, Athayde paintings, and chinoiserie panelling. Its exterior is considered the most beautiful in Mariana by some. Unfortunately this church was damaged by fire in early 1999. ■ *Daily 1400-1700.* Across Rua Dom Silvério is the **Casa da Câmara e Cadéia** (1768), at one time the Prefeitura Municipal. It, too, is a superb example of civic colonial construction, but was under restoration in 1997.

Proceed up Rua Dom Silvério, passing the **Colégio Providência** at No 61, the first college for boarding students in Minas Gerais (part of it is now a hotel, see below). Also on this street is the **Igreja da Arquiconfraria** and, nearing the top of the hill, the **Chafariz de São Pedro**. On the Largo de São Pedro is the church of **São Pedro dos Clérigos** (founded by Manuel da Cruz, first bishop of the town, 1748-64, begun in 1753), one of the few elliptical churches in Minas Gerais. The façade is convex, with two towers set back, and two ellipses contain the nave and chancel. It is unadorned, although there is a painting by Athayde of 'A Entrega do Menino Jesus a Santo Antônio'. The altar is made of cedar, ungilded or painted, and has not been affected by termites. Look for the cockerel, carved in memory of the biblical verses about St Peter betraying Christ before the cock has crowed three times. The altar was made by José Pedro Aroca. The church was only opened to the public in 1988; for many years it was left unfinished, then bishops maintained it as a private chapel. Ask to see the view from the bell tower. Restoration is under way. The guide is called Domingos.

Capela de Santo Antônio, wonderfully simple and the oldest in town, is on Rua Rosário Velho. It is some distance from the centre. Overlooking the city from the north, with a good viewpoint, is the church of **Nossa Senhora do Rosário**, Rua do Rosário (1752), with work by Athayde and showing Moorish influence.

Outside the centre, to the west, but within easy walking distance, is the **Seminário Menor**, no longer a seminary but the Instituto de Ciencias Históricas e Sociais of the Federal University.

South of the river, Avenida Getúlio Vargas leads to the new Prefeitura Municipal. It passes the Ginásio Poliesportivo and, across the avenue, the railway station. This is a romantic building with a clock tower, but it is rapidly falling into disrepair. No trains run on the line any more.

Excursions The small village of Antônio Pereira, 24 kilometres north, is where the imperial topaz is mined. Tours can be made of an interesting cave with stalactites: pay local children a small fee to show you round. ■ *3 buses a day from Mariana Monday-Friday, 0800, 1200, 1445, plus 1100, 1750 and 2100 on Saturday.*

B *Pousada Solar dos Corrêa*, R Josefá Macedo 70 and R Direita, T/F5572080. Central, **Sleeping** with breakfast, parking. **B** *Faísca*, R Antônio Olinto 48, T5571206. Also central, including breakfast. **C** *Central*, R Frei Durão 8, T/F5571630. **D** without bath, on the attractive Praça Gomes Freire, pleasant, quiet. Recommended but avoid downstairs rooms. **C** *Pousada do Chafariz*, R Cônego Rego 149, T5571492. Parking, breakfast included, family atmosphere. Recommended. **C** *Providência*, R Dom Silvério 233, T5571444. Run by nuns, small rooms, pool, quiet. **D** *Müller*, Av Getúlio Vargas 34, T5571188, across the river from the Terminal Turístico. Recommended. The modern service station (*Posto Mariana*) on the highway above the town offers good clean rooms with hot showers.

Mangiare della Mamma, D Viçoso 27. Italian. Recommended. *Tambaú*, R João **Eating** Pinheiro 26. Regional food. *Engenho Nôvo*, Praça da Sé 26, T5571312. Bar at night, English spoken by the owners and clients. Recommended. *Panela de Pedra* in the Terminal Turístico serves food by weight at lunchtime.

Carnival and *Holy Week* are celebrated in the town. **29 June** *São Pedro*. In July, **Festivals** Mariana shares some events of the *Festival do Inverno da UFMG* with Ouro Preto.

Buses These leave **Ouro Preto** from beside the Escola de Minas, for Mariana, every **Transport** 30 minutes, US$0.60, all passing Minas de Passagem (buses also leave from Ouro Preto rodoviária). Ouro Preto buses stop at the new rodoviária, out of town on the main road, then at the *Posto Mariana*, before heading back to the centre of Mariana at Praça Tancredo Neves. Many buses seem to go only to the *posto* above the town, but it's a long walk from the centre. A bus from the rodoviária to the centre via the *posto* and Minas de Passagem costs US$0.40. Buses from Mariana to Ouro Preto can be caught by the bridge at the end of Rua do Catete.

Bus from **Belo Horizonte** (via Ouro Preto), US$4.50, 2¼ hours. Buses for **Santa Bárbara** (near Caraça) leave from the rodoviária.

Banks *Bemge* at *Ginásio Poliesportivo*, Av Getúlio Vargas, across the river from Praça Tancredo **Directory** Neves. **Communications** Post office: Corner of R Frei Durão and Praça Gomes Freire, also in *Ginásio Poliesportivo* (see above). **Telecommunications:** in *Ginásio Poliesportivo*. **Tourist information** *Terminal Turístico Manoel Costa Athayde*, Praça Tancredo Neves, houses the local guides' association (AGTURB, T5571158), who run tours for US$40. There is also a small tourist office; map US$1.50. A free monthly booklet, *Mariana Agenda Cultural*, has details of the historical sites, accommodation, restaurants, shopping, transport etc, plus articles, poems and a calendar of events.

From Ouro Preto to Congonhas do Campo: the *Útil* bus takes the paved **Conselheiro** Rodovia dos Inconfidentes and turns south to Itabirito. After this town the **Lafaiete** road is unpaved, passing through rolling farmland and mines. One mining *Population: 94,500* town, with a railway junction, has a huge church. The paving starts again near *Phone code: 031* the large mines and reservoir before Ouro Branco and Açominas. Whether coming from Ouro Preto or Rio de Janeiro to Congonhas, there is no direct bus; you have to change buses at Conselheiro Lafaiete.

Sleeping **B** *Carumbé*, Av Telésforo Cândido de Rezende 212, T7631555. **B** *Cupim*, on main Rio road, 18 km, T/F7241200. **B** *Newton*, Av Telésforo Cândido de Rezende 266, T/F7215644. **C** *Rhud's Palace*, R José Nicolau de Queiroz 11, opposite the rodoviária, T7214199, F7212957. Two-star.

Transport **Buses**: there is a frequent service to **Congonhas do Campo**, US$1.

Congonhas do Campo

Population: 36,000
Phone code: 031
Altitude: 866m
Colour map 4, grid C3

This hill town is connected by a paved 3½ kilometre road with the Rio-Belo Horizonte highway. Most visitors spend little time in the town, but go straight to the Sanctuary of Bom Jesus de Matosinhos on a hill above the town. This masterpiece of colonial art can be visited in a day, but there are other things to see in the area should you decide to stay overnight.

In the 18th century, Congonhas was a mining town. Today, in addition to the business brought by the tourists and pilgrims who come to the Sanctuary, its industries include mining and handicrafts.

Sights
0700-1900
Tuesday-Sunday

O Santuário de Bom Jesus de **Matosinhos**, the great pilgrimage church, and its Via Sacra dominates the town. The idea of a sanctuary belonged to a prospector, Feliciano Mendes, who promised to erect a cross and chapel in thanks to Bom Jesus after he had been cured of a serious illness. The inspiration for his devotion came from two sources in Portugal, the cult of Bom Jesus at Braga (near where Mendes was born) and the church of Bom Jesus de Matozinhos, near Porto. Work began in 1757, funded by Mendes' own money and alms he raised. The church was finished in 1771, six years after Mendes' death, and the fame that the sanctuary had acquired led to its development by the most famous architects, artists and sculptors of the time as a Sacro Monte. This involved the construction of six linked chapels, or *pasos* (1802-18), which lead up to a terrace and courtyard before the church. On this terrace (designed in 1777) stand 12 prophets, sculpted by Aleijadinho between 1800 and 1805.

There is a wide view of the country from the church terrace, below which are six small chapels set in an attractive sloping area with grass, cobblestones and palms. Each chapel shows scenes with life-size Passion figures carved by Aleijadinho and his pupils in cedar wood. In order of ascent they are: the chapel of the Last Supper, the chapel of the Mount of Olives, the chapel of the taking, or betrayal of Christ, the chapel of the flagellation and the crowning with thorns, the chapel of Jesus carrying the Cross and the chapel of Christ being nailed to

Santuário de Bom Jesus de Matosinhos

Adro dos Profetas detail

Prophets

1 Abdias	7 Isaías
2 Amós	8 Jeremias
3 Baruc	9 Joel
4 Daniel	10 Jonas
5 Ezquiel	11 Naum
6 Habacuc	12 Oséias

N

Not to scale

the Cross. Many of the statues, especially those of Christ and the main actors in each scene, are attributed to Aleijadinho, while the other figures were made by his assistants.

On the terrace stand the 12 prophets sculpted by Aleijadinho (thought of as his masterpieces). Carved in soapstone with dramatic sense of movement, they constitute one of the finest works of art of their period in the world. Note how Aleijadinho adapted the biblical characters to his own cultural references. All the prophets are sculpted wearing leather boots, as all important men in his time would have done. Daniel, who entered the lion's den, is represented with the artist's own conception of a lion, never having seen one himself: a large, maned cat with a face rather like a Brazilian monkey. Similary, the whale which accompanies Jonah is an idiosyncratic interpretation. Each statue has a prophetic text carved with it. The statues "combine in a kind of sacred ballet whose movements only seem uncoordinated; once these sculptures cease to be considered as isolated units, they take on full significance as part of a huge composition brought to life by an inspired genius." (*Iberian-American Baroque*, edited by Henri Stierlin, page 178.) The beauty of the whole is enhanced by the combination of church, Via Sacra and wide landscape over which the prophets seem to preside.

Inside the church, there are paintings by Athayde and the heads of four sainted popes (Gregory, Jerome, Ambrose and Augustine) sculpted by Aleijadinho for the reliquaries on the high altar. Other artists involved were João Nepomuceno Correia e Castro, who painted the scenes of the life and passion of Christ in the nave and around the high altar, João Antunes de Carvalho, who carved the high altar, and Jerônimo Félix and Manuel Coelho, who carved the crossing altars of Santo Antônio and São Francisco de Paula. Despite the ornate carving, the overall effect of the paintwork is almost muted and naturalistic, with much use of blues, greys and pinks. Lamps are suspended on chains from the mouths of black dragons.

To the left of the church, as you face it, the third door in the building alongside the church is the Room of Miracles, which contains photographs and thanks for miracles performed.

On the hill are a tourist kiosk, souvenir shops, the *Colonial Hotel* and *Cova do Daniel* restaurant. There are public toilets on the Alameda das Palmeiras. From the hotel the Alameda das Palmeiras sweeps round to the **Romarias**, a large, almost oval area surrounded by buildings. This was the lodging where the pilgrims stayed. It now contains the Espaço Cultural, the headquarters of the local tourist office (*Fumcult*), workshops, the museums of mineralogy and religious art, the Memória da Cidade, the *Estalagem* restaurant and a *lanchonete*. A winter festival is held here for one week in July.

Transport A bus marked Basílica runs every 30 minutes from the centre of the rodoviária to Bom Jesus, 5 km, US$0.45. A taxi from the rodoviária will cost US$5 one-way, US$10 return including the wait while you visit the sanctuary. The information desk at the bus station will guard luggage. In town, the bus stops in Praça JK. You can walk up from Praça JK via Praça Dr Mário Rodrigues Pereira, cross the little bridge, then go up Ruas Bom Jesus and Aleijadinho to the Praça da Basílica.

Other churches The oldest church here is **Nossa Senhora do Rosário**, Praça do Rosário, built by slaves at the end of the 17th century. The **Igreja Matriz de Nossa Senhora da Conceição**, in Praça 7 de Setembro, dates from 1749; the portal is attributed to Aleijadinho, while parts of the interior are by Manuel Francisco Lisboa. There are two 18th century chapels, **Nossa Senhora da Ajuda**, in the district of Alto Maranhão, and the church at Lobo Leite, 10 kilometres away.

Sleeping & eating **B** *Colonial*, Praça da Basílica 76, opposite Bom Jesus, T7311834. Good and comfortable but noisy, breakfast extra, most rooms have bathroom (**D** pp without bath), fascinating restaurant (*Cova do Daniel*) downstairs is full of colonial handicrafts and good local food. **D** *Freitas*, R Marechal Floriano 69, T7311543. Basic, with breakfast, **E** without bath. *Estalagem Romaria*, 2 minutes from *Hotel Colonial* in the Romarias. Good restaurant and pizzeria, reasonable prices.

Festivals Congonhas is celebrated for its *Holy Week* processions, which have as their focus the Bom Jesus church. The most celebrated ceremonies are the meeting of Christ and the Virgin Mary on the Tuesday, and the dramatized Deposition from the Cross late on Good Friday. The *pilgrimage season*, first half of **September**, draws many thousands. 8 December, *Nossa Senhora da Conceição*.

Transport **Buses** The Rodoviária is 1½ km outside town; bus to town centre US$0.40; for Basílica, see above. To/from **Belo Horizonte**, 1½ hours, US$3, 8 times a day. To **São João del Rei**, 2 hours, US$3.60, tickets are not sold until the bus comes in. To **Ouro Preto**, go via Belo Horizonte, Murtinho or Conselheiro Lafaiete.

Directory **Tourist information** *Fumcult*, in the Romarias, T7311300, ext 114, or 7313133, very helpful.

The road from Congonhas do Campo to São João del Rei goes through São Brás do Suaçuí, whose smart church, painted blue and white, dominates the town. The countryside is hilly, given over to farming. There are frequent, wide views. The town of Entre Rios de Minas is the birthplace of the Campolina horse. This breed, like the Manga Larga, also bred in southern Minas Gerais, has a gait which keeps three feet on the ground, one in the air, instead of the usual trot.

Just past Lagoa Dourada is the turning (12 kilometres) for **Prados**, a town known for its musical and handicrafts traditions. This pleasant place maintains its historical church music (see under São João del Rei, below). Its chief tradition is leatherwork, especially saddles (some say this dates back to the time when mule trains had to be equipped – Prados was one of the earliest places to produce gold). The forge produces the ironwork (bits etc) and another workshop produces the frames for the saddles. In this and other shops animals are carved in wood. Excellent leather clothing can also be found, good prices from *Mara e Café*, Rua Magalhães Gomes 90. Other crafts include crochet and sisal carpets.

Two *fazendas* in the vicinity breed Pega donkeys, *Fazenda do Vau* and *Fazenda do Engenho Velho*, which is 10 kilometres from Lagoa Dourada and difficult to get to. Both also produce *pinga* (*cachaça*).

Barbacena An alternative route to São João del Rei is to turn off the BR-040 at Barbacena,
Population: 102,000 71 kilometres south of Conselheiro Lafaiete. The town has an important horse
Phone code 032 and cattle fair, and a rose festival in October. A paved road runs west from Barbacena for 62 kilometres to São João.

Sleeping A *Grogotá*, R Cruz das Almas, on a hill overlooking the road to Rio, T3317755, F3314430. Excellent, operated by Senac. There is a *fazenda* which takes guests, reached by turning off the BR-040 12½ km after Cupim, which is between Conselheiro Lafaiete and Barbacena **AL** *Estalagem Fazenda Lazer*, Carandaí, T3611425, reservations in Belo Horizonte, Av Cristovão Colombo 519, sala 103, Savassi, 30140-140, T031-2813715, F031-2814933, estalagem@cyberdock.com.br, http://www.cyberdock.com.br/ estalagem. (member of *Ametur*, see under Belo Horizonte **Tour companies and travel agents**), suites and chalets, typical restaurant, bar, pool, sports facilities, walking, within easy reach of Congonhas, São João del Rei and Tiradentes.

Directory Tourist information *Cenatur*, in the rodoviária.

São João del Rei

The colonial city of São João del Rei is at the foot of the Serra do Lenheiro. The streets are paved with fossilized plants: 'almost sacrilegious to walk on them'. A good view of the town and surroundings is from Alto da Boa Vista, where there is a Statue of Christ (Senhor dos Montes). São João del Rei is a pleasant city, very lively at weekends.

Population: 75,500
Phone code: 032
Colour map 4, grid C3

Before gold was discovered in this part of Minas, what is now São João del Rei was an important point on one of the main routes between the existing goldfields and the coast. It was known as the Porto Real da Passagem. Once gold was found here, the settlement of Arraial Novo de Nossa Senhora da Pilar was set up. In this neighbourhood one of the decisive actions of the Guerra dos Emboabas took place (see **History**, page 258), in which the Paulistas were ambushed and murdered by the outsiders at the Capão da Traição (the Hedge of Treason). In another episode so many were killed that the river running between modern-day São João del Rei and Tiradentes was renamed the Rio das Mortes (the River of the Deaths). When the town was named São João del

History

Minas Gerais & Espírito Santo

São João del Rei

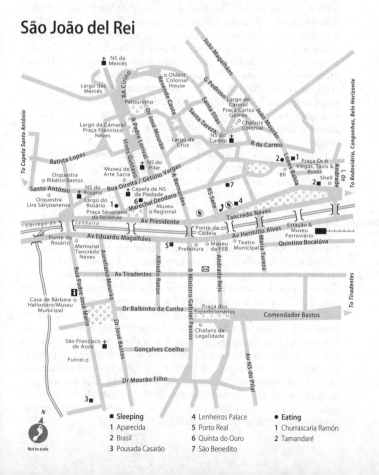

■ Sleeping	4 Lenheiros Palace	● Eating
1 Aparecida	5 Porto Real	1 Churrascaria Ramón
2 Brasil	6 Quinta do Ouro	2 Tamandaré
3 Pousada Casarão	7 São Benedito	

N
Not to scale

Rei in 1713, it became the seat of the judiciary for the district which took the name of the Rio das Mortes. It remained a commercial centre after the decline in gold mining, the main activities being livestock raising and agriculture. It became a city in 1833. Two English travellers in the 19th century visited and wrote about this area (among others), Captain Richard Burton, *The Highlands of Brazil* (1869), and the Reverend J Walsh, *Notices of Brazil* (1830).

The town is known as the land of Tiradentes and Tancredo Neves. The former has been mentioned frequently already in this section, but it is worth mentioning here that Joaquim José da Silva Xavier's place of birth was the Fazenda de Pombal, about 15 kilometres downstream from Tiradentes on the Rio das Mortes. After his execution, the Fazenda was confiscated. It is now an experimental station owned by Ibama. Another of the Inconfidentes, Bárbara Heliodora Guilhermina da Silveira, wife of Ignacio José Alvarenga, was born in the town (see below). Tancredo Neves, to whom there is a memorial in the town (see also below), was the man who would have become the first civilian president of Brazil after the military dictatorships of the mid-20th century, had he not died before taking office.

Sights Through the centre of town runs the Corrego do Lenheiro, a stream with steep grassy banks. Across it are two fine, stone bridges, A Ponte da Cadeia (1798) and A Ponte do Rosário (1800). There are several other modern bridges, including three footbridges, one called A Ponte dos Suspiros (the bridge of sighs). Both sides of the river have colonial monuments, which are interspersed with modern buildings. On the north side are many streets with pleasant houses, but in various states of repair. Rua Santo Antônio has many single-storey colonial houses which have been restored and painted. Rua Santo Elias has several buildings all in the same style. Behind the church of Nossa Senhora do Pilar (see below), the Largo da Câmara leads up to Mercês church, which has quite a good view. Throughout the city you will see locked portals with colonial porticos. These are *passinhos*, shrines that are opened in Holy Week. They can be seen for instance on Largo da Cruz and Largo do Rosário.

Many streets and squares seem to have more than one name, which can be a little confusing, but as the town centre is not large, it is hard to get lost. One such is the street across the Ponte da Cadeia from Rua Passos; it has three names: Rua da Intendência, Manoel Anselmo and Artur Bernardes.

Churches
There are 5 18th-century churches in the town, 3 of which are splendid examples of Brazilian colonial building

São Francisco de Assis (1774), Praça Frei Orlando: Stierlin and Bottineau in *Iberian-American Baroque* describe the design for the façade as Aleijadinho's highest achievement, "which is richly ornamented, yet, at the same time, simple and poetic in feeling". The towers are circular, the doorway intricately carved and the greenish stone frames the white paint to beautiful effect. In front is a balustrade with steps down to the Praça Frei Orlando, in which are 19 palm trees, 12 of which are very tall. Inside are two sculptures by Aleijadinho, and others of his school. The six side altars are in wood; restoration has removed the plaster from the altars, revealing fine carving in sucupira wood. Their artistry is wonderful and the three pairs of altars mirror each other, each pair in a different style (note, for instance, the use of pillars and the different paintings which accompany each altar). Two pulpits, also in wood, face each other. The overall shape of the nave is elliptical; its white paint, greenish-grey stone and brown wood contrast with the white and gold altar with its spiralling columns and five-tiered altar. An adoring St Francis kneels atop the altar. ■ *0830-1200 and some afternoons, US$1.*

Basílica de Nossa Senhora do Pilar (the Cathedral, Rua Getúlio Vargas – formerly Rua Direita), built in 1721, has a 19th-century façade which replaced the 18th century original. It has rich altars and a brightly painted ceiling (Madonna and Child in the middle, saints and bishops lining the sides). The chancel has a tiled floor and walls with blue paintings. Note the androgynous gold heads and torsos within the eight columns set into the walls either side of the main altar. There is a profusion of cherubs and plants in the carving. This abundance and angelic innocence contrasts with the suffering of the Passion and the betrayal of the Last Supper (two pictures of which are before the altar), all common themes in Brazilian baroque. In the sacristy are portraits of the Evangelists. ■ *Open afternoons.*

Nossa Senhora do Carmo, Praça Dr Augusto Viegas (Largo do Carmo), very well restored, is all in white and gold. Construction commenced in 1733. The façade is outlined in lights at night. ■ *Open afternoons.*

There are three other churches in town: the **Igreja do Rosário**, Largo do Rosário, in its present form dates from 1753, but the first chapel on the site was put up in 1719. It is all white, except for silver angels. ■ *Open afternoons.* The **Igreja de Santo Antônio**, Rua Santo Antônio, is a chapel built in the 1760s. The **Igreja das Mercês**, on the hill behind the Cathedral, is again a later construction than the original chapel. The present building is of 1853, just over 100 years younger than its predecessor.

Museums

Almost opposite São Francisco is the house of **Bárbara Heliodora** (1759-1819), Rua Padre José Maria Xavier, which also contains the **Museu Municipal Tomé Portes del Rei**, with historical objects and curios. In the same building is the Instituto Histórico e Geográfico; downstairs is the tourist office. Next door is the Biblioteca Municipal and the Acadêmia das Letras.

Museu de Arte Sacra, Praça Gastão da Cunha 8, by Nossa Senhora do Pilar, is small but recommended; it has sculptures, vestments and a room full of silver. ■ *Tuesday-Sunday 1100-1700, US$1.*

The **Memorial Tancredo Neves**, Rua Padre José Maria Xavier 7, is a homage to the man and his life. An eight-minute video on São João del Rei is shown. It also holds exhibitions and has a bookshop. ■ *Wednesday-Friday 1300-1800, weekends and holidays 0900-1700, US$1.*

The **Museu de Arte Regional do Patrimônio Histórico**, in Praça Severiano de Resende, in a fine three-storey building (1859), has 18th and 19th century furniture and pictures and an archive of documents pertaining to the city. ■ *Tuesday-Sunday, 0800-1200, 1330-1730, US$1.*

Museu da FEB (or **dos Ex-Combatentes**), Avenida Hermílio Alves, entrance on Avenida Tiradentes, in the Círculo Militar, houses items from the Second World War. ■ *Thursday-Saturday 1200-1700, Sunday 0900-1300.*

The **Museu Ferroviário/railway museum**, Avenida Hermílio Alves 366, is well worth exploring. The museum traces the history of railways in general and in Brazil in brief. There is an informative display of the role of Irineu Evangelista de Souza, Barão de Mauá, who was a pioneer of both industry and the railways following his visit to England in 1840. The locomotive that ran on the first railway from Rio de Janeiro to the foot of the Serra do Mar was called *A Baronesa* after his wife. The railway to São João, the Estrada de Ferro Oeste de Minas was not a success, but it was instrumental in the development of the region.

In the museum is an 1880 Baldwin 4-4-0 locomotive from Philadelphia (No 5055) and a 1912-13 VIP carriage. Outside, at the end of the platforms are carriages and a small Orenstein and Koppel (Berlin) engine. You can walk along the tracks to the round house, in which are several working engines in superb condition, an engine shed and a steam-operated machine shop, still working.

It is here that the engines get up steam before going to couple with the coaches for the run to Tiradentes. On days when the trains are running, you can get a good, close-up view of operations even if not taking the trip; highly recommended. ■ *T3718004, US$0.50, see below for the train to Tiradentes.*

Music São João del Rei has two famous orchestras which play baroque music which dates back to colonial times. In those days, the music master not only had to provide the music for mass, but also had to compose new pieces for every festival. All the music has been kept and the **Riberio Bastos** and **Lira Sanjoanense** preserve the tradition. Both have their headquarters, rehearsing rooms and archives on Rua Santo Antônio (at nos 54 and 45 respectively). The Orquestra Ribeiro Bastos plays at mass every Sunday in São Francisco de Assis at 0915, as well as at many religious ceremonies throughout the year (for example Holy Week). The Orquestra Lira Sanjoanense plays at Mass every Thursday in Nossa Senhora do Pilar at 1900 and on Sunday in Nossa Senhora do Rosário at 0830 and Nossa Senhora das Mercês at 1000, as well as on other occasions. It is best to check at their offices for full details.

There are similar orchestras in Prados (see above) and Tiradentes, but the latter is not as well supported as those in São João.

Worth a visit is the **pewter factory** (with exhibition and shop), Avenida Leite de Castro 1150, 10 minutes' walk from the rodoviária. Run by Englishman John Somers and his son Gregory. ■ *0900-1800, T3718000, F3717653.*

The nearby town of **Resende Costa** (30 kilometres north) is known for its textile handicrafts.

Sleeping A *Lenheiro Palace*, Av Pres Tancredo Neves 257, T/F3718155. Modern hotel with
■ *on map, page 291* good facilities, parking, cheaper in low season, teahouse, breakfast. A *Pousada Quinto do Ouro*, Praça Severiano de Resende 4, above the restaurant of the same name, T3712565. Cheaper in low season, fan. **B** *Porto Real*, Av Eduardo Magalhães 254, T/F3717000. Modern, comfortable, sizeable rooms, good restaurant. **B** *Pousada Casarão*, Ribeiro Bastos 94, opposite São Francisco church, T3717447, F3711224. Firm beds, pool, games room, in a converted mansion, delightful. **C** *Aparecida*, Praça Dr Antônio Viegas 13, T3712540. Central, by the bus and taxi stop, has a restaurant and *lanchonete*. **D** *Brasil*, Av Pres Tancredo Neves 395, T3712804. In an old house full of character, on the opposite side of the river from the railway station, cheap. Recommended but basic, no breakfast. **D** *do Hespanhol*, R Mcal Deodoro 131, T3714677. Also central, price varies according to room. **E** pp *Pousada São Benedito*, R Mcal Deodoro 254, T3717381. Shared rooms only, shared bath.

Eating *Quinto do Ouro*, address as *pousada* above. Good regional food, reasonable prices;
● *on map, page 291* also on Praça Severiano de Resende is *Churrascaria Ramón*, No 52. Good. *Portal del Rey*, Praça Severiano de Rezende 134, *comida à kilo*, Minas and Arabic food, very good. By the railway station is *Churrascaria e Pizzaria Chafariz*. For breakfast, go up Lopes Bahia from Av Pres Tancredo Neves and on the corner opposite the BR filling station is *Tamandaré*, with a *padaria* next door at No 9.

Festivals April, *Semana Santa*; 15-21 *Semana da Inconfidência*. May or June, *Corpus Christi*. First 2 weeks of **August**, *Nossa Senhora da Boa Morte*, with baroque music (*novena barroca*). Similarly, **12 October**, *Nossa Senhora do Pilar*, patron saint of the city. **8 December**, founding of the city. FUNREI, the university (on R Padre José Maria Xavier), holds *Inverno Cultural* in **July** each year.

Buses The rodoviária is 2 km west of centre of São João; it has a phone office, toilets, **Transport** luggage store, lanchonetes and a tourist information office. Buses to **Rio**, 5 daily with *Paraibuna* (3 on Saturday and Sunday), 5 hours, US$10-12. *Cristo Rei* to **São Paulo**, 8 hours, 5 a day (also to Santos), and *Translavras*, 4 a day (also to Campinas), US$12.50. **Belo Horizonte**, 3½ hours, US$6.60. To **Juiz de Fora**, US$5.40, at least 8 a day with *Transur*. Frequent service to **Tiradentes** with *Meier*, 8 a day, 7 on Saturday, Sunday and holidays, US$0.65; on the return journey to São João, the bus stops outside the railway station before proceeding to the rodoviária.

Banks *Bemge*, Av Pres Tancredo Neves 213. Has exchange, 1100-1600. **Directory** **Communications** Telecommunications: Av Pres Tancredo Neves 119. 0700-2200. **Tourist information** *Secretaria de Turismo*, in the house of Bárbara Heliodora, T3717833. 0900-1700, provides a free map.

Tiradentes

The centre of this charming little town, 15 kilometres from São João, with its *Population: 5,000* nine streets and eight churches, at the foot of the green Serra São José, at first *Phone code: 032* glance hardly belongs to this century. Look behind the colonial façades, *Colour map 4, grid C3* though, and you will see galleries, *ateliés*, antique shops, *pousadas* and restaurants. This is a mark of its popularity as a tourist centre, but in no way mars its attractiveness. The town is very busy during Holy Week, when there are numerous religious processions.

In 1938, Tiradentes' rich architectural and artistic heritage was recognized and it was declared a national monument. Since then it has been carefully restored.

Tiradentes stands on the site of yet another *bandeirante* encampment, the Arraial de Santo Antônio do Rio das Mortes. It prospered and was founded as an autonomous town with the name São José del Rei on 14 January 1718. During the 18th century its fortunes rested on mining and, as elsewhere, the wealthy lay orders spared no expense on their churches. After independence, when the mines had become exhausted, São José fell into decay which not even the coming of the railway in 1881 could remedy. It was after the ousting of the emperor in 1889 that the town was renamed in honour of the martyr of the Inconfidência, see page 276. Tiradentes was not the only Inconfidente associated with the place, though. Also resident was Carlos Correia de Toledo Pisa (Padre Toledo), a priest.

Churches The **Igreja Matriz de Santo Antônio**, first built in 1710 and **Sights** enlarged in 1736, contains some of the finest gilded wood carvings in the country. The main church is predominantly white and gold. Lamps hang from the beaks of golden eagles. The symbols on the panels painted on the ceiling of the nave are a mixture of Old Testament and medieval Christian symbolism (for instance the phoenix, and the pelican). A carved wooden balustrade separates the seating in the nave from richly carved side chapels and altars. The principal altar is also ornately decorated, as are the walls and ceiling around it. The church has a small but fine organ brought from Porto in the 1790s; it and its loft are painted in pinks and blues. On a scroll beside it are verses from Psalm 150: "Laudate eum in tympano & choro; laudate eum in chórdis, & órgano". The upper part of the reconstructed façade is said to follow a design by Aleijadinho. In front of the church, on the balustrade which overlooks the main street and the town, are also a cross and a sundial by him. ■ *Daily 0900-1700.*

Minas Gerais & Espírito Santo

The charming **Nossa Senhora do Rosário** church, on a small square on Rua Direita, has fine statuary and ornate gilded altars. On its painted ceiling colonnades rise to heaven; two monks stand on a hill and the Virgin and Child are in the sky. Other ceiling panels depicting the life of Christ are in poor shape. The church contains statues of black saints, including São Benedito, patron saint of cooks; in one of the statues he is holding a squash. The church dates from 1727, but building by the Irmandade dos Pretos Cativos (black slave brotherhood) began as early as 1708. ■ *Thursday-Monday 1200-1600; entry US$0.50.*

São João Evangelista is on the Largo do Sol, a lovely open space. It is a simple church, built by the Irmandade dos Homens Pardos (mulattos). Predominantly white inside, it has paintings of the four evangelists and a cornice painted in an elaborate pattern in pink, blue and beige. ■ *Thursday-Monday 0900-1700.*

Nossa Senhora das Mercês (18th century), Largo das Mercês, has an interesting painted ceiling and a notable statue of the Virgin. ■ *Sunday 0900-1700.*

There are other churches and chapels in the town, including the **Igreja de Bom Jesus da Pobreza**, on the Largo das Forras. **Santuário da Santíssima Trindade**, on the road which leads up behind the Igreja Matriz de Santo Antônio is well worth seeing. The chapel itself is 18th century while the room of miracles associated with the annual Trinity Sunday pilgrimage is modern. On the grassy Morro de São Francisco is the small chapel of **São Francisco de Paula** (mid-18th century).

Secular buildings and a suggested tour From the main Praça, Largo das Forras, take Rua Resende Costa up to the Largo do Sol (Igreja São João Evangelista – see above). Beside the church is the **Museu Padre Toledo**, the house of this leader of the Inconfidência Mineira. It exhibits some good pieces of furniture. See also the roof which depicts the Five Senses. The house belongs to the Fundação Rodrigo Mello Franco de Andrade, as does the **Casa de Cultura** in the row of 18th century houses on Rua Padre Toledo, which leads from Largo do Sol to the Igreja Matriz de Santo Antônio. From this church you

Tiradentes

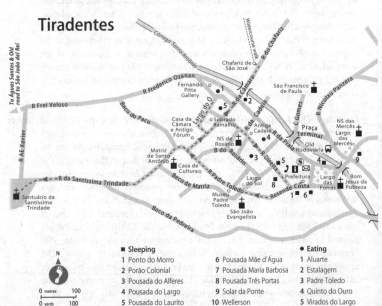

■ Sleeping		● Eating
1 Ponto do Morro	6 Pousada Mãe d'Água	1 Aluarte
2 Porão Colonial	7 Pousada Maria Barbosa	2 Estalagem
3 Pousada do Alferes	8 Pousada Três Portas	3 Padre Toledo
4 Pousada do Largo	9 Solar da Ponte	4 Quinto do Ouro
5 Pousada do Laurito	10 Wellerson	5 Virados do Largo

can make a detour to the chapel of Santíssima Trindade. From Santo Antônio, head down the Rua da Câmara, past the **Casa da Câmara e Antigo Fórum**. Here the road divides, the left hand street, Jogo de Bola, leading to the Largo do Ó (which rejoins the main street), while Rua da Câmara goes to the crossroads with Rua Direita. At this junction is the **Sobrado Ramalho**, said to be the oldest building in Tiradentes. It is believed to be where the gold was melted down and has a lot of soapstone carving inside. It has been beautifully restored as a cultural centre.

Before taking Rua Direita back to Largo das Forras, you can carry straight on to the river and cross the bridge to the magnificent **Chafariz de São José** (the public fountain), installed in 1749. The water is brought by a stone aqueduct from springs in the forest at the foot of Serra São José. It is still used for drinking, clothes washing and watering animals.

Rua Direita has some interesting old buildings. Opposite the Praça Padre Lourival, on which stands Nossa Senhora do Rosário, is the **Antiga Cadeia** (18th-19th century) which now contains the **Museu de Arta Sacra**. Rua Direita meets the Largo das Forras at the **Prefeitura Municipal**, a two-storey building with an extra room under the roof. It now houses the tourist, post and phone offices.

The **train** on the line between São João del Rei and Tiradentes (13 kilometres) **Excursions** has been in continuous operation since 1881, using the same locomotives and rolling stock, running on a 76 centimetres gauge track, all lovingly cared for. The maximum speed is 20 kilometres per hour: tickets cost US$13 return *interior*, US$6.50 return *meia*. The train runs on Friday, Saturday, Sunday and holidays, 1000 and 1415 from São João del Rei, returning from Tiradentes at 1300 and 1700. To get to the railway station from the centre of the village you have to cross the river and head out of town on the Rua dos Inconfidentes. Follow this road until it becomes the Rua Antônio Teixeira Carvalho, which carries on to the bridge over the Rio das Mortes. (In 1997 a new bridge was being constructed here.) On the opposite bank is a small park and the station. The railway museum at the railway station in São João del Rei is described above.

Walks The forest on the Serra de São José is now protected. Easiest access is from behind the Chafariz, where a black door in the wall is opened at 0730 (Wednesday-Sunday). In just five minutes you are in the forest, following the watercourse, and monkeys and birds can be seen.

From behind the Mercês church you can walk up into the Serra; ask for directions. Similarly, it is recommended to take a guide if you wish to walk along the top of the Serra.

There is a good one to two hour walk from Tiradentes to the **Balneário de Águas Santas**. It involves crossing the Serra. At the Balneário is a swimming pool, also a

R Silvio
Vasconcelos

R F de Mortes

2
3

R dos Inconfidentes
10

Antônio Carvalho

R Henrique Diniz

7

To Train Station & São João del Rei

Praça
da Estação

Rio Das
Mortes

- - ▶ - - Walking tour

lake and a *churrascaria*, *Senzala*. A map can be obtained from the *Solar da Ponte*, or ask locally for directions (taxi US$15). On the way you pass a Parque Municipal which is in the process of being set up, **Parque Frei Mariano Vellozo**, which contains the Cachoeira do Mangue falls. It is busy at weekends and can be reached by car on the old road to São João.

Sleeping

■ *on map, page 296*
Price codes: see inside front cover
see inside front coverg
Prices are generally lower in the more expensive hotels Sun-Thu

AL *Solar da Ponte*, Praça das Mercês T3551255, F3551201. Has the atmosphere of a country house, run by John and Anna Maria Parsons, the price includes breakfast and afternoon tea, only 12 rooms, fresh flowers in rooms, bar, sauna, lovely gardens, swimming pool, light meals for residents only, for larger meals, the hotel recommends 5 local restaurants. Highly recommended (it is in the Roteiros de Charme group, see page 57). **A** *Pousada Três Portas*, R Direita 280A, T3551444, F3551184.There are more expensive suites, has sauna, thermal pool, hydromassage, heating. **A** *Pousada Mãe D'Água*, Largo das Forras 50, T3551206, F3551221. Including breakfast but not tax. Very nice. **A** *Candonga da Serra*, Estr Velha Tiradentes towards São João del Rei, T/F3551483. Out of town, calls itself 'ecológico', big rooms with firm beds but spartan, no TV, restaurant/bar, pool. **A** *Pousada Maria Barbosa*, R Antônio Teixeira Carvalho 144, near the bridge that leads out of town, T/F3551227. Pool, very pleasant, at the weekend the price includes breakfast, lunch and evening snack. In the same group is *Hotel Wellerson*, R Foco Simbólico 218, T3551226. Also not in the centre, but closer than *Maria Barbosa*. **B** *Porão Colonial*, R dos Inconfidentes 447, T3551251. Looks pleasant, pool, sauna, parking. **C** *Hotel Ponto do Morro*, Largo das Forras 2, T3551342, F3551141. With pool, sauna, also has 2 chalets, the hotel has a nice entry. **C** *Pousada do Alferes*, R dos Inconfidentes 479, T3551303. **C** *Pousada do Largo*, Largo das Forras 48, T/F3551219. With TV, pool, sauna. **C** *Pousada do Laurito*, R Direita 187, T3551268.

Eating

● *on map, page 296*

Local food *Quinto de Ouro*, R Direita 159. Recommended. *Virados do Largo*, Largo do Ó. Good food and service. *Estalagem*, R Min Gabriel Passos 280. *Padre Toledo*, R Direita 202. *Aluarte*, Largo do Ó 1. Bar with live music in the evening, nice atmosphere, US$4 cover charge, garden, sells handicrafts. Recommended. There are many other resturants, snack bars and lanchonetes in town and it is a small enough place to wander around and see what takes your fancy.

Entertainment

Art galleries *Fernando Pitta*, Beco da Chácara, T/F3551475, produces fascinating work, painting, mixed media and sculture, worth a visit. *Oscar Araripe*, R da Câmara, paints Tiradentes and other local scenes in bright colours, popular and commercial.

Transport

Buses Last bus back to **São João del Rei** is 1815, 2230 on Sunday; fares are given above. **Taxis** to **São João del Rei** costs US$10. See **Excursions** above for the **train** between the 2 towns.

Around town there are pony-drawn taxis; ponies can be hired for US$5. For horse-riding treks, contact John Parsons at the *Solar da Ponte*.

Directory

Communications The combined post and telephone office is on the Largo das Forras in the Prefeitura Municipal, R Resende Costa 71. It closes at 1200 for lunch. **Tourist information** In the Prefeitura, R Resende Costa 71.

The most remote of the colonial cities to the north of Belo Horizonte is reached from Belo Horizonte by taking the paved road to Brasília (BR-040). Between Caetanópolis and Paraopeba is the *Flora Eunice Leite ao Pé de Vaca*, a small private botanic garden and zoo with contented animals, recommended. There is also a snack bar with good toilets. Nineteen kilometres beyond Paraopeba is a turning northeast to **Curvelo**, a lively town, **A** *Hotel*

Sagarana, very good; *Restaurant Denise* with accommodation, on the main highway. Beyond Curvelo the road passes through the impressive rocky country of the Serra do Espinhaço.

Diamantina

The centre of a once active diamond industry, Diamantina has excellent colonial buildings. Its churches are difficult to get into, except for the modern Cathedral, and are not as grand as those of Ouro Preto. It is, however, possibly the least spoiled of all the colonial mining cities, with carved overhanging roofs and brackets. It is a friendly, beautiful town situated in the deep interior, amid barren mountains, and it is lively at weekends.

Population: 46,000
Phone code: 038
Altitude: 1,120m
Colour map 4, grid B3

In 1720 diamonds were discovered at Arraial do Tijuco, the first settlement of gold prospectors who had come to the region. Within 14 years it had become important enough to be made the administrative capital of the Distrito de Diamantina. Since the Portuguese crown made the same impositions on diamond mining as on gold, there was a similar resentment among those people who saw no chance of improvement in their living conditions. One such was Padre José da Silva de Oliveira Rolim (Padre Rolim), who joined the Inconfidência Mineira. Nevertheless, the town was one of the most wealthy in 18th century Brazil. It was elevated to the status of city, and renamed Diamantina, in 1838.

History

President Juscelino Kubitschek, the founder of Brasília, was born here. His house, Rua São Francisco 241, has been converted into a museum.

Churches The oldest church in Diamantina is **Nossa Senhora do Rosário**, Largo Dom Joaquim, built by slaves in 1728. **Nossa Senhora do Carmo**, Rua do Carmo, dates from 1760-65 and was built by João Fernandes de Oliveira (see below) for the Carmélite Third Order. It is the richest church in the town,

Sights

Minas Gerais & Espírito Santo

Diamantina

To Belo Horizonte

with fine decorations and paintings and a pipe organ, covered in gold leaf, made locally. According to some of the tourist literature, the tower is at the back of the church to please Chica da Silva (see below), who did not like to hear the sound of the bells.

São Francisco de Assis, Rua São Francisco, just off Praça JK, was built between 1766 and the turn of the 19th century. It is notable for its paintings. Other colonial churches are the **Capela Imperial do Amparo** (1758-76), **Nossa Senhora das Mercês** (1778-1784) and **Nossa Senhora da Luz** (early 19th century), erected to fulfil the vow of a Portuguese lady, Dona Tereza de Jesus Perpétuo Corte Real, who survived the 1755 Lisbon earthquake.

The **Catedral Metropolitana de Santo Antônio** on Praça Correia Rabelo, was built in the 1930s in neo-colonial style to replace the original cathedral.

Secular buildings After repeated thefts, the diamonds of the **Museu do Diamante**, Rua Direita 14 in the house of Padre Rolim, have been removed to the Banco do Brasil. The museum does house an important collection of the materials used in the diamond industry, plus other items from the 18th and 19th centuries. ■ *US$1*. Diamonds are still sought; see traditional methods at Guinda, seven kilometres away. Other local industries are the making of Portuguese Arraiolos-style tapestry carpets by hand, at a cooperative in the centre, and etchings on leather.

At Rua Quitanda 48 is the **Biblioteca Antônio Torres**, also known as the **Casa Muxarabi**. This name derives from the enclosed balcony, of Moorish design, on one of the windows of this 18th century house.

The **Casa de Chica da Silva**, is at Praça Lobo Mesquita 266. Chica da Silva was a slave in the house of Padre Rolim's father. She became the mistress of João Fernandes de Oliveira, a diamond contractor. They had 14 children and lived in luxury until Fernandes returned to Portugal in 1772 when his last contract ended. Chica, who died on 15 February 1796, has become a folk heroine among Brazilian blacks. ■ *Entrance free.*

Behind the 18th century building which now houses the **Prefeitura Municipal** (originally the diamonds administration building, Praça Conselheiro Matta 11), is the **Mercado Municipal** or **dos Tropeiros** (muleteers), Praça Barão de Guaicuí. It was built in 1835 as a residence and trading house before being expanded; it has wooden arches. The **Casa da Glória**, Rua da Glória 297, is in fact two houses on either side of the street connected by an enclosed bridge. Among its earlier inhabitants was the first bishop of Diamantina. It now contains the Instituto Eschwege de Geologia.

Excursions Walk along the **Caminho dos Escravos**, the old road built by slaves between the mining area on Rio Jequitinhonha and Diamantina. A guide is essential and also cheap, ask at the Casa de Cultura; beware of snakes and thunderstorms.

Nine kilometres from town is the **Gruta de Salitre**, a big cave with a strange rock formation. There is no public transport, you have to take a taxi or walk. It is a good walk and you can find some interesting minerals along the way. Ask the tourist office for directions. Closer to the town is the **Cachoeira da Toca**, a 15 metre waterfall which is good for swimming.

Along the river bank it is 12 kilometres on a dirt road to **Biribiri**, a pretty village with a well-preserved church and an abandoned textile factory. It also has a few bars and at weekends it is a popular, noisy place. About half-way, there are swimming pools in the river; opposite them, on a cliff face, are animal paintings in red, age and origin unknown. The plantlife along the river is interesting and there are beautiful mountain views.

A *Pousada do Garimpo*, Av da Saudade 265, T/F5312523, pgarimpo@diaman- **Sleeping**
tina.uemg.br. **B** *Diamante Palace*, Av Sílvio Felício dos Santos 1050, T/F5311561.
B *Pousada Jardim da Serra*, R das Rosas 65, T/F5311607. **B** *Tijuco*, R Macau do Melo
211, T/F5311022. Good food. **C** *Dália*, Praça JK (Jota-Ka) 25, T5311477. Fairly good.
D *JK*, opposite the rodoviária. With good breakfast, clean, friendly, hot showers.
E *Pensão Comercial*, Praça M Neves 30. Basic. Wild camping is possible near the
waterfall just outside town.

Capistrana, R Campos Carvalho 36, near Cathedral square. Recommended. *Santo* **Eating**
Antônio in the centre has a good self-service *churrasco* and salad for US$3 during
the week.

Serestas (serenades) are sung on Friday and Saturday nights. Many young people **Bars &**
hang out in the bars in Beco da Mota. *Taverna de Gilmar* is recommended for a good **nightclubs**
mix of music, although it gets packed quickly. *Cavernas Bar*, Av Sílvio Felício dos
Santos, is good for *pagode* on Saturday and Sunday from late afternoon.

Carnival is said to be very good here and the town is trying to establish another festi- **Festivals**
val in September. **12 September** is *O Dia das Serestas*, the Day of the Serenades, for
which the town is famous; this is the birthday of President Juscelino Kubitschek, who
was born here. Religious festivals: *Semana Santa*; *Corpus Christi* (**May-June**); *Santo*
Antônio (**13 June**); *O Divino Espírito Santo* (50 days after Pentecost), a major 5-day
feast; *Festa do Rosário* (first half of **October**).

Buses Six buses a day to **Belo Horizonte**, via Curvelo, with *Pássaro Verde*, 2½ hours **Transport**
to **Curvelo**, US$3, to **Belo Horizonte**, US$10, 5½ hours. There are daily *Gontijo* buses
at 1600 to **São Paulo**, 16-17 hours, US$19.25 but it is an uncomfortable journey; the
journey ends at the Bresser terminal. It is better to go to Belo Horizonte and change
buses there if you want to arrive at Tietê in São Paulo.

Routes If *en route* to Bahia, take the *Gontijo* Belo Horizonte-Salvador bus to **Araçuaí**
and change there, the fare is US$11.50 but you have to check an hour or so beforehand
to see if there is space in the bus. The bus passes Diamantina at about 1330-1400, or
0200. It's a very bumpy ride through Couto de Magalhães de Minas and Virgem da Lapa.
At Araçuaí is **D** *Pousada Tropical*, opposite the rodoviária behind the policlínica,
T7311765. With bath, clean and friendly. From there you can take a bus to Itaobim
(US$2.65, 2 hours, Rio Doce company) then make an onward connection to Vitória da
Conquista (US$5.50, 4 hours, same company – see page 316). The BR-116 passes inter-
esting rock formations at Pedra Azul before crossing the border with Bahia.

Banks *Banco do Brasil*, Praça Cons Mata 23. **Tourist information** *Departamento de Turismo* in **Directory**
the Casa de Cultura in Praça Antônio Eulálio 53, 3rd floor, T5311636, F5311857. Pamphlets and a
reliable map are available, also information about churches' opening times, friendly and helpful. The
office will arrange a free tour of churches with guide who has access to keys (tip guide). *Passeio a*
Diamantina, an excellent guide, is written by the author of *Passeio a Sabará*. **Voltage** 110 AC.

Ninety two kilometres by paved road from Diamantina and reached by bus **Serro**
from there or from Belo Horizonte is this unspoiled colonial town on the Rio *Population: 20,500*
Jequitinhonha. It has six fine baroque churches, a museum and many beautiful *Phone code: 038*
squares. It makes *queijo serrano*, one of Brazil's best cheeses, being in the centre of a prosperous cattle region. The most conspicuous church is **Santa Rita**,
on a hill in the centre of town, reached by a long line of steps. On the main
Praça João Pinheiro, by the bottom of the steps, is **Nossa Senhora do Carmo**,
arcaded, with original paintings on the ceiling and in the choir. The town has

Minas Gerais & Espírito Santo

two large mansions: those of the **Barão de Diamantina**, Praça Presidente Vargas, now in ruins, and of the **Barão do Serro** across the river on Rua da Fundição, beautifully restored and used as the town hall and Casa de Cultura (Tuesday-Saturday 1200-1700, Sunday 0900-1200); there are old mine entrances in the hillside behind the courtyard. The **Museu Regional Casa dos Ottoni**, Praça Cristiano Ottoni 72, T9411440, is an 18th century house now containing furniture and everyday objects from the region. The Ottoni brothers, who were born here, were prominent naval officers turned politicians in the 19th century. For tourist information, contact *Secretaria de Turismo*, Chácara do Barão do Serro, T5411368 extension 234.

Just by the Serro turn-off is the town of **Datas**, whose spacious church (1832) decorated in red and blue, contains a striking wooden image of Christ with the crown of thorns.

Sleeping A *Pousada Vila do Príncipe*, R Antônio Honório Pires 38, T/F5411485. Very clean, in an old mansion containing its own museum, the artist Mestre Valentim is said to have been born in the slave quarters. There are other cheaper hotels.

Eating *Itacolomi*, Praça João Pinheiro 20. Fair. *Churrascaria Vila do Príncipe*, Praça Dom Epaminondas 48.

Northern Minas Gerais

Rio São Francisco

Passenger services on the river have been discontinued but masters of cargo boats in the port may permit passage. The regular stops are at **Januária** (famous for Brazil's reputed best *cachaça*) and **Bom Jesus da Lapa** in Bahia (a pilgrimage centre with a church built in a grotto inside a mountain, but a very poor town; there are hotels and a choice of bars on the river beach).

Tres Marias
Population: 24,000
Phone code: 038

Some 240 kilometres northwest of Belo Horizonte is a lake five times as large in area as Rio de Janeiro bay, formed by the **Três Marias dam** on the upper reaches of the São Francisco River. The town is at the lake's northern end.

Sleeping A *Mar Doce*, on the BR-040 towards Belo Horizonte, 4 km from town, T7541399, F7541294. B *Grande Lago*, Acampamento de Cemig, on BR-040. T7541050, F7541286.

Transport *Sertaneja* bus from **Belo Horizonte** at 1615, US$9.

Pirapora
Population: 48,500
Phone code: 038

North of Três Marias is the terminus for boat journeys on the Rio São Francisco (see also page 470). The cutting down of trees, in part as fuel for the boats, and the low rainfall in recent years, has greatly reduced the flow. The town itself is a tourist attraction because of the falls in the river which make for excellent fishing. The fishermen use punt-like canoes. The sandy river beaches are used for swimming. The riverboats' grotesque figureheads, *carrancas*, are made in the workshops of Lourdes Barroso, Rua Abaeté 390.

Sleeping and eating B *Pirapora Palace*, Praça Melo Viana 61, 7 blocks west and 1 block south of the rodoviária, T7413851. Ask for room on the garden, safe. B *Canoeiras*, Av Salmeron 3, T7411933. Used by river-tour parties. D *Daila*, Praça JK 13. With breakfast but without bath. D *Grande*, R da Quitanda 70. With bath but without breakfast. *Lá em Casa*, 'meals by the kilo, huge *caipirinhas*, excellent value'.

Between Pirapora and Januária is the colonial fishing town of São Francisco, with many attractive houses and a good handicraft market in the town hall. Of the two remaining wood-burning stern-wheel boats, allegedly built for Mississippi services in the 1860s and imported from the USA in 1922 to work on the Amazon, one, the *Gaiola*, was restored for services on the Rio São Francisco. The town is popular during Semana Santa, Festas Juninas and a carnival in July. A *Hotel Green Fish*, R Min Hermenegildo de Barros 560, T/F6311106.

São Francisco
Population: 50,500
Phone code: 038

The largest city in the north of Minas Gerais, Montes Claros is a pleasant town and an important transport hub between Brasília and Bahia. There are folklore festivals in May and August as well as a **Museu do Folclore**, R Ângelo de Quadros 1057.

Monte Claros
Population: 271,500
Phone code 038

Sleeping and eating A Dimas Lessa, R Pires e Alberquerque 291, T2222800, F2225757. **D** *Giovanni*, close to the rodoviária. Clean, modern. For eating, *Peixaria do Nélson*, Av João XXIII 1168. Try the *moqueca do surubim*.

Transport Buses: from **Belo Horizonte** with *Transnorte*, 9 times a day, US$15-18, *leito* at midnight, US$24.) To get to **Bahia** take a bus to Almenara (12 hours) and from there to Salto da Divisa (2½ hours; hotel facing the bus station), then take a bus to Porto Seguro. An alternative route to Bahia is the daily 1000 bus to Vitória da Conquista (see page 316, *Gontijo* US$6.50); an interesting journey through hilly country, pine and eucalyptus plantations, and many remote towns. See also above for the route from Diamantina to Bahia.

Eastern Minas Gerais

This region is a centre of semi-precious stone processing and crystal carving, and also contains the Serra do Caparaó, where are found several of Brazil's highest mountains. The two principal towns, Governador Valadares and Teófilo Otôni, are both on the BR-116 inland Rio-Salvador road, and both have good connections with Belo Horizonte.

Through *Focus Tours* (see **Tours and tour operators**, page 30) the private **Caratinga Biological Station** be visited, 880 hectares of mountainous, inland Atlantic forest which is home to four rare primates: the muriqui (formerly called the woolly spider monkey, the largest primate in the Americas and the largest mammal endemic to Brazil – also one of the world's most endangered primates), the black-capped capuchin, the brown howler monkey and the buffy-headed marmoset. Also at the station are brown-throated three-toed sloths and an incredible array of birds. The primates and many of the birds are not bothered by human presence. Entrance fee is US$15 per person per day (payable only in reais).

The **Parque Estadual do Rio Doce** is 248 kilometres east of Belo Horizonte in the municipalities of Dionísio, Timóteo and Marliéria. Between 230 metres and 515 metres above sea level and covering almost 36,000 hectares, this is the largest tract of Mata Atlântica in southeast Brazil. As well as forest there are a number of lakes, on which boat trips are possible, besides swimming and fishing. The park is home to a great many birds and animals. There is an information centre, a campsite six kilometres into the park and trails have been laid out for hiking. ■ *T8223006, or phone the Instituto Estadual de Florestas T3307013/2951655. Access is by the roads BR-262 or 381, either of which you have to turn off onto dirt roads to get to the park.*

Rio Doce

Minas Gerais & Espírito Santo

Parque Nacional Caparaó

The park features rare Atlantic rainforest in its lower altitudes and Brazilian alpine on top; this is good walking country

In the park are the Pico da Bandeira (2,890 metres), Pico do Cruzeiro (2,861 metres) and the Pico do Cristal (2,798 metres). From the park entrance (where a small fee has to be paid) it is six kilometres on a poorly-maintained road to the car park at the base of the waterfall. From the hotel (see below) jeeps (US$20 per jeep) run to the car park at 1,970 metres (2½ hours' walk), then it's a three to four hour walk to the summit of the Pico da Bandeira, marked by yellow arrows; plenty of camping possibilities all the way up, the highest being at Terreirão (2,370 metres). It is best to visit during the dry season (April-October). It can be quite crowded in July and during Carnival.

Park essentials Contact via Caixa Postal 17, alto Jequitibá, MG, CEP 36976-000, T255, via operator on 101-PS 1, Alto do Caparaó. Otherwise seek information from Ibama, T2916588, ext 119/122.

Sleeping B *Caparaó Parque*, 2 km from the park entrance, 15 minutes' walk from the town of Caparaó, nice, T7412559. Ask where **camping** is permitted in the park. In **Manhumirim**: D *São Luiz*, good value, but *Cids Bar*, next door, Trav 16 do Março, has better food.

Transport Caparaó National Park is 49 km by paved road from Manhuaçu (about 190 km south of Governador Valadores) on the Belo Horizonte-Vitória road (BR-262). There are buses from Belo Horizonte (twice a day with Pássaro Verde), Ouro Preto or Vitória to **Manhumirim** (*population* 27,625), 15 km south of Manhuaçu. From Manhumirim, take a bus direct to Caparaó, 0930, 1630 US$1, or to Presidente Soares (several, seven kilometres), then hitch 11 km to Caparaó. By car from the BR-262, go through Manhumirim, Presidente Soares and Caparaó village, then 1 km further to the *Hotel Caparaó Parque*.

Governador Valadares

Population: 231,000 Phone code: 033 Colour map 4, grid B4

A modern planned city, 324 kilometres from Belo Horizonte, Governador Valadares is a good place to break the Belo Horizonte-Salvador journey. It is a centre of gemstone mines and lapidation, as well as for the cut-crystal animals one finds in tourist shops all around Brazil.

Sleeping & eating **A** *Governador Palace*, Av Minas Gerais 550, T2717474, F2714750. **A** *Real Minas*, Praça Serra Lima 607, T2716751, F2711089. **B** *Panorama*, Mcal Floriano 914, T/F2717840. Many cheap hotels near the bus station. A recommended eating place is *JB*, R Bárbara Heliodoro 384.

Sports At the top of the Pico de Ibituruna, 1123m, there are ramps for hang gliding and parapenting, T2214725. There is also a hang gliding championship held around Carnival.

Transport **Air** The airport is on the BR-381, 6 km from the city centre, T2771800. Flights to **Belo Horizonte** and **Ipatinga**. **Buses** 5½ hours from **Belo Horizonte** with *Gontijo*, US$11.50, US$21 *leito*.

Directory **Airline offices** *Nordeste*, T2711522; *Pantanal*, T2772020. **Banks** *Banco do Brasil*, R Paulo Deslandes 35. *Bradesco*, Av Minas Gerais 395.

Situated 138 kilometres from Governador Valadares, this is a popular buying spot for dealers of crystals and gemstones, with the best prices in the state. There are various hotels (**B**) and *Pousada Tio Miro* (**C**), R Dr Manoel Esteves 389, T5214343, which has a relaxed atmosphere. Recommended.

Teófilo Otôni
Population: 127,500
Phone code: 033

Transport Buses: from **Belo Horizonte** with *Gontijo*, US$15.50, *leito* US$29; to **Porto Seguro** via **Nanuque** (can break Belo Horizonte-Salvador journey here; **D** *Hotel Minas*, at the rodoviária, adequate, and others nearby).

Southern Minas Gerais

Juiz de Fora

The pleasant city of Juiz de Fora lies on the Paraibuna River, in a deep valley between the Mar and Mantiqueira mountain chains. It is a good stopover on the route between Rio de Janeiro and the colonial cities or Belo Horizonte.

Juiz da Fora used to be known as the Manchester Mineira because it was the first city in Brazil to industrialize, principally through textiles. Another reason for the nickname was the widespread use of red brick as a building material. Nowadays there is no sign of the early industries nor of red brick; new industries like Mercedes Benz are being attracted to the city and Juiz is growing and changing fast. Architecturally, though, it is of little note.

The city centre is very busy commercially and the central streets are a maze of shopping galleries. See especially the food shops selling sausages, fish and cheese.

Population: 424,500
Phone code: 032
Altitude: 695m
117 km S of Barbacena
184 km N of Rio
Colour map 4, grid C3

The main thoroughfare through the city centre is Avenida Barão do Rio Branco. Where this avenue meets Rua Halfeld is the Parque Halfeld. The junction is a major urban bus stop. Rua Halfeld is pedestrianized from Avenida Rio Branco to Avenida Getúlio Vargas; it is the banking as well as the main shopping street in the centre. The **Banco do Brasil** has a building close to the Rio Branco/Halfeld junction which was designed by Oscar Niemeyer (Banco do Brasil has another branch at the junction of Halfeld and Getúlio Vargas). Also on Rua Halfeld is the **Teatro Municipal** (No 1179, T2155255), opposite the Edifício São Joaquim.

Sights

Praça da Estação has good examples of Belle Epoque architecture, the station hall, the hotels *Príncipe* and *Renascença* and the Associação Comercial building. Also in this part of the city, at the railway end of Rua Halfeld, is the **Espaço Cultural Mascarenhas**, Avenida Getúlio Vargas 200 (T2297208). See the Portinari mural of tiles in the foyer of Edifício Clube Juiz de Fora, on Rua Halfeld.

On Avenida Rio Branco is the **Centro Cultural Pró-Música**, at No 2329, T2153951. It has a concert hall and art gallery. Each July, in conjunction with the Prefeitura and the business community, the centre promotes a festival of Música Colonial Brasileira, which is recommended. At No 3146 is the **Círculo Militar**, which is an interesting building. The **Centro de Estudos Murilo Mendes**, Avenida Rio Branco 3372, T2133931, is a small cultural centre which holds exhibitions, lectures, film shows, etc. It is part of the Universidade Federal de Juiz da Fora. It is dedicated to the work of the poet, Murilo Mendes, and has an exhibition on his links with famous painters (Picasso, Miró, Léger, Guignard, Portinari) and other poets (Cecília Meireles, Jorge de Lima). ■ *Monday-Friday 1300-1700.*

Minas Gerais & Espírito Santo

Museums The **Museu Mariano Procópio**, Mariano Procópio sem número, in beautiful wooded grounds, has collections covering various stages of Brazilian history up to the New Republic. The room on Tiradentes, for example, has a huge painting by Pedro Américo de Figueiredo e Melo of his quartered body (1893). There are a great many objects and portraits from the Imperial period. It also houses some natural history, geology (including types of stones), paintings and sculpture. It is an enormous exhibition and a guide would be helpful to explain it all. In the grounds are a *cantina*, playground, lake, monkeys on an island and caged birds. ■ *Museum: Tuesday-Sunday 1200-1800, US$1; grounds: Tuesday-Sunday 0800-1730, T2111145. The pedestrian entrance is on Rua Mariano Procópio, opposite the Mariano Procópio railway station. To get back to the centre, take any bus going to Avenida Rio Branco, for example No 606.*

There is a **railway museum** at Avenida Brasil 2001, next to the station. ■ *Tuesday-Friday 1300-1800, Saturday-Sunday 1400-1800.* The Universidade Federal has a **Museu do Folklore** at Rua Santo Antônio 1112. ■ *Monday-Friday 1400-2100.*

Excursions An attractive train journey (25 kilometres) from Estação Mariano Procópio (opposite the museum, Monday-Saturday), runs to South America's first hydro-electric power station at **Matias Barbosa** (return by bus, hourly).

Santos Dumont, 47 kilometres north, is a town named after the aviator (see page 164). Seventeen kilometres away is the *Fazenda Cabangu*, where he was born.

Juiz da Fora

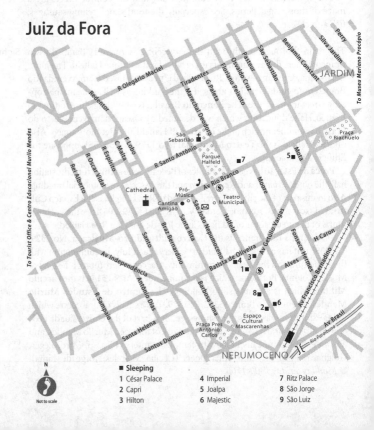

■ Sleeping

1 César Palace	4 Imperial	7 Ritz Palace
2 Capri	5 Joalpa	8 São Jorge
3 Hilton	6 Majestic	9 São Luiz

Mar de Espanha, 62 kilometres east, is a charming 19th century town with tame sloths in the trees. To get there, take a bus from Juiz da Fora rodoviária, one hour, six a day, US$4.50. Rio Novo, 48 kilometres northeast, has colonial architecture and is renowned for its dairy produce.

AL *César Park*, Av Getúlio Vargas 181, T/F2154898. Sauna, pool, parking, accepts **Sleeping** credit cards. **A** *Ritz Palace*, Av Barão do Rio Branco 2000, T2157300, F2151892. Sauna, pool, parking, takes all credit cards except Amex. **A** *Joalpa*, R Afonso Pinto da Motta 29, between Av Rio Branco and Av Getúlio Vargas, T2156055, F2152694. Sauna, pool, parking, credit cards accepted. **A** *César Palace*, Av Getúlio Vargas 335, T2156599, F2162117. Central, parking. **B** *Imperial*, R Batista de Oliveira 605, T2157400, F2163766. Popular business hotel in the centre, **C** without bath. **C** *São Luiz*, R Halfeld 360, T2151155. Art deco lobby, winter garden, TV, fridge, parking, good, helpful. **D** *Hilton*, Av Getúlio Vargas 483-99, near the junction with Batista de Oliveira, T2158112. Clean, polite. **D** *Majestic*, R Halfeld 284, T2155050. TV, cheaper without bath; also on this block of Halfeld are *São Jorge* and *Capri*. Many cheaper hotels on Av Getúlio Vargas, in **E** range, mostly short-stay.

Berttu's, R Santo Antônio 572. Very good, *mineira* and international food. *Cantão* **Eating** *Suíço*, R Santa Rita 557/59. Good self-service. *Cantina do Amigão*, R Santa Rita 552. Italian, good, including pizzas, T2152179 for home delivery. Others on same street and R São João Nepomuceno. *Le Beau Bistrot*, R Delfim Moreira 22. French bar/restaurant. *Brasão*, Av Rio Branco 2262. Very smart. *Belas Artes*, Galeria Tte Belfort Arantes 26, entrance at Halfeld 631. Good. There is a *McDonalds* at R Halfeld 823.

Best nightclub is *Clube Noturno Vila das Tochas*, R Roberto Stiegert 4, Bairro São **Bars &** Pedro. American bar, crêperie, dance floor. *Bar do Bené*, Pres Costa de Silva 2305, **nightclubs** Bairro São Pedro. Friendly. *Prova Oral*, R A Braga 210. Highly recommended bar with live music. For lots of bars, restaurants, pizzerias and nightlife, visit the Bairro São Mateus, bounded by Av Independência, R São Mateus, R Padre Café, R Monsenhor Gomes Freire with R Manoel Bernardino running down the middle.

Priscila Jóias, Galeria Solar, loja 228, gold and silver workshop. Many interesting **Shopping** antique shops; plentiful regional foods.

Air Flights arrive at the small but modern airport, Av Guadalajara, T2331315. Flights **Transport** to **Belo Horizonte**, **Ipatinga** and **São Paulo**. Bus 520 on the hour to the centre.

Buses Local: town buses charge US$0.40. It is difficult to tell the routes because the route plaques are beside the back door entrance and cannot be seen as the bus approaches; you need to know the route numbers.

Long distance: the rodoviária is outside town on Av Brasil 4501, T2157696. Take bus 630 to town. Taxi to centre US$5. To/from **Rio**, many daily, *Útil*, US$5.50 *convencional*, US$6.75 *super* (a spectacular trip through mountains and tropical forest on an excellent, dualled highway); *Útil* to **Belo Horizonte**, frequent, US$9.15-11 (*Viaçao Útil*, T2153976, Rodoviária, or in town R Henrique Surerus 22, T2156759, Monday-Friday 0800-1800, Saturday 0800-1200). To **São João del Rei** via Barbacena, 6 hours, US$5; to **Conselheiro Lafaiete** (for Congonhas do Campo), US$5.75. To **Petrópolis**, 7 a day, 2 hours, US$4.25. *Frota Nobre* to **Teresópolis** and **Nova Friburgo** once a day, US$4.80 and US$7.35 respectively. To **Foz do Iguaçu** with *Pluma*, US$40, via Londrina, Maringá and Cascavel, Tuesday, Thursday, Sunday 0800.

Directory   **Airline offices** *Nordeste/Rio Sul*, T2159184. *TAM*, T2331360. **Banks** *Banco 24 Horas*, Av Rio
Branco 700. **Communications** Post office: at São João Nepomuceno 291. **Telecommunications:**
Av Rio Branco 2288. Another branch at R Halfeld 804. 0700-2200 Mon-Fri, 0700-1400 Sat.
Security Take care if walking between Av Getúlio Vargas and the railway at night. **Tour
companies & travel agents** *Serra do Ibitpoca*, R Braz Bernardino 105, loja 212, Braz Shopping,
T/F2163657, ibitipoc@nutecnet.com.br, www.jfa.nutecnet.com.br/local/ibitipoca. *Serra Branca*, R
Aristóteles Braga 186, Cidade Universitária, T2311245. Local tours and to further afield in Minas
Gerais. *Beijaflor*, Shopping Santa Cruz, loja 1148, T2150249. French, Italian, some English spoken.
Tourist information *Secretaria de Desenvolvimento Econômico*, Av Rio Branco 3029, CEP
36010-012, T/F2155931, www.pjf.jfa.mg.gov.br.

Parque Florestal de Ibitipoca

Altitude: 1,760m   This park, 85 kilometres from Juiz de Fora, contains quartzite caves, interesting
rock formations, many waterfalls, rivers, different types of vegetation, orchids,
bromeliads, cactus and lots of lichens and flowers, such as purple *quaresmeiras*.
Evidence suggests that it was under the sea at one time. In more recent times, it
was on the *bandeirantes'* trails. A little gold was found, but it was mostly micah
which was taken out (there is quartzite everywhere you look).

Ibitipoca preserves birds and animals (including monkeys, which you will
hear but not see). The French botanist Auguste St-Hilaire visited the area in
1822. To see all that the park has to offer takes four days. There are a number of
trails of varying length; on the longest be prepared for stretchces of up to eight
hours (take water and protection against the sun). ■ *US$2, 0800-1600, but
you can stay overnight (see below).*

The nearest village, Conceição de Ibitipoca, is one of the oldest in Minas
Gerais. Its church was built in 1768 and has original paintings on the ceiling.
There is a statue of São Sebastião and a separate bell tower. The key for the
church is at *Ibiti-Bike*. Mass is said once a month. Modern building in the village is giving it a messy look, however the park is definitely worth visiting.

Transport   By unpaved road, 27 km, from Lima Duarte to Conceição de Ibitipoca. The
road is rough and difficult in the wet, but in the dry season especially, ordinary cars
can make it. From Conceição it is a 3 km walk (or hitchhike) to the park. Bus Frota
Nobre from Juiz da Fora to Lima Duarte, 8 a day, US$2.10; bus Lima Duarte-Ibitipoca
daily at 0700 and 1600. You can also take a tour from Juiz da Fora with the agency
Serra do Ibitipoca, address above.

Sleeping   **Conceição**: there are various lodgings, including **C** pp *Estrela da Serra*, more expensive with TV and fridge, price includes breakfast and dinner; lunch costs US$10. A
4-star hotel is under construction outside the village. **Campsite** *Ibiti-Lua*, in the park
itself is a campsite for 50 tents, with toilets, showers, restaurant/bar and car park.
There are also various eating places. The local speciality is *pão de canela*. Also in the village, hand-dyed and woven bedspreads and handicrafts in wood are made.

Transport   **Routes**   From Juiz da Fora to Petrópolis or Rio de Janeiro, the BR-040 crosses the
Minas Gerais/Rio de Janeiro state border; it is dual carriageway and in good condition.
There is a toll at Km 814/5 (leaving Minas) and at Km 46 (entering Rio, US$2.25). At the
state border the road follows the Rio Paraíba for about 7 km, with deforested hills on
either side. The hills become steeper, more forested and with granite outcrops as one
approaches Itaipava (see under **Petrópolis**).

Towns and spas of southwestern Minas

A group of popular spas are easily reached by road from Rio de Janeiro and São Paulo. Most of the hydro resorts lie south of the Dutra Highway (BR-381, Belo Horizonte-São Paulo). These are Cambuquirá, Lambari, São Lourenço and Caxambu, south of the town of Três Corações, which also gives access to the mystical centre of São Tomé das Letras. Further west and north, on the Minas/São Paulo border is the much larger resort of Poços de Caldas. Some 240 kilometres southwest of Belo is the huge lake formed by the Furnas dam. It can be seen from the BR-381 road to São Paulo.

December-March is the high season

Tres Corações

Eight kilometres east of the BR-381 is Tres Corações, in southern Minas, a convenient place for making connections to the spas. It is the birthplace of Pelé, the legendary football star, to whom there is a statue in Praça Coronel José Martins. He holds the Jules Rimet trophy aloft and, on the plinth, are the names of the other players in the World Cup teams in which he played.

Population: 61,000
Phone code: 035
Colour map 4, grid C2

The rodoviária is beside the old railway station; a steam engine is on show (the railway is used but there is no passenger traffic). From the rodoviária, cross the river to Avenida Getúlio Vargas which leads past the Casa de Cultura Godofredo Rangel (Departamento de Turismo e Cultura and Library) at No 154 to Praça Odilon Rua de Andrade. On this square are the post office and *Banco do Brasil* (no exchange facilities). Turn left off this Praça on Rui Barbosa for one block to the statue of Pelé. Just off Praça Coronel Martins is a *Telemig* phone office.

From Praça Martins Avenida Julião Arbex leads steeply uphill to a statue of Christ on top of a chapel on Praça Monsenhor Fonseca.

Back at Praça Andrade, go uphill one block and turn left up the pedestrianized Rua Luciano Pereira Penha to the small Praça Coronel V Resende. In this square are two trees which, at dusk, become the roost for hundreds of sparrows. The trees become alive and the noise is incredible; it can be heard a couple of blocks away. Turn right to the Praça C Zeferino Avelar, on which is the main church, completely painted inside by Pedro Zogbi in the 1930s (but in need of restoration because of damp). Around this square are some older, tiled buildings, but it is mostly a modern city.

The spas of Minas Gerais & São Paulo

Minas Gerais & Espirito Santo

Sleeping **B** *Cantina Calabreza*, R Joaquim Bento de Carvalho 65, T/F2311183. Pool, sauna, has a reasonable restaurant (Italo-Brasileira), has a takeaway service. **D** *Capri*, Av Getúlio Vargas 111, not far from the bridge across the river, T2311427. With or without bath, simple but OK, TV in the more expensive rooms; nearer the bridge, at No 55, is the older *Avenida*. There are other, more basic hotels near the rodoviária.

Eating Opposite the *Cantina Calabreza* is the *Xodó*. *Quinta da Bock*, Av Getúlio Vargas, just up from *Hotel Capri*, open air restaurant and beer place. Opposite, above Bemge, is *Pizzaria Per Tutti*. Further up Av Getúlio Vargas, beyond the Praça at No 363 is *Pizzaria Jardins*, cheap, good *executivo* menu and other dishes, popular, on 1st floor.

Transport There are 3 daily buses (2 on Sunday) to **São Tomé das Letras**, US$1.65, 1½ hours (the first 30 minutes is on a paved road). To **Belo Horizonte**, *Gardénia*, 4 a day (3 on Sunday), US$10.50, 5½ hours, roadworks permitting. To **São Paulo**, *Transul*, 7 a day, US$8.10. *Beltour* runs buses to **Rio de Janeiro**; *Cristo Rei* to **Santos**.

São Tomé das Letras

Population: 5,750
Phone code: 035
Colour map 4, grid C2

São Tomé das Letras, 35 kilometres from Três Corações, is a beautiful hilltop town. At 1,291 metres it is one of the five highest places in Brazil. The average maximum temperature is 26°C and the minimum is 14°C. The rainy season is October-March. A quarry town since the beginning of the 20th century, there is evidence of the industry everywhere you look.

History Settlement in colonial times dates from the mid to late 18th century when the *bandeirantes* from São Paulo moved into this area, displacing the indigenous Indians. Rock paintings found in caves were attributed to the Indians, but in fact the pictures have been dated to about 2,000 BC. The inscriptions have lent the town a mystical reputation, attracting 'new age' visitors. Even before the 20th century 'alternative' arrivals, the hill acquired a legend: at the end of the 18th century, an escaped slave hid in a cave for a long time. A finely dressed man appeared, asking him why he was living there. On hearing the slave's story, the man gave him a message on a piece a paper which, on presentation to his master, would earn the slave forgiveness. The slave duly did as the man said and the master, impressed by the writing and the paper, went to the cave to seek the mysterious man for himself. He found no one, but instead a statue of São Thomé (St Thomas). The master therefore built a chapel at the site, which was replaced by the Igreja Matriz in 1784, now standing beside the cave. The inscriptions, in red, can just about be seen in the cave; they are the 'Letras' of the town's name.

Sights The town is almost at the top of the hill. Behind it are rocky outcrops on which are the Pyramid House, the Cruzeiro (Cross, 1,430 metres, with good 360° views), the Pedra da Bruxa and paths for walking or, in some parts, scrambling.

The main road into town is Rua Virgílio Mastrogiovanni. The bus stops at the main Praça, on which is the frescoed 18th century **Igreja Matriz** beside the fenced cave. A second church, the **Igreja das Pedras** (Nossa Senhora do Rosário – 18th century) is on a Praça to the left as you enter town (Rua Ernestina Maria de Jesus Peixoto). It is constructed in the same style as many of the charming old-style buildings, with slabs of the local stone laid on top of each other without mortar.

In the surrounding hills are many caves: Sobradinho, 12 kilometres; **Tours**
Carimbado, five kilometres; Gruta do Feijão, a short walk from town; Gruta da
Bruxa, six kilometres. Seven waterfalls are also close by, including: Cachoeira
de Eubiose, four kilometres; Véu de Noiva, 12 kilometres; Paraíso, near Véu
de Noiva; Vale das Borboletas; da Lua, eight kilometres; and do Flávio, six
kilometres. Also rapids such as Shangri-lá, 17 kilometres, and Vale dos
Gnomos, near the Vale das Borboletas. Some of these places make a good hike
from the town, but you can also visit several in a day on an organized tour (car
with four passengers): for example the waterfalls Flávio, Eubiose, Paraíso and
Véu de Noiva, US$50; Shangri-lá, US$70; Vale das Borboletas, Gruta do
Carimbado and Ladeira do Amendoim (a slope on which cars appear to run
uphill when in neutral – like the one in Belo Horizonte), US$50. T2371283 or
enquire at *Néctar* shop on Rua José Cristiano Alves. Tours run on weekends
and holidays from the Praça at 1000 and 1400 to waterfalls, caves, etc,
T2371353 and ask for Jaime or Iraci.

São Tomé is very popular at weekends. The mystical nature of the place
involves not just the cave inscriptions. Many believe it is a good vantage point
for seeing UFOs (some claim that the inscriptions are extraterrestrial in origin). There are believed to be many places with special energies. The
Carimbado cave is especially rich in myths and legends: its passages lead to an
underground civilization; its powers form an energy source linked to Machu
Picchu in Peru. Shangri-lá, which is a beautiful spot, is also called the Vale do
Maytréia. The shops reflect this atmosphere and the hotels are classified by
UFOs instead of stars! Someone in town said that to walk to Carimbado
requires a degree of physical fitness and of spiritual fitness (if you are not in the
right frame of mind, you may have a long wait for anything to happen). For
others, São Tomé is 'uncontrolled' Brazilian 'ecotourism'. Whatever your
point of view, it is certainly an unusual place.

There are lots of *pousadas* and rooms to let all over town. **Sleeping**

C *Pousada Arco-Iris*, R João Batista Neves 19, T/F2371212. Rooms and chalets, *Note that streets are*
sauna, swimming pool. **D** pp *Sonhos II* (do Gê), Trav Nhá Chica 8, T2371235. Very nice, *hard to follow because*
restaurant, swimming pool, sauna, television in rooms. Recommended. **E** pp *their names seem to*
change almost from one
Hospedaria dos Sonhos I, R Gabriel Luiz Alves. With bath, no TV, restaurant, shop, *block to the next;*
groups accommodated. Here is a selection of others: *Pousada Casarão e Restaurante* *numbering is also*
Dona Tereza, behind the cemetery on R Armando Duplesis Vilela, in the next block is *chaotic*
Pousada Resende, R Capt João de Deus, T2371230; almost opposite is *Pousada Serra*
Branca, at No 7, T2371200. On Capt José Martins (or maybe its continuation)
Hospedaria Sol e Lua, keys from No 24, and *Pousada Serra do Leão*; on a different
part of this street

Youth hostel *Mahã Mantra*, R Plínio Pedro Martins 48, T9895563, F2371264. IYHA,
open all year. *Pousada Baraunas*, R João Cristiano Alves 19, T3461330 and, next door,
Pousada Novo Horizonte, at No 10. All are priced in the **E** range pp.

On the main Praça is the shop of the *Fundação Harmonia*, whose headquarters
are downhill, on the road to Sobradinho (4 km), Bairro do Canta Galo, São Tomé das
Letras, CEP 37418-000, T2371280, or T0XX11-2043766 in São Paulo. The community
emphasizes several disciplines and principles for a healthy lifestyle, for mind and
body, 'new age', workshops, massage, excursions, vegetarian food, clean accommodation (**D** pp). Eight kilometres on the road to Sobradinho is *Rancho Paraíso*,
T2371342. Lodging, campsite, restaurant, garden and trekking.

Minas Gerais & Espírito Santo

Eating *O Alquimista*, R Capt Pedro Martins 7. *das Magas*, R Camilo Rosa. *Ximama*, Martins at the corner of G L Alves, pizzas. *Veranda Pôr-do-Sol*, R Plínio Pedro Martins, *comida caseira*, pizza. Two *Padarias Bom Dia*, 1 opposite the bus stop on the main Praça. There are many other restaurants and bars.

Transport If driving to the town, take care at the unsigned road junctions. After the pavement ends, at the next main junction, turn right. If going by bus, take the one that leaves Três Corações at dawn to see the mist in the valleys; schedule and fare are given under Três Corações.

Directory **Bank** *Bemge* in the main Praça. **Communications** Post office: in the group of buildings at the top right of the Praça, facing the Gruta São Tomé. **Tourist information** R José Cristiano Alves 4.

Hydro resorts

Cambuquirá
Population: 12,000
Phone code: 035
Altitude: 946m

Twenty kilometres south of Três Corações by paved road, Cambuquirá's Parque das Águas is very popular. The town is hilly and has a pleasant atmosphere. Horse-drawn taxis ferry visitors around. Nearby *fazendas* sell *cachaça*. **C** *Santos Dumont*, Av Virgílio de Melo Franco 400, T2511466, F2511012. The São Paulo-Três Corações bus (*Gardênia*) passes through, US$8.10.

Lambari
Population: 17,500
Phone code: 035
Altitude: 900m

This is another hilly town, 27 kilometres south of Cambuquirá. The Parque das Águas has seven mineral springs and mineral water swimming pools on Praça Conselheiro João Lisboa. ■ *Daily 0600-1800*. There are boat trips on the Lago Guanabara and to Ilha dos Amores. The resort has a casino. There is also **A** *Parque Hotel*, R Américo Werneck 46, in the centre of town, T2712000 and **B** *Itaici*, R Dr Jos dos Santos 320, T/F2711366. Four buses a day run from Bresser station in São Paulo, US$8.10.

São Lourenço
Population: 33,750
Phone code: 035
Altitude: 850m

Sixty two kilometres southeast of Lambari, São Lourenço is easily accessible from Rio de Janeiro (five to six hours by bus) or São Paulo (six to seven hours by bus). There is a splendid park, tennis, boating, swimming, a flying field, and fishing. Its rich mineral waters are used in the treatment of stomach, liver, kidney and intestinal complaints. The famous carbo-gaseous baths are unique in South America and can be found at Parque das Águas, Praça Brasil. ■ *Daily 0800-1700*. There is a grand ride through fine scenery to the Pico de Buqueré at 1,500 metres.

Sleeping A *Emboabas*, Al Jorge Amado 350, T3324600, F3324392. Restaurant. There are many others in all price ranges. **Camping** *Fazenda Recanto das Carvalhos*, BR-460 towards Pouso Alto, 10 km from town, T3322098.

Caxambu
Population: 21,000
Phone code: 035
Altitude: 900m

The waters at Caxambu, 31 kilometres northeast of São Lourenço, are used for treating stomach, kidney and bladder diseases, and are said to restore fertility (the Parque das Águas is closed on Monday). The waters seemed to work for Princess Isabel, daughter of Dom Pedro II, who produced three sons after a visit. The little church of Santa Isabel da Hungária (1868) stands on a hill as a thanks-offering. The mountains and forests around are very beautiful. There is a view over the city from Morro Caxambu, 1,010 metres. Three kilometres out of town is the charming **B** *Pousada Canto do Sabiá*, BR-354 towards Itamonte, T3413499. It has chalets and serves excellent breakfast. There are many other good hotels.

Routes Caxambu to Rio de Janeiro state: the BR-354 to Engeheiro Passos (see page 177) is the highest road in Brazil, paved and impressive, but narrow. The Registro Pass is 1,680m and near the secondary entrance to the Itatiaia National Park. Along the road are excellent, reasonably priced farm-hotels. Recommended is **L** *Casa Alpina*, BR-354, Km 721, about 3 km before the Registro Pass, alpine-style, beautiful surroundings, price is full board (T/F3631230/1231).

The BR-381, in the process of being made into a dual carriageway and in bad shape in parts, runs through southwest Minas Gerais into São Paulo state. Some buses make a detour off the highway to Pouso Alegre, which has a steam locomotive outside the town. Around Cambuí there are fields of strawberries. The last towns in Minas are Camanducaia, Itapeva and Extrema. From Camanducaia a paved road runs 32 kilometres to the hill resort of Monte Verde in the Serra Mantiqueira with a temperate climate and plenty of opportunities for walking in the hills. In July and August temperatures can fall below freezing. A lot of the architecture and cuisine is German.

Monte Verde
Population: 3,000
Phone code: 035
Altitude: 1,600m

Sleeping and eating AL *Meissner Hof*, R da Pedra 2, T4381515, F4381543. A Roteiro de Charme hotel (see page 57) Apartments and chalets, restaurant, saunas, gym, sports facilities. **A** *Pousada Pedra Partida*, R dos Orions 520, T/F4381396. Chalets. **Youth hostel E** pp *Torre Branca*, R Pau Brasil 28, Camanducaia, T4381833. IYHA.

Eating places include *Bavária*, Av Monte Verde 659. German, closed Mondays and Thursdays. *Paulo das Trutas*, R da Floresta 810. Fish.

Poços de Caldas

The city is in a different part of southwestern Minas, 105 kilometres northwest of Pouso Alegre. It is right on the São Paulo state border, some 150 kilometres north of the hydro resorts around Lindóia. It is sited at 1,180 metres on the crater of an extinct volcano in a mountainous area. Venetians from Murano settled here and established a crystal-glass industry. The resort, a traditional honeymoon centre, has thermal establishments for the treatment of rheumatic, skin and intestinal diseases; you need a local doctor's certificate to use these facilities. The climate is excellent.

Population: 122,000
Phone code: 035
272 km to São Paulo
507 km to Rio
510 km to Belo
Horizonte
Colour map 4, grid C2

These include the Véu das Noivas with its three waterfalls illuminated at night; the tall statue of Cristo Redentor at 1,678 metres, which can be reached by cable car, hang gliders fly from here; Pedra Batão, an 80 metre granite rock; and the Japanese teahouse at the Recanto Japonês. Arts and handicrafts fair is held every Saturday and Sunday in Praça Pedro Sanches.

Excursions

A *Palace*, Praça Pedro Sanches, T7223636, F7221922. Old fashioned but well run, with sulphur baths. **A** *Novo Hotel Virgínia*, R Minas Gerais 506, T7222664. Good. Many others in this range, very few under US$50 a night (many more above it).

There are plenty of restaurants. All the good hotels have dining rooms. Local specialities are smoked cheese, sausages, sweets and jams (try squash-and-coconut).

Sleeping & eating
There are some 80 hotels and pensións

Carnival; *São Benedito* **1-13 May**; the *Festa UAI*, of popular *mineira* music and dance, foods and handicrafts is held in the second half of **August**.

Festivals

Air The town has an airport. A monorail runs down the main avenue, Av Francisco Sales, to the cable car station. **Buses** The rodoviária is 3 km from centre. **Rio**, 8 hours, US$13.25; **São Paulo**, 4½ hours, US$7.25.

Transport

Minas Gerais & Espírito Santo

Western Minas Gerais

Araxá
Population: 74,500
Phone code: 034
Altitude: 997m
374 W of Belo Horizonte

Situated in the Minas Triangle, Araxá has thorium and radioactive waters, sulphur and mud baths. The *Grande Hotel Araxá* (where the springs and the ruins of the *Hotel do Rádio* are located) is eight kilometres from the town at Estâncio do Barreiro. The hotel has been completely renovated while maintaining its 1940s-50s style and gardens designed by Burle Marx. It is now run by the Tropical chain (Av Paulista 1765, 1 andar, 01311-200, São Paulo, T/F0XX11-2532003, or T0XX34-6628001 for the thermal resort.

Sleeping A *Colombo*, Estâncio do Barreiro, T/F6624016. Pool, sports facilities. **A** *Virgilius Palace*, R Dr Franklin de Castro 545, T/F6625000. Restaurant. **C** *Imbiara*, Av Imbiara 356, T/F6612500.

Transport Bus from **Belo Horizonte**, *Gontijo*, US$12.65-23.50, depending on service. There is an airport.

Parque Nacional da Serra da Canastra

South of Araxá is the Serra da Canastra National Park, in which the Rio São Francisco rises. It is a cool region (temperatures in May and June average 18°C), comprising two ranges of hills, the Serra da Canastra and the Serra das Sete Voltas, with the Vale dos Cândidos between. The altitude ranges from 900 metres to 1,496 metres above sea level and the vegetation is mostly grassland, rising to high altitude plants on the uplands. Animals include the maned wolf, the great anteater, armadillos and deer. Birds that can seen in the park are rheas, owls, seriema, king vulture and the diving duck. There are also birds of prey, partridges and tinamous. Besides the source of the Rio São Francisco (6½ kilometres from the São Roque park entrance), visitors can also see the two parts of the Casca d'Anta waterfall.

Park essentials Details on visiting the park can be obtained from Ibama in Belo Horizonte, Avenida do Contorno 8121, Cidade Jardim, CEP 30110-120, Belo Horizonte, T2916588, ext 119/122, or from Caixa Postal 01, CEP 37928-000 São Roque de Minas, T031-4331195. The park has a visitors' centre just inside the park, at the São Roque de Minas entrance. There are 3 other entrances, Casca d'Anta, São João Batista and Sacramento. All gates close at 1800.

Transport The park is best reached from Piumhi, on the MG-050, 267 km southwest of Belo Horizonte (this road heads for Ribeirão Preto in São Paulo). From Piumhi you go to São Roque de Minas (60 km).

Uberaba

Population: 232,500
Phone code: 034
485 km to São Paulo
Colour map 4, grid B1

From Araxá the BR-262 heads 120 kilometres west to Uberaba, also in the Minas Triangle on the Rio da Prata. It is an important road junction on the direct highway between São Paulo and Brasília and serves a large cattle raising district. At the beginning of April each year the Rural Society of the Minas Triangle holds a famous cattle and agricultural exhibition at Uberaba.

Excursions Between Uberaba and Ponte Alta (31 kilometres east on the BR-262) is **Peirópolis**, which is one the world's most important palaeontological sites, with dinosaur remains, including eggs. The **Centro de Pesquisas Paleontológicas – Museu do Dinossauro** is 23 kilometres east of Uberaba, at Km 784.5. ■ *0800-1800, 1100-1700 weekends, T9720023.*

Sleeping A *Novotel*, Av Filomena Cartafina 150, off BR-050, 5 km from town, T3364288, F3364297. Pool, restaurant. **A** *Pousada São Francisco*, on BR-330, 7 km from town, T3145553. Horse riding. **B** *Karajá*, Av Fernando Costa 146, T3361000, F3366167. **C** *Porto Bello*, Av Barão do Rio Branco 1000, T/F3366701.

Transport Bus from **Belo Horizonte**, US$15 (*leito* US$30), 7 hours.

About 100 kilometres north of Uberaba is Uberlândia, founded in 1888 as São Pedro do Uberabinha. It is a fast growing city with good communications by air and road. Several major bus routes (eg Campo Grande-Brasília) pass through here.

Uberlândia
Population: 439,000
Phone code: 034

Sleeping AL *Plaza Inn Master*, R da Bandeira 400, T2398000, F2398100. Restaurant. **A** *Estância das Flores*, Km 166 BR-050, T2340120. Horse riding, fishing. **B** *Super S*, Av Marcos de Freitas Costa 1225, T/F2382434. **D** *Hotel Nacional*, Higino Guerra 273, opposite the rodoviária, T2354983. With view (cheaper without), shower and breakfast.

Transport Air: Airport 8 km from town, T2125192. **Buses**: To **Brasília**, 6 hours, US$9; To **Belo Horizonte**, 9 hours, US$15; To **São Paulo**, US$18).

Directory Airline offices *Rio-Sul*, T2361414. *TAM*, T2531000. **Tourist information** Kiosk in the rodoviária. Helpful.

Espírito Santo

The coastal state of Espírito Santo is sandwiched between Rio de Janiero, Minas Gerais and Bahia. All three attract more visitors than Espírito Santo, so it is relatively little known, except by mineiros *heading for the coast for their holidays. Espírito Santo has many beaches, but they are overshadowed by those in its northern and southern neighbours. There are a number of nature reserves and turtle breeding grounds in the state, which are detailed below, and European immigration has given the towns a distinctive atmosphere. The state capital is also the main industrial and commerical centre, the port of Vitória. People here are known as Capixabas, after a former Indian tribe.*

Background

Espírito Santo was one of the original captaincies created by the Portuguese in the 16th century, but their colony was very precarious in its early days. During the struggle for supremacy, the son of Mem de Sá (the governor in Bahia) was killed, but, as elsewhere, the invaders eventually prevailed. It was not as successful as some of the other captaincies because the Portuguese were unable to gain a foothold other than on the coastal plains. When the focus of attention moved away from the coast to the mines in Minas Gerais in the 18th and subsequent centuries, the state became strategically important. Initially it was not on the gold exporting route, but after iron mining began, a route from Belo Horizonte to Vitória was created. This remains one of the major economic corridors in the country. The state population is 2.6 million, the largest concentration of inhabitants being around Vitória.

History

Minas Gerais & Espírito Santo

Geography Espírito Santo has a hot, damp seaboard with a more-or-less straight, low coastline. Long beaches are open to the Atlantic. In the south the vegetation is mainly of the *restinga* type, while the north is the broad coastal plain of the Rio Doce valley. In the far north of the state is an area of sand dunes. A mountainous interior in the south, the Serra da Chibata, gives way to the Rio Doce valley in the north. Espírito Santo used to be an important grower of coffee, especially in the 1850-1900 period. New coffee areas opened up after 1950, but cattle and pig farming are also important now. There are industrial centres at Vitória, Cachoeira de Itapemirim, Linhares and Colatina and, in the south, there is offshore oil-drilling.

Climate Tropical with temperatures ranging throughout the year from an average maximum of 28°C to a minimum of 20°C (18°C in the south of the state and lower still at the higher southern altitudes). Rainfall is about 750-1500 millimetres a year (higher in the north), with the rainy season being October to December.

Vitória

Population: 266,000
Phone code: 027
Colour map 4, grid C5

Five bridges connect the island on which Vitória stands with the mainland. The town is beautifully set, its entrance second only to Rio's, its beaches quite as attractive, but smaller, and the climate is less humid.

A rail connection westwards with Minas Gerais transports for export iron ore, coffee and timber. Port installations at Vitória and nearby Ponta do Tubarão have led to some beach and air pollution at places nearby.

Vitória dates from 1551 and takes its name from a battle won by the Portuguese over the Indians. There are a few colonial remnants, but it is largely a

Vitória

modern city and port. The upper, older part of town, reached by steep streets and steps, is much less hectic than the lower harbour area which suffers dreadful traffic problems.

On Avenida República is the huge **Parque Moscoso**, an oasis of quiet, with a lake, playground and tiny zoo. Other parks are the **Morro da Fonte Grande**, a state park from whose summit of 312 metres there are good views, and the **Parque dos Namorados**, six kilometres from the centre at Praia do Canto. Two islands reached by bridge from Praia do Canto are **Ilha do Frade** and **Ilha do Boi**.

Colonial buildings still to be seen in the city are the **Capela de Santa Luzia**, Rua José Marcelino in the upper city (1551), now an art gallery; the church of **São Gonçalo**, Rua Francisco Araújo (1766) and the ruins of the **Convento São Francisco** (1591), also in the upper city. In the **Palácio do Governo**, or **Anchieta**, Praça João Climaco (upper city) is the tomb of Padre Anchieta, the 16th century Jesuit missionary and one of the founders of São Paulo. The **Catedral Metropolitana** was built in 1918 and stands in Praça Dom Luís Scortegagna. The **Teatro Carlos Gomes**, on Praça Costa Pereira, often presents plays, also jazz and folk festivals.

Vila Velha, reached by a bridge across the bay, has an excellent beach, but it is built up and noisy: take a bus from Vitória marked Vilha Velha. See the mostly ruined, fortified monastery of **Nossa Senhora da Penha**, on a high hill above Vila Velha; the views are superb. The Dutch attacked it in 1625 and 1640. There is also a pleasant ferry service to Vila Velha.

Urban beaches such as **Camburi** can be affected by pollution (some parts of it are closed to bathers), but it is quite pleasant, with fair surf. South of the city is Vila Velha (see above), but for bigger waves go to **Barra do Jucu**, which is 10 kilometres further south.

Visit **Santa Leopoldina** or **Domingos Martins**, both around 45 kilometres from Vitória, less than an hour by bus (two companies run to the former, approximately every three hours). Both villages preserve the architecture and customs of the first German and Swiss settlers who arrived in the 1840s. Domingos Martins (also known as Campinho) has a Casa de Cultura with some items of German settlement. (Hotels include **AL** *Pedra Azul*, BR-262 Km 88, T2481101, F2481201, which is part of the Roteiro de Charme hotel group, see page 57, and **B** *Imperador*, Praça Duque de Caxias 275, T/F2681115). Santa Leopoldina has an interesting museum covering the settlers' first years in the area. ■ *Tuesday-Sunday, 0900-1100 and 1300-1800*.

Santa Teresa is a charming hill town, a beautiful journey of 2½ hours, 90 kilometres by bus, from

Population: 20,000

Morro da Fonte Grande

R Alziro Viana
R Pereira Pinto

Rua do Rosário
Itapemirim

R Wilson Freitas
Souza

G Dias
Av Governador Bley
J Prado
P Blase
A D Santos

Av Princesa Isabel

Praça Getúlio Vargas
Pinto Pacca

To Camburi, Tubarão & Airport

Praça Pio XII

Av Marcechal Mascarenhas de Moraes

Baía de Vitória

Minas Gerais & Espírito Santo

Vitória (US$6). Among the hotels is **B** *Pierazzo*, Avenida Getúlio Vargas 115, T/F2591233, and there are many restaurants.

There is a unique hummingbird sanctuary at the **Museu Mello Leitâo**, Avenida José Ruschi 4, which is a library including the works of the hummingbird and orchid scientist, Augusto Ruschi. Hummingbird feeders are hung outside the library. ■ *0800-1200, 1300-1700, T2591182*. Also in the municipality is the **Dr Augusto Ruschi Biological Reserve** (formerly the Nova Lombardia National Biological Reserve), a forest rich in endemic bird species, including several endangered humming birds, Salvadori's antwren, cinnamon-vented Piha, russet-winged spadebill, Oustalet's tyrannulet, rufous-brown solitaire and hooded berryeater. Previous permission must be obtained to visit from **Ibama**, Av Marechal Mascarenhas de Moraes 2487, Caixa Postal 762, Vitória ES, CEP 29000.

Sleeping **AL** *Best Western Porto do Sol*, Av Dante Michelini 3957, Praia de Camburi, T3372244, F3372711. Overlooking the sea 7 km from the centre, with restaurant. **A** *Senac Ilha do Boi*, R Bráulio Macedo 417, Ilha do Boi, T3450111, F3450115. Government-run hotel school, luxurious, swimming pool, restaurant, on the ocean. **B** *Pousada da Praia*, Av Saturnino de Brito 1500, Praia do Canto, T/F2250233. Pool. **C** *Avenida*, Av Florentino Avidos 350, T2234317. With breakfast. Recommended. **C** *Vitória*, Cais de São Francisco 85, near Parque Moscoso. Excellent restaurant, changes money. Recommended. **D** *Europa*, 7 de Setembro, corner of Praça Costa Pereira. Noisy but cheap, good value restaurant (nearby is a good value vegetarian restaurant and a money changer, ask at the hotel). Adequate hotels can be found opposite the rodoviária. Other hotels are located in beach areas, Camburi to the north, Vila Velha to the south, both about 15 minutes from city centre.

Youth hostels *Jardim da Penha*, R Hugo Viola 135, take Universitário bus, get off at the first University stop, T3240738, F3256010. *Praia da Costa*, R São Paulo 1163, Praia da Costa, Vila Velha, T3293227, F2231135. IYHA. *Príncipe Hotel*, Av Dario Lourenço de Souza 120, Ilha do Príncipe, T3222799, F2233392. IYHA.

Eating A local speciality is *Moqueca capixaba*, a seafood dish served in an earthenware pot. It is a variant of the *moqueca* which is typical of Bahia. *Lareira Portuguesa*, Av Saturnino de Brito 260, Praia do Canto, T3450329. Portuguese, expensive. *Pirão*, R Joaquim Lírio 753, Praia do Canto. Regional food. *Mar e Terra*, opposite the rodoviária. Good food, live music at night. *Lavacar* and many others at Praia Camburi offer food and live music.

Transport **Car hire** *Localiza*, Praça do Aeroporto, T3270211; at the airport T0800-992000; *Vila Velha*, Av Carlos Lindemberg 2707, T2004466.

Air Eurico Salles airport at Goiaberas, 11 km from the city, T3270811. There are flights to Belém, Belo Horizonte, Brasília, Guarapari, Maceió, Porto Alegre, Recife, Rio de Janeiro, Salvador and São Paulo.

Trains Daily passenger service to **Belo Horizonte**, 14 hours, US$17.50 *executivo* (very comfortable), US$11.50 1st class, US$7.80 2nd.

The rodoviária is 15 mins walk W of the centre

Buses Rio, 8 hours, US$15 (*leito* 25). **Belo Horizonte**, US$14.50 (*leito* 29). **Salvador**, 18 hours, US$27; **Porto Seguro** direct 11 hours with lots of stops, US$18 (also *leito* service); alternatively, take a bus to Eunápolis, then change to buses which run every hour.

Hitchhiking To hitch to **Salvador**, take a bus to Serra, which is 13 km beyond Carapina, itself 20 km north of Vitória; alight where the bus turns off to Serra.

Directory **Airline offices** *Rio Sul/Nordeste*, Av NS dos Navegantes 2091, conj 102, T2271588. *TAM*, Av Fernando Ferrari 3055, Goiaberas, T3270868. *Transbrasil*, R José Teixeira 300, Praia do Canto, T2253922/9055, airport T3270308. *Varig*, Av Jerônimo Monteiro 1000, loja 3, at airport T3270304.

Vasp, R Desembargador Sampaio 40, T3241499, at airport, T3270236. **Communications** Post office: Av Jerônimo Monteiro, between R Gonçalves Ledo and R Quintino Bocaiúva. Telecommunications: Palácio do Café, Praça Costa Pereira 52. **Embassies & consulates** *Denmark*, R do Sol 141, Sala 210, T2224075, open 0900-1300, 1500-1900. *Finland*, Av NS dos Navegantes 675, Edif Palácio do Café, Enseada do Suá, T3254066, F2276051. *Spain*, R Aristides Freire 22, Centro, T2232846. **Hospitals & medical services** *Santa Casa*, R Dr Jones de Santos Neves 143, T3220074. **Tour companies & travel agents** *Saytur*, Av Des Santos Neves 1425, T3251899, F3251391. American Express representative. **Tourist information** *Cetur*, Av Princesa Isabel 54, T3228888, at airport T3278855 and at rodoviária (friendly, good free map). Also *Instituto Jones dos Santos Neves*, Av Marechal Campos 310, 3rd floor, Edif Vitória Center, CEP 29040-090, T3222033, ext 2215, F3222033, ext 225.

South of Vitória

The ES-060 road hugs the coast from Vitória to the Rio de Janeiro state border, south of Marataízes whilst the BR-101 runs inland for those in a hurry (traffic permitting) to get to Campos (see page 160) in Rio de Janeiro State. The highway passes 12 kilometres from **Cachoeiro do Itapemirim** (*population* 150,000), a busy city on both banks of the fast-flowing Rio Itapemirim. **Cachoeira Alta** with a natural swimming pool is 38 kilometres away on the road to Castelo.

Sleeping and eating A *Mirante*, R Antônio Caetano Gonçalves 45, T/F5215588. **A** *Rio Grande*, Av Beira-Rio 199, T/F5211980. **A** *San Karlo*, Av Beira-Rio 65, T5210755, F5225737. Restaurant. For eating, try *Belas Artes*, Praça Jerônimon Monteiro 77.

Directory Banks: *Banco do Brasil*, Praça Jerônimon Monteiro 26. *Bradesco*, R Capt Deslandes 68.

Fifty four kilometres south of Vitória on the coast road is Guarapari whose beaches are the closest to Minas Gerais, so they get very crowded at holiday times. The busiest time is mid-December to end-February. The beaches also attract many people seeking cures for rheumatism, neuritis and other complaints, from the radioactive monazitic sands. Information about the sands can be found at the Casa de Cultura (see below), the former seat of the prefeitura, which was built in 1749 (open from 1300), and at the Antiga Matriz church on the hill in the town centre, built in 1585 by Padre Anchieta.

Guarapari
Population: 74,000
Phone code: 027

Sleeping AL *Flamboyant*, Km 38 Rod do Sol, T/F2290066. Fazenda hotel with fishing and horse riding. **A** *Atlântico*, Av Edísio Cirne 332, Praia dos Namorados, T/F3611551, atlantic@escelsa.com.br. Recommended. **A** *Best Western Porto do Sol*, Av Beira Mar 1, Praia do Morro, T3611100, F2612929. Mediterranean-style village on a rocky point overlooking a calm beach, pool, sauna. Recommended. **A** *Vieira*, R Joaquim da Silva Lima 310, T3611122, F2611056. Recommended. **B** *do Angelo*, R Pedro Caetano 254, T/F2610230. Restaurant. Recommended. **B** *Costa Sul*, R Getúlio Vargas 101. Breakfast, loads of mosquitoes, otherwise recommended. **B** *Bom Jesus*, R Pedro Caetano 156, T2611184. Breakfast, fan, simple, central, good. Recommended. **Youth hostel** IYHA hostel at *Guara Camping*, R Antônio Guimarães s/n, quadra 40, Praia de Itapessu, T2610475, F2610448: turn left out of the rodoviária, then right and right again, past *Pousada Lisboa*, 2 blocks, across a dual carriageway (Av Jones de Santos Neves), 1 block to the campground, US$10 with good breakfast. Recommended.

Camping *Camping Clube do Brasil*, Setiba beach, 9 km from centre, T2621325.

Eating *Guaramare*, Km 65 Rod do Sol, T2721300. Fish, expensive. Regional food at Praia de Meaípe, 8 km south: *Cantinho do Curuca*, Av Santana 96 and *Gaeta*, Av Santana 46.

Minas Gerais & Espírito Santo

Transport Buses: Alvorada has a separate rodoviária from Itapemirim/Penha, Sudeste, São Gerardo and others. They are close together, 15 minutes' walk from the city centre or US$5 by taxi. Penha tickets are sold at *R-Tur Turismo*, in the centre at R Manoel Severo Simões and R Joaquim da Silva Lima where air tickets, free brochures, maps, and hotel addresses can also be obtained. To **Vitória**, 1 hour with *Sudeste*, US$2. To **Rio** with *Itapemirim*, 2 a day, US$12.

Directory Banks: *Banco 24 Horas*, Praça do Coronado, Praia da Areia. *Banco do Brasil*, R Joaquim da Silva Lima 550. *Bradesco*, R Henrique Coutinho 901. **Tourist information**: at R Davino Matos, Praça da Gratidão, T2612151. *Setuc*, in the Casa de Cultura, Praça Jerônimo Monteiro, T2613058.

A little further south (20 kilometres) is the fishing village of **Ubu** with calm waters and clear sand.

Sleeping and eating A *Pousada Aba Ubu*, R Manoel Miranda Garcia, T/F3450187, abaubu@tropical.com.br. Restaurant, half board. B *Pontal de Ubu*, R Gen Oziel 1, T2613111. Good regional food at *Peixada do Garcia*, Av Magno Ribeiro Muqui and *Peixada do Menelau Garcia*, Av Mário Neves.

Eight kilometres further down the coast is **Anchieta**, with the **Igreja de NS da Assunão** (1569) and a museum. Nearby Praia de Castelhanos is five kilometres east, on a peninsula. One of the attractions of Anchieta is to take a boat up the Rio Benaventes at dusk to see the egrets coming in to roost. The trip takes about 15 minutes and boatmen from the Colônia da Pesca charge about US$20 there and back.

Sleeping A *Pousada dos Castelhanos*, Rod do Sol 2679, T/F5361427. A *Thanharu Praia*, R Jovina Serafim dos Anjos, T/F5361246. Half-board, good. B *Porto Velho*, Av Carlos Lindenberg 183, T/F5361181.

Close by is **Iriri**, a small village in a beautiful setting with two beaches, Santa Helena and Inhaúma. There are a few hotels (**A-B**) at Praia Costa Azul. Lodging in private houses is possible. A regular bus runs from Guarapari.

The next spot down the coast, five kilometres, is **Piúma**, a calm, little-visited place, renowned for its craftwork in shells. The skill has been passed down through generations of craftsmen and women. The name derives from the Indian word *pium*, meaning mosquito. It is 100 kilometres south of Vitória. Three kilometres north of the village is Pau Grande beach, where you can surf.

Sleeping B *Solar de Brasília*, Av Eduardo Rodrigues 15, Praia Acaiaca, T/F5201521. B *Pousada Haras Monte Agha*, R das Castanheiras, T/F5201363. Fazenda hotel with horse riding. **Campsite** *Mar a Mar*, Av Beira Mar 645, Praia da Piúma, T5201463.

The resort town of **Marataízes**, with good beaches, is 30 kilometres south of Piúma. It is just north of the Rio state border.

Sleeping A *Saveiros Palace*, Av Miramar 119, on the beach, T5321413, F5321285. A *Praia*, Av Atlântica 99, on the beach, T5322144, F5323515. B *Dona Judith*, Av Lacerda de Aguiar 353, T5321436, F5321305. **Camping** Municipal site on Praia do Siri, 9 km south of the centre, T3252202.

Directory Banks: *Banco do Brasil*, Av Lacerda de Aguiar 356.

North of Vitória

The ES-010 road follows the coast from Vitória north to the mouth of the Rio Doce. It passes beaches such as Manguinhos and Jacaraípe and the town of Nova Almeida before reaching **Santa Cruz**, 60 kilometres north of the state capital. The town, at the mouth of the Rio Piraquê-Açu, depends economically on cellulose factories, which have been the subject of an international outcry over child labour. It is a simple place, with few facilities. The coast around Santa Cruz, called Aracruz, has several good beaches, mostly undeveloped, which are tranquil and uncrowded.

A *Pousada dos Cocais*, Praia de Sauê, T/F2501515, Restaurant, pool. **B** *Coqueiral*   **Sleeping**
Praia Park, Praia do Coqueiral, 6 km along the road to Barra do Riacho, T2501214. A/c,
TV, restaurant, pool, pretty location. **C** *Pousada das Pedras*, Praia dos Padres,
T2501716. There are *pousadas* at Praia Formosa, 3 km south of town, and campsites at
Barra do Sahy, Praia do Putiry and Formosa beaches.

Turtle beaches

The **Reserva Biológica Comboios**, 44 kilometres north of Santa Cruz, is designed to protect the marine turtles which frequent this coast. Three species use this long stretch of sand backed by *restinga* to lay their eggs, the leatherback, the green (*araunã*) and the *cabeçuda*, for which this is the prime nesting ground on the Brazilian seaboard. ■ *Contact Ibama in Vitória, Avenida Marechal Mascarenhas 2487, CP 762, CEP 29000 or telephone T2641452.*

    Regência, at the mouth of the Rio Doce, 65 kilometres north of Santa Cruz, is part of the reserve and has a regional base for **Tamar**, the national marine turtle protection project. On the north shore of the mouth of the Rio Doce is Povoação, which also has a Tamar office, Caixa Postal 105, CEP 29900-970, Lagoa do Monsorá, Povoação, Linhares, ES. Regência is popular with sailors, anglers, divers and surfers.

    Linhares (*population* 103,500), 143 kilometres north of Vitória on the Rio Doce, has good hotels and restaurants. It is a convenient starting place for the turtle beaches. Besides those at the mouth of the Rio Doce, there is another Tamar site at **Ipiranga**, which is 40 kilometres east of Linhares by an unmade road. ■ *For information on the turtles, also contact Tamar at Caixa Postal 105, CEP 29900-970, Linhares, ES.*

B *Pratti Park*, R Rufino de Carvalho 793, T/F3711866. Pool. **B** *Linhatur*, R Augusto   **Sleeping**
Pestana 1274, T3710300, F3711445. **C** *Virgínia*, R Gov Santos Neves 919, T/F2641699.
At Pontal do Ipiringa: **C** *Paraíso*, Av do Sol, T9843477. Pool

Linhares is close to two other **nature reserves**: the **Linhares Reserve** owned   **Linhares &**
by CVRD (the former state-owned mining company, now privatized) is possi-   **Sooretama**
bly the largest remaining lowland tract of Atlantic forest; permission from the   **reserves**
reserve's director must be obtained to visit. There is very good birdwatching in the reserve; specialities include red-billed curassow, minute hermit, rufous-sided crake, blue-throated (ochre-cheeked) parakeet, black-billed scythebill and black-headed berryeater.

    The **Sooretama Biological Reserve**, some 45 kilometres north of Linhares and 65 kilometres south of Conceição da Barra, on the BR-101, protects tropical Atlantic rain forest and its fauna and birds (it contains several bird species not found in the Linhares Reserve). Much of the wildlife is rare and endangered. Both Sooretama and Linhares have orchids apparently not found anywhere else. It was protected in 1969. With year-round tropical humidity, vegetation here is dense with ancient trees reaching over 40 metres in height. Two rivers, the Barra Seca and the Cupido, cross the reserve and, together with Lagoa Macuco, provide marshlands which attract migratory birds as well as numerous resident flocks. The reserve is strictly monitored by Ibama and is not open to the public, but drivers and cyclists can cut across it by road. For authorization to visit, researchers should phone T3740016.

São Mateus, 88 kilometres north of Linhares, is a pleasant town. It is 13 kilometres from good beaches at Guriri, which is another Tamar base – Caixa Postal 130.153, CEP 29930-000 São Mateus, T027-7611267.

Conceição da Barra
Population: 25,500
Phone code: 027

The most attractive beaches in the State, however, are around Conceição da Barra 261 kilometres north of Vitória. Corpus Christi (early June) is celebrated with an evening procession for which the road is decorated with coloured wood chips. It is an organized town which welcomes visitors. Many come in summer and for Carnival, otherwise it is quiet. Viewed from its small port, the sunsets are always spectacular.

Sleeping and eating There are pleasant beach hotels. **D** *Caravelas*, Av Dr Mário Vello Silvares 83, 1 block from the beach, T7621188. Basic, shared bathroom, light breakfast. Recommended. **E** *Pousada Pirámide*, next to rodoviária, T7621970. Owner Lisete Soares speaks English, good value, 100m from beach. Recommended. *Camping Clube do Brasil* site with full facilities, Rod Adolfo Serra, Km 16, T7621346. *Tia Teresa*, R Dr Mário Vello Silvares 135. Brazilian food, self-service, good value.

Itaúnas, 27 kilometres north by road, or 14 kilometres up the coast (some *pousadas* and a small campsite), is an interesting excursion. The small town has been swamped by sand dunes, 30 metres high. The theory is that the sudden encroachment of the sands, in the 1970s, was caused by massive deforestation of the surrounding area. From time to time, winds shift the sand dunes enough to reveal the buried church tower. Itaúnas has been moved to the opposite river bank. There is now a fantastic landscape of huge dunes and deserted beaches. The coast here, too, is a protected turtle breeding ground (Tamar, Caixa Postal 53, Conceição da Barra, T7621124). Buses three to four times a day from Conceição da Barra.

Meleiras beach, three kilometres south, is accessible only on foot or by boat (one of a number of pleasant trips). It is 12 kilometres long and offers fabulous diving and fishing. **Guaxindiba**, three kilometres north, is partially developed, with hotels and restaurants, but the natural vegetation is still intact.

Sleeping A *Barramar Praia*, Av Atlântica 3000, T7621311, F7621312. **A** *Praia da Barra*, Av Atlântica 350, T/F7621100. **B** *Pousada Gandia*, Av Atlântica 1054, T/F7621248. **B** *Pousada Mirante*, Av Atlântica 566, T/F7621311.

Transport Buses: bus from the *padaria* in Conceição da Barra at 0700, returns 1700.

Iguaçu Falls
and the South

Iguaçu Falls and the South

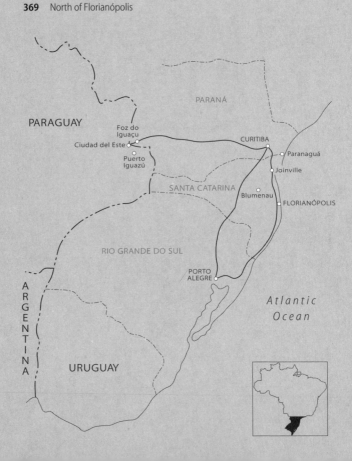

The states of Paraná, Santa Catarina and Rio Grande do Sul form the subtropical south, where European immigration has had a strong influence. The Iguaçu Falls, one of Latin America's major natural attractions, should not be missed. Nearby is the Itaipu dam, one of the world's largest manmade constructions. One of the continent's most scenic railways, from Curitiba to Paranaguá, runs through the coastal range of mountains. The area around Florianópolis has some wonderful beaches, especially for surfers. Inland is the town of Blumenau, with its German architecture and lively Oktoberfest. The wine region of Caxias do Sul and the beautiful scenery around Canela are both popular. The pampas cowboy culture of the Gaúchos is strong around Port Alegre and the borders with Uruguay and Argentina. In the west there are the remains of the Jesuit missions long abandoned by their founders.

Paraná

Paraná has one of the premier tourist sites in South America, the Iguaçu Falls. No guidebook can do justice to the spectacle of the magnificent cataratas; they are a must on any itinerary to Brazil, or Argentina for that matter. The state has a short coastline and its main port, Paranaguá, is connected with the capital, Curitiba, by one of the best railways in South America. Curitiba itself is a progressive city and very pleasant to visit. The culture of Paraná has been heavily influenced by its large immigrant communities and its economy is principally agricultural.

The area of what is now Paraná was neglected by the Portuguese until the beginning of the 17th century. At this time gold was discovered and, together with the need to find new Indians to enslave, interest was awakened. The region fell under the control of São Paulo, but there was no great success in the extraction of gold, partly because Indian labour was unavailable to work the finds (they had all been sent elsewhere or had died of disease). As soon as the Minas Gerais gold was discovered, this aspect of Paraná's economy was abandoned. Instead, the colonists turned to agriculture and cattle-raising and in the 18th and 19th centuries *fazendeiros* and drovers were the dominant people of Paraná. Until 1853, the area was controlled from São Paulo. When the new province was created, cattle and *mate* growing were the most important activities, but to this was added timber at the end of the 19th century, with the coming of the railways.

It was realized in the second half of the 19th century that the province of Paraná would not develop without a major increase in the population. Consequently, an official immigration policy was launched. The Italians were first in Paraná, but later settlers came from Germany, Poland, the Ukraine, France, England, Holland, and since the beginning of the 20th century from Japan, Syria, the Lebanon and Jews.

Paraná is now the leading producer of wheat, rye, potatoes and black beans, but its population, 8,415,660, no longer expands as quickly as it did, partly because of the displacement of rural workers following the uprooting of coffee plants in the more frost-prone areas and the turning of the land over to cattle. The recent boom crop, soya, also employs fewer workers throughout the year than coffee.

Curitiba

Population: 1,476,500
Phone code: 041
Altitude: 908m
Colour map 5, grid A4

Situated in the Serra do Mar, Curitiba is regarded as one of Brazil's model cities for quality of life. It is well organized and an extremely pleasant base for exploring the coast and the surrounding mountains.

The state capital Curitiba was founded on 29 March 1693 in the spot which is now Praça Tiradentes, and was known as Vila Nossa Senhora da Luz dos Pinhais. For many years it was used as a stopping place for cattle herders travelling from Rio Grande do Sul to cattle fairs in São Paulo state and on to the mining towns of Minas Gerais, In 1842 it was elevated to the rank of city and given the name of Curitiba, and on 29 August 1853 it was made the state capital.

Viagra

The world famous anti-impotency drug Viagra is big business in Brazil – but one wily mayor took it upon himself to distribute the pills free of charge in a desperate bid to boost his town's flagging population.

Elcio Berti, mayor of Bocaiuva do Sul in the southern state of Paraná, hoped to secure the city a bigger slice of federal cash, shared among municipalities according to their size.

"'Enlarging the local population is the only way to get a larger chunk of the federal fund", the Brazilian daily newspaper

O Globo quoted Berti as saying.

Not only did he claim to be footing the US$30,000 dollar bill himself, but he also personally oversaw the distribution of the drug to prevent an invasion of lusty citizens from neighbouring towns, eager to procure one of the US$25 tablets free of charge.

His plan was an improvement on an earlier attempt to increase the town's population of 10,000 – he had previously passed a municipal law banning the sale of condoms, a move quickly cancelled by a judge on the grounds of unconstitutionality.

Robin Eveleigh

Getting there International and domestic flights usually arrive at Afonso Pena Airport. There are buses to the centre and bus station as well as taxis. International and interstate buses arrive at the Terminal Rodoviário on Av Afonso Camargo.

Ins & outs

Getting around There is an integrated transport system with several types of bus route, pick up a map for details.

Town planning

With the influx of European immigrants in the 19th and 20th centuries, it has now become a modern city on the plateau of the Serra do Mar. It has won a prize as one of the three cleanest cities in Latin America, it has extensive open spaces with a rate of green area per inhabitant as high as 52 square metres per one, and has some exceptionally attractive modern architecture: the new opera house, Rua 24 Horas, the green house in the Botanical Garden and several of the larger 'tubo' bus stations all share the same semi-circular arch-steel-tube-and-glass style. Parks are well-manicured and the 'tubo' bus system, somewhat metrô like, trades a little in speed for more complete coverage of the entire city. The city clearly benefits from the Itaipú hydroelectric plant in terms of spending on public works, but it has also benefited from integrated urban planning, which has made it one of the more pleasant Brazilian cities in which to live. In outlying areas of the city, **Ruas da Cidadania**, citizenship streets, or malls, are being built next to bus stops so that municipal services, shops, crèches and child care, sports and leisure activities are provided and local people avoid the need to travel to the centre. These streets are of a colourful, vibrant design, the first of which was built at **Boqueirão**. Another, more central, is **Rua da Cidadania da Matriz**, which was inaugurated in 1997 next to the Praça Rui Barbosa transport terminal, with the added innovation of having 20 computer terminals for access to the internet.

Sights

A panoramic view can be had from the glass observation deck of the telecommunications tower, **Torre Mercês**, built by Telepar and so also called the **Telepar Tower**, Rua Jacarezinho, on the corner with Rua Professor Lycio Veloso 191. The height of the tower is 109.5 metres and it stands at an elevation of 940.5 metres above sea level. The observatory is actually 95 metres high and

Iguaçu Falls & the South

there is a map of the city on the floor so that you can locate key sites. ■ *1230-2030, Tuesday-Friday, 1030-2030 Saturday, Sunday and holidays, US$1.50, T3228080.*

The commercial centre is the busy Rua 15 de Novembro, part of which is a pedestrian area called **Rua das Flores**, where there are Saturday morning painting sessions for children. Since urban planning first began in 1720, the Rua das Flores has always been a place for street happenings and is now well decorated with flowers and trees, with benches, cafés and restaurants, cinemas and shops. The **Boca Maldita** is a particularly lively part, a good meeting place. Another pedestrian area is behind the cathedral, near Largo da Ordem, with a sacred art museum, flower clock and old buildings, very beautiful in the evening when the old lamps are lit – nightlife is concentrated here. There is an art market on Saturday morning in the **Praça Rui Barbosa**, and an even better one on Sunday morning in **Praça Garibáldi**, beside the attractive Rosário church.

The **Centro Cívico** is at the end of Avenida Dr Cândido de Abreu, two kilometres from the city centre: a monumental group of five buildings dominated by the **Palácio Iguaçu**, headquarters of the state and municipal governments.

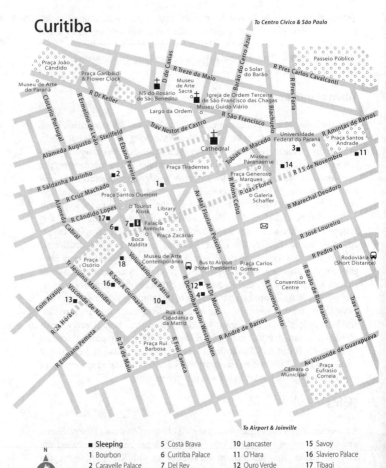

Curitiba

To Centro Cívico & São Paulo

To Airport & Joinville

■ Sleeping	5 Costa Brava	10 Lancaster	15 Savoy
1 Bourbon	6 Curitiba Palace	11 O'Hara	16 Slaviero Palace
2 Caravelle Palace	7 Del Rey	12 Ouro Verde	17 Tibagi
3 Cervantes	8 Itamarati	13 Rayon	18 Tourist Universo
4 Climax	9 King's	14 Regência	

N

Not to scale

In a patio behind it is a relief map to scale of Paraná. The **Bosque de João Paulo II**, behind the Civic Centre on Rua Mateus Leme, was created in December 1980 after the Pope's visit to Curitiba. It also contains the **Memorial da Imigração Polonesa no Paraná** (Polish immigrants memorial): both are worth a visit, T3218375 (museum), T2544816. In contrast to the Civic Centre is the old municipal government building in French Art Nouveau style, now housing the Museu Paranaense in Praça Generoso Marques.

All that remains of the magnificent old **Palácio Avenida**, on Travessa Oliveira Belo 11, T3216249, is the façade, which was retained during remodelling works in 1991. Nowadays it has a completely modern interior, with banks, offices, an auditorium for 250 people and various cultural activities. Christmas is the time to visit, for **Natal no Avenida**, when the building is decorated and illuminated and crowds gather outside for celebrations. The **Solar do Barão** is another old building, built in 1880-83 as a home for the Baron of Serro Azul. Today it is used as a centre for art and leisure, with concerts in the auditorium, exhibitions and courses, Rua Presidente Carlos Cavalcanti 533, T3221525. The **Teatro Paiol**, south of the centre on Rua Coronel Zacarias next to Praça Guido

Viaro, was built in 1906 as a depository for gunpowder, and its round construction definitely has a defensive, military feel to it. It has been a theatre since 1971 and can hold an audience of 220. ■ *T3221525*. In contrast, the **Teatro Guaíra** has always been a theatre. First built in 1884 as the Teatro São Teodoro, the present building dates from 1953. It has three auditoria of different sizes to cater for different shows. ■ *Rua 15 de Novembro, T3222628*.

The **Ópera de Arame** and the **Pedreira Paulo Leminski** lie north of the centre on the site of an old stone quarry. The pit has been transformed into a site of major cultural importance where open air shows and concerts are held. It has a capacity to entertain up to 70,000 people and it was here that the tenor, José Carreras, gave his first performance in Brazil in March 1993, to celebrate Curitiba's 300th anniversary. The opera house itself is a beautiful tubular structure, circular, with a glass and metal dome, which radiates light when performances are held at night.

Another fine example of the use of tubular steel and glass is **Rua 24 Horas**, where the whole street is protected by an arched roof. The street's two clocks use the 24-hour system and the shops, bars and restaurants never close. The theme of light, glass and space is developed further in education. Attached to several schools are **Faroles de Saber**, lighthouses of knowledge, which are modular 5,000-book libraries with a lighthouse tower, a beacon on top and a guard. The first one was opened in 1994 in Bairro Mercês, but 48 are planned.

Parks The most popular public park is the **Passeio Público**, in the heart of the city (closed Monday). Inaugurated in 1886, it has three lakes, each with an island, and a playground.

On the northeast edge of the city is **Parque do Barigüi**, take bus 450 'São Braz' from Praça Tiradentes. The park contains an exhibition centre, amusement park, football, volleyball, churrascarias, a lake and lots of other entertainments. Near the shores of Lagoa Bacacheri, on the northern edge of the city (Rua Nicarágua 2453), is an unexpected Egyptian temple. Visits can be arranged to the Brazilian centre of the Rosicrucians; take Santa Cândida bus to Estação Boa Vista, then walk.

Four kilometres east of the rodoferroviário, the **Jardim Botânico Fanchette Rischbieter** is worth visiting, particularly for its very fine glass house, again with domes, curves and lots of steel, inspired by Crystal Palace in London. The gardens are in the French style and there is also a **Museu Botánico**, Rua Ostoja Roguski (Primeira Perimetral dos Bairros), T3218646/3621800 (museum). It can be reached by the orange *Expreso* buses from Praça Rui Barbosa.

Of the many other *parques* and *bosques* around the city, of interest are: **Bosque João Carlos Hartley Gutierrez**, access along Rua Jacarezinho between Vista Alegre and Mercês, where there is a memorial to Chico Mendes; **Bosque de Portugal**, along Rua Osório Duque Estrada at the corner with Rua Fagundes Varela, with Portuguese architecture and some lovely, hand painted tiles; **Bosque Alemão**, between Ruas Franz Schubert, Nicollo Paganini and Francisco Schaffer, where there is an Oratório Bach, used for concerts, and murals in tiles depicting the Hansel and Gretel fairy tale; **Parque Regional do Iguaçu – Zoológico**, on Avenida Marechal Floriano Peixoto, T3781221, where there is a zoo but other parts of the park are devoted to sport, waterbased activities such as rowing or fishing (take *bi-articulado* bus to Terminal Boqueirão, then direct bus to the zoológico, entry free); **Parque Tingüi**, between Ruas Fredolin Wolf and José Valle (T3352112), created in 1994 and named after an Indian tribe who lived in the area, it contains a **Memorial da Imigração Ucraniana**, in honour of one of the main sources of immigration to the city, and also a replica of the church of São Miguel Arcanjo.

Churches On Praça Tiradentes is the **Cathedral**. It was originally a small wooden chapel, which was elevated to the Primeira Igreja Matriz in 1715, but improvements in the colonial style of construction led to cracks appearing and in 1875 it had to be demolished. The present cathedral, built in neo-gothic style and inaugurated in 1893, was restored in 1993 and promoted to Catedral Basílica Menor de Curitiba. ■ *Rua Barão do Serro Azul 31, T2221131*.

The oldest church in Curitiba is the **Igreja de Ordem Terceira de São Francisco das Chagas**, built in 1737 in Largo da Ordem. Its most recent renovation was in 1978-80. In its annex is the **Museu de Arte Sacra**. ■ *T2237545*. The **Igreja de Nossa Senhora do Rosário de São Benedito** was built in the Praça Garibáldi in 1737 by slaves and was the Igreja dos Pretos de São Benedito. It was demolished in 1931 and a new church was inaugurated in 1946. There is a mass for tourists, Missa do Turista, which is held on Sundays at 0800.

Museu Paranaense, Praça Generoso Marques, was founded in 1876 by **Museums** Agostinho Ermelino de Leão, although it has not always been at this location. The collection of exhibits includes documents, manuscripts, ethnological and historical material, stamps, works of art, photographs and archaeological pieces. ■ *Tuesday-Friday 1000-1800, other days 1300-1800, closed first Monday of each month*. **Museu de Arte Contemporânea**, Rua Desembargador Westphalen 16, Praça Zacarias, displays Brazilian contemporary art in its many forms, with an emphasis on artists from Paraná. ■ *Tuesday-Friday 0900-1900, Saturday-Sunday 1400-1900, T2225172*. **Casa Romário Martins**, Largo da Ordem 35, is a colonial building of the 18th century and the second oldest in the city, next to the oldest, the Igreja da Ordem. Exhibitions of art by Paranaense artists. ■ *T3221525*. **Casa Andersen**, Rua Mateus Leme 336, is the painter's house. ■ *Monday-Friday, 0900-1200, 1400-1800*. **Museu de Arte do Paraná**, in the Palácio São Francisco, was built in the 1920s for the Garmatter family and used in 1938-53 as the Governor's palace. The museum dates from 1987 and exhibits the work of many of Paraná's artists. ■ *T2343172*. **Museu da Imagem e do Som**, Rua Barão do Rio Branco 395, was created with the aim of preserving audiovisual and photographic memories of Paraná. ■ *T2329113*. **Museu do Expedicionário**, Second World War Museum, is maintained by the Legião Paranaense do Expedicionário (Paraná Expeditionary Legion) made up of ex-combatants of Paraná who served in the Brazilian Expeditionary Force, Praça do Expedicionário. ■ *Daily 0800-1800, T2643931*. **Museo do Automóvel**, Avenida Cândido Hartmann 2300, has a collection of cars dating from as early as 1910 to the McLaren of Emerson Fittipaldi. ■ *Saturday 1400-1800, Sunday 1000-1200, 1400-1800*. **Museu de História Natural**, Rua Benedito Conceição 407, is a natural history museum with lots of zoology and scientific collections of things like spiders, insects and parasites, which also has details on endangered species in the State. ■ *T3663133*.

Excursions

Twenty kilometres west of Curitiba at Km 119 on the road to Ponta Grossa is the **Museu Histórico do Mate**, an old water-driven mill where mate was prepared. ■ *Free*.

The beautiful **Ouro Fino** estate, 34 kilometres west, is open to the public 0700-1700 every day except Monday, December-March, and every second Sunday the rest of the year. It has parkland and woods, walking trails, mineral water swimming pool, and barbecues. The nearest bus stop is 16 kilometres away at Campo Largo, so car is the best way to get there. Advance permission needed, T3232025/8481300.

Joinville, in Santa Catarina (see page 375), is within easy reach of Curitiba. If taking this route, *La Dolce Vita* at Tijucas do Sul, T/F8341214, is a pleasant and convenient place to stay and is 33 kilometres from Curitiba, take turning at Km 655 on the BR-376. It is part of the *Roteiros de Charme* group (see page 57).

Iguaçu Falls & the South

Essentials

Sleeping
■ *on map, page 328*
Price codes: see inside front cover
There are some 90 places to stay in Curitiba; contact the tourist office for a full list

Note that although prices are high, most hotels will give you a discount of 10%-30% (some even 40%) if you pay in cash or with a cheque, but not normally if you use a credit card. Nearly all hotels include morning coffee, if not full breakfast. Service charge is usually 10%.

L *Bourbon & Tower*, R Cândido Lopes 102, T3224001, F3222282. Most luxurious in centre. **L** *Grand Hotel Rayon*, R Visconde de Nacar 1424, T3226006, F3224004. **AL** *Lancaster*, R Voluntários da Pátria 91, T/F2238953. Tourist class. **AL** *Slaviero Palace*, Sen Alencar Guimarães 50, T3227271, F2222398. Central. **A** *Caravelle Palace*, R Cruz Machado 282, T3225757, F2234443. First class. **A** *Climax*, R Dr Murici 411, T3227887, F2256165. Good value, popular. **A** *Condor*, Av 7 de Setembro 1866, T/F2620322. Breakfast. Recommended. **A** *Curitiba Palace*, R Ermelino de Leão 45, T3228081, F3223356. Central, airy modern hotel with vast rooms, 24-hour restaurant, pool, great value. Highly recommended. **A** *Del Rey*, R Ermelino de Leão 18, T/F3223242. Good restaurant. **A** *Doral Torres*, R Mariano Torres 951, T3622424, F2647929. Good breakfast. **A** *Jaraguá*, Av Pres Afonso Camargo 279, T3622022, F2647763. Noisy, good breakfast. Recommended. **A** *Ouro Verde*, R Dr Murici 419, T3225454, F2256165. Standard class. **A** *Savoy*, R João Negrão 568, T/F2237191. **A** *Tourist Universo*, Praça Gen Osório 63, T3220099, F2235420. Satellite TV, good restaurant. Recommended. **B** *Costa Brava Palace*, R Francisco Torres 386, T2627172. Restaurant. Well recommended. **B** *Filadélfia*, R Gen Carneiro 1094, 4 blocks from station through market, T2645244. Good breakfast. **B** *Tibagi*, R Carlos de Carvalho 9, T2233141, F2331811. Central business hotel. **C** *Cervantes*, R Alfredo Bufrem 66, T2229593. Amazing breakfast. Recommended. **C** *King's*, Av Silva Jardim 264, T3228444. Good apartment hotel, secure. Highly recommended. **C** *Nova Lisboa*, Av 7 de Setembro 1948, T2641944. With breakfast, bargain for cheaper rates without breakfast. Recommended. **C** *O'Hara*, R 15 de Novembro 770, T2326044. Good location, fan, excellent breakfast, parking. **C** *Paraty*, R Riachueto 30, T2231355. Central, apartments with kitchen, with breakfast, clean, spacious, good. **C** *Regência*, R Alfredo Bufrem 40, T2234557. With breakfast, good value, excellent. **D** *Inca*, R João Negrão 370, T2238563. Breakfast OK, clean, friendly, safe, German spoken, good. **D** *Itamarati*, Tibagi 950, T2229063. Fan, garage, good breakfast, showers can be dangerous, rather run down. **E** *Lusitano*, R João Negrão 420, T3232232. Basic, clean, front rooms noisy. **E** *Solar*, Jaime Reis 445. Basic but adequate. **F** *Pensão*, R Gen Carneiro 657. Basic, clean, good. There are good hotels southeast of the centre in the vicinity of the Rodoferroviária, but the cheaper ones are close to the wholesale market, which operates noisily throughout the night (there are many hotels so don't settle for a bad one).

Youth hostels **E** pp *AJ de Curitiba*, Av Padre Agostinho 645, Mercês, Curitiba PR, CEP 80430-050, T2332746, F2332834, ajcwb@uol.com.br. IYHA. Youth hostel association for Paraná is located here. For those with ISIC student cards try **E** *Casa dos Estudantes*, Parque Passeio Público, north side. Four nights or more. **E** *Casa do Estudante Luterano Universitario*, R Pr Cavalcanti, T2238981. Good.

Camping *Camping Clube do Brasil*, BR-116, Km 84, 16 km in the direction of São Paulo, T3586634.

Eating

Arabic *Clube Sírio Libanês*, R Padre Germano Mayer 1347, Alto da XV, T2626981. *Oriente Arabe*, R Ebano Pereira 26, 1st floor, T2232708. Excellent, huge Arab lunch.

Churrasco *Badida*, Av Batel 1486, Batel, T2430473. *Boi Gordo*, Av Victor Ferreira do Amaral 1088, Tarumã, T2623711. *Churrascão Colônia*, Av Manoel Ribas 3250, Vista Alegre, T3358686. *Devon's*, R Lysimaco Ferreira da Costa 436, Centro Cívico, T2547073. *OK*, Av das Torres 4600, Uberaba, T2762615. *Paiol*, R João Negrão 2400, Prado Velho, T3323830. *Per Tutti*, Av das Torres 2958, Guabirotuba, T2785422.

French *Boulevard*, R Voluntários da Pátria, T2248244. Closed Sunday. Good but pricey. *Île de France*, Praça 19 de Dezembro 538, T2239962. Expensive, closed Sunday. *Le Pistou*, R Col Dulcídio 333, Batel, T2234964. French restaurants also in the hotels *Rayon, Bourbon* and *Slaviero Palace*.

German *Cantina do Eisbein*, Av dos Estados 863, Água Verde. Owner Egon is friendly, duck specialities. Highly recommended (US$15 for 2). Closed Mondays. *Scharzwald*, Lg da Ordem 63. Evenings only except Sundays.

Italian *Bologna – Famiglia Caliceti*, R Carlos de Carvalho 1367, Batel, T2237102. Good food. *Cascatinha*, Av Manoel Ribas 4455. *Dom Antônio*, Av Manoel Ribas 6121. Excellent. *Famíglia Fadanelli*, Av Manoel Ribas 5667. *Porta Romana*, Av Manoel Ribas 4330. *Madalosso*, Av Manoel Ribas 5875. Enormous Italian self-service, allegedly the second largest in the world, cheap. Recommended. *A Sacristia*, R João Manuel 197. Pizzeria, bar, very good. *Salão Italiano*, R Padre G Mayer 1095, Cristo Rei. Good Brazilian and Italian food. *Scavollo*, R Emiliano Perneta 924, Batel, T2252244. *Velho Madalosso*, Av Manoel Ribas 5852, T2731014. *Veneza*, Av Manoel Ribas 6860.

Nearby Santa Felicidade, northeast of the centre, is a good area for Italian food and local red wine

Oriental *China Express*, R Mcal Deodoro 791. Chinese and Japanese, good buffet, pay by weight. *Mali*, R Padre Germano Mayer 1480, Hugo Lange, T2649152. Japanese. *Mikado*, R São Francisco 126. Good Japanese, vegetarian, lunch only. *Nakaba*, R Nunes Machado 56. Huge set Japanese meal under US$10. *Tung Lock*, R Prudente de Morais 175, Mercês, T3359399. Chinese.

Portuguese *Adega do Marquês*, Al Dr Muricy 135, T2245724. In the centre. *Alpendre*, R Visconde do Rio Branco 1046, in the centre, T2245694. Good food. *Camponesa do Minho*, R Padre Anchieta 978, Mercês, T3361312.

Seafood *Albatroz*, R Mateus 2869, Taboão, T2539309. *Ancoradouro*, Av Água Verde 663, Água Verde, T2428551. *Marinheiro*, R Bispo Dom José 2315, Batel, T2433828. *Peixe Frito*, Av Manoel Ribas 5438, Santa Felicidade, T2732630.

Swiss *Helvétia*, R Ubaldino do Amaral 1191, Alto da XV, T2627383. *Matterhorn*, Mateus Leme 575, São Francisco, T2336115. *Challet Suisse*, R Francisco Dallalibera 1428, Santa Felicidade, T2731223. *Chez Artur*, Av Des Hugo Simas 2617, Pilarzinho, T3386758.

Vegetarian *Greenland*, R 15 de Novembro 540, T2323813. Recommended. *Panini*, R da Glória 307. Recommended for buffet lunches (US$4 with meat; US$2.50 vegetarian) in a charming house. *Super Vegetariano*, R Pres Faria 121, T2236277, Cruz Machado 217, R Dr Murici 315. Lunch and dinner Monday-Friday, very good and cheap buffet. *Vherde Jante*, R Pres Faria 481, Centro, T2251627. Very good, open in evening.

Most closed at night

Fast food *Kisco*, 7 de Setembro near Tibagi. Good, huge *prato do dia*, US$4, friendly. Cheap food also near the old railway station and good meals in the bus station. Close to the Rodoferroviária is the market, where there are a couple of *lanchonetes*. Hot sweet wine sold on the streets in winter helps keep out the cold. For addicts, there are *McDonald's*, and takeaway Chinese and pizzas. Restaurants offering buffets are usually good value at around US$12.

Rua 24 Horas, see above, an indoor street full of bars and cafés, open 24 hours. *London Pub*, São Francisco 350, São Francisco. Recommended.

Bars & nightclubs

Cinema *Shopping Curitiba*, Praça Oswaldo Cruz 2698, T3261412. *Shopping Novo Batel*, T2222107. *Shopping Center Água Verde*, T2428741. *Shopping Crystal*, R Comendador Araújo 731, T3233061, and other places show films from all over the

Entertainment

Iguaçu Falls & the South

world. Tickets are usually US$4-5 Monday-Thursday, and US$6-8 at weekends. Best to look in the newspaper for music and what's on in the bars, clubs and theatres. *Gazeta do Povo* has an arts and what's on section called *Caderno*.

Theatre Teatro Guaíra, R 15 de Novembro, T3222628. Plays and revues (also has free events – get tickets early in the day). Teatro Paiol, in the old arsenal, R Col Zacarias, T3221525. Ópera de Arame, R João Gava, T2529637; Opera house. Teatro Universitário de Curitiba (TUC). Teatro Novelas Curitibanas, R Carlos Cavalcanti 1222, T2338552. Teatro Fernanda Montenegro, Shopping Novo Batel, T2244986.

Festivals *Ash Wednesday* (half-day); *Maundy Thursday* (half-day); **8 September** Our Lady of Light.

Shopping For souvenirs and handicrafts, try *Lojas Leve Curitiba*, at several locations, R 24 Horas, Afonso Pena airport, Ópera de Arame, Jardim Botánico, Memorial de Curitiba. *Lojas de Artesanato*, Casa de Artesanato Centro, R Mateus Leme 22, T3524021. *Lojas de Artesanato 'Feito Aquí'*, Dr Muricy 950, International Airport and Shopping Mueller. Feira de Arte e Artesanato, Praça Garibáldi, Sunday 0900-1400. Curitiba is a good place to buy clothes and shoes. *H Stern* jewellers at Mueller Shopping Centre. Bookshop: *O Livro Técnico*, Shopping Itália, R João Negrão and Mcal Deodoro.

Sports **Golf** Graciosa Country Club, Av Munhoz da Rocha 1146. Nine holes.

Transport **Local Car hire**: *Localiza*, at the airport and Av Cândido de Abreu 336, T2530330; *Interlocadora*, at the airport, T3811370, F3324648.

Buses: there are several route types on the integrated transport system and you are advised to pick up a map with details. There are 25 transfer terminals along the exclusive busways and trunk routes, allowing integration between all the different routes. **Express** are red, often articulated, and connect the transfer terminals to the city centre, pre-paid access, they use the 'tubo' bus stops; **Feeder** orange conventional buses connect the terminals to the surrounding neighbourhoods; **Interdistrict** green conventional or articulated buses run on circular routes, connecting transfer terminals and city districts without passing through the centre; **Direct or speedy** silver grey buses use the 'tubo' stations (3 km apart on average), to link the main districts and connect the surrounding municipalities with Curitiba; **Conventional** yellow buses operate on the normal road network between the surrounding municipalities, the Integration Terminals and the city centre; **City circular** white mini buses circle the major transport terminals and points of interest in the traditional city centre area. There are 221 'tubo' bus stops with covered, circular shelters, which allow ground level, pre-paid boarding and are no problem for wheelchairs; all bus stops have maps, but often in a rather poor condition.

Long distance Air: there are 2 airports: Afonso Pena, 21 km away for international and national flights, T3811515, and Bacacheri for military and commercial flights, T2562121. There are buses to the centre and bus station as well as taxis. Bus 208 goes to Afonso Pena airport every 25 minutes, US$0.60, 30 minutes from hotels *Presidente* and *Araucária* with a stop near the bus terminal.

Flights to Campinas, Cascavel, Foz do Iguaçu, Joinville, Londrina, Maringá, Porto Alegre, Rio de Janeiro and São Paulo.

Trains: Rodoferroviária, Av Afonso Camargo, T3229585, T3234007 (Serra Verde Express). Passenger trains to **Paranaguá**, see below.

Buses: short-distance bus services within the metropolitan region (up to 40 km) begin at Terminal Guadalupe at R João Negrão, T3218611. The Terminal Rodoviário/Estação Rodoferroviária is on Av Afonso Camargo, T3224344/4846, for other cities in Paraná and other states. There are restaurants, banks, bookshops, shops, phones, Post Office, pharmacy, tourist agency, tourist office and other public services.

Frequent buses to **São Paulo** (6 hours, US$10.25-12.50) and **Rio de Janeiro** (12 hours, US$25). To **Foz do Iguaçu**, 10 a day, 10 hours, US$15; **Porto Alegre**, 10 hours; **Florianópolis**, 4½ hours; **Blumenau** 4 hours, US$5.50, 3 daily with *Penha/Catarinense*; good service to most destinations in Brazil. *Pluma* bus to **Buenos Aires** and to **Asunción**. *TTL* runs to **Montevideo**, 26 hours, 0340 departure (*semi-cama*).

Road: if travelling by car to **Porto Alegre** or **Montevideo**, the inland road (BR-116) is preferable to the coastal highway (BR-101). The BR-116 from Curitiba to São Paulo is being made into a dual carriageway. Where this work is incomplete, the road is tortuous, dangerous and full of huge trucks.

Directory

Banks *ABN/AMRO*, Av Cândido Abreu 304, Centro Cívico, T2522233. Changes TCs, Dutch bank, also arranges money transfer from Netherlands, paid in *reais* (2-3 days). *Bradesco*, R 15 de Novembro, Visa ATM. *Citibank*, R Mcal Deodoro 711, T2216703. *Credicard*, R Saldanha Marinho 1439, Bigorrillo. Cash with Mastercard. *Diplomata*, R Pres Faria 145 in the arcade. *Transoceânica*, R Mcal Deodoro 532, English and German spoken. *Triangle Turismo Travel*, Praça Gen Osório 213. Cash and TCs. *Sydney Turismo*, R Mcal Deodoro 301.

Communications Post Office: Main post office is at Mcal Deodoro 298. Branches at R 15 de Novembro and R Pres Faria. *UPS*, T2626180. **Telecommunications:** Galeria Minerva, R 15 de Novembro. Information, T102. **Internet:** *Tripp's Bar*, Av NS Aparecida 405, Seminário.

Cultural centres *Sociedade Brasileira de Cultura Inglesa* (British Council), R Gen Carneiro 679, CP 505. *Instituto Goethe*, R Schaffenberg, near Military Museum, Mon-Thu 1500-1900, Library, Mon-Tue till 2130.

Embassies & consulates *Austria*, R Cândido Hartmann 570, Edif Champagnat, 28th floor, T3361166. Mon-Fri 1000-1300. *Denmark*, R Prof Francisco Ribeiro 683, Caixa Postal 321, T8432211, F8431443. *Germany*, Av J Gualberto 1237, T2524244. *Netherlands*, R Mcal Floriano Peixoto 96, conj 172, T2220097. Consul Tony Bruinjé, open 1400-1700, except emergencies. *Switzerland*, Av Mcal F Peixoto 228, Edif Banrisul, conj 1104/5, T2237553. *Uruguay*, R Voluntários da Pátria 475, 18th floor.

Hospitals & medical services Emergency, T192 or T100. *Cajuru Hospital*, Av São José 300, T3621100. *Evangélico*, Al Augusto Stellfeld 1908, T3224141. Both deal with emergencies.

Laundry R C Laurindo 63, next to theatre. US$3 for 5 kg.

Tour companies & travel agents *BMP Turismo* (American Express), R Brig Franco, 1845, T2247560. *Stella Barros* (Thomas Cook), Av Visconde de Guarapuava 5170, T3424080, F3421266.

Tourist information The Department of Tourism is at R da Glória 362, 3rd floor, T3524021, with an information kiosk at R das Flores Galeria Schaffer. *Paranatur*, R Deputado Mário de Barros 1290, 3rd floor, Centro Cívico, Edif Caetano Munhoz da Rocha, T2546933, F2546109. www.pr.gov.br/turismo, for the west coast, www.pr.gov.br/westcoast, and for the east coast, www.pr.gov.br/plitoral. For the Disque Turismo, T2541516. There are also booths at R das Flores, Loja 18, at the Rodoferroviária and the airport, helpful, English spoken, but no maps. Free maps from R Ebano Pereira 187, 5th floor. Free weekly leaflet, *Bom Programa*, available in shops, cinemas, paper stands etc. *Guía Turística de Curitiba e Paraná*, annual, US$4, on sale at all kiosks, has been recommended.

Useful addresses Federal police, Dr Muricy 814. For visa extensions 1000-1600.

Voltage 110 V 60 cycles.

Iguaçu Falls & the South

Curitiba to Paranaguá

The most spectacular railway journey in Brazil gives access to Parana's Atlantic coast. Popular expeditions during the summer are by paved road or rail to Paranaguá. There are numerous tunnels with sudden views of deep gorges and high peaks and waterfalls as the train rumbles over dizzy bridges and viaducts. Near Banhado station (Km 66) is the waterfall of Véu da Noiva; from the station at Km 59, the mountain range of Marumbi can be reached, see below.

Transport There are 2 trains running on the line from Curitiba to Paranaguá: the *Litorina*, a modern a/c railcar with on board service with bilingual staff, which stops at the viewpoint at the Santuário da Nossa Senhora do Cadeado and Morretes; hand luggage only; tickets can be bought 2 days in advance; departs Friday, Saturday, Sunday 0900, returns 1700, US$11 one-way; and the *Trem Classe Turística*, which stops at Marumbi and Morretes, buy tickets 2 days in advance, departs 0800 daily except Monday, returns 1600, *convencional* US$8.50, *turístico* US$10, *executivo* US$11 (with English-speaking guide). Schedules change frequently; check times in advance. For information and reservations, *Serra Verde Express*, T3234007, T/F3234009. Tickets sold at the Rodoferroviária, Portão 8, Curitiba, 0800-1200, 1330-1800. Sit on the left-hand side on journey from Curitiba. On cloudy days there's little to see on the higher parts. The train is usually crowded on Saturday and Sunday. Many travellers recommend returning by bus (1½ hours, buy ticket immediately on arrival, US$6.50), if you do not want to stay 4½ hours. A tour bus meets the train and offers a tour of town and return to Curitiba.

Antonina and Morretes

Colour map 5, grid A5

You can also visit the port of **Antonina** (*population* 18,500), which is not on the main route, and **Morretes** (*population* 15,000), which is on the main route. These two sleepy colonial towns can be reached by bus on the old Graciosa road, which is almost as scenic as the railway. Fourteen kilometres north of Morretes is the beautiful village of **São João de Graciosa**, two kilometres beyond which is a flower reserve. The Graciosa road traverses the **Marumbi** range for 12 kilometres, with six rest stops with fire grills, shelters and camping. Marumbi, a state park and area of special tourist interest, is very beautiful. You can also hike the original trail which follows the road and passes the rest-stops. Take food, water and plenty of insect repellent.

Curitiba environs

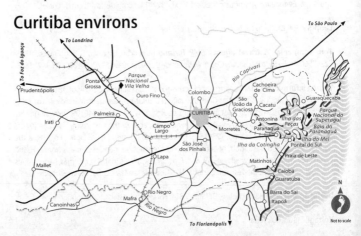

Morretes **B** *Porto Real Palace*, R Visc do Rio Branco 85, T4621344. **C** *Nhundiaquara*, R Gen Carneiro, in town centre, T4621228. Well located but hot and cramped, good restaurant. Try *barreado*, beef cooked for 24 hours. A highly recommended eating place is *Armazém Romanus*, R Visconde do Rio Branco 141.

Sleeping & eating

Transport Buses from **Paranaguá** to Morretes at 1830, US$1, to Antonina, stopping *en route* at Morretes, 6 a day (US$1.50). Twelve buses daily Morretes-Curitiba US$2; 11 buses a day Curitiba-Antonina.

Paranaguá

Chief port of the state of Paraná and one of the main coffee-exporting ports, Paranaguá was founded in 1585. It is on a lagoon 29 kilometres from the open sea and is approached via the Baia de Paranaguá, dotted with picturesque islands. Paranaguá is also a free port for Paraguay.

Population: 115,500
Phone code: 041
268 km S of Santos
Colour map 5, grid A5

The fort of **Nossa Senhora dos Prazeres** was built in 1767 on a nearby island; one hour's boat trip. The former Colêgio dos Jesuitas, a fine baroque building, has been converted into a **Museu de Arqueologia e Artes Populares**. ■ *Tuesday-Sunday 1200-1700, US$1*. Other attractions are a 17th-century fountain, the church of **São Benedito**, and the shrine of **Nossa Senhora do Rocio**, two kilometres from town. There are restaurants and craft shops near the waterfront. The part of town between the waterfront, railway station and new bus station has been declared a historic area.

Sights

There are cruises on Paranaguá Bay by launch, daily from Cais do Mercado.
   Matinhos (*population* 11,500), 40 kilometres south, is a medium sized Mediterranean-style resort, invaded by surfers in October for the Paraná surf competition. *Praia e Sol* (**B**), R União 35, T4521922, has been recommended. There is the basic, cheap *Bolamar* and four campsites in the vicinity.
   Eight kilometres south is **Caiobá**, at the mouth of a bay, the other side of which is **Guaratuba** (*population* 32,000), which is less built up than Caiobá. The ferry between the two towns is frequent and is a beautiful crossing, free for pedestrians, US$1.50 for cars. Both towns have a few hotels but most close in winter; there is also camping at Guaratuba. The *Sol Nascente* restaurant, R Vicente Machado 967, is superb.

Excursions

AL *Camboa*, R João Estevão, in the Centro Histórico, T/F4232121. **A** *Portofino*, Av Atlântica 4409, Balneário Porto Fino, T/F4581488. Very nice. **C** *Auana*, R Correia de Freitas 110, T4226531. Good value. Recommended. **E** *Karibe*, F Simas 86, T4221177. Good value, shared bath, with breakfast. **D** *Litoral*, R Correia de Freitas 66. Without breakfast, comfortable. **Camping** *Arco Iris*, Praia de Leste, on the beach, 29 km south of Paranaguá, T4582001.

Sleeping

Aquárius, Av Gabriel de Lara 40. Good but not cheap seafood. *Bela Vista*, on the waterfront. Open in the evenings when many places shut, good, typical atmosphere, good food at reasonable prices, *prato do mar* US$8.50 for 1 person, US$12 for 2. *Bobby's*, Faria Sobrinho 750. Highly recommended, especially for seafood. *Casa do Barreado*, R Antônio da Cruz 9. Good local food and drink. *Danúbio Azul*, 15 de Novembro 91. Good fish and view of river. There are cheap restaurants in the old market building, and plenty of cheap ones near the markets on the waterfront. The *Yacht Club*, beyond *Danúbio Azul*, is impressive and has a good bar.

Eating

Iguaçu Falls & the South

Transport   **Car hire** *Interlocadora*, T4234425, F3324648. **Buses** All operated by *Graciosa*. To Curitiba, US$4, many, 1½ hours (only the 1500 to Curitiba takes the old Graciosa road); direct to **Rio** at 1915, 15 hours, US$23. Eight buses a day to **Guaratuba** (US$1, 2 hours), **Caiobá** and **Matinhos**. The buses to Guaratuba go on the ferry, as do direct buses to Joinville, 0740, 1545.

Directory   **Banks** *Banco do Brasil*, Largo C Alcindino 27. *Bradesco*, R Faria Sobrinho 188. *Câmbio*, R Faria Sobrinho. For cash. **Tourist information** *Funcultur*, R Des Hugo Simas 373, T4232155. Kiosk outside the railway station.

Ilha do Mel

Colour map 5, grid A5   Ilha do Mel is at the mouth of the Baía de Paranaguá and was of strategic use in the 18th century. The Fortaleza da Barra was built in 1767 on the orders of King José I of Portugal, to defend what was one of the principal ports in the country. In 1850, a British warship captured three illegal slave trading ships, giving rise to a battle known as *Combate Cormorant*. The lighthouse, Farol das Conchas, was built in 1872 to guide shipping into the bay. The Gruta das Encantadas is surrounded with myths and legends about beautiful mermaids, enchanting all who came near them.

The island is now an ecological reserve (no cars permitted and visitors limited to 5,000 per day), but is well-developed for tourism and is accessible by boat from Paranaguá or Pontal do Sul. Its four villages, **Nova Brasilia, Praia das Encantadas, Praia da Fortaleza** and **Farol**, are linked by pathways. Bicycles and kayaks can be hired. The beaches, caves, bays and hill walks are beautiful. The hike to the fort is very rewarding. April-October are very rainy months here and there are very persistent *mutucas* (biting insects) in November, so December-March is the best time to visit. Electricity on the island 1000-0200. From Praia das Encantadas to Nova Brasília there are boats (US$10, or US$2 per person if more than five), or you can walk on a track (1½-2 hours) or follow the coast, walking in the sea. From Nova Brasília, a 20-minute walk leads to El Farol for good views.

Beaches   Praia das Encantadas is more suitable for swimming than Nova Brasília. Praia Grande is a deserted, horse shoe shaped beach on the east side with the best surfing. Fortaleza is one of the most popular beaches and can be crowded, with restaurants and *pousadas*. In between Praia de Fora and Praia das Encantadas, on the south point, is the Gruta das Encantadas, the rocky area of natural pools where mermaids are said to lurk (see above).

Sleeping   **Praia do Farol** **B** *Pousadinha*, Praia das Conchas, T973366. Good beds, fan, bath, mosquito nets, staff speak various languages, excellent breakfast, delightful rooms. **B** *Pousada Praia do Farol*, in front of the pier, T9783433. With breakfast. **C** *Estalagem Ancoradouro*. With breakfast. At Praia das Encantadas: **C** *Pousada Estrela do Mar*, T9782010. **C** *Pousada Tia Maria*, in front of the pier, T9783352. You can rent a fisherman's house – ask for *Valentim's Bar*, or for Luchiano. Behind the bar is *Cabanas Dona Maria*, shared showers, cold water; food available if you ask in advance.

Praia Nova Brasília B *Pousada Pôr do Sol*, Praia do Limoeiro, T9781038. **C** *Estalagem Pirata*, wonderful house on the beach, music, easy atmosphere, run by Roberto and Darlene. *Pousada Portal*, T9783534. With breakfast. Good.

Praia da Fortaleza B *Parque Hotel Ilha do Mel*, T9783322.

Praia das Encantadas Many *pousadas* and houses with rooms to rent (shared kitchen and living room). Shop around, prices from about US$10 double, low season, mid-week.

Camping There are mini campsites with facilities at Encantadas, Farol and Brasília. Camping is possible on the more deserted beaches (good for surfing). If camping, watch out for the tide, watch possessions and beware of the *bicho de pé* which burrows into feet (remove with a needle and alcohol) and the *borrachudos* (discourage with Autan repellent).

Eating *Forró do Zorro* (see below). Expensive restaurant. *Lanchonete Paraíso*, nice meeting place, good food and music. *Toca do Abutre*, Restaurant 1 km from Nova Brasília.

Bars & nightclubs In summer and at holiday times the island is very crowded with an active nightlife and Forró dancing, whilst at other times it is very quiet. Bars *Barbeira* and *Forró do Zorro*, Praia das Encantadas. Dancing Thursday-Sunday, lively and popular.

Transport There are 2 ways of getting to Ilha do Mel: By ferry from Paranaguá, Saturday at 1000, Monday and Friday at 1500, 1 hour 40 minutes, boats with a capacity of 40, 60 or 80 passengers leave from R Gen Carneiro (R da Praia) in front of the Tourist Information kiosk; by ferry from Pontal do Paraná (Pontal do Sul), daily from 0800 to 1800 (last boat from island to mainland) every hour at weekends, less frequently in the week. From Paranaguá, take the bus to Pontal do Sul (many daily, 1½ hours, US$0.60), then wait for the ferry, US$3.25. At the ferry point are souvenir and handicraft stalls. The last bus back to Paranaguá leaves at 2200. Alternatively, go to the small harbour in Paranaguá and ask for a boat to Ilha do Mel, US$5 one-way (no shade). Make sure the ferry goes to your chosen destination (Nova Brasília or Encantadas are the most developed areas).

Ilha do Mel

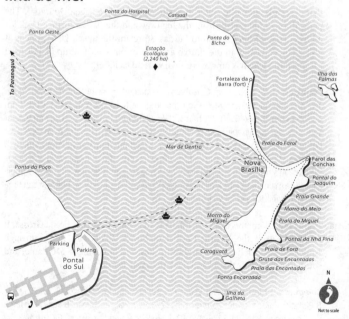

Iguaçu Falls & the South

Superagui National Park The islands of Superagui and Peças, 21,400 hectares together, form one of the principal stations for research into Atlantic rainforest, its flora and fauna. Just north of Ilha do Mel, the park is reached by regular boat service from Guarequeçaba, an interesting trip through the mangroves which separate the islands from the mainland, or from Paranaguá (negotiate a fare by fishing boat at the docks near the Mercado do Café). Boats disembark at Superagui village, which has no electricity, a simple restaurant and a small *pousada*. It is also possible to rent a room from villagers, and camping is allowed at various sites. Many threatened and migratory species of birds are seen here – kingfishers, storks, herons and parrots among others – and animals such as the rare yellow-fronted alligator, otters, jaguars and black-faced monkeys. There is superb swimming from deserted beaches, but watch out for stinging jelly fish. Contact Ibama on the island, two kilometres out of the village, for information. Commercially organized tours are available, T2520180/3387060.

Guarequeçaba is also an environmental protection area, preserving Atlantic coastal forest, a lagoon estuary complex, archaeological sites and traditional communities. For information T041-3336163, Instituto Ambiental do Paraná. Guarequeçaba is hard to reach by road. It is best to take a boat from Paranaguá, 1½ hours.

Vila Velha On the road to Ponta Grossa is Vila Velha, now a state park, 97 kilometres from Curitiba, 10 from Ponta Grossa: the sandstone rocks have been weathered into most fantastic shapes. Many have also been defaced by thoughtless tourists. The Lagoa Dourada, surrounded by forests, is close by. Nearby are the Furnas, three waterholes, the deepest of which has a lift (US$1 – not always working) that descends almost to water level (the same level as Lagoa Dourada). The park office is 300 metres from the highway and the park a further 1½ kilometres. The entrance is also to Furnas, so retain the ticket, US$1; opens at 0800. You can camp in the church grounds or put your tent up in a disused campground which is now overgrown with no facilities.

Transport Take a bus from **Curitiba** to the national park, not to the town 20 km away. Ask the bus driver where you should get off. *Princesa dos Campos* bus from Curitiba at 0730 and 0930, 1½ hours, US$5.65 (return bus passes park entrance at 1600); it may be advisable to go to Ponta Grossa and return to Curitiba from there. Last bus from Vila Velha car park to Ponta Grossa at 1800. Bus from Vila Velha at 1310, 1610 and 1800, US$1, 4½ km to turn-off to Furnas (another 15 minutes' walk) and Lagoa Dourada (it's not worth walking from Vila Velha to Furnas because it's mostly uphill along the main road). Allow all day if visiting all 3 sites (unless you hitch, or can time the buses well, it's a lot of walking).

Ponta Grossa
Population: 253,500
Phone code: 042
Altitude: 969m

About 117 kilometres from Curitiba, the road inland reaches Ponta Grossa. It now calls itself the 'World Capital of Soya'. Roads run north through Apucarana, which has hotels and campsites, and Londrina to São Paulo, and south to Rio Grande do Sul and the Uruguayan border.

Sleeping and eating A *Vila Velha Palace*, R Balduíno Taques 123, T/F2252200. **B** *Planalto Palace*, R 7 de Setembro 652, T2252122. Plain and clean. **B** *Scha Fransky*, R Col Francisco Ribas 104, T2252499, F2222794. Very good breakfast. **C** *Central*, R Col Francisco Ribas 162. With fan and basin. **C** *Gravina*, R Col Bittencourt 92, T2240503. With bath. **D** *Esplanada*, in bus station. With bath and breakfast, quiet, safe. **E** *Luz*, near railway station. Basic. **E** *Casimiri*, next door. Often full.

Casa Verde, near the *Central*. Lunch only. Recommended. There are cheap restaurants near the railway station.

Transport Car hire: *Localiza*, Av Visconde de Mauá 1950, T2293161. **Buses**: *Princesa dos Campos* to **Curitiba**, 6 a day, 2 hours, US$4.25; same company to **Iguaçu**, 4 daily, 9 hours, US$24. To **Vila Velha** at 0700 and 0900 (return bus at 1800).

If driving from Curitiba to Foz do Iguaçu (or vice versa), **Guarapuava** makes a useful stopover town. It is 258 kilometres from Curitiba and 389 kilometres from Foz. There is *Hotel América* (**C**), which is excellent value, and others. A number of bus services from Paraná state to Porto Alegre (*Aguia Branca, Unesul*) and to Campo Grande, Cuiabá and Porto Velho (*Eucatur*), commence at **Cascavel** (*population* 220,000) further south on the Curitiba-Iguaçu road. It has hotels including *Grand Prix* (**B**), Av Brasil 5202, T/F2254949, safe, good breakfast, parking, and *Rodotur* (**D**), RC Gomes, one block south of Av Brasil (turn at the two-metre high gold thumb in mid-street), cheaper without TV, clean, safe, parking, good. It takes 27 hours between Curitiba and Cascavel and costs US$25.

Northwest Paraná

In Alto Paraná in the extreme northwest of the State, connections have traditionally been with São Paulo rather than with Curitiba. In 1930 four Japanese and two Germans arrived in Londrina, later developed by a British company. Today it is a city with skyscrapers, modern steel and glass cathedral, and wide streets. There is a small museum at Sergipe and Rio de Janeiro.

Londrina
Population: 412,500
Phone code: 043

Sleeping AL *Crystal Palace*, R Quintino Bocaiúva 15, T/F3212526, crystal@inbrapenet.com.br. Restaurant, convention centre. **B** *Coroados*, Sen Souza Naves 814, T3237690. Standard. **B** *Triúnfo*, R Prof João Cândido 39, T3235054. Laundry, restaurant. **D** *Cravinho*, R Minas Gerais 88. Clean, friendly. **Youth hostel** R Gomes Carneiro 315, Centro Esportivo Moringão.

Transport Car hire: *Localiza*, Av Juscelino Kubitschek 2245, Londrina, T3377979. **Buses**: Londrina and Maringá are good points for connections between the south (**Porto Alegre**), **Foz do Iguaçu** and Mato Grosso do Sul (**Campo Grande**). Bus Londrina-Porto Alegre takes 22 hours; to Campo Grande 11 hours, via Presidente Prudente (see page 254). Londrina-Ponta Grossa, US$12, 5½ hours.

Eighty kilometres west of Londrina, Maringá was founded in 1947 and is now an important centre for textiles. About a third of the town is Japanese. There is a small conical cathedral and Parque Ingá is shady, with a Japanese garden.

Maringá
Population: 268,000
Phone code: 044

Sleeping and eating A *Deville*, Av Herval 26, next to the cathedral, T2261001, F2261977. **D** *Fatima*, Av Brasil, T2242321. With breakfast, clean, hot shower, TV. *Casa Portuguesa, Com Certeza*, R Santos Dumont 3226, T2246160, serves good Portuguese food.

Iguaçu Falls & the South

Iguaçu Falls

The Iguaçu Falls (As Cataratas do Iguaçu, spelt Iguazú in Spanish) are the most overwhelming and spectacular waterfalls in South America. They are also one of, if not the, major natural attractions in Brazil. Situated on the Rio Iguaçu/Iguazú (in Guaraní guazú is big and I is for water), the border between Argentina and Brazil, they lie 19 kilometres upstream from the confluence of the Rio Iguaçu with the Rio Alto Paraná. Bridges connect the Brazilian city of Foz do Iguaçu with the Argentine town of Puerto Iguazú and the Paraguayan city of Ciudad del Este.

History The first European visitor to the falls was the Spaniard Alvar Núñez Cabeza de Vaca in 1541, on his search for a connection between the Brazilian coast and the Río de la Plata: he named them the Saltos de Santa María. Though the falls were well known to the Jesuit missionaries, they were forgotten, except by local inhabitants, until the area was explored by a Brazilian expedition sent out by the Paraguayan president, Solano López, in 1863.

In the 20th century, the falls have become recognized globally as a major attraction. This did not impress Malcolm Slesser in the 1960s, though: "Except for a night on the tiles in Rio de Janeiro, Brazil's greatest tourist attraction is the Iguaçu falls where Argentina, Brazil and Paraguay meet. This huge cataract eclipses Niagara. These falls are a splendid frolic of 300 falls, 270 feet high, almost three miles wide, filling the place with spray. Here is a large government hotel, luxurious with absolutely nothing to do except eat, drink and lounge – and look at the falls. We did not go, on the principle that a waterfall was a waterfall." (*Brazil: Land without Limit*; London: George Allen and Unwin, 1969, pages 151-2). Don't follow his example!

Geography
The falls are 20m higher than Niagara and about half as wide again

The Iguaçu river basin extends over some 62,000 square kilometres. The river rises in the Brazilian hills near Curitiba at an altitude of around 1,200 metres, from where it flows for some 1,300 kilometres across the Paraná Plateau, a thick layer of very hard basalt lava formed as a result of a massive Triassic volcanic eruption over 100 million years ago. On its way it receives the waters of about 30 rivers before reaching the falls which lie at an altitude of 160 metres at the edge of the plateau. Above the main falls the river, sown with wooded islets, opens out to a width of four kilometres. There are rapids for 3½ kilometres above the falls: a 60 metres precipice over which the water plunges in 275 falls over a frontage of 2.7 kilometres at an average rate of 1,750 cubic metres a second (in 1992, after heavy rains, the rate rose to 29,000 cubic metres a second). The most spectacular part is the Garganta del Diablo, visited from the Argentine side (see below). Downstream is a 28 kilometre long gorge, stretching to the Río Alto Paraná and formed as the river has eroded its way back up the river.

Above the impact of the water, upon basalt rock, hovers a perpetual 30 metres high cloud of mist in which the sun creates blazing rainbows. Viewed from below, the tumbling water in its setting of begonias, orchids, fern and palms, with toucans, flocks of parrots and cacique birds, great dusky swifts dodging in and out of the very falls, and myriad butterflies (at least 500 different species), is majestically beautiful, especially outside the cool season (when the water is much diminished, as are the birds and insects).

Most of the falls lie in Argentina, but there are national parks on both sides of the falls: transport between the two parks is via the Ponte Tancredo Neves, as there is no crossing at the falls themselves.

The Brazilian park offers a superb panoramic view of the whole falls and is best visited in the morning when the light is better for photography. The Argentine park (which requires a day to explore properly) offers closer views of the individual falls and of the forest with its wildlife and butterflies, though to appreciate these properly you need to go early and get well away from the

How to visit

Between Oct–Feb daylight saving dates change each year, Brazil is 1 hr ahead of Argentina and, from Dec, 2 hrs ahead of Paraguay

Iguaçu Falls

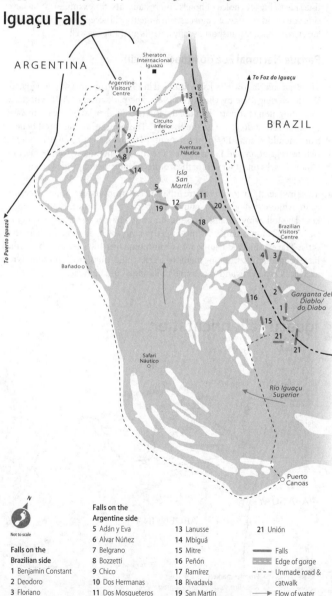

ARGENTINA

Sheraton Internacional Iguazú

▲ To Foz do Iguaçu

Argentine Visitors' Centre

B R A Z I L

13
10
6
Circuito Inferior
9
Aventura Náutica
17
8
14
Isla San Martín
5
11
12
20
19
18
Brazilian Visitors' Centre
4 3
Bañado
7
2
16
Garganta del Diablo/ do Diabo
1
15
21
21

To Puerto Iguazú

Safari Náutico

Rio Iguaçu Superior

Puerto Canoas

Rio Iguaçu Inferior

Iguaçu Falls & the South

N

Not to scale

Falls on the Brazilian side

1 Benjamin Constant
2 Deodoro
3 Floriano
4 Santa Maria

Falls on the Argentine side

5 Adán y Eva	13 Lanusse
6 Alvar Núñez	14 Mbiguá
7 Belgrano	15 Mitre
8 Bozzetti	16 Peñón
9 Chico	17 Ramírez
10 Dos Hermanas	18 Rivadavia
11 Dos Mosqueteros	19 San Martín
12 Escondido	20 Tres Mosqueteros

21 Unión

━━━ Falls
▬▬▬ Edge of gorge
----- Unmade road & catwalk
──▶ Flow of water

visitors areas. Both parks can, if necessary, be visited in a day, starting at about 0700, but the brisk pace needed for a rapid tour is exhausting for the non-athletic in the heat. Sunset from the Brazilian side is a worthwhile experience.

Busiest times are holiday periods and on Sunday, when helicopter tours over the falls from the Brazilian side are particularly popular. Both parks have visitors' centres, though the information provided by the Argentine Centre is far superior to that in the Brazilian Centre.

There are many advantages in staying in Foz and commuting to the Argentine side (a bigger choice of hotels and restaurants, for example). Whichever side you decide to stay on, most establishments will accept *reais*, pesos or dollars. Cross-border transport usually accepts guaraníes as well.

Parque Nacional Foz do Iguaçu (Brazil)

The Brazilian National Park was founded in 1939 and the area was designated a World Heritage Site by Unesco in 1986. The park covers 170,086 hectares, extending along the north bank of the Rio Iguaçu, then sweeping northwards to Santa Tereza do Oeste on the BR-277. The subtropical rainforest benefits from the added humidity in the proximity of the falls, creating an environment rich in vegetation and fauna. Given the massive popularity of the falls, the national parks on either side of the frontier are surprisingly little visited.

Fauna Most frequently encountered are little and red brocket deer, South American coati, white-eared opossum, and a sub-species of the brown capuchin monkey. The following are also present, but much harder to see: jaguar, ocelot, jaguarundi, puma, margay, white-lipped peccary, bush dog and southern river otter. The endangered tegu lizard is common. Over 100 species of butterflies have been identified, among them the electric blue *Morpho*, the poisonous red and black *heliconius* and species of Papilionidae and Pieridae.

Iguaçu Falls orientation

Related maps
A Iguaçu Falls,
page 343

Not to scale

▲ **Frontier markers** 2 Brazilian
1 Argentine 3 Paraguayan

The Macuco Safari

After about 20 minutes ride on the trailer, you get off and begin hiking your way down the side of the Iguaçu gorge to the Macuco Falls, which cascade into a deep dark plunge pool. Steps cut into the rock allow you to descend to the foot of the falls, but beware: they are slippery and steep. Stout walking shoes are a must. The tour is taken at a relaxed pace and there is no pressure to rush back up those steps. After the falls, you descend to the banks of the river, where you take to water in inflatable rafts capable of carrying 20 people. The ride is bumpy, but make sure you look up at the

steep sides of the gorge. As the boat comes up to the edge of the falls, there is a deafening roar from above as the boat begins to turn and the spray is so powerful you have to shut your eyes. You will get very wet. Plastic raincoats are sold at the launch site and plastic bags are provided for cameras if you ask. The view of the falls is unbeatable. Once back on dry land, you are whisked up to the top of the canyon by jeep to rejoin the trailer to the entrance. From here, a free shuttle bus transfers you through the park to the top of the falls.
Naomi Peirce

The birdlife is especially rewarding for birdwatchers. Five members of the toucan family can be seen: toco and red-breasted toucans, chestnut-eared araçari, saffron and spot-billed toucanets. In the bamboo stands you may see: spotted bamboowren, grey-bellied spinetail, several antshrikes, short-tailed ant-thrush. In the forest: rufous-thighed kite, black-and-white hawk-eagle, black-fronted piping-guan, blue ground dove, dark-billed cuckoo, black-capped screech-owl, surucua trogon, rufous-winged antwren, black-crowned tityra, red-ruffed fruitcrow, white-winged swallow, plush-crested jay, cream-bellied gnatcatcher, black-goggled and magpie tanagers, green-chinned euphonia, black-throated and utlramarine grosbeaks, yellow-billed cardinal, red-crested finch. (Bird and mammal information supplied by Douglas Trent, *Focus Tours*; see **Tours and tour operators**, page 30.)

From opposite the *Hotel das Cataratas* a 1½ kilometre paved walk runs part of the way down the cliff near the rim of the falls, giving a stupendous view of the whole Argentine side of the falls. It ends up almost under the powerful Floriano Falls: from here an elevator carries visitors to the top of the Floriano Falls (from 0800; US$0.50) and to a path leading to Porto Canoa (if there is a queue, it is easy and quick to walk up). A catwalk at the foot of the Floriano Falls gives a good view of the Garganta do Diabo. There are toilets and a lanchonete/restaurant on the path down and more toilets at the top of the elevator.

The **Macuco Safari Tour**, US$30 (Amex accepted), leaves from near the falls, with trailers taking the visitors down the trail (see box); guides speak Portuguese, English and Spanish; take insect repellent, highly recommended. *Macuco Safari de Barco*, Caixa Postal 509, 85851-001, Foz do Iguaçu, Paraná, T0XX45-5744464. Expeditions can also be organized, by prior arrangement, for photographers, botanists and others, and boat hire can be arranged for up to 80 people, by the hour, or by the day.

Helicopter tours over the falls leave from *Hotel das Cataratas*, US$60 per person, 10 minutes. Apart from disturbing visitors, the helicopters are also reported to present a threat to some bird species which are laying thinner-shelled eggs: the altitude has been increased, making the flight less attractive.

Park entry is US$3 (six *reais*, payable only in Brazilian currency), payable at the entrance. There is a *Banco do Brasil câmbio* at the entrance (0800-1900). If possible, visit on a weekday when the walks are less crowded. **NB** The Brazilian side of the falls is closed on Monday until 1300 for maintenance. Non-residents can eat at the *Hotel das Cataratas*, mid-day and evening buffets.

Iguaçu Falls & the South

Transport Buses: these leave Foz do Iguaçu, from the *Terminal Urbana* on Av Juscelino Kubitschek, opposite the Infantry Barracks. The green Transbalan service (marked 'Cataratas') goes to the falls every hour, 0715-1800, past the airport and *Hotel das Cataratas*, 40 minutes US$0.80 one-way, payable in *reais* only (the driver waits at the park entrance while passengers purchase entry tickets, which are checked by a park guard on the bus); the Parque Nacional bus runs every 22 minutes, US$0.40, to the park entrance only (from where you will need to take a 'Cataratas' bus the rest of the way, which works out more expensive). Both buses can also be picked up at any of the stops on Av Juscelino Kubitschek. Return buses 0800-1900. **Taxis**: US$4, plus US$5.50 per hour for waiting.

Many hotels organize tours to the falls: these have been recommended in preference to taxi rides. If visiting the Brazilian side from Puerto Iguazú by bus, ask the driver to let you off shortly after the border at the roundabout for the road to the falls (BR-469), where you can get another bus.

Parque Nacional Iguazú (Argentina)

Created in 1934, the park extends over an area of 67,620 hectares, most of which is covered by the same sub-tropical rainforest as on the Brazilian side. It is crossed by Route 101, a dirt road which runs southeast to Bernardo de Yrigoyen on the Brazilian frontier. Buses operate along this route in dry weather, offering a view of the park.

Fauna As in Brazil, very little of the fauna in the park can be seen around the falls: even on the nature trails described below you need to go in the early morning. Fauna include jaguars, tapirs, brown capuchin monkeys, collared anteaters and coatimundi. Among over 400 species of birds, the most commonly visible are the following: the black-crowned night heron, the black vulture, the plumed kite; the white-eyed parakeet; the blue-winged parrolet, the greater ani, the great dusky swift, the scale throated hermit, the suruca trogon, the Amazon kingfisher, the toco toucan, the tropical kingbird, the boat-billed flycatcher, the red-rumped cacique which builds hanging nests on pindo palms, and fruiteaters like the magpie tanager and the colourful purple-throated euphonia.

The falls From the Visitors' Centre, two sets of catwalks (the *Circuito Inferior*) lead down to the lower falls, but the catwalks to the **Garganta del Diablo** (Devil's Throat) were damaged by floods, most recently in 1986. Instead boats (US$4) link Puerto Canoas with the remains of the catwalks which lead to a viewing platform above the Garganta, particularly recommended in the evening when the light is best and the swifts are returning to roost on the cliffs, some behind the water. The catwalks and platform get very crowded in mid-morning after tour buses arrive. Puerto Canoas can be reached by bus – see below – or by car (parking US$1). Projects to renew the entire catwalk network and to build a railway line from the Visitors' Centre to Puerto Canoas have been approved.

Below the falls, a free ferry leaving regularly, subject to demand, connects the Circuito Inferior with **Isla San Martín**. A path on the island leads to the top of the hill, where there are trails to some of the less visited falls and rocky pools (take bathing gear in summer to cool off).

Other attractions There are two nature trails near the falls: the **Sendero Macuco**, four kilometres, starting from near the Visitors' Centre and leading to a natural pool (El Pozón), fed by a waterfall and good for swimming; the **Sendero Yacaratiá**, leading from near the start of the Macuco trail and leading to Puerto Macuco (this has been criticized as not being a 'serious' nature trail).

A number of activities are offered, both from the Visitors' Centre and through **Activities**
agencies in Puerto Iguazú. These include: *Aventura Náutica*, a journey by
launch along the lower Río Iguazú, US$15 per person; *Safari Náutico*, a four
kilometre journey by boat along the Río Iguazú above the falls, US$15 per per-
son; *La Gran Aventura*, a boat trip down the lower Río Iguazu to Puerto
Macuco, followed by a trip back in a four-wheel drive vehicle along the
Yacaratiá Trail, US$33 per person; *Full Day*, which includes the *safari náutico*,
aventura náutica, US$30 per person (five hours), or US$45 with *gran aventura*
(seven hours), lunch extra (November 1999 prices from *Iguazú Jungle
Explorer* at the *Hotel Sheraton Iguazú*, T421600, F420311; also have an office in
the bus terminal, local 3, T422722).

There are also night-time walking tours between the *Hotel Sheraton* and the
falls when the moon is full; on clear nights the moon casts a blue halo over the
falls. Mountain bikes and boats can also be hired, US$3 an hour. For serious
birdwatching and nature walks with an English speaking guide, contact Daniel
Samay (*Explorador* agency) or Miguel Castelino, Apartado Postal 22, Puerto
Iguazú (3370), Misiones, T420157, FocusTours@aol.com, highly recommended. A useful guidebook is *Iguazú, The Laws of the Jungle* (in Spanish,
Iguazú, las leyes de la selva), by Santiago G de la Vega, Contacto Silvestre
Ediciones (1999).

Clothing In the rainy season, when water levels are high, waterproof coats or swim-   **Park essentials**
ming costumes are advisable for some of the lower catwalks and for boat trips. Cam-
eras should be carried in a plastic bag. Wear shoes with good soles, as the rocks can be
very slippery in places.

Services The park is open 0800-1900 every day. Entry US$5, payable in pesos or dol-
lars only (guests at *Hotel Sheraton* should pay and get tickets stamped at the hotel to
avoid paying again). The Visitors' Centre includes a museum of local fauna and an
auditorium for periodic slide shows (on request, minimum 8 people), no commentary, only music; it also sells a good guide book on Argentine birds. Food and drinks
are available in the park but are expensive, so it is best to take your own. There is a
Telecom kiosk at the bus stop. **Camping** Camping Puerto Canoas, 600m from Puerto
Canoas; tables, but no other facilities, nearest drinking water at park entrance.

Transport *Transportes El Práctico* buses run every hour from Puerto Iguazú bus terminal, stopping at the national park entrance for the purchase of entry tickets and
continuing to Puerto Canoas. Fares US$4 return to Visitors' Centre, a further US$0.50
to Puerto Canoas, payable in pesos, dollars, guaraníes or reais. First bus 0740, last
1940, last return 2000, journey time 30 minutes. These buses are sometimes erratic,
especially when it is wet, even though the times are clearly indicated. There are fixed
rates for taxis, US$15 one-way, up to 5 people. A tour from the bus terminal, taking in
both sides of the falls, costs US$40. Hitchhiking to the falls is difficult, but you can hitch
up to the Posadas intersection at Km 11, then it is only a 7 km walk. For transport
between the Argentine and Brazilian sides see under Foz and Puerto Iguazú, below.
Motorists can park overnight in the national park, free.

Foz do Iguaçu (Brazil)

Population: 232,000
Phone code: 045
Colour map 5, grid A2

This is a rapidly developing and improving town 28 kilometres from the falls, with a wide range of accommodation and good communications by air and road with the main cities of southern Brazil and Asunción in Paraguay.

Excursions

Artificial beaches on Lake Itaipu (see below for the Itaipu dam itself) The closest to Foz de Iguaçu are at Bairro de Três Lagoas, at Km 723 on BR-277, and in the municipality of Santa Terezinha do Itaipu, 34 kilometres from Foz. The leisure parks have grassed areas with kiosks, barbecue sites and offer fishing as well as bathing, US$2.50. It is also possible to take boat trips on the lake.

The **Parque das Aves** bird park, entrance US$8, at Rodovia das Cataratas Km 18, just before the falls, has received frequent good reports. It contains Brazilian and foreign birds in huge aviaries through which you can walk, with the birds flying and hopping around you. There is also a butterfly house. For a guided tour T5231007. The Parque is within walking distance of the *Hotel San Martin*; the *Paudimar* youth hostel (see below) offers a discount for its guests.

Sleeping
Many hotels offer excursions to the falls

If you know which hotel you wish to stay in (there is a wide selection), note that touts may say it no longer exists, or quote room rates below what is actually charged. In high season (eg Christmas-New Year) you will not find a room under US$15, but in low season there are many good deals.

Foz do Iguaçu

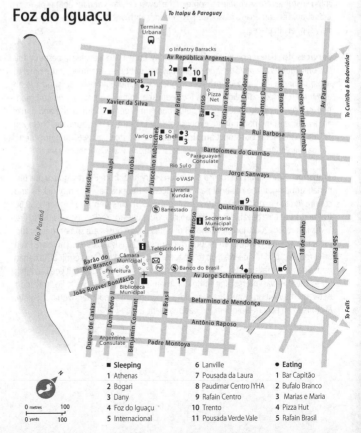

To Itaipu & Paraguay

■ Sleeping	6 Lanville	● Eating
1 Athenas	7 Pousada da Laura	1 Bar Capitão
2 Bogari	8 Paudimar Centro IYHA	2 Bufalo Branco
3 Dany	9 Rafain Centro	3 Marias e Maria
4 Foz do Iguaçu	10 Trento	4 Pizza Hut
5 Internacional	11 Pousada Verde Vale	5 Rafain Brasil

0 metres 100
0 yards 100

Hotels outside Foz do Iguaçu L-AL *Hotel das Cataratas*, directly overlooking the Falls, 28 km from Foz, T5217000, F5741688, 40% discount for holders of the Brazil Air Pass. Generally recommended but caters for lots of groups, attractive colonial-style building with pleasant gardens (where a lot of wildlife can be seen at night and early morning) and pool. Receipt of email for guests only. Check the exchange rate if paying in dollars. Non-residents can eat here, mid-day and evening buffets (mixed reports); also *à-la-carte* dishes and dinner with show. On the road to the falls (Rodovia das Cataratas) are **L** *Bourbon*, Km 2.5, T5231313, F5741110. Top quality, excellent buffet dinner, open to non-residents (US$12). **L** *San Martin*, Km 17, T5232323, F5743207, www.fnn.net/hoteis/sanmartin/new. Four-star, a/c, TV, pool, sports, nightclub, several eating options, luxury, comfortable (any problems ask for Miguel Allou). Recommended. **AL** *Carimã*, Km 10, T5231818, F5743531. Four-star, pool, restaurant, bars. Very good value. Recommended. **A** *Colonial*, Km 16, T5231777, F5258585, 1 km from the airport. Pool, fine location, price includes breakfast and mediocre dinner, no English, credit cards accepted, packages including transport and tours can be booked with a good discount at hotel booking office at the airport. **A** *Panorama*, Km 12, T5231200, F5231456. Good value, pool.

Hotels in Foz do Iguaçu L *Internacional*, Almte Barroso 2006, T5214100/4159, F5745201. Very well-appointed and decorated, good. **A** *Lanville Palace*, Av Jorge Schimmelpfeng 827, T/F5231511. Restaurant, bar, pool. **A** *Rafain Centro*, Mcal Deodoro 984, T/F5231213. Good restaurant, pool. **A** *Recanto Park*, Av Costa e Silva 3500, T/F5223000. Comfortable accommodation with restaurant, coffee shop, pool, sauna. **A** *Suiça*, Av Felipe Wandscheer 3580, T5253232, F5253044. Swiss manager, helpful, pool. **A** *Bogari*, Av Brasil 106, T5232243, F5722123, bogari@fnn.net. Excellent restaurant, swimming pool, a/c, safe. **B** *Foz do Iguaçu*, Av Brasil 97, T5234455, F5741775, hotelfoz@purenet.com.br. Good, expensive laundry, luggage store. **B** *Foz Presidente*, R Xavier da Silva 1000, T/F5724450. Restaurant, pool, with breakfast, convenient for buses. Recommended. **B** *Foz Presidente II*, R Mcal Floriano Peixoto 1851, T5232318. Smaller but a little more expensive, also with pool, bar and restaurant. **C** *Dany*, Av Brasil 509, T/F5231530, danyhotel@danyhotel.com.br. Comfortable, a/c, TV, good buffet breakfast. **C** *Luz*, Av Costa e Silva Km 5, near Rodoviária, T5223535, F5222474. Recommended. **C** *San Remo*, Kubitschek e Xavier da Silva 563, T5722956. A/c, good breakfast. Recommended. **D** *Minas*, R Rebouças 809, T5745208. Basic, hot water, safe, no breakfast. **D** *German Pension*, R Rebouças 1091, T5745603. Recommended. **D** *Maria Schneider*, Av Jorge Schimmelpfeng 483, T5742305. German spoken. **D** *Ortega*, Av Brasil 1140, T5231288. Good breakfast. **D** *Pousada Evelina Navarrete*, R Irlan Kalichewski 171, Vila Yolanda, T/F5743817. Lots of tourist information, English, French, Italian, Polish and Spanish spoken, helpful, lots of information, good breakfast and location, near Chemin Supermarket, near Av Cataratas on the way to the falls. Warmly recommended. **D** *Pousada da Laura*, R Naipi 671, T/F5723374. Good breakfast, hot water, bathroom, central, friendly, secure, kitchen, laundry facilities, good place to meet other travellers, Spanish, English, Italian and French spoken, excellent. **D** *Tarobá*, R Tarobá 1048, T5743670/3890. Helpful, a/c, clean, small pool, good breakfast. Recommended. **E** *Athenas*, R Almte Barroso 2215 e Rebouças, T5742563. Good value, special rates for backpackers, some rooms with shared bath, fan, breakfast extra. **E** *Trento*, R Rebouças 829, T5745111. A/c, with bath, without breakfast, noisy, but recommended. **E** *Pousada Verde Vale*, R Rebouças 335, T5742925. Cramped, cheap, very basic, open high season only. **Youth hostel** There are 2 branches of the *Paudimar* youth hostel, both **F** pp (in high season IYHA members only): *Paudimar Campestre*, Av das Cataratas Km 12.5, Remanso Grande, near airport, T/F5722430, paudimarcampestre@paudimar.com.br. From airport or town take Parque Nacional bus (0530-0100)and get out at Remanso Grande bus stop, by *Hotel San Juan*, then take the free shuttle bus (0700-1900) to the hostel, or 1.2 km walk from main road. IYHA, camping as well, pool, soccer pitch, quiet, kitchen and communal meals, breakfast. Very friendly and highly recommended. For assistance, ask for Gladis. *Paudimar Centro*, R Rui Barbosa 634, T/F5745503, paudimarcentro@paudimar. com.br. Safe, laundry, kitchen, TV, central, convenient for buses to falls, also very friendly. Recommended. For assistance, ask for Lourdes. English, Spanish and Portuguese spoken. Hostel will pay half taxi fare from rodoviária or airport if staying more than 2 days. Both hostels have telephone, fax and internet for use of guests. You can stay at one hostel and use the facilities of the other; tours run to either side of the falls. *Paudimar* desk at rodoviária.

Camping Pretty cold and humid in winter. *Camping Pousada Internacional*, R Manêncio Martins, 600m from turnoff. For vehicles and tents. *Camping Clube do Brasil*, by the National Park entrance 17 km from Foz, T5238599, US$10 pp (half with International Camping Card), pool, clean. Park vehicle or put tent away from trees in winter in case of heavy rainstorms, no restaurants, food there is not very good, closes at 2300. Camping is not permitted by the *Hotel das Cataratas* and falls. Sleeping in your car inside the park is also prohibited.

Eating Many stay open till midnight and accept a variety of currencies. *Bufalo Branco*, R Rebouças 530. All you can eat churrasco for US$15, good salad bar. *Cabeça de Boi*, Av Brasil 1325. Live music, buffet. Churrasco, but coffee and pastries also. *Rafain*, Av das Cataratas, Km 6.5, with Paraguayan harp trio, good *alcatra* (meat), excellent buffet, US$25 for all you can eat. *Rafain Brasil*, Brasil 157, a collection of food stalls for different tastes and budgets, with live music and dancing 2000 to 0200, bingo, lively. Recommended. *Scala*, Santos Dumont and Xavier da Silva. Good atmosphere and value. *Sorvete Italia*, Av Kubitschek 553. Very good ice cream. *Tropicana*, Av Juscelino Kubitschek 228. All-you-can-eat pizza or *churrascaria* with salad bar, good value. *Vira Lata*, Av Juscelino Kubitschek e Jorge Sanways. Good value. *Zaragoza*, R Quintino Bocaiúva 882, T5743084. Spanish. *Marias e Maria*, Av Brasil 50. Good *confeitaria*.

Bars & nightclubs *Oba! Oba!*, Av das Cataratas 3700, T5742255/5724217 (Antigo Castelinho). Live samba show Monday-Saturday 2315-0015, very popular, US$9 for show and 1 drink. *Churrascaria Rafain Cataratas*, Av das Cataratas Km 6.5. With floor show and food, see **Eating** above. *Capitão Bar*, Av Schimmelpfeng 288 y Almte Barroso, T5721512, popular nightspot for drinks, open from 1730.

Entertainment **Cinema** On Barão do Rio Branco beside the former *Hotel Salvatti*.

Sports **Fishing** For *dourado* and *surubi* fishing, contact Simon Williams at Cataratas late Club, Av Gen Meira, Km 5, T5232073.

Shopping *Kunda Livraria Universitária*, R Almte Barroso 1473, T5234606. Guides and maps of the area, books on the local wildlife, novels etc in several languages, including French and English.

Transport **Car hire** *Localiza* at airport, T5234800, Av Juscelino Kubitschek 2878, T5221608, and Rodovia das Cataratas Km 2.5, *Hotel Bourbon*, T5231632.

Air Iguaçu international airport, 18 km south of town near the falls. In Arrivals is *Banco do Brasil* and *Caribe Tours e Câmbio*, car rental offices, tourist office (see below) and an official taxi stand, US$10 to town centre (US$11 from town to airport). Transbalan (Parque Nacional) town bus for US$0.50, first at 0530, does not permit large amounts of luggage but backpacks OK. Many hotels run minibus services for a small charge. Daily flights to **Rio**, **São Paulo**, **Curitiba** and other Brazilian cities.

Buses For transport to the falls, see above under Parque Nacional Foz do Iguaçu. Long distance terminal (*Rodoviária*), Av Costa e Silva, 4 km from centre on road to Curitiba; bus to centre, any bus that says 'Rodoviária', US$0.65. Book departures as soon as possible. As well as the tourist office (see below), there is a Cetreme desk for tourists who have lost their documents, Guarda Municipal (police) and luggage store. To **Curitiba**, *Pluma, Sulamericana*, 9-11 hours, paved road, US$15; to **Guaíra** via Cascavel only, 5 hours, US$10; to **Florianópolis**, *Catarinense* and *Reunidas*, US$22, 16 hrs; *Reunidas* to **Porto Alegre**, US$30; to **São Paulo**, 16 hours, *Pluma* US$30, *executivo* 6 a day, plus 1 *leito*; to **Rio** 22 hours, several daily, US$38. To **Asunción**, *Pluma, RYSA* (direct at 1430), US$11.

Iguaçu Falls & the South

Airline offices *Rio Sul*, J Sanways 779. *TAM*, T5238588 (offers free transport to Ciudad del Este for its flights, all cross-border documentation dealt with). *Transbrasil*, Av Brasil 1225, T5743836. *Varig*, Av Juscelino Kubitschek 463, T5232111. *Vasp*, Av Brasil 845, T5232221.

Banks It is difficult to exchange on Sunday, but quite possible in Paraguay where US$ can be obtained on credit cards. There are plenty of banks and travel agents on Av Brasil. *Banco do Brasil*, Av Brasil 1377. High commission for TCs. *Bradesco*, Av Brasil 1202. Cash advance on Visa. *Banespa*, Av Barroso and Av Schimmelpfeng, good rates for Visa, quick service. *Banestado*, Av Juscelino Kubitschek e Bocaiúva, has *câmbio*. *Banco 24 Horas* at Oklahoma petrol station. *Itaú* ATM at airport.

Communications Post Office: Praça Getúlio Vargas 72. **Telecommunications:** Phone calls from *Telescritório* 606, R Rio Branco 606, T5232167, also fax, email (US$2.50 per hr), telescritorio@ foznet.com.br, open Mon-Fri 0730-2230, Sat-Sun 0800-2200. Phone calls also from *Telepar* on Edmundo de Barros. **Internet:** *Cafe PizzaNet*, R Rebouças 950, T/F5232122, www.foznet.com.br. 0900-2300, US$4 per hr; also phone and fax. See also *Telescritório* above.

Embassies & consulates *Argentina*, Travessa Eduardo Bianchi 26, T5742969. Open Mon-Fri 1000-1430. *France*, R Federico Engels 48, Villa Yolanda. *Paraguay*, Bartolomeu de Gusmão 480, T5232898.

Hospitals & medical services There is a free 24-hr clinic on Av Paraná, opposite Lions Club. Few buses: take taxi or walk (about 25 mins).

Security Av Juscelino Kubitschek and the streets south of it, towards the river, have a reputation as being unsafe at night as a favela is nearby. Take care if walking after dark. Taxis are only good value for short distances when you are carrying all your luggage.

Tour companies & travel agents Beware of overcharging for tours by touts at the bus terminal. There are many travel agents on Av Brasil. *Caribe Tur* at the international airport and *Hotel das Cataratas*, T5231230, runs tours from the airport to the Argentine side and *Hotel das Cataratas*. Recommended guides, *Wilson Engel*, T5741367, friendly, flexible. *Ruth Campo Silva*, STTC Turismo, Hotel Bourbon, Rodovia das Cataratas, T5743849, F5743557 (American Express). *Chiderly Batismo Pequeno*, R Almte Barroso 505, Foz, T5743367.

Tourist information 24-hr kiosk on Rua Rio Branco s/n, by Praça Getúlio Vargas. *Secretaria Municipal de Turismo*, Almte Barroso 1300, T5230222, T/F5742196. There is a 24-hr tourist help line number, T0800-451516. Very helpful. Kiosk on Av Brasil, by Ponte de Amizade (helpful), books hotels. Airport tourist information is also good, open for all arriving flights, gives map and bus information. Helpful office, free map, at the rodoviária, English spoken. A newspaper, *Triplice Fronteira*, carries street plans and other tourist information.

Voltage 110 volts AC.

Directory

This crossing via the Puente Tancredo Neves is straightforward. If crossing on a day visit, no immigration formalities are required. If leaving to stay in Puerto Iguazú, you must visit Brazilian immigration to get your exit stamp. Then visit Argentine immigration on the Argentine side to get your entry stamp (if staying in Puerto Iguazú for only 24 hours, Argentine officials may not give you a stamp). *Libres Cambio* beside Argentine immigration.

Frontier with Argentina

Be sure you know when the last bus departs from Puerto Iguazú for Foz (usually 2000) and remember that in summer Argentina is an hour earlier than Brazil

Transport Buses: to **Puerto Iguazú** run every 20 minutes from the Terminal Urbana, crossing the frontier bridge; 20 minutes' journey, no stops for border formalities, three companies: *Itaipu*, *Pluma* and *Três Fronteiras*, US$1.50, or 2 *reais*. If you have to get out of the bus to get your passport stamped at immigration, you can take any following bus to the end of the line without paying extra. To get to the Argentine side of the falls without going into Puerto Iguazú, get out of the bus from the frontier bridge at the first traffic lights and cross the road for the bus to the falls. To **Buenos Aires**, *Pluma* daily 1230 and Friday 1300, 18 hours, US$45. It is cheaper to go to **Posadas** via Paraguay. **Taxis**: Foz to the border, waiting for Brazilian immigration, US$10; Foz-Argentina US$35, US$45 to *Hotel Sheraton Iguazú*.

Puerto Iguazú

Population: 19,000
Phone code: 03757

The town is situated 18 kilometres northwest of the falls, high above the river on the Argentine side near the confluence of the Ríos Iguazú and Alto Paraná. A modern town which serves mainly as a centre for visitors to the falls, its prosperity has varied in relation to the difference in prices between Argentina and Brazil. The port lies to the north of the town centre at the foot of a hill: from the port you can follow the Río Iguazú downstream towards Hito Argentino, a *mirador* with views over the point where the Ríos Iguazú and Alto Paraná meet and over neighbouring Brazil and Paraguay. There are souvenir shops, toilets and *La Barranca* pub here; bus US$0.50. Puerto Iguazú is an easy town to walk around and it is less frenetic than Foz.

Museums **Museo Mbororé**, San Martín 231, has an exhibition on Guaraní culture and also sells Guaraní made handicrafts, cheaper than shops. ■ *Monday-Saturday 1700-2100, US$1*. **Museo Imágenes de la Selva**, Calle Los Cedros y Guatambú, one block west of Av Victoria Aguirre, displays the sculptures in wood of Rodolfo Allou, mostly from materials found in the forest. He was related to Jules Verne. ■ *0800-1200, 1500-1800, US$2*.

Other sites **La Aripuca** is a large wooden structure housing a centre for the appreciation of the native species and their environment. Turn off Ruta 12 just after *Hotel Cataratas*, T423488, English and German spoken. At **Güira Oga** (Casa de los Pájaros), birds that have been injured are cured and reintroduced to the wild. There is also a trail in the forest and a breeding centre for endangered species. Turn off Ruta 12 at *Hotel Orquídeas Palace*; Cell15670684.

Sleeping

Crowded during summer (Jan-Feb), Easter and July holiday periods. Accommodation is expensive but there is plenty of choice; outside the high season be prepared to shop around and to bargain

LL-L *Sheraton Internacional Iguazú Resort*, T421600, F491800, T0800-8889180, in Buenos Aires T0XX11-43189390, F43189394, www.sheraton.com. Five-star, pool, casino, good restaurants, business facilities, overlooking the falls, being completely remodelled, rooms with garden views cost less, excellent, check-out can take ages. *Cataratas*, Route 12, Km 4, T421100, F421090, www.fnn.net/hoteis/cataratas-ar. Five-star, pool, gymnasium. **L** *Esturión*, Av Tres Fronteras 650, T420020. Last hotel before Hito Argentino, clean, comfortable, swimming pool, good restaurant. **A** *Las*

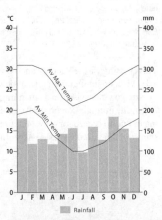

Rainfall

Climate: Puerto Iguazú

Orquídeas, Ruta 12, Km 5, T420472. Very comfortable. **A** *Saint George*, Córdoba 148, T420633, F420651, www.hotelsaintgeorge.com. With breakfast, comfortable, pool and garden, good, expensive restaurant, close to bus station. Highly recommended. **B** *Alexander*, Córdoba 685, opposite bus station, T420249, T420566. With breakfast, a/c, pool. Recommended. **B** *Hostería Casa Blanca*, Guaraní 121, 2 blocks from bus station, T421320. **C** in low season, with breakfast, fan, large rooms with phone. Recommended. **B-C** *Hostería Los Helechos*, Amarante 76, off Córdoba, behind *Saint George*, T/F420338. With breakfast, cheaper rooms have no TV, owner speaks German, pleasant, a/c or fan, pool. **B** *El Libertador*, Bompland 110, T/F420984. Modern, central, helpful, large bedrooms and public rooms, rooms at back have balconies overlooking garden and swimming pool. **B** *Residencial Lilian*, Beltrán 183, T420968. Two blocks from bus terminal, with breakfast, a/c, cheaper with fan, TV, helpful, safe. Recommended. **C** *King*, Aguirre 915, T420360. Pool, hot showers, good value. **C** *Residencial Paquita*, Córdoba 158, opposite terminal, T420434. Some rooms with terrace, a/c extra, nice setting. Recommended. **C** *Residencial Ríoselva*, San Lorenzo 140, at end of street, T421555. Laundry facilities, large garden, pool, communal barbecue. Highly recommended. **C** *Residencial San Fernando*, Córdoba y Guaraní, near terminal, T421429. With bath and breakfast, popular. **C** *Tierra Colorada*, Córdoba y El Urú 28, T420649, F420572. Fan or a/c, cheaper without breakfast, pool, trips arranged. Very good. **E** pp *Bompland*, Av Bompland 33, T420965. **D** with a/c, with bath, barbecue, central. **E** pp *Residencias Gastón*, Félix de Azara 590, T423184. With bath, breakfast, a/c, youth hostel style, by river. **F** pp *Noelia*, Fray Luis Beltrán 119, T420729. Not far from bus terminal, good value, with bath. **Youth hostel D** pp *Hospedaje Uno*, Beltrán 116, T420529. With bath and breakfast, **E** in dormitory accommodation, IYHA,

Puerto Iguazú

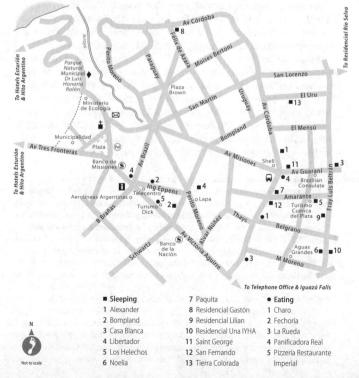

■ **Sleeping**	7 Paquita	● **Eating**
1 Alexander	8 Residencial Gastón	1 Charo
2 Bompland	9 Residencial Lilian	2 Fechoría
3 Casa Blanca	10 Residencial Una IYHA	3 La Rueda
4 Libertador	11 Saint George	4 Panificadora Real
5 Los Helechos	12 San Fernando	5 Pizzería Restaurante
6 Noelia	13 Tierra Colorada	Imperial

N

Not to scale

Iguazú Falls & the South

friendly, clean. Recommended. Tour to Itaipú, Foz de Iguaçu and Brazilian side of the falls. The Tourist Office has a list of family accommodation (**E** pp), though it may be reluctant to find private accommodation unless the hotels are full.

Camping For the site in the National Park see above. Municipal site, Corrientes y Entre Ríos. Reported as 'grim'. *Camping El Pindo*, Av Aguirre, Km 3 at the southern edge of town, US$1.50 pp, plus charge for tent and for use of pool, friendly, but very run down. There are also facilities at *Camping El Yaguarete*, Route 12, Km 5, T420168. Opposite is *El Viejo Americano*, which also has camping. Pool open to non-guests, US$2.50. In pleasant, wooded gardens, but no food; US$3 pp, US$3 per car, US$3 per tent.

Eating *La Rueda*, Córdoba 28. Good food at reasonable prices. *El Charro*, Córdoba 106. Good food, *pizzería* and *parrilla*, popular with locals, no credit cards. *El Criollito*, Tres Fronteras 62. Recommended. *Jardín de Iguazú*, Córdoba y Misiones, at bus terminal. Good. *Fechoría*, Ingeniero Eppens 294. Good *empanadas*. On Aguirre, next to *Turismo Dick* is a group of restaurants: *Pizzería y Restaurante Imperial, Fast Food* (*tenedor libre*, ie fixed price), *Blanco Paraíso parrillada*. *Panificadora Real*, Córdoba y Guaraní. Good bread, open Sunday evening; another branch at Victoria y Brasil in the centre.

Transport **Car hire** *Avis* at airport. *Localiza*, at airport and Aguirre 279, T0800-9992999. Cars may be taken to the Brazilian side for an extra US$5. **Radio taxis** T420973/421707, fares: to airport US$15, to Argentine falls US$15, to Brazilian falls US$20, to centre of Foz US$15, to Ciudad del Este US$20, to Itaipu US$30 return, to Wanda gem mines with wait US$35.

Air Airport is south of Puerto Iguazú near the Falls. *Expreso del Valle* buses (T420348) between airport and bus terminal connect with plane arrivals and departures, US$3. Check times at Aerolíneas Argentinas office. Taxis charge US$10 to *Hotel Sheraton*, at least US$18 to Puerto Iguazú, US$14 to Foz do Iguaçu and US$25 to the Brazilian airport. Aerolíneas Argentinas and Lapa fly direct to Buenos Aires, 2 hours, flights are very crowded. For the best view on landing, sit on the right side of the aircraft.

Buses The bus terminal, at Av Córdoba y Av Misiones, has a phone office, a Municipalidad office, various tour company desks (see below) and bus offices. To **Buenos Aires**, 21 hours, *Expreso Singer, Tigre Iguazú, Crucero del Norte, ViaBariloche*, daily, US$33-40 *semi cama*, US$50 *cama* (some offer student discounts). It is cheaper to take a local bus to Posadas and then rebook. To **Posadas**, stopping at San Ignacio Miní, frequent, 5 hours, US$19, *expreso*, 7 hours, US$16 *servicio común*; to **San Ignacio Miní**, US$16 *servicio común*. *Agencia de Pasajes Noelia*, local 3, T422722, can book tickets beyond Posadas for other destinations in Argentina, ISIC discounts available.

Directory **Airline offices** *Aerolíneas Argentinas*, Brasil y Aguirre, T420194. *Lapa*, Perito Moreno casi Bompland, T420390. **Banks** Several *cambios* on Aguirre near the outskirts of town towards the Falls. *Turismo Dick* (address below) changes TCs at high commission (up to 10%). Rates vary so shop around. Alternatively pay in US$. Nowhere to get cash on Visa. **Communications** *Telecentro*, Victoria Aguirre y Horacio Quiroga, T420177, phone, fax, post office and Banelco ATM. **Embassies & consulates** Brazil, Av Guaraní 70, T/F420131. **Tour companies & travel agents** *Turismo Dick*, Aguirre 226, T420778, turismodick@interiguazu.com.ar, open Mon-Sat 0830-1300, 1630-2000. *Turismo Caracol*, Aguirre 563, T420064. All-day tour of both sides of falls, including good meal in Brazil, but mainly for 'non-English speaking clients with an interest in shopping'. *Turismo Cuenca del Plata*, Amarante 76, T421330, F421458, cuencadelplata@fnn.net, 10% discount to ISIC and youth card holders on local excursions. *IGRTur*, Terminal de Omnibus, local 5, T/F422983, all tours sold, mountain bike hire US$3 per hr, 2-hr circuit in forest on quadbikes US$30, information on hostels and other accommodation. *Aguas Grandes*, Mariano Moreno 58, T421140, F423096, www.aguasgrandes.com.ar, tours to both sides of the falls and further afield: Saltos de Moconá, 5,000m wide (overnight US$190 all included); Puerto Península, using old logging trails, rope ladders in trees and abseiling down (US$40 pp); Sendero de los Saltos, giant ferns, abseiling down waterfalls, swimming; Raíces Guaraníes to an indigenous community (US$25 pp); bilingual and local guides, flexible. *Cabalgatas por la Selva*, Ruta 12, just after the Rotonda for the road to the international bridge, Cell15542180. For horse riding. *Exploradaor Expediciones*, Perito Moreno 217, 1 B, T/F421632 and in *Hotel Sheraton*. Trips in the forest leaving from the Visitors' Centre 1030 and 1500, photographic safaris. Recommended taxi-guide, Juan Villalba, T420973 (radiotaxi 044). Good value, speaks basic English. Agencies arrange day tours to the Brazilian side (lunch in Foz), Itaipú and Ciudad del Este (US$25), though more time is spent shopping than at the falls, and to a gem mine at Wanda, the Jesuit ruins at San Ignacio Miní and a local zoo (10 hours driving time, US$30, not including entry fees, may be cheaper for more than 2 in a taxi or hired car). **Tourist information** Aguirre 396, T420800. Mon-Fri 0800-1300, 1400-2000, Sat-Sun 0800-1200, 1630-2000.

The crossing is via the Puente Tancredo Neves. When leaving Argentina, Argentine immigration is at the Brazilian end of the bridge. The Brazilian consulate is at Guaraní y Esquiú, Puerto Iguazú, 0800-1400.

Frontier with Brazil

Transport Buses: these leave Puerto Iguazú terminal for Foz do Iguaçu every 20 minutes, US$1.50 or 2 *reais*. The bus goes straight through the Argentine side and stops at the Brazilian end of the bridge for both Argentine and Brazilian formalities. If you need stamps, get out of the bus with your luggage and go to both immigration offices. The bus has to wait for an Argentine official to check those bus passengers who do not get off, so if you are quick you may get back on the same bus. If not, wait for the next one (about 20-30 minutes) or walk up to the main road, which is not far, and catch a bus there. **Taxis**: between the border and Puerto Iguazú US$15; between the border and *Hotel Sheraton Iguazú* US$35.

The *Ponte de Amizade/Puente de Amistad* (Friendship Bridge) over the Río Paraná, six kilometres north of Foz, leads straight into the heart of Ciudad del Este. Crossing is very informal but keep an eye on your luggage and make sure that you get necessary stamps – if the volume of traffic is great it can be difficult to stop, especially with the traffic police moving you on. Pedestrians from Brazil cross on the north side of the bridge, allowing easier passage on the other side for those returning with bulky packages. Since the devaluation of the real, the attraction of Ciudad del Este as a mecca for cheap shopping for Brazilians has diminished.

Frontier with Paraguay

Immigration Paraguayan and Brazilian immigration formalities are dealt with at opposite ends of the bridge. There is a US$3 tourist charge to enter Paraguay. **NB** Remember to adjust your watch to local time. If only intending to visit the national parks, crossing by private vehicle presents no problems.

Transport Buses (marked Cidade-Ponte) leave from the Terminal Urbana, Av Juscelino Kubitschek, for the Ponte de Amizade (Friendship Bridge), US$0.65. Buses do not stop for formalities.

From Argentina Ferry service from the port in Puerto Iguazú to Tres Fronteras is for locals only (no immigration facilities). Crossing to Paraguay is via Puente Tancredo Neves to Brazil and then via the Puente de la Amistad to Ciudad del Este. Brazilian entry and exit stamps are not required unless you are stopping in Brazil. The Paraguayan consulate is at Bompland 355, Puerto Iguazú.

Transport Direct *Nuestra Señora de la Asunción* buses (non-stop in Brazil) leave Puerto Iguazú terminal every 20 minutes, US$2, 45 minutes, liable to delays especially in crossing the bridge to Ciudad del Este. Taxis charge US$35 to Ciudad del Este bus station and US$45 to Ciudad del Este airport.

Iguaçu Falls & the South

Itaipu

The Itaipu dam, on the Río Paraná 12 kilometres north, is the site of the largest single power station in the world built jointly by Brazil and Paraguay. Construction of this massive scheme began in 1975 and it came into operation in 1984. The main dam is eight kilometres long, creating a lake which covers 1,400 square kilometres. The 18 turbines have an installed capacity of 12,600,000 Kw and produce about 75 billion Kwh a year, enough electricity to power the whole of Southern Brazil and much of Rio de Janeiro, São Paulo and Minas Gerais. The Paraguayan side may be visited from Ciudad del Este. Both governments are proud to trumpet the accolade, 'one of the seven wonders of the modern world' (the only one in South America), which was given to it by the American Society of Civil Engineering in *Popular Mechanics* in 1995.

Tours of Itaipu Buses No 110 or 120 from Terminal Urbana (stand 50 Batalhão) go every 13 minutes to the Public Relations office at the main entrance (US$0.40), 110, Conjunto C Porto Meira, 120 via Sul goes within 250 metres. Visits are free, but in groups only. In the Visitors' Centre (T5206999) is a short video presentation with stunning photography and amazing technical information, apparently available in English but usually only in Portuguese. The height of the main dam is equivalent to a 65-storey building, the amount of concrete used in its construction is 15 times more than that used for the Channel Tunnel between England and France. The spillways are capable of discharging the equivalent of 40 times the average flow of the Iguaçu Falls. If you are lucky, the spillways will be open. After the film and a brief visit to the souvenir shop where an English guidebook is available, a coach will take you to the dam itself. As it crosses the top, you get a stomach-churning view of the spillways and really begin to appreciate the scale of the project. There are several tours daily at 0800, 0900, 1000, 1400, 1500 and 1600 (closed between 1100 and 1400). The 'executive' bus and agency tours are an unnecessary expense. If it's sunny, go in the morning as the sun is behind the dam in the afternoon and you will get poor photographs. Website: www.itaipu.gov.br.

The **Ecomuseu de Itaipu** (Av Tancredo Neves, Km 11, T5205813/6034, Tuesday-Saturday 0900-1130, 1400-1700, Monday 1400-1700) and Iguaçu Environmental Education Centre are geared to educate about the preservation of the local culture and environment, or that part which isn't underwater (free with guide, recommended). A massive reforestation project is underway, with over 14 million seedlings having already been planted. On the lake's shore, six biological refuges have been created. Whatever your views on the need for huge hydroelectric projects, it is worth visiting Itaipu to gain a greater understanding of the scale and impact of such constructions, then make up your own mind.

Ciudad del Este

Population: 133,893
Phone code: 061

Founded as Ciudad Presidente Stroessner in 1957, the city grew rapidly during the construction of the Itaipú hydroelectric project. Described as the biggest shopping centre in Latin America, it attracts Brazilian and Argentine visitors in search of bargain prices for electrical goods, watches, perfumes etc. Dirty, noisy, unfriendly and brashly commercial, it is worth a visit just for the people watching, but you should be careful with valuables and be particularly cautious after dark.

Excursions The Paraguayan side of the **Itaipú** hydroelectric project can be visited (see above). Buses run from Rodríguez y García, outside the terminal, to the

Shop till you drop

As you enter the city across the bridge from Brazil you see hunched figures struggling back into Brazil, dwarfed by the massive bags strapped on their backs. Nearing the border control, many bundle their bags over the side of the bridge, jump down onto the riverbank after them and clamber back up the slope with their valuables, undoubtedly worth more than the US$150 allowed duty-free by the law, but unchecked by the customs officers who watch the spectacle with disinterest.

The streets of the city itself are narrow and congested. On every side you are bombarded by street vendors trying to convince you to buy steak knives, hair clippers, massaging hair brushes, sweatshirts ... the list is endless and is accompanied by a cacophony of shouting in Spanish, Portuguese, Guaraní and English. To get a more distant view of the action, try the Fleur de Lys bar on the main street: it accepts almost any currency, offers a good range of drinks and snacks and allows you to watch Ciudad del Este in action down below.

By comparison, the Mona Lisa department store is a haven of peace and tranquility: air conditioned and with polished marble floors, but unless you have lots of money and airplane luggage space to spare, you will find little to tempt you.

Though hardly on every traveller's list of destinations, Ciudad del Este is well worth a visit if you are in the area. Its streets are dirty, it can be hot and smelly, and you may find it annoying to be pestered every 30 seconds, but you will come away humbled by the experience: most of the street vendors work harder every day and for less money than any of us ever will.

Naomi Peirce

Visitors' Centre. ■ *Monday-Saturday 0730-1200, 1330-1700, Sundays and holidays 0800-1200, 1330-1630. Free conducted tours of the project include a film show (versions in several languages – ask) 45 minutes before bus tours, which start at 0830, 0930, 1030, 1400, 1500, 1600, check times in advance. Take your passport.* On the way to Itaipú is **Flora y Fauna Itaipú Binacional**, containing animals and plants rescued from the area when the dam was built. It is about two kilometres from the visitors' centre on the road back to Cuidad del Este. ■ *0830-1030, 1330-1630.*

Cascada de Monday (Monday Falls), where the Río Monday drops into the Paraná gorge, is a worthwhile trip; there is good fishing below the falls. It is 10 kilometres south of Ciudad del Este. Return fare by taxi US$20.

A *Convair*, Adrián Jara y García, T500342. Comfortable, cheaper rooms without bath. **A** *Executive*, Adrián Jara y Curupayty, T500942/3. With breakfast – restaurant recommended. **A** *Residence de la Tour* at Paraná Country Club, 5 km from centre, T60316. Superb, Swiss-owned, excellent restaurant (US$12-16 pp), swimming pool, gardens, beautiful view. **B** *Catedral*, C A López 838, several blocks from commercial area, T500378. With breakfast, TV, a/c, large, modern with pool, restaurant. **B** *Gran Hotel Acaray*, 11 de Septiembre y Río Paraná, T/F511471/5. Pool, casino, nightclub, restaurant. **B** *San Rafael*, Abay y Adrián Jara, T68134. Large rooms, with breakfast, German and English spoken. **C** *Itaipú*, Rodríguez y Nanawa, T500371. With breakfast, a/c. **C** *Munich*, Fernández y Miranda, T500347. With breakfast, a/c, garage. Recommended. **C** *Puerta del Sol*, Rodríguez y Boquerón, just off the main street, T500798. A/c. **C-D** *El Cid*, Recalde 425, T512221. With breakfast, a/c, cheaper with fan. **D** *Austria* (also known as *Viena*), Fernández 165, above restaurant, T500883. With good breakfast and a/c, Austrian family, good views from upper floors. Warmly recommended. **D** *Tripolis*, San Blas 331, T512450. A/c. Poor restaurant, unhelpful, unsafe. **E** *Caribe*, Emiliano Fernández, opposite *Austria*, a/c, hot water, nice garden, helpful owner. Recommended.

Sleeping
■ *on map, page 358*
Price codes: see inside front cover
Accommodation is generally expensive

Iguaçu Falls & the South

Eating
Many restaurants close on Sunday

Coreio, San Blas 125. Good Korean food. *Osaka*, Adrián Jara. Good Japanese. *New Tokyo*, Adrián Jara 202. Authentic Japanese. *Seoul*, Curupayty y Adrián Jara. Good *parrillada*. *Mi Ranchero*, on Adrián Jara, good food, service and prices, well-known. *Hotel Austria/Viena*. Good Austrian food, clean, good value. Cheaper restaurants can be found along García and in the market.

Shopping Prices are decidedly high for North American and European visitors. The leather market is well worth a visit, be sure to bargain. Don't buy perfume at tempting prices on the street, it's only coloured water. Make sure that shops which package your goods pack what you actually bought. Also watch the exchange rates if you're a short term visitor from Argentina or Brazil.

Transport **Air** To Asunción, *Arpa*, 3 flights Monday-Saturday, 1 on Sunday. Also *TAM* daily *en route* to São Paulo.

Buses The terminal is on the southern outskirts. No 4 bus from the centre goes there, US$0.50 (taxi US$3.50). Many buses (US$17.50 *rápido*, 4½ hours, at night only; US$10 *común*, 6 hours) to and from **Asunción**. *Nuestra Señora* and *Rysa* recommended. To **Encarnación** (for Posadas and Argentina), along a fully paved road, frequent, 3 hours, US$7.50 (cheaper than via Foz do Iguaçu).

Ciudad del Este

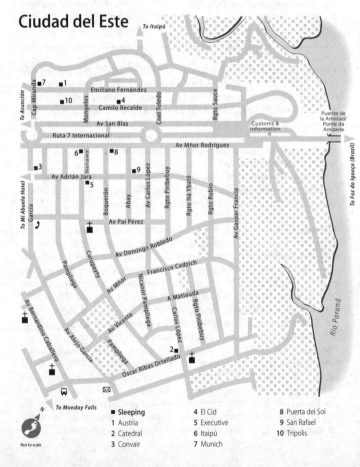

To Itaipú
To Asunción
To Mi Abuela Hotel
To Monday Falls
To Foz do Iguaçu (Brazil)

Emiliano Fernández
Camilo Recalde
Av San Blas
Ruta 7 Internacional
Av Mñor Rodríguez
Av Adrián Jara
Av Pai Pérez
Av Domingo Robledo
Francisco Cedzich
A Matiauda
Óscar Ribas Ortellado

Cap Miranda · Mongelos · Cnel Toledo · Rgto Sauce · Nanawa · Boquerón · Abay · Av Carlos López · Rgto Piribebuy · Rgto Itá Ybaté · Rgto Rubio · Av Gaspar Francia · García · Pampliega · Curupayty · Av Mñor · Nicanor Pampliega · Av Vicente · Pampliega · Av Bernardino Caballero · Av Alejo García · Carlos López · Rgto Piribebuy · Río Paraná

Customs & Information
Puente de la Amistad/ Ponte da Amizade

Not to scale

■ Sleeping	4 El Cid	8 Puerta del Sol
1 Austria	5 Executive	9 San Rafael
2 Catedral	6 Itaipú	10 Tripolis
3 Convair	7 Munich	

To Brazil International bus from outside the terminal to the new long-distance terminal (*Rodoviária*) outside Foz. Local buses from the terminal run along Av Adrián Jara and go to the city terminal (*terminal urbana*) in **Foz** every 15 minutes, 0600-2000, US$0.65. Most buses do not wait at immigration, so disembark to get your exit stamp, walk across the bridge (10 minutes) and obtain your entry stamp; keep your ticket and continue to Foz on the next bus free. Paraguayan taxis cross freely to Brazil (US$20), but it is cheaper to walk across the bridge and then take a taxi, bargain hard. You can pay in either currency.

To Argentina Direct buses to **Puerto Iguazú**, frequent service by several companies from outside the terminal, US$2, you need to get Argentine and Paraguayan stamps (not Brazilian); the bus does not wait so keep your ticket for the next bus.

Airline offices *TAM*, Edif SABA, Monseñor Rodríguez. **Banks** Local banks open Mon-Fri 0730-1100. Dollars can be changed into *reais* in town. *Banco Holandés Unido*, cash on Mastercard, 5% commission. Several exchange houses: *Cambio Guaraní*, Monseñor Rodríguez, changes TCs for US$0.50. Branch on Friendship Bridge has good rates for many currencies, including dollars and *reais*. *Tupi Cambios*, Adrián Jara 351. *Cambios Chaco*, Adrián Jara y Curupayty. *Casa de cambio* rates are better than street rates. Money changers (not recommended) operate at the bus terminal, but not at the Brazilian end of the Friendship Bridge. **Communications** Telecommunications: *Antelco*, Alejo García and Pai Pérez, near the centre on the road to the bus terminal. **Embassies & consulates** *Brazil*, C Pampliega 337, corner of Pai Perez, T561500984, F56163283. **Directory**

Guaíra

In the far northwest of the state, also on the Rio Paraná, were the tremendous waterfalls known in Brazil as Sete Quedas (the Seven Falls), and in Spanish Latin America as the Salto de Guaíra; they were drowned by the filling of the lake behind the Itaipu dam in 1982. The 1978 *South American Handbook* described Sete Quedas thus: "The great river, nearly five kilometres wide, hurls itself through the rocky gorges of the falls with a tremendous roar. Rocky islands between the falls are connected by wooden suspension bridges; the whole area can warrant a whole day. Many of the falls are from 30 to 40 metres high. This is the most enormous volume of falling water in the world; it is double Niagara's."

Population: 29,000
Phone code: 044
Colour map 5, grid A2

Guaíra, about 130 kilometres north of Iguaçu by air or road, has not been flooded, but much of its agricultural land and its clay beds have. The four kilometres from Guaíra to the lake can be walked or done by car (US$2.50 one way, return taxi up to US$12). Entrance to the park is US$0.50. There is a small museum three blocks from Guaíra's rodoviária. ■ *0800-1100 and 1400-1700*.

A *Deville*, R Paraguai 1205, T/F6421617. Restaurant, pool. **C** *Palace Hotel*, Rui Barbosa 1190, near the rodoviária, T6421325. **D** *Majestic*, opposite rodoviária. With or without bath, with breakfast, good. **D** *Sete Quedas*, Otávio Tosta 385. With breakfast and sandwich lunch, not too clean. For eating, try *O Chopão*, Thomaz Luiz Zebalhos 427. Pleasant. **Sleeping & eating**

Transport Buses: to **Campo Grande**, buy a ticket (US$25) at the Guaíra rodoviária, take a ferry from the Porto da Paragem at the end of Av Almte Tamandaré to Porto Ilha Grande in Mato Grosso do Sul, then bus to Mondo Novo, change bus there for Campo Grande. Morning and night bus, 12 hours in all. There is a bus service between **Curitiba** and Guaíra, US$15, 10 hours. To **São Paulo**, US$30, 16 hours. Other destinations include **Iguaçu** (bumpy, but interesting), 5 hours, but may be cancelled in the wet, US$10.

Embassies & consulates *Brazil*, Av Pres Stroessner 259, T/F546305. *Paraguay*, T6421505. **Directory**

Frontier with Paraguay

Immigration and transport There is an hourly passenger ferry service from Porto de Lanchas and Porto Guaíra to Salto Del Guayra on the Paraguayan side, US$0.50, and an hourly car ferry from Porto Guaíra (US$4 for car with 2 people). The car ferry runs until 1830 (Brazilian time). Customs and immigration for documentation close at 1700. There is a time change when you cross the Paraná. The area is intensively patrolled for contraband and stolen cars, ensure that all documentation is in order.

Santa Catarina

Today's mix of beach tourism, agriculture and industry give no indication of Santa Catarina's turbulent past. The old town of Laguna is especially interesting in this respect. Famous for its beaches and popular with Argentine and Paraguayan holidaymakers in high summer, this is one of the best beaches on the Brazilian coast for surfing. Immigrant communities, such as German, give a unique personality to many towns and districts. Rural tourism is becoming increasingly important and the highlands just in from the coast are among the coldest in Brazil, giving winter landscapes reminiscent of Europe, or Brazil's southern neighbours, rather than the tropics.

Background

History
The coast of Santa Catarina was known to both Portuguese and Spanish explorers in the 16th century; the name was given to the island that still bears it by Sebastian Cabot in 1526. The interior was only visited, not settled, by a few colonists and Jesuit priests. The first towns grew up in the mid-17th century: São Francisco, Nossa Senhora do Desterro (now Florianópolis), Laguna. The captaincy of Santa Catarina was created in 1738, first under the influence of São Paulo, then Rio de Janeiro. In 1777 the Spanish invaded and destroyed Ilha de Santa Catarina, but were forced to leave under the Treaty of Santo Ildefonso. After independence, the new province was caught up in the Farroupilha revolt (see box, page 383) and the proclamation of the Juliana Republic; the government forces regained all of Santa Catarina in 1840.

European immigration was encouraged in the second half of the 19th century, with the foundation of towns like Dona Francisca (now Joinville), Blumenau and Brusque. When the Republic was declared, the state governor rebelled, leading to two years of fighting which ended in harsh repression for the rebel *catarinenses*. Another conflict was the *Contestado* movement (see the same box as above) and there was more unrest during the 1930 revolution.

Immigration
Santa Catarina today, with a population of 4,750,000, has a varied history of settlement which is still in evidence. As well as each region having its own climate and scenery, it also has a distinctive culture depending on its immigrants. The Portuguese from the Azores settled along the coast, the Germans moved along the Itajaí Valley, the Italians headed for the south and into Rio Grande do Sul, while in the north there are Ukrainians, Japanese, Africans, Hispanics and Indians. Each group maintains its traditions and festivals, its architecture, food and language or accent. The vast majority of people today can trace their origin to these ethnic origins.

In Santa Catarina, a state of smallholdings, the farmer owns his land and cattle: the familiar European pattern of mixed farming worked by the family. Sixty percent of the population is rural. There are 260 cities, but only eight of them have more than 100,000 residents. There is coal in the south, and flourishing food processing (notably poultry, pork, rice, fruit), ceramics, plastics, high-tech and textile industries. Itajaí and São Francisco do Sul are the main ports, handling 90 percent of the trade. Tourism is now a major source of income and employment, attracting 1.5 million visitors to the 170 beaches just in the summer alone, mostly from Brazil, Argentina and Uruguay, while one million visit the Oktoberfest in Blumenau. Except for the summer months of January and February, the beaches of Santa Catarina are pleasant and uncrowded. The best months to visit are April and May. Only 100 kilometres away from the beaches the mountains rise to 1,000 metres and the temperature drops substantially, with some areas receiving snow in winter.

Economy & climate

Florianópolis

Half way along the coast of Santa Catarina is the state capital Florianópolis, founded in 1726 on the Ilha de Santa Catarina. The natural beauty of the island, beaches and bays make Florianópolis a popular tourist centre ; only January and February are very crowded and expensive.

Population: 271,500
Phone code: 048
Colour map 5, grid B5

The island is joined to the mainland by two bridges, one of which is Ponte Hercílio Luz, the longest steel suspension bridge in Brazil (now pedestrian only and closed for repairs – 1999). The newer Colombo Machado Salles bridge has a pedestrian and cycle way beneath the roadway. It is a port of call for coastal shipping, 725 kilometres from Rio de Janeiro and 420 kilometres from Santos. The southern beaches are usually good for swimming, the east for surfing, but be careful of the undertow. 'Floripa' is accepted as a shortened version of Florianópolis, with the people known as 'Floripans', although they like to call themselves 'Ilhéus', or Islanders.

Getting there International and domestic flights arrive at Hercílo Luz airport. Buses from international destinations and from other Brazilian cities arrive at the Rita Maia rodoviária on the island.

Ins & outs

Getting around Florianópolis is a small city, quite hilly but easy and safe to walk around. To explore the island you need to use the good bus services; standard buses and more expensive yellow micro buses run to nearly every important point on the island.

Sights

In the 1960s Florianópolis port was closed and the aspect of the city's southern shoreline was fundamentally changed, with land reclaimed from the bay. The two main remnants of the old port area are the late 19th-century **Alfândega** and **Mercado Público**, both on Rua Conselheiro Mafra, fully restored and painted ochre. In the Alfândega is a handicraft market. ■ *Monday-Friday 0900-1900, Saturday 0900-1200, T2246082.* The market is divided into *boxes*, some are bars and restaurants, others shops. ■ *Monday-Friday 0600-1830, Saturday 0600-1300, a few fish stalls open on Sunday, T2253200.* The **Cathedral** on Praça 15 de Novembro was completed in 1773. It is built on the site of the first chapel erected by the founder of the city, Francisco Dias Velho. Inside is a life-size sculpture in wood of the flight into Egypt, originally from the Austrian Tyrol.

Iguaçu Falls & the South

Forte Santana (1763), beneath the Ponte Hercílio Luz, houses a **Museu de Armas Major Lara Ribas,** with a collection of guns and other items, mostly post Second World War. ■ *Tuesday-Sunday 0830-1200, 1400-1800 (Monday 1400-1800), free, T2296263.* There are four other museums. The **Museu Histórico,** in the 18th-century Palácio Cruz e Souza, on Praça 15 de Novembre, contains furniture, documents and objects belonging to governors of the state. ■ *Tuesday-Friday 0800-1900, Saturday 1300-1900, Sunday 1530-1900, T2213504.* The **Museu de Antropologia,** at the Trindade University Campus,

Florianópolis

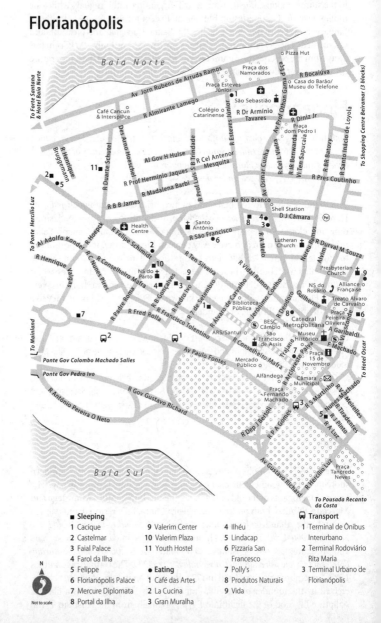

■ **Sleeping**
1 Cacique
2 Castelmar
3 Faial Palace
4 Farol da Ilha
5 Felippe
6 Florianópolis Palace
7 Mercure Diplomata
8 Portal da Ilha

9 Valerim Center
10 Valerim Plaza
11 Youth Hostel

● **Eating**
1 Café das Artes
2 La Cucina
3 Gran Muralha

4 Ilhéu
5 Lindacap
6 Pizzaria San Francesco
7 Polly's
8 Produtos Naturais
9 Vida

🚍 **Transport**
1 Terminal de Ônibus Interurbano
2 Terminal Rodoviário Rita Maria
3 Terminal Urbano de Florianópolis

has a collection of stone and other archaeological remains from the cultures of the coastal Indians. ■ *Monday-Friday 0900-1200, 1300-1700, T3318821.* The **Museu do Homem Sambaqui**, at the Colégio Catarinense, Rua Esteves Júnior 711, exhibits pieces from the *sambaqui* culture and fossils. ■ *Monday-Friday 1330-1630, T2249190.* At the end of 1999 a **Museu do Telefone** opened in the Casa do Barão, R Bocaiúva e Avenida Gama D'Eça. There is a look-out point at **Morro da Cruz** (take Empresa Trindadense bus, US$0.60, waits 15 minutes, or walk). On the north shore, outside the perimeter road, the mangroves of the **Mangue do Itacorubi** are being protected. Lookout points above the trees, with a connecting path, are being built.

Excursions

See below for a description of the island and excursions to beaches and other local attractions. Boat trips can be made from Florianópolis in the bay with *Scuna Sul*, T2221806, www.scunasul.com.br, from US$7.50.

Essentials

Sleeping A *Baía Norte Palace*, Av Beira Mar Norte 220, T2253144, F2253227. On the main road, a/c, TV, safe, pool, business facilities, restaurant. A *Castelmar*, R Felipe Schmidt 1260, T2253228, F2250360, 3126, www.iaccess.com.br/castelmar. Pool, a/c, TV, laundry, restaurant. A *Faial*, R Felipe Schmidt 603, T2252766, F2250435. Good restaurant. A *Florianópolis Palace*, R Artista Bittencourt 14, T2249633, F2230300. Recommended. A *Mercure Diplomata*, Av Paulo Fontes 1210, T2244455, F2255082. Very good views, 4-star hotel but prices sometimes negotiable. **A-B** *Valerim Plaza*, R Felipe Schmidt 705, T/F2253388. Three-star, more modern than *Valerim Center*, buffet restaurant open till 2300.

B *Baia Sul*, R Tiradentes 167, near Praça 15 de Novembro, T2232269, F2240810. With breakfast, a/c, safe, good. **B** *Farol da Ilha*, R Bento Gonçalves 163, T2252766, F2250435. New, a/c, TV, not far from rodoviária. **B** *Oscar*, Av Hercílio Luz 760, T2220099, F2220978. A/c, TV, safe, central. **B** *Porto da Ilha*, R Dom Jaime Câmara 84, T3220007, F3220144. Central, comfortable. Recommended. **B** *Valerim Center*, R Felipe Schmidt 554, T2251100. Two-star, large rooms, hot water, hard beds.

C *Pousada Recanto da Costa*, R 13 de Maio 41. With breakfast, hot water, laundry facilities, parking, 15 minutes' walk from centre.

D *Cacique*, R Felipe Schmidt 423, same owners as *Valerim*, T2225359. No breakfast but clean and friendly, good value but rooms vary. **D-E** *Felippe*, R João Pinto 132, 1 block from 15 de Novembro, by Terminal Urbano, T2224122. Small rooms, some with no windows, breakfast is just a cup of coffee, dirty bathrooms.

Youth hostels **E** pp *Ilha de Santa Catarina*, R Duarte Schutel 227, T2253781, F2251692. IYHA. Recommended, breakfast included, cooking facilities, clean, some traffic noise, very friendly, will store luggage. Prices rise in December-February; more expensive for non-members. See under Canasvieiras, page 368.

Camping *Camping Clube do Brasil*, São João do Rio Vermelho, north of Lagoa da Conceição, 21 km out of town; also at Lagoa da Conceição, Praia da Armação, Praia dos Ingleses, Praia Canasvieiras. 'Wild' camping allowed at Ponta de Sambaqui and Praias Brava, Aranhas, Galheta, Mole, Campeche, Campanhas and Naufragados; 4 km south of Florianópolis, camping site with bar at Praia do Sonho on the mainland, beautiful, deserted beach with an island fort nearby. 'Camping Gaz' cartridges from *Riachuelo Supermercado*, on R Alvim and R São Jorge.

Eating Take a walk along Rua Bocaiúva, east of R Almte Lamego, to find the whole street filled with Italian restaurants, barbecue places and an exclusive fish restaurant, *Toca da Garoupa* (turn on to R Alves de Brito 178). *Don Pepé Forno a Lenha* is a great place to go for a quiet romantic meal with a *serenador* (cover charge added to bill for singer). *Papparella*, Almte Lamego 1416. Excellent giant pizzas. Shrimp dishes are good everywhere. A popular place to start a night out (after 2100) is the *Nouvelle Vague*, more commonly known as *A Creperia*, buzzing every weekend, wide selection of sweet and savoury pancakes. *Macarronada Italiana*, Av Beira Mar Norte 2458. Good. Next door is *Pizza da Piedra*. *Casa de Coimbra*, Av Beira Mar Norte 2568. Specializes in chicken with polenta and salad, Portuguese, good. Next door is *Kayskidum* lanchonete and crêperie, very popular. *Café das Artes*, nice café at north end of R Esteves Junior, No 734. With excellent cakes. *Churrascaria Ataliba*, Av Irineu Bornhausen 5050, Agronômico district. Excellent *rodízio*. *Lindacap*, R Felipe Schmidt 1132 (closed Monday). Recommended, good views. *Pim-Pão*, R Deodoro. Good cheap breakfast, lunches. *Pizzaria San Francesco*, R São Francisco 2000, opens at 1800. Good service, popular, quite expensive. *Polly's*, Praça 15 de Novembro 151, 1st floor. Good food and service, reasonable prices. *Mirantes*, R Alvaro de Carvalho 246, Centro. Buffet self-service, good value. Recommended; also on R Vidal Ramos opposite Produtos Naturais. *A Grande Muralha*, Av Osmar Cunha 323. Chinese, good, cheap.

    Vegetarian *La Cucina*, R Padre Roma 291. Buffet lunch, Monday-Saturday, pay by weight, good, vegetarian choices. Recommended. *Vida*, R Visc de Ouro Preto 298, next to Alliance Française. Good. *Produtos Naturais*, R Vidal Ramos 127. Breads, cereals, nuts, café next door sells pizzas, *asteis*, vegetable and fruit dishes (and some chicken), juices. *Panino in Due*, Vidal Ramos 79, near Trajano, also sells vegetarian snacks, breads, salads. For a wide selection of juices and snacks (not vegetarian): *Cía Lanches*, Ten Silveira e R Trajano, downstairs, and, in Edif Dias Velho al R Felipe Schmidt 303, *Laranja Madura*, *Sabor e Sucos* and *Lanchonete Dias Velho*.

Bars & The Mercado Público in the centre, which is alive with fish sellers and stalls during the
nightclubs day, has a different atmosphere at night; the stall, *Box 32*, is good for seafood and becomes a bar specializing in *cachaça* for hard working locals to unwind. *Restaurant Pirão* overlooks the market square with a quieter view and live Brazilian music on Tuesday, Thursday and Friday. The *Alfândega* bar is right in the middle of the market and a good place to mix with locals. *Empórium*, Bocaiúva 79, is a shop by day and popular bar at night. Other clubs and bars may need a car: *Café Matisse*, Av Irineu Bornhausen 5000, inside the Centro Integrade de Cultura, *Dizzy* nightclub (O Centro) and the hotspots at the beaches. To find out about events and theme nights check the Beiramar centre for notices in shop windows, ask in surf shops or take a trip to the University of Santa Catarina in Trindade and check out the noticeboards. The news-paper *Diário Catarinense* gives details of bigger events, eg Oktoberfest.

    Nightclubs *Baccarat*, R Bocaiúva. Opens its doors around 2300 at the weekend, Greek-style building with 2 dance floors, 1 for live bands, 1 for popular music, crème de la crème of clubs in town with prices to match. *Ilhéu*, Av Prof Gama d'Eça e R Jaime Câmara. Bar and club open until early hours, tables spill outside, very popular with locals, fills up quickly, music a mixture of 1980s and 1990s hits but dance floor shamefully small. *Café Cancun*, Av Beira Mar Norte, T2251029. Wednesday-Saturday from 2000, bars, restaurant, dancing, sophisticated.

Entertainment **Cinema** The 3-screen cinema at Shopping Centre Beiramar has international films with subtitles. **Music** Free open air concert every Saturday morning at the market place near the bus terminal.

In **December** and **January** the whole island dances to the sound of the *Boi-de-Mamão*, **Festivals**
a type of dance which incorporates the puppets of Bernunça, Maricota (the Goddess of
Love, a puppet with long arms to embrace everyone) and Tião, the monkey. The Portuguese brought the tradition of the bull, which has great significance in Brazilian celebrations. Around **Easter** is the Festival of the Bull, *Farra de Boi*. It is only in the south that,
controversially nowadays, the bull is killed on Easter Sunday. The festival arouses fierce
local pride and there is much celebration around this time.

Shopping Centre Beiramar is a famous shopping centre which attracts bus loads of **Shopping**
eager shoppers from outside the state. There are many things on offer, from surf-
boards to fashion items. The 3-screen cinema is here. There are many smaller shopping malls dotted aroung the resorts, Ingleses, Centro da Lagoa. However, bargain
hunters are better off bartering in the family run businesses in the Mercado Público.

Local Car hire: *Auto Locadora Coelho*, Felipe Schmidt 81, vehicles in good condition. **Transport**
Localiza at the airport, T2361244, and at Av Paulo Fontes 730, T2255558. *Interlocadora*,
T2360179 at the airport, F2361370, rates from US$40 a day before supplements.
 Buses: there are 3 bus stations for routes on the island, or close by on the main-
land: Terminal de Ônibus Interurbano between Av Paulo Fontes and R Francisco
Tolentino, west of the Mercado Público; Terminal Urbano between Av Paulo Fontes
and R Antônio Luz, east of Praça Fernando Machado; a terminal at R Silva Jardim and R
José da Costa. Yellow micro buses (Transporte Ejecutivo), starting from the south end
of Praça 15 de Novembro and other stops, charge US$0.75-US$1.45 depending on
destination. Similarly, normal bus fares vary according to destination, from US$0.65.

Long distance Air: international and domestic flights arrive at Hercílio Luz airport,
Av Deomício Freitas, 12 km from town, T2360879. Take Ribeiroense bus 'Corredor
Sudoeste' from Terminal Urbano.

Buses: international and buses from other Brazilian cities arrive at the rodoviária Rita
Maia on the island, at the east (island) end of the Ponte Colombo Machado Salles.
 Regular daily buses to **Porto Alegre** (US$16, 7 hours), **São Paulo**, 9 hours
(US$23.75, *leito* US$36.25), **Rio**, 20 hours (US$31 *convencional*, US$42 *executive*, 55
leito), **Brasília** (at 0300, US$48); to **Foz do Iguaçu** (US$22, continuing to **Asunción**
US$30), to most other Brazilian cities. To **São Joaquim** at 1145, 1945 with *Reunidos*,
1815 with *Nevatur*, 5-6 hours, US$9.30; to **Laguna** US$5.25; to **Caxias do Sul**, *Eucatur*
via **Porto Alegre** at 0800, or go to Lages and change there. No direct bus to Corumbá,
change at Campo Grande.
 International buses: Montevideo, US$52, daily, by *TTL*. **Buenos Aires**, US$55,
Pluma, buses very full in summer, book 1 week in advance.

Road: the coastal highway (BR-101) is preferred as an alternative to the congested
inland BR-116; it runs close to Florianópolis, but either side of the turn-off to the city it
is undergoing major roadworks and long delays are possible. North of Florianópolis
the BR-101 is largely dual carriageway.

Airline offices *Aerolíneas Argentinas*, R Tte Silveira 200, 8th floor, T2247835, F2227267. **Directory**
Nordeste/Rio Sul, Jerônimo Coelho 185, sala 601, T2247008, airport T2361779. *TAM*, at airport,
T2361812. *Transbrasil*, Praça Pereira Oliveira 64, T2237177. *Varig*, R Felipe Schmidt 796,
T2247266, F2222725. *Vasp*, Av Osmar Cunha 105, T2241122, F2242970. **Banks** *Banco do Brasil*,
Praça 15 de Novembro, exchange upstairs, 1000-1500, huge commission on cash or TCs. Lots of
ATMs downstairs, some say Visa/Plus. *Banco Estado de Santa Catarina*, (BESC) câmbio, R Felip,
Schmidt e Jerônimo Coelho, 1000-1600, no commission on TCs. *Lovetur*, Av Osmar Cunha 15, Ed
Ceisa and *Centauro Turismo* at same address. *Açoriano Turismo*, Jaime Câmara 106, T2243939,
takes Amex. Money changers on R Felipe Schmidt outside BESC. ATM for Mastercard/Cirrus at

Banco Itaú, Shopping Centre Beiramar (not in the centre, bus Expresso). **Communications** Post Office: Praça 15 de Novembro 5. **Telephones:** Praça Pereira Oliveira 20. **Internet:** *Intersp@ce*, Café Cancun (see **Nightclubs** above), Av Beira Mar Norte 1344, T2251220. Mon-Fri 0900-2000, US$3 per hr. **Embassies & consulates** *Austria*, R Luiz Delfino 66, apto 501, T2225952/2691379, open Mon-Fri, 1500-1700, phone in advance. *Chile*, R Alvaro de Carvalho 267, 6th floor, Edif Mapil, T2233383. *France*, Alliance Française, T2227589, Fri 0900-1200. *Spain*, R Almte Alvim 24, Casa 9, T2221821, F2241018. *Uruguay*, R Prof Walter de Bona Castela 26, T2344645, 0800-1200, 1400-1800. **Laundry** *Lav e Lev*, R Felipe Schmidt 706, opposite *Valerim Plaza*. **Tour companies & travel agents** *Ilhatur Turismo e Cambio*, R Jerónimo Coelho 185, T2246333, F2236921. **Tourist information** *Setur*, head office at Portal Turístico de Florianópolis, mainland end of the bridge, Av Eng Max de Souza 236, Coqueiros, T2445822/5960, 0800-2000 (Sat/Sun 1800). Near the Cathedral, Praça 15 de Novembro, Centro, T2229200, 0800-1800 (2200 in high season), reliable for leaving messages. At rodoviária, Av Paulo Fontes, T2232777, and airport, 0700-1800 (0800 Sat/Sun), maps available, free. www.guiafloripa.com.br or www. hipernet. ufsc.br/floripa. *Santur*, Edif ARS, R Felipe Schmidt 249, 9th floor, T2245862/6300, F2221145, helpful, www.ciasc.gov.br and www.sc.gov.br/santur. A good series of bilingual books on all of southern Brazil is published by *Mares do Sul*, R Luiz Pasteur, Trindade, T/F3331544, www.maresdosul.com.br. **Voltage** 220 volts AC.

Ilha de Santa Catarina

There are 42 beaches around the island, so there is no shortage of choice. The most popular are the surfers' beaches such as Praia Mole, Joaquina or Barra da Lagoa; for peace and quiet, try Campeche or the southern beaches; for sport, the Lagoa de Conceição has jet skis and windsurfing. You can walk in the forest reserves, hang glide or paraglide from the Morro da Lagoa, sandboard in the dunes of Joaquina, or surf. Surfing is prohibited 30 April-30 July because of the migration of the island's largest fish, the *tainha*. Note that the temperature in the north can differ from the south of the island by several degrees. Almost all the beaches are easily reached by public buses: you need to ask at the Terminal Interurbano and the Terminal Urbano for the bus you need, or get a schedule from the Tourist Office. Buses (US$1) run hourly to virtually every place on the island.

Lagoa da Conceição is worth visiting for its beaches, sand dunes, fishing and the church of Nossa Senhora da Conceição (1730). It also has a market every Wednesday and Saturday and post office. For tandem hang gliding, contact *Lift Sul Vôo Livre*, T2320543. You can take a boat ride on the lagoon; from the Centro da Lagoa on the bridge there are daily boat trips to Costa da Lagoa which run until about 1830, check when you buy your ticket, US$4 return; the

Ilha de Santa Catarina

1 Forte Nossa Senhora da Conceição
2 Forte São José da Ponta Grossa
3 Morro da Cruz
4 Universidade Federal

Iguaçu Falls & the South

service is used mostly by the local people who live around the lake and have no other form of public transport. The ride is spectacular and there is a charming restaurant to greet you at the end of a thirsty journey. A recommended meal is the local fish, *tainha*, with salad, chips and an abundance of rice.

Across the island at **Barra da Lagoa** is a pleasant fishing village and beach, lively in the summer season, with plenty of good restaurants. You can walk across the wooden suspension bridge to one overlooking the bay, which is in a spectacular setting for a meal; it can be reached by Transol bus No 403, every 15 minutes from Terminal Urbano, 55 minutes, US$0.75. The same bus goes to beaches at **Mole**, which is a soft sand beach, good for walking. South of Mole is **Joaquina**, where surfing championships are held in January.

There is a pleasant fishing village at **Ponta das Canas**, walk one kilometre to Praia Brava for good surfing, and the beach at **Canasvieiras** is good, with many watersports on offer (bus US$0.75). Also in the north of the island is **Praia dos Ingleses** (bus 602), which gets its name from an English ship that sank in 1700. Dunes separate it from **Santinho**, where Carijó inscriptions can be seen on the cliffs. Both are surfing beaches. Other northern beaches: Jureré, Daniela and Forte. **Forte São José da Ponta Grossa** is here, beautifully restored with a small museum of its history. ■ *US$1.50.* Buses to Jureré and Daniela come here, one hour.

On the west side, north of the city, you can visit the 'city of honey bees' with a Museo da Apicultura, closes 1600 Saturday, and the Church of Santo Antônio Lisboa; take Trindadense bus 331 or any bus going north, to the turn off, on the way to Sambaqui beach and fishing village (fare US$0.65).

In the south of the island are **Praia do Campeche**, 30 minutes by bus (Pantano do Sul or Costa de Dentro) from Florianópolis; offshore is an island with a beach which is good for diving. Just inland from **Praia da Armação** is **Lagoa do Peri**, a protected area. After Armação look for a bar by the roadside called *Lanchonette e Bar Surf.* Just before the bar there is a road to the left. Walk up a red clay path and after about 200 metres you should see a path (unsignposted) on the left, leading up into the hills. A steady walk of up to two hours will lead you over two *montes* with a fabulous view from the top, down to **Praia da Lagoinha de Leste**. This is a beach rarely visited by the hoards and you can get away from the crowds even in the summer months. Camping is permitted. Further south is **Pantano do Sul**, an unspoilt and relaxed fishing village with a long, curved beach and lovely views across to the Três Irmãs islands. There are several *pousadas*, bars and restaurants, though not much nightlife. For **Praia dos Naufragados**, take bus to Caieira da Barra do Sul and walk for an hour through fine forests. **Forte Nossa Senhora da Conceição** is on a small island just offshore. It can be seen from the lighthouse near Praia dos Naufragados or take a boat trip with Scuna Sul from Florianópolis.

Lagoa da Conceição D *Pousada Zilma*, R Geral da Praia da Joaquina 279, T2320161. Quiet, safe. Recommended. *Ricardo*, R Manoel S de Oliveira 8, CEP 88062, T220107, rents self-contained apartments, can arrange houses also. Recommended restaurant: *Oliveira*, R Henrique Veras. Excellent seafood dishes. **Sleeping**

    Barra da Lagoa A *Cabañas Verde Limão*, on the beach. Small cabins with bath, fan, fridge. **A** *Pousada 32*, on beach. Comfortable apartments, helpful. **C** *Mini-Hotel Caiçara*, good, near beach. **C** *Pousada Floripaz*, Estrada Geral (across hanging bridge at bus station), T2323193. Book in advance, safe, family-run, helpful owners, will organize tours by boat and car on island. Highly recommended. **D** *Pousada-Lanchonete Sem Nome*, Praia do Moçambique. In 4-bunk rooms, bathrooms separate, kitchen, laundry. Recommended. **D** *Albergue do Mar*, basic, good for lone travellers. *Pousada Sol Mar* operates as a youth hostel but only 2 bathrooms for all. *Camping da Barra*,

T2323199. Beautiful site clean, helpful owner. Restaurant: *Meu Cantinha*, R Orlando Shaplin 89. Excellent seafood.

Joaquina A *Hotel Cris*, T2320380, F2320075. Luxurious. Recommended.

Ponta das Canas A *Hotel Moçambique*, T/F2661172, in centre of village. Noisy at weekends; houses to let from Frederico Barthe, T2660897.

Canasvieiras L *Lexus-Hotel*, RHG Pereira 745, T2660909, F2660919, on beach. Friendly, good breakfast, studio apartments. **Youth hostel**: *Albergue da Juventude Canasvieiras*, R Dr João de Oliveira 100, esq Av das Nações, T2662036, F2660220. IYHA, 2 blocks from sea, convenient, good, open from mid-December.

Praia dos Ingleses A *Sol e Mar*, T2621271. Excellent. Recommended.

Praia de Campeche A *Hotel São Sebastião da Praia*, Av Campeche 1373, T/F2374247/4066. Resort hotel on splendid beach, offers special monthly rate April to October, excellent value. *Natur Campeche Hotel Residencial*, T2374011. Ten minutes' walk from beach.

Near Pantano do Sul B *Pousada dos Tucanos*, Estr Geral da Costa de Dentro 2776, T2375084, Caixa Postal 5016. English, French, Spanish spoken, spacious bungalows in garden setting. Excellent organic food. Very highly recommended. Take bus to Pantano do Sul, walk 6 km or telephone and arrange to be picked up by German owner.

Bars & nightclubs Throughout the summer the beaches open their bars day and night. The beach huts of Praia Mole invite people to party all night (bring a blanket), while the Club *Seven* (in the Boulevard) and *L'Equinox* bar (Joaquina) are more for clubbers who don't mind 'sand in their shoes'. *Seven* offers theme nights and is very popular with surfers. Any bars are worth visiting in the Lagoon area (around the Boulevard and Barra da Lagoa) where the great Brazilian phrase '*cualquer lugar é lugar*' fits perfectly. This means whichever place is the place to be, reflecting the laid back Brazilian mood at the beach. Other clubs and bars generally require a car: *Latitude 27*, near Praia Mole, *Ilhéus* bar (Canasvieras) and the popular *Ibiza* nightclub in Jureré.

Spas near Florianópolis The BR-282 heads west from the capital to Lages (see page 381), which is a junction with the BR-116 running north-south through the state from Curitiba to Porto Alegre. About 12 kilometres along the BR-282, you come to the hot springs at **Caldas da Imperatriz** (41°C) and **Águas Mornas** (39°C). There are two spa hotels at Caldas da Imperatriz. *Caldas da Imperatriz* (**A**), T2451388, including meals and baths, was built in 1850 under the auspices of Empress Teresa Cristina and houses public baths. *Plaza Caldas da Imperatriz* (**AL**), T2451333, has baths and swimming pools and is very well appointed. At Águas Mornas, the *Aguas Mornas Palace Hotel* (**L**), T2451315, is on the site of the springs, baths open to the public Monday-Friday morning only.

The **Parque Estadual da Serra do Tabuleiro** is just south of the BR-282, with the BR-101 to the east. It is the largest protected area in Santa Catarina, covering 87,405 hectares, or nearly one percent of the state. Apart from its varied and luxuriant flora which is home to many birds and animals, it is also important to Florianópolis for its water supply. There is a small reserve near the park headquarters (near Paulo Lopes, Km 252, BR-101), where animals and birds previously in captivity are rehabilitated before being released into the wild. ■ *Daily 0800-1700*.

Italian Crosses and Saints

In 1889, Padre Jesuíta Luís Maria Rossi decided to commemorate the new century by erecting crosses on the highest hills above Nova Trento. Padre Alfredo Russel, a missionary, promised to put a statue of Nossa Senhora do Bom Socorro beside the highest cross, which eventually came to pass in 1901 on Morro da Cruz; a sanctuary was later built there.

Nova Trento's most famous inhabitant was Madre Paulina, who was beatified by the Pope in 1991. Born in Trento, Italy, in 1865, the young Amabile Visintainer emigrated to Brazil with her family in 1875 and they were given land in Nova Trenta. Amabile cared for the sick and her charitable works led her to a religious calling and the founding of the Sisters of the Immaculate Conception. She took the name of her Sister Pauline, leading a humble life until her death in 1942. Since then several miracles have been claimed in her name, which led to her beatification.

North of Florianópolis

Porto Belo

On the coast north of Florianópolis there are many resorts. They include Porto Belo, a fishing village on the north side of a peninsula settled in 1750 by Azores islanders, with a calm beach and a number of hotels and restaurants. Around the peninsula are wilder beaches reached by rough roads: Bombas, Bombinhas (both with the same sort of accommodation as Porto Belo), Quatro Ilhas (quieter, good surfing, 15 minutes' walk from Bombinhas), Mariscal, and, on the southern side, Zimbros (or Cantinho). Many of the stunning beaches around **Bombinhas** are untouched, accessible only on foot or by boat. Its clear waters are marvellous for diving.

Population: 7,500
Phone code: 047
Colour map 5, grid B5

Southwest of Porto Belo, reached by turning off the BR-101 at Tijucas and going west for 30 kilometres, is **Nova Trento**, a small town in a valley first colonized by Italians and still showing heavy Italian influence. The local cuisine includes cheese, salami and wine such as you might find in Italy. There are several Italian restaurants and wine producers where you can buy *vinho artesanal*. A good view of the area, down the Tijucas valley and even as far as the sea (on a clear day), can be had from the top of Morro da Cruz, at 525 metres.

Excursions
See box

B *Baleia Branca*, Al Nena Trevisan 98, T3694011, F3694114. Three-star, with camping. **D** *Pousada Trapiche*, no breakfast. **Youth hostel** *Porto Belo*, R José Amâncio 246, T0XX47-3694483, F2431057. IYHA. Lots of apartments, mostly sleep 4-6, in **B** range, good value for a group.

West of Porto Belo is **Praia de Perequê**, with a handful of hotels: *Blumenauense*, Av Sen Atílio Fontana, T3694208. With bath and breakfast, on beach. *Perequê Praia*, R Ida Ceni Lorenzi 100, T3694279. **Zimbros B** *Pousada Zimbros*, R da Praia 527, T3693225/1225. Cheaper off season, on beach, sumptuous breakfast, restaurant. Highly recommended. Spear fishing guide. **Camping** There are lots of campsites around the peninsula.

Sleeping

Buses Florianópolis to Porto Belo, several daily with *Rainha*, US$3, fewer at weekends, more frequent buses to **Tijucas**, **Itapema** and **Itajaí**, all on the BR-101 with connections. Buses from Porto Belo to the beaches on the peninsula.

Transport

Iguaçu Falls & the South

On the BR-101, 10 kilometres up the coast from Porto Belo, you get to **Itapema**, 60 kilometres from Florianópolis, and another former fishing village on a wide sweep of sandy beach now dominated by tourism. In high season the town accommodates around 300,000 visitors. The *Plaza Itapema Resert e Spa*, all-inclusive, is the best such establishment on this part of the coast, T3682222, F3682111. Around the headland there are several smaller and quieter beaches, Praia Grossa being one of the best, with good surf. Between Itapema and Camboriú, a tunnel is being built for the BR-101, to prevent further damage to the last vestiges of Mata Atlântica here.

Camboriú
Population: 25,500
Phone code: 047

Eighty kilometres north of Florianópolis is Camboriú, once beautiful, but now the most concentrated urban development on Brazil's southern coast. From 15 December to late February it is very crowded and expensive; the resort is popular with Argentines. In the low season it is popular with retired people. Avenida Atlântica is a wide pedestrian street along the shore. A few kilometres south, at Lojas Apple, there is Parque Cyro Gevaerd, a museum (archaeology, oceanography, fishing, local arts and crafts etc), zoo and aquarium; and Meia Praia, which is quieter and cleaner than Camboriú. A *teleférico* (cable car) has been built to Praia Laranjeiras, previously deserted; US$5 return from Barra Sul shopping centre to Laranjeiras via Mata Atlântica station. Pinho beach, 15 kilometres out of the city, is one of Brazil's few legal nudist beaches; two campsites and a small hotel. Between Itajaí and Camboriú is the beautiful, deserted (and rough) beach of Praia Brava. Note that from mid-July to mid-August it can be chilly.

Sleeping There are a huge number of modern hotels, 4-star and downwards, and aparthotels. From March-November it is easy to rent furnished apartments by the day or week. **Youth hostel E** pp *Alpino*, R Estados Unidos 180, Nacões, T/F3673332. IYHA.

Transport Buses: from **Florianópolis** (US$3.85), **Joinville** and **Blumenau**. *TTL* buses Montevideo-São Paulo stop here at about 1800, a good place to break the journey (US$68 from Montevideo).

Porto Belo beaches

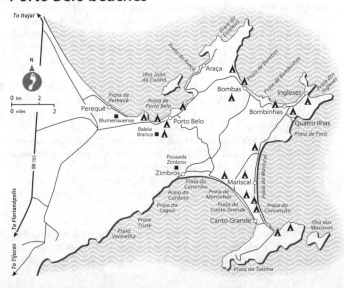

Ninety four kilometres up the coast, north of Florianópolis, by the paved BR-101 is the most important port in Santa Catarina at the mouth of the Rio Itajaí-Açu. It is the largest exporter of chicken in the country and the fourth largest container port. It has thriving fishing and shipbuilding industries and is the centre of a district largely colonized by Germans and Italians, although the town itself was founded by immigrants from the Azores.

Itajaí
Population: 135,000
Phone code: 047

Despite the port, tourism is heavily promoted and in summer the population triples. Itajaí celebrates a Marejada festival in October in honour of Portugal and the sea. It is held in the Centro de Promoções Itajaí Tur, where there are musical and folkloric festivities, a pavilion for dancing and shows, and a pavilion for food (lots of different ways of preparing *bacalhau* and masses of seafood). For tourist information, contact the Centro de Promoções Itajaí Tur, T3481080/3322.

The local beaches are Atalaia, Geremias and Cabeçudas (within walking distance, quiet and small), but within the municipality there is also Praia do Morcego which is considered a health resort because of the large amount of minerals in the water. There is also a cave here, the Caverna do Morcego, about which there are many myths and legends. About 50 kilometres southwest of Itajaí is the **Caverna de Botuverá**, which you enter through a dripping tunnel which can flood in the wet season. The first gallery is like a cathedral, with stalactites and rock formations, one of which is called the organ, and the guide will play a sort of tune for you. There are several galleries, not all of which are fully explored, but pillars of 20 metres have been found, making the cave extremely old. It is believed that it takes 10,000 years for one metre of rock to form. To get to Botuverá, take the road to Brusque off the BR-101, where there is tourist information and they can give you directions and other details. Botuverá is 10 kilometres from Brusque.

Sleeping A *Grande*, R Felipe Schmidt 198, T3480968, F3482179. Good value. **B** *Marambaia Cabeçudas*, Praça Marcos Konder 46, Praia de Cabeçudas, 6 km out of town, T/F3487373, 3-star. **Bars & nightclubs** *Trudys*, on riverfront at end of main street. Good place for changing cash.

Twenty kilometres north of Itajaí is Penha (*population* 15,000), another resort along the BR-101, with a broad, curved, sandy beach with rocky headlands at either end, offering smaller coves for swimming, surfing and fishing. The town was founded by Portuguese fishermen in the 18th century and fishing is still important as elsewhere along the coast. However, tourism took off in the 1970s and during the high season the population rises to 100,000. Its major claim to fame is the **Beto Carrero World**, opened in 1991 on Praia de Armação, the largest theme park in Latin America and the fifth largest in the world. Penha even offers themed shopping, at the Shopping Temático on Avenida Eugênio Krause, where you can visit different countries in different ages.

There are several fiestas and events in Penha, starting with a seafood festival in February, Carnival, the Festa do Divino (procession and crowning of the Emperor) in May or June, and the Festa de São João e São Pedro, 24-29 June (a tradition from the Azores). There are hotels, *pousadas* and camping.

Other resorts north of Itajaí include **Piçarras**, with sandy beaches interspersed with rocky headlands (ideal for fishing, several hotels), and **Barra Velha**, with a good, cheap hotel, *Hotel Mirante*, with a restaurant, and two more expensive hotels.

Iguaçu Falls & the South

Blumenau

There is a 61 kilometre paved road from Itajaí to Blumenau, 47 kilometres up the Rio Itajaí-Açu. It is in a prosperous district settled mostly by Germans; the first to arrive were the philosopher Herman Bruno Otto Blumenau and 16 other German explorers, who sailed up the river in 1850. Work soon began to build schools, houses and the first plantations, and the city soon became a notable textile centre. Today, high-tech and electronics industries are replacing textiles as the town's economic mainstay. A clean, orderly city with almost caricatured Germanic architecture, the German Enxaimel design (exposed beams and brickwork) typifies some of the more famous buildings such as the Museum of the Colonial Family (1868), the Mayor's Residence and the Molemann Shopping, which resembles a medieval German castle. Blumenau offers a charming alternative to the less-organized Brazilian way of life.

Sights See the **German Evangelical Church**, also the **Museu da Família Colonial**, German immigrant museum, on Avenida Duque de Caxias 78. ■ *Monday-Friday, 0800-1130, 1330-1730, Saturday morning only, US$0.15.* The houses, now **museums**, of **Dr Bruno Otto Blumenau** and of **Fritz Müller** are worth a visit. Müller, a collaborator of Darwin, bought the Blumenau estate in 1897 and founded the town. ■ *Both museums: 0800-1800.*

Excursions The **Parque Ecológico Spitzkopf** is a pleasant day trip for hiking, with very nice trails through the forest, passing waterfalls, natural pools, up to the Spitzkopf Peak at 936 metres,5½ kilometres from the entrance, from where you get a wonderful view of the region. If you are not up to hiking up hills, there are paths around the lower slopes which will take you half a day. Get the 'Garcia' bus from Avenida 7 de Septembro via Rua São Paulo to Terminal Garcia, then change to 'Progresso' until the end of the paved road, US$0.60 each bus. Then 1½ kilometres walk to the park entrance (US$1.50), German spoken, small zoo, cabins to rent, **D** *Pousada Ecológoca Spitzkopf*, R Bruno Schreiber 3777, bar but no restaurant, pool, heating, beautiful, clean, extremely quiet, T3365422.

You can also visit Timbó and Pomerode (from the riverside road opposite the Prefeitura), by bus past rice fields and wooden houses set in beautiful gardens. At **Pomerode** (*population* 21,500), 33 kilometres west of Blumenau, there is an interesting zoo, founded in 1932 and the oldest in the state. It can be found on Rua Hermann Weege 160, and houses over 600 animals of different species. The tourist office can be contacted on T3872627. Next door to the Prefeitura Municipal is the Associação dos Artistas e Artesãos de Pomerode, where you can find exhibitions of local arts and crafts and a shop. The north German dialect of Plattdeutsch is still spoken here and there are several folkloric groups keeping alive the music and dance of their ancestors: *Alpino Germánico, Pomerano, Edelweiss* and *Belgard*. Shooting and hunting is also traditional in the area and there are 16 Clubes de Caça e Tiro which are active at all festivities. The men compete for the title of Rei do Tiro Municipal in July and the women compete for the Rainha do Tiro Municipal in November. Other activities include parapenting (T3870803), a jeep club (T3872328), horse riding (T3872290) and swimming pools with waterslides. The Museu Pomerano, Rodovia SC 418, Km 3, T3870477, tells the story of the colonial family. Museu Ervin Kurt Theichmann, Rua 15 de Novembro 791, T3870282, has sculptures. The *Confeitaria Torten Paradies*, Rua 15 de Novembro 211, serves excellent German cakes.

Blumenau's Oktoberfest

In 1983, Blumenau suffered a great flood. After its destructive impact, the idea was born to introduce a German-style 'traditional' Oktoberfest beer-festival to motivate people to reconstruct the city. The festival celebrating German music, beer and the German way of life was started in 1984 here, and was expected to become the second largest in the world after Munich's (bands come from Germany for the event). It is the second largest street party in Brazil, after Carnival. It is set next to the São Francisco de Assis National Park and usually held in the first half of October. During the day the narrow streets are packed around the Molemann Centre, which is where many locals like to begin their festivities before the Oktoberfest Pavilion opens. The centre contains a mixture of bars, live music and, of course,

Chopp. At 1900 the doors open and you will find four decorated pavilions, each holding different events from drinking competitions to the 'sausage Olympics', all accompanied by non-stop traditional German music. The cultural pavilion holds traditional dress and cake making competitions, as well as getting the audience involved in the singing, which grows steadily worse as the evening rolls on. There is also a fun fair and folk dancing shows. Food around the stalls is German and half a litre of Chopp will cost you around US$2. Brazilian popular bands are slowly being introduced, much to the disapproval of the older inhabitants. Visitors report it is worth attending on weekday evenings but weekends are too crowded. It is repeated, but called a 'summer festival', in the three weeks preceding Carnival.

Sleeping **C** *Schroeder*, R 15 de Novembro 514, T3870933. A/c, TV, phone, fridge, pool. **D** *Pousada Max*, R 15 de Novembro 257, T3870598. Apartment with satellite TV, fridge, a/c, parking.

Transport *Coletivos Volkmann* (T3871321), Blumenau-Pomerode, 10 daily buses Monday-Friday, 9 on Saturday and 6 on Sundays and holidays. There are also buses from Pomerode to Jaraguá do Sul, Joinville, São Bento do Sul, Florianópolis, São Paulo, Curitiba and other local places with Rex (T3870387), *União*, *Reunidas* and *Penha/Itapemirim* (T3870387).

Half-day excursion to Gaspar (15 kilometres) to visit the cathedral, Igreja Matriz São Pedro Apóstolo, set high above the river (Verde Vale bus company from stop outside the huge supermarket on Rua 7 de Setembro in the centre, office at Rua Angêlo Dias 220, sala 207, Blumenau, T3266179/3716, www.braznet.com.br/~verdetur/index.html). There are two water parks in Gaspar with waterslides and other amusements: Parque Aquático Cascanéia, on Rua José Patrocínio dos Santos, T3390690, with chalets, parking, restaurants, and Cascata Carolina, Estrada Geral da Carolina-Belchior Alto, T3390779, with water coming straight from the rocks. *Fazenda Park Hotel* is new, with a swimming pool, fishing, walking and riding, on the Estrada Geral do Gasparinho 2499, T3265696.

Further west along the Rio Itajaí-Açu, around Ibirama, the river is good for whitewater rafting. You can take a break between rapids to bathe in the waterfalls.

A *Garden Terrace*, R Padre Jacobs 15, T3263544, F3260366. **A** *Glória*, R 7 de Setembro 954, T3261988, F3265370. German-run, excellent coffee shop. **A** *Himmelblau Palace*, R 7 de Setembro 1415, T/F3265800. **A** *Plaza Hering*, R 7 de Setembro 818, T3261277, F3229409. Four-star, heating. **C** *Blumenau Turist Hotel*, R Francisco Margarida 67, T3234640, 200m from bus station. Helpful (all aforementioned hotels have heating in

Sleeping
Reservations essential during Oktoberfest

rooms). **D** *Central*, R 7 de Setembro 1036, T322057. Basic, **E** without bath, both without breakfast, clean. **D** *City*, R Ángelo Dias 263, T3222205. **D** *Herrmann*, central, Floriano Peixoto 213, T3224370, F3260670. One of the oldest houses in Blumenau, clean, rooms with or without bath, excellent big breakfast, German spoken. Many cheap hotels do not include breakfast. **Youth hostel** *Pousada Albergue da Juventude Dusseldorf*, R São Paulo 2457, T3234332. **Camping** Municipal campsite, 3 km out on Rua Pastor Osvaldo Hesse; Paraíso dos Poneis, 9 km out on the Itajaí road, also Motel; Refúgio Gaspar Alto, 12 km out on Rua da Glória.

Eating Good German food at *Frohsinn*, Morro Aipim (panoramic view) and *Cavalinho Branco*, Av Rio Branco 165. Huge meals. International eating at *Moinho do Vale*, Paraguai 66. *Amigo*, Peixoto 213, huge cheap meals. *Caféhaus Glória*, in *Hotel Glória*. Excellent coffee shop. *Deutsches Eck*, R 7 de Septembro 432. Recommended. Especially *carne pizzaiola*. *Gruta Azul*, Rodolfo Freygang 8. Good, popular, not cheap. *Internacional*, Nereu Ramos 61. Chinese, very good, not particularly expensive. *Chinês*, R 15 de Novembro 346, near Tourist office. Good.

Entertainment **Theatre** *Teatro Carlos Gomes*, 15 de Novembro between Kennedy and N Deeke; is also an exhibition centre; public library open 0800-1800.

Shopping German bookshops, *Librerias Alemãs*, at bus station and R 7 de Setembro (also stocks English books), and 15 de Novembro. Craft shop, *Casa Meyer*, 15 de Novembro 401.

Transport **Car hire** *Localiza*, R 7 de Setembro 255, T3220843. **Buses** Bus to the rodoviária from Av Pres Castelo-Branco (Beira Rio). There are good bus connections in all directions from Blumenau. To **Curitiba** and **Rio** with *Penha*, US$35; to *Curitiba* alone, US$5.50, 4 hours, 3 daily (*Penha* and *Catarinense*). Blumenau to **Caxias do Sul** at 1930 only, arrives 0400, US$9.50.

Directory **Banks** At *Câmbios*/travel agencies: *Vale do Itajaí Turismo e Cambio*, Av Beira Rio 167. Very helpful, German spoken. *Tilotur Turismo*, Al Rio Branco e 15 de Novembro, 2nd floor. **Communications** **Telephones**: corner of Av Brasil and República Argentina, also a kiosk near the Prefeitura. **Tourist information** 15 de Novembro, on the corner of R Ângelo Dias. Helpful.

West of Blumenau

To Iguaçu As an alternative to a direct bus, daily from Florianópolis and Itajaí to Iguaçu via Blumenau, you can travel through rich and interesting farming country in Santa Catarina and Rio Grande do Sul, stopping at the following places. **Joaçaba** (*population* 28,000) is a town of German immigrants, in the centre of the Vale do Contestado (see box, page 383). For information, T5223000. **Erexim** has a strong *gaúcho* influence. **Iraí** (*population* 11,500) is a town with thermal springs, situated in an Italian immigrant area. The town is good for semi-precious stones. From any of these places you can go to Pato Branco and Cascavel and thence to Foz do Iguaçu.

Treze Tílias
Population: 4,500
Phone code: 049

Two hours from Joaçaba is Treze Tílias, a village where 19th century Tyrolean dialect is still spoken and the immigrant culture is perfectly preserved. It was settled in 1933 by a group led by Andreas Thaler, who had been the Austrian Minister of Agriculture. Dairy farming is the main economic activity and children are taught German and Portuguese in school. The style of architecture has been lifted straight from the Alps. The major festivity of the year is the four-day Tirolerfest in October, celebrating the customs of the Tirol, with food, sculpture and art. Tourist information is at Praça Andreas Thaler 25, T/F5370176.

Sleeping **B** *Dreizhnlinden*, R Leoberto Leal 392, T5370297, F5370539. **B** *Tirol*, R São Vicente de Paula III, T5370125. **C** *Alpenrose*, R Min João Cleophas 340, T5370273. **D** *Áustria*, R Tirol 5, T5370132.

Located 80 kilometres up the coast, at the mouth of the Baia de Babitonga, São Francisco do Sul is the port for the town of Joinville, 45 kilometres inland at the head of the Rio Cachoeira. It is the country's third oldest city (Binot Paulmier de Gonneville landed here in 1504), after Porto Seguro in Bahia and São Vicente in Rio de Janeiro. There is an interesting **Museu Nacional do Mare** reflecting Brazil's seafaring history. ■ *Rua Manual Lourenço de Andrade, T4441868. Tuesday-Friday 0900-1800, Saturday-Sunday 1100-1800, US$1.* The colonial centre has over 150 historical sites and has been protected since 1987. The **cathedral**, Nossa Senhora da Graça, was built between 1699 and 1719 and still has its original walls made with sand, shells and whale oil. The **Museu Histórico de São Francisco do Sul** is on Rua Coronel Carvalho, in the 18th-century Cadeia Pública. There is a tourist information desk in the cinema behind the Prefeitura. Not far from the historical centre is the modern port. Petrobrás has an oil refinery here.

There are about 13 excellent **beaches** nearby, such as Ubatuba, Enseada, which has good nightlife, hotels, pensions and three campsites, Prainha (surf championships are held here) and Cápri. Quieter waters can be found at Ingleses, Figueiras, Paulas and Calixtos but, being in the bay, the sea is polluted. A ferry crosses the Baia de Babitonga from Bairro Laranjeiras, eight kilometres from the centre, to Estaleiro, 30 minutes. The historic town of Vila da Glória (six kilometres from Estaleiro) can be visited. See under Joinville for the *Príncipe de Joinville* boat trip. For schooner trips T9747266. Take mosquito repellent.

São Francisco do Sul
Population: 27,000
Phone code: 047

Sleeping **B** *Kontik*, Babitonga 211, T4442232. In historic centre, view of bay. **AL-A** *Zibamba*, R Fernandes Dias 27, T/F4442020. Central, pleasant, a/c, pool, good restaurant.

Transport Bus terminal is 1½ km from centre. Direct bus (*Penha*) daily to **Curitiba** at 0730, US$6, 3½ hours.

Joinville

The state's largest city lies two kilometres from the main coastal highway, BR-101, by which Curitiba and Florianópolis are less than two hours away. Joinville is known as the 'city of the princes' for its historical connections with royalty, although it is also nicknamed the 'city of flowers', the 'city of bicycles' or even 'Manchester Catarinense'.

Population: 500,000
Phone code: 047
Colour map 5, grid B5

Twenty five square leagues of land in the north of Santa Catarina was the dowry of Dona Francisca Carolina, the sister of Emperor Pedro II, when she married the Prince of Joinville, the son of the King of France. However, political problems led to the Prince seeking refuge in Hamburg, where interest in exploring the land took hold. The couple never visited, and in 1849 ceded eight square leagues to the Colonizing Society of Hamburg. The first party of immigrants was organized by the senator Christian Mathias Schroeder. A military engineer, Hermann Güenter, chose the site and on 9 March 1851 the new community was founded. The first immigrants were a group of 118 German and Swiss, to be followed later by 74 Norwegians and some other Europeans. The colony was first known as Dona Francisca but was changed in 1852 to Joinville. The city now has an area of 1,183 square kilometres with a population of 270,000 in the urban area, and is one of the most important in the state.

History

Iguaçu Falls & the South

Sights At **Expoville**, four kilometres from the centre on BR-101 (continuation of 15 de Novembro), is an exhibition of Joinville's industry, although it is used for many other exhibitions and festivals as well. The new, multifunctional, Centreventos Cau Hansen has been built to house sporting activities, shows, festivals, conferences and other events. It will have the first Bolshoi Ballet School outside Moscow. The tiled mural around the entrance, by Juarez Machado, depicts a circus. There are some 600 industries in the manufacturing park, many of which are substantial exporters. The industry does not, however, spoil the considerable charm of the city.

Museums **Museu Nacional da Imigração e Colonização**, in the Palácio dos Príncipes, Rua Rio Branco 229, has a collection of objects and tools from the original German settlement and other items of historical interest. ■ *Tuesday-Friday 0900-1800*. **Arquivo Histórico de Joinville**, Avenida Hermann August Lepper 65, houses a collection of documents dating from the town's foundation. ■ *Monday-Friday 0830-1200, 1330-2000, T4222154*. There is also the **Museu de Fundição**, Rua Helmuth Fallgatter 3345, with around 800 items, including books, documents, photographs, old equipment and tools, minerals and artistic items. ■ *Monday-Friday 0800-1200, 1330-1700, T4320133*. The interesting **Museu de Artes de Joinville** is in the old residence of Ottokar Doerfell, Rua 15 de Novembro 1400. It promotes temporary exhibitions by local and other Brazilian artists. ■ *Tuesday-Sunday, 0900-2100*. The **Casa da Cultura** (Galeria Municipal de Artes 'Vistor Kursansew'), Rua Dona Fransisca 800, also contains the School of Art 'Fritz Alt', the School of Music 'Vila Lobos' and the School of Ballet. ■ *Monday-Friday 0900-1800, Saturday 0900-1300*. **Casa Fritz Alt**, Rua Aubé, is the home of the sculptor, exhibiting his works of art and personal possessions; several of his monuments are on display in the town. ■ *0900-1200, 1400-1800, closed Monday*. **Museu Nacional dos Bombeiros**, Rua Padre Carlos, is dedicated to the Brazilian fire service. ■ *T4332495*.

The **Museu Arqueológico do Sambaqui**, Rua Dona Francisca 600, has a collection dating back to 5000 BC, with an exhibition of Sambaqui man, his way of life, eating habits, funereal customs and sculpture. ■ *Tuesday-Sunday, 0900-1200, 1400-1800, T4330114*. There are also two archaeological reserves: **Sambaqui do Rio Comprido**, carbon dated to BC 2865, and **Sambaqui Morro do Ouro**.

The **Alameda Brustlein** is better known as the **Rua das Palmeiras**. This most impressive avenue of palm trees, leading to the **Palácio dos Príncipes**, was planted in 1873 by Frederico Brustlein with seeds brought in 1867 by Louis Niemeyer. They have been protected since 1982. The **Railway Station** on Rua Leite Ribeiro dates from 1906 and is a fine example of the German style of architecture (T4222550), and the **Mercado Municipal**, Praça Hercílio Luz, is in the enxaimel style. At the other end of the spectrum, the **Cathedral**, on Avenida Juscelino Kubitscheck with Rua do Príncipe (T4333459), is futuristic with spectacular windows recounting the story of man. The **Cemitério dos Imigrantes**, on Rua 15 de Novembro 978, is interesting and a quiet place; the attached **Casa da Memória do Imigrante** has information on the town's history, with audiovisual and documentary displays. ■ *Monday-Friday 1400-1730*. The **Parque Zoobotânico**, 15 minutes' walk in the direction of Mirante, on Rua Pastor Guilherme Rau 462, is a good zoo and park, with many local species of birds and animals and a children's park. ■ *0900-1800, closed Mondays, T4331230*. From here it is another 25 minutes' walk to the **Mirante** for a beautiful view of the town and the bay. The tower on the top is at an altitude of 250 metres and you can walk up a spiral staircase on the outside for a panoramic view. There is an **Orchid Farm** in Boa Vista which is open to the public for sales or just to look around, on Rua Helmuth Fallgatter 2547, opposite the Terminal de Integração Tupy. ■ *0800-1200, 1330-1800.*

You can take a boat trip on the *Príncipe de Joinville III* at 1000 from Lagoa **Excursions**
Saguaçú, Bairro Espinheiros (nine kilometres from the centre), past several
islands to São Franciso do Sul, visit the Museu Nacional do Mar, the port, have
lunch at a fish restaurant and return with a stop on Ilha da Rita and Ilha das
Flores, getting back at 1600. ■ *US$10 pp, T4550824/9844570.*

Four daily buses go to **Ubatuba** beach, a weekend resort (see above under
São Francisco do Sul).

Guaratuba (see page 337) by bus, 1¼ hours, US$2 (connections to
Paranaguá).

The **festival of São João** in June can be seen best in Santa Catarina at **Campo Alegre**, the first town on the road inland to Mafra. There are bonfires, a lot

Joinville

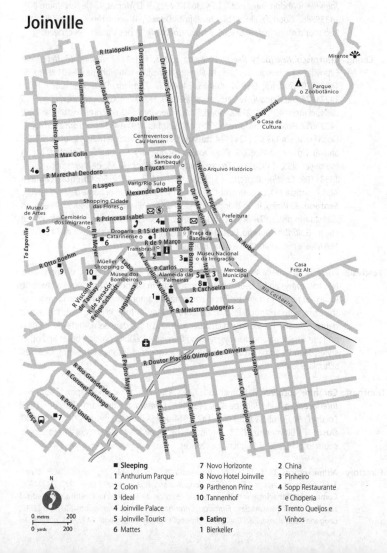

Iguaçu Falls & the South

■ Sleeping	7 Novo Horizonte	2 China
1 Anthurium Parque	8 Novo Hotel Joinville	3 Pinheiro
2 Colon	9 Parthenon Prinz	4 Sopp Restaurante
3 Ideal	10 Tannenhof	e Choperia
4 Joinville Palace		5 Trento Queijos e
5 Joinville Tourist	● Eating	Vinhos
6 Mattes	1 Bierkeller	

N

0 metres 200
0 yards 200

of (German) folk dancing, and large quantities of *quentão* and *pinhões* (see under Gramado, **Eating**, below). It is a beautiful climb on the road from the BR-101 to Campo Alegre. The road continues through São Bento do Sul and Rio Negrinho to Mafra, from where a good road (the BR-116) goes to Curitiba.

Sleeping
■ *on map, page 377*
Price codes: see inside front cover

A *Parthenon Prinz Suite*, R Otto Boehm 525, T/F4339111. Pool, sauna, gym, squash, conference rooms, restaurant, café, bar. **A** *Anthurium Parque*, R São José 226, T/F4336299. Colonial building, once home to a bishop, good value, English spoken, pool, sauna, part of the Roteiro de Charme hotel group, see page 57. **A** *Colon Palace*, R São Joaquim 80, T4336188, F4332969, colon@netville.com.br. Three-star, pool, bar, restaurant. **A** *Tannenhof*, R Visc de Taunay 340, T/F4338011. Four-star, pool, gym, traffic noise, excellent breakfast, restaurant on 14th floor. **B** *Joinville Palace*, R do Príncipe 142, T4336111, F4338123. A/c, heating, TV, Visa accepted. **B** *Joinville Tourist*, R 7 de Setembro 40, T4331288, F4331500. Pool, bar, restaurant. **B** *Novo Hotel Joinville*, R Abdon Batista 237, T/F4336112. A/c, TV. **D** *Mattes*, 15 de Novembro 801, T4339886. Good facilities, big breakfast. **D** *Ideal*, R Jerônimo Coelho 98, near Rodoviário Municipal, T4223660. **E** *Novo Horizonte*, at bus station. Basic, clean.

Eating
● *on map, page 377*

Churrasco *Rex (Baby Beef)* , Blumenau 3097, T4351722. *Ataliba (Buffet)*, near Expoville, 5 km out on Rua 15 de Novembro at the junction with the BR-101 at Km 39, T4531870. *Rudnick*, BR-101, Km 25, T4641122. *Familiar*, R Dr João Colin 1872, T4271474. *Via Piana II*, Av Getúlio Vargas 1169, T4227994. **German** *Bierkeller*, R 15 de Novembro 497, T4221360. *Sopp*, R Mcal Deodoro 640, on corner with R Jaraguá, T4223637. *Recanto do Marreco*, R 15 de Novembro 3791, T4332975. *Tante Berta*, Estr Dona Francisca 11757, T4241324. **Italian** *O Fornão*, R Visc de Taunay 240, T4227866, and at No 299, T4338028. *Pizza rodízio*, good, very reasonable. *Fatirella*, R Eng Niemeyer 255, T4338136. *Trento Queijos e Vinhos*, R 15 de Novembro 2973, T4531796. *Cantina Richetti*, R Dr João Colin 1163, T4222156. **Oriental** *China*, R Abdon Batista 131, opposite the Cathedral, T4223323. Eat in or home delivery service. **Seafood** *Pinheiro*, R Rio Branco 299, T4551254. Well worth a visit for excellent fish and shrimp dishes. *Tritão*, R Visc de Taunay 902, T4334816. Very good seafood, not cheap. *Golfinho Dourado*, Praça Hercílio Luz, annex to Mercado Municipal, T4227494. The Müeller Shopping has a good food hall.

Festivals
There is an annual flower festival in **November** (mostly orchids, disappointing, US$1.50 entry) and a beer festival, *Fenachopp*, in **October**. Shooting is a favourite local past time and there are lots of competitions among the 2,000 or so members of the clubs, with an annual festival, *Fenatiro*, in **May**. In **July**, Joinville hosts the largest dance festival in the world, which attracts around 4,000 dancers who stay for 12 days and put on shows and displays, ranging from jazz, folklore, classical ballet and other styles, seen by some 30,000 spectators in a variety of locations: theatres, factories, schools, squares.

Transport
Car hire *Localiza*, R Blumenau 1728, T4339393, or at the airport T4671020; *Interlocadora*, R do Príncipe 839, T4227888; *Olímpia*, R 9 de Março 734, T4331755; *Locasul*, Av Getúlio Vargas 695, T4221514. **Air** Airport 5 km from city, T4671000. **Buses** To Blumenau, US$3, 2¼ hours. The rodoviária is 2½ km outside the town, south exit, T4332991 (regular bus service).

Directory
Airline offices *TAM*, T4332033. *Transbrasil*, R São Joaquim 70, *Hotel Colon* annex, T/F4226060, at airport T/F4671023. *Varig/Rio Sul*, R Alexandre Dohler 277, T4332800. **Communications** Internet: *Biernet Bar*, R Visconde de Taunay 456. **Hospitals & medical services** 24-hr pharmacies: *Farmacia Catarinense*, R 15 de Novembro 503, T4222318. *Drogaria Catarinense*, Filial Boa Vista, in front of the Hospital Regional, T4372355, or Filial São

South of Florianópolis

Two beaches south of Florianópolis which are worth a stop are **Pinheira** and **Guarda do Embaú**, which you get to by crossing a river in a canoe. The surfing is excellent here and Guarda is a favourite spot of surfers from Rio and São Paulo (surfing is not permitted in the *tainha* fishing season, 15 May-15 July). **Garopaba**, 89 kilometres south of Florianópolis, is a village of 11,000, which swells to 100,000 during the holiday season. Its Carijó Indian name 'Y-Gara-Paba' means 'much water, many fish and many hills'. There is a simple colonial church and a sandy coast. **B** *Pousada da Lagoa*, Rua Rosalina de Aguiar Lentz 325, T/F2543201. There is also a youth hostel, **E** per person, *Praia do Ferrugem*, Estr Gerals do Capão, T0XX48-2540035, IYHA.

Silveira, three kilometres east, is considered one of Brazil's finest surfing spots. Swimming can be risky, though, because of the surf and sudden drops in the ocean floor. There is good fishing for *tainha*, lobster, anchovy and other varieties. **Praia da Rosa**, 18 kilometres south, is a 3½ kilometre beach with good swimming, fishing, diving and pleasant coastal walks. It is also one of Brazil's prime whale-watching sites, with right whales coming to the bay to calve between June and November. The headquarters of the Baleia Franca project is *Pousada Vida Sol e Mar*, T3540041, pousadavidasolemar@zaz.com.br, www.vsmar.com.br; trips cost US$42 in a boat, US$20 on land. The *pousada* also has cabins for rent, with kitchen, TV, restaurant, sushi bar, tennis, surf school (**L**).

Sleeping Praia da Rosa: **A** *Caminho do Rei*, Caminho do Morro, T/F3556062. **A** *Morada do Bouganvilles*, Estr Geral do Morro, T3556100, F3556179. **B** *The Rosebud*, Estr Geral do Morro, T3556101.

At the port of **Imbituba** (*population* 33,000) there is a carbo-chemical plant, from which air pollution is very bad. The rail link between Imbituba and Tubarão to the south was one of the busiest steam services in South America, but is now closed. Imbituba is now a popular resort with extensive beaches, lakes and lively surf. Just south of the town there are a few *pousadas* at **Vila Nova**, on the beach, further south along the BR-101 is *Quinta do Bucanero*, Estrada Geral do Rosa, T/F3556056, which is part of the Roteiro de Charme hotel group, see page 57; at **Itapirubá**, about 10 kilometres further south, there is the four-star *Hotel Itapirubá*, on the beach, T/F6460294.

Laguna

Fifteen kilometres from Tubarão is the small fishing port of Laguna in southern Santa Catarina. The town, which was founded in 1676, was a focal point of defence against Spanish invasions and still retains vestiges of its turbulent past. Now Laguna serves mainly as a holiday resort, perched between the ocean and a chain of three lakes. In 1839, Laguna was the capital of the Juliana Republic, a short-lived separatist movement led by Italian idealist Guiseppe Garibáldi. At that time he met a devoted lover, Ana Maria de Jesus Ribeiro, who followed him into battle, was taken prisoner, escaped and rejoined Garibáldi at Vacaria. Their first son, Menotti, was born in Rio Grande do Sul, but the family moved

Population: 43,500
Phone code: 048
124 km S of Florianópolis
Colour map 5, grid B4

Iguaçu Falls & the South

to Montevideo in 1841, where they lived in poverty. They later moved to Argentina and then to Italy, where they fought for the unification of the peninsula. Ana Maria (or Anita) died near Ravenna in 1849 while they were fleeing to Switzerland from the Austrian army. She became a heroine in both Brazil and Italy and there are monuments to her in Rome, Ravenna, Porto Alegre, Belo Horizonte, Florianópolis, Juiz da Fora, Tubarão and Laguna. At Laguna is the **Anita Garibáldi Museum**, containing documents, furniture, and her personal effects.

Laguna's beach, two kilometres from the centre, is not very good, but 16 kilometres away (by ferry and road) are beaches and dunes at **Cavo de Santa Marta**. Also from Laguna, take a *Lagunatur* or *Auto Viação São José* bus to **Farol** (four buses a day Monday-Friday, one on Saturday, US$1.50, beautiful ride). You have to cross the mouth of the Lagoa Santo Antônio by ferry (10 minutes) to get to Farol; look out for fishermen aided by dolphins (*botos*). Here is a fishing village with a lighthouse, the Farol de Santa Marta; the largest lighthouse in South America with the third largest view in the world. It was built by the French in 1890 of stone, sand and whale oil. Guided tours available (taxi, US$10, not including ferry toll). It may be possible to bargain with fishermen for a bed, or there are campsites at Santa Marta Pequena by the lighthouse, popular with surfers.

Sleeping A *Laguna Tourist*, Praia do Gi, 4 km, T6470022, F6470123. Five-star, first-class. B *Hotel Farol de Santa Marta*, Farol, 18 km away, T9861257, F6441944. C *Turismar*, Av Rio Grande do Sul 207, T6470024, F6470279. Two-star, view over Mar Grosso beach, TV. D *Recanto*, Av Colombo 17, close to bus terminal. With breakfast, modern but basic. D *Beiramar*, 100m from *Recanto*, opposite Angeloni Supermarket, T6440260. No breakfast, clean, TV, rooms with view over lagoon. Also nearby, D *Farol Palace*, R Gustavo Richard.

Transport **Buses** To Porto Alegre, 5½ hours, with *Santo Anjo Da Guarda*; same company goes to Florianópolis, 2 hours, US$5.25, 6 daily; to Tubarão, every hour with *Alvorada*, US$2.75, 50 minutes.

Tubarão
Population: 83,500
Phone code: 048

Some 75 kilometres north of Araranguá is the coalfield town of Tubarão. Inland from the main road are the coalfields of Criciúma and Içara, with good beaches nearby. Tubarão has a railway museum with a large collection of steam engines used in South America. Trips are run once a month to Urussaga (see below), April-October, and to Imbituba and Jaguaruna, November to March. ■ *T9761257*. **Termos do Gravatal** can be visited from Tubarão for its mineral pools. It is a quiet and peaceful area.

Sleeping Gravatal: **AL** *Internacional do Gravatal*, Av Pedro Zappelini 882, T6482155, F6482101, 4-star. **AL** *Gravatal Termas*, Av Pedro Zappelini 285, T6482122, F6482056, 3-star. **A** *Cabanas Termas*, Av Pedro Zappelini, T6482082, F6482147.

North of Gravatal are the towns of **Armazém**, settled by Germans, where agriculture and livestock are the main economic activities, and **São Martinho**, with enxaimel architecture brought by German immigrants. West of Gravatal is **São Ludgero**, also colonized by Germans and a major producer of cheese and fruit. Along the same road and about 60 kilometres inland from Tubarão is **Orleães**, first colonized in 1883 by Italians, followed by the Germans, Portuguese and Polish. Its museum has an original water-powered workshop and sawmill, complete with waterwheel. It dates from the original settlers, and is still in working order. To get there one must get off the bus at the junction about three kilometres from the town. From here you can continue inland to the west through **Lauro Müller** and up into the mountains, or south to **Urussanga**, where the Italian influence is very strong, and down to Cruciúma and the coast.

Continuing down the coast on the BR-101, you come to Araranguá, 13 kilometres from which is the beautiful beach of **Arroio do Silva**. Also reached from here is another beach resort, **Morro dos Conventos**, with hotels and campsites.

Araranguá
Population: 51,000
Phone code: 048

Sleeping Arroio do Silva: **B** *Scaini Palace*, Av Mondardo 130, T/F5261266. Good food. Recommended. **C** *Hotel Paulista*, R Dionizio Mondardo 58, T/F5261244.

Bars and nightclubs *Bar Nabar*, Av Getulio Vargas 970, close to beach. Cheap drinks, English speaking owners, live music. Recommended.

Just before you get to the border with Rio Grande do Sul (but not on the BR-101) is **Praia Grande**, which has a hotel and a good, cheap *churrascaria* just off the praça (see page 395 for access to Parque Nacional de Aparados da Serra).

São Joaquim

Buses from Tubarão go inland to Lauro Müller, then over the Serra do Rio do Rastro (beautiful views of the coast in clear weather, really spectacular) to **Bom Jardim da Serra**, which has an apple festival every April. The road continues to São Joaquim. At 1,360 metres, it is the highest town in Southern Brazil, with regular snowfalls in winter. It is a very pleasant town with an excellent climate. Eleven kilometres outside the town, on the way to Bom Jardim da Serra, is the **Parque Ecológico Vale da Neve** (Snow Valley). It is an easy hike and very beautiful, the entrance is on the main road, US$3, and there is a restaurant. The owner is American and an English speaking guide will take you for a 1½ hour walk through the forest. From São Joaquim, northeast over Pericó to Urubici is unpaved. These roads go around the **Parque Nacional de São Joaquim** (33,500 hectares) in the Serra Geral. It has canyons containing subtropical vegetation, and araucaria forest at higher levels. There is no bus (local *Ibama* office, T048-2226202, *Secretaria de Turismo de São Joaquim*, T2330258).

Population: 22,000
Phone code: 049
Colour map 5, grid B4

B *Pousada Caminhos da Neve*, Av Irineu Bornhausen, T/F2330385. **C** *Incomel Park*, Av Ivo Silveira 340, 1 km from centre towards Lages, T2330980, F2330281. Heating, accepts Visa. **D** *Nevada*, R Manuel Joaquim Pinto 213, T/F2330259. Expensive meals. **E** *Maristela*, R Manoel Joaquim Pinto 220, 5 minutes' walk from Rodoviária, T233007. French spoken, no heating so can be cold, friendly, helpful, good breakfast. **Camping** *Clube do Brasil* site.

Sleeping

Buses To **Florianópolis** 0700 and 1700 via Bom Retiro (*Reunidos*) and 0800 via Tubarão (*Nevatur*), 5½ hours, US$9.30. Several daily buses to **Criciúma**, **Tubarão**, **Cascavel** and **Foz do Iguaçu**.

Transport

West of Florianópolis, 212 kilometres by paved road (BR-282), is Lages (formerly spelt Lajes), a convenient stopping place on the BR-116 between Caxias do Sul and Curitiba. The route can also be done on poorer roads via São Joaquim (80 kilometres from Lages), which is perhaps the most interesting journey in the State, with scenery changing as the road climbs out of coastal forest.

Lages
Population: 140,000
Phone code: 049

Iguaçu Falls & the South

Sleeping A *Grande*, R João de Castro 23, T/F2223522. Good. **B** *Presidente*, Av Pres Vargas 101, T/F2240014. One of the 3 hotels near the rodoviária is **D** *Rodeio*, T2232011, with or without bath, good breakfast. In the same building is a good *churrascaria*, open in the evening, US$7.50.

Transport Bus station in 30 minutes' walk southeast of the centre. Bus to the centre (Terminal Municipal), 'Rodoviária' runs Monday-Friday only, or 'Dom Pedro II' every 40 minutes at weekends. To Florianópolis 6-8 buses daily on the direct road (BR282), 5 hours, US$10; to Caxias do Sul, 3¾ hours, US$5.60.

The area around Lages is particularly good for 'rural tourism', with lots of opportunities for hiking, horse riding, river bathing, working on a farm and other activities. The weather can get really cold in winter and even the waterfalls have been known to freeze. Many of the local *fazendas* are open for visitors and offer accommodation. This is gaúcho country and you will get gaúcho hospitality, culture and food.

Sleeping On average, prices are **A**, including all meals, all on working farms: *Fazenda Pedras Brancas*, Rod SC 438, Km 10, Parque das Pedras Brancas, T2232073, 2222262. Horses, shooting, fishing, pool, sauna, heating, games room, river beach. *Fazenda do Barreiro*, Rod SC 438, Km 43, T2223031. Games room, library, horses, pool, fishing, boats, TV. *Fazenda Rancho do Boqueirão*, BR-282, Km 4, Saída São José do Cerrito, T2260354/0282, F2260354. Heating, TV, library, games room pool, horses, bicycles, good walking, fishing. *Fazenda Ciclone*, BR-116, Km 276, localidade Vigia, T2223382. Horses, fishing, table tennis, billiards, river beach. *Fazenda Aza Verde*, Antiga BR-2, Soroptimista 13, T2220277. Horses, fishing, boats, games room, heating, pool. *Fazenda Refúgio do Lago*, Rod SC 438, Km 10, Pedras Brancas, T2221416. Pool, games room, library, horses, shooting, fishing, boats, river beach. *Fazenda Dourado Turismo Rural*, Estr Lages-Morrinhos Km 14, T2930360. *Fazenda Nossa Senhora de Lourdes*, R Aristiliano Ramos 565, T2220798. Pool, games room, library, horses, fishing, good walking.

Rio Grande do Sul

This is gaúcho (cowboy) country; it is also Brazil's chief wine producer. The capital, Porto Alegre, is the most industrialized city in the south, but in the surroundings are good beaches, interesting coastal national parks and the fine scenery of the Serra Gaúcha. On the border with Santa Catarina is the remarkable Aparados da Serra national park. In the far west are the remains of Jesuit missions. Look out for local specialities such as comida campeira, te colonial *and* quentão. *From Rio Grande do Sul there are various routes into Uruguay and one crossing to Argentina.*

The Great Escarpment runs down the coastal area as far as Porto Alegre. South of Tubarão to the borders of Uruguay, the hills of southern Rio Grande do Sul, which never rise higher than 900 to 1,000 metres, are fringed along the coast by sand bars and lagoons. In southern Rio Grande do Sul, south and west of the Rio Jacuí (draining into the Lagoa dos Patos), there are great grasslands stretching as far as Uruguay to the south and Argentina to the west. This is the

Southern rebellions

In the 1830s a number of violent rebellions occurred in Brazil, largely as a reaction to the abdication of Dom Pedro I and the uncertain direction of the republic. There was the Cabanagem in Pará (see page 609), the Sabinada in Bahia (1837-38) and the Balaiada in Maranhão (1838-42). A fourth revolt took place in Rio Grande do Sul between 1835-45. It was called the Farroupilha and involved estancieiros, the producers of charque (dried beef and hides), the local military and the forces of the central government. The leader was Bento Gonçalves, a landowner, mason and colonel, who favoured a federation between Rio Grande do Sul, the recently independent Uruguay and Argentina. There were strong links between the three regions, especially through the cattle trade. Whether all the rebels sought separation from Brazil is a debatable issue, but the declaration of the independence of the province in 1836 was one of the catalysts of the war. It was during the conflict that the Italian Garibaldi lent his support with the formation of the Juliana Republic (see page 379). As far as the central government was concerned, Rio Grande do Sul was an important buffer against the volatile Río de la Plata region and a major supplier of taxes (on the cattle industry, on cross-border trade) and food for other parts of the country. The war dragged on for 10 years, causing a decline in the cattle economy. This, plus the fact that neither side was able to press for outright victory, led to the rebellion eventually petering out.

Rio Grande do Sul also played an instrumental part in the 1930 Revolution, which brought the First Republic to an end. The political representatives of the state formed a large bloc in the Liberal Alliance with those of Minas Gerais and the Democrats of São Paulo; among their main aims was to shift power away from those states and politicians for whom coffee was the dominating interest. At the time, the governor of Rio Grande do Sul was Getúlio Vargas, who became the president of Brazil after the events of 1930 brought an end to the oligarchic system which had ruled the country for so many years (see **History**, page 745).

The South also had its own religious movement to rival the Canudos and Joazeiro revolts of the Northeast. This was the Contestado movement (1911-16), led by José Maria de Santo Agostinho, who was declared a saint by his followers after his death early in the rebellion. The action took place in Paraná and Santa Catarina and the main participants, as well as the government forces intent upon its destruction, were rural workers, urban unemployed who had worked on a number of construction projects but had been abandoned at the end of their contract, and criminals. The townships which grew up during the movement stressed communal reward for labour, equality and support for the monarchy. The combination of religious belief and the organization of rural communities into an alternative way of life was perceived as a serious threat to the established elite. So, as at Canudos before it, the Contestado Movement was ruthlessly destroyed by the army.

See Brazil, Empire and Republic 1822-1930 (edited by Leslie Bethell), chapters 2 and 6; Modern Brazil, Elites and Masses in Historical Perspectives (edited by Michael L Conniff and Frank D McCann).

distinctive land of the *gaúcho*, or cowboy (pronounced ga-oo-shoo in Brazil), of the flat black hat, of *bombachas* (the baggy trousers worn by the *gaúcho*), of the poncho and *ximarão* (also spelt *chimarrão*, it is *mate* without sugar), the indispensable drink of southern cattlemen. There are many millions of cattle, sheep and pigs, rice production is on the increase, and some 75 percent of all Brazilian wine comes from the state. Its population (who all call themselves *gaúchos*) now number over nine million. The *gaúcho* culture is increasingly developing a sense of distance from the African-influenced culture of further north. This separatist strain was most marked in the 1820s and 1830s when

Iguaçu Falls & the South

the Farroupilha movement, led by Bento Gonçalves, proclaimed the República Riograndense in 1835. The subsequent war with the federal government ended with the Treaty of Ponche Verde in February 1845 (see box).

Although it is true that *gaúchos* come of mainly European ancestry, essentially Brazilian blends are evident everywhere. A lot of people in this state are tall, with light brown skin and hair and intensely green eyes: a striking combination indeed. When travelling even slightly off the beaten track, it can be quite startling to discover that traditional *gaúcho* dress: baggy trousers with a heavy sash and wide-brimmed hat for men and long, full, belted skirts for women, is worn by many citizens of all ages. Folk dances, unchanged since early settlers brought them from Europe, are still practised, both for tourists' benefit and privately, at celebrations which often take place in the open air. A favourite all-purpose *gaúcho* exclamation, which means nothing but is used all the time, is '*Tchê*'!

There are three sharply contrasted types of colonization and land owning in Rio Grande do Sul. During the colonial period, wars with the Spaniards of Uruguay were frequent, and the Portuguese government brought into the grasslands of the south a number of military settlers from the Azores; these soldiers inter-married with the Brazilian herdfolk in the area. In the colonial period, also, the Jesuits built several settlements to acculturate the local Indians; relics of this process include the impressive ruins of the **Sete Povos das Missões Orientais** (São Borja, São Nicolau, São Luiz, São Lourenço, São Miguel, São João, Santo Ângelo).

At São Leopoldo, north of Porto Alegre, a group of Germans were settled in 1824 on their own small farms, and during the next 25 years over 20,000 more were brought into the area by the Brazilian government. The Germans concentrated on rye, maize and pigs. Between 1870 and 1890, settlers from northern Italy arrived, bringing viticulture with them, and settled north of the Germans at Alfredo Chaves and Caxias do Sul.

Porto Alegre

Population: 1,289,000
Phone code: 051
Colour map 5, grid B3

Not a usual tourist destination, Porto Alegre is nonetheless one of Brazil's most important cities. As capital of the southern frontiers, it is the hub through which extensive trade is conducted with other Mercosul countries such as Argentina and Uruguay. It is a good base for exploring the rest of Rio Grande do Sul's natural beauty and historical sites.

The capital of Rio Grande do Sul lies at the confluence of five rivers (called Rio Guaíba, although it is not a river in its own right) and thence into the great freshwater lagoon, the Lagoa dos Patos, which runs into the sea. The freshwater port, one of the most up-to-date in the country, handles ocean-going vessels up to 7,000 tonnes and 4.87 metres draught. Porto Alegre is the most important commercial centre south of São Paulo and one of the most heavily industrialized cities in Brazil. Standing on a series of hills and valleys on the banks of the Guaíba, it has a temperate climate through most of the year, though the temperature at the height of summer can often exceed 40°C and drop below 10°C in winter. Mosquitoes are plentiful. The city centre juts out into the water on a promontory. The surrounding suburbs are pleasant. The city's many bars and clubs cluster around the Zona Norte.

Getting there International and domestic flights arrive at Salgado Filho airport. There are regular buses to the rodoviária and a metrô service to the city centre. International and interstate buses arrive at the terminal at Largo Vespasiano Júlio Veppo, on Av Mauá with Garibáldi.

Ins & outs
See also Transport, page 390

Getting around First-class minibuses (*Lotação*), painted in a distinctive orange, blue and white pattern, stop on request. Safer and pleasanter than normal buses, fare about US$1. The Trensurb metrô runs from the southern terminal at the Mercado Público (station beside the market), going as far north as Sapucaia do Sul. The second station serves the rodoviária and the fifth the airport (10 minutes), 0500-2300, single journey US$0.50.

Sights

The older residential part of the town is on a promontory, dominated previously by the **Palácio Piratini** (Governor's Palace) and the imposing modern **cathedral** on the **Praça Marechal Deodoro** (or da Matriz). Also on, or near this square, are the neoclassical **Theatro São Pedro** (1858), the **Solar dos Câmara** (1818, now a historical and cultural centre) and the **Biblioteca Pública**, but all are dwarfed by the skyscraper of the **Assembléia Legislativa**. Down Rua General Câmara from Praça Marechal Deodoro is the **Praça da Alfândega**, with the old customs house, the Museu de Arte de Rio Grande do Sul (see below), the old post office and the Banco Meridional. A short walk east of this group, up Rua 7 de Setembro, is Praça 15 de Novembro, on which are the neoclassical **Mercado Público**, next to the Prefeitura, the Chalé da Praça XV bandstand and café and the Fonte Talavera de la Reina fountain.

Do not miss that section of the **Rua dos Andradas** (Rua da Praia) that is now permanently closed to traffic. It is the city's principal outdoor meeting place, the main shopping area, and by around 1600 it is jammed full of people. Going west along Rua dos Andradas, you pass the pink **Casa Cultural Mário Quintana** in the converted Hotel Majestic (see **Entertainment**, below) and the wide stairway that leads up to the two high white towers of the church of **Nossa Senhora das Dores**. Many tall buildings in this part of the city rise above the fine, sometimes dilapidated, old houses and the streets are famous for their steep gradients. At the end of the promontory, the **Usina do Gasômetro** has been converted from a thermoelectric station into a cultural centre. Its enormous chimney has become a symbol for the city. In the **Cidade Baixa** quarter are the colonial **Travessa dos Venezianos** (between Ruas Lopo Gonçalves and Joaquim Nabuco) and the **house of Lopo Gonçalves**, Rua João Alfredo 582, which houses the **Museu de Porto Alegre Joaquim José Felizardo**, a collection on the history of the city. ■ *0900-1700 Tuesday-Sunday, free.*

Museu Júlio de Castilhos, Duque de Caxias 1231, has an interesting historical collection about the state of Rio Grande do Sul. ■ *Tuesday-Sunday 0900-1700.* **Museu de Arte do Rio Grande do Sul,** Praça Senador Florêncio (Praça da Alfândega), is interesting. It specializes in art from Rio Grande do Sul, but also houses temporary exhibitions. ■ *Tuesday*

Museums

Climate: Porto Alegre

1000-2100, Wednesday-Sunday 1000-1700, free. **Museu de Comunicação Social**, Rua dos Andradas 959, in the former *A Federação* newspaper building, deals with the development of the press in Brazil since the 1920s. ■ *Monday-Friday 1200-1900, T2244252.*

Parks   Porto Alegre is well endowed with open spaces and, according to the Prefeitura, there are over one million trees along the streets, many of them the flowering varieties, such as jacarandas and flamboyants. There are seven parks and 700 squares in the city, of which the most traditional is the **Parque Farroupilha** (called Parque Redenção), a fine park near the city centre. It has a triangular area of 33 hectares between Avenida Osvaldo Aranha, Avenida José

Porto Alegre

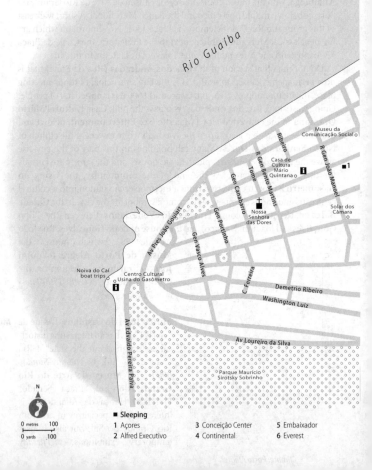

■ Sleeping
1 Açores	3 Conceição Center	5 Embaixador
2 Alfred Executivo	4 Continental	6 Everest

Bonifácio and Avenida João Pessoa, and contains a lake, minizoo, amusement park, bicycle hire, the Araújo Viana auditorium and a monument to the *Expedicionário*. On Sundays there is a *feira* of antiques, handicrafts and all sorts at the José Bonifácio end, where locals walk, talk and drink *chimarrão*, the traditional gaúcho drink. **Parque Moinhos de Vento** is popular for jogging and you can see lots of fit people around who train in the gym of the same name nearby. There is a replica of a windmill in the middle of the park, but there used to be plenty of working mills, which gave the *bairro* its name. The riverside drive, Avenida Edvaldo Pereira Paiva, around Parque Maurício Sirotsky Sobrinho, is closed to traffic on Sunday, for cycling, skating, jogging and strolling. **Marinho do Brasil** is another large park between the centre and the *zona*

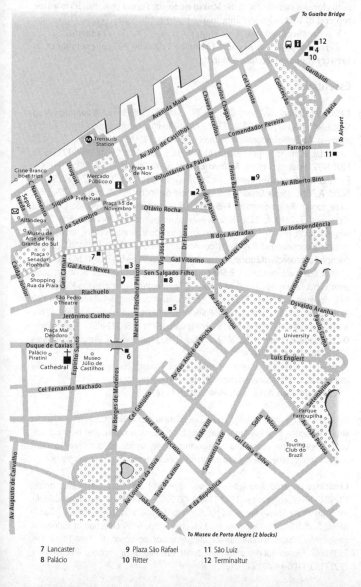

To Museu de Porto Alegre (2 blocks)

7 Lancaster	9 Plaza São Rafael	11 São Luiz
8 Palácio	10 Ritter	12 Terminaltur

sul, where there are lots of sporting activities. The **Jardim Botânico**, the **Botanic Garden** (Bairro Jardim Botânico, bus 40 from Praça 15 de Novembro), is on Rua Salvador França 1427, *zona leste*.

The five-kilometre wide **Rio Guaíba** lends itself to every form of boating and there are several sailing clubs. Two boats run trips around the islands in the estuary: *Cisne Branco*, from Cais do Porto, near Museu de Arte de Rio Grande do Sul, T2245222, several sailings on Sunday, fewer mid-week, one hour, US$5; and *Noiva do Caí*, from the Usina do Gasômetro, T2117662, several on Sunday, fewer mid-week, one hour, US$3.50 (check winter schedules). Jetskiers jump the wake of the tour boats. **Ipanema beach**, on the southern banks of the river, has spectacular sunsets. You can see a good view of the city, with glorious sunsets, from the **Morro de Santa Teresa** (take bus 95 from the top end of Rua Salgado Filho, marked 'Morro de Santa Teresa TV' or just 'TV'). Another good sunset-viewing spot is the Usina do Gasômetro.

Cervejaria Brahma, Avenida Cristovão Colombo 545, offers tours of its brewery (but not December-March).

Essentials

Sleeping
■ *on map, page 386*
Price codes: see inside front cover
There are many good restaurants

L *Plaza São Rafael*, Av Alberto Bins 514, T2115767, F2216883. Pool. **A** *Continental*, Lg Vespasiano Júlio Veppo 77, T2112344, F2285024. High standards, pool, gym. Recommended. **AL** *Embaixador*, R Jerônimo Coelho 354, T2156600, F2285050. Four-star, comfortable, unexciting restaurant. **AL** *Everest*, R Duque de Caxias 1357, T2159500, F2284792. Business centre. **A** *Alfred Executivo*, Av Otávio Rocha 270, T2218966, F2262221. **A** *Conceição Center*, Av Sen Salgado Filho 201, T2257774, F2256135. Good. **A** *Porto Alegre Residence*, R Des André da Rocha 131, T2258644, F2240366. Large rooms. Recommended. **A-B** *Ritter*, Lg Vespasiano Júlio Veppo 55, opposite rodoviária, T2284044, F2281610, www.ritterhoteis.com.br. Four-star and 3-star wings, English, French, German spoken, bar, small pool, sauna. Fine restaurant, good service. Recommended. **B** *Açores*, R dos Andradas 885, T2217588, F2251007. Central, cramped but friendly. **B** *Lancaster*, Trav Acelino de Carvalho 67, T2244737, F2244630. Central, quiet, a/c, restaurant. **B** *São Luiz*, Av Farrapos 45, T2281722. Spotless, good service, but near rodoviária so a bit noisy. **C** *Terminaltur*, Lg Vespasiano Júlio Veppo 125, opposite rodoviária, T2271656. A/c, breakfast, heating, small rooms and tiny bathrooms, not too comfortable. **C** *Palácio*, Av Vigário José Inácio 644. Central, hot water. Recommended. **C** *Savoy*, Av Borges Medeiros 688, T2240511. Good value. **D** *Curitibano*, R Dr Barros Cassal 82, T2282343. Recommended. **E** *Uruguay*, Dr Flores 371. Simple but recommended.

Hotels in the area around R Garibáldi and Voluntários da Patria between Av Farrapos and rodoviária are overpriced and used for short stays.

Camping Praia do Guarujá, 16 km out on Av Guaíba.

Eating

Gaúcho cooking features large quantities of meat, while German cuisine is also a strong influence. Regional farm (*campeiro*) food, now a dying art, uses plenty of rice, vegetables, and interesting sauces. Vegetarians might try some of the *campeiro* soups and casseroles, otherwise stick to Italian restaurants or *churrascaria* salad bars.

Churrasco *Capitão Rodrigo*, Av Albert Bins 514 (in *Plaza São Rafael* hotel), T2216100. Self service, open 1200-1430, 1900-2300, closed Monday. *Galpão Crioulo*, Av Loureiro da Silva (Parque da Harmonia or Maurício Sirotsky Sobrinho, Cidade Baixa), T2268194. Show and dancing, 1130-1600, 1900-0100. *Gauchão*, at Rodoviária. Inexpensive, live entertainment nightly. *Moinhos de Vento*, R Dona Laura 424, T3311847. Closed Sunday afternoon. *Santo Antônio*, R Dr Timotéu 465, Floresta, T2223130, 1100-1430, 1900-2400.

General *Chalé da Praça 15*, Praça 15 de Novembro. Average food but recommended for early evening drinks and snacks. *Komka*, Av Bahia 1275, San Geraldo, T2221881. Recommended.

German *Chopp Stübel*, R Quintino Bocaiúva 940, Moinhos de Vento, T3328895. Open 1800-0030, closed Sunday, Recommended. *Hannover*, Av C Colombo 2140, Floresta, T2227902. Closed Monday. Recommended. *Sociedade Germânia*, Av Independência 1269, 6th floor, T2229094. Saturday night dinner dance, closed Monday, Saturday lunch, Sunday evenings. Recommended. *Wunderbar*, R Marquês do Herval 5981, Moinhos de Vento, T2224967. Very busy 1900-0100. Recommended.

Italian *Al Dente*, R Mata Bacelar 210, Auxiliadora, T3431841. Expensive northern Italian cuisine. *Atelier de Massas*, R Riachuelo 1482, Excellent, not cheap. *Spaguetti Express*, Centro Comercial Nova Olária, Lima e Silva 776. Good.

Regional *Recanto do Tio Flor*, Av Getúlio Vargas 1700, Menino Deus, T2336512. *Comida campeira*. Recommended, 1130-1400, 1900-0100. *Pulperia*, Trav do Carmo 76, Cidade Baixa, T2271172. Inexpensive, music, opens till 0400, closed Sunday lunch. *Porky's*, Av Cristóvão Colombo 1971, Floresta, T2227552. Serves wild boar and buffalo, closed Sunday. Recommended. *Farroupilha*, Fernando Machado 973 (corner of Borges de Medeiros). Delicious *prato feito*.

Vegetarian *Associação Macrobiotica*, R Mcal Floriano 72, T2254784. Weekdays only. *Ilha Natural*, R Gen Câmara 60. Self-service, cheap, lunch only Monday-Friday.

Bars & nightclubs

Cía Sandwiches, Getúlio Vargas 1430. Beer, sandwiches and music. *João de Barro*, R da República 546, Cidade Baixa. Good jazz. *Sargeant Peppers*, Dona Laura 329. There is a pleasant bar at the Casa de Cultura Mário Quintana, R dos Andradas 736. Gay bars include *Fly*, R Gonçalvo de Carvalho 189. Predominantly male, attractive bar with art exhibition, sophisticated, open 2100-0200, closed Tuesday. *Doce Vício*, R Vieira de Castro 32. Three floors with games room, bar, restaurant, 1830-0230, closed Monday. *We Cia*, R Mostadeiro 462. Predominantly female, bar and club, 1200-0300, closed Monday-Tuesday. *Bar do Goethe*, R 24 de Outubro 112, Moinhos de Vento, T2222043, www.compuserv.com.br/bardogoethe/. Reunion each Tuesday, 2030, for foreign language speakers. *Crocodillo's*, 24 de Outubro, Auxiliadora. Recommended disco. *Descretu's*, Venâncio Aires 59. Gay club, shows at 0230. *Gaúchos* congregate at late-night bars such as *Amsterdam*, Av Nilo Peçanha 1690 (3 Figueras), 1900-0200, closed Sunday, sophisticated. *Best Bier*, Av C Colombo 3000, corner R Germano Petersen Júnior, Higienópolis. Monday-Friday 1800-0100, weekends 2000-0200, mixed crowd, live music, choice of ambiences. *Barong*, R Mostadeiro 517, T2221663. Balinese style, Indian snack food, varied music, closed Sunday.

Entertainment

Art galleries *Casa de Cultura Mário Quintana*, R dos Andradas 736. A lively centre for the arts, with exhibitions, theatre etc, open 0900-2100, 1200-2100 Saturday-Sunday. Bookshop sells Englsih books. **Theatre** *São Pedro*, Praça Mcal Deodoro. Free noon and late afternoon concerts Saturday, Sunday, art gallery, café.

Festivals

The main event is on **2 February** (a local holiday), with the festival of *Nossa Senhora dos Navegantes* (Iemanjá), whose image is taken by boat from the central quay in the port to the industrial district of Navegantes. *Semana Farroupilha* celebrates *gaúcho* traditions with parades in traditional style, its main day being on **20 September**. The Carnival parade takes place in Av A do Carvalho, renamed Av Carlos Alberto Barcelos (or Roxo) for these 3 days only, after a famous carnival designer.

Shopping

H Stern jewellers at Shopping Center Iguatemi and international airport. The Praia de Belas shopping centre, claimed to be the largest in Latin America, is a US$1.50 taxi ride from town. There is a street market (leather goods, basketware etc) in the streets around the central Post Office. Good leather goods are sold on the streets. Sunday

Iguaçu Falls & the South

morning handicraft and bric-a-brac market (plus sideshows) Av José Bonifácio (next to Parque Farroupilha). There is a very good food market.

Bookshops *Livraria Kosmos*, R dos Andradas 1644 (international stock). *Livraria Londres*, Av Osvaldo Aranha 1182. Used books in English, French and Spanish and old *Life* magazines. *Saraiva Megastore*, in Shopping Praia de Belas. *Siciliano*, R dos Andradas 1273 and other branches. Each year a *Feira do Livro* is held in Praça da Alfândega, October-November.

Sports **Gyms** Weights and aerobics at *Academia do Parcão*, 24 de Outubro 684. **Golf** Porto Alegre Country Club, Av Líbero Badaró 524, Bela Vista, 18 holes, closed to non-members. Several 9-hole courses in nearby towns. **Swimming** Forbidden from the beaches near or in the city because of pollution, except for Praia do Lami, in the south of the city, which has been cleaned up. Over the next few years it is planned to improve Belém Novo and Ipanema as well. See **Beaches**, below.

Transport
See also Ins & outs, page 385

Car hire *Localiza* at airport, T0800-992000, and Av Carlos Gomes 230, T3285122. **Air** The international airport is on Av dos Estados, 8 km from the city, T3421082. A regular bus runs from the rodoviária, as well as a metrô service from the centre (see Ins and outs, page 385).

Buses The rodoviária is on Lg Vespasiano Júlio Veppo, connected to the city centre by metrô (just outside), T2868230, www.rodoviaria-poa.com.br. There are good facilities, including a post office and long-distance telephone service until 2100. There are 2 sections to the terminal; the ticket offices for interstate and international destinations are together in 1 block, beside the municipal tourist office (very helpful). The intermunicipal (state) ticket offices are in another block; for travel information within the state, ask at the very helpful booth on the station concourse.

To **Rio**, US$48.50 (*leito* 85), 24 hours; **São Paulo**, US$66.50 (*leito* 60), 18 hours; **Brasília**, US$66.50, 33 hours; **Uruguaiana**, US$13, 8 hours; **Florianópolis**, US$16, 7 hours with *Santo Anjo* or *Eucatur* (take an *executivo* rather than a *convencional*, which is a much slower service); **Curitiba**, from US$21 *convencional* to US$37 *leito*, coastal and *serra* routes, 11 hours; **Rio Grande**, US$10, every 2 hours from 0600, 4½ hours. **Foz do Iguaçu**, US$30, 15 hours. Many other destinations. To **Cascavel** (Paraná) for connections to Campo Grande, Cuiabá and Porto Velho: daily with *Unesul*, 19 hours, US$23. To **Jaguarão** on Uruguayan border at 2400, 6 hours, US$10.

Take your passport & tourist card when purchasing international bus tickets

International buses To **Montevideo**, with *TTL* (daily 1700 and 2000, US$39, US$56 *leito*; see page 405), alternatively take bus to border town of Chuí at 1200 daily, 7½ hours, US$13, then bus to Montevideo (US$13). To **Asunción** with *Unesul* at 1900, Tuesday, Friday, 18 hours via **Foz do Iguaçu**, US$35. **Santiago**, *Pluma* 0705, Tuesday and Friday, US$89.

There are bus services to **Buenos Aires**, US$45, 19 hours (depending on border) with *Pluma*, 1805 daily, route is Uruguaiana, Paso de los Libres, Entre Ríos and Zárate. For **Misiones** (Argentina), take 2100 bus (not Saturday) to Porto Xavier on the Río Uruguay, 11 hours, US$15, get exit stamp at police station, take a boat across to San Javier, US$2, go to Argentine immigration at the port, then take a bus to Posadas (may have to change in Leandro N Além).

Roads Good roads radiate from Porto Alegre, and Highway BR-116 is paved to Curitiba (746 km). To the south it is paved (mostly in good condition), to Chuí on the Uruguayan frontier, 512 km. In summer visibility can be very poor at night owing to mist, unfenced cows are a further hazard. The paved coastal road to Curitiba via Itajaí (BR-101), of which the first 100 km is the 4-lane Estrada General Osório highway, is much better than the BR-116 via Caxias and Lajes. The road to Uruguaiana is entirely paved but bumpy.

Banks Exchange on Av Borges de Medeiros, good rate, cash only. *Platino Turismo*, R dos **Directory**
Andrades and Av Borges de Medeiros (only one to change TCs, Amex, but 6% less than cash).
Exprinter, Sen Salgado Filho 247 (best for cash). *Mastercard*, cash against card, R 7 de Setembro
722, 8th floor, Centro. For other addresses consult tourist bureau brochure. *Lloyds Bank*, R Gen
Câmara 249. 1000-1630. *Banco do Brasil*, Uruguai 185, 9th floor. 1000-1500, good rates for TCs.
Bradesco, Praça Sen Florência, Visa machine. *Citibank*, R7 de Setembro 722, T2208619.

Communications Post office: R Siqueria Campos 1100, Centro, Mon-Fri 0800-1700, Sat
0800-1200. *UPS*, T434972/424602 (Alvaro). **Telephones:** R Siqueira de Campos 1245. **Internet**:
.Com Cyber Café, Rua da Praia Shopping, S17, T2864244, US$4 per hr. *Ciber Café*, Câncio Gomes e
C Colombo 778, T3463098, open 0900-2300. *Livraria Saraiva Megastore*, Shopping Praia de
Belas, T2316868, www.livrariasaraiva.com.br, open Mon-Sat 1000-2200.

Cultural centres *Sociedade Brasileira da Cultura Inglesa*, Praça Mauricio Cardoso 49,
Moinhos de Vento. *Instituto Goethe*, 24 de Outubro 122. Mon-Fri, 0930-1230, 1430-2100,
occasional concerts, bar recommended for German *Apfelkuchen*. See also Casa de Cultura Mário
Quintana and Usina do Gasômetro, above.

Embassies & consulates *Argentina*, R Prof Annes Dias 112, 1st floor, T2246799. *Germany*, R
Prof Annes Dias 112, 11th floor, T2249255, F2264909. *Italy*, Praça Marechal Deodoro 134,
T2282055. 0900-1200. *Japan*, Av João Obino 467, Alto Petrópolis, T3341299, F3341742.
0900-1230, 1500-1700. *Portugal*, R Prof Annes Dias 112, 10th floor, T2245767. 0900-1530. *Spain*, R
Ildefonso Simões Lopes 85, T3381300, F3381444. *Sweden*, Av Sen Salgado Filho 327, Apdo 1303,
T2271289. 0900-1100. *UK*, R Itapeva 110, Sala 505, Edif Montreal, Bairro Passo D'Areia,
T/F3410720. 0900-1200, 1430-1800. *Uruguay*, R Siquera Campos 1171, 5th and 6th floors,
T2243499, F2242644.

Language courses Portuguese and Spanish, Matilde Dias, R Pedro Chaves Barcelos 37, Apdo
104, T331-8235, intermm@pro.via-rs.com.br. US$15 per hr.

Laundry Several along Av Andre da Rocha including *Lavandería Lav-Dem*, No 225. US$1.50
per kg wash and dry.

Security The market area in Praça 15 de Novembro and the bus terminal are dangerous at
night; thefts have been reported in Voluntários da Pátria and Praça Parcão.

Tour companies & travel agents *Klift Tur*, R Mcal Floriano 270, T2254733, F2287959.
American Express; also *Mercatur*, Av Salgado Filho 97, T2258055, F2256954. *Stella Barros*, R Dom
Pedro II, T3426563, F3433843. Thomas Cook. Several tour companies offer trips to Foz do Iguaçu
and Ciudad del Este, overnight journey each way (12 hrs in Paraguay). Three-day trips with 1
night's hotel accommodation, US$55 including sightseeing (time at the falls may be limited). See
Turismo section in 'Zero Hora' classifieds (Thu, Sat, Sun) for tour companies' advertisements.

Tourist offices *Central de Informações Turísticas*, R Vasco da Gama 253, Bom Fim,
T3115289, open daily 0900-2100. *Setur*, Borges de Medeiros 1501, 10th floor, T2287377,
F2281311; also at Salgado Filho airport, friendly; interstate bus station, very helpful (free city
maps); Casa de Cultura Mário Quintana, open Tue-Fri 0900-2100, Sat-Sun 1200-2100; Usina do
Gasômetro, open daily 1000-1800; Mercado Público, Mon-Sat 0900-1600. On Sun there are
guided walks from Praça da Alfândega and on Sat from Praça da Matriz, at 1500 or 1600, free,
T3115289 or contact the tourist office at Vasco da Gama 253, or in the Mercado Público. *Touring
Clube do Brasil*, Av João Pessoa 623.

Voltage 110-120 AC 50 cycles.

Beaches around Porto Alegre

The main beach resorts of the area are to the east and north of the city. Heading **Tramandaí**
east along the BR-290, 112 kilometres from Porto Alegre is **Osório**, a pleasant *Population: 28,000*
lakeside town with a few hotels. From here it is 18 kilometres southeast to the *Phone code: 051*
rather polluted and crowded beach resort of **Tramandaí**. The beaches here are
very popular, with lots of hotels, bars, restaurants, and other standard seaside
amenities. Extensive dunes and lakes in the region provide an interesting variety
of wildlife and sporting opportunities. The beach resorts become less polluted the further north you travel, and the water is clean by the time you reach
Torres (see below).

Iguaçu Falls & the South

Sleeping Osório: **C** *Ibiama*, R Dr Mário Santo Dani 1161, T/F6632822. **Camping**: *Pinguela Parque*, BR-101, 22 km, T6288080. **Tramandaí**: **B** *Beira-Mar*, Av Emancipação 521, T6611234, F6611133. Thermal pool, sports facilities. **C** *São Jorge*, F Amaral 19, T6611154. Quiet. Recommended. **Youth hostel**: **E** pp *Tramandaí*, R Belém 701, T2283802, F2265380. IYHA. **Camping**: *Lagoa e Mar*, RS-030, 5 km, T9882885.

Transport Bus Porto Alegre-Tramandaí, 5 a day, US$3.50.

The BR-101 heads north, just inland of the coast from Osório to Florianópolis and beyond. A series of lakes separates the road from the coastal belt and the beach resorts, but there is another road running all along the coast from Tramandaí to Torres and the border with Santa Catarina. Between the two towns are the resorts (heading south to north) of **Atlântida do Sul**, **Capão da Canoa**, **Arroio Teixeira** and **Arroio do Sal** (*Casa da Sogra*, good food). At **Capão da Canoa** there is surfing at Atlântida beach, while the Lagoa dos Quadros, inland, is used for windsurfing, sailing, water-skiing and jet-skiing.

Sleeping Capão da Canoa: **A** *Kolman*, R Sepé 1800, T6252022, T6252021. Pool. **B** *Napoli*, Av Paraguassu 3159, T/F665-2231. **Camping**: *Marina Park*, RS-389, 7 km, T3016150. **Arroio Teixeira** (18 km further north up the coast): **Camping**: *Alvorada*, on the beach, T6221242. Good facilities, café, only open December-March. *Camping Clube do Brasil*, RS-03, T6221209. Good. *Parque*, Estr Interpraias 2222, T/F6221163. At Arroio do Sal: **D** *Hotel D'Itália*, Av Assis Brasil 11, on beach. Highly recommended.

Torres

Population: 25,500
Phone code: 051
Colour map 5, grid B4

Torres is a well developed resort, with a number of beaches, several high class, expensive hotels, a wide range of restaurants, professional surfing competitions and entertainment. There is a lively club scene during the holidays. There is no lack of cheap accommodation, but from Christmas to Carnaval rooms are hard to find. Torres holds a ballooning festival in April. There is an annual independence day celebration, when a cavalcade of horses arrives in town on 16 September from Uruguay.

Torres gets its name from the three huge rocks, or towers, on the town beach, Praia Grande. Two kilometres long, the beach is safe for swimming and there is surf near the breakwater. Fishing boats can be hired for a trip to

Porto Alegre coast

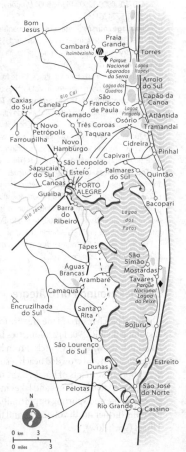

Iguaçu Falls & the South

Ilha dos Lobos, a rocky island two kilometres out to sea, where sea lions spend the winter months. During May, dolphins visit Praia dos Molhes, north of the town. On the edge of Rio Mampituba, which marks the state boundary, this beach is good for net fishing and has restaurants. Two kilometres south of Torres, past rocky little Prainha, is Cal (*Pradise Dunas* campsite, December-February only), popular with surfers. A further two kilometres south, passing the Praia da Guarita leisure development, is Itapeva, with a campsite open December-March. The water here is calm, good for swimming, and there are bars and cafés.

A *Continental Torres*, R Plínio Kroeff 465, Mampituba, T6641811, F6641090. Two pools, 1 of which is thermal, sauna, children's playground. **A** *Dunas Praia*, Praça Marechal Deodoro 48, Praia Grande, T6641011, F6642080. Pool. **A** *A Furninha*, R Joaquim Porto 281, T/F6641655. Good service. **B** *Pousada Brisa do Mar*, R Júlio de Castilhos and R Borges de Medeiros, T6642019. Good breakfast. Recommended. **B** *Grande Hotel Torres*, R Júlio de Castilhos 124, T6641887. Balcony and breakfast. **C** *Central*, R Borges de Medeiros 296, T6642580. Good breakfast. **C** *Oceano Hotel*, Av Barão do Rio Branco 400, T6641154. Recommended. **C** *Salth*, R Borges de Medeiros 209, T6641881. Good December-February. **Youth hostel E** pp *São Domingos*, R Júlio de Castilhos 875, T6641865, F6641022. IYHA, clean. Closed out of season. **Camping** At Praia de Itapeva, 5 km, T6055112.

Bom Gosto, R Rio Branco 242. Churrasco. *Sol Macrobiótico*, R Júlio de Castilhos 746. Good cheap vegetarian with a cosy, personal atmosphere.

Sleeping & eating

Hotels tend to be very full during the summer season

Transport Bus Porto Alegre-Torres, 6 a day, US$6.60.

Banks *Banco do Brasil* and at Rodoviária. **Tourist information** R Rio Branco 315, T6641219.

Directory

There is a paved road running south from Tramandaí (mostly prohibited to trucks) along the coast to Quintão, giving access to many beaches. One such beach is **Cidreira**, 26 kilometres south of Tramandaí. It is not very crowded and has *Hotel Farol* on the main street (**D** with bath). Bus from Porto Alegre US$3.40. A track continues to **Mostardas**, thence along the peninsula on the seaward side of the Lagoa dos Patos to São José do Norte, opposite Rio Grande (see below, Rio Grande **Excursions**). There is accommodation in **Palmares do Sul** (across the peninsula from Quintão) and Mostardas. South of Mostardas is **Tavares**, with a recommended hotel , the red house on the Praça (no sign). There are several buses a week from Tavares to São José do Norte (130 kilometres) via Bojuru and several daily to Porto Alegre. Tavares is on the **Lagoa do Peixe**, a national park, which is a resting place for migrating birds (details from Praça Luís Martins 30, Mostardas, CEP 96270-000, T6731464). The road to the park is called the Estrada do Inferno.

Tramandaí to São José do Norte

Another popular beach area is south of Porto Alegre, around Cassino, near Rio Grande (see page 400). Forty kilometres to the south (towards Rio Grande) begins the Costa Doce of the Lagoa dos Patos; noted bathing points are Tapes, Barra do Ribeiro, Arambaré, São Lourenço do Sul and Laranjal. São Lourenço is a good place to enjoy the lake, the beaches, fish restaurants and watersports. The town hosts a popular four-day festival in March. Bus from Porto Alegre US$6.50, six a day.

São Lourenço do Sul

Population: 42,500
Phone code: 053

Sleeping B *Camussi*, R Dr Pio Ferreira 159, T2513180, F2513180. **C** *Vilela*, R Almte Abreu 428. Family hotel, clean, friendly. **Camping** At Lagoa dos Patos, T2513002 extension 221. Also at Reponte by the beach. Good facilities.

The Serra Gaúcha

Inland is the pleasant Serra Gaúcha, the most beautiful scenery being around the towns of Gramado and Canela, about 130 kilometres from Porto Alegre to the north. There is a distinctly Bavarian flavour to many of the buildings in both towns. In spring and summer the flowers are a delight, and in winter there are frequently snow showers.

This is excellent walking and climbing country among hills, woods, lakes and waterfalls. For canoeists, the Rio Paranhana at Três Coroas is renowned, especially for slalom. It is 25 kilometres south of Gramado. In both towns it is difficult to get rooms in the summer/Christmas. Local crafts include knitted woollens, leather, wickerwork and chocolate.

Gramado

Population: 25,500
Phone code: 054
Colour map 5, grid B4

Gramado is renowned for its fine climate and surroundings and lives almost entirely by tourism. Among its fine parks are Parque Knorr and Lago Negro, and Minimundo, a collection of miniature models such as European castles, T2861334. ■ *1300-1700, closed Monday.* In the summer, hundreds of hydrangeas (*hortênsias*) bloom. The locally made chocolate is a good buy. Each August, Gramado holds a festival of Latin American cinema.

Sleeping **AL** *Serra Azul*, R Garibáldi 152, T2861082, F2863374. Two pools, 1 of which is thermal, sauna, massage, tennis. **A** *Estalagem St Hubertus*, R da Carriere 974, Lago Negro, T/F2861273. Part of the *Roteiro de Charme* hotel group, see page 57. **A** *Gramado Parque*, R Leopoldo Rosenfeldt 818, T/F2862588. Bungalows, good breakfast, reasonable laundry service. **A** *Ritta Höppner*, R Pedro Candiago 305, T2861334, F2863129. Cabins with TV and fridge. Very good value, friendly, good breakfasts. German owners, pool and miniature trains in grounds, closed in May. **B** *Pequeno Bosque*, R Piratini 486, located in wood close to Véu da Noiva waterfall, T2861527, F2861771. Good breakfast. **B** *Pousada Zermatt*, R da Fé 187, Bavária, T/F2862426. Recommended. **C** *Luiz*, Sen Salgado Filho 432, T2861026. Good breakfast. **D** *Dinda*, R Augusto Zatti 160, T2861588. One of the cheapest. **D** *Planalto*, Av Borges de Medeiros 2001, opposite rodoviária, T2861210. Clean and friendly, a private house, Av Borges de Medeiros 1635, rents rooms. Recommended.

Eating *Gasthof Edelweiss*, R da Carriere 1119, T2861861. Good German food. *Nápoli*, Av Borges de Medeiros 2515. Good Italian. *Lancheira*, R Garibáldi 321. Cheap and good. *Tia Nilda*, Av das Hortênsias 765. Coffee shop 1300-2130, Sunday 1100-2130, closed Wednesday. *Pyp*, Av S Diniz 1030. Yoghurt factory with snack bar serving health food sandwiches and yoghurt. The local speciality is *café colonial*, a 1700 meal of various dishes, including meats, recommended, at *Café da Torre*, Av das Hortênsias 2174. 1300-2200. A local speciality is hot *pinhões*, nuts from the Paraná pine, and *quentão* – hot red wine, cachaça, ginger, cloves, sugar and cinnamon, often topped with gemada – egg yolks and sugar.

Transport **Buses** Frequent bus service to Canela, 10 minutes. Bus from Porto Alegre US$4.35.

Directory **Banks** *Banco do Brasil*, R Garibáldi corner Madre Verónica. **Tourist information** At Av das Hortênsias (Pórtico) and Praça Maj Nicoletti/Av Borges de Medeiros 1674, T2861418.

Canela

The town is equally popular as a tourist centre for the Serra Gaúcha, with many good hotels and restaurants, adventure sports and famous Christmas celebrations. Six kilometres from Canela is the **Parque Estadual do Caracol**; a well-marked nature trail leads to the foot of the falls, which are 130 metres high (allow 1½ hours of daylight), and to smaller falls above Caracol. From the high point at Ferradura, seven kilometres from the park, there is a good view into the canyon of the Rio Cai. Good views also from Morro Pelado at 600 metres; follow signs from behind the town for pleasant four kilometre walk through the forest. In Canela, tourist information is on Praça João Correia, T2821287, with good maps and hotel lists.

Population: 31,000
Phone code: 054
Colour map 5, grid B4

AL *Laje de Pedra*, Av Pres Kennedy Km 3, T2824300, F2824400. Restaurant, pool, thermal pool, sauna, tennis. **A** *Vila Suzana Parque*, R Col Theobaldo Fleck 15, T2822020, F2821793. Chalets, heated pool. Attractive. **B** *Bela Vista*, Av Oswaldo Aranha 160, near rodoviária, T/F2821327. Good breakfasts. **C** *Canela*, Av Osvaldo Aranha, 223, T2822774. Breakfast, English speaking staff. Recommended. **D** *Central*, Av Júlio de Castilhos 146. Safe. Recommended. **Youth hostels** *Pousada do Viajante*, R Ernesto Urbani 132, behind rodoviária (street name changed in late 1999), T2822017. Kitchen facilities. Recommended. **Camping** *Camping Clube do Brasil*, 1 km from waterfall in Parque do Caracol, 1 km off main road (signposted), 8 km from Canela, T282431. Excellent honey and chocolate for sale here. Highly recommended. *Sesi*, R Francisco Bertolucci 504, 2½ km outside Canela, T/F2821311. Cabins also available, restaurant, clean. Recommended.

Sleeping

Transport Buses: several daily Canela-**Caxias do Sul**, 2 hours, US$2. From **Florianópolis**, you have to go via Porto Alegre. Porto Alegre-Canela US$4.15.

Eighty eight kilometres from São Francisco de Paula (138 kilometres east of Canela, 117 kilometres north of Porto Alegre) is the **Parque Nacional de Aparados da Serra**, where the major attraction is the 7.8-kilometre canyon, known locally as the Itaimbezinho. Here, two waterfalls cascade 350 metres into a stone circle at the bottom. There is a free campsite and a restaurant, which has a few rooms, in the park. For experienced hikers (and with a guide) there is a difficult path to the bottom of Itaimbezinho. One can then hike 20 kilometres to Praia Grande in Santa Catarina (see page 381). An extension, the **Parque Nacional da Serra Geral**, was opened in 1992. Its main attractions are the Malacara and Fortaleza canyons. As well as the canyons, the parks and surrounding region have several bird specialities. Red-legged Seriema, a large conspicuous bird, can be seen on the way to the park, and there are two fox species.

Parque Nacional de Aparados da Serra

Park essentials There are tourist excursions, mostly at weekends, from São Francisco de Paula. At other times, take a bus to Cambará do Sul, get off at the crossroads, from where it is 18 km, unpaved, to the park entrance at Guarita Gralha Azul – walk or hitchhike if you're lucky. Gralha Azul is 20 km by unpaved road from Praia Grande. From Cambará do Sul to the Fortaleza canyon is 23 km on an unmade road. Aparados da Serra is open Wednesday to Sunday 0900-1700, entry US$3 plus US$2.50 for a car, T2511262. Serra Geral is open all year, daily, and has no infrastructure. The best time to visit is May-August. Rain is heaviest in September. For more information, Ibama, R Miguel Teixeira 126, Cidade Baixa, Caixa Postal 280, Porto Alegre, CEP90050-250, T2252144. For guides in Cambará do Sul T2511265 and in Praia Grande T0XX48-5320330.

Sleeping São Francisco de Paula: **A** *Veraneio Hampal*, RS-235 road to Canela, Km 73, T6441363. **Cambará do Sul**: **C** *Mirão*, R Benjamin Constant. Breakfast, rooms and apartments. Recommended.

Nova Petrópolis

Population: 15,000
Phone code: 054

Twenty four kilometres west of Gramado (bus US$1) is another city with strong German roots. Nova Petrópolis has a Parque do Imigrante, an open-air museum of German settlement. North of Nova Petrópolis is **Jammerthal**, a valley in the Serra Gaúcha with German farms, many of whose inhabitants still speak German; go to Joanette and walk from there.

Sleeping B *Petrópolis*, R Col Alfredo Steglich 33, T2811091, F2811644. Rooms and chalets, pool. **B** *Recanto Suíço*, Av 15 de Novembro 2195, on Parque dos Imigrantes, T/F2811229. Rooms, chalets or cabins, pool. **B** *Veraneio Schoeller*, RS-235, Km 8.5, T2811778. Pool, tennis, lake. **Youth hostel E** pp *Bom Pastor*, RS-235 Km 14, Linha Brasil, T2988066, F2811376. IYHA.

Caxias do Sul

Population: 326,000
Phone code: 054
Colour map 5, grid B3

This expanding and modern city, 122 kilometres from Porto Alegre, is the centre of the Brazilian wine industry. Caxias' population is principally of Italian descent. Vines were first brought to the region in 1840, but not until the end of the century and Italian immigration did the industry develop.

Sights

The church of **São Pelegrino** has paintings by Aldo Locatelli and five metre high bronze doors sculptured by Augusto Murer. There is a good **Muséu Municipal** at Rua Visconde de Pelotas 586, with displays of artefacts of the Italian immigration. ■ *Tuesday-Saturday, 0830-1130, 1330-1700, Sunday 1400-1700, T2212423*. Italian roots are again on display in the **Parque de Exposições Centenário**, five kilometres out on Rua Ludovico Cavinato, where a replica of Caxias do Sul in 1885 has been set up, with a light and sound show at 2000 about the migration from Italy. January and February is the best time to visit.

Excursions

Caxias do Sul's festival of grapes is held in February and March. Many *adegas* accept visitors, but they do not always give free tastings. Good tour and tasting of six wines at *Adega Granja União*, Rua Os 18 de Forte 2346. Visit also the neighbouring towns and sample their wines.

Farroupilha (*population* 47,000; *altitude* 783 metres), 20 kilometres from Caxias do Sul, is a good place to buy shoes and jerseys direct from the factory.

A good *adega*, with free tasting, is *Cooperativa Viti Vinícola Emboaba Ltda*, in **Nova Milano**, six kilometres away (bus to Farroupilha, then change – day trip).

At **Bento Gonçalves** (*population* 77,337; *altitude* 691 metres), 40 kilometres from Caxias do Sul, you can visit the *Adega Aurora*, Rua Olavo Bilac 500, T4514111, free, including tasting. There are about six others offering guided tours, tasting and sales. About 13 kilometres from Bento Gonçalves, at **Colônia São Pedro**, is the **Caminho de Pedra**, restored stone and wooden houses typical of the northern Italian style of architecture and artefacts and fabrics of the first wave of Italian colonization, very interesting and in beautiful landscape. There is no public transport so rent a car, or a bicycle, the latter from Beto Bicicletas, Rua São Paulo 543, T4512211, US$5 per day. Other Italian colonial towns just over one hour from Bento Gonçalves, which can be reached by frequent buses, are **Veranópolis** and **Nova Prata**, both set in lovely countryside. A pleasant trip through vineyards is to **Monte Belo do Sul**, where you can find pleasant walks through the hills and vineyards; buses US$1.50, 45

The legend of Negrinho do Pastoreio

There used to be a cruel landowner in Rio Grande do Sul; greedy and evil-tempered, he treated the many slaves on his estância very badly. Delimited only by natural boundaries, his property was enormous. Animals could roam more or less as they wished, but in those days it was normal to assign a slave to shepherd duties, keeping the livestock within reach of the farm.

The slave assigned to the task on this property was known as Negrinho, because he was a little Negro. One day he lost an animal. Furious, the boss beat him until he bled, then tied him to a plank of wood and sent him out to find the animal. Barely able to walk, Negrinho searched all day. When night fell, he was sent out again. To light his way, his boss gave him a candle-end and an armful of cinders from the fire, still smoking.

Returning at dawn without the lost animal, Negrinho was tied once more to a plank. He was tied so tightly that he died – or, he seemed dead. The boss sent his broken little body away, with instructions that it should be stuffed into the centre of a live ant hill.

Next day, the boss took a party to look at the ant hill. When they opened it up, there was Negrinho the shepherd, safe and well, with the lost animal by his side.

To this day, Negrinho do Pastoreio is the patron 'saint' of lost things. All he charges for his service is the stub of a candle, or some smoke. The most widespread of gaúcho legends, the story is valued as a reminder of a shameful era in the region's history.

minutes, **D** *Hotel Brasil* with bath, very quiet. Tourist information is in Bento Gonçalves at the town entrance at Pipa Pórtico and is very helpful, unlike the Secretaria de Turismo in the centre, who have limited information. Currency exchange at Banco do Brasil, also travellers' cheques, US$15 commission.

Garibáldi (*population* 26,771; *altitude* 617 metres) has a dry ski slope and toboggan slope – equipment hire, US$5 per hour. Garibáldi is smaller than the other towns, but has more old colonial buildings than Bento Gonçalves and a nice atmosphere. There are some *adegas/vinícolas* in town which you can visit (*Adega Le Cantier, Cooperative Vinícola Garibáldi* etc), and the town is known as the capital of Brazilian champagne with some other good wines as well.

A restored steam train leaves Bento Gonçalves Wednesday and Saturday at 1400 for **Carlos Barbosa**; called '*a rota do vinho*' (the wine run), it goes through vineyards in the hills and terminates at a modern station outside town, rather than at the beautiful old railway station in the centre. US$25 round trip, including wines, with live band; reserve in advance through *Giodani Turismo*, Rua Emy H Dreher 197, T4512788. It is often fully booked by groups, particularly on Saturday. For information on the local *Vinícolas* which can be visited in the **Vale dos Vinhedos**, contact Aprovale, Travessa Guaiba 75, T4524901, English spoken.

Another good excursion is to **Antônio Prado**, 1½ hours by *Caxiense Bus*. The town is now a World Heritage Site because of the large number of original buildings built by immigrants in the Italian style. Some to look out for are the **Casa de Neni** (1930) on Praça Garibáldi, **Farmácia Palombini** (1930) on Avenida Valdomiro Bocchese 439, and the **Prefeitura**, Praça Garibáldi. The **Museu Municipal** is also devoted to Italian immigration, Praça Garibáldi 77. There are two hotels on the main street. At *Restaurant Italia*, the churrasco lunch for US$6 is excellent.

AL *Alfred Palace*, R Sinimbu 2302, T/F2218655. **A** *Alfred* at No 2266, T/F2262555. **A** *Cosmos*, 20 de Setembro 1563, T/F2214688. **A** *Samaura Alfred*, 10 km out on RS-122, road to Farroupilha, T2272222, F2271010. Lots of sporting facilities, tennis,

Sleeping

Iguaçu Falls & the South

football, pool etc. **A** *Volpiano*, Ernesto Alves 1462, T2214744, F2214445. **B** *Itália*, Av Júlio de Castilhos 3076, T/F2251177. **D** *Peccini*, R Pinheiro Machado 1939. Shared bath, good breakfast. **D** *Pérola*, corner Ernesto Alves and Marquês de Herval 237. Good value. **D** *Hotel Praça*, R Cândido Mendes 330, T5213782. Good. Hotels fill up early in the afternoon.

Farroupilha **B** *Don Francesco*, R Dr J Rossler 88, T2611132. **A** *Concatto*, R 13 de Maio 730, T2612574, F2613411. **D** *Grande*, R Independência, T/F2611025, 2 blocks from the church where the buses from Caxias do Sul stop. No breakfast, clean.

Bento Gonçalves **A** *Dall'Onder*, R Erny Hugo Dreher 197, T/F4513555. Away from the centre. Under the same ownership is **B** *Vinocap*, R Barão do Rio Branco 245, T4521566. **E** *Pousada Somensi*, R Siba Paes 367, T4531254, near the Pipa Pórtico and Cristo Rei church in the upper town. Bath, without breakfast, good new rooms, friendly; 6 km out of town in Vale dos Vinhados is **B** *Pousada Casa Valduga*, at the *adega*, T4524338, F4526204. Beautiful, pool. **Youth hostel** *Pousada Casa Mia*, Travessa Niterói 71, T4511215. IYHA.

Garibáldi **A** *Casacurta*, R Luís Rogério Casacurta 510, T4622166, F4622354. **A** *Mosteiro São José*, R Buarque de Macedo 3590, T/F4621703. **C** *Pietá*, João Pessoa 47, T2621283. Rather run down. **Camping** *Palermo*, 5 km out on BR-116 at Km 118, T2227255. *Recanto dos Pinhais*, on BR-453 towards Lajeado Grande at Km 23, T2831144. At Garibáldi, Camping Clube do Brasil, estrada Gen Buarque de Macedo, 4 km.

Eating Good restaurants include *Cantina Pão e Vino*, R Ludovico Cavinato 1757, Bairro Santa Catarina, T2215557. 1130-1400, 1900-2300, closed Monday, *refeição colonial*. *Cantina Honda*, R Francisco Paglioli 984, in Saint Etiene, T2222359. 1900-2300, closed Sunday, Italian. *Belaria*, R Marquês do Herval 1124, T2230100. Italian, excellent meat and pasta, open 1130-1400, 1900-2330, closed Sunday. *Dom Rafael*, Praça Rui Barbosa.

Transport **Buses** Rodoviária, R Ernesto Alves 1341, T2223000. Fifteen-minute walk from the main square, but many buses pass through the centre. Bus fare from Porto Alegre to both Caxias do Sul and Bento Gonçalves is US$5.25.

Directory **Banks** *Banco do Brasil*, Exchange and TCs, US$20 charge. **Tourist information** Kiosk in Praça Rui Barbosa.

South of Porto Alegre

Pelotas

Population: 304,500
Phone code: 053
Colour map 5, grid C3

On the BR-116, 271 kilometres south of Porto Alegre, 56 kilometres north of Rio Grande, Pelotas is the second largest city in the State of Rio Grande do Sul, a river port on the Rio São Gonçalo which connects the Lagoa dos Patos with the Lagoa Mirim. Early colonial architecture, among the usual flat-fronted buildings, enhances the city's air of being stuck in a time warp; it is sleepy yet prosperous, with much typically Brazilian charm. It has an array of shops, which are easy to browse in the pedestrianized town centre, and pleasant parks with plenty of green (testament to the region's warm, damp climate). Pelotas is famous for its cakes and sweets; preserved fruits from the many small confectioners are worth trying.

Excursions Within a radius of 60 kilometres, about an hour's drive, there are numerous excursions to the farms of settlers of German descent in the hilly countryside, where you can find simple and clean accommodation, with cheap, good and plentiful food.

The **Lagoa dos Patos** is very shallow; at low tide it is possible to walk one kilometre out from the shore. During heavy rain, saltwater entering the lake brings with it large numbers of crabs which are a local delicacy. Fishermen are generally happy to take tourists out on sightseeing or fishing trips for a small fee (best to go in a group). **Praia do Laranjal** is full of locals' beach houses and there are several friendly bars. A recommended nightclub is *Rabo de Peixe* on the beach strip, next to the *Reticência* bar. **Barro Douro** is very green with no beach, but is the site of a big local festival for *Iemanjá* on 1-2 February, well worth visiting, campsite, *Ze3* buses (or taxi US$30) from Pelotas.

South of Pelotas, on the BR-471, is the **Taim** water reserve on the Lagoa Mirim. The road cuts the reserve in two and capibaras, killed by passing traffic, are sadly a common sight along the route. Many protected species, including black-necked swans and the *quero-quero* bird, migrate to the Taim for the breeding season. There is a small, very simple, restaurant on the reserve, but no other facilities. Visitors should stay in Rio Grande, 80 kilometres distant, or in Pelotas. Five kilometres from Taim there is an ecological station with a small museum of regional animals; there is some accommodation for scientists or other interested visitors. ■ *Information from Ibama in Porto Alegre, T0XX51-2267211/2252144.*

Sleeping A *Manta*, R Gen Netto 1131, T2252411, F2259911. Pool. B *Plaza Ipiranga*, Av Fernando Osório 8079, on the BR-116 north, 12 km out of town, T/F2736677. Pool. B *Pousada Lagoa Azul*, Av Antônio Augusto de Assumpção, 9805, T2261266. Cabins. B *Tourist Executive*, 7 km out of town on the BR-116 going north, T2719440. Luxury hotel in park setting, pool, tennis.

Eating *El Paisano*, R Mcal Deodoro 1093, T2271507. *Churrasco* meat comes from Uruguay and is cooked Uruguayan style, closed Monday, opening hours vary seasonally. *Lobão*, Av Bento Gonçalves 3460, T2256197. Churrasco *rodízio*. *Vila do Conde*, R Andrade Neves 1321, T2224612. 1100-1400, 1900-2300, closed Monday, Portuguese food.

Transport **Taxis** Radio taxi *Princesa*. Recommended. T2258466. **Air** Flights to Porto Alegre and Rio Grande. **Buses** Rodoviária is far out of town, with a bus every 15 minutes to the centre. Frequent daily buses to **Porto Alegre**, 244 km (US$8.15, 3-4 hours, paved road); **Rio Grande**, 90 minutes (paved but in poor condition), buses stop at Praça 20 de Setembro; Jaguarão, on the frontier with Río Branco, Uruguay, paved; and inland to **Bagé** and other towns. The road to the Uruguayan frontier at **Chuí** (paved), has international bus service, but only a couple of daily buses Pelotas-Chuí. *TTL* bus services (Montevideo-Porto Alegre) stop at the bus station for Montevideo (R Chile and R Venezuela); tickets must be purchased from an agency during the day. Bus service to Buenos Aires via Uruguaiana. From Bagé, where there is a police post, the Uruguayan company Núñez runs buses 3 times a week to Melo, via Aceguá. Good direct road northwest to Iguaçu via **São Sepé**, which has a very friendly hotel (**C** *Trevo Parque Hotel*, with a/c), Santa Maria (see page 403) and São Miguel mission ruins (see below).

Directory Banks *Banco do Brasil* will change TCs. It is difficult to change money at weekends. **Tourist information** *Integrasul*, Praça Col Pedro Osório 6, main square, has information on Pelotas and the entire southern region.

Iguaçu Falls & the South

Sonhos (Dreams)

The South of Brazil is very fond of sweets, combining mostly Germanic and Portuguese influences with a taste of Africa to produce a seemingly endless array of cakes and desserts. Sonhos, from Rio Grande, are tiny, light dumplings traditionally served with coffee.

Guava jelly (goiabada), sold cheaply everywhere in Brazil, is hard to come by elsewhere: try Portuguese or Caribbean grocers. Otherwise, substitute a very stiff fruit conserve. Recipe makes about 25 sonhos.

Ingredients
200g plain flour
50g cornflour
pinch of salt
180ml water
160ml milk
45g butter
30g sugar
The grated peel of 1 lime
4 eggs
Oil (eg sunflower or grapeseed) for deep frying

Filling
25 squares guava jelly, about 1 cm square
Caster sugar for dusting

Method
Mix the flour, cornflour and salt in a bowl. Put water, milk and butter together in a pan and boil until all the butter has melted. Remove the pan from the heat, throw all the flour mixture into the liquid and, using a wooden spoon, beat vigorously until it forms a ball of sticky dough. (This takes quick reactions and some determination!) Put the pan over a low heat and keep mixing vigorously. When the dough has dried out enough, it should come away from the sides of the pan, leaving a smooth film behind. Transfer the dough to a large bowl and let it cool completely.

Then beat the dough together with the sugar and lime peel in a food processor. Add the eggs gradually: allow each egg to become completely absorbed before adding the next one. Return the mixture to the bowl and leave covered for 1 hour.

Heat the oil to a depth of about 6 cm in a large, heavy pan. Use a soup spoon to form bite-sized balls of dough, with a square of jelly inside each one. Make sure the jelly is not exposed. Fry 3 or 4 sonhos at a time: when they're firm and crisp on the outside, store them on kitchen paper in a low oven while you cook the others. Sprinkle with sugar and serve, still warm.

Rio Grande

Population: 178,500
Phone code: 053
Colour map 5, grid C3

At the entrance to the Lagoa dos Patos, 274 kilometres south of Porto Alegre, is Rio Grande, founded in 1737. The city lies on a low, sandy peninsula, 16 kilometres from the Atlantic Ocean. Today it is the distribution centre for the southern part of Rio Grande do Sul, with significant cattle and meat industries.

During the latter half of the 19th century, Rio Grande was an important centre, but today it is a rather poor town, notable for the charm of its old buildings. The **Catedral de São Pedro** dates from 1755-75. **Museu Oceanográfico**, has an interesting collection of 125,000 molluscs. ■ *Daily, 0900-1100, 1400-1700, T2313496, 2 km centre on Avenida Perimetral; bus 59 or walk along waterfront.* At Praça Tamandaré is a small zoo.

Excursions **Cassino** is a popular seaside town with hotels and shops, 24 kilometres from Rio Grande via a good road. There are several beaches within easy reach of Cassino, but they have no facilities. A wrecked ship remains on the shore where it was thrown by a storm in 1975; unfortunately the road is used as a roadway. Travelling south, the beaches in order are Querência (five kilometres), Stela Maris (nine kilometres), Netuno (10 kilometres), all with surf.

The breakwater (the Barra), five kilometres south of Cassino, no bus connection, through which all vessels entering and leaving Rio Grande must pass, is a tourist attraction. Barra-Rio Grande buses, from the east side of Praça Ferreira, pass the Superporto. Very good fishing. The coastline is low and straight, lacking the bays to the north of Porto Alegre. One attraction is railway flat-cars powered by sail, settle the price in advance; the railway was built for the construction of the breakwater.

Across the inlet from Rio Grande, the little visited settlement of **São José do Norte** makes a pleasant trip (see above, **Tramandaí to São José do Norte**). Founded in 1725 and still mostly intact, the village depends on agriculture and crab fishing. There are only three hotels, a good campsite, *Caturritas*, T2381476, in pine forests five kilometres from the town, and several long beaches. Frequent ferries (two hours approximately) link São José with Rio Grande; there are also three car ferries daily, T2321500. Tourist information from R Gen Osorio 127.

Sleeping A *Charrua Rio Grande*, R Duque de Caxias 55, T/F2313833. Recommended, good value. B *Europa*, R Gen Neto 165, main square, T/F2313933. D *Paris*, R Mcal Floriano 112. Old, charming. At Cassino: A *Atlântico*, Av Rio Grande, 387, T2361350. Clean, refurbished, special rates for students. B *Marysol*, Av Atlântica 700, T2361240, near beach. Friendly. Private campsite on Av 33, on the way out to Rio Grande. Camping Clube do Brasil site near town.

Eating *Recanto Doce*, Silva Paes 370. Cheap. *China Brasil*, R Luís Loréa 389. Good, but not cheap. *Pescal*, Mcal Andréa 389. For fish, fairly expensive. *Caumo's*, Dr Nascimento 389. Good churrascaria. *Jensen*, Al Abreu 650, near rodoviária. Good and cheap. *Bar Brejeiro*, Andrades 193. Jazz upstairs. *Tia Laura*, 29 km from town on, BR-392 north to Pelotas. Excellent, specializes in home cooking and *café colonial*.

Transport **Buses** Frequent daily buses to and from **Pelotas** (56 km), **Bagé** (280 km), **Santa Vitória** (220 km) and **Porto Alegre** (US$10, 4½ hours). To **Itajaí**, 14 hours, US$15. All buses to these destinations go through Pelotas. Road to Uruguayan border at **Chuí** is paved, but the surface is poor (5 hours by bus, at 0700 and 1430). Bus tickets to **Punta del Este** or **Montevideo** at *Bentica Turismo*, Av Silva Paes 373, T321321/321807. **Boats** Boat trip across mouth of Lagoa dos Patos, to pleasant village of São José do Norte, every hour from Porto Velho.

Directory Communications Telephones: R Andrade Neves 94. **Embassies & consulates** *Denmark*, R Mcal Floriano 122, CP 9296200, T2324422, open 0800-1200, 1330-1800. *UK*, R Francisco Marques 163, Caixa Postal 455, Centro, 96-200 Rio Grande, T2327107. **Tourist information** R Riachuelo, on the waterfront, behind the Câmara de Comércio and beneath the Hidroviária; good map and information.

Western Rio Grande do Sul

Passo Fundo
Population: 156,500
Phone code: 054

Northwest of Porto Alegre by 328 kilometres is Passo Fundo, regarded as 'the most *gaúcho* city in Rio Grande do Sul', so much so that the town's square boasts a statue of a maté gourd and bombilla. There is an international *rodeio* in December. The town has several hotels (**A-B**).

Jesuit Missions

Santo Ângelo
Population: 75,500
Phone code: 055

West of here are the **Sete Povos das Missões Orientais** (see page 384). Santo Ângelo is the town with the best infrastructure for visiting the missions. The

The Jesuit aldeia

The typical plan of a Jesuit aldeia (also called a redução) was rectangular, built around a large praça de armas. To the rear of the plaza stood the church. On one side of the church was the cemetery and on the other the claustro, where the Jesuits themselves lived and studied. Near this were the workshops (ateliês) in which the works of art etc were produced. Behind the church were the gardens. Around the other sides of the plaza were the houses in which the Indians lived. The streets between the buildings were at right angles to each other and the settlement could easily be expanded along this plan. Chapels were sometimes built on the sides of the plaza. Other buildings included the cabildo, the municipal building of the Indians, the cotiguazu, a house for widows, a prison, a hospital and an inn for visitors.

(See Yves Bottineau and Henri Stierlin (ed), Iberian-American Baroque, page 176; plan taken from Folha de São Paulo, 30 June 1997.)

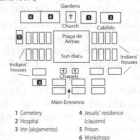

1 Cemetery
2 Hospital
3 Inn (alojamento)
4 Jesuits' residence (claustro)
5 Prison
6 Workshops

only considerable Jesuit remains in Brazilian territory are the very dramatic ones at **São Miguel das Missões**, some 50 kilometres from Santo Ângelo. At São Miguel, now a World Heritage Site, there is a church, 1735-45, and small museum. ■ *0900-1800*. A *son et lumière* show in Portuguese is held daily, in winter at 1900, and a different time in summer, although all times rather depend on how many people there are. The show ends too late to return to Santo Ângelo. The only place to stay in São Miguel is *Hotel Barichello* (**C**), which is nice, clean and quiet. It also has a restaurant, *Churrasco* for lunch. It is difficult to find a place to eat in the evening; you could try a snack bar for hamburgers. *Gaúcho* festivals are often held on Sunday afternoons, in a field near the Mission (follow the music).

Sleeping **A** *Maerkli*, Av Brasil 1000, T/F3122127. Recommended. **B** *Avenida II*, Av Venâncio Aires 1671, T3133011. **D** *Hotel Nova Esperança*, behind bus station. No breakfast. **D** *Brasil*, Av Vernáncio Aires. **E** *Comércio*, Av Brasil. A bit run down but good for the price, clean, friendly. Hotel next door, also **E**, is more than basic. There are other cheap central hotels on or near Praça Rio Branco, fairly near old railway station.

Transport Bus Porto Alegre-Santo Ângelo, 5 *convencional* daily, 6 hours, US$15, and *executivo* at 1830, US$19.50.

Directory **Banks** *Banco do Brasil* charges a commission of US$15 for TCs. Good rates for cash at the garage with red doors opposite *Hotel Maerkli* on Av Brasil.

To the Argentine missions You can continue into Argentina to see the mission ruins at San Ignacio Miní by getting a bus from Santo Ângelo at 0615 or 1300 to **Porto Xavier**, four hours. Buses also to Porto Xavier on the Rio Uruguay and frontier with Argentina, from Porto Alegre, one daily, and Santa Maria. Porto Xavier is a quiet town, with one hotel, **D** *Rotta*, on the main street near the praça, with or without a/c, and/or TV, bath, breakfast, good restaurant closed Saturday and Sunday evening; good *pizzaria* on the terrace on the main square. The hotel is about 10 minutes' walk from the ferry at the end of the main street. The Policia Federal post for the entry and exit stamps is about 200 metres north of the ferry in a white building, friendly.

Inland routes to Uruguay and Argentina

Rail and road to the west and southwest of Rio Grande do Sul go through Santa Maria. The town has a university and is an important commercial and farming centre. There is a Saturday morning fruit and veg market, R 13 de Maio. Nearby **Parque Balneário Oásis** on the BR-158 has nature trails, lakes and a minizoo.

Santa Maria
Population: 226,500
Phone code: 055

Sleeping and eating A *Itaimbé Palace*, R Venâncio Aires 2741, T2221144, F2212051. Good breakfast, pool. Recommended. **D** *Jantzen*, R Rio Branco. Central, noisy on disco nights. **D** *Imperial*, R Manoel Ribas 1767, near station. Clean, garden. **D** *Popular*, also near station. Clean but basic. Restaurant *Augusto*, R F Peixoto 1356. Traditional, chicken a speciality.

Directory Laundry *Lave Só*, R F Peixoto 876.

In the extreme west are Uruguaiana, a cattle centre 772 kilometres from Porto Alegre, and its twin Argentine town of Paso de los Libres with a casino. A 1,400 metre bridge over the Rio Uruguai links the two cities.

Uruguaiana
Population: 121,500
Phone code: 055

    Brazilian immigration and customs At the end of the bridge, five blocks from the main praça. Exchange and information in the same building. Exchange rates are better in the town than at the border.

Sleeping A *Fares Turis*, Av Pres Vargas 2939, T4123358. May let you leave your bags while you look around town. **A** *Glória*, R Domingos de Almeida 1951, T4124422, F4124804. Good. **D** *Palace*, Praça Rio Branco. No breakfast.

Transport Taxi or bus across the bridge about US$3.50. Buses connect the bus stations and centres of each city every 30 minutes. If you have to disembark for visa formalities, a following bus will pick you up without extra charge. There are bus services to **Porto Alegre**. *Planalto* buses run from Uruguaiana via Barra do Quaraí/Bella Unión (US$4.50) to Salto and Paysandú in Uruguay.
    If wishing to break the journey between Uruguaiana and Porto Alegre, **Alegrete** (130 kilometres east of the border) is a good place, with several hotels, eg **D** *Grandense*, near rodoviária, shared bath, TV, friendly. Good restaurant, *La Piazza*, on praça, excellent beef.

Directory Banks: if you arrive in Uruguaiana from Porto Alegre in the early hours of the morning and need money, cross the border with Pluma bus, wait in Paso de los Libres until opening time (0730) and then go to the Visa ATM in Banco Francés for cash.

The crossing furthest west is **Barra do Quaraí** to **Bella Unión**, via the Barra del Cuaraim bridge. This is near the confluence of the Rios Uruguai and Quaraí. **Bella Unión** (*population* 12,000) has three hotels and a campsite in the Parque Fructuoso Rivera (T0642-2261). Brazilian Consulate, Calle Lirio Moraes 62, T/F7392054; buses to Salto and Montevideo.
    Thirty kilometres east is another crossing from **Quaraí** to **Artigas** (*population* 40,000), in a cattle raising and agricultural area. Brazilian consulate, Calle Lecueder 432, T86422504, F86424504. Artigas has hotels, a youth hostel and campsites. Buses also run to Salto and Montevideo.
    There are two further crossings at **Aceguá**, 60 kilometres south of Bagé, 59 kilometres north of the Uruguayan town of Melo, and further east, **Jaguarão/Rio Branco**. The 1½ kilometre long Mauá bridge across the Rio Jaguarão joins these two towns. The police post for passport checks is three kilometres before the bridge; customs are at the bridge.

Iguaçu Falls & the South

Frontier with Uruguay
For road traffic, at Chuy is better than Río Branco or Aceguá

Before crossing into Uruguay, you must visit Brazilian Polícia Federal to get an exit stamp; if not, the Uruguayan authorities will send you back. **Brazilian consulates** are at Melo: R Del Pilar 786, T0462-2136. At Río Branco: Lavalleja and Palomeque. Exchange rates are usually better at Melo than at the frontier.

Santana do Livramento

Population: 85,500
Phone code: 055
Colour map 5, grid C2

The southern interior of the state is the region of the real *gaúcho*. Principal towns of this area include Santana do Livramento. Its twin Uruguayan city is Rivera (see below). All one need do is cross the main street, but by public transport this is not a straightforward route between Brazil and Uruguay. For motorists there are three customs offices in Santana do Livramento, about 30 minutes needed for formalities.

Sleeping

A *Jandaia*, R Uruguai 1452, T2422288. Recommended. **A** *Portal*, Av Tamandaré 2076, T2423244. Parking, clean. Recommended. **C** *Uruguaiana*, close to bus station. **Youth hostel E** pp *Palace*, R Manduca Rodrigues 615, T2423340, F2423110. With breakfast, single rooms available, old and grimy.

Transport

Buses Rodoviária is at Gen Salgado Filho and Gen Vasco Alves. To **Porto Alegre**, 2 daily, 7 hours, US$20; 3 daily to **Urugaiana** (4 hours, US$10), services also to **São Paulo** and other destinations.

Directory

Banks *Banco do Brasil*, Av Sarandí. Best rates for Amex TCs at *Val de Marne*.

Into Uruguay
You must have a Brazilian exit stamp to enter Uruguay and a Uruguayan exit stamp to enter Brazil

Uruguayan immigration is in the new Complejo Turístico at Sarandí y Viera, 14 blocks, two kilometres, from the border (take bus along Agraciada). There is also a tourist office here. **Uruguayan customs** Luggage is inspected when boarding buses out of Rivera; there are also three check points on the road out of town.

Rivera
Population: 55,500
Phone code: 0622

Rivera has a park, the Plaza Internacional and the nearby Cañapirú dam. There is also a casino and many duty-free shops.

Sleeping A *Casablanca*, Sarandí 484, T3221. With breakfast, comfortable, pleasant. **B** *Comercio*, Artigas 115. Comfortable, **C** without bath. **B** *Sarandí*, Sarandí 777, T3521. Fan, good, **C** without bath. **C** *Uruguay-Brasil*, Sarandí 440,

Santana do Livramento & Rivera

BRAZIL

URUGUAY

Not to scale

■ Sleeping
1 Casablanca
2 Comercio
3 Estrela Palace
4 Ferrocarril
5 Sarandí
6 Tamoio
7 Uruguay-Brasil
8 Verde Plaza
9 Youth Hostel

T3068. A/c, breakfast. **D** *Ferrocarril*, Lavalleja and Uruguay, T3389. Without bath, basic, quiet. **Youth hostel** Uruguay and Brasil. **Camping** In Municipal site near AFE station, T3803, and in the Parque Gran Bretaña 7 km south along Route 27.

Transport Air: flights to **Montevideo**. **Trains** Passenger service to **Tacuarembó**. **Buses** To **Montevideo** and other Uruguayan towns.

Directory Banks: there are plenty of exchange houses. **Embassies & consulates**: *Argentina*, Ituzaingó 524, T3257. *Brazil*, C Ceballos, 1159, T3278, F4470.

Coastal route to Uruguay

Chuí (Chuy)

On the Brazilian side of the border is Chuí, a tranquil town, whilst on the Uruguayan side is Chuy. The BR-471 from Porto Alegre and Pelotas skirts the town and carries straight through to Uruguay, where it becomes Ruta 9. Each country's immigration is outside the town (see below); if you are staying in town you can walk anywhere as long as you do not go beyond the immigration posts. The main street is Avenida Internacional: on the Brazilian side it is called Avenida Uruguaí and on the Uruguayan side Avenida Brasil. Each side carries two-way traffic. On the Brazilian side the shops are mainly clothes, shoes and household goods, while the Uruguayan side has duty-free shops and a casino. São Miguel fort, built by the Portuguese in 1737, now reconstructed with period artefacts, is worth a visit. A lighthouse 10 kilometres west marks the Barro do Chuí inlet, which has uncrowded beaches and is visited by sea lions. **NB** From October to February, Brazil is one hour ahead of Uruguay (GMT-2; Uruguay GMT-3).

Population: 3,000
Phone code: 053
Colour map 5, grid C2

A *Bertelli Chuí*, BR-471, 2 km from town, T2651266, F2651207. Comfortable with pool. *Turis Firper*, Av Samuel Prilliac 629, T2651398, F2651068. A/c, TV, bar. **D** *Bianca*, Chile 1620, T2651500 or 0474-2189, F0474-2911. With bath. **D** *Rivero*, Colômbia 163-A, T2651271. With bath, without breakfast. **E** *San Francisco*, Av Colômbia and R Chile. Restaurant, with bath.

Sleeping

Rodoviária on R Venezuela. Buses run from Chuí to **Pelotas** (6-7 daily, US$6.60, 4 hours), **Rio Grande** (0700, 1400, 5 hours, US$6.10) and **Porto Alegre** (1200, 2400, 7¾ hours, US$13); also from Chuí to **Santa Vitória do Palmar** nearby, US$0.60, where there are a few hotels and rather quicker bus services to the main cities.

Transport

Banks *Cambios* on the Uruguayan side, see below. *Banco do Brasil*, Av Uruguaí, 3 blocks west of post office. Change all remaining Uruguayan pesos into *reais* before leaving Uruguay, since not even black marketeers in Brazil want them. **Communications Post Office:** Av Uruguaí, between Colômbia and Argentina. **Telephones:** Corner of R Chile and Av Argentina.

Directory

Brazilian immigration Immigration is about 2½ kilometres from the border, on BR-471, road to Pelotas. All buses, except those originating in Pelotas, stop at customs on both sides of the border; if coming from Pelotas, you must ask the bus to stop for exit formalities. International buses, for example *TTL* from Porto Alegre, make the crossing straightforward: the company holds passports; hand over your visitors card on leaving Brazil and get a Uruguayan one on entry. Have luggage available for inspection. Make sure you get your stamp, or you will have trouble leaving Brazil.

Frontier with Brazil
Tourists may freely cross the border in either direction

Iguaçu Falls & the South

Uruguayan immigration Uruguayan passport control is 2½ kilometres before the border on the road into Chuy, US$2.50 by taxi, officials are friendly and co-operative. If travelling by bus, make sure the driver knows you want to stop at Uruguayan immigration, it will not do so automatically. If you stay overnight in Chuy you cannot get your exit stamp in advance. You may only do so immediately prior to leaving the country.

Entering Brazil From Uruguay, on the Uruguayan side, the bus will stop if asked, and wait while you get your exit stamp (with bus conductor's help); on the Brazilian side, the appropriate form is completed by the rodoviária staff when you purchase your ticket into Brazil. The bus stops at Polícia Federal (BR-471) and the conductor completes formalities while you sit on the bus. Customs officials may ask you to open your luggage for inspection. Also, if entering by car, fill up with petrol in Brazil, where fuel is cheaper.

Entering Uruguay To enter Uruguay, you must have a Brazilian exit stamp and a Uruguayan entry stamp, otherwise you will not be permitted to proceed. Those requiring a visa must have a medical examination before a visa can be issued in Chuí, cost about US$20 and US$10 respectively.

Into Uruguay
Population: 9,000
Phone code: 0474

The Uruguayan town of **Chuy** is 340 kilometres from Montevideo.

Excursions On the Uruguyan side, on a promontory overlooking Laguna Merín and the gaúcho landscape of southern Brazil, stands the restored fortress of **San Miguel**, dating from 1752 and surrounded by a moat. It is set in a park in which many plants and animals are kept. (Bus from Chuy US$0.45, entry US$0.20, closed Monday.) The hotel nearby, **A** *Parador San Miguel*, is excellent, beautiful rooms, fine food and service, highly recommended. Tours (US$10 from Chuy) end for the season after 31 March.

Sleeping and eating B *Nuevo Hotel Plaza*, Gral Artigas y Arachanes, T/F0474-2309. On plaza, central, helpful, with breakfast, TV, *El Mesón de la Plaza* restaurant. **B-C** *Alerces*, Laguna de Castillos 578, T0474-2260. Heater, bath, TV, breakfast, nice. **C** *International*, Río San Luis 121, T0474-2055. TV, breakfast extra. **D** *Madrugada*, C S Priliac y India Muerta, T0474-2346. Clean, quiet. *Hospedaje El-Cort*, Lago de los Patos 287. With bath, parking. *Brisas*, Laguna Negra y Lago Castillos, T0474-2708. **Camping** From Chuy, buses run every 2 hours to the Barra del Chuy campsite, Ruta 9 Km 331, turn right 13 km, T2425. Good bathing, many birds. *Cabañas* for up to 4 persons cost US$20 daily or less, depending on amenities. Most restaurants are on Av Brasil. A good one is *Parrillada Jesús* at the corner of L Olivera. Also *Parrillada/Pizzería Javier*, Arachanes 589, OK, and *Los Leños*, Av Gral Artigas, for meat and pizzas.

Transport Buses: to Montevideo (*COT, Cynsa*, both on Av Brasil between Olivera and Artigas, or *Rutas del Sol*, on L Oliveria) US$13, 5 hours.

Directory Banks: several *cambios* on Av Brasil, eg *Cambio Gales*, Gral Artigas y Brasil, Mon-Fri 0830-1200, 1330-1800, Sat 0830-1200; in World Trade Center 1000-2200. Also *Los Aces* and *Val*, either side of Gales. All change TCs at US$1 per cheque and 1% commission and give similar rates, without commission, for cash (pesos, dollars and *reais*). On Sun, try the casino, or look for someone on the street outside the *cambios*. Brazilian currency can be bought here. *Banco de la República Oriental Uruguay*, Gral Artigas, changes TCs. **Communications** Telephones: Antel, S Priliac, between C L Olivera and C Gen Artigas, 0700-2300. **Embassies & consulates** *Brazil*, A Fossati, T0474-2049.

Bahia

7

Bahia

This state, often dubbed 'Africa in exile', was the heart of colonial Brazil and Salvador its first capital. The slave trade brought cheap labour for the sugar plantations, as well as a culture that has endured over the years and is still evident in the religion, cuisine and racial mix today. The city's colonial architecture has been restored and the historic centre is a maze of bars, restaurants, workshops and music in the streets. There are fine beaches, particularly at Morro de São Paulo and in the south around Porto Seguro. Inland there is the Chapada Diamantina National Park, to be explored on foot or on horseback. Colourful festivities and street carnivals are held throughout the year to the beat of the massed drummers of Olodum, Ilê Aiye and other African cultural groups.

Bahia

Background

History Santa Cruz Cabrália, in the south of the state, is believed to be the site of the first landing in Brazil by Portuguese explorer Pedro Álvares Cabral in 1500. Later, under the division of Brazil into captaincies by King João III, Bahia was given to Francisco Pereira Coutinho who landed in 1535. Initial relations with the Tupinambá Indians were good, largely because a Portuguese man, Diogo Álvares, known as Caramuru, was living with them. The Portuguese soon soured the relationship with excessive demands and then fell out among themselves. Ten years after his arrival, Coutinho left, unable to stop the fighting between rival groups of Portuguese and their Indian allies. The Tupinambá, eager for a return of their source of arms and metals, invited Coutinho back. As he sailed back into the bay in 1547, he was shipwrecked at Itaparica and the survivors were ceremonially killed and eaten by the Indians (John Hemming, *Red Gold*, gives more details on this disastrous episode).

Despite this inauspicious start to the colony, it was recognized that the Bahia de Todos Os Santos was strategically important. It was therefore chosen as the place from which the new colony of Brazil was to be governed. Once the threat of Indian attack had been removed, the Portuguese quickly made the most of a land and climate which was ideal for sugar cultivation.

Geography & climate Bahia is the southernmost of the states in the northeastern bulge of Brazil, with a population of about 13 million in an area the size of France. Most people live along the coast, but there are many other smaller towns in the interior. The Recôncavo is a fertile area surrounding the Bahia dos Todos os Santos, once extensively cultivated for sugar and tobacco. The Rio São Francisco traverses the harsh Sertão, linking Minas Gerais to the Atlantic Ocean at the border of Sergipe and Alagoas.

Economy Tourism is extremely important for the state and the capital has become a centre for Bahian music, which is now popular throughout the country. Cacao is grown almost entirely in southern Bahia, inland from the port of Ilhéus, although crop pests have caused problems lately. Some of Brazil's main oilfields are in the State of Bahia and there has been more investment in industrial production in the state recently, with interest from foreign companies attracted by lower labour costs.

Salvador

Population: 2.5 million
Phone code: 071
Colour map 4, grid A6

The capital of the State of Bahia is the third largest city in Brazil and is also often referred to as Bahia, rather than Salvador. Salvador is one of the must see tourist points of Brazil and it is quite easy to spend a whole vacation here without leaving this heady mix of colonial buildings, beautiful beaches, African culture and pulsating musical rhythms.

Salvador stands on the magnificent Bahia de Todos os Santos, a sparkling bay dotted with 38 islands. The bay is the largest on the Brazilian coast covering an area of 1,100 square kilometres. Rising above the bay on its eastern side is a cliff which dominates the landscape and, perched on top, 71 metres above sea level, are the older districts of Salvador, with buildings dating back to the 17th and 18th centuries.

The Bahians

Bahia is perceived in the south of the country as being a place where life moves at a different pace. The word preguiça (laziness) will inevitably creep into a conversation with paulistas and cariocas when the topic is Salvador. This slightly malicious accusation from the southerners cannot take away the great infectious joy for life, so obvious in Bahians.

Bahians have a great propensity for partying; there is even a popular carnival song that says that every day is party day in Bahia. The cycle of massive street festivals throughout the year is evidence of this.

There is no doubt that Bahians have a different slant on time keeping. For instance, the clock in the main bus station is officially seven minutes fast as Bahians will almost always be late. The weekend and carnival are among the few events that start early: the former on Thursday night, the latter four days before anywhere else in the country. If you want someone to turn up for an appointment on time you will need to emphasize that you are expecting them at 'horário británico'. Another popular saying is that it takes nine months to leave the womb, so why hurry now! While this laid back attitude can be frustrating, Bahians are very open, warm, hospitable, endearing people to spend time with, willing to try to understand, either in words or gestures. People still have time to talk to one another in this town.

Conor O'Sullivan

Ins and outs

Air Domestic and international flights arrive at Dois de Julho Airport, 32 km from the city centre. An a/c bus service leaves every 25 minutes between 0620 and 2230 from the airport to the centre along the coast road, stopping at hotels *en route*, US$2. Also ordinary buses, US$0.50. 'Special' taxis (buy ticket at the airport desk), US$40; normal taxis, US$20, bus-taxi service, US$15. Taxis from the airport to the city are controlled by certain drivers.

Getting there
See also Transport, page 435

Buses Interstate buses arrive at the rodoviária near Iguatemi Shopping Centre. There are regular bus services to the centre (US$0.50); bus RI or RII 'Centro-Rodoviária-Circular' stops at the foot of the Lacerda lift (see below); buses also go to Campo Grande; the journey can take up to 1 hour, especially at peak periods. An executive bus (US$1.50, weekdays only) to Praça da Sé or the lower city (Comércio) via the coast road leaves from outside the shopping centre (reached from the bus station by a walkway but be careful at night). Taxi to the centre, US$10.

The broad peninsula on which the city of Salvador is built is at the mouth of the Bahia de Todos Os Santos. On the opposite side of the bay's entrance is the Ilha de Itaparica (described below). The commercial district of the city and its port are on the sheltered, western side of the peninsula; residential districts and beaches are on the open, Atlantic side. The point of the peninsula is called Barra, which is itself an important area.

Getting around

The centre of the city is divided into 2 levels, the Upper City (or Cidade Alta) where the Historical Centre lies, and the Lower City (Cidade Baixa) which is the commercial and docks district. The 2 levels are connected by a series of steep hills called *ladeiras*. The easiest way to go from 1 level to the other is by the *Lacerda* lift, which connects Praça Municipal (Tomé de Sousa) in the Upper City with Praça Cairu and the famous Mercado Modelo. There is also the Plano Inclinado Gonçalves, a funicular railway which leaves from behind the Cathedral going down to Comércio, the commercial district.

Most visitors limit themselves to the centre, Barra, the Atlantic suburbs and the Itapagipe peninsula, which is north of the centre. The roads and avenues between these areas are straightforward to follow and are well-served by public transport. Other parts of the city are not as easy to get around, but have less of tourist interest. If going to these areas, a taxi may be advisable until you know your way around.

Climate It rains somewhat all the year, but the main rainy season is between May and September. The climate is pleasant and the sun is never far away. Temperatures range from 25°C to 32°C, never falling below 19°C in winter.

Safety

Tourist Police: R Gregório de Matos 16, T2422885. Delegacia de Proteção ao Turista, R Gregório de Matos 1, T2423504

Be very careful of your money and valuables at all times and in all districts. Avoid the more distant beaches out of season, when they are empty (eg Itapoã, Piatã, Placafor); on Sunday they are more crowded and safer. There have been reports of armed muggings on the sand dunes surrounding Lagoa do Abaeté. Do not visit them alone. At night, the area around and in the lifts and buses are unsafe. On no account change money on the streets; this is a guaranteed way to be robbed. Leave valuables securely in your hotel, particularly at night (including wristwatch and cameras if possible: disposable cameras are widely available). Carry a small amount of money that you can hand over if you are threatened. One is warned not to walk down any of the links between the old and new city, especially the Ladeira de Misericôrdia, which links the Belvedere, near the Lacerda Lifts, with the lower city. Should a local join you at your table for a chat, leave at once if drugs are mentioned. The civil police are reported to be very sympathetic and helpful and more resources have been put into policing the

Salvador orientation

Related maps
A Salvador Centro Histórico, page 415
B Praça Castro Alves to Vitória, page 416
C Porto da Barra, page 418

N
Not to scale

■ **Sleeping**
1 Bahia Othon Palace
2 Enseada das Lajes
3 Meridien

old part of the city and Barra, which are now well-lit at night. Police are little in evidence after 2300, however.

History

On 1 November 1501, All Saints Day, the navigator Amérigo Vespucci sailed into the bay. As the first European to see it, he named it after the day of his arrival. When Martim Afonso was sent by the Portuguese crown to set up a permanent colony in Brazil, he decided against the Bahia de Todos Os Santos in favour of São Vicente in present-day São Paulo, even though the bay was one of the finest anchorages on the coast and a favourite port of call for French, Spanish and Portuguese ships. It was also a known export point for *pau brasil*.

This strategic importance was finally recognized and it was chosen as the place from which the new colony of Brazil was to be governed when the first Governor General, Tomé de Sousa, arrived on 23 March 1549, to build a fortified city to protect Portugal's interest from constant threats of Dutch and French invasion. Salvador was formally founded on 1 November 1549 and

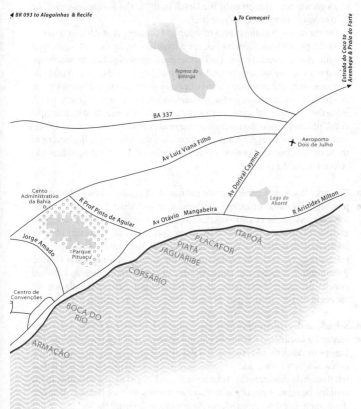

Bahia

 Ochente!

The rest of Brazil tends to find the northeastern accent funny: in common with the poorest and oldest regions of many countries, it retains outmoded structures, expressions and pronunciations which, language historians claim, recall the Portuguese spoken by the earliest settlers. It is an attractive accent, with rising cadence that lends a sing-song quality to the language (considered downmarket in Southerners) – and is easy for visitors to manage, since it is spoken comparatively slowly and clearly.

The minute you arrive in the northeast, you are likely to hear the local all-purpose exclamation: "Ochente!", probably at maximum decibels. Meaning everything from "You don't say!" to the unprintable, it's a particularly satisfying yell, capable of a thousand inflections, and is almost impossible not to adopt. The short version, "Oshh!", is reserved for situations where hushed tones are required – as in "She didn't!"

remained the capital of Brazil until 1763. One short-lived disruption in the city's growth was its capture by the Dutch in 1624. The Portuguese, with the help of Spain, recaptured it a year later.

On the strength of the export of sugar and the import of African slaves to work the plantations, Salvador became a wealthy city. By the 18th century, it was the most important city in the Portuguese Empire after Lisbon, ideally situated in a safe, sheltered harbour along the trade routes of the 'New World'. Its fortunes were further boosted by the discovery of diamonds in the interior, but this could not compensate for the eventual decline in the sugar industry, which led to the loss of capital status and the rise of Rio de Janeiro as Brazil's principal city. Until the introduction of 20th century industries such as tourism and petrochemicals, the local economy could not rival the gold and coffee booms of the Southeast, but the city always played an influential part in the political and cultural life of the country.

African presence

The city's first wealth came from the cultivation of sugar cane and tobacco, the plantations' workforce coming from the west coast of Africa. For three centuries, Salvador was the site of a thriving slave trade. Even today, Salvador is described as the most African city in the Western hemisphere and the University of Bahia boasts the only chair in the Yoruba language in the Americas. The influence permeates the city: food sold on the street is the same as in Senegal and Nigeria, Bahian music is fused with pulsating African polyrhythms, men and women nonchalantly carry enormous loads on their heads, fishermen paddle dug out canoes in the bay, and the pace of life is a little slower than elsewhere.

Modern Salvador

Salvador today is a city of 15 forts, 166 Catholic churches, 1,000 *candomblé* temples and a fascinating mixture of old and modern, rich and poor, African and European, religious and profane. It is still a major port, exporting tropical fruit, cocoa, sisal, soya beans and petrochemical products. Its most important industry, though, is tourism; after Rio it is the second largest tourist attraction in the country, being very popular with Brazilian tourists who see Bahia as an exotic destination. Local government has done much to improve the fortunes of this once rundown, poor and dirty city, and most visitors feel that the richness of its culture is compensation enough for any problems they may encounter.

Major investments are being made in infrastructure and public health areas. A new comprehensive sewage system has been installed throughout the city, with a view to improving living conditions and dealing with pollution.

The once forgotten Lower City, Ribeira and the Itapagipe Peninsula districts have received major facelifts. Bahia has become more industrialized, with major investments being made by multinational firms in the automotive and petrochemical industries, principally in the Camaçari complex, 40 kilometres from the city. The Bahian economy is currently the fastest growing in the country.

Sights

There is much more of interest in the Upper than in the Lower City (see **Getting around**, page 411). From Praça Municipal to the Carmo area, two kilometres north along the cliff, is the Centro Histórico (Historical Centre), now a national monument and also protected by UNESCO. It was in this area that the Portuguese built their fortified city and where today stand some of the most important examples of colonial architecture in the Americas. The historic centre is undergoing a massive restoration programme, funded by the Bahian state government and Unesco. The colonial houses have been painted in pastel colours. Many of the bars have live music which spills out onto the street on every corner. Patios have been created in the open areas behind the houses, with open air cafés and bars. Artist ateliers, antique and handicraft stores have brought new artistic blood to what was once the bohemian part of the city. Many popular traditional restaurants and bars from other parts of Salvador have opened new branches in the area.

Centro Histórico

Salvador Centro Histórico

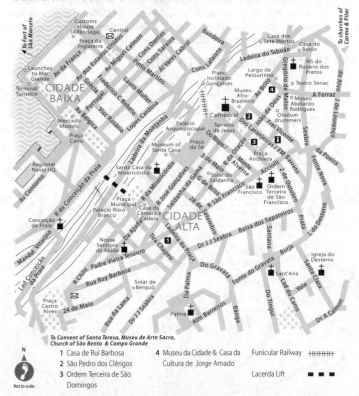

N

Not to scale

1 Casa de Rui Barbosa
2 São Pedro dos Clérigos
3 Ordem Terceira de São Domingos
4 Museu da Cidade & Casa da Cultura de Jorge Amado

Funicular Railway
Lacerda Lift

Praça Municipal, Praça de Sé & Terreiro de Jesus Dominating the **Praça Municipal** is the old Casa de Câmara e Cadeia or **Paço Municipal** (Council Chamber – 1660), while alongside is the **Palácio Rio Branco** (1918), once the Governor's Palace and now the headquarters of Bahiatursa, the state tourist board. Leaving it with its panoramic view of the bay, Rua Misericôrdia goes north passing the **Santa Casa Misericôrdia** (1695 – see the high altar and painted tiles) to **Praça da Sé**.

This praça, with its mimosa and flamboyant trees, is now pedestrianized on all but one side – with accompanying benches. There is a statue of Salvador's founder, Thomé da Souza, as well as a coffee bar and viewing space, which gives the best view of the bay. On the platform, there is a permanent installation called the Cruz Caido, by the sculptor Mario Cravo. It is dedicated to the old Igreja da Se, which was pulled down in 1933 and whose remaining foundations have been uncovered. One of the viewing pits displays the remains of slaves and mariners who were buried in the churches' grounds in the 16th century.

The next square is **Terreiro de Jesus**, a picturesque praça named after the church which dominates it. Built in 1692, the **church of the Jesuits** became the property of the Holy See in 1759 when the Jesuits were expelled from all Portuguese territories. The façade is one of the earliest examples of baroque in Brazil, an architectural style which was to dominate the churches built in the 17th and 18th centuries. Inside, the vast vaulted ceiling and 12 side altars in baroque and rococo frame the main altar completely leafed in gold. The tiles in blue, white and yellow in a tapestry pattern are also from Portugal. It houses the tomb of Mem de Sá. The church is now the city Cathedral (**Catedral Basílica**). ■ *Tuesday to Sunday, 0800-1100, 1500-1800*. Across the square is the church of **São Pedro dos Clérigos**, which is beautifully renovated. ■ *Sunday 0800-0930*. Alongside is the church of the **Ordem Terceira de São Domingos** (Dominican Third Order), which has a beautiful painted wooden ceiling. ■ *Monday-Saturday 0700-1100, Sunday 0700-1000, US$0.25*.

Praça Castro Alves to Vitória

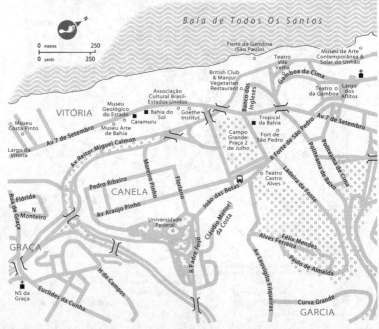

Facing Terreiro de Jesus is Praça Anchieta and the church of **São Francisco**. Its simple façade belies the treasure inside. The entrance leads to a sanctuary with a spectacular painting on the wooden ceiling, by local artist José Joaquim da Rocha (1777). The main body of the church is the most exuberant example of baroque in the country. The cedar wood carving and later gold leaf was completed after 28 years in 1748. The cloisters of the monastery are surrounded by a series of blue and white tiles from Portugal. ■ *0800-1115 and 1400-1700 (entry to cloisters US$0.20, church free).* Next door (and with the same opening hours, entry US$0.20) is the church of the **Ordem Terceira de São Francisco** (Franciscan Third Order – 1703), with its façade intricately carved in sandstone. Inside is a quite remarkable Chapter House, with striking images of the Order's most celebrated saints.

São Francisco

Leading off the Terreiro de Jesus is Rua Alfredo Brito, a charming, narrow cobbled street lined with fine colonial houses painted in different pastel shades. This street leads into the **Largo do Pelourinho** (Praça José Alencar), which was completely renovated in 1993. Considered the finest complex of colonial architecture in Latin America, it was once the site of a pillory where slaves were publicly punished and ridiculed. It was also the site of the slave market. After the cleaning of the area, new galleries, boutiques and restaurants are opening, and at night the Largo is lively, especially on Tuesday (see **Nightlife** below). **Nosso Senhor Do Rosário Dos Pretos** church, the so-called Slave Church, dominates the square. It was built by former slaves, with what little financial resources they had, over a period of 100 years. The side altars honour black saints. The painted ceiling is very impressive, the overall effect being one of tranquillity in contrast to the complexity of the Cathedral and São Francisco. ■ *Small entrance fee.*

Largo do Pelourinho

At the corner of Alfredo Brito and Largo do Pelourinho is a museum to the work of Jorge Amado (**Casa da Cultura Jorge Amado**, mainly photos, book covers and a lecture room), who lived in, and set many of his books, in this section of the city. ■ *Monday-Friday 0900-1800.* A good way to get a feel of the city and its people is to read *Dona Flor and her two husbands, Dona Flor e seus dois Maridos* (1966). The Carmo Hill is at the top of the street leading out of Largo do Pelourinho. The **Carmo** (Carmelite Third Order) church (1709) houses one of the sacred art treasures of the city, a sculpture of Christ made in 1730 by a slave who had no formal training, Francisco Xavier das Chagas, known as O Cabra. One of the features of the piece is the blood made from whale oil, ox blood, banana resin and 2,000 rubies to represent the drops of blood. ■ *Monday-Saturday 0800-1130 and 1400-1730, Sunday 1000-1200, US$0.30.* **Museu do Carmo**, in the Convento do Carmo, has a collection of icons and colonial furniture. ■ *Monday-Saturday 0800-1200, 1400-1800, Sunday 0800-1200, US$0.10.*

Bahia

South of the
Praça Municipal
In the direction of the mouth of the bay is the more modern section of the city, with many skyscrapers. Rua Chile leads to **Praça Castro Alves**, with its monument to Castro Alves, who started the campaign which finally led to the Abolition of Slavery in 1888. Two streets lead out of this square, Avenida 7 de Setembro, busy with shops and street vendors selling everything imaginable, and, parallel to it, Rua Carlos Gomes. **São Bento** church (rebuilt after 1624, but with fine 17th century furniture) is on Avenida 7 de Setembro. ■ *Monday-Saturday 0630-1230 and 1600-1900, Sunday 0700-1130 and 1700-1900.*

Campo Grande
to Barra
Both eventually come to **Campo Grande** (also known as Praça Dois de Julho). In the centre of the praça is the monument to Bahian Independence, 2 July 1823. The British Club is just off the square on Rua Banco dos Ingleses. Avenida 7 de Setembro continues out of the square towards the Vitória area. There are some fine 19th century homes along this stretch, known as Corredor da Vitória (Vitória Corridor). From Praça Vitória, the avenue continues down Ladeira da Barra (Barra Hill) to **Porto da Barra**. The best city beaches are in this area. Also in this district are the best bars, restaurants and nightlife. A little further along is the **Forte de Santo Antônio**, 1580, built on the spot where Amérigo Vespucci landed in 1501. It is right at the mouth of the bay where Bahia de Todos Os Santos and the South Atlantic Ocean meet. The **Museu Hidrográfico** has been recently restored and is housed in the upper section of the Forte de Santo Antônio, with fine views of the bay and coast, recommended. ■ *Tuesday-Saturday 1300-1800, US$1.*

The Barra section of town, for many years neglected, has received a major facelift with the installation of a new lighting system, which has transformed the

Porto da Barra

neighbourhood. The pavements/sidewalks fill with people day and night, exercising, strolling, or simply watching the world go by. Many sidewalk restaurants and bars are open along the strip from Porto da Barra, as far as the Cristo at the end of the Farol da Barra beach. The beaches are very busy at night with people playing football and volleyball and swimming. Great attention to security is now given, with high profile policing on the streets. Once the centre of nightlife, Barra is beginning to regain its previous importance in daily Salvador life.

The promenade leading away from the fort and its famous lighthouse is called Avenida Oceânica, which follows the coast to the beach suburbs of Ondina, Amaralina and Pituba. The road is also called Avenida Presidente Vargas, but the numbering is different. Beyond Pituba are the best ocean **beaches** at Jaguaripe, Piatã and Itapoã (take any bus from Praça da Sé marked Aeroporto or Itapoã, about one hour). *En route* the bus passes small fishing colonies at Amaralina and Pituba, where *jangadas* can be seen. A *jangada* is a small raft peculiar to the northeastern region of Brazil, used extensively as well as dug out canoes. Near Itapoã is the **Lagoa do Abaeté**, surrounded by brilliant, white sands. This is a deep, freshwater lake where local women traditionally come to wash their clothes and then lay them out to dry in the sun. The road leading up from the lake offers a panoramic view of the city in the distance, the coast, and the contrast of the white sands and freshwater less than a kilometre from the sea and its golden beaches. **NB** See **Security**, above.

Near the lighthouse at **Itapoã** are two campsites on the beach. A little beyond the campsites are the magnificent ocean beaches of Stella Maris and Flamengo, both quiet during the week but very busy at the weekends. Beware of strong undertow at these beaches.

Atlantic beach suburbs

See also the famous church of **Nosso Senhor do Bonfim** on the Itapagipe peninsula in the suburbs north of the centre, whose construction began in 1745; it draws endless supplicants (particularly on Friday and Sunday) offering favours to the image of the Crucified Lord set over the high altar; the number and variety of ex-voto offerings is extraordinary. ■ *Monday 0630-0800, Tuesday to Sunday 0600-1200 and 1400-2000.* The processions over the water to the church on the third Sunday in January are particularly interesting. Also on the Itapagipe peninsula is a colonial fort on **Monte Serrat** point, and at Ribeira the church of **Nossa Senhora da Penha** (1743). The beach here has many restaurants, but the sea is polluted (bus from Praça da Sé or Avenida França).

Bonfim & Itapagipe

The **Museu de Arte Moderna**, converted from an old estate house and outbuildings off Avenida Contorno, is only open for special exhibitions. The good restaurant(*Solar do Unhão*) is still there, and the buildings are worth seeing for themselves (take a taxi there as access is dangerous). ■ *Tuesday-Friday 1300-2100, Saturday 1500-2100 and Sunday 1400-1900, T3209433.*

Museums
Many guides offer their services in museums, but their English is poor and their expectations of a tip high

Museu de Arte Sacra is in the 17th century monastery and church of Santa Tereza, at the bottom of the steep Ladeira de Santa Tereza, at Rua do Sodré 276 (off Rua Carlos Gomes). Many of the 400 carvings are from Europe, but a number are local. Among the reliquaries of silver and gold is one of gilded wood by Aleijadinho (see page 783). ■ *Monday-Friday 1130-1800, US$0.40.* The collection of treasures which used to be in the Casa de Calmon, Avenida Joana Angélica 198, are well worth a visit. Opposite is **Tempostal**, a private museum of postcards, which is at Rua do Sodré 276. The proprietor is Antônio Marcelino do Nascimento. ■ *Tuesday-Friday 0900-1830, Saturday-Sunday 0900-1800.*

Bahia

Religion

Bahians pray at many different altars and like to blend several religions together. The first synagogue in South America was in Salvador and the city is home to several great baroque Catholic churches, dating back to the 18th century when Rome invested heavily in the new territories acquired by Spain and Portugal. In candomblé rituals, ancestral Yoruba spirits from Africa are worshipped; there are a multitude of centres following the writings of the French spiritist Allan Kardec; shamanism and other Amerindian belief systems attract great interest, along with the União Vegetal and Santo Daime cults which use the ayahuasca roots from the Amazon (see also Religion, page 763). The very name given to the immense bay where the city is situated reflects the multiplicity of religious beliefs.

Mysticism and religion are also strong in rural Bahia, mainly in the sertão semi-arid region, especially in Juazeiro, Canudos and Monte Santo (see page 471).

Closer to Salvador is the river port town of Cachoeira, steeped in African religious traditions. The festivities there for the Festa da Boa Morte is one of the most important celebrations in Bahia's spiritual calendar (see Cachoeira, page 442).

Conor O'Sullivan

Museu Abelardo Rodrigues, Solar Ferrão, Pelourinho (Rua Gregório de Mattos 45), is a religious art museum, with objects from the 17th, 18th and 19th centuries, mainly from Bahia, Pernambuco and Maranhão. ■ *Daily 0900-1845 except Monday*. **The Pelourinho Renovation Exhibition**, Rua Gregório de Matos (next door), contains pictures showing houses before and after the renovation.

Museu Afro-Brasileiro is in the former Faculty of Medicine building, Terreiro de Jesus. It compares African and Bahian Orixás (deities) celebrations, beautiful murals and carvings, highly recommended. ■ *Monday-Friday 0900-1700, US$1*.

Museu Arqueológico e Etnográfico, in the basement of the same building, houses archaeological discoveries from Bahia, such as stone tools, clay urns, an exhibition on Indians from the Alto Rio Xingu area, including artefacts, tools, photos; recommended. There is a museum of medicine in the same complex – **Memorial de Medicina**. ■ *Monday 1400-1700, Tuesday-Friday 0900-1230*.

Casa do Benin, below NS do Rosario dos Pretos, shows African crafts, photos, a video show on Benin and Angola. ■ *Monday-Friday 1000-1800*.

Museu da Cidade, Largo do Pelourinho, has exhibitions of arts and crafts and old photographs. From the higher floors of the museum you can get a good view of the Pelourinho. ■ *Weekdays except Tuesdays 0930-1830, Saturday 1300-1700, Sunday 0930-1300, free*.

Museu Carlos Costa Pinto, Avenida 7 de Setembro 2490, Vitória, www.guasar.com.br/mccp/mccp.htm, is a modern house with collections of crystal, porcelain, silver, furniture etc. It also has the only collection of *balangandãs* (slave charms and jewellery), highly recommended. ■ *Monday, Wednesday-Friday 1430-1900, Saturday-Sunday 1500-1800, US$4*.

Museu de Arte da Bahia, Avenida 7 de Setembro 2340, Vitória, has interesting paintings of Brazilian artists from the 18th to the early 20th century.

Candomblé

The pulse of the city is candomblé, a religion brought over by slaves from West Africa and syncretized with Catholicism and indigenous belief-systems (see **Religion**, page 763). The pantheon of deities (orixás) worshipped in temples (terreiros) which can be elaborate, decorated halls, or simply someone's front room with tiny altars to the orixá. Ceremonies are divided into two distinct parts. The first is when the orixás are invoked through different rhythms, songs and dances. Once the dancers have been possessed by the orixá, they are led off in a trance-like state to be changed into sacred, often very elaborate costumes, and come back to the ceremonial area in a triumphant procession in which each one dances separately for their deity. Overseeing the proceedings are mães or pães de santo, priestesses or priests.

Candomblé ceremonies may be seen by tourists, usually on Sundays and religious holidays. The ceremonies can be very repetitive and usually last several hours, although you are not under pressure to remain for the duration. Appropriate, modest attire should be worn; visitors should not go in shorts, sleeveless vests or T-shirts. White clothing is preferred, black should not be worn especially if it is combined with red. Men and women are separated during the ceremonies, women always on the left, men on the right. No photography or sound recording is allowed. Most temples are closed during Lent, although each one has its own calendar. Bahiatursa often has information about forthcoming ceremonies, but accurate information on authentic festivals is not always easy to come by.

Conor O'Sullivan

■ *Tuesday-Friday 1400-1900, Saturday-Sunday 1430-1830, US$3.* The **Museu Geológico do Estado** is at Avenida 7 de Setembro 2195, Vitória. ■ *Tuesday-Friday 1330-1830, Saturday-Sunday 1400-1800.*

The **Casa da Musica** at Parque Metropolitano de Abaete, Itapoan, houses the original Trio Eletrico truck from 1950, belonging to Dodo and Osmar. ■ *Tuesday-Sunday 1000-1900, T2499665.*

Thirty six kilometres from the city is the **Museu do Recôncavo** (Museu do Vanderlei do Pinho) in the old Freguesia mill (1552), in which one can find artefacts and pictures of three centuries of the economic and social life of this region. The Casa Grande e Senzala (the home of the landowner and the combined dwelling and working area of the slaves) is still intact. It is a peaceful way to spend an afternoon, but difficult to get to by public transport; the museum is near the town of São Francisco do Conde, seven kilometres from the main highway. ■ *Tuesday, Thursday and Sunday 0900-1700, T3209382, F3209410.*

Culture

The Bahianas – black women who dress in traditional 18th century costumes – are street vendors who sit behind their trays of delicacies, savoury and seasoned, made from the great variety of local fish, vegetables and fruits.

See Capoeira, a sport developed from the traditional foot-fighting technique introduced from Angola by African slaves. The music is by drum, tambourine and *berimbau*; there are several different kinds of the sport (see box, **Music and dance**, page 431). If you want to attempt Capoeira, the best school is Academia de Mestre Bimba, Rua das Laranjeiras, T3220639, open 0900-1200, 1500-2100, basic course US$25 for 20 hours. It has a small boutique at the bottom of the stairs. Other schools are Associação Brasileira de Capoeira (ABCA), Rua

Gregorio de Mattos, 38, Monday-Saturday 1000-2000, *Roda* takes place every Friday evening, US$2, and Academia de Mestre Pastinha, Rua Castro Rabelo. Classes on Monday, Wednesday and Friday 1900-2100, Saturday-Sunday 1500-1700. Classes are held in the evening (if you want to get the most out of it, knowledge of Portuguese is essential). There are two more schools in Forte de Santo Antônio behind Pelourinho. Exhibitions take place in the Largo do Pelourinho, very picturesque, in the upper city (cost: US$2). You can also see the experts outside the Mercado Modelo on most days, around 1100-1300, and at Campo Grande and Forte de Santo Antônio on Sunday afternoons; they often expect a contribution. Negotiate a price before taking pictures or demands may be exorbitant. At the Casa da Cultura at Forte de Santo Antônio there is also free live music on Saturday night.

Excursions

From the lower city the train (Trem do Leste) leaves Calçada for a 40 minute journey through the bayside suburbs of Lobato, Plataforma (canoes and motor boats for Ribeira on the Itapagipe peninsula), Escada (17th century church), Praia Grande, Periperi and Paripe (take a bus for the 17th century church at São Tomé de Paripe). The train runs Monday-Friday only; the same trip can be made by bus, less picturesquely, but much more comfortably.

Essentials

Sleeping

A 10% service charge is often added to the bill. Check which credit cards are accepted. All luxury hotels have swimming pools

Luxury hotels L *Enseada das Lajes*, Av Oceânica 511, Rio Vermelho, T3361027, F3360654. Family-run, 9 rooms in former private house, period furniture and works of art, wonderful setting (owned by the singer Gal Costa and may become a private residence). **L** *Fiesta Bahia*, Av Antônio Carlos Magalhães, Itaigara, T3520000, F3520050. Caters for business travellers, excellent pool area, very comfortable. Highly recommended. **L** *Tropical Hotel da Bahia*, Praça 2 de Julho 2, Campo Grande, T3360102, F3369725. Well-run, owned by *Varig*, convenient for city centre theatres and museums, swimming pool, sauna, gym, beauty parlour, can be noisy. Highly recommended. **L** *Transamérica*, R Morro do Conselho 505, Rio Vermelho, T3302233, F3302200. Newest luxury hotel in Salvador, pool, tennis, gym. **L** *Bahia Othon Palace*, Av Oceânica 2456, Ondina, T2471044, F2454877. Five-star, nice rooms and views, excellent swimming pool, next to beach. **L** *Marazul*, Av 7 de Setembro 3937, Barra, T3362110, F2352121. Four-star, near Farol and Porto da Barra beaches, discounts for longer stays. Highly recommended. **L** *Meridien*, R Fonte do Boi 216, Rio Vermelho, T3358011, F2488902. Five-star, well-run, ocean views, beach 100m away suitable for swimming, a larger beach is a further 100m away, for other beaches taxis must be used. **L** *Ondina Apart Hotel*, Av Oceânica 2400, Ondina, T2038000. Five-star, self-contained apartments, on beach. Highly recommended. **L** *Sofitel* (Quatro Rodas), R da Passargada, Farol de Itapoã, T3749611, F3746946. Five-star, a complete resort hotel 22 km from the city centre, extensive grounds, peaceful but plenty of activities available, eg golf, tennis etc, shuttle bus to city centre. Close by is **L** *Catussaba*, R Alameida da Praia, T3740555, F3741666. The only beachfront hotel in Salvador, beware of ocean currents when swimming.

A *Do Farol*, Av Oceânica 68, T3366611, F2454436. Good views, on seafront, a little noisy. **A** *Itapoã Praia*, R AD Gomes 4, Jardim Itapoã, Placafor, T3759988, F2487111. Three-star, 20 km from the centre near excellent beaches. **A** *Portobello Ondina Praia*, Av Oceânica 2275, Ondina, T3361033, F2453742. Near beach. **A** *San Marino*, Av Oceânica 889, Barra, T3364363. Three-star, on ocean. **A** *Caesar Towers*, Av Oceânica 1545, Ondina, T3318200, F2374668. Sauna, pool, coffee shop. **A** *Salvador Praia*, Av Pres Vargas 2338, T2455033, F2455003. Pool, bar.

City centre B *Palace*, R Chile 20, T3221155, F2431109. English spoken, good break- *This includes the old city* fast. Recommended. Opposite is **D** *Chile*, No 7, T3210245. Big rooms, some have har- *and the main* bour view. **C** *Imperial*, Av 7 de Setembro 751, Rosário, T/F3293127. A/c, helpful, *shopping area* breakfast. Recommended. **C** *Pousada da Praça*, Ruy Barbosa 5, T3210642. Breakfast not included, rooms with and without bath. Recommended. **D** *Internacional*, R Sen Costa Pinto 88, T3213514. Convenient, good value. **D** *Paris*, R Rui Barbosa 13, T3213922. A/c rooms more expensive, shared showers, breakfast, restaurant in same building. Recommended. **D** *São Bento*, Largo de São Bento 3, T2437511. Good cheap restaurant. Cheaper hotels on Av 7 de Setembro: **E** *São José*, No 847, T321492. Safe. Recommended. **F** pp *Pousada*, No 2349. Warmly recommended.

There are many hotels near the Praça da Sé. The following have been recom- mended: **C** *Pelourinho*, R Alfredo Brito 20, T2432324. Run down but central and charismatic. **C** *Pousada Villa del Carmo*, R do Carmo 58, T/F2413924. Fan, good breakfast, many European languages spoken. **D** *Solara*, R José Alencar 25, Largo do Pelourinho, T3264583. With shower, toilet, breakfast, laundry facilities. **D** *Themis*, Praça da Sé 398, Edif Themis, 7th floor, T3296955. Fan, wonderful views over bay and old city. Recommended restaurant with French chef. **E** *Ilhéus*, Ladeira da Praça 4, 1st floor, T3227240. Breakfast.

Campo Grande/Vitória A *Bahia do Sol*, Av 7 de Setembro 2009, T3367211, F3367776. *This is a much quieter* Comfortable, safe and frigobar in room, family run, good breakfast and restaurant, Bureau *area, still central and* de change. Highly recommended (no swimming pool). **A** *Vila Velha*, Av 7 de Setembro *convenient for museums* 1971, T3368722, F3365663. **D** *Caramuru*, Av 7 de Setembro 2125, Vitória, T3369951. Breakfast, safe parking. Recommended. **D** *Do Forte*, R Forte de São Pedro 30, Campo Grande, T/F3294080. Breakfast, bath. **D** *Santiago* at No 52, T2459293. Breakfast, bath.

Santo Antônio B *Pousada das Flores*, R Direita de Santo Antônio 442, near Santo *Quiet residential district* Antônio fort, T/F2431836. Brazilian/French owners, excellent breakfast, beautiful old *NE of Pelourinho* house. Highly recommended. **C** *Pousada do Boqueirão*, R Direita do Santo Antônio 48, T2412262, F2418064. Family-run, beautiful house overlooking the bay, relaxed atmosphere, most European languages spoken, great food, especially breakfast. Highly recommended.

Barra There are many restaurants in all price ranges. Barra was once the focal point *Barra offers many* of nightlife in Salvador, but has fallen from grace a little in recent years. The bars *budget hotels, in a good* around Porto da Barra have become meeting places for prostitutes and drug dealers, *location close to the* but efforts are being made to stop their activities. Taxis are recommended after dark. *beaches at Farol da* Care should be taken on Sundays when the beaches are extremely busy. On Av 7 de *Barra and Porto da* Setembro: **B** *Barra Turismo*, No 3691, Porto da Barra, T2457433. Breakfast, a/c, fridge, *Barra, which are very* on beach. Recommended. **C** *Porto da Barra*, No 3783, Porto da Barra, T2477711. *popular* Some rooms very small, on beach. **C** *Pousada Malu*, No 3801, T2374461. Small with breakfast, on beach, cooking facilities and laundry service. **B** *Barra Praia*, Av Almte Marqués do Leão 172, Farol da Barra, T2350193, F2477364. A/c, 1 street from beach. Recommended. **B** *Pousada Hotel Ambar*, R Afonso Celso 485, T3321507, F2356956. Good service, nicely decorated, excellent breakfast, convenient, run by Paulo and Christine (French, also speaks English). Warmly recommended. **C** *Villa Romana*, R Lemos Brito 14, T3366522, F2476748. Good location, pool, a/c. Highly recommended. **C** *Enseada Praia da Barra*, R Barão de Itapoã 60, Porto da Barra, T2359213. Breakfast, safe, money exchanged, accepts credit cards, laundry bills high, otherwise good value, near beach. **C** *Seara Praia*, R Belo Horizonte 148, Barra, T/F3310105. Good breakfast. **D** *Bella Barra*, R Afonso Celso 439, T2378401, F2354131. A/c. Recom- mended. **E** Rooms to let in private apartments: *Carmen Simões*, R 8 de Dezembro 326. Safe, helpful. *Gorette*, R 8 de Dezembro 522, Apt 002, Edif Ricardo das Neves, Graça, T2643016, gorete@e-net.com.br. Recommended.

Bahia

This modern suburban area runs along the coast from Ondina to Itapoã for 20 km towards the airport. Best beaches are after Pituba

Atlantic Suburbs A *Catharina Paraguaçu*, R João Gomes 128, Rio Vermelho, T2471488. Charming, small, colonial-style, tastefully decorated. Recommended. **A** *Ondina Plaza*, Av Pres Vargas 3033, Ondina, T2458158, F2477266. A/c, pool, good value, on beach. Recommended. **A** *Mar A Vista*, R Helvécio Carneiro Ribeiro 1, Ondina, T/F2473866. With restaurant and bar. **C** *Mar*, R da Paciência 106, Rio Vermelho, T3312044, F2454440. Good nightlife in the area. Recommended.

Pituba: **D** *Pituba*, Av Manoel Dias da Silva 1614, T2480197/5469. No breakfast, near the excellent beach.

Placaford: **B** *Praia Dourada*, R Dias Gomes 10, T3759639. A/c. Recommended.

Patamares, 17 km from the city: **A** *Sol Bahia Atlântico*, R Manoel Antônio Galvão 100, T3709000, F3709001, near one of the best beaches in Salvador, set high on the hill with great views of the coastline. Recommended.

Itapoã: **B** *Praia da Sereia*, Av Dorival Caymmi 14, T/F3754523. Very good, pool, safe. **A** *Villa do Farol*, Praia do Pedra do Sol. Small Swiss-run *pousada*, pool, homely, great restaurant, 1 block from beach. Highly recommended. **B** *Grão de Areia*, R Arnaldo Santana 7, Piatã, T3754818. A/c, pool, near good beach. **C** *Europa*, R Genibaldo Figueiredo 53, T3759344. Breakfast. **D** *Pousada Glória*, R do Retiro 46, T/F3751503. No breakfast, near beach.

Near the bus station B *Portal Da Cidade*, Av Antônio Carlos Magalhães 4230, next to rodoviária, T3710099, F3711419. A/c, pool.

Self-contained apartments with fully equipped kitchen and a/c, with all the facilities of hotels, rented by the day. Standards are generally high

Apartment hotels *Bahia Flat*, Av Pres Vargas 235, Barra, T3394140, F3394200. On beach, pool, sauna. *Barra Apart Service*, R Marquês de Caravelas 237, Barra, T2475844. *Flat Jardim de Alá*, Av Otávio Mangabeira 3471, Armação, T3715288, beautiful location by beach. Pool, sauna. Recommended. *Parthenon Farol da Barra Flat*, Av Oceânica 409, Barra. Pool, sauna, on beach. Recommended. *Porto Farol*, R Milton de Oliveira 134, Barra, T2475566, F2476555. Recommended. *Pituba Apart Hotel*, R Paraíba 250, Pituba, T2407077, F3458111. Pool, sauna; all in **A** range. Recommended. *Lucia Arleo*, R Miguel Bournier 59, Apto 203, 2372424. Specially furnished apartments near the beach. Recommended.

Youth hostels Albergues de Juventude, **D-E** pp including breakfast, but sometimes cheaper if you have a IYHA membership card. Prices are higher and hostels very full at carnival.

Pelourinho: *Albergue das Laranjeiras*, R Inácio Acciolli 13, T/F3211366. Independent hostel, with breakfast, cooking facilities, English spoken. Warmly recommended. *Albergue Solar*, R Ribeiro dos Santos 45-47, T/F2410055. *Albergue do Peló*, same street No 5, T/F2428061. IYHA, laundry facilities. *Albergue do Passo*, No 3, T3261951, F3513285. Clean, safe, group rates available, English, French and Spanish spoken. Highly recommended. *Pousada Gloju*, R das Laranjeiras 34, T3218249. No breakfast but stunning views of Pelourinho, clean rooms, en suite bathrooms, warm showers. *Vagaus*, R Alfredo Brito 25, Pelourinho, T3216398, F3221179, vagaus@elitenet.com.br. Independent youth hostel, all rooms collective with breakfast, internet access available. Recommended.

On the beaches: *Albergue do Porto*, R Barão de Sergy 197, T2646600, F2643131, albergue@e-net.com.br. One block from beach, short bus ride or 20 minutes on foot from historical centre. IYHA hostel in beautiful turn-of-the-century house, breakfast, convenient, English spoken, double room with a/c and bath available, kitchen, laundry facilities, safe, TV lounge, games room, courtyard. Highly recommended. *Casa Grande*, R Minas Gerais, 122, Pituba, T2480527, F2400074. IYHA, laundry and cooking facilities. *Pousada Azul*, R Praguer Fróis 97, Barra, T2649798, pousada@provider.com.br. Youth hostel-style, near beach, airport transfers. *Pousada Marcos*, Av Oceânica 281, T2355117. Youth hostel-style, great location near the lighthouse, very busy, notices in Hebrew for potential travelling companions, efficient.

Pensionatos are places to stay in shared rooms (up to 4 persons per room); part or full board available. Houses or rooms can be rented for US$5-35 a day from Pierre Marbacher, R Carlos Coqueijo 68A, Itapoã, T2495754 (Caixa Postal 7458, 41600 Salvador), he is Swiss, owns a beach bar at Rua K and speaks English. At Carnival it's a good idea to rent a flat; the tourist office has a list of estate agents (eg José Mendez, T2371394/6). They can also arrange rooms in private houses; however, caution is advised as not all householders are honest.

Camping *Camping Clube do Brasil*, R Visconde do Rosario 409, Rosario, T2420482. *Camping de Pituaçu*, Av Prof Pinto de Aguiar, Jardim Pituaçu, T2317143. *Ecológica*, R Alameida da Praia, near the lighthouse at Itapoã, take bus from Praça da Sé direct to Itapoã, or to Campo Grande or Barra, change there for Itapoã, about 1 hour, then 30 minutes walk, T3740201. Bar, restaurant, hot showers. Highly recommended. *Igloo Inn*, Terminal Turistico de Buraquinho, Praia Lauro de Freitas, T3792854.

Sea bathing is dangerous off shore near the campsites

Pelourinho (historical centre) *Cantina da Lua*, Terreiro De Jesus. Open daily, popular but hangers-on can sometimes be a nuisance. *Todo Na Brasa*, R Alfredo Brito 11 (upstairs). Open Monday-Saturday, 1100-2330, Sunday 1800-2330, good seafood, meat, English spoken. *Quilombo do Pelô*, R Alfredo Brito 11, T3224638. Jamaican cuisine, bar and restaurant, open daily 1100-0100, good food and reggae. *Maria Mata Mouro*, R Inácio Acciolli 8, T3213929. International menu, excellent service, relaxing atmosphere, a quiet corner in bustling Pelourinho. Highly recommended. *Bargaço*, R das Laranjeiras 26, T2426546. Traditional seafood restaurant, Bahian cuisine, open daily except Tuesday. *Senzalla*, R João de Deus 9, T3215172. Good salad bar, very popular, the best pay-by-weight restaurant in the Pelourinho, open for lunch only. Highly recommended. *Pizzeria Micheluccio*, R Alfredo Brito 31, T3215884. Best pizzas in Pelourinho, open daily 1200 till late. Recommended. *Senac*, Praça José Alencar 8, Largo do Pelourinho. State-run catering school, a selection of 40 local dishes, buffet, lunch 1130-1530, dinner 1830-2130, all you can eat for US$16, inconsistent quality but very popular, folkloric show Thursday-Saturday 2030, US$5. *Casa do Benin*, Praça José Alencar 29. Afro-Bahian restaurant, great surroundings, try the shrimp in the cashew nut sauce, closed Monday, open 1200-1600, 1900-2300, expensive. Highly recommended.
　　Near the Carmo church: *Casa da Roça*, R Luis Viana 27. Pizzas, caipirinhas and live music at weekend. *Axego*, R do Carmo 36. Good views.

Eating

Atelier Maria Adair, R J Castro Rabelo 2. Specializing in coffees and cocktails, owner Maria is a well known artist whose highly original work is on display. Recommended. Good wholemeal snacks and juices at *Bar da Tereza*, No 16, open daily 0900-2330. Recommended. *Dona Chika-Ka*, No 10. 1100-1500 and 1900-0200, good local dishes. Open gates beside *Dona Chika-Ka* lead to an open square, Largo de Quincas Berro d'Água (known locally as Quadra 2M), with many bars and restaurants. Recommended here is *Quincas Berro D'Agua*, T3215472. Bahian cuisine, expensive. On the next block down is *Tempero da Dadá*, R Frei Vicente 5. Open daily 1130 till late, closed Tuesday, Bahian cuisine, owners Dadá and Paulo are genial hosts, extremely popular. Across the street is *Quereres*, a restaurant and bar with good live music. *Kilinho*, Ribeiro dos Santos 1. Fresh salads, popular with locals. Recommended. *Restaurante e lanchonete Xango*, Praça Cruzeiro de São Francisco. Good for fruit juices. *Carvalho*, R Conselheiro Cunha Lopez 33, Centro, T7413249. *Comida a kilo*, tasty, excellent fish, cheap. Recommended.

Uauá, R Gregório de Matos 36 (upstairs). 1130-1500 and 1900-2330, closed Tuesday, excellent northeastern cuisine, try the *carne de sol (sun-dried beef)*, very reasonably priced. Highly recommended. *Casa da Gamboa*, R João de Deus 32, 1st floor. 1200-1500 and 1900-2400, closed Monday; also at R Newton Prado 51 (Gamboa de Cima), beautifully located in old colonial house overlooking the bay, good reputation,

Bahia

Bahian cuisine

Bahian cooking is spiced and peppery. The main dish is moqueca, *seafood cooked in a sauce made from coconut milk, tomatoes, red and green peppers, fresh coriander and* dendê *(palm oil). It is traditionally cooked in a wok-like earthenware dish and served piping hot at the table. Served with* moqueca *is* farofa *(manioc flour) and a hot pepper sauce which you add at your discretion, it's usually extremely hot so try a few drops before venturing further. The* dendê *is somewhat heavy and those with delicate stomachs are advised to try the* ensopado, *a sauce with the same ingredients as the* moqueca, *but without the palm oil.*

Nearly every street corner has a Bahiana selling a wide variety of local snacks, the most famous of which is the acarajé, *a kidney bean dumpling fried in palm oil which has its origins in West Africa. To this the Bahiana adds* vatapá, *a dried shrimp and coconut milk paté (also delicious on its own), fresh salad and hot sauce (pimenta). For those who prefer not to eat the palm oil, the* abará *is a good substitute. Abará is steamed, wrapped in banana leaves. Seek local advice on which are most hygienic stalls to eat from.*

Recommended Bahianas are Chica, *at Ondina beach (in the street behind the Bahia Praia Hotel) and in Rio Vermelho,* Dinha *(who serves* acarajé *until midnight, extremely popular) and* Regina *at Largo da Santana (very lively in the late afternoon), and* Cira *in Largo da Mariquita. Bahians usually eat* acarajé *or* abará *with a chilled beer on the way home from work or the beach at sunset. Another popular dish with African origins is* Xin-Xin de Galinha, *chicken on the bone cooked in* dendê, *with dried shrimp, garlic and squash.*

open Monday to Saturday 1200-1500 and 1900-2300, not cheap. Good *feijoada* at **Alaide do Feijão**, R Francisco Muniz Barreto 26. Open daily 1100-2400. Also at **da Dinha** on Praça José Alencar 5, Monday-Saturday 0800-2000. **Encontro dos Artistas**, R das Laranjeiras 15, T3211721, Ribeiro do Santos 10. Passo – Pelourinho, cheap.

Between the Historical Centre and Barra *Chez Bernard*, R Gamboa de Cima, 11. French cuisine, open daily except Sunday. Recommended. At Praça da Sé, **Café Brasil**, good breakfast. Also **Recanto das Coroas**, underneath the *Hotel Themis* (see above), looks uninviting but the food is excellent. **Bar Padrão**, R José Gonçalves, near Praça da Sé. Recommended. There are some good snack bars on Av 7 de Setembro: **Nosso Cantinho**, near *Hotel Madrid*. Good value. **Kentefrio**, No 379. The best, clean, counter service only, closed Sunday. Recommended. **Casa D'Italia**, corner of Av 7 and Visconde de São Lourenço. Reasonable prices, good service. **Grão de Bico**, No 737. Very good vegetarian. Another good vegetarian restaurant is **Nutrebem**, Av Joana Ângélica 148. An excellent Japanese restaurant is **Beni-Gan**, Praça A Fernandes 29, Garcia, intimate atmosphere, Tuesday-Sunday 1900 till midnight. Recommended. The best *churrascaria* in Salvador is **Baby Beef**, Av AC Magalhães, Iguatemi. Top class restaurant, excellent service, extremely popular, not expensive. Highly recommended, open daily 1200-1500 and 1900-2300.

At the bottom of the Lacerda Lift is Praça Cairu and the famous **Mercado Modelo**: on the upper floor of the market are 2 very good restaurants, **Camafeu De Oxossi** and **Maria De São Pedro**, both specializing in Bahian dishes, great atmosphere, good view of the port, daily 1130 till 2000, Saturday lunchtime is particularly busy. Opposite the Mercado Modelo, the Paes Mendonça supermarket self-service counter is good value, 1100-1500, 1st floor. **Divino Gula**, Av Francia 414, 400m from the *Mercado Modelo* is good and frequented by locals. On Av Contorno, **Solar Do Unhão**, a beautiful manor house, formerly a sugar mill, on the edge of the bay, lunch and dinner with the best folklore show in town, expensive.

Moqueca de Peixe

There are as many recipes for this marinaded fish dish, as there are cooks in Brazil. Named after the main Indian method of barbecuing fish wrapped in banana leaves, developed in the great plantation houses of the sugar zone, the dish is now cooked on top of the stove in a pan. Many cooks add coconut milk, giving the sauce a Caribbean flavour typical of the Northeast. In this recipe, the fish flavour is fresh and sharp, balanced by coconut rice.

To serve 6

Marinade ingredients

1 kg fillets of mixed, fresh white fish
1 chopped medium onion
50ml dendê (palm) oil or olive oil
2 fresh hot chillis, seeded and chopped
2 large peeled tomatoes, chopped

1 crushed clove of garlic
A handful of fresh coriander leaves
3 tbsp lime juice
Salt

Method

Crush the marinade ingredients to a purée in a mortar, or use a blender. Cut the fish into five centimetre pieces, mix with the purée in a non-metallic bowl and leave for one hour. Transfer to a saucepan. Add 75 millilitres water and half the oil. Cover and simmer until the fish is cooked (about 10 minutes). One minute before serving, add the rest of the oil and turn up the heat.

Serve with hot pepper and lime sauce (see **Feijoada** recipe in Essentials, page 72) and coconut rice.

Barra *Ban Zai*, Av 7 de Setembro 3244, Ladeira da Barra, T3364338, by the yacht club. Sushi bar, always busy, open daily except Monday. *Oceânia*, Av Oceânica. Street café, noisy, good people watching, open every day until late. Almost next door is *Don Vitalone Pizzaria*, No 115. Excellent pizzas. *Don Vitalone Trattoria*, T2357274, is a block away. Part of the same chain, great Italian food, open daily for lunch and evening meal. Highly recommended. There are a number of restaurants specializing in crab, something of a tradition throughout coastal northeastern Brazil, along the seafront promenade. *Caranguejo do Farol*, Av Oceânica 231. Raised above the road, specializing in crab, extremely busy, young clientèle, you might have to wait for a table. A little further along is *Restaurante do Sergipe*, also very busy. Across the road is *Barravento*, great view but food can vary in quality, good for sunset views. *Yan Ping*, on R Airova Galvão, T2456393. Good Chinese, open daily 1100 until midnight, reasonably priced, very generous portions, clean. Recommended. On R Marques de Leão parallel to the promenade at No 77 is *Pizzaria Il Forno*, T2477287. Italian food at a good price, good service, open daily for lunch and evening meal. *Mediterrânio*, at No 262. Pay by weight, open daily. *Zobbi Ilê*, open for lunch, good pay by weight restaurant, good salads and cooked dishes, busy, cheap. Recommended. Another good pay by weight restaurant nearby is *Bem Barra*, on R Recife 98, Jardim Brasil, T2358420. Wednesday-Sunday for lunch and dinner, closes at 2200, more expensive but good quality and variety of food, very clean. Highly recommended. On R Afonso Celso, 2 blocks back from the seafront, *A Porteira*, No 287, T2355656. Open for lunch only, pay by weight northeastern Brazilian food. On the same street is *Firmino do Bacalhau*, specializing in codfish, a delicacy in Brazil, the Barra branch of a traditional restaurant, open for lunch and evening meal. Half a block away is *Ki-Moqueca*, T2350764, the only Bahian cuisine restaurant in Barra, open 1100 till 2300. *Xangai*, Av 7 de Setembro 1755 (Vitória). Chinese, reasonable. *Nan Hai*, No 3671. Good Chinese, lunch and dinner (Porto da Barra). Good cheap snacks at the Goethe Institute and the American Institute. *Tiffany's*, Barão do Sergy 156. 1900-2400, French. Recommended. On the same street are *Alface e Cia*, a wide range of salads and juices. *Via Brera*, No 162. T2476973, upmarket Italian. *Unimar* supermarket, good cheap meals on second floor.

Near the lighthouse at the mouth of the bay (Farol Da Barra area) are a number of good fast food places: *Micheluccio*, Av Oceânica 10. Good pizza, always busy.

Bahia

Recommended. Next door is *Baitakão*, good hamburgers and sandwiches. *Mon Filet*, R Afonso Celso 152. Good steaks, pastas, open 1830 till midnight; on the same street, *Pastaxuta*, pizza, pasta, reasonable prices, and a number of other good cheap restaurants, eg *Maná*, opens 1100 till food runs out, different menu each day, closed Sunday, popular, owner Frank speaks a little English. Also *Luar da Barra*, No 447. Shopping Barra has good cheapish places to eat, *Pizza e Cia* on the ground floor, good selection of fresh salads, also good pizzas, good value. Recommended. Opposite is *Perini*, great ice cream, chocolate, savouries and cakes. *Saúde Brasil*, on the top floor (L3), for very good wholefood snacks, cakes and a wide variety of juices. Recommended. The best Bahian restaurant in the area is *Frutos Do Mar*, R Marquês de Leão 415. A very good vegetarian restaurant is *Rama*, R Lord Cochrane, great value. *Don Vitalone*, D M Teixeira 27, near the lighthouse, off the seafront. Excellent Italian, open daily for lunch and evening meal. Highly recommended.

Ondina *Double Gula* in *Mar A Vista Hotel*. For excellent meat. Further along Av Oceânica, towards the Rio Vermelho district, is *Sukiyaki*, No 3562. Excellent Japanese, open 1200-1500, 1900 till midnight, not cheap. Recommended. *Extudo*, Largo Mesquita 4, T2374669. Good varied menu, lively bar at night, attracts interesting clientèle, open 1200-0200, closed Monday, not expensive. Recommended. *Manjericão*, R Fonte do Boi (the street leading to *Meridien Hotel*). Excellent wholefood menu, Monday-Saturday 1100-1600. Highly recommended. *Marisco*, at Paciência Beach nearby. Good seafood, 1100-1500, 1800-2100, good value. *Margarida*, R Feira de Santana, Parque Cruz Aguiar. Open daily for lunch 1130-1500, original dishes, pasta, seafood, meat, imaginative salads, pay by weight, great desserts, very friendly owners, attracts interesting clientèle. Highly recommended. *Postudo*, R João Gomes 87, T2455030. Over a small shopping mall called *Free Shop*, open daily except Sunday, reasonably priced good food in an interesting setting, always busy. Across the street, at the base of the hill in Largo da Santana, is **Santana Sushi Bar**, T2375107. Open Tuesday-Saturday, authentic. Recommended.

There is an interesting fish market at Largo da Mariquita with a number of stalls serving food from noon until the small hours, clean, good atmosphere, popular with locals. A good kiosk is *Riso e Nega* (kiosk with green tables), friendly, good basic food. Nearby is *Brisa*, R Augusto Severo 4. Monday-Saturday 1100-1500, excellent wholefood restaurant, small, simple, cheap, owner Nadia is very friendly. *Cantina Famiglia-Salvatore*, Largo da Mariquita 45. Delicious, authentic Italian pasta, 2 other branches. Recommended.

Jardim *Armação Yemanjá*, a 20-minute taxi ride from the centre. Excellent Bahian seafood, open daily from 1130 till late, very typical, always busy, reasonably priced, good atmosphere. Highly recommended. Nearby is *Tamboril*, busy seafood restaurant, 1200-1600 and 1900-2400. *Deutsches Haus*, Av Otávio Mangabeira 1221. Good German cooking. Highly recommended for Bahian cuisine is *Bargaço*, open daily 1200-1600 and 1900-2400. Great selection of starters, oyster, lobster, freshwater shrimp, crab meat etc, expensive but worth it. *Rodeio*, Jardim dos Namorados, Pituba, T2401762. Always busy, good value 'all you can eat' *churrascaria*, open daily from 1130-midnight. Also nearby is *Rincão Gaúcho*, R Pedro Silva Ribeiro, Jardim Armação, T2313800. Excellent *churrascaria*, huge selection of salads, many different cuts of meat, very popular with locals. Highly recommended.

A Porteira, at Boca do Rio, specializes in northeastern dishes including *carne de sol*, 1200-1600 and 1800-2300, seafood dishes also served. Nearby on the same street is *Bar Caribe* (more commonly known as *Pimentinha*), this is where Fellini meets Bahia, zany décor, very little offered in the line of comfort, hard to believe that it could be so busy, originally became a popular place where the weekend could continue, becoming extremely busy on Monday (its best night), tables on the street, blessings given by the owner, a *pai de santo*, there is no other bar like this anywhere, food served, healthy portions, expect delays though, not to be missed but go only Monday. In Itapoã near the lighthouse, 2 good restaurants are *Mistura Fina*, R Prof Souza Brito 41, T2492623. Seafood, pasta dishes, open daily 1000-midnight and *O Lagostão*, R Agnaldo Cruz 12, T3753646, Bahian cuisine, open daily 1100 till midnight. Both recommended. *Casquinha De Siri* at Piatã beach. Daily from 0900, live music every night, cover charge US$2, very popular. The beaches from Patamares to Itapoã are lined by *barracas*, thatched huts serving chilled drinks and freshly cooked seafood dishes, ideal for lunch and usually very cheap. Try *Ki-Muqueca*, Av Otávio Mangabeira 36 (Av Oceânica). For large helpings of excellent Bahian food in attractive surroundings. *Restaurant Uauá*, Av Dorival Caymmi 46, open Thursday to Sunday, Friday and Saturday are very busy with forró dancing till 0400.

See box, page 431, for times and venues of the *bloco* rehearsals. The best time to hear and see artists and groups is during carnival, but they are also to be seen outside the carnival period.

There is free live music every night throughout the summer in the other squares of Pelourinho (Quincas Berro d'Água and Pedro Arcanjo). Saturday nights are very busy, a popular band being the *Fred Dantas Orchestra* which plays a fusion of big band music and Latin rhythms. Monthly printed handouts can be found in most hotels or check with Bahiatursa.

Reggae hangs in the air of Pelourinho with many reggae bars such as *Bar do Reggae*, *Casa do Olodum* and *Bar do Olodum*, all within a short walk of each other.

A good jam session takes place every Saturday night (August-March) in the grounds of the *Solar do Unhão* on Av Contorno. Guest musicians are welcome. It is best to go there by taxi as bus connections are difficult.

Pelourinho Good bars are *Atelier Maria Adair* (see above), *Casa do Olodum*, *Estação Pelô* and *Alamabique Cachaçaria*, all on R João de Deus, the latter has a great selection of *cachaças* from all over Brazil, watch out for the steep stairs, especially after a few *cachaças*! Also good is *Café Impresso*, R João de Deus 3, interesting clientèle. Recommended. Many bars on the Largo de Quincas Berro d'Água (see above), *Dom Crepe*, *Habeas Copos* are very busy. There is often live music in this square. *Cafelier*, R Inácio Acciolli 16 and *Bar Museum* next door, are both good 'artcafés'. Good café and great chocolate at *Cailleur*, R Gregório de Matos 17, open daily 0930-2100, bar service continues till 0100. A popular disco is *Gueto*, R Alfredo Brito, plays techno mainly, but does vary. *Bataclan do Pelo*, R João de Deus 28, dance and Bahian music.

Barra *Mordomia Drinks*, Ladeira Da Barra. Enter through a narrow entrance to an open air bar with a spectacular view of the bay, very popular. Most Barra nightlife happens at the Farol da Barra (lighthouse). R Marquês de Leão is very busy, with lots of bars with tables on the pavement: *Habeas Copos*, R Marquês de Leão 172. Famous street side bar, very popular. Also *Aladim*, *Bali*, *Ponte de Safena* and *Psicoanalista*, all busy. In the next street, R Afonso Celso, is *Casco Grosso*. *Barril 2000*, on Av Oceânica is very busy, with live music (MPB – popular Brazilian music) at weekends. *Barra Vento 600* is a popular open air bar on the beachfront. Bar in the ICBA (Goethe Institute), has good light snacks, attracts a young bohemian clientèle, closes 2300, very pleasant courtyard setting. Further along the coast at Ondina is the *Bahia Othon Palace Hotel* with a good disco called *Hippotamus*, busy at weekends.

Rio Vermelho This district was once the bohemian section of town and where Jorge Amado and Caetano Veloso still have houses. The nightlife in this region rivals Pelourinho. *Alambique* is a good dance bar (especially on Saturday night US$10). *Chico*

Bars & nightclubs
Much of the nightlife is concentrated in the historical centre. Busy nights in the Pelourinho are Tuesday and weekends

Bahia

Rocco, *Azurri* and *Barcelona* are along the same strip. *Rio de Janeiro Bar*, Largo Mesquita. A small bar attracting bohemian clientèle, few tables, most people drink in the street, Thursday-Saturday, 1900-0300. *Via Brasil*, rooftop bar in *Bahia Park Hotel*, Largo da Mariquita. Open Wednesday-Sunday 2130-0300, live music, cover charge. In the same square, *Bar Canoa* at the *Meridien Hotel* has live music every night, jazz, popular Brazilian music, cover charge US$6, 2100 till 0100. Dancing at *Carinhoso*, Av Otávio Mangabeira, T2489575. *Champagne* at *Salvador Praia Hotel*, T2455033. *New Fred's*, Av Visconde de Itaboraí 125, T2484399 (middle-aged market, singles bar). *Bell's Beach* disco at Boca Do Rio. Open Tuesday-Saturday 2200-0400, up-market, expensive.

Entertainment **Cinema** *Cinema do Museu* in the Museu de Geólogia on Corredor da Vitória shows art movies with subtitles Wednesday-Sunday. The main shopping malls at Barra, Iguatemi, Itaigara and Brotas, and *Cineart* in Politeama (Centro), run more mainstream movies. The impressive Casa do Comércio building near Iguatemi houses the *Teatro do SESC* with a mixed programme of theatre, cinema and music Wednesday-Sunday.

Theatre *Castro Alves*, at Campo Grande (Largo 2 de Julho), seats 1400 and is considered one of the best in Latin America. It also has its own repertory theatre, the *Sala de Coro*, for more experimental productions. The theatre's *Concha Acústica* is an open-air venue used frequently in the summer, attracting the big names in Brazilian music. *Teatro da Gamboa*. *Teatro Vila Velha*; Márcio Meirelles, the theatre's director works extensively with Grupo Teatro Olodum; although performed in Portuguese, productions here are very visual and worth investigating. *Senac*; *Instituto Cultural Brasil-Alemanha* (ICBA) and the *Associação Cultural Brasil Estados Unidos* (ACBEU), both on Corredor de Vitória, have a varied programme, the former with a cinema; *Teatro Santo Antônio*, part of the Escola de Teatro da Universidade Federal da Bahia; *Teatro de Arena*. The Universal English Course (UEC) has recently opened the 400-seat *Teatro Jorge Amado* in Pituba. Recently opened in the Pelourinho is the *Teatro XVIII*, an experimental theatre. *Teatro Gregorio de Matos* in Praça Castro Alves offers space to new productions and writers.

The Fundação Cultural do Estado da Bahia edits a monthly brochure listing the main cultural events for the month. These can be found in most hotels and Bahiatursa information centres. Local newspapers *A Tarde* and *Correio da Bahia* have good cultural sections listing all events in the city.

Festivals 6 January (Epiphany); **Ash Wednesday** and **Maundy Thursday**, half-days; **2 July** (Inde-
See box, page 432, for pendence of Bahia); **30 October**; **Christmas Eve**, half-day. An important local holiday is
Carnival information the *Festa do Nosso Senhor do Bonfim*; it takes place on the 2nd Sunday after Epiphany, but the washing or *lavagem* of the Bonfim church, with its colourful parade, takes place on the preceding Thursday (usually mid-January). The *Festa da Ribeira* is on the following Monday. Another colourful festival is that of the fishermen of Rio Vermelho on **2 February**; gifts for Yemanjá, Goddess of the Sea, are taken out to sea in a procession of sailing boats to an accompaniment of *candomblé* instruments. The *Holy Week* processions among the old churches of the upper city are also interesting.

Sports **Football** *Esporte Clube Bahia* and *Vitória* play at the Otávio Mangabeira Stadium, Trav Joaquim Maurício, Nazaré, T/F2423322. The stadium holds 90,000 and is better known as the Fonte Nova. It is 10 minutes away from the Pelourinho, and the Barroquinha terminal.

Swimming *Wet 'n' Wild Bahia*, Av Luiz Viana (also known as Av Paralela), 10 km from Iguatemi, 6 km from the airport, T3678900. This new water theme park, a franchised US chain, is extremely well-run, with great attention to safety and comfort: wave pool, toboggan, waterslides and chutes, great fun. Highly recommended,

Bahia

Music in Bahia

Walking the streets of the old town on busy nights is like surfing the wavebands of your radio. A short walk from one bar and you hear the music coming from the next. Grupo Cultural Olodum began life in 1980 as a carnival option for the inhabitants of Pelourinho, then a much neglected area. Every Tuesday night Banda Olodum, a drumming troupe made famous by their innovative powerhouse percussion and involvement with Paul Simon, Michael Jackson and Branford Marsalis, rehearse in the Largo Teresa Batista (starts 1930, US$10) in front of packed crowds. They also rehearse free of charge in the Largo do Pelourinho on Sunday, T3215010.

Ilê Aiyê is just as much revered for its socio-political profile as its musicality; it still maintains its original pure percussion format. Established in Liberdade, the largest suburb of the city, Ilê Aiyê is a thriving cultural group dedicated to preserving African tradition, which under the guidance of its president Vovô is deeply committed to the fight against racism. Rehearsals take place mid-week at Boca do Rio and on Saturday nights on the street in front of their headquarters at Ladeira do Curuzu in Liberdade. You don't need to understand the words to be moved by the sheer joy in the air.

Araketu hails from the sprawling Periperi suburb in the Lower City. Once a purely percussion band, Araketu has travelled widely and borrowed on various musical forms (samba, candomblé, soukous etc) to become a major carnival attraction and one of the most successful bands in Bahia. Rehearsals take place on Wednesday nights on Avenida Contorno. These get very full and it is best to buy tickets in advance from Avenida Oceânica 683, Barra Centro Comercial, Sala 06, T2476784.

Neguinho do Samba was the musical director of Olodum until he founded Didá, an all-woman drumming group based along similar lines to Olodum. They rehearse on Friday nights in the Praça Teresa Batista, Pelourinho (starts 2000, US$10).

Faithful to their traditions are Filhos de Gandhi, the original African drumming group and the largest, formed by striking stevedores during the 1949 carnival. The hypnotic shuffling cadence of Filhos de Gandhi's afoxé rhythm is one of the most emotive of Bahia's carnival.

Carlinhos Brown is a local hero. From humble beginnings he has become one of the most influential musical composers in Brazil today, mixing great lyrics, innovative rhythms and a powerful stage presence. He played percussion with many Bahian musicians, until he formed his own percussion group, Timbalada. His first album, Alfagamabetizado, is perhaps the most successful fusion album in Brazilian music. Ever faithful to his background in the poor Candeal district, he has invested heavily in his old neighbourhood, both socially and culturally. He has created the Candy All Square, a centre for popular culture where the Timbalada rehearsals take place every Sunday night (1830, US$10) from September to March. Not to be missed.

During the winter (July-September), ring the blocos to confirm that free rehearsals will take place.

Artists and bands using electronic instruments and who tend to play in the trios eléctricos draw heavily on the rich rhythms of the drumming groups, creating a new musical genre known as Axé. The most popular of such acts is Daniela Mercury, following the steps to international stardom of Caetano Veloso, Maria Bethânia, João Gilberto and Gilberto Gil. Other newer, interesting acts are Margareth Menezes, who has travelled extensively with David Byrne. Gerónimo was one of the first singer/songwriters to use the wealth of rhythms of the Candomblé in his music and his song 'E d'Oxum' is something of an anthem for the city. All of the above have albums released and you can find their records easily in most record stores. See Shopping, page 432. Also try Billbox in the Shopping Barra on the third floor.

Conor O'Sullivan

Bahia

☞ **Carnival in Bahia**

The **pre-Carnival festive season** begins towards the end of November with São Nicodemo de Cachimbo (penultimate Sunday of November), then comes Santa Bárbara (4 December), then the Festa da Conceição da Praia, centred on the church of that name (normally open 0700-1130) at the base of the Lacerda lift. (8 December is the last night – not for those who don't like crowds!) The last week of December is the Festa da Boa Viagem in the lower city; the beach will be packed all night on 31 December. On 1 January is the beautiful boat procession of Nosso Senhor dos Navegantes from Conceição da Praia to the church of Boa Viagem, on the beach of that name in the lower city. The leading boat, which carries the image of Christ and the archbishop, was built in 1892. You can follow in a sailing boat for about US$1; go early (0900) to the dock by the Mercado Modelo. A later festival is São Lázaro on the last Sunday in January.

Carnival officially starts on Thursday night at 2000 when the keys of the city are given to the Carnival King 'Rei Momo'. The unofficial opening though is on Wednesday with the Lavagem do Porto da Barra, when throngs of people dance on the beach. Later on in the evening is the Baile dos Atrizes, starting at around 2300 and going on until dawn, very bohemian, good fun. Check with Bahiatursa for details on venue, time etc (see under Rio for carnival dates).

Carnival in Bahia is the largest in the world and encourages active participation. It is said that there are 1½ million people dancing on the streets at any one time.

There are two distinct musical formats. The **Afro Blocos** are large drum based troupes (some with up to 200 drummers) who play on the streets, accompanied by singers atop mobile sound trucks. The first of these groups was the Filhos de Gandhi (founded in 1949), whose participation is one of the highlights of Carnival. Their 6,000 members dance through the streets on the Sunday and Tuesday of Carnival dressed in their traditional costumes, a river of white and blue in an ocean of multicoloured carnival revellers. The best known of the recent **Afro Blocos** are Ilê Aiye, Olodum, Muzenza and Malê Debalê. They all operate throughout the year in cultural, social and political areas. Not all of them are receptive to foreigners among their numbers for Carnival. The basis of the rhythm is the enormous surdo (deaf) drum with its bumbum bumbum bum anchorbeat, while the smaller repique, played with light twigs, provides a crack-like overlay. Ilê Aiye take to the streets around 2100 on Saturday night and their departure from their headquarters at Ladeira do Curuzu in the Liberdade district is not to be missed. The best way to get there is to take a taxi to Curuzu via Largo do Tanque, thereby avoiding traffic jams. The ride is a little longer but much quicker. A good landmark is the Paes Mendonça supermarket on the corner of the street, from where the bloco leaves. From there it's a short walk to the departure point.

The enormous **trios eléctricos**, 12 metre sound trucks with powerful sound systems that defy most decibel counters,

US$20 per day. Open daily (during summer months closed in off season), 1000-1800. Tickets can be purchased in most hotels, including free shuttle bus during the summer months. Towel and locker rental is available upon payment of a small deposit.

Shopping *H Stern*, jewellers at *Hotels Meridien*, *Othon Palace* and *Bahia*, also at Barra and Iguatemi Shopping centres and at the airport. The Barra and Iguatemi shopping centres are big, modern and air-conditioned, with big department stores. Quality *artesanato* at the 3 official FIEB-SESI shops: Av Tiradentes 299 (Bonfim); Av Borges dos Reis 9 (Rio Vermelho); Av 7 de Setembro 261 (Mercês).

Pelourinho The major carnival *afro blocos* have boutiques selling T-shirts etc. *Boutique Olodum*, on Praça José Alencar, *Ilê Aiyê*, on R Francisco Muniz Barreto 16, and *Muzenza* next door. On the same street is *Modaxé*, a retail outlet for clothes

are the second format. These trucks, each with its town band of up to 10 musicians, play songs influenced by the **afro blocos** and move at a snail's pace through the streets, drawing huge crowds. Each **Afro Bloco** and **bloco de trio** has its own costume and its own security personnel, who cordon off the area around the sound truck. The **bloco** members can thus dance in comfort and safety.

The traditional Carnival route is from Campo Grande (by the Tropical Hotel da Bahia) to Praça Castro Alves near the old town. The **blocos** go along Avenida 7 de Setembro and return to Campo Grande via the parallel Rua Carlos Gomes. Many of the trios no longer go through the Praça Castro Alves, once the epicentre of Carnival. The best night at Praça Castro Alves is Tuesday (the last night of Carnival), when the famous 'Encontro dos Trios' (Meeting of the Trios) takes place. Trios jostle for position in the square and play in rotation until the dawn (or later!) on Ash Wednesday. It is not uncommon for major stars from the Bahian (and Brazilian) music world to make surprise appearances.

There are grandstand seats at Campo Grande throughout the event. Day tickets for these are available the week leading up to Carnival. Check with Bahiatursa for information on where the tickets are sold. Tickets are US$10 (or up to US$30 on the black market on the day). The blocos judged as they pass the grandstand and are at their most frenetic at this point. There is little or no shade from the sun so

bring a hat and lots of water. Best days are Sunday to Tuesday. For those wishing to go it alone, just find a friendly barraca in the shade and watch the blocos go by. Avoid the Largo da Piedade and Relógio de São Pedro on Avenida 7 de Setembro: the street narrows here, creating human traffic jams.

The other major centre for Carnival is Barra to Ondina. The **blocos alternativos** ply this route. These are nearly always **trios eléctricos**, connected with the more traditional blocos who have expanded to this now very popular district. Not to be missed here is Timbalada, the drumming group formed by the internationally renowned percussionist Carlinhos Brown (see box, page 431).

Recommended Blocos Traditional Route (Campo Grande): Mel, T245-4333, Sunday, Monday, Tuesday; Cameleão, T336-6100, Sunday, Monday, Tuesday; Pinel, T336-0489, Sunday, Monday, Tuesday; Internacionais, T245-0800, Sunday, Monday, Tuesday; Cheiro de Amor, T336-6060, Sunday, Monday, Tuesday. **Afro Blocos**: Araketu: T237-0151, Sunday, Monday, Tuesday; Ilê Aiye, T388-4969, Saturday, Monday; Olodum, T321-5010, Friday, Sunday. **Blocos Alternativos**: Timbalada, T245-6999, Thursday, Friday, Saturday; Nana Banana, T245-1000, Friday, Saturday; Melomania, T245-4570, Friday, Saturday.

Prices range from US$180 to US$450. The quality of the **bloco** often depends on the act that plays on the **trio**. See box, page 431.

Bahia

manufactured by street children under the auspices of the Projeto Axé, expensive, but these are the trendiest T-shirts in town. Also on this street at No 18 is **Brazilian Sound**, for the latest in Brazilian and Bahia music, CDs mainly. Another good music shop is **Mini Som** in the nearby Praça da Sé. The record shop at the Rodoviária is good for regional Bahian music.

Instituto Mauá, R Gregorio de Matos 27 (T3215638), open Tuesday-Saturday 0900-1800, Sunday 1000-1600, good quality Bahian handicrafts at fair prices, better value and better quality for traditional crafts than the Mercado Modelo. A similar store is **Loja de Artesanato do SESC**, Largo Pelourinho (T3215502), Monday-Friday 0900-1800 (closed for lunch), Saturday 0900-1300.

Trustworthy, reliable jewellery stores are **Lasbonfim** (T2429854) and **Simon** (T2425218), both in the Terreiro de Jesus. They both have branches in the nearby

☞ The Sand Captains

Bahia's most famous son is Jorge Amado, the internationally renowned author. In his earlier works he campaigned for the oppressed. One of his personal favourite novels is Capitães de areia (the Sand Captains), which is about the daily life of a group of abandoned street children in Salvador. This continues to be a problem, with the treatment of the children at the hands of the authorities and vigilante groups sometimes making international headlines.

The Projeto Axé (pronounced ash-ay, Yoruba for 'life source') was begun by Cesare Florio de la Rocca and an Italian NGO, Terra Nuova, to reach out to children and adolescents living on their wits in the streets of Salvador.

Using a team of highly professional educators and sociologists, the Projeto Axé won the trust of the children who had hitherto seen any approach from adults as being potentially threatening. Once initial contact had been made, the children would gain confidence and seek further contact with the project where they would be offered the opportunity to take part in activities such as capoeira, dance, percussion and circus skills. A number of local companies offer them work experience and training programmes monitored by the project. There is a paper recycling unit and a clothes manufacturing unit, where all stages, from design to the final finished product, are taught. Goods such as T-shirts and paper products can be purchased in the project's store in Rua Francisco Muniz Barreto das Laranjeiras. All proceeds go to the project. There is a visitor centre in Rua Professor Lemos Brito in Barra, where there is more information in English.

The Projeto Axé is a shining example of a major social problem being dealt with in a non-patronizing way, laying real foundations in the future instead of the sands of the past.

Conor O'Sullivan

Carmo district. Excellent hand-made lace products at **Artesanato Santa Bárbara**, R Alfredo Brito 7. For local art the best stores are **Atelier Portal da Cor**, Ladeira do Carmo 31 (T2429466), run by a co-operative of local artists, Totonho, Calixto, Raimundo Santos, Jô, good prices. Recommended. Also across the street at **Casa do Índio**, Indian artefacts and art, restaurant and bar open here till late, good surroundings. Good wood carvings on R Alfredo Brito next to *Koisa Nossa* (No 45), by a cooperative of sculptors – Palito and Negão Barão being the most famous. **Shopping do Pelô**, R Francisco Muniz 02 (T3214200), is run by SEBRAE, the Brazilian small business authority, open daily until 1800, stalls with varied goods, clothes, jewellery etc.

Handmade traditional percussion instruments (and percussion lessons) at **Chez Lua**, Alfredo Brito 27, made by percussionist Dilson Lua. Also percussion lessons at **Oficina de Investigação Musical**, Alfredo Brito 24 (T3210339), Monday-Friday, 0800-1200 and 1300-1600.

Confectionery *Feitiço Baiano*, R Inácio Acioly 09, T2410775. Makes sweets and liqueurs from every tropical fruit imaginable. Recommended. *Marrom Marfim Chocolates*, R Gregório de Matos 17, also make delicious sweets.

Bookshops *Livraria Brandão*, R Ruy Barbosa 104, Centre, T2435383, second-hand English, French, Spanish and German books. *Livraria Civilização Brasileira*, Av 7 de Setembro 912, Mercês, and in the Barra, Iguatemi and *Ondina Apart Hotel* shopping centres have some English books. Also *Graúna*, Av 7 de Setembro 1448, and R Barão de Itapoã 175, Porto da Barra, many English titles. *Livraria Planeta*, Carlos Gomes 42, loja 1, sells used English books. The bookshop at the airport has English books and magazines.

Markets The *Mercado Modelo*, at Praça Cairu, lower city, offers many tourist items such as wood carvings, silver-plated fruit, leather goods, local musical instruments. Lace items for sale are often not handmade (despite labels), are heavily marked up, and are much better bought at their place of origin (eg Ilha de Maré, Pontal da Barra and Marechal Deodoro, see page 483). *Cosme e Damião*, musical instrument sellers on 1st floor, has been recommended, especially if you want to play the instruments. Bands and dancing, especially Saturday (but very much for money from tourists taking photographs), closed at 1200 Sunday. There is a photograph exhibition of the old market in the basement. (Many items are often cheaper on the Praça da Sé.) The largest and most authentic market is the *Feira de São Joaquim*, 5 km from Mercado Modelo along the seafront: barkers, trucks, *burros*, horses, boats, people, mud, all very smelly, every day (Sunday till 1200 only), busiest on Saturday morning; interesting African-style pottery and basketwork; very cheap. (The car ferry terminal for Itaparica is nearby.) *Iguatemi Shopping Centre* sells good handicraft items, it is run by the government so prices are fixed and reasonable; similarly at Instituto Mauá, Porto da Barra. Every Wednesday from 1700-2100 there is a **handicrafts fair** in the 17th century fort of Santa Maria at the opposite end of Porto da Barra beach. On Friday from 1700-2100, there is an open air market of handicrafts and Bahian food in **Porto da Barra**, a popular event among the local young people. Daily market of handicrafts in **Terreiro de Jesus** in the old city from 1000-1800. Mosquito nets from *Casa dos Mosquiteros*, R Pedro Sá 6F, Calçada, T2260715.

Photography *Pepe*, R da Ajuda, Ed Triúnfo, 1st floor, Centre. *Maxicolor*, R Estados Unidos (Mercado Modelo), for cut-price developing. *Fotocolor*, R da Misericórdia 3, a recommended place for slide film. *Gil Filmes*, R Chile 7, recommended for Fujichrome and Ektachrome (well priced).

Videotapes *HAL Vídeo Produçoes*, R da Paz 1 (near Largo da Graça), T3317946, copies produced for US$15 per tape or US$20 including new tape, *transcodificação* (Brazilian NTSC – European PAL system) US$25. *Videovic*, Av Centenário 945, sala 905, T2373041, copying and *transcodificação* US$25-30.

Local Car hire: *Avis*, Av 7 de Setembro 1796, T2370155, also at airport, T3772276 (toll free 0800-118066). *Budget*, Av Pres Vargas 409, T2373396. *Hertz*, R Baependi, T2458364. *Interlocadora*, at airport, T3772550/2041019, in the centre T3774144. *Localiza*, at airport, T0800-992000, Oceânica 3869, T3321999, and Av Otávia Mangabeira 29, T3368377. *Unidas*, Av Oceânica 2456, Ondina, T3360717. If renting a car check whether credit card or cash is cheapest.

Transport
See also Ins & outs, page 411

Buses: US$0.70, *frescões* (or *executivos*) US$1.40, US$1.5 or US$3 depending on the route. On buses and at the ticket sellers' booths, watch your change and beware pickpockets (one scam used by thieves is to descend from bus while you are climbing aboard). To get from the old city to the ocean beaches, take a 'Barra' bus from Praça da Sé to the Barra point and walk to the nearer ones; the Aeroporto *frescão* (last 2130) leaves from R Chile, passing Barra, Ondina, Rio Vermelho, Amaralina, Pituba, Costa Azul, Armação, Boca do Rio, Jaguaripe, Patamares, Piatã and Itapoã, before turning inland to the airport. The glass-sided Jardineira bus goes to Flamengo beach (30 km from the city), following the coastal route; it passes all the best beaches; sit on the right hand side for best views. It leaves from the Praça da Sé daily 0730-1930, every 40 minutes, US$1.50. For beaches beyond Itapoã, take the *frescão* to Stella Maris and Flamengo beaches. These follow the same route as the Jardineira. During Carnival, when most streets are closed, buses leave from Vale do Canela (O Vale), near Campo Grande.

Taxis: meters start at US$0.50 for the 'flagdown' and US$0.10 per 100m. They charge US$15 per hour within city limits, and 'agreed' rates outside. Taxi Barra-Centro US$3 daytime; US$4 at night. Watch the meter, especially at night; the night-time charge should be 30% higher than daytime charges. Teletaxi (24-hour service), T3219988.

Long distance Air: Dois de Julho Airport is located 30 km from Salvador. International flights to Amsterdam, London, Paris and Rome. Domestic flights to Aracaju, Barreiras, Belo Horizonte, Brasília, Ilhéus, Maceió, Paulo Afonso, Petrolina, Porto Seguro, Recife, Rio de Janeiro, São Paulo and Vitória da Conquista. A/c buses leave from Praça da Sé via the coast road between 0630 and 2100, US$2, 1¼ hours (1 hour from Barra). Ordinary buses 'Aeroporto' from same stop US$0.50. Taxis from the city to the airport are less restricted, but still can be expensive, US$20.

There are frequent **Buses**: the Rodoviária is 5 km from the city with regular bus services, US$0.70, take
services to the majority bus RI or RII, 'Centro-Rodoviária-Circular', get on in the Lower City at the foot of the
of destinations; a large Lacerda lift (the journey can take up to 1 hour especially at peak periods). A quicker
panel in the main hall of executive bus from Praça da Sé or Praça da Inglaterra (in front of McDonalds),
the terminal lists Comércio, run to Iguatemi Shopping Centre, US$1.50, weekdays only, from where
destinations and the there is a walkway to the rodoviária (take care in the dark, or a taxi, US$10).
relevant ticket office

To **Belém** US$48 *comercial* with *Itapemirim*. To **Recife**, US$18-25, 13 hours, 2 a day and 1 *leito*, *Itapemerim*, T3580037. To **Rio** (28 hours, US$45.50, *leito* US$91, *Itapemirim*, good stops, clean toilets, recommended). To **São Paulo** (30 hours) US$51, *leito* US$64 (0815 with *Viação Nacional*, 2 in afternoon with *São Geraldo*, T3580188). To **Fortaleza**, 19 hours, US$33 at 0900 with *Itapemerim*. To **Ilhéus**, 7 hours, *Aguia Branca*, T3587044, *comercial* US$14.50, *leito* US$29, several. To **Lençóis** at 2200, 8 hours, US$12 with *Real Expresso*, T3581591. To **Belo Horizonte**, *Gontijo*, T3587448, at 1700, US$40 *comercial*, US$50 *executivo*, *São Geraldo* at 1800. To **Foz do Iguaçu**, 52 hours, US$66 *comercial*. There are daily bus services to **Brasília** along the fully paved BR-242, via Barreiras, 3 daily, 23 hours, *Paraíso*, T3581591, US$27.

Hitchhiking: out of Salvador, take a 'Cidade Industrial' bus from the rodoviária at the port; it goes on to the highway.

Directory **Airline offices** *Aerolineas Argentinas*, R da Belgica 10, Loja D, T3410217. *Air France*, Edif Regente Feijo, R Portugal 17, T3516631. *Alitalia*, Av Tancredo Neves 3343, Sala 503, T3415831. *American Airlines*, Trav Marques de Leão 13, T2454077. *British Airways*, T0800-996926. *KLM*, Av Tancredo Neves 3323, Pituba, T3410217. *Lufthansa*, Av Tancredo Neves 805, Sala 601, Iguatemi, T3415100. *Nordeste/Rio-Sul*, R Almte das Espatodias 100, Caminho das Arvores, T3591666. *TAM*, Praça Gago Coutinho, T3774747. *TAP*, Edif Ilheus, sala 401, Av Estados Unidos 137, T2436122. *Transbrasil*, R Almte Marques de Leão 465, Barra, T3397766. *Varig*, R Carlos Gomes 6, T3249000. *Vasp*, R Chile 27, T0800-998277.

Banks Don't change money on the street (see below), especially in the Upper City where higher rates are usually offered. Changing at banks can be bureaucratic and time-consuming. Banks are open 1000-1600. All major banks have exchange facilities but these are only available at selected branches. *Citibank*, R Miguel Calmon 555, Comércio, centre, good rates, will change large denomination TCs into smaller ones with a commission, does not have ATM, but branch at R Almte Marquês de Leão 71, Barra, does. *Banco Econômico*, R Miguel Calmon 285, Comércio is the American Express representative (also in Ondina, under *Ondina Apart Hotel*). Visa ATM at *Banco do Brasil*, Av Estados Unidos 56, Comércio, in the shopping centre opposite the Rodoviária (also a *câmbio* here), very high commission on TCs, at the airport (open 0830-1530 and 1600-2100 Mon-Fri and 0900-1600 Sat, Sun and holidays); branches in Barra, R Miguel Bournier 4, in Shopping Barra and in Ondina. *Banespa*, Av dos Estados Unidos, changes TCs without commission. Mastercard at *Credicard*, 1st floor, Citibank building, R Miguel Calmon 555, Comércio. *Tours Bahia*, R João de Deus 2, 2nd floor, T3223676, for cash and TCS in Pelourinho. *Figueiredo*, opposite *Grande Hotel da Barra* on Ladeira da Barra, will exchange cash at good rates. *Shopping Tour* in Barra Shopping centre changes dollars, as will other tour agencies. If stuck, all the big hotels will exchange, but at poor rates.

Communications **Post Office:** Main post office and poste restante is in Praça Inglaterra, in the Lower City, open Mon-Fri 0800-1700, Sat 0800-1200, F2439383 (US$1 to receive fax). Other offices are at Praça da Sé in Ed Associação Bahiana de Imprensa on R Guedes de Brito 1, T2406222; R Alfredo

Brito 43, Mon-Sat 0800-1700, Sun 0800-1200, has a philatelic section; Rodoviária, Mon-Sat 0800-1800 (till 1200 on Sun); airport; Barra and Iguatemi Shopping Malls (Mon-Fri); Av Princesa Isabel, Barra, and R Marquês de Caravelas; in Ondina by the hotels there is a booth by the beach next to *Ondina Apart Hotel*. **Telecommunications:** *Embratel*, R do Carro 120. *Telemar* has branches at Campo da Pólvora, on Trav Joaquim Mauricio (0630-Midnight), airport (daily 0700-2200), Porto da Barra (1200-2200 daily) and Rodoviária (0700-2200 daily). **Internet:** *Novo Tempo*, Ladeira do Carmo 16, Centro Histórico, T/F2431241. *Standard Internet*, Ladeira do Passo 1, 1st floor. T2418903, www.svn.com.br/standard. Open 0900-2000 Mon-Fri and 0900-1800 Sat, US$5 per hr.

Cultural centres *British Club*, Esquina Inglesa 20B, just off Campo Grande, T3367802. *Cultura Inglesa*, R Plínio Moscoso 357, Jardim Apipema. *Associação Cultural Brasil-Estados Unidos*, Av 7 de Setembro 1883, has a library and reading room with recent US magazines, open to all, free use of internet for 30 mins. At No 1809 on the same avenue is the German *Goethe Institut*, also with a library and reading room.

Embassies & consulates *Austria*, R Almte Marques de Leão 46, room 33, Barra, T2311017, Mon/Wed/Fri 1400-1700. *Belgium*, Centro Empresarial Iguatemi, Bloco B, Sala 804, Iguatemi, T3588907, Tue/Fri 0830-1230. *British Vice-Consulate*, Av Estados Unidos 4, Salas 1109, Edif Visconde de Cairu, Caixa Postal 38, Comércio, T2439222, Mon-Thu, 0900-1100, 1400-1600, Fri 0900-1100. *Denmark*, Av 7 de Setembro 3959, Barra, T2479667. Mon-Fri 0900-1200, 1400-1700. *Finland*, Jardim Ipiranga 19, T2473312, Mon-Fri 0800-1000 and after 1900. *France*, Trav Francisco Gonçalves 1, Comércio, T2410168, Mon/Tue/Thu 1430-1700. *Germany*, R Lucaia 281, Sala 204, Rio Vermelho, T2477106, Mon-Fri 0900-1200. *Holland*, Av Tancredo Neves 1283, Ed Omega, Sala 201, T3710410, Mon-Fri 0800-1200. *Italy*, Av 7 de Setembro 279, Centro, T3218335, Mon, Wed, Fri 1500-1800. *Norway and Sweden*, R Quintino de Carvalho 145, Apdo 601, Jardim Apipema, T2470528, Mon-Fri 0900-1200, 1400-1600. *Portugal*, Praça da Piedade, T2411633, Mon-Fri 0800-1400. *Spain*, R Mcal Floriano 21, Canela, T3361937, Mon-Fri 0900-1400. *Switzerland*, Av Tancredo Neves 3343, 5th floor, sala 507, T3715827. *USA*, Edif Cidadela Center 1, room 410, Av ACM, T3589166, Mon-Fri, 0900-1130, 1430-1630.

Hospitals & medical services Clinic: Barão de Loreto 21, Graça. *Dr Argemiro Júnior* speaks English and Spanish. First consultation US$40, second free. *Dr Manoel Nogueira* (from 1000-1200), Av Joana Angélica 6, T2412377, English-speaking. **Doctors:** German-speaking doctor, *Dr Josef Stangl*, R Conselheiro Pedro Luiz 179, Rio Vermelho, T2371073. **Health:** Yellow fever vaccinations free at *Delegação Federal de Saúde*, R Padre Feijó, Canela. Ensure that a new needle is used. Israeli travellers needing medical (or other) advice should contact *Sr Marcus* (T2475769), who speaks Hebrew.

Language courses *Casa do Brasil*, R Milton de Oliveira 231, Barra, T2455866, Portuguese for foreigners. *Superlearning Idiomas*, Av 7 de Setembro 3402, Ladeira da Barra, T3372824, www.allways.com.br/spl.

Laundry *Kit Lavaderia*, Av Amaralina 829, Amaralina. *Laundromat*, R Oswaldo Cruz, Rio Vermelho. *Lav e Lev*, Av Manoel Dantas da Silva 2364, loja 7. *Unilave*, Av Magalhães Neto 18, Pituba.

Tour companies & travel agents Bus tours are available from several companies: *LR Turismo*, *Itaparica Turismo*, *Bahia Tours* and *Alameda Turismo*, city tour US$25 pp. Bahiatours' Bahia by

Bahia

Night includes transport to the *Senac* restaurant, a show, dinner and a night-time walk around Pelourinho (US$45 pp). All day boat trip on Bahia de Todos Os Santos, last from 0800-1700 including a visit to Ilha dos Frades, lunch on Itaparica (US$10 extra), US$35 pp. *Tatur Turismo*, Av Tancredo Neves 274, Centro Empresarial Iguatemi, Bloco B, Sala 228, Iguatemi, Salvador, T4507216, Mobile 9729322 (urgent only), F4507215, tatur@svn.com.br, run by Irishman, Conor O'Sullivan. He speaks English, specializes in Bahia, arranges private guided tours and can make any necessary travel, hotel and accommodation arrangements. Highly recommended. *Submariner*, R de Paciência 223, Rio Vermelho, T2374097. Hires diving equipment, friendly. *Kontik*, Av Tancredo Neves 969, room 1004, T3412121, F3412323, is American Express representative. *Turitravel*, Av Centenário 2883, Ed Vitória Center, Sala 1106, T2459345 or 2374596, Helpful, English spoken. *Gregorio Barreto*, Ladeira da Barra 3495, T9710591, F2350591, offers visits to candomblé ceremonies. A recommended guide who speaks German, English and Portuguese is *Dieter Herzberg*, T3341200.

Tourist offices *Bahiatursa*, R Francisco Muniz Barreto 12, Historical Centre, T3212463, open daily 0830-1930; rodoviária, T3580871, good, English spoken; airport, T2041244, open daily 0800-2000, friendly; in the Mercado Modelo, T2410242, Mon-Fri 0800-1800, Sat 0800-1200; Porto da Barra, T2473195, Mon-Fri 0800-1800, Sat-Sun 0800-1200, the offices also have details of travel throughout the State of Bahia, T131-06000030 for tourist information in English, visitors can obtain a weekly list of events and itineraries (on foot or by car) planned by the city, well worth doing, Bahiatursa has lists of hotels and accommodation in private homes, Map, US$2, good, offices have noticeboards for messages. *Emtursa*, at airport, T3772262, Mon-Sat 0800-2200, is helpful and has good maps. **Maps:** from *Departamento de Geografia e Estadística*, Av Estados Unidos (opposite Banco do Brasil, Lower City): also from news-stands including the airport bookshop, US$1.50. A website with information of culture, tourism and history is http://www.bahiabeat.com.br.

Useful addresses **Immigration:** Polícia Federal, Av O Pontes 339, Aterro de Água de Meninos, Lower City, T3196082. Open 1000-1600. For extensions of entry permits show an outward ticket or sufficient funds for your stay, visa extension US$15.

Voltage 110-220 AC, 60 cycles.

Islands in the bay

Small boats go 25 kilometres to **Ilha da Maré** between 0900 and 1100, connecting the island's villages of Itamoaba, Praia Grande and Santana (US$1.70); the boat returns next day from Santana at 0400-0500. The departure point is near the naval base: take a 'Base Naval/São Tomé' bus from the foot of the Lacerda Lift; follow a path that leads off from the left hand side of the naval base gate. Santana is a centre for lace making, Praia Grande for basket-weaving. None of the villages has a hotel, but there are restaurants and bars and camping is possible. From São Tomé de Paripe, near the naval base at Aratu, irregular boats go to **Ilha dos Frades**, sparsely populated, no electricity, one *pousada* (**C** *Ponta de Nossa Senhora de Guadalupe*, beachfront, T071-2458536). The beach is busy at lunchtimes with excursions from Salvador, but otherwise is quiet, with good snorkelling.

Itaparica

Phone code: 071
Colour map 4, grid A6

Across the bay from Salvador lies the island of Itaparica, 29 kilometres long and 12 kilometres wide. The town of Itaparica is very picturesque, with a fair beach in the town, and well worth a visit. Take a bus or kombi by the coast road (Beira Mar) which passes through the villages of Manguinhos, Amoureiras and Ponta de Areia. The beach at Ponta de Areia is one of the best on the island and is very popular. There are many *barracas* on the beach, the best and busiest is *Barraca Pai Xango*, always very lively.

In Itaparica there are many fine residential buildings from the 19th century, plus the church of **São Lourenço**, one of the oldest in Brazil, a delightful walk through the old town. During the summer months the streets are ablaze with the blossoms of the beautiful flamboyant trees. The beaches at Mar Grande are fair but can be dirty at times. There are many *pousadas* in Mar Grande and at the nearby beaches of Ilhota and Gamboa (both to the left as you disembark from the ferry).

From Bom Despacho there are many buses to other towns such as Nazaré das Farinhas, Valença (see below) and also **Jaguaribe**, a small, picturesque colonial port. Both of these towns are on the mainland connected by a bridge on the southwest side of the island, turn off between Mar Grande and Cacha Pregos (bus company is Viazul). There are good beaches across the bay on the mainland, but a boat is needed to reach these (US$12).

Sleeping

A good simple *pousada* at Amoureiras is **C** *Pé na Praia*, T8311389, good breakfast, good sized rooms, English and French spoken. There is a popular *Club Med* on the island (Fazenda Boca do Rio, 44470 Vera Cruz, Bahia, T8807141, F2410100).

There are a few *pousadas* in the town. The best is **A** *Quinta Pitanga*, T8311554. Beautifully decorated by the owner Jim Valkus, 3 suites and 2 singles, beachfront property, a retreat, excellent restaurant, expensive but highly recommended, accepts day visitors. **A** *Grande Hotel da Itaparica*, Av Beira Mar, T8311120. **D** *Pousada Santa Rita*, and **D** *Restaurant/Pousada Cantinha da Ilha*, T8821380. **D** *Icarai*, Praca da Piedade, T8311110. Charming, good location. **D** *Zula*, R Monsenhor Flaviano 3, near the fort, T/F8313119, taiike@hotmail.com. With breakfast, laundry facilities, email available, manager Henrique speaks English and Spanish.

Mar Grande **A** *Pousada Arco Iris*, Estr da Gamboa 102, T8331130. Magnificent building and setting in mango orchard, expensive, good if slow restaurant, *Manga Rosa*. Recommended, they have camping facilities next door, shady, not always clean. **D** *Pousada Estrela do Mar*, Av NS das Candeias 170, T8331108. Good rooms, fan or a/c. Recommended. **D** *Lagoa e Mar*, R Parque das Dunas, 01-40, T/F8231573. Very good breakfast, spacious bungalows, swimming pool, 200m to beach, restaurant, helpful. Highly recommended. **D** *Pousada Scórpio*, R Aquárius, T8231036. Breakfast, beach, swimming pool, simple rooms, weekend restaurant. Recommended. **D** *Água no Toco*, Av Atlántica, T8231190, 20m to beach. Restaurant, weekend busy. Recommended. **D** *Pousada Sonho do Verão*, R São Bento 2, opposite *Pousada Arco Iris*. Chalets and apartments, cooking facilities, French and English spoken, T8331616. Like other *pousadas* they rent bicycles (US$3 per hour); they also rent horses (US$5 per hour). Near the church in the main praça is the **D** *Pousada Casarão da Ilha*, T8331106. Spacious rooms with a great view of Salvador across the bay, swimming pool, a/c. Recommended. **E** *Pousada Samambaia*, Av NS das Candeias 61. Good breakfast, French spoken. Recommended.

Ilha de Itaparica

Bahia

Gamboa **C** *Hotel Pousada Ponta Caieira*, T8331080. Beachfront, take bus to Gamboa and it's a 5-minute walk to the *pousada*, quiet.

Aratuba D *Pousada Zimbo Tropical*, Estrada de Cacha Pregos, Km 3, R Yemanjá, T/F8381148. French/Brazilian run, good breakfast, evening meals available. Recommended. There is an excellent hostel, **E** *Albergue da Juventude*, **F** (for students), on the beach, shady. Recommended.

Cacha Pregos *Hotel Village Sonho Nosso*, T8371040 or 2261933. Very clean huts on clean beach, good service, collect you from anywhere on the island – also Bom Despacho Kombis stop in front of entrance, a 5-minute walk. Recommended. **D** *Pousada Cacha Pregos*, next to the supermarket, T8371013. With fan, bath, no breakfast, good. Also **C** *Pousada Babalú*, T8371193. Spacious bungalows, frigobar, fan, good breakfast. Recommended.

Eating Good restaurants in Mar Grande are *Philippe's Bar and Restaurant*, Largo de São Bento. French and local cuisine, information in English and French. *O Pacífico* is peaceful. *Restaurant Rafael* in the main praça for pizzas and snacks. Also pizzas at *Bem Me Quer*, opposite *Pousada Samambaia*, down an alley. There are many Bahianas selling *acarajé* in the late afternoon and early evening, in the main praça by the pier.

Transport **Ferries** The island is reached from the main land by 2 ferries. The main passenger ferry leaves for Bom Despacho from São Joaquim (buses for Calçada, Ribeira stop across the road from the ferry terminal; the 'Sabino Silva-Ribeira' bus passes in front of the Shopping Barra). The first ferry from Salvador leaves at 0600 and, depending on demand, the ferries leave at intervals of 45 minutes. The last ferry from Salvador is at 2230. Returning to Salvador, the first ferry is at 0515 and the last one is at 2230. During the summer months the ferries are much more frequent. Enquiries at the Companhia de Navegação Bahiana (CNB), T3217100 from 0800 to 1700. A one-way ticket for foot passengers on Monday-Friday is US$1.20, Saturday-Sunday US$1.80. There is also a catamaran service departing for Bom Despacho at 0740, US$10.

Mar Grande can be reached by a smaller ferry (*Lancha*) from the Terminal Marítimo, in front of the Mercado Modelo in Salvador. The ferries leave every 45 minutes and the crossing takes 50 minutes, US$1.80 return.

Road From Bom Despacho there are many buses, kombis and taxis to all parts of the island. The best beaches are at Ponta de Areia, Mar Grande (US$1 by kombi), Berlinque, Aratuba and Cacha Pregos. Kombi and taxis can be rented for trips around the island but be prepared to bargain, US$30 for a half-day tour.

Tours of the bay

Small boats for trips around the bay can be hired privately at the small port by the Mercado Modelo, called Rampa do Mercado. A pleasant trip out to the mouth of the bay should take 1½ hours as you sail along the bottom of the cliff. When arranging to hire any boat, ensure that the boat is licensed by the Port Authority (Capitânia dos Portos) and that life-jackets are on board. The Companhia de Navegação Bahiana (T3217100) sails five times a week to **Maragojipe** on the Rio Paraguaçu to the west (see page 442). The trip takes three hours. It sails across the bay and then up the valley of the river. There are some very beautiful views along the trip. The ship makes two stops along the way, at Barra do Paraguaçu and at Mutuca, where locals row out to the ship in dug outs to disembark passengers. A good trip would be to continue to Cachoeira by bus from Maragojipe and return to Salvador the following day. Departures from Salvador from the Terminal Turístico in front of the Mercado Modelo, Monday-Thursday 1430 (1530 in summer). Friday departure is at 1130. Departures from Maragojipe Monday-Thursday 0500 and Friday 0830, US$4.50.

American yachtsman Steve Lafferty is highly recommended for enjoyable sailing trips, for up to four people: R do Sodré 45, apt 301, T2410994.

Sixty kilometres inland from Itaparica, Nazaré das Farinhas is reached over a bridge by bus from **Bom Despacho**. This 18th-century town is celebrated for its market, which specializes in the local ceramic figures, or *caxixis*. There is a large market in Holy Week, particularly on Holy Thursday and Good Friday. Twelve kilometres from Nazaré (taxi US$4.25, also buses) is the village of **Maragojipinha**, which specializes in making the ceramic figures. Bus from Salvador, 1530, takes five hours.

Nazaré das Farinhas
Population: 25,000
Phone code: 075

The Recôncavo

The area around Salvador, known as the Recôncavo Baiano, was one of the chief centres of sugar and tobacco cultivation in the 16th century. The town of Cachoeira, with fine examples of colonial buildings and friendly inhabitants, is also famous for its many interesting festivals. There are also small fishing villages on the bay such as Bom Jesus dos Pobres and the decaying ruins of the once productive engenhos (sugar plantations), which can be visited.

Leaving Salvador on the Feira road, at Km 33, one forks left on the BR-324 to the **Museu do Recôncavo Vanderlei de Pinho** (see page 421). Further west, round the bay, is **São Francisco do Conde**, 54 kilometres from Salvador, with a church and convent of 1636 and the ruins of Don Pedro II's agricultural school, said to be the first in Latin America.

At 60 kilometres from Salvador, the BA-026 road branches off the BR-324 to Santo Amaro, Cachoeira and São Félix.

Santo Amaro da Purificação

Seventy three kilometres from Salvador is Santo Amaro da Purificação, an old sugar centre sadly decaying. It is noted for its churches, which are often closed because of robberies, municipal palace (1769), fine main praça, birthplace of the singers Caetano Veloso and his sister Maria Bethania and ruined mansions including Araújo Pinto, former residence of the Barão de Cotegipe. Other attractions include the splendid beaches of the bay, the falls of Vitória and the grotto of Bom Jesus dos Pobres. The festivals of **Santo Amaro**, 24 January to 2 February, and **Nossa Senhora da Purificação** on 2 February itself, are interesting. There is also the **Bembé do Mercado** festival on 13 May. Craftwork is sold on the town's main bridge. There are no good hotels or restaurants.

Population: 56,500
Phone code: 075
Colour map 4, grid A6

Three kilometres beyond Santo Amaro on BR-420, turn right onto BA-878 for **Bom Jesus dos Pobres**, a small, traditional fishing village with a 300-year history. There is one good hotel, *Água Viva* (**A**), T075-6991178, reservations T071-3591132, on the beach front, with chalets or apartments, air conditioning or fan, good breakfast and restaurant, on one of the oldest farms in the region, good beach, recommended. Bus from Salvador rodoviária four a day (Camurjipe), US$3.

Bahia

Cachoeira and São Félix

Phone code: 075
Colour map 4, grid A6

At 116 kilometres from Salvador, and only four kilometres from the BR-101 coastal road, are the towns of Cachoeira (Bahia's 'Ouro Preto', *population* 28,255), and São Félix (*population* 12,095), on either side of the Rio Paraguaçu below the Cachoeira dam.

History
The impressive colonial architecture, particularly its fine examples of baroque and rococo churches, have made Cachoeira a UNESCO heritage site

Set deep in the heart of some of the oldest farmland in Brazil, Cachoeira was once a thriving riverport that provided a vital supply link with the farming hinterland and Salvador to the east. The region was the centre of the sugar and tobacco booms which played such an important role in the early wealth of the colony. The majestic *saveiro*, a gaff-rigged boat, traditionally transported this produce down the Rio Paraguaçu to Salvador across the bay. These boats can still be seen on the river at Cachoeira. The town was twice capital of Bahia: once in 1624-25 during the Dutch invasion, and once in 1822-23 while Salvador was still held by the Portuguese. With the introduction of roads and the decline of river transport and steam, the town stopped in its tracks and thus maintains its special charm. As in Salvador, *candomblé* plays a very important part in town life. Easy access by river from Salvador allowed the more traditional *candomblé* temples to move in times of religious repression. Cachoeira was the birthplace of Ana Néri, known as 'Mother of the Brazilians', who organized nursing services during the Paraguayan War (1865-70). There are beautiful views from above São Félix.

Sights

Cachoeira's main buildings are the **Casa da Câmara e Cadeia** (1698-1712), the **Santa Casa de Misericórdia** (1734 – the hospital; someone may let you see the church), the 16th-century **Ajuda** chapel (now containing a fine collection of vestments) and the Convent of the **Ordem Terceira do Carmo**, whose church has a heavily gilded interior. Other churches are the **Matriz**, with five metre high *azulejos*, and **Nossa Senhora da Conceição do Monte**. There are beautiful lace cloths on the church altars. All churches are either restored or in the process of restoration.

The **Museu Hansen Bahia**, on Rua Ana Néri, houses fine engravings by the German artist who made the Recôncavo his home in the 1950s, recommended. There is a great wood-carving tradition in Cachoeira. The artists can be seen at work in their studios. Best are Louco Filho, Fory, both in Rua Ana Néri, Doidão in front of the Igreja Matriz, and J Gonçalves on the main praça. A 300-metre railway bridge built by the British last century spans the Rio Paraguaçu to São Felix, where the Danneman cigar factory can be visited to see hand-rolling in progress. A trail starting near the Pousada do Convento leads to some freshwater bathing pools above Cachoeira.

Excursions

Six kilometres from Cachoeira, on the higher ground of the Planalto Baiano, is the small town of **Belém** (the turning is 2½ kilometres on the road to Santo Amaro), a healthy spot where people from Salvador have summer homes. **Maragojipe** (*population* 39,000), a tobacco exporting port 22 kilometres southeast of Cachoeira along a dirt road (BA-123), can also be reached by boat from Salvador. See the old houses and the church of São Bartolomeu, with its museum. The main festival is **São Bartolomeu**, in August. Good ceramic craftwork is sold in the town. The tobacco centre of Cruz das Almas can also be visited, although transport is poor.

Sleeping

Cachoeira A *Pousada do Convento de Cachoeira*, T7251716. In a newly restored 16th-century convent, good restaurant. *Pousada do Guerreiro*, 13 de Maio 14,

Bahia

The Sisters of Good Death

The Sisterhood of the Boa Morte (Good Death) was formed nearly two centuries ago in the senzalas (slave quarters), where slaves would gather to discuss abolition and pray for those killed in the struggle for emancipation. Once freed, ex-slaves would often form religious associations under the mantle of the Catholic church. The real purpose of these associations, however, was to free other slaves from captivity, help them to survive in the free world and preserve the traditions handed down orally from generation to generation. To this day they still continue the tradition of only admitting women of African descent. Each August they parade through the streets of Cachoeira with the image of Nossa Senhora da Boa Morte. The sisterhood worships iyá's, the female spirits of the dead. The sisters were expelled from the Catholic Church for refusing to surrender their statue of Nossa Senhora to the Vatican. At one point they were reduced to only 25 members, but the sisterhood has managed to survive through the support of African American solidarity groups from Bahia and the USA, and through the promotion of the ceremony as a tourist attraction by the state government. The sisters are a living document of the African Diaspora in the Americas.

The first procession takes place on the Friday after 15 August, on the Feast of the Assumption of the Virgin Mary, and is followed by a banquet. On the Saturday, after prayers, a funeral procession takes place, accompanied by a local brass band. On the Friday and Saturday, ceremonies begin at 1800. The following morning, after a night's vigil and a ceremony in the Casa da Irmandade at 1000, the sisters and novices parade through the town in their finery with the miraculously reborn Nossa Senhora carried aloft. Then the celebrations begin as the sisters dance Samba de Roda, a spinning samba danced in beautifully coloured skirts which create a kaleidoscope effect as the sisters twirl to the music. This form of samba originated in Cachoeira and is seldom seen anywhere else. During the festival weekend there are also displays of Capoeira and top Brazilian reggae stars often play to honour the sisterhood and the town.

T7251104. No restaurant. **D** *Pousada do Pai Tomaz*, R 25 de Junho 12, T7251288. **D** *Santo Antônio*, near the rodoviária, T7251402. Basic, safe, laundry facilities. Recommended. **E** *Pousada Tia Rosa*, near Casa Ana Neri, T7251692. With breakfast, very basic. **E** Youth hostel at Av Parnamirim 417, T2684844/3390.

São Félix D *Pousada Paraguassu*, Av Salvador Pinto 1, T7252550. Pretty riverside pousada, with breakfast.

Cabana do Pai Thomaz, 25 de Junho 12. Excellent Bahian food, good value, also a **Eating** hotel, **C** with private bath and breakfast. *Gruta Azul*, Praça Manoel Vitorino. Lunch only. *Do Nair*, R 13 de Maio. Delicious food and sometimes Seresta music. *Casa do Licor*, R 13 Maio 25. Interesting bar, try the banana-flavoured spirit. *Bahiana's Point*, good riverside bar, although open irregularly.

São Félix *Xang-hai*, good, cheap food, warmly recommended, try the local dish, maniçoba (meat, manioc and peppers).

São João (**24 June**) 'Carnival of the Interior' celebrations include dangerous games **Festivals** with fireworks, well-attended by tourists. The festival of *Nossa Sehora da Boa Morte* is held in **mid-August**, see box on page 443. A famous *candomblé* ceremony at the Fonte de Santa Bárbara is held on **4 December**.

Buses From **Salvador** (Camurjipe) every hour or so from 0530. To **Feira Santana**, 2 **Transport** hours, US$3.

Bahia

Directory **Banks** *Bradesco*, in the main square, Cachoeira, ATM accepts Visa credit but not debit cards, open Mon-Fri 0830-1700. **Communications** **Post office:** in the main square, Cachoeira, open Mon-Fri 0900-1700. **Tour companies & travel agents** Local tour guide *Claudio*, doesn't speak much English, but is friendly and knowledgeable, T9826080. **Tourist office** In the Casa de Ana Néri, Cachoeira.

The Chapada Diamantina

Colour map 4, grid A5 *The road from Salvador to Brasília passes through Feira de Santana, famous for its Micareta, an extremely popular out of season carnival, before arriving at Lençóis. This small colonial town, once a main centre for diamond prospectors, is now an excellent base for exploring the Chapada Diamantina national park, with its many waterfalls and rock formations.*

Motorists to Brasília can save a little time by taking the ferry to Itaparica, book in advance to avoid long queues, and then going across country to Itaberaba for the BR-242 highway. The journey can be broken at Itaberaba, Lençóis (see below) or Ibotirama on the Rio São Francisco; at Barreiras on the Rio Grande,

Chapada Diamantina

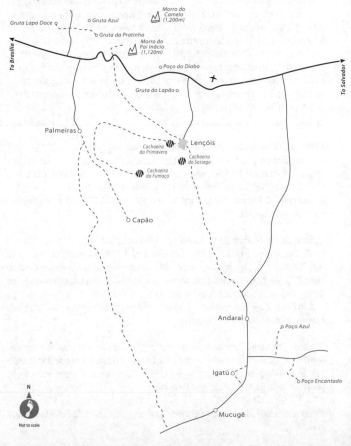

where buses stop for two to three hours; or at Posse or Alvorada do Norte (Goiás). All have hotels of varying quality. The road is paved from Salvador to Brasília, but it is reported poor between Salvador and Lençóis and full of potholes between Barreiras and Alvorado do Norte.

Located 112 kilometres northwest of Salvador on both the coastal BR-101 and the inland BR-116 roads to Rio, Feira de Santana is the centre of a great cattle breeding and trading area. Its Monday market, known as Feira do Couro (leather fair), is said to be the largest in Brazil and attracts great crowds to its colourful display of local products. The permanent Artesanato market in the centre, however, has a bigger selection, including leather, than the Monday market. The rodoviária has an interesting wall of painted tiles (made by Udo-Ceramista, whose workshop is in Brotas, Avenida Dom João VI 411, Salvador). The *Micareta* held in late April is the biggest out of season carnival in Bahia and attracts many popular *Axé* music groups from Salvador. Bus from Salvador every 20 minutes, 1½ hours, US$3.

Feira de Santana
Population: 450,500
Phone code: 075

Sleeping and eating A *Feira Palace*, Av Maria Quitéria 1572, T2215011, F2215409. A *Luxor*, Km 437, BR-116 South, T2215922. B *Flecha*, Km 171, BR-101, 20 km away, T2215999. B *Senador*, R Sen Quintino 10, T/F6235111. Recommended. Several cheap hotels in Praça da Matriz and near the rodoviária (both are quite near the centre). *Panela de Barro*, R Sen Quintino 259, good Bahian food.

Directory Banks: *Banco 24 Horas*, Av Senhor dos Passos 1332. *Banco do Brasil*, Av Getúlio Vargas 897.

Lençóis

On the BR-242, 400 kilometres west of Salvador, is Lençóis, a historical monument and a colonial gem, founded in 1844 to exploit the diamonds in the region. The tents assembled by the prospectors who first arrived there looked like sheets, *lençóis* in Portuguese, when seen from the hills, hence the name. There are still some *garimpeiros* left. In the town, *Artesanato Areias Coloridas*, Rua das Pedras, owned by Taurino, is the best place for local sand paintings made in bottles. These are inexpensive and fascinating to see being done. They will make one as you wait. For ceramic work, the most original is *Jota*, who has a workshop which can be visited. Take the steps to the left of the school near the *Pousada Lençóis*. The market on Monday and Friday mornings is recommended. There are Artesanato stalls in the main square, open every evening. It is difficult to change money in Lençóis.

Population: 10,000
Phone code: 075
Colour map 4, grid A5

A *Canto de Águas*, Av Senhor dos Passos, T/F3341154. Comfortable, good location, swimming pool, a/c or fan, good service. Recommended. A *Portal de Lencois*, R Chacara Grota, at the top of the town, T071-3710099. Luxury, fridge, pool, breakfast, tours arranged. A *Pousada de Lençóis*, R Altinha Alves 747, T/F3341102. With breakfast, swimming pool. Recommended. B *Aguas Claras*, opposite tourist office, 100m from the rodoviaria, T3341236. TV, fridge, pool, breakfast, excellent view. B *Fazenda Guaxo*, Estr da Granja, by first bridge before town, T3341356. Quiet. C *O Casarão*, Av 7 de Setembro 83, T3341198. Breakfast, fridge, a/c. Recommended. C *Estalagem de Alcino*, R Gen Vieira de Morais 139, T3341171. Shared bath, beautiful, restored 19th-century house, superb breakfast. Highly recommended. C *Pousada Village Lapão*, T3341117. Ten chalets of various size, quiet. C *Pousalegre*, R Boa Vista 95, T3341124. Dormitories only, good regional breakfast, safe, hot showers, good vegetarian restaurant.

Sleeping

D *Casa da Geleia*, R Gen Viveiros 187, T3341151. Two excellent chalets set in a huge garden at the entrance to the town, English spoken, good breakfast (Ze Carlos is a keen birdwatcher and an authority on the region, Lia makes excellent jams). D *Casa de Hélia*, R da Muritiba, T3341143. English and some Hebrew spoken, good facilities, legendary breakfast. Recommended. D *Por do Sol*, R Boa Vista, T3341163. Next door, good breakfast, safe. Recommended. D *Roncador*, R da Baderna 41, T3341133, cirtur@neth.com.br. D *Tradição*, R José Florêncio, T3341137. TV, breakfast, fridge, mosquito net, pleasant. E *Pousada dos Duendes*, R do Pires, T/F3341229. Shared bath, with breakfast, run by Olivia Taylor, an Englishwoman whose agency *Saturno* on R Miguel Calmon arranges tours and treks from 1 to 11 days and more. **Camping** *Alquimia*, 2 km before Lençóis, T3341213, and *Camping Lumiar*, near Rosário church in the town centre, T3341241. Popular restaurant. Friendly, recommended. There are also houses to rent in the town. Most of these are basic, with cooking and washing facilities. Juanita on R do Rosário rents rooms with access to washing and cooking facilities, US$3.50 pp. Claudia and Isabel, R da Baderna 95, T3341229, rent a house on the main praça in front of the Correios, US$4 pp without breakfast.

Eating *Lajedo*, good food with good view of town, popular meeting place at night. *Via Terra*, R Silva Jardim 89. Creative menu, pastas. Recommended. *Picanha na Praça*, on main praça. Best steak in town. *Artistas da Massa*, R Miguel Calmon, Italian. *Goody*, R da Rodoviária, good simple cooking. *Saravá*, great *muqueca*. *Lanchonette Zacão*, on main praça, natural yoghurts, juices and *bolinhos de queijo*, fried balls of dough filled with melted cheese. Recommended.

Bars & nightclubs The busiest spot at weekends is *Amigo da Onça*, R José Florêncio, near the municipal market. Lambada, forró and samba-reggae until the small hours, good fun. *Bar Lençóis* on the main praça. Recommended. *Clube Sete*, R das Pedras. Nightclub open Friday and Saturday nights.

Transport **Air** Airport, Km 209, BR-242, T6256497. **Buses** *Real Expresso* from **Salvador** 0730, 1200 and 2200, US$12, *comercial*. **Feira de Santana**, returns at 0900, 2100. Buses also from Recife, Ibotirama, Barreiras or Brasília, 16 hours, US$33 (take irregular bus to Seabra, then 2 a day to Brasília).

Directory **Banks** *Bank of Brazil*, 0900-1700 Mon-Fri, Visa ATM and changes TCs and US$ cash (high commission). There are no facilities for Mastercard. **Communications** **Post Office**: on main square. Open 0900-1700 Mon-Fri. **Telephone**: Open daily 0800-2200. **Internet**: *Cirtur*, address under **Tour companies**, below, US$0.15 per min. **Tourist information** *Sectur*, on Praça Oscar Maciel, next to the church across the river from town, T3341214.

Parque Nacional da Chapada Diamantina

Palmeiras Fifty kilometres from Lençóis is this headquarters of the Parque Nacional da Chapada Diamantina (founded 1985), which contains 1,500 square kilometres of mountainous country. It forms part of the Brazilian shield, like the Guayana Highlands, a geological remnant of when the world comprised only one land mass. There is an abundance of endemic plants, waterfalls, large caves (take care, and a strong torch, there are no signs and caves can be difficult to find without a guide), rivers with natural swimming pools and good walking tours. ■ *Information, T075-3322175, or Ibama, Av Juracy Magalhães Junior 608, CEP 40295-140, Salvador, T071-2407322.*

Trekking The most essential item for any trek is a flashlight with strong beam. Some of the walking may be after nightfall, but guides take trouble to avoid this. Carry mosquito repellent as there are a lot of them around in the encampment areas. It is highly advisable to bring a sleeping bag and/or a blanket and a roll-up mattress. Nights in the 'winter' months can be cold. Sometimes, guides can arrange these.

A tent is useful but optional; many camps are beside reasonably hospitable caves. Matches and paper for kindling campfires, as well as a first aid kit, are necessary.

The trails are often not on specially marked routes, and can involve a lot of clambering over rocks and stepping stones. A reasonable level of physical fitness is advisable. Walking boots are preferable but good training shoes are adequate. Avoid using new shoes, which give less grip on rocks.

Cirtur, R da Baderna 41, T3341133, cirtur@neth.com.br. *Lentur*, Av 7 de Setembro 10, **Tour companies**
T/F3341271, speak to Paulo and Eliane, open daily 0730-1200 and 1500-2200, organizes day trips to nearby caves and to see the sunset at Morro do Pai Inácio. *Pé de Trilha Turismo Aventura*, R Boa Vista 140, T3341124, guiding, trekking, rents camping equipment etc, can make reservations for most of the *pousadas* in the Chapada Diamantina (see below), represented in Salvador by *Tatur Turismo* (T0XX71-4507216, F071-4507215).

There are many guides offering their services at most *pousadas*, about US$20-30 per **Guides**
trip; most of them are very young. Recommended are: *Trajano*, Contact via Casa da Helia, T3341143, speaks English and some Hebrew, a good-humoured guide for treks to the bottom of the Cachoeira da Fumaca. *Edmilson* (known locally as Mil), R Domingos B Souza 70, T3341319, he knows the region extremely well and is very knowledgeable and reliable. *Roy Funch*, T/F3341305, royfunch@gd.com.br, the ex-director of the Chapada Diamantina National Park, is an excellent guide and has written a visitors' guide to the Chapada Diamantina, currently in translation into English. It is recommended as the best for information on the geography and trails of the Chapada. *Luiz Krug*, contact via Pousada de Lençóis, T3341102, an independent guide specializing in geology and espinology (the study of caves), speaks English. Christina, lives near the rodoviaria, T3341308, speaks French, English and Portuguese. *Índio*, contact at *Pousada Diangela*, R dos Minheiros 60, Centro Histórico. Specialist bird watching guides are *Andre*, Alto do Bonfim, T3341340, and *Ereas*, R Jose Florencio 60, T3341155. Abseiling can be organized by Ze Americo and Ze Augusto, T3341314.

Near Lençóis, visit the **Serrano** with its wonderful natural pools in the **Excursions**
riverbed, which give a great hydro massage. A little further away is the **Salão de Areia**, where the coloured sands for the bottle paintings come from. **Ribeirão do Meio** is a 45-minute walk from town, here locals slide down a long natural watershute into a big pool (it is best to be shown the way it is done and to take something to slide in). **Gruta do Lapão**, three hours from Lençóis, guide essential, is in quartz rock and therefore has no stalagmites. Some light rock climbing is required. **Cachoeira da Primavera**, two very pretty waterfalls close to town, recommended. **Cachoeira Sossego**, two hours from town, a 'picture postcard' waterfall, swimming in pool, recommended.

Morro de Pai Inácio, 30 kilometres from Lençóis, has the best view of the Chapada, recommended at sunset (bus from Lençois at 0815, 30 minutes, US$1). In the park is the **Cachoeira da Fumaça** (Smoke Waterfall, also called **Glass**), 384 metres, the highest in Brazil. To see it, go by car to the village of **Capão** and walk two and a half hours. The view is astonishing; the updraft of the air currents often makes the water flow back up, creating the 'smoke' effect. Olivia Taylor at the *Pousada dos Duendes* offers a three-day trek seeing the falls from top and bottom, the village of Capão and Capivara and Palmital falls from US$45.

Bahia

Other excursions are: **Lapa Doce**, a cave with fine stalagmites and stalactites, 70 kilometres, **Andaraí**, 101 kilometres, and the diamond ghost town of **Igatu**, a further 14 kilometres on the other side of the Rio Paraguaçu. There is a bridge across the river. The town has a good *pousada*. A good day trip from Lençóis is to **Poço Encantado** (23 kilometres southeast of the Chapada itself, 55 kilometres from Andaraí), a mountain cave with a lake of crystal clear water, 60 metres deep, which is spectacular. From April to August, the sunlight enters the cave from the mountain side, hits the water and is dispersed into the colours of the spectrum. A visit is recommended and can be followed by a trip to Igatu on the return to Lençóis. Southeast of the park is **Mucugé** (*Hotel Mucugé*, opposite the rodoviária, good food, basic, take mosquito coils), lovely walks among hills or along the Rio Paraguaçu. Buses from Mucugé to Seabra run Tuesday, Thursday, Saturday at 0500, frequent service from there to Lençóis and Palmeiras.

Sleeping Capão: **C** *Candombá*, good breakfast, excellent food, home-grown vegetables, run by Claude and Suzana (Claude speaks French and English and guides in the region), F075-3322176, or through *Tatur Turismo* in Salvador (address above). **D** *Pousada Verde*, at entrance to town, very good breakfast. Recommended. **E** *Pouso Riacho do Our*, friendly. Recommended. **E** *Tatu Feliz*, no breakfast.

Transport From Salvador you can get a bus to Lençois, US$16, 3 times daily, last bus from Salvador departs 2200, arrives 0430 via Alto Paraíso. **NB** Book in advance. Local guides can often arrange transport to the more remote excursions, certainly this is possible when groups are involved.

The Southern Coast

From Feira da Santana, the BR-116 (known as the Rio-Bahia) runs south to Minas Gerais, passing the towns of Jequié and Vitória da Conquista. The BR-101 runs parallel to the coast but slightly inland, passing Itabuna, Eunápolis, Itamaraju and Teixeira de Freitas before entering Espírito Santo. On the coast south of Salvador are the popular tourist centres of Valença, Ilhéus and Porto Seguro.

Jequié
Phone code: 073

This centre for distribution of petroleum products to the surrounding states is 374 kilometres from Salvador. The town, however, has fairly good accommodation for those making the long three-day journey to Rio de Janeiro, including *Itajubá* (**A**), Praça Col João Borges, T5252111, F5251779 and *Rex* (**B**), Praça Rui Barbosa 26, T/F5252541. There is a *Banco do Brasil*, Rua da Itália 28 and *Bradesco*, Rua 2 de Julho 66.

Vitória da Conquista
Population: 242,500
Phone code: 077

This busy town, 527 kilometres from Salvador, has a large market Monday-Saturday and a man-made lake with fountains and waterfalls. It is an important stopping place on the inland Rio-Bahia route and on routes from Minas Gerais to Bahia. It is also the only place to change money in this part of southern Bahia and northern Minas Gerais.

Sleeping C *Fenix*, R 2 de Julho 182, T/F4245992. **C** *Hotel Livramento*, Praça Barão do Rio Branco, T4241906. Restaurant. **Camping** *Camping Clube do Brasil*, Km 831, BR-116.

Transport Air: airport, Av Parana, T4212080. Flights to Montes Claros and Salvador. **Bus**: bus station, south of centre on BR-116, T4241379. To **Salvador**, 8 hours, US$15.

Directory Banks: *Banco 24 Horas*, Praça Barão do Rio Branco 169. *Banco do Brasil*, Praça Barão do Rio Branco 43.

Valença

On an asphalted road, 271 kilometres from Salvador, is this small, attractive town at the mouth of the Rio Una. Two old churches stand on rising ground. The views from Nossa Senhora do Amparo are recommended. The town is in the middle of an area producing black pepper, cloves and *piaçava* (used in making brushes and mats). Other industries include the building and repair of fishing boats (*saveiros*). The Rio Una enters an enormous region of mangrove swamps. The main attractions of Valença are the beaches on the mainland (Guabim, 14 kilometres north) and on the island of Tinharé. Avoid touts at the rodoviária; it's better to visit the friendly tourist office opposite.

Population: 75,000
Phone code: 075
Colour map 4, grid A5

A *Portal Rio Una*, R Maestro Barrinha, T/F7415050. Pool. **B** *do Porto*, Av Maçônica 50, T/F7412383. Clean, helpful, safe, good breakfast, good restaurant. **B** *Guabim*, Praça da Independência, T7411110. Modest, good. Recommended. **C** *Rafa*, T7411816. Large rooms. Well recommended. **D** *Valença*, R Dr H Guedes Melo 15, T7411807. Comfortable, good breakfast. Recommended. For eating, try *Akuarius*, Praça da Independência. *Recanto do Luiz*, Km 43, BA-001, good seafood.

Sleeping & eating

Buses Long distance buses run from the new rodoviária, Av Maçônica, T7411280, while the old one is for local buses. Eight buses a day to/from **Salvador**, 5 hours, US$6, *Camarujipe* (T071-3580109) and *São Jorge* companies. São Jorge to **Itabuna**, 5 hours, US$5, very slow. For the shortest route to Valença, take the ferry from São Joaquim to Bom Despacho on Itaparica island, from where it is 130 km to Valença via Nazaré das Farinhas (see page 441). To/from **Bom Despacho** on Itaparica, *Camarujipe* and *Águia Branca* companies, 16 a day, 1 hour 45 minutes, US$3.60.

Transport

Morro de São Paulo

Tinharé is a large island separated from the mainland by the estuary of the Rio Una and mangrove swamps, so that it is hard to tell which is land and which is water. The most popular beaches and *pousadas* are at Morro de São Paulo. Immediately south is the island of **Boipeba**, separated from Tinharé by the Rio do Inferno. On this island, too, there are lovely beaches and a small fishing village, also called Boipeba.

Phone code: 075

Morro de São Paulo is situated on the headland at the northernmost tip of Tinharé, lush with ferns, palms and birds of paradise. The town is dominated by the lighthouse and the ruins of a colonial fort (1630), built as a defence against European raiders. This did not stop the Dutch and French using the waters around the island as hiding places for attacks on the Portuguese.

The village has a landing place on the sheltered landward side, dominated by the old gateway of the fortress. From the lighthouse a path leads to a ruined lookout with cannon, which has panoramic views. The fort is a good point to watch the sunset from. Dolphins can be seen in August. Fonte de Ceu waterfall is reached by walking along the beach to **Gamboa**, then inland. Watch the tide; it is best to take a guide. Alternatively, take a boat back to Morro (US$0.50-1). All roads are unmade and no motor vehicles are allowed on the island. The beaches are good and, at low tide, saltwater pools appear in which you can swim or watch fish. Fish to eat can be bought from the fishermen in summer, or borrow a pole and catch your own at sunset. Second-hand books (English, German, and others) are sold at the back of the craft shop. On 7 September there is a big fiesta with live music on the beach.

The place is expensive December-March, but cheaper and more tranquil during the rest of the year. Morro de São Paulo gets very crowded during public holidays and with the influx of more tourists it is not the paradise it once was. Beware of prostitutes, drugs and theft at the busiest times. There is a port tax of US$1 payable at the *prefeitura* on leaving the island, which is resented by many.

Sleeping *Pousada da Tia Glória*, quiet. Next door is **C** *Pousada da Praça*, fan. Recommended. There are many cheap *pousadas* and rooms to rent near the fountain (Fonte Grande), but this part of town is very hot at night, eg **D** pp *Pousada Mare Sol*, simple. Recommended. Senhora Preta rents rooms (**D**), ask at the quay. **C** *Pousada Village da Ponte*, R da Fonte Grande, T071-2482699. A/c, fridge, fan. Recommended. **D** pp *Pousada Trilha do Riacho*, without breakfast, fan. **D** pp *Pousada Escorregue no Reggae*, with breakfast, reggae played all day. Recommended. Highly recommended are **B** *Pousada Porto da Cima* (200m past **A** *Pousada Casarão*) chalets with fans. **C** *Pousada Gaúcho*, huge breakfast, shared bath. A little further along and up some steep steps to the left is **B** *Pousada Colibri*, cool, always a breeze blowing, excellent views, only 6 apartments, Helmut, the owner, speaks English and German. Highly recommended.

Beach hotels The beaches on Morro de São Paulo are at the bottom of the main street where one turns right on to the first beach (Primeira Praia). **A** *Pousada Vistabella*, owner Petruska is extremely welcoming, good rooms, those to the front have good views and are cooler, all have fans, hammocks. Recommended. T073-7831001. **B** *Pousada Farol do Morro*, all rooms with sea view, cool, T7831038, or T071-2434144, F2434207. **C** *Pousada Ilha da Saudade*, good breakfast, simple. **C** *Pousada Ilha do Sol*, good views. Recommended. On the second beach (Segunda Praia) is **C** *Pousada Oxum*, on third beach (Terceira Praia) **B** *Pousada Guaiamú*, T071-7831073, F7831035. Fourteen rooms, in lush tropical setting, secluded. Nearby is **A** *Pousada Fazenda Caeira*, large grounds, private, well stocked library with snooker and other games, T7411272. Both of these are recommended. **A** *Hotel Ville Gaignon*, swimming pools, games rooms, convention rooms etc. **D** *Pousada Aradhia*, balconies with ocean view. Highly recommended. *Albatroz*, T7831185, managed by Johny, big rooms, good breakfast, good value. **E** *Pousada Govinda*, simple, good breakfast, other meals available, English and Spanish spoken. Recommended. On 4th beach (Quarta Praia) is **A** *Pousada Catavento*, T/F7831052.

Boipeba A *Pousada Tassimirim*, T/F071-9724378 (R Com Madureira 40, 45400-000, Valença). Bungalows, bar, restaurant, includes breakfast and dinner, secluded. **D** pp *Pousada Tropical*, lunch available. Highly recommended. **D** *Pousada Luar das Águas*, T7412238. Simple, good.

Eating *Restaurant Gaúcho* for good, reasonably priced, typical regional cooking. *Ebano* offers a good varied menu. *Belladonna* on the main street is a very good Italian restaurant with great music, a good meeting point, owner Guido speaks Italian, English and French, and is a willing source of information on the Morro, open daily from 1800 till the small hours. *Pizzas!*, across the street. *Morena Bela*, good for *moqueca*. *Casablanca* is a good simple restaurant, open daily till late, good breakfasts at *Doceria da Paula* on main street and at *Pousada Natureza*, near the church, US$5. *Comida Natural*, on the main street, *comida a kilo*, good juices. Recommended. *Bahiana*, on the main square, good food. Recommended.

Good pasta dishes at *Club do Balango* on the second beach, which is the liveliest with many beach huts offering cool drinks and meals. *Barraca Caita* opens till late with good music at weekends. They have snorkelling equipment for hire, popular meeting point, potent cocktail parties every night! Another *barraca* is *Ponto da Ilha* alongside. There are many other *barracas* on the third beach, but a short walk to the fourth beach is *Barraca da Piscina*, good swimming in front, good ambience, dominos, draughts etc, reasonable seafood menu, open till late during summer months.

Ferries From **Salvador**, a direct ferry service sails from the Terminal Marítimo in front of the Mercado Modelo to Morro de São Paulo (*Lancha Executiva*): daily in high season, Friday, Saturday, Sunday in low season, 0830, returns 1730, US$30 1-way, 2½ hour trip. Also, the *Bonanza III* from Rampa do Mercado Modelo, US$15, daily at 1300, 4 hours, T2267523 (Salvador), T7831062 (Morro de São Paulo). Part of the trip is on the open sea, which can be rough.

    Boats leave every day from **Valença** for Gamboa (1½ hours) and Morro de São Paulo (1½ hours) from the main bridge in Valença 5 times a day (signalled by a loud whistle). The fare is US$2.50. A *lancha rápida* taking 25 minutes travels the route between Valença and Morro, US$8. Only buses between 0530 and 1100 from Salvador to Valença connect with ferries. If not stopping in Valença, get out of the bus by the main bridge in town, don't wait till you get to the rodoviária, which is a long way from the ferry. Private boat hire can be arranged if you miss the ferry schedule. A responsible local boatman is Jario, T75-7411681; he can be contacted to meet travellers arriving at the rodoviária for transfer to the Morro. He also offers excursions to other islands, especially Boipeba. Overnight excursions to the village are possible. There is a regular boat from Valença to Boipeba on weekdays 1000-1230 depending on tide, return 1500-1700, 3-4 hours.

Transport

South of Valença, 46 kilometres along the BA-250, is Ituberá, on a deep inlet. To explore the beaches here it is best to go by boat. A further 27 kilometres south is Camamu, where the 16th century settlers took refuge from the Aimoré Indians (see Ilhéus, below). There are still some colonial buildings, such as the church of Nossa Senhora da Assunção (1631). Trips to beaches and around the bay can be made by boat. At the mouth of the bay is Ponta do Mutá, with fine beaches at Barra Grande. A dirt road runs up the peninsula to the point from **Ubaitaba**, a town on the BR-101 on the north bank of the Rio de Contas. (The BA-250 runs 42 kilometres inland from Camamu to join BR-101 at Travessão, 19 kilometres north of Ubaitaba.)

Ituberá & Camumu
Phone code: 073

The picturesque fishing village of Itacaré is at the mouth of the Rio de Contas, 56 kilometres from Ubaitaba on the south bank. It is a beautiful area with a protected beach, with crystal-clear water to the right of town; across the river there are beaches with good surfing. Other surfing beaches are Tiririca to the south and Farol at the rivermouth.

Itacaré
Phone code: 073

Sleeping C *Pousada Litoral*, R de Souza 81, 1 block from where buses stop. Owner João Cravo speaks English and can organize tours to remote beaches, hiring fishing boats. Recommended. **C** *Sage Paint*, Cuban owner, Ana Cubana, oceanfront *pousada*, showers, outings organized to nearby beaches. Recommended.

Transport Buses to Ilhéus, 3-4 hours, US$7. To Salvador, change at Ubaitaba (3 hours, US$3), Ubaitaba-Salvador, 6 hours, US$12, several daily.

Ilhéus

At the mouth of the Rio Cachoeira, 462 kilometres south of Salvador, the port of Ilhéus serves a district which produces 65 percent of all Brazilian cocoa. Shipping lines call regularly. A bridge links the north bank of the river with Pontal, where the airport is located. The local beaches are splendid, but the central beach is polluted.

Population: 242,500
Phone code: 073
Colour map 4, grid A5

Bahia

History Everyone is happy to point out that Ilhéus is the birthplace of Jorge Amado (1912) and the setting of one of his most famous novels, *Gabriela, cravo e canela* (*Gabriela, Clove and Cinnamon*, 1958; see box, page 782). While Amado's birth could possibly be the most important event in the city's recent history, its past stretches back to the earliest days of Portuguese colonization. Ilhéus was one of the captaincies created by King João III in 1534, south of the Baía de Todos Os Santos. Porto Seguro, further south, was another. The town was founded in 1536; its first church, São Jorge, was completed in 1556. An earlier church, though, is Santana at Rio do Engenho, 20 kilometres south, which dates from 1537, one of the oldest in Brazil. The Indians of this region, the Tupinikin, at first welcomed the Portuguese, but the relationship was soon undermined by slavery and disease. The sugar mills which the colonizers established flourished for a while, but by the end of the 16th century, both Ilhéus and Porto Seguro had been reduced to desperately fortified towns on the coast, facing attack from the fierce Aimoré Indians who descended from the forested coastal hills. After the pacification of the Aimoré in the 17th century, Ilhéus relied on sugar as its mainstay.

In 1881, a new crop was introduced from Pará, *cacau*, cocoa, which rapidly replaced the ailing sugar plantations. The first years of the cocoa boom were a time of lawlessness and violence, as owners of *fazendas* (the *coronéis*) jockeyed

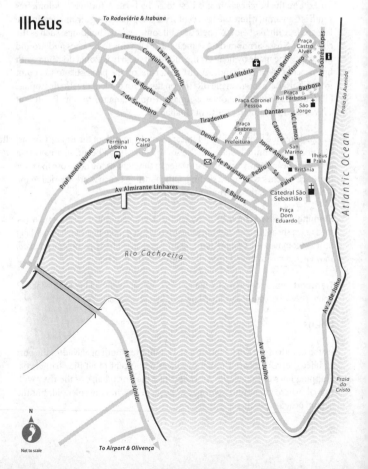

Ilhéus

for dominant positions in the new industry. Things settled down and the area around Ilhéus became one of the richest agricultural regions of the state and the city a major exporting harbour. Jorge Amado chronicled life on the cocoa plantations in two novels, *Cacau* (written in 1933) and the much better known *Terras do Sem Fim* (1942 – *The Violent Lands*), whose principal themes are 'terras, dinheiro, cacau e morte': land, money, cocoa and death. A later novel, *São Jorge dos Ilhéus* (1944), continues the story.

The church of **São Jorge** (1556), the city's oldest, is on the Praça Rui Barbosa; **Sights** it has a small museum. The cathedral of **São Sebastião**, on the Praça Dom Eduardo, near the seashore, is a huge, early 20th-century building. In Alto da Vitória is the 17th century **Nossa Senhora da Vitória**, built to celebrate a victory over the Dutch. Ask in travel agencies for trips to Rio de Engenho to visit the church of **Santana** (see above). Tourist information is situated on the beach opposite Praça Castro Alves (a few minutes' walk from the cathedral), friendly, maps US$2, recommended.

North of Ilhéus, two good beaches are Marciano, with reefs offshore and good **Beaches** surfing, and Barra, one kilometre further north at the mouth of the Rio Almada. South of the river, the beaches at Pontal can be reached by 'Barreira' bus; alight just after the *Hotel Jardim Atlântico* (the hotel, in our **AL** range, has sports facilities, restaurant, bar etc, T6322222, F6322223). Between Ilhéus and **Olivença** are a number of fine beaches, eg Cururupe, Batuba (good surfing) and Cai n'Água in Olivença itself (also a surfers' beach). The Balneário de Tororomba, on the Rio Batuba, 19 kilometres from Ilhéus, has hot, mineral baths. São Jorge or Canavieiras buses go there and frequent buses also go to Olivença. Youth hostel *Fazenda Tororomba* is in the centre of Olivença, Rua Luiz Eduardo Magalhães s/n, T2691139, F2691150.

Buses run every 30 minutes to **Itabuna** (32 kilometres, *population* 192,255), the **Excursions** trading centre of the rich cocoa zone (also many lumber mills). Ceplac installations at Km 8, on the Itabuna-Ilhéus road, show the whole processing of cocoa (T2143000, open Monday-Friday 0830-1230). Tours of cocoa plantations can be arranged through the *Ilhéus Praia* hotel. Also at Km 8, the Projeto Mico-Leão Baiano at the **Reserva Biológica del Una** is dedicated to the *mico-leão da cara dourada* (golden-faced tamarin); T2143024. This is the wettest part of Bahia (most notably in October). Visits to the reserve are not encouraged; information from Ibama in Salvador. Bus from Salvador, 6½ hours, US$12. The paved BA-415 links Itabuna to Vitória da Conquista (275 kilometres) on the BR-116.

A *Hotel Barravento*, on Malhado beach, R NS das Graças 276, T/F6343223. Ask for the **Sleeping** penthouse – usually no extra charge, includes breakfast and refrigerator. A *Ilhéus Praia*, Praça Dom Eduardo (on beach), T6342533. Pool, helpful. Recommended. A *Pontal Praia*, Av Lomanto Júnior 1358, Praia do Pontal, T/F6343033. Swimming pool, outside city but frequent buses passing. B *Pousada Sol Atlântico*, Av Lomanto Júnior 1450, Pontal T2318059. Good view over bay, fan, TV, balcony. B *São Marino*, 28 de Junho 29, T2316511 and at No 16. C *Britânia*, T2311722. Plenty of cheap hotels near the municipal rodoviária in centre. Also D *Hotel Atlântico Sul*, R Bento Berilo 224, Centro, T2314668. Good bar/restaurant. Recommended.

Camping *Estância das Fontes*, 19 km on road south to Olivença, T2122505. Cheap, shady. Recommended.

Itabuna A *Itabuna Palace*, Av Cinqüentenário 1061, T/F6131233. The best in town, restaurant. A *Príncipe*, Av Amelia Amado 5, T6133272, F2113374. B *Imperial*, R Miguel Calmon 234, T2115764. B *Lord*, Quintino Bocaiúva 1017, T/F2111233.

Eating *Os Velhos Marinheiros*, Av 2 de Julho, on the waterfront. Recommended. *Come Ben*, near Praça Cairu. Cheap and good. *Vesúvio*, Praça Dom Eduardo, next to the cathedral, made famous by Amado's novel (see above), now Swiss-owned, very good but pricey. *Nogar*, Av Bahia 377, close to the sea, good pizzas and pasta. Local drink, *coquinho*, coconut filled with cachaça, only for the strongest heads! Also try *suco de cacau* at juice stands.

Festivals *Festa de São Sebastião* (**17-20 January**), *Carnival*, *Festa de São Jorge* (**23 April**), *Foundation day* (**28 June**) and *Festa do Cacau* (throughout **October**).

Transport **Buses** Rodoviária is 4 km from the centre on Itabuna Rd, but Itabuna-Olivença bus
Insist that taxi drivers goes through the centre of Ilhéus. Several daily to **Salvador**, 7 hours, US$14.40 (*leito*
have meters and US$29, Expresso São Jorge), 0620 bus goes via Itaparica, leaving passengers at Bom
price charts Despacho ferry station on the island – thence 50-minutes ferry to Salvador. To **Itacaré**, 4 hours, US$5. To **Eunápolis**, 5 hours, US$5.40, this bus also leaves from the central bus terminal. Other destinations also served; local buses leave from Praça Cairu.

The paved coastal road continues south of Olivença, through Una, near the **Reserva Biologica de Una** (see above). The road ends at **Canavieiras**, a picturesque town which benefited from the cocoa boom. It has several beaches.

Porto Seguro

Population: 65,000 About 400 kilometres south of Ilhéus on the coast is the old town of Porto
Phone code: 073 Seguro. The town is a popular holiday resort with many charter companies fly-
Colour map 4, grid B5 ing in directly from Rio de Janeiro and São Paulo. It is now Bahia's second most popular tourist destination. The state government has invested heavily in the region; the airport has been enlarged to take jet aircraft and a major water theme park has recently opened. Since the 1980s there have been proposals to make the area an open museum of discovery, the Museu Aberto do Descubrimento. This whole region is certain to attract a great deal of foreign and national tourists in the year 2000, when the dual celebrations of the millennium and the 'discovery' of Brazil take place.

Building is subject to controls on height and materials, in keeping with traditional Bahian styles (colonial or Indian). In the area are remains of original Atlantic coastal forest, with parrots, monkeys, marmosets and snakes.

History Pedro Álvares Cabral is credited with being the first European to lay eyes on Brazil, sighting land at Monte Pascoal south of Porto Seguro. Upon anchoring on 22 April 1500, he sent out an advance party and the first contact with the indigenous Indians was made. But the sea here was too open to offer a safe harbour. After two days, Cabral sailed his fleet north in search of a secure protected harbour, entering the mouth of the Rio Burnahém to find the harbour he later called Porto Seguro (safe port). The first mass was celebrated by Frei Henrique de Coimbra; a cross marks the spot on the road between Porto Seguro and Santa Cruz Cabrália. A tourist village, Coroa Vermelha, has sprouted at the site of Cabral's first landfall, 20 minutes by bus to the north of Porto Seguro. It has souvenir shops selling Pataxó-Tupi Indian items, beach bars, hotels and rental houses, all rather uncoordinated.

Gonçalo Coelho's expedition of 1503 established the first settlement at this point on the coast, and in 1534 Porto Seguro became a captaincy. Thereafter, its history mirrored that of Ilhéus as far as relations between Portuguese and Indians went. It did not, however, share in the cocoa boom of the late 19th century. Instead Porto Seguro had to wait until the second half of the 20th century to see its fortune rise, when it was discovered by the tourist industry.

Bahia

The Festival of Nossa Senhora da Pena

The cult of Nossa Senhora da Pena began in Leiria, Portugal, a century after the reconquest of the country from the Moors. It arrived in Porto Seguro in 1535 when a Portuguese noble, Donatário Pero do Campo Tourinho (a recipient of one of Brazil's 16th century capitanias), brought with him a small image of Nossa Senhora da Pena (Our Lady of Suffering). He named his captaincy 'Villa de Nossa Senhora da Pena de Porto Seguro' and built a small church to house his favourite saint. The church was rebuilt in the 18th century.

Nossa Senhora da Pena is the patron saint of Art and Literature and her day is celebrated on 8 September in the historic city on the cliff, overlooking the beach hotels of the modern resort of Porto

Seguro. Devotees of the cult called 'romeiros' travel great distances to her shrine and the surrounding area becomes a huge campsite of tents, caravans and tour buses.

The festival resembles a cross between a Brazilian street party and market, with cheap clothes, household goods, as well as the usual ice-cold beer and barbecued meat on sale. During the weekend there are displays of capoeira *and nightly dances of* pagôde *and* forró *are held during the festival period. After prayers on the afternoon of the eighth, the festival is officially closed with a religious procession through the streets of this beautiful colonial town.*

Mick Day

From the roundabout at the entrance to Porto Seguro take a wide, steep, **Sights** unmarked path uphill to the historical city (**Cidade Histórica**), three churches (Nossa Senhora da Misericórdia-1530, Nossa Senhora do Rosário-1534 and Nossa Senhora da Pena-1718), the former jail and the stone monument marking the landfall of Gonçalo Coelho; a small, peaceful place with lovely gardens and panoramic views.

There are *borrachudos*, little flies that bite feet and ankles in the heat of the day; coconut oil keeps them off; at night mosquitoes can be a problem (but there is no malaria, dengue or yellow fever).

Guided tours of the area can be arranged with *BPS*, at the Shopping Centre, **Excursions** T2882373. *Companhia do Mar* (Praça dos Pataxós, T2882981) does daily trips by schooner to coral reefs off the coast. The most popular is to Recife de Fora, with good snorkelling; it leaves daily at 1000, returns at 1630, about US$18, US$3 extra for snorkelling gear. Dugout canoes fish on the Rio Burnahém and trips can be taken by canoe to explore the mangroves.

The best beaches are north of the town along the road to Santa Cruz de **Beaches** Cabrália (known as Avenida Beira Mar – BR-367). Most popular beaches are *The beaches in the town* Itacimirim, Curuípe, Mundaí and Taperapuã. Regular buses (*Expresso* *are not recommended* *Brasileiro*) run along this busy road from Praça dos Pataxós, with many stops on the seafront in the town. Porto Belo and Santa Cruz Cabrália buses go to the beaches frequently from the port. There are many *barracas* on these lively beaches. The biggest (and busiest) are *Barra Point*, *Toá Toa*, *Axé Moi*, *Vira Sol* and *Barramares*. Most of these have jet-ski and other watersports facilities for hire. Some cater mainly for coach groups from the larger charter companies, so expect crowds. Then again, being in a crowd is an important part of the Brazilian way of having fun. Other beaches north of Porto Seguro include Rio dos Mangues (nine kilometres) and Ponta Grande (12 kilometres – three kilometres before Coroa Vermelha). For beaches south of the Rio Buranhém, see below under Arraial d'Ajuda and points further south.

Bahia

Sleeping

Prices rise steeply Dec-Feb and July. Off-season rates can drop by 50%, negotiate for stays of more than 3 nights

Room capacity of the local hotel industry is greater than that of Salvador. Outside December-February, rooms with bath and hot water can be rented for about US$150 per month.

AL *Paradise Resort Hotel*, Praia do Apaga Fogo, T8751010, F8751016. Five-star luxury resort with all watersport facilities, 10 minutes by free exclusive shuttle from Porto Seguro. **A** *Pousada Imperador*, Estr do Aeroporto, T2882759, F2882900. Four-star, all facilities, interesting architecture, above the city, great views from pool deck. **A** *Pousada Gaivota*, Av dos Navegantes 333, Centro, T/F2882826. A/c, pool, sauna, parking facilities. **A** *Estalagem Porto Seguro*, R Mcal Deodoro 66, T2882095, F2883692. In an old colonial house, relaxing atmosphere, a/c, TV, pool, good breakfast. Highly recommended. **A** *Pousada Abaltroz*, Av dos Navegantes 600, Centro, T2882394, F2882047. Pool, TV, a/c. **A** *Pousada Casa Azul*, 15 de Novembro 11, T/F2882180. TV, a/c, good pool and garden, quiet part of town. **A** *Pousada Coqueiro Verde*, R Alameda do Coqueiro Verde 11, T2882621, F2882387. TV, a/c, sauna, pool. **A** *Pousada Alegrete*, Av dos Navegantes 567, T/F2881738. All facilities, very friendly. Recommended. **B** *Pousada Las Palmas*, Praça Antônio Carlos Magalhães 102, T/F2882643. A/c, TV, no pool. Highly recommended. **C** *Pousada Jandaias*, R das Jandaias 112, T2882611, F2882738. Fan, great breakfast, tranquil. Highly recommended. **C** *Pousada Coral*, R Assis Chateaubriand 74, T/F2882630. A/c, TV, good location. Recommended. **C** *Pousada Da Orla*, Av Portugal 404, T/F2881131. Fan, good breakfast, great location. Highly recommended. **C** *Pousada do Francês*, Av 22 de Abril 180, T/F2882469. A/c, TV, breakfast. Recommended. **B** *Pousada dos Raizes* (**D** without breakfast), Praça dos Pataxós 196, T/F2884717. Clean, friendly. Recommended. **C** *Pousada Mar e Sol*, Av Getúlio Vargas 223, T/F2882137. Fan in most apartments, a/c in a few, family run. **C** *Pousada Alcantara*, R das Papagaias 70, T/F2881657. Fan, clean, central. **C** *Pousada dos Navegantes*, Av 22 de Abril 212, T2882390, F2882486, navegantes@portonet.com.br, www.portonet.com.br/navegantes. A/c, with bathroom, TV, pool. **D** *Pousada da Praia*, Av Getúlio Vargas 153, T/F2882908. A/c, TV, pool, breakfast, comfortable. **D** *Pousada Aquarius*, R Pedro Álvares Cabral 174, T/F2882738. No breakfast, clean, family run, friendly, central. Recommended. **D** *Estalagem da Ivonne*, R Mcal Deodoro 298, T2881515. Some rooms with a/c. **E** *Porto Brasília*, Praça Antônio Carlos Magalhães 234. Fans, mosquito nets, with breakfast. **E** *Rio do Prado*, R Portugal 228, T2881019. **E** *Pousada Sapucaia*, Av Getúlio Vargas 397, T2882331. Without breakfast.

Youth hostels D pp *Porto Seguro*, R Cova da Moça 720, T/F2881742. *Maracaia*, Coroa Vermelha, on road to Santa Cruz Cabrália, T8721155, F8721156. Both IYHA.

Camping *Camping dos Marajas*, Av Getúlio Vargas, central. *Camping Gringa*, Praia do Cruzeiro, T2882076. Laundry, café, pool, excellent, US$5 per night. *Camping Mundaí Praia*, US$8 per night, T8792287. *Camping do Sítio*, R da Vala. Mosquitoes can be a problem here. *Tabapiri Country*, BR-367, Km 61.5, next to the Rodoviária on the road leading to the *Cidade Histórica*, T2882269.

Eating

Cruz de Malta, R Getúlio Vargas 358. Good seafood. *Preto Velho*, on Praça da Bandeira. Good value à la carte or self-service. Good breakfast at *Pau Brasil*, Praça dos Pataxós. On Praça Pataxós: *da Japonêsa*, No 38. Excellent value with varied menu, open 0800-2300. Recommended. *Ponto do Encontro*, No 106. Good simple food, owners rent rooms, open 0800-2400. *Prima Dona*, No 247. Italian, good. *Anti-Caro*, R Assis Chateaubriand 26. Good. Recommended. Also antique shop, good atmosphere. *Les Agapornis*, Av dos Navegantes 180. Wide selection of crêpes and pizzas. *Tres Vintens*, Av Portugal 246. Good imaginative seafood dishes. Recommended. *Ninô*, 22 de Abril 100. Good pizzas. *Vida Verde*, R Dois de Julho 92, T2882766. Good vegetarian, open 1100-2100 except Sunday. Recommended.

Porto Seguro is famous for the *lambada* (see box on page 458 and **Music and Dance**, **Bars &** page 771). A good bar for live music is *Porto Prego* on R Pedro Álvares Cabral, small **nightclubs** cover charge. *Sotton Bar*, Praça de Bandeira, is lively, as are *Pronto Socorro do Choppe*, *Doce Letal 50* and *Studio Video Bar*. There are bars and street cafés on Av Portugal.

Diving *Portomar Ltda*, R Dois de Julho 178, equipment hire, also arranges diving **Sports** and snorkelling trips to the coral reefs offshore, professional instructors.

Local **Car hire**: *Itapoã*, Av Portugal 1350, T2882710. *Localiza*, at airport, T2883106, **Transport** and R Cova da Moça 620, T2881488. Motorcycles at *Lupa Motos*, Praça dos Pataxós, T2882868, expensive, heavy deposit required. Bicycles, *Oficina de Bicicleta*, Av Getúlio Vargas e R São Pedro, about US$10 for 24 hours, also at Praça de Bandeira and at 2 de Julho 242.

Porto Seguro

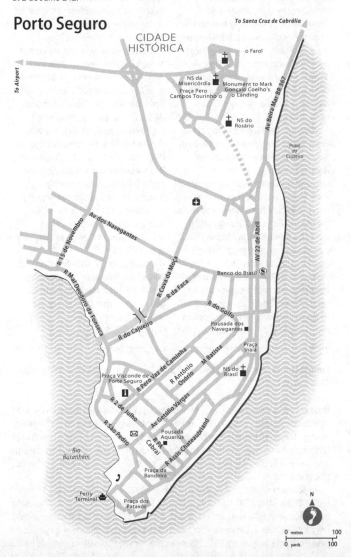

Night out in Porto Seguro

The night has always been one of the main attractions in Porto Seguro. It was here that the lambada craze boomed. Although now pretty much a thing of the past, it is still possible to see the lambada being danced and to try your hand, or feet, at learning the steps. Couples twist and swirl, glued together, at breakneck speed. They sometimes unglue when males fling their female partners about with wild abandon in a mesmerizing display of technique, swing and stamina. All important here is the ability to requebrar (from the word quebrar, to break) as you break to the left or right, and then break again (re-break) in the same direction. There is a lot of standing on locals' feet involved before the requebra is finally conquered and then the floor, and the night, is yours.

A night out will inevitably start at the Passarela do Álcool (roughly translated as Alcohol Broadway), a short section of Avenida Portugal, the seafront promenade, where most of the nightlife of Porto Seguro is centred. Houses from the last century have been transformed into a multitude of bars and restaurants. A long row of stalls (barracas) to one side sell a staggering array of lethal cocktails made from exotic tropical fruit. They do not taste like potent drinks but be warned. Most of these stalls specialize in capeta, a slang word for devil. The drink is made from vodka, cachaça or conhaque, condensed milk, guaraná and fruit of your choice. The

result is devilish, the effect too. Each stall tries to outdo their competitors with wonderful fruit arrangements that would do Carmen Miranda proud. The most popular barraca is Barraca de Macelinho, halfway along the passarela, always busy.

The latest craze is lambaérobica, as the name would suggest, a mixture of the dance and aerobics. The essential energy for this is helped along with the assistance of a local liqueur called guaraxaça, a potent blend of the natural stimulant from the guaraná berry, and cachaça (sugar cane rum). This concoction is not to be underestimated though. It is also seen as something of an elixir. Potency, in all its forms, is claimed to be its main attribute. It can be bought from Thia Siessa, Avenida Passarela do Álcool, 228. No prescription required.

The night continues in the barracas of the Avenida Beira Mar towards Santa Cruz de Cabrália. Barra Point, Toá Toa, Axé Moi, Vira Sol and Barramares all have intense nightlife, the most popular being Barramares, Toá Toa and another, Jungle Bar, at Mundaí. During the low season each one of the above is open on a particular night, in the high season many open each night.

Monday: Axé Moi, **Wednesday**: Barramares, **Thursday**: Toá Toa, *Friday*: Jungle Bar, **Saturday**: Barra Point. It is good to check with locals though for any changes.

Conor O'Sullivan

Long distance Air: flights to Belo Horizonte, Rio de Janeiro, Salvador and São Paulo. Taxi to airport US$7.

At Brazilian holiday times, all transport north or south should be booked well in advance

Buses: there is a new rodoviária, with reliable luggage store and lounge on the third floor, on the road to Eunápolis, 2 km from the centre, regular bus service (30 minutes) through the city to the old rodoviária near the port. Local buses US$0.30. Taxis charge US$5 from the rodoviária to the town or ferry (negotiate at quiet times). For local trips a taxi is an economic proposition for 2 or more passengers wishing to visit various places in a day.

To **Salvador** (*Águia Branca*), daily, 12 hours, US$22.25. To **Vitória**, daily, 11 hours, US$18. **Ilhéus**, daily 0730, 5½ hours, US$11. To **Eunápolis**, 1 hour, US$2. For **Rio** direct buses (*São Geraldo*), leaving at 1745, US$35 (*leito* 70), 18 hours, from Rio direct at 1600 (very cold a/c, take warm clothes), or take 1800 for Ilhéus and change at Eunápolis. To **Belo Horizonte** daily, direct, US$33 (*São Geraldo*). To **São Paulo** direct, 1045, 25 hours, not advisable, very slow, much better to go to Rio then take Rio-São Paulo express. Other services via Eunápolis (those going north avoid Salvador) or Itabuna (5 hours, US$9). (For the routes from Vitória see page 318 and from Belo Horizonte page 269.)

(For the routes from Vitória see page 318 and from Belo Horizonte page 269.)

Banks *Banco do Brasil*, Av Beira Mar open 1000-1500, changes TCs and US$ cash, also Visa ATMs. *Bradesco*, Av Getulio Vargas, Visa ATMs. *Deltur*, in the new shopping centre, near Banco do Brasil. *Agência do Descobrimento*, Av Getúlio Vargas, also arranges flight tickets and house rental. **Communications** Post Office: In the mini-shopping on the corner of R das Jandaias and Av dos Navegantes. **Telephone:** Shopping Av, open 0700-2300, corner of Av dos Navegantes and Av Beira Mar, also at Praça dos Pataxós, beside ferry terminal. Open daily 0700-2200, cheap rates after 2000, receives and holds faxes, F2883915. **Laundry** *New Porto*, Shopping Av, open 0900-2230, priced per item. **Tour companies & travel agents** *Brazil travel*, Av 22 de Abril 200, T2881824, F2883436, braziltravel@portonet.com.br, Dutch-run travel agency, all types of trips organized. **Tourist offices** *Casa de Lenha*, Praça Visconde de Porto Seguro, near the port, has basic information but is keen to sell tours.

Directory

Santa Cruz Cabrália

Ten minutes north of Coroa Vermelha, Santa Cruz Cabrália is a delightful small town at the mouth of the Rio João de Tiba, with a splendid beach, river port, and a 450-year-old church with a fine view.

Phone code: 073
Colour map 4, grid B5

A good trip from here is to Coroa Alta, a reef 50 minutes away by boat, passing along the tranquil river to the reef and its crystal waters and good snorkelling. There is a daily departure at 1000. A recommended boatman is Zezé (T/F2821152) on the square by the river's edge, who is helpful and knowledgeable. The trip costs around US$15 without lunch. The company next door is less helpful.

A river crossing by ferry to a new road on the opposite bank gives easy access to the deserted beaches of **Santo André** and **Santo Antônio**. As yet few tourists make it to here, but the new road is certain to change this. There are two pousadas: *Victor Hugo*, T9855292 (cellular), and *Tribo da Praia*, T2821002, with a helpful American owner. Hourly buses from Santa Cruz to Porto Seguro (23 kilometres).

A *Baía Cabrália*, R Sidrack de Carvalho 141, in the centre, T/F2821111. Sauna and gym. **C** *Pousada Coroa Alta*, T/F2821148. A/c, waterfront. **C** *Pousada do Mineiro*, T2821042. A/c, pool, sauna, friendly, also good churrascaria. Recommended. **C** *Pousada Arakakaí*, fan, comfortable. **C** *Pousada Estrela do Paz*, T2821258. On the hill overlooking the town: **C** *Pousada Atobá*, T/F2821131. A/c, pool, sauna. A good cheap restaurant is the *Coqueiro Verde*. Try the *pitu*, a kind of crayfish.

Sleeping & eating

Arraial da Ajuda

Across the Rio Buranhém, south from Porto Seguro, is the village of Arraial da Ajuda, the gateway to the idyllic beaches of the south coast. Set high on a cliff, there are great views of the coastline from behind the church of Nossa Senhora da Ajuda in the main square. Each August there is a pilgrimage to the shrine of Nossa Senhora da Ajuda (1549). In the church is an interesting room full of ex-voto offerings. There are fine views from behind the church. Legend has it that a spring miraculously appeared during mass, aiding the construction of the Jesuit church. The spring can be seen at the foot of the steep hill leading up to the town.

Phone code: 073
Colour map 4, grid B5

Ajuda has become very popular with 'younger' tourists and there are many *pousadas*, from the very simple to the very sophisticated, restaurants, bars and small shops. There is also a *capoeira* institute; ask for directions. It has become

Bahia

known as a 'hippie' resort: drugs are said to be widely available, but easily avoided. Parties are held almost every night, on the beach or in the main street, called the *Broadway*. At Brazilian holiday times (especially New Year and Carnival) it is very crowded and, with the coastline up for sale, it may become overdeveloped in a few years.

The beaches, several protected by a coral reef, are splendid. The nearest is 15 minutes' walk away. During daylight hours those closest to town (take Rua da Praia out of town to the south) are extremely busy; excellent *barracas* sell good seafood, chilled drinks, and play plenty of music. The best beaches are Mucugê, Pitinga ('*bronzeamento irrestrito*' or nude sunbathing) and Taipé.

Sleeping

At busy times such as New Year's Eve and Carnival, don't expect to find anything under US$15 pp in a shared room, for a minimum stay of 5-7 days

In the price list below, those shown as **D** will be at the uppermost end of that range. Camping is best at these times. Out of season, some *pousadas* change hands, so the following recommendations may change. **A** *Pousada Pitinga*, Praia Pitinga, T8751067, F8751035. Bold architecture amid Atlantic forest, a hideaway, great food and pool, member of the *Roteiros de Charme* group, see page 57. Highly recommended. **A** *Pousada Canto d'Alvorada*, on road to Ajuda, T8751218. **C** out of season, Swiss run, 7 cabins, restaurant, laundry facilities. **A** *Pousada das Brisas*, T8751033, F8751147. Panoramic views. **B** *Pousada Caminho do Mar*, Estr do Mucugê 246, T/F8751099. Owners helpful. Highly recommended. **B** *Pousada do Robalo*, T8751053/1528, F8751078. Good grounds, welcoming, good pool. **B** *Pousada Arquipélago*, T/F8751123. Every room decorated differently, reading library, relaxed atmosphere. Highly recommended. **B** *Ivy Marey*, near centre on road to beach, T8751106. Four rooms and 2 bungalows, showers, nice décor, good bar, French/Brazilian owned. Recommended. Nearby is **B** *Le Grand Bleu*, T8757272. Same owner, good *pizzaria*. Recommended. **B** *Sole Mio*, T8751115, just off the beach road leading from the ferry to Arraial. French owners, English spoken, laid back, 4 chalets, excellent *pizzaria*.

C *Pousada Erva Doce*, Estr do Mucugê 200, T8751113. Good restaurant, well appointed chalets. Highly recommended. **C** *Pousada Natur*, T2882738. Run by a German environmentalist. Recommended, English spoken. **C** *Pousada Porto do Meio*, Estr D'Ajuda 2476, 1 Km before Arraial da Ajuda, T/F8751017, close to beach. A/c, pool, laundry facilities, Swiss run, English and German spoken. **C** *Pousada Torrorão*, Estr do Mucugê 306, T8751260. Restaurant. Recommended. **C** *Pousada Tubarão*, R Bela Vista, beyond the church on the right, T8751086. Good view of the coastline, cool, good restaurant. Recommended. **C** *Vila do Beco*, beautiful garden, good value. **C** *Pousada Mar Aberto*, Estr do Mucugê 554, T/F8751153, very near Mucugê beach, 400m from centre of village. Set in lush gardens. Highly recommended.

D *Pousada Flamboyant*, Estr Mucugê 89, T8751025. Pleasant, good breakfast. Recommended. **D** *Pousada Flor*, on square, T8751143. Owner Florisbela Valiense takes good care of female guests. Warmly recommended. **D** *Pousada Gabriela*, Trav dos Pescadores, T8751237. With breakfast. Recommended. **D** *Pousada Le Cottage* (across the ferry from Porto Seguro, but before Ajuda, T8751029). French owner, Sr Georges, **C** in chalet. **D** *Lua Cheia do Amor*, T8751533. Cosy, owners Dino and Mariana are very helpful. **D** *Pousada do Mel*, Praça São Bras, T8751309. Simple, clean, good breakfast. Recommended. **D** *Pousada Vento Sul*, Caminho da Praia, T8751294. Hammocks, ocean view. On the way to the beach are: **D** *Pousada Corujão*, T/F8751508. Bungalows, cooking facilities, laundry, restaurant and book exchange. **D** *Pousada Mangaba*, bath, laundry facilities, without breakfast. Recommended. **D** *Pousada Nova Esperança*, nearby, without breakfast, bath. Recommended. **D** *Pousada Tamarind*, on Praça Brig Eduardo Gomes, near the church, without breakfast, bath. **D** *Pousada Tio Otto*, without breakfast, next to *Pousada Aconchego*, opposite Telebahia post.

Camping *Praia*, on Mucugê Beach. Good position and facilities. *Chão do Arraial*, 5 minutes from Mucugê beach. Shady, good snack bar, also hire tents. Recommended. Generally, Arraial da Ajuda is better for camping than Porto Seguro.

Bahia

São João, near the church, is the best typical restaurant. *Mão na Massa*, an excellent **Eating**
Italian restaurant, behind the church. Recommended. *Paulinho Pescador*, open
1200-2200, excellent seafood, also chicken and meat, one price (US$5), English spo-
ken, good service, *bobó de camarão* highly recommended, very popular, there are
often queues for tables. *Los Corales*, Trav dos Pescadores 167. Spanish, *paella* a speciality. Recommended *barracas* are *Tem Q Dá* and *Agito* on Mucugê beach, as well as
Barraca de Pitinga and *Barraca do Genésio* on Pitinga.

At the *Jatobar* bar the *lambada* is danced, on the main square, by the church (opens **Bars &**
2300 – *pensão* at the back is cheap, clean and friendly). *Gringo Louco* is a good bar as **nightclubs**
is *Duere*, great dance bar. Highly recommended. Many top Brazilian bands play at the
beach clubs at Praia do Parracho during the summer, entry is about US$20. Entry to
other beach parties is about US$10.

Ferries Across the Rio Buranhém from Porto Seguro takes 10 minutes to the south **Transport**
bank, US$0.60 for foot passengers, US$3.60 for cars, every 30 minutes day and night. It
is then a further 5 km to Arraial da Ajuda, US$0.50 by bus, kombis charge US$0.75 pp,
taxis US$5.

Banks There is a mobile *Banco do Brazil* in the main square during the high season periods. **Directory**
There are several bars on Broadway which change US$ cash, but rates are poor. Best to go to Porto
Seguro for money. **Communications** Post Office: Praça São Bras. **Telephone:** There is a service
post on the main square, open 0800 until 2200, number for receiving faxes is F8751309, US$1.
Tour companies & travel agents *Arraial Turismo*, T9856140, various excursions. *Arco-Iris
Turismo*, T8751580, specializes in boat trips.

Trancoso

Twenty five kilometres to the south of Porto Seguro and 15 kilometres from   *Phone code: 073*
Ajuda is Trancoso. It is a three-hour walk along the beach, but watch out for   *Colour map 4, grid B5*
the tides. This simple village, with its beautiful beaches (Praia dos Nativos is
recommended, Pedra Grande is nudist), is popular with Brazilian tourists and
many Europeans have built or bought houses there. There are good restaurants around the main square. From the end of Praça São João there is a fine
coastal panorama. Trancoso has a historic church, São João Batista (1656).
Between Ajuda and Trancoso is the village of Rio da Barra.

A *Caipim Santo*, to the left of the main square, T8681122. Has the best restaurant in **Sleeping**
Trancoso (natural cuisine). Recommended. **A** *Hotel de Praça*, games room, good
breakfast, in São Paulo, TXX011-2112239. **A** *Pousada Brasília*, Estr do Arraial,
T8681128. **B** *Pousada Calypso*, Parque Municipal, T8681113. Good apartments, comfortable, rooms at lower price also available, good library, German and English spoken. Recommended. **B** *Pousada Terra do Sol*, on the main square, T/F8681036. Good.
Recommended. **C** *Pousada Canto Verde*, T024-2437823. Restaurant only in high season. Recommended. **C** *Gulab Mahal*, on the main square. Oriental style, lovely garden, vast breakfast. Highly recommended. **C** *Pousada do Bosque*, on the way to the
beach. English, German and Spanish spoken, with breakfast, camping facilities also
available, good value. **D** *Pousada Lagoa*, T9856862. Bungalows, with breakfast.
About 500m inland, away from main square (known as the 'quadrado'), lies the newer
part of Trancoso (known as the 'invasão'), with 2 good value *pousadas*: **D** *Pousada
Quarto Crescente*, English, German, Dutch and Spanish spoken, cooking facilities,
laundry, helpful owners, library. Highly recommended. About 15 minutes from beach.
D *Luna Pousa*, further along on the left. Well ventilated. Recommended. **E** *Pousada
Beira Mar*, with bath, restaurant serving *prato feito*. There are many houses to rent,

Bahia

very good ones are rented by Clea who can be contacted at *Restaurant Abacaxi* on the main square on the right. You can leave a message for any one of the above mentioned *pousadas* by calling the Telebahia service post, T8671116, most people in town check there for messages daily.

Eating   *Urano*, just before the main square. Recommended. Good portions. *Rama* has also been recommended, as has *Silvana e Cia* in the historical centre. *Abacaxi* on the main square does good breakfasts, light snacks and very good crêpes. *Galub Mahal* for Eastern dishes. Good breakfast also at *Pé das Frutas*, *Maré Cheia* next door for good simple dishes, great *moqueca*. *Pacha* on the seafront does a good *prato feito*. Good ice cream at *Tão Vez*. Apart from restaurants which serve breakfast, most others open at 1500 until 2200 or so.

Transport   **Buses** Trancoso can be reached by bus (1 every hour, from 0800, last returns at 1800, US$1.25, 1 hour, more buses and colectivos in summer), colectivo, or by hitchhiking. Colectivos run from Trancoso to Ajuda (US$1.15).

Caraíva

Phone code: 073
Colour map 4, grid B5

This peaceful town, 65 kilometres south of Porto Seguro, is on the banks of the Rio Caraíva. There are no wheeled vehicles, no electricity nor hot water, but this fishing village has marvellous beaches and is a real escape from the more developed Trancoso and Porto Seguro. Between Trancoso and Caraíva is **Espelho**, near Curuípe, good for diving. The owner of *Pará's* bar does boat trips to Curuípe. Also good for diving and snorkelling is the reef at **Pedra de Tatuaçu**, 15 minutes by boat from Caraíva. Ponto Satu, three kilometres to the north, has a beautiful palm-fringed beach. Praia de Barra Velha in the **Parque Nacional Monte Pascoal** (see below) is reached by walking along the beach for six kilometres, or by boat. There is an Indian village here. Excellent horse riding through the Indian reserve can be arranged at *Fazenda Edwiges*.

Sleeping & eating   **B** *Pousada Lagoa*, T/F9856862. Chalets and bungalows under cashew trees in an area of 7,000 sq m good restaurant, always a cool breeze, has its own generator; the owner, Hermínia, speaks English, is very helpful and can arrange local trips and excursions. **E** *Pousada do Bill*, by football pitch. Recommended. *Bar Astral* for *prato feito*. *Deca* for vegetarian food. Good restaurant next to O Carrefour supermarket. *Bar do Sol* on the beach and *Netuno* are the best bars. There is forró music and dancing in the village bars late into the night.

Transport   Caraíva is reached by boat (4 hours from Porto Seguro with Cia do Mar, T8751170), by dirt road from Arraial da Ajuda and Trancoso, 2 buses daily 0800 and 1500 from the Ajuda side of the Rio Buranhém ferry crossing, 2½ hours (a

Porto Seguro environs

To Itabuna & Salvador

Santo Antônio
Gualú
Santo André
Santa Cruz Cabrália
Coroa Vermelha
Eunápolis
BR 367
Ponta do Mutá
Recife de Fora
Curuípe
Rio Buranhém
Arraial de Ajuda
Porto Seguro
Mucugé
Itabela
Pitinga
Lagoa Azul
Rio da Barra
Rio dos Frades
Trancoso
Caraíva
Parque Nacional de Monte Pascoal
Ponta do Corumbau
Itamaraju
Barra do Caí
Curumuxatiba
Praia das Ostras
Atlantic Ocean
BR 101
Prado
Guaratiba
Parque Nacional Marino de Abrolhos
Teixeira de Freitas
Rio Itanhém
Alcobaça
N
To Linhares & Vitória
Barra de Caravelas
Caravelas
0 km   20
0 miles   20

Bahia

bumpy journey due to the quality of the road!), or from the BR-101, turning off just before Itabela (Km 753) and following the signs to Fazenda Santa Rita. Buses from Eunápolis take 2½ hours also, 0600 and 1400.

South of Porto Seguro, reached by a 14 kilometres paved access road at Km 796 of the BR-101, is the Parque Nacional de Monte Pascoal, set up in 1961 to preserve the flora, fauna and birdlife of the coastal area in which Europeans made landfall in Brazil (Caixa Postal 076, CEP 45830-000 Itamaraju, T2812419). The Pataxó Indian reservation is located at Corombau village, on the ocean shore of the park. Corombau can be reached by schooner from Porto Seguro. A small luxury resort has been built at Corombau. From Caraíva there is a river crossing by boats which are always on hand. Buses run from Itamaraju 16 kilometres to the south, at 0600, Friday-Monday only.

Parque Nacional de Monte Pascoal

From Itamaraju (93 kilometres south of Eunápolis) are the coastal towns of Curumuxatiba and Prado. The latter has some 16th-century buildings and beautiful beaches north and south. It is 214 kilometres south of Porto Seguro via Eunápolis.

Curumuxatiba & Prado
Phone code: 073

Sleeping Curumuxatiba: **D** *Pousada Guainamby*, R Bela Vista, CEP 45983. German and Brazilian owned, small, clean, comfortable chalets, good views to long beach, good breakfast and fish and Italian meals. Recommended. Also reached from Itamaraju is the *Jacotoka* holiday village, which offers diving, surfing and riding in a tropical paradise, US$50 per day, reservations at 7 de Setembro 149, Porto Seguro, T2882291, F2882540, it can also be reached by boat from Porto Seguro. **Youth hostel**: *Praia de Cumuruxatiba*, Av Beira Mar s/n, T8731020, F8731004.
    Prado: The proprietors of the *Casa de Maria*, R Seis, Novo Prado, T2981377, claim to serve the best breakfast in the region. **D** *Pousada Talipe* (1125 Central Ave, 23rd St, Los Alamitos, T5556539, USA). Friendly, good breakfast. Recommended.

Further south still, 107 kilometres from Itamaruju, is this charming little town, rapidly developing for tourism, which was a major trading town in the 17th and 18th centuries. Caravelas is in the mangroves; the beaches are about 10 kilometres away at Barra de Caravelas (hourly buses), a fishing village.

Caravelas
Phone code: 073

Sleeping A *Marina Porto Abrulhos*, on the beach front. Very luxurious. **C** *Pousada Caravelense*, 50m from the rodoviária, T2971182. TV, fridge, good breakfast, excellent restaurant. Recommended. **D** *Shangri-la*, Barão do Rio Branco 216. Bath, breakfast. **Barra de Caravelas**: **C** *Pousada das Sereias*, French-owned. **E** *Pousada Jaquita*, use of kitchen, big breakfast, bath, airy rooms, the owner is Secka who speaks English. There are some food shops, restaurants and bars.

Transport Buses to Texeira de Freitas (4 a day), Salvador, Nanuque and Prado. Flights from Belo Horizonte, São Paulo and Salvador to Caravelas; otherwise fly to Porto Seguro. Rail connection to Minas Gerais.

Directory Banks: *Banco do Brasil*, Praça Dr Imbassahi, does not change money. **Tourist offices**: helpful tourist information at *Ibama Centro de Visitantes*, Barão do Rio Branco 281. **Tour companies & travel agents**: Teresa and Ernesto (from Austria) organize boat trips (US$40 per day), jeep and horse hire (turn left between the bridge and the small supermarket). 'Alternative' beach holidays (organic vegetarian food, yoga, meditation, other activities) with Beky and Eno on the unspoilt island of Coçumba, recommended, contact *Abrolhos Turismo*, Praça Dr Imbassahi 8, T2971149, also rent diving gear and arrange boat trips.

Bahia

Parque Nacional Marinho dos Abrolhos The Parque Nacional Marinho dos Abrolhos is 70 kilometres east of Caravelas. Abrolhos is an abbreviation of Abre os olhos, 'Open your eyes', from Amérigo Vespucci's exclamation when he first sighted the reef in 1503. Established in 1983, the park consists of five small islands (Redonda, Siriba, Guarita, Sueste, Santa Bárbara), which are volcanic in origin, and several coral reefs. Darwin visited them in 1830 and Jacques Cousteau studied the marine environment here. The islands and surrounding reefs are home to goats, birds, whales, fish, turtles and giant fire corals. The warm current and shallow waters (eight to 15 metres in depth) make a rich undersea life (with 160 species of fish) and good snorkelling. The park is best visited October-March, when underwater visibility reaches 30 metres. The waters are warmest and calmest at this time too. Humpback whales breed and give birth from July-December. Diving is best December-February.

The archipelago is administered by Ibama and a navy detachment mans a lighthouse on Santa Bárbara, which is the only island that may be visited. Permission from Parque Nacional Marinho dos Abrolhos, Praia do Kitombo, Caravelas, Bahia 45900, T2971111, or Ibama, Av Juracy Magalhães Junior 608, CEP 40295-140, Salvador, T071-2407322. Visitors are not allowed to spend the night on the islands, but may stay overnight on schooners.

Transport The journey to the islands takes between 1 and 6 hours, depending on the boat. Mestre Onofrio Frio in Alcobaça, Bahia, T2932195, is authorized by the Navy to take tourists. Tours also available from *Abrolhos Turismo*, see above, Caravelas (about US$170 for a slow 2½ day tour by *saveiro*). One-day tours can be made in a faster boat (US$100) from Abrolhos or the Marina Porto Abrolhos. Three-day, 2-night packages from São Paulo cost around US$700, including return flights.

The Northern Coast

The paved BA-099 coast road, from near Salvador airport, is known as the Estrada do Coco (Coconut Highway, because of the many coconut plantations) and for 50 kilometres passes some beautiful beaches. The best known from south to north are Ipitanga (with its reefs), Buraquinho, Jauá, Arembepe, Guarajuba, Itacimirim, Castelo Garcia D'Ávila (with its 16th century fort) and Forte. North of Praia do Forte, the road is called the Linha Verde as it runs along another beautiful stretch of coast.

Buses serve most of these destinations. The Estrada do Coco was extended in 1994 to the state of Sergipe. The road is called the Linha Verde (Green Line), because of the concern of disturbing the environment as little as possible.

Arembepe Forty five kilometres north of Salvador, this former fishing village is now a
Phone code: 071 quiet resort. There is an 'alternative' village of palm huts, 30 minutes' walk along the beach, behind the sand dunes, with a café and swimming. The best beaches are two kilometres north of town. A popular music festival is held the weekend after Carnaval. There is *Pousada da Fazenda* (**B**), on the beach, which has thatched huts and good but expensive seafood. At *Mar Aberto* (**D**), Lg de São Francisco 43, T8241257, English and French are spoken and it has very good food. Recommended. Try *pastel de banana* at *Verá's* restaurant. Bus from Terminal Francês, Salvador, every two hours, 1½ hours, US$2, last one back at 1700. Buses also run from Itapoã.

Praia do Forte

The fishing village, 80 kilometres north of Salvador, takes its name from the castle built by a Portuguese settler, Garcia D'Ávila, in 1556, to warn the city to the south of enemy invasion. Garcia D'Ávila was given a huge area of land, from Praia do Forte to Maranhão, on which he made the first farm in Brazil. He brought the first head of cattle to the country, cleared the virgin Atlantic forest and brought the first coconut and mango trees to Brazil.

Phone code: 071
Colour map 4, grid A6

Praia do Forte is now a tranquil resort, with a strong emphasis on preservation of the local flora and fauna. Inland from the coast is a *restinga* forest, which grows on sandy soil with a very delicate ecosystem. Near the village is a small *pantanal* (marshy area), which is host to a large number of birds, caymans and other animals. Birdwatching trips on the *pantanal* are rewarding. The Tamar Project was set up to preserve the sea turtles which lay their eggs in the area. Address is Caixa Postal 2219, Rio Vermelho, Salvador, Bahia CEP 40210-990, T8761045, F8761067. Praia do Forte is now the headquarters of the national turtle preservation programme and is funded by the Worldwide Fund for Nature. There is a visitors' centre at the project (US$1.50 to visit the turtle sanctuary). Praia do Forte is also ideal for windsurfing and sailing, owing to constant fresh Atlantic breezes.

Linha Verde

LL *Praia do Forte Eco-resort*, Av do Farol, T8761111, F8761112, reservas@pfr.com. br. Pools, sauna, creche, gym, tours arranged. **A** *Pousada Praia do Forte*, Av do Farol, T8761050, F8761033. Chalets in peaceful setting, more private than larger *Resort Hotel*. Recommended. **A** *Pousada Solar da Lagoa*, R do Forte, T8761271. Good location, spacious rooms. **A** *Sobrado da Vila*, Al do Sol, T/F8761088. Balcony, pleasant, good value restaurant. **A** *Solar dos Arcos*, on the beach. Two-bedroom apartments with pool, gardens, lawns. Warmly recommended. **B** *Pousada Tatuapara*, T8761015. Friendly. **B** *Pousada João Sol*, R da Corvina, T8761054. Owner speaks English, Spanish and German, good. Recommended. Only 6 apartments, great breakfast. **B** *Pousada da Sereia*, R da Corvina, T8761032. Fan, good breakfast. **B** *Pousada Sol Nascente*, on the street parallel to the main street. Good, bath, frigobar, fan, breakfast. **C** *Tia Helena*, Helena being the motherly proprietor who provides an excellent meal and enormous breakfast, nice rooms, price reduced for 3 day stays. Highly recommended. **Youth Hostel D** *Albergue Praia do Forte*, R da Aurora 3, T8761094, praiadoforte@ albergue.com.br. Private bathroom, fan, breakfast, kitchen and shop, more expensive for non-IYHA members.

Sleeping
Prices rise steeply in the summer season. It can be difficult to find cheap accommodation

Bahia

Eating *Bar Da Souza*, on the right as you enter the village. Best seafood in town, open daily, live music at weekends. Highly recommended. Reasonably priced. *Brasa Na Praia*, grilled seafood and meat, open daily, peaceful setting. Recommended. *La Crêperie*, excellent crêpes, Tuesday to Sunday, good music, popular, owner Klever very friendly. Highly recommended. *Pizzaria Le Gaston*, good pizza and pasta, also good home-made ice creams, open daily. In a lively square just off R da Aurora are *BarForte Creperia* and *Mundo Blu*, Italian food. *Cafe Tango*, pleasant tea and coffee bar, family atmosphere, great pastries and cakes. *Pernetas*, good value pizzaria. *Tutti-Frutti*, recommended ice cream parlour. There are many other restaurants in the village: good ones include *Pousada Solar Da Lua*, open daily until late, *Nora*, on the main street, and *Restaurant Tropical*.

Shopping *Kennedy Bahia*, gallery run by a family of Irish-Brazilian artists. Recommended. *Boutique Ogum Marinho* for excellent wood carvings. *Afro-Bahia* for good T-shirts.

Transport **Buses** To Praia do Forte from **Salvador**: Santa Maria/Catuense leaves 5 times daily from the rodoviária, 1½ hours, US$2.15.

Directory **Tour companies & travel agents** *Bahia Adventure*, T8761262, F8761018, baadventure@ svn.com.br, eco-tourism, abseiling and Land Rover trips. *Odara Turismo*, in the *Resort Hotel*, T8761080, F8761018, imaginative tours to surrounding areas and outlying villages and beaches using 4WD vehicles, very friendly and informative, recommended; owners, Norbert and Papy, speak English and German.

To the Sergipe border

The **Linha Verde** runs for 142 kilometres to the Sergipe border; the road is more scenic than the BR-101, especially near Conde. There are very few hotels or *pousadas* in the more remote villages. Amongst the most picturesque are **Subaúma** (*pousada*) and **Baixio** (very beautiful, where the Rio Inhambupe meets the sea).

Phone code: 071   Fourteen kilometres from Praia do Forte is the simple village of **Imbassaí**, with its beach at the mouth of the Rio Barroso. Other nearby beaches are Praia de Santo Antônio, four kilometres away, with its sand dunes and small fishing village, and **Porto Sauípe**, 22 kilometres north, with a hotel (**B**).

Sleeping **Imbassaí B** *Pousada Caminho do Mar*, T/F8322499. Bungalows with a/c, restaurant, German-run. **B** *Pousada Imbassaí*, T/F8761313. Chalets and apartments. **C** *Pousada Lagoa da Pedra*, T2485914. Large grounds, some English spoken, friendly. **D** *Pousada Anzol de Ouro*, T3224422. Chalets, fan, pool.

Phone code: 075   Situated on the coast, six kilometres from Conde, **Sítio do Conde** is a site for *Projeto Tamar* (see above). The beaches are not very good but it's an ideal base to explore other beaches at Barra do Itariri, 12 kilometres south, at the mouth of a river, which has fine sunsets. The road passes unspoilt beaches; the best are Corre Nu and Jacaré. You can also go to Seribinha, 13 kilometres north of Sítio do Conde. The road goes along the beach through coconut groves and mangroves; at Seribinha are beach huts serving cool drinks or food, one *pousada* reported on beach. Bus from Salvador to Conde with *São Luís*, T071-3584582, three a day, four on Friday, US$7.25.

Sleeping and eating A *Hotel Praia do Conde*, T4291129, in Salvador T071-3212542. A/c, pool. **C** *Pousada Oasis*, T4212397. Simple. **C** *Pousada Beira Mar*. **D** *Pousada do Boliviano*. **E** *Pousada de Dona Dulce*. *Bar e Restaurante Zeca*, local dishes. *Pizzaria Marcos*. *Restaurante Harmonioso*.

The last stop on the Linha Verde is **Mangue Seco**. Access from Sergipe is by boat or canoe on the Rio Real from Pontal (10 minute crossing). A steep hill rising behind the village to tall white sand dunes offers a superb view of the coastline. The encroaching dunes have caused the mangrove to dry up. The town was immortalized in Jorge Amado's book '*Tieta*'. In the main square is *Pousada Mangue Seco* (**B**), T071-3598506. Further away, on the left from the boat landing, 15 minutes' walk, is *Village Mangue Seco* (**B**), Praia do Rio Real, T079-2242965, with a pool. Seafood restaurants can be found at the boat landing.

Phone code: 075

The Sertão

The harsh beauty of the Sertão and its hospitable people are the reward for those wanting to get off the beaten track. The region has been scarred by droughts and a violent history of bandits, rebellions and religious leaders. Euclides da Cunha and Canudos are good places to start to explore this history. The Raso da Catarina, once a hiding place for Lampião, and the natural beauty of the Falls of Paulo Afonso, can both be visited from the town of Paulo Afonso located on the Rio São Francisco. This important river continues through the Sertão, linking agricultural settlements such as Juazeiro, Ibotirama and Bom Jesus de Lapa before entering northern Minas Gerais. For those wanting to get off the Bahia tourist trail, the less developed beaches of the northern coast along the Linha Verde, as well as the harsh beauty and small but hospitable towns of the Sertão, are good options.

Phone code: 075

Situated 250 kilometres from Salvador, surrounded by the dry Bahian *sertão*, are the spa towns of **Cipó**, on the banks of the Rio Itapicuru and nearby **Caldas do Jorro**. Both are popular for their thermic springs and have hotels: **C** *Grande Hotel Caldas de Cipó*, Praça Juraci Magalhães, T/F4351312, Cipó, and **A** *Caldas Palace*, Av José Carlos Arleo 210, T2561103, F2561134, Caldas do Jorro.

North of Feira da Santana, by 225 kilometres on the BR-116 road to Fortaleza, is Euclides da Cunha (*phone code* 075), a good base for exploring the Canudos area.

Euclides da Cunha

Sleeping **B** *do Conselheiro*, Av Mcal Juarez Tvora 187, T271814. *Lua*, T27111108, simple. *Varanda do Sertão*, T2711164. **C** *Grapiuna*, Praça Monsenhor Berenguer 401, T2751157. Cheaper without bath. Recommended.

The bus station is on the BR-116, T2711365. Thirty eight kilometres west is the famous hill shrine of **Monte Santo** in the Sertão, reached by 3½ kilometres of steps cut into the rocks of the Serra do Picaraça (about 45 minutes' walk each way – set out early). This is the scene of pilgrimages and great religious devotion during Holy Week. The shrine was built by an Italian who had a vision of the cross on the mountain in 1765. One block north of the bottom of the stairs is the **Museu do Sertão**, with pictures from the 1897 Canudos rebellion.

Canudos itself is 100 kilometres away at the junction of the BR-116 and BR-235. Religious rebels, led by Antônio Conselheiro, defeated three expeditions sent against them in 1897 before being overwhelmed (see box, page 468). The Rio Vaza Barris, which runs through Canudos, has been dammed, and the town has been moved to Nova Canudos by the dam. Part of the old town is still located 10 kilometres west in the Parque Estadual de Canudos, created in 1997. For tourist information, contact the *Prefeitura*, T8942165. There are direct buses to Canudos from Salvador. In Nova Canudos is **E** *Brasil*, with bath, fan, clean, simple, cheaper without breakfast.

Canudos

Bahia

Antônio Conselheiro and the Canudos rebellion

Much has been written about this 'extravagant mystic', 'indifferent paranoic', or 'crude gnostic', as described by Euclides da Cunha, the author of Os Sertões about the Canudos uprising. Yet being a leader of a messianic cult is not a title which sits easily with Antônio Conselheiro; rather, it is a label which has been thrust upon him to suit other people's ideas about him.

From the 1960s, Roman Catholicism in the northeast underwent a spiritual revival among both the laity and the clergy and there was renewed interest, particularly among the lower classes. During 1871-93, Antônio Vicente Maciel, later known as Antônio Conselheiro, a lay preacher, roamed the sertão (backlands) on a permanent pilgrimage and attracted a large band of followers. Known as a beato, he was a wandering servant of the Church, reconstructing abandoned churches, chapels and cemeteries, while also building roads and dams. Hardly a town existed which did not materially benefit from the labour gangs he directed and the financial support he obtained from wealthy landowners, eagerly encouraged by local priests. His control over large numbers of workers made him sought after by landowners and politicians, for labour and potential votes, increasingly valuable when set in the context of the abolition of slavery, the devastating droughts in the northeast in 1877-1915 which crippled agriculture for 12 of those years, and the competition for workers from the booming rubber and coffee plantations elsewhere. His habit of

preaching from pulpits brought him into conflict with the Church hierarchy, but he never rebelled against the Church and never questioned its doctrines, sacraments or spiritual authority.

He was not a monarchist, but Antônio Conselheiro was, however, staunchly opposed to the Republic when it separated Church and State, annulled the Church's jurisdiction over marriages and burials and introduced religious tolerance. In 1893 he became caught up in local political rivalries which eventually brought his downfall. Antônio Conselheiro led a demonstration in Bom Conselho against the Republic, dramatically burning tax edicts in the main square. A 30-man contingent of police was eventually despatched from Salvador to arrest him and disperse his followers. They found the beato at Masseté, but after a brief skirmish Antônio Conselheiro and his followers retreated to Canudos, an abandoned fazenda, which became their base. Despite his treason, there were deputies in the Bahian legislature who defended him against police brutality, or at least argued for his removal by non-violent means. The incident at Bom Conselho came hard on the heels of a major split in the leadership of the one-party system which had governed Bahia since 1889. The monolithic Partido Republicano Federalista-Bahia fell apart when Luiz Vianna (soon to be Governor of Bahia) rejected the leadership of his traditional allies, José Gonçalves and Cícero Dantas Martins (the Baron of Geremoabo), during

The BR-235 runs west from Canudos to Juazeiro; alternatively, from Salvador go to Feira de Santana, take the paved BR-324, then the BR-407, which continues through Petrolina to Picos in Piauí (see page 580), the junction for Fortaleza or Teresina.

Senhor do Bonfim
Population: 84,500
Phone code: 074

On the BR-407, 124 kilometres south of Juazeiro, is Senhor do Bonfim, a busy market town with lots of life and a good place to buy leather goods. The **Catedral do Senhor do Bonfim** is in Praça Juracy Magalhães and there is a jewellery school specializing in emeralds 25 kilometres from the town. Popular festivals are *Senhor do Bonfim* in January and *São João* in June. The bus station is at Km 124, BR-407, T8413839. Twenty five kilometres from town is *Rio das Pedras* (**B**), Praça Frei Lino, Campo Formosa, T/F8451307.

a mid-year legislative session. Control of the state's municípios was the major issue, but there was also rivalry between Gonçalves and Vianna over the former's candidacy for a federal senate seat. Factionalism erupted violently throughout the backlands as Viannistas and Gonçalvistas campaigned for local allies. The burning of decrees was a tactic employed by the minority Viannista partisans in several other municípios, as well as Bom Conselho. The police mission was therefore an attempt by Vianna's opponents, who briefly had a majority in the assembly, to eliminate their enemy's backland ally. Antônio Conselheiro tried to escape from the consequences of rapid change in Bahian politics by settling in Canudos with his followers.

Canudos grew into one of the largest towns in the northeast. At its peak it had 5,200 rudimentary houses and a population of 25,000-30,000, mostly mestiços drawn from all over the northeast looking for a better life and salvation. They brought their families and in fact women outnumbered men. Traditional Catholicism was practised, with the mysticism which was endemic throughout the northeast, but it was not a messianic cult and Antônio Conselheiro did not proclaim himself to be sent from God. However, the charismatic orator was a political innocent and his separatist movement was soon at odds with the politicians and landowners. He was branded a 'restorationist' and a monarchist. Meanwhile, Vianna triumphed in the polls despite opposition accusations that he exploited Antônio Conselheiro's movement for his own ends, and was inaugurated as Governor of Bahia in May 1896. Five months later, backland officials urgently requested that he send a force against Canudos, but he hesitated. He was accused of delaying because of elections due in December, finally bowing to pressure and despatched troops. News of their surprise defeat reached Salvador in November and after that, Salvadorans joined with Vianna's opponents in demanding Antônio Conselheiro's blood. Vianna now judged it expedient to sacrifice his political ambitions in the backlands and from January 1897 sent out a succession of troops, who met with a succession of surprise defeats at the hands of the ill-equipped inhabitants of Canudos. However, by October it was all over, with Canudos dynamited and burned to the ground, leaving an estimated 5,000 soldiers and 20,000 sertanejos dead. The body of Antônio Conselheiro was exhumed, decapitated and his head sent to Salvador, to determine whether he was mad.

The events at Canudos inspired one of the most famous books written in Brazil, the aforementioned Os Sertões by Euclides da Cunha (see **Literature**, page 777). It also spawned a more recent, fictionalized account, La guerra del fin del mundo, by the Peruvian novelist Mario Vargas Llosa. A film has also been made, which can be accessed on the Internet: http://www.canudos.com.br/filme.htm.

Bahia

Directory Banks: *Banco do Brasil*, Praça Dr José Gonçalves 210. **Hospitals & medical services**: *Regional*, Praça Duque de Caxias 172, T8414122.

A further 112 kilometres from Senhor do Bonfim and 344 kilometres from Salvador is the friendly and interesting agricultural town of Jacobina. Once a major mining centre, gold, diamonds and emeralds are still found in the surrounding hills. There is *Serra do Ouro* (**B**), Lg Monte Tabor, T6213325, with air conditioning, good views of the city, pool and restaurant.

Jacobina
Phone code: 074

Paulo Afonso

Population: 94,000
Phone code: 075
Colour map 2, grid C5

Part of the northern border of Bahia is the Rio São Francisco. On the opposite bank are Pernambuco and Alagoas. From Salvador, the paved BR-110 runs 471 kilometres north to the river at Paulo Afonso, also linked to Recife, by a paved road and partially paved to Maceió (306 kilometres). The town was founded in 1913 during the construction of the dam and is some distance from the falls in the Parque Nacional de Paulo Afonso. Handicrafts (embroidery, fabrics) are available from *Núcleo de Produção Artesanal*, Av Apolônio Sales 1059. Nearby is the **Raso da Catarina**, a series of trails in the caatinga which was used as a hide-out by the bandit Lampião; guides and a four-wheel drive vehicle are recommended due to the heat and lack of shade – for information, T2813347.

Sleeping & eating **B** *Belvedere*, Av Apolônio Sales 457, T2813314. A/c, pool. **B** *Palace*, Av Apolônio Sales (next door to Belvedere), T2814521. A/c, pool, 'best value in town'. *Da Parada*, Qd E1, good regional food.

Transport **Air** Airport, 4 km from town. Flights to Recife and Salvador. **Buses** Bus station, Av Apolônio Sales, T2814769. To **Aracaju** with *Bonfim*. To **Maceió** via Palmeira dos Índios with *Real Alagoas*. To **Recife** with *Progresso*, 7 hours, US$9.65. To **Rio** with *Itapemirim*. To **Salvador** with *Viazul*. To **São Paulo** with *São Geraldo*.

Directory **Airline offices** *Rio-Sul*, T2813260. **Banks** *Banco do Brasil*, Av Landulfo Alves 46. **Tourist information** R Apolônio Sales, T2812757, guides available.

Parque Nacional de Paulo Afonso About 25 kilometres northwest of Paulo Afonso is the Parque Nacional de Paulo Afonso. The Falls of Paulo Afonso, once one of the great cataracts of the world but now exploited for hydroelectric power, are 270 kilometres from the mouth of the São Francisco river, which drains a valley three times the size of Great Britain. There are 2,575 kilometres of river above the Falls to its source in Minas Gerais. The 19th-century British linguist and explorer, Sir Richard Burton, took a 1,500 mile expedition down the river and negotiated some of its treacherous rapids. Below the Falls is a deep, rock gorge through which the water rushes. The national park is an oasis of trees and the lake amid a desert of brown scrub and cactus. The best time to visit the Falls is in the rainy season (January-February); only then does much water pass over them, as almost all the flow now goes through the power plant. The best view is from the northern (Alagoas) bank.

The Falls are in a security area with admission from 0800-1100 only by car or taxi, accompanied by a guide from the tourist information office, T2821717, two hours, US$6 per car. There is the *Grande Hotel de Paulo Afonso* (**B**), T2811914, F2811915, which has a pool as well as a guesthouse (apply for room in advance) at the Falls.

Travel on the Rio São Francisco

The São Francisco River is navigable above the Falls from above the twin towns (linked by a bridge) of Juazeiro, in Bahia, and Petrolina, in Pernambuco, thriving towns compared to many on the upper São Francisco. Navigation is possible as far as Pirapora in Minas Gerais, linked by road to the Belo Horizonte-Brasília highway (see page 302).

Juazeiro is located at an important crossroads where the BR-407 meets the Rio São Francisco. For information on river transport, T075-8112465. On the opposite bank in Pernambuco is Petrolina (see page 514). The local economy revolves around agriculture and its exportation. There is a market on Friday and Saturday. Bus to Canudos, five hours, is crowded; buy ticket early to get a seat. The second half of the route is unpaved.

Juazeiro
Population: 172,500
Phone code: 074

Sleeping and eating A *Grande Hotel*, R José Pititinga, T8117710. Also *União* (recommended) and *Oliveira* in R Conselheiro Saraiva. **B** *Pousada de Juazeiro*, 6 km south on BR-407, T8117820, F8116547. A/c, pool, restaurant, bar, pleasant. A unique restaurant known as the *Vaporzinho* is high and dry on the riverfront, a side-wheel paddle steamer (poor food), the *Saldanha Marinho*, built at Sabará in 1852.

The next major town upriver is **Xique-Xique**, an agricultural town 587 kilometres from Salvador. The remains of possibly pre-Neanderthal man have been found in the nearby Grotto of the Cosmos, whose cave paintings suggest that it was used as an observatory. *Carranca Grande* hotel (**B**) with a pool and restaurant is at Km 1, BA-052, T/F6611674.

Phone code: 074

The next town upriver, **Ibotirama**, 650 kilometres from Salvador on the BR-242, is famous for its fishing especially for *Surubim* and *Pocomã*. There are a few hotels with restaurants (**B-C**).

Phone code: 077

An important stop on the Rio São Francisco and 148 kilometres from Ibotirama on the BR-242 is **Bom Jesus de Lapa**. The **Igreja NS da Soledad** is situated within a grotto near to Praça da Bandeira. This sanctuary discovered by a monk in the 17th century is the centre of a romaria between July and September, bringing thousands of visitors to the town. There are a few places to stay. The airport is at Av Manuel Novais, T4814519.

Phone code: 077

Directory Airline offices: *Abaeté*, T4814264. **Banks**: *Banco do Brasil*, R Avelino Bastos 264. **Hospitals & medical services**: *Carmela Dutra*, Av Manuel Novais, T4814714.

Bahia

Recife and the Northeast Coast

8

Recife and the Northeast Coast

Sergipe and Alagoas are the first states encountered on the coast road north. There are good beaches near their capitals Aracaju and Maceió, as well as historic Penedo on the mouth of the Rio São Francisco. Pernambuco, with the colonial gem of Olinda near to its capital Recife, also has the Atlantic archipelago of Fernando de Noronha. Inland is the handicraft and market centre of Caruaru. Brazil's most easterly point is located near the pleasant city of João Pessoa in Paraíba. Campina Grande on the edge of the Sertão is renowned for one of Brazil's liveliest São João festival.

Recife & the Northeast Coast

Sergipe

This state has beautiful beaches around its capital Aracaju, as well as some interesting towns such as colonial São Cristóvão and imperial Laranjeiras, making it worth at least a short visit when travelling on the coastal highway between Salvador and Recife.

In the 16th century, the Sergipe river formed the boundary between the captaincies of Bahia and Pernambuco and as such, it was a troubled area. This was not because of rivalry between the two captaincies, but because the French had some influence there and because the Jesuits gave protection to Indians fleeing slavery and epidemics of European diseases. Things came to a head in the 15 years from 1575 to 1590. The colonists, anxious to recapture their runaway slaves and sensing a good opportunity to take more slaves from the missions, promoted a war, which they regarded as just, but which the Portuguese crown did not. By 1590, the Indians had been defeated, Bahia and Pernambuco were united and the French lost their foothold.

The land which Sergipe now occupies fell into Dutch hands in the early 17th century (see box, page 492). After the Portuguese had regained their territory, Sergipe remained under the influence of the large colonial centre of Bahia until it was made a province and took on an identity of its own.

Sergipe has a population of about 1,680,000 mainly living near the coast. The Rio São Francisco forms the border between Sergipe and Alagoas to the north, whilst the Rio Real defines the southern border with Bahia. The area of *sertão* is quite small in this state compared with other parts of the northeast.

Aracaju

Population: 428,500
Phone code: 079
Colour map 2, grid C5

The state capital, 327 kilometres north of Salvador, founded 1855, is a clean and friendly town. It stands on the south bank of the Rio Sergipe, about 10 kilometres from its mouth.

Sights In the centre is a group of linked, beautiful parks: **Praça Olímpio Campos**, in which stands the cathedral, **Praça Almirante Barroso**, with the Palácio do Governo, and **Praças Fausto Cardoso** and **Camerino**. Across Avenida Rio Branco from these two is the river. The streets are clean and parts of Laranjeiras and João Pessoa in the centre are reserved for pedestrians. There is a handicraft centre, the **Centro do Turismo** in the restored Escola Normal, on Praça Olímpio Campos, Rua 24 Horas; the stalls are arranged by type (wood, leather etc). ■ *0900-1300, 1400-1900.* The commercial area is on ruas Itabaianinha and João Pessoa, leading up to Rua Divina Pastora and Praça General Valadão. At Rua Itabaianinha 41 is the **Instituto Geográfico e Histórico de Sergipe.** ■ *Monday-Friday 0800-1200, 1400-1700.*

Beaches A 16 kilometre road leads to the fine **Atalaia** beach: there are oil-drilling rigs offshore. Beaches continue south down the coast along the Rodovia Presidente José Sarney. This long stretch of sand is between the mouths of the Rios Sergipe and Vaza Barris; the further you go from the Sergipe, the cleaner the water. There is an even better beach, **Nova Atalaia**, on Ilha de Santa Luzia across the river. The beach is 30 kilometres long. It is easily reached by boat from the Hidroviária (ferry station), which is across Avenida Rio Branco from Praça General Valadão. Boats cross the river to **Barra dos Coqueiros** every 15 minutes (US$0.50); the boats at a quarter past the hour combine with a bus to Nova Atalaia (US$0.60). Buses return to Barra on the hour. Services are more frequent at weekends, when it is very lively. The river at Barra dos Coqueiros is busy with fishing and pleasure craft.

Twenty three kilometres northwest from Aracaju is **Laranjeiras** (*population* **Excursions** 21,500), a small pleasant town, with a ruined church on a hill. It is reached by the São Pedro bus, from the old rodoviária in the centre of Aracaju, 30-60 minutes. It has several churches from the imperial period, when it was an important sugar producer, although it was originally founded in 1605. The 19th century Capela de Sant'Aninha has a wooden altar inlaid with gold. It has three museums: **Museu Afro-Brasileiro**, Rua José do Prado Franco 70 (Tuesday-Friday 1000-1700, weekends 1300-1700); **Museu Sacro**, Praça Dr H Diniz Gonçalves (Tuesday-Sunday 1000-1700); and the **Centro de Cultura**, João Ribeiro. Its main festival is **São Benedito** in the first week of January. Hotels include *Pousada Vale dos Outeiros* (**B**), Av José do Prado Franco 124, T2811027, 10 rooms, restaurant. Recommended.

Seventy kilometres west of Aracaju is **Itabaiana**, which has a famous gold market on Saturday. There are a few hotels in the centre (**D**). See below for São Cristóvão.

Atalaia (Velha) Many hotels and aparthotels, mostly mid- to high-price range. **Sleeping** **L** *Parque dos Coqueiros*, Atalaia beach, RFR Leite Neto 1075, T/F2431511. Large pool, luxurious, attractive, only hotel on beach. **A** *Beira Mar*, Av Rotary, T2431921,

Recife & the Northeast Coast

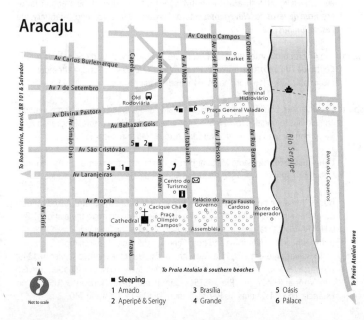

Aracaju

N
Not to scale

To Praia Atalaia & southern beaches

■ **Sleeping**
1 Amado
2 Aperipê & Serigy
3 Brasília
4 Grande
5 Oásis
6 Pálace

F2431153, beiramar@eibeiro.com.br. **C** *Cali Praia*, Av Oceânica 500, T2431521, F2431542. **C** *Pousada da Praia*, R Niceu Dantas 667, T2231700. **D** *Aracaju Praia*, Av Santos Dumond, T/F2432521. **D** *Costa do Mar*, R Niceu Dantas 325, T2431349. **Atalaia Nova** **AL** *Da Ilha*, T2621221, F2621359. Also **D** *Casa Lavrada*, T2601221.

Centre **A** *Palace de Aracaju*, Praça Gen Valadão, T2245000. Three-star, a/c, TV, fridge, central, restaurant, pool, parking. **A** *Grande*, R Itabaianinha 371, T/F2111383. A/c, TV, fridge, central, *Quartier Latin* restaurant. **A** *Aperipê*, R São Cristóvão 418, T2111880. Central, a/c, phone, fridge, restaurant. **A** *Serigy*, R Santo Amaro 269, T2111088. Same management and facilities, comfortable. **B** *Brasília*, R Laranjeiras 580, T2248022. Good value, good breakfast. Recommended. **B** *Oásis*, R São Cristóvão 466, T2242125. Good breakfast, hot water, fair, a bit tatty. **C** *Amado*, R Laranjeiras 532. A/c (less with fan), laundry facilities. **D** *Turista*, R Divina Pastora 411, noisy, mosquitoes, no hot water or breakfast, friendly.

Camping *Camping Clube do Brasil*, Av Santos Dumont, T2431413.

Eating Very many in Atalaia; on Av Oceânica try *Chapéu de Couro*, No 128. Recommended. *Cantinha da Bahia*, No 180. Recommended for fresh crab. In town, there is a good bar and restaurant, *Cacique Chá*, in the cathedral square. Lively at weekends. Also on Praça Olímpio Campos is *Rancho Gaúcho*, No 692. Quite good, very friendly. *Bar e Lanchonete Dom Qui Chopp*, Laranjeiras opposite *Telemar*. Popular. *Gonzaga*, R Santo Amaro 181. Lunch only, good value, very popular, excellent traditional dishes.

Bars & nightclubs *Augustu's*, T2432274. Nightclub, closed Mon. *Espaço Ernes*, Av Tancredo Neves 225, T2319138. Venue for live shows. *Gonzagao*, Av Heraclito Rollemberg. Live shows, especially Forró.

Entertainment **Cinema** Ten-screen *Cinemark*, in Shopping Jardins.

Festivals On **8 December** there are both Catholic (Nossa Senhora da Conceição) and Umbanda (Iemenjá) religious festivals. Other festivals are: the procession on the river on **1 January**, *Bom de Jesus dos Navegantes*; *Santos Reis*, on the first weekend in **January**; the *Festas Juninas*.

Shopping The *Artesanato* is interesting: pottery figures and lace particularly. See above for the *Centro de Turismo*. A fair is held in Praça Tobias Barreto every Sunday afternoon. The municipal market is a block north of the Hidroviária.

Transport **Local** **Buses**: Look for route plates on the side of buses and at bus stations in town. The old bus terminal in town is at Santo Amaro and Divina Pastora, Praça João XXIII. Buses from here to Laranjeiras and São Cristóvão (45 minutes, US$1.25).

Long distance **Air**: Santa Maria airport is 11 km from the centre, on Av Sen Júlio César Leite, Atalaia, T2431388. Flights to Maceió, Rio de Janeiro and Salvador.

Buses: Interstate buses arrive at the rodoviária, 4 km from the centre, linked by local buses from the adjacent terminal (buy a ticket before going on to the platform). Bus 004 'T Rod/L Batista' goes to the centre, US$0.50. Buses go from Praça João XXIII, the terminal near the Hidroviária and from Capela at the top of Praça Olímpio Campos.

To **Salvador**, 6-7 hours, 11 a day with *Bonfim*, US$11, executive service at 1245, US$14, saves 1 hour. To **Maceió**, US$9 with *Bonfim*. Many coastal destinations served; also **Vitória** (US$26.50), **Rio** (US$51), **São Paulo, Belo Horizonte** (US$35). To **Estância**, US$2, 1½ hours. To **Recife**, 7 hours, US$12-14, 1200 and 2400.

Airline offices *Transbrasil*, T2431155. *Varig*, T2433464. *Vasp*, T2432535. **Banks** Visa ATMs at   **Directory**
Shopping centres, *Banco do Brasil*, Praça Gen Valadão and *Bradesco* in the city centre. Mastercard
ATMs at *Banco 24 horas*, Av Francisco Porto and Av Geraldo Sobral, in the city centre close to the
Shell gas station. **Communications Post Office:** Laranjeiras and Itabaianinha. **Telephones:**
Laranjeiras 296, national and international calls until 2200, also at rodoviária. **Embassies &
consulates** *France*, T2248610. *Italy*, T2433814. *Portugal*, T2226662. **Hospitals & medical
services** *Clinica São Domingos Savio*, T2111344, casualty department. *São Lucas*, R Col Stanley
Silveira 33, São Jose, T2111738. **Dental emergencies:** *Pronto Odonto*, Av Barão de Maruim,
T2222927. **Tourist offices** *Bureau de Informações Turísticas de Sergipe*, R 24 Horas, T2245168,
very friendly, helpful, abundant leaflets. *Emsetur*, Trav Baltazar Gois 86, Edif Estado de Sergipe,
11th-13th floors, T2228373, F2243403, emsetur@prodase.com.br, www.prodase.com.br/emsetur
In the centre, go to *Aracatur*, R Maruim 100, Sala 10, T2241226, F2243537, which has leaflets and
maps such as *Aracaju no bolso* and *Onde?*, helpful, English spoken.

São Cristóvão

The old state capital of Sergipe, 17 kilometres southwest of Aracaju on the road   *Population: 57,500*
to Salvador, was founded in 1590 by Cristóvão de Barros. It is the fourth oldest   *Phone code: 079*
town in Brazil. Built on top of a hill, its colonial centre is unspoiled, the major-   *Colour map 2, grid C5*
ity of buildings painted white with green shutters and woodwork.

There are no hotels, but families rent rooms near the rodoviária at the bottom of the hill. *Senzala do Preto Velho*, R Messias Prado 84, recommended for
Northeastern specialities.

Festivals celebrated here are *Senhor dos Passos*, held 15 days after Carnival
and *Nossa Senhora de Vitória*, the patron saint's day on 8 September. In
November the town holds a *Festival de Arte*, but check the date as it sometimes
falls in October.

The **Museu de Arte Sacra e Histórico de Sergipe** contains religious and other   **Sights**
objects from the 17th to the 19th centuries; it is in the **Convento de São Francisco**. ■ *Tuesday-Friday 1000-1700 and Saturday-Sunday 1300-1700.* Also
worth visiting (and keeping the same hours) is the **Museu de Sergipe** in the
former **Palácio do Governo**; both are on Praça de São Francisco. Also on this
square are the churches of **Misericórdia** (1627) and the **Orfanato Imaculada
Conceição** (1646, permission to visit required from the Sisters), and the
Convento de São Francisco.

On Praça Senhor dos Passos are the churches of **Senhor dos Passos** and
Terceira Ordem do Carmo (both 1739), while on the Praça Getúlio Vargas (for-
merly Praça Matriz) is the 17th century **Igreja Matriz Nossa Senhora da Vitória**.
■ *All are open Tuesday-Friday 1000-1700 and Saturday-Sunday 1500-1700.*

Also worth seeing is the old **Assembléia Legislativa** on Rua Coronel
Erundino Prado.

Buses *São Pedro* buses depart from the old rodoviária in the centre of Aracaju, see   **Transport**
above. **Trains** A tourist train runs between Aracaju and São Cristóvão each Saturday
and Sunday, 0900, 3½ hours, T2113003 to check that it is running – a minimum of 15
passengers is needed.

The Rio São Francisco marks the boundary between Sergipe and Alagoas.
The BR-101 between Aracaju and Maceió – the next port to the north – is
paved, crossing the São Francisco by bridge between Propriá and Porto Real
do Colégio.

The Poet (?)

The bus from Aracaju stops at the bottom of the hill. It's a short, steep climb up to the centre of São Cristóvão. Arriving in the late afternoon the town is quiet, the streets quite empty and, below, the rays of the setting sun glint on the waving fronds of the banana plantations. Tourist information being in short supply, I had not known that, at my chosen time of visiting, all the churches would be closed, but, no matter, it was pleasant wandering through the streets, enjoying the tranquillity of the green and white façades after the modernity of the city down the road. An old man sitting in a doorway greeted me, asked me who I was and where I was from and we struck up a conversation. He was, he told me, "the poet J Jorge". Sadly, at that time, my knowledge

of Brazilian poets was very limited, being more interested in prose fiction then. It appeared that I hid my ignorance well enough because, after enquiring if I was married, he wrote a short poem for my wife. (It's personal, so I shall keep its contents between her and me.)

Of course, I had to find out who this generous J Jorge was. Had I met J G Araújo Jorge, the lyric poet, opponent of the military dictatorship, holder of several important political posts in the MDB and the PDT? One of his poems was, suitably, 'Poema ao Turista e à Kodak', part of which you will find at the front of this book. It would have been great, wouldn't it? But J G Araújo Jorge died in Rio de Janeiro in 1988, several years before I was in São Cristóvão.

Estância
Population: 57,000
Phone code: 079

Estância is 247 kilometres north of Salvador, on the BR-101, almost midway between the Sergipe-Bahia border and Aracaju. It is one of the oldest towns in Brazil. Its colonial buildings are decorated with Portuguese tiles (none are open to the public). Its heyday was at the turn of the 20th century and it was one of the earliest places to get electricity and telephones. Estância is also called Cidade Jardim because of its parks. The month-long festival of *São João* in June is a major event. Many buses stop at the rodoviária, on the main road. Bus from Salvador 4 hours, US$12-14.

There are pleasant hotels

Sleeping **C** *Jardim*, Praça Joaquim Galazans 202, T5221638. Modern, a/c, huge buffet breakfast. Recommended. **C** *Turismo Estanciano*, Praça Barão do Rio Branco 176, T5221404. **D** *Dom Bosco*, bath and breakfast. **D** *Magnus*, T5222453. Breakfast, TV, fridge. **D** *Praia Abais*, T7510020. Breakfast, TV, pool. **D** *Sawana*, T9851570. With own restaurant.

Alagoas

The state has a pleasant capital in Maceió with its many beaches. There is also the interesting river culture of Penedo at the mouth of the important Rio São Francisco, which flows from Minas Gerais through the arid interior to meet the Atlantic Ocean.

After the Portuguese had regained their territory from the Dutch invasion during the 17th century, Alagoas remained under the influence of the larger colonial centre Pernambuco until it was made a province and took on an identity of its own.

Alagoas, with a population of about 2,690,000, is one of the poorest and least developed states. Most people live near the coastal strip and in the capital. The arid interior is quite small and not particularly habited.

Maceió

The state capital is 294 kilometres northeast of Aracaju by road, and 285 kilometres south of Recife. Maceió is a friendly city with a low crime rate. It is mainly a sugar port, although there are also tobacco exports and a major petrochemical plant. A lighthouse stands in a residential area of town (Farol), about one kilometre from the sea. The commercial centre stretches along the seafront to the main dock and climbs the hills behind.

Population: 725,000
Phone code: 082
Colour map 2, grid C6

Getting there Flights arrive at Campos dos Palmares airport, 20 km from the centre. Taxi to the centre about US$20. Interstate buses arrive at the rodoviária, 5 km from the centre. Luggage store is available. Take bus marked 'Ouro Preto p/centro' (taxi quicker, US$7) to Pajuçara.

Ins & outs
See also Transport, page 485

    Getting around The commercial centre is easy to walk around but you need to take a bus to the main hotel and beach area of the city at Pajuçara. Frequent buses, confusingly marked, serve all parts of the city. Bus stops are not marked: it is best to ask where people look as if they are waiting. The ferroviária is in the centre, R Barão de Anádia 121. Train services are suburban.

Sights

Two of the city's old buildings, the **Palácio do Governo**, which also houses the Pierre Chalita museum (see below), and the church of **Bom Jesus dos Mártires** (1870 – covered in tiles), are particularly interesting. Both are on the Praça dos Martírios (or Floriano Peixoto). The recently restored **cathedral**, Nossa Senhora dos Prazeres (1840), Praça Dom Pedro II, is also worth a visit.

Instituto Histórico e Geográfico, Rua João Pessoa 382, T2237797, has a good small collection of Indian and Afro-Brazilian artefacts. **Fundação Pierre Chalita**, in the Palácio do Governo, Praça Floriano Peixoto 44, in the centre, T2234298, houses Alagoan painting and religious art. ■ *Monday-Friday 0800-1200, 1400-1800.*

Museums
All close Saturday & Sunday

    Lagoa do Mundaú, a lagoon, whose entrance is two kilometres south at **Pontal da Barra**, limits the city to the south and west: excellent shrimp and fish are sold at its small restaurants and handicraft stalls; a nice place for a drink at sundown. Boats make excursions in the lagoon's channels, T2317334.

Beaches

Beaches fronting the old city, between the Salgema terminal and the modern port area (Trapiche, Sobral), are too polluted for swimming. Beyond the city's main dock, the beachfront districts begin; within the city, the beaches are more exclusive the further from the centre you go. The first, going north, is Pajuçara where there is a nightly craft market. At weekends there are wandering musicians and entertainers and patrols by the cavalry on magnificent Manga Larga Marchador horses. There are periodic *candomblé* and *axé* nights and rituals to the goddess Iemanjá. Next is Ponta Verde, then Jatiúca, Cruz das Almas, Jacarecica (nine kilometres from the centre), Guaxuma (12 kilometres), Garça Torta (14 kilometres), Riacho Doce (16 kilometres), Pratagi (17 kilometres)

For beaches beyond the city, see Excursions below

Recife & the Northeast Coast

and Ipioca (23 kilometres). Jatiúca, Cruz das Almas and Jacarecica are all good for surfing. The beaches, some of the finest and most popular in Brazil, have a protecting coral reef a kilometre or so out. Bathing is much better three days before and after a full or new moon, because tides are higher and the water is more spectacular.

There is a natural swimming pool two kilometres off Pajuçara beach (**Piscina Natural de Pajuçara**), at low tide you can stand on the sand and rock reef (beware of sunburn). You must check the tides, there is no point going at high tide. *Jangadas* cost US$5 per person per day (or about US$20 to have a *jangada* to yourself). On Sunday or local holidays in the high season it is overcrowded. At weekends lots of *jangadas* anchor at the reef, selling food and drink.

Transport Taxis from town go to all the northern beaches (for example 30 minutes to Riacho Doce), but buses run as far as Ipioca. The Jangadeiras bus marked 'Jacarecica-Center, via Praias' runs past all the beaches as far as Jacarecica. From there you can change to 'Riacho Doce-Trapiche', 'Ipioca' or 'Mirante' buses for Riacho Doce and Ipioca. These last 3 can also be caught in the centre on the seafront avenue below the Praça Sinimbu (US$0.50 to Riacho Doce). To return take any of these options, or take a bus marked 'Shopping Center' and change there for 'Jardim Vaticana' bus, which goes through Pajuçara.

Maceió orientation

To Cruz das Almas, Jacarecica, Riacho Doce & Ipioca

Related map
A Maceió centre,
page 484

Not to scale

■ **Sleeping**
1 Buon Giorno
2 Casa Grande da Praia & Hotels Sete Coqueiros & Velamar
3 Enseada
4 Othon Pajuçara
5 Tambaqui Praia

Recife & the Northeast Coast

Excursions

Twenty two kilometres south, by bus past Praia do Francês, is the attractive colonial town and former capital of Alagoas, **Marechal Deodoro** (*population* 28,215), which overlooks the Lagoa Manguaba. The 17th century **Convento de São Francisco**, Praça João XXIII, has a fine church (Santa Maria Magdalena) with a superb baroque wooden altarpiece, which has been badly damaged by termites. You can climb the church's tower for views, but if you want to take photos you will have to collect your camera from the baggage store at the entrance. Adjoining it is the **Museu de Arte Sacra**. ■ *Monday-Friday 0900-1300, US$0.30, guided tours available, payment at your discretion.* Also open to visitors is the **Igreja Matriz de Nossa Senhora da Conceição** (1783). Remains of other 18th century churches include Nossa Senhora do Rosário, do Amparo and the Convento do Carmo.

The town is the birthplace of Marechal Deodoro da Fonseca, founder of the Republic; the modest house where he was born is on the Rua Marechal Deodoro, close to the waterfront. ■ *Monday-Saturday, 0800-1700, Sunday 0800-1200, free.*

The *Restaurant São Roque* is simple but good. Good local lacework can be bought. **NB** Schistosomiasis is present in the lagoon.

On a day's excursion, it is easy to visit the town, then spend some time at beautiful **Praia do Francês**. The northern half of the beach is protected by a reef, the southern half is open to the surf. Along the beach there are many *barracas* and bars selling drinks and seafood; try *agulhas fritas*.

To Northern Beaches

Sleeping and eating **A** *Cumaru*, T260-1110, three-star, good. **A** *Pousada Le Baron*, Av Caravelas, T2601165. On the road from the beach to the highway, good. **B** *Pousada Bougainville e Restaurant Chez Patrick*, T2601251. A/c, TV, pool, seafood and international cooking, very nice. **C** *O Pescador*, T2316959. Restaurant, beach huts, chalets with fridge, TV, 40 metres from Praia do Frances beach, T2601306 for information. Eating places include *Panela Mágica*. Recommended.

Further out from Maceió is the beach of **Barra de São Miguel**, entirely protected by the reef. It gets crowded at weekends. You can make excursions to other beaches. Several good, cheap *barracas* serve food and drink (*da Amizade*, recommended). Carnival here has a good reputation. At the *Village Barra Hotel* (**A**), R Sen Arnon de Mello, T2721207, is a pool, restaurant, excursions run. The *Pousada da Barra* is good.

Sleeping

■ *on map, page 482*
Price codes: see inside front cover
There are many hotels on Praia Pajuçara, mostly along Av Dr Antônio Gouveia and R Jangadeiros Alagoanos

AL *Enseada*, Av A Gouveia 171, T2314726, F2315394, enseada@vircom.com.br. Recommended. **AL** *Pajuçara Othon*, R Jangadeiros Alagoanos 1292, T3276200, F2315499. **AL** *Sete Coqueiros*, Av A Gouveia 1335, T2318583, F2317467. 3-star, a/c, TV, phone, popular restaurant, pool. Next door is the smaller **A** *Velamar*, No 1359, T3275488, F2316849. A/c, TV, fridge, safes in rooms.

There are many good *pousadas* on R Jangadeiros Alagoanos, 1 block back from the beach (it can be hard to find a room during the December-March holiday season, when prices go up): **A** *Laguna Praia*, No 1231, T2316180. Highly recommended. **A** *Maceió Praia*, No 3, T2316391. Highly recommended. **A** *Pousada Sete Coqueteiros*, No 123, T2315877. Recommended. **A** *Verde Mar*, No 1, T2312669. A/c, hot water, TV, very good. **B** *Buongiorno*, No 1437, T2317577, F2312168. A/c, fridge, English-speaking owner, helpful. **C** *Casa Grande da Praia*, No 1528, T2313332. A/c, TV, cheaper without. Recommended. *Amazona*, No 1095. Great breakfast. **C** *Costa Verde*, No 429, T2314745. Bath, fan, good family atmosphere, English, German spoken, rooms on first floor are best. **C** *Pousada Maramar*, No 34. Bright, some rooms with sea view, exchange library. **C** *Pousada Quinta Pruma*, No 597, T2316065. **C** *Pousada Shangri-La*, Antônio de Mendonça 1089, T2313773. Safe. **D** *Pousada Saveiro*, No 805. A/c, bath, TV, clean, simple, good value, cheaper without a/c. *Mandacaru*, Almte Maranenhas 85, 2 corners from the beach. Safe, good value.

Ponta Verde beach L *Tambaqui Praia*, R Eng Mário de Gusmão 176, T2310202. A/c, TV, phone, restaurant. **B** *Dos Corais*, R H Guimarães 80. Helpful. **B** *Hotel do Mar*, Av R Kennedy 1447, T2313171. Good. **C** *Baleia Azul*, Av Sandoval Arroxeias 822. A/c, fridge, TV. **C** *Sol de Verão*, R Eng Mário do Gusmão 153, **D** in small rooms without bath. **C** *Pousada Bela Vista*, Av Eng Mário de Gusmão 1260, T2318337. Well situated, excellent breakfast, a/c, TV. Recommended.

Further from the centre, **L** *Matsubara*, on Cruz das Almas beach, Av Brig Eduardo Gomes 1551, T2353000, F2351660. Pool, tennis, all facilities. Recommended. **C** *Hospedaria de Turismo Costa Azul*, Av João Davino and Manoel Gonçalves Filho 280, T2316281. Shower, fan, English spoken, discounts for stays over a week. **C** *Pousada Cavalo Marinho*, R da Praia 55, Riacho Doce (15 km from the centre), facing the sea, T2351247, F2353260. Use of bicycle, canoes and body boards included, hot showers, German and English spoken, tropical breakfasts, Swiss owner. Very highly recommended (nearby is *Lua Cheia*, good food and live music at night).

Maceió centre

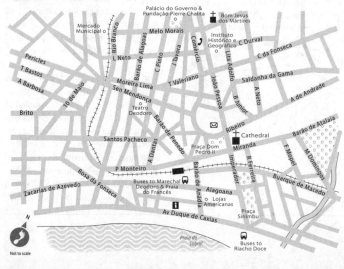

Centre B *Beiriz*, R João Pessoa 290, T2211080, F2233455. Comfortable, pool. **C** *Parque*, Praça Dom Pedro II 73, T2219099. A/c. **C** *Pousada Sol e Mar*, Av Rosa da Fonseca, T2212615. Helpful owners, safe. Recommended. **D** *Golf*, R Prof Domingos Moeda 38A (near the Cathedral). Clean. Cheap hotels (mostly without windows) in R Barão de Atalaia.

Youth hostels *Nossa Casa*, R Pref Abdon Arroxelas 327, Ponta Verde, T2312246. IYHA. *Pajuçara*, R Quintino Bocaiúva 63, Pajuçara, T2310631. *Stella Maris*, Av Des Valente de Lima 209, Mangabeiras, T3252217. All require reservations December-February, July and August.

Camping There is a *Camping Clube do Brasil* site on Jacarecica beach, T2353600. A 15-minute taxi drive from the town centre. *Camping Pajuçara*, Largo da Vitória 211, T2317561. Clean, safe, food for sale. Recommended.

Eating *Spettus*, Av R Kennedy 1911, Ponta Verde, *churrascaria rodízio*. *Ao Lagostão*, Av Duque de Caxias 1348. Seafood, fixed price (expensive) menu. *Pizzeria Sorrisa*, Av Alagoana and J Pessoa Imperador. Very cheap and good food, popular with Brazilians. *Bar das Ostras*, R Cruzeiro do Sul 487, Vergel do Lago. Expensive but good. **Vegetarian**: *O Natural*, R Libertadora Alagoana (R da Praia) 112. *Nativa*, Osvaldo Sarmento 56. Good views. Many good bars and restaurants in Pajuçara: recommended places on Av Antônio Gouveia are: *Paraíso*, No 631, vegetarian, open late. *O Dragão*, No 21, Chinese. *Comes e Bebes*, No 981, Italian and Arabic, good, takeaway service. *Tempeiro Paulista*, No 1103, regional food, good service, cheap. *Massarella*, Jangadeiras Alagoanas 1255, Italian, small, good. *Mello's Bar*, R Epaminondas Gracindo 194, excellent food and value.

The beaches for 5 km, from the beginning of Pajuçara to Cruz das Almas in the north, are lined with *barracas* (thatched bars) providing music, snacks and meals until midnight (later at weekends). Vendors on the beach sell beer and food during the day; clean and safe. There are many other bars and *barracas* at Ponto da Barra, on the lagoon side of the city.

Local specialities include oysters, *pitu*, a crayfish (now becoming scarce), and *sururu*, a kind of cockle. Local ice cream, *Shups*, is recommended.

Bars & nightclubs
These are relaxed & varied

Popular *barracas* are **Bar Lampião** (or *Tropical*) and **Ipaneminha** on Pajuçara (Brazilian pop), and **Fellini** on Ponta Verde (varies: good blues and jazz). There are nightclubs to suit most tastes. *Calabar*, in Pajuçara, for *forró* and *lambada*, *Lambadão* at Cruz das Almas (excellent *lambada*, weekends only). *Bar Chapéu de Couro*, José Carneiro 338, Ponto da Barra, is a popular music bar for young people.

Entertainment **Cinema** *Cinema São Luiz*, R do Comércio, in the centre. *Arte 1 and 2*, Pajuçara and Iguatemi shopping centres. **Theatre** *Teatro Deodoro*, Praça Mcal Deodoro, in the centre.

Festivals 27 August: *Nossa Senhora dos Prazeres*; 16 September: *Freedom of Alagoas*; 8 December: *Nossa Senhora da Conceição*; 15 December: *Maceiofest*, "a great street party with *trios elêctricos*"; *Christmas Eve*; *New Year's Eve*, half-day.

Transport
See also Ins & outs, page 481

Local Car hire: *Localiza*, Av Alvaro Otacilio 6445, Jatiuca, T3256565/6553. *Rotacar*, R Quintino Bocauiva 123, Pajucara, T3273388.

Buses: the 'Ponte Verde/Jacintinho' bus runs via Pajuçara from the centre to the rodoviária, also take 'Circular' bus (25 minutes Pajuçara to rodoviária, the stop in Pajuçara is opposite the petrol station by Bompreço supermarket); 'Feitosa' also goes to the rodoviária, by a different route. See also **Beaches**, above. Buses and kombis to Marechal Deodoro, Praia do Francês and Barra de São Miguel leave from R Barão de Anádia, outside the ferroviária, opposite *Lojas Americanas*: bus US$0.75, kombi US$1 to Marechal Deodoro, 30 minutes, calling at Praia do Francês in each direction. Last bus back from Praia do Francês to Maceió at 1800.

Recife & the Northeast Coast

Trains: 5 trains a day, Monday-Saturday, from 0630-1855 to Rio Largo (35 km, US$0.25), via Fernão Velho, Satuba and Utinga. Worth taking in one direction at least since it passes the Lagoa Mundaú, through places where buses do not go.

Long distance   Air: airport, BR-101, 20 km north, T3221300. Flights to Aracaju, Recife, Rio de Janeiro, Salvador and São Paulo. Taxi about US$25. Buses to airport from near *Hotel Beiriz*, R João Pessoa 290 or in front of the Ferroviária, signed 'Rio Largo'; alight at Tabuleiro dos Martins, then 7-8 minutes walk to the airport, bus fare US$0.75.

Buses: the rodoviária is on a hill with good views and cool breezes. Bus to **Recife**, 10 a day, 3½ hours express (more scenic coastal route, 5 hours), US$9. To **Aracaju**, US$9, 5 hours (potholed road). To **Salvador**, 10 hours, 4 a day, US$20 (*rápido* costs more). Buses to most large cities including Belém, Fortaleza, Brasília, Belo Horizonte (US$41), Rio (US$60.50) and São Paulo.

Directory   **Banks** Open 1000 to 1500. Good rates at *Banespa*. Cash against Mastercard at *Banorte*, R de Comércio, 306, Centro. **Communications** Post Office: R João Pessoa 57, Centro, 0700-2200. **Telephones:** R do Comércio 508, almost opposite *Bandepe*. There is a small post on Pajuçara beach, opposite the *Othon* hotel. Also at the rodoviária. **Embassies & consulates** *France*, T2352830. *Portugal*, T3364564. *Spain*, T2412516. **Hospitals & medical services** *Unimed*, Av Antonio Brandao 395, Farol, T2211177, used to be São Sebastião hospital. *Pediatria 24 horas*, R Durval Guimaraes 519, Ponta Verde, T2317742/7702. **Dentist:** *Pronto Socorro Odontologico de Maceio*, Av Pio XV11, Jatiuca, T3257534. **Laundry** *Lave-Sim*, R Jangadas Alagoanas 962, Pajuçara. *Washouse*, R Jangadas Alagoanas 698, Pajuçara. **Tour companies & travel agents** *Aeroturismo*, R Barão de Penedo 61, T3262020, F2214546, American Express representative. **Tourist offices** *Ematur* (*Empresa Alagoana de Turismo*), Av da Paz 2014, Centro, T2219465, F2218987, also at the airport and rodoviária (latter not always open). The office is helpful, has good maps and leaflets. The municipal tourist authority is *Emturma*, R Saldanha da Gama 71, Farol, T2234016; information post on Pajuçara beach, opposite *Hotel Solara*. The *Secretaria da Indústria, Comércio e do Turismo* has an office at Av Duque de Caxias 1108, centre, T2214480. **Voltage** 220 volts AC, 60 cycles.

Penedo

Population: 54,500
Phone code: 082
Colour map 2, grid C5

A more interesting crossing into Alagoas can be made by boat from **Neópolis** in Sergipe, to Penedo some 35 kilometres from the mouth of the Rio São Francisco.

Penedo is a charming town, with a nice waterfront park, Praça 12 de Abril, with stone walkways and walls. Originally the site of the Dutch Fort Maurits (built 1637, razed to the ground by the Portuguese), the colonial town stands on a promontory above the river. Among the colonial architecture, modern buildings such as the Associação Comercial and *Hotel São Francisco*, both on Avenida Floriano Peixoto, do not sit easily.

Sights   On the Praça Barão de Penedo is the neoclassical **Igreja Matriz** (closed to visitors) and the 18th-century **Casa da Aposentadoria** (1782). East and a little below this square is the Praça Rui Barbosa, on which are the **Convento de São Francisco** (1783 and later) and the church of **Santa Maria dos Anjos** (1660). As you enter, the altar on the right depicts God's eyes on the world, surrounded by the three races, one Indian, two negroes and the whites at the bottom. The church has fine *trompe-l'oeil* ceilings (1784). The convent is still in use. Guided tours are free.

The church of **Rosário dos Pretos** (1775-1816), on Praça Marechal Deodoro, is open to visitors as are **Nossa Senhora da Corrente** (1764), on Praça 12 de Abril, and **São Gonçalo Garcia** (1758-70) on Avenida Floriano Peixoto between 0800-1200, 1400-1700 weekdays only. Also on Avenida

Floriano Peixoto is the pink **Teatro 7 de Setembro** (No 81) of 1884. ■ *Weekdays 0800-1200, 1400-1730, Saturday morning only, closed Sunday.* Between it and the old covered market are fruit and vegetable stalls.

The **Casa de Penedo**, at Rua João Pessoa 126 (signs point the way up the hill from F Peixoto), displays photographs and books on, or by, local figures. ■ *T5512516; Tuesday-Sunday 0800-1800.*

Very few of the long two-masted sailing vessels that used to cruise on the river **River traffic** can be seen now, although there are plenty of smaller craft. Boats can be rented at the waterfront for excursions to the river islands, the mouth of the river and to beaches. Arrange boat trips with owners in Penedo, or in Piaçabuçu, 28 kilometres east. Boats go to the mouth of the São Francisco and out into the Atlantic (the currents can be tricky at the river mouth). Beaches in Sergipe (for example, Arambipe) or Alagoas (for example, Peba) can be reached by boat; the latter also by road. Either side of the river mouth are turtle nesting grounds which are protected. For information contact the **Fundação Pró-Tamar**, Reserva Biológica de Santa Isabel, CEP 49190-000, Pirambu, SE, T079-2761201, F2761217.

A *São Francisco*, Av Floriano Peixoto, T5512273, F5512274. Standard rooms have no **Sleeping** a/c, others have a/c, TV, fridge. Recommended except for poor restaurant. **B** *Pousada Colonial*, Praça 12 de Abril 21, T5512355, F5513099. *Luxo* and suite have phone, TV and fridge, suites have a/c, spacious, good cheap restaurant, front rooms with view of Rio São Francisco. **D** *Turista*, R Siqueira Campos 143, T5512237. With bath, fan, hot water. Recommended.

Forte da Rocheira, R da Rocheira (take either of the alleys running west off the hill **Eating** between Praças Barão de Penedo and 12 de Abril, turn right), T5513273. Good food, especially *ensopada de jacaré* (alligator stew). Continue along the cliff walkway to the riverside for *Churrascaria O Scala*, at the end of R 15 de Novembro.

Daily market on streets off Av Floriano Peixoto, good hammocks. Ceramics for sale **Shopping** outside Bompreço supermarket on Av Duque de Caxias.

Buses Salvador, 451 km (US$12-14, 6 hours, by daily bus at 0600, book in advance), **Transport** at same time for **Aracaju** (US$6); buses south are more frequent from Neópolis, 6 a day (0630-1800) to Aracaju, 2 hours, US$3.60. **Maceió**, 115 km, 5 buses a day in either direction, US$5.40-6.60, 3-4 hours. One bus to **São Paulo** daily, 2 a day to **Recife**. The Penedo rodoviária is on Av Duque de Caxias, behind Bompreço, little information; timetables are posted in *Pousada Colonial*.

Ferries Frequent launches for foot passengers and bicycles across the river to **Neópolis**, 25 minutes, US$0.50. The dock in Penedo is on Av Duque de Caxias, below Bompreço. The ferry makes 3 stops in Neópolis, the second is closest to the rodoviária (which is near the Clube Vila Nova, opposite the Texaco station). There is also a half-hourly car ferry (US$3, take care when driving on and off).

Banks Open 0830-1300. *Banco do Nordeste do Brasil*, on Av Floriano Peixoto. *Banco do Brasil* **Directory** and *Bradesco* on Av Duque de Caxias, opposite Bompreço supermarket. *Restaurant e Bar Lulu*, Praça 12 de Abril, will change cash if conditions suit the owner, fair rates. **Communications** Post Office: Av Floriano Peixoto, opposite *Hotel Imperial*. **Telephones:** On Barão de Penedo. **Tourist offices** In Casa da Aposentadoria, Praça Barão de Penedo (if open), T5512827, ext 23.

The slave state of Palmares

From the introduction of African slaves to northeast Brazil, fujões or runaways would disappear into the interior and set up villages or mocambos. Between the 1630s and the end of 17th century the mocambos prospered – especially during times of crisis such as the Dutch invasion in 1630 – and together formed quilombos, free territories which accepted not only runaway slaves but also freed ones and whites who had fallen out with the re-established Portuguese colony. The most famous of these quilombos, established in what is now the state of Alagoas, was called Palmares after the large number of palm trees in the area. It consisted of 30,000 people living in several mocambos in an area of 17,000 square miles (44,000 square kilometres). According to reports from Bartholomeus Lintz, the leader of a Dutch expedition in 1640, the largest settlement in Palmares had 220 buildings, a church, four smithies and a meeting house.

The political and social structures were very similar to those found in West Africa, and although Catholicism was practised, so was polyandry, mainly due to the lack of women in the republic. The leader of Palmares was one Ganga-Zumba who was revered like a king. But it appears he was killed by his followers in 1680 after making some concessions to the Portuguese two years earlier; he was succeeded by the republic's brave military commander, Zumbi. The existence of Palmares was a constant thorn in the side of Portuguese domination of Brazil and dozens of attempts were made to destroy it. However, Zumbi managed to defend the republic until it was finally smashed by the Portuguese with bandeirante help in 1695. Zumbi was killed and his decapitated head was put on display in Recife to discourage other potential runaways and prove that he was not immortal as his followers believed. He is still remembered every year on 20 November, Brazil's Black Conciousness Day. He has also become a popular theme at Carnival time.

The site of the Palmares Republic is situated on the Serra da Barriga, close to modern União do Palmares in Alagoas state, reached by driving north out of Maceió on the BR-101, turning left after Messias and driving for 40 kilometres along a paved road. There is one hotel, Parque Hotel dos Quilombos, T2811135, on the BR-104 towards Recife, TV, a/c, fridge, restaurant.

North of Maceió

There are many interesting stopping points along the coast between Maceió and Recife. At **Paripueira**, 40 minutes bus ride from Maceió (Rodoviária), the beach is busy only during high season. As at Pajuçara (see above), low tide leaves lots of natural swimming pools.

Barra de Santo Antônio Forty five kilometres north is this busy fishing village, with a palm fringed beach on a narrow peninsula, a canoe ride away. Boats also go to the Ilha da Croa. The beaches nearby are beautiful: to the south, near the village of Santa Luzia, are Tabuba and Sonho Verde. To the north is Carro Quebrado, from which you can take a buggy to Pedra do Cebola, or further to Praia do Morro, just before the mouth of the Rio Camaragibe.

Sleeping and eating D *São Geraldo*, simple, very clean, restaurant. *Pousada Buongiorno* has 6 modest rooms to rent in a farmhouse, bathrooms but no electricity, many fruit trees (in Maceió T2317577, F2312168). Accommodation can be found through local people. *Peixada da Rita*, try prawns with coconut sauce. Recommended for local seafood. *Estrela Azul*, more expensive, good, popular with tourists.

Beyond Barra do Camaragibe, a coastal road, unpaved in parts, runs to the Pernambuco border and São José da Coroa Grande. The main highway, BR-101, heads inland from Maceió before crossing the state border to Palmares.

Pernambuco

This state, which once produced all of the world's sugar, today offers a variety of attractions from beaches, traditional culture, colonial cities and museums. Recife, the state capital, is the main industrial and commercial centre with an international airport. Olinda offers its colonial elegance and imposing churches. Towns such as Caruaru in the agreste, *the region between the coast and the Sertão have distinctive regional fairs selling clay, straw and leather handicrafts. The archipelago of Fernando de Noronha (reached by daily flights) is rich in nature and a must for diving and other watersports. Pernambuco is saturated in music, from the rustic forms of forró to the urban mixes of maracatu with modern pop which spawned bands that have influenced mainstream Brazilian music and fortified Northeastern pride. Carnival here is distinctive, mixing the party atmosphere with African cultural processions, all set to the backdrop of breathtaking colonial architecture.*

Background

When King João III divided Brazil into captaincies, Pernambuco was given to **History** the donatory Duarte Coelho. He was keen to make his territory succeed, but he and his two sons who followed him had to struggle to hold onto their possession in the face of constant Indian opposition. Sugar estates were created as the forests were cleared and Indians enslaved to work them. The colony prospered, its two main towns being Olinda and Igaraçu. By the end of the 16th century, Pernambuco was the most profitable of the Portuguese captaincies, with more sugar *engenhos* than anywhere else, a sizeable population of colonists, its frontiers largely won from the Indians such as the Caeté, Tobajara and Potiguar, and French influence removed. It was thus a rich prize for the Dutch when they took possession of northeastern Brazil during the years that Portugal was being ruled by Spain. One of the main theatres of the vicious fighting between the Dutch, the Portuguese and each one's Indian allies was Recife.

By the middle of the 17th century, Brazil's dominance in world sugar production was undermined by the new plantations of France and England in their Caribbean colonies, but Pernambuco was able to maintain much of its economic importance through the additional cultivation of cotton. Some colonists in the province, dissatisfied with subordination to Rio de Janeiro and Lisbon, proclaimed an independent Pernambuco in 1817, but it lasted no more than 2½ months. The movement did, however, point the way for Pernambuco's swift acceptance of the declaration of independence in 1822. Not everyone was in favour, though. In 1832, following a brief military uprising in favour of the restoration of Dom Pedro I to the throne, a popular rebellion with the same aim fought against the new empire for three years. Known as the **War of the Cabanos**, it involved members of all levels of society, from landowners to slaves. The rebels' leader was Vicente Ferreira de Paula and the Cabanos had the support of merchants in Recife and politicians in Rio de

Janeiro who wanted to see Dom Pedro I back in control. The abdicated king's death in 1834 helped persuade many Cabanos to give in, but the last of the rebels held out in the forests against the government forces until 1835.

Through much of the 19th century, political debate centred around differences between liberals and conservatives, but by the 1870s the Republican movement was gaining adherents in Pernambuco. There was strong resentment for what was seen as neglect for the Northeast by the administration in Rio. Nevertheless, the change to the Brazilian Republic did not halt the shift of economic and political power more and more into the pockets and hands of São Paulo and Minas Gerais. The value of the commodity exports upon which Pernambuco had been built, sugar and cotton, had dwindled to a mere fraction of what they once were by the beginning of the 20th century. The loss of economic power, together with declining political influence, meant that Pernambuco's leaders had to forge alliances with other northeastern states to exert any power at a federal level. This, however, has not been an easy task throughout the 20th century.

Geography & climate The population is about 7,520,000. Pernambuco's climate is humid tropical and the geography is, like the other states on Brazil's northeastern part, divided into three parts, the *Zona da Mata/Litoral*, the *Agreste* and the *Sertão*. The *Litoral* is the area of large plantations, mostly sugar, and the few remaining pockets of *mata atlântica*; the *sertão* is characterized by drought-resistant plants such as *jurema, xique-xique, madacaru, macambira, umburana* and *marmeleiro*. The *agreste* is the transitional zone between these two. In the *agreste*, only Caruaru has any significant population. An important factor in this region is the presence of the Rio São Francisco, which forms the southern border of Pernambuco with Bahia.

Recife

Population: 1,350,000
Phone code: 081
Colour map 2, grid B6

Recife is one of the principal cities of the Northeast and a popular tourist destination thanks to its beaches, historical monuments and international airport. The culture and in its close neighbour Olinda is quite distinct, and spending carnival here is a good choice.

Ins and outs

Getting there
See also Transport, page 500

Air International and domestic flights arrive at Guararapes airport, 12 km from the city. Bus to airport, No 52, US$0.60. Taxis at the airport charge US$5 to Boa Viagem. There is a bank desk before customs which gives much the same rate for dollars as the moneychangers in the lobby.

Buses Long distance buses arrive at the Terminal Integrado dos Passageiros, or TIP (pronounced 'chippy'), 12 km outside the city. There is a 30 minute metrô connection to the central railway station. The train to the centre is much quicker than the bus.

Getting around

Buses City buses cost US$0.30-0.60; they are clearly marked and run frequently until about 2230. Many central bus stops have boards showing routes. On buses, especially at night, look out for landmarks as street names are written small and are hard to see. Integrated bus-metrô (see **Trains** below) routes and tickets (US$1) are explained in a leaflet issued by CBTU Metrorec, T2515256. See below for buses to Olinda and other destinations outside the city. Trolleybuses run in the city centre. Taxis are plentiful; fares double on Sunday.

Trains Commuter services, known as the **Metrô** but not underground, leave from the central station; they have been extended to serve the rodoviária (frequent trains, 0500-2300, US$0.30 single, US$0.50 return). If going to Boa Viagem from the rodoviária, get off the Metrô at Joanna Bezerra (20 minutes from the rodoviária) and take a bus or taxi (US$10) from there.

About 285 kilometres north of Maceió and 839 kilometres north of Salvador is the state capital Recife, founded on reclaimed land by the Dutch prince Maurice of Nassau in 1637 after his troops had burnt Olinda, the original capital. The city centre consists of three portions: Recife proper, Santo Antônio and São José, and Boa Vista and Santo Amaro. The first two are on islands formed by the rivers Capibaribe, Beberibe and Pina, while the third is made into an island by the Canal Tacaruna, which separates it from the mainland. The centre is always very busy by day; the crowds and the narrow streets, especially in the Santo Antônio district, can make it a confusing city to walk around. Recife has the main dock area, with commercial buildings associated with it. South of the centre is the residential and beach district of Boa Viagem, reached by bridge across the Bacia do Pina. Olinda, the old capital, is only seven kilometres to the north (see page 503).

Sights

Forte do Brum (built by the Dutch in 1629) is an army museum. ■ *Tuesday-Friday 0900-1600, Saturday-Sunday 1400-1600, donation optional.* **Forte das Cinco Pontas** was built by the Dutch in 1630 and altered by the Portuguese in 1677. The two forts jointly controlled access to the port at the northern and southern entrances respectively. Within Forte das Cinco Pontas is the **Museu da Cidade do Recife**, which houses a cartographic history of the settlement of Recife. ■ *Monday-Friday 0900-1800, Saturday-Sunday 1300-1700, US$0.50 donation preferred.*

The first Brazilian printing press was installed in 1706 and Recife claims to publish the oldest daily newspaper in South America, *Diário de Pernambuco*, founded 1825 (but now accessible on the Internet). The building is on the Praça da Independência.

The artists' and intellectuals' quarter is based on the **Pátio de São Pedro**, the square round São Pedro dos Clérigos. Sporadic folk music and poetry shows are given in the square on Friday, Saturday and Sunday evenings, and there are pleasant little restaurants, with good atmosphere, at nos 44, 46 and 47, and No 20 *Caldeira de Cana e Petisqueira Banguê*. The square is an excellent shopping centre for typical northeastern craftware; clay figurines are cheapest in Recife.

Not far away off Avenida Guararapes, two blocks from the central post office, is the **Praça do Sebo**, where the city's second-hand booksellers concentrate; this Mercado de Livros Usados is off the Rua da Roda, behind the Edifício Santo Albino, near the corner of Avenida Guararapes and Rua Dantas Barreto. You can also visit the city markets in the São José and Santa Rita sections.

The former municipal prison has now been made into the **Casa da**

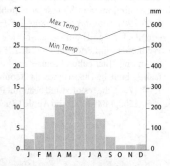

Climate: Recife

The Dutch in Brazil

At the beginning of the 17th century, the Dutch were looking for ways of expanding their influence on the western hemisphere. It seemed to them that controlling land in Brazil would be the ideal place to start. Not only would they obtain rich, sugar-producing territory, they would also have a good base from which to raid the treasure fleets of Spain and eventually attack the Spanish colonies of Peru and Mexico. Moreover, the Portuguese crown, nominal overlord of Brazil, was in the power of Spain, which itself was too busy protecting its own far-flung colonies to pay much attention to defending Brazil.

In 1624, the Dutch captured Bahia, but the next year they lost it. Five years later (1630) they turned their attention to Olinda and Recife, successfully took them and, by 1634, had control of a stretch of the coast from Rio Grande do Norte to Cabo de Santo Agostinho. The Dutch position was strengthened by the arrival in 1637 of Johan Maurits of Nassau-Siegen (1604-79) as governor. He fell in love with Brazil, and his desire to win the trust of the Indians and his tolerance towards Jews (and Catholics) was markedly different from that of most of the Portuguese colonists. Johan Maurits' job, however, was military. With Bahia still in Portuguese hands, there was constant tension with Pernambuco. He attacked Salvador in 1638, but failed. In the following year, a Spanish armada was sent to attack the Dutch, but the two sides did not engage until 1640, after which the Spanish gave up all thought of attacking Recife.

When the Portuguese threw the Spanish out of Lisbon late in 1640, the Portuguese in Brazil were delighted. In the following year, the Portuguese and Dutch signed a truce, covering Europe, Africa, the East Indies and Brazil, but ratification was slow in coming, during which time the Dutch and Portuguese in Brazil were engaged in a bitter war. Johan Maurits extended Dutch control to São Luís do Maranhão in 1641, but he was not able to capitalize on the possession. In 1644 he returned to Holland, partly because his rule was economically unviable. The West India Company, which controlled a large part of the trade of Brazil, resented the cost of supporting Recife. Too much sugar was being cultivated (trade which was handled by free traders, not the Company), too little other produce was being grown to feed the city and Johan Maurits had failed to secure the countryside. A year after his departure, fighting intensified and, because the Dutch had no real power base outside their main cities, the Portuguese gradually won back their territory. Dutch supremacy at sea and their heavily defended forts meant that neither side could win outright victory and the war dragged on until 1654. By this time, the Dutch were also at war with England, which weakened their navy in Brazilian waters. They surrendered on 26 January 1654. The last real threat to Portuguese rule in Brazil was over.

Cultura, with many cells converted into art or souvenir shops and with areas for exhibitions and shows (also public conveniences). ■ *Monday-Friday 0900-1900, Saturday 0900-1800, Sunday 0900-1400.* Local dances such as the ciranda, forró and bumba-meu-boi are held as tourist attractions on Monday, Wednesday and Friday at 1700. ■ *T2842850 to check in advance.*

Among other cultural centres are Recife's three traditional **theatres: Santa Isabel**, built in 1850 (Praça da República, open to visitors Monday-Friday 1300-1700), the restored and beautiful **Parque** (Rua do Hospício 81, Boa Vista, 0800-1200, 1400-1800) and **Apolo** (Rua do Apolo 121, 0800-1200, 1400-1700).

The best churches are **Santo Antônio do Convento de São Francisco** (1606), which has beautiful Portuguese tiles, in the Rua do Imperador, and adjoining it the finest sight of all, the **Capela Dourada**, or Golden Chapel (1697). ■ *Daily 0800-1130: US$0.25, no flash photography; entry through the Museu Franciscano de Arte Sacra, US$1.*

São Pedro dos Clérigos in São José district (1782) should be seen for its façade, its fine wood sculpture and a splendid *trompe-l'oeil* ceiling. ■ *Daily 0800-1130 and 1400-1600.* **Nossa Senhora da Conceição dos Militares**, Rua Nova 309 (1771), has a grand ceiling and a large 18th century primitive mural of the battle of Guararapes. There is a museum next door. ■ *Daily 0700-1600 and 1700-1900.*

Other important churches to be seen are **Santo Antônio** (1753-91), in Praça da Independência, rebuilt in 1864 (daily 0800-1200 and Monday-Friday 1400-1800, Sunday 1700-1900); **Nossa Senhora do Carmo**, Praça do Carmo (1663) (Monday-Friday 0800-1200 and 1400-2000, Saturday-Sunday 0600-1200); **Madre de Deus** (1715), in the street of that name in the district of Recife, with a splendid high altar, and sacristy (daily 0800-1100 and 1400-1600); the **Pilar Church** (1680), Rua do Pilar, Recife district; the **Divino Espírito Santo** (1689), the original church of the Jesuits, Praça 17 in Santo Antônio district (Monday-Friday 0800-1630, Saturday 0800-1400, Sunday 1000-1200); **São José do Ribamar** (19th century), in São José (Thursdays only). There are many others.

Fourteen kilometres south of the city, a little beyond Boa Viagem and the airport, on Guararapes Hill, is the historic church of **Nossa Senhora dos Prazeres**. ■ *Tuesday to Friday 0800-1200 and 1400-1700, Saturday 0800-1200, closed to tourists on Sundays.* It was here, in 1648-49, that two Brazilian victories led to the end of the 30-year Dutch occupation of the Northeast in 1654. The church was built by the Brazilian commander in 1656 to fulfil a vow. Boa Viagem's own fine church dates from 1707.

Churches
Many of them are closed to visitors on Sunday because of services

The **Museu do Homem do Nordeste**, Avenida 17 de Agosto 2223, Casa Forte, comprises the **Museu de Arte Popular**, containing ceramic figurines (including some by Mestre Alino and Zé Caboclo); the **Museu do Açúcar**, on the history and technology of sugar production, with models of colonial mills, collections of antique sugar bowls and much else; the **Museu de Antropologia**, the **Nabuco Museum** (at No 1865) and the modern museum of popular remedies, **Farmacopéia Popular**. ■ *Tuesday-Friday 1100-1700, Saturday-Sunday 1300-1700, T4415500, entry US$1.*

Museums

Take the 'Dois Irmãos' bus (check that it's the correct one, with 'Rui Barbosa' posted in window, as there are two) from outside the Banorte building near the post office on Guararapes, 30 minutes' ride, 10 kilometres outside the city to the **zoo** (US$0.20, not very good) and **botanical gardens**; it passes the museum complex, and together with the zoo they make a pleasant day's outing. It is easier to get to the museum complex by taxi.

The **Museu do Estado**, Avenida Rui Barbosa 960, Graças, has excellent paintings by the 19th century landscape painter, Teles Júnior. ■ *Tuesday-Friday 0900-1800, Saturday-Sunday 1400-1800.* **Museu do Trem**, Praça Visconde de Mauá, is small but interesting, especially the Henschel locomotive. ■ *Tuesday-Friday 0900-1200, 1400-1700, Saturday 0900-1200, Sunday 1400-1700.* **Museu de Imagem e Som**, on the Rua da Aurora 379, Boa Vista, has exhibitions of photographs, films and temporary shows. ■ *Monday-Friday 0900-1700.*

Recife orientation

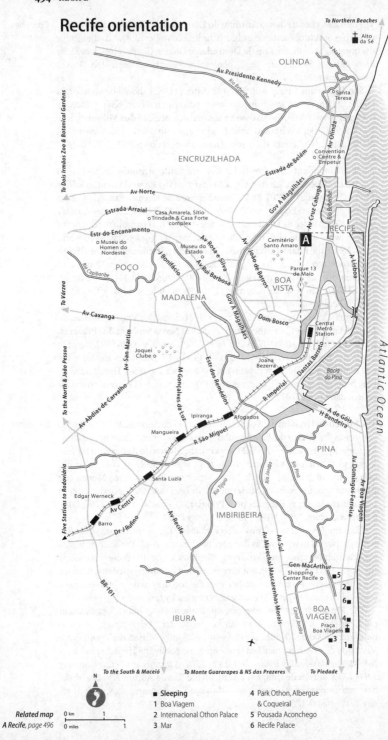

To Northern Beaches

Alto da Sé

J Nabuco

OLINDA

Av Presidente Kennedy

Rio Beberibe

Santa Teresa

Av Olinda

ENCRUZILHADA

Estrada de Belém

Gov A Magalhães

Av Cruz Cabugá

Rio Beberibe

RECIFE

Convention Centre & Empetur

To Dois Irmãos Zoo & Botanical Gardens

Av Norte

Estrada Arraial

Casa Amarela, Sítio o Trindade & Casa Forte complex

Estr do Encanamento

o Museu do Homen do Nordeste

Av Rosa e Silva

Av João de Barros

Cemitério Santo Amaro

A

A Lisboa

Museu do Estado

Av Rui Barbosa

Parque 13 de Maio

POÇO

J Bonifácio

Rio Capibaribe

To Várzea

MADALENA

BOA VISTA

Av Caxanga

Gov A Magalhães

Dom Bosco

Central Metrô Station

Joquei Clube o

Av San Martim

Estr dos Remédios

Joana Bezerra

Dantas Barreto

Atlantic Ocean

Bacia do Pina

To the North & João Pessoa

M Gonçalves da Luz

R Imperial

Av Abdias de Carvalho

Ipiranga

Afogados

A de Góis H Bandeira

Mangueira

R São Miguel

PINA

Av Domingos Ferreira

Av Boa Viagem

Santa Luzia

Rio Tijipó

Rio Jordão

Rio Pina

Edgar Werneck

Av Central

Av Recife

Five Stations to Rodoviária

Barro

Dr J Rufino

IMBIRIBEIRA

Rio Jordão

BR 101

Av Sul

Av Marechal Mascarenhas Morais

Canal Jordão

Gen MacArthur

Shopping Center Recife o

5

IBURA

BOA VIAGEM

2
6
4

Praça Boa Viagem

3   1

To the South & Maceió

To Monte Guararapes & NS das Prazeres

To Piedade

N

0 km   1
0 miles   1

■ Sleeping
1 Boa Viagem
2 Internacional Othon Palace
3 Mar

4 Park Othon, Albergue
  & Coqueiral
5 Pousada Aconchego
6 Recife Palace

Boa Viagem

This is the main residential and hotel quarter. The eight kilometre promenade commands a striking view of the Atlantic, but the beach is crowded at weekends and not very clean. During the January breeding season, sharks come close to the shore. You can go fishing on *jangadas* at Boa Viagem with a fisherman. The main *praça* has a good market on Saturday, with *forró* dancing.

Buses To get there by bus from the centre, take any marked 'Boa Viagem'; from Nossa Senhora do Carmo, take buses marked 'Piedade', 'Candeias' or 'Aeroporto' – they go on Avenida Domingos Ferreira, two blocks parallel to the beach, all the way to Praça Boa Viagem (at Avenida Boa Viagem 500). Back to the centre take buses marked 'CDU' or 'Setubal' from Avenida Domingos Ferreira.

Excursions

Any bus going south of Boa Viagem passes the **Ilha do Amor**; ask a fisherman to row you out to it and collect you at a set time, US$5. Walk across the island (10 minutes) to the Atlantic side for a fine, open, uncrowded beach. Take care here as it is a little isolated. For beaches south of Recife, see below.

    Carpina (*population* 55,000), 63 kilometres from Recife, is well known for its carnival and for the traditional **Epiphany festival** early in January, and also for the carpets made in the nearby village of Lagoa do Carro. There is a historical museum, several hotels (**B**) and restaurants.

    Tracunhaém (*population* 12,500) is a peaceful town where fine ceramics are made; there are two interesting early 19th century churches. It is just north of Carpina, on to the road to Nazaré da Mata.

Essentials

Hotels in the Santa Rita area are not recommended as this area is dangerous at night. Many hotels sell 5-day Carnival packages (at high prices), which you must take regardless of the length of time you wish to stay. Shop around.

    Centre A *Recife Plaza*, R da Aurora 225, T2311200. Boa Vista, 3-star, overlooking the Rio Capibaribe, every comfort. Highly recommended, fine restaurant (very popular at lunchtime). **B** *4 de Outubro*, R Floriano Peixoto 141, Santo Antônio, T4244477, F4242598. Four standards of room, hot water, TV, phone, a/c. **C** *Hotel Park 13 de Mayo* (not the same as Hotel Parque nearby, both opposite park), R do Hospicio. Under new management, safe, OK. **D** *América*, Praça Maciel Pinheiro 48, Boa Vista, T2211300. Two-star, with a/c (cheaper without), front rooms pleasanter, quiet. **D** *Interlaine*, R do Hospício 186, T4232941. Good value in town centre. Highly recommended. **D** *Lido*, R do Riachuelo 547, T2224660. Good breakfast, hot water. Recommended. **D** *Nassau*, Largo do Rosário 253, T2243977. Hot showers, but a bit noisy (breakfast only, served on seventh floor, with a balcony overlooking the city). **D** *Recife*, R do Imperador 310, T2240799. Cheaper without bath, central, OK but grubby. **E** *Brasiliense*, R do Hospício 179. Good value, clean, safe, breakfast, TV.

    Boa Viagem AL *Mar*, near the beach at R Barão de Souza Leão 451, T4624444, F4624445. Five-star. **AL** *Recife Palace*, Av Boa Viagem 4070, T4656688, F4656767. Five-star. Two *Othon* hotels: **A** *Praia*, Av Boa Viagem 9, T4653722, F4651500 and *Park*, R dos Navegantes 9, T/F4654666. **A** *Savaroni*, Av Boa Viagem 3772, T4654299, F3264900. Four-star, good, pool. **A** *Do Sol*, Av Boa Viagem 978, T4654299, F4655278. Four-star. **A** *Recife Monte*, corner of R Petrolina and R dos Navegantes 363, T4657422, F4658406. Good value. Recommended. **B** *Aguamar Praia*, R dos Navegantes 492, T3264317, F3264604. A/c, TV, safe, good breakfast. **B** *Arcada*, Av Conselheiro Aguiar 3500,

Sleeping
■ *on map*
Price codes: see inside front cover
For Olinda hotels, see page 504

T/F4656499. Fondue restaurant and travel agency with exchange. **B** *Setúbal*, R Setúbal 932, T3414116. Helpful, good breakfast. **B** *Uzi Praia*, Av Conselheiro Aguiar 942, T3252741. A/c. Recommended. **C** *Aconchego*, Félix de Brito 382, T3262989, F3268059.

Recife

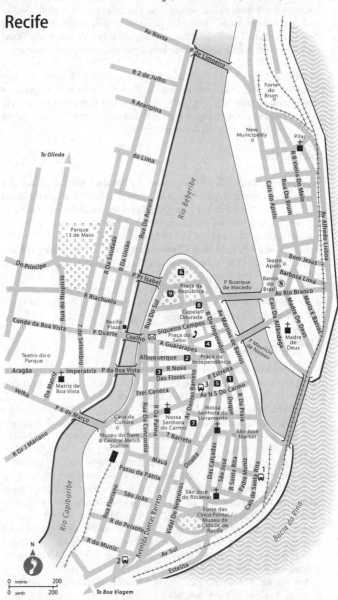

1 Church of Espírito Santo
2 Church of Santo Antônio
3 Conceição dos Militares
4 Diário de Pernambuco
5 Nossa Senhora do
   Rosário dos Pretos
6 Palácio do Campo das

Princesas (Governor's Palace)
7 Pátio de São Pedro
   & São Pedro dos Clérigos
8 Santo Antônio do Convento
   de São Francisco
9 Teatro de Santo Isabel

🚌 Buses
1 To Itamaracá
   & Igarassu
2 To Porto da Galinhas
3 To Boa Viagem

Three levels of tariff, a/c, pleasant, swimming pool, good meals, safe is closed on Sunday and in evening, English-speaking owner, will collect you from the airport. **C** *Casa Grande e Senzala*, Av Conselheiro Aguiar 5000, T/F3417646. Three-star. **C** *Praia Mar*, Av Boa Viagem 1660, T4653759. Small. Recommended. **C** *Coqueiral*, R Navegantes 43, T3265891. Dutch-owned (Dutch, English, French spoken), a/c, small. Recommended. **D** *Guest House Pousada*, Luis Marquês Teixeira 155, T3410559. A/c, secure, proprietor Ricardo Teixeira is a Sevagtur guide, helpful, English and German spoken. Recommended. **D** *Pousada da Julieta*, R Prof Jose Brandao 135, T3267860. **D** *Pousada da Praia*, Alcides Carneiro Leal 66, T3267085. A/c, fridge, TV, safe, rooms vary (some tiny), helpful. **D** *Solar da Tia Cléo*, R Joaquim Carneiro da Silva 48, T3261090, no sign outside. Fans, family atmosphere, fine garden, English spoken. Recommended.

Praia de Piedade L *Sheraton Petribu*, Av Bernardo Vieira de Melo 1624, at the end of Boa Viagem, on the beach, T4681288, F4681118. All services and excellent restaurant. Very high quality and recommended. **C** *Casa da Praia*, Av Beira Mar 1168, T4611414. On a quiet street, with garden, good breakfast, owner speaks French. Recommended.

Youth hostels D *Albergue Mandacaru*, R Maria Carolina 75, T3261964. Stores luggage, English and German spoken, good breakfast. Recommended. *Maracatus do Recife*, R Maria Carolina 185, T3261221, F3252645. *IYHA*, pool, clean, safe, friendly, membership not needed, good breakfast. Recommended. **E** *Albergue do Mar*, R dos Navegantes 81, T3262196. Good breakfast and atmosphere.

Camping *Paraíso Camping Clube*, Av Dantas Barreto 512, loja 503, T2243094. Can give information on camping throughout the state.

Private accommodation Paulo Bezerra de Mello, DHL, R do Riachuelo 201, T2212000. Rents an apartment for 3 at Boa Viagem. Recommended. During Carnival and for longer stays at other times, private individuals rent rooms and houses in Recife and Olinda; listings can be found in the *Diário de Pernambuco*, or ask around the streets of Olinda. This accommodation is generally cheaper, safer and quieter than hotels.

Be careful of eating the local small crabs, known as *guaiamum*; they live in the mangrove swamps which take the drainage from Recife's *mocambos* (shanty towns).

City centre *Leite* (lunches only), Praça Joaquim Nabuco 147/53 near Casa de Cultura. Old and famous, good service, smart (another branch in Boa Viagem, at Prof José Brandão 409). *Le Buffet*, R do Hospício 147-49. Good, helpful, English speaking owner. *Fuji*, No 354. Economical Japanese, good tofu dishes. *Lisboa á Noite*, R Geraldo Pires 503. Good, reasonable prices, open Sunday evenings (unlike many). *Tivoli*, R Matias de Albuquerque, Santo Antônio. Lunches downstairs, a/c restaurant upstairs, good value. *Galo D'Ouro*, Gamboa do Carmo 83. Recommended, good value. At No 136, *Casa de Tia*. Lunch only, must arrive by 1215, try *cosido*, a meat and vegetable stew, enough for 2. Highly recommended. *O Vegetal*, R Cleto Campelo and Av Guararapes (second floor) behind Central Post Office. Lunch only. Highly recommended, closed Saturday-Sunday. *Casa dos Frios*, da Palma 57, loja 5. Delicatessen/sandwich bar, salads, pastries etc, very good. *Buraquinho*, Pátio de São Pedro. Lunch only, all dishes good, generous servings of caipirinha, friendly. Recommended.

Boa Viagem Main hotels. *Maxime*, Av Boa Viagem 21. Where the locals eat seafood. *Oficina da Massas*, No 2232. Italian. Pizzas at *Mr Pizza*, Av Conselheiro Aguiar 3553 and *Fiorentino*, R Laete Lemos 60 (another branch at Av Bernardo Vieira de Melo 4738, Candeias). *Mediterráneo*, R Setúbal, 100m from *Hotel Setúbal*. Italian, pasta, fish, reasonable. Recommended. *Biruta*, Bem-te-vi 15, Pina. Seafood, reasonable prices, beachfront. *Picanha de Tio Dada*, Av Bernardo Vieira de Melo 1188. Smart. *Shangai Palace*, Av Domingos Ferreira 4719. Excellent Chinese, plenty of food, another branch at Av Boa Viagem 5262. *China Especial*, Av Domingos Ferreira 3470. Good value, large helpings. *Futuba*, R Manoel de Brito 44. A tiny side street towards beach from Av Conselheiro Aguiar 1313, Japanese, good. *Chinés*, Herculano Bandeiro 875, Pina (just after the bridge, on the Boa Viagem side). Good value, another branch at Av Bernardo

Eating
There are many good restaurants, at all prices, in the city, and along beach at Boa Viagem

Recife & the Northeast Coast

Recife's New Wave

If Bahia produced Brazil's musical innovations in the late 1980s and early 1990s, more recent steps forward have been taken by Pernambucans. It is again a case of outside influences mixing well with Brazilian rhythmic flair. As in Bahia, where Olodum took reggae and added it to 'afoxe' rhythms, a local band called Chico Science & Nacão Zumbi took Pernambucan popular music forms including maracatu, baião and ciranda, and welded them to modern dance forms such as hip-hop, electro and jungle. The fusion became known as Mangue-Beat, best translated as 'Mangroove', after a 1991 manifesto written by a local DJ, Renato Lins, summed up the local music scene and the local mangrove swamps with the same word: stagnant.

Chico Science was killed in February 1997, casting a shadow over the carnival of that year, but, in 1999, Nacão Zumbi returned with a reshuffled line-up to prove,

with devastating new material, that their intention was always to carry on Chico's work. Although there are also innovative and exciting rock bands like Eddie, River Raid and Supersoniques, the so-called 'Mangue -Beat' sees to it that talent scouts from Rio and Sao Paulo-based record companies still descend on Pernambuco regularly, in the hope of finding new stars.

Three major festivals take place each year which showcase new bands. February sees Carnival's Rec-Beat in Recife take over the Rua da Moeda in the renovated old town. In April, the Pro-Rock festival is to be found at the Pernambuco State Convention Centre between Recife and Olinda – Sepultura played in 1999 – and in July each year, Pe-No-Rock takes place at the Circo Maluco Beleza in the Aflitos district of Recife. At least there aren't any awkward dance steps to learn.

Marc Starr

Vieira de Melo, Piedade. *Prá Vocês*, Av Herculano Bandeira 115, Pina (town end of Boa Viagem beach). Good but pricey seafood. *Snack Bar Flamingo*, Av Conselheiro Aguiar 542. Good hamburgers and ice cream. *Churrascaria o Laçador*, R Visconde Jequitinhonha 138. Good meat, superb salads of all kinds. Recommended. *Churrascaria Porcão*, Av Eng Domingos Ferreira 4215. Good. *Bargaço*, Av Boa Viagem 670. Typical northeastern menu.

Cafés *Cafe Cordel*, R Domingos Jose Martins. Northeastern dishes, cordel litera-ture, regional books (some in English), good CD collection with requests accepted. *Savoy*, Av Guararapes, open since 1944 and a haunt of Pernambucan intellectuals, Simone De Beauvoir and Jean Paul Sartre once ate there according to a book written on the bar, poetry all over the walls.

Bars & nightclubs The historic centre of Recife Antigo has been restored and is now an excellent spot for nightlife. Bars around R do Bom Jesus such as *London Pub* are the result of a scheme to renovate the dock area. Similarly, *Downtown*, R Vigário Tenório, English pub, live music. The Graças district, west of Boa Vista, on the Rio Capibaribe, is popular for bars and evening entertainment. Recommended bars are *Capibar*, Aflitos, on River Capibaribe. *Depois do Escuro*, R da Amizade 178, Graças. *Shoparia*, 2 doors from *Maxime* restaurant, good beer and atmosphere, live rock music after 2200. Disco-theques tend to be expensive and sophisticated – a good area is Casa Forte. Best times are around midnight on Friday or Saturday, take a taxi.

The Pina zone, north of the beginning of Boa Viagem, is one of the city's major hang-out areas with lively bars, music and dancing. Suggested nightclubs are *Calypso Club*, R do Bom Jesus and *Planeta Maluco*, R do Apolo; however, most bars stay open until dawn.

Also visit a typical northeastern *Forró* where local couples dance to typical music, very lively especially on Friday and Saturday, several good ones at Candeias.

Theatre *Recife Ballet*, shows in the Recife/Olinda Convention Center, US$10, tradi- **Entertainment**
tional dances in full costume. Recommended.

Music Brazil's better known bands play at *Funhouse*, Torre, T2274466. Live music also at *Circo Maluco Beleza*, Av Rui Barbosa, Espinheiro, T4271654. Live regional music at *O Catedral da Seresta*, R Real da Torre 1435, Bairro Torre, T2280567. *O Pirata*, Av 17 de Agosto 1738, Bairro Casa Forte.

1 January, *Universal Brotherhood*. **12-15 March**, parades to mark the city's founda- **Festivals**
tion. **Mid-April**, *Pro-Rock Festival*, a week-long celebration of rock, hip-hop and *For Carnival, see box on page 500*
manguebeat at Centro de Convenções, Complexo de Salgadinho and other venues. Check *Diário de Pernambuco* or *Jornal de Comércio* for details. **June**, *Festejos Juninos*, see Box. **11-16 July**, *Nossa Senhora do Carmo*, patron saint of the city. **August** is the *Mes do Folclore*. **October**, *Recifolia*, a repetition of the carnival over a whole weekend; dates differ each year. **1-8 December** is the festival of *Iemanjá*, with typical foods and drinks, celebrations and offerings to the goddess; also **8 December**, *Nossa Senhora da Conceição*.

Diving Offshore are some 20 wrecks, including the remains of Portuguese galleons; **Sports**
the fauna is very rich. *Expedição Atlântico*, R Comendador Bento Aguiar 520/101, Madalena T2270458, F4455233. Ask for Penenha.

Football Recife's 3 clubs are *Sport*, *Santa Cruz* and *Nautico*. Sport play at Ilha do Retiro, T2271213, take Torrões bus from Central Post Office on Av Guararapes. Santa Cruz play at Arruda, T4416811, take Casa Amarela bus from Central Post Office. Nautico play at Aflitos, T4238900, take Água Fria or Aflitos bus. **NB** Local derbies are sometimes full beyond safe capacities. Avoid 'Arquibancada' tickets for Santa Cruz-Sport games. For games at Arruda, dress down.

Golf *Caxangá Golf Clube*, Av Caxangá 5362, T2711422. Nine holes. **Racing** *Pernambucan Jockey Club*, T2274961. **Yachting** *Recife Yacht Club*, T4652002. *Itamaraca Yacht Club*, T2212648.

Markets The permanent craft market is in the **Casa da Cultura** (see above); prices **Shopping**
for ceramic figurines are lower than Caruaru (see below). *Mercado São José* (1875) for local products and handicrafts. *Hippy fair* at Praça Boa Viagem, on the sea front, lifesized wooden statues of saints (a good meeting place is the *Bar Lapinha* in the middle of the square). Saturday craft fair at *Sítio Trindade*, Casa Amarela: during the feast days of 12-29 June, fireworks, music, dancing, local food. On 23 April, here and in the Pátio de São Pedro, one can see the *xangô* dance. Herbal remedies, barks and spices at Afogados market. *Cais de Alfândega*, Recife Barrio, market of local artisans work, first weekend of every month. *Domingo na Rua*, weekly market in Recife Barrio, with stalls of local artesanato and performances.

Shopping malls *Shopping Center Recife* is a large mall between Boa Viagem and the airport, www.shopping-recife.com.br. *Shopping Tacaruna*, a new development in Santo Amaro, buses to/from Olinda pass it.

Bookshops *Livraria Brandão*, R da Matriz 22 (used English books and some French and German), and bookstalls on the Rua do Infante Dom Henrique. *Livro 7*, a huge emporium with a very impressive stock, R Sete de Setembro 329. *Saraiva*, R Sete de Setembro 280, T2316613, best selection of Brazilian literature in the city. *Sintese*, Riachuelo 202, T2214044. *Almanque Livros*, Largo do Varadouro 418, loja 58, bohemian atmosphere, sells food and drink. *Sodiler* at Guararapes airport has books in English, newspapers, magazines; also in the *Shopping Center Recife*. *Livraria do Nordeste*, between cells 118 and 119, Ralo Leste, Casa da Cultura, for books in Portuguese on the Northeast. *Livraria Nordeste*, R Imperatriz 43, Boa Vista. A great local character, *Melquísidec Pastor de Nascimento*, second-hand bookseller, at R Bispo Cardoso Aires, 215; also has a second-hand stall at Praça do Sebo (see page 491).

Recife & the Northeast Coast

Carnival in Pernambuco

Carnival in Pernambuco encompasses *trios eléctricos and samba schools as well as having its own distinctive dances and rhythms such as Maracatu and Frevo. Avenida Guararapes in Recife, Pina near Boa Viagem, Largo do Amparão and Mercado Eufrásio Barbosa (Varadouro) in Olinda are the main centres for the festivities.*

There is a pre-carnavalesca week which starts with the 'Bloco da Parceria' in Boa Viagem bringing top Axé music acts from Bahia and the 'Virgens de Bairro Novo' in Olinda which features men in drag. These are followed by Carnival balls such as Baile dos Artistas (popular with the gay community) and the Bal Masque held at the Portuguese club, Rua Governador Agamenon Magalhães, T2315400. On the following Saturday morning the bloco Galo da Madrugada with close on a million participants officially opens carnival (wild and lively), see the local press for routes and times. The groups taking part are maracatu, caboclinhos, troças, tribos de índios, blocos, ursos, caboclos de lança, escolas de samba and frevo. Usually they start from Rua Conde da Boa Vista and progress along Rua do Hospício, Rua da Imperatriz, Ponte da Boa Vista, Praça da Independência, Rua 1° de Março and Rua do Imperador. This is followed by the main days Sunday to Tuesday. During Carnival (and on a smaller scale throughout the year) the Casa de Cultura has frevo demonstrations where visitors can learn some steps of this unique dance of Pernambuco (check press for details of Frevioca truck and frevo orchestras during Carnival in the Pátio de São Pedro). The best place to see the groups is from the balconies of Hotel do Parque or Recife Palace Hotel. Seats in the stands and boxes can be booked up to a fortnight in advance at the central post office in Avenida Guararapes.

The Maracatu groups dance at the doors of all the churches they pass; they usually go to the Church of Nossa Senhora do Rosário dos Pretos, patron saint of the slaves (Rua Estreita do Rosário, Santo Antônio), before proceeding into the downtown areas. A small car at the head bears the figure of some animal and is

Transport **Local** **Car hire**: *Interlocadora*, T4651041. *Localiza*, Av Visconde de Jequitinhonha 1145, T3410477, and at Guararapes airport, T0800-992000. *Budget*, T3412505. *Hertz*, T4623552.

Long distance **Air**: Guararapes airport, 12 km from the city. International flights to Lisbon and Milan. Domestic flights to Brasília, Campina Grande, Fernando de Noronha, Fortaleza, João Pessoa, Juazeiro do Norte, Maceió, Natal, Paulo Afonso, Petrolina, Rio de Janeiro, Salvador and São Paulo.

Buses: the rodoviária, mainly for long distance buses, is 12 km outside the city at São Lourenço da Mata, T4521999/1163. There is a 30-minute metrô connection from the central railway station, entrance through Museu do Trem, opposite the Casa da Cultura, 2 lines leave the city, take train marked 'Rodoviária'. From Boa Viagem a taxi all the way costs US$25-35, or go to Joana Bezerra Metrô station and change there. Bus US$1, 1 hour, from the centre or from Boa Viagem.

Bus tickets are sold at Cais de Santa Rita (opposite EMTU) and *Fruir Tur*, at Praça do Carmo, Olinda.

To **Salvador**, daily 1930, 12 hours, US$18-25, 4 a day (all at night) (1 *leito*, 70). To **Fortaleza**, 12 hours, US$20 *convencional*, US$30 *executivo*. To **Natal**, 4 hours, US$9. To **Rio**, daily 2100, 44 hours, US$58-65. To **São Paulo**, daily 1630, 50 hours, US$60-70. To **Santos**, daily 1430, 52 hours, US$60. To **Foz do Iguaçu**, Fri and Sun 1030, 55 hours, US$90. To **Curitiba**, Fri and Sun, 52 hours, US$76. To **Brasília**, daily 2130, 39 hours, US$49-60. To **Belo Horizonte**, daily 2115, 34 hours, US$41. To **São Luís**, 28 hours,

followed by the king and queen under a large, showy umbrella. The bahianas, who wear snowy-white embroidered skirts, dance in single file on either side of the king and queen. Next comes the dama do passo carrying a small doll, or calunga. After the dama comes the tirador de loas who chants to the group which replies in chorus, and last comes a band of local percussion instruments.

Still flourishing is the dance performance of the caboclinhos. The groups wear traditional Indian garb: bright feathers round their waists and ankles, colourful cockades, bead and animal teeth necklaces, a dazzle of medals on their red tunics. The dancers beat out the rhythm with bows and arrows; others of the group play primitive musical instruments, but the dance is the thing: spinning, leaping, and stooping with almost mathematical precision. Further information from Casa da Carnaval, office of Fundação da Cultura de Recife, Pátio de São Pedro, lojas 10-11. Galo da Madrugada, Rua da Concórdia, Santo Antônio, T2242899.

Festejos Juninos In the June festas, the days of Santo Antônio (13 June), São João (24 June), São Pedro and São Paulo (29 June), form the nuclei of a month-long celebration whose roots go back to the Portuguese colony. Intermingled with the Catholic tradition are Indian and African elements. The annual cycle begins in fact on São José's day, 19 March, historically the first day of planting maize; the harvest in June then forms a central part of the **festejos juninos**. During the festivals the forró is danced. This dance, now popular throughout the Northeast, is believed to have originated when the British builders of the local railways held parties that were for all. This is one aspect of the festivities which makes Pernambuco's **festejos juninos** distinct from those that celebrated all over Brazil.

The Prefeitura and Secretaria de Turismo has published three booklets on História Junina, História de Carnaval and História do Folclore, all by Claudia Lina, which provide a good introduction to these topics.

Progresso at 1430 and 1945, US$75. To **Belém**, 34 hours (*Boa Esperança* bus recommended). To **João Pessoa**, every 30 minutes, US$2.50. To **Caruaru**, every hour, 3 hours, US$3. To **Maceió**, US$9, 3½ hours (express), 6 hours (slow), either by the main road or by the coast road daily via 'Litoral'.

Buses to the nearby destinations of **Igarassu** (every 15 minutes) and **Itamaracá** (every 30 minutes) leave from Av Martins de Barros, in front of *Grande Hotel*. To **Olinda**, see below; those to the beaches beyond Olinda from Av Dantas behind the post office. To **Cabo** (every 20 minutes) and beaches south of Recife from Cais de Santa Rita.

Airline offices *TAM*, reservations T425011, at airport, T4624466. *TAP Air Portugal*, Av **Directory** Conselheiro de Aguiar 1472, Boa Viagem T4658800, at airport T3410654. *Transbrasil*, Av Conde de Boa Vista 1546, T4232656, Av Conselheiro de Aguiar, Boa Viagem, T4650450, at airport, T4650333. *Nordeste/RioSul*, Av Domingos Ferreira 801, loja 103-5, T4656799 (*RioSul* T4658535), at airport, T3413187. *United*, R Progreso 465/802, T4232444. *Varig*, R Conselheiro de Aguiar 456, Boa Viagem, T4644440, R J E Favre 719, T3392998, at airport 3414411, cargo T4658989. *Vasp*, R da Palma 254, Santo Antônio, T4213088, R Dr Nilo Dornelas Câmara 90, Boa Viagem, T4213611, F3253434, at airport, T3417742.

Banks *Banco do Brasil*, R Barão da Souza Leão 440, Boa Viagem, Av Dantas Barreto, Santo *Open 1000-1600, hours* Antonio, exchange between 1000-1600, US$20 commission, credit/debit cards, TCs. *Bandepe*, Av *for exchange vary* Dantas Barreto 1110, Santo Antonio. MasterCard ATMs. *Banorte*, Av Domingos Ferreira and Av *between 1000 and 1400,* Conselheiro Aguiar, Boa Viagem. *Bradesco*, Av Cons Aguiar 3236, Boa Viagem, Av Conde de Boa *sometimes later* Vista, Boa Vista, R da Concordia 148, Santo Antônio, 24-hr VISA ATMs, but no exchange. *Citibank*, Av Marquês de Olinda 126, T2161262, takes Mastercard. *Edifício Bancomércio*, 3rd floor, R Matias de Alberquerque 223, takes cash and TCs. *Lloyds Bank*, R A.L. Monte 96/1002. *Mastercard*, Av Conselheiro Aguiar 3924, Boa Viagem, cash against card. **Money changers:** *Anacor*, Shopping Center Recife, loja 52, also at Shopping Tacaruna, loja 173. *Monaco*, Praça Joaquim Nabuco, cambio, TCs and cash, all major currencies, no commission but poor rates. *Norte Cambio Turismo*, Av Boa Viagem 5000, also at Shopping Guararapes, Av Barreto de Menezes.

Communications **Post Office:** Poste Restante at Central Correios, Av Guararapes 250, next to Rio Capibaribe. Open 0900-1700, outgoing mail leaves at 1500 each day. Also has a philately centre. Another on R 24 de Maio 59. Poste Restante also with American Express representative *Souto Costa*, R Félix Brito de Melo 666, T4655000, also at Av Conselheiro Aguiar, Boa Viagem. **Telephones:** *Embratel*, Av Gov Agamenon Magalhães, 1114, Parque Amorim. Also at Praça da Independencia. International calls at phone centres on Av Conselheiro Aguiar, Boa Viagem, Av Herculano Bandeira, 231, Pina and Av Conde da Boa Vista, open 0800-1800, phone cards sold, faulty cards replaced. The news-stand on the corner of Av Guararapes and Dantas Barreto is an official vending point. Also at R Diario de Pernambuco 38 and airport, second floor.

Cultural centres *British Council*, Av Domingos Ferreira 4150, Boa Viagem, CEP 51021-040, T4657744, F4657271, recife@britcoun.org.br, www.britcoun.org/br. Open 0800-1500, reading room with current British newspapers, very helpful. *Instituto Brasileiro Alemão*, R do Sossego 364. *Alliance Française*, R Amaro Bezerra 466, Derby, T2220918.

Embassies & consulates *Denmark*, Av Marques de Olinda 85, Edif Alberto Fonseca 2nd floor, CP 3450030, T2240311, F2240997, open 0800-1200, 1400-1800. *Finland*, R Ernesto de Paula Santos 1327, T4652940, F4652859. *France*, Av Conselheiro Aguiar 2333, 6th floor, T4653290. *Germany*, Av Dantas Barreto 191, Edif Santo Antônio, 4th floor, T4243488, T4242660. *Japan*, Av Dantas Barreto 191, 3rd floor, T2241930. *Netherlands*, Av Conselheiro Aguiar 1313/3, Boa Viagem, T3268096. *Spain*, R Sirinhaem, 105, 2nd floor, T4657474. *Sweden*, Av Conde de Boa Vista 1450, T2312581. *Switzerland*, Av Conselheiro Aguiar 4880, loja 32, Boa Viagem, T3263144. *UK*, Av Eng Domingos Ferreira 4150, Boa Viagem, T4650230, open 0800-1130. *USA*, R Gonçalves Maia 164, Boa Vista, T4212441, F2311906.

Hospitals & medical services *Hospital Santa Joana*, R Joaquim Nabuco 200, Graças, T4213666. *Unicordis*, Av.Conselheiro Aguiar 1980, Boa Viagem, T3265237 and Av Conselheiro Rosa de Silva 258, Aflitos, T4211000, equipped for cardiac emergencies. *Unimed*, Av Bernardo Vieira de Melo 1496, Guararapes, T4621955/4611530, general medical treatment, general practitioners. **Dental:** R Ademar da Costa Almeida, 130, Piedade, Jaboatao, T3413341. **NB** Dengue has been resurgent in Recife. Previous sufferers should have good insurance as a second infection can lead to the haemorhagic form, requiring hospitalization.

Laundry Av Conselheiro Aguiar 1385, Boa Viagem.

Places of worship *Episcopalian church*, R Carneiro Vilela 569, nearest bus stop at Club Nautica, service in Portuguese but friendly welcome from English speakers.

Security Opportunistic theft is unfortunately common in the streets of Recife and Olinda (especially on the streets up to Alto da Sé). Keep hold of bags and cameras, and do not wear a watch. Prostitution is reportedly common in Boa Viagem, so choose nightclubs with care. **Tourist Police**, T3269603.

Tour companies & travel agents *Jacaré e Cobra de Água Eco-Group*, T4473452, Mobile 9687360, ribeiros@truenet.com.br, www.truenet.com.br\jacare&cobradagua, regular excursions in Pernambuco. *Souto Costa Viagens e Turismo Ltda*, R Felix de Brito Melo 666, T4655000, and Aeroporto de Guararapes (American Express representative). *Stella Barros* (Thomas Cook), R Monsenhor Ambrosino Leite 93, Graças, T/F2315201. *Student Travel Bureau (STB)*, R Padre Bernardino Pessoa 266, T4654522, F4652636, stbmaster@stb.com.br, ISIC accepted, discounts on international flights but not domestic Brazilian flights. *Trilhas*, T2226864, recommended for ecologically oriented excursions.

Tourist offices *Empetur*, main office, Centro de Convenções, Complexo Rodoviário de Salgadinho, T4278000, F2419601, between Recife and Olinda, branch at airport, T4624960. Open

24 hrs (will book hotels, helpful but few leaflets, English spoken). Maps are available, or can be bought at newspaper stands in city; also sketch maps in monthly guides *Itinerário Pernambuco* and *Guia do Turista*. **Secretaria de Turismo do Recife**, T2247198/4242070. The Prefeitura has a project, *Recife 2000*, currently in operation, for details contact the **Secretaria de Desenvolvimento Económico, Turismo e Esportes**, Cais do Apolo 925, 5th floor, T4258460/8605, F4258070, www.emprel.gov.br. Hours of opening of museums, art galleries, churches etc are published in the *Diário de Pernambuco* and *Jornal do Comercio*.

Voltage 220 volts AC, 60 cycles.

Olinda

Seven kilometres north of Recife is the old capital, founded in 1537 and named a 'Patrimônio da Humanidade' by UNESCO in 1982. A programme of restoration, partly financed by the Netherlands government, was initiated in order to comply with the recently conferred title of National Monument. Despite adoption by UNESCO and the Dutch, the need for restoration and cleaning has grown.

Population: 350,000
Phone code: 081
Colour map 2, grid B6

Of particular interest are: on Rua São Bento, the **Prefeitura**, once the palace of the viceroys, and the monastery of **São Bento**, founded 1582 by the Benedictine monks, restored 1761, the site of Brazil's first law school and the first abolition of slavery (paintings, sculpture, furniture; the monastery is closed to anyone without written permission to visit); the convent of **Santa Teresa** (1687), Avenida

Sights
None of the historic buildings has fixed opening hours

Olinda

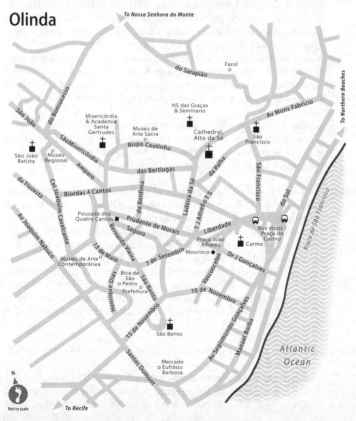

Olinda 570; the **Convento de São Francisco** (1585), with splendid woodcarving and paintings, superb gilded stucco, and azulejos, in Capela de São Roque (entry US$1); the church of **Nossa Senhora das Neves**, Ladeira de São Francisco (visits permitted only with prior written application); the **Igreja da Misericórdia**, built 1540, Rua Bispo Coutinho, fine tiling and gold work, and Académia Santa Gertrudes; the **Cathedral** (1537), Alto da Sé, the first church to be built in the city, of simple and severe construction; the **Graças** church (seminary) built 1552, also in Alto da Sé; **São João Batista dos Militares** (19th century), Rua da Saudade, closed to the public; **Nossa Senhora do Monte**, built late 16th century; the **Carmo** church (1581) overlooking Praça Carmo (under restoration, guides may be able to get you in), and the colonial public fountain, the **Bica de São Pedro**, Rua Joaquim Cavalcanti.

There are some houses of the 17th century with latticed balconies, heavy doors and pink stucco walls, including a house in Moorish style at Praça João Alfredo 7, housing the *Mourisco* restaurant. There is a colony of artists and excellent examples of regional art, mainly woodcarving and terracotta figurines, may be bought in the Alto da Sé, the square on top of the hill by the cathedral, or in the handicraft shops at the **Mercado da Ribeira**, Rua Bernardo Vieira de Melo (Vieira de Melo gave the first recorded call for independence from Portugal, in Olinda in 1710). Handicrafts are also sold at good prices in the Mercado Eufrásio Barbosa, by the junction of Avenida Segismundo Gonçalves and Santos Dumont, Varadouro; the bars serve good value meals. There is a **Museu de Arte Sacra** in the former Palácio Episcopal (1696) at Alto da Sé 7. ■ *Monday-Friday, 0800-1230.* At Rua 13 de Maio 157, in the 18th century jail of the Inquisition, is the **Museu de Arte Contemporânea**. ■ *Tuesday-Friday 0900-1700, Saturday-Sunday 0930-1700.* The **Museu Regional**, Rua do Amparo 128, is excellent (same hours). **Museu do Mamulengo**, Amparo 59, houses Pernambucan folk puppetry. ■ *Daily 0900-1700.* **Corredor Artístico do Amparo**, formally identified as the cultural and artistic zone, has artists workshops, while the **Casa dos Bonecos** houses papier mache giants; there are also many restaurants.

Guides Guides with identification cards wait in Praça do Carmo. They are former street children and half the fee for a full tour of the city (about US$20) goes to a home for street children. If you take a guide you will be safe from mugging which, unfortunately, occurs (see below).

Beaches The beaches close to Olinda are reported to be seriously polluted. Those further north from Olinda, beyond Casa Caiada, are beautiful, usually deserted, palm-fringed; at **Janga**, and **Pau Amarelo**, the latter can be dirty at low tide (take either a 'Janga' or 'Pau Amarela' bus, Varodouro bus to return). At many simple cafés you can eat *sururu* (clam stew in coconut sauce), *agulha frita* (fried needle-fish), *miúdo de galinha* (chicken giblets in gravy), *casquinha de carangueijo* (seasoned crabmeat) and *farinha de dendê* (served in crabshells). Visit the Dutch fort on Pau Amarelo beach; small craft fair here on Saturday nights. Near the fort is *Bar Lua Cheia*, which has music and dancing. *Veneza Water Park*, Av Claudio Gueiros Leite 10050, Maria Farinha, T4363850, bus Pau Amarelo.

Sleeping **NB** Hotels on Rua do Sol and in Bairro Novo are below the old city and on the roads
At Carnival, the price of heading north.
accommodation rises   **Historic city** **B** *Pousada dos Quatro Cantos*, R Prudente de Morais 441, T4293333,
steeply. Houses or rooms F4291845. In a converted mansion, very good. Highly recommended, prices rise to **L** for
may be rented at this 5-night package during Carnival, sometimes has live entertainment, expensive
time for 5-10 days

restaurant. **B** *7 Colinas*, Ladeira de Sao Francisco 307, T/F4396055, 7colinas@hotel7 colinasolinda.com.br. New hotel in beautiful grounds, fridge, telephone, TV, pool and sauna, excursions arranged. **C** *Pousada d'Olinda*, P João Alfredo 178, T/F4391163. Happy. Warmly recommended. Discount of 10% for owners of *Footprint Handbooks*, 5 luxury a/c apartments, 2 colonial suites, 16 rooms with shared bath, 2 communal rooms with good view, pool, breakfast, other meals if requested in advance, English, French, German and Spanish spoken. **C** *Pousada do Amparo*, R do Amparo 191, T4391749. Relatively new *pousada* in the heart of Olinda; gives excellent view of carnival parades in an 18th century house, beautiful rooms with a/c and bath, some with fridge, nice garden, pool, sauna, good view, very helpful, English spoken, in the *Roteiros de Charme* group (see page 57). Warmly recommended. **C-D** *Pousada Peter*, R do Amparo 215, T/F4392171. With bath, a/c, clean, small pool, German owner, family atmosphere, good value. **E** *Sete Colinas*, Ladeira de São Francisco 307, T/F4396055, 7colinas@hotel7 colinasolinda.com.br. Pool, excursions.

Outside the historic centre B *Oh! Linda Pousada*, Av Ministro Marcos Freire 349, Bairro Novo, T4392116. Recommended. **B** *Pousada São Francisco*, R do Sol 127, T4292109, F4294057. Comfortable, pool. Recommended, modest restaurant. **C** *Cinco Sóis*, Av Ministro Marcos Freire 633, Bairro Novo, T/F4291347. A/c, fridge, hot shower, parking. **C** *Hospedaria do Turista*, Av Marcos Freire 989, Bairro Novo, T4393717, Mobile 9632961. Excellent. **C** *Olinda Bellomonte*, Av Beira Mar 1414, T4290409, F4214176. **D** *Cinco Sois*, Av Ministro Marcos Freire 633, Bairro Novo, T/F4291347. A/c, fridge, hot shower, parking. **D** *São Pedro*, Praça Conselheiro João Alfredo 168, T4292935. Cosy, helpful, laundry, Danish run, English spoken. Recommended. **E** *Jangada*, R 15 de Novembro 98, T4294747.

Youth hostels E *Albergue da Olinda*, R do Sol 233, T4291592, F4212110. Rooms with bath as well as communal bunk rooms, laundry facilities. Highly recommended. **D** *Cheiro do Mar*, Av Min Marcos Freire 95, T4290101. IYHA, more expensive for non-members, very good small hostel with some double rooms (room No 1 is noisy from the disco), cooking facilities, ask driver of 'Rio Doce/Piedade' or 'Bairra de Jangada/Casa Caiada' bus (see below) to drop you at Albergue de Juventude on the sea front.

Camping *Olinda Camping*, R Bom Sucesso 262, Amparo, T4291365. US$5 pp, space for 30 tents, 5 trailers, small huts for rent, quiet, well-shaded, town buses pass outside. Recommended.

Eating *Cantinho da Sé*, lively, good view of Recife, views just as good and prices lower upstairs. *Creperia*, R Prudente Moraes, 168. French restaurant. *Donana*, on seafront near Praça do Carmo. Good, quite cheap. *Grande Pequim*, Av Min Marcos Freire 1463, Bairro Novo. Good Chinese food. *Império dos Camarões*, Av Min Marcos Freire 2895. Fish restaurant. *Leque Moleque*, Av Sigismundo Goncalves 537. Good for Pernambucan specialities. *Mourisco*, R João Alfredo 7. Calm and pleasant, discotheque attached. *Oficina do Sabor*, R do Amparo. Nice décor, food served in hollowed-out pumpkins. *Samburá*, Av Min Marcos Freire 1551. With terrace, try *caldeirada* and *pitu* (crayfish), also lobster in coconut sauce or daily fish dishes, very good. *Stillus*, Av Min Marcos Freire 1571, churrascos and carne do sol. *Tony*, 2 blocks from Praça do Carmo towards Recife. Good, reasonable prices. *Chin Lee*, excellent Chinese food. Maison do Bomfim, R do Bomfim 115, French chef, the food is Franco-Pernambucan, excellent. Many others, mostly for fish.

Local specialities The traditional Olinda drinks, *Pau do Índio* (which contains 32 herbs) and *Retetel*, are both manufactured on R do Amparo. In Olinda also try *tapioca*, a local dish made of manioc with coconut or cheese.

Entertainment At Janga beach on Friday and Saturday, you can join in a *ciranda* (a round dance) at the bar-restaurant *Ciranda de Dona Duda*. For the less active, there is the *Casa da*

Recife & the Northeast Coast

Seresta (serenade), also in Janga on the beach side of the main road. On Praça do Carmo is *Clube Atlântico*, a *forró* dance hall. *Centro Cultural Luiz Freire*, 27 de Janeiro, holds club events in its garden at weekends, US$2-3, high-energy parties and gigs.

Beginning at dusk, but best after 2100, the Alto da Sé becomes the scene of a lively street fair, with arts, crafts, makeshift bars and barbecue stands, and impromptu traditional music; even more animated at Carnival.

Festivals At Olinda's *Carnival* thousands of people dance through the narrow streets of the old city to the sound of the *frevo*, the brash energetic music which normally accompanies a lively dance performed with umbrellas. The local people decorate them with streamers and straw dolls, and form themselves into costumed groups (*blocos*) which you can join as they pass (take only essentials). Among the best-known *blocos*, which carry life-size dolls, are *O homem da meia-noite* (Midnight Man), *A Corda* (a pun on The Rope and "acorda" – wake up!), which parades in the early hours, *Pitombeira* and *Elefantes*. Olinda's carnival continues on Ash Wednesday, "a quarta-feira do Batata" (Potato's Wednesday, named after a waiter who claimed his right to celebrate carnival after being on duty during the official celebrations). The streets are very crowded with people dancing and drinking non-stop. The local cocktail, *capeta* (guaraná powder, sweet skimmed milk and vodka) is designed to keep you going. (With thanks to Jorn Seemann, Fortaleza). *Foundation Day* is celebrated with 3 days of music and dancing, **12-15 March**, night-time only.

Transport **Buses From Recife**: take any bus marked 'Rio Doce', No 981, which has a circular route around the city and beaches, or No 33 from Av Nossa Senhora do Carmo, US$0.60, or 'Jardim Atlântico' from the central post office at Siqueira Campos; from Boa Viagem, take bus marked 'Piedade/Rio Doce' or 'Bairra de Jangada/Casa Caiada' (US$0.60, 30 minutes). Change to either of these buses from the airport to Olinda: take 'Aeroporto' bus to Av Domingos Ferreira, Boa Viagem, and ask to be let off; and from the Recife Rodoviária: take the metrô to Joana Bezerra station and then change. In all cases, alight in Praça do Carmo. Taxis between Olinda and Recife put their meters onto higher rates at the Convention Centre (between the 2 cities), so it's best to start a journey either way there (taxi to Recife US$6, US$12 to Boa Viagem at night).

Directory **Banks** *Banco do Brasil*, R Getulio Vargas 1470. *Bandepe*, Av Getulio Vargas, MasterCard ATMs. *Bradesco*, R Getulio Vargas 729, Visa ATMs. **Communications Post Office:** Praça do Carmo, open 0900-1700. **Telephone:** Private booths and international phones in Praça do Carmo across the road from the bus stop, open Mon-Sat 0900-1800. **Laundry** *Cooplav*, Estr dos Bultrins, cost per weight of laundry, easily visible from main road, take Bultrins bus from Olinda. **Hospitals & medical services** *Prontolinda*, R Jose Augusto Moreira 1191, T4321700, general, but also equipped for cardiac emergencies. **Security** Olinda has been severely afflicted by rapidly worsening poverty, the effects of which are perhaps more noticeable in this attractive and comparatively prosperous area. Please exercise caution, and sympathy. **Tour companies & travel agents** *Felitur*, Rua Getulio Vargas 1411, Bairro Novo, T/F4391477. *FruirTour*, Av Segismundo Gonçalves, close to Praça do Carmo, T4294099. Bus tickets sold, recommended. *Viagens Sob O Sol*, Prudente de Moraes 424, T/F4293303, Mobile 9718102, English spoken, transport offered to all parts, all types of trip arranged, contact Mauro. **Tourist offices** *Secretaria de Turismo*, R de São Bento 160, T4291927.

Biological reserves For information on Pernambuco's two reserves, contact **Ibama**, Avenida 17 de Agosto 1057, Casa Forte, CEP 52060-590, T4415033, F4411380, Recife. They are **Saltinho**, in the south of the state, which preserves some of the last vestiges of Atlantic Forest in the Northeast, and **Serra Negra**, in the centre of the state, which has some of the last remaining forest at higher altitude in the interior.

The Southern Coast

About 30 kilometres south of Recife, beyond Cabo, is the beautiful and quiet **Gaibu** beach, with scenic Cabo de Santo Agostinho on the point five kilometres east of town. It has a ruined fort. In 1996 surfing in this area was banned owing to the danger of shark attacks. To get there, take bus 'Centro do Cabo' from the airport, then frequent buses – 20 minutes – from Cabo. Places to stay include *Pousada Beto Qualhado*, *Oliver y Daniel*, Av Laura Cavalcante 20, German, very relaxed, *Pousada Águas Marinhas* (**C**), Belgian-Brazilian owned, beautiful garden and location, highly recommended. There are cheap restaurants. One kilometre on foot from Gaibu is **Praia Calhetas**, which is very nice. **Itapuama** beach is even more empty, both reached by bus from Cabo. **Cabo** (*population* 140,765), Pernambuco's main industrial city, has interesting churches and forts and a **Museu da Abolição**, and at nearby **Suape** are many 17th-century buildings and a biological reserve.

Further south still is a beautiful beach. It has cool, clean water, and waves. For diving and canoeing trips, as well as excursions to Santo Aleixo island, contact *Porto Point Diving*, Praça Principal de Porto de Galinhas, T5521111. Also *AICA Diving*, Nossa Senhora do Ó, T/F5521290 or Mobile 9684876, run by Mida and Miguel. Porto de Galinhas is reached by bus from the far end of Av Dantas Barreto, eight a day, seven on Sunday, 0700-1700, US$1.25.

Porto de Galinhas
Phone code: 081

Sleeping and eating **A** *Solar Porto de Galinhas*, on the beach, T/F5521211 or T3250772. Many facilities, a beautiful place. **B** *Pousada Beira Mar*, Av Beira Mar 12, T/F5521052, www.pousadabeiramar.com.br. On beach, pleasant, comfortable. *Pousada Som das Ondas*, in Ipojuca, T/F5521339, somdasondas@portodegalinhas. com.br. Run by Jean-Marc, five European languages spoken. **C** *Morada Azul*, Loteamento Recanto Porto de Galinhas, Lote 5, Ipojuca, T5521143. Several other options, eg **C** *Maracatu*, ½ block from beach, cool, bath, TV, nice rooms and, next door, **D** *Meninão*, above bakery, includes breakfast and dinner. Both recommended. *Pousada of Dona Benedita*, in the street where the bus stops. Very basic, clean.

Directory **Tourist office**: T5521480. Also contact Roberto, T5521514, for information and assistance on all aspects of Porto Galinhas' attractions. He can also give lifts to Recife and Olinda. Alternatively, Sylvie, a well known French local guide, speaks 5 languages and knows the area well.

Further south (80 kilometres from Recife) are the beaches of **Barra do Sirinhaém**, with some tourist development, three hotels including **D** *dos Cataventos*; fishermen make trips to offshore island (good views).

The Northern Coast

Thirty nine kilometres north of Recife on the road to João Pessoa, Igarassu has the first church built in Brazil (SS Cosme e Damião, built in 1535), the Livramento church nearby, and the convent of Santo Antônio with a small museum next door. The church of Sagrado Coração is said to have housed Brazil's first orphanage. Much of the town, which was founded in 1535, has been declared a National Monument; it is an attractive place, with a number of colonial houses and Brazil's first Masonic hall.

Igarassu
Population: 77,500
Phone code: 081
Colour map 2, grid B6

There is a hotel, *Fazenda Praia da Gavoa* (**A**), Estrada do Ramalho (Nova Cruz), T/F5431413. *Camping Clube do Brasil* has a site nearby at Engenho Monjope, an old sugar estate, now a historical monument (it is five kilometres before Igarassu coming from Recife – bus US$1 – alight at the 'Camping' sign and walk 5-10 minutes, T5430528, US$5). Igarassu buses leave from Cais de Santa Rita, Recife, 45 minutes, US$1.

Itamaracá
Population: 14,000
Phone code: 081

North of Igarassu you pass through coconut plantations to Itapissuma, where there is a bridge to **Itamaracá** island, where, the locals say, Adam and Eve spent their holidays (so does everyone else on Sunday now). It has the old Dutch **Forte Orange**, built in 1631; an interesting penal settlement with gift shops, built round the 1747 sugar estate buildings of Engenho São João, which still have much of the old machinery; charming villages and colonial churches, and fine, wide beaches. At one of them, **Praia do Forte Orange**, Ibama has a centre for the study and preservation of manatees (*Centro Nacional de Conservação e Manejo de Sirênios* or *Peixe-boi*). ■ *Tuesday to Saturday 1000-1600, T5441056, F5441835.*

There are pleasant trips by *jangada* from Praia do Forte Orange to **Ilha Coroa do Avião**, a recently formed sandy island (developing wildlife and migratory birds – for which there is a research station) with rustic beach bars. **Praias do Sossego** and **da Enseada** are quiet, with some bars but relatively undiscovered. The crossing is three kilometres north of Itamaracá town, recommended for sun worshippers.

Further north again, two hours from Recife by bus, is **Pontas de Pedra**, an old fishing village, nice beach, fishing and diving expeditions, lots of bars.

Sleeping and eating B *Casa da Praia*, Av da Forte Orange, T5441255. With breakfast, pool, minibar, breakfast and optional dinner. **B** *Itamaracá Parque*, Estr do Forte, T5441030, F5441854. **C** *Pousada Itamaracá*, R Fernando Lopes 205/210, T5441152. Pool, some minutes from the beach. **C** *Pousada Jaguaribe*, R Rios 355 (close to bus terminal), close to the beach. Fans and mosquito nets in all rooms, kitchen, laundry facilities, swimming pool. Those with a car and above budget means should have lunch and a swim at charming *Vila Velha* (Call T9712962, ask for Newton Bezerra, dealer for artist Luis Jasmim. Visit them, and any purchase comes with an offer of lunch included in the deal), allow all afternoon. *Bar da Lia*, R do Jaguaribe, close to the Forte Orange, weekends feature Cirandas danced at the bar, led by the well known singer, Dona Lia, and her band.

Transport Buses from **Recife** (Av Martins de Barros opposite *Grande Hotel*, US$1.10, very crowded) and **Igarassu**.

Goiana
Population: 67,250
Phone code: 081

Situated on the Recife-João Pessoa road and founded in 1570, Goiana is an important town for ceramics. The **Carmelite church** and monastery, founded 1719, is impressive but poorly restored. **Matriz Nossa Senhora do Rosário dos Brancos** (17th century), on Rua Direita, is only open for 1800 mass. Also worth a visit are the **Convento da Soledade** (1735), on Rua da Soledade; **Nossa Senhora do Amparo dos Homens Pardos** (1681), Rua do Amparo, with a sacred art museum; and **dos Milagres da Misericórdia** church (1723), Rua da Misericórdia.

Visit the workshop of Zé do Carmo, opposite the *Buraco da Giá* restaurant (excellent seafood; owner has a tame crab which will offer you a drink), Rua Padre Batalha 100. *Hotel Dois Irmãos* (**D**) is in the town centre.

At the Pernambuco-Paraíba border, a 27 kilometre dirt road goes to the fishing village of **Pitimbu**, with *jangadas*, lobster fishing, surf fishing, and lobster-pot making. There are no tourist facilities but camping is possible; food from *Bar do Jangadeiro*. Bus from Goiana, US$1.

West of Recife

Gravatá

Eighty two kilometres west of Recife, by the paved BR-232 road that passes through the Serra dos Russos, is Gravatá, known as the Switzerland of Pernambuco for its scenery and good hill climate. On one of its hills is a replica of the Cristo Redentor of Rio de Janeiro. The former municipal prison on Rua Cleto Campelo has been made into a Casa da Cultura and historical centre. ■ *Monday-Friday.*

Population: 62,000
Phone code: 081
Colour map 2, grid B6

Sleeping

L *Casa Grande Gravatá*, BR-232 Km 82, T4653011/5330920, F5330812. Four-star, very comfortable, restaurant serving regional food, excellent breakfast, swimming pool and waterslides, English-speaking owner, splendid gardens, sauna, hydromassage. **A** *Portal de Gravatá*, BR-232 Km 82, T2270345/5330288, F5330610. Three-star, comfortable, a/c, TV, phone, restaurant with regional food, good breakfast, pool, large gardens, bar. **In the cheaper categories** *da Serra*, BR-232 Km 77, T5330014. The first hotel in Gravatá, 2-star, a/c, TV, phone, swimming pool, bar, garden, English-speaking owner. *Petur-Hotel Centro Gravatá*, BR-232 Km 77, T5330016/0252, F5330075. Two-star, small, no bar or restaurant, a/c, TV, phone, swimming pool.

Eating

There are many good restaurants with regional and international food; fondue is very good in Gravatá. *Faisão Dourado*, BR-232 Km 82. Old and famous, Swiss architecture, good service, international and regional food, T5330054, open Saturday and Sunday. *Taverna Suíça*, BR-232 Km 78. Old, Swiss style, good service, international food (fondue a speciality), good wine list, English, French and Italian spoken by the owner, T5330299. *Picanha da Serra*, R 15 de Novembro 1472, T9629960. Good service, regional food, good value, closed Monday.

Festivals

In Holy Week, *Semana Santa*, there is dancing, music and a *vaquejada* (rodeo) at Km 78 on the BR-232, Haras da Serra. In **June**, the feast of *São João* is celebrated with fireworks, music, dancing and local food throughout the city. In **October** there is the *Strawberry festival of the Northeast*, with more typical food, drink, music and dancing.

Transport

Buses To **Recife** and **Caruaru** run every hour; the rodoviária is at Km 80 on the BR-232, T5330691.

Directory

Banks *Banco do Brasil*, in the centre of town, open 1000-1600, very helpful, English-speaking manager, T5330388. **Tourist offices** *Secretaria de Turismo*, R Cleto Campelo, open Mon-Fri.

Bezerros

Population: 52,000

About 15 kilometres further west on the BR-232 is Bezerros, on the Rio Ipojuca. It has some old houses, fine praças and churches. Some, like the Igreja de Nossa Senhora dos Homens Pretos, São José and the Capela de Nossa Senhora, date from the 19th century. The former railway station has been converted into the **Estação da Cultura**, with shows and other cultural performances. The city's main attraction is handicrafts, which are found in the district of **Encruzilhada de São João**; items in leather, clay, wood, papier maché and much more. The best known artist and poet is J Borges (born 1935), whose work has been exhibited internationally. Most typical are the Papangu masks, made of painted papier maché (see below). The masks are used at carnival, as interior decoration, even as key-holders. Wooden toys are also popular. About 10 kilometres from the centre of Bezerros, near the village of Serra Negra, a small ecotourism park,

Serra Negra ecological tourism trail, has been set up. Trails lead to caves and springs; the flora is typical of the *agreste*.

Carnival here is famed throughout Brazil and is known as *Folia do Papangu*. The Papangu characters wear masks that resemble a cross between a bear and a devil and are covered from head to foot in a costume like a bear skin (a variant is an all-covering white tunic). Other celebrations in the year are *São João* in June, and Christmas.

For tourist information contact the *Departamento de Turismo*, Praça Duque de Caxias 88, Centro, CEP 55660-000, T281286, F7281316. *Associação dos Artesãos de Bezerros*, the Artisans' Association, is at the same address.

Caruaru

Population: 232,000
Phone code: 081
Altitude: 554m
Colour map 2, grid B6

Situated 134 kilometres west of Recife, the paved road there passes through rolling hills, with sugar cane and large cattle *fazendas*, before climbing an escarpment. As the road gets higher, the countryside becomes drier, browner and rockier. Caruaru itself is a busy, modern town, one of the most prosperous in the *agreste* in Pernambuco. It is also culturally very lively, with excellent local and theatre and folklore groups.

Worth a visit are the **Espaço Cultural Tancredo Neves**(known as the Forro Village), which has an exhibition space, **Museu do Barro e da Cerâmica**, which does contain works by Vitalino and other clay sculptors and **Museu da Fábrica de Caroá**, with an art gallery, music school and headquarters of the municipal tourist office. **Casa da Cultura José Condé**, in Parque 18 de Maio, contains the **Museu José Condé** and a **museum of Forró**, as well as an art gallery, the municipal library and a theatre.

The little clay figures (*figurinhas* or *bonecas de barro*) originated by Mestre Vitalino (1909-63), and very typical of the *Nordeste*, are the local speciality; most of the local potters live at **Alto da Moura** six kilometres away, where a house once owned by Vitalino is open (the **Casa Museu Mestre Vitalino**), with personal objects and photographs, but no examples of his work. Unesco has recognized the area as the largest centre of figurative art in the Americas. There is a bus, 30 minutes, bumpy, US$0.50.

Sleeping
■ *on map, page 511*
A large number of cheap hospedarias are around the central square, Praça Getúlio Vargas

A *Grande Hotel São Vicente de Paulo*, Av Rio Branco 365, T7215011, F7215290. Good, central, a/c, laundry, garage, bar, restaurant, pool, TV, houses the local cinema. A *Village*, BR-232 Km 135, 3 km out, T7215974/7225544, F7227030. Clean, quiet, pleasant, 5 minutes from rodoviária, 15 minutes from the centre, a/c, TV, fridge, phone. Food recommended. B *do Sol*, 3 km outside town at Cidade Alta, T7213044, F7211336. Three-star on hill, good restaurant, pool. C *Centenário*, 7 de Setembro 84, T7224011, F7211033. Also has more expensive suites, good breakfast, pool, in the town centre so not very quiet, otherwise recommended. C *Central*, R Vigario Freire 71, T7215880. Suites or rooms, all with a/c, TV, good breakfast, in the centre. Recommended.

Eating
Lots of cheap lunch restaurants in the centre near Banco do Brasil (US$3-4), recommended are A *Massa*, R Vidal de Negreiros. Excellent pizzas, reasonably priced. *Costela do Baiano*, close to Igreja do Rosário. Very good value. *Tia Teta*, Av Agamenon Magalhães. Good for dinner. For drinks, *Catracho's*, close to the São Sebastião hospital. Has a Caribbean feel and the Honduran owner mixes great cocktails with salsa. Alto da Moura is a real tourist spot so it gets very busy, but good places to eat are *Bode de Luciano*, on the left as you enter, barbecued goat. *Tengo Lengo*, 1 km up from Bode de Luciano. Traditional Pernambucan dishes.

17 December-2 January, *Festas Natalinas*; *Semana Santa*, Holy Week, with lots of **Festivals** folklore and handicraft events. **18-22 May**, *city's anniversary*. **13 June,** *Santo Antônio* and **24 June** *São João*, the latter a particularly huge *forró* festival, are part of Caruaru's **Festas Juninas**. The whole town lights up with dancing, traditional foods, parties like the Sapadrilha, when the women dress as men, and the Gaydrilha, where the men dress as women, and there is even a Trem do Forró which runs from Recife to Caruaru, rocking the whole way to the rhythms. **September**, *Micaru*, a street carnival;

Caruaru

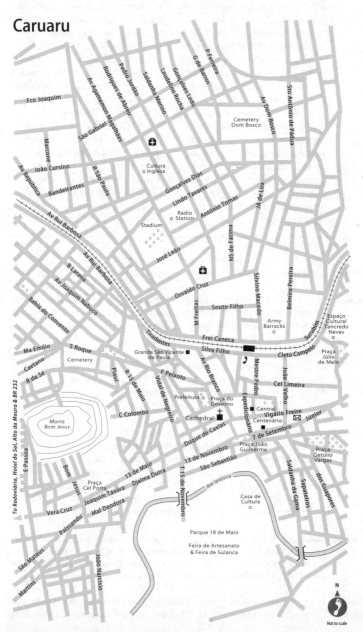

São João and the Festas Juninas

As well as the Brazilian equivalent to Valentine's Day falling on 12 June, St John is one of the three saints homaged in the Festas Juninas (June Festivals). The first official party on the Brazilian calendar after Lent, these winter celebrations take up the month of June with the main celebration on the eve of St John's Day, 23 June. Potential visitors to Brazil with a fear of fireworks should take note: this is when the streets of northeastern cities fill with stalls offering their bangers, catherine wheels and rockets.

In June, the rural areas of Brazil provide the entertainment. The region's many maize-based recipes such as pamonha and canjica are traditionally eaten and washed down with a drink known as quentão, pinga heated with cloves and cinnamon. The cities of Caruaru, Pernambuco and Campina Grande, Paraíba have built up a reputation for staging the wildest parties, with a million people descending on Caruaru. The Pernambucan town possesses a 'Forró Village', a full mock-up of a Sertão town complete with a bank and a post office which are fully functional throughout the festivities. The most exciting way to arrive must surely be the 'forró trains' from Recife's central station to Caruaru, which promise live forró trios to entertain the passengers. Brazil's biggest forró bands and singers perform in all the major cities. The festival will always be the best setting to hear the music of Forró king, Luiz Gonzaga, who died in 1989 but whose classic São João song, 'Olha pro Céu' (Look to the Sky), is sung to this day. Gonzaga tells of falling for a girl at a São João party and, in the song, he tells her to look to the sky... purely for her to admire the fireworks, of course.

Marc Starr

also in September, *Vaquejada* (a Brazilian cross between rodeo and bull fighting), biggest in the Northeast.

Shopping Caruaru is most famous for its markets which, combined, are responsible for about 70% of the city's income. The *Feira da Sulanca* is basically a clothes market supplied mostly by local manufacture, but also on sale are jewellery, souvenirs, food, flowers and anything else that can go for a good price; in one part, electronic goods are sold (this is called the *Feira de Paraguaí*, or the illegal import market). The most important day is Monday. There is also the *Feira Livre* or *do Troca-Troca* (free, or barter market). On the same site, Parque 18 de Maio, is the *Feira do Artesanato*, leather goods, ceramics, hammocks and basketware, all the popular crafts of the region; it is tourist-oriented but it is on a grand scale and is open daily 0800-1800.

Transport The rodoviária is 4 km from the town; buses from Recife stop in the town centre. Alight here and look for the *Livraria Estudantil* on the corner of Vigário Freire and R Anna de Albuquerque Galvão. Go down Galvão, turn right on R 15 de Novembro to the first junction, 13 de Maio; turn left, cross the river to the Feira do Artesanato. Bus from the centre, at the same place as Recife bus stop, to rodoviária, US$0.40. Many buses from TIP in **Recife**, 2 hours express, US$3. Bus to **Maceió**, 0700, 5 hours, US$9. Bus to **Fazenda Nova** 1030, 1 hour, US$2, returns for Caruaru 1330.

Directory **Banks** *Banca Terceiro Mundo*, a magazine stall which exchanges dollars, in front of the new Cathedral, will tell you what's going on. **Cultural centres** *Cultura Inglesa*, Av Agamenon Magalhães 634, Maurício de Nassau, CEP 55000-000, T7214749, cultura@netstage.com.br, will help any visitors with information. **Useful information** The local press, *Vanguarda* newspaper, is weekly.

Fazenda Nova & Nova Jerusalém During Easter Week each year, various agencies run package tours to the little country town of Fazenda Nova, 23 kilometres from Caruaru. Just outside the town is Nova Jerusalém, where, from the day before Palm Sunday up to Easter Saturday, an annual passion play, suggested by Oberammergau, is enacted. The site is one third the size of the historic quarter of Jerusalem, with nine permanent stages on which scenes of the Passion are presented; 50 actors and 500 extras re-enact the story. The latest sound and lighting effects are used in the performance. The audience moves from one stage to another as the story unfolds. Performances begin at 1800, lasting around three hours. Also in Fazenda Nova is a sculpture park, where gigantic figures carved from blocks of stone represent motifs of *Nordeste* culture. The best hotel in Fazenda Nova is *Grande* (**E**), Av Poeta Carlos Penha Filho, T7321137.

Good roads via Caruaru or Palmares run to the city of Garanhuns, 209 kilometres southwest of Recife. Its claims to be the best holiday resort in the Northeast are attributed to its cool climate – it stands at 890 metres, and has an average temperature of 21°C – its mineral waters and its beautiful landscapes and parks.

Garanhuns
Population: 110,000
Phone code: 081

Sleeping **B** *Tavares Correia*, Av Rui Barbosa 296, T7610900, F7611597. Four-star. **C** *D'Nyl*, Praça Dom Moura 302, T/F7610998. Telephone, TV, minibar, breakfast included, also serves optional dinner. **C** *Village*, Av Santo Antônio 149A, T7613624. Central, 15 mintues' walk from rodoviária, good, bath, fridge, TV, fan (cheaper than a/c). **D** *Diplomata*, R Dr Jose Mariano 194. Telephone, shower, TV, minibar, breakfast included. **Camping** *Camping Treze*, BR-432, Km 105.

About 126 kilometres west of Caruaru (bus 2½ hours, US$6) is **Arcoverde**, a market town in the Sertão, with a market every Saturday; it is cool at night. There are various hotels (**C-D**).

About 200 kilometres west of Arcoverde, via Serra Talhada, is this delightful small town in the Serra de Borborema. It has a good climate and a great variety of crops, flowers and fruits. There is also a sugar mill that can be visited (Engenho Boa Esperança), waterfalls (eg Cachoeira do Pingas, six kilometres, signposted; if there has been no rain waterfalls may be dry, ask), sounding rocks, the convent of São Boaventura, and the Museu do Cangaço, showing the lives and relics of the traditional bandits of the *Nordeste*.

Triúnfo
Population: 15,000
Phone code: 081

Sleeping **C** *Fazenda Calugi*, Estr Santa Tereza, T8461183. TV, pool, minibar, breakfast. Recommended. **D** *Lar Santa Elizabeth*, opposite church on hill near rodoviária, T8461236. The sisters offer lodging and profits support social work, good, bath, fan, balcony, clean, patio. **D** *Pousada Baixa Verde*, R Manoel Paiva dos Santos 114, T/F8461103. Nice rooms, good breakfast.

Transport Two Progresso buses daily to and from **Recife** (10 hours). It is quicker to take a bus from Recife to Serra Talhada, then a colectivo to Triunfo (US$2). In Truinfo colectivos leave from the lakeside. To Triúnfo from **Caruaru**, 1 bus per day, 0830, US$10.

The Sertão

Beyond Serra Talharda the BR-232 continues to Salgueiro, where it meets the BR-116 heading north to Fortaleza. The BR-232 becomes the BR-316 and heads northwest to Araripina before entering Piauí. This part of Pernambuco was the haunt of the bandit Lampião until his death in 1938. Even today the area is still quite lawless and buses are often escorted by armed police. Also cultivation of marijuana in the area between Salgueiro and Floresta means that visitors are not generally welcome.

☞ *The Great Western of Brazil Railway*

At its height, the Great Western of Brazil Railway Company Ltd ran the entire railway network in four states in Northeast Brazil – Rio Grande do Norte, Paraíba, Pernambuco, and Alagoas. This network, known popularly as the 'gretueste', eventually comprised more than 1,600 kilometres of railway track, and is credited with opening up the interior of the four states through which it ran and joining together the four state capitals of, respectively, Natal, João Pessoa (Parahyba), Recife (the headquarters) and Maceió.

Construction began on the original GWBR line in 1879, during the time of the Brazilian Empire when these present day States were known as provinces, and three years later 95 kilometres of track were operational from Recife to Limoeiro, with a branch line to Nazaré. The choice of `Great Western' as the name of the company was justified by the north-westerly direction taken by the line from Recife, but undoubtedly it was also hoped that this famous name would attract shareholders on the stock markets in Britain. In fact, the GWBR had no connection whatsoever with the Great Western Railway in England. Rather, it resulted from the ambition of the Pernambuco Provincial government in the 1850s to link the important agricultural area around Limoeiro to the coast for the transport of its sugar, cotton, cattle, vegetables and cereals.

English investors met in 1872 to incorporate a company with a total stock of over £1,000,000, with the intention of exploiting a concession given to a Brazilian Baron – the Barão da Soledade. In 1874, the Baron obtained from the Imperial and Provincial governments confirmation that seven percent interest would be paid yearly on the capital invested – a guarantee that attracted several English capitalists to Brazil – and the following year he transferred this concession to the GWBR. The contract with the government offered many advantages, including free land in a privilege zone extending 20 kilometres on either side of the track, exemption from import tax, and exclusive use for 90 years. A further clause, common to all the foreign railway concessions, had a lasting effect on Brazil. This clause prohibited the use of slaves both in the construction and in the operation of the railway, and, in the words of Brazil's foremost sociologist Gilberto Freyre, "contributed to the breaking up of the feudal and slave-based conditions of manual and field work hitherto dominant among us". It should be remembered that slavery was abolished in Brazil only in 1888.

Of the several foreign owned lines that existed at the beginning of this century, the GWBR was the only profitable company – not surprising given the generous terms on which companies were enticed to invest in railways in Brazil – and it was invited by the then Republican government to rent out the existing regional network in a series of takeovers expected to last 60 years, but which ended in expropriation in 1950. One of the lines rented to the GWBR, in 1901, was the famous Recife and São Francisco Railway which was the second railway to open to traffic in Brazil (1858), the first railway built with foreign capital, and the first railway of economic importance in Brazil.
Eddie Edmundson

Petrolina
Population: 173,500
Phone code: 081

Located on the Rio São Francisco which forms the southern border of Pernambuco, Petrolina is best visited from Juazeiro in Bahia (see page 471). Like Pirapora, Petrolina is famous for the production of *carrancas* (boat figureheads, mostly grotesque) of wood or ceramic. Petrolina has its own airport and close to this is the small **Museu do Sertão** – relics of rural life in the northeast and the age of the 'coronéis' and the bandit Lampião (see page 545). Hotels include *Pousada da Carranca* (**D**), BR-122, Km 4, T9613421, and *Hotel Neuman* (**C**), Av Souza Filho 444, T9610595, (overpriced, small room, bath, a/c, clean). *Hotel Central* is not recommended.

Fernando de Noronha

This small archipelago, 345 kilometres off the northeast coast, was declared a *Phone code: 081* Marine National Park in 1988. Only one island is inhabited. The island, which is dominated by a 321-metre peak, has many unspoilt beaches and interesting wildlife, especially in the waters that surround it. Scuba-diving and snorkelling are excellent. It is part of the state of Pernambuco administered from Recife.

The islands were discovered in 1503 by Amérigo Vespucci and were for a time a pirate lair. (In some descriptions, the name is given as Fernando de Loronha.) In 1738 the Portuguese built the Forte dos Remédios, later used as a prison in this century, and a church to strengthen their claim to the islands. Remains of the early fortifications still exist. One of the more famous prisoners in the 20th century was Luís Carlos Prestes, who led the famous long march, the Prestes Column, in 1925-27.

Vila dos Remédios is where most people live and socialize. It is near the north coast, which is the one most frequented by locals and visitors. At the northeast end is Baía de Santo Antônio, which has a jetty. Some of the beaches on this side are Conceição, Boldró, Americano, Bode, Baía dos Porcos (a beautiful cove at the beginning of the marine park) and Baía do Sancho. Beyond is the Baía dos Golfinhos, with a lookout point for watching the spinner dolphins in the bay. On the south, or windward side, there are fewer beaches (for example Praia do Leão, Baía do Sueste, Atalaia), higher cliffs and the whole coastline and offshore islands are part of the marine park. As with dive sites, Ibama restricts bathing in low-tide pools and other sensitive areas to protect the environment.

Ibama has imposed rigorous rules to prevent damage to the nature reserve and everything, from development to cultivation of food crops to fishing, is strictly administered, if not forbidden. Many locals are now dependent on tourism and most food is brought from the mainland; prices are about double. Entry to the island has been limited to 100 tourists per day because of the serious problems of energy and water supply. A maximum of 420 tourists is

Fernando de Noronha

allowed on the island at any one time. Moreover, there is a tax of US$13, payable per day for the first week of your stay. In the second week the tax increases each day. Take sufficient *reais* as dollars are heavily discounted. For information, contact the park office, Paranamar-FN, T6191210.

The rains are from February to July; the island turns green and the seawater becomes lovely and clear. The dry season is August to March, but the sun shines all year round. The time is one hour later than Brazilian Standard Time. Repellent is not available for the many mosquitoes.

Essentials

Sleeping **L** *Pousada Esmeralda*, T/F6191355. The only establishment classified as a hotel, rates are full board, it is none too comfortable, its location used to be an airbase, packages from mainland travel agents usually place visitors in the *Esmeralda*. **AL** *Solar dos Ventos*, T6191347, F6191253. Large a/c apartments full board. Recommended. Ask for 'o capitanão'. **B** *Estrela do Mar*, T6191366. With breakfast, excursions arranged. Independent travellers can go much cheaper as many local families rent out rooms with full board, ranging from US$50-75 pp per day. The best known is that of Suzanna and Rocha, T6191227, rooms with fan and bathroom. Vanilda across the street has been highly recommended. There are plenty of others and the home owners have an association, *Associação das Hospedarias Domiciliares de Fernando de Noronha*, T6191142 for information.

Eating There are 3 restaurants, *Anatalício*, *Ecológico* and *Miramar*. The speciality of the island is shark (*tubarão*), which is served in bars and at the port (Noronha Pesca Oceânica). There aren't many bars, but a good one is *Mirante Bar*, near the hotel, with a spectacular view over Boldró beach, it has loud music and at night is an open-air disco. *Bar do Cachorro* is a popular new bar.

Sports **Scuba-diving** Diving is organized by *Atlantis Divers*, T6191371, *Águas Claras*, T6191225, in the hotel grounds, and *Noronha Divers*, T6191112. Diving costs between US$50-75 and equipment rental from US$50. This is the diving mecca for Brazilian divers with a great variety of sites to explore and fish to see. Further details will be found in the **Adventure sports**, page 30. Enquire in advance if it is possible to swim with the dolphins at the Baía dos Golfinhos. If it is not allowed they can be seen from the beach. Similarly, sharks and turtles can be seen without entering the water. For details on the turtles, contact Fundação Pró-Tamar, Caixa Postal 50, CEP 53990-000, Fernando de Noronha, T6191269, F6191386.

Transport **Air** Daily flights from Recife, with Nordeste and Transporte Regional do Interior Paulista and with the latter from Nata, 1 hour 20 minutes from Recife, 1 hour from Natal, US$400 and US$300 return respectively.

Directory **Tour companies & travel agents** Boat trips and jeep tours around the island are available; it is also possible to hire a beach buggy (US$100 a day without a driver, US$30 with driver). Motorbikes can be rented for US$80 a day. You can hitch everywhere as everyone stops. There are good hiking, horse riding and mountain biking possibilities, but you must either go with a guide or ranger in many parts.

Paraíba

This state has a historic and pleasant capital with a rich cultural heritage. There are some wonderful beaches beside the turquoise waters of the Atlantic Ocean. The most easterly point in Brazil is to be found at Ponta das Seixas. Inland is the town of Campina Grande on the edge of the dry Sertão and famous for its very lively São João celebrations in June.

The Portuguese did not gain a foothold on this part of the northeast coast until the very end of the 16th century. Their fort grew until the city of Filipéia (the third in Brazil), renamed Parahyba, then João Pessoa. The Dutch took control in 1634, but after 1644 exercised little influence over the region until their expulsion 10 years later. After this, Portuguese Indian hunters and Jesuit missionaries penetrated far into the interior. Drought in colonial times, as today, severely affected the state's economic development.

The state has a population of about 3,350,000. A coastal strip was once covered in dense tropical forest which now only survives in patches. Where forest used to grow, the land is now given over to agriculture, mainly monocultures like sugar. The seaboard is marked for much of its length by offshore reefs. Inland from the coastal plain, which is called the *Zona da Mata*, is an abrupt line of hills and plateaus, a transitional region between the moist coast and the much drier interior. Here the rainfall is less, but still sufficient for smaller scale, multi-crop agriculture. The vegetation of this zone, called the *Agreste*, is also transitional, sharing some of the characteristics of the *zona da mata* with a greater variety of palms and the plants of the *caatinga*, the scrub forest of the *sertão*. Population distribution mirrors rainfall in that the drier the land the fewer people per square kilometre. Most people live in the *zona da mata*, especially in and around the state capital and a couple of other industrial centres. In the *agreste*, only Campina Grande has a significant concentration of inhabitants.

João Pessoa

It is a bus ride of two hours through sugar plantations over a good road from Recife (126 kilometres) to João Pessoa, the state capital, on the Rio Paraíba. It retains a small town atmosphere.

Population: 550,000
Phone code: 083
Colour map 2, grid B6

Ocean-going ships load and unload at Cabedelo (see **Excursions** below). Founded in 1585 as Nossa Senhora das Neves, it became Friederikstaadt during the Dutch occupation (1634-54) and was only given its current name in 1930 in memory of a governor who was killed in Recife.

Sights

The well preserved **Centro Histórico** has several churches and monasteries which are worth seeing. The São Francisco Cultural Centre (Praça São Francisco 221), one of the most important baroque structures in Brazil, includes

Recife & the Northeast Coast

the beautiful 16th century church of **São Francisco** and the Convento de Santo Antônio, which houses the **Museu Sacro e de Arte Popular**, with a magnificent collection of colonial and popular artefacts. ■ *Tuesday-Saturday 0800-1100, Tuesday-Sunday 1400-1700, T2212840.* This is also the best point to see the sun set over the forest.

Other tourist points include the **Casa da Pólvora**, an old gunpowder store which has become the city museum, and **Museu Fotográfico Walfredo**

João Pessoa orientation

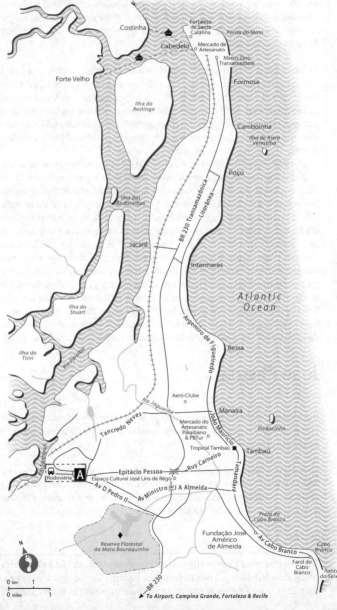

Related map
A João Pessoa centre,
page 521

0 km 1
0 miles 1

To Airport, Campina Grande, Fortaleza & Recife

Rodríguez, Ladeira de São Francisco. ■ *Monday-Friday 0800-1200 and 1330-1700*. The **Teatro Santa Roza** at Praça Pedro Américo, Varadouro, was built in 1886 with a wooden ceiling and walls. ■ *Monday-Friday 1400-1800, T2411230*. The **Espaço Cultural José Lins de Rego**, Rua Abdias Gomes de Almeida 800, Tambauzinho, a cultural centre named after the novelist (see **Literature**, page 777), includes an art gallery, history and science museums, several theatres, cinema and a planetarium. ■ *T2441360*. The **Fundação José Américo de Almeida**, Avenida Cabo Branco 3336, Cabo Branco, should be visited by those interested in modern literature and politics; it is in the former house of the novelist and sociologist.

João Pessoa prides itself in being a green city and is called **Cidade Verde**. Its parks include the 17-hectare **Parque Arruda Câmara**, also known as Bica, located north of the centre in the neighbourhood of Roger; it has walking trails, an 18th century fountain, an aviary and a small zoo. **Parque Solon de Lucena** or **Lagoa** is a lake surrounded by impressive palms in the centre of town, the city's main avenues and bus lines go around it. **Mata** or **Manancial do Bouraquinho** is a 471-hectare nature reserve of native *mata atlântica*, one of the largest urban forest reserves in Brazil. It is located south of the centre and administered by Ibama (T2441626), which organizes guided walks; access is otherwise restricted.

Urban beaches

The beachfront stretches for some 30 kilometres from Ponta do Seixas (south) to Cabedelo (north); the ocean is turquoise green and there is a backdrop of lush coastal vegetation. By the more populated urban areas the water is polluted, but there are also parts away from town which are reasonably clean, some spots are calm and suitable for swimming while others are best for surfing. Seven kilometres from the city centre, following Avenida Presidente Epitáceo Pessoa, is the beach of **Tambaú**, which has many hotels, restaurants and the state tourism centre. The pier by *Hotel Tambaú* affords nice views (bus No 510 'Tambaú' from outside the rodoviária or the city centre, alight at *Hotel Tropical Tambaú*). South of Tambaú are Praia de Cabo Branco and Praia do Seixas and to the north are the beaches of Manaíra, Bessa, Intermares, Poço and Camboinha, before reaching the port of Cabedelo.

Excursions

Fourteen kilometres from the centre, south down the coast, is the **Cabo Branco** lighthouse at Ponta do Seixas, the most easterly point of continental Brazil and South America (34° 46' 36"W) and thus the first place in the Americas where the sun rises; there is a panoramic view from the cliff top. **Cabo Branco** is much better for swimming than **Tambaú**. Take bus 507 'Cabo Branco' from outside the rodoviária to the end of the line; hike up to the lighthouse. At low tide you can walk from Tambaú to Ponta do Seixas in about two hours.

The port of **Cabedelo** (*population* 29,000), on a peninsula between the Rio Paraíba and the Atlantic Ocean, is 18 kilometres north by road or rail. Here, Km 0 marks the beginning of the Transamazônica highway. At the tip of the peninsula are the impressive, but somewhat rundown, walls of the 17th-century fortress of Santa Catarina, amid oil storage tanks and the commercial port. The **Mercado de Artesanato** is at Praça Getúlio Vergas, Centro.

The estuary of the Rio Paraíba has several islands; there is a regular boat service between Cabedelo and the fishing villages of **Costinha** and **Forte Velho** on the north bank; Costinha had a whaling station until the early 1980s.

The beaches between João Pessoa and Cabedelo have many bars and restaurants and are very popular with the locals on summer weekends. *Portal das Cores*, Rua da Ensenada 876, Praia Ponta de Campina, Intermares, have drinks and food, very nice location and atmosphere, live music on weekend nights; *Bar do Sumé*, Rua Beira Mar 171, Praia Ponta do Mato, Cabedelo, has good fish and seafood. Take bus marked Cabedelo-Poço for the beach as most Cabedelo buses go inland along the Transamazônica; taxi Tambaú-Cabedelo US$24.

At Km 3 of the Transamazônica, about 12 kilometres from João Pessoa, is the access to **Jacaré**, a nice beach on the Rio Paraíba (take Cabedelo bus and walk 1½ kilometres or take the train and walk one kilometre, taxi from Tambaú US$10). There are several bars along the riverfront where people congregate to watch the lovely sunset to the sounds of Ravel's Bolero. Here you can hire a boat along the river to visit the mangroves or ride in an ultralight aircraft (Flaviano Gouveia, T9821604, US$19 for eight-minute ride or US$115 for an hour). Brian Ingram, originally from Kent, England, runs *Sea Tech* (PO Box 42, João Pessoa, 56001-970, T2451476, F2452302), a boat yard and frequent port of call for international yachtspeople plying the Brazilian coast.

From Tambaú tour boats leave for **Picãozinho**, a group of coral reefs about 700 metres from the coast which at low tide turn into pools of crystalline water, suitable for snorkelling (US$15 per person). Further north, across from Praia de Camboinha (boats leave from here), is **Areia Vermelha**, a large sandbank surrounded by corals. This becomes exposed at low tide, around the time of the full and new moon, and is a popular bathing spot (US$20 per person tour, US$5 per person transport in a *jangada*). Floating bars are set up at both locations, travel agencies arrange trips.

Essentials

Sleeping **Central hotels A** *Guarany*, R Almeida Barreto 181 and 13 de Maio, T/F2412161 (**B** without a/c and TV, cheaper still in low season). Safe, good value, good breakfast. **B** *JR*, Rodrigues Chaves 87, T2412104. With bath, cheaper with fan and in low season. **B** *Pousada dos Estrangeiros*, Alberto Falco 67 and Epitácio Pessoa, Miramar, T2264667, F2262787. Bath, a/c. **C** *Aurora*, Praça João Pessoa 51, T2412204, a/c, cheaper with fan. Recommended. **C** *Princesa Isabel*, Princesa Isabel 885, T2413630, near Mercado Central. With bath, a/c, cheaper with fan. **D** *Ouro Preto*, Idaleto 162, T2215882, Varadouro near rodoviária. With bath, fan. Cheaper hotels can be found near the rodoviária.

Tambaú L *Ouro Branco Praia*, Av Nossa Senhora dos Navegantes 999, T2471010, F2266274. A/c, fridge, pool (**AL** in low season). **L** *Tropical Tambaú*, Av Alm Tamandaré 229, T2473660, F2471070. A distinctive round building with an obelisque in the centre, looks like a rocket launching station and is a landmark in town, comfortable, good service, recommended, price varies according to standard of rooms. **AL** *Caiçara*, Av Olinda 235, T/F2472040. A/c, pool, restaurant. **A** *Victory Business Flat*, Av Tamandaré 310, T2451196, F2473100. Furnished apartments, pool, sauna, cheaper in low season. **A** *Royal Praia*, Coração de Jesus, T2473006, F2264346. A/c, fridge, pool. **A** *Sol-Mar*, Rui Carneiro 500, T2261350, F2263242. Pool, superb restaurant. Highly recommended (reduced to **C** in low season). **B** *Brisa Mar*, Av Rui Carneiro 577, T2265400, F2263061. A/c, fridge, includes dinner. **B** *Costa Bela Praia*, Av Négo 131, T2261570. With bath, a/c, small. Recommended. **B** *Villa Mare Apartment Hotel*, Av Négo 707, T2262142. Apartments for 2 or 3 people, US$500-600 per month, helpful. Recommended. **D** *Pousada Canta-Maré*, Osório Paes 60, T2471047, near Mercado de Artesanato. Good value.

Manaíra AL *Ponto do Sol*, Av João Maurício 1861, T2463100, F2462782. A/c, pool, nice location (**A** low season). **A** *Gameleira*, Av João Maurício 157, T2261576, F2262360. Good breakfast, dirty, noisy at night, **C** with fan, cheaper in low season. **A** *Pousada Casa Grande*, Av Édson Ramalho 530, T2265622. A/c, fridge, pool.

Cabo Branco L *Littoral*, No 2172, T2471100, F2471166. Full service, luxury, low *All are across from the* season discounts available. **AL** *Xênius*, No 1262, T2263535, F2265463. A/c, fridge (low *beach, along Av Cabo* season reductions). **A** *Veleiros*, No 3106, T/F2261332, F2261332. A/c, fridge. **B** *Escuna* *Branco unless* *Praia*, No 1574, T2265611. A/c, fridge. **B** *Pouso das Águas*, No 2348, T2267268, *otherwise noted* F2265103. A/c, fridge, pool. **B** *Pousada Casa Rosada*, No 1710, T2472470. With bath, fan, **C** with shared bath, family run, new in 1997. Accommodation can also be found in the outer beaches such as Camboinha and Seixas, and in Cabedelo.

Youth hostels *Albergue de Juventude Cabo Branco*, R Padre José Tringuero 104, Cabo Branco, T2472221, F2263628, IYHA. *Albergue de Juventude Tambaú*, Bezerra Reis 83, Manaíra, T2265460. US$8 pp. Also at Av das Trincheiras, at Palácio dos Esportes, T2217220/1.

Camping *Camping Clube do Brasil*, Praia de Seixas, 13 km from the centre, T2472181.

Adega do Alfredo, Coração de Jesus, Tambaú. Pricy, good, Portuguese. *Recanto do* **Eating** *Picuí*, Feliciano Dourado 198, Torre. Good *carne de sol* and regional. *Tábua de Carne*, Av Pres Epitáceo Pessoa 4975 and Av Sen Rui Carneiro 648, Tambaú. Grill. *Churascaria Picanha de Ouro*, Av Pres Epitáceo Pessoa 5102, Tambaú. Regional grill. *Cheiro Verde*, R Alverga 43, Tambaú. Self service. *Sagaranda*, Av Tamandaré near *Hotel Tambaú*. Very good *cozinha criativa* (akin to *nouvelle cuisine*). *Olho de Lula*, Av Cabo Branco 2300, Cabo Branco, straw hut by the beach. Varied menu. *Apetito Tratoria*, Osório Paes 35, Tambaú. Very good Italian, charming. *Sapore d'Italia*, Av Cabo Branco 1584, Italian, pizza. *Palhoça do Seixas*, Pescadores 43, Praia do Seixas, straw hut on the beach, past the Cabo Branco lighthouse. Seafood, meats, daytime only. *Naturoasiss*, Parque Solon de Lucena 2216, Centro. Health food. *Barriga Cheia*, Duque de Caxias 533, Centro. Self service.

There are many open bars on and across from the beach in Tambaú and Cabo Branco; **Bars &** the area known as *Feirinha de Tambaú*, on Av Tamandaré by the *Tambaú Hotel* and **nightclubs** nearby streets, sees much movement on weekend nights, other beachfront

João Pessoa centre

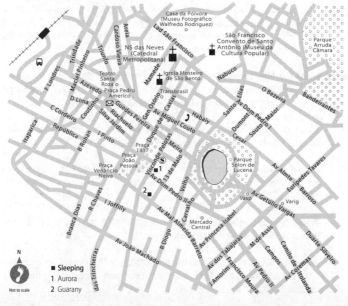

Recife & the Northeast Coast

Coconut rice with shellfish

Use condensed or dried coconut milk, or the solid concentrate available from Asian grocers. Make it up, according to the instructions, to a milky (not creamy) consistency. Quantity serves 6-8.

Ingredients:
350g long-grain rice
50 ml olive oil
1 finely chopped medium onion
350 ml coconut milk
1 tomato, peeled, seeded and chopped
1 tbsp lime or lemon juice
2 handfuls fresh coriander, chopped
24 clams or mussels (fresh, canned or preserved in water)
Water to make the fish juice up to 350 ml

Method:
In a heavy saucepan, sauté the onion with the oil over a medium heat. When it is soft and transparent, add the rice. Stir for a few minutes until the rice is coated with oil, but not brown. Add the coconut milk with the fish water, the tomato, and some salt if needed. Bring to the boil, then reduce the heat and simmer until the rice is tender and the liquid all absorbed (about 30 minutes). Pour the lime juice over the shellfish. Five minutes before the rice has finished cooking, stir in the shellfish and herbs.

---

neighbourhoods also have popular bars (see excursions above). **Bahamas**, Av J Maurício, Tambaú, young crowd. **Marinas**, Av Cabo Branco 4924, pleasant atmosphere. Suggested nightclubs are **Brumas**, Av Nossa Senhora dos Navegantes 1105, Tambaú. **Casa Blanca**, Praça Santo Antônio 22, Tambaú, fancy.

Festivals Pre-carnival celebrations in João Pessoa are renowned: the bloco *Acorde Miramar* opens the celebrations the Tuesday before **Carnival** and on Wednesday, known as *Quarta Feira de Fogo*, thousands join the *Muriçocas de Miramar*, forming a bloco second only to Recife's *Galo da Madrugada* with as many as 300,000 people taking part in the celebrations. The street celebrations for the patroness of the city, **Nossa Senhora das Neves**, take place for 10 days around **5 August**, to the rhythm of frevo.

Shopping Regional crafts, including lace-work, embroidery and ceramics, are available at the following centres: **Mercado de Artesanato**, Centro de Turismo, Almte Tamandaré 100, Tambaú. **Mercados de Artesanato I e II**, Av Rui Carneiro, Tambaú. **Bosque dos Sonhos**, by the Cabo Branco lighthouse.

Transport **Local Car hire**: *Localiza*, Av Epitácio Pessoa 4910, T2474030, and at the airport, T0800-992000. *Locarauto*, Tito Silva 23, Miramar, T2263335, F2262713. *Loca Buggy*, T9824545. *Tempo*, Almte Tamandaré 100, at the Centro de Turismo, T2471288.

Buses: all city buses stop at the rodoviária and most go by the Lagoa (Parque Solon de Lucena). Take No 510 for Tambaú, No 507 for Cabo Branco.

Long distance Air: domestic flights arrive at Presidente Castro Pinto airport, 11 km from centre, T2321200. Flights to Recife and Rio de Janeiro. Taxi to centre costs US$10, to Tambaú US$17.

Trains: ferroviária at Av Sanhauá, Varadouro, T2214257. Regional service west to Bayeux and Santa Rita and Cabedelo to the north.

Buses: rodoviária is at R Francisco Londres, Varadouro, 10 minutes from the centre, T2219611. Luggage store and PBTUR information booth, helpful. Taxi to the centre US$2, to Tambaú US$8.

Xinxim de Galinha

Almost a definitive northeastern dish, this chicken in shrimp and peanut sauce is an exotic combination of Guaraní Indian influences, African and Portuguese. Dendê (palm) oil is available from Brazilian and African shops; dried shrimp is also sold by Asian grocers. This recipe serves 4.

Ingredients:
4 chicken quarters
The juice of 2 lemons
2 crushed garlic cloves
2 tbsp olive oil
1 finely chopped onion
50g dried, ground shrimp
50g ground peanuts
1 small chilli, seeded and chopped
150 ml chicken stock
3 tbsp dendê

Method:
Sprinkle the lemon juice, garlic and some salt over the chicken pieces. Put the onion, shrimp powder, peanuts and chilli pepper in a heavy pan with the olive oil. Stir constantly over a low heat for 5 minutes to make a paste. Add the chicken and its liquid to the pan. Pour in the stock and mix thoroughly, bringing it to a simmer. Cover and allow to cook on a low heat for about 40 minutes, until the chicken is tender. Turn the chicken once during cooking, and add more stock if needed. Before serving, add the dendê and increase the heat for a couple of minutes. Serve with Brazilian rice and farofa (see **Feijoada** recipe, page 72).

To **Recife** with *Boa Vista* or *Bonfim*, every 30 minutes, US$2.50, 2 hours. To **Natal** with *Nordeste*, every 2 hours, US$4.25 *convencional*, US$5.40 *executivo*, 3 hours. To **Fortaleza** with *Nordeste*, 4 daily, 10 hours, US$15. To **Campina Grande** with *Real*, every 30 minutes, US$3, 2 hours. To **Juazeiro do Norte** with *Transparaíba*, 2 daily, US$14, 10 hours. To **Salvador** with *Progresso*, 4 weekly, US$20, 14 hours. To **Brasília** via Campina Grande, with *Planalto*, 2 weekly, US$57, 48 hours. To **Rio de Janeiro** with *São Geraldo*, daily, US$65.50 *convencional*, US$78 *executivo*, 42 hours. To **São Paulo** with *Itapemirim*, daily, US$63 *convencional*, US$76 *executivo*, 47 hours. To **Belém** with *Boa Esperança*, daily, US$47.50, 36 hours.

Directory

Airline offices *TAF*, at airport, T2322747. *Transbrasil*, Gen Osório 177, Centro, T2412822, F2412829. *Varig*, Av Getúlio Vargas 183, Centro, T2211140, F2216580. *Vasp*, Parque Solon de Lucena 530, Centro, T2211140, F2223879, at airport, T2321757. **Banks** *Banco do Brasil*, Praça 1817129, 3rd floor, Centro, Isidro Gomes 14, Tambaú, behind Centro de Turismo, helpful but poor rates. *Mondeo Tour*, Av Négo 46, Tambaú, T2263100. Open 0900-1730, cash and TCs. *PB Câmbio Turismo*, Visconde de Pelotas 54C, Centro, T2414555, open Mon-Fri 1030-1630, cash and TCs. **Communications** Post Office: main office is at Praça Pedro Américo, Varadouro; central office is at Parque Solon de Lucena 375; also by the beach at Av Rui Carneiro, behind the Centro de Turismo. Telephones: Calling stations at: Visconde de Pelotas and Miguel Couto, Centro; Centro de Turismo, Tambaú; Av Epitácio Pessoa 1487, Bairro dos Estados; rodoviária and Airport. **Tour companies & travel agents** *Roger Turismo*, Av Tamandaré 229. *Hotel Tambaú*, T2471856, F2471533, local and regional tours, airport transfers. *Preocupação Zero Turismo*, Av Cabo Branco 2566, T2264859, F2264599, local and regional tours, floating bars. *Navegar*, Artur Monteiro de Paiva 97, Bessa, T/F2462191, buggy tours (US$25 to Jacumã). *Cabo Branco*, Des Souto Maior 186, Centro, T2215044, F2224023. *Comvitur*, Cecília Miranda 20, T2223742, F2411354, tours to Tambaba. **Stella Barros**, Av Epitácio Pessoa 2230, Tambauzinho, T2244989, F2251165, Thomas Cook representative. **Tourist offices** *PBTUR*, Centro de Turismo, Almte Tamandaré 100, Tambaú, at rodoviária and airport, all open 0800-2000, for information, T1516. **Voltage** 220 volts AC, 60 cycles.

Recife & the Northeast Coast

The Paraíba Coast

The Paraíba coastline has 117 kilometres of beautiful beaches and coves, surrounded by cliffs and coconut groves. These are among the least developed of the Northeast.

Tambaba

Colour map 2, grid B6 The best known beach of the state is **Tambaba**, the only official nudist beach of the Northeast and one of only two in Brazil. It is located 49 kilometres south of João Pessoa in a lovely setting: the green ocean, warm water, natural pools for swimming formed by the rocks, cliffs up to 20 metres high full of caves, palms and lush vegetation. Two coves make up this famous beach: in the first bathing-suits are optional, while the second one is only for nudists. Strict rules of conduct are enforced, unaccompanied men are not allowed in this area and any inappropriate behaviour is reason enough to be asked to leave. The only infrastructure is one bar (meals available).

Between Jacumã and Tambaba are several nice beaches such as **Tabatinga**, which has many summer homes built on the cliffs, and **Coqueirinho**, surrounded by nice vegetation, good for bathing, surfing and exploring caves.

Sleeping **B** *Pousada Corais de Carapebus*, Av Beira Mar, Carapebus, T2901179, a few kilometres south of Jacumã. With bath, pool, restaurant, nice breeze since it is located on a cliff across from the ocean. **B** *Chalé Suiço*, R Chalé Suiço 120, Tabatinga, T9812046. Small, shared bath, restaurant, upstairs rooms with balconies towards the ocean. **B** *Vivenda Ocean*, R Sidine C Dore 254, Carapebus, T2266017. Chalets for 5, restaurant. **C** *Vallhalla*, R Niterói, Jacumã, T2901015. Away from the beach, simple, fan, nice views, Swedish-run, restaurant with varied menu. *Solemar*, Jacumã, T2901032. **Camping** is possible in Tambaba with permission from the guards, also in Coqueirinho, no infrastructure in either.

Transport Access to Jacumã is via the BR-101, 20 kilometres south from João Pessoa to where the PB-018 goes 3 km east to Conde and continues 11 km to the beach of Jacumã; from here a dirt road goes 12 km south to Tambaba. There are hourly buses from the João Pessoa rodoviária (0530-1900) to Jacumã; in the summer, dune buggies can be hired at Jacumã to go to Tambaba. Buggy from João Pessoa to Tambaba US$25 pp return (leave 0930, return 1730). Day trip in a taxi US$95.

Near the border with Pernambuco is the 10 kilometres long beach of **Pitimbu**, see page 508.

Campina

The nicest beaches of northern Paraíba are in the vicinity of the fishing village of **Campina**; although there is little infrastructure in this area, the shore is worth a visit. Access is via a turnoff to the east at Km 73.5 of the BR-101, 42 kilometres north of João Pessoa. It is 28 kilometres along a dirt road (PB-025) to Praia Campina, with a wide beach of fine sand, palms and hills in the background. Nearly three kilometres south is **Praia do Oiteiro**, in which the white sand stands out in contrast with the multicoloured cliffs and the calm blue ocean. About two kilometres north of Campina is **Barra do Mamanguape**, where Ibama runs a centre for the preservation of the marine manatee.

Eighty five kilometres from João Pessoa is **Baia da Traição**, a fishing village and access point for a number of beaches. Its name refers to a massacre of 500 residents of a sugar plantation in the 16th century. There is an Indian reserve near town where wood and string crafts are made. An annual festival, **Festa do Toré** (an Indian dance), takes place on 19 April. Inho, a fisherman, offers tours by sea to the more inaccessible beaches in the area (US$15 per person). **Barra de Camaratuba**, some 17 kilometres north of Baia da Traição, is a popular surfing beach.

Sleeping C *Pousada Ponto do Sol*, Dom Pedro II 537, Baia da Traição, T2961050. With bath, fridge, restaurant. On the same street are the simpler pousadas *Alvorada* and *2001*, T2961043. Several others in town. **Barra de Camaratuba** C *Pousada Porto das Ondas*, T2472054. Bath, fan, restaurant.

The Sertão

The Transamazônica runs due west of João Pessoa as the BR-230, along the axis of the state of Paraíba and through the heart of the *sertão*.

Campina Grande

Located in the Serra da Borborema at 551 metres above sea level and 130 kilometres west of João Pessoa, the second city in Paraíba has a very pleasant climate. Known as the *porta do sertão*, it is an important centre for light industry and an outlet for goods from most of the northeast. In the 1920s it was one of the most important cotton producing areas in the world; a decline in this industry brought a decrease in prosperity in the 1940s and 1950s and the diversification of industry to areas such as sisal and leather. The city's two universities have been instrumental in technological development and reactivation of the local economy.

Population: 340,500
Phone code: 083
Colour map 2, grid B6

Sights Avenida Floriano Peixoto is the main street running east-west through the entire city, with Praça da Bandeira at its centre. The **Museu de Arte Assis Chateaubriand**, Parque do Açude Novo, has a collection of paintings and etchings by Brazilian artists and temporary exhibits. ■ *Monday-Friday 0900-1200, Monday-Sunday 1400-2200, T3413300*. **Museu Histórico de Campina Grande**, Avenida Floriano Peixoto 825, Centro, is the city museum housed in a 19th century building, with a photo and artefact collection reflecting the cycles of prosperity and poverty in the region. ■ *Daily 0800-1130, 1300-1645*. **Museu da História e Tecnologia do Algodão**, Centro Nacional de Produção do Algodão, Oswaldo Cruz 1143, Centenário, has machines and related equipment used in the cotton industry in the 16th and 17th centuries. ■ *Monday-Friday 0730-1130 and 1330-1730, Saturday-Sunday 0800-1200, T3413608*. **Museu Regional de São João**, Largo da Estação Velha, Centro, houses a collection of objects and photographs pertaining to the June celebrations. ■ *Daily 0800-1300, T3412000*.

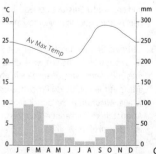

Climate: Sertão

(Recife & the Northeast Coast)

Teatro Municipal Severino Cabral, Avenida Floreano Peixoto, is a modern theatre where there are regular performances. The main parks in town are: the **Parque do Açude Novo** (Evaldo Cruz), a green area with playgrounds, fountains and restaurants; the nearby **Parque do Povo** with its *forródromo*, where the main festivities of the city take place; and the **Açude Velho**, a park around a dam south of the centre. The **Mercado Central**, where a large roof has been built over several blocks of old buildings, has regional crafts and produce; interesting and worth a visit.

Excursions Thirty five kilometres east of Campina Grande, off the road to João Pessoa, is Ingá, site of the **Pedra de Itacoatiara** archaeological centre, where inscriptions dated as 10,000 years old were found on a boulder 25 metres long and three metres high; a small museum at the site has fossils of a giant sloth and a tyrannosaurus. During the June festivities there is a train service to Itacoatiara.

Seventy kilometres southeast of town is the **Boqueirão** dam on the Rio Paraíba, where locals flock on holidays for watersports; there is a hotel-fazenda, T3911233.

To the north, 46 kilometres of Campina Grande, is **Areial** (*population 28,500*), main city of the *Brejo Paraibano*, a scenic region of green hills and valleys, with a pleasant climate, where colonial sugar plantations have been transformed into hotels like *Bruxaxá* (**A**), Floriano Peixoto, T3622423, with a pool and restaurant. Ten kilometres north from Campina Grande is Lagoa Seca, where figures in wood and sacking are made and there is a **Museu do Índio**.

Sleeping
Many hotels are clustered around Praça da Bandeira

A *Serrano*, Tavares Cavalcante 27, T3413131, F3210635. Luxury, pool, restaurant, discounts for cash. **A** *Ouro Branco*, João Lourenço Porto 20, T3412929, F3225788. Cheaper rooms available, discounts for cash. **B** *Souto Maior*, Floriano Peixoto 289, T3218043, F3212154. With bath, a/c, fridge. **B** *Mahatma Gandi*, Floriano Peixoto 338, T/F3215275. With bath, a/c (**C** with fan), fridge. **C** *Pérola*, Floriano Peixoto 258, T3415319. With bath, a/c, **D** with fan, parking, very good breakfast. **C** *Regente*, Barão do Abiaí 80, T3213843, F3213843. With bath, a/c (**D** with fan), fridge. **D** *Verona*, 13 de Maio 232, T3411926. With bath, fan, good value, friendly. **D** *Avenida*, Floriano Peixoto 378, T3411249. With fan, good value, cheaper with shared bath. **D** *Eliu's*, Maciel Pinheiro 31B, 1st floor, T3214115. Clean, friendly, a/c and bath (cheaper with fan, **E** without bath), good value, no breakfast. **E** *Aurora*, 7 de Setembro 120, T3214874. Shared bath, very basic, run down.

Eating R 13 de Maio by Rui Barbosa in the centre has several good restaurants including: *La Nostra Casa*, *Pizza & Cia* and *Pizzarella* for Italian; *Carne & Massa*, churrasco and by weight; *Possidônio*, varied menu; *Vila Antiga*, popular by weight, restaurant also at Maciel Pinheiro 305; *Manoel da Carne de Sol*, Félix de Araújo 263, regional specialties; *Lanchonette Casa das Frutas*, Marquês de Herval 54, good value meals, fruit juices and snacks; *La Suissa*, Dep João Tavares 663. Good savory and sweet snacks. Many bars near Parque do Povo, busy at weekends.

Festivals Campina Grande boasts the largest *São João* celebrations in Brazil; from the beginning of **June** into the first week of **July** the city attracts many visitors; there are bonfires and *quadrilhas* (square dance groups) in every neighbourhood; *forró* and invited artists at the Parque do Povo; *quentão*, *pomonha* and *canjica* are consumed everywhere. *Micarande*, the out-of-season Salvador-style carnival, takes place in **April**. In **August** there is an annual *Congresso de Violeiros*, which gathers singers and guitarists from all of the Nordeste.

Car hire On R Tavares Cavalcante are *Intermezzo*, No 27, T3214790, F3210835. **Transport**
Kelly's, No 301, T/F3224539. *Localiza*, R Dr Severino Cruz 625, T3414034, and at the
airport, T3314594.

Air Airport João Suassuna, 7 km south of centre on the road to Caruaru, T3311149.
Daily flights to Recife with Nordeste. Taxi to airport US$7. City bus *Distrito Industrial*
from Praça Clementino Procópio, behind Cine Capitólio.

Buses Rodoviária is at Av Argemiro de Figueiredo, a 20 minute ride from the
centre, T3215780. To **João Pessoa**, with *Real*, every 30 minutes, US$3, 2 hours. To
Souza with *Transparaíba*, 6 daily, US$7, 6 hours. To **Juazeiro do Norte** with
Transparaíba, 2 daily, US$10, 9 hours. To **Natal** with *Nordeste*, 0800 daily, US$6, 18
hours. To **Rio** with *Itapemirim*, 1600 daily, US$65, 42 hours. To **Brasília** with *Planalto*,
2 weekly, US$55, 46 hours.

Banks *Banco do Brasil*, 7 de Setembro 52, cash and travellers' cheques at poor rates. *Mondeo* **Directory**
Tour, R Índios Cariris 308, T/F3216965, cash at good rates and TCs, Mon-Fri 1000-1600.
Communications Post Office: R Marquês do Herval, Praça da Bandeira. **Telephone:** Floriano
Peixoto 410 by Praça da Bandeira, in the industrial district and at the rodoviária. **Tourist**
offices *PBTUR*, T156 for information. *DEMTUR* (Municipal), T3413993.

West of Campina Grande the landscape turns to vast, flat expanses, flanked by **Patos**
rolling hills and interesting rock formations; very scenic when green, but a sad *Population: 84,500*
sight during the prolongued *sertão* droughts. Situated 174 kilometres from
Campina Grande is Patos, centre of a cattle ranching and cotton growing area,
and an access point for the Serra do Teixeira 28 kilometres away, which
includes Pico do Jabre, the highest point in the state, at 1,130 metres above sea
level. There are various hotels and restaurants in Patos.

West of Patos by 130 kilometres is this pleasant *sertão* town, with hot tem- **Souza**
peratures year-round, which is gaining fame for the nearby dinosaur tracks *Population: 59,000*
and pre-historic rock carvings. The **Igreja do Rosário** at the Praça Matriz *Phone code: 081*
has paintings dating to the Dutch occupation of the area. It currently func-
tions as a school. Three kilometres from the centre, atop a hill, is a statue to
Frei Damião, an important religious leader of the northeast who died in
1997. Frei Damião was an Italian friar who came to Brazil in the 1930s and
stayed to become an inspiration for the faith of its most recent generation of
dispossessed. He is seen very much as belonging to the same tradition as O
Conselheiro and Padre Cícero.

Fossilized dinosaur prints, of as many as 90 different species which inhabited
the area between 110 and 80 million years ago, are found in a number of sites in
the Souza region. These were extensively studied by the Italian Palaeontologist
Giussepe Leonardi in the 1970s and 1980s. The **Vale dos Dinossauros**, on the
sedimentary river bed of the Rio do Peixe, is one of the closest sites to Souza; it
has some impressive Iguanodontus prints; access is four kilometres from town
along the road north to Uiraúna; the best time to visit is the dry season, July to
October. The area has no infrastructure and is best visited with someone who
can guide you. Contact Robson Marques of the *Movisaurio Association* (Rua
João Rocha 7, Souza, PB 58800-610, T5221065), he worked with Leonardi and is
very knowledgeable; or contact the Prefeitura Municipal.

Sleeping and eating **B** *Gadelha Palace*, Trav Luciana Rocha 2, T5211416. With bath,
a/c, fridge, pool, restaurant. **B** *Santa Terezinha*, R Col Zé Vicente 101, T5211412. With
fan, bath, overpriced. **C** *Dormitório Sertanejo I*, R Col Zé Vicente. With bath, fan, clean,
no breakfast, good value. Recommended. **E** *Dormitório Aguiar*, R João Gualberto. Very
basic. Several restaurants on R Col Zé Vicente. *Diagonal*, Getúlio Vargas 2. Pizza.

Recife & the Northeast Coast

Transport The rodoviária is 1 km from the centre, there are no city buses, walk (hot), take a moto-taxi (US$1) or a taxi (US$5). To **Campina Grande** with *Transparaíba*, 6 daily, US$7, 6 hours. To **João Pessoa** with *Transparaíba*, 6 daily, US$10, 8 hours. To **Juazeiro do Norte** with *Transparaíba* or *Boa Esperança*, 4 daily, US$4, 3½ hours. To **Mossoró**, RN, with *Jardinense*, 4 daily, US$6, 4½ hours.

Cajazeiras
Population: 51,000

Thirty seven kilometres west of Souza, the Transamazônica (BR-230) reaches Cajazeiras, centre of a cotton growing area, with an impressive looking tower on the main church and various hotels. This is an access point for the **Brejo das Freiras** thermal, mineral baths 32 kilometres to the north, an oasis with natural springs in the middle of the *sertão*: **A** *Estância Termal Brejo das Freiras*, São João do Rio do Peixe, T5221515, rooms or chalets with bath, a/c, fridge, pool, restaurant. There is no money exchange in Cajazeiras. Hotels: **C** *Regente*, in centre, 15 minutes' walk from rodoviária, air conditioning, cheaper without, TV, bath. **E** *Cacique*, near rodoviária, cheaper without air conditioning.

From Cajazeiras the Ceará border is reached in 17 kilometres, the Transamazônica continues west across the *sertãos* of Ceará and Piauí and on to Maranhão, Tocantins and Pará. Southwest of Cajazeiras by 118 kilometres is Juazeiro do Norte, an important pilgrimage centre, see page 569.

Fortaleza and the North Coast

9

Fortaleza and the North Coast

The beautiful dunes of Natal, in Rio Grande do Norte, are already well known to tourists. Fine beaches are also to be found at Fortaleza and the isolated Canoa Quebrada and Jericoacoara on the coast of Ceará. Inland lies the harsh and arid Sertão but with much of cultural interest in towns such as Juazeiro do Norte. Piauí is home to archaeological remains in the Capivara National Park and the natural beauty of the Parnaíba delta leading to the Lençóis Maranhenses in Maranhão. This state, where the Northeast meets Amazônia, has historic Alcântara and São Luis, Brazil's reggae capital. The state interior also has spectacular mountain scenery and waterfalls around Carolina.

Fortaleza & the North Coast

Rio Grande do Norte

This state is famous for its beaches and their dunes, especially around Natal. The people are called 'Potiguares', after an Indian tribe that once resided in the state. The local accent is quite distinct from other northeastern states, being clear and crisp and often easier for outsiders to understand.

Like its neighbour to the south, Rio Grande do Norte was not taken into Portuguese possession until the end of the 16th century, but here the impediment was French and Indian resistance. Only after the construction of the Forte dos Reis Magos and a year-long struggle did the Portuguese prevail in 1599. The Dutch domination during 1630-50 saw the expansion of salt production, sugar cane and cattle rearing, the first and last of which became chief activities when the Portuguese won back control. In the late 17th and early 18th centuries a rebellion, by Indians against enslavement, the Confederação dos Cariris, affected Rio Grande and the neighbouring provinces. It was put down by troops led by *bandeirantes*. In the mid-18th century, the Portuguese crown banned the export of salt and dried beef, which decimated the economy; it did not recover until Brazilian independence removed the prohibition. Throughout its history, drought (as in 1877 and 1975-76) has been a determining factor in Rio Grande do Norte's fortunes.

The state has a population of about 2,620,000. The coastline begins to change here, becoming gradually drier and less green with many sand dunes, as it shifts from running north/south to east/west. The vast sugar-cane plantations and a few remaining strands of *mata atlântica* (coastal forest) are replaced by the dry *caatinga* vegetation and *caju* orchards.

The state has three main paved roads radiating from Natal: south to João Pessoa and Recife (BR-101), southwest to Caicó (BR-226 and BR-427) and west to Mossoró and Fortaleza (BR-304). There are many secondary paved roads and dirt roads throughout the state.

Natal

Population: 657,000
Phone code: 084
Colour map 2, grid B6

The state capital is located on a peninsula between the Rio Potengi and the Atlantic Ocean and is one of the most attractive cities of Brazil's northeast coast, as well as a popular destination for those seeking sun and good beaches. Located 185 kilometres to the north of João Pessoa and 537 kilometres northeast of Fortaleza, it is known as the Cidade do Sol *and* Cidade das Dunas.

Ins & outs
See also Transport, page 537

Getting there Flights arrive at Augusto Severo airport, 15 km south from centre. Taxi US$25 to centre, US$20 to Ponta Negra. Bus every 30 minutes to the old rodoviária near the centre, US$0.65. Interstate buses arrive at the rodoviária, 6 km southwest of the centre. Luggage store. City bus 'Cidade de Esperança Avenida 9', 'Areia Preta via Petrópolis' or 'Via Tirol' to centre. Taxi US$6 to centre, US$10 to Ponta Negra.

Getting around Unlike most Brazilian cities, in Natal you get on the bus in the front and get off at the back. The old rodoviária on Avenida Junqueira Aires, by Praça Augusto Severo, Ribeira, is a central point where many bus lines converge. Buses to some of the beaches near Natal also leave from here.

Sights

The oldest part of the city is the **Ribeira** along the riverfront where a process of renovation has been started, which can be seen on Rua Chile (not safe at night) and in public buildings restored in vivid art-deco fashion, such as the **Teatro Alberto Maranhão** (built 1898-1904, Praça Agusto Severo, T/F2229935) and the **Prefeitura** (Rua Quintino Bocaiuva, Cidade Alta). The **Cidade Alta**, or Centro, is the main commercial centre and Avenida Rio Branco its principal artery. The main square is made up by the adjoining **praças: João Maria, André de Albuquerque, João Tibúrcio** and **7 de Setembro**. At Praça André de Albuquerque is the old cathedral (inaugurated 1599, restored 1996). The modern cathedral is on Avenida Deodoro, Cidade Alta. The church of **Santo Antônio**, Rua Santo Antônio 683, Cidade Alta, dates from 1766, and has a fine, carved wooden altar and a sacred art museum. ■ *Tuesday-Friday 0800-1700, Saturday 0800-1400.*

The **Museu Câmara Cascudo**, Avenida Hermes de Fonseca 1440, Tirol, has exhibits on archaeological digs, Umbanda rituals and the sugar, leather and petroleum industries. ■ *Tuesday-Friday, 0800-1100, 1400-1600, Saturday 1000-1600, US$1.90, T2122795.*

The 16th-century **Forte dos Reis Magos** is at Praia do Forte, the tip of Natal's peninsula; between it and the city is a military installation. It is possible to walk along the beach to the fort, or to go on a tour, or by taxi; it is worth it for the views. ■ *Daily 0800-1645, US$1.90.*

Museu do Mar, Avenida Dinarte Mariz (Via Costeira), Praia de Mãe Luiza, has aquariums with regional sea life and exhibits with preserved specimens. ■ *Monday-Friday, 0800-1100, 1400-1700, T2213611.* At Mãe Luiza is a lighthouse with beautiful views of Natal and surrounding beaches (take a city bus marked Mãe Luiza; get the key from the house next door).

The **Via Costeira** runs south along the ocean beneath the towering sand dunes of **Parque das Dunas** (access restricted to protect the nine kilometres of dunes), joining the city to the neighbourhood and popular beach of **Ponta Negra**; a cycle path parallels this road and provides great views of the coastline.

Urban beaches

East of the centre, from north to south are: Praia do Forte, do Meio, dos Artistas, de Areia Preta, Mãe Luzia, Barreira d'Água (across from Parque das Dunas) and Ponta Negra; the first two have reefs offshore, therefore little surf, and are appropiate for windsurfing. The others are urban beaches and local enquiries regarding pollution are recommended before bathing. **Ponta Negra**, 12 kilometres from the centre, is the most popular and has many hotels (see below). It is 20 minutes by bus from the centre; pleasant and quaint atmosphere; the northern end of the beach is good for surfing, while the southern end is calmer and good for bathing. At the south end of the beach is **Morro do Careca**, a 120 metre high dune with a sand skiing slope surrounded by vegetation. It is crowded on weekends and holidays, but it is not safe to wander alone when deserted, as there are robberies.

Natal has excellent beaches, some of which are also the scene of the city's nightlife

Fortaleza & the North Coast

Excursions

See also the Southern Coast and the Northern Coast, pages 538 and 541 respectively

The coastline near Natal has beautiful beaches, good for day trips and longer stays. Beach lovers can find innumerable beaches to enjoy year-round. There are developed beaches with hotel and restaurant infrastructure, as well as pristine ones accessed only by foot. Those closer to Natal are built-up with beach

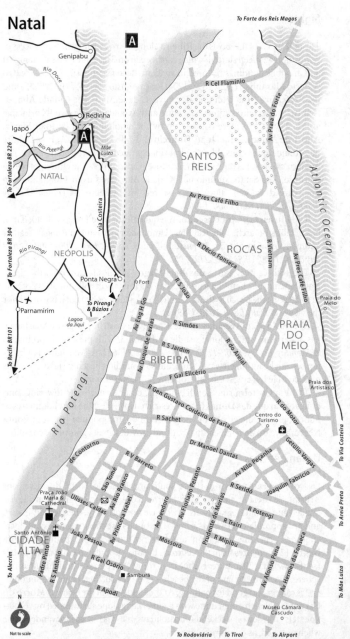

Natal

To Forte dos Reis Magos

Genipabu

Rio Doce

A

Redinha

Igapó

To Fortaleza BR 226

Rio Potengi

NATAL

Mãe Luiza

R Cel Flamínio

Av Praia do Forte

SANTOS REIS

Atlantic Ocean

Av Pres Café Filho

Via Costeira

To Fortaleza BR 304

Rio Pirangi

NEÓPOLIS

R Décio Fonseca

R Vietnam

Av Pres Café Filho

ROCAS

Ponta Negra

o Fort

To Pirangi & Búzios

To Recife BR 101

Parnamirim

Lagoa da Jiqui

Av Eng H Go

R S João

R Simões

R do Areial

Praia do Meio

PRAIA DO MEIO

R S Jardim

RIBEIRA

F Gal Elicério

Praia dos Artistas o

Rio Potengi

R Gen Gustavo Cordeiro de Farias

R do Motor

R Sachet

Centro do Turismo

Getúlio Vargas

de Contorno

R V Barreto

Dr Manoel Dantas

Av Nilo Peçanha

To Via Costeira

Av Duque de Caxias

São Tomé

Av Rio Branco

R Serido

Joaquim Fabrício

To Areia Preta

Praça João Maria & Cathedral

Ulisses Caldas

Av Princesa Isabel

Av Deodoro

Av Floriano Peixoto

Prudente de Morais

R Potengi

R Trairí

Santo Antônio

João Pessoa

Massoró

R Mipibu

CIDADE ALTA

Padre Pinto

R S Antônio

R Gal Osório

Samburá

Av Afonso Pena

Av Hermes da Fonseca

To Alecrim

R Apodi

Museu Câmara Cascudo o

To Mãe Luiza

N

Not to scale

To Rodoviária   To Tirol   To Airport

homes and get busy during the summer holidays (December to Carnival), when dune-buggy traffic can become excessive. The coast north of the city is referred to as *Litoral Norte*, that to the south as *Litoral Sul*; dune buggies are a popular way to travel here. Tours are available through travel agencies. See page 538 for details.

Pirangi do Norte, 25 kilometres south, or 30 minutes by bus from new rodoviária, is popular for watersports and has the world's largest cashew-nut tree (*cajueiro*), see page 538. A number of good beaches and attractive villages may be found along this coast. North of Natal are extensive cashew planta-tions. Land or boat tours of the Litoral Sul usually include a stop at Pirangi.

Boat tours on the Rio Potengi and along the nearby beaches of the Litoral Sul are available from *Albacora Azul* (T2392160, F2382204) or *Marina Badauê* (T2382066, F2382166); a two-hour tour includes hotel pick-up, a snack, and allows time for a swim, US$15 per person. Boat trips to Barra do Cunhaú, 86 kilometres south of Natal, go through mangroves, visit an island and a salt mine (*Passeio Ecológico Cunhaú*, T2111123/9816346); see beaches below.

Ultralight flights over the Rio Potengi and sand dunes and beaches north of Natal are available for US$29 per person including hotel pick-up (Ultraleve, T9827348).

The **Centro de Lançamento da Barreira do Inferno**, launching centre for Brazil's space programme, is located 11 kilometres south of Natal on the road to Pirangi; visits by appointment on Wednesday starting 1400, T2114799.

Essentials

As a popular holiday destination, Natal has a large hotel infrastructure, busy between December and Easter and quiet at other times, when the prices are about 20% lower. The Via Costeira and Ponta Negra are nice places to stay, but economical hotels are easier to find in the city proper.

Sleeping

Via Costeira L *Ocean Paláce*, Km 11, near Ponta Negra, T2194144, F2193081. Full service luxury hotel, 5-star. **L** *Vila do Mar*, No 4233, Km 8, Parque das Dunas, T2116000, F2021899. Full service, 4-star, pool, restaurant. **AL** *Marsol Natal*, No 1567, Km 7, Parque das Dunas, T/F2021300. Four-star (**A** in low season). **AL** *Imirá Plaza*, No 4077, T2114104, F2115722, **A** in low season. On beach, pool, tennis. Recommended.

Natal L *Maine*, Av Salgado Filho 1741, Lagoa Nova, T2065774, F2065707. Full ser-vice, 4-star, restaurant. **L** *Sol Potengi Natal*, Potengi 521, Petrópolis, T2113088, F2113006. Luxury suites, **AL** in low season, a/c, pool, restaurant. **A** *Natal Center*, R Santo Antônio 665, Centro, T2212355, F2212351. A/c, fridge. **A** *Praia do Sol*, Av Pres Café Filho 750, Praia do Meio, T2114562, F2226571. Opposite beach, renovated, quiet, a/c, TV. Recommended. **A** *Reis Magos*, Av Café Filho 822, Praia do Meio, T2021991, F2023288, by the sea, **B** in low season. A/c, fridge, pool. **B** *Casa Grande*, R Princesa Isabel 529, Centro, T2110555. A/c, cheaper without bath (also low season discounts), good breakfast, pleasant, excellent value. Recommended. **B** *Oassis Swiss*, R Joaquim Fabrício 291, Casa 08, Petrópolis, T/F2022455. Swiss-owned, a/c, cheaper with fan (cheaper still in low season), pool, massive breakfasts, exceptional value. **B** *Pousada Centromar*, Av Rodrigues Alves 544, Petrópolis, T/F2215177. A/c, fridge. **B** *Samburá*, R Prof Zuza 263, T2210611. Recommended. **C** *Parque das Dunas*, R João XXIII 601 (take Bus 40, alight at Farol, 40 minutes from the centre), T2021820. Excellent break-fast, safe, **D** in low season. **C** *Pousada Ibérica*, R Fabrício Pedrosa 98, Petrópolis, T2022224. Fan, TV. **D** *Beira Mar*, Av Pres Café Filho, Praia dos Artistas, T2224256, on the beach front, with breakfast, but no a/c, small, good value, popular. **D** *Bom Jesús*, Av Rio Branco 384. Good value, popular. **D** *Fenícia*, Av Rio Branco 586, Centro,

T2114378. (More with a/c), with breakfast and shower, English spoken, low season discount. **D** *Le Bateau*, Praia de Areia Preta, on beachfront. Helpful, good breakfast, English and French spoken. **D** *Natal*, Av Rio Branco 740, Centro, T2222792, F2220232. A/c, cheaper with fan, basic, good value. **D** *Pousada Marina*, at No 860, T2220678. A/c, TV, fridge, 'lovely'. **D** *Pousada Terra do Sol*, Av Pres Café Filho, 11, Praia dos Artistas, T2114878. Noisy, arranges good Passeio de Buggy. Recommended. **D** *Pousada Zur Kurve*, Av Sílvio Pedrosa 97, Praia Areia Preta, T2023477, F2220626. Good breakfast, safe. Recommended. *Papa Jerimum*, R Rodrigues Dias 445, Praia do Meio. English spoken. Recommended. **E** pp *Pousada Ponta do Morcego*, R Valentin de Almeida 10, Praia dos Artistas, T2022367. Dorm style.

Across from the rodoviária are **B** *Pousada Esperança*, Av Capt Mor Gouveia 418, T2051955. With bath, a/c, cheaper with fan, cheaper without bath. **D** *Cidade do Sol*, Piancó 31, T2051893. With bath, a/c, cheaper with fan. **E** *Pousada Beth Shalom*, R Patos 45, T2051141. Fan, friendly. **E** *Pousada Macario's*, R Patos 33, T2052517. Fan.

Ponta Negra **L** *Manary Praia*, R Francisco Gurgel 9067, T/F2192900, manary@ digi.com.br. A/c, safe in room, pool, by the beach, charming, member of the *Roteiro de Charme* group, see page 57. **A** *Village Ponta Negra*, R da Praia 150, T2362424, F2362425. A/c, pool. **A** *Bella Napoli*, Av Erivan França 3188, T2192666. A/c (**B** in low season), fridge. **A** *Chalés Suíço*, R Luiz Esteves 2272, T2363090. Furnished cabins for up to 5 persons, **C** in low season. **A** *Hotel e Pousada O Tempo e o Vento*, R Elias Barros 66, T/F2192526, www.digicom.br/otempoeovento. A/c (**B** in low season), fridge, cheaper with fan, pool, clean, *luxo* rooms are very comfortable. Recommended. **B** *Caminho do Mar*, R Des HH Gomes 365, near Ponta Negra beach, T2193363. **B** *Flat*, R 31 de Março, Morro de Careca, T2192541. Breakfast, fridges in rooms, fans, hot showers and a nice garden, discounts for longer stays, warmly recommended, another flat belongs to Joel de Queiroz Amorim, T7411833 (opposite *Pousada Flor*, Morro de Careca), 3 bedrooms, 2 bathrooms, kitchen, safe parking, helpful owner, US$450 per month, but may be negotiable on a daily basis. **B** *Maria Bonita 2*, Estrela do Mar 2143, T2362941, F2192726. With a/c, **C** with fan. Recommended. **B** *Miramar*, Av da Praia 3398, T2362079. **B** *Ponta Negra Beach*, R Des João V da Costa 8896, T/F2193264. Pool. Recommended. **B** *Pousada do Mar*, T2362509. Pool. **C** *Pousada Porta do Sol*, R Francisco Gurgel 9057, T2362555, F2052208. Room with bar, TV, excellent breakfast, pool, steps down onto beach, good value. Recommended.

Youth hostels **D** pp *Lua Cheia*, R Dr Manoel Augusto Bezerra de Araújo 500, Ponta Negra, T2363696, luacheia@digi.com.br, www.luacheia.com.br. IYHA, includes breakfast. *Verdes Mares*, R das Algas 2166, Conj Algamar, Ponta Negra, T2362872, F2362872. IYHA, includes breakfast, discount in low season. **E** *Ladeira do Sol*, R Valentin de Almeida 10, Praia dos Artistas, T2215361. *Meu Canto*, R Manoel Dantas 424 Petrópolis, T2113954. Highly recommended.

Camping *Camping Clube do Brasil* site at Sítio do Jiqui, Pirangi, T2172603. Expensive. Vale das Cascatas, Via Costeira Km 8.5, Ponta Negra beach. Little shade, swimming pool, leisure facilities.

Eating **Churrasco** *Tereré*, Estr de Pirangi 2316, Ponta Negra. Good *rodízio*. **International** *Xique Xique*, Av Afonso Pena 444, Petrópolis. *Chaplin*, Av Pres Café Filho 27, Praia dos Artistas. Good seafood. *Doux France*, R Otávio Lamartine, Petrópolis. Very good French food. *Raro Sabor*, R Seridó 722, Petrópolis. Exclusive. *Companhia do Alimento*, Av Afonso Pena 529, Petrópolis. Good, self-service. *Saint Antoine*, R Santo Antônio 651, Cidade Alta. Self-service by kilo. **Oriental** *Thin-San*, Av Hermes da Fonseca 890, Tirol. Chinese, quite good, not expensive. *Guinza*, R Ana Porto 04 (Via

Costeira), Ponta Negra. Japanese. **Italian** *Mamma Italia*, Av Gov Sílvio Pedrosa 43, Praia de Areia Preta. *Bella Napoli*, Av Hermes da Fonseca 960, Tirol and Av Erivan França, Ponta Negra. Good. **Regional food** *Casa de Mãe*, R Pedro Afonso 153 (Petrópolis). Recommended. *Bom Demais*, R Princesa Isabel 717C, Centro. Cheap, good. *Carne de Sol Benigna Lira*, R Dr José Augusto Bezerra de Medeiros 09, Praia do Meio. **Seafood** *Camarões*, Via Costeira 2610, Ponta Negra and Natal Shopping Centre. Very good seafood. *Peixada da Comadre*, R Dr José Augusto Bezerra de Medeiros 4, Praia dos Artistas. Popular with visitors. *Calamar* and others between Praias dos Artistas and da Areia Preta. **Vegetarian** *A Macrobiótica*, Princesa Isabel 524, Centro (with shop). For snacks try the stalls on Praia do Meio, there are also various restaurants along the beach road nearby, where itinerant musicians play.

Bars & nightclubs A number can be found on Av Pres Café Filho, in Praia do Meio, in Praia dos Artistas, also by the Ponta Negra beach and some in Petrópolis such as *Don Quixote*, R Seridó 706. Several nightclubs on Av Eng Roberto Freire in Ponta Negra. Dance is an important pastime in Natal. The *Casa da Música Popular Brasileira* has dancing on Friday and Saturday night and Sunday from 1700, very popular. Daily shows also at *Mandacarú*, Av Ayrton Senna 201, Neópolis, T2173008 (US$8), and *Zás-Trás*, R Apodi 500, Tirol, T2111457; the *Centro de Turismo* (see shopping below) has *Forró com Turista*, a chance for visitors to learn this fun dance, Thursday at 2200; many other enjoyable venues where visitors are encouraged to join in.

Festivals In **January** is the *Festa de Nossa Senhora dos Navegantes* when numerous vessels go to sea from Praia da Redinha, north of town. In mid-October there is a country show, Festa do Boi, bus marked Parnamirim to the exhibition centre, it gives a good insight into rural life. **Mid-December** sees *Carnatal*, the Salvador-style out of season carnival, a lively 4-day music festival with dancing in the streets.

Shopping *Centro de Turismo*, R Aderbal de Figueiredo, off R Gen Cordeiro, Petrópolis, T2122267. A converted prison with a wide variety of handicraft shops, art gallery, antique shop and tourist information booth, offers good view of the Rio Potengi and the sea, open daily 0900-1900, Thursday 2200. *Forró com Turista* (see Bars & nightclubs above), access bus No 46 from Ponta Negra or No 40 from rodoviária. *Centro Municipal de Artesanato*, Av Pres Café Filho, Praia dos Artistas. Daily 1000-2200. Sand-in-bottle pictures are very common in Natal.

Transport *See also Ins & outs, page 532* **Local Car hire**: *Dudu Locadora*, Av Rio Branco 420, Centro, T2117000, F2214694. *Buggy Mille*, Av Praia de Ponta Negra 8848, T2363373, F2362382. *Localiza*, Av Nascimento de Castro 1792, T2065296, or at airport, T0800-992000. Several in Capim Macio along Av Eng Roberto Freire including *Companhia do Buggy*, No 1432. *Avis*, No 3083, T2177300, F2177153. *Clean Car*, No 1536, T2175206, F2172301. Buggy tour of dunes US$60, to Pipa US$115.

Long distance Air: Aeroporto Augusto Severo, in Parnamirim. Flights to Belém, Brasília, Fernando de Noronha, Fortaleza, Recife, Rio de Janeiro, Salvador and São Paulo.

Buses: rodoviária, Av Capitão Mor Gouveia 1237, Cidade da Esperança, T2054377. Regional tickets are sold on street level, interstate on the second floor.

To **Recife** with *Napoles*, 5 daily, US$6.60 *convencional*, US$9 *executivo*, 4 hours. With *Nordeste* to **Mossoró**, US$6 *convencional*, US$10 *executivo*, 4 hours. To **Aracati**, US$7.50, 5½ hours. To **Fortaleza**, US$11 *convencional*, US$15.50 *executivo*, US$25 *leito*, 8 hours. To **João Pessoa**, every 2 hours, US$4 *convencional*, US$5 *executivo*, 3 hours. With *São Geraldo* to **Maceió**, buses both direct and via Recife, US$14 *convencional*, US$20 *executivo*, 10 hours. To **Salvador**, US$32.50 *executivo*, 20 hours.

Fortaleza & the North Coast

To **Rio de Janeiro**, US$69.65. To **São Paulo**, US$66 *convencional*, US$84 *executivo*, 46-49 hours. With *Boa Esperança* to **Teresina**, US$26 *convencional*, US$31.25 *executivo*, 17-20 hours. To **Belém**, US$45, 32 hours.

Directory **Airline offices** *Nordeste*, at airport, T2726814. *TAM*, at airport, T2722236, F2722624. *Transbrasil*, Av Deodoro 429, Petrópolis, T2211805, F2216025, at airport T2722235. *Varig*, R Vigário Bartolomeu 635, Centro, T2211535, F2211531, at airport, T2722224. *Vasp*, R João Pessoa 220, Centro, T2214453, F2213548, at airport, T2722236.

Banks *Banco do Brasil*, Av Rio Branco 510, Cidade Alta, US$ cash and TCs at poor rates, cash advances against Visa, Mon-Fri 1000-1600. *Banespa*, Av Rio Branco 704, Cidade Alta, US$ cash and TCs at *dolar turismo* rate, Mon-Fri 1000-1430. *Sunset Câmbio*, Av Hermes da Fonseca 628, Tirol, T2122552, cash and TCs, 0900-1700. *Dunas Câmbio*, Av Roberto Freire 1776, Loja B-11, Capim Macio (east of Parque das Dunas), T2193840, cash and TCs, 0900-1700. *Norte Câmbio*, Natal Shopping Centre, Neópolis, T2358159, cash and TCs, 1000-2200.

Communications **Post Office:** R Princesa Isabel 711, Centro; Av Rio Branco 538, Centro, Av Engenheiro Hildegrando de Góis 22, Ribeira, Av Praia de Ponta Negra 8920, Ponta Negra. **Poste restante** is in Ribeira, near the old rodoviária, at Av Rio Branco and Av General Gustavo Cordeiro de Farias, hard to find. **Telephone:** R Princesa Isabel 687 and R João Pessoa, Centro; Av Roberto Freire 3100, Ponta Negra, Shopping Cidade Jardim, Av Roberto Freire, Ponta Negra; and rodoviária.

Embassies & consulates *Canada*, Av Roberto Freire 2951, Bloco 01, Loja 09-CCAB Sul, Ponta Negra, T2192197. *Germany*, R Gov Sílvio Pedrosa 308, Areia Preta, T2061396. *Italy*, R Auta de Souza 275, Centro, T2226674. *Spain*, R Amintas Barros 4200, Lagoa Nova, T2065610.

Security Tourist police: *Delegacia do Turista*, T2363288, 24 hrs.

Tour companies & travel agents A city tour costs US$15; if it includes the northern beaches US$20-25, including southern beaches US$30-35; buggy tours US$50-120, depending on the destination. *Manary Ecotours*, R Francisco Gurgel 9067, Ponta Negra, T/F2192900, manary@digi.com.br, tours to beaches and interior. *Eventur*, R Jureino Barreto 257, Ribeira, T/F2210415, tours, transport to beaches. *Nataltur*, Av Deodoro 424, Centro, T2110117, F2116325. *Marsol*, Via Costeira 1567, Km 7, T/F2021300. *China's*, Av Deodoro 755, T2115179, F2214520, American Express representative.

Tourist offices *Secretaria Estadual de Turismo (SETUR)*, main office, Centro de Convenções, Via Costeira sem número, T2194226, F2363101. Information booths at *Centro de Turismo* (see Shopping above), Av Pres Café Filho sem número, Praia dos Artistas, Cajueiro de Pirangi (see Excursions above), rodoviária and airport. For information T1516 or 2194216. SETUR publishes a list of prices for tourist services such as tours, taxi fares, food and drinks.

Voltage 220 volts AC, 60 cycles.

The Southern Coast

Rota do Sol

The *Rota do Sol/Litoral Sul* (RN-063) follows the coastline for some 55 kilometres and is the access to beaches south of Ponta Negra (bus from Natal: Campos, in summer every 30 minutes, from both rodoviárias, US$1 to Pirangi, one hour; US$1.50 to Tabatinga, 1¼ hours). **Praia do Cotovelo**, 21 kilometres from Natal, offers a view of the Barreira do Inferno rocket launching centre to the north. At the south end it has some cliffs and coconut palms where camping is possible.

Pirangi do Norte, 25 kilometres from Natal, has calm waters, is popular for watersports and offshore bathing (500 metres out) when natural pools form between the reefs. It is near the world's largest cashew-nut tree (*cajueiro*); branches springing from a single trunk cover an area of some 7,300 square metres. From Natal (Viação Campos), US$0.60, five times a day from 0630 to 1815, three on Sunday, 0730, 0930, 1645; the snack bar by the tree has schedules of buses back to Natal. Pirangi has a lively Carnival. Lacemakers here offer good bargains for clothing and tableware.

Caju!

CAJU! Although you may be tempted to respond "God bless you", this is not a sneeze, it is the Brazilian term for cashew. The northeastern states of Ceará and Rio Grande do Norte are the country's largest growers of this internationally prized delicacy and important export product. The municipality of Serra do Mel (RN) alone produces some 20 to 40 tonnes of cashews every year.

The cashew tree (Anacardium occidentalis) thrives in the dry soil and extreme heat of Brazil's northeast coast; being broad and bushy it provides much welcome shade. The flowers are small and unimpressive but the pungent, pepper shaped, fruits are quite remarkable in that a single large seed hangs off them, on the outside. In season, their characteristic aroma fills the warm night air.

The cashew fruit (without the seed) has an entirely unique flavour. Tangy, almost astringent, it is guaranteed to pucker even the most reserved of lips. It is commonly used to make excellent juices, ice-cream and sweets.

The cashew seed is the familiar crescent-shaped nut known throughout the world, but beware of trying some fresh off the tree, it is poisonous! Raw cashew nuts are impregnated in an irritating oil which can cause painful lesions of the mouth and lips, as well as a generalized skin reaction. The nuts are roasted to burn off this oil and kilns are scattered among the orchards. During the harvest season, their acrid black smoke may fill the air, making eyes water and everybody sneeze. CAJU!

Robert and Daisy Kunstaetter

Búzios, 35 kilometres from Natal, has a pleasant setting with vegetation-covered dunes and coconut palms, the ocean is mostly calm and the water clear; good for bathing.

Barra de Tabatinga, 45 kilometres from Natal, is surrounded by cliffs used for parasailing; waves are strong, making it a popular surfing beach.

Camurupim and **Barreta**, 46 and 55 kilometres from Natal respectively, have reefs near the shore, where bathing pools form at low tide; this area has many restaurants specializing in shrimp dishes. Beyond Barreta is the long, pristine beach of **Malenbar** or **Guaraíra**, access walking or by 10-minute boat ride accross the Rio Tibau to the south end. Buggy tour from Natal US$100.

Cotovelo A *Cotovelo Apart-hotel*, R Estrela D'Alva 34, T2372051. Kitchenette, pool. **Sleeping**
A *Colinas Chalés*, Estr de Pirangi, T2372168. Cabins, fridge, restaurant, pool. **B** *Portal do Kutuvelo*, Estr para Búzios, T2372121. Kitchen, pool. *Pousada do Francês*, R Belém do Pará, T/F2372161.

Pirangi do Norte A *Varandas de Pirangi*, Av Dep Márcio Marinho 5264, T/F2382243. A/c, kitchenette, restaurant. *Chalés de Pirangi*, R Sebastião 56, T2382241. **B** *Pousada Esquina do Sol*, R Dom Bosco and Av Dep Márcio Marinho, T2382078, F2115637. Rooms and cabins for four, no breakfast. *Posada Pirangi*, R Projetada 24. **B** *Pousada Vista do Atlântico*, R do Cajueiro 141, T2312586. Away from shore, upstairs rooms better ventilated, good views. Across the river in **Pirangi do Sul B** *Barreira do Sol*, Estr para Búzios, T2382230. With bath. *Enseada das Pedras*, R Pedra Grande 200, T2392240, F2392202.

Búzios B *Balneário Rio Doce*, pool, games. Highly recommended. **B** *Pousada da Lagosta*. Recommended. *Amaris Apart-hotel*, R Chico Mendes 10. *Enseada de Pirambúzios*, R da Pedra Grande, T/F2116645. *Mar de Búzios*, Praia de Búzios, T2215939. **B** *Varandas de Búzios*, Estr Principal, T2392121. Cabins with fridge, pool, restaurant.

Camurupim *Pousada Pontal de Camurupim*, Estr de Tabatinga.

Tibau do Sul and environs

Population 6,124
Colour map 2, grid B6

One of the most visited areas of the southern coast, because of its great natural beauty, is that surrounding Tibau do Sul. Lovely beaches circled by high cliffs, lagoons, Atlantic forest and dolphins are among its attractions. Access is via the BR-101, south from Natal or north from João Pessoa, as far as **Goianinha**, then east 18 kilometres to Tibau do Sul.

The fishing town of Tibau do Sul is located atop a 38 metre high cliff, overlooking the ocean and the scenic Lagoa Guaraíra where fishing boats are anchored; boat tours to the secluded Praia de Malenbar (see above) are available. Hotels in Tibau do Sul include *Marinas Tibau Sul* (**A**), T/F5022323. Cabins for four, pool, restaurant, watersports, horse riding, dock.

South of town there are fine, wide, white-sand beaches, separated by rocky headlands, set against high cliffs and coconut groves. **Praia do Madeiro** or **dos Golfinhos**, five kilometres south of Tibau do Sul, has a few upmarket hotels in a very scenic setting at the top of the cliffs. *Village Natureza*, Estr para Pipa Km 5, T/F5022325, has chalets overlooking the sea, **A** in low season, air conditioning, pool, nice grounds, lovely views. *Ponta do Madeiro* (**A**), Estr para Pipa Km 3, T/F5022377, has chalets with air conditioning, fridge, pool, restaurant, good views.

The ocean is calm and clear and dolphins can often be seen here, with the best chance being in early morning. Access to the shore is down the steps built by hotels or walking along the beach for an hour from Pipa at low tide. There are boat tours to see the dolphins from Pipa, US$5 per person.

Praia da Pipa, located three kilometres further south (85 kilometres from Natal), is a resort popular with Brazilians and foreigners alike. Just north of town, on a 70 metre high dune, is the **Santuário Ecológico de Pipa**, a 60 hectare park created in 1986 to conserve the *mata atlântica* forest; there are several trails and lookouts over the cliffs which afford an excellent view of the ocean and dolphins. ■ *0800-1600, US$3.* South of town is **Praia do Amor**, a good surfing beach, secluded by the cliffs. Bike rentals from *Blue Planet*, US$5 half day, US$10 full day; buggy rentals, US$50 south to Barra de Cunhaú, US$100 to Paraíba border, US$80 north to Barra de Tabatinga.

Sleeping
In Pipa more than 30 pousadas and many private homes offer accommodation

AL *Sombra e Água Fresca*, Praia do Amor, T9823803, **A** in low season. A/c, fridge, pools, restaurant with beautiful view especially at sunset. **A** *Toca da Coruja*, T5022333. Comfortable chalets and rooms (**A** – cheaper in low season), with bath, hot water, a/c, fridge, member of the *Roteiros de Charme* group, see page 57. **A** *Hotel Pousada da Pipa*, Praia do Amor, T/F5022323. With bath, restaurant, pool. **A** *Pousada da Ladeira*, T/F5022310. A/c, fridge, pool. **A** *Marajoara*, T9826348. A/c, fridge, cheaper with fan, pool, nice views. **A** *Pousada da Bárbara*, T2215548. With bath, pool. *Pousada Sítio Verde*, T9824623. Chalets, pool, spacious grounds. **C** *Pousada do Golfinho*, T9813087. With bath, fan, restaurant. **D** *Vera-My house*, T9885154/2723800. With bath, US$5 pp in dormitory, use of kitchen, no breakfast. Good value, friendly. Recommended. **D** *Tropical*, T9832642. Good food. Recommended. **D** *Pousada da Pipa*, T981090. Bath in room. **Youth hostel** *Albergue de Juventude Enseada dos Golfinhos*, at entrance to town, T2723800. Dormitories, clean, use of kitchen, US$8, breakfast US$2. **Camping** *Espaço Verde*, behind restaurant, T9885145, US$3 pp. Sandy lot with some shade.

Eating

Pipa Many restaurants along the main street. For seafood *Casarão* (good views), *Embarcação*, *O Jangadeiro* (also regional specialties), *Barraca do Ernandes* (shrimp specialities). For pizza *Caligula* and *Pipa Brasil*. *Espaço Verde*, self-service by kilo. *Bocca Ratton* for soups.

Buses From **Natal** *Queiroz e Melo*, from new rodoviária, 0800 and 1515, to Tibau do **Transport** Sul, US$3, 2 hours. To Pipa, US$4, 2¼ hours, return from Pipa 0500, 1600. Minivans also do this run. They are easiest to catch from the beach to Natal. Buggy tour Natal-Pipa US$115.

Praia da Barra de Cunhaú is located at the mouth of the Rio Curimataú. The **Praia da Barra** five kilometre beach is wide and the ocean calm, there is a small beachcomber **de Cunhaú** village by the river and some shrimp ponds. Access is via the BR-101 as far as **Canguaretama**, then 12 kilometres northeast. For boat tours from Natal, see Excursions above. Hotels include *Caribe Sul* (**A**), T5022624, with bath, pool and restaurant. Mirante (**C**), T2412313/9811205, has chalets by the beach and a restaurant. There are seafood restaurants by the beach.

There are many beautiful fishing villages along the coast in southern Rio **Baía Formosa** Grande do Norte and northern Paraíba, often difficult to reach. One of the most popular is Baía Formosa, in a bay surrounded by forest; its name 'beautiful bay' was given by the Portuguese who were charmed by the area. Located 97 kilometres south of Natal, access is via the BR-101, seven kilometres south of Canguaretama, then east 18 kilometres on the RN-062 (bus from Natal: *Queiroz e Melo*, from the new rodoviária, US$3, 2½ hours). The beach, popular for surfing, is almost 15 kilometres long, interrupted periodically by reddish outcrops of rock.

South of Baía Formosa is **Sagi**, an isolated beach just before the state border, with coconut groves and small dunes, reached only by foot or dune buggy.

Sleeping & eating **B** *Pousada Sonho Meu*, R Dr Manuel Francisco de Melo 143, T9821704. With bath, a/c, fridge, restaurant. Several fish restaurants including *Elila* at Praça da Conceição.

The Northern Coast

The coast north of Natal is known for its many impressive, light-coloured sand dunes, reaching up to 50 metres in height. There are fixed dunes which are protected and should not be disturbed and shifting dunes popularly used for joy rides with buggies. Those encroaching on the edge of a lake or the ocean are favourites for tobogganing.

A 25 minute ferry crossing on the Rio Potengi, or a 16 kilometre drive along the **Redinha** *Rota do Sol/Litoral Norte*, takes you from Natal to Redinha, the nearest beach *Colour map 2, grid B6* on the north coast. It is an urban beach, with ocean and river bathing, the local delicacy is fried fish with tapioca, served at the market, buggies can be hired here. Five kilometres north of Redinha on a point is **Santa Rita**. From its high dunes there is a great view of the nearby coastline.

Sleeping and eating **A** *Atlântico Norte*, Av Litorânea, Redinha Nova, T2242002, F2242001. Luxury, a/c, fridge, pool, restaurant. **A** *Redinha Praia*, Av Litorânea, Redinha Nova, T2242130, F2242109. A/c, fridge, pool, safe, restaurant.

Transport **Ferries**: frequent ferry service for Redinha from Cais Tavares de Lira, Ribeira, weekdays 0530-1900, weekend and holidays 0800-1830, US$0.50 pp, US$3 for car. **Buses**: regular bus service from the old rodoviária, last bus back starting at Genipabu at 1830.

Genipabu

A must for visitors
to Natal

The best known beach in the state is Genipabu, 30 kilometres north of the city; access from Redinha via RN-304. Its major attractions are very scenic dunes, the Lagoa de Genipabu (a lake surrounded by cashew trees and dunes, tables are set up on a shoal in the water, drinks served) and many bars and restaurants on the sea shore. Buggy rental from Associação dos Bugueiros, T2252077, US$35 for dune tour, ultralight flights available.

North of Genipabu, across the Rio Ceará Mirim, are several beaches with coconut groves and dunes. They have fishing villages combined with summer homes owned by people from Natal; access is via the town of Extremoz. One of these beaches, **Pitangui**, 35 kilometres from Natal, is six kilometres long and has a cristaline lake where colourful schools of fish can be seen in the water. **Jacumã**, 49 kilometres from Natal, has a small waterfall (Cachoerinha). Inland is Lagoa de Jacumã, a lake surrounded by dunes where sand skiing is practised.

Muriú, 44 kilometres from Natal, is known for its lovely green ocean where numerous small boats and *jangadas* anchor, the beach has nice palms (buggy tour from Natal, including shifting dunes US$100). Five kilometres to the north is **Prainha** or **Coqueiro**, a beautiful cove with many coconut palms and strong waves.

Lovely beaches continue throughout the state's coastline; as you get further away from Natal these are more distant from the main highways and access is somewhat more difficult. Eighty three kilometres north of Natal, by **Touros** (*population* 28,407), centre of a coconut and lobster producing region, the coastline veers east-west.

Sleeping & eating

Genipabu A *Genipabu*, Estr de Genipabu, 2 km from beach, T2252072. Marvellous views, isolated. A *Aldeia*, R Principal, Estr de Genipabu, T/F2252219. Five luxury bungalows and a restaurant. Several *pousadas* on R da Igreja including B *Mar-Azul*, T2252065. With bath, fridge, restaurant. B *Casa de Genipabu*, on beach, T2252141. With bath, fridge, pool. B *Pousada Villa do Sol*, Loteamento Tabú, Quadra 09, T2252132, F2252037. With bath, restaurant, pool. C *Pousada da Coruja*, R Principal 100, T2252092. With fan. C *Tabuão*, R Principal, T2252134. Furnished bungalows, no breakfast. E *Pousada Porta Alberta*, on beach. Good breakfast. Several restaurants serving seafood and regional dishes on R da Igreja by the beach.

Pitangui C *Pousada Marruá*, Av Beira Mar 438, T2022404. Simple.

Muriú *Bangalôs Muriú*, T/F2193731. Furnished chalets. Several self-service restaurants at the beach including *Guiomar* and *Marina's Muriú*.

Touros A *Rio do Fogo*, Praia Rio do Fogo, 9 km south of town, T2215872. With bath, pool. B *do Gostoso*, Praia Ponta de Santo Cristo, 27 km west of town, T2214399. Chalets, restaurant. B *Barra do Punau*, Praia Zumbi, 27 km south of town at the mouth of the Rio Punau, T2312875. Chalets, restaurant. *Chalés de Touros*, Estr de Carnaubinha, T2113252.

Mossoró

Population: 206,000
Phone code: 084
Colour map 2, grid B6

About half-way between Natal (277 kilometres) and Fortaleza (262 kilometres) along the BR-304 is Mossoró, the second city of Rio Grande do Norte, commercial centre for the largest salt and land-based petroleum-producing region in the country. The area also produces natural gas, cashew nuts, carnauba wax, fruits and minerals. Temperatures are high all year, mean 30°C.

Mossoró Mix-up

It could not have been any hotter. The shimmer off the black ribbon of asphalt, known as highway BR-304, conjured up many a mirage but no relief. We were taking a bus on the long haul from Fortaleza to Recife and drinking water was in short supply. The air conditioning had failed and everybody's patience wore thin.

"Dez minutos," grumbled the driver as we lurched into the Mossoró rodoviária, still in a haze. Bathrooms ... a line-up ... a shop for água mineral ... tem não? ... another shop ... Oh my God, the bus has gone! We could see it pulling away, but our sprint and acrobatics attracted no-one's attention. Still well in sight, it accelerated along the endless BR with all our gear onboard. At the crowded Recife bus terminus it would quickly disappear.

What do we do now? A taxi, "Follow that bus!", and so we did, but the fusca (VW Beetle) was no match for the motor coach on the open highway. In an hour that seemed an eternity we managed to overtake it, only because it had made another stop along the way. The

bleary-eyed bus driver didn't even seem surprised to see us. We breathed a transient sigh of relief until the taxi driver presented us with the bill.

How much was an hour-long break-neck chase worth? How much was our luggage worth? Regardless, we didn't have enough at hand. The bus driver wanted to be on his way, the taxi driver wanted his money (or we were going back with him to visit the Mossoró jail) and we were feeling increasingly desperate when someone came forward, sweat dripping from his brow. "These estrangeiros are lost. We've passed the hat among the passengers and collected enough to pay for the cab. Let's get going!"

It would be many years before we understood the complex meaning of o jeitinho brasileiro, 'the Brazilian way' (out of any predicament), but we had certainly experienced it that day outside Mossoró, where the heat of the climate was only matched by the warmth of the people.

Robert and Daisy Kunstaetter

Sights

The *Hotel Thermas Mossoró*, a resort with a hot, mineral water pool system, 10 pools, each on a terrace, with temperatures ranging from 54°C at the top to 30°C at the bottom, water-slide, spa, sports facilities, restaurant, is open to the public. ■ *0700-2300, US$14 pp.* While drilling for thermal water here in 1979 oil was struck, and this first derek in the area is still working and can be seen at the hotel.

The **Museu Histórico Lauro da Escossia**, Praça Antônio Gomes 514, Centro, has a small but interesting display, with the highlights of the region's history and an extensive photo collection relating to the *Cangaço* (see page 549). ■ *Tuesday-Friday 0700-1800, Saturday 0800-1100 and 1400-1700, Sunday 0800-1100, free.* The Escola Superior de Agricultura de Mossoró (ESAM), which concentrates on agricultural and veterinary studies specific to semi-desert areas, runs a park, **Parque Zoobotânico Onélio Porto**, with species of the Sertão, T3215755.

Excursions

Grossos, 46 kilometres to the north, is the centre of the important salt mining industry. The white salt dunes extending into the horizon against the blue sky and turquoise ocean are very scenic and worth a visit; an Antarctic landscape in the tropical heat. Official tours can be hired at *Hotel Thermas* or arranged with the different companies' headquarters in Mossoró (for example, Salina Maranhão, T3211290, Monday-Saturday), just walking around can be very interesting. Bus from Mossoró weekdays 0630 and 1330, US$1.50, leaves from near *Hotel Zenilândia*.

From Grossos there is a ferry across the Rio Mossoró (every 30 minutes, Monday-Friday 0730-1630, Saturday until 1700, Sunday until 1730, US$5 car, US$1 per person) to **Areia Branca**, the main port for salt exports and access to the Costa Branca, 42 kilometres of beaches to the east. The area remains undeveloped for the time being, with pleasant coves and some fishermen's villages, but tourist development may not be far off. Areia Branca is also accessed directly by road from Mossoró via the BR-110 (50 kilometres). There are several places to stay in Areia Blanca.

The main beach resort for Mossoró is **Tibau**, 44 kilometres to the north, just on the Ceará border, set in a lovely palm-fringed bay. A village of 5,000 inhabitants, its population swells to 35,000 during the peak vacation period between December and Carnival. The town is particularly lively in January during Mossoró's *Fest Verão* and during Carnival. The beach here is wide, has good waves and is popular for surfing. Beach homes continue to the east at Praia das Manoelas, beyond where access is by buggy to several beaches with good fishing. Ricardo Lopes, *Alibi Turismo*, T3262398, offers tours in this area and has very good photographs of the region. The local handicraft is coloured sand arrangements in bottles. Bus from Mossoró leaves near *Hotel Zenilândia*, 0630 and 1330, returns 1130 and 1630, US$1.60, 40 minutes. *Dunas Praia* (**B**), Praia das Manoelas, T3262304, F3173185, is friendly and has chalets, fridge and restaurant. *Leiria Mar* (**B**), Tibau, T3262541, has air conditioning, fridge, pool, restaurant. *Panorama* (**D**), Tibau, with bath, more with fan, restaurant. There are several other *pousadas* in town and many restaurants and bars along the beach.

Essentials

Sleeping   **L** *Hotel Thermas Mossoró*, Av Lauro Monte 2001, by entrance to town from Fortaleza, T3181200, F3182344. Luxurious resort, a/c, fridge, friendly management (see above). **A** *Imperial*, R Santos Dumont 47, Centro, T3216351, F3173524. A/c, fridge, modern, very clean, restaurant. **B** *Ouro Negro*, Av do Contorno, on BR-304, near rodoviária, T/F3172070. With bath, a/c, fridge, modern, restaurant, parking, small pool. **B** *São Luiz Plaza*, R Dionísio Filgueira 125, Centro, T3216580. With bath, a/c. **B** *Scala*, R Dionísio Filgueira 220 (across from market), T3213034. With bath, a/c, **C** with fan. **D** *Zenilândia*, Praça Souza Machado 89, Centro, T3212949. With fan, bath, **E** with shared bath, breakfast not included.

Eating   *Churrascaria A Gauchinha*, R Bezerra Mendes 99, Centro. Grill, closed Sunday. *Drago*, Av Dix-Sept Rosado 190, Centro, Chinese. *O Severino*, R Felipe Camarão 2975 (road to Apodi, by airport). Regional specialities. *La Gôndola*, R Amaro Duarte 450, near rodoviária. Italian. *Flavio's*, Av Pres Dutra, Ilha de Santa Luzia. Varied. *Taberna D'Angelo*, R Wenceslau Braz 468, São José. Pizza.

Bars & nightclubs   *Cheiro Nordestino*, R Wenceslau Braz 817, São José. Drinks and snacks, pleasant atmosphere, live music on weekends. *Acapulco's*, R Chico Linhares, quadra 7. Snacks and drinks, open Wednesday-Sunday.

Festivals   3-13 December, *Santa Luzia*, 10 days of fairs and celebrations closed by a large procession; *Fest Verão* in January sees much movement during the local *Carnaval fora de época*.

Transport   **Car hire**   *Yes*, Av Pres Dutra 2020, Alto de São Manoel, T3214526.

     Buses The rodoviária is at Av do Contorno (BR-304); bus to centre 'Boa Vista' or 'Circular', US$0.50, taxi US$6. With *Nordeste* to Natal, US$6 *convencional*, US$10 *executivo*, 4 hours. To Fortaleza, US$5, 4 daily, 4 hours. To Aracati, US$2.50, 2 hours,

Cangaço

Were they subversives, common criminals or heroes? The debate rages on about the armed band led by Virgulino Ferreira da Silva, better known as Lampião. He is regarded by some as a Robin Hood of the Northeast, stealing from the coroneis (wealthy landowners with almost feudal powers) and urban gentry, to give to the ubiquitous poor of the Sertão. Others look on Lampião and his followers as nothing more than common criminals; looting, raping and killing as they terrorized town after town in the Northeast during the 1920s and 1930s. This was the Cangaço, the reign of banditry, which inspired so much fear and fascination throughout Brazil and attracted worldwide attention.

The controversial religious leaders of the Sertão were also involved (see page 570). Lampião claimed the spiritual protection of Padre Cícero and the legacy of the Cangaço retains an unusual religious dimension. The tomb of Jararaca, for example, one of Lampião's lieutenants who was captured during the band's unsuccessful 1927 siege of Mossoró, and supposedly buried alive, is attributed miraculous powers and has become a site of pilgrimage. Yet Jararaca is reputed to have been a ruthless killer.

There was even a middle eastern connection. Several early cinematographers from the US, Germany and France tried to film Lampião and his band, but only Lebanese-born Benjamin Abrahão was sufficiently taken into his confidence to do so. Abrahão spent almost seven months recording the day-to-day life of the cangaceiros. His footage was considered so subversive that he was subsequently murdered under mysterious circumstances and his film confiscated by the government of Getúlio Vargas. It languished in an official vault for 20 years, much of it destroyed by time and the elements.

Today the Sociedade Brasileira de Estudos do Cangaço is one of the organizations which collects data, anecdotes and artefacts from this important episode in the region's and the nation's history. It also carries on the unresolved debate as to whether the cangaceiros were really heroes or villains.
Robert and Daisy Kunstaetter

not all buses bound for Fortaleza will let you off at Aracati, enquire before. *Guanabara* to Recife. *São Geraldo* for main cities in the south. Several regional carriers for points in the interior.

Banks *Banco do Brasil*, Praça Dix-Sept Rosado. **Communications** Post Office: Praça Rafael Fernandes. **Telephone:** Av Dix-Sept Rosado 56, Centro, national and international calls, 0730-1130 and 1330-1730. **Directory**

The Sertão

The interior of Rio Grande do Norte, like that of its neighbours, is a combination of semi-desert sertão, *with hilly areas covered in green vegetation and pleasant temperatures oscillating between 16°C and 25°C. The state is rich in archaeological sites and numerous caves, with primitive paintings having been found.*

In the mountainous south-central region of the state is **Acari**, with an 18th-century church of Nossa Senhora da Guia. It is the access point for the Serra do Bico de Arara and is 221 kilometres from Natal and 224 kilometres from Mossoró. South of town, in the **Seridó** area, are multicoloured cave paintings. Human remains dating back 11,000 years were discovered here. Five kilometres from Acari is *Pousada do Gargallheiras* (**C**), Açude Marechal Dutra, with

Population: 11,000

bath, restaurant. Twenty seven kilometres south of Acari is *Conceição Palace Hotel*, R Otávio Lamartine 432, Jardim do Seridó, T4722249, one-star.

In the centre of the state, on the east shore of the Armando Rua Gonçalves dam, is **São Rafael**, a town surrounded by granite mountains on top of which are natural waterholes, up to three metres deep, containing countless fossils of giant fauna of the Pleistocene period; there are also rock paintings and engravings in boulders in this area. Larger towns nearby are **Açu** (*population* 43,539) 20 kilometres north and **Caicó** (*population* 53,196) 100 kilometres south.

Seventy six kilometres southwest of Mossoró along the BR-405 is **Apodi**, a town with colonial mansions, where people live from agriculture, ceramics and lime extraction. Ten kilometres from town is **Lajedo de Soledade**, a limestone shelf, one kilometre wide by two kilometres in length, weathered into canyons, grottos and interesting formations, where paintings of animals and geometric figures, dated between 3,000 and 5,000 years, have been found in the caves. On the BR-405, Km 76, is Passeio Hotel, T3332031, one-star. In Apodi is *Pousada Chapado*, R Dep Dauto Cunha 30, Apodi, T3332049, with bath, air conditioning, fridge and a restaurant serving regional food.

Eighty three kilometres beyond Apodi is **Pau dos Ferros**, the main centre for southwest Rio Grande do Norte, from where the road continues to Cajazeiras, Paraíba. *Pousada do Jatobá* is on the BR-405, Km 01, T/F3512211.

Ceará

Known as terra da luz *(the land of light) since 1990, the state has become one of the most important tourist destinations in the northeast, popular with both Brazilian and international tourists. Its well known beaches are the main attraction, with 2,800 hours of sunshine per year. Local handicrafts are renowned and the interior has several sites of natural and cultural interest such as Juazeiro de Norte. Other good beaches are to be found at Jericoacoara and Canoa Quebrada.*

It was only during the period of Dutch rule that efforts were made to populate the interior of Ceará. Many Portuguese, fleeing the Dutch from all parts of the Northeast, moved into the *sertão* to raise cattle. Beef and leather came to typify the region. The Cearenses participated in the republican movements that flared up in the Northeast in the early 19th century, but real development did not begin until the second half of that century. Ceará was one of the foremost provinces in the drive to abolish slavery. It remains largely underdeveloped, although it has been the focus of several successful health and educational programmes.

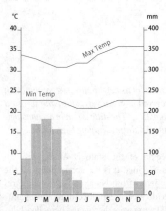

Climate:
Ceará State

The state has a population of about 7,010,000. The coast has many dunes whilst inland is the harsh *sertão*. The main centre of population is around the capital Fortaleza.

Ceará has 573 kilometres of coastline, beaches are usually long and straight, the ocean warm with average temperatures of 29°C and a constant breeze makes the temperature pleasant. One third of the coast is east of Fortaleza in the *Litoral Leste* or *Costa Sol Nascente* (Sunrise Coast), which has a fair concentration of towns and fishing villages. Two thirds of the coastline is west of Fortaleza in the *Litoral Oeste* or *Costa Sol Poente* (Sunset Coast), which has some beautiful undeveloped stretches.

The main access roads are the BR-304 southeast to Natal (537 kilometres, 800 kilometres to Recife), paved and in good condition; the BR-222 west to Sobral (230 kilometres) and the Piauí border, paved with a few poor sections. It is 634 kilometres to Teresina, 1,070 kilometres to São Luís and 1,600 kilometres to Belém; the BR-020 southwest to Picos (Piauí, 486 kilometres) and on to Brasília (2,285 kilometres), paved; the BR-116 south to the Pernambuco border and on to Salvador (1,389 kilometres), mostly paved, but with several stretches in poor condition; the CE-004 or *litorânea*, joining the coastal towns to the southeast as far as Aracati (142 kilometres), paved. There are many paved secondary roads and fair dirt roads throughout the State.

Fortaleza

The fifth largest city in Brazil and capital of the State of Ceará, Fortaleza is 537 kilometres from Natal, northwest along the coast and 634 kilometres northeast of Teresina. It is a busy metropolis with many high-rise buildings, an important clothes manufacturing industry, many hotels and restaurants and a lively nightlife. Fishermen's jangadas still dot the turquoise ocean across from the beach.

Population: 1,975,000
Phone code: 085
Colour map 2, grid A5

The city is spread out, its main attractions are in the centre and along the seashore, transport from one to the other can take a long time. The midday sun is oppressive, tempered somewhat by a constant breeze, evening temperatures can be more pleasant, especially by the sea.

Getting there International and domestic flights arrive at Pinto Martins airport, 6 km south of the centre. Bus 404 from the airport to Praça José de Alencar in the centre, US$0.90. Expresso Guanabara minibus runs to the rodoviária and Beira-Mar (US$1.50). Taxi to Praia de Iracema US$10. Interstate buses arrive at the rodoviária, 6 km south from the centre. No luggage store, only lockers.

Ins & outs
See also Transport, page 555

    Getting around The city bus system is efficient if a little rough. Fare US$0.90. Vans ("topic") also charge US$0.90. The cheapest way to get to know the city is to take the *Circular 1* (anti-clockwise) or *Circular 2* (clockwise) buses which pass Avenida Beira-Mar, the Aldeota district, the University (UFC) and the city centre and cathedral; fare US$0.90. Alternatively, take the new *Top Bus* of Expresso Guanabara, a/c minibus starting at Av Abolição, US$1.50, T0800-991992.

Sights

Walking through the centre of Fortaleza, it is hard to ignore the city's history, dating back to the 17th century. **Praça do Ferreira**, from which pedestrian walkways radiate, is the heart of the commercial centre. **Fortaleza Nossa Senhora da Assunção**, originally built in 1649 by the Dutch, gave the city its name (Avenida Alberto Nepomuceno). ■ *Daily 0800-1100, 1400-1700,*

Fortaleza & the North Coast

T2315155. Near the fort, on Rua Dr João Moreira, is the 19th-century **Passeio Público** or Praça dos Mártires, a park with old trees and statues of Greek deitiese. West of here a neoclassical former prison (1866) houses a fine tourist centre, the **Centro de Turismo do Estado** (Emcetur), with museums, theatre and craft shops on Avenida Senador Pompeu 350, near the waterfront, T2313566. Further west along Rua Dr João Moreira, at **Praça Castro Carreira**, is the nicely refurbished train station **Estação João Felipe** (1880).

The **Teatro José de Alencar**, on the praça of the same name, was inaugurated in 1910. It is a magnificent iron structure imported from Scotland and decorated in neo-classical and art nouveau styles, and is worth visiting. It also houses a library and art gallery. ■ *Monday-Friday, 0800-1700, hourly tours, some English speaking guides available, US$1, Wednesday entry free, T2522324.* The mausoleum of President Castelo Branco (1964-67) may be visited, it is part of the **Palácio da Abolição**, a former state government building on Avenida Barão de Studart 505. ■ *Daily 0800-1800.* The **Praça dos Leões** or **Praça General Tibúrcio** on Rua Conde D'Eu has bronze lions imported from France. Around it stand the 18th-century **Palácio da Luz**, former seat of the state government; the **Igreja Nossa Senhora do Rosário**, built by slaves in the 18th century; and the former provincial legislature, dating from 1871, which houses the Museu do Ceará. The new **cathedral**, completed in 1978, in gothic style but built in concrete, stands beside the new **Mercado Central**, with beautiful stained glass windows on Praça da Sé, Avenida Alberto Nepomuceno.

Fortaleza

Sleeping
1 Cabana Praia
2 Caxambu
3 Chevalier
4 Colonial Praia
5 Esplanada Praia
6 Imperial Othon Palace
7 Nordeste Palace
8 Nossa Pousada
9 Novotel

At the Centro de Turismo are the **Museu de Arte e Cultura Populares**, which **Museums**
is the most interesting, and the **Museu de Minerais**. ■ *Monday-Friday,*
0800-1700, Saturday 0800-1400, US$0.50.

Museu do Ceará, Rua São Paulo, next to Praça dos Leões, has displays on
history and anthropology. ■ *Tuesday-Friday 0830-1730, Saturday 0830-1400;*
T2511502; take bus marked 'Dom Luís'.

Museu das Secas, Pedro Pereira 683, houses collections of photographs
and anti-drought equipment. ■ *Tuesday-Friday 1330-1700, T2816444.*
Museu do Maracatu, Rufino de Alencar 231, at Teatro São José, has costumes
of this ritual dance of African origin.

Museu de Arte da Universidade Federal do Ceará, Avenida da
Universidade 2854, is a fine arts museum. ■ *Monday-Friday, 0800-1200,*
1400-1800.

Museu Artur Ramos (Casa de José de Alencar), Avenida Perimetral,
Messejana, 15 kilometres from the centre, displays artefacts of African and
indigenous origin collected by the anthropologist Artur Ramos, as well as documents from the writer José de Alencar, see below. ■ *Tuesday-Sunday*
0800-1200, 1400-1730, Monday 1400-1730, T2291898.

Museu de Fortaleza, Avenida Vicente de Castro, Praia de Mucuripe,
housed in a lighthouse, has photographs and artefacts relating to the city's history. There are good views of the coast and nearby beches from the top.
■ *Monday-Friday 0800-1700, Saturday-Sunday 0800-1200, free, T2631115.*

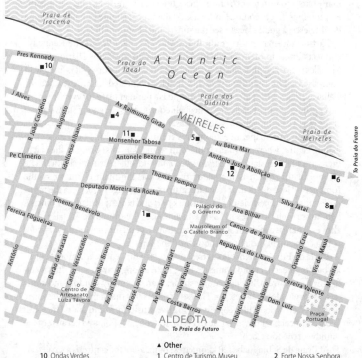

10 Ondas Verdes	▲ Other	2 Forte Nossa Senhora
11 Pousada da Praia	1 Centro de Turismo, Museu	da Assunção
12 Zen Praia	de Arte e Cultura Populares,	3 Mercado Central
	Museu de Minerais & Tourist Office	

Fortaleza & the North Coast

Centro Cultural Dragão do Mar, R Dragão do Mar 81, Praia de Iracema, houses a contemporary art museum (Museu de Arte Contemporânea do Ceará), planetarium and a cultural memorial (Memorial da Cultura Cearense) with a highly recommended folk arts collection. There are also several temporary exhibitions and shows as well as cafés and bookshops. ■ *Tuesday-Thursday 1000-1730, Friday-Sunday 1400-2130, US$1 (free Sunday), T4888600.*

Parks   The main green area in the city is **Parque do Cocó**, a 446-hectare park with forest and mangroves along the Rio Cocó, on Avenida Engenheiro Santana Jr and Rua Andrade Furtado, in the south of the city; there are sports fields, an amphitheatre and snack bars. Nearby on Avenida Pontes Vieira, Bairro Dionísio Torres, is **Parque Adahil Barreto**, where boat rides on the Rio Cocó can be arranged.

Urban beaches

Fortaleza has 25 km of   Those beaches between Barra do Ceará (west) and Ponta do Mucuripe (east)
beaches, many of which   are considered polluted and not suitable for swimming. *Jardineira* buses are a
are the scene of the   special transport service from the centre and from Avenida Beira Mar to the
city's nightlife   beaches (US$2).

Eastern beaches   To Praia do Futuro, take a bus marked 'Caça e Pesca', which passes all southeast beaches on its route.

Just east of the centre is **Praia de Iracema**, one of the older beach suburbs, with some original turn-of-the-century houses. It is a popular nightspot with many bars and restaurants; one of these, the *Estoril*, housed in one of the earliest buildings, has become a landmark. At the shore is Ponte Metálica or Ponte dos Ingleses, a good place to see the sunset and view dolphins.

East of Iracema, the **Avenida Beira Mar** (Avenida Presidente Kennedy) connects Praia do Meireles (divided into Praia do Ideal, dos Diários and do Meireles proper) with Volta da Jurema and Praia do Mucuripe; it is lined with high-rise buildings and most luxury hotels are located here. A *calçado*, or walkway, follows the palm-lined shore and is a popular place for evening walks and cycling; on the beach are volleyball courts, bars, open air shows and a crafts fair. The atmosphere is quite pleasant.

Praia do Mucuripe, five kilometres from the centre, is Fortaleza's main fishing centre, where *jangadas* (rafts with triangular sails) bring in the catch; there are many restaurants serving *peixada* and other fish specialities. The symbol of this beach is the statue of Iracema, the main character of the romance by José de Alencar (see **Literature** section, page 777); from the monument there is a good view of Mucuripe's port and bay. At Mucuripe Point is a lighthouse built by slaves in 1846, which houses the Museu de Fortaleza (see above). There is a lookout at the new lighthouse, good for viewing the *jangadas* which come in, in the late afternoon, and the sunset.

Praia do Futuro, eight kilometres southeast of the centre, is the most popular bathing beach, eight kilometres long, with strong waves, sand dunes and freshwater showers, but no natural shade; there are many vendors and straw shacks serving local dishes. On Thursday nights it is the main nightlife centre of the city, crowded with people enjoying live music, *forró* and crab. The south end of the beach is known as Caça e Pesca; water here is polluted because of the outflow of the Rio Cocó.

At **Praia de Sabiaguaba**, 20 kilometres southeast of the centre, is a small fishing village known for its seafood; the area has mangroves and is good for fishing.

Twenty nine kilometres southeast of the centre is **Praia Porto das Dunas**, a pleasant beach popular for watersports including surfing. Buggies and ultralight tours can be arranged. The main attraction is **Beach Park**, the largest water park in South America, with pools, water toboggans, sports fields, restaurants (admission US$20; *jardineira* bus from centre or Avenida Beira Mar).

Western beaches Northwest of the centre is **Praia Barra do Ceará**, eight kilometres, where the Rio Ceará flows into the sea (take a Grande Circular 1 bus). Here are the ruins of the 1603 Forte de Nossa Senhora dos Prazeres, the first Portuguese settlement in the area, partially covered by dunes; sunsets are very beautiful. The beaches west of the Rio Ceará are cleaner, are lined with palms and have strong waves. A bridge across this river has been built, making the area more accessible and open to development, as at **Praia de Icaraí**, 22 kilometres to the northwest, and **Tabuba**, five kilometres further north.

Beyond Tabuba, 37 kilometres from Fortaleza, is **Cumbuco**, a lively beach, dirty in high season, with bars, buggies, horse riding, jangadas, dunes which you can slide (known locally as *Skibunda*) down into a freshwater lake (Lagamar de Cauípe), palm trees. You can also walk five kilometres to Cauípe. Take the *Jardineira* bus, US$1, 45 minutes, from Avenida Rui Barbosa next to *Ideal Clube*, Fortaleza, which passes Icaraí, Tabuba and Cambuco. Best to take 0815, 0900 or 1030 departures, returning at 1530, 1700 or 1745 (last bus), for information T2521402. The restaurant at the final bus stop has lockers, US$0.50 per day, and provides tours. Buggy tour, US$7 per person, is recommended. There is a wide range of accommodation and places to eat in Cumbuco and all the beaches closer to the city.

Excursions

Sailing boat or yacht tours along the coast leave from Praia do Mucuripe (see **Tour companies** below). There are diving possibilities off the coast, including Pedra da Risca, off Mucuripe, rich in shoals of colourful fish and rays; shipwrecks across from Pecém northwest of the city and Portal de Maceió to the southeast. There are 14 dive sites along the state's coast; regular weekend outings, guides and equipment from *ASPA* or *Projeto Netuno* (see **Sports** below).

Train tours on the *Litorina*, a railcar, go on Saturday (0720) to **Praia da Lagoinha** to the northwest, 64 kilometres by train to Croatá and 43 kilometres by bus. This beach is very scenic, see page 563 for details (tour US$30).

Another train/bus combination tour on the *Litorina* goes on Sunday (0710) to the **Maciço de Baturité**, a scenic highland area with many waterfalls and much history. It is 103 kilometres by rail to the town of Baturité, then by bus up the massif (tour, including lunch at Estância das Flores, Pacoti, US$40). Information from *Turistar* at the railway station, T2113090, F2122456, see **Interior of Ceará** below.

The **Serra de Maranguape** (*altitude* 890 metres) with tropical growth and distant views back to the city, is 30 kilometres inland from Fortaleza along a paved road (CE-020); there are some resorts with swimming possibilities. The path to the top starts from *Pousada Serra Verde* (**B**, Sítio São José, green surroundings, nice views, at the end of a five-kilometre cobblestone road from the town centre). It's a two-hour walk and a rewarding climb. Frequent buses from rodoviária or from the centre, near the train station, US$3.

Another possible day trip is to the **Serra da Aratanha** (775 metres) in Pacatuba, southeast of Maranguape. Passing a colonial church and *Pousada das Andreias* (**B**) it's a two-hour walk to the top through plantations of banana, mango and jack-fruit trees. There is a waterfall half-way (see the turbines from a 1980s plane crash). Near the top is a house with a pond where you should ask for permission or help to continue to the summit and the Pedra de Letreiro, with ancient inscriptions, views of metropolitan Fortaleza and a colony of vultures. Bus from rodoviária one hour, US$2.50.

Those interested in crafts should visit **Aquiraz** (*population* 48,286), 31 kilometres southeast of Fortaleza, and the nearby beaches of **Prainha** (six kilometres north) and **Iguape** (18 kilometres south), where crafts-people can be seen using the techniques of *bilro* and *labirinto* with amazing speed, to create beautiful lacework; several hotels and restaurants in all these locations, see **Eastern Coast** below.

Essentials

Sleeping
■ *on map, page 548*
Price codes: see inside front cover
Most hotels offer reduced prices in the low season. Where 2 rates are indicated, the first letter refers to luxo, the second standard rooms

LL *Ceasar Park*, Av Beira Mar 3980, Mucuripe, T2631133, F2631444. Full luxury hotel, 5-star, pool, Brazilian, French and Japanese restaurants, heliport. **L** *Esplanada Praia*, Av Beira Mar 200, Meireles, T/F2248555. Five-star, pool, restaurant. **L** *Praia Verde*, Av Dioguinho 3860, Praia do Futuro, T2345233, F2340808. Five-star luxury, pool, restaurant. **L** *Imperial Othon Palace*, Av Beira Mar 2500, Meireles, T2429177, F2427777. Five-star, beach front location (recommended *feijoada* on Saturday). **L** *Marina Park*, Av Pres C Branco 400, Jacarecanga, T2525253, F2531803. Huge 5-star luxury leisure complex with all facilities, modern mooring for yachts at reasonable prices, day rates available for non-residents. Strongly recommended. **L** *Seara Praia*, Av Beira Mar 3080, Meireles, T2429555, F2641666. Luxury 4-star, covered pool, restaurant. **AL** *Praiano Palace*, Av Beira Mar 2800, Meireles, T2449333, F2443333. Four-star, restaurant, pool. **AL** *Beira Mar*, Av Beira Mar 3130, Meireles, T2449444, F2615659. Four-star, swimming pool. **AL** *Novotel Magna*, Av Beira Mar 2380, Meireles, T2449122, F2612793. Four-star, pool, restaurant. **A** *Samburá Praia*, Av Beira Mar 4530, Meireles, T2631999, F2632177. Cheaper than most beach hotels. **A** *Colonial Praia*, R Barão de Aracati 145, Iracema, T2119644, F2523501. Four-star, pleasant grounds and big pool, laundry service (10 minutes' walk from Av Beira Mar). **A** *Ibis Praia*, Atualpa Barbosa de Lima 660, Iracema, T2192121, F2190000. A/c, fridge, restaurant, pool. **A** *Paraíso da Praia*, R dos Pacajus 109, Iracema, T2313387. Small, on beach, helpful, good. **A** *Praia Mar*, Av Beira Mar 3190, Meireles, T/F2449455. A/c, fridge, restaurant. **A** *Pousada Jardim*, Ildefonso Albano 950, Aldeota, T2317991, F2263256, www.hoteljardim.com.br. No sign outside, by Iracema beach, nice garden, excursions arranged, many languages spoken, 20% discount for owners of *Brazil Handbook*. Warmly recommended. **A** *Pousada da Praia*, Av Monsenhor Tabosa 1315, Iracema, 2 blocks from beach, T2245935, F2611104, **B** with fan. Recommended. Bus stop for centre outside. **A** *Praia de Iracema*, Av Raimundo Giro 430, Iracema, T2542299, F2314356. A/c, fridge. **A** *Cabana Praia II*, at R João Lourenço 441, Aldeota, T2611399, F2242798 and No I at Av Rui Barbosa 555, T2614954. Both small. **A** *Sunflower*, R Silva Paulet 300, Meireles, T2482427, F2480602, info@sunflower-hotel.com, www.sunflower-hotel.com. **A** *Zen Praia*, Av Abolição 1894, Meireles, T2443213, F2612196. A/c, pool, restaurant. Recommended.

B *Apart-hotel Aquidabá*, Av Raimundo Girão 630, at beginning of Praia Iracema, T2319733, F2319697, 20 minutes' walk from centre. With bath, pool and bar, quiet. **B** *Chevalier*, Av Duque de Caxias 465, T2314611. Fan, pleasant. **B** *Caxambu*, Gen Bezerril 22, T2310339. A/c, with breakfast, central (opposite Cathedral). **B** *Nordeste Palace*, R Assunção 99 in centre, T2211999, F2211999. Large rooms, good value. **B** *Ondas Verdes*, Av Beira Mar 934, Iracema, T2260871. Fan, TV. Recommended. **B** *Pousada d'Antonietta*, Carlos Vasconcelos 660, T2243454. Quiet, 5 minutes from beach, buses nearby. **B** *Pousada Jangada da Praia*, Silva Paulet 155, Aldeota, T2612263. Near the beach, a/c, good breakfast. **C** *Passeio*, R Dr João Moreira 221,

Centro, T2522104. Fan, good breakfast, safe, storage, good value. **C** *Pousada Central*, Av Dom Manuel 470, near Costa Barrios, T2525040, F2274640. Good value. **C** *Pousada Village Mar e Sol*, R Idelfonso Albano 614, Praia Iracema, T2523206. With or without bath. Recommended. **C** *Pousada Vida da Praia*, José Vilar 252, in Aldeota district, T2610444, F2681243. Safe, helpful, English spoken. **C** *Big*, Gen Sampaio 485, in centre by train station, T2511066. With bath, fan, **D** with shared bath, clean, friendly, good value, caution recommended at night. **C** *Nossa Pousada*, Av Abolição 2600, Meireles, T2614699. Without bath, near beach, helpful, has good value *churrasco*. **C** *Pousada Abril em Portugal*, Av Almte Barroso 1006, Iracema, T2319508. With bath, breakfast, fan, good value. Recommended. **C** *Pousada da França D'Eloise*, Av Monsenhor Tabosa 2623, Meireles, T/F2274640. Cheaper without a/c, 5 minutes from beach. **C** *Pousada Casa Grande*, Av Monsenhor Tabosa 1320, Meireles, T2245164, F2247052. **C** *Pousada Jambo*, R Antonia Augusto 141, Praia de Iracema, T2193873, Mobile 9929481. A/c, cheaper with fan, Swiss run, very friendly, changes cash and travellers' cheques. **C** *Pousada Santa Maria*, Almte Barroso 617, T2444019. Laundry, kitchen, English-run. Recommended. **D** *Pousada Kalahara*, R Raimundo Esteves 41, Praia do Futuro, T2623144, near beach. Big rooms, pool, friendly. Recommended. Several hotels along R Senador Pompeu, eg **D** *Universo*, at No 1152. Without breakfast, may rent by the bed (ie single sex clients 3 to a room), smokers not welcome, some rooms have mosquito nets. Try student houses on Av Universitários, cheap or even free.

Youth hostel **D** *Albergue Praia de Iracema*, Av Almte Barroso 998, T2193267, F2193720. Good location, mixed reports. *Albergue de Fortaleza*, R Rocha Lima 1186, Aldeota, T2441850. Separate men and women dormitories, 1 room for couples, cheaper for members. *Coqueiro Verde*, R Frei Mansueto 531, 5 blocks from Beira-Mar, Meireles, T2671998. Dormitories, kitchen, laundry facilities.

Camping *Fortaleza Camping Club*, R Pedro Paulo Moreira 505, Parque Manibura, Água Fria, 10 km, T2732544. Many trees for shade, US$7 pp. *Barra Encantada*, Praia do Barro Preto, 42 km southeast, T2441916 (office Av Barão de Studart 2360, s 1607). US$9 pp, Camping Club members US$4 pp, see **East Coast** below. *Fazenda Lago das Dunas*, Uruaú (115 km southeast), T2442929. US$4 pp for Camping Club members, US$9 pp others, also rents rooms, see Beberibe, **East Coast** below.

Several good fish restaurants at Praia de Mucuripe, where the boats come ashore between 1300 and 1500. Recommended on Av Beira Mar, Meireles are: *Alfredo* (good fish), No 4616, and, next door, No 4632, *Peixada do Meio*. *Colher de Pau*, R Federico Borges 204, Varjota. Recommended regional food, in Varjota district (others here, too), also at R dos Tabajaras 412, Iracema. *Carneiro de Ordones*, R Azevedo Bolão 571, Parquelândia, near North Shopping. Crowded with locals at weekends for every kind of lamb dish (try *buchada*, a kind of haggis). *Plato*, Av Barão de Studart 2360, Aldeota. Revolving restaurant, good views, expensive. Cheaper options in Aldeota: *A Tia Neto*, R Tabosa 937, *Churrascaria Picanha de Veras*, R Carlos Vasconcelos 660, good for chicken, *Dom Pastel*, R Carlos Vasconcelos 996, pay-by-weight, and *Tropicália*, Av Santos Dumont 1815, very popular, good quality. *Estoril*, R dos Tabajaras 397, Iracema. Varied food, restaurant and school. *Nossa Casa*, Aracati 15, Iracema. Cearense food, good value.

Italian *La Trattoria*, R dos Pacajus 125, Iracema. Good. *Sandras*, Av Engenheiro Luis Vieirra 555, Praia do Futuro. Lobster has been recommended, as has *Francés-Italiano*, Av Des Moreira 155. *Parque Recreio*, Rui Barbosa 2727. For good *churrasco*.

German *Hofbräuhaus*, Costa Barros 1080, good food.

Chinese *Hong Kong*, Av Beira Mar 4544, Meireles.

Japanese *Mikado*, Av Barão de Studart 600, Aldeota.

Eating
At Praia de Iracema, good outdoor nightlife and a collection of cafés on the beach, serve good fast food and great coffee

Fortaleza & the North Coast

Vegetarian *Alivita*, Barão do Rio Branco 1486. Good for fish, lunch only, Monday-Friday. *Fonte de Saúde*, R Pedro 339. Excellent vegetarian food, sold by weight, and a wide range of fruit juices. *Belas Artes*, Maj Facundo 82, just up from Passeio Público. Good.

Other Cheap meals at the railway station. Emcetur restaurant, *Xadrez*, in the old prison, good atmosphere, overpriced, open to 2400, reported safe to 2100. Good view of Fortaleza from *Restaurant Panorámico*, R Mirante, in Mucuripe district, near the lighthouse. *Tropical* ice cream parlour, several branches, try *murici*, *cajá* and other northeast flavours.

Bars &
nightclubs
Fortaleza is renowned
for its nightlife and
prides itself with having
the liveliest Monday
night in the country

Some of the best places for entertainment, with many bars and restaurants are: the Av Beira Mar, Praia de Iracema, *El Mirante*, the hill above Praia de Mucuripe and Av Dom Luís. Some recommended bars: *Mucuripe Club*, on Av Beira Mar, popular. *Bar Mirabilis*, R Barão de Aracati 142, near *Hotel Colonial*, Iracema, German and Swiss newspapers and sports results. *Espaço Cultural Diogo Fontenelle*, R Gustavo Sampaio 151, art gallery and bar with live music. *Sirigüella Banana*, R dos Tremembés 100, Iracema.

Forró is the most popular dance and there is a tradition to visit on specific nights certain establishments where the action concentrates. **Monday** *Forró* is danced at the *Pirata Bar*, US$5, recommended, and other establishments along R dos Tabajaras and its surroundings, at Praia de Iracema. **Tuesday** Music and comedy at *Subindo ao Céu*, Praia do Futuro. Live golden oldies at *Boate Oásis*, Av Santos Dumont 6061, Aldeota. **Wednesday** Regional music and samba-reggae at *Clube do Vaqueiro*, city bypass, Km 14, by BR-116 south and E-020, at 2230. **Thursday** Live music, shows and crab specialities at the beach shacks in Praia do Futuro, *Chico do Caranguejo*, lively bar. Recommended. **Friday** Singers and bands play regional music at *Parque do Vaqueiro*, BR-020, Km 10, past city bypass. **Saturday** *Forró* at *Parque Valeu Boi*, R Trezópolis, Cajueiro Torto, *Forró Três Amores*, Estrado Tapuio, Euzébio and *Cantinho do Céu*, CE-04, Km 8. **Sunday** *Forró* and *música sertaneja* at *Cajueiro Drinks*, BR-116, Km 20, Euzébio.

Entertainment **Cinema** For information about cinema programming, T139. **Theatre** In the centre are *Teatro José de Alencar*, Praça José de Alencar (see **Sights** above), and *Teatro São José*, R Rufino de Alencar 363, T2315447, both with shows all year.

Festivals *6 January*, *Epiphany*; *Ash Wednesday*. *19 March*, *São José*; *Christmas Eve*; *New Year's Eve*, half-day.

A festival, the *Regata Dragão do Mar*, takes place at Praia de Mucuripe on the last Sunday in *July*, during which the traditional *jangada* (raft) races take place. Also during the last week of July, the out-of-season Salvador-style carnival, *Fortal*, takes place along Av Almte Barroso, Av Raimundo Giro and Av Beira Mar.

In Caucaia, 12 km to the southeast, a *vaquejada*, traditional rodeo and country fair, takes place during the last weekend of **July**.

On **15 August**, the local Umbanda *terreiros* (churches) celebrate the **Festival of Iemanjá** on Praia do Futuro, taking over the entire beach from noon till dusk, when offerings are cast into the surf. Well worth attending (members of the public may 'pegar um passo' – enter into an inspired religious trance – at the hands of a *pai-de-santo*). Beware of pick-pockets and purse-snatchers.

Sports **Diving** Diving trips (see Excursions above), lessons and equipment rental from: *ASPA (Atividades Subaquáticas e Pesquisas Ambientais)*, R Eduardo Garcia 23, s 13, Aldeota, T2682966/9874341; or *Projeto Netuno*, R do Mirante 165, Mucuripe, T/F2633009. **Golf** The *Ceará Golf Club* has 9 holes. **Surfing** Surfing is popular on a number of Ceará beaches, including those by the towns of Paracurú and Pecém to the west of Fortaleza and Porto das Dunas to the east. *Projeto Salva Surf*, a surfers rescue service operated by the fire department, may be reached by dialling 193. **Trekking** The Fortaleza chapter of the *Trekking Club do Brasil* has walks once a month to different natural areas, visitors are welcome to join, US$20 for transport and T-shirt, T2122456. **Windsurfing** Due to constant trade winds, a number of Ceará beaches are excellent for windsurfing. Equipment can be rented in some of the more popular beaches such as Porto das Dunas and in the city from *Windclub*, Av Beira Mar 2120, Praia dos Diários, T9825449. Lessons also available.

Fortaleza has an excellent selection of locally manufactured textiles, which are among **Shopping** the cheapest in Brazil, and a wide selection of regional handicrafts. The local craft specialities are lace (mostly hand-made) and embroidered textile goods; also hammocks (US$15 to over US$100), fine alto-relievo wood carvings of northeast scenes, basket ware, leatherwork and clay figures (*bonecas de barro*). Bargaining is OK at the **Mercado Central** near Praça da Sé, and the *Emcetur Centro de Turismo* in the old prison (more expensive). Leather, lacework and cashew nuts at the Mercado Central are excellent.

Crafts are also available in shops near the market (eg *Itaparica*, R Conde D'Eu 434). The *SINE* shop, at R Dr João Moreira 429, is part of a state government initiative to promote small independent producers. Every night (1800-2300), there are stalls along the beach at Praia Meireiles, lively, fair prices. *Ceart*, Av Santos Dumont 1589, Aldeota, is good but expensive. Crafts also available in the commercial area along Av Monsenhor Tabosa as it approaches the beach. Clothes boutiques along Monsenhor Tabosa are closer to the centre, between Sen Almino and João Cordeiro.

Local Car hire: *HM*, R Vicente Leite 650, Aldeota, T2617799, cars and buggies. *Avis*, Av **Transport** Barão de Studart 1425, Aldeota, T2616785. *Localiza*, Av Antônio Justa 2400, T2424255, *See also Ins & outs,* or airport T0800-992000. *Loc Autos*, Av Abolição 1840, Mucuripe, T2244494. *Loc Car*, Av *page 547* Virgílio Távora 206, Aldeota, T2248594, cars and buggies. *Loca Buggy*, Av Beira Mar 2500, Meireles, T/F2616945. **Trains**: Station at Praça Castro Carreira in the centre, T2114255. Commuter service southwest to Caucaia and south to Maracanaú. Tourist trains run on Saturday to Croatá, plus bus trip to Praia da Lagoínha and on Sunday to Baturité, plus bus to the mountains; see **Excursions** above.

Long distance Air: Aeroporto Pinto Martins, Praça Eduardo Gomes, 6 km south of centre, T2726166. International flights to Lisbon, Milan and Rome. Domestic flights to Belém, Natal, Juazeiro do Norte, Parnaíba, Recife, São Luís and Teresina.

Buses: rodoviária at Av Borges de Melo 1630, Fátima, 6 km south from centre, T186, many city buses (US$0.65) including 'Aguanambi' 1 or 2 which go from Av Gen Sampaio, 'Barra de Fátima-Rodoviária' from Praça Coração de Jesus.

Nordeste to **Aracati**, many daily, US$4, 2 hours; to **Mossoró**, 9 daily, US$5 *convencional*, US$7.50 *executivo*, 4 hours; to **Natal**, 7 daily, US$11 *convencional*, US$15.50 *executivo*, US$25 *leito*, 8 hours; to **João Pessoa**, 3 daily, US$15 *convencional*, 10 hours. Guanabara to **Recife**, 5 daily, US$20 *convencional*, US$30 *executivo*, US$40 *leito*, 12 hours, book early for weekend travel. Itapemirim to **Salvador**, US$33, 21 hours. Penha to **Rio de Janeiro**, US$76.50 *convencional*, US$96 *executivo*, 48 hours, to **São Paulo**, US$76.50 *convencional*, US$96 *executivo*, 48 hours. Timbira, Guanabara and Boa Esperança to **Teresina**, several daily, US$13.50, 10 hours (or Top Bus, US$18, *leito* US$27); to **Belém**, 5 daily, US$35 *convencional*, US$40 *executivo*, 23 hours (*Expresso Timbira* also sells Belém-Manaus boat tickets). Piripiri, to **Parque Nacional de Sete Cidades**, US$11, 9 hours, a good stop *en route* to Belém. Guanabara to **São Luiz**, 3 daily, US$23.50, 16 hours. Rápido Juazeiro to **Juazeiro do Norte**, 4 daily, US$13.50, 9 hours. Guanabara to **Campina Grande**, US$15, 13 hours.

Fortaleza & the North Coast

Beaches: *Redençao* to **Gijoca** and **Jericoacoara**, daily 0900, 2100, US$7.50 to Gijoca, US$8.50 to Jericoacoara, 7 hours, book ahead in high season. For eastern beaches near Fortaleza (Prainha, Iguape, Barro Preto, Batoque) and towns such as Aquiraz, Eusébio or Pacajus, you must take *São Benedito* buses from Av Domingos Olímpio 184 (10 minutes' walk from downtown), not from the rodoviária. At the rodoviária buses leave for Caponga and further on (Morro Branco, Aracate, etc). Details are given below.

Directory **Airline offices** On Av Santos Dumont, Aldeota are: *Varig*, No 2727, T2668000, F2440500. *Vasp*, No 3060, sala 803, T2446222, F2723046. *Transbrasil*, No 2813, T2682866, F2441560. *TAM*, R Oswaldo Cruz 1101, Aldeota, T2613232, F2615317. *TAF* (*Transportes Aéreos Fortaleza*), T2727333, flights to Juazeiro do Norte and other places in the interior.

Open 0900-1630 **Banks** *Banco do Nordeste*, R Major Facundo 372, a/c, helpful, recommended. *Banco Excel*, R Major Facundo 322, T2111834, sells TCs on Amex card. TCs exchanged and cash with Visa at *Banco do Brasil*, R Barão do Rio Branco 1500, also on Av Abolição. *Banco Mercantil do Brasil*, R Mayor Facundo 484, Centro, Praça do Ferreira, cash against Mastercard. Exchange at *Tropical Viagens*, R Barão do Rio Branco 1233, T2213344, English spoken. *Libratur*, Av Abolição 2794, recommended. *ACCtur* has exchange booths for dollars (cash and TCs) throughout the city, main office Av Dom Luís 176, Aldeota, T2619955. *Rudy Constantino* has automatic exchange machines for several currencies, eg Av Virgílio Távora 150, Meireles, T2617288 and Av Desembargador Moreira 1155. *IJB Câmbio*, Av Dom Luís 655, Aldeota, T2617466.

Communications **Post Office:** Main branch at R Senador Alencar 38, Centro; Av Monsenhor Tabosa 1109, Iracema; at train station. Parcels must be taken to Receita Federal office at Barão de Aracati 909, Aldeota (take 'Dom Luiz' bus). **Telephone:** International calls from Emcetur hut on Iracema beach and from *Telemar* offices: R Floriano Peixoto 99, corner of R João Moreira, Centro; R José Vilar 375, Aldeota; Av Beira Mar 736, Iracema; Av Beira Mar 3821, Meireles; Av César Cals 1297, Praia do Futuro; at rodoviária and airport. Public phones take phone cards.

Embassies & consulates *Belgium*, R Eduardo Garcia 609, Aldeota, T2641500. *British*, Praça da Imprensa, Aldeota, T4668888 (consul is Annette, her secretary Eunice). *Denmark*, R Inácio Capelo 50, Colônia, T2285055, open 0800-1800. *France*, R Bóris 90, Centro, T2542822. *Germany*, R Pedro Borges 33, s 1135, Centro, T2314366. *Italy*, Miguel Dibe 80, cj Wash Soares, T2786352. *Portugal*, R Pedro Borges 33, Ed Palácio Progresso, Centro, T2542900. *Sweden* and *Norway*, R Leonardo Mota 501, Aldeota, T2420888. *Switzerland*, R Dona Leopoldina 697, Centro, T2269444. *USA*, Nogueira Acioli 891, Centro, T2521539.

Hospitals & medical services *Instituto Dr José Frota* (*IJF*), R Barão do Rio Branco 1866, T2555000, recommended public hospital.

Laundry *Laundromat*, Av Abolição 3038, Meireles.

Security Tourists should avoid the Serviluz *favela* between the old lighthouse (Av Vicente de Castro), Mucuripe and Praia do Futuro; the *favela* behind the railway station; the Passeio Público at night; Av Abolição at its eastern (Nossa Senhora da Saúde church) and western ends. Generally, though, the city is safe for visitors.

Tour companies & travel agents City and beach tours, airport transfers at *Lavila*, Rui Barbosa 1055, T2614777. Recommended. *Eurotur*, Av Abolição 2686, very helpful, good tours to beaches for US$30. *Lafuente Turismo*, Av Sen Virgílio Tavora 496, T2448558. *Petrelli Turismo*, R Barbosa de Freitas 1440, T2611222, F2444335. *Beach Sun*, Av Anto Justa 2666, Meireles, T2644022, F2247667. *Planet Tur*, Eduardo Garcia 23, loja 1, Aldeota, T2616022, F2610642. In the same building is *Duplatour*, loja 2, T2642810, F2612656. *Nettour*, R Tte Benévolo 1355, Aldeota, T2683099, F2682724. Tours to Jericoacoara with *Pousada Ondas Verdes*, recommended, and *Duplatour*, see above. *Hippopotamus*, João Carvalho 800, Aldeota, T2449191, F2240043. *Magia Turismo*, R Dep Moreira Rocha 329, Meireles, T/F2522217. Boat tours with *Ceará Saveiro*, Av Beira Mar 4294, T2631085, sailboat and yacht trips, daily 1000-1200 and 1600-1800 from Praia de Mucuripe. *Martur*, Av Beira Mar 4260, T2631203, sailing boat and schooner trips, from Mucuripe, same schedule as above. *Marina Park Hotel*, T2525253, boat trips with minimum 30 passengers, daily

1600-1800. Tours to the interior by rail and bus with *Turistar*, Praça Castro Carreira at the railway station, T2123090/9824675, F2122456, helpful with general information (see **Excursions** above). *BIC*, R Barão do Rio Branco 772, T2641406, F2441186, American Express representative. *Stella Barros*, Av Dom Luís 55, Aldeota, T/F2445427, Thomas Cook representative.

Tourist offices *Setur* (*Secretaria do Turismo*), state tourism agency, main office at Centro Administrativo Virgílio Távora, Cambeba, T2181177, F2181167, for information T1516, information booths at Centro de Turismo, in ex-municipal prison, helpful, has maps (sometimes), information about beach tours (0700-1830, Sunday 0700-1300), rodoviária (0600-1800 daily), airport (24 hrs) and Museu de Fortaleza, old lighthouse, Mucuripe (0700-1620). *Fortur* municipal agency; main office at Av Santos Dumont 5335, Papicu, T2651177, F2653430, for information T2521444, information booths at Praça do Ferreira, Av Beira Mar (*calçado* at Praia do Meireles, very informative and friendly, several languages spoken) and at the airport, www.ceara.net.

Voltage 220 volts AC, 60 cycles.

The Eastern Coast

The most prominent feature of the eastern coast is the impressive coloured sand cliffs, used in the production of crafts; there are also sweet-water springs near the shore, palm groves and mangroves. Lobster fishing is one of the main activities.

Aquiraz

Thirty one kilometres east of Fortaleza is the first capital of Ceará, which conserves several colonial buildings and has a religious art museum. It is also the access point for the beaches of Prainha, do Presídio, Iguape and Barro Preto.

Population: 52,500
Phone code: 085
Colour map 2, grid A5

Six kilometres east of Aquiraz is **Prainha**, a fishing village and weekend resort with a 10 kilometre long beach and dunes. The beach is clean and largely empty and the waves are good for surfing. You can see *jangadas* coming in daily in the late afternoon. The village is known for its lacework; you can see the women using the *bilro* and *labirinto* techniques at the **Centro de Rendeiras**. In some of the small restaurants it is possible to see displays of the *Carimbó*, one of the North Brazilian dances. Just south of Prainha is **Praia do Presídio** with calm surf, dunes, palms and *cajueiros* (cashew trees).

Eighteen kilometres southeast of Aquiraz is **Praia Iguape**, another fishing and lacework village. The beach is a large, elbow-shaped sandbank, very scenic especially at Ponta do Iguape. Nearby are high sand dunes where skiing is popular. There is a lookout at Morro do Enxerga Tudo; trips on *jangadas* one hour for US$8.50. Lacework is sold at the **Centro de Rendeiras**. Locals are descendants of Dutch, Portuguese and Indians, some traditions such as the *coco-de-praia* folk dance are still practised. Three kilometres south of Igape is **Praia Barro Preto**, a wide, tranquil beach, with sand dunes, palms and lagoons.

Prainha **L** *New Life*, Alto da Prainha, T3621314. Weight reduction centre, with fridge, pool, restaurant. **A** *Aquiraz Praia e Escola de Hotelaria*, Estr da Prainha, Km 5, T3621006. With bath, fridge, pool, restaurant. **B** *Da Prainha*, R Berlim, Alto da Prainha, T3621122. With bath, rooms in top floor have more air, nice views. **B** *Prainha Solar*, R Principal, T3621355, F3621366. With fridge, restaurant, pool, comfortable. **C** *Pousada*, R Principal near rodoviária. No name and no breakfast, owner lives on the beach, noisy but clean; fishermen also rent space in their homes. Good fish restaurant, *O Leonção*, R Principal. There are several small, cheap and good restaurants along the beach (*barracas de praia*), crab, shrimp, lobster and fish figure prominently in the menu (eg *Mar Aberto*, *Mar e Sol*).

Sleeping & eating

Praia do Presidio **B** *Do Sol*, T3701222. Large rooms with bath, a/c, a couple of chalets, pool, restaurant. **B** *Iguape Hotel de Turismo*, R 8, T3701444. Cabins, pool with springwater, restaurant. **B** *Jangadeiro Praia*, T3701039. With bath, fridge, restaurant, pool.

Iguape **B** *Sol Leste*, R São Pedro, T/F3701233. With bath, fridge, pool, restaurant, sports fields. Other hotels and *pousadas* also available. *Peixada do Iguape*, Av Stuart at the beach. Fish specialities. *O João do Camarão*, Av Stuart. Fish and seafood. *O Caldinho*, Estr do Iguape. Regional food.

Barro Preto **A** *Marina Barro Preto*, R Francisco das Chagas 10, T3701166. With bath, fridge, pool, restaurant. **B** *Chalés Barra Encantada*, R Francisco das Chagas 13, T3701466. Cabins for up to 6, fridge, pool, restaurant, large camping area with palms, US$9 pp, Camping Club members US$4 pp. **B** *Recanto da Fantasia*, R Francisco das Chagas, T2394943. Equipped cabins for up to 4, no breakfast.

Transport **Buses** Daily service to all these beaches from the terminal at Av Domingos Olímpio 184, **Fortaleza**. For information T2721999; **Prainha**, 11 daily, US$1; **Iguape**, hourly between 0600 and 1900, US$1.10.

Caponga and Águas Belas

Cascavel (*population* 48,497) is 62 kilometres southeast of Fortaleza and has a Saturday crafts fair by the market. It is the access point for the beaches of Caponga and Águas Belas, where traditional fishing villages coexist with fancy weekend homes and hotels.

Phone code: 085   **Caponga**, 15 kilometres northeast of Cascavel, has a two kilometre long beach which is wide and lined with palms. *Jangadas* set sail in the early morning; arrangements can be made to accompany fishermen on overnight trips, 90-minute ride by beach, US$14 for up to five people. There is a fish market and crafts sales (ceramics, embroidery and lacework) on the beach.

A 30-minute walk south along the white-sand beach leads to **Águas Belas**, on the mouth of the Rio Mal Cozinhado, offering a combination of fresh and saltwater bathing (access also by road, 15 kilometres from Cascavel, four kilometres from Caponga). The scenery here, and five kilometres further east at Barra Nova, changes with the variations of the tide. A walk north along the beach for six kilometres takes you to the undeveloped Praia do Batoque, which is surrounded by cliffs and dunes.

It is possible to hike along much of the eastern coast. From Prainha to Águas Belas, for example, is seven hours (take plenty of water and sun protection). Where rivers have to be crossed, there is usually a boatman. Fishing villages have accommodation or hammock space.

Sleeping & **Caponga** **A** *Village Barra Mar*, T/F3351088. Chalets with a/c, fridge, restaurant, **eating** pool, nice grounds, watersports. **B** *Summer House*, a/c, pool, restaurant. **B** *La France*, T3351100, F3351016. Fridge, pool, restaurant. On R Laureano de Paula Santana are **B** *JS*, T3351006. With bath, restaurant. **C** *Fateixa*, No 555, T3351122. With bath, pool, garden. **C** *Coqueiral*, No 537, T3351073. With bath, porch with hammocks. *Caponga Praia*, on the beach front. Simple rooms and good meals. **C** *Mon Kapitan*, R Pedro Moita on the square, T3351031. Large rooms with bath, very helpful, good restaurant. *Bybloss*, by beach, T3351045. Shared bath, horse and buggie rental, restaurant. **D** *Versailles*, R J Irineu Araujo, 1.5 km from the beach, T3351071. With small bath, breakfast extra. Snacks from *Gula-Gula*, Estr de Caponga. Varied menu at *Aqui Agora*, R Antonio Camilo and *Na Boca do Povo*, Av Henrique Rodrigues, Centro.

Águas Belas **B** *Praia Águas Belas*, T3351060. Room with bath and cabins, pool, restaurant. **B** *Le Paradis*, T3351050, F3351289. With bath, pool, restaurant. Fishermen

Life's a beach

With almost 7,500 kilometres of Atlantic coastline, it is little wonder that beaches are an integral part not only of Brazil's geography but also of its mentality. For many Brazilians, the term férias (vacation) is synonymous with praia (beach). Those unfortunate souls who live deep inland must get by finding a river, lake or dam to which to flock at weekends and holidays. And if that is still not good enough, places like Manaus' five-star Hotel Tropical have built a wave-pool; an artificial beach within sight of the Amazon.

While the seashore is attractive throughout almost all of its length, the beaches of the northeast are among the country's most famous, and justifiably so. Their towering sand dunes, turquoise lagoons, coloured sand cliffs, coconut palms, quiet fishing villages and lively resorts attract countless Brazilians and foreigners alike.

With so many to choose from, how does one select a beach? There is something for almost every taste: Jericoacoara (CE), with its famous sand dunes and sunsets, Canoa Quebrada (CE), the ultimate party beach, Tambada (PB) and its strictly controlled nudist colony, havens for surfers, sailors and divers; as well as thousands of others that have yet to be 'discovered'. Even the big city beaches can have their charm, sports or cultural events and nightlife, although they are frequently too polluted for bathing.

Brazil's beaches also call for appropriate precautions. Sun protection is vital (some reports suggest that ultraviolet radiation may have increased by as much as 45 percent between 1996 and 1997). Always enquire locally about tides, the strength of the surf, currents and undertows before swimming. Don't go wandering off on your own amid sand dunes, it is easy to get lost. Always protect your valuables, especially on crowded urban beaches.

A general description of the better beaches is provided throughout this Handbook. Hard-core beach bums may wish to obtain the 4-Rodas Guia de Praias, published annually and available at most news-stands (US$15), with detailed descriptions and satellite photos of each and every beach in Brazil. Surely no other country has such a publication!

Robert and Daisy Kunstaetter

offer housing in their homes. Cheaper seafood restaurants are available in the village. **Barra Nova D** *Encontro das Águas*, no sign, friendly.

Buses Direct *Pratius* bus to Caponga from **Fortaleza** rodoviária (hourly, fewer on Sunday, US$1.50) or take a bus to Cascavel from terminal at Av Domingos Olímpio 184 (not rodoviária, 80 minutes) then a bus from Cascavel (20 minutes); bus information in Fortaleza, T2721999, in Caponga T3341485. Bus from Av Domingos Olímpio 184, Fortaleza, direct to Barra Nova, 0900, or go to Cascavel and change there. **Transport**

Morro Branco and Praia das Fontes

Beberibe (*population* 36,989), 78 kilometres from Fortaleza, is the access point for Morro Branco and Praia das Fontes, some of the better known beaches of the east coast. *Phone code: 085*

Four kilometres from Beberibe is Morro Branco, with a spectacular beach, coloured craggy cliffs and beautiful views. *Jangadas* leave the beach at 0500, returning at 1400-1500, lobster is the main catch in this area. The coloured sands of the dunes are bottled into beautiful designs and sold along with other crafts such as lacework, embroidery and straw goods. *Jangadas* may be hired for sailing (one hour for up to six people US$30). Beach buggies (full day US$100) and taxis are also for hire. There are summer homes along the beach which can get very crowded at holiday times.

Fortaleza & the North Coast

South of Morro Branco and six kilometres from Beberibe is Praia das Fontes, which also has coloured cliffs with sweet-water springs; there is a fishing village and at the south end a lagoon. Near the shore is a cave, known as Mãe de Água, visible during low tide. Buggies and ultralight aircraft can be hired on the beach. A luxury resort complex has been built here, making the area expensive.

South of Praia das Fontes are several less developed beaches including **Praia Uruaú** or **Marambaia**, about six kilometres from Praia das Fontes along the beach or 21 kilometres by road from Beberibe, via Sucatinga on a loose sand road. The beach is at the base of coloured dunes; there is a fishing village with some accommodation. Just inland is Lagoa do Uruaú, the largest in the state and a popular place for watersports. Buggy from Morro Branco US$45 for four.

About 50 kilometres southeast of Beberibe is **Fortim**, access point to **Pontal de Maceió**, a reddish sand point on the mouth of the Rio Jaguaribe, from where there is a good view of a large section of the eastern coast. In the winter the river is high and shrimp is fished, while in the summer it dries up, forming islands and sweet-water beaches; boats go to the islands from Fortim. A fishing village is about one kilometre from the ocean; there are bars, restaurants and small *pousadas*.

Sleeping & eating

Morro Branco B *Recanto Praiano*, T2247118. Good breakfast. Recommended. **B** *Pousada dos Ventos*, T3301137. Chalets, pool, restaurant. **B** *Cabana do Morro*, Av Beira Mar, T3300140. Mosquitoes, fan, shower, restaurant, pool, porch with hammocks. **B** *Pousada do Morro Branco*, T3301040. Fridge, pool, restaurant. **C** *Pousada Sereia*, on the beach, T3301144. Good breakfast. Highly recommended. **D** *Rosalias'*, T3301131. With use of kitchen, 50m from bus stop, somewhat run down. You can rent fishermen's houses. Meals can also be arranged at beach front bars (try *O Jangadeiro*). Double room at **D** *Bar São Francisco*, or 7-room house for rent.

Praia das Fontes L *Praia das Fontes*, Av A Teixeira 1, T3381179, F3381087. Luxurious resort, watersports, horses, racket games, spa. Recommended. **B** *Das Falésias*, T3381018, F3011117, clean, German owner, fridge, pool, restaurant.

Camping *Lago das Dunas*, access 9 km south of Beberibe on CE-004, then east from Sucatinga 5 km on a poor dirt road; large area with grass and palms for shade, pool, restaurant, sports fields, it is 1 km through dunes to Praia Marambaia or Uruaú, US$4 pp Camping Club members, US$9 pp non members; also rents rooms with shared bath (US$45 room for 4, US$55 room for 6).

Transport

Buses *São Benedito* bus from **Fortaleza** to Morro Branco, US$2.15; 2½ hours, 5 a day; information in Fortaleza, T2721999. To get to **Natal**, take 0600 bus to Beberibe, then 0800 bus (only one) to Aracati, US$0.60, then on to Natal.

Aracati

Population: 57,000
Phone code: 088

Situated on the shores of the Rio Jaguaribe, Aracati is the access point to the southeastern-most beaches of Ceará; it is along the main highway (BR-304), 142 kilometres from Fortaleza and 90 kilometres from Mossoró. The city is best known for its Carnival, the liveliest in the state, and for its colonial architecture, including several 18th-century churches and mansions with Portuguese tile façades; there is a religious art museum (closed lunch time and Sunday afternoon) and a Saturday morning crafts fair on Avenida Coronel Alexandrino. On the same street is **B** *Pousada Litorânea*, R Col Alexandrino 1251, T4211001, with air conditioning, **D** with fan, near rodoviária. **C** *Beira Rio* is on Trav Senhor do Bonfim, T4211881, with bath and fan.

Transport Bus Natal-Aracati via Mossoró, 6 hours, US$7.50; from Mossoró US$2.50, 2 hours; Fortaleza-Aracati, São Benedito, Guanabara or Nordeste many daily, US$4, 2 hours; Aracati-Canoa Quebrada from General Pompeu e João Paulo, US$0.60; taxi US$3.60.

Canoa Quebrada

Ten kilometres from Aracati is Canoa Quebrada on a sand dune, famous for its *labirinto* lacework and coloured sand sculpture, for sand-skiing on the dunes, for the sunsets, and for the beaches. An isolated fishing village until 1982, when a road was put through, it is now a very popular resort known for its easygoing party atmosphere (there have been reports of drug problems here). There are many bars, restaurants and *forró* establishments. Fishermen have their homes in Esteves, a separate village also on top of the cliff; they still live off the sea and rides on *jangadas* can be arranged at the beach. To avoid biting insects (*bicho do pé*) it is best to wear shoes or sandals. There is nowhere to change money except *Banco do Brasil* in Aracati. In the second half of July the *Canoarte* festival takes place, which includes a *jangada* regatta and music festival.

Phone code: 088
Colour map 2, grid A5

Excursions South of Canoa Quebrada and 13 kilometres from Aracati is **Majorlândia**, a very nice village, with many-coloured sand dunes (used in bottle pictures and cord crafts) and a wide beach with strong waves, good for surfing; the arrival of the fishing fleet in the evening is an important daily event; lobster is the main catch. It is a popular weekend destination with beach homes for rent and Carnival here is quite lively. About five kilometres south along the beach is the village of **Quixaba** on a beach surrounded by coloured cliffs; there are reefs offshore and it is considered a good place for fishing (*Pousada Lúcia*, T4211576). At low tide you can reach Lagoa do Mato, some four kilometres south. Between Canoa Quebrada and Majorlândia is **Porto Canoa**, a resort town (opened 1996), fashioned after the Greek islands. It includes beach homes and apartments, shopping areas, restaurants and hotels, and there are facilities for watersports, horse riding, ultralight flights, buggy and *jangada* outings.

Buggy rentals are available at Canoa Quebrada beach; a popular destination going through the dunes is **Lagoa do Mato**, about 12 kilometres southeast, a pristine beach, surrounded by dunes, cliffs and palms (buggy US$30 for four). There is a hotel with a restaurant. **Ponta Grossa**, about 30 kilometres southeast, is another beautiful beach, where there is a natural lookout on the cliffs (buggy US$75 for four, four hours). The fishing community here has many inhabitants of Dutch origin, following a shipwreck in the 19th century. To the south are the beaches of **Redonda** and **Barreiras**, good for surfing, with a hotel.

Sleeping **Canoa Quebrada** **A** *Tranqüilândia*, T339. Fridge, restaurant. **A** *Falésias Praia*, T335. A/c, fridge. **B** *Pousada Latitude*, R Dragão do Mar, T323. A/c, fridge, cheaper with fan, restaurant. **B** *Pousada Lua Estrela*, R Nascer do Sol 106, T333, F2347472. IYHA affiliated. Fan, fridge, hot shower. **B** *Pousada Logus*, at entrance to town, T9641416. A/c, fridge, quiet. **C** *Pousada do Rei*, R Nascer do Sol 112, T316. Fan, fridge. Highly recommended. **C** *Pousada Maria Alice*, R Dragão do Mar, T4211852. Fan, restaurant, safe. **C** *Pousada Alternativa*, R Francisco Caraço, T335. With or without bath, central. Recommended. **C** *Pousada Via Láctea*, off the main street (so quieter), beautiful view of beach which is 50m away. Some rooms with hot shower, fridge, fan, good breakfast, safe parking, horse and buggy tours, English spoken. Highly recommended. **C** *Tenda do Cumbe*, at end of the road on cliff, T4211761. Thatched huts, restaurant. Warmly recommended. **D** *Pousada 3 de Junho*, L Bezerra with access to beach, T2136510. No breakfast. **D** *Pousada Novo Horizonte*, R Dragão do Mar, T322, above souvenir shops. With bath, breakfast extra, restaurant. **D** *Beco's*, R José Melancia 2300, T328. With bath, inner courtyard with porch and hammocks. **D** *Pousada do Holandês*, R Nascer do Sol, rooms without bath (**E**). No breakfast, use of kitchen. Villagers will let you sling your hammock or put you up cheaply. Verónica is recommended, European books exchanged. Sr Miguel rents good clean houses for US$10 a day.

Town's calling centre:
T4211401 & T4211761,
3-digit numbers
indicated below are
extensions on these
central lines

Town's calling centre: T4211748, 3-digit numbers indicated are extensions on this central line

Majorlândia C *Pousada Esquina das Flores*, T188. Nice. C *Pousada Dunas Praia*, T4211846. With bath, restaurant. **D** *Pousada do Gaúcho*, R do Jangadeiro 323, T195. With bath, restaurant, friendly. **D** *Apartamentos Beira Mar*, on beach, T134. Furnished apartments, no breakfast. **D** *Pousada e Restaurante Requinte*, 100m before beach on main road. Airy rooms, use of kitchen, rooms with or without bath. Recommended. *Majorlândia Praia Hotel*, T4211748. **D** *Pousada a Sereia*, T130. With bath, fridge, restaurant. *Pousada Beira Mar*, T134. With bath, fridge. *Restaurant O Gilberto*, for fish.

Redonda **D** *Pousada O Pescador*, T0XX88-4321127, and 2 others.

Eating Bars and restaurants, vegetarian food in *Espácio Cultural*, cheap seafood (don't drink the water). *Casaverde*, R Dragão do Mar. Good food – Chinese, Mexican and typical Brazilian – good atmosphere, cards and darts available, good music. Home cooking at *Estrela do Mar*, R Dragão do Mar, *Bom Apetite* and *Rasgo de Lua*, both on R José Melancia. Several shacks along the descents to the beach serving *peixe na telha*, the local fish speciality.

Transport **Buses** Fortaleza-Canoa Quebrada, *São Benedito*, 3 daily, US$4.25. Fortaleza-Majorlândia, *São Benedito*, 4 daily, US$4.25. Bus information in Fortaleza, T2270385, 2721999. To **Redonda**: no direct bus, but 4 daily from Fortaleza to Icapuí (US$8), ask the driver to stop about 6 km before the town at a *jangada* which serves as a roadsign at the access road, unpaved, to Redonda, 5 km.

The Western Coast

The coast northwest of Fortaleza has many wide beaches, near fixed or shifting dunes, surrounded by coconut groves. The main roads are some distance from the shore, making access to the beaches somewhat more difficult than on the eastern coast. Hence the fishing villages retain a traditional lifestyle and responsible travel can be especially important.

Pecém & Taíba
Population: 5,500 (Pecém)
Phone code: 085

Fifty eight kilometres northwest of Fortaleza is Pecém, a village set by a cove with a wide beach, dunes, inland lagoons and a strong surf; here and in Taíba, a 14 kilometre long beach to the north (19 kilometres by road), there are surfing and fishing championships; by Taíba, a long point filled with palms extends into the sea. Nearby is **Siupé**, a village that maintains colonial characteristics, where embroidered hammocks, a trademark of Ceará, are made.

Town's calling centre: T3441064 & T3401328, 3-digit numbers indicated are extensions on these central lines

Sleeping and eating **Pecém B** *Pecém Praia*, R São Luís, T189. Fridge, pool. *Pousada Isca do Sol*, Colônia de Férias, T112. Chalets or rooms with bath, pool, restaurant with Swiss specialties. *Pousada do Gaúcho*, Colônia de Férias, T173. With bath, fan. Restaurant. *O Manoel*, R São Luís. Fish dishes. At the Colônia de Férias are several beach shacks including *Joselito*, seafood specialities. *Porto Alegre*, meat, pizza, snacks.

Taíba **E** *Pousada Vitória*, T2235715, good value. *Le Petit Resto Bar*, lobster, shrimp, fish. *O Barão*, regional specialities, *carne de sol*, lamb.

Transport From **Fortaleza** rodoviária, to Pecém 11 daily, US$1.75. To Taíba 4 daily, US$3, information T2521402.

Northwest of Fortaleza by 106 kilometres, and two hours by bus, is Paracuru, a fishing port which has the most important Carnival in the northwest coast, including street dancing and parades, decorated boat parades, sports championships and a beauty contest. It has some lovely deserted white sand beaches with good bathing and surfing, and the people are very friendly. There are several *pousadas* in the centre. Restaurant *Ronco do Mar* has good fish dishes. *Boca do Poço* bar has *forró* at weekends. There are eight buses daily from Fortaleza rodoviária, US$3, information in Fortaleza, T2724483.

West of Paracuru, about 120 kilometres from Fortaleza and 12 kilometres from the town of Paraipaba, is Lagoinha, a very scenic beach with hills, dunes and palms by the shore; a fishing village is on one of the hills. Nearby are some small but pleasant waterfalls and three kilometres west of town Lagoa da Barra, a lake surrounded by dunes. Local legend says that one of the hills, Morro do Cascudo, has a hidden treasure, left by French pirates.

Sleeping and eating Lagoinha: **C** *O Milton*, T102. Cabins, outdoor restaurant. **C** *Ondas do Mar*, T146. With bath, porch with hammocks, restaurant. **C** *Sol e Mar*, small rooms with bath, restaurant, large portions. **C** *Monalisa*, T126. Large rooms with bath. Beach shacks serve fish.

Transport Bus service from **Fortaleza** rodoviária to Lagoinha, 3 daily, US$3.15, information T2724483, train tours from Fortaleza on Saturday, see **Excursions**, page 551.

Fleixeiras

Further northwest, some 135 kilometres from Fortaleza, is **Trairi**, access point to a series of beaches which conserve a natural beauty and, until the mid-1990s, were untouched by tourism. North of Trairi, 15 kilometres by road, is Fleixeiras, where at low tide, pools, good for snorkelling, form near the beach. There are strong waves for surfing and wind for windsurfing as well as dunes by the wide beach. In the village there is a *jangada* repair shop, a good place to learn about these crafts, and a needlework workshop, where lacework and embroidered clothing and linen are made.

About five kilometres west is **Imboaca**, a scenic beach with interesting rock formations and shifting dunes. Further west, at the mouth of the Rio Mundaú, is **Mundaú**, another nice beach, with palms, dunes and an old working lighthouse. A common sport here is fishing for *camurupim*, a large fish, good for eating. Access roads from Imboaca and Cana to the south are often impassable because of shifting dunes; at low tide it is possible to reach it along the beach from Fleixeiras. A fishing village is near the beach; there are some *pousadas* and restaurants. From Fortaleza to Fleixeiras there are three buses daily, US$3.85, information T2724128.

You can cross the Rio Mundaú and walk eight kilometres to Baleia, a developing beach resort with plenty of *pousadas* (**C** *Maresia*, Swiss-run; **C** *Som das Águas*, OK). There is one daily bus from Fortaleza, 1300, five hours, US$10). For another 40 kilometres there are beautiful dune landscapes and fishing villages, how Canoa Quebrada and Jericocoara must have been 30 years ago. Icaraí de Amontada is in a windy bay, good windsurfing, simple accommodation (**D**). There is one daily bus from Fortaleza, 0900, six "horrible" hours, US$12.

Paracuru & Lagoinha
Population: 23,500 (Paracuru)
Phone code: 085

Lagoinha's calling centre: T3631232, 3-digit numbers indicated are extensions on this central line

Phone code: 085
Colour map 2, grid A4

Fortaleza & the North Coast

Sleeping & eating

Calling centres: Fleixeras, T511184, Mundaú, T3511210; 3-digit numbers indicated are extensions on this central line

Fleixeiras **A** *Solar das Fleixeiras*, T136. With bath, pool, restaurant. On R São Pedro are **C** *Da Célia*, T105. With bath, no breakfast. **C** *O Coqueiro*, T125. With bath. On Av Beira Mar are several restaurants including *O Edmar*, varied menu and *São Pedro*, seafood.

Mundaú **A** *Mundaú Dunas*, T3511020, x197. Fridge, pool, restaurant. **B** *Sombra dos Coqueiros*, T200. With bath, restaurant. **D** *Brisa do Mar*, small rooms with bath, breakfast extra. **E** *Casa de Retiro Estrela do Mar*, T3511220, x154. Priest's retreat home, must reserve ahead, rooms with hammocks, some with bath, use of kitchen.

Almofala

Colour map 2, grid A4

Some seven hours by bus and 230 kilometres from Fortaleza is the sleepy fishing village of Almofala, home of the Tremembés Indians who live off the sea and some agriculture. There is electricity, but no hotels or restaurants, although locals rent hammock space and cook meals. Bathing is better elsewhere, but the area is surrounded by dunes and is excellent for hiking along the coast to explore beaches and lobster-fishing communities. In Almofala, the church, with much of the town, was covered by shifting sands and remained covered for 50 years, reappearing in the 1940s; it has since been restored. From Fortaleza there are buses at 0700 and 1530 daily, US$6, information on Fortaleza, T2722728.

Jijoca de Jericoacoara

Phone code: 088
Colour map 2, grid A4

Northwest of Fortaleza by 294 kilometres is Jijoca de Jericoacoara (alternate spelling: Gijoca), near the south shore of scenic Lagoa Paraíso (or Lagoa Jijoca). It is the access point for Jericoacoara, one of the most famous beaches of Ceará and all Brazil. Lagoa Paraíso is turquoise and a good place for swimming and watersports; there are some nice hotels by the lake, from town it is one kilometre along the shore when the lake is low, or three kilometres along the road with high water, taxi (pick-up truck) US$5.

Sleeping & eating

Town's calling centre: T6114244, for hotel reservations

On the lakeshore are **B** *Jardim do Paraíso*, small, with bath, restaurant, windsurfing equipment. **C** *Capitão Tomaz*, rooms and chalets, sports equipment, boat trips. **C** *Pousada do Paulo*, 4 km from town, nice chalets, pleasant, restaurant. **C** *Paraíso da Lagoa*, chalets, area for camping. In town are **C** *Pousada da Lagoa*, with bath. **D** *Pousada dos Corsos*, T6691144, friendly, excellent, Corsican food. **E** *Pousada São Sebstião*, R Vicente Paulo 146, shared bath, basic. There are a couple more *pousadas*. *Restaurante Central* is recommended.

Transport A *jardineira* (open-sided four-wheel drive truck) does the 23 km, 1½ hours, trip from Jijoca to Jericoacoara. A rough but very pretty ride through sand dunes and hills, sadly criss-crossed by vehicle tracks which have damaged the fragile *caatinga* vegetation (four-wheel traction and high clearance are necessary on this road).

Directory **Banks** *Banco do Brasil* does not change foreign currency in Jijoca.

Jericoacoara

Nestled in the dunes, 317 kilometres from Fortaleza and 165 kilometres before the border with the state of Piauí, is the fishing community of Jericoacoara, or Jerí as the locals call it. It is popular with both Brazilian and international travellers, crowded at weekends mid-December to mid-February, in July and during Brazilian holidays. Despite the large influx of visitors, it remains a tranquil and safe town. The visitor is rewarded with towering sand dunes, deserted beaches with little shade, cactus-covered cliffs rising from the sea, interesting rock formations and a pleasant atmosphere. Watching the sunset from the top of the large dune just west of town, followed by a display of capoeira *on the beach, is a tradition among visitors well worth preserving. There is* forró *nightly in high season, Wednesday and Saturday at other times.*

Phone code: 088
Colour map 2, grid A4

Excursions

Jericoacoara is part of an environmental protection area which includes a large coconut grove, lakes, dunes and hills covered in *caatinga* vegetation. A youth group publishes *Força Jovem Jericoacoara*, a monthly newspaper with information for visitors and general issues of environmental protection in the area. There are several possibilities for walks, horse riding (US$2-3 per hour) and dune-buggy trips (many for hire, ask for recommendations as some drivers are considered unsafe). Take water and sun protection, it gets very hot and there is no shade; several hotels offer tours.

Going west along the beach takes you through a succession of sand dunes and coconut groves; the views are beautiful. In two kilometres you reach the beach of **Mangue Seco**, and two kilometres beyond an arm of the ocean which separates it from **Guriú** (bridge across), where there is a village atop a fixed dune. Some of the best scenery in the area is by **Nova Tatajuba** (see below), about 35 kilometres west of Jerí, reached by land from Camocim, or along the beach by dune-buggy including a river crossing on a barge (US$20 per person, minimum four) or by sea, three hours (US$100); there are basic *pousadas*, see details below.

A 45-minute walk to the east takes you to the *pedra fourada*, a stone arch sculpted by the sea, one of the symbols of Jerí, accessible only at low tide (check the tide tables at *Casa do Turismo*). In the same direction, but just inland, is *Serrote*, a large hill with a lighthouse on top; it is well worth walking up for the magnificent views.

About 15 kilometres east along the shore (43 kilometres by road via Jijoca and Caiçara) is **Praia do Preá**, with light sand and blue ocean (**D** *Pousada Azul do Mar*, T6601238, with bath, no electricity), and 10 kilometres beyond (62 kilometres by road) is the beach of **Barrinha**, access to the scenic *Lagoa Azul*.

Ten kilometres inland through the dunes (20 kilometres along the road), to *Lagoa Paraíso* or *Jijoca*, is a turquoise, sweet-water lake, great for bathing (buggy US$10 per person).

Essentials

There are 47 establishments operating during high season, about half close at other times when hotel prices go down some 30%. **A** *Avalon*, R Principal, T2245677 (Fortaleza). Nice rooms with fan, pleasant, restaurant; **A** *Hippopotamus*, R do Forró, T085-2449191 (Fortaleza). Nice, with pool, light, fan, restaurant, tours. **A** *Matusa*, R São Francisco. Pool, restaurant and bar. **B** *Capitão Tomáz*, on east end of beach,

Sleeping
Town's calling centre: T88-6210544; you can leave a message for most hotels through this number

Fortaleza & the North Coast

T6691185. Good. Recommended apart from breakfast. **C** *Acoara de Jerico*, R Principal, by beach. Gas lamps, restaurant. **C** *Casa Nostra*, R das Dunas. Nice rooms with bath, good breakfast, friendly service, can pay with US$ or German marks, money change, Italian spoken. Recommended. **C** *Casa do Turismo*, R das Dunas, T088-6210211, jericoacoara@secrel.com.br. Nice cabins, information, tours, horse rental, bus tickets, telephone calls, post office, exchange, friendly. **C** *Isabel*, R do Forró by beach. Light and shower. Recommended. **C** *Isalana*, R São Francisco. Light and shower. **C** *Papagaio*, Beco do Forró, T/F2682722 (Fortaleza). With bath, recommended, tours. **C** *Pousada Renata*, bath, patio with hammocks, breakfast, English, Italian and German spoken. **D** *Pousada Paraíso*, R Principal. Friendly, clean. **D** *Calanda*, R das Dunas, T6211144. With bath, solar energy, Swiss run, good rooms, good breakfast, good views, helpful, German, English and Spanish spoken. Warmly recommended. **D** *do Coqueiro*, R Principal. **D** *Pousada do Véio*, R Principal. With and without bath (**E**), **camping** in shady area US$3 per tent, tours. **E** *Por do Sol*, Bairro Novo Jerí, 1 street west of R das Dunas, behind main dune. Basic, good value, with bath.

Eating

There are several restaurants serving vegetarian and fish dishes: *Alexandre*, *Isabel*, both on the beach, good seafood, pricey. *Acoara do Jerico*, R Principal by the beach, reasonable. *Avalon*, R Principal. Crêpes a speciality, good. Home cooking all on R Principal *Samambaia*, good value. *Catavento*, good. *Espaço Aberto* also recommended for breakfast. *Sorrisa de Natureza*, cheap, tasty food. Recommended. Italian food and pizza at: *Pizza Banana*, R Principal. Good. *Senzala*, same street. Nice, pleasant atmosphere (allows **camping** in its grounds). *Cantinho da Masa*, R do Forró. Good. *Casinha da Barra*. Several shops sell basic provisions, so camping is possible.

Bars & nightclubs

Nightlife is interesting: *Forró* nightly in high season at R do Forró, Wednesday and Saturday in low season, starts about 2200. Action moves to the bars when *forró* has stopped about 0200. *Bar Barriga da Lua* and *Pizza Reggae*, opposite *forró*. There are also frequent parties to which visitors are welcome. About once a week in high season there is a folk dance show which includes *capoeira*.

Transport

If on a motorcycle, it is not possible to ride from Jijoca to Jericoacoara (unless you are an expert in desert conditions). Safe parking for bikes in Jijoca is not a problem

A *jardineira* (open-sided four-wheel drive truck) meets *Redenção* bus from/to **Fortaleza**, at Jijoca: 1½ hours, US$1.05, from Jijoca at 1400, 0200, from Jericoacoara at 0600, 2200, from Rua das Dunas by *Casa do Turismo*. At other times pick-ups can be hired in Jijoca, US$6 pp. For a direct connection take the *Redenção* bus leaving Fortaleza at 0900 (arrive Jerí 1600) or 2100 (arrive Jerí 0330); the 0600 bus from Jerí arrives in Fortaleza 1430, the 2200 bus arrives between 0430 and 0600, from the rodoviária it goes to Praia Iracema; night buses are direct, while daytime ones make many stops; Fortaleza-Jericoacoara US$8.50. Two or 3-day tours from Fortaleza are available, book through travel agencies in Fortaleza. You can also get there by boat, 'seasickness guaranteed'. If coming from Belém or other points north and west, go via Sobral (from Belém US$28.25, 20 hours), where you change for Cruz (Sobral-Cruz: Monday-Saturday at 1200; Cruz-Sobral: Monday/Wednesday/Friday at 0400, Tuesday/Thursday/Saturday at 0330; US$7.25; 3-4 hours), several *pousadas* (see below) continue to Jijoca the next day (Cruz-Jijoca, daily about 1400, US$1.25, meets Jardineira for Jerí, Cruz-Jericoacoara, US$2.20).

An alternative from the west, especially if going through Parnaíba, is by bus from **Camocim** approximately 45 km west along the beach (see below); a private bus goes most days Jijoca-Camocim, about 0230, return Camocim-Jijoca at 1130, US$4.25; pickups also do the run for US$4.25-7.75 pp, depending on demand; alternatively you can go through Sobral, a much longer trip, or hire a buggy along the beach, beautiful scenery, Jericoacoara-Camocim US$72.50 for 4; from Camocim there is a regular bus service to Parnaíba. If you are looking for more adventure, take a truck from Camocim to Guriú where hammock space can be found. The village musician sings his own songs in the bar. Walk 4 hours, or take a boat across the bay to Jericoacoara.

Forty kilometres east of Jijoca is Cruz, an obligatory stop if travelling by bus **Cruz**
from Sobral to Jericoacoara. It is a pleasant small town, surrounded by a *carnauba* palm forest (used in making brooms). At the south end is a large
wooden cross dating from 1825, nearby is a statue to São Francisco. There is a
lively market on Sunday when, at dawn, *pau d'arara* trucks, mule carts and
bicycles converge on the town. There are two very basic hotels (**F**) with shared
bath, *Hotel Magalhães*, R Teixeira Pinto 390, friendly, meals available and
Hospedaria, R 6 de Abril 314, as well as *Pousada Ideal*, R Teixeira Pinto.
Churrascaria Casa do Sol Nascente is near the cross at the south entrance to
town. The bus to Jijoca goes through about 1400, US$2 or US$3.50 to
Jericoacoara, wait for the bus by 1330.

Northwest of Fortaleza by 360 kilometres is this regional centre with some **Camocim**
industry, an important fishing port and crafts centre. In the area there are many *Population: 51,500*
lagoons and unspoilt beaches such as Maceió, 28 kilometres west, and Nova *Phone code: 088*
Tatajuba, 40 kilometres east, access requires a vehicle with good traction. **Nova
Tatajuba** has magnificent scenery, it is on the west margin of the outflow of
Lagoa Grande; the beach is wide, dunes follow the shore, the ocean is clear and
calm; there is a fishing village with a few basic *pousadas*. The town was built to
replace old Tatajuba which was buried by the shifting sands. The area has been
'discovered' and tourism development is expected to increase rapidly. For transport see Jericoacoara above, bus information in Fortaleza, T2272999.

Sleeping and eating Camocim: **C** *Hotel Municipal*, Av Beira Mar, T6210274. With
bath, pool. **D** *Hotel Lusitania. Dimas Restaurant*, Av Beira Mar, 2 km from centre.
Varied menu. **Nova Tatajuba**: **B** *Tatajuba*, basic, rooms with and without bath, no
electricity, meals served in proprietor's home included in the price. **D** *Verde Folha*,
adapted fisherman's home, one room with bath, two shared bath (**E**), restaurant,
breakfast extra.

The Sertão

*Two types of area characterize the interior of Ceará, the serras, highlands and
tablelands with a pleasant climate and green scenery, and the sertões, arid
expanses of semi-desert. Although there are some very scenic and interesting sites,
infrastructure for tourism in the interior is still limited, especially when compared
with the coast. Some of the tourism is of a religious nature, to important shrines
and pilgrimage sites.*

Baturité

At 105 kilometres south of Fortaleza is Baturité, a town surrounded by hills *Population: 29,500*
and waterfalls, which conserves some colonial buildings; there is a historical *Phone code: 085*
museum. It is home of the *Pingo de Ouro* distillery which can be visited; there *Altitude: 171m*
are hotels and restaurants. You can also stay in the Jesuit Seminary where a few *Colour map 2, grid A5*
monks still work in the local community and tend the cloister garden (**E** per
person full board, ask for 'Jesuitas' if taking a taxi, or walk up; T3470362 in
advance, Irmão João Batista). Baturité is the largest town in the **Maciço de
Baturité**, an irregular massif with beautiful scenery. Nineteen kilometres
northwest of Baturité and at 365 metres above sea level is **Guaramiranga**, centre of a fruit and flower growing area, home of the *Festival Nordestino de
Teatro*, held in September. In the area is a remnant of native forest, now a
nature reserve. Nearby is Pico Alto (1,115 metres above sea level), which offers

Fortaleza & the North Coast

Pau de Arara

Pau de Arara, *a parrot's perch. This very descriptive term refers to an unusual vehicle which has become part of the culture of the Northeast. A large flat-bed truck, with narrow wooden slats for seats, it may have a tattered tarpaulin stretched overhead for shade. Lurching over the rutted back-roads of the Sertão, passengers impregnated with dust from head to toe, they were for decades the staple of rural public transport throughout the region. They were also the only affordable conveyance for legions of drought-stricken nordestinos, fleeing to the industrialized south. Today, better roads and improved fleets of buses are making the pau de arara increasingly rare, but custom remains more important than comfort in some places. Hence the anachronistic sight of the latest-model truck, complete with a sophisticated sound system and air conditioning for the cab, but fitted with the traditional narrow wooden slats of a pau de arara at the back.*
Robert and Daisy Kunstaetter

special views and sunsets. Seven kilometres further north is **Pacoti**, with large botanical gardens (*horto forestal*), trails and several waterfalls; good for a dip and for viewing the highland flora.

Sleeping **A** *Estância Vale das Flores*, Sítio São Francisco, Pacoti, T3251233. Chalets and rooms, price includes lunch, fridge, restaurant, pool, sauna, lake, horses. **B** *Remanso Hotel da Serra*, 5 km north of Guaramiranga, T3251222. Bath, restaurant, pool, lake, sports fields. **B** *Hotel Escola de Guaramiranga*, in Guaramiranga, T/F3211106. Bath, fridge, hot water, restaurant, pool, atop a hill in an 8-hut estate which includes forest, orchards and an old convent, it doubles as a tourism school, run by the state agency SETUR.

Transport *Redenção* bus from Fortaleza rodoviária, mornings only, 3 hours. Also a tourist train round trip, Sunday (US$22 including museum, bus to Guaramiranga and lunch at *Hotel da Serra*).

Canindé The pilgrimage centre of Canindé, 108 kilometres southwest of Fortaleza along the BR-020, is located in the *Sertão Central* of Ceará. A large modern church stands on a hill; it has carved baptistery doors, many ex-votos. It receives hundreds of thousands of pilgrims from all over the northeast between 26 September and 3 October; devotees of São Francisco das Chagas, '*O pobrezinho de Asis*', many of them dressed like Franciscan priests. The faithful flock to town on foot, by bus and mostly on *pau de arara* trucks (see box). There is a regional museum with artefacts representative of northeast culture and several restaurants. There is a daily bus service from Fortaleza rodoviária with *Viação Nova Esperança*, three hours, interesting dry-land vegetation along route.

Quixadá
Population: 64,500
Phone code: 088

Southeast of Canindé and 152 kilometres from Fortaleza is Quixadá, on the **Serra do Estevão**, rocky dry hills representative of the central *sertão*. The town has a dam built during the empire by order of Dom Pedro II, following the terrible drought of 1877-79. The scenery around the dam is very nice, with interesting rock formations including the *galhina choca* (brooding hen). The area is popular for sports such as hang gilding. There is a historical museum. Twenty one kilometres from town is Gruta do Pajé, a complex of religious buildings dating from the early 1900s, which includes the **A** *Casa de Reposo São José*, today a popular hotel run by nuns (T8120155, with bath).

Forty three kilometres southwest of Quixadá is **Quixeramobim**, an important regional centre, with nearby archaeological sites with ancient inscriptions on boulders (contact Sr Simão, R Mons Salviano Pinio 233, T6380000). The regional dam has been used for irrigation with good results. In August it has an important musical event, the *Festival de Violas e Violeiros*, drawing participants from far and near, and in September the *Grande Vaquejada de Quixeramobim* (a typical *sertão* rodeo). *Redenção* bus from Fortaleza rodoviária to Quixadá, three hours, US$4.50. Same company to Quixeramobim, 0900, four hours, US$7.

Because of the Rio Jaguaribe, 20 percent of the agricultural land of the state is concentrated in the east, in the region known as the **Vale do Jaguaribe**. Using irrigation, the *sertão* becomes quite fertile, with rice and beans as the main crops here. Among the towns are **Morada Nova**, 161 kilometres from Fortaleza and **Limoeiro do Norte**, 201 kilometres from Fortaleza; just south of Limoeiro is **Tabuleiro do Norte**, where an important religious pilgrimage takes place in honour of Nossa Senhora da Saúde, 11-15 August. Festivities include processions, musical shows and much *forró*. The area is rich in crafts made with *carnauba* palm thatch, including fine basketry and hats. The town of **Jaguaruana**, 185 kilometres from Fortaleza, is an important producer of hammocks. A deeply rooted tradition in this area is the *vaquejada* (rodeo), accompanied by country guitar music (*violeiros*) and regional food.

> **Vale do Jaguaribe**

South of the Vale do Jaguaribe is the area known as the **Sertões do Salgado**, in the Rio Salgado valley. The most prominent feature here is the **Orós** dam, with a capacity of 2.1 billion cubic meters; the reservoir has 300 islands and is used for watersports. Some of the towns in the area are **Orós** (403 kilometres from Fortaleza), **Icó** (372 kilometres from Fortaleza) and **Iguatu** (378 kilometres from Fortaleza), all historical cities with well preserved colonial structures; and **Lavras de Mangabeira** (432 kilometres from Fortaleza), surrounded by rocks, caves and a canyon formed by the Rio Salgado, four kilometres from town.

Juazeiro do Norte

The south of the state is known as the Cariri region, the name of an indigenous Indian group which lived in the interior and resisted Portuguese colonization for a long time. The main centre in this area is Juazeiro do Norte, located 528 kilometres south of Fortaleza. It is the second city in Ceará. Along with its two satellites, Crato and Barbalha, 10 kilometres to the west and south respectively, they form an oasis of green in the dry sertão.

> *Population: 190,000*
> *Phone code: 088*
> *Colour map 2, grid B4*

Juazeiro do Norte was the home of Padre Cícero Romão Batista, a controversial and very popular priest who advocated the interests of the city and its most dispossessed inhabitants from the 1870s through the 1930s (see box, page 570). Even before his death, Padre Cícero had become a legend and Juazeiro do Norte an important pilgrimage site, drawing the faithful from throughout the northeast and increasingly nationwide. Today it is the most important pilgrimage centre of the region: there are six main annual pilgrimages but visitors arrive all year round. Religious tourism is the main source of income in this otherwise poor area; prices rise during pilgrimages and there are many beggars at all times. Another cultural manifestation seen throughout the Cariri region is the *bandas cabaçais ou de pífaros*, musical groups which participate in all celebrations; in addition to playing, they dance, imitating animals, performing a game or fight.

Padre Cícero

Padre Cícero Romão Batista came to Juazeiro in 1872 as a young priest where he worked for many years, gaining respect in his pastoral duties and caring for the poor. However, his life was dramatically changed with the occurrence on 1 March 1889 of a miracle during a communion service at which he was presiding. One of the congregation, Maria de Araújo, received the host and immediately collapsed, as it turned to blood which dripped on to the communion cloth and down to the floor. This event was repeated several times over the next few months and Padre Cícero was confused as to what was happening. He contacted the bishop in Fortaleza, Dom Joaquim, who initially ignored what was going on in the hope that it would go away, but after a doctor published an article saying that it was impossible to find a scientific explanation for the host turning to blood, the bishop sent two priests to investigate. It is probable that Dom Joaquim hoped that they would uncover a fraud being perpetrated in this poor and backward part of the state, but they returned agreeing that the events were miraculous. Only the Vatican claimed that the miracles were a sham and put it down to local superstition, but by that time the ball had started to roll and Padre Cícero's name was spreading far and wide. Brazilians were convinced that miracles were happening in the town and that Padre Cícero was a living saint.

Pilgrims started arriving to ask his blessing. He cared for the poor and the dispossessed, using the money donated by pilgrims to invest in schools and orphanages. His ability to attract large numbers of workers drew him to the attention of political bosses, with whom he reached an understanding (unlike Antônio Conselheiro at Canudos). Most of the pilgrims were, and still are, poor farmers and workers from nearby states such as Pernambuco and Alagoas. Some spend days travelling through the arid sertão before reaching the green valley of Juazeiro: a geographical and spiritual oasis. Before he died aged 90 in 1934, he contributed further to the mysticism surrounding him by saying, "I am not going to die. I am going on a journey. I will come back in a while".

Although the Church still regards prayers to Padre Cícero as superstitious and refuses to beatify him, his popularity remains undimmed and appeals to Brazilians' strong spiritual and syncretic traditions. Today's pilgrims are still convinced of his miracles, believing that he restores people to health and is the cause of unexplained recoveries. Many come to Juazeiro to carry out promessas, promises made to Padre Cícero in their prayers that if they survived an illness, or overcame a problem, they would make a pilgrimage to give thanks. In the museum dedicated to Padre Cícero, the walls are lined with photographs and messages from grateful people, while in the next room there are piles of ex-votos, carvings of limbs in wood or wax, representing the parts of the body which prayers to Padre Cícero have cured.

Since the death of Padre Cícero, the legends surrounding his miraculous powers have spread. Here is one example: "A war broke out here and many soldiers came to attack Juazeiro. So then my Padrinho Cícero assembled his followers in order to repel them. He planted a ring of macambira (a form of cactus) which encircled the city, two feet high, overnight. The soldiers would not pass. When they started to fire their guns, the bullets did not hit anyone but went bounding back at them. Many soldiers died but here in Juazeiro there were only two - an old man and a boy – who did not respect my Padrinho's word and who died on the spot."

Further reading: The story is taken from Candace Slater, Trail of Miracles. Stories from a Pilgrimage in Northeastern Brazil (Berkeley, Los Angeles, London: University of California Press, 1986), page 93. See also Ralph Della Cava, Miracle at Joaseiro (New York and London: Columbia University Press, 1970).

Sights

Memorial Padre Cícero, Praça do Cinquentenário, is a museum featuring photographs and religious artefacts; a good selection of books is on sale. ■ *Monday-Friday 0730-1130 and 1330-1730; Saturday-Sunday 0800-1200, free.* Nearby is the **Chapel of Nossa Senhora do Perpétuo Socorro**, which houses Padre Cícero's tomb. A 27 metre high statue to him stands in the Logradouro do Horto, a park overlooking the town; either take the pilgrim trail up the hill (one hour, start early because of the heat) or take the Horto city bus. Also worth seeing is the **Church of Nossa Senhora das Dores** with the adjacent pilgrimage grounds, roughly fashioned after St Peter's Square in Rome.

Excursions

The **Chapada do Araripe**, a tableland about 850 metres high, is south of Juazeiro do Norte and extends from east to west for 220 kilometres. The area is believed to have been uplifted and numerous fossilized plants and animals including giant sloths have been found. It has one of the main native forest reserves in the state, the **Floresta Nacional do Araripe**, 20 kilometres from Crato, with grottos, palaeontological sites, springs and cloud forest with ferns and orchids. Twenty two kilometres south of Juazeiro do Norte, within the Chapada, is *Balneário do Caldas*, a pool fed with natural springwater (0700-1700), access through Barbalha; here is **A** *Hotel das Fontes*, T5321060, with bath, fridge, restaurant.

In the area of **Jardim**, 34 kilometres south of Barbalha, there are several natural springs, while by **Missão Velha**, 22 kilometres east of Barbalha, are the rapids on the Rio Salgado and a nice waterfall. Another access to the Chapada is through **Santana do Cariri**, 60 kilometres west of Juazeiro do Norte. Its main attraction is the **Nascente dos Azedos**, a natural spring good for bathing. There is also a palaeontology museum, one basic hotel; transport with *Pernambucana*, daily at 1430, returning 0600, US$2.50, two hours.

Crato is an older city which lost its limelight in the region, owing to the increased importance of Juazeiro do Norte. It has several nice praças and a small **Museu de Fósseis**, Praça da Sé 105, housing an impressive collection of fossils from the Cretaceous period gathered in the Chapada do Araripe. ■ *Monday-Friday 0800-1200 and 1400-1800, free.* There is the friendly *Crato* (**B**), R Bárbara de Alencar 668 near Praça Cristo Rei, T5212824, with bath, a/c, **D** with fan, restaurant, as well as two other simpler hotels in town.

Population: 90,360

Essentials

A *Verde Vales Lazer*, Av P A Castelo, 3 km from town on the road to Barbalha, T/F5712544. Pool, restaurant. **B** *Panorama*, Santo Agostinho 58, T5213100, F5123110. Pool, restaurant, good value. **C** *Viana Palace*, São Pedro 746, T5112585, F5112476. With bath, a/c, fridge, **D** with fan. **C** *Municipal*, São Francisco 220, Praça Padre Cícero, T5122899. Comfortable large rooms, good value, cheaper with fan. Recommended. **C** *Plaza*, Padre Cícero 148, T5110493. With bath, a/c, **D** with fan and cheaper still with shared bath. **D** *Aristocrata*, São Francisco 402, T5111889. With bath, fan, cheaper without bath, basic, family run, restaurant. **D** *Guanabara*, São José 202, T5111857. With bath and fan. **D** *Maceió*, São José 208, T5112930. With bath, fan, cheaper with shared bath. **D** *Magnata*, São Francisco 381, T5111720. With bath, a/c, cheaper with fan, restaurant. **D** *Pousada Cariri*, São José 218, T5122079. With bath, **E** without breakfast, basic, friendly, family run, good restaurant. Many basic hotels and *hospedarias* for pilgrims on R São José and around Nossa Senhora das Dores Basilica.

Sleeping
You can expect prices to be higher during pilgrimages

Fortaleza & the North Coast

Eating *Cheiro Verde*, S Cândido 72, varied menu. Several restaurants around Praça Padre Cícero, more economical ones on R São José; *Pousada*, tasty food.

Festivals The following pilgrimage dates are listed in decreasing order of importance: **1-2 November**, *Finados*, the city receives some 600,000 visitors for the *All Saints Day* pilgrimages; **10-15 September**, *Nossa Senhora das Dores*, the city's patron saint; **2 February**, *Candeias, Nossa Senhora da Luz*; **20 July**, *Padre Cícero's death*; **24 March**, *Padre Cícero's birth*; **6 January**, *Reis Magos, Epiphany*.

Transport **Car hire** *Unidas*, Av Padre Cícero, Km 2 on road to Crato, T5711226, F5711855. *IBM*, Santo Agostinho 58, T5110542. *Localiza*, Airport and Av Padre Cícero Km 03, No 3375, T5712668.

    Air Airport is 7 km from the centre along Av Virgílio Távora, T5112118. Flights to Fortaleza, Petrolina and Recife. Taxi from centre US$5.75, motorcycle taxi US$3; taxi from rodoviária US$8.40.

    Buses Rodoviária, Av Dalmiro Gouveia, on the road to Crato, T5112868. Taxi from the centre US$3, motorcycle taxi US$0.60. To **Fortaleza** with *Rio Negro*, 2 daily, US$13.50 *convencional*, US$17.50 *executivo*, 8 hours. To **Picos** with *Boa Esperança*, 2 daily, US$5.75, 5 hours. To **Teresina** with *Boa Esperança, Progresso* or *Aparecida*, 3 daily, US$11-12, 11 hours. To **São Luís** with *Progresso*, US$20, 16 hours. To **Belém** with *Boa Esperança*, 1 daily (often full), US$30, 25 hours. To **Campina Grande** with *Transparaiba*, 2 daily, US$9, 9 hours. To **João Pessoa** with *Braga*, 1 daily, US$12, 10 hours. To **Recife** with *Braga*, 1 daily, US$14, 11 hours. To **Salvador** with *Itapermirim*, 2 weekly, US$17.50, 14 hours. To **São Paulo** with Itapemirim, 1 daily, US$63, 40 hours.

Directory **Airline offices** *TAF* (*Táxi Aéreo Fortaleza*), T5110699. **Banks** *Banco do Brasil*, R São Francisco, near Praça Pradre Cícero, poor rates, Mon-Fri 1100-1600. No *câmbios* in town. **Communications** Post Office: R Conceição 354 and at rodoviária. **Telephone:** R São Pedro 204, half a block from Praça Padre Cícero and at rodoviária.

Juazeiro do Norte is 45 kilometres west of the BR-116, which joins it with Fortaleza in the north and the State of Pernambuco in the south. It is 50 kilometres south of the Transamazônica (BR-230), which joins it with Campina Grande 505 kilometres to the east. The route west from Juazeiro do Norte

Juazeiro do Norte

Not to scale

(CE-090) goes via Crato and Nova Olinda along the Chapada do Araripe and is very scenic. As it descends into the flatlands it gets very hot. At **Campos e Sales**, about eight kilometres before the Piauí border (**D** *Pousada e Churrascaria Denis*, one kilometre west of town), the road joins the BR-230 which continues west to Picos, Piauí.

Western Ceará

Sobral

The road west from Fortaleza to Sobral and Teresina, BR-222, is paved but in poor condition between Apazível, 23 kilometres west of Sobral, and Piripiri in Piauí. Sobral, 238 kilometres west of Fortaleza, the principal town in western Ceará, is the supply centre for an agricultural area. The city has some well preserved colonial buildings including the Catedral da Sé, Teatro São João and a mansion on the Praça da Sé. There is a **Museu Diocesano** at Praça São João, a Cristo Redentor Statue and a monument to the 1919 solar eclipse. Near town is the Parque Ecológico Lagoa da Fazenda. Sobral is the access point to beaches in the west of the state.

Population: 139,000
Phone code: 088
Colour map 2, grid A4

Sleeping A *Ytacaranha*, 18 km from town on road northwest to Meruoca, T6134000, in the highlands. Full service, pool, restaurant, sports. **A** *Beira Rio*, R Conselheiro Rodrigues 400 across from the rodoviária, T6131040. A/c, **A** with fan, fridge. **A** *Visconde*, Av Lúcia Saboia 473, 10 minutes from the rodoviária, T6114222, F6114197. Friendly, a/c, cheaper with fan, good breakfast. **B** *Cisne*, Trav do Xerez 215, T/F6110171. A/c, cheaper with fan, friendly. **B** *Vitória*, Praça Gen Tibúrcio 120, T6131566. Bath, a/c, cheaper with fan, some rooms without bath (**C**), restaurant. **D** *Francinet's*, R Col Joaquim Ribeiro 294. With fan, bath, cheaper with shared bath. *Casa Grande o Louro*, R Tabelo Idelfonso Cavalcante 611. Good meat. *Hotel Vitória*, good lunch buffet. Recommended. *Churrascaria Gaúcho*, Av Dom José, meat. *Chico 1000* and *2000*, varied menu. *Lataro*, self-service.

Northwest of Sobral is the **Serra da Meruoca**, a highland area with nice scenery, forest, trails, small rivers and waterfalls. The main towns in the area, both at about 700 metres above sea level, are **Meruroca** and **Alcântaras**, 42 and 37 kilometres from Sobral respectively; they are known for their straw crafts, as well as home-made sweets and liqueurs.

Chapada de Ibiapaba

In the **Chapada de Ibiapaba**, an area of tablelands, caves, rock formations, rivers and waterfalls, is **Tianguá** (*population* 45,888; *altitude* 900 metres), 330 kilometres west of Fortaleza on the Teresina road. The town is surrounded by waterfalls; three kilometres to the north is Cachoeira de São Gonçalo, a good place for bathing; five kilometres from town are natural pools at the meeting place of seven waterfalls. Sixteen kilometres from town on the edge of the BR-222 is Cana Verde, a 30 metre high waterfall surrounded by monoliths and thick vegetation. Two kilometres from town is *Serra Grande* hotel (**A**), BR-222 Km 311, T6711818, F6711477, all amenities, good. In Tianguá is **D** *Hotel Gean*, on the central praça. Bus from Fortaleza US$10, from Belém US$30.

Thirty kilometres north of Tianguá is **Viçosa do Ceará**, a colonial town also within the Chapada, known for its ceramics. The Igreja de Nossa Senhora das Vitórias, a stone church on top of the 820 metre high Morro do Céu, is reached walking up 360 steps. There is an excellent view of the town, the surrounding highlands and the *sertão* beyond. Near the town are interesting rock formations such as the 100 metre wide Pedra de Itagurussu with a natural spring. There is good walking in the area.

Parque Nacional Ubajara

Colour map 2, grid A4 Eighteen kilometres south of Tianguá is **Ubajara** (*population* 23,729), with an interesting Sunday morning market selling produce of the *sertão*; buses to Fortaleza.

Three kilometres from town is Ubajara National Park, the smallest of Brazil's national parks, with 563 hectares of native highland (similar to that found in the *planalto central*) and *caatinga* brush. The park's main attraction is the Ubajara cave on the side of an escarpment. Fifteen chambers totalling 1,120 metres have been mapped, of which 400 metres are open to visitors, well worth seeing. Access is along a footpath and steps (two to three hours, take water) or with the *bondinha*, a cablecar which descends the cliff to the cave entrance, 0830-1630, US$4. Lighting has been installed in nine caverns of the complex, but a torch and spare batteries may be useful. An Ibama guide leads visitors in the cave; the Ibama office at the park entrance, five kilometres from the caves, is not always helpful and not always open, T6341388. The views of the *sertão* from the upper cablecar platform are superb; beautiful walks among forest and waterfalls and old sugar-mills are scattered around the plateau. To walk all the way up to the top of the plateau takes 14 hours, if you want to do this take plenty of water.

Sleeping & eating **Near the park** B *Pousada da Neblina*, Estr do Teleférico, 2 km from town, T6341270, in beautiful cloud forest. Swimming pool, with breakfast and private shower (**C** without breakfast), restaurant open 1100-2000, meals recommended, campsite (US$15 per tent). Opposite is **C** *Pousada Gruta da Ubajara*, with bath, rustic, restaurant. Recommended. **D** *Sítio do Alemão*, take Estr do Teleférico 2 km from town, after the Pousada da Neblina turn right, 1 km to Sítio Santana, in the coffee plantation of *Herbert Klein*, on which there are three small chalets. Warmly recommended, with full facilities, excursions, walking maps, bicycle hire offered, homemade jams, if chalets are full the Kleins accommodate visitors at their house.

Ubajara town **C** *Le Village*, on Ibiapina road 4 km south from town, T6341364. Restaurant, pool, sauna, good value. **D** *Ubajara*, R Juvêncio Luís Pereira 370, T6341261. Small restaurant. Most restaurants US$10, big meals in the old market cost US$3.

The Chapada de Ibiapaba continues south from Ubajara for some 70 kilometres. Other towns along the highlands are: **Ibiapina**, with the nearby Cachoeira da Ladeira, reached by a steep trail, a good place for bathing; **São Benedito**, known for its straw and ceramic crafts (**B** *Pousada de Inhuçu*, R Gonçalo de Freitas 454, T6261173, pool, restaurant); **Carnaubal**, with waterfalls and a bathing resort; and **Ipu**, with a 180 metre high waterfall, site of the legendary love affair between the Indian, Iracema, and the founder of Fortaleza (**E** *Hotel Ipu*, in upper town, basic, friendly; there is a *pousada* at the waterfall).

Monsenhor Tabosa, in the centre of the state, has the highest peak in Ceará. This remote town is very friendly, with three hotels: *dos Viajantes* and *São Sebastião*, both contactable through the phone exchange, 0XX88-8261150, and *Márcia's Buffet*, T0XX88-8261213, ask for Márcia or Honório Júnior. Honório will draw rough walking maps and, if asked, can arrange for the *forró* band to play. It can get very wet in the rainy season (around March). The easiest way to get there is by car or Horizonte bus on the CE032 from

Dancing in the dust

Travelling by bus about the Northeast of Brazil in the course of my work, I developed a strange kind of familiarity with the Sertão. I gained little knowledge of the individual settlements, but a kind of overall impression – of dry heat, isolation and desperate hopefulness – which has stayed with me, and, indeed, coloured my view of life, ever since.

I had never visited a desert before I came to the Sertão. I had expected vistas of sand, maybe a few rocks, and dramatic horizons. What I found was a seemingly unbroken plain of brown, dead-looking thorn bushes from east to west. Everything was brown: reddish-brown earth, dusty brown roads, and sad little villages of brown clay houses. Outside the houses, thin, brown-skinned, strikingly dignified people tended their few animals and attempted to cultivate their land. For the first time I saw the truth in the phrase 'scratching a living': how can you farm dry earth with only a hand-made hoe?

The faster the bus marched over this monotonous landscape, the hotter the air rushing through the window seemed. My contact lenses stuck to my eyes, I drank gallons of bottled water, and, eventually, I adjusted to the climate. Any event was a drama. One house had a well-watered tree, in full crimson blossom, which broke up the prevailing colour scheme so effectively that the whole bus was speculating on how the residents managed to maintain their water supply. Ubajara, rising suddenly out of the desert with all its lush green forest, seemed like a miracle. We passed inexplicable lone pedestrians, some of them obviously distressed, but we stopped only to let passengers board, to give lifts to ragged children, and at postos where we could wash and buy refreshments.

Drivers on these routes were paid less than those in urban areas, so they supplemented their wages by any number of scams. One memorable day my bus halted at a tiny café, which had no roof, in the middle of nowhere. We were all invited to descend and enjoy a few cold drinks – for an hour or two. While the driver and his friend proceeded to remove all the tyres from the bus (he was exchanging them for reconditioned tyres, at an illegitimate profit), the bartender put on a cassette and his huge wife decided to give me my first lesson in Samba dancing. Most of the other passengers found this so entertaining that they all joined in: I learned to wiggle my hips in a figure of eight, at an impromptu party by a roadside bar, shuffling in the dust somewhere on the BR-316.

Cherry Austin

Canindé, but there are roads from Nova Russas, south of Ipu, and the BR-020 from Boa Viagem (very rough).

Continuing south, the greenery of the Chapada de Ibiapaba eventually gives way to the dry **Sertão dos Inhamuns**. One of the main towns in this area is **Crateús** (*population* 66,635), about 210 kilometres south of Sobral, a remote town with rich folkloric traditions seen during festivals in August (*Mergulho Folclórico*) and September (*Festival de Repentistas*); nearby are archaeological sites with rock inscriptions. There is the very reasonable and clean *Crateús Palace Hotel* (**D**), with breakfast, good restaurant. *Churrascaria Pequena Cabana* is at the back of the hotel. There is a regular bus service on the paved road to Fortaleza (347 kilometres). Bus service from Crateús over a very bad road to Teresina, every two days.

Fortaleza & the North Coast

Piauí

Piauí is possibly the poorest state in Brazil. Its population is about 2,710,000, but many leave to seek work elsewhere. The economy is almost completely dependent upon agriculture and livestock, both of which in turn depend on how much rain, if any, falls.

The history of Piauí springs from cattle farmers who moved into the interior from Bahia, beginning in the 17th century. Until the early 19th century, though, the state was under the control of Maranhão. At independence, there was bitter fighting between the Portuguese supporters of the colony and the Brazilians who sought their freedom.

Teresina

Population: 598,450
Phone code: 086
Colour map 2, grid A3

About 435 kilometres up the Rio Parnaíba is the state capital. There are paved road and rail connections (freight only) with the neighbouring state capitals. The city itself is reputed to be the hottest after Manaus, with temperatures up to 42°C.

Teresina

■ **Sleeping**
1 Luxor Hotel do Piauí   3 Royal Pálace   5 São José
2 Real Pálace   4 Sambaíba   6 Teresina Pálace

Cabeça-de-Cuia

Crispim was a fisherman who lived at the confluence of the rivers Poti and Parnaíba, in Teresina. One day, returning home after a hard day's fishing with no catch whatsoever, he discovered that there was no food in the house. Infuriated, he grabbed a large bone which was lying nearby and beat his mother to death. Her dying curse was that Crispim should live out his days as a hideous monster with an enormous head.

A young and single man, Crispim was driven to despair by his now terrifying appearance. He drowned himself in the Parnaíba. Legend has it that Crispim will be restored to life, and his good looks, when he has managed to eat seven virgins named Maria. Young laundresses, when they go to the river, are still afraid of him.

Cabeça-de-Cuia means 'head of a gourd'. Carvings of this strange figure are a common sight in Teresina.

Sights

The **Palácio de Karnak** (the old governor's palace), just west of Praça Frei Serafim, contains lithographs of the Middle East in 1839 by David Roberts RA. ■ *Monday-Friday, 1530-1730*. Also see the **Museu do Piauí**, Praça Marechal Deodoro. ■ *Tuesday-Friday 0800-1730, Saturday, Sunday, 0800-1200, US$0.60*.

There is an interesting open market by the Praça Marechal Deodoro and the river is picturesque, with washing laid out to dry along its banks. The market is a good place to buy hammocks, but bargain hard. Every morning along the river bank there is the **troca-troca**, where people buy, sell and swap. An undercover complex, **Mercado Central do Artesanato**, has been built at Rua Paissandu 1276, Praça Dom Pedro II. ■ *Monday-Friday 0800-2200*. Most of the year the river is low, leaving sandbanks known as *coroas* (crowns).

Essentials

L *Rio Poty*, Av Mcal Castelo Branco 555, Ilhota, T2231500, F2226671. Five-star. Recommended. **L** *Luxor Hotel do Piauí*, Praça Mcal Deodoro 310, T2214911, F2215171. A/c, pool, restaurant. **A** *Real Pálace*, R Lizandro Nogueira 1208, T2212768, F2217740. A/c, pool, restaurant. **A** *São José*, João Cabral 340, T2232176, F2232223. Reasonable restaurant. **B** *Royal Pálace*, R 13 de Maio 233N, T/F2217707. A/c, restaurant. **B** *Sambaíba*, R Gabriel Ferreira 230-N, T2226711. Two-star, central, good. **B** *Teresina Pálace*, Paissandu 1219, T2212770, F2214476. A/c, pool, restaurant. **D** *Fortaleza*, Felix Pacheco 1101, Praça

25° Batalhão Barracks

Coelho de Resende

Pires de Castro

Av Frei Serafim

1° de Maio

Gov. A de Vasconcelos

19 de Novembro

Avendia Miguel Rosa

To Airport & Fortaleza

To Rodoviária, Picos & Recife

Saraiva, T2222984. Fan, basic. Recommended. **D** *Santa Terezinha*, Av Getúlio Vargas 2885, opposite rodoviária, T2195918. With a/c, cheaper with fan, clean, friendly. Many other cheap hotels and *dormitórios* around Praça Saraiva. **D** *Grande*, Firmino Pires 73. Very friendly and clean. Many cheap ones in R São Pedro and in R Alvaro Mendes. **D** *Glória*, at 823 (clean, best), blocks 800 and 900 on each street.

Eating

Many places for all budgets in Praça Dom Pedro II

For fish dishes, *Pesqueirinho*, R Domingos Jorge Velho 6889, in Poty Velho district. *Camarão do Elias*, Av Pedro Almeida 457, T2325025. Good seafood. *Sabores Rotisserie*, R Simplício Mendes 78, Centro. By kilogram, good quality and variety.

Festivals

Teresina is proud of its *Carnival*, which is then followed by *Micarina*, a local carnival in **March**. There is much music and dancing in **July** and **August**, when there is a Bumba-meu-Boi, the Teresina dance festival, *Festidanças*, and a convention of itinerant guitarists.

Shopping

Teresina is an excellent, and cheap source, of northeastern *artesanato*, for which Piauí is renowned throughout Brazil. Panels of carved and painted hardwood, either representing stylized country scenes or of religious significance, are a good buy, as are clay or wooden models of traditional rural characters. Many of these eccentric figures come from the region's rich fund of myths and legends. Hammocks, straw and basket ware are also varied, interesting and well made here.

Supermarket on Praça Mcal Deodoro 937, clean, good, fresh food. Local handicrafts include leather and clothes.

Transport

Local Taxis: *Rádio Táxi*, T2222222. **Trains**: local services only, on a diesel service called the 'metrô'.

Long distance Air: flights to Fortaleza, Brasília, Rio de Janeiro, São Paulo, Goiânia, São Luís. Buses from outside the airport run straight into town and to the rodoviária.

Buses: the bus trip to Fortaleza is scenic and takes 9 hours (US$13.50). There are direct buses to **Belém** (13 hours, US$23.40), **Recife** (16 hours, US$27) and **São Luís** (7 hours, US$12). To **Picos**, US$6, 4 hours.

Directory

Banks Banks with ATMs *Banco do Brasil* and *Unibanco*, Av Nossa Senhora de Fátima, in front of Caixa Econômica Federal. *Itaú*, in same avenue at P Center Shopping. *Bradesco*, Av Frei Serafim, at corner of 1 de Maio. *Mirante Câmbio*, Av Frei Serafim 2150, T2233633. *Alda Tur*, R A de Abreu 1226. Larger hotels may be helpful. **Tourist offices** *Piemtur*, R Álvaro Mendes 2003, Caixa Postal 36, information office at R Magalhães Filho (next to 55 N, English spoken); also at R Acre, Convention Centre, T2217100, kiosks at rodoviária and airport. *Singtur* (Sindicato dos Guías de Turismo de Piauí), R Paissandu 1276, T2212175, has information booths at the Centro de Artesanato, Praça Dom Pedro II, helpful, friendly, the Encontro das Águas, Poty Velho and on the shores of the Rio Poty. *Ana Turismo*, R Álvaro Mendes 1961, Centro, T/F2233970.

Leaving Teresina

A very bad road leads inland to Porto Franco and Imperatriz on the Belém-Brasília highway (see page 591); daily bus takes 26-40 hours for the trip to Imperatriz, depending on the state of the road; these buses are very crowded. Another main road runs southeast to Picos (see below). From there a good road runs via Salgueiro (many *pousadas*) to Recife (800 kilometres), another to Petrolina, on the Rio São Francisco opposite the Bahian town of Juazeiro, and a third east to Juazeiro do Norte. Buses from Petrolina/Juazeiro (see page 471) run southeast to Salvador.

Parque Nacional de Sete Cidades

Some 190 kilometres northeast of Teresina and 12 kilometres from Piracuruca, just off the Fortaleza-Teresina road, is this interesting park, with its strange eroded rock formations. From the ground it looks like a medley of weird monuments. The inscriptions on some of the rocks have never been deciphered; one theory suggests links with the Phoenicians, and the Argentine Professor Jacques de Mahieu considers them to be Nordic runes left by the Vikings. Within the 20 square kilometres of the park, there is plenty of birdlife and iguanas, which descend from their trees in the afternoon. If hiking in the park, beware of rattlesnakes. Ibama provides a free bus (see below), or else walk (it takes all day, very hot, start early).

Colour map 2, grid A3

Ibama, Av Homero Castelo Branco 2240, Teresina, CEP 64048-400, T2321142. Small booklet with sketch map (not really good enough for walking), entrance US$3. There are camping facilities (US$2) and two natural swimming pools, although during drought years the level can be low. Local food is limited and monotonous: bring a few delicacies, and especially fruit. Guided tours with *Tropicália Turismo*, Piracuruca, T086-3431347. Fifty kilometres away, **Pedro Segundo** is a good place to buy opals.

Park essentials

Situated 6 km from the park entrance is **B** *Hotel Sete Cidades*, Km 63 on BR-222, T086-2762222. Chalets with private bath, swimming pool, good restaurant and bicycle or horse transport; also has a free pick-up to the park (and a most unpleasant zoo). In the park is an Ibama hostel, T3431342, **E** pp. Rooms with bath, pleasant, good restaurant, natural pool nearby, camping. Recommended.

Sleeping

    Piripiri Located 26 km from the park (*population* 59,665); several good ones, including **E** *Novo Hotel Central*, in the centre. With fan, bath, breakfast and safe parking, friendly. Recommended. Also **D** pp *Martins*, T2761273. Others can be found near bus offices and behind the church. Exchange at the bank only.

Piripiri is a cheap place to break the Belém-Fortaleza journey, 26 km from the park

A free bus service leaves the Praça da Bandeira in Piripiri (in front of Telemar office), at 0700, passing *Hotel Fazenda Sete Cidades* at 0800, reaching the park 10 minutes later; return at 1630, or hitchhike. Taxi from Piripiri, US$15, or from Piracuruca, US$20. Bus Teresina-Piripiri and return, throughout the day 2½ hours, US$4. Bus São Luís-Piripiri, 1200, 1630, 2130, 10 hours, US$15. Several daily buses Piripiri-Fortaleza, 9 hours, US$11. Bus Piripiri-Ubajara (see above), marked 'São Benedito,' or 'Crateús', 2½ hours; US$4, first at 0700 (a beautiful trip).

Transport

Parnaíba

Between the states of Maranhão and Piauí runs the Rio Parnaíba. Near the river mouth is the anchorage of Luís Correia, where ships unload for final delivery by tugs and lighters at Parnaíba; 15 kilometres upriver, the collecting and distributing centre for the trade of Piauí: tropical products and cattle. It is partly encircled by shifting sands in white dunes up to 30 metres high. The town is a relaxed, friendly place. If crossing the delta, buy all provisions here. There is a regular connection here to Tutóia, for boats across the Parnaíba delta (see page 590); a tour in the delta costs US$20 per person.

*Population: 124,500
Phone code: 086
Colour map 2, grid A3*

There are beaches at Luís Correia, 14 kilometres from Parnaíba, with radioactive sands (**A** *Rio Poty Praia*, Av dos Magistrados 2350, T/F3671277, bar, restaurant, pool). Eighteen kilometres from Parnaíba is Pedra do Sal, with dark blue lagoons and palm trees. At Lagoa de Portinho, 12 kilometres from Parnaíba, there are bungalows, a bar and restaurant, and it is possible to camp;

Beaches

Fortaleza & the North Coast

canoes for hire. Praia do Coqueiro is a small fishing village with natural pools formed at low tide (**A** *Aimberê Resort*, T3661144, F3661204. *Alô Brasil* and *Bar da Cota* for seafood).

Sleeping **L** *Jardim das Araras*, BR-343, Km 5, Zona Urbana, T3223580, F3223916. Bungalows situated in a large out-of-town park, clean, spacious, restaurant, many sports facilities. **L** *Cívico*, Av Gov Chagas Rodrigues 474, T3222470, F3222028. Restaurant, pool, good breakfast. Recommended. **A** *Pousada dos Ventos*, Av São Sebastião 2586, Universidade, T3222177, F3224880. Pool. Recommended. **D** *Rodoviária*, and other basic hotels in the centre.

Eating *Recanto Gaúcho*, Trav Costa Fernandes, next to university, churrasco. *Renatinho*, Av das Nações Unidas, Beira Rio. Crab and seafood. *Sorveteria Araújo*, R Pires Ferreira 615. Good ice cream from local fruits.

Bars & *Centro Cultural Porto das Barcas*, a pleasant shopping and entertainment complex
nightclubs with several good restaurants and a large open-air bar on the riverside.

Shopping *Artesanato de Parnaíba*, R Dom Pedro II 1140 and *Cooperativa Artesanal Mista de Parnaíba*, R Alcenor Candeira, for local handicrafts.

Directory **Banks** *Banco do Brasil*, Praça da Graça 340. *Bradesco*, Av Pres Getúlio Vargas 403. **Communications** Post office: Praça da Graça. **Telephone:** Av Pres Getúlio Vargas 390. **Hospital & medical services** *Pró-Médica*, Av Pres Vargas 799, T3223645. 24 hr emergency ward. **Tourist offices** *Piemtur*, T3211532, and *Secretaria de Turismo e Meio Ambiente*, T3231715, both at Porto das Barcas (see above).

Southern Piauí

Picos

Population: 63,500
Phone code: 086
Colour map 2, grid B3

Located 330 kilometres south of Teresina at an important crossroads of the BR-407 from Bahia, BR-316 from Pernambuco and the BR-020 from Fortaleza, is the very hot town of Picos. The BR-407 is reported unsafe near the border with Pernambuco due to robberies of vehicles travelling this route. Across from the rodoviária in Picos is *Hotel Picos* (**C**), Av Brasil 400, T4221344, F4223620, with air conditioning, **D** with fan, very clean, restaurant, good breakfast. There is a *Banco do Brasil*, Av Brasil, in the rodoviária.

West of Picos by 93 kilometres is the town of **Oeiras** (*population* 51,890), the old capital of Piauí, where the state government is restoring some of the old buildings, such as the bishop's palace and the church of Nossa Senhora da Vitória.

Parque Nacional Serra da Capivara

Colour map 2, grid B3

About 500 kilometres south of Teresina is this 130,000 hectare park, established in 1979 and now on the Unesco World Heritage list. Some 30,000 prehistoric rock paintings on limestone have been found, dating to between 6,000 and 12,000 years ago. The paintings are of daily life, festivities and celebrations, as well as hunting and sex scenes. Excavations by Brazilian and French archaeologists have uncovered fossilized remains of extinct animals such as the sabre-toothed tiger, giant sloths larger than elephants and armadillos larger than a compact car.

Nearly 400 archaeological sites have been identified in the park since research began in 1970. Twenty two of those sites have been set up to receive tourists. Roads and all-weather paths allow visitors to view the site with ease. Specially trained guides are available. The area is good for hiking in the *caatinga*, with its canyons and mesas. It is also possible to see much of the *caatinga* wildlife, in particular the birds.

Much investment has gone into the park, not just for visitors' facilities, but also in educating the local population about protecting the paintings and establishing a beekeeping project to provide income in times of drought. The main organization is the **Fundação do Homem Americano** (Fumdham), Rua Abdias Neves 551, CEP 64770-000, São Raimundo Nonato, Piauí, T5821612/1389, F5821656, which has a museum for scientists. For further information on the park and reservations in local hotels, contact Dr Niéde Guidon, Fumdham Parque Nacional, at the address above.

Transport Access is from São Raimundo Nonato on the BR-324, or from Petrolina in Pernambuco (the nearest airport, 290 km away). Taxi from Petrolina airport will cost about US$200 one way, or there are buses. An airport is planned at Remanso in Bahia, 96 kilometres away; another is scheduled for São Raimundo Nonato.

In the far southwest of the state, near **São Gonçalo do Piauí**, is one of the best places for seeing hyacinth macaws. The Hyacinth Site is on private land, 20 kilometres from São Gonçalo, in a region of *cerrado* with red sandstone cliffs where the macaws nest. This used to be an area in which the illegal bird trade flourished, but the local people now guard the site, which is supported by the Kaytee Avian Foundation (USA) and others. Many other *cerrado* birds may be seen, together with black-and-gold howlers and, less commonly, maned wolf and giant anteaters. Accommodation is in very simple huts with mosquito nets, sand floors and shared bath. Meals are served at the site. Access is via the airport at Barreiras in Western Bahia, 340 kilometres south, five or six hours' drive away. Tours are only possible through *Focus Tours*, see **Tours and tour operators**, page 30.

Maranhão

The colonial centre of São Luís, with its use of ceramic tiles as exterior decoration, has been restored and is now part of Unesco's list of sites of worldwide cultural importance. The coast to the east, stretching to the Parnaíba delta, contains an area of sand dunes and freshwater lakes, the Lençóis Maranhenses, which deserves a visit for its beauty and remoteness. The area around Carolina, south of Imperatriz, is renowned for its mountain scenery and spectacular waterfalls. As for culture, the Bumba-Meu-Boi is typical of the region and the African influence harks back to the days when slaves were imported in the city, which is also considered Brazil's Reggae capital.

Initially, the Portuguese did not show much interest in this part of the Northeast, so the French were the first to bring in colonists. By the end of the 16th century, the Portuguese took over, but this was interrupted by a brief period of Dutch dominance in the early 1640s. The Companhia Geral do Comércio do

Fortaleza & the North Coast

Maranhão e Grão-Pará, 1685-1777, was the major influence in the area, but after its demise, there was unrest until Maranhão finally bowed to the Independence movement. Since agriculture relied heavily on slave labour, the abolition introduced a period of decline, but this was reversed with increased industrialization and improvements in babaçu, sugar and rice cultivation. Following José Sarney's term as Governor in the 1960s, efforts have been made to develop the state through public works.

Maranhão state is about the size of Italy, with a population of 5,360,000. Its land is flat and low-lying, with highlands to the south. The Atlantic coastline – a mass of sandbanks and creeks and sandy islands on one of which stands São Luís – is 480 kilometres long. The wet season lasts from January to March and the temperature is generally between 24 and 34°C throughout the year.

A quarter of Maranhão is covered with *babaçu* palms, the nuts and oil of which are the state's most important products. Rice comes a poor second. There are salt pans along the coast. The huge Boa Esperança hydroelectric plant on the Parnaíba River now provides the State with energy, and some petroleum has been discovered.

São Luís

Population: 802,000
Phone code: 098
1,080 km W of Fortaleza
830 km SE of Belém
Colour map 2, grid A2

The capital and port of Maranhão state, founded in 1612 by the French and named after St Louis of France, stands upon São Luís island between the bays of São Marcos and São José. The urban area extends to São Francisco island, connected with São Luís by three bridges. An old slaving port, the city has a large black population and has retained much African culture. It is located in a region of heavy tropical rains, but the surrounding deep forest has been cut down to be replaced by babaçu palms.

Sights

The old part, on very hilly ground with many steep streets, is still almost pure colonial. Part of it, known as the **Reviver**, has been restored with generally splendid results: the damp climate stimulated the use of ceramic tiles for exterior walls, and São Luís shows a greater variety of such tiles than anywhere else in Brazil; in Portuguese, French and Dutch styles. The commercial quarter (Rua Portugal, also called Rua Trapiche) is still much as it was in the 17th century; best shopping area is Rua de Santana near Praça João Lisboa.

The **Palácio dos Leões** (Governor's Palace), Avenida Dom Pedro II, has beautiful floors of dark wood (*jacarandá*) and light (*cerejeira*). There are marvellous views from the terrace and the old slave market. ■ *Monday, Wednesday and Friday 1500-1800.* The restored **Fortaleza de Santo Antônio**, built originally by the French in 1614, is on the bank of the Rio Anil at Ponta d'Areia. The **Fonte do Ribeirão**, Largo do Ribeirão, was begun in 1796.

The **Fábrica Canhamo**, Rua São Pantaleão 1232, Madre de Deus, near Praia Grande, is a restored factory and houses an arts and crafts centre. ■ *Monday-Friday 0900-1900, T2322187.* The **Centro da Creatividade Odylo Costa Filho**, Rua da Alfândego 200, Praia Grande, is an arts centre with theatre, cinema, exhibitions, music etc, with a bar and café; a good meeting place. ■ *Monday-Friday 0800-2200, T2314058.* Near the Travessa Ladeira there is live music at night.

The best colonial churches are the **Cathedral** (1629) on Praça Dom Pedro II, **Churches**
and the churches of **Carmo** (1627), Praça João Lisboa, **São João Batista** (1665),
Largo São João, **Nossa Senhora do Rosário** (1717 on Rua do Egito), and the
18th-century **Santana**, Rua de Santana. On Largo do Desterro is the church of
São José do Desterro, which was finished in 1863, but has much older parts.

The **Cafua das Mercês**, Rua Jacinto Maia 43, is a museum housed in the old **Museums**
slave market. It is well worth the effort to find it: a small building opposite the
Quartel Militar. ■ *Monday-Friday 1330-1700.* Also worth a visit is the Casa dos
Negros next door. The **Museu Histórico e Artístico do Estado**, in a fine early
19th-century mansion (complete with slave quarters) at Rua do Sol 302, is
closed for renovations (since January 1995). Also on the Rua do Sol is the **Teatro
Artur Azevedo** (1816). **Museu de Artes Visuais**, Avenida Portugal 289, shows
ceramics and post-war art. ■ *Monday-Friday 0800-1300, 1600-1800.*

Excursions

Calhau is a huge beach, 10 kilometres away. **Ponta D'Areia** is nearer to São
Luís but more crowded. **Raposa**, a fishing village built on stilts, is a good place
to buy handicrafts. There are a few places to stay on Av Principal. It is an hour's
bus ride with *Viação Santa Maria*, every 30 minutes from the Mercado Central, São Luís. Another fishing village is **São José de Ribamar**, whose church
dedicated to the patron saint is a centre for *romeiros* in September. There is
Hotel Sol e Mar, Av Gonçalves Dias 320, with a restaurant; many bars on the
seafront serve local specialities such as fried stonefish. It is a 30 minute bus ride
with *Maranhense* from in front of the market, São Luís.

São Luís historical centre

Fortaleza & the North Coast

Essentials

Sleeping

L *Sofitel*, Av Avicênia, Praia do Calhau, 8 km from centre on the beach, T2354545, F2354921, sofitel@elo.com.br. Excellent, restaurant, pool, sports facilities. **L** *Vila Rica*, Praça Dom Pedro II 299, T2323535, F2327245, www.hotelvilarica.com.br. Central, pool, business centre with internet connection. Recommended. **AL** *Praia Mar*, Av São Marcos, Ponta d'Areia, on the beach, T2352328. **AL** *La Ravadière*, Av Mcal Castelo Branco 375, São Francisco, T2352255, F2352217. Pool, restaurant, sauna. **A** *Panorama Palace*, R dos Pinheiro 15, São Francisco, T2354292, F2274474. **A** *São Francisco*, R das Figueiras, São Francisco, T2355544, F2352128. **B** *Deodoro*, R de Santaninha 535, T2315811. A/c, parking, good. **B** *Pantheon*, R da Santaninha 550, T2215657. **B** *Ponta D'Areia*, Av dos Holandeses, Ponta D'Areia, T2353232, F2272892. Pool. **B** *Pousada Colonial*, R Afonso Pena 112, T2322834. In a beautiful restored, tiled house. Recommended. **B** *Pousada do Francês*, R 7 de Setembro 121, T2314844, F2320879. Bar and restaurant, a/c. **B** *São Marcos*, R da Saúde 178, T2323768, F2317777. Restored colonial house, a/c, family-run. Recommended. **C** *Lord*, R de Nazaré 258, facing Praça Benedito Leite, T/F2214655. A/c, comfortable, good value, good breakfast. Recommended. **C** *Pousada Central*, R de Nazaré 340, T2211649. A/c. **D** *Hotel Casa Grande*, R Isaac Martins 94, Centro, T2322432. Clean, basic, single, double or triple rooms. Recommended. **D** *Estrela*, R da Estrela 370, Centro, T2327172. A/c, cheaper with fan, noisy, not too clean, safe. **D** *Pousada Turismo Jansen Müller*, R Jansen Müller 270, T2310997. With breakfast and bath. Many cheap hotels can be found in R das Palmas, very central, and R Formosa. Students may be able to use *Casa do Estudante*, R do Passeio, 2 km from centre.

Eating

Bases are good for home cooking in simple surroundings, although most are found away from the centre and beaches

Regional food Typical dishes are *arroz de cuxá* and *torta de camarão*. Desserts and liquors are made from local fruits. Try the local soft drink called *Jesús* or *Jenève*. *Base do Edilson*, R Joao Damasceno 21, Ponta do Farol. Excellent for prawns. *Base do Germano*, Av Venceslau Brás, Camboa. Excellent *caldeirada de camarão* (shrimp stew). *Base da Lenoca*, Av Dom Pedro II 181. Good view, big portions. *Senac*, R Nazaré 242, next to hotel *Lord*. Tourism school restaurant, good food in a beautifully restored mansion. *Tia Maria*, Av Nina Rodrigues 1, Ponta d'Areia. Recommended for fried fish with *castanha* and *caju*.

Oriental *Daruma*, R 33, Ponta D'Areia. *Oriental*, Av Mcal Castelo Branco 47, São Francisco, just across bridge. Good Chinese.

Churrasco *Pavan*, Av dos Holandeses, Calhau.

Italian *Internacional*, Av Mcal Castelo Branco, São Francisco. Pizzeria.

Other *Beiruth 2*, Av Mcal Castelo Branco 751B. Recommended. *Naturalista Alimentos*, R do Sol 517. Very good, natural food shops and restaurants, open till 1900.

Bars & nightclubs

Many bars in Praia Grande such as *Antigamente* with live music from Thursday-Saturday. *Poeme-Sei*, R João Gualberto 52, Praia Grande is a bar/gallery open in the evening, good atmosphere, no food. Piano bar in *Senac* (see above) from Thursday-Saturday. Reggae is extremely popular. Good places are *Tombo da Ladeira*, Praia Grande on Wednesdays, and *Coqueiro Bar*, Av dos Holandeses, Praia da Ponta D'Areia on Thursdays. A good nightclub is *Extravagance*, Av Conselheiro Hilton Rodrigues, Calhau.

Entertainment

Cinema *Colossal*, Av Mcal Castelo Branco 92, São Francisco. *Passeio*, R Oswaldo Cruz 806. **Theatre** *Teatro Artur Azevedo*, see **Sights** above. *Teatro Viriato Correa*, Av Getúlio Vargas, Monte Castelo, T2189019.

Bumba-Meu-Boi

Throughout the month of June the streets of São Luís are alive to the sound of tambores and dancers recreating the legend of Catirina, Pai Francisco and his master's bull. Although this mixture of African, indigenous and Portuguese traditions exists throughout the North it is in Maranhão that it is most developed with around 100 groups in São Luís alone. Here there are various styles called sotaques, *which have different costumes, dances, instruments and* toadas. *These are* Boi de Matraca da Ilha *and* Boi de Pindaré, *both accompanied by small percussion instruments called* matracas, Boi de Zabumba *marked by the use of a type of drum, and* Boi de Orquestra *accompanied by string and wind instruments. Although there are presentations throughout June the highpoints are the 24th (São João) and the 29th (São Pedro) with the closing*

ceremony lasting throughout the 30th (São Marçal), particularly in the bairro *João Paulo. The shows take place in an* arraial, *which are found all over the city, with the ones at* Projeto Reviver *and* Ceprama *being more geared towards tourists (however be aware that a livelier more authentic atmosphere is to be found elsewhere in other* bairros, *such as Madre Deus). The Centro de Cultura Popular Domingos Vieira Filho at Rua do Giz 221, Praia Grande is the place to learn more about these variations as well as many other local festivals and traditions such as Tambor de Crioula or* Cacuriá, *both sensual dances derived from Africa. A good location to see these dances and capoeira practised is* Labouarte, *Rua Jansen Muller, Centro (*Cacuriá de Dona Tetê *is particularly recommended with participation encouraged).*
Mick Day

On **24 June** (São João) is the **Bumba-Meu-Boi**, see box, above. For several days before the festival street bands parade, particularly in front of the São João and São Benedito churches. There are dances somewhere in the city almost every night in June. In **August**, *São Benedito*, at the Rosário church. Festival in **October**, with dancing, at Vila Palmeira suburb (take bus of same name).

Festivals

The *Parque do Bom Menino*, Av Jaime Tavares, has a running track and sports courts. **Gyms** *Vida e Sade*, R Rio Branco 174. *São Francisco*, Av Mcal Castelo Branco 120.

Sports

Ceprama, R de São Pantaleão 1232, Madre Deus, handicraft shops in an old colonial house.

Shopping

Air Marechal Cunha Machado airport, 15 km from centre, Av Santos Dumont, T2451688. Flights to Belém, Fortaleza, Imperatriz, Parnaíba and Teresina. *São Cristovão* buses to city until midnight, US$0.75. Taxi to city US$12.50.

Transport

Buses Rodoviária is 12 km from the centre on the airport road, 'Rodoviária via Alemanha' bus to centre (Praça João Lisboa), US$0.50. To **Fortaleza**, US$23.50, 4 a day, 18 hours. To **Belém**, 13 hours, US$20, *Transbrasiliana* at 1900 and 2000 (no *leito*). Also to **Recife**, US$45, 25 hours, all other major cities and local towns. To **Rio de Janeiro**, US$80.

Ferries These cross the bay daily from Porto do Itaqui to Porto do Cujupe. T2228431 for times. US$3 foot passenger, US$15 car.

Trains Three trains a week on the Carajás railway to Parauapebas, 13½ hours, 890 km, leave São Luís 0800, Monday, Wednesday, Friday, return 0800, Tuesday, Thursday, Saturday (crowded, take your own food). For the station take 'Vila Nova' or 'Anjo da Guarda' bus.

Fortaleza & the North Coast

Directory **Airline offices** *TAM*, T2440461. *Transbrasil*, Praça João Lisboa 432, T2321414. *Varig/Nordeste*, Av Dom Pedro II 267, T2315066. *Vasp*, R do Sol 43, T2314422. **Banks** *Banco do Brasil*, Praça Deodoro, for TCs and Visa ATMs. *BFB*, R do Sol 176. *Agetur*, R do Sol 33A. **Communications** Post office: Praça João Lisboa 292. **Telephone:** *Embratel*, Av Dom Pedro II 190. **Internet:** *HCG*, R Paparaúbas 11, São Francisco. **Embassies & consulates** *Denmark*, Av Colares Moreira 444, Monumental Shopping, Sala 220, T2357033. *France*, R Santo Antônio 259, T2314459. *Germany*, Praça Gonçalves Dias 301, T2327766. *Italy*, R do Genipapeiro, Jardim São Francisco, T2270270. *Spain*, Praça Duque de Caxias 3, João Paulo, T2232846. *USA*, Av Daniel de La Touche, Jardim Buriti, T2481769. **Hospitals & medical services** *Clínica São Marcelo*, R do Passeio 546, English speaking doctor. *Hospital Monte Sinai*, R Rio Branco 156, T2323260, 24 hrs. **Language courses** *Senhora Amin Castro*, T2271527, for Portuguese lessons. Recommended. **Laundry** *Nova China*, *R da Paz 518*. **Libraries** *Arquivo Púúblico*, R de Nazaré 218, rare documents on local history. **Tourist offices** *Fumtur*, Praça Benedito Leite, T2225281, also at airport. *Maratur*, Praça João Lisboa 66, opposite the post office, T2210880, F2327641, maratur@geplan.ma.gov.br. Dial T2312000 for tourist information. **Tour companies & travel agents** *Taguatur*, R do Sol 141, loja 15, T2320906, F2321814. *Babaçu Viagens*, Av Dom Pedro II 258, lojas A/B/C, T/F2314747, good.

Leaving São Luís

There is a direct paved road to **Belém** via **Santa Inês** (convenient stopping place, **C** *Pousada San Antônio*, on street with same name, breakfast. **D** *Hotel Novo Horizonte*, near rodoviária) and **Alto Bonito**, in reasonable condition (sometimes washed out but still passable – fascinating swamplands). Petrol stations are not far apart; about nine hours' driving with a lunch stop.

Alcântara

Population: 4,000 (city),
19,800 (municipality)
Phone code: 098
Colour map 2, grid A2

Some 22 kilometres away by boat is Alcântara, the former state capital, on the mainland bay of São Marcos. Construction of the city began at the beginning of the 17th century and is now a historical monument. There are many old churches (for example, the ruined **Matriz de São Matias**, 1648) and colonial mansions (see the **Casa**, and **Segunda Casa, do Imperador**, also the old cotton barons' mansions with their blue, Portuguese tiled façades). In the Praça da Matriz is the traditional pillory, the **Pelourinho** (1648), also a small museum (0900-1330, US$0.75), and the **Forte de São Sebastião** (1663), now in ruins. See also the **Fonte de Mirititiua** (1747). Principal festivals are *Festa do Divino*, at Pentecost (Whitsun); 29 June, *São Pedro*; early August, *São Benedito*.

Canoe trips go to **Ilha do Livramento**, where there are good beaches and walking around the coast (can be muddy after rain). Watch out for mosquitoes after dark. A rocket launching site has been built nearby.

Sleeping & eating **B** *Pousada dos Guarás*, Praia da Baronesa, T3371339. Bungalows with bath, good restaurant, canoe hire. **C** *Pousada do Mordomo Régio*, R Grande 134, T3371197. TV, fridge, good restaurant. **D** *Pousada Pelourinho*, Praça da Matriz 55, T3371257. Breakfast, good restaurant, communal bathroom. Recommended. *Pousada do Imperador*, Beco Escuro. *Pousada da Josefa*, R Direita, T3371109. Restaurant. Ask for hammock space or rooms in private houses, friendly but no great comfort, provide your own mineral water. *Bar do Lobato*, Praça da Matriz. Pleasant with good, simple food, fried shrimps highly recommended. The restaurants are about US$10 per meal. In R Direita, *Copos e Bocas* and *Pôr do Sol*.

Boats Lancha Diamantina leaves São Luís dock at about 0700 and 0930, returning **Transport**
from Alcântara about 0815 and 1615: check time and buy the ticket at the *hidroviária*,
west end of R Portugal, T2320692, the day before as departure depends on the tides.
The journey takes 90 minutes, return US$15. The sea can be very rough between
September and December. Old wooden boats, the *Newton Bello* and *Mensageiro da
Fé*, leave São Luís at 0630 and 1600, returning at 0730 (1½ hours, US$5 return).
There are sometimes catamaran tours bookable through tour operators in São Luís,
meals not included.

Banks *Banco do Estado do Maranhão*, R Grande 76, exchanges US$ cash and TCs. **Directory**
Communications **Post Office:** R Direita off Praça da Matriz. **Telephone:** *Telemar*, R Grande,
0700-2200 daily.

Parque Nacional Lençóis Maranhenses

To the east of São Luís, on the Atlantic Coast, is the **Parque Nacional Lençóis** *Phone code: 098*
Maranhenses, 155,000 hectares of beaches, lakes and dunes, with very little *Colour map 2, grid A3*
vegetation and largely unstudied wildlife.

A strange landscape of shifting white dunes, stretching about 140 kilometres along the coast between **Tutóia** and Primeira Cruz, west of
Barreirinhas, has created a unique and delicate ecosystem which was protected in 1981. The sand, which extends from the coast up to 50 kilometres

Alcântara

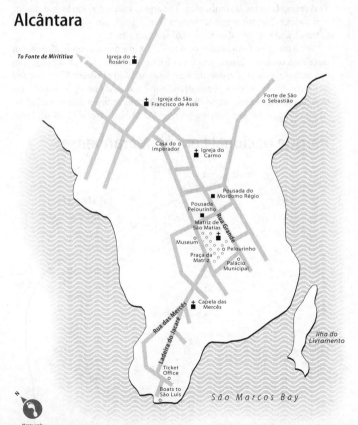

Fortaleza & the North Coast

inland, is advancing by as much as 200 metres a year in some places. Dumped by the sea and blown by the wind, it forms ridges 50 metres high in long flowing patterns which change constantly. The best time to visit is during the rainy season (June-September), when the dune valleys fill with water. Reflections of the sky make the water appear vivid blue, a spectacular contrast against brilliant white sand.

Barely visited until recently, Lençóis Maranhenses provides a refuge for severely endangered species: giant turtles come here to lay their eggs; among the mammals are *paca*, some deer, sea cow;``` and there are almost-extinct varieties of fish such as the *camurupim*, which likes both salt and freshwater. The dunes are a breeding ground for migratory birds and recent studies have shown the sparse vegetation to include grasses unknown elsewhere. Excavations were begun in 1995 on the supposed site of a Jesuit settlement which, according to persistent local rumour, was buried intact by a sandstorm.

Despite its remoteness, Lençóis Maranhenses (which means 'sheets of Maranhão') is not too difficult to visit. Travellers with a few days to spare are rewarded as much by the amazing panorama of watery dunes, reaching from horizon to horizon, as by deserted beaches, boat rides on the aptly-named Rio Preguiça (Lazy River) and tiny, quiet hamlets where strangers are still a novelty. Interest in the region among Brazilian holidaymakers – and developers – is growing fast, so explorers would be well advised to go there soon.

Traversing Lençóis Maranhenses The area to the west of Rio Preguiça is the park proper. The dunes east of the river form a 'protected area' which is easier to travel, and has several small, friendly settlements.

Along the coast from Barreirinhas to Tutóia in either direction, allow about three days on foot. Camping is permitted, but you must take all supplies with you including water, since some dune lakes are salty. Because of the hot and sandy conditions, this is a punitive trek, only for the very hardy. Do not try the treacherous hike inland across the dunes. By horse: contact Ibama, see below. Allow two days by jeep, staying overnight at Paulino Neves (US$20). From

Parque Nacional Lençóis Maranhenses

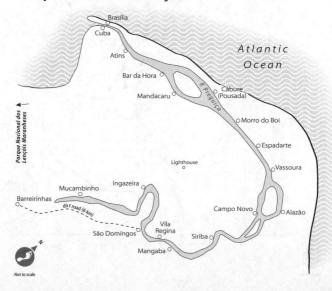

Tutóia, José Neves Rodrigues, known as 'O Anjo' (the Angel), does the trip for around US$40 per passenger. By boat: a regular river-boat service plies between Tutóia and Paulino Neves/Rio Novo; another from there goes to Barreirinhas (both four hours, US$10). It is also possible to hire a speedboat, or get a ride from a fisherman. A very bad road passing inland links Tutóia and Barreirinhas: hardy drivers could stop at Rio Novo and explore the dunes from there.

Ribamar at Ibama, Avenida Jaime Tavares 25, São Luís, T2223066/3006, is helpful on walks and horse rides along lesser routes; other Ibama address, Avenida Alexandre Mowa 25, Centro, T2313010, F2314332, or T2212063/3070. Agencies in São Luís are *Nasaturismo*, T2354429; *Baluz Turismo*, T2226658; *Jaguarema*, T2224764; *Sunset Turismo* at the airport; *Maratur*, T2211231. At Barreirinhas, *Pousada Lins* (but see below); *Parna Lençóis Maranhenses*, director Sr Edson; *Pocof Barreirinhas*, director José de Ribamar Santos Silva, both at Rua Cazuza Ramos 3, T3491155. Barreirinhas residents are generally keen to help tourists out.

Park essentials & tours

Tutóia *Tutóia Palace Hotel*, Av Paulino Neves 1100, T4791115, F4791247. Attractive. **D** *Pousada Em-Bar-Cação*, R Magalhães de Almeida 1064, T4791219, on the beach. Breakfast US$3, friendly, recommended for good food and *tiquira*, a drink made of manioc. There are *pousadas* and restaurants at Rio Novo and Paulino Neves.

Barreirinhas D *Pousada Lins*, Av Joaquim Soeiro de Carvalho, T3491203. Restaurant, good, but shop around before taking their tours. **D** *Pousada do Baiano*, R Col Godinho, T3491110. Many others.

Sleeping

Buses Parnaíba-Tutóia: bus, 4 hours, US$6; river boat up the Parnaíba delta, 8 hours, US$6. Recommended. Private boat hire is also possible. São Luis-Barreirinhas: bus, 8 hours on an awful road, US$12; private tour buses, US$24, are more comfortable but cannot improve the road, organized bus tours cost US$72.50; plane (single propeller), 1 hour, US$75. Recommended. A fabulous experience, giving panoramic views of the dunes, pilot Amirton, T2252882. Agencies charge about US$200 for a tour with flight.

Transport

Boats Excursions from/to Barreirinhas: regular boat service between Barreirinhas and Atins (7 hours return, US$5): boat along Rio Preguiça, 4 hours then 1 hour's walk to the dunes, US$12. Highly recommended. **Speedboats**, about US$100 for 5 people, from Cláudio, T5491183, or Sr Carlos, T3491203. They also have a Kombi, US$150 for up to 15 people. The only forms of transport that can get across the dunes right into the park are a **jeep** or a **horse**, both about US$15. It is a 2-3 hour walk from Barreirinhas to the park; you will need at least another 2 hours in the dunes. At Mandacaru, a popular stop on tours of the area, the lighthouse gives a very impressive view.

The Parnaíba delta

The extensive Parnaíba delta, its 70 islets variously covered in forest, palms or dunes, is the only sea-water delta in the Americas: river and saltwater flow side by side among its channels. Catch a boat on the riverside in Parnaíba, hook up your hammock, and pass a desultory five to eight hours watching herons nesting in the trees, fishermen asleep in their rowing-boats and admiring the daily crab harvest.

When you arrive at the delta mouth you have the choice between stopping at **Ilha do Caju**, which gets its name from the hundreds of cashew trees that grow there (www.ilhadocaju.com.br), or continuing to **Tutóia**, where millions of birds populate freshwater lakes, formed by rain collecting between massive white dunes. Both are protected areas of outstanding natural beauty. Good food and accommodation are available on the island and in Tutóia, but many people in this region live as they have done for generations, in adobe

See box on page 590 for Ilha do Caju

Ilha do Caju

After dozing for five hours in a hammock slung across the river-boat from Parnaíba, fresh ocean breezes woke me up when the delta mouth suddenly opened out. We docked at the island's little wooden jetty. I heaved my bag over the side and followed the guide to a waiting jeep. In the blazing sunshine, the only sounds were birdsong and the waves. Mário drove at breakneck speed along a track over rough fields, studded with thousands of cashew trees – I had no idea there were so many varieties. For the next few days, their fresh and fruity scent would perfume all the air I breathed.

Virtually unchanged for four centuries, Ilha do Caju has an astonishing variety of terrain, with lakes, forest, marshes and an expanse of white dunes to the northwest. Much of the water, including the sea, is salobre – a mixture of fresh and salty. Swimming from a vast, shimmering beach, through alternating currents of sea and river water, is an experience I would heartily recommend.

There are lakes, caused by flooding, in which trees killed by the brine content stand, bleached and knotted, an unnerving image of lifelessness surrounded by vigorous vegetation. I was taken by rowing boat across another lake, full of nesting herons and peregrines, which took off in clouds of flashing green feathers as we passed. Tiny, long-legged cafézinho birds hopped from leaf to leaf on the water lilies. Walking alone in the forest that surrounded the lake, myriad butterflies hovered around my head, while every step I took startled flurries of birds and small animals. At the woodman's house, his teenaged son scaled a coconut tree to provide us with fresh juice.

Although I lost all track of time, it was four days before I returned to Parnaíba by a different route: speedboat to the pretty fishing village of Porto dos Tatus, then a truck ride through babaçu palm plantations, where locals put every part of the tree to use; we passed many tired-looking old couples bearing huge piles of leaves on their heads, on bicycles or on mule carts. Sleepy Parnaíba almost seemed like a humming metropolis by comparison.

The island has a population of 70, many still living in rustic adobe houses where the stove is made of baked earth. The pousada's owner, Ingrid, has introduced a teacher and a doctor, and offers training to islanders who want to work on her farm or at the pousada.

Sleeping **A1** Pousada Ecológica Ilha do Caju, contact address: Av Presidente Vargas 235, Centro, 64-200-200, Parnaíba, Piauí, T086-3222380, F3211308, helpful, welcoming staff; the owner, Ingrid, and senior staff speak English. Children must be aged 12 or over.

The pousada is an attractive converted farmhouse with thatched guesthouses in the grounds; each has its own hammock outside, but inside there is a huge bed, hand-made by the same craftsmen who made much of the pousada's highly individual furniture. There was an unexpected feature in my bathroom: a family of small green frogs made regular use of my shower, hopping across the floor and out the window whenever they felt like it. Because the whole island is environmentally protected, no chemical pesticides are used.

Cherry Austin

houses, on a diet of fish cooked in baked-earth ovens. Illiteracy is the norm. Travel is by jeep, or, more commonly, by horse. There is no mains electricity and the nearest shopping is at Parnaíba.

Transport Crossing the Parnaíba delta, which separates Piauí from Maranhão, is possible by boat, arriving in **Tutóia**; an interesting trip through swamps sheltering many birds. Trucks from Tutóia go to Barreirinhas, gateway to the **Parque Nacional dos Lençóis Maranhenses**, a vast protected area of sand dunes with rare birds and other wildlife (see above).

The main road from Teresina passes through the Maranhense town of Caxias, a battle site during the Balaiada rebellion in 1838. It has a good churrascaria, *Selva do Braz*, Avenida Central 601, with live music in the evening. Three kilometres from the town on the Buriti Bravo road is a spring for medicinal bathing, with a restaurant serving regional food.

Caxias
Population: 149,500

Southern Maranhão

Imperatriz

On the Eastern bank of the Rio Tocantins, at Maranhão's western border with Tocantins, is Imperatriz, a city serving a large cattle region. Founded in 1851, the **Igreja de Santa Tereza D'Ávila** in Rua 15 de Novembro is dedicated to the city's patron saint. River beaches appear between July and October when the river is low.

Population: 295,000
Phone code: 098
Colour map 2, grid A1

A *Posseidon*, R Paraíba 740, T7232323. Central, best, pool. Recommended. A *Imperatriz Park*, BR-010, Km 1347, opposite rodoviária, T7232950. Pool. *Fogão Mineiro*, Av Getúlio Vargas 2234. *Rafaello Grill*, in Imperatriz Shopping, Av Dorgival Pinheiro Sousa 1400. Self-service. *Fly Back Disco Club*, Beira Rio, north of the ferry crossing. Two dance floors, one fast, one slow (for couples only), good.

Sleeping & eating
There are many cheap hotels near the rodoviária

Car hire *Interlocadora*, Av Dorgival Pinheiro de Souza 990, T7223050. *Localiza*, BR-010, Setor Rodoviária, T7214507, and at airport, T7218611.

Transport

   Air Airport, T7224666. Flights to Altamira, Araguaína, Belém, Brasília and São Luís. Air Taxi: *Heringer*, at airport, T7223009.

   Buses Lying on the BR-010 **Belém-Brasília** highway, Imperatriz has bus connections with both cities; there is a slow, crowded bus service to **Teresina**. To get to **Marabá** on the Transamazônica, you can either take a Transbrasiliana bus direct, 7-10 hours (starting on the Belém highway, the bus then turns west along a poorer road, passing finally through destroyed forest, new *fazendas* and unplanned cities), or a faster route, involving taking a ferry across the river in the early morning (0600-0700) to catch a pick-up on the other side, takes about 5 hours, but is more expensive. To get to the ferry across the river, go along R Luís Domingues, which runs parallel to Av Getúlio Vargas.

   Trains Station, T7232260. Trains to Pará and other towns in Maranhão.

Airline offices *Penta*, R Luís Domingues 1420, T7231073. *TAM*, R Ceará 678, T7223148. *Varig/RioSul*, R Luís Domingues 1471, T7232155. **Banks** *Banco do Brasil*, Av Getúlio Vargas 1935. **Communications** Telephone: R Rio Grande do Norte 740, a side street off Av Getúlio Vargas, near *Hotel Posseidon*, 0630-2400. **Hospital & medical services** *Santa Mônica*, R Piauí, T7223415, 24 hrs emergency ward. **Security** The town can be quite a rough place and it is wise to exercise caution, especially at night.

Directory

South of Imperatriz, also on the Rio Toncantins, is Carolina, set in an area of spectacular waterfalls and mountain scenery. Near to the **Cachoeira da Prata**, on the Rio Farinha, is **Morro das Figuras**, which has rock inscriptions. Access is by unmade road from the BR-230, requiring a four-wheel drive. Thirty five kilometres south of Carolina, on the road to Estreito, is **Cachoeria de Pedra Caída**.

Carolina
Population: 26,000
Phone code: 098

Sleeping and eating *Pousada Pedra Caída*, BR-010 Km 30, T7311318. Chalets with fan, restaurant, natural pool and 3 waterfalls. *Pousada do Rio Lages*, BR-230 Km 2, T7311499. Chalets with a/c. *Cafuné*, BR-230 Km 2. Local food.

Fortaleza & the North Coast

Transport Bus station, R Lias Barros, Nova Carolina, T7311195.

Directory Banks: *Banco do Brasil*, A Mascarenhas 159. **Communications**: Telephone: Av E Barros, open 0730-2230. **Hospital & medical services**: *FNS*, R Benedito Leite 57, T7311271. **Tourist offices**: *Secretaria de Turismo*, R Duque de Caxias 522, T7311613, Mon-Fri 0800-1300.

The Amazon

10

594

The Amazon

The mighty Amazon stretches from the Atlantic to the Peruvian and Colombian borders. The river, its tributaries and the forests through which they flow, make up over half of Brazil's national territory. In this vast area there are only a few centres for visiting Amazônia. At the river's mouth is Belém, the capital of Pará. It's a good place to begin or end a river journey, with its fascinating market, its historical associations and its famous festival of candles. Riverboats ply the route from here to Manaus in Amazonas via Santarém.

On the north bank of the delta is Macapá, the capital of Amapá. Santarém, near the confluence of the Tapajós and Amazon rivers, makes an ideal stopping place on the long haul from the coast to Manaus, 1,600 kilometres inland. This city grew rich in the rubber boom and is an excellent starting point for tours into the jungle. North of Manaus, on the Venezuelan border, is the state of Roraima and its capital Boa Vista. In the far southwest of Amazônia, towards the Bolivian border, is the state of Acre and its capital Rio Branco. Porto Velho, capital of Rondônia, is the crossroads of river and road connections from Amazônia and the Centre West of Brazil. A legendary railway, the Madeira-Mamoré, is an attraction in the west of the state. The new state of Tocantins, with its modern capital, includes the Ilha de Bananal, a huge river island with good opportunities for fishing. Indian culture remains strong in the region and is expressed in the Festa de Boi, held on Parantins island. Many types of rare animals, birds and plants can be encountered on trips into the rainforest.

The Amazon

Background

History A Spanish conquistador was the first person to travel across the region. In 1541 Francisco de Orellana successfully journeyed from Quito to the island of Marajó, close to the mouth of the Amazon. The river and its environs were called the 'Land of the Amazons' after the chronicler for the journey, Gaspar de Carvajal, described how the party had come across warlike women who resembled in temperament the Amazons of Greek mythology. In the 16th and 17th centuries the 'Green Hell' of the Amazon became the most likely site of the mythical 'El Dorado' and a number of expeditions were launched there by fortune-seeking Europeans, including Sir Walter Raleigh. In the 17th century the Portuguese consolidated their hold of the Amazon by establishing a fort at Belém in 1616 and one at Barra, the site of Manaus, in 1669. In 1638 Pedro de Teixera, the governor of the Pará captaincy, succeeded in travelling in the opposite direction, from Belém to Quito. He also returned by the same route to Belém the following year, the first person to do so.

During the 18th and 19th centuries the Amazon attracted the gaze of European scientists, botanists and philosophers who debunked the myth of the warrior women, but discovered more than enough realities to inspire further exploration and settlement. The British botanists Alfred Russel Wallace and Henry Walter Bates spent four and 11 years in the Amazon basin respectively, collecting species for the Natural History Museum which would help to provide evidence for the theory of evolution. During his travels of the Amazon Basin, Charles Marie de la Condamine described how the natives used the resin of the 'heve' tree to make balls, syringes and pumps and to waterproof their canoes. The inventions of the vulcanization process and the pneumatic tyre in Europe meant that the race for rubber was on.

Economy Successive modern Brazilian governments have made strenuous efforts to develop Amazônia (see box, page 620). Roads have been built parallel to the Amazon to the south (the Transamazônica), from Cuiabá in Mato Grosso, northwards to Santarém in Pará, and northeast from Porto Velho through Humaitá to the river bank opposite Manaus. Some maps show a road north of the Amazon, marked Perimetro (or Perimetral) Norte; this road does not exist, never has and probably never will. Unsuccessful attempts were made to establish agricultural settlements along these roads; major energy and mining projects for bauxite and iron ore are bringing rapid change. More environmental damage has been caused to the region by gold prospectors (*garimpeiros*), especially by their indiscriminate use of mercury, than by organized mining carried out by large state and private companies using modern extraction methods. The most important cause of destruction, however, has been large-scale deforestation to make way for cattle ranching, with logging for hardwoods for the Asian markets coming a close second.

It is estimated that 600,000 square kilometres, an area the size of France, has now been shed of its forest cover, with more destruction occurring in the last three decades than in the last four centuries. To make a more regional comparison, an area the size of the state of Sergipe is lost every year to the chainsaw and match. A lot of the destruction occurred in the 1980s. It slowed down in the early 1990s, but with the recovery of the Brazilian economy and very dry weather in the mid-1990s the destruction sped up again. In 1995, for example, 29,000 square kilometres of forest were destroyed, the highest figure ever. The rate of deforestation fell to 18,000 square kilometres in 1996, still about the same rate as in the 1970s and 1980s, but in the absence of any government schemes which encouraged deforestation. The forest fires prior to the late arrival of the rains in

The enchanted river dolphin

The Brazilian Amazon is no doubt one of the richest repositories of folklore in the world. Ancient Indian legends have mingled with the myths that were brought to the region by foreigners and the results are often amazing.

One of the most fascinating myths is the Enchanted River Dolphin, a story that exists throughout the entire Amazon region of South America. The people who live on the Amazon firmly believe that a certain species of river dolphin, the boto cor-de-rosa (Inia geoffrensis), has strange, magical powers. It is said that these pink, freshwater mammals can temporarily become human beings at night, leaving the river to socialize with us. Normally they assume the shape of a handsome young man, wearing a white suit and always sporting a hat. This covers the blow-hole at the top of his head (the only visible sign that he really is a dolphin). He loves parties and knows how to dance, sing and play the guitar and, above all, his favourite occupation is seducing pretty young girls, be they single or married.

The enchanted dolphin is reputed to be an extremely creative and ardent lover, at least for one night, because after sleeping with the girl he loses interest and, next morning, simply takes his normal shape and dives back into the nearest river, never to return. Most women get pregnant in these relationships and in the Amazon region people call any child of a single mother, or of an unknown father, filho de boto (dolphin's child).

So, a word of advice to any girls travelling in the Amazon who don't want to be seduced by this gallant chap: at night-time parties always keep a needle attached to your dress in a visible place. The enchanting, handsome (enchanted) young man will avoid you because he knows that even the smallest of nicks that draws blood will make him recover his dolphin form in an instant.

Fábio Sombra

1997 created a haze of smog over Manaus. Worse still, fires in Roraima, started by farmers clearing land in January 1998, spread over 55,000 square kilometres of land, destroying open savannah and rainforest. By March 1998 the fires had entered the Yanomami Indian Reserve and thousands of cattle had died. Prolonged drought as a result of El Niño, warm winds, high temperatures and the slowness of the federal government to react to the emergency allowed the fires to affect a vast area. At the very end of March, rains arrived, proving more effective at putting out the blaze than the belated human efforts.

There is a gradually growing awareness among many Brazilians that their northern hinterland is a unique treasure and requires some form of protection, and recently some encouraging moves have been made. At the end of 1997 the **Amanã Sustainable Development Reserve** (SDR) was set up, linking two other reserves to form the world's largest protected rainforest area. The Amanã SDR surrounds Lake Amanã north of Tefé and covers 23,500 square kilometres. It is sandwiched between the Jaú National Park to the east and the Mamiraua SDR to the west, forming a 640-kilometre long corridor. It is hoped that whole ecosystems will be preserved and that local inhabitants will be able to find sustainable work in the reserve's management. Also in January 1998, Congress passed a law which creates 'environmental crimes' for the first time, which will help in the punishment of illicit logging.

Much attention has been focused on ecotourism as a potentially non-destructive source of income for the region. But these are early days. It has been estimated that less than five percent of the earnings from Brazil's billion dollar tourist industry comes from 'ecotourism' in the Pantanal and the Amazon. In comparison, Costa Rica, about 10 percent the size of Amazônia, has a number of well maintained and, on the whole, environmentally friendly national parks, which earned US$600m from tourism in the same year. The high cost of internal flights has meant that approximately less than one percent of Brazil's foreign tourists make a visit to Manaus.

Anyone interested in the Amazonian development programme and its ecological, social, economic and political effects should read Richard Bourne's masterly *Assault on the Amazon* (London, Gollancz, 1978), *Dreams of Amazonia*, by Roger D Stone (Penguin, 1986), or *Amazon*, by Brian Kelly and Mark London (Harcourt Brace Jovanovich, New York, 1983). *The Fate of the Forest*, by Suzanne Hecht and Alexander Cockburn (Penguin, 1991), has also been recommended.

Geography & climate

The area is drained by the Amazon, which in size, volume of water – 12 times that of the Mississippi – and number of tributaries has no equal in the world. Between 80 and 90 million years ago the world supercontinent Gondwanaland split and South America, then a massive island, drifted away from Africa. At this time, Amazônia's only outlet to the sea was towards the Pacific. The Andes had not yet formed and the Guiana and Brazilian Highlands were joined together in the east, barring access to the Atlantic. In *Amazon – The Flooded Forest* (BBC Books 1989), Michael Goulding states that the ancestors of the stingrays that are found today in the turbid waters of the Amazon came from the Pacific, not the Atlantic. About 15 million years ago the South American continental plate crashed into the Nazca plate, forming the Andes. The Amazon became a huge swamp. During the Pliocene period 10 million years ago, the Amazon eventually found a course to the Atlantic between the Guiana and Brazilian highlands. Nowadays at the base of the Andes, far to the west, the Amazonian plain is 1,300 kilometres in width, but east of the confluences of the Madeira and Negro rivers with the Amazon, the highlands close in upon it until there is no more than 80 kilometres of floodplain between them. Towards the river's mouth – about 320 kilometres wide – the plain widens once more, and extends along the coast southeastwards into the state of Maranhão and northwards into the Guianas.

Brazilian Amazônia, much of it still covered with tropical forest, is 56 percent of the national area. Its jungle is the world's largest and densest rain forest, with more diverse plants and animals than any other jungle in the world. It has only eight percent of Brazil's population, and most of this is concentrated around Belém (in Pará), and in Manaus, 1,600 kilometres up the river. The population is sparse because other areas are easier to develop.

The rainfall is heavy, but varies throughout the region; close to the Andes, up to 4,000 millimetres annually, under 2,000 at Manaus. Rains occur throughout the year, but the wettest season is between December and May; the driest month is October. The humidity can be extremely high and the temperature averages 26°C. There can be cold snaps in December in the western reaches of the Amazon basin. The soil, as in all tropical forest, is poor.

River transport

Although air services are widespread throughout the region and road transport is gradually increasing, rivers remain the arteries of Amazônia for the transport of both passengers and merchandise. The two great ports of the region are Belém at the mouth of the Amazon and Manaus at the confluence of the Rio Negro and Rio Solimões. Manaus is the hub of river transport, with regular shipping services east to Santarém and Belém along the lower Amazon, south to Porto Velho along the Rio Madeira, west to Tabatinga (the border with Colombia and Peru) along the Rio Solimões, northwest to São Gabriel da

Cachoeira along the Rio Negro, and more sporadically north to Caracaraí (for Boa Vista) along the Rio Branco. There is also a regular service connecting Belém and Macapá, on the northern shore of the Amazon Delta, Santarém and Macapá, as well as Santarém and Itaituba, south along the Rio Tapajós. All of the above services call at many intermediate ports and virtually every village has some form of river boat service.

The size and quality of vessels varies greatly, with the largest and most comfortable ships generally operating on the Manaus-Belém route; acceptable conditions can be found, however, on some boats to almost all destinations. In 1999 hygiene, food and service were reasonable on most vessels, but overcrowding was a common problem. Many of the larger ships offer air-conditioned berths and even suites with double beds and private bath, in addition to first class (upper deck) and second class (lower deck) hammock space (on many routes this distinction does not apply). Most boats have some sort of rooftop bar serving expensive drinks and snacks.

River boat travel is no substitute for visiting the jungle. Except for a few birds and the occasional dolphin, little wildlife is seen. However, it does offer an insight into the vastness of Amazônia and a chance to meet some of its people, making a very pleasant experience.

The vessels operate on a particular route and their schedules are frequently changing; it is generally not possible to book far in advance. Extensive local inquiry and some flexibility in one's schedule are indispensable for river travel. The following are some suggestions on how to choose a river boat. Refer to the appropriate city sections for details of port facilities in each. **Choosing a river boat**

Agencies on shore can inform you of the arrival and departure dates for several different ships, as well as the official (highest) prices for each; they are sometimes amenable to bargaining. Whenever possible, however, see the vessel yourself and have a chat with the captain or business manager to confirm departure date and time, length of voyage, ports of call, price etc. Inspect cleanliness in the kitchen, toilets and showers. All boats are cleaned up when in port, but if a vessel is reasonably clean upon arrival then chances are that it has been kept that way throughout the voyage. You can generally arrange to sleep on board a day or two before departure and after arrival, but be sure to secure carefully your belongings when in port. If you take a berth, lock it and keep the key even if you will not be moving in right away. If you are travelling hammock class, board ship at least six to eight hours before sailing in order to secure a good spot (away from the toilets and the engine and check for leaks in the deck above you). Be firm but considerate of your neighbours as they will be your intimate companions for the duration of the voyage. Always keep your gear locked. Take some light warm clothing, it can get very chilly at night.

Compare fares for different ships and remember that prices may fluctuate with supply and demand. As a general rule of thumb they will be about one-third of the prevailing one-way airfare, including all meals. (Drinks not included. Most ships sail in the evening and the first night's supper is not included.) Empty cabins are sometimes offered to foreigners at reduced rates once boats have embarked. Payment is usually in advance. Insist on a signed ticket indicating date, vessel, class of passage, and berth number if applicable.

All ships carry cargo as well as passengers, and the amount of cargo will affect the length of the voyage because of weight (especially when travelling upstream) and loading/unloading at intermediate ports. All but the smallest boats will transport vehicles, but these are often damaged by rough handling. Insist on the use of proper ramps and check for adequate clearance. Vehicles can also be transported aboard cargo barges. These are usually cheaper and

The Amazon

Bates on the Amazon

> *"The birds were astir, the cicadas had begun their music, and the Urania Leilus, a strange and beautiful tailed and gilded moth, whose habits are those of a butterfly, commenced to fly in flocks over the tree-tops. Raimundo exclaimed 'Clareia o dia!' – 'The day brightens!' The change was rapid: the sky in the east assumed suddenly the loveliest azure colour, across which streaks of thin white clouds were painted. It is at such moments as this that one feels how beautiful our world truly is! The channel on whose waters our little boat was floating was about 200 yards wide; others branched off right and left, surrounding the group of lonely islands which terminate the land of Carnopijó. The forest on all sides formed a lofty hedge without a break: below, it was fringed with mangrove bushes, whose small foliage contrasted with the large glossy leaves of the taller trees, or the feather and fan-shaped fronds of the palms."*
>
> Henry Walter Bates, The Naturalist on the River Amazon, 1863. (This extract is taken from Abroad. A Miscellany of English Travel Writing 1700-1914, compiled by Alan Wykes, London: Macdonald & Jane's, 1973.)

passengers may be allowed to accompany their car, but check about food, sanitation, where you will sleep (usually in a hammock slung beneath a truck), and adequate shade.

The following are the major shipping routes in Amazônia, giving a selection of vessels and indicating intermediate ports, average trip durations, and fares. Not all ships stop at all intermediate ports. There are many other routes and vessels providing extensive local service. All fares shown are one-way only and include all meals unless otherwise stated. Information is generally identical for the respective reverse voyages (except Belém-Manaus, Manaus-Belém).

Belém-Manaus via Breves, Almeirim, Prainha, Monte Alegre, Curua-Uná, Santarém, Alenquer, Óbidos, Juruti and Parintins on the lower Amazon. Five days upriver, 4 days downriver, including 18-hour stop in Santarém, suite US$500 upriver, US$400 down, double berth US$300 upriver, US$260 down, hammock space US$85 upriver, US$75 down. Vehicles: small car US$320, combi US$420 usually including driver, other passengers extra, four-wheel drive US$600 with 2 passengers; motorcycle US$100. *Nélio Correa* is best on this route. *Defard Vieira*, very good and clean, US$87. *São Francisco* is largest, new and modern, but toilets smelly. *Cisne Branco* of similar quality. *Cidade de Bairreirinha* is the newest on the route, a/c berths. *Lider II* has good food and pleasant atmosphere. *João Pessoa Lopes* is also recommended. *Enasa* has one sailing per week 2000 Thursday, US$54 pp including meals. The Belém-Manaus route is very busy. Try to get a cabin if you can.

Belém-Santarém, same intermediate stops as above. Two days upriver, 1½ days downriver, fares berth US$200, hammock US$61 upriver, US$55 down. All vessels sailing Belém-Manaus will call in Santarém.

Santarém-Manaus, same intermediate stops as above. Two days upriver, 1½ days downriver, fares berth US$100, hammock US$35. All vessels sailing Belém-Manaus will call in Santarém and there are others operating only the Santarém-Manaus route, including: *Cidade de Terezinha III* and *IV*, good. *Miranda Dias*, family run and friendly. In 1997 speedboats (*lanchas*) were introduced on this route, 16 hours sitting, no hammock space, US$35.

Belém-Macapá (Porto Santana) non-stop, 8 hours on fast catamaran, *Atlântica*, US$30, 3 days a week, or 24 hours on large ships, double berth US$120, hammock space US$30 pp, meals not included but can be purchased onboard (expensive), vehicle US$100, driver not included. *Silja e Souza* (Wednesday) is best. *Comandante Solon*

(Saturday) is state run, slightly cheaper, crowded and not as nice. Same voyage via Breves, 36 to 48 hours on smaller river boats, hammock space US$25 pp including meals. *ENAL* (Saturday); *Macamazônia* (every day except Thursday), slower and more basic; *Bartolomeu I* of Enavi, food and sanitary conditions OK, 30 hours; *Rodrigues Alves* has been recommended. *Golfinho do Mar* is said to be the fastest.

Macapá (Porto Santana)-Santarém via Vida Nova, Boça do Jari, Almeirim, Prainha, and Monte Alegre on the lower Amazon (does not call in Belém), 2 days upriver, 1½ days downriver, berth US$150, hammock US$48. Boats include *Viageiro V* (nice), *São Francisco de Paula*.

Santarém-Itaituba along the Rio Tapajós, 24 hours (bus service on this route is making this river trip less common).

Manaus-Porto Velho via Borba, Manicoré, and Humaitá on the Rio Madeira. Four days upriver, 3½ days downriver (up to 7 days when the river is low), double berth US$200, hammock space US$79 pp. Recommended boats are *Almirante Moreira II*, clean, friendly owner; *Lord Scania*, friendly; *Ana Maria VIII*, modern. The *Eclipse II* is a very nice boat which sails Manaus-Manicoré (2 days, US$120 double berth, US$30 hammock). Many passengers go only as far as Humaitá and take a bus from there to Porto Velho, much faster.

Manaus-Tefé via Codajás and Coari, 24 to 36 hours, double berth US$80, first class hammock space US$30 pp, second class hammock space US$25 pp. *Capitão Nunes* is good. *Jean Filho* also OK. Note that it is difficult to continue west from Tefé to Tabatinga without first returning to Manaus.

Manaus-Tabatinga via Fonte Boa, Foz do Mamaria, Tonantins, Santo Antônio do Içá, Amataura, Monte Cristo, São Paulo de Olivença and Benjamin Constant along the Rio Solimões. Up to 8 days upriver (depending on cargo), 3 days downriver, double berth US$250, hammock space US$75 pp (can be cheaper downriver). When going from Peru into Brazil, there is a thorough police check some 5 hours into Brazil. *Voyagers*, *Voyagers II* and *III* (T2363782) recommended; *Almirante Monteiro*, *Avelino Leal* and *Capitão Nunes VIII* all acceptable; *Dom Manoel*, cheaper, acceptable but overcrowded.

Manaus-Caracaraí (for Boa Vista) along the Rio Branco, 4 days upriver, 2 days downriver, many sandbars, impassable during the dry season. Now that the BR-174 (Manaus-Boa Vista) has been paved, it is almost impossible to get a passage on a boat. The only tourist boat is erratic.

Manaus-São Gabriel da Cachoeira via Novo Airão, Moura, Carvoeiro, Barcelos, and Santa Isabel do Rio Negro along the Rio Negro. Berth US$240, hammock US$80, most locals prefer to travel by road. Boats on this route: *Almirante Martins I* and *II*, *Capricho de Deus*, *Manoel Rodrigues*, *Tanaka Netto* departing from São Raimundo dock, north of main port.

What to wear

Light cotton or poplin clothing for the day and at night put on a sweater or coat, for it gets quite cold. Wear long trousers. Leather sandals fall apart in the wet, rubber ones are better, but proper shoes or boots are best for going ashore: there are many foot-attacking parasites in the jungle. Two pairs of trainers, so you always have a dry pair, is a good idea. Also take a hat and rain gear, such as a poncho with hood.

A hammock is essential on all but the most expensive boats; it is often too hot to lie down in a cabin during the day. Light cotton hammocks seem to be the best solution. Buy a wide one on which you can lie diagonally; lying straight along it leaves you hump-backed. A climbing carabiner clip is useful for fastening hammocks to runner bars of boats. It is also useful for securing baggage, making it harder to steal.

The Amazon

Health   There is a danger of malaria in Amazônia. Mosquito nets are not required when in motion as boats travel away from the banks and are too fast for mosquitoes to settle, though repellent is a boon for night stops. From April to October, when the river is high, the mosquitoes can be repelled by Super Repelex spray or K13. A yellow fever inoculation is strongly advised; it is compulsory in some areas and may be administered on the spot with a pressurized needle gun. The larger ships must have an infirmary and carry a health officer. Drinking water is generally taken on in port (ie city tap water), but taking your own mineral water is a good idea.

Food   This is ample but monotonous, better food is sometimes available to cabin passengers. Meal times can be chaotic. Fresh fruit is a welcome addition; also take plain biscuits, tea bags, seasonings, sauces and jam. Fresh coffee is available; most boats have a bar of sorts. Plates and cutlery may not be provided. Bring your own plastic mug as drinks are served in plastic beakers which are jettisoned into the river. A strong fishing line and a variety of hooks can be an asset for supplementing one's diet; with some meat for bait, *piranhas* are the easiest fish to catch. Negotiate with the cook over cooking your fish. The sight of you fishing will bring a small crowd of new friends, assistants, and lots of advice – some of it useful.

    Local specialities Inevitably fish dishes are very common, including many fish with Indian names, eg *pirarucu, tucunaré* and *tambaqui*, which are worth trying. Also shrimp and crab dishes (more expensive). Specialities of Pará include duck, often served in a yellow soup made from the juice of the root of the manioc with a green vegetable (*jambu*); this dish is the famous *pato no tucupi*, highly recommended. Also *tacaca* (shrimps served in *tucupi*), *vatapá* (shrimps served in a thick sauce, highly filling, simpler than the variety found in Salvador), *maniçoba* (made with the poisonous leaves of the bitter cassava, simmered for eight days to render it safe – tasty). *Caldeirada*, a fish and vegetable soup, served with *pirão* (manioc puree), is a speciality of Amazonas. There is also an enormous variety of tropical and jungle fruits, many unique to the region. Try them fresh, or in ice creams or juices. Avoid food from street vendors.

Exchange   Facilities are sparse in Amazônia: banks and exchange can be found in Belém, Macapá, Santarém and Manaus. Small amounts of US dollars cash can usually be exchanged in many other towns, but some boat captains will not take US dollars.

Amapá

Sometimes called the Brazilian Guyana, this isolated frontier state has developed close links with its neighbours. Once exploited for its natural resources, it is now gaining recognition both inside and outside of Brazil for its efforts at sustainable development. Located near the European Union territory of Guyane with its cheap air link to Paris, it is another good port of entry into Northern Brazil. Tourist infrastructure outside the capital Macapá is negligible, but for the adventurous there are opportunities for ecotourism such as the Cabo Orange national park.

The region that is today Amapá was given to Bento Manuel Parente in 1637. However, Portuguese ownership was disputed by the Dutch, English and French until the treaty of Utrecht in 1713 established the border between Brazil and French Guiana. The discovery of gold and the high price of rubber caused another French invasion in 1895, but possession of the region was awarded to Brazil in 1900 and it was incorporated into the state of Pará. In 1945 manganese deposits were discovered in Serra do Navio and mining began in 1957. A standard gauge railway, 196 kilometres long and the only one in Brazil, was built from the mining camp Icomiland to the port at Santana. During the 1960s the region was responsible for 80 percent of the world's manganese supply. After a period as a Federal Territory under military control, Amapá finally became a state in 1988. Today its main industries are coal, timber and agriculture, especially fishing.

The state is one-quarter the size of France but with an estimated population of 600,000. The Rio Oiapoque forms the border with Guyane. The northern channel of the Rio Amazonas and the Rio Jari define the borders with Pará, while the Atlantic Ocean washes the eastern coast. In the northwest is the Serra do Tumucumaque, reaching 500 metres in parts. The wet season lasts from December to June, followed by the hot dry season for the rest of the year. Temperatures vary between 25-30°C. The state still retains some 70 percent of its forest coverage. Malaria is rampant in the interior, especially in the areas mined by gold prospectors.

Macapá

The capital of Amapá is a pleasant city on the banks of the northern channel of the Amazon Delta. It has an impressive fortress as well as a monument to the equator that divides the city and is worth visiting for a couple of days. There is a museum detailing the research being carried out in the rain forest and nearby Curiaú, a village formed by escaped slaves.

Population: 315,000
Phone code: 096
Colour map 1, grid A5

The town was founded around the first Forte de São José do Macapá, built in 1688. In 1751 more settlers from the Azores arrived to defend the region from Dutch, English and French invasions and the aldea became a Vila in 1758. Many slaves were later brought from Africa for the construction of the Fortaleza.

The Amazon

Ins & outs
See also Transport, page 606

Getting there Flights arrive at the airport close to the city. There are also international connections from Cayenne and Paramaribo. The centre is a short taxi ride from the airport. There are also buses. Boats from Belém and Santarém arrive at nearby Porto Santana, which is linked to Macapá by bus or taxi. Buses from Oiapoque pass through the centre of Macapá after a long and uncomfortable journey over mainly unsurfaced roads. This journey can take even longer during the rainy season from January-May.

Getting around There is an air taxi service to some towns. Towns are linked by trucks, community minibuses and the main bus companies. These leave from various locations in Macapá until the new rodoviária is completed on the BR-156 north of Macapá. Car hire is readily available. The centre and the waterfront are easily explored on foot. Buses to other parts of the city leave from a bus station near the Fortaleza.

Sights

Each brick of the **Fortaleza de São José do Macapá**, built between 1764 and 1782, was brought from Portugal as ballast. There is a museum and the Fortaleza is used for concerts, exhibits and colourful festivities on the anniversary of the city's founding on 4 February. **São José Cathedral**, inaugurated by the Jesuits in 1761, is the city's oldest landmark. The **Centro de Cultura Negra**, in Rua General Rondon, has a museum and holds frequent events. The **Museu do Desenvolvimento Sustentável**, in Avenida Feliciano Coelho 1509, exhibits research on sustainable development and traditional community life in Amazônia. ■ *Tuesday-Friday 0830-1200, 1500-1800, Monday and Saturday 1500-1800.*

The riverfront has been landscaped with trees, lawns and paths. It is a very pleasant place for an evening stroll. The **Complexo Beira Rio** has food and drink kiosks and a nice lively atmosphere. The newly rebuilt pier (*trapiche*) is a lovely spot for savouring the cool of the evening breeze, or watching sunrise over the Amazon.

Macapá

■ **Sleeping**
1 Açai Palace
2 Glória
3 Macapá
4 Pousada Ekinox

There is a monument to the equator, **Marco Zero** (take Fazendinha bus from Avenida Mendonça Furtado). The equator also divides the nearby football stadium in half, aptly named O Zerão. The Sambódromo is located nearby. South of these, on Rodovia Juscelino Kubitschek, are the **zoo** and **botanical gardens**. ■ *Tuesday-Sunday 0900-1700.* Nearby **Fazendinha** is a popular local beach, which is very busy on Sunday, with many seafood restaurants. **Curiaú**, a town eight kilometres from Macapá, is inhabited by the descendants of African slaves who have maintained many of the customs of their ancestors. They are analogous to the Bush Negroes of Suriname, but apparently the only such village in Brazil. Popular at weekends for dancing and swimming, the surrounding area is an environmental reserve with many water buffalo.

Essentials

A *Atalanta*, Av Coaracy Nunes 1148, T/F2331612. Laundry service, bar. **A** *Ekinox*, R Jovino Dinoá 1693, T2224378, F2237554, jef@brasnet.online.com.br. Library, French spoken, helpful, excellent restaurant. Highly recommended. **A** *Frota Palace*, Av Tiradentes 1104, T2233999, F2224488. Airport pick-up. **A** *Macapá*, Av Azarias Neto 17, on waterfront, T2231144, F2231115. Pool, tennis courts, convention centre. Recommended. **A** *Marabaixo*, R Cândido Mendes 340, T2237853, F2232157. Apartment hotel, meals available. **B** *Açai Palace*, Av Antônio Coelho de Carvalho 1399, T2234899, 20 minutes from centre. Cheaper without a/c. Recommended. **B** *Gloria*, Leopoldo Machado 2085, T2220984. **B** *Mara*, R São José 2390, T2220859, F2234905. A/c, TV, fridge, good. **C** *Santo Antônio*, Av Coriolano Jucá 485, T2220226, **D** in dormitory, near main praça. Fan, good breakfast extra. **D** *Mercúrio*, R Cândido Mendes 1300, 2nd floor, T2231699, close to Praça São José (where bus from Porto Santana stops).

Sleeping

Cantino Bahiano, *Martinho's Peixaria* and *Peixaria Amazonas* are good fish restaurants on Av Beira-Rio, south of the Fortaleza. *Chalé*, Av Pres Vargas 499. Good food and nice atmosphere. *Le Chateau*, Av 13 de Setembro 2022, corner of Barão de Mauá, T2422481. Small and intimate but a long way from the centre. *Soho*, Av Capt Pedro Baião, 2201. Chinese. *Zero Grau*, R Leopoldo Machado 2405. Pizzas. *Bom Paladar Kilo's*, Av Pres Vargas 456. Pay by weight buffet. Excellent ice cream made from local fruits, try *cupuaçu*, *Sorveteria Jesus de Nazare*, R Leopoldo Machado 737. *Sorveteria Macapá*, R São José 1676.

Eating

Rithimus, R Odilardo Silva 1489, T2222354. Good for local rhythm *Brega*. *Arena*, R Hamilton Silva. Food and drink kiosks in *Complexo Beira Rio* have live music most evenings.

Bars & nightclubs

Art galleries *Cândido Portinari*, corner of R Cândido Mendes and Av Raimundo Álvares da Costa. Exhibits of local art. **Cinemas** In *Macapá Shopping*, R Leopoldo Machado 2334. **Theatre** *Teatro das Bacabeiras*, R Cândido Mendes. Concerts, poetry and plays.

Entertainment

Marabaixo is the traditional music and dance festival held for 40 days after *Easter*. 14 August, *Festa de São Joaquim* held in Curiaú. The Sambódromo has parades of Escolas de Samba at *Carnival* and Quadrilhas during *São João* in June.

Festivals

Macapá and Porto Santana (*population*: 105,000) were declared a customs-free zone in 1992. There are now many cheap imported goods available from shops in the centre. In the handicraft complex *Casa do Artesão*, Av Azárias Neto, Monday-Saturday 0800-1900, craftsmen produce their wares onsite. A feature is pottery decorated with local manganese ore, also woodcarvings and leatherwork.

Shopping

The Amazon

Transport
See also Ins & outs, page 604

Car hire *Localiza*, R Independência 30, T2232799, and airport T2242336. *Sila Rent a Car*, Av Procópio Rola 1346, T2241443.

Air Airport, 4 km from centre, T2232323. International flights to Cayenne and Paramaribo. Domestic flights to Belém, Belo Horizonte, Boa Vista, Brasília, Breves, Manaus, Oiapoque, Rio de Janeiro, Santarém and São Paulo. Air taxi service with *Rio Norte*.

Boats To **Belém**, *Atlântica*, fast catamaran 8 hours, 3 times a week, US$30, reservations at *Martinica*, Jovino Dinoá 2010, T2235777, F2223569. Slower but slightly cheaper boats are *Bom Jesus*, *Comandante Solon*, *São Francisco de Paulo*, *Silja e Souza* of Souzamar, Cláudio Lúcio Monteiro 1375, Santana, T2811946, car ferry with *Silnave*, T2234011. Purchase tickets from offices 2 days in advance (*Agencia Sonave*, R São José 2145, T2239090, sells tickets for all boats). Also smaller boats to **Breves** as well as a regular direct service to **Santarém** (see **River transport**, page 598).

Buses New rodoviária on BR-156, north of Macapá. *Estrela de Ouro*, office on the main square, in front of the cathedral, leaves daily at 2000, and *Cattani*, office on Nunes between São José and Cándido Mendes, leaves daily at 0630 to **Amapá** (US$20), **Calçoene** (US$25, 7 hours) and **Oiapoque** (12 hours – dry season – with several rest stops, 14-24 hours in rainy season, US$35). The Oiapoque bus does not go into Amapá or Calçoene and it is therefore very inconvenient to break the trip at these places.

Pick-up trucks run daily to various locations throughout Amapá, crowded on narrow benches in the back, or pay more to ride in the cab. Despite posted schedules, they leave when full. To **Oiapoque** at 0800, 10-12 hours, US$35 cab, US$15 in back, to **Lourenço** at 0900.

Trains Limited services from Porto Santana to Serra do Navio.

Directory **Airline offices** *META*, Av Mendonça Júnior 18, T2234628. *Penta*, Av Mendonça Júnior 13D, T2235226. *Rio Norte*, at airport, T2220033. *TAM*, at airport, T2232688. *Varig*, R Cândido Mendes 1039, T2234612. *Vasp*, R Independência 146, T2241016. **Banks** *Banco do Brasil*, R Independência 250, and *Bradesco*, R Cândido Mendes 1316, have Plus ATMs for VISA withdrawals. *Câmbios* (cash only): *Casa Francesa*, R Independência 232. *Monopólio*, Av Isaac Alcoubre 80. Both US$ and French francs can be exchanged here. Best to buy francs in Belém if heading for Guyane as *câmbios* in Macapá are reluctant to sell them and they are more expensive and hard to obtain at the border. **Communications** Post Office: Av Corialano Jucá. Telephone: R São José 2050. Open 0730-2200. Internet: *@llnet* in Macapá Shopping. **Embassies & consulates** *France*, at Pousada Ekinox (see above). Visas are not issued for non-Brazilians. **Hospitals & medical services** *Geral*, Av FAB, T2126127. *Hospital São Camila & São Luiz*, R Marcelo Candia 742, T2231514. **Libraries** R São José, next to cathedral. **Tour companies & travel agents** *Amapá Turismo*, in *Hotel Macapá*, T2232667. *Fénix*, R Cândido Mendes 374, T/F2238200, and R Jovino Dinoá 1489, T2235353. **Tourist offices** *Detur*, Av Raimundo Álvares da Costa 18, Centro, CEP 68906-020, T2230627, F2230567, mcp10009@zaz.com.br. Branch at airport. **Useful addresses** *Ibama*, R Hamilton Silva 1570, Santa Rita, CEP 68906-440, Macapá, T/F2141100.

North of Macapá

The road north to the Guyane border (BR-156) is due to be completely paved by 2001. Although precarious in places, it is open throughout the year with buses and pick-ups operating even in the wet season. At all times, however, take food and water for the journey as services are scarce. Gasoline and diesel (not alcohol) are available along the road, but drivers should take extra fuel from Macapá.

Daniel Ludwig and the Jari Project

In the 1960s, the American billionaire and supertanker magnate, Daniel K Ludwig, investigated the possibilities of converting an area of Amazon rainforest into a large-scale, commercially viable plantation, producing wood for pulp and timber. His experts had convinced him that a tree called Gmelina arborea *(originally from Burma and India) would grow in sufficient volume, and fast enough in an equatorial climate, to fulfil Ludwig's dream of supplying the world's wood pulp needs before the end of the 20th century. Politically and, apparently, agriculturally, conditions favoured Brazil, so Ludwig bought four million acres of land (at only US$1 per acre) on the northern shore of the Amazon and the east and west banks of the Rio Jari, which forms the border between Amapá and Pará. As two lengthy articles by Dr Jerry A Shields in the* South American Explorer *magazine in January and April 1993 show, the project was beset with difficulties and delays, not least the failure of the* Gmelina *to grow quickly enough in the rainforest soil. Controversy surrounded every aspect of Jari, environmental, political/nationalistic, social and economic, and Ludwig had to sink an enormous amount of money into the land that he had cleared of jungle. Parallel with the forestry project were agricultural schemes (for example, huge rice paddies), kaolin production and bauxite mining. Ludwig himself ran out of enthusiasm in 1981, when he put Jari up for sale. The Brazilian government, which had initially encouraged the project, had to garner funds from a wide variety of public and private sources to buy Ludwig out and cover Jari's debts. By 1993 the pulp plant was operating profitably, but whether it could be called a success is a matter of debate. Loren McIntyre, in the June 1993 issue of the* South American Explorer, *in which he updated Shields' report and questioned some of his conclusions, was not pessimistic about the future. Daniel Ludwig himself died in 1992, aged 95.*

North of Macapá the road divides at **Porto Grande**, and a branch heads northwest to Serra do Navio where manganese extraction has now ended (*Hotel Serra do Navio* and several bars and restaurants). The BR-156 continues north, passing the turn-offs for two jungle hotels, *Recanto Ecológico Sonho Meu*, Km 108, T2341298, and *Pontal das Pedras* (**B**), Km 109, T2512781, restaurant, fishing, boat trips, ecological trail, popular at weekends, recommended. The road goes to **Ferreira Gomes** on the shores of the Rio Araguari, where the pavement ends. Further on is **Amapá**, formerly the territorial capital and location of a Second World War American airbase. There are a few hotels, *Hotel Amapá* (**C**), T4211108, and another, which is clean and comfortable, one block from the square towards docks, turn right, second house on the left. Beyond Amapá is **Calçoene**, with a government-owned hotel (**D**) by the bus stop, which serves expensive food in an adjoining canteen; very cheap sleeping space is also advertized in a café on the Oiapoque road. North of Calçoene a road branches west to **Lourenço**, whose gold fields continue to produce even after various decades of prospecting. The main road continues north across the Rio Caciporé and on to the border with French Guyane at Oiapoque, on the river of the same name. Seven kilometres to the west is Clevelândia do Norte, a military outpost and the end of the road in Brazil.

The Amazon

Oiapoque

This is a remote place, 90 kilometres inland from Cabo Orange, Brazil's north-ernmost point on the Atlantic coast, with its share of contraband, illegal migration and drug trafficking. It is also the gateway to gold fields in the interior of both Brazil and Guyane. It is quite a rough place and the visitor should be cautious, especially late at night. Prices here are high but still lower than in neighbouring Guyane. The **Cachoeira Grande Roche** rapids can be visited, upstream along the Oiapoque River, where it is possible to swim, US$30 by motor boat. Mountain bikes can be rented at Jance de Aluguel in the street parallel to the riverfront for US$10 daily. The Associação dos Povos Indígenas de Oiapoque, in front of the *Banco do Brasil*, gives information about the indigenous peoples in the area, such as the Uaçá Indian Reserve.

Sleeping & eating   **C** *Trânsito*, Av Joaquim Caetano da Silva, on the riverfront. Clean, with breakfast, fridge, TV, restaurant. **D** *Kayama*, on the same street, No 760, T5211448. A/c and bath, **E** with fan, good, international calls. Another, **F**, next door, basic. **D** *Pousada Central*, one street back from the river. A/c, bath, **E** with fan and shared bath. Also **F** *Sonho Meu*, basic. Other cheap hotels along the waterfront are mainly used by Brazilians waiting to cross to Guyane. *Restaurant Paladar Drinks*, 1 block up from the river, expensive. *Pantanal Bar*, next to the monument at riverfront, has dancing at weekends.

Transport   **Air** Flights to Macapá 3 times a week. **Buses** *Estrela de Ouro* leaves for **Macapá** from the waterfront, daily at 1000, 12 hours (dry season), 14-24 hours (wet season), US$35, also Cattani. Pick-up trucks depart from the same area when full, US$35 in cab, US$15 in the back. **Boats** Occasional cargo vessels to Belém or Macapá (Porto Santana).

Directory   **Banks** It is possible to exchange US$ and reais to francs, but dollar rates are low and TCs are not accepted anywhere. *Banco do Brasil*, Av Barão do Rio Branco, open 1000-1500, reais to francs and Visa facilities. Visa users can also withdraw reais at *Bradesco*, exchanging these to francs. Gold merchants, like *Casa Francesa* on the riverfront and a *câmbio* in the market, will sell reais for US$ or French francs. Rates are even worse in St-Georges. Best to buy francs in Belém, or abroad. **Communications** Post Office: Av Barão do Rio Branco, open 0900-1200, 1400-1700. **Useful addresses** Immigration: Polícia Federal for Brazilian exit stamp is on the road to Calçoene, about 500m from the river.

Frontier with Guyane   Motorized canoes cross to St-Georges de L'Oyapock, 10 minutes downstream, F20 per person, slightly cheaper in reais, bargain. A vehicle ferry will operate until a bridge is eventually built. *Catraias* (decrepit canoes) carry illegal migrants for night landings, expensive, dangerous, definitely not recommended.

    Into Guyane An unmade road from St-Georges to Cayenne has been cut through the jungle, but it is best to fly or take a boat. For more details, see the *South American Handbook*.

Pará

This northern state has many places of ecological interest, such as the fluvial island of Marajó in the Amazon Delta and the Amazônia national park on the River Tapajós. It is an extremely good location for sport fishing and the local cuisine is based around the many varieties of fish and fruits available in the region. The capital Belém is a good place to begin or end a journey on the River Amazon, and Santarém with its nearby river beaches is an excellent place to spend a few days while changing boats.

Belém was established because of its strategic position in 1616 as part of the Portuguese drive to claim the territory to the west of its Atlantic seaboard possessions, and to prevent French, Dutch and English incursions into the area. During the following 10 years, the Portuguese engaged in a war with the Tupinambá Indians, which, together with disease and enslavement, saw to the decimation of the indigenous peoples of Pará. It was not long before Belém became the centre for slaving expeditions into the Amazon basin, but at the same time it was the starting-point for Brazilian expansion beyond the line drawn by the Treaty of Tordesillas. For instance, Pedro Teixeira set out in October 1637 from Belém on a journey which took him all the way to Quito and back. The Portuguese of Pará, together with those of Maranhão, treated the Indians abominably. Being remote from the longer-established colonies, and having stronger links with distant Portugal itself, both places were relatively lawless. In 1655, the Jesuits, under Antônio Vieira, attempted to lessen the abuses, while enticing the Indians to 'descend' to the *aldeias* around Belém. This eventually led to further misery when smallpox spread from the south, striking the Pará *aldeias* in the 1660s.

Soon after Brazil's independence, the Revolta da Cabanagem, a rebellion by the poor blacks, Indians and mixed-race *cabanos* (who lived in *cabanas*), was led against the Portuguese-born class that dominated the economy. The movement began in 1823 when the Provincia do Grão Pará was proclaimed independent. It came to an end in 1840 when the *cabanos* finally surrendered, but the worst years of violence were 1835-36. Some estimates say 30,000 were killed. The state's strategic location once again became important during the Second World War, when Belém was used as an airbase by the Americans to hunt German submarines in the Atlantic.

Today, with a population of around 5,770,000 and an area of 1,253,164 square kilometres, Pará is the second largest state in the union. It possesses some 40 percent of Brazil's inland waters, including the majority of the rivers Amazon, Tapajós, Tocantins and Xingu. The more isolated parts of the state are linked by air as road travel can be difficult during the rainy season from December to May.

It is prominent in many economic activities. The dam at Tucuruí provides hydroelectric power. Mining of bauxite, iron, gold and copper amongst other minerals takes place in large quantities. Agriculture and fishing is another extremely important sector.

Belém

Population: 1,500,000
Phone code: 091
Colour map 1, grid A6

Belém do Pará, 145 kilometres from the open sea and slightly south of the equator, is the great port of the Amazon. With mean temperatures of 26°C, it is hot, but frequent showers freshen the streets. The city has much of cultural interest and its nightlife is also very good.

Ins & outs
See also Transport, page 615

Getting there Val-de-Cans airport is 12 km from the city. Buses take 40 minutes to the centre and charge US$0.50. Taxis charge US$10. Belém can be reached from Cayenne, Miami and Paramaribo as well as from Brasília, Rio de Janeiro and other cities in Brazil by air. There are road connections from São Luis and the northeastern coast as well as a 3-day bus link from São Paulo via Brasília. Thr rodoviária for interstate buses is 3 km from the centre; bus US$0.50, taxi US$5-7 to the centre. Boats arrive at the port fom Macapá, Manaus and Santarém as well as other parts of the Amazon region and delta.

Getting around The city centre is easily explored on foot. City buses and taxis run to all the sites of interest and transport hubs away from the centre.

History

Belém was founded by Francisco Caldeira de Castelo Branco on 12 January 1616. The first settlement was based on the Forte do Presépio, now Forte do Castelo; as the town grew it was called Santa Maria de Belém do Grão Pará. Other than its importance as a slaving port, Belém was not a wealthy colonial possession until, in the mid-18th century, the Portuguese government encouraged the import of African slaves to work new agriculture ventures in which it was investing. The population rose from 4,000 to 10,000 as settlers came to make the area thrive. The expansion lasted only until the end of the century. The Revolta da Cabanagem (see above) brought disaster to the city; a memorial designed by Oscar Niemeyer stands at the eastern entrance to Belém. Further devastation came in 1850 in an epidemic of yellow fever. The city's fortunes dramatically revived during the rubber boom (see below under Manaus), which accounts for the French belle-epoque appearance of much of the city centre. Decline followed the collapse of the rubber trade, but there was a brief revival during the Second World War. The city's importance as a port and gateway between the Atlantic and Amazon should not be forgotten, and the waterfront, with its docks and markets, exhibits the continuity between the earliest days of exporting Amazonian produce and today's merchants. It is, as one local guide puts it, a synthesis of the Amazon world.

Sights

There are some good squares and fine buildings set along broad avenues. Belém used to be called the 'City of Mango Trees' and there are still many such trees remaining. There was much renovation of public places in 1985-87, and a building boom in the early 1990s sent up many new apartment towers.

The largest square is the **Praça da República**, where there are free

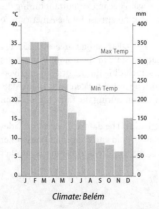

Climate: Belém

afternoon concerts; the main business and shopping area is along the wide Avenida Presidente Vargas, leading to the river and the narrow streets which parallel it.

The neoclassical, recently restored, **Teatro da Paz** is one of the largest theatres in the country. It was built between 1868 and 1874. It stages performances by national and international stars and also gives free concert and theatre shows; worth visiting. ■ *Tuesday-Friday 0900-1800, tours cost US$1.50.*

Visit the **Cathedral** (1748) on Praça Frei Caetano Brandão, another neoclassical building which contains several remarkable paintings. ■ *Monday 1500-1800, Tuesday-Friday 0800-1100, 1530-1800.* The Cathedral stands directly opposite the 18th-century **Santo Aleixandre** church, now being restored, which is noted for its wood carving.

The 17th-century **Mercês** church (1640), near the market, is the oldest church in Belém. It forms part of an architectural group known as the Mercedário, the rest of which was heavily damaged by fire in 1978 and is now being restored.

The **Basílica of Nossa Senhora de Nazaré** (1909), built from rubber wealth in romanesque style, is an absolute must for its beautiful marble and stained glass windows. It is on Praça Justo Chermont, Avenida Magalhães Barata. ■ *Monday-Saturday 0500-1130, 1400-2000, Sunday 0545-1130, 1430-2000.* A museum at the Basílica describes the Círio de Nazaré religious festival (see below).

The **Palácio Lauro Sodré** and **Museu do Estado do Pará**, on Praça Dom Pedro II, is a gracious 18th-century Italianate building. It contains Brazil's largest framed painting, 'The Conquest of Amazônia', by Domenico de Angelis. The building was the work of the Italian architect Antonio Landi who also designed the Cathedral and was the administrative seat of the colonial government. During the rubber boom many new decorative features were added. ■ *Monday-Friday 0900-1800, Saturday 1000-1800.* Also on Praça Dom Pedro II is the **Palácio Antônio Lemos**, which houses the **Museu de Arte de Belém** as well as the **Prefeitura**. It was originally built as the Palácio Municipal between 1868 and 1883, and is a fine example of the imperial neoclassical style. In the downstairs rooms there are old views of Belém; upstairs the historic rooms, beautifully renovated, contain furniture, paintings etc, which are all well explained. ■ *Tuesday-Friday 0900-1200, 1400-1800, Saturday-Sunday 0900-1200.*

The Belém market, known as **Ver-o-Peso**, was the Portuguese Posto Fiscal, where goods were weighed to gauge taxes due, hence the name: 'see the weight'. It now has lots of gift shops selling charms for the local African-derived religion, *umbanda*; the medicinal herb and natural perfume stalls are also interesting. You can see giant river fish being unloaded around 0530, with frenzied wholesale buying for the next hour; a new dock for the fishing boats was built just upriver from the market in 1997. The area around the market swarms with people, including many armed thieves and pickpockets.

One of the most varied and colourful markets in South America

In the old town, too, is the **Forte do Castelo**, Praça Frei Caetano Brandão 117. The fort overlooks the confluence of the Rio Guamá and the Baía do Guajara and was where the Portuguese first set up their defences. It was rebuilt in 1878. ■ *Entry on request, T2230041.* Also on the site is a good restaurant, *Círculo Militar* (entry US$1; drinks and *salgadinhos* served on the ramparts from 1800 to watch the sunset). At the square on the waterfront below the fort, the *açaí* berries are landed nightly at 2300, after being picked in the jungle. *Açaí* berries, ground up with sugar and mixed with manioc, are a staple food in the region.

The **Bosque Rodrigues Alves**, Avenida Almirante Barroso 2305, is a 16 hectare public garden (really a preserved area of original flora), with a small

The Amazon

animal collection. ■ *0800-1700 closed Monday, T2262308, yellow bus marked 'Souza' or 'Cidade Nova' (any number) 30 minutes from Ver-o-Peso market, also bus from Cathedral.* The **Museu Emílio Goeldi**, Avenida Magalhães Barata 376, takes up a city block and consists of the museum proper (with a fine collection of Marajó Indian pottery, an excellent exhibition of Mebengokre Indian lifestyle), a zoological garden (including manatees) and botanical exhibits including Victoria Régia lilies. ■ *Tuesday-Thursday 0900-1200, 1400-1700, Friday 0900-1200, Saturday and Sunday 0900-1700, US$1, additional charges for specialist areas, now renovated. Take a bus from the Cathedral.* The **Murucutu** ruins, an old Jesuit foundation, are reached by the Ceará bus from Praça da República, through an unmarked door on the right of the Ceará bus station.

Excursions

A passenger ferry (*foca*) to the small town of **Barcarena** makes an interesting half-day trip, departures from Ver-o-Peso, US$1. A return trip on the ferry from Ver-o-Peso to **Icaoraci** provides a good view of the river. Several restaurants here serve excellent seafood; you can eat shrimp and drink coconut water and appreciate the breeze coming off the river. Icaoraci is 20 kilometres east of the city and is well known as a centre of ceramic production. The pottery is in Marajoara and Tapajonica style. Take the bus from Avenida Presidente Vargas to Icoaraci (one hour). Artisans are friendly and helpful, will accept commissions and send purchases overseas. ■ *Open all week, but best on Tuesday-Friday.*

The nearest beach is at **Outeiro** (35 kilometres) on an island near Icoaraci, about an hour by bus and ferry (the bus may be caught near the Maloca, an Indian-style hut near the docks which serves as a nightclub). A bus from

Belém orientation

Icoaraci to Outeiro takes 30 minutes. Further north is the island of **Mosqueiro** (86 kilometres), accessible by bridge and an excellent highway, with many beautiful sandy beaches and jungle inland. It is popular at weekends when traffic can be heavy (also July) and the beaches can get crowded and polluted. Buses Belém-Mosqueiro every hour from rodoviária, US$1.50, 80 minutes. There is also a ferry from Porto do Sal, on the street between Forte de Castelo and the cathedral. It takes about two hours. There are many hotels and weekend villas at the villages of Mosqueiro and Vila, which are recommended, but these may be full weekends and July. *Farol* (**B**), on Praia Farol, T7711219, 1920s architecture in good repair, small restaurant, good views. Restaurants at Mosqueiro include *Hotel Ilha Bela*, Av 16 de Novembro 409, recommended for fish, no evening meals. Highly recommended at Praia Chapeu Virado is *Marésia*. *Sorveteria Delícia*, Av 16 de Novembro, serves good local fruit ice creams and the owner buys dollars. Camping is easy.

Essentials

L *Hilton*, Av Pres Vargas 882, T2426500, F2252942. Pool, sauna, restaurants. **AL** *Equatorial Palace*, Av Braz de Aguiar 612, Nazaré, T2412000, F2235222, equatorial@belemnet.com.br. Gym, pool. **A** *Itaoca*, Av Pres Vargas 132, T2413434, F2410891. New, charming, but some rooms are noisy. **A** *Novotel*, Av Bernardo Sayão 4808, T2497111, F2497808. Pool, unprepossessing neighbourhood, far from centre (take Universidade bus). **A** *Regente*, Av Gov José Malcher 485, T2411222, F2420343, hregente@libnet.com.br. Modest but comfortable, good breakfast, some English-speaking staff. **A** *Sagres*, Av Gov José Malcher 2927, T2469556, F2268260, opposite rodoviária. Good meals, pool and gym. **A** *Vila Rica*, Av Júlio César 1777, T2571522, F2570222, 9 km from town. Free airport transfer, good rooms and service. **A** *Zoghbi Park*, R Padre Prudêncio 220, T/F2411800.

B *Le Massilia*, R Henrique Gurjão 236, T2247147. Also has French restaurant. **B** *Novo Avenida*, Av Pres Vargas 404, T2429953, F2238893, central. A/c, fridge, cheaper with fan. **C** *São Geraldo*, Trav Padre Prudêncio 56, T2234800, central. Recommended. **C** *Vidonho's*, R Ó de Almeida 476, T2421444, F2247499. A/c, fridge, good breakfast, in a side street.

D *Central*, Av Pres Vargas 290, T2423011, F2417177. Under same ownership as *Vidonho's*, with a/c (**E** without bath), some rooms noisy, but comfortable, good meals, a must for art-deco fans. Recommended. **D** *Esmeralda*, Trav Padre Prudêncio 407, T2228916, hotgege@interconect.com.br. French and English spoken. **D** *Sete-Sete*, Trav 1 de Março 677, T2227730, F2242346. Clean, comfortable, safe, with breakfast. Recommended. **D** *Ver-o-Peso*, Av Castilho França 208, T2412022, opposite Ver-o-Peso market. Rooftop restaurant, TV and fridge in room. Recommended. **D** *Vitória Rêgia*, Trav Frutuoso Guimarães 260, T/F2122077. With breakfast, more with a/c, bath, fridge (**E** without), safe. Recommended. **E** *Fortaleza*, Trav Frutuoso Guimarães 276. Very basic (will put you in contact with boat agent), but recommended for what is offered. **E** *Palacio das Musas*, Trav Frutuoso Guimarães 275, T2254022. Big rooms, clean, shared bath.

Camping Nearest at Mosqueiro, 86 km away.

Sleeping
■ *on map, page 614*
Price codes: see inside front cover
All hotels are fully booked during Círio (see box, page 615).
There are many cheap hotels close to waterfront, none too safe. There are several others near the rodoviária, which are generally OK

All the major hotels have good but expensive restaurants. The *Açaí* at the *Hilton*, T2426500. Recommended for regional dishes, daily lunch, dinner with live music and Sunday brunch. *Círculo Militar*, Praça Ferreira Cantão, situated in the grounds of Forte do Castelo, T2234374. Recommended for Belém's best Brazilian food and view over river (wide selection, try *filetena brasa*). *Churrascaria Rodeio*, Rodovia Augusto Montenegro Km 4, T2483223. Excellent meat, salad bar, reasonable prices. *Churrascaria Tucuruvi*, Trav Benjamin Constant 1843, Nazaré. Good value, generous

Eating
There are many street and market vendors who, although they should be viewed with care, often sell delicious local food

The Amazon

portions, tasty. *Roxy Bar*, Av Sen Lemos 231, T2244514. Delicious dishes named after Hollywood stars, pleasant, nice music, no a/c, open late, reasonable prices. *Casa Portuguesa*, R Sen Manoel Barata 897, T2424871. Good, inexpensive. *Lá em Casa*, Av Gov José Malcher 247, T2231212. Try *menu paraense*, good cooking, fashionable, expensive. *Okada*, R Boaventura da Silva 1522, past R Alcindo Cacela, T2463242. Japanese, excellent, try 'Steak House', various types of meat, rice and sauces, vegetables, all you can eat, also try *camarão à milanesa com salada*, good prices. *Miako*, Trav 1 de Março 766, behind Praça de República, T2422355. Very good medium-priced oriental food. Recommended. *Germania*, R Aristides Lobo 604. Munich-style, mid-price. Recommended. *Pizzaria Napolitano*, Praça Justo Chermont 12, T2225177. Pizzas and Italian dishes. *Cantina Italiana*, Trav Benjamin Constant 1401, T2252033. Very good Italian. Enthusiastically recommended. *Nectar*, Av Gentil Bittencourt, Trav Padre Eutíquio 248, pedestrian zone. Good vegetarian, lunch only. *Casa dos Sucos*, Av Pres Vargas, Praça da República. Serves 41 types of juice (including Amazonian fruits) and delicious chocolate cake (vegetarian restaurant upstairs, recommended for lunches). Specially recommended are some very good snack-bars (mostly outdoors in Belém), where you can buy anything up to a full meal, much cheaper than restaurants: *Charlotte*, Av Gentil Bittencourt 730, at Trav Quintino Bocaiúva. Best *salgadinhos* in the city, also good desserts, very popular. Many buffet-style restaurants along R Santo Antônio pedestrian mall and elsewhere in the *Comércio* district, including *Doce Vida Salgado*, Trav 1 de Março 217. Good food and prices, generally lunch only, good variety, pay by weight, prices average US$4 per kilo.

Belém

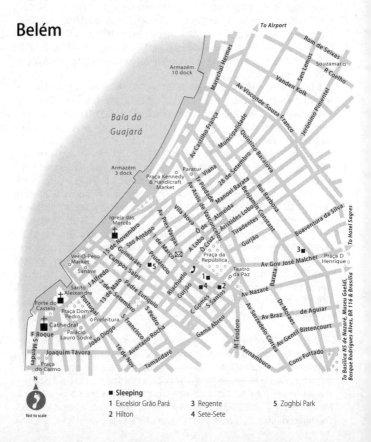

■ **Sleeping**
1 Excelsior Grão Pará
2 Hilton
3 Regente
4 Sete-Sete
5 Zoghbi Park

Not to scale

The Festival of Candles

Círio, the Festival of Candles in October, is based on the legend of the Nossa Senhora de Nazaré, whose image was found on the the site of her Basílica around 1700. On the second Sunday in October, a procession carries a copy of the Virgin's image from the Basílica to the cathedral. On the Monday, two weeks later, the image is returned to its usual resting place. There is a Círio museum in the crypt of the Basílica, enter at the right side of the church; free entry. The festival, which is *'cheio de coração' (full of heart)*, has attracted many major Brazilian artists and musicians. It has developed into a massive national festival and is highly recommended. The biggest carnival performers attend, along with important rock groups and an increasing contingent of international artists. The non-religious element of the festival is known as Carnabelém. For dates check with Paratur, T2233130.

Cherry Austin

African Bar, Praça Waldemar Henrique 2. Rock or Samba, weekends only. *Bar do Parque*, Praça da República, next to Municipal Theatre. *Bora Bora*, R Bernal do Couto 38, MPB and Pagode from 2100 until late Thursday-Sunday. *Cosanostra Caffé*, Trav Benjamin Constant 1507. 'Pub' atmosphere, a/c, expensive. *Colarinho Branco*, Av Visconde de Souza Franco, near the river. Popular. *Escapóle*, Rodovia Augusto Montenegro 400. Huge dance hall with various types of music, live and recorded, frequented by all age groups, open Wednesday-Saturday from 2200 (take a radio taxi for safety), no a/c, dress informally. *Olê Olá*, Av Tavares Bastos 1234. Disco, live music and dance floor. *Rhinos*, Av Nazaré 400. Good discotheque. **Bars & nightclubs**

Art galleries *Debret*, R Arcipreste Manoel Theodoro 630, Batista Campos, T2224046. Contemporary painting and sculpture, also has library specializing in art and philosophy. **Cinema** *Olímpia*, Av Pres Vargas 918. In existence for over 80 years and was the first cinema in Belém. **Theatre** *Margarida Schiwwazappa*, Av Gentil Bittencourt 650, T2222923. **Entertainment**

Maundy Thursday, half-day; *Good Friday*, all shops closed, all churches open and there are processions; **9 June**, *Corpus Christi*; **15 August**, accession of Pará to independent Brazil; **7 September**, *Independence Day*, commemorated on the day with a military parade, and with a students' parade on the preceding Sunday (morning); *Círio* through **October** (see box); **30 October**, half-day; **2 November**, *All Souls Day*; **8 December**, *Immaculate Conception*; *Christmas Eve*, half-day. **Festivals**

Iate Clube do Pará, Av Bernardo Sayão 3324. Swimming pools and sports courts. **Sports**

Shopping Iguatemi, Trav Padre Eutique 1078. Indian handicrafts shop, Praça Kennedy, set in a garden with Amazonian plants and animals. *Parfumaria Orion*, Trav Frutuoso Guimarães 268. Has a wide variety of perfumes and essences from Amazonian plants, much cheaper than tourist shops. The *Complexo São Brás* on Praça Lauro Sodré. Has a handicraft market and folkloric shows in a building dating from 1911. Belém is a good place to buy hammocks, look in the street parallel to the river, 1 block inland from Ver-o-Peso. Bookshop with English titles in the arcade on Av Pres Vargas. **Camera repairs** *Neemias Teixeira Lima*, R Sen Manoel Barata 274, Sala 211, T2249941. **Shopping**

Car hire *Localiza*, Av Governador José Malcher 1365, T2122700, and at airport T0800-992000. **Transport**
See also Ins & outs, page 610

The Amazon

Air International flights to Cayenne, Miami and Paramaribo. Domestic flights to Altamira, Brasília, Breves, Carajás, Fortaleza, Imperatriz, Macapá, Manaus, Marabá, Monte Dourado, Rio de Janeiro, Santarém, São Luís and São Paulo. Bus 'Perpétuo Socorro-Telégrafo' or 'Icoaraci', every 15 minutes from the Prefeitura, Praça Felipe Patroni, to the airport, 40 minutes, US$0.50. Taxi to airport, US$10 (ordinary taxis are cheaper than Coop taxis, buy ticket in advance in Departures side of airport). The airport has a hotel booking service but it is operated by, and is exclusive to, 5 of the more expensive hotels, discounts offered.

Buses The rodoviária is at the end of Av Gov José Malcher, 3 km from the centre, take Aeroclube, Cidade Novo, No 20 bus, or Arsenal or Canudos buses, US$0.50, or taxi, US$5 (day), US$7 (night) (at rodoviária you are given a ticket with the taxi's number on it, threaten to go to the authorities if the driver tries to overcharge). It has a good snack bar and showers (US$0.10) and 2 agencies with information and tickets for riverboats. Regular bus services to all major cities. To **Marabá**, US$20 (16 hours) on the Transamazônica, direct with Transbrasiliana. To **Santarém**, via Marabá once a week (US$45, more expensive than by boat and can take longer, goes only in dry season). To **São Luís**, 2 a day, US$20, 13 hours, interesting journey through marshlands. To **Fortaleza**, US$35-40 (24 hours), several companies. To **Salvador**, US$50. To **Rio de Janeiro**, US$85. To **Cuiabá**, US$65, direct with *Açailândia*.

Boats River services to Santarém, Manaus, and intermediate ports (see **River transport**, page 598). The larger ships berth at Portobrás/Docas do Pará (the main commercial port), either at Armazém (warehouse) No 3 at the foot of Avenida Pres Vargas, or at Armazém No 10, a few blocks further north (entrance on Avenida Marechal Hermes, corner of Avenida Visconde de Souza Franco). The guards will sometimes ask to see your ticket before letting you into the port area, but tell them you are going to speak with a ship's captain. Ignore the touts who approach you. Smaller vessels (sometimes cheaper, usually not as clean, comfortable or safe) sail from small docks along the Estrada Nova (not a safe part of town). Take a Cremação bus from Ver-o-Peso.

To **Macapá** (Porto Santana) daily service. *Silja e Souza* of **Souzamar**, Trav Dom Romualdo Seixas, corner of R Jerônimo Pimentel, T2220719, and *Comandante Solon* of **Sanave** (Serviço Amapaense de Navegação, Av Castilho Franca 234, opposite Ver-o-Peso, T2227810). Via Breves, *ENAL*, T2245210. There are 2 desks selling tickets for private boats in the rodoviária; some hotels (eg *Fortaleza*) recommend agents for tickets. Purchase tickets from offices 2 days in advance. Smaller boats to Macapá also sail from Estrada Nova.

Hitchhiking Going south, take bus to Capanema, 3½ hours, US$2.30, walk 500m from the rodoviária to BR-316 where trucks stop at the gas station.

Directory **Airline offices** *Penta*, Av Sen Lemos 4700, T2447777. *Surinam Airways*, R Gaspar Viana 488, T2127144, F2247879. English spoken, helpful with information and documentation. *Taba*, Av Dr Freitas 1191, international airport, T2574000. *Transbrasil*, Av Pres Vargas 780, T2126977. *Varig*, Av Pres Vargas 768, T2243344, airport T2570481. *Vasp*, Av Pres Vargas 345, T2122496, airport T2570944.

Banks open 0900-1630, but foreign exchange only until 1300 **Banks** Exchange rates are generally the best in the north of the country, although you can't get cash against MasterCard anywhere. French francs are readily available, but rates vary markedly between different *câmbios* and change rapidly. *Banco do Brasil*, Av Pres Vargas, near *Hotel Central*, good rates. *Banco de Amazônia* (Basa), on Pres Vargas, good rates for TC (Amex or Citicorp only), but does not change cash. *Itaú*, R Boaventura 580, good TC and cash rates. *Banorte*, R Cons João Alfredo 331, Centro. *Colombo*, Av Gov José Malcher 815, T2424092, F2411103. American Express representative. *American Express*, R Gen Gurjão and Av Pres Vargas, No 676, also representative office in *Hilton Hotel*, helpful. *Casas de câmbio*: *Carajás*, Av Presidente Vargas 762, Galeria da Assambléia Paraense, Loja 12, also at Pres Vargas 620. *Casa Francesa*, Trav Padre Prudêncio 40.

The Amazon

Monopólio, Av Pres Vargas 325, térreo do Ed Palácio do Rádio. *Turvicam*, Av Conselheiro Furtado 1558A, also at Av Pres Vargas 640, Loja 03. *Ourominas*, R 28 de Setembro 79. *Loja Morpho*, Pres Vargas 362. *Hilton, Central* (cash only), *Ver-o-Peso* (cash and cheques, reasonable rates) and *Victória Rêgia Hotels*.

Communications Post Office: Av Pres Vargas 498. Also handles telegrams and fax. **Telephone:** *Telemar*, Av Pres Vargas. Internet: *Convert*, Shopping Iguatemi, 3rd floor, US$3 per hr.

Embassies & consulates *Denmark* (Consul Arne Hvidbo), R Senador Barata 704, sala 1503, T2235888 (PO Box 826). *Finland*, Rodovia Arthur Bernardes 1393, Bairro Telégrafo, T2330333. *France*, R Pres Pernambuco 269, T2246818 (also for French Guiana, South Africans must apply in South Africa). *Germany*, Edif Comendador Pinho, Trav Campos Sales 63, room 404, T2225666. *Italy*, R Gaspar Viana 253, 1st floor, T2416489. *Netherlands*, Av Cláudio Saunder 1694, T2245811. *Sweden*, R Santo Antônio 316, mailing address Caixa Postal 111, T2224788, open 1600 1800. *UK*, Robin Burnett, Edif Palladium Centre, room 410, Av Gov José Malcher 811, T2225074. *USA*, Trav Padre Eutíquio 1309, T2230800. *Venezuela*, opposite French Consulate, R Pres Pernambuco 270, T2226396 (Venezuelan visa takes 3 hrs, costs US$30 for most nationalities, but we are told that it is better to get a visa at Manaus; latest reports indicate that a yellow fever vaccination certificate is not required but it is best to check in advance – see also **Health**, next paragraph).

Hospitals & medical services Health: a yellow fever certificate or inoculation is mandatory. It is best to get a yellow fever vaccination at home (always have your certificate handy) and avoid the risk of recycled needles. Medications for malaria prophylaxis are not sold in Belém pharmacies. You can theoretically get them through the public health service, but this is hopelessly complicated. Such drugs are sometimes available at pharmacies in smaller centres, eg Santarém and Macapá. Bring an adequate supply from home. *Clínica de Medicina Preventativa*, Av Bras de Aguiar 410 (T2221434), will give injections, English spoken, open 0730-1200, 1430-1900 (Saturday 0800-1100). *Hospital da Ordem Terceira*, Trav Frei Gil de Vila Nova 59, T2122777, doctors speak some English, free consultation. The British consul has a list of English-speaking doctors.

Language schools *Unipop*, Av Sen Lemos 557, T2249074. Portuguese course for foreigners.

Laundry *Lav e Lev*, R Dr Moraes 576.

Libraries *UFPA*, Av Augusto Correa 1, T2111140, university library with many titles on Amazônia.

Security Police: for reporting crimes, R Santo Antônio and Trav Frei Gil de Vila Nova. Belém has its share of crime and is prone to gang violence. Take sensible precautions especially at night.

Tour companies & travel agents *Amazon Star*, R Henrique Gurjão 236, T/F2126244, Mobile 9827911, amazstar@interconect.com.br. French run, good half-day boat tour with jungle walk, as well as tours to Marajó. *Angel*, in Hilton Hotel, T2242111, F2242030, angel@datanetbbs.com.br, tours and events, issues ISIC and IYHA cards. *Gran-Para*, Av Pres Vargas 676, T2123233, F2415531, good for airline bookings.

Tourist offices *Belemtur*, Av Gov José Malcher 592, T2420900, F2413194, belemtur@cinbesa.com.br, also at airport T2116151. *Paratur*, Praça Kennedy on the waterfront, T2232130/2126601, F2236198, by the handicraft shop, helpful, many languages spoken, has a good map of Belém in many languages (but some references are incorrect), town guidebook, US$2.75.

Useful addresses *Ibama*, Av Conselheiro Furtado 1303, Batista Campos, CEP 66035-350, T2412621/2245899, F2231299.

Voltage 110 AC, 60 cycles.

The Amazon

Around Belém

Marajó

Colour map 1, grid A5 This is the world's largest river island, a claim disputed by the Bananal, which is flooded in the rainy season December-June. It provides a suitable habitat for the water buffalo, which are said to have swum ashore after a shipwreck. They are now farmed in large numbers; try the cheese and milk. Marajó is also home to many birds, crocodiles and other wildlife, and has several good beaches. It is crowded at weekends and in the July holiday season. The island was the site of the pre-Columbian Marajoaras culture.

Ponta de Pedras Boats leave Belém, near Porto do Sal, most days for the five-hour crossing to Ponta de Pedras. Seats are US$3.60, two-berth cabins US$38. Buses for Soure or Salvaterra meet the boat. In Ponta de Pedras is *Hotel Ponta de Pedras* (**D**), which serves good meals. Bicycles can be hired at US$1 per hour to explore beaches and the interior of the island. Fishing boats make the eight-hour trip to Cachoeira do Arari (one hotel, **D**), where there is a Marajó museum. A 10-hour boat trip from Ponta de Pedras goes to the Arari lake where there are two villages: Jenipapo (one *pousada*, **E**), built on stilts, forró dancing at weekends; and Santa Cruz, which is less primitive, but less interesting; a hammock and a mosquito net are essential. There is a direct boat service to Belém twice a week.

Soure The capital of the island is Soure. There are fine beaches: Araruna, two kilometres
Population: 17,500 away; take supplies and supplement with coconuts and crabs, beautiful walks along the shore; do Pesqueiro (bus from Praça da Matriz, 1030, returns 1600, eat at *Maloca*, good, cheap, big, deserted beach, 13 kilometres away); and Caju-Una (15 kilometres). A ferry from Belém sails weekends, only departing from the old Enasa dock near the Ver-o-Peso market (four hours, US$5). Small craft await passengers from the Enasa boats, for Salvaterra village (good beaches and bars: seafood), US$12, 10 minutes, or trips are bookable in Belém from Mururé, T2410891. There is a ferry from the 'escalinha' at the end of Avenida Presidente Vargas to Porto do Cámara (three hours, US$10). Then take a bus to Salvaterra and a ferry to Soure. Boats return from Cámara at 0800 and 1100. There is a taxi-plane service to Soure.

Changing money is only **Sleeping and eating** **A** *Pousada das Guarás*, Av Beira Mar, Salvaterra, T/F7651133.
possible at very poor Well-equipped, on beach. **B** *Hotel Ilha do Marajó*, 8a Rua 10, Matinha, T7411315
rates. Take plenty of (Belém 2245966). **D** *Pousada Parque Floresta*, good meals. **C** *Cosampa*, Trav 14,
insect repellent T2293928. Hot showers, free transfer from docks. **C** Soure (3a Rua, Centro), walk straight on from Enasa dock, then take third street on left, a/c, basic. **C** *Waldeck*, Trav 12, T7411414. Only 4 rooms. **E** *Pensão* at 2a R 575 (*Bar Guaraní*). Simple. Recommended. *Canecão*, Praça da Matriz. Sandwiches, meals. Recommended.

East and south of Belém

A good asphalted road, BR-316, leads east out of the city. A branch goes north to the coast town of Salinópolis, some 223 kilometres, at the extreme end of the eastern part of the Amazon Delta. Various paved roads branch off: 118 kilometres out of Belém the BR-010 turns right, the paved highway south to Brasília (2,120 kilometres). Straight on, the road leads to Bragança, the centre of an early, unsuccessful, attempt in the 1900s to transfer the population to Amazônia. At Capanema, 120 kilometres from Belém, 54 kilometres before Bragança, the BR-316 for São Luís, Teresina, Fortaleza and Recife branches right.

This seaside resort has many small places where you can eat and drink at night by the waterfront and a fine sandy beach nearby (buses and cars drive on to the beach). It is a peaceful place mid-week and is best during the holiday month of July. Atalaia, an island opposite Salinópolis, is pleasant and can be reached by taxi (US$6) or with a fisherman. Salinópolis is four hours from Belém by bus on a good road, US$6.

Salinópolis
Population: 28,500

Sleeping and eating A *Atalaia*, on Atalaia island, 15 km from Salinópolis, T/F8241122. Simple, beautiful setting, reserve in advance, take a taxi. **A** *Solar*, Av Beira Mar, T8231823. With bath, best in town, good restaurant. **A** *Jeanne d'Arc*, Av João Pessoa 555, T/F8231422. With breakfast. *Bife de Ouro*, Av Dr Miguel Santa Brígida, opposite filling station. Simple, but excellent fish and shrimp, always crowded for lunch. *Gringo Louco*, further out than Atalaia, 15 km (take taxi or hitch), at Cuiarana beach, follow signs. Gringo owner serves good, unusual dishes, and some 'wild' drinks known as 'bombs', popular.

This is a pleasant city and a good place to stop if you prefer not to stay in Belém *en route* to São Luís. *Diolindina* (**B**), Av Pres Médici 424, T8211667, has small clean rooms with fridge and bath, air conditioning, breakfast buffet and safe parking. Recommended. There are good restaurants and supermarket a opposite. Not as good is *São Luís* (**D**).

Capanema

    Tomé-Açu, south of Belém on the Rio Acará-Mirim, affords a view of life on a smaller river than the Amazon; three buses a day from Belém, US$8. *Hotel Las Vegas*, owner Fernando is very friendly. Boat back to Belém on Sunday at 1100, arriving 1800, US$5.

Along the Transamazônica

The Transamazônica, about 5,000 kilometres in length, represents the greater part of a direct road connection between Brazil's furthest east and furthest west points. It skirts the southern edge of the Amazonian plain, linking Estreito (junction with the Belém-Brasília highway, north of Araguaína, see page 676), Marabá (on the Tocantins river), Altamira (on the Xingu), São Luís do Tapajós, near Itaituba (on the Tapajós), Jacarèacanga, Humaitá (on the Madeira), Rio Branco and Japim, in the far west of the State of Acre. It was officially opened in December 1973. Parts of it have been paved, but the harsh climate and inadequate maintenance have caused much deterioration. Some sections are often totally impassable throughout the rainy season (for example, Santarém to the Belém-Brasília Highway). Others may require a four-wheel drive and winch. There are stretches with regular truck traffic and scheduled bus services, but as conditions are constantly changing, detailed local inquiry is essential before heading out. The journey along the Transamazônica can be dangerous and speaking some Portuguese is essential. Also ensure that you have sufficient *reais*.

The Amazon

Marabá

Near Marabá are beaches on the Tocantins and Itacaiúnas rivers, which are best visited June-October. With the filling of the Tucuruí dam, the town has been moved; even so, it suffers from flooding. There is a bridge across the Tocantins at Marabá. There are essentially three parts of Marabá: Marabá Velha (also called Marabá Pioneira), Marabá Nova and Cidade Nova. The distance between Marabá Nova and Velha is about 2½ kilometres. A good travel

Population: 150,000
Altitude: 84m
Colour map 1, grid B5

The roads of the Amazon

In the early 1970s, Brazil's military rulers became increasingly unnerved by what they saw as foreign designs upon the resources of the Amazon basin. This real or imaginary fear of invasion was not only directed against the rich, developed countries, but also Brazil's neighbours who the Brazilians felt were slowly encroaching upon the country's borders. In the early 1960s, Peru's President Fernando Belaunde Terry had proposed the construction of the Carretera Marginal in order to link Peru's jungle with the rest of the country. Under the slogan of 'Integrar para não entregar' (takeover not handover), the Brazilian military announced the construction of the Transamazônica Highway. The road was originally designed to link João Pessoa, Paraíba, with Acre, thence to link up with the Peruvian road system to complete a road route across South America to the Pacific and open up Brazilian products to Asian markets. The Transamazônica itself would be 5,400 kilometres, and would integrate Amazônia from east to west and unify it with the rest of the nation. In addition, it would give opportunities for people from the northeast to resettle in areas not affected by drought and to become economically active in small agricultural schemes. In the often-quoted words of President Emílio Garrastazu Médici, it would move 'Homens sem terra para terras sem homens' (men without land to land without men). All along the highway, purpose-built 'agrovilas' would offer Brazil's poor a new life. The project was proposed in 1970; huge financial investment failed to make the project work. Not only did fewer than anticipated northeasterners take up the offer, but those that did found that the Amazonian soils did not permit the type of rewards that they had been led to expect. The colonizers also found that social infrastructure did not meet their needs and the road itself began to deteriorate as the whole project wound down. By the

late 1980s, a Movement for Survival along the Transamazônica had been set up by the farmers.

Another road which was intended to promote development in the Amazon region was the BR-364, from Cuiabá to Acre state. The government in the mid-1970s hoped that it would reinvigorate settlement in the Amazon, in a way that the Transamazônica had failed to do. Like the latter, the BR-364 was supposed to encourage small landholders to follow the building of the main highway and its feeder roads, but in Rondônia the main colonizers were cattle ranchers and land speculators who speeded up the process of deforestation and land conflicts with the traditional cultivators, forest farmers and indigenous people.

A third road in the Amazon which has come to grief, even more so than the other two, is the BR-319 from Manaus to Humaitá on the Transamazônica. Planned in 1960 and opened to traffic in 1975, the road has become a route from nothing to nowhere. The people living along it have been deserted, the only maintenance being the occasional team from Embratel who come to look at the telephone lines which follow the road. Initially there were farms, hotels, petrol stations and restaurants along the BR-319. Most have now gone. Access to health clinics and schools is all but impossible and the only public transport on the southern part of the road is a once-weekly truck. The only people to benefit are the shipping owners who take the traffic, which would have used the road, on barges along the Rio Madeira. The journalist Giuliano Cedroni tried to take the BR-319 in the late-1990s. He and his companions made it through, but not without a tow from the weekly truck after their jeep broke down. One inhabitant of the region pleaded with him, "Tell the people down there [in the south] what is happening in the north. This here is not a life."

agent is *IBR Travel* on the main street of Marabá Velha. *Banco do Brasil* will not cash travellers' cheques; the parallel market operates in larger stores; for example, *Supermercado Bato Logo*.

The **Serra Pelada** gold mines are now worked by heavy machinery. This massive excavation was the scene of much human misery and also some fabulous fortunes. To get there, take a bus to Km 6 and change for the Serra Pelada bus, US$6, three hours, last bus back 1400. Eleven kilometres before the town is a police post: search for weapons and alcohol (forbidden); second search at the airport two kilometres from the mine. No prior permission is needed to visit the mines. **Excursions**

A *Vale do Tocantins*, Folha 29, Cidade Nova, 7 km, T3222321, F3221841. Modern, restaurant, travel agency. **A** *Itacaiúnas*, Folha 30, Cidade Nova, T3221326. **A** *Del Príncipe*, Av Marechal Rondon 95, Cidade Nova, T3241175. A/c. **B** *Bahia*, Nova Marabá, next to the rodoviária. **B** *Dallas*, Nova Marabá, next to rodoviária. Recommended. **B** *Plaza*, Folha 32, Quadra 10, Lote 06, T3221610/1611/1612. Fan, quiet, helpful, very good breakfast, some English spoken. Recommended. **D** *Serra de Ouro*, all of wood, shower. Others near rodoviária. **Sleeping**

Kome Aki no Chikão, Av Antônio Maia 997, central. A/c, modest, 1200-1500, 1800-2300 (in theory). *Bambu*, Pedro Cameiro 111, Cidade Nova, 3 km. Mainly fish, clean, good value, 1100-1500, 1800-2300. Good *Churrascaria* in the main square near the public TV set, juice bars and *DiscoTony* discotheque. *Lanchonete Domino*, opposite the rodoviária. Recommended. **Eating**

Air Airport in Cidade Nova, 3 km. There are no direct flights to Altamira or Santarém, only via Belém with *Brasil Central* or *Varig*. *Brasil Central* flies to several local destinations, eg São Luís, Imperatriz. **Transport**

Buses Rodoviária in Nova Marabá, 4 km on PA-150, T3211892. Buses leave daily for **Belém** (654 km, paved, US$20), for **Santarém** (34 hours) and many daily for **Imperatriz** (7-10 hours, US$10, there is also a pick-up to the bank of the Tocantins opposite Imperatriz, 5 hours, but more expensive); buses can be caught going south at Tocantinópolis, opposite Porto Franco on the Belém-Brasília road. Also a bus can be taken to **Araguaína**, 12½ hours, US$20; bus Marabá-Goiânia (change at Araguaína). Bus to **Santa Inês** (Maranhão, on the Belém-Teresina road), 19 hours, US$55. *Transbrasiliana* bus to **Altamira** daily, 1300 (if road is passable), 15 hours, US$30. There are direct buses to **Rio** and **São Paulo**. On these bus trips take plenty of food and drink as local supplies are expensive. From the rodoviária to the railway station for trains on the São Luís-Parauapebas line (see below), take a colectivo bus US$0.75 from opposite the rodoviária to Km 6 (a kind of suburb of Marabá), then another colectivo bus, US$0.75, to the Estação Ferrovia. The colectivos are not frequent but are crowded. Alternatively taxis, which can be shared, cost US$15 from the railway station to town.

Boats Trips to **Belém** (24 hours) and **Santarém** (18 hours).

Airline offices *TAM*, T3243644. *Varig*, T3221965. **Banks** *Banco do Brasil*, Praça Duque de Caxias 966. **Hospitals & medical services** *Celina Gonçalves*, T3221031. **Directory**

Carajás

Companhia Vale Rio Doce (CVRD) operates the very impressive iron mine at Carajás, which looks like a giant red hole in a green jungle. The ore is almost pure iron oxide and is therefore extremely profitable. It is ground, washed and shipped to São Luís by trains up to two kilometres long, without further *The largest mineral development in Brazil*

treatment or chemical processing. Apart from iron, other metals like manganese are also mined by the CRVD in the area. A city has built up around Carajás, but most of it is within CVRD bounds. To get into Carajás (the Núcleo and to visit the mine) and to pass the checkpoint 35 kilometres from the project, you must have a permit, available from CVRD, phone locally 0XX91-3275300, or enquire in Marabá, São Luís, São Paulo or Rio: Avenida Graça Aranha 26, 16° andar, Centro, Rio 20030000 – attention Dr Hugo Mourão (hotel bookings handled here too); apply in advance and have a good reason for visiting.

Parque Zoo-Botânico is a very pleasant zoo with local animals, and like everything else in the region is run by CVRD. The animals have very spacious, quasi-natural cages. There is a lot to see, including a small shop with Funai articles from the local indians.

Thirty seven kilometres before the mine is **Parauapebas**. Originally intended as a temporary settlement for the Carajás construction workers, it is now a big city and still growing. Both Parauapebas and Núcleo Carajás are expensive, especially Carajás. In the dry season, summer, there are frequent bush fires in the region, ignited mainly by *fazendeiros*. The old part of Parauapebas is where the colourful fruit market, shops and banks are situated and is very busy.

Sleeping **Parauapebas A** *Almaribe*, T3461048. Very pleasant, manager Alipio speaks excellent English, some French and German, safe, a/c, fridge, TV, good breakfast, restaurant, gym machines, good atmosphere. Highly recommended. **C** *Ouro Verde*, Rio Verde district near market. Basic. Recommended. *Florida Bar*, T3461038. Good cocktails and food, the friendly owner Neuma speaks good Austrian/German, opens from 2000, closed Monday and Tuesday. Recommended. *Pit Dog*, on main street. Fast food and live music. Recommended.

Santarém environs

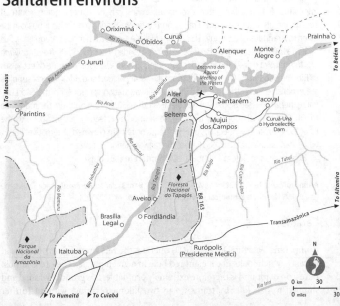

Air There are flights to Carajás from Belém, Marabá and Tucuruí. **Trains** Parauapebas **Transport**
is the final station of the Carajás railway line. To **Marabá**, departs 1930, 2 hours,
US$4. To **São Luís**, see page 585. **Buses** There are 8 daily buses to Marabá between
0545 and 1900. There is a daily bus to **Conceição de Araguaia**. Direct buses from
Rio, **São Paulo** and **Vitória** to Parauapebas with *Aguia Branca*. Plenty of
Transbrasiliana buses daily Marabá-Carajás, 4-5 hours, US$6. Military police check
for weapons and drugs at Curianópolis.

The Transamazônica crosses the Rio Xingu at Favânia, 41 kilometres east of **Altamira**
Altamira, a busy, booming Amazônian town with many gold dealers. A road is *Population: 120,000*
being paved 46 kilometres north to the fishing village of Vitória on the lower
Xingu, from which boats go to Belém; a good place to watch the *garimpeiros*
working below the last rapids. There are no organized trips but a boat can be
hired, US$25 per day, for a trip up the Xingu, which is highly recommended.
Many animals can be seen. The area is an Assurine Indian reservation and it is
not allowed to enter villages; buy food in Altamira.

Sleeping and eating B *Alta Palace*, Av Tancredo Neves 3093. Bar/restaurant, a/c,
good, T5152057. C *Pãe e Filho*, simple. Recommended. C *Requinte*. Recommended.
C *Lisboa*, Lindolfo Aranha 405. A/c, TV, good value, slightly better than C *Imperatriz*, R
Beto Somez near market. Bath, a/c. Recommended.
   Good *churrascos* and shopping in the market. *Restaurante Casa Grande*, R
Anchieta, centre. Good *churrascos*, cheap, 1130-1430, 1930-2330. *Restaurante
Esquina*, next to hotel *Lisboa*. Good *sucos*, closed Sunday. Recommended.

The next major town, **Rurópolis** (Presidente Medici), lies at the junction of
the Transamazônica and the Santarém highway. There is a hotel run by Incra.

This *garimpeiro town* is the jumping-off place for the **Amazônia National** **Itaituba**
Park. See Father Paul Zoderer, who may help to arrange a visit, at the church
on the waterfront – nearest Ibama information, Avenida Marechal Rondon,
CEP 681811-970, Itaituba, T5181530. **NB** Malaria is present in Itaituba. In
Itaituba is *Hotel Central Plaza* (**B**), recommended, and *Hotel 3 Poderes* (**D**),
clean, friendly, recommended. The *Transbrasiliana* company has a rodoviária
on the Rio Tapajós, near the ferry docks. Bus to Marabá, about 34 hours,
US$45. Bus to Santarém via Rurópolis, 11 hours, US$20. The road continues
to Jacarèacanga, crosses the border with Amazonas and finally reaches
Humaitá on the Rio Madeira (see page 650).

Southern Pará

South of Marabá are many ranches and new townships such as **Xinguara** (*popu-* **Redenção**
lation 40,000 already; **D** *Hotel Rio Vermelho*, OK) and Redenção, where timber *Population: 60,000*
as well as ranching is important. There are several hotels on Av Santa Tereza:
Inácio's (**A**), T4241334, F4241168, restaurant, and *Magnum* (**B**), T4241540,
with air conditioning. The airport is five kilometres from the centre. Air taxi with
Carajás, T4241390. The bus station is on Av Alceu Veroneze, T4241231.

Directory **Airline offices**: *BRC*, T4241157. **Banks**: *Banco do Brasil*, Av Santa Tereza. *Bradesco*,
Av Alacid Nunes 525. **Hospitals & medical services**: *São Vicente*, Av Pedro Paulo Barcui,
T4240818. **Security**: these places are raw, dusty and not very safe for tourists, especially at night.

These fast-developing frontier regions between the lower Araguaia and Xingu
rivers are connected to the Brasília-Belém road. There is now a soaring concrete

The Amazon

bridge spanning the Araguaia just south of Conceição do Araguaia, which is the only bridge across the Araguaia between Barra dos Garças and Marabá.

Conceição do Araguaia

Population: 50,000
Phone code: 091
Colour map 1, grid B5

The town, once a centre for rubber extraction, still has a frontier atmosphere, although mudhuts are being replaced by bricks, cowboy hats, battered Chevrolet pick-ups, skinny mules and a red light district.

Sleeping & **B** *Taruma Tropical*, Av Brasília 2120, T/F4211205. Pool, conference centre, garage,
eating sauna, frigobars, expanded restaurant, clean and functioning bathrooms, a/c – when it works, the hotel is well patronized by ranchers and absentee landowners from Brasília. **B** *Pousada do Sol*, R Couto de Magalhães 2942, T4211483. A/c, bar, pool. Also *Marajoara*, Av JK 1587, T4211220. Some a/c, safe parking, breakfast. *Araguaia*, R Couto de Magalhães 2605. Breakfast, both small. *Café Taboquinha*, Av Francisco Vitor. Well-prepared fish, open 1200-1500, 1800-2300.

Transport Airport, 14 km southwest on the road to Guaraí. Bus station, Av Araguaia, T4211322.

Directory **Airline offices** *BRC*, T4211467. **Banks** *Banco do Brasil*, Av 7 de Setembro 626. **Hospitals & medical services** *Modelo*, R D Sebastião Tomás 32, T4211599.

The Amazon River

The Amazon system is 6,577 kilometres long, of which 3,165 kilometres are in Brazilian territory. Ships of up to 4-5,000 tons regularly negotiate the Amazon, for a distance of about 3,646 kilometres up to Iquitos, Peru. Distances upstream from the river mouth to Manaus in nautical miles are: Belém 80, Narrows (entrance) 225, Narrows (exit) 330, Gurupá 334, Prainha 452, Santarém 538, Óbidos 605, Parintins 694, Itacoatiara 824, Manaus 930.

A few hours up the broad river the region of the thousand islands is entered. The passage through this maze of islets is known as 'The Narrows', perhaps the nicest part of the journey. The ship winds through 150 kilometres of lanes of yellow flood, with equatorial forest within 20 metres or 30 metres on both sides. Here local children paddle toward the passing riverboats in their small dugout canoes, hoping for a handout. Passengers will often throw used clothing (in plastic bags), plastic utensils, containers and similar items overboard for them. If you wish to do likewise, be sure that your gift is genuinely useful and that it will float.

See also box, page 625
On one of the curious flat-topped hills after the Narrows stands the little stucco town of **Monte Alegre**, an oasis in mid-forest (airport; some simple hotels, **E**). There are lagoon cruises to see lilies, birds, pink dolphins; also village visits (US$25-40 per day). A recommended guide Nelce Cideq lives next door to a small brown and white hotel, near the end of the terrace at the east side of the docks.

Santarém

Population: 243,000
Phone code: 091
Colour map 1, grid B4

Two to three days upstream on the southern bank is this city, standing at the confluence of the Rio Tapajós with the Amazon, half-way between Belém and Manaus. It was founded in 1661 as the Jesuit mission of Tapajós. It also had a fort. In 1758, the name was changed to Santarém, but it was another 90 years before it was large enough to be called a city. Today it is the third largest town

Monte Alegre

Monte Alegre is the site of archaeological discoveries, which have threatened to alter radically views of the spread of civilization in South America. Dr Anna C Roosevelt, of the Field Museum of Natural History, Chicago, found in the early 1990s pottery fragments in a cave which, according to radio-carbon dating, appear to be from 7000 to 8000 BC. This predates by some 3,000 years what was thought to be the earliest ceramic ware in South America (from Colombia and Ecuador). Subsequent artefacts discovered here, however, have radio-carbon dates of 15000 BC, which calls for a significant rethink of the original idea that people moved from the Andes into the Amazon Basin. If nothing else, these finds suggest that the story of the people of the Americas is more diverse than hitherto understood. The cave which Dr Roosevelt excavated is called Caverna da Pedra Pintada. Also in the area are pictographs, with large designs of human and animal figures and geometrical shapes. Trips can be arranged.

We are grateful to Philip W Hummer, who sent us a description of a tour to the region, led by Dr Anna Roosevelt.

on the Brazilian Amazon, but it is small enough to walk around. Its attractive colonial squares overlook the waterfront. Most visitors arrive from either Manaus or Belém by boat or air. There is a road southwards to Cuiabá (Mato Grosso), meeting the Transamazônica at Rurópolis (see page 623).

Sights The yellow Amazon water swirls alongside the green-blue Tapajós; the **meeting of the waters**, in front of the market square, is nearly as impressive as that of the Negro and Solimões near Manaus. A small **Museu dos Tapajós** in the old city hall on the waterfront, now the **Centro Cultural João Fora**, downriver from where the boats dock, has a collection of ancient Tapajós ceramics, as well as various 19th-century artefacts and publications. The unloading of the fish catch between 0500 and 0700 on the waterfront is interesting. There are good beaches nearby on the Rio Tapajós. **Prainha**, a small beach, is between town and the port, by a park with many mango trees which provide much welcome shade (Floresta-Prainha bus from centre); on the outskirts of town is Maracanã, with sandy bays (when the Tapajos is low) and some trees for shade (Maracanã bus from centre, 20 minutes).

Excursions **Alter do Chão** is a friendly village on the Rio Tapajós, at the outlet of Lago Verde, 34 kilometres west. Of particular interest is the **Centro do Preservação da Arte Indígena**, Rua Dom Macedo Costa, which has a substantial collection of artefacts from tribes of Amazônia and Mato Grosso (call David Richardson for further information, T5271110). Good swimming in the Tapajós from the beautiful, clean beach. Close to Alter do Chão (30 minutes by boat), the conjunction of the Rio Tapajós with the Aruã and the Arapiuns creates an island surrounded by clean rivers of differing colours, each teeming with life. The forested island, already popular, is being developed as an ecopark, **Parque Ecoturístico Arapiuns**, with accommodation for visitors. Monkeys and birds inhabit the woodlands, which are protected more for commercial reasons than any other. Permission was given in 1995 for a simple complex of bungalows for tourists, which could provide a level of comfort without compromising the environment unduly. In 1999 lack of funds has prevented further development of this project. For information, contact Paratur in Belém, T2232130.

Sleeping and eating B *Pousada Tupaiulândia*, R Pedro Teixera 300, T5271157, a/c, unimpressive but OK, very friendly and helpful, good breakfast for US$5, next to telephone

The Amazon

Santarém: the Confederates and other newcomers

In 1978, the American poet, Elizabeth Bishop, described the city thus:
"Two rivers full of crazy shipping – people
all apparently changing their minds, embarking,
disembarking, rowing clumsy dories.
(After the Civil War some Southern families
came here; here they could still own slaves.
They left occasional blue eyes, English names,
and oars. No other place, no one on all the Amazon's four thousand miles does anything but paddle.)"
('Santarém' from New Poems, 1979; Complete Poems – London: Chatto and Windus, 1991)

She was referring to the Confederates who came in 1867, but the immigration had nothing like the impact of that of other people who came to Brazil in the 19th century and later. More successful, though, was another foreign resident in the 19th century, Henry Wickham (see page 630), the Englishman who smuggled the first rubber seeds out of Brazil. Santarém shared in the rubber boom, first in the late 19th and early 20th centuries, then again during the Second World War. It was just south of here that Henry Ford set up his company's plantations; see Belterra and Fordlândia, below. The discovery of gold on the Upper Tapajós in 1959 sparked a gold rush which still continues. The city has become the jumping off point for the prospectors in the Mato Grosso territories to the south.

office opposite bus stop. **D** *Alter do Chão*, R Lauro Sodré 74, T5271215, restaurant and orchid garden. **D** *Tia Marilda*, Trav Agostinho Lobato, T5271144, a/c, cheaper with fan. *Lago Verde*, Praça 7 de Setembro, good fresh fish, try *calderada de tucunaré*.

Transport Tickets and information from the bus company kiosk opposite *Pousada Tupaiulândia*. From Santarém: bus stop on Av São Sebastião, in front of Colégio Santa Clara, US$1, about 1 hour.

Sleeping **A** *Amazon Park*, Av Mendonça Furtado 4120, T5232800, F5222631. Swimming pool, friendly, recently renovated, 4 km from centre, taxi US$5. **B** *Brasil Grande Hotel*, Trav 15 de Agosto 213, T5225660. Family-run with restaurant. **B** *New City*, Trav Francisco Corrêa 200, T/F5224719. A/c, frigobar, will collect from airport. **B** *Rio Dourado*, R Floriano Peixoto 877, T5223764. Modern, a/c, also collects from airport. **B** *Santarém Palace*, Rui Barbosa 726, T5232820, F5221779, close to city centre. **C** *Brisa*, Av Senador Lameira Bittencourt 5, T/F5221296. A/c, **E** with fan and without bath, on waterfront. **D** *Brasil*, Trav dos Mártires 30, T5226665. Includes breakfast, communal bath, good food, good service. **D** *Horizonte*, Trav Senador Lemos, T5225437. With a/c, **E** with fan, modern, clean.

Eating *Mascote*, Praça do Pescador 10, T5232844. Open 1000-2330. *Xodó do Amazonas*, Av Tapajós 2061, T5232356. Churrasco and fish. *Mascotinho*, Praça Manoel de Jesus Moraes, on riverfront. Bar/pizzeria, popular, good view. *Luci*, Praça do Pescador. Good juices and pastries. Recommended. *Sombra do Jambeiro*, Trav 15 de Novembro. Bar and restaurant, excellent and cheap meals.

Entertainment **Cinema** Av Rui Barbosa 183.

Festivals 22 June, *Foundation of the city*; 29 June, *São Pedro*, with processions of boats on the river and boi-bumbá dance dramas; 8 December, *NS da Conceição* (the city's patron saint). In *Alter do Chão*: second week in July, *Festa do Sairé*, religious processions and folkloric events. Recommended.

Muiraquitã, R Lameira Bittencourt 131. Good for ceramics, wood carvings and baskets. **Shopping**

Local Buses: US$0.30 and taxis US$3 link the port with the centre. **Transport**

Long distance Air: 15 km from town. Internal flights only, to Alta Floresta, Almerim, Altamira, Belém, Boavista, Breves, Cuiabá, Imperatriz, Itaituba, Macapá, Manaus, Marabá, Monte Dourado, Óbidos, Oiapoque, Oriximiná, Parantins, Porto de Moz, Porto Trombetas, Rurópolis, Sinop and Urucu. Buses run to the centre or waterfront. From the centre the bus leaves in front of the cinema in Rui Barbosa every 80 minutes from 0550 to 1910, or taxis (US$12 to waterfront). The hotels *Amazon Park*, *New City* and *Rio Dourado* have free buses for guests; you may be able to take these.

Buses: rodoviária is on the outskirts, take 'Rodagem' bus from the waterfront near the market, US$0.35. Santarém to **Itaituba**, US$12.50, 11 hours, 2 a day. To **Marabá** on the Rio Tocantins (via Rurópolis US$9, 6 hours, and **Altamira** US$25, 28 hours), 36 hours (if lucky; can be up to 6 days), US$50, with *Transbrasiliana*. Also to **Imperatriz**, via Marabá; office on Av Getúlio Vargas and at the rodoviária. Enquire at the rodoviária for other destinations. (Beware of vehicles that offer a lift, which frequently turn out to be taxis.) Road travel during the rainy season is always difficult, often impossible.

Santarém

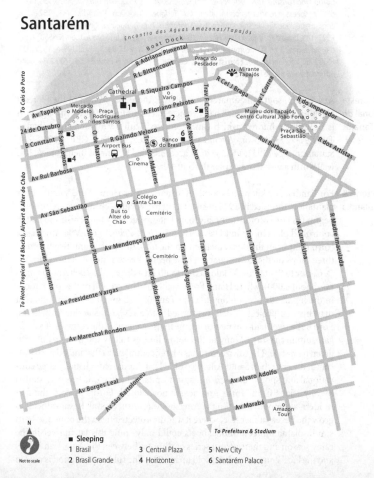

N
Not to scale

■ **Sleeping**
1 Brasil
2 Brasil Grande
3 Central Plaza
4 Horizonte
5 New City
6 Santarém Palace

The Amazon

Boats: shipping services to **Manaus**, **Belém**, **Macapá**, **Itaituba**, and intermediate ports (see **River transport**, page 598). Boats to Belém and Manaus dock at the Cais do Porto, 1 km west, take 'Floresta-Prainha', 'Circular' or 'Circular Externo' bus; taxi US$4. Boats to other destinations, including Macapá, dock by the waterfront by the centre of town. Local service to **Óbidos**, US$10, 4 hours, **Oriximiná** US$12.50, **Alenquer**, and **Monte Alegre** (US$10, 5-8 hours).

Directory | **Airline offices** *META*, R Siquiera Campos 162, T5226222. *Penta*, Trav 15 de Novembro 183, T5232532. *TAVAJ*, Trav dos Mártires 161, T5221418. *Varig/Nordeste*, R Siqueira Campos 277, T5221951. **Banks** *Banco do Brasil*, Av Rui Barbosa 794, exchanges TCs and cash, also withdrawals on Visa. Exchange cash at *Farmácia Java*, opposite *Coruá-Una Turismo*, Trav 15 de Novembro, or *Ouro Minas*, a gold dealer, Trav dos Mártires 198A; also try travel agencies. **Communications** Post office: Praça da Bandeira 81. **Telephone:** *Posto Trin*, R Siquiera Campos 511. Open 0700-1900 Mon-Sat, 0700-2100 Sun. **Internet:** *Tapajos On Line*, Mendonça Furtado 2454, US$3.50 per hr. **Hospitals & medical services** *Hospital São Raimundo Nonato*, Av Mendonça Furtado 1993, T5231176. **Laundry** *Storil*, Trav Turiano Meira 167, 1st floor. **Tour companies & travel agents** *Amazon Tours*, Trav Turiano Meira 1084, T5221928, Mobile 9751981, F5221098, amazontours@amazonriver.com, www.amazonriver.com, owner Steve Alexander is very friendly and helpful who can give you lots of hints on what to do, he also organizes excursions for groups to Bosque Santa Lúcia with ecological trails, recommended. *Coruá-Una Turismo*, Trav 15 de Novembro 123A, T5226611, F5232670, offers various tours, Pierre d'Arcy speaks French, recommended. *Gil Serique*, Praça do Pescador 131, T5225174, English-speaking guide, recommended. *Santarém Tur*, R Adriano Pimental 44, T5224847, F5223141, branch in *Amazon Park Hotel* (above), friendly, helpful, also group tours (US$50 pp per day for a group of 5), recommended. *Tapam Turismo*, Trav 15 de Agosto, 127 A, T5223037, F5232055, recommended. **Tourist offices** *Comtur*, R Floriano Peixoto 343, T/F5232434, good information available in English.

Floresta Nacional do Tapajós | At Km 123, south of Santarém on BR 163, there is a section of the Floresta Nacional do Tapajós which has a vehicle track running due west through it. It is beautiful rainforest which can be entered with permission from Ibama, T0XX91-2245899, or Avenida Tapajos 2267, Aldeia CEP 68010-000, Santarém, T5223032, F5223476, if accompanied by one of their guides. It is well worth a visit if only to see the butterflies.

Belterra & Fordlândia | Fordlândia, 300 kilometres south of Santarém, was Henry Ford's first rubber plantation, founded in 1926 in an attempt to provide a cheaper source of rubber for his Ford Motor Company than that produced by the British and Dutch controlled plantations in Malaya. There is *Hotel Zebu*, in old Vila Americana (turn right from the dock, then left up the hill), one restaurant, two bars and three shops on the town square. A little pebble beach is north of the town.

Closer to Santarém, 37 kilometres south on a dirt road, is Belterra (*population* about 8,000), where Henry Ford established his second rubber plantation, in the highlands overlooking the Rio Tapajós and much closer to Santarém than his first project, which was turned into a research station. At Belterra, Ford built a well laid-out new town; the houses resemble the cottages of Michigan summer resorts. Many of the newer houses follow the white paint with green trim style. The town centre has a large central plaza that includes a bandstand, the church of Santo Antônio (c1951), a Baptist church and a large educational and sports complex. A major hospital, which at one time was staffed by physicians from North America, is now closed. Ford's project, the first modern attempt to invest in the Amazon, was unsuccessful. It was difficult to grow the hevea rubber tree, where it was unprotected from the rains and hard sun in plantation conditions; boats could only come this far upriver in the rainy season and there were a series of disputes between the American bosses and the local employees. Ford sold up in 1945. The rubber plantation is now in bad condition. There is **E** *Hotel Seringueira* in Belterra, with about eight rooms and a pleasant restaurant.

Transport Bus from **Santarém** to Belterra (from Trav Silvino Pinto between Rui Barbosa and São Sebastião), 1000 and 1230, Monday-Saturday, return 1300 and 1530, US$4, about 2 hours. **NB** There is a 1 hour time difference between Santarém and Belterra, so if you take the 1230 bus you'll miss the 1530 return bus. Boats from Santarém to Itaituba stop at Fordlândia if you ask (leave Santarém 1800, arrive 0500-0600, US$12 for first class hammock space); ask the captain to stop for you on return journey, about 2300. The alternative is to take a tour with a Santarém travel agent.

Óbidos

Population: 42,500
Phone code: 091

Upriver from Santarém, 110 kilometres or five hours by boat, Óbidos is located at the narrowest and deepest point on the river, where millions of years ago the Amazon squeezed through the gap in the Guyana and Brazilian Highlands to meet the Atlantic. It was a strategic point in the Portuguese expansion of the Amazon. The **Forte Pauxi** (1697) is a reminder of this fact (Praça Coracy Nunes). Today, Óbidos is a picturesque and clean city with many beautiful, tiled buildings and some pleasant parks. Worth seeing are the **Prefeitura Municipal**, the cuartel and the **Museu Integrado de Óbidus**, Rua Justo Chermont 607. ■ *Monday-Friday 0700-1100, 1330-1730*. There is also a **Museu Contextual**, a system of plaques with detailed explanations of historical buildings througout town. Boating and fishing trips can be made and there is a popular beach at **Igarapé de Curuçambá** (buses go there). A poor road runs east to Alenquer, Monte Alegre and Prainha and west to Oriximiná, impassable in the wet season. The small airport has flights to Manaus, Santarém and Parintins.

Sleeping and eating **C** *Braz Bello*, R Corrêia Pinto, on top of the hill. Shared bath, clean, full board available. **C** *Pousada Brasil*, R Correia Pinto. Basic with bath, cheaper without. *Pousada Curiô*, R Antônio Brito de Souza, in the upper town. *Pousada Casa Grande*, R Raimundo Chaves, near Prefeitura. *Restaurante Tucuruvi*, Praça Santana, fish.

Oriximiná

Population: 12,000

About eight to 10 hours by boat from Santarém and 24 hours from Manaus on the lower Rio Trombetas, a tributary on the north shore, Oriximiná is the regional centre for an area dedicated to ranching, timber extraction and brazil nut cultivation; on the upper Trombetas is a large bauxite mine. It has daily boat service to Santarém and regular service to Manaus and Belém. An excursion can be taken to Porteira on the upper Trombetas, 15 hours upriver; the Prefeitura runs a boat on Tuesday, returning Sunday; alternatively, it is four hours by speedboat (Sr Bonina, returning the same day or staying overnight, US$250 return). There is a small village without an infrastructure, visitors can hang their hammocks at the Electronorte camp or camp on the beach, take food and all supplies; nearby is the scenic Porteira waterfall. The area is malarial, take all necessary precautions.

Sleeping and eating **C** *Tropicão*, R 24 de Dezembro by the waterfront. With a/c and bath, cheaper shared bath and fan. **C** *Tapuyu*, with bath, fan, cheaper with shared bath, fan, basic. *Restaurante Josinara* and a few other simple restaurants.

Directory **Banks**: neither *Banco do Brasil* nor *BASA* change money.

The Amazon

Amazonas

This is the main centre for ecotourism in Brazil with new areas such as the Mamiraúá sustainable development reserve, north of Tefé, being opened to visitors. Stays in jungle lodges, riverboat trips and treks in the rainforest can all be easily arranged in Manaus. The world's largest river archipelagos are located on the Rio Negro and are havens for wildlife. The region's Indian influence manifests itself in the Festa da Boi held on Parintins Island and in many other folklore festivals throughout the year.

This is the largest state in Brazil (1.6 million square kilometres), but with a population of only about 2½ million. Half of the inhabitants live in the capital Manaus, with the rest spread out amongst remote communities mainly linked by air and river only. Having borders with Venezuela, Colombia and Peru, this state has the longest frontier in the union.

Colonization by the Portuguese of what is now Amazonas began in the mid-17th century when 'ransom troops' (slave-gathering expeditions accompanied by priests) first set up camp at the mouth of the Rio Tarumã. The Indians at first co-operated with the Portuguese, providing them with slaves from Indian groups they themselves had captured, but relations soured in the 1720s. The Portuguese, suspecting the Manau chief, Ajuricaba, of dealing also with the Dutch in nearby Dutch Guiana, began attacking and enslaving the Manau and in very few years had subdued them and their neighbours completely. By the 18th century, the whole Rio Negro region had become a major source of Indian slaves, but Christian settlements were few and far between.

As demand for rubber in the rapidly industrializing world grew, so the need for labour to extract and export it rose. First came Indians from Peru and Bolivia, then Cearenses, fleeing the drought of 1877-79. Seekers of the 'black gold of the forests' spread far and wide across the region. The Amazon's monopoly of the rubber trade ended when the rubber plants smuggled out of the region by the Englishman, Henry Wickham, were cultivated into successful plantations in the British possessions in Ceylon and Malaya.

Although the British rubber industry came to dominate, it was held that rubber from the wild was of better quality than that produced on plantations. CR Enock, writing in 1920, said that "One of the evils of the Malaysian system is that whereby coolie labour is brought in without their women, and consequently no family life is possible among these coloured workers, in the Amazon Valley there are no such restrictions, and under better auspices the native rubber gatherers could prosper and multiply. Herein lie important matters for the future, especially for that fortunate part of civilized mankind that rides on the rubber tyres of the motor car" (*Spanish America*, volume II, page 104). What would Chico Mendes (page 671) have made of that statement?

Manaus

The next city upstream from Santarém, Manaus, was at one time an isolated urban island in the jungle. It is the collecting point for the produce of a vast area which includes parts of Peru, Bolivia and Colombia. Though 1,600 kilometres from the sea, it is only 32 metres above sea level. The city sprawls over a series of eroded and gently sloping hills divided by numerous creeks (igarapés). It is an excellent port of entry for visiting the Amazon. Less than a day away are river islands and tranquil waterways. The opportunities for canoeing, trekking in the beautiful forest and meeting local people should not be missed and, once you are out of reach of the urban influence, there are plenty of animals to see.

Population: 1,158,000
Phone code: 092
Mean temp: 27°C
Colour map 1, grid B3

The road from Porto Velho is very difficult and often impassable, making river or air travel essential. The road north to Boa Vista has been paved, bringing the frontiers of Venezuela and Guyana within easy reach.

Getting there From the airport, which is 9 km from the city, a taxi to the centre costs US$18, fixed rate. Buses to the city cost US$0.70, but there are none between 2200 and 0700. Manaus rodoviária is 5 km out of town at the intersection of Av Constantino Nery and R Recife. The only long-distance route arriving here is that from Boa Vista and the Venezuelan border. Boat passengers arrive at the floating dock with access to R Marquês de Santa Cruz, just down form the Praça da Matriz.

Ins & outs
See also Transport,
page 639

   Getting around The city centre is easily explored on foot. Buses serve the entire urban area and there are taxis. Other towns in the state are best visited by air or boat, especially during the December to June wet season when road travel is almost impossible.

   NB Manaus time is 1 hour behind Brazilian standard time (2 hours behind during October-March when the rest of Brazil is on summer time).

History

The town was formed in 1669 around São José do Rio Negro fort, built on the news that Dutch invaders were penetrating into the area from present-day Suriname. The name changed to Fortaleza da Barra (also Lugar, Vila and Cidade da Barra do Rio Negro, Barra meaning bar or river mouth) and remained so until 1856, when it became a city with the present name. Manaus derives from an Indian tribe called the Manau, or Manao, who lived on the middle Rio Negro, higher upstream than the site of the city.

   Rubber boom A visitor to Manaus in 1879 estimated its population at 5,000, a port wholly inadequate to accommodate the wealth that traders were beginning to recognize could be harvested from the surrounding forest. Manaus became the chief collecting point for rubber and by the turn of the century, 50,000 people were living in the city, whose boom time was 1890-1920. The opulence of the inhabitants' lifestyle was matched by the speed of development. Manaus was the first Brazilian

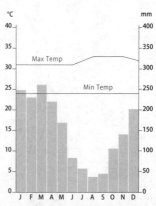

Climate: Manaus

The Amazon

city to have electricity, water and sewage treatment, trams (now replaced by buses), streets and pavements, all imported from Britain. Architecture, fashion and taste were all dictated by Europe, the opera house (Teatro Amazonas, see below) being the prime example. After the loss of the market to plantations in Asia (see above), the Brazilian rubber trade collapsed and so did Manaus.

Duty-free Zone Manaus' fortunes were revived eventually in 1967 with the creation of the Zona Franca de Manaus (ZFM), decreed by President Castelo Branco to bring industry and progress to the region and to lower the cost of living. Initially it was a success, with Brazilians from the south flocking to buy consumer goods at free port prices. In the 1980s, however, protectionist policies led to the restriction of imports free of duty, which limited the attractiveness of Manaus for shoppers, especially since it is so far from the country's main centres of population.

Today, Manaus is building fast, with 20-storey modern buildings rising above the traditional flat, red-tiled roofs. Under recent municipal

Manaus orientation

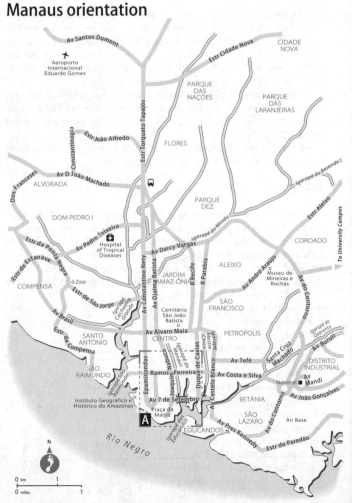

*Related map
A Manaus centre,
page 634*

administrations the city, including the Zona Franca, old commercial district, port area and nearby markets, has been kept relatively clean and orderly. New markets have been built and a few old buildings restored.

Sights

Dominating the centre is a **Cathedral**, built in simple Jesuit style on a hillock; there is nothing distinguished inside or out. Nearby is the main shopping and business area, the tree-lined Avenida Eduardo Ribeiro, crossed by Avenida 7 de Setembro and bordered by ficus trees. This area is pedestrianized.

Other main attractions include the **Teatro Amazonas**, on Praça São Sebastião, which was completed in 1896 during the great rubber boom, following 17 years of construction. It was rebuilt in 1929. It seats 685 people. The designs on the backdrop inside the theatre and the paving in the praça at the front of the building represent the meeting of the waters. ■ *Monday-Saturday 0900-1600, 20 minute guided tour US$7, students US$2.50, recommended, same price to attend a concert. Information on programmes, T6222420.*

Another interesting historic building is the **Mercado Adolfo Lisboa**, Rua dos Barés. It was built in 1882 as a miniature copy of the now-demolished Parisian Les Halles. The wrought ironwork, which forms much of the structure, was imported from Europe and is supposed to have been designed by Eiffel.

The remarkable **harbour installations**, completed in 1902, were designed and built by a Scottish engineer to cope with the Rio Negro's annual rise and fall of up to 14 metres. The large passenger ship floating dock is connected to street level by a 150 metre-long floating ramp, at the end of which, on the harbour wall, can be seen the high water mark for each year since it was built. When the water is high, the roadway floats on a series of large iron tanks measuring 2½ metres in diameter. The material to build the large yellow **Alfândega** (customs building) near the harbour was brought block by block from Scotland as ballast. ■ *Daily 0730-2000 for tourists.*

The **Centro Cultural Pálacio Rio Negro** in Avenida 7 de Setembro was the residence of a German rubber merchant until 1917 and later the state government palace. It now holds various cultural events, exhibitions, shows, films; there is also a café. ■ *Tuesday-Sunday 1600-2100, T2324450.*

The **Biblioteca Pública** (Public Library) at Rua Barroso 57 is well stocked and worth a visit. ■ *Monday-Friday 0800-1700, T2340588.*

There is a curious little church, **Igreja do Pobre Diabo**, at the corner of Avenidas Borba and Ipixuna in the suburb of Cachoeirinha. It is only four metres wide by five metres long, and was built by a worker (the 'poor devil' of the name). ■ *Take Circular 7 de Setembro Cachoeirinha bus from the cathedral to Hospital Militar.*

Instituto Geográfico e Histórico do Amazonas, Rua Bernardo Ramos 117 **Museums** (near Prefeitura), is located in a fascinating older district of central Manaus. It houses a museum and library of over 10,000 books, which thoroughly document Amazonian life through the ages. ■ *Monday-Friday 0800-1200, T2327077, US$0.20.*

Museu do Índio, Rua Duque de Caxias (near Avenida 7 Setembro), is run by the Salesian missionaries. It has an interesting collection that includes handicrafts, ceramics, clothing, utensils and ritual objects from the various Indian tribes of the upper Rio Negro and an excellent craft shop, recommended. ■ *Monday-Friday 0830-1200 and 1400-1700, Saturday 0800-1130, closed Sunday, T2341422, US$3.*

The Amazon

Museu do Homem do Norte, Avenida 7 de Setembro 1385 (near Avenida Joaquim Nabuco), reviews the way of life of the Amazonian population. Social, cultural and economic aspects are displayed with photographs, models and other pieces. ■ *Monday-Thursday 0900-1200, 1300-1700, Friday 1300-1700, T2325373, US$1.*

Museu do Porto de Manaus, Rua Vivaldo Lima 61 (near harbour), contains various historical items, documents, letters, diaries and charts. ■ *Monday-Saturday 0700-1100 and 1300-1700, Sunday 1200-1700, T2320096.*

Museu Tiradentes, on Praça da Polícia, is run by the military police and holds selected historical items and old photographs. ■ *Monday 1400-1800, Tuesday-Friday 0800-1200 and 1400-1800, T2347422.*

The **Centro de Artes Chaminé**, in Rua Isabel near Rua Quintino Bocaiúva bridge, has occasional art exhibitions mounted in a restored water treatment works built by the British in 1896. ■ *Monday-Friday 0830-1330, T2347877.*

Manaus centre

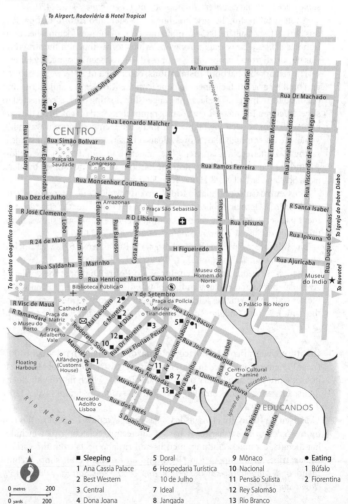

■ Sleeping		● Eating
1 Ana Cassia Palace	5 Doral	9 Mônaco	1 Búfalo
2 Best Western	6 Hospedaria Turística	10 Nacional	2 Fiorentina
3 Central	10 de Julho	11 Pensão Sulista	
4 Dona Joana	7 Ideal	12 Rey Salomão	
	8 Jangada	13 Rio Branco	

0 metres 200
0 yards 200

The Amazon

Museu de Minerais e Rochas, Estrada do Aleixo 2150, has a large collection of minerals and rocks from the Amazon region. ■ *Monday-Friday 0800-1200 and 1400-1800, T2361582.*

Museu de Ciências Naturais da Amazônia has a pavilion with insects and fish of the region and is located at Al Cosme Ferreira, Colonia Cachoeira Grande, 15 kilometres away. ■ *Monday-Saturday 0900-1700, US$4, T6442799, difficult to get to, take 'São José-Acoariquarape/Tropolis' bus 519 to Conjunto Petro, then 2 km walk, best to take a taxi.*

Botanic Gardens, **Instituto Nacional de Pesquisas Amazonas** (INPA), Estrada do Aleixo at Km 3, is not far from the Natural Science Museum. It is worth a visit and is good for birdwatchers. It has named trees and manatees (best seen Wednesday and Friday mornings when the water is changed), caimans and giant otters. ■ *US$2, Monday-Friday 0900-1100, 1400-1630, Saturday-Sunday 0900-1600, T6433377/6433192, take any bus to Aleixo.*

Jardim Botânico 'Chico Mendes' (Horto Municipal), Avenida André Araujo sem número, contains a collection of plants from the Amazon region. ■ *Daily 0800-1200 and 1400-1700, take a bus 'Aleixo' or 'Coroado'.*

The **Zoo**, Estrada Ponta Negra 750 (no sign), is run by CIGS, the Brazilian Army Unit specializing in jungle survival. About 300 Amazonian animals are kept in the gardens (reported as run-down with small cages). ■ *Tuesday-Sunday 0900-1630. Entry for foreigners, US$3, free on Sunday, T6252044, take bus 120 or 207 (marked 'Ponta Negra'), US$0.70, every 30 minutes from Rua Tamandaré, opposite the cathedral in the centre, alight 400m past the first Jungle Infantry Barracks (a big white building), look for the sentries.* There is also a small zoo at the *Hotel Tropical*, see below.

Excursions

About 15 kilometres from Manaus is the confluence of the yellow-brown Solimões (Amazon) and the blue-black Rio Negro, which is itself some eight kilometres wide. The two rivers run side by side for about six kilometres without their waters mingling. Tourist agencies run boat trips to this spot (US$60-160). The simplest route is to take a taxi or No 713 'Vila Buriti' bus to the Careiro ferry dock, and take the car ferry across. The ferry, which is very basic with no shelter on deck and no cabins, departs at 0700 returning 1000, and 1500 returning 1800 (approximately). Small private launches cross, a 40 minute journey costing about US$10-15 per seat, ask for the engine to be shut off at the confluence. You should see dolphins especially in the early morning. Alternatively, hire a motorized canoe from near the market (US$15 approximately; allow three to four hours to experience the meeting properly). A two kilometre walk along the Porto Velho road from the Careiro ferry terminal will lead to a point from which Victoria Regia water lilies can be seen in April-September in ponds, some way from the road.

Meeting of the waters
See also Tours, page 641

This typical Amazon small market town is situated on the Solimões west of Manaus. It has three basic hotels and *Il Maccarone* pizzeria, Avenida Eduardo Ribeiro 1000. It is 84 kilometres on AM-070 by bus, four daily, US$5, two hours including ferry crossing.

Manacapuru

This village on the Rio Mamori has plenty of wildlife close at hand. Canoes can be hired. It is three hours by No 11 bus from the rodoviária in the direction of Castanho; the journey includes the ferry at the confluence of the Negro and Solimões (fare to Araça US$1.50, bus leaves 0600 and 1100). Three buses a day return to Manaus.

Araça

The Amazon

Arquipélago de Anavilhanas This is the second largest archipelago in a river in the world. It is located in the Rio Negro, some 100 kilometres upstream from Manaus, near the town of Novo Airão. There are hundreds of islands, covered in thick vegetation. When the river is low, white sand beaches are revealed, as well as the roots and trunks of the trees. Tour companies arrange visits to the archipelago (US$160-200, one day).

Essentials

Sleeping
■ *on map, page 634*
Price codes: see inside front cover
Luxury hotels often give up to 50% discounts during low season

There is a hotel booking service at the airport. When taking a taxi from the airport, insist on being taken to the hotel of your choice, and not to the one which pays the driver commission. The Zona Franca is reported to be safer than the area around Av Joaquim Nabuco and R dos Andradas.

L *Tropical*, Estr da Ponta Negra 9015, T6585000, F6585026. Lavish 5-star hotel 20 km outside the city (taxi to centre, US$25), 12% service tax added to bill, discount when arriving on *Varig* flights, *churrascaria* by pool, 24-hour coffee shop open to well-dressed non-residents, take minibus from R José Paranaguá in front of Petrobras building at the corner of Dr Moreira, US$6 return, 0830, 0930, 1130 to hotel, 1200, 1400, 1500, 1800 to town, or take Ponta Negra bus, US$0.80, then walk. Collects guests from airport. It is rarely full, except in January-February. Parkland setting, wave pools, small zoo with animals in small cages, beach with new dock, departure point for many river cruises, tennis courts, poor exchange rates in lobby. **L** *Taj Mahal* Av Getúlio Vargas 741, T6331010, F2330068, tajmahal@internext.com.br, near to centre. Awaiting Holiday Inn accreditation, has own tour agency. **L** *Adrianópolis*, R Salvador 275, T6332001, F6333992. Fully furnished aparthotel, pool, sauna, includes breakfast. **A** *Ana Cassia Palace*, R dos Andradas 14, T6223637, F6224812. **A** *Best Western*, R Marcílio Dias 217, T6222844, F6222576, bwmanaus@internext.com.br. A/c, with good breakfast and service. **A** *Central*, R Dr Moreira 202, T6222600, F6222609, hcentral@zaz.com.br. Modern, friendly, safe, quiet, good breakfast. **A** *Da Vinci*, R Belo Horizonte 240, 3 km from centre, T6631213, F6113721. Pool. **A** *Mônaco*, R Silva Ramos 20, T6223446, F6223637. Rooms have good view, pleasant (some rooms noisy), rooftop restaurant/bar, delicious breakfast. **A** *Novotel*, Av Mandií 4, in the Industrial Area, T6631211, F6131094. Four-star, luxurious, pool, US$3 taxi ride from centre. **A** *Plaza*, Av Getúlio Vargas 215, F2327766, F2340647, plazahot@internext. com.br. **A** *Rei Salomão*, R Dr Moreira 119, T2347374. With breakfast. A highly recommended aparthotel is **A** *Saint Paul*, R Ramos Ferreira 1115, T6222131, F6222137. Suites with bath, kitchen, living room, has pool, gym and sauna. **C** *Aquários*, R Guilherme Moreira 116, T2330039. A/c, fridge, basic but good location and view from terrace. **C** *Ideal*, R dos Andradas 491, T/F2339423. A/c, **D** with fan, bath, pleasant, modern, bar. **C** *Nacional*, R Dr Moreira 59, T2329206. Fridge, a/c, safe. **C** *São Rafael*, Dos Barés and Leovegildo Coelho. A/c, fridge, TV, not too clean. **D** *Dona Joana*, R dos Andradas 553, T2337553. A/c, fridge, good value, the hotel is safe although the area is not. **D** *Doral*, Joaquim Nabuco 647, T2324102. With breakfast, bath, TV, a/c, OK. Next door is **E** *Rondovia*. No bath, no window, small room. **D** *Hospedaria de Turismo 10 de Julho*, R Dez de Julio 679, T2326280. A/c, good breakfast. Recommended. **D** *Jangada*, R dos Andradas 473, T2322248. A/c, **E** with fan, without bath, basic, breakfast, cooking facilities and laundry (beware rats). **D** *Paradise*, R 10 de Julho 685, T2324840. A/c. **D** *Pensão Sulista*, Av Joaquim Nabuco 347, T2345814. A/c, **E** with fan, breakfast, run-down, outside showers, parking, not a safe area. There are others on this avenue. **D** *Rio Branco*, R dos Andradas 484, T/F2334019. Safe, laundry facilities, a/c, **E** with fan, popular. Recommended, but avoid damp rooms on ground floor.

Iranduba A small but growing town 10 km southwest of the city, cheaper than Manaus, with a good beach. **D** *Hotel Verdes Matas*, T3671133. Recommended. An easy bus ride from Manaus, includes ferry crossing.

Camping   There are no campsites in or near Manaus; it is difficult to find a good, safe place to camp wild.

Novotel serves a recommended *feijoada completa* on Saturday. *Restaurant Tarumã*   **Eating**
in Tropical Hotel. Dinner only. *Canto da Peixada*, R Emílio Moreira 1677 (Praça 14 de
Janeiro), T2343021. Superb fish dishes, lively atmosphere, unpretentious, close to
centre. *La Barca*, R Recife 684, T2367090. Wide variety of fish dishes, classy, popular,
often has live music. *São Francisco*, Blvd Rio Negro 195, 30 minutes walk from centre
(or bus 705), in Educandos suburb. Good fish, huge portions. Highly recommended.
Panorama next door, No 199, T6244626. Also good for fish, balcony overlooking river,
cheap. Highly recommended. *Peixaria Moronguêtá*, R Jaith Chaves, Vila da
Felicidade, Porto da Ceasa, T6153362. Good fish and view. *Caçarola*, R Maués 188,
Cachoeirinha, T2333021, and *Paramazon*, R Santa Isabel 1176, Cachoeirinha,
T2337768. Both very good local fish dishes (take a taxi). Japanese at *Miako*, R São Luís
230, also *Suzuran*, Boulevard Álvaro Maia 1683, Adrianópolis, good, closed Tuesday,
take taxi. *Búfalo*, *churrascaria*, Av Joaquim Nabuco 628. Best in town, US$5, all you can
eat. *Mania de Comer*, R Quintino Bocaiúva 472. Good self-service, cheaper after 1400.
Encontro dos Amigos, R Pedro Botelho 163. Good. *Fiorentina*, R José Paranaguá 44,
Praça da Polícia. Italian, very good, great Feijoada on Saturday, half price on Sunday.
Fiorella, R Pará 640, good Italian. *Olinda*, Pedro Botelho 93, near Miranda Leão. Good
regional dishes, *caldeirada* recommended. *Frangolandia*, Joaquim Nabuco near 7 de
Setembro. Good grill. *Chapaty*, Saldanho Marinho 429B; also R Costa Azevedo 105.
Vegetarian, closed in the evening. *Mandarim*, Av Eduardo Ribeiro 650. Chinese, pay
by weight, closed Sunday. Recommended. *Skina dos Sucos*, Eduardo Ribeiro e 24 de
Maio. Recommended for juices. Pizzeria next door is also good. *Casa do Guaraná*, R
Marcílio Dias. Marvellous juices mixed with *guaraná*. *Casa dos Sucos*, 7 de Setembro
between Joaquim Nabuco and G Vargas. Regional fruit juices and snacks. *Maté
Amargo*, R Saldanha Marinho 603. Good buffet, all you can eat. *Veneza*, Av Getúlio
Vargas 570. Good Saturday *feijoada*. *Jangada Bar*, near port, good snacks. *Alemã*,
cafetería, R José Paranaguá, Praça da Polícia. Good for juices, sandwiches. *Sorveteria
Glacial*, Av Getúlio Vargas 161 and other locations. Highly recommended for ice
cream. *Restaurante Natalia*, Av Epaminondas, downtown. With garden, has Pagode
music and dancing on Friday nights. *Vegetariano*, 7 Setembro. Vegetarian kilo buffet,
good. Many restaurants close on Sunday nights and Monday. City authorities grade
restaurants for cleanliness: look for A and B. Good juice bars along Av Joaquim
Nabuco, try *cupuaçu*.
   The fishing catch is brought to the waterfront between 2300-0100, including the
giant *pirarucu*.

Spectrum, R Lobo D'Almada 322. Very young. Cachoeirinha has a number of bars   **Bars &**
offering music and dancing, liveliest at weekends. The nightclub in the *Tropical Hotel*   **nightclubs**
attracts Manaus's wealthy citizens on Thursday-Saturday, as does its bingo club;
nearby Ponta Negra beach becomes extremely lively late on weekend nights and during holidays, with outdoor concerts and samba in the summer season. *Studio 5* disco,
R Contorno, Distrito Industrial, T2378333.

Theatre   For *Teatro Amazonas*, see above. **Cinema**   In R 10 de Julho and 6 screens at   **Entertainment**
Amazonas shopping centre, bus Cidade Nova 5, or 204, 207, 208, 307. Most foreign
films are shown with original soundtrack and Portuguese sub-titles. Afternoon performances are recommended as long queues often form in the evenings.

6 January: *Epiphany*; *Ash Wednesday*, half-day; *Maundy Thursday*; 24 June: *São*   **Festivals**
João; 14 July; 5 September; 30 October; 1 November, *All Saints Day*, half-day;
Christmas Eve; *New Year's Eve*, half-day. February: *Carnival* in Manaus has

The Amazon

spectacular parades in a sambadrome modelled on Rio's, but with 3 times the capacity. Tourists may purchase grandstand seats, but admission at ground level is free (don't take valuables), with every samba school member guaranteed entrance. Carnival dates vary – 5 days of Carnival, culminating in the parade of the Samba Schools. Third week in **April**: *Week of the Indians*, Indian handicraft. In **June**: *Festival do Amazonas*; a celebration of all the cultural aspects of Amazonas life, indigenous, Portuguese and from the northeast, especially dancing; Festival Marquesiano also in June; mostly typical dances from those regions of the world which have sent immigrants to Amazonas, performed by the students of the Colégio Marquês de Santa Cruz; **29 June**: *São Pedro*, boat processions on the Rio Negro. In **September**: *Festival de Verão do Parque Dez*, second fortnight, festival with music, fashion shows, beauty contests, local foods etc, Centro Social Urbano do Parque Dez; *Festival da Bondade*, last week, stalls from neighbouring states and countries offering food, handicrafts, music and dancing, SESI, Estr do Aleixo Km 5. **October**: *Festival Universitário de Música – FUM*, the most traditional festival of music in Amazonas, organized by the university students, on the University Campus. **8 December**: *Processão de Nossa Senhora da Conceicão*, from the Igreja Matriz through the city centre and returning to Igreja Matriz for a solemn mass.

Sports　**Swimming**　At Ponta Negra beach (Soltur bus, US$0.70), though the beach virtually disappears beneath the water in April-August. Good swimming at waterfalls on the Rio Tarumã, where lunch is available, shade, crowded at weekends; take Tarumã bus from R Tamandaré or R Frei J dos Inocentes, 30 minutes, US$0.70 (very few on weekdays), getting off at the police checkpoint on the road to Itacoatiara. There is also superb swimming in the natural pools and under falls of clear water in the little streams which rush through the woods, but take locals' advice on swimming in the river; electric eels and various other kinds of unpleasant fish, apart from the notorious *piranhas*, abound, and industrial pollution of the river is growing.

Shopping　**Bookshops**　*Livraria Nacional*, R 24 de Maio. Stocks some French books. *Usados CDs*
All shops close at 1400　*e Livros*, Av Getúlio Vargas 766. Good selection of used books, English, German,
on Saturday and all day　French and Spanish. *Valor*, R Ramos Ferreira 1195. Some English classics stocked.
Sunday　**Markets & souvenirs**　Go to the *Mercado Adolfo Lisboa* (see above) early in the morning when it is full of good quality regional produce, food and handicrafts, look out for *guaraná* powder or sticks, scales of *pirarucu* fish (used for manicure), and its tongue used for rasping *guaraná* (open daily 0500-1800). See the 2 markets near the docks, best in the early morning. In Praça da Saudade, R Ramos Ferreira, there is a Sunday *Festa de Arte* from 1700; try prawns and calaloo dipped in *tacaca* sauce. In the Praça do Congresso, Av E Ribeiro, there is a very good Sunday craftmarket. Ponta Negra beach boasts a small 'hippy' market, very lively at weekends. There is a good supermarket at the corner of Av Joaquim Nabuco and R Sete de Setembro. The *Central Artesanato*, R Recife, near Detran, has local craft work. *Casa de Beija-Flor*, in the *Hotel Tropical*, is good. The souvenir shop at the INPA has some interesting Amazonian products on sale. *Selva Amazônica*, Mercado Municipal. For wood carvings and bark fabric. For hammocks go to R dos Andradas, where there are many shops.

　　Since Manaus is a free port, the whole area a few blocks off the river front is full of electronics shops.

　　Photographic　Highly recommended for camera repairs, *Oficina Kawasky*, Ilidio Lopes 750, in the Japanese quarter, taxi US$15 return. Film processing at *Studio Universal*, R 24 de Maio 146, cheap, good quality.

Local Car hire: *Localiza*, R Major Gabriel 1558, T2334141, and airport, T6521176. **Bicycle repairs**: there are 3 shops on R Com Clementino, near Av Alvaro Maia. **Buses**: all city bus routes start below the cathedral in front of the port entrance; just ask someone for the destination you want.

Transport
See also Ins & outs, page 631

Long distance Air: Eduardo Gomes airport is 9 km from the city. There are international flights to Guayaquil, La Paz, Mexico City, Miami, Orlando, Santa Cruz and Quito. To the Guyanas, a connection must be made in Belém. Domestic flights to Belém, Boa Vista, Brasília, Cruzeiro do Sul, Macapá, Parantins, Porto Velho, Rio Branco, Rio de Janeiro, Santarém, São Paulo, Tabatinga, Tefé and Trombetas.

Make reservations as early as possible, flights may be full. Do not rely on travel agency waiting lists; go to the airport 15 hours early and get on the airport waiting list. Domestic airport tax US$7.

Taxi fare to airport US$7.25, fixed rate, or take bus marked 'Aeroporto Internacional' from Marquês de Santa Cruz at Praça Adalberto Vale, near the cathedral, US$0.70, or from Ed Garagem on Av Getúlio Vargas every 30 minutes. No buses 2200-0700. Taxi drivers often tell arrivals that no bus to town is available, be warned! It is sometimes possible to use the more regular, faster service run by the *Tropical Hotel*; many tour agencies offer free transfers without obligation. Check all connections on arrival. **NB** Check in time is 2 hours in advance. Allow plenty of time at Manaus airport, formalities are very slow especially if you have purchased duty-free goods. The restaurant serves good à la carte and buffet food throughout the day. Many flights depart in the middle of the night and while there are many snack bars there is nowhere to rest. Local flights leave from airport terminal 2: make sure in advance of your terminal.

Buses: rodoviária is 5 km out of town at the intersection of Av Constantino Nery and R Recife; take a local bus from centre, US$0.70, marked 'Aeroporto Internacional' or 'Cidade Nova' (or taxi, US$5).

Roads The road north from Manaus to Boa Vista (770 km) is described on page 655. **Hitchhiking** with truckers is common, but not recommended for women travelling alone. To hitch, take a Tarumã bus to the customs building and hitch from there, or try at 'posta 5', 2 km beyond the rodoviária.

The Catire Highway (BR-319), from Manaus to Porto Velho (868 km), has been officially closed since 1990. Several bridges are out and there is no repair in sight. The alternative for drivers is to ship a car down river on a barge, others have to travel by boat (see below).

To **Itacoatiara**, 285 km east on the Amazon, with Brazil-nut and jute processing plants (bus service 8 a day, 4 hours); now paved route AM-010, 266 km, through Rio Preto da Eva.

Boats: to Santarém, Belém, Porto Velho, Tefé, Tabatinga (for Colombia and Peru), São Gabriel da Cachoeira, and intermediate ports. Almost all vessels now berth at the first (downstream) of the floating docks, which is open to the public 24 hours a day. Bookings can be made up to 2 weeks in advance at the ticket sales area by the port's pedestrian entrance (bear left on entry). The names and itineraries of departing vessels are displayed here as well as on the docked boats themselves. Touts will engulf you when you arrive at the pedestrian entry; be calm, patient and friendly. Travellers still recommend buying tickets from the captain on the boat itself. The port is relatively clean, well organized, and has a pleasant atmosphere.

See also River transport, page 598

ENASA (the state shipping company) sells tickets for private boats at its office in town (prices tend to be high here), T6333280. Local boats and some cargo barges still berth by the concrete retaining wall between the market and Montecristi. Boats for São Gabriel da Cachoeira, Novo Airão, and Caracaraí go from São Raimundo, up river

The Amazon

from the main port. Take bus 101 'São Raimundo', 112 'Santo Antônio' or 110, 40 minutes; there are 2 docking areas separated by a hill, the São Raimundo *balsa*, where the ferry to Novo Airão, on the Rio Negro, leaves every afternoon (US$10); and the Porto Beira Mar de São Raimundo, where the São Gabriel da Cachoeira boats dock (most departures Friday). For Caracaraí cargo barges go year round, but don't take passengers. **NB** From Manaus-São Paulo is cheaper by boat Manaus-Porto Velho, then bus to São Paulo, than by flying direct or by boat to Belém then bus. Departures to the less important destinations are not always known at the Capitânia do Porto, Av Santa Cruz 265, Manaus. Be careful of people who wander around boats after they've arrived at a port: they are almost certainly looking for something to steal.

Immigration For those arriving by boat who have not already had their passports stamped (eg from Leticia), the immigration office is on the first of the floating docks next to the tourist office. Take the dock entrance opposite the cathedral, bear right, after 50m left, pass through a warehouse to a group of buildings on a T section.

Directory   **Airline offices** *American Airlines*, Av Eduardo Ribeiro 664, T6333363. *Lloyd Aéreo Boliviano*, Av 7 de Setembro 993, 1st floor, T6334200. *Transbrasil*, R Guilherme Moreira 150, T6221705. *Varig*, R Marcílio Dias 284, T6214522. *Vasp*, Av 7 de Setembro 993, T6223470.

Banks *Banco do Brasil*, R Mcal Deodoro (5th floor), and airport changes US$ cash, 8% commission, Visa withdrawals at Praça Dom Pedro II (in front of the docks), 2nd floor, efficient (PIN necessary); many local branches, open 0900-1600. Most offices shut in the afternoon; foreign exchange operations 0900-1200 only, or even as early as 1100. Thomas Cook TCs changed by *Banespa* (good rates, TCs and cash). *Bamerindus*, R Marcílio Dias 196, TCs only, fast and friendly service. *Banco Amazonas*, R Henrique Martins Cavalcante, good rates. *Bradesco*, Av 7 de Setembro 895/293, for Visa ATM. *Credicard*, Av Getúlio Vargas 222 for Diner's cash advances. *American Express* for money transactions and mail at *Selvatur* (see **Tours** below). Cash at main hotels; *Câmbio Cortez*, 7 de Setembro 1199, converts TCs into US$ cash, good rates, no commission. Do not change money on the streets.

Communications Post Office: Main office including poste restante on Mcal Deodoro. On the 1st floor is the philatelic counter where stamps are sold, avoiding the long queues downstairs. Staff don't speak English but are used to dealing with tourists. For airfreight and shipping, Alfândega, Av Marquês Santa Cruz (corner of Marechal Deodoro), Sala 106. For airfreight and seamail, Correio Internacional, R Monsenhor Coutinho e Av Eduardo Ribeiro (bring your own packaging). *UPS* office, T2329849 (Custódio). **Telephone:** International calls at *Telemar*, Av Getúlio Vargas 950. **Internet:** *Internext*, Rio Negro Centre, corner of R 24 de Maio and Av Eduardo Ribeiro, US$4 per hr. At *SESC*, R Henrique Martins, 2nd floor in library, US$1.50 per hr. Internet access at the college on 7 de Setembro just before Câmbia Cortez.

Embassies & consulates Most open in the morning only. *Austria*, R 5, Qd E, No 4, Jardim Primeravera II, T6421939, F6421582. *Belgium*, Conj Murici, Qd D 13, Parque 10, T2361452. *Bolivia*, Av Efigênio Sales 2226, Qd B, No 20, T2369988. *Colombia*, R Dona Libânia 62, near opera house, T2346777, check whether a Colombian tourist card can be obtained at the border. *Denmark*, Estr da Refinaria, T6151555, also handles Norway. *Finland*, R Marcílio Dias 131, T6226686. *France*, Av Joaquim Nabuco 1846, T2336583. *Germany*, R 24 Maio 220, Edif Rio Negro Centre, sala 812, T2349045, 1000-1200. *Italy*, R Belo Horizonte 240, Adrianópolis, T6114877. *Japan*, R Ferreira Pena 92, T2322000. *Netherlands*, R Miranda Leão 41, T6221366. *Peru*, R A, Casa: 1, Conj Aristocrático, Chapada, T6563267. *Portugal*, R Terezina 193, T6331577. *Spain*, Al Cosme Ferreira 1225, Aleixo, T6443800. *UK*, Av Eduardo Ribeiro 520, Sala 1501, T6223879. *USA*, R Recife 1010, Adrianópolis, T6334907, will supply letters of introduction for US citizens. *Venezuela*, R Ferreira Pena 179, T2336004, F2330481, 0800-1200, everyone entering Venezuela overland needs a visa. The requirements are 1 passport photo, an onward ticket and the fee, usually US$30 (check in advance for changes to these regulations – it is reported that a yellow fever certificate is not needed). Takes 24 hrs.

Hospitals & medical services *Hospital of Tropical Medicine*, Av Pedro Teixeira (D Pedro I), T2381711, treatment free, some doctors speak a little English. Take buses 201 or 214 from Av Sete de Setembro in the city centre.

Laundry *Lavlev*, Blvd Alvaro Maia 1400. Another on Paranaguá between Botelho and J Nabuco. Can negotiate on price. Also a good cheap laundry opposite the cemetery, open Sun.

Security Manaus is a friendly, if busy city. Unemployment and a depressed local economy have been responsible for a rise in crime, but Manaus is a good deal safer than the big cities of southern Brazil. As in any city, the usual precautions against opportunist crime should be taken (see **Essentials** chapter). Bars along R Joaquim Nabuco are reported particularly unsafe due to drugging of drinks. A tourist police force, *Politur*, has been created in an effort to assist visitors.

Tour companies & travel agents *Tarumã Turismo*, Av Eduardo Ribeiro 664, T6333363, taruma@taruma.com, www.taruma.com, packages to Parintins festival, flights, hotels and car hire. See below for advice on choosing a jungle tour.

Tourist offices *Secretaria de Estado da Cultura e Turismo*, Av 7 de Setembro 1546, Vila Ninita, T6332850, F2339973, Mon-Fri 0700-1900, Sat 0700-1300. *FUMTUR*, Av 7 de Setembro 157, T6224986, F2327025, fumtur@internext.com.br, www.internext.com.br/fumtur. There is a tourist office at the airport. Town map from *Amazon Explorers*, or from news kiosks. *Guide Book of Manaus*, US$3, in English, useful, available from *Selvatur*. *A Crítica*, newspaper, lists local entertainments and events. *Mananara Guia*, a very detailed Manaus street index and guide, is available from news kiosks, US$18.

Useful addresses **Visas**: Take bus from Praça Adalberto Vale to Kissia Dom Pedro for Polícia Federal post, people in shorts not admitted.

Voltage 110 volts AC; some hotels 220 volts AC, 60 cycles.

Tours

There are many different kinds of tours: 'luxurious', which are comfortable but 'set up' for tourists; some aiming at seeing lots of animals, and others at seeing how the people in the jungle live. Be sure to ascertain in advance the exact itinerary of the tour, that the price includes everything (even drink and tips), that guides are knowledgeable and will accompany you themselves and that there will be no killing of anything rare. Ensure that others in your party share your expectations and are going for the same length of time. Choose a guide who speaks a language you can understand. A shorter tour may be better than a long, poor one. Packaged tours, booked overseas, are usually of the same price and quality as those negotiated locally. **Choosing a tour**

NB There are many hustlers at the airport and on the street (particularly around the hotels and bars on Joaquim Nabuco and Miranda Leão), but it is not wise to go on a tour with the first friendly face you meet. Make enquiries and check credentials personally. *Secretaria de Estado da Cultura e Turismo* (see **Directory** above) can help you find a company you will be comfortable with. Do not employ freelance guides touting at the airport or the river port and it is potentially very dangerous to go with an unknown guide. When you are satisfied that you have found a reputable company, book direct with the company itself. Ask for a detailed, written contract. Your hotel may be able to help with recommendations, but employees may earn commission from those they suggest to you.

Bill Potter, resident in Manaus, writes: "opposite Manaus, near the junction of the Rio Negro and the Rio Solimões, lies the **Lago de Janauri**, a small nature reserve. This is where all the day or half-day trippers are taken, usually combined with a visit to the 'meeting of the waters'. Although many people express disappointment with this area because so little is seen and/or there are so many **Tour duration & itinerary**

The Amazon

'tourist-trash' shops, for those with only a short time it is worth a visit. You will see some birds and with luck dolphins. In the shops and bars there are often captive parrots and snakes. The area is set up to receive large numbers of tourists, which ecologists agree relieves pressure on other parts of the river. Boats for day trippers leave the harbour constantly throughout the day, but are best booked at one of the larger operators such as *Amazon Explorers* or *Selvatur*. Remember that in the dry season, one-day tours may not offer much to see if the river is low."

Those with more time can take the longer cruises and will see various ecological environments. To see virgin rainforest, a five-day trip by boat is needed. Most tour operators operate on both the Rio Solimões and the Rio Negro. The Rio Negro is considered easier to navigate, generally calmer and with fewer biting insects. This area has more visible upland rainforest and larger animals, whilst the Solimões is flooded for six months of the year. On the Rio Solimões there are more birds, piranha and alligators, but you're likely to be constantly fighting the mosquitoes and sandflies!

Another alternative is to go up river to one of the jungle hotels. From the base, you can then take short trips into the forest or along the river channels. Flights over the jungle give a spectacular impression of the extent of the forest.

Taking a transport boat from Manaus is not a substitute for a tour as they rarely get near to the banks and are only interested in getting from A to B as quickly as possible.

Generally, between April and September excursions are only by boat; in the period October-March, the Victoria Regia lilies virtually disappear. Fishing is best between September and March (no flooding). If using a camera, do remember to bring a fast film as light is dim.

Prices vary. The recommended companies charge within the following ranges (per person): one day, US$60-95; two days, for example to Lago

Manaus environs

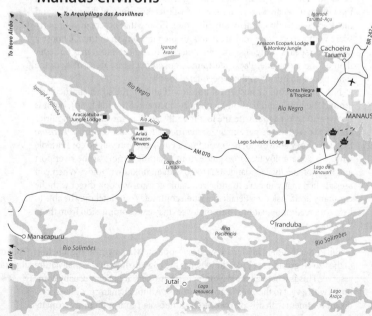

Salvador, US$260 including lodging; fishing trips US$250. Longer, special-ized, or more luxurious excursions will cost significantly more. It is more eco-nomical to incorporate the meeting of the waters in a longer trip than to make a separate excursion.

Many kinds of birds can be seen in and around the grounds of the *Hotel Tropical* such as fly catchers – kingbirds and kiskadees – swallows, yellow-browed spar-rows, aracaris – member of the toucan family – woodpeckers, woodcreepers, thrushes, anis, three species of tanager, two of parrots – the dusky and blue headed. Sloths and monkeys may also be seen. For further information, contact Moacir Fortes or Andrew Whittaker, birding@internext.com.br.

Birdwatching

Essentials

There are several lodges within a few hours boat or car journey from Manaus. Most emphasize comfort rather than a real jungle experience, and you are more likely to enjoy a nice buffet in pleasant company than come face to face with rare fauna. Nev-ertheless the lodges are good if your time is limited and you want to have a brief taste of the Amazon rainforest. Agencies for reservations are also listed. **L** *Acajatuba Jungle Lodge*, Lago Acajatuba, 4 hours up the Rio Negro from Manaus. Forty apartments with shower, bar, restaurant, contact office at R Dr Almino 36, Centro, T2337642. **L** *Ariaú Amazon Towers*, Rio Ariaú, 2 km from Archipélago de Anavilhanas, 60 km from Manaus on a side channel of the Rio Negro, 140 apartments with shower, restaurant, beach (September-March), 40m high lookout, walkway across a swamp, museum, orchidarium, herbarium, trips to the Anavilhanas islands in groups of 10-20, rates start at US$280 for a 2-day/1-night package, standard is US$400 pp, 3 nights/4 days, including transfers, meals, all excursions, bilingual guides, has a new 'cosmic suite' with planetarium and 24-hour internet connection (family size, US$2,000 per night all inclusive). Strongly recommended. Con-tact *River Jungle Hotel*, R Silva Ramos 20, Centro, T2347308, F2335615, treetop@internext.com.br, www.ariautowers.com.br, in Rio T/F021-2348779, in USA, Jill A Siegel, 17 Schenck Av 2C, Great Neck, NY 11021, T/F718-5230041, 1-800-4707636 (access 21), jsananda@aol.com. **L** *Amazon Ecopark Lodge*, Igarapé do Tarumã, 20 km from Manaus, 15 minutes by boat. Sixty apartments with shower, bar, restaurant, contact T2340939, F2340027. Nearby is the **Amazon Monkey Jungle**, an ecological park where many monkey species are treated and rehabilitated in natural sur-roundings. The *Living Rainforest Founda-tion*, which administers the *Ecopark*, also offers educational jungle trips and over-night camps (bring your own food), entrance US$15. **L** *Amazon Village*, Lago do Puraquequara, 60 km from Manaus. A comfortable lodge on dry land, with nice cabins, 32 apartments with cold shower, restaurant. Recommended. Contact T6331444, F6333217. **A** *Amazon Lodge*,

Lodges

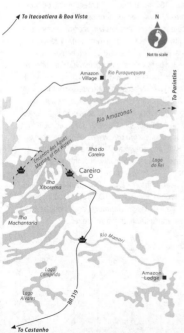

a floating lodge on Lago do Juma, 80 km from Manaus, 30 minutes by Careiro ferry, then 1½ hours by bus, then 2 hours by boat. Twelve basic apartments with cold shower, restaurant, good excursions. Highly recommended. Contact T6565464, F6566101. **A** *Boa Vida Jungle Resort*, 53 km from Manaus by route AM-10, direction Itacoatiara. Seven apartments and 6 chalets, shower, fridge, bar, restaurant, fishing, boating, contact T2345722, F2322482. *Pousada dos Guanavenas* on Ilha de Silves, 300 km from Manaus on the road to Itacoatiara, then by boat along the Rio Urubu. Views of Lago Canacari, 33 rooms, a/c, fridge, electric showers, contact *Guanavenas Turismo*, Av Constantino Nery 2486, Flores, T6561500, F2381211, aristides@internext.com.br, www.guanavenas.com.br. **A** *Lago Salvador Lodge*, Lago Salvador, 30 km from Manaus, 40 minutes by boat from the *Hotel Tropical*. Twelve apartments, cold shower, bar, restaurant, contact T6584221. **A** *Rainforest Lodge*, on the banks of Lago Januacá, 4 hours from Manaus. Fourteen bungalows with fans, pool, restaurant, snack bar, contact T2339182. **C** *Zequinho* (José dos Santos Lima), on Rio Araçá, 3 hours from Manaus, contact Antônio José dos Santos Lima, São Joaquim 48, T6291821, or through *Green Planet* (see **Tour companies**, below). Simple wooden family house, piranha fishing, caiman hunting (the animal is returned to the water), José is a highly recommended guide.

Directory **Tour companies & travel agents** *Alternatur*, R Col Salgado 63, Aparecida, T2345915, F6337094, alternatur@internext.com.br, run by French researcher Thérèse Aubreton. *Amazon Explorers*, R Nhamundá 21, Praça NS Auxiliadora, T6333319, F2345753, www.amazonexplorers.com.br, day tour including 'meeting of the waters', Lago do Janauari, rubber collecting and lunch has been highly recommended by most users (US$60), boat *Amazon Explorer* available for hire at about US$230 per day. *Amazon Travel Service*, Av Joaquim Nabuco 1626, sala 201/203, Centro, T6222788, F6222715, atstur@amazonet.com.br. *Fontur*, in *Tropical Hotel*, Estr da Ponta Negra, Km 18, T6583052, F6583512, fontur@manaus.br, www.fontur.com.br. *Green Planet Tours*, Room 104 (in *Hotel Aquarius*), R Guilherme Moreira 116, T/F2321398, Mobile 9894889, g.planet@usa.net, arrange tours to jungle lodges including Rio Araçá. *Selvatur*, Praça Adalberto Vale 17, T6222577, F6222177, selvatur@manaus.br, Rio Negro trip, 0800-1500, with lunch at *Janaurylândia* floating hotel. *Swallows and Amazons*, R Quintino Bocaiúva 189, andar 1, Sala 13, enter through *Guarana do Primo*, T/F6221246, swallows@internext.com.br, www.overlookinn.com, Mark and Tania Aitchison offer a wide range of riverboat, adventure and speciality tours and accommodation (up to 14 days); they have their own houseboat (with hammocks), covered motorized canoe and 12-bed private jungle lodge just before the Anavilhanas islands, very comprehensive service. **Guides:** Those listed below have been recommended by travellers, but bear in mind that different tourists have different expectations and recommendations can change. Guides sometimes work individually as well as for various tour agencies. Some will only accompany longer expeditions and often subcontract shorter trips. *Carlos Colares*, Av Atlântica 91, Raiz, T2371961, excursions with fishing, hunting and exploring in the more remote regions of the Rio Negro, speaks English. *Carlos Damasceno* (*Jaguar Adventure Tours*, R Marciano Armond, Vila Operária 23A, Cachoeirinha, T/F6632998, Mobile 9827285, jaguartours@objetivonet.com.br, www.objetivonet.com.br/jaguartours), serious deep jungle exploration with an ecological slant and visits to remote historical and Indian settlements, speaks English and German, very highly recommended. *Moacir Fortes* (R Miguel Ribas 1339, Santo Antônio, Manaus, T2327492, or through *Amazônia Expeditions Ltd*, Houston, T713-6608115) has his own 19m boat *Amazônia Expedition*, speaks English and German. *Gerry Hardy* (*Jungle Experience*, contact via Chris Gomes at *Hotel Ideal*, T2332000), speaks English, very warmly recommended. *Soares* (*Amazonas Indian Turismo*, R dos Andradas 311, T/F6335578), Indian guides who speak Portuguese and Spanish, cheap, mixed reports.

The Amazon

Down the Amazon River

Just before the Amazonas-Pará border, between Manaus and Santarém, is Parintins, a town on the Ilha Tupinambana. Boat trips can be taken to river beaches in the dry season and to nearby lakes.

Parintins
Population: 72,000
Phone code: 092

Here, on the last three days of June each year, the *Festa do Boi* draws some 40,000 visitors. Since the town has only two small hotels, everyone sleeps in hammocks on the boats that bring them to the festival from Manaus and Santarém (a large vessel will charge about US$130 per person, including breakfast, for the duration). The *Festa do Boi de Parintins* consists of lots of folkloric dancing, but its main element is the competition between two rival groups, the Caprichoso (whose colour is blue) and the Garantido (red), in the *bumbódromo*, built in 1988 to hold 35,000 spectators. There are about 2,500 competitors, but many more participants. During the festival, Mãe Catirina, Pai Francisco and Cunhãporanga (the beautiful woman) are major characters in this particular *boi-bumbá* drama. A preview of the festival is held in the *Hotel Tropical* in Manaus in the middle of June. Parintins' other main festival is the *Pastorinhas*, from 24 December to 6 January.

Transport Boats call on the Belém-Manaus route: 60 hours from Belém, minimum 10, maximum 26 from Manaus (depending on boat and if going up or down river). There are irregular sailings from Óbidos (ask at the port), 12-15 hours. A boat from Santarém takes 20 hours. There is also a small airport with flights to Manaus (1¼ hours), Óbidos and Santarém (1 hour 20 minutes).

Up the Rio Solimões

The river route from Manaus to Colombia and Peru can take as much as a week upriver. This journey will let you experience life on one of the world's great waterways.

Tefé is approximately halfway between Manaus and the Colombian border. The waterfront consists of a light sand beach. The waterfront market is on Monday morning. The nuns at the Franciscan convent sell handicrafts and embroidery.

Tefé
Population: 26,000

Sleeping and eating There are 3 small hotels and 5 pensions. **D** *Anilce*, Praça Santa Teresa 294. Clean, a/c, do not leave valuables in your room, very helpful. *Hotel Panorama*, recommended, good restaurant. Restaurant *Au Bec d'Or* by the port, French/Amazonian cuisine.

Transport Airport has a connection to Manaus. If travelling on to Tabatinga, note that Manaus-Tabatinga boats do not usually stop at Tefé. You must hire a canoe to take you out to the main channel and try to flag down the approaching ship.

Situated on the frontier with Peru, Benjamin Constant is served by boat services from Manaus, seven days or more; to Manaus, four days or more. Colombian territory is on the opposite bank of the river.

Benjamin Constant
Population: 15,000

Sleeping and eating **B** *Benjamin Constant*, beside ferry. All rooms a/c, some with hot water and TV, good restaurant, arranges tours, postal address Apdo Aéreo 219, Leticia, Colombia. *Mar Azur*, a/c, friendly. **D** *Benjamin*, very basic. **D** *Márcia Maria*, bath, a/c,

The Amazon

fridge, clean, friendly. Recommended. **E** *São Jorge*, meals available. Recommended. **E** *Hotel Lanchonete Peruana*, good food. *Pensão Cecília. Bar-21 de Abril*, cheaper.

Tabatinga
Population: 28,000

Four kilometres from Leticia (Colombia) is Tabatinga. The Port Captain here is reported as very helpful and speaking good English. The port area is called Marco. A good hammock will cost US$15 in Tabatinga (try Esplanada Teocides) or Benjamin Constant. A mosquito net for a hammock is essential if sailing upstream from Tabatinga; much less so downstream.

Sleeping and eating *Hotel Martins*, good but expensive. **D** *Residencial Aluguel Pajé*, with bath, fan, clean. **D** *Solimões*, run by the military – close to the airport – with breakfast, other meals available if ordered in advance, excellent value, clean – some taxi drivers are unaware that this hotel accepts non-military guests, but there is a VW colectivo minibus from the barracks to town centre, harbour and Leticia. *Três Fronteiras*, excellent restaurant. *Canto do Peixado*, on main street. Highly recommended.

Transport Airport to Tabatinga by minibus, US$1. Flights to Manaus and Tefé. Regular minibus to Leticia, US$0.60.

Directory **Banks**: it is difficult to change TCs in Tabatinga (try *Casa Branca*, *Casa Verde* or *Casa Amarela* on the main road, or the general manager of the main shopping centre), and far harder to purchase Peruvian soles than in Leticia. Good rates can be found at *Câmbio Cortez*, Av da Amizade 2205 (near *Banco do Brasil*).

Amazon border area with Colombia & Peru

Frontier with Colombia and Peru

It is advisable to check all requirements and procedures before arriving at this multiple border. As no foreign boat is allowed to dock at the Brazilian, Colombian and Peruvian ports, travellers should enquire carefully about embarkation/disembarkation points and where to go through immigration formalities. If waiting for transport, the best place for accommodation, exchange and other facilities is Leticia, Colombia. Travel between Colombia and Brazil and Peru is given below. Travel from/into Colombia is given under Leticia (see below).

There are no customs formalities for everyday travel between Leticia and Tabatinga

Brazilian immigration Entry and exit stamps are given at the Polícia Federal, 10 minutes' walk from the Tabatinga docks, opposite *Café dos Navegantes* (walk through the docks and follow the road to its end, turn right at this T-junction for one block to a white building). ■ *Monday-Friday 0800-1200, 1400-1800; also at the airport, open Wednesday and Saturday only. Proof of US$500 or an onward ticket may be asked for.* There are no facilities in Benjamin Constant, although it is possible to buy supplies for boat journeys. One-week transit in Tabatinga is permitted. In this frontier area, carry your passport at all times. If coming from Peru, you must have a Peruvian exit stamp and a yellow fever certificate.

Brazil

NB When crossing these frontiers, check if there is a time difference (for example Brazilian summer time, usually mid-October to mid-February). The **Colombian consulate** is near the border on the road from Tabatinga to Leticia, opposite *Restaurant El Canto de las Peixadas* (0800-1400). Tourist cards are issued on presentation of two passport photos.

Transport Taxis: travel between Tabatinga and Leticia is very informal; taxis between the 2 towns charge US$5 (more if you want to stop at immigration offices, exchange houses etc; beware of taxi drivers who want to rush you expensively over the border before it 'closes'), or US$0.80 in a colectivo (more after 1800). It is not advisable to walk the muddy path between Tabatinga and Leticia; robbery occurs here.

Boats: from Manaus-Benjamin Constant, boats normally go on to Tabatinga and start from there when going to Manaus. They usually wait 1-2 days in both Tabatinga and Benjamin Constant before returning to Manaus; you can stay on board. Tabatinga and Leticia are 1½-2 hours from Benjamin Constant (ferry/*recreio* US$2; 25 minutes by speedboat, US$4 pp, cheaper if more passengers).

For information on boats to/from Manaus, see Boats, page 639, and River transport, page 598

Colombian immigration *DAS,* C 9, No 8-32, T27189, Leticia, and at the airport. Exit stamps to leave Colombia by air or overland are given only at the airport. If flying into Leticia prior

Colombia

The Amazon

to leaving for Brazil or Peru, get an exit stamp while at the airport. Check both offices for entry stamps before flying into Colombia.

Entering Colombia To enter Colombia you must have a tourist card to obtain an entry stamp, even if you are passing through Leticia en route between Brazil and Peru (the Colombian consul in Manaus may tell you otherwise; try to get a tourist card elsewhere). The Colombian Consular Office in Tabatinga issues tourist cards; 24-hour transit stamps can be obtained at the DAS office. If visiting Leticia without intending to go anywhere else in Colombia, you may be allowed to enter without immigration or customs formalities (but travellers' cheques cannot be changed without an entry stamp).

Consulates *Brazilian,* C 11, No 10-70, T27531, 1000-1600. Open Monday-Friday, efficient, helpful; onward ticket and 2 black-and-white photos needed for visa (photographer nearby); allow 36 hours. *Peruvian,* Cra 11, No 6-80, T27204, F27825. Open 0830-1430; no entry or exit permits are given here.

Peru   **Peruvian immigration** Entry/exit formalities take place at Santa Rosa. Every boat leaving Peru stops here. There is also an immigration office in Iquitos (Malecón Tarapacá 382), where procedures for leaving can be checked. **Exchange** is available at Islandia (see below).

     Consulates In Iquitos there are consulates for Brazil (C Sargento Lores 363, T005194-232081) and Colombia (C Putumayo 247, T231461).

Transport Boats sail from Iquitos to a mud bank called Islandia, on the Peruvian side of a narrow creek, a few metres from the Brazilian port of Benjamin Constant. The journey time is a minimum of 2 days upstream, 8-36 hours downstream, depending on the speed of the boat. In ordinary boats, fares range from US$30-40 pp, depending on standard of accommodation, food extra. Speedboats charge US$75 pp, 3 a week run by *Amazon Tours and Cruises.* Passengers leaving Peru must visit immigration at Santa Rosa when the boat stops there. For entry into Brazil, formalities are done in Tabatinga; for Colombia, in Leticia. Boats to Peru leave from Islandia, calling at Santa Rosa (2-3 days upstream to Iquitos). *Amazon Tours and Cruises* also operate a luxury service between Iquitos and Tabatinga leaving Sunday, returning from Tabatinga on Wednesday, US$695 pp in the *Río Amazonas.* Also M/V *Arca* US$495 pp, return journey Wednesday-Saturday.

Leticia

Population: 23,000
Phone code: 9819
Colour map 1, grid B1

The city is clean, modern, though run down, and is situated near the river. It is rapidly merging into one town with neighbouring Marco in Brazil. There is a modern, well-equipped hospital. The best time to visit the area is in July or August, the early months of the dry season. At weekends, accommodation may be difficult to find. Leticia is a good place to buy typical products of Amazon Indians, and tourist services are better than in Tabatinga or Benjamin Constant.

Sights   Museum at Cra 11 y Calle 9, set up by *Banco de la República,* covers local ethnography and archaeology, in a beautiful building with a library and a terrace overlooking the Amazon. There is a small Amazonian zoo, entry US$1, and botanical garden on the road to the airport, within walking distance of town (20 minutes). Reports in 1999 state that this has closed and may not reopen.

AL *Anaconda*, Cra 11, No 7-34, T27119. Large a/c rooms, hot water, restaurant, good **Sleeping** terrace and swimming pool. **AL** *Parador Ticuna*, Av Libertador (Cra 11), No 6-11, T27241. Spacious apartments with bath, hot water, a/c, sleep up to 6, swimming pool, bar and restaurant. Under same ownership: **B** *Colonial*, Cra 10, No 7-08, T27164. A/c or fans, swimming pool, cafetería, noisy. **C-D** *Residencias Fernando*, Cra 9, No 8-80, T27362. Well equipped, clean. Recommended. **D** *Residencias Marina*, Cra 9 No 9-29, T27201/9. TV, some a/c, cold water, good breakfast and meals at attached restaurant, clean. **D** *Residencias La Manigua*, C 8, No 9-22, T27121. Bath, fan, clean, friendly. **E** *Residencia Internacional*, Av Internacional, between centre and Brazilian border. Basic, bath, fan, friendly, hard beds, clean. **E** *Primavera*, C 8 between Cras 9 and 10. Bath and fan, noisy. **F** *Residencias Colombia*, Cra 10 y C 8. Good value, shared bath.

Sancho Panza, Cra 10, No 8 72. Good value, good meat dishes, big portions, Brazilian **Eating** beer. Several small sidewalk restaurants downtown, good value *plato del día*. *Señora Mercedes*, C 8 near Cra 11. Good, cheap meals until 1930. Cheap food (fried banana and meat, also fish and pineapples) is sold at the market near the harbour. Also cheap fruit for sale. Many café/bars overlook the market on the river bank. Take your own drinking water and anything stronger that you desire.

Air The airport is 1½ kilometres from town, taxi US$1.60; small terminal, few facilities. **Transport** Expect to be searched before leaving Leticia airport, and on arrival in Bogotá from Leticia. To Bogotá, Monday and Friday, SAM (Tabatinga airport if Leticia's is closed).

Banks *Banco de Bogotá*, will cash TCs, has ATM on Cirrus network, good rates for Brazilian *reais*. **Directory** Apart from at this bank, TCs are hard to change, impossile at weekends. There are street money changers, plenty of *cambios*, and banks for exchange. Shop around. **Communications** Post Office: Avianca office, Cra 11, No 7-58. **Telephone:** Cra 11/C 9, near Parque Santander. **Tourist offices** Tourist office at C 10, No 9-86. *MA* (Ministerio del Medio Ambiente), Cra 11, No 12-05, for general information on national parks.

Up the Rio Negro

It is possible to get a launch from Manaus up the Rio Negro; see **River transport**, page 598. There are hardly any villages of more than a few houses, but these places are important in terms of communications and food resources. It is vital to be self-sufficient in food and cash and to be able to speak Portuguese or have a Brazilian guide. **Nova Airão**, on the west bank of the Negro, is about two days upstream. It has a large boat-building centre at the south end, and a fish and vegetable market at the north end. Ice and bread can also be purchased here. It has a telephone (from which international calls can be made – after a fashion). There is road access and a bus service from Manaus.

Nova Airão is the starting point for the **Parque Nacional Jaú**, contact the Ibama office in Manaus, Rua Ministro João Gonçalves de Souza, BR-319, Km 01, Distrito Industrial, Caixa Postal 185, CEP 69900, T2373718/3710, F2375177.

Moura is about five days upstream from Manaus. It has basic medical facilities and the military base has an airstrip (only usable September to December) and telecommunications. About a day further upstream is **Carvoeira**, almost opposite the mouth of the Rio Branco. There is a vibrant festival in the first week of August. More than a day beyond is **Barcelos**, with an airstrip (Hotel *Oasis*, German spoken; *Macedo*).

The Amazon

Are you sure you want to climb this mountain?

If you are tempted to climb Pico da Neblina, you will face plenty of discouraging factors before you set out. It is in an area of national strategic importance, with lots of minerals, including radioactive elements – in the surrounding soils. There is also gold in the neighbourhood, so garimpeiros are thick on the ground and they may not be too welcoming. The peak is in a Yanomami reserve and a permit is needed from Funai to enter. Similarly, a permit is required from Ibama to enter the national park. This can be a long-winded procedure in Manaus, where it is supposed to be done, although it may be a lot easier in São Gabriel da Cachoeira. Next, you have to get there, an expedition in itself, unless you go by helicopter like the Brazilian scientific and military teams (even then, choppers can't land on the top because of cross winds). Finally, there is the small matter of the climate. Almost 100 percent humidity, fierce heat until you get to the summit and, as Kevin Haight so delicately put it in South American Explorer, No 47, Spring 1997 (pages 9-15), a "four-letter word. Rain". The rain is torrential and can turn the rock faces into 'mini-Niagaras' in a matter of minutes. If you are happy to put up with all that, don't forget the insects – on Pico da Neblina itself there are countless species that haven't been catalogued yet.

São Gabriel da Cachoeira A great distance further upstream is São Gabriel da Cachoeira, from where you can continue to Venezuela. In São Gabriel, Tom Hanly, an Irish Salesian brother, is helpful, friendly and informative. There are beautiful white beaches and, in the river, rapids for 112 kilometres. São Gabriel is near the **Pico da Neblina National Park**. Pico da Neblina is the highest mountain in Brazil, 3,014 metres. Contact the Ibama office in Manaus for more information, see above. In São Gabriel there are two banks but no exchange facilities and *Valpes* hotel (**E**). There is a better class hotel on the island, restaurant. Recommended.

Cargo boats ply to **Cucuí** at the border between Brazil, Colombia and Venezuela. Also twice-weekly bus, US$5 (one hotel, ask for Elias, no restaurants). From Cucuí there are daily boats to Guadalupe (Colombia) and infrequent boats to Santa Lucía (Venezuela).

Warning The upper Rio Negro can be a rough area due to gold prospecting and drug running. Obtain local information and exercise caution when travelling in this region.

South on the Rio Madeira

Manicoré
Population: 37,000

Manicoré is a pleasant town. The Praça da Bandeira is at the corner of Avenida Getúlio Vargas and Avenida Pedro Tinoco (one block to the left of the road that goes up from the dock). There is a hotel (**E**) and, one block from the Praça at the floating dock, a slow but good restaurant, *Restaurant Tapuia*. The fruit market is on Av Vargas. See page 662 for transport from Porto Velho, to Manaus.

Humaitá
Population: 25,000
Phone code: 092

Humaitá is situated at the crossroads of the Rio Madeira with the Transamazônica highway and the BR-319 north to Manaus. Cattle ranching has begun in the area around the town. There are several basic hotels on the eastern edge of town (**C-D**). The Soltur rodoviária is in the centre.

There is very little traffic on the Transamazônica from Humaitá east to Itaituba (1,025 kilometres); local drivers may give lifts. A ferry crosses the Rio Aripuanã at Vila do Carmo. The road is good for about 350 kilometres from Humaitá, then it deteriorates badly. It is hilly, narrow, and the jungle usually

grows over the side of the road. Bus to **Apuí** (**E** *Hotel Goaino*, basic), 458 kilometres, about 12 hours, US$36, bus to Jacarèacanga erratic service, another
222 kilometres (the town is eight kilometres off the highway). One must stay
overnight and catch the Transbrasiliana bus to Itaituba (24 hours, schedule
erratic, the bus is replaced occasionally by a truck). **D** *Hotel São Cristóvão*,
with good restaurant, or try the filling station on the Transamazônica near the
Jacarèacanga turn-off, for hammock space. Travel times depend on the
weather conditions, the condition of the bus, and whether the driver decides to
stop somewhere for the night. There are flights Jacarèacanga-Itaituba (see
page 623). Boat, not daily, ticket from filling station, US$25, 1½ days, very
basic, hammock space only. Seventy kilometres before Itaituba there are rapids; the rest of the journey is done by pickup, US$10.

Roraima

*This extreme northern state is little visited by travellers, except those making the
journey between Manaus and the frontiers with Venezuela and Guyana. Mount
Roraima, after which the Territory is named, is possibly the original of Sir Arthur
Conan Doyle's 'Lost World'.*

Land grants in the 1970s to encourage agricultural development caused the
population to grow quickly from only 25,000 in 1960. In the late 1980s a gold
rush in the northwest of Roraima drew prospectors from all over the country.
The mining took place on the Yanomami Indian Reserve, causing much disruption to their traditional way of life. Further tragedy came in January 1998
when forest fires spread across the state, causing massive destruction until
extinguished by rains in March.

The state's population is now only 300,000 in an area nearly twice the size of
England. The forest cover gives way to grasslands in the northeast and there is
a pronounced dry season. The Várzea (flood plain) along the main rivers irri-
gates the southeast of the state. Cattle ranching is important as is rice cultivation on the flood plain of the Rio Branco. Other crops are maize, beans,
manioc and banana. Some gold mining still continues but at a reduced level.

Boa Vista

The state capital, 759 kilometres north of Manaus, has a modern functional plan,
which often necessitates long hot treks from one function to another. South of
town is an industrial estate; northwest is a new government district. It has an
interesting modern cathedral; also a museum of local Indian culture (poorly
kept). There is swimming in the Rio Branco, 15 minutes from the town centre
(too polluted in Boa Vista), reachable by bus only when the river is low. Under
heavy international pressure, the Brazilian government expelled some 40,000
gold prospectors (*garimpeiros*) from the Yanomami Indian Reserve in the west
of the state in the early 1990s. The economic consequences were very severe for
Boa Vista, which went from boom to bust. An increase in cattle ranching in the
area has not taken up the slack.

Population: 154,000
Phone code: 095
Colour map 1, grid A3

The Amazon

Essentials

Sleeping
Accommodation is generally expensive

A *Aipana Plaza*, Praça Centro Cívico 53, T2244800, F2244116, aipana@tecbet.com.br. Restaurant, pool, good service. **B** *Uiramutam Palace*, Av Capt Ene Garcez 427, T/F2249912. Restaurant, pool. **C** *Eusébio's*, R Cecília Brasil 1107, T6230300. Always full, book ahead, demand a single if on your own, pool, free transport to rodoviária or airport, very good restaurant. Recommended. **C** *Beija-Flor*, Av NS da Consolata 939 W, Bairro, near rodoviária, T2248241, F2248270. Includes breakfast, run by a Belgian Jean and his Brazilian wife Néia. Highly recommended. **C** *Roraima*, Av Benjamin Constant 284, T2249843. Recommended. The restaurant opposite is also recommended. **C** *Três Nações*, Av Ville Roy 1885, T2243439, close to the rodoviária. Some rooms a/c, refurbished, basic. Often recommended. **D** *Imperial*, Av Benjamin Constant, between R Ajuricaba and R Cecília Brasil. With bath, fan or a/c, welcoming, safe motorcycle parking. Recommended. **D** *Joelma*, Av NS da Consolata 1870, corner of Av Gulana S Vincento, T2245404. With bath, near rodoviária. **D** *Lua Nova*, R Benjamin Constant 591, T2242142. Without a/c, more expensive with, English spoken, noisy, seedy, often full. **D** *Monte Líbano*, Benjamin Constant 319 W, T2247232. Without a/c, dearer with (bus from rodoviária to centre passes by). **D** *Brasil*, next door at No 331, west near Drogafarma. Good meals (do not confuse with dirty, overpriced *Hotel Brasa* in the same street). At Av Ville Roy 1906-24, Carlos Alberto Soares lets a

Boa Vista

room, warm shower. Recommended. **E** *Terraço*, Av Cecília Brasil 1141. Without bath, noisy, friendly. **E** hotel opposite rodoviária, OK, clean, with bath, a/c, TV, quiet, cheap churrascaria 20m away on same street.

Camping Rio Caaumé, 3 km north of town (unofficial site. Small bar, clean river, pleasant).

Senzala, Av Castelo Branco 1115. Where the town's high society eats. *Café Pigalle*, R   **Eating**
Cecília Brasil, just off central square, next to *Eusébio's*. Good food, drinks and atmosphere, open late. *Góndola*, Benjamin Constant and Av Amazonas. Good. *Vila Rica*, R Ville Roy, near the rodoviária. Good cheap lunch. Snacks at *Top Set*, Av Jaime Brasil. *Catequeiro*, Araújo Filho and Benjamin Constant. Recommended *prato feito*. *M'Drinks*, Av das Guianas 1203. Bar.

Local Car hire: *Localiza*, Av Benjamin Constant 291E, T/F2245222 and *Yes*, Av Maj Wil-   **Transport**
liams 538, T/F2243723. **Buses**: The local bus terminal is on Av Amazonas, by R Cecília Brasil, near the central praça. **Taxis**: radio taxis with *Tupã*, R Monte Castelo 318, T2249150.

Long distance Air: international airport is 4 km from the centre. Taxi to rodoviária, US$9, to centre US$12, Bus 'Aeroporto' to/from the centre is US$0.40, 45 minutes' walk. No left luggage, information or exchange facilities at the airport. Flights to Belém, Brasília, Macapá, Manaus, Santarém and São Paulo. Confirm flights before reaching Boa Vista as they are often fully booked. Aircraft maintenance, baggage checking and handling are unreliable. Air taxis with *Rondônia*, Praça Santos Dumond, T2245068.

Buses: rodoviária, Av das Guianas, 3 km out of town at the end of Av Ville Roy,   *See also Border*
T2240606. Taxi to centre, US$5, bus US$0.45, 10 minutes. Note that it is difficult to get   *crossings below*
a taxi or bus to the rodoviária in time for early morning departures; as it's a 25 minute walk, book a taxi the previous evening.

To **Manaus**, with *União Cascavel*, US$32.50, 18 hours, 4 a day each way, can be very crowded, advisable to book because sometimes buses are fully booked days in advance, but extra buses may run when the scheduled service is full, check times, especially in the wet season. Buses often run late, and the night bus has to wait up to 4 hours for the Rio Branco ferry. To **Caracaraí** US$9, 3 hours. *Amatur* to **Bonfim**, daily 0730, 1430, 1700, 2 hours, US$3.70.

Hitchhiking: to **Santa Elena**, Venezuela is not easy; either wait at the bridge and police checkpoint on the road to the border, or try to find a Venezuelan driver on the square. Hitching from Boa Vista to **Manaus** is fairly easy on the many trucks travelling south; try from the service station near the rodoviária. You may have to change trucks at Caracaraí. At the ferry crossing over the Rio Branco there is usually a long queue of waiting hikers; try to arrange a lift on the ferry. Truck drivers ask for approximately half the bus fare to take passengers in the cab, which is a bargain, much cheaper or free in the back. The view from the truck is usually better than from the bus and you can see the virgin forest of the Indian Reserve in daylight. Take some food and water.

Airline offices *Penta*, T2246849. *META*, Praça Santos Dumond 100, T2247677. *Varig*, T2242269.   **Directory**
Banks US$ and Guyanese notes can be changed in Boa Vista. TCs and cash in *Banco do Brasil*, Av Glycon Paiva 56, 1000-1300 (minimum US$200). There is no official exchange agency and the local rates for bolívares are low: the *Banco do Brasil* will not change bolívares. *Bradesco*, Jaime Brasil e Getúlioi Vargas. Visa ATM. Best rate for dollars, *Casa Pedro José*, R Araújo Filho 287, T2244277, also changes TCs and bolívares. *Timbo's* (gold and jewellery shop), on the corner of R Cecília Brasil e Av Getúlio Vargas, will change money. **Embassies & consulates** *Venezuela*, Av Benjamin Constant 525E, Boa Vista, T2242182, Mon-Fri 0830-1300, but may close earlier. **Hospitals & medical services** *Geral*, Av Brig Eduardo Gomes, T6232068. Yellow fever inoculations are free at a clinic near the hospital. **Tourist offices** R Col Pinto 241, Centro,

T6231230, F6231831. Also at rodoviária, T6231238 and airport. **Guides:** Boat trips on Rio Branco and surrounding waterways (jungle, beaches, Indian reservations), *Acqua*, R Floriano Peixoto 505, T2246576, guide Elieser Rufino is recommended.

The Rio Branco

The Rio Branco is yellowish in colour, and less acidic than the Negro. Biting insects and their associated diseases are more prevalent outside the wet season. The river is better for fishing, though, and there is more wildlife to see. About two days up the Rio Branco from Manaus, on the way to Caracaraí, is **Santa Maria de Boiaçu**, a village with a military airstrip (in use in July and August), very basic medical facilities and an indirect radio link with Manaus. Three small shops sell basic necessities (frequently closed), and there are several tiny, but lively, churches.

Caracaraí

This busy port, with modern installations, is connected to Manaus with river traffic and is also on the Manaus-Boa Vista road (see below). The river banks are closer, so there is more to see than on the Amazon and stops in the tiny riverside settlements are fascinating.

Sleeping & eating **D** *Maroca*, opposite fuel tanks, 1 street back from the river. Clean and friendly. **E** *Caracaraí*, down the street from the rodoviária. Friendly but dirty. *Sorveteria Pizzaria Lidiany*. Recommended.

Transport **Buses** From Caracaraí to Boa Vista costs US$9, 3 hours. **NB** The Perimetral Norte road marked on some maps from Caracaraí east to Macapá and west to the Colombian frontier does not yet exist; it runs only about 240 km west and 125 km east from Caracaraí, acting at present as a penetration road. **Boats** Passengers are rarely allowed on boats now that the Manaus-Boa Vista has been paved.

Directory **Banks** Silas in the Drogaria on the south side of town will change US$.

The Rio Branco

The Amazon

To Venezuela and Guyana

The road which connects Manaus and Boa Vista (BR-174 to Novo Paraíso, then the Perimetral, BR-210, rejoining the BR-174 after crossing the Rio Branco at Caracaraí, ferry as long as there is traffic) is fully paved and regularly maintained. There are service stations with toilets, camping etc, every 150-180 kilometres, but all petrol is low octane. At Km 100 is Presidente Figueiredo, with shops and a restaurant. About 100 kilometres further on is a service station at the entrance to the **Uaimiri Atroari Indian Reserve**, which straddles the road for about 120 kilometres. Private cars and trucks are not allowed to enter the Indian Reserve between sunset and sunrise, but buses are exempt from this regulation. Nobody is allowed to stop within the reserve at any time. At the northern entrance to the reserve there are toilets and a spot to hang your hammock (usually crowded with truckers overnight). At Km 327 is the village of Vila Colina with *Restaurante Paulista*, good food, clean, you can use the shower and hang your hammock. At Km 359 there is a monument to mark the equator. At Km 434 is the clean and pleasant *Restaurant Goaio*. Just south of Km 500 is *Bar Restaurante D'Jonas*, a clean, pleasant place to eat, you can also camp or sling a hammock. Beyond here, large tracts of forest have been destroyed for settlement, but already many homes have been abandoned.

Boa Vista has road connections with the Venezuelan frontier at Santa Elena de Uairén, 237 kilometres away. The road is paved, but the only gasoline available is 110 kilometres south of Santa Elena. Boa Vista is also linked to Bonfim for the Guyanese border at Lethem. Both roads are open all year.

Frontier with Venezuela

Immigration & customs Border searches are thorough and frequent at this border crossing. Ensure in advance that you have the right papers for entering Brazil before arriving at this frontier. It may be possible to get your passport stamped in Manaus, but you may be fined. Everyone who crosses the border must have a visa for Venezuela; current procedure is to take filled out visa form, onward ticket, one passport photo and deposit slip from *Banco do Brasil* (US$30) to the Venezuelan consulate in Boa Vista, be prepared to wait an hour, but it may be possible to get a visa at the border; check requirements in advance. There is also a Venezuelan consulate in Manaus which issues one-year, multiple entry visas (see page 640).

Sleeping On the Brazilian side there are a basic hotel, *Pacaraima Palace*, a guesthouse, camping possibilities and a bank.

Transport Buses leave Boa Vista rodoviária at 0730, 1000 and 1400 for Santa Elena de Uairén, stopping at all checkpoints, US$7.50, 3½-6 hours, take water. Buses from Santa Elena to Boa Vista leave at 0830, 1200, 1500 and 1600. It is possible to share a taxi.

Santa Elena de Uairén (*population* 7,500) is the gateway to the Venezuelan Guiana Highlands for those entering the country from Brazil. It is a growing, pleasant frontier town, 10-12 hours by bus from Ciudad Bolívar, itself nine hours from Caracas. The road is paved all the way. There are also flights. The landscape is beautiful, an ancient land of flat-topped mountains and waterfalls. The road skirts the Parque Nacional Canaima, in which is the highest fall in the world, Salto Angel (Angel Falls). Not far north of Santa Elena is the route to Mount Roraima.

In Santa Elena are plenty of hotels and places to eat, money changing facilities, a phone office with international connections and tour companies for trips into the Gran Sabana – as the region is known. The bus station is on Calle Mcal Sucre. Buses south to Ciudad Bolívar are run by several companies throughout the day, earliest at 0700, last at 1930 (10-12 hours). The Brazilian consulate is near the bus terminal opposite the Corpoven gas station; open 0800-1200, 1400-1800. Full details on this region, and the rest of the country, can be found in the *Venezuela Handbook*.

Frontier with Guyana

The main border crossing between Brazil and Guyana is from Bonfim, 125 kilometres northeast of Boa Vista, to Lethem. The towns are separated by the Rio Tacutu, which is crossed by small boats for foot passengers; vehicles cross by pontoon, or can drive across in the dry season. The river crossing is 2½ kilometres from Bonfim, about 1½ kilometres north of Lethem. Formalities are generally lax on both sides of the border, but it is important to observe them as people not having the correct papers may have problems further into either country.

There is another border crossing at Laramonta from where it is a hard, but rewarding, walk to the Guyanese town of Orinduik.

Brazilian immigration At Polícia Federal (closed for lunch): from the rodoviária in Bonfim take a taxi, otherwise it's a long, dusty walk to the police checkpoint. Obtain an exit stamp at the Polícia Federal, then take the path to the river which leads to the right (going straight on also leads to the river, but not to the crossing point). After 10-15 minutes you reach the canoes which go to Guyana. Once across, keep to the right, on the road to the airport. For immigration formalities, do not go to the Guyanese police, but to a building on the road to *Cacique* guesthouse. Ask directions. The office is someone's front room.

Brazilian customs At Ministério da Fazenda checkpoint, before entering Bonfim; jeeps from here charge US$1 to immigration.

Sleeping & eating
Electricity is officially turned off between 2200 and 0700; take a torch or candles

D *Bonfim*, owned by Mr Myers, who speaks English and is very helpful, fan, shower. *Domaia*. There is a café at the rodoviária, opposite the church, whose owner speaks English and gives information. *Restaurante Internacional*, opposite the rodoviária, on other side from church. Another restaurant, a bit further from the rodoviária, serves good food. English-speaking teacher, Tricia Watson, has been helpful to bewildered travellers.

Transport **Buses** Boa Vista-Bonfim 3 a day, US$3.70. Weekly jeep Boa Vista-Laramonta US$30. **Boats** To cross the river, take a canoe (see above) US$0.25 (no boats at night).

Directory **Banks** Reais can be changed into Guyanese dollars in Boa Vista. There are no exchange facilities in Lethem, but reais are accepted in town. **Embassies & consulates** *Guyana*, there is no consul in Boa Vista, so if you need a visa for Guyana, you must get it in São Paulo or Brasília.

The Amazon

Bonfim

Rondônia

Rondônia is a state peopled by immigrants from other parts of Brazil. There is no regional accent. Foreigners are welcomed without question or curiosity. A local academic described the state as "a land where nobody has a name and everyone can have a dream". Most visitors tend to arrive via the BR-364 from Cuiabá or the Rio Madeira from Manaus.

In the early days of Portuguese occupation of what is now Brazil, it was thought that the land they had found was an enormous island. The Madeira and Guaporé rivers marked the northwest/southwest water-boundary: the Madeira joined with the Amazon to make the northern edge and the Guaporé was thought, erroneously, to link with the Rio Paraguay on the southwestern side. **History**

A group of Tupinambá Indians, who fled from the Portuguese colonists on the Atlantic coast, migrated up the Rio São Francisco, across Mato Grosso, to the Madeira. There they encountered Spanish colonists, so they moved north, down the Madeira, settling eventually on the Ilha de Tupinambaranas near the river's mouth. It was probably their accounts of the rivers in this region which encouraged the idea that the Amazon and Río de la Plata systems were linked, making Brazil an island.

Slave and gold hunters in the 18th century used the Guaporé and Madeira rivers for their expeditions. The rivers were also areas of settlement for Jesuit missions. Being also a frontier area between Portuguese and Spanish colonization, the rivers were scenes of tension between the opposing powers as well as the conflicts between Indians and slave-traders, and *bandeirantes* and Jesuits.

One Jesuit was Father João de Sampaio. He set up *aldeias* the length of the Madeira. One such was Santo Antônio das Cachoeiras, near the modern city of Porto Velho (see **Excursions**, below).

What is now Rondônia was originally the Territory of Guaporé. It became a state in 1981 after the central government's push to open up the unpopulated, undeveloped far west brought roads and settlers to the region. The destructive effects of this are well-documented. The BR-364 highway, being one of those roads prompted by plans for exaggerated growth, led to widespread deforestation and erosion of the way of life of many indigenous groups. Ironically, the name given to the state was that of the founder of the **Indian Protection Service (SPI)** in 1910, **Colonel Cândido Mariano da Silva Rondon.** (The SPI was replaced by the National Indian Service, Funai.) Rondon was part Indian himself and the policies which he incorporated into the SPI included respect for the Indians' institutions, the guarantee of permanent ownership by the Indians of their land, the right to exclusive use of natural resources on their land and the protection of the Indians against rapid change once contact between indigenous and 'civilized' worlds had been made. As an explorer of the Amazon and the builder, over eight years from 1907, of a telegraph wire out of Cuiabá to the northwest frontier, Rondon came into contact with many indigenous groups. The pressures of contact between Indians and the people who subsequently encroached on their world – ranchers, gold-prospectors, rubber-tappers, Brazil-nut gatherers and so on – made the SPI's task very difficult.

The River of Doubt

In 1913, Colonel Rondon invited the former US president Theodore Roosevelt to accompany him on one of his surveys. Together they explored the Rio da Dúvida – the River of Doubt – in 1914, following it to the Rio Aripuanã, thence to the Madeira. On the expedition they suffered great difficulties on the river itself, and Roosevelt contracted a fever which incapacitated him on the voyage and from which he never fully recovered. Rondon rechristened the Rio da Dúvida the Rio Roosevelt. The former president's account is told in Through the Brazilian Wilderness *(London: John Murray,*

1914), which contains photographs of the expedition; Missão Rondon, *notes on the project of the Mato Grosso ao Amazonas telegraph by Coronel Cândido Mariano da Silva Rondon, 1907-15, with photos, includes an account of the Roosevelt-Rondon expedition, pages 377 ff; Sam Moses, 'Down the River of Doubt' (Travelers' Tales Brazil, pages 351-9), gives an account, written in 1993, of an expedition in Roosevelt's footsteps, highlighting the effects of the late 20th-century mahogany trade on the Cinta Larga tribe who live on the Rio Roosevelt.*

When **Claude Lévi-Strauss** was travelling in Rondon's footsteps in the 1930s, researching *Tristes tropiques*, he described the Colonel's telegraph wire thus:

"Running through the totally virgin countryside, the cutting of the path, the twisted silhouettes of the posts, the loops of the wire connecting them, are as incongruous objects floating in the emptiness as one would see in a painting by Yves Tanguy" (chapter XXVI, 'Sur la ligne').

Geography & climate The Rio Madeira on which Porto Velho, the state capital, stands is one of the Amazon's major tributaries. The four main rivers which form it are: the Madre de Dios, rising a short distance from Cusco (Peru); the Beni, coming from the southern Cordillera bordering Lake Titicaca; the Mamoré, rising near Sucre, Bolivia; and the Guaporé, coming out of Mato Grosso, in Brazil.

Rondônia falls within the same climatic zone as the rest of western Amazônia, with average temperatures of 24-26°C and between 2,000 and 3,000 millimetres of rain a year. The wettest months are November-April, the driest June-August. Acre is slightly drier, with 1,500-2,000 millimetres of rain a year. Rondônia can be subject to the phenomenon known as the *friagem*, a sudden drop in temperature, to about 6°C, as a result of low pressure over the Amazon Basin attracting polar air from the South Atlantic. The cold weather can last for a week or more and occurs in the winter months. It is said to be an effect of El Niño, the changing patterns in ocean currents in the Pacific at Christmas time.

Economy The chief mineral extracted is cassiterite (a brown, tin oxide). Gold is also sought by *garimpeiros*. Timber is an important contributor to the economy, but the logging of mahogany for export to the United States and Europe is a controversial trade. The reason for this is that mahogany trees grow singly, not in stands, so to cut down and drag out one tree involves the destruction of many others, let alone the fact that more trees have been cut down than are being regenerated. More traditional economic activities in the forest are rubber-tapping (see below) and the harvesting of Brazil nuts (*castanho-do-pará*). Cattle-rearing has been introduced over large areas of both states. Associated with it is forest clearance to make pastures and a consequent alteration in climatic patterns: temperatures rise, rainfall decreases and the land becomes impoverished. Given that over 80 percent of Rondônia's soil is classified as of poor quality, these factors have made it hard for the settlers who rushed to the state in the 1970s from southern Brazil to earn a living. Some have turned to other activities, such as gold prospecting. On Rondônia's fertile soils, cocoa and coffee are grown.

Porto Velho

Porto Velho stands on a high bluff overlooking a curve of the Rio Madeira. The city has seen the rubber, gold and timber booms come and go. Service and IT industries are now major employers. Today the city is a large sprawl of streets, laid out in blocks stretching eight kilometres into the interior. The lack of town planning means that many of the best shops, hotels and banks are now a fair distance from the old centre near the river. **NB** Malaria is common. The drinking water is contaminated with mercury from gold panning.

Population: 294,500
Phone code: 069
Colour map 1, grid B2

Getting there Domestic flights arrive at the airport, 8 km west of town. Taxi to downtown US$15. Interstate buses from Rio Branco and Cuiabá arrive at the rodoviária on Jorge Teixeira.

Ins & outs
See also Transport, page 662

   Getting around Urban bus services are good. Consider hiring a car if you're going to stay for some time. Be patient as local residents get confused themselves by directions. Taxis in town are cheap and plentiful, *Radio Taxi Mamoré*, T2247070. Find your favourite driver and stick with him, all have mobile phones and work with partners to give prompt 24 hour service.

Sights

At the top of the hill on Praça João Nicoletti is the **Cathedral**, built in 1930, with beautiful stained glass windows; the **Prefeitura** (town hall) is across the street. The principal commercial street is Avenida 7 de Setembro, which runs from the railway station and market hall to the upper level of the city, near the rodoviária. The centre is hot and noisy, but not without its charm, and the port and old railway installations are interesting. As well as the **Museu Ferroviário**, there is a **Museu Geológico** at the old railway yards, known as Praça Madeira-Mamoré. ■ *Both are open 0800-1800.* See page 665 for the Madeira-Mamoré railway. Also in the Praça Madeira-Mamoré is the **Casa do Artesão** (see **Shopping** below) and a promenade with bars by the river, a wonderful place to watch the sunset.

   A neoclassical **Casa do Governo** faces Praça Getúlio Vargas, while Praça Marechal Rondon is spacious and modern. There are several popular viewpoints overlooking the river and railway yards: **Mirante I** (with restaurant) is at the end of Rua Carlos Gomes; **Mirante II** (with a bar and ice cream parlour) is at the end of Rua Dom Pedro II; **Mirante III** (with restaurant), at the end of Benjamin Constant.

Excursions

The **Cachoeira de Santo Antônio**, rapids on the Rio Madeira seven kilometres upriver from Porto Velho, is a popular destination for a swim during the dry season; in the rainy season the rapids may be underwater and swimming is dangerous. Access is by boat, taking a tour from Porto Cai N'Água, one hour; or by train on Sundays (see Madeira-Mamoré railway, below); or by bus, take city bus No 102, *Triângulo*, which runs every 50 minutes from the city bus terminus or from the bus stop on Rua Rogério Weber, across from Praça Marechal Rondon. Gold dredges may be seen working near Porto Velho, ask around if interested.

The Amazon

The **Banho do Souza** is a bar, restaurant and swimming area, 36 kilometres out of town on the BR-364. A coolbox of beers and soft drinks is left by your table and you pay for what you've drunk at the end of the afternoon, swimming is free.

Essentials

Sleeping **AL** *Vila Rica*, Av Carlos Gomes 1616, T/F2243433. Tower block, restaurant, pool, sauna, flashy but efficient. **A** *Rondon Palace*, Av Gov Jorge Teixeira, corner R Jacy Paraná, away from the centre, T/F2246160. Restaurant, pool, travel agency. **B** *Central*, R Tenreiro Aranha 2472, T2242099, F2245114, www.enter-net.com.br/hcentral. A/c, TV, fridge, good breakfast, clean and friendly. Highly recommended. **C** *Vitória Palace*, R Duque de Caxias 745, T219232. A/c, cheaper with fan, basic, clean and friendly. **D** *Líder*, Av Carlos Gomes near rodoviária. Honest, welcoming, reasonably clean, fan, coffee. Recommended. **E** *Tía Carmen*, Av Campos Sales 2995, T2217910. Very good, honest, good cakes in *lanche* in front of hotel. Highly recommended. From the rodoviária, take bus No 301 'Presidente Roosevelt' which goes to the railway station at the riverside, then along Av 7 de Setembro as far as Av Marechal Deodoro, passing: **C** *Pousada da Sete*, No 894, T2218344. A/c, cheaper with fan, **D** with shared bath. **D** *Guaporé Palace*, Av G Vargas 1553, T2212495. A/c, restaurant. **D** *Cuiabano*, Av 7 de Setembro 1180, T2214084. Good, a/c, cheaper with fan, **E** with shared bath, no break-fast. Recommended. **D** *Nunes*, Av 7 de Setembro 1195, T2211389. Fan, basic. **E** *Laira*, Joaquim Nabuco, just off 7 de Setembro, good, cheap.

Porto Velho

■ Sleeping		
1 Aline Park	3 Cuiabano	5 Sonora
2 Central	4 Nunes	6 Vila Rica

To BR 364, Rio Branco & Cuiabá

Arabic *Almanara*, R José de Alencar 2624. Good authentic Lebanese food, popular, not cheap. Recommended. **Churrascarias** *Assados na Brasa*, Av Carlos Gomes 2208. Similar. *Natal*, Av Carlos Gomes 2783. Good meat and chicken. *Ponto Certo*, Av Rio Madeira 45. Excellent view of river, best in town, closed Monday. **Italian/pizzas** *Bella Italia*, Av Joaquim Nabuco 2205. Italian, pizza and *comida caseira*. *Mister Pizza II*, Av Carlos Gomes and José de Alencar. Good. *Pizza & Cia* (known as Lady Pizza), Av Joaquim Araújo Lima 1625, T2219953. Delivery available, best in town, some English spoken. *Tutti Frutti Pizza*, Tenreiro Aranha I, Apt 201. Pizzas not recommended but rest of menu is excellent, no talking encouraged during evening soap operas! **Oriental** *Gengis Kan*, Av Pinheiro Machado 590. Reasonably priced Japanese. There is a good Chinese at Av Joaquim Nabuco 2264, oriental food. **Other** *Bar do Dico*, Av Joaquim Nabuco 955. Best fish in town, lively in evenings. *Carovela do Madeira*, R Jos Camache 104. Expensive, popular with businessmen. There are a number of good restaurants around the intersection of Dom Pedro II and Av Joaquim Nabuco, such as *Champagne*. Recommended for pizzas. **Fast food** Many *lanches* in town: recommended are *Petiskão*, Av 7 de Setembro and Joaquim Nabuco. Excellent juices. *Caffé*, Av Carlos Gomes 1097. Excellent and cheap pay-by-kilo buffet with vegetarian choice, friendly service. Highly recommended. *Chá*, Av Pres Dutra 3024. By kilo buffet, pricey. *Panificadora Popular*, Av Mcal Deodoro between 7 de Setembro and Dom Pedro II. Good juices and soups. *Xalezinho*, opposite, for an even bigger bowl of soup. *Banana Split*, Av 7 de Setembro. Popular, good pay-by-kilo meals. Also *Sorvette Pinguim* for ice creams.

Eating
Avoid eating too much fish because of mercury contamination

Tom Brasil club at *Peixe Noturnos*, near airport (Taxi US$15 essential to book return fare). Every Sunday night from 2200, US$3 entry for men. *Maria Fumaça* collective, T2244385. Organizes regular raves, concerts and festas around town. Check radio and newspapers for details. *Mirantes I* (see above), lively bar and a popular meeting place, excellent bar snacks and live acoustic music.

Bars & nightclubs

Indian handicrafts at *Casa do Índio*, R Rui Barbosa 1407 and *Casa do Artesão*, Praça Madeira-Mamoré, behind the railway station. Open Thursday-Sunday 0800-1800. Hammocks are more expensive than in Manaus.

Shopping

Markets There is a clean fruit and vegetable market at the corner of R Henrique Dias and Av Farquhar and a dry goods market 3 blocks to the south, near the port. On Sundays there is a general market off Av Rogério Weber near port, excellent bargains but no souvenirs. Watch out for pickpockets. **Rocha e Costa**, Av Brasília 2235. Out of town hypermarket, selling everything from fruit to outboard motors.

Bookshop *Livraria da Rose*, Av Rogério Weber 1967, opposite Praça Marechal Rondon. Exchanges English paperbacks, Rose, the proprietor, speaks English, friendly. Other bookshops nearby.

To Airport & BR 319 to Humaitá

Arquimedes
Calama
Abunã
Senador Álvaro Maia
Av Dr Rafael Vaz e Silva
Av Elias Gorayes
Av Gov Jorge Teixeira
Av Miguel Chakian
Herbert de Azevedo
Benjamin Constant
Av João Goulart
Av Guanabara
Quintino Bocaiúva
Av Pinheiro Machado
Duque de Caxias
Carlos Gomes
Dom Pedro II
Afonso Pena
Av 7 de Setembro
Paulo Leal
Almirante Barroso

To BR 364 & Rio Branco

● Eating
1 Mirante I
2 Mirante II

The Amazon

Supermercado Maru, 7 de Setembro and Joaquim Nabuco. **Camping** supplies and gas at *Casa do Pescador*, Joaquim Nabuco and Pinheiro Machado.

Photography *Casa do Fotógrafo*, Av Mcal Deodoro 2361, T2246696, and *Fotógrafo Elmir* sell and develop film, expensive but quick and reliable. Film developing also at 7 de Setembro and José de Alencar.

Transport
See also Ins & outs, page 659

Car hire *Localiza*, R Dom Pedro II 1208, T2246530, F2231968, friendly and good service, US$50 per day. Recommended. Also at airport. *LeMans*, Av Nações Unidas 1200, T2242012. *Silva Car*, R Almte Barroso 1528, T2211423/6040. *Ximenes*, Av Carlos Gomes 1055, T2245766.

Air Airport, 8 km west of town, T2251755. Flights to Brasília, Manaus and Rio Branco. Take bus marked 'Aeroporto' (last one between 2400 and 0100).

Buses Rodoviária is on Jorge Teixeira between Carlos Gomes and Dom Pedro II. From town take 'Presidente Roosevelt' bus No 301 (if on Av 7 de Setembro, the bus turns at Av Mcal Deodoro); 'Aeroporto' and 'Hospital Base' (No 400) also go to rodoviária. Health and other controls at the Rondônia-Mato Grosso border are strict. To break up a long trip is much more expensive than doing it all in one stretch.

Bus to **Humaitá**, US$5, 3 hours. To **São Paulo**, 60-plus hours, US$75. To **Cuiabá**, 23 hours, US$45, expensive food and drink is available en route. To **Rio de Janeiro** US$90, 72 hours. **Belo Horizonte** US$70, 44 hours. **Curitiba** US$95, 52 hours. **Fortaleza** US$120, 72 hours. To **Guajará-Mirim**, see below. To **Rio Branco**, *Viação Rondônia*, 5 daily, 8 hours, US$12.50. Daily bus with *Eucatur* from **Cascavel** (Paraná, connections for Foz do Iguaçu) via Maringá, Presidente Prudente, Campo Grande and Cuiabá to Porto Velho (Porto Velho-Campo Grande 36 hours, US$60). To **Cáceres** for the Pantanal, 18 hours, US$30. There is no bus service to Manaus as the road remains closed.

Hitchhiking This is difficult, try the gasoline stations on the edge of town.

Roads Cuiabá (BR-364 – Marechal Rondon Highway) is 1,550 km, fully paved; see below and page 720; Rio Branco, 554 km, BR-364, poorly paved; north to Humaitá (205 km) on the Madeira river, BR-319, paved, connecting with the Transamazônica, BR-230 (frequently closed, ascertain conditions before travelling). The BR-319 north from Humaitá to Manaus is closed indefinitely. Road journeys are best done in the dry season, the second half of the year.

Boat See **River transport**, page 598. Passenger service from *Porto Cai N'Água* (which means 'fall in the water', watch out or you might!), for best prices buy directly at the boat, avoid touts on the shore. The Rio Madeira is fairly narrow, so the banks can be seen and there are several 'meetings of waters'. Shipping a car: São Matheus Ltda, Av Terminal dos Milagros 400, Balsa, takes vehicles on pontoons, meals, showers, toilets, cooking and sleeping in your car is permitted. Wait at the Capitânia do Porto in the centre of town for a possible passage on a cargo boat; these boats leave from the Porto Brás docks, down river from Porto Velho.

Boats usually call at Humaitá (paved road and regular bus service from Porto Velho, see above, first class hammock Humaitá-Manaus US$60), Manicoré (see page 650), Novo Aripuanã, Borba and Nova Olinda. Passengers can disembark or embark at these ports, if that is your intention confirm the itinerary beforehand; if embarking at an intermediate port you will not have your choice of hammock space.

Six days a week a boat leaves at 1800 for Manaus from Manicoré, at the confluence of the Rios Madeira and Manicoré, 2 nights and 1 day's journey, food included; boats from Porto Velho to Manicoré on Monday, Wednesday and Saturday (1800, arrives

0200, but you can sleep on the boat), connecting with Manicoré-Manaus boats (a recommended boat is *Orlandina*).

Directory

Airline offices *Varig*, Av Campos Sales 2666, T2242262, F2242278, English spoken. *Vasp*, R Tenheiro Aranha 2326, T2244566. *TAM*, R J Castilho 530, T2242180. *Tavaj*, T2252999. **Banks** Open in the morning only. *Banco do Brasil*, Dom Pedro II 607 and Av José de Alencar, cash and TCs with 2% commission, minimum commission US$10, minimum amount exchanged US$200. *Marco Aurélio Câmbio*, R José de Alencar 3353, T2232551, very quick, efficient, good rates for US$ cash, Mon-Fri 0900-1500. *Parmetal* (gold merchants), R Joaquim Nabuco 2265, T2211566, cash only, good rates, open Mon-Fri 0730-1800, Sat 0730-1300. Local radio news and papers publish exchange rates. Exchange is difficult elsewhere in Rondônia. **Communications** Post Office: Av Pres Dutra 2701, corner of Av 7 de Setembro. **Telephones:** Av Pres Dutra 3023 and Dom Pedro II, 0600-2300 daily. **Hospitals & medical services** *Hospital Central*, R Júlio de Castilho 149, T/F2244389, 24 hr emergencies. Dentist at Carlos Gomes 2577; 24-hr clinic opposite. **Laundry** *Lavanderia Marmoré*, Pinheiro Machado 1455B. **Security** Although with rising unemployment, crime has increased in the city and outside, the city is relatively safe for tourists. Caution is recommended in the evenings and at all times near the railway station and port. **Tourist offices** *Funcetur*, Av 7 de Setembro, above Museu Estadual, T2211881, F2211831, seplan@ronet.com.br, very helpful, publishes free annual events list *Calendario do Porto Velho*. *Departamento de Turismo*, R Padre Chiquinho 670, Esplanada das Secretarias, CEP 78904-060, T2211499, F2252827/2232276. *Fundação Cultural do Estado de Rondônia (Funcer)* is at the same address. Street maps are hard to find. For a free map go to the *Teleron* Office, Av Pres Dutra 3023, between 0600 and 2300, and ask for the *Guia de Porto Velho* which includes a map and city services listings. **Voltage** 110 volts AC, Guajará-Mirim also, elsewhere in Rondônia 220 volts.

Along the BR-364

The Marechal Rondon Highway, BR-364, runs 1,550 kilometres from Porto Velho to Cuiabá in Mato Grosso. A result of the paving of this road is the development of farms and towns along it; cattle ranches can be seen all along the road, with least population density in the south between Pimenta Bueno and Vilhena.

In Ariquemes, 202 kilometres from Porto Velho, are *Ariquemes*, Av Capt Sílvio 1141, T5352200, F5353602, with air conditioning, fridge and parking. *Valérius Palace* (**D**) is at Av Tancredo Neves 3113, T5353311. There are buses to/from Porto Velho hourly from 0600, three to four hours. There is a *Banco do Brasil*. Further south are Nova Vida (200 kilometres), Jaru (257 kilometres) and Ouro Preto d'Oeste (297 kilometres).

Ariquemes
Population: 69,000
Phone code: 069

About 250 kilometres south of Porto Velho, it is possible to stay on a working *fazenda*, *Pousada Ecológica Rancho Grande* (**A**) at Caixa Postal 361, Ariquemes, Rondônia 78914, T/F5354301, pousada@ariquemes.com.br. About 450 bird species and numerous mammals can be seen on the 20 kilometres of trails, Harald Schmitz speaks English, German and Spanish, highly recommended, especially for butterfly lovers. Reservations and tours can be arranged through *Focus Tours*, see **Tours and tour operators**, page 30.

Situated on the shores of the Rio Machado is Ji Paraná, 376 kilometres from Porto Velho. It is a pleasant town with a small riverside promenade, which has several bars, lively at night. There is swimming at the river, beware of the current; a telegraph museum is on Avenida Marechal Rondon.

Ji Paraná
Population: 95,500
Phone code: 069

Sleeping **A** *Transcontinental*, R Júlio Guerra 258, centre, T4221212, F4222064. Restaurant, pool, overlooking the river. Recommended. **B** *Vitória Regia*, R Júlio Guerra 172, centre, T4221432, F4221767. A/c, fridge, TV, parking, view of the river. **B** *Plaza*, R Martins Costa 336, across the bridge from the centre, T4222524. A/c, fridge, TV, parking. **C** *Nova Era*, Av Marechal Rondon 1845, 2 blocks from the rodoviária. With bath,

The Amazon

a/c, TV, cheaper with fan, parking, good value. Recommended. **D** *Sol Nascente*, R Dr Osvaldo 101, across the bridge from the centre, T4211997, with *churrascaria*. *Casablanca*, R Padre Rohl 465, centre, T4215894. With bath, a/c, fridge, TV, cheaper with fan. Cheap hotels in front of the rodoviária are filthy – not recommended.

Transport Air: airport, 12 km from centre on Av Brasil. Air taxi with *Eucatur*, T4222030. **Buses**: bus station, R dos Mineiros, T4222233. To **Porto Velho**, US$16.25, 16 hours. To Cuiabá, 15 hours, US$28. **Car hire**: *Localiza*, airport and R Dr Osvaldo 38, T4223221.

Directory Airline offices: *TAM*, T4221373. **Banks**: *Bradesco*, Av Mcal Rondon 385. **Hospitals & medical services** *Pró-Saúde*, R Almte Barroso 99, T4221545. **Tour companies & travel agents**: *Transcontinental*, R Júlio Guerra 258, T4221433, F4222064.

Cacoal
Population: 72,500

Further southeast is Cacoal, 481 kilometres from Porto Velho, which is a coffee, cacau and timber exporting centre. The bus station is at Av Sergipe 396, T4412233.

Sleeping and eating B *Estoril Palace*, R São Luís 1065, T/F4414810. A/c, parking, pool. **B** *Cacoal Palace*, R Gen Osório 937, T4415011. A/c, parking. *Zeppelin*, Av 2 de Junho 2518. Fish restaurant.

Directory Banks: *Bradesco*, Av Porto Velho 2091. **Hospitals & medical services**: *Cristo Rei*, Av Guaporé 2270, T4412483.

Vilhena
Population: 43,000

The next town, 530 kilometres from Porto Velho, is **Pimenta Bueno** (*population* 50,000), with a gasoline station, rodoviária and hotels), whilst on the Rondônia-Mato Grosso border is **Vilhena**, 704 kilometres from Porto Velho (bus US$40, 11 hours), 752 kilometres from Cuiabá (bus US$21, 11 hours), a good place to break the Cuiabá-Porto Velho trip.

Sleeping and eating A *Mirage*, Av Maj Amarantes 3536, on the main commercial street, T/F3222166. Parking, pool. **A** *Diplomata*, R Francisco Tildre 63, T3213173, F3213233. Parking, pool. **B** *Santa Rosa Palace*, R Dal Toé 191, T3213900. A/c, fridge, TV, parking, **C** with fan. **C** *Comodoro*, Av Capt Castro 3663, in the centre, T/F3221244. A/c, parking. In Nova Vilhena ('Circular' bus to the centre), near the rodoviária, are: **D** *Vitória*, at No 117, T3213918. With fan, cheaper with shared bath, parking. On Av Sabino Bezerra de Queiroz are: **B** *Campinense*, No 5227, T/F3213156. Fan, parking, **D** with shared bath, good value. Recommended. **B** *Nacional*, No 5363, T3213952. A/c, TV, fridge, **C** with fan, parking. **C** *Rover Pálace*, No 5423, T/F3212253. With fan, TV, parking, simpler rooms **D**. **D** *Luz*, No 5341, T/F3211825. With fan, parking, good value. **D** *Rodoviário*, No 5537, T3213785. With fan, **E** with shared bath, basic, run down.

By the rodoviária are *Tókio*, Av Sabino Bezerra de Queiroz 5489, oriental, and *Bom Papão II*, Av Sabino Bezerra de Queiroz, 5261. Good *comida caseira*.

Transport Air: airport, 8 km from centre. **Buses**: bus station, BR-346 Km 690, T3222233. **Car hire**: *Interlocadura*, T3211050.

Directory Airline offices: *Pantanal*, T3212051. *TAM*, T3213823. **Hospitals & medical services** *Santa Helena*, Av Liberdade 2832, T3213259. At the Mato Grosso state border, proof of yellow-fever inoculation is required: if no proof is presented, a new shot is given.

Pacaás Novos National Park

This park of 765,800 hectares lies west of the BR-364 in a transitional zone, between open plain and Amazonian forest. The majority of its surface is covered with *cerrado* vegetation and the fauna includes jaguar, brocket deer, puma, tapir and peccary. The average annual temperature is 23°C, but this can fall as low as 5°C when the cold front known as the *friagem* blows up from the South Pole. Details from Ibama, Avenida Jorge Teixeira 3477, CEP 78904-320, T2232599/3597, Porto Velho, T2233607/3598, F2218021, or Rua João Batista Rios, CEP 78958-000 Pacaás Novas-RO. Also enquire here about the Jaru Biological Reserve in the east of the state.

On the Rio Guaporé is the Guaporé Biological Reserve, Avenida Limoeira, CEP 78971, Guaporé-RO, T6512239, in which is the Forte Príncipe da Beira, begun in 1777 as a defence of the border with Bolivia. The fort, which is being restored, can be reached from Costa Marques (20 kilometres by road), which is some 345 kilometres by unpaved road west of **Rolim de Moura**. This unplanned town (*population* 43,930), 40 kilometres west of Pimenta Bueno, relies on agriculture, livestock and a small furniture industry.

Sleeping and eating Rolim de Moura: **B** *Transcontinental*, R Jaguaribe 5104, T4421722, F4421729 and **C** *Iguaçu Palace*, Av 25 de Agosto 4430, T/F4421414. *Restaurant Caribe*, Av João Pessoa 4925.

Transport Bus station, Av São Paulo, T4422397.

Directory Hospitals & medical services: *Bom Jesus*, Av Macapá 5040, T4422463.

Porto Velho was the terminus of the Madeira-Mamoré railway (see box, page 666). It was supposed to go as far as Riberalta, on the Rio Beni, above that river's rapids, but stopped short at Guajará Mirim. The line works all week, but tourist excursions to Santo Antônio are on Sunday only, departures at 0800, 1115 and 1430, returning at 0915, 1500 and 1600, US$3 return, crowded with people going to bathe at the falls during the dry season – good fun; there are dolphins at Santo Antônio. The roundhouse, recently restored, has two other antique locomotives on display. Mr Johnson at the station speaks English.

The Madeira-Mamoré railway

Guajará Mirim

From Porto Velho, the paved BR-364 continues 220 kilometres southwest to Abunã (with a few hotels, **E**), where the BR-425 branches south to Guajará Mirim. Nine kilometres east of Abunã is a ferry crossing over the Rio Madeira, where it receives the waters of the Rio Abunã. The BR-425 is a fair road, partly paved, which uses the former rail bridges in poor condition. It is sometimes closed March-May. Across the Mamoré from Guajará Mirim is the Bolivian town of **Guayaramerín**, which is connected by road to Riberalta, from where there are air services to other Bolivian cities.

Population: 37,500
Phone code: 069
Colour map 1, grid C2

Guajará Mirim is a charming town. The **Museu Municipal** is at the old Guajará Mirim railway station beside the ferry landing; interesting and diverse, highly recommended. ■ *0500-1200, 1400-1800, T5413362*. An ancient stern wheeler plies on the Guaporé; 26-day, 1,250 kilometre trips (return) can be made on the Guaporé from Guajará Mirim to Vila Bela (see page 728) in Mato Grosso, the fare includes food.

C *Jamaica*, Av Leopoldo de Matos 755, T/F5413721. A/c, fridge, parking. **C** *Lima Palace*, Av 15 de Novembro 1613, T5413421, F5412122. A/c, fridge, parking. *Central Palace*, Av Mcal Deodoro 1150, T5412610. Recommended. **C** *Mini-Estrela*, Av 15 de Novembro 460, T5412399. A/c, parking. **D** *Chile*, Av Q Bocaiúva. Includes breakfast, good value. Recommended. **D** *Fénix Palace*, Av 15 de Novembro 459, T5412326. Highly recommended. **D** *Mamoré*, R Mascarenhas de Moraes 1105, T5413753. Clean, friendly. **Youth hostel** *Centro Deportivo Afonso Rodrigues*, Av 15 de Novembro,

Sleeping & eating

The Madeira-Mamoré railway

The Brazilian government agreed to build a railway between the rivers Madeira and Mamoré, to compensate Bolivia for the annexation of Acre in 1903. This was not, however, the first time that such a scheme had been proposed. In the mid-19th century, the demand for rubber was growing fast. It was discovered that the region of Brazil and Bolivia, around the rivers Madeira, Mamoré, Abunã and Guaporé, had plentiful supplies of trees, but that the only route out, the Rio Madeira, had some 400 kilometres of rapids and cataracts between Porto Velho and Guajará-Mirim, which made transport of the rubber almost impossible. The rubber barons were forced to trust to chance that their boats and cargo would get through this dangerous stretch. In the late 1860s surveys were made to see if a route on land was possible, and in 1871-72 the American George Church made his first attempt to build a railway between the Madeira and Mamoré. He went bankrupt within a year as the difficulty of the terrain and appalling loss of life from fever drained his resources. In 1878, Church tried a second time and, again, the heat and the multitude of insects and the diseases they carried defeated him.

The contract for the third attempt at a railway between the Madeira and Mamoré was won after the Treaty of Petrópolis (1903), by another American, Percival Farquhar, who had successfully carried out engineering projects in Cuba and Guatemala. Construction began in August 1907 and was completed on 15 July 1912. The project cost US$33 million. At least 3,600 men died building the 367 kilometres of track (popular estimates say that each one hundred sleepers cost one human life). The cost, though, was in vain because by the time the line was operational, the British had successfully cultivated rubber in their Asian colonies. Farquhar's scheme did bring some improvements to the region in terms of health care, social infrastructure and respect for the indigenous people, but he was involved in other projects in Brazil and when the railway's business plummeted, his empire soon followed. His reputation changed from that of pioneer to exploiter in many Brazilians' perception, although when he died in 1953 most hostility had evaporated.

The Madeira-Mamoré railway had about a year of full operation before the combination of the collapse of rubber prices, the opening of a railway from Bolivia to the Pacific via Chile and of the Panama Canal rendered it uneconomic. From 1919 to 1931 it was managed by a British group and then the Brazilian government kept it going until 1972. The BR-364 took over many of the railway bridges, leaving what remained of the track to enthusiasts to salvage what they could for tourist excursions. An attempt to reopen the line was made in 1980-84. In the 1990s the situation is that, from Porto Velho, trips run seven kilometres to Santo Antônio. From Guajará-Mirim, 16 kilometres of line have been renovated to Bananeiras, with work continuing to Yata. The regional branch of the Preservation Association plans to recuperate four steam locomotives for the project: the Baldwin 4-8-2 (loco No 20), which is in Guajará-Mirim; another Baldwin 4-8-2 (loco No 50) in Porto Velho; an Alco 2-8-2 (loco No 15) in Porto Velho; and a Schwartzkopf 2-8-0 (loco No 18).

With thanks to Martin Cooper, BBC York, for the historical information, and Eddie Edmundson, the British Council, Recife, for the latest preservation details.

T5413732. There is a basic *dormitório*, **E**, opposite the rodoviária. Best restaurant is *Oásis*, Av 15 de Novembro 464. Recommended (on main dishes, 10% service charge is added). *Lanchonates*, self-service, good value. Recommended.

Transport Buses from **Porto Velho**, 5½ hours or more depending on season, 8 a day with *Viação Rondônia*, US$18. Taxi from Porto Velho rodoviária, US$25 pp for 4-5, 3 hours, leaves when full.

Directory

Banks *Banco do Brasil*, foreign exchange in the morning only. *Loja Nogueira*, Av Pres Dutra, corner Leopoldo de Matos, cash only. There is no market in Brazil for bolivianos. **Communications** Post Office: Av Pres Dutra. **Telephone:** Av B Ménzies 751. **Embassies & consulates** *Bolivia*, Av C Marquês 495, T5412862, visas are given here. **Hospital & medical services** *Regional*, Av Mcal Deodoro, T5412651. **Tour companies & travel agents** *Alfatur*, Av 15 de Novembro 106, T/F5412853.

Frontier with Bolivia

Immigration Brazilian exit/entry stamps from Polícia Federal, Avenida Pres Dutra 70, corner of Avenida Quintino Bocaiúva, T5414021.

Transport Speedboat across the Rio Mamoré (border), US$1.65, 5-minute crossing, operates all day, tickets at the waterside; ferry crossing for vehicles, T5413811, Monday-Saturday 0800-1200, Monday-Friday 1400-1600, 20-minute crossing.

The Bolivian town of **Guayaramerín** is a cheerful, prosperous little town (*population* 35,000), on the bank of the Río Mamoré. It has an important *Zona Libre*. There are flights to Trinidad, La Paz, Cobija, Cochabamba and Santa Cruz, as well as buses to La Paz, Santa Cruz, Trinidad, Cobija and other destinations, but the roads are in poor shape and appalling in the wet season. Boats sail to Trinidad. For more details, see the *Bolivian Handbook* or *South American Handbook*.

Acre

This intriguing state, rich in natural beauty, history and the seringueiro culture, is still very much off the beaten track. The area is beginning to develop its considerable tourist potential for adventure tourism and historians, as links are opened up with neighbouring Peru and Bolivia.

In the mid-19th century, what is now Acre was disputed land between Brazil and Bolivia. The Treaty of Ayacucho, 1866, gave the territory to Bolivia but allowed the Bolivians to use the Brazilian Amazon river system to transport their goods, rather than traverse the Andes to the Pacific Ocean. The onset of the rubber boom in the 1880s upset this arrangement because many of the landowners who were exporting rubber from Acre and down the Rio Madeira were Brazilian. They resented the fact that the Bolivian government had nominal control, exacting duties, but had signed economic rights over to North American interests. Many *Nordestinos* also migrated to this western frontier at the time in search of fortune. In 1899 the Brazilians rebelled. Four years later the Bolivian government yielded the territory to Brazil under the Treaty of Petrópolis and the American company received US$2m compensation. The other concession which the Brazilians made was the construction of the Madeira-Mamoré railway to allow Bolivian goods to be transported east. In 1913, Rio Branco became capital of the new Território Federal do Acre, which attained statehood in 1962.

Acre has a population of only 500,000, but as its land is much more productive than its neighbour, Rondônio, there has been a flood of immigrants in the 1990s. The future of Acre's forests depend largely on whether any effort is made to improve the lot of the landless of the south, who constitute the majority of the migrants into the far northwest.

The Amazon

The chief industries remain rubber and *castanho-de-pará* (Brazil nut) extraction, but timber and ranching are becoming increasingly important and improved road access is putting the state's tropical forests at considerable risk.

Rio Branco

Population: 229,000
Phone code: 068
Colour map 1, grid B2

The state capital is 544 kilometres from Porto Velho on the BR-364. **NB** Rio Branco time is one hour behind Porto Velho and Manaus time (therefore two hours behind Brazilian Standard Time).

Sights

The Rio Acre is navigable upstream as far as the Peru and Bolivia borders. It divides the city into two districts called Primeiro (west) and Segundo (east), on either side of the river. In the central, Primeiro district, are **Praça Plácido de Castro**, the shady main square; the **Cathedral**, Nossa Senhora de Nazaré, along Avenida Brasil; the neo-classical **Palácio Rio Branco** on Rua Benjamin Constant, across from Praça Eurico Gaspar Dutra. Two bridges link the districts. In the Segundo district is the **Calçadão da Gameleira**, a pleasant promenade along the shore, with plaques and an old tree marking the location of the original settlement. The airport and rodoviária are in the Segundo district. There are several large parks in the city: the **Horto Forestal**, popular with joggers, in Vila Ivonete (1° distrito), three kilometres north of the centre ('Conjunto Procon' or 'Vila Ivonete' city-buses), has native Amazonian trees, a small lake, walking paths and picnic areas; the **Parque Zoo-Botânico**, on the UFAC campus (1° distrito), is five kilometres from the centre, along BR-364.

Museums **Museu da Borracha** (Rubber Museum), Avenida Ceará 1177, is housed in a lovely old house with a tiled façade. It has information about the rubber boom, archaeological artefacts, a section about Acreano Indians, documents and memorabilia from the annexation and a display about the Santo Daime doctrine (see Excursions below), recommended. ■ *Monday-Friday 0900-1700*. **Casa do Seringueiro**, Avenida Brasil 216, corner of Avenida Getúlio Vargas, has a good exhibit on rubber tappers and on **Chico Mendes** in particular; the Sala Hélio Melo has a display of Melo's paintings, mainly on the theme of the forest. ■ *Monday-Friday 0700-1200, 1400-1700*.

Excursions

Eight kilometres southeast of town, upriver along the Rio Acre, is **Lago do Amapá**, a U-shaped lake good for boating and watersports; access is by river or by land via route AC-40. Two kilometres beyond along the AC-40 is **Praia do Amapá**, a bathing beach on the Rio Acre; an annual arts festival is held here in September. Excursions can be made to **rubber plantations** and rubber extraction areas in native forest (*seringais nativos*).

Thirteen kilometres from Rio Branco is **Colônia Cinco Mil** (access along AC-10), a religious centre of the followers of the Santo Daime doctrine: its members, many originally from outside Acre and Brazil, live a communal life, working in agriculture and producing crafts made of latex. The religion centers around the use of *Ayahuasca*, a hallucinogenic potion adopted from local Indians. Visitors are usually welcome, but enquire beforehand.

Essentials

1° distrito (west bank) **A** *Pinheiro Palace*, R Rui Barbosa 91, T2247191, F2245726, pinheiro@mdnet.com.br. Pool. Recommended. **B** *Rio Branco*, R Rui Barbosa 193, by Praça Plácido de Castro, T2241785, F2242681. A/c, fridge, TV, nice but simple. **C** *Inácio Palace*, R Rui Barbosa 72, T2246397 (same fax and email address as Pinheiro Palace above). A/c, fair restaurant. **C** *Triângulo*, R Floriano Peixoto 727, T2249265, F2244117. A/c, TV, fridge, restaurant (see below). **C** *Albemar*, R Franco Ribeiro 99, T2241938. A/c, fridge, TV, good breakfast, good value. Recommended. **D** *Xapuri*, Nações Unidas 187, T2257268. Shared bath, fan, basic, 15 minutes' walk from the centre.

2° distrito (east bank), in Cidade Nova by the rodoviária **B** *Rodoviária*, R Palmeiral 268, T2244434. A/c, fridge TV, **D** with shared bath, fan, good value. **C** *Skina*, Uirapuru 533, T2240087. A/c, fridge, TV, fan. **D** *Nacional*, R Palmeiral 496, T2244822. Fan, both cheaper with shared bath.

Youth hostel *Fronteira Verde*, Trav Natanael de Albuquerque, 2° distrito, T2257128.

Sleeping
There are few economical hotels in the centre, but a reasonable selection by the rodoviária

Kaxinawa, Av Brasil at the corner of Praça Plácido de Castro. The best in town for Acreano regional food. *Pizzaria Tutti Frutti*, Av Ceará 1132, across from the Museu da Borracha. Pizzas, ice cream, not cheap. *Casarão*, Av Brasil 310, next to the telephone office. Good food and drink. *Churrascaria Triângulo*, R Floriano Peixoto 727. As much charcoal-grilled meat as you can eat. Recommended. *Remanso do Tucunaré*, R José de Melo 481, Bairro Bosque. Fish specialities. *Anexos*, R Franco Ribeiro 99, next door to *Albemar Hotel*. Popular for meals and drinks.

A local delicacy is tacacá: a soup served piping hot in a gourd (*cuia*), it combines manioc starch (*goma*), cooked *jambu* leaves which numb the mouth and tongue, shrimp, spices and hot pepper sauce; recommendation from Sra Diamor, Blvd

Eating
There are boats on the river serving cheap but good local food

The Amazon

Rio Branco

■ **Sleeping**
1 Albemar
2 Inácio Palace
3 Pinheiro Palace
4 Rio Branco

To 2° Distrito, Rodoviária, Airport & Porto Velho

0 metres   100
0 yards   100

The seringueiros

After the abolition of slavery, in northern Brazil merchants dominated the rubber economy. They obtained the rubber from seringueiros, rubber-tappers, who exchanged their crop for the supplies they were required to live on. However, the high cost of the rubber tappers' basket of necessities meant that they were forced into debt peonage and were obliged to live on the rubber estates until they cleared their debts, which they were unable to do. After the collapse of the rubber boom (see under Manaus), the businessmen who had built up large rubber estates allowed their properties to decline. Their place was taken by intermediaries, marreteiros (itinerant traders), who continued the system of exchange and credit, but increasingly the seringueiros became the owners of their own rubber trees. Rubber-tapping is no longer a lucrative business, but the tappers' livelihood was put under threat by outside landowners in the 1970s and 1980s, who were given incentives to create huge cattle ranches by the military government. Confrontations, called empates, between seringueiros and the workers sent to clear the forest, were largely peaceful and prevented the

destruction of many trees in Acre. In addition, the tappers set up a national council, the Conselho Nacional dos Seringueiros (CNS), to represent their interests in the continuing struggle to hold on to their traditional lands.

Lévi-Strauss describes a typical seringueiro's day: Each morning, early, the seringueiro sets out on one of his rounds, armed with his faca, a curved knife, and lighting his way with his coronga, a lamp fixed to his hat like a miner's. His incisions in the seringas are delicate, in order to prolong the productivity of the tree; 150 to 180 trees have been visited by about 1000. After breakfast, the seringueiro returns to his round to collect the latex which has seeped out of the trunk, into the zinc cup fixed to the bark. This he then pours into his cotton sack which is impregnated with rubber. About 1700 in the afternoon, he returns home to add the latex to the ball of rubber (the borracha) which is suspended on a rod over a fire. The smoke makes the latex coagulate into thin layers on the ball, which is considered complete when it has reached a weight of between 30 and 70 kilos (depending on the region). This can take several weeks.

Augusto Monteiro 1046, Bairro 15 in the 2° distrito (bus Norte-Sul from the centre), other kiosks in town, ask around.

For ice cream **Sorveteria Arte Sabor**, Trav Santa Inés 28, corner Aviario, 1° distrito, 15 minutes' walk from the centre. Excellent home-made ice cream, many jungle fruit flavours. Highly recommended. **Sorvete & Cia**, Av Brasil 394. Ice cream by the kilo and fix-it-yourself hot dogs.

Shopping Arts and crafts fair in Praça do Seringueiro on Sunday evenings. Market in 1° distrito, off R Epaminondas Jácome.

Transport **Car hire** *Locabem*, Rodovia AC-40, Km 0, 2° distrito, T2233000, F2245222. *Localiza*, R
Car rentals with Rio Grande do Sul 310, T2247746, airport T2248478. *Unidas*, T2245044.
nationwide agencies are
higher in Acre than
other states **Air** The airport is on AC-40, Km 1.2, in the 2° distrito, T2246833. Taxi from the airport to the centre US$20 flat rate, but going to the airport the meter is used, which usually comes to less. By bus, take 'Norte-Sul' or 'Vila Acre'.

Flights to Porto Velho, Manaus, Brasília, São Paulo, Cuiabá and Campo Grande; once a week to Cruzeiro do Sul. Oriente Redes Aéreas, T2232390 (airport), 2242830 (manager, Pasco at home), operates a twin engine Bandeirante with capacity for 18, to Puerto Maldonado, Peru, irregular departures (1-3 per week), US$100 (payable in US$ cash or *reais*), an interesting hour's flight over the jungle; Puerto Maldonado

Chico Mendes – the first eco-martyr

The most famous seringueiro *was Francisco (Chico) Alves Mendes, born in 1944. Chico's father had come to Acre from northeast Brazil as a* soldado da borracha, *engaged in providing rubber for the Allies during the Second World War. Chico learnt the trade of his father, became a leader of the Xapuri Rural Workers' Union and was a founder member of the CNS. He was instrumental in setting up a number of 'extractive reserves', parcels of land preserved for sustainable exploitation by those that lived there. He was shot dead on 22 December 1988 by cattle ranchers, to whose land-grabbing Mendes was in open opposition. He was by no means the only* seringueiro *who had been killed in such circumstances (he was the 90th rubber-tapper to be killed in 1988 alone), but his murder was the culmination of a decade of* fazendeiro-seringueiro *confrontation. Over 4,000 people attended his funeral; the world's media latched onto the story and Chico Mendes became the*

first globally-recognized eco-martyr. He was honoured by the United Nations for his efforts in stopping the destruction of the rainforest. The universal outcry at his assassination led to the arrest, trial and imprisonment of his killers, members of the family of Darly Alves da Silva, a rare event in the history of Amazon land disputes. His death inspired changes in government policy over environmental protection, greater involvement of rubber-tappers and other forest workers in local organizations and the development of extractive reserves, first promoted in 1985 as protected areas for the seringueiros. *Father Andre Ficarelli, assistant to the Bishop of Acre, said that Mendes' murder was like "the lancing of a tumour, exposing all the corruption and problems which the government [chose] to ignore". To others it was an opportunity to portray the whole affair in Hollywood-style melodrama; there was fierce competition for the film rights of Mendes' life story.*

office, González Prada 360, T571656; the Polícia Federal are at the airport for exit/entry stamps when these international flights operate. Air Taxi with *Céu Azul*, R G Bastos 174, T2243242.

Buses Rodoviária on Av Uirapuru, Cidade Nova, 2° distrito (east bank), T2241182. City bus 'Norte-Sul' to the centre. To **Porto Velho**, *Viação Rondônia*, 5 daily, 8 hours, US$12.50. To **Guajará Mirim**, daily with Rondônia at 1130 and 2200, 5-6 hours, US$10; or take *Inácio's Tur* shopping trip, 3 per week. To **Brasiléia** with *Acreana*, daily at 0600, 1115 and 1300, 5 hours in the wet season, faster in the dry, US$10, continuing to **Assis Brasil** in the dry season only.

Airline offices *Varig*, T2242719. **Communications Post Office:** On the corner of R Epaminondas Jácome and Av Getúlio Vargas. **Telephone:** Av Brasil between Mcal Deodoro and Av Getúlio Vargas, long delays for international calls. **Embassies & consulates** *Brazil*, C 10 de Junio 379, T84652003, F84652816. **Hospital & medical services** *Santa Casa*, R Alvorada 178, T2246297. **Security** Despite improved air and road links, Rio Branco remains at the 'end of the line', a frontier outpost whose depressed economy, high unemployment and prevalent drug-running make the city unsafe at night, and some caution is advised at all hours. **Tour companies & travel agents** *Nilce's Tour*, R Quintino Bocaiúva 20, T/F2232611, for airline tickets, helpful, 15 mins' walk from the centre. *Serra's Tur*, R Silvestre Coelho 372, T2244629. *Inácio's Tur*, R Rui Barbosa 91, at *Hotel Pinheiro*, T2249626. **Tourist offices** *SIC/AC, Secretaria de Indústria e Comércio*, Av Getúlio Vargas 659, Centro, or Departamento de Turismo, BR-364, Km 05, Distrito Industrial, for either T2243997/2231901.

Directory

The Amazon

From Rio Branco, the BR-364 continues west (in principle) to Cruzeiro do Sul and Japim, with a view to reaching the Peruvian frontier further west when

The legend of the rubber tree

Once upon a time, an Amazonian Indian called Maitá was unfairly accused of theft. As a punishment, the chief of his tribe condemned him to a very peculiar and cruel task: to empty a small lake by using a wicker basket. The work was of course extremely unproductive, as the water always flowed through the holes of the basket. Maitá soon realized that he would have to work for the rest of his life and still never empty the lake.

Knowing that Maitá was innocent, a forest fairy approached the poor Indian and asked him to follow her. They walked in the jungle until they reached a very large tree. There, she showed Maitá how to make some cuts in the tree and as he did, he noticed that a milk-like liquid started to

flow. The tree was a rubber tree and the liquid was natural latex. Then the fairy told him to spread the sticky liquid over the basket and wait for a while. As the liquid started to dry, he realized that a thin layer of a water resistant material (rubber) was covering all the holes. On returning to the lake, he was very pleased to see that he had no problem in scooping out large amounts of the lake's water. He gratefully thanked the fairy and finished his task in a few days.

As in all good fairy tales, there was a happy ending. The chief discovered he had made a mistake and apologized to Maitá on his return to the tribe. A big party was held to celebrate Maitá's return and, most of all, an important secret had been revealed: the secret of the rubber tree.

completed; it is hoped that it will be continued by the Peruvians to Pucallpa. It is very difficult to get from Rio Branco to Cruzeiro do Sul by road because there is no bus service, but the occasional truck goes mainly in the dry season. The road is frequently impassable; it is open, on average, 20 days a year.

Cruzeiro do Sul This is an isolated Amazonian town on the Rio Juruá in western Acre. Cheap
Population: 65,000 excursions can be made on the river, for example to the village of Rodrigues Alves, two to three hours, return by boat or by road, 15 kilometres. In the jungle one can see rubber-tapping, and collecting the latex into *borrachas*. Money changing is very difficult in Cruzeiro do Sul.

Sleeping and eating D *Savonne*, Av Col Mncio Lima 248, next to the cathedral, T3222481. Recommended. **E** *Novo do Acre*. A/c. Recommended. **E** *Flor de Maio*, facing river. Showers, full board available. Several other hotels and restaurants.

Transport Air: besides the scheduled *Varig* flight to **Rio Branco**, air taxis go to Rio Branco (Tavaj) and Pucallpa (Tasa). **Boats**: in the rainy season, river transport to **Manaus** is possible.

Frontier with Bolivia and Peru

The BR-317 from Rio Branco heads south and later southwest, parallel to the Rio Acre; it is paved as far as **Xapuri**. Here is the Fundação Chico Mendes, one very basic lodging and two restaurants. The road continues to **Brasiléia** opposite the Bolivian town of Cobija on the Rio Acre. In Brasiléia are three hotels, two basic lodgings, several restaurants; Polícia Federal give entry/exit stamps. There are three buses daily to Rio Branco, five hours in the wet, US$10. It is possible to stay in Epitaciolândia (**D** *Hotel Kanda*, five minutes' walk from the police post) and cross the border into Bolivia early in the morning. There are two official crossings between Cobija and Brasiléia. One is by ferry to Cobija's boat wharf, just off Calle Bolívar, at the west end of town. The other is via the international bridge, east of the ferry. The former is often quicker, and certainly cheaper (US$0.35), as taxis are expensive (US$12). All visitors must carry a yellow fever certificate.

The road ends at Assis Brasil, where the Peruvian, Bolivian and Brazilian frontiers meet. Across the Rio Acre are Iñapari (Peru), where the border crossing is difficult, even out of the wet season, and Bolpebra, Bolivia. A bus service operates only in the dry season beyond Brasiléia to Assis Brasil, access in the wet season is by river. In **Assis Brasil** there is one basic but clean hotel, **E**, two restaurants, some shops, a bank which does not change US dollars. The hotel owner may be persuaded to oblige. You get between Iñapari and Assis Brasil by wading across the river. **NB** There is no Polícia Federal in the village, get entry/exit stamps in Brasiléia.

Cobija is roughly 500 kilometres northwest of La Paz and there are air and road connections. The town is popular with both Brazilians and Peruvians for duty-free shopping. For more details, see the *Bolivia Handbook* or the *South American Handbook*.

Tocantins

Tocantins is not yet on the tourist track, other than for its share in the fishing bonanza (September-October and March-April are the best times) around the Ilha do Bananal, one of the largest river islands in the world. There are some opportunities for ecotourism in the Parque Nacional do Araguaia (park entrance is at Santa Terezinha in Mato Grosso, see page 731). However, most visitors to this state are likely to be only passing through on the long road journey between Brasília and Belém.

The first separatist movement began in 1809 from Comarca de São João de Palma, located at the junction of the Rio Palma and Rio Parana. Joaquim Teotônio Segurado declared an autonomous government in 1821, but this was soon suppressed. The new state was finally created in the 1988 constitution with its separation from Goiás. Today the economy is based around commerce, light industry and agriculture – mainly rice, soya and livestock.

It is the most southeastern of the northern states, with 278,420 square kilometres and a population of nearly a million. There are *chapadas* in the north of the state and the *savanas* are well irrigated by the many rivers such as the Araguaia and Tocantins. The climate is humid, with temperatures of around 36°C during the dry season between May to September, and a rainy season between October and April with lower temperatures of 22°C.

Palmas

Brazil's newest city is an interesting detour on the highway between Belém (1,282 kilometres away) and Brasília (973 kilometres). There are waterfalls in the surrounding mountains and beaches on the River Tocantins, which make for a relaxing stop on an otherwise long drive. The BR-153 is close to the city and provides a good road connection, both north to Maranhão, Pará, and south to Goiás.

Population: 130,000
Phone code: 063
Colour map 1, grid B5

The Amazon

The new capital is a planned city, with wide, long avenues and modern public buildings. Construction began on 20 May 1989 and the state government was transferred on 1 January 1990. The choice of name was partly influenced by the large numbers of palm trees in the area. The city is divided into four sectors: Noroeste (NO), Nordeste (NE), Sudoeste (SO) and Sudeste (SE). Like Brasília, the different blocks are named by use and location. Some address abbreviations are Área Central (AC), Área de Comércio and Serviço Urbano (ACSU) and Área Administrativa (AA).

The **Palácio Araguaia**, in Praça dos Girassóis, is an impressive modern building. The **Catedral de Nossa Senhora das Mercês** was built by the Dominicans from rocks from the Rio Tocantins. The **Parque da Cidade** is south of the city centre. See also **Praça do Bosque**, ARSE 51. The **Cachoeira de Taquarussu**, located near the city in the Serra do Carmos, is worth visiting.

Excursions Eight kilometres away at Canelas is **Praia da Graciosa**, a river beach on the Rio Tocantins – popular at weekends. There are floating bars, sports courts, shows, and camping is possible. Along the Estrada do Rio Negro at Km 18 is the **Reserva Ecológica do Lajeado**, 1,500 square kilometres of *caatinga*, *cerrado* and humid forest. The Morro do Governador, near the entrance, offers good views. Further along the road at Km 36 there are trails along the river **Brejo da Lagoa**, until the 60 metre-high **Cachoeira do Roncador** and other waterfalls are reached.

Essentials

Sleeping & eating **A** *Dos Buritis*, Av JK (ACNO 1), Conj 1, Lt 4/6, T/F2151936. Restaurant, pool. **A** *Rio do Sono*, Av Teotônio Segurado (ACSUSO 10), Conj 1, Lt 10, T/F2151733. Restaurant, pool, convention centre. **B** *Eldorado Plaza*, Av JK (ACSO 1), Conj 1, Lt 11A, T/F2152808. A/c, pool. **B** *Pousada dos Girassóis*, ACSO 1, Conj 3, Lt 43, T2151187, F2152321. A/c, restaurant, pool, sauna. **B** *Turim Palace*, ACNO 1, Conj 2, Lt 37/40, T2151484, F2152890. A/c, restaurant, sauna, pool, convention centre. **C** *Casa Grande*, Av Joaquim Teotônio Segurado (ACSUSO 20), Conj 1, Lt 1, T/F2151813. A/c, restaurant, pool.

Bela Palma, ACSUSO 40, Conj 1, Lt 19. Pizzas. *Estrela do Sul*, ACNO II, Conj 4, Lt 38/42. Churrasco, lunchtime only. *Minuano*, ACSUSE, Conj 9, Lt11/12.

Bars & nightclubs *Boulevard*, Av JK. *Carangueijos Bar*, Av Joaquim Teotônio Segurado (ACSUSE 40). *Consulado*, ACSO 1. *Phaeton Club*, ACSE 1, Conj 3, Lt 19.

Palmas

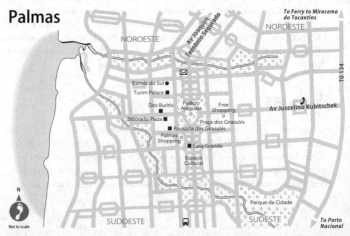

Cinema *Cine Blue, Palmas Shopping*, ACSU 10. **Theatre** *Espaço Cultural*, Av Teotônio Segurado, also has a library.

Entertainment

Gym *Academia Corpus*, ACNO 1 Conj 2, Lt 11.

Sports

Free Shopping, Av JK. *Palm Blue Shopping*, ACSUSO 10, Conj 2, Lt 10.

Shopping

Local City **buses** are plentiful and cheap. **Taxis** with *Rádio Táxi Palmas*, T2132001. **Car hire** *Hertz*, Av Nossa Senhora, T9781900, F2151900, and *Localiza*, ACSO 11-CL02, lote 41, Setor comercial, T2161104, and airport. *Rentauto*, Av Joaquim Teotônio Segurado (ASUSE10), Conj 1, Lt 6, T/F2151900.

Transport

   Long distance   Air: airport, Av NS 5, 2 km from centre, T2161237. Air taxi with *Nobre*, T2161500, and *Aeropalmas*, T2161716. Flights to Belém and Brasília, Goiânia, São Paulo. **Buses**: bus station, ACSUSO 40, T2161603. **Boat**: port is 9 km from the city. Ferries to Miracema do Tocantins and Paraíso do Tocantins.

Airline offices *Passeredo*, T2161515. *TAM*, T2161969. **Communications** Post office: Av Joaquim Teotônio Segurado. **Telephone:** Av JK. **Hospital & medical services** *Hospital Regional*, Praça ARSE, Qd 51, Setor Serrano, T2141424. **Dentist:** Dra Adriana Helena Toledo, ACNO 11, Conj 3, Lt 38, T2153201. **Tour companies & travel agents** *Batista Pereira Turismo*, ACSO 1, Conj 1, Lt 41, T2151228, F2151414. **Tourist office** ACSE 1, Conj 4, Lt 10, Edif Jamir Resende, 2nd floor, CEP 77100-100, T2151481, F2151494.

Directory

Towns in Tocantins

This is the second most important city in Tocantins, due to industrialization. Located on the BR-153, 90 kilometres north of the Tocantins border, it has been recommended as a pleasant place to break the journey. Entry to the Bananal is not permitted from here.

Gurupi
Population: 65,000

Sleeping A *Veneza Palace*, Av Pará 1823, T/F7123500, bar, restaurant, sauna, pool. **B** *Açaí Garden*, Av Pará 2432, T/F7124444, a/c, restaurant, pool. **B** *Transhotel*, BR-153, Km 572, T/F7141100, a/c, restaurant, pool. **B** *Gurupi Palace*, R Min Alfredo Nasser 650, T/F8511262, a/c, pool. **E** Hotel near the rodoviária. *The Club*, Av Pr Norte 438, nightclub.

Transport   Air   Flights to Porto Nacional, São Félix do Araguaia and Vila Rica in Mato Grosso. **Buses**   Bus station, R 19, T8511544. **Car hire**   *Localiza*, R Pres Castelo Branco 1464-A, T7121451. *Unidas*, Av Pará 1340, T/F7121121.

Directory Airline offices: *TAM*, T8512468. **Banks:** *Banco do Brasil*, Av Pará 1328. **Hospitals & medical services:** *Regional*, Av Pernambuco 1710, T7122800. **Tour companies & travel agents:** *Gurutur Viagens e Turismo*, R 4 No 1695, Centro, T7121820.

At Fátima, on the BR-153, a paved road heads east 52 kilometres to a new bridge over the Rio Tocantins to Porto Nacional. From here a road runs north to Palmas, 55 kilometres, a few kilometres from the village of Canela (which is opposite Molha – ferry across the Tocantins). The church of Nossa Senhora das Mercês (1903) is on the main square. The festival of Nossa Senhora das Mercês is on 24 September. Two-hour boat trips up the Tocantins from the old ferry port go to the Carreira Comprida rapids and island beaches (best May-September).

Porto Nacional
Population: 46,000

Sleeping and eating   *Meridional*, Av Luis Leite Ribeiro 5, T8631121, F8631720. *São Judas Tadeu*, Av Pres C Branco, T8631242. *Shelton*, Av Jq Aires 2662, T8631696. There are 3 restaurants.

The Amazon

Transport There is an airport with regional flights. Bus station, Praça do Peso Boiadeiro. Taxis with *Pioneiro*, Praça Centenário, T8631004.

Directory Banks: There are 7 banks. **Hospitals & medical services**: there is a regional hospital. **Tour companies & travel agents**: *Halleytur*, Av Associação, T8631224.

Miracema do Tocantins
Population: 17,500

Upriver from Palmas, 77 kilometres on the west bank of the Rio Tocantins, is the previous state capital Miracema do Tocantins, 23 kilometres from the BR-153. There is sightseeing at nearby Cachoeira do Lajeado Grande. On the road to Miranorte is *Mira-Rio* (**C**), Av Tocantins 3075, T/F8661327, with air conditioning and a pool. In Miracema do Tocantins are *Grande*, Av L Solino 1341, T8661124, and *Miracema Palace*, Av Tocantins 2678, T8661161. There is an airport. The bus station is at Av Tocantins 1376, T8661281. There is a 24-hour ferry to Tocantínia on the east bank. Ferry and boats to Palmas.

Directory Banks: *Banco do Brasil*, Praça Fued Sebba 410. **Hospitals & medical services**: *Regional*, Av Irmã Emma Rudolph Navarro, T8661220.

Paraíso do Tocantins
Population: 33,000

Continuing north on the BR-153, 176 kilometres from Gurupi, is this agricultural centrea, good stopping place for those not wishing to divert to Palmas. There is *Serrano's Park* (**B**), Av Bernardo Sayão 250, T6021410, F6021866, with air conditioning, a bar and pool, and *Saches*, Av Bernardo Sayão 535. There is an airport and a ferry to Palmas. The bus station is at R Alfredo Nasser, T6026644.

Directory Banks: *Banco do Brasil*, Av Tocantins 367. **Hospitals & medical services**: *Modelo*, R Tapajós 260, T8611115.

At **Guaraí** the road forks, one branch continuing west to cross the Rio Araguaia at Conceição do Araguaia, then turning north to Marabá on the Transamazônica. The other branch goes to Araguaína, whereafter the BR-226 goes to Estreito in Maranhão, from where the BR-010 runs north through Imperatriz to Belém. A pleasant overnight stop on the road to Araguaína is the hilly town of **Uruaçu**, cheap hotels near the rodoviária.

Araguaína

This town (*population*: 106,000, *phone code*: 063) is a good stopping place. It is located on the Brasília-Belém road, Brasília, 1,102 kilometres; Belém, 842 kilometres; Imperatriz, 174 kilometres.

Sleeping and eating **B** *Olyntho Estância*, BR-153 Km 125, T/F8131377. A/c, restaurant, pool. **B** *Transhotel*, BR-153 Km 120, T/F8141222. A/c, restaurant, pool. Several other hotels near rodoviária. *Maresia's*, R das Mangueiras 868, fish restaurant.

Transport Air: airport, 9 km south off the BR-153, T8131168. Flights to Brasília, Imperatriz, Uberaba and São Paulo. **Buses**: bus station, T8131663. Buses leave Araguaína for Marabá 0700 and 1400. Ordinary bus to Goiânia takes 24 hours: try to get an express. If travelling to Belém or Brasília by bus, reservations are not normally accepted: be at the terminal 2 hours before scheduled departure as buses tend to leave early; as soon as the bus pulls in, follow the driver to the ticket counter and ask if there are seats. Brasília 1200, 2400, US$50 (22 hours). Buses also to Santarém. **Car hire**: *Localiza*, Av Santos Dumont 985, T/F8131212, and at airport T8131431.

Directory Airline offices: *Passeredo*, T8143636. *Varig/Rio-Sul*, T8144222. **Banks**: *Banco do Brasil*, R 15 de Novembro 1537. **Hospitals & medical services**: *Comunitário*, R 13 de Maio 1336, T8141144. **Tour companies & travel agents**: *Tropicália Turismo*, R Santa Cruz 662, T8143097.

Brasília and the Pantanal

11

Brasília and the Pantanal

Distrito Federal

The Distrito Federal and the states of Goiás, Mato Grosso and Mato Grosso do Sul make up the Centre West region of Brazil. Brasília is the capital of the union and this city of politicians, with its purpose-built late 20th-century design, is now a Unesco world heritage site. Goiás itself has many historic mining towns such as Pirenópolis and Goiás Velho. Its capital Goiânia is famous for its outdoor cafés and bars with live music. The Chapada dos Veadeiros and Emas national parks are also excellent for trekking and viewing wildlife.

Further west are the states of Mato Grosso do Sul and Mato Grosso, in which is located the Pantanal, one of Brazil's premier wildlife destinations. The Pantanal, a large area of wetland, is a mecca for wildlife tourism and fishing. The seasonal variation in the water levels make a great difference to the practicalities of getting there and what you will experience, whether you are land or river based. This is the heart of the Brazilian interior, and on heading north you pass Cuiabá en route to the ancient landscapes of the Chapada dos Guimarães. To the south is Campo Grande and the lovely area around Bonito near the Paraguayan border. To the west is Corumbá and the border with Bolivia.

Distrito Federal

The creation of an inland capital had been urged since the beginning of the 19th century, but it was finally brought into being after President Juscelino Kubitschek came to power in 1956. He personally oversaw the project to completion and the city was inaugurated on 21 April 1960.

The Federal District has an area of 5,814 square kilometres, with a population of around 1,920,000. The climate is mild and the humidity refreshingly low, but trying in dry weather. The noonday sun beats hard, but summer brings heavy rains and the air is usually cool by night.

Brasília

Population: 1.7 million
Phone code: 061
Colour map 4, grid A2

Although not generally viewed as a tourist attraction, Brasília is nonetheless on the Unesco list of world heritage sites for its innovative modern design. It is well worth undertaking a city tour when passing through, and its central position makes it a natural crossroads for visiting the north and interior of Brazil.

Brasília orientation

Getting there Flights arrive at the international airport. Taxi to centre US$10 after bargaining. Left luggage facilities at airport (locker tokens, US$0.50). Interstate buses arrive at the rodoferroviária beside the railway station. Bus 131 between rodoviária, the municipal terminal, and rodoferroviária, US$1.25. Both bus stations have large luggage lockers.

Ins & outs
See also Transport,
page 688

Getting around A good and cheap way of seeing Brasília is by taking bus rides from the municipal rodoviária at the centre: the destinations are clearly marked. The circular bus routes 106, 108 and 131 go round the city's perimeter. If you go around the lake by bus, you must change at the Paranoá dam; to or from Paranoá Norte take bus 101, 'Rodoviária', and to and from Sul, bus 100, bypassing the airport. It is worth telephoning addresses away from the centre to ask how to get there. An urban railway, Metrô, to the southwest suburbs, should have recently been completed.

History and design

Brasília is 960 kilometres away from Rio de Janeiro at 1,171 metres on undulating ground in the unpopulated uplands of Goiás, in the heart of the undeveloped Sertão. The official name for central Brasília is the Plano Piloto. A competition for the best general plan was won by Professor Lúcio Costa, who laid out the city in the shape of a bent bow and arrow. It is also described as a bird, or aeroplane, in flight.

Along the curve of the bow are the residential areas made up of large six-storey apartment blocks, the 'Super-Quadras'. They lie on either side (east and west) of the 'bow' (the Eixo Rodoviário) and are numbered according to their relation to the Eixo and their distance from the centre. Thus the 100s and 300s lie west of the Eixo and the 200s and 400s to the east; Quadras 302, 102, 202 and 402 are nearest the centre, and 316, 116, 216 and 416 mark the end of the Plano Piloto. The numbering applies equally on either side of the centre, the two halves of the city being referred to as Asa Sul and Asa Norte (the north and south wings). Thus, for example, 116 Sul and 116 Norte are at the extreme opposite ends of the city. Each Super-Quadra houses 3,000 people and has a primary school and playgroup. Each group of four Super-Quadras should have a library, police station, club, supermarket and secondary school. All Quadras are separated by feeder roads, along which are the local shops. There are also a number of schools, parks and cinemas in the spaces between the Quadras (especially in Asa Sul), though not as systematically as was originally envisaged. On the outer side of the 300s and extending the length of the city is the Avenida W3, and on the outer side of the 400s is the Avenida L2, both of these being similarly divided into north and south according to the part of the city they are in.

Asa Sul is almost complete and Asa Norte is growing very fast, with standards of architecture and urbanization that promise to make it more attractive than Asa Sul in the near future. The main shopping areas, with more

Oscar Niemeyer and Brasília

Oscar Niemeyer Soares Filho (born 1907 in Rio de Janeiro) was educated at the Escola Nacional de Belas Artes and in 1936 joined the group of architects charged with developing Le Corbusier's project for the Ministry of Education and Health building in Rio de Janeiro. His first international project was the Brazilian pavilion at the New York International Fair in 1939 in partnership with Lúcio Costa. In the 1940s he was one of the main designers of Pampulha (see under Belo Horizonte) and in 1947 he worked on the United Nations headquarters in New York. This was the period in which he affirmed his style, integrating architecture with painting and sculpture. He transformed utilitarian constructions with the lightness of his designs, his freedom of invention and the use of complex, curved surfaces. Throughout the 1950s he was commissioned to design a wide variety of national and international projects, but it was the years 1956-59 which stamped his signature on the architectural world. This was when he worked on Brasília, specifically the Palácio da Alvorada, the Ministries, the Praça dos Três Poderes, the Cathedral, University and, in 1967, the Palácio dos Arcos e da Justiça. After Brasília Niemeyer continued to work at home and abroad; among his more famous later projects were the Sambódromo in Rio (1984) and the Memorial da América Latina in São Paulo (1989). The Royal Institute of British Architects awarded him the prestigious Royal Gold Medal for Architecture in March 1998.

Many of Brazil's most famous architects, sculptors and designers were involved in Brasília. The city was built during Juscelino Kubitschek's term as president, 1955-1960, and was unparalleled in scale and architectural importance in Latin America at that time. A description of the city, and its effect on the economy at the time of its construction are dealt with elsewhere in the book. Niemeyer was appointed chief architecture and technical adviser to Novacap, the government authority which oversaw the new capital. But while it is common knowledge who the famous names were, it is also worth noting that 30,000 workers were involved in bringing the plan to reality. Most of them came from the Northeast. The city has been honoured not just for its architecture, but also for being the first purpose built capital of the 20th century. In 1987 it was named a Unesco World Cultural Heritage Site, the first contemporary city to gain such protection from the United Nations.

Niemeyer himself has said "The modern city lacks harmony and a sense of occasion. Brasília will never lack these". And it is true that the principal buildings, and the overall plan itself, are strikingly powerful. The whole enterprise is deeply rooted in the 20th century, not just in its design, but also in the idea that it is a city you jet into and out of. If you arrive by road (which most people do not), the experience is even more fantastic. After hours and hours in the bus, travelling across the unpopulated central plateau, you come to this collection of remarkable buildings and sculptures in the middle of nowhere. The vastness of the landscape demands a grand city and yet, for all its harmony, it is almost as if not even Brasília can compete with the sky and the horizon.

cinemas, restaurants and so on, are situated on either side of the old bus station (rodoviária). There are now several parks, or at least green areas. The private residential areas are west of the Super-Quadras, and on the other side of the lake.

At right angles to these residential areas is the 'arrow', the eight-kilometre long, 250 metres wide **Eixo Monumental**. The main north-south road (Eixo Rodoviário), in which fast-moving traffic is segregated, follows the curve of the bow; the radial road is along the line of the arrow – intersections are avoided by means of underpasses and cloverleaves. Motor and pedestrian traffic is segregated in the residential areas.

Sights

A fine initial view of the city may be had from the **television tower**, which has a free observation platform at 75 metres up; also bar and souvenir shop; closes for maintenance on Monday mornings. If the TV tower is closed, the nearby *Alvorada* hotel has a panoramic terrace on the 12th floor (lift to 11th only): ask at reception. Tours, from 1300-1700, start from the downtown hotel area and municipal rodoviária (US$12-20). Many hotels arrange city tours (see also **Tour companies**, page 689). Weekends have little to occupy the tourist except sightseeing (car needed) or visiting the market at the base of the TV tower.

Some buildings are open 1000-1400 Saturday-Sunday, with guided tours in English; well worth going

At the tip of the arrow, as it were, is the **Praça dos Três Poderes**, with the Congress buildings, the Palácio do Planalto (the President's office), the Palácio da Justiça and the Panteão Tancredo Neves. Nineteen tall Ministry buildings line the Esplanada dos Ministérios, west of the Praça, culminating in two towers linked by a walkway to form the letter H, representing Humanity. They are 28 storeys high: no taller buildings are allowed in Brasília. Where the bow and arrow intersect is the city bus terminal (rodoviária), with the cultural and recreational centres and commercial and financial areas on either side. There is a sequence of zones westward along the shaft of the arrow; a hotel centre, a radio city, an area for fairs and circuses, a centre for sports, the **Praça Municipal** (with the municipal offices in the Palácio do Buriti) and, lastly (where the nock of the arrow would be), the combined new bus and railway station (rodoferroviária) with the industrial area nearby. The most impressive buildings are all by Oscar Niemeyer (see box, page).

The **Palácio da Alvorada**, the President's official residence (not open to visitors), with a family of emus on the lawn, is on the the lakeshore. The 80-kilometre drive along the road, round the lake to the dam, is attractive. There are spectacular falls below the dam in the rainy season. Between the Praça dos Três Poderes and the lake are sites for various recreations, including golf, fishing and yacht clubs, and an acoustic shell for shows in the open air. The airport is at the eastern end of the lake. Some 395 hectares between the lake and the northern residential area (Asa Norte) are reserved for the Universidade de Brasília, founded in 1961. South of the university area, the Avenida das Nações runs from the Palácio da Alvorada along the lake to join the road from the airport to the centre. Along it are found all the principal embassies. Also in this area is the attractive vice-presidential residence, the **Palácio do Jaburu**, not open to visitors. This area is very scenic.

Congress Visitors may attend debates when Congress is in session (Friday morning). The building also has excellent city views from the 10th floor in Annex 3. ■ *Monday-Friday 0930-1130 and 1400-1700 (take your passport), guides free of charge (in English 1400-1600).* The **Palácio do Planalto** may be visited on special occasions only. The guard is changed ceremonially at the Palácio do Planalto on Tuesday every two hours. The President attends if he is available. Opposite the Planalto is the Supreme Court building, **Supremo Tribunal Federal**. The marvellous building of the Ministry of Foreign Affairs, the **Itamarati**, has modern paintings and furniture and beautiful water gardens. ■ *Guided visits Monday, Wednesday, Friday 1500-1700, free.* Opposite the Itamarati is the **Palácio da Justiça**, with artificial cascades between its concrete columns. ■ *Monday-Friday, 0900-1130, 1500-1700.*

Official buildings
Town clothes (not shorts or minis) should be worn when visiting these buildings

The **Catedral Metropolitana**, on the Esplanada dos Ministérios, is a spectacular circular building in the shape of the crown of thorns. Three aluminium angels, suspended from the airy, domed, stained-glass ceiling, are by the

Churches

Brasília & the Pantanal

sculptor Alfredo Scesciatte, who also made the four life-sized bronze apostles outside. The baptistery, a concrete representation of the Host beside the cathedral, is connected to the main building by a tunnel, open Sundays only. The outdoor carillon was a gift from the Spanish government: the bells are named after Columbus's ships. ■ *0800-1800, T2244073.*

South of the TV tower on Avenida W3 Sul, at Quadra 702, is the Sanctuary of **Dom Bosco**, a square building with narrow windows filled with blue glass mosaics, purple at the four corners; the light inside is most beautiful.

The **Templo da Boa Vontade**, Setor Garagem Sul 915, lotes 75/76, is a seven-faced pyramid topped by the world's largest crystal, a peaceful place dedicated to all philosophies and religions. ■ *T2451070, take bus 151 from outside the Centro do Convenções or on Eixo Sul to Centro Médico.*

Other religious buildings worth seeing are the **Igreja Nossa Senhora de Fátima** church (the Igrejinha) in the Asa Sul at Quadras 307-308, the **Santuário Nossa Senhora de Fátima**, the 'orange caterpillar' on Avenida W5, Quadra 906, a little south of the Dom Bosco sanctuary, and the chapel (**Ermida**) of Dom Bosco, on the other side of the lake opposite the Alvorada, though the site is not well maintained.

Memorials & military buildings
Some 15 kilometres out along the Belo Horizonte road is the small wooden house, known as **O Catetinho**, in which President Kubitschek stayed in the late 1950s during his visits to the city when it was under construction; it is open to visitors and is most interesting. A permanent memorial to Juscelino

Brasília: Plano Piloto

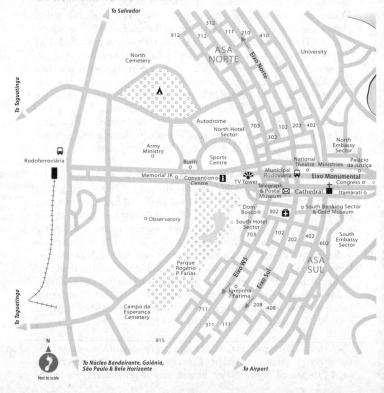

Kubitschek, the **Memorial JK**, contains his tomb and his car, together with a lecture hall and exhibits. ■ *Daily except Monday 0900-1800, entry US$0.50, with toilets and lanchonete.* The **Quartel-General do Exército**, Brazilian Army headquarters designed by Oscar Niemeyer, is interesting. The **Panteão Tancredo Neves** is a 'temple of freedom and democracy', built 1985-86 by Niemeyer. It includes an impressive homage to Tiradentes (see box, page 276). **Espaço Lúcio Costa** contains a model of Plano Piloto, sketches and autographs of the designer's concepts and gives the ideological background to the planning of Brasília. The **Monumental Parade Stand** has unique and mysterious acoustic characteristics (the complex is north of the Eixo Monumental, between the 'Memorial JK' and the rodoferroviária). There are remarkable stained glass panels, each representing a state of the Federation, on the ground floor of the Caixa Econômica Federal.

Museu Histórico de Brasília, Praça dos Três Poderes, is really a hollow monument, with tablets, photos and videos. ■ *Daily 1000-1800.* **Museu de Valores** at the Banco Central exhibits old and new notes and coins and gold prospecting in Brazil. ■ *Tuesday-Friday 1000-1730, Saturday 1400-1800.* **Museu Postal e Telegráfico da ECT**, Setor Comercial Sul, Ed Apolo, quadra 13 bloco A, has displays of stamps, telegraphic equipment etc. ■ *Tuesday-Friday 0900-1800, Saturday 0900-1300, US$0.30.* **Museu da Imprensa Nacional**, Setor de Indústrias Gráficas, Quadra 6; houses old printing and embossing equipment etc. ■ *Monday-Friday 0800-1700, Saturday, Sunday and holidays 1300-1800, free; bus 152 from municipal rodoviária.*

Museums

Brasília is famous for its wealth of modern sculpture. Examples are: 'Cultura' (on the University campus), 'Meteoro' (above the Itamarati water-mirror), and 'Os Candangos', in front of the Planalto, which pays homage to the pioneer workers who built Brasília on empty ground – all by Bruno Giorgi; 'A Justiça' (in front of Supremo Tribunal Federal), the four evangelists in front of the Cathedral and 'As Banhistas' (The Water-Nymphs, above the Alvorada water-mirror) – all by Alfredo Scesciatte; 'Rito dos Ritmos' (Alvorada gardens), by Maria Martins; and the beautiful 'Sereia' (Mermaid), in front of the Navy Ministry on the Esplanada dos Ministérios. A statue of Juscelino Kubitschek stands above the 'Memorial JK'. A short distance west of here is a huge wooden cross marking the site of the first Mass said in Brasília (3 May 1957), at the city's highest point.

Sculptures

Brasília & the Pantanal

Essentials

Sleeping

Prices include breakfast, but 10% must be added. Weekend discounts of 30% are often available but must be requested. The tourist office has a list of pensões

Southern Sporting Sector LL *Academia de Tênis*, SCES, Trecho 04, Conj 05, Lt 1B, T3166161, F3166268. Sports facilities, pools, conference facilities, good restaurant, heavily booked in advance.

Southern Hotel Sector L *Carlton*, Qd 5 bloco G, T2248819, F2268109. Four-star, excellent, pool, good views from rooms but building work nearby. L *Nacional*, Qd 1 bloco A, T3217575, F2239213. Five-star, pool, expensive, old-fashioned. Recommended. A *Alvorada*, Qd 4 bloco A, T3321122, F2253130. Good view from roof terrace. Recommended. A *Bristol*, Qd 4 bloco F, T3216162, F3212690. Three-star, pool. A *Planalto*, Qd 3 bloco A, T3221828, F2258050. Rooms in front noisy, city tours.

Moderately priced hotels can be found in this sector only

Northern Hotel Sector AL *Eron Brasília*, Qd 5 bloco A, T3294000, F3292698. Five-star. AL *Aracoara*, Qd 5 bloco C, T3289222, F3289067. Four-star. The same road gives access to: A *Aristus*, Qd 2 bloco O, T3288675, F3265415. Good, TV, phone, money exchange, small restaurant. A *Casablanca*, Qd 3 bloco A, T3288586, F3288273. Some rooms noisy. A *Diplomat*, Qd 2 bloco L, T/F3262010. Good value. B *El Pilar*, Qd 3 bloco F, T2245915. A/c or fan, TV. C *Mirage*, Qd 2 lote N, T2257150. Fan, good value. D *Cury's Solar*, Av W3 Sul, HIGS 707, bloco I, casa 15, T1136252/2441899, curyssolar@conectanet.com.br, www.conectanet.com.br/curyssolar. Cramped but helpful, safe, around 30 minutes from the centre (Eixo Monumental) along W3 Sul. Recommended. D *Pensão da Zenilda*, W3 Sul Qd 704, bloco Q, casa 29, T2247532, safe. Teresa Tasso, SQN312-'K'-505, T2734844/2724243, tasso@tba.com.br, offers accommodation in an apartment in the Asa Sul at US$20 pp (sleeps 5, kitchen, bath, laundry facilities). Excellent value, Teresa gives city tours for US$15-20 pp for 3-4 hours, and will collect you at the airport if you phone in advance (bus to flat from centre, 5 minutes). Rooms to let (**D-C**) from: Getúlio Valente. Warmly recommended. Av W3 Sul, HIGS 703, Bl I, casa 73, near the TV tower, good, cheap meals available, Portuguese speakers, T2268507/9639 and Getúlio will pick you up; otherwise, turn right off Av W3 Sul between 703 and 702, then take first left (an unpaved driveway). Nearby is J Araújo, HIGS 703, Bl G, C35, T2264059.

The hotels outside the city in **Taguatinga** (take 102 or 106 bus, EIXO, 304 or 306 from rodoferroviária, taxi from airport US$33) and Núcleo Bandeirante, though fairly basic, are more economical, but it is difficult to get single rooms. Taguatinga is more pleasant than the Núcleo, which is full of shanties. There are many cheap hotels and restaurants of a reasonable standard, eg: A *Colorado*, Setor Hoteleira, Projeção B, T/F5613500. Price includes breakfast and taxes, with bath, fridge, TV, good, friendly, no English spoken, no credit cards, good food, huge portions enough for 2, in the centre. C *Pousada Brasília*, next door at Projeção L, T5625055. C *Globo*, CNB4, lote 1, T5611716. Without breakfast, basic. D *Solar*, C 7, lote 13, sobreloja, T5635660, near Pão de Açúcar Supermarket, basic and clean. Bus 'Estrutural' from Brasília rodoferroviária to Taguatinga Rodoviária where you change, without extra charge, to 700 bus which passes, in order: C *Camará*, QNE 16, lt 8, T5612597 (hourly rentals also). C *Palace*, CNB 11, basic, hot water. Bus 700 or 800 (marked 'Eixo') goes from opposite Pão de Açúcar Supermarket in Taguatinga to old rodoviária in Brasília. Very cheap accommodation in Formosa (see page 541).

Camping The city's main site is 2 km out, by the Centro Esportivo, near the motor-racing track, with room for 3,100 campers, mixed reports. Take bus 109 (infrequent) from municipal rodoviária. *Água Mineral Parque*, 6 km northwest of city, direct buses only at weekend; mineral pool, showers. *Associação Brasileira de Camping* (Edif Márcia, 12th floor, Setor Comercial Sul, T2258768) has 2 sites: 1 at Km

19 on the Belo Horizonte Rd and 125 km northeast of Brasília at Sobradinho. *Camping Clube do Brasil* has a site at Itiquira waterfall, 100 km northeast of the city, near Formosa; information from Edif Maristela, room 1214, Setor Comercial Sul, T2236561.

The following are classified by their speciality:

Eating

International *Aeroporto*, terrace of international airport, pleasant, very good. Most of the big hotels' restaurants. *Restaurant Gaf*, Centro Gilberto Salomão, Lago Sul (very good, especially meat, but expensive). **Brazilian** There are several *churrascarias*, eg *Churrascaria do Lago*, SHTN, Conj 1-A, by Palácio da Alvorada, a number of Brazilian restaurants and some serving Amazonian food. **Seafood** *Panela de Barro*, Galeria Nova Ouvidor, Setor Comercial Sul, Quadra 5. **Portuguese** *Cachopa*, Galeria Nova Ouvidor, loja 127. **Spanish** *O Espanhol*, Av W3 Sul, quadra 506, bloco A. **French** *Le Français*, Av W3 Sul, quadra 404, bloco B. *La Chaumière*, Av W3 Sul, quadra 408, bloco A. **Italian/Pizzerias** *Kazebre 13*, Av W3 Sul, quadra 504. *Roma*, Av W3 Sul, quadras 501 and 511. Good, quite cheap. **Chinese** *China*, Av W3 Sul, quadra 103 bloco D. *New China*, Av W3 Sul 209, bloco A. *Fon Min*, Av W3 Sul 405; *Fon Pin*, Av W3 Sul 402. **Japanese** *Nipon*, Av W3 Sul 413 and at 112. **Arabic** *El Hadj*, in Hotel Torre Palace, Setor Hoteleiro Norte, quadra 4 bloco A. Very good. **Vegetarian** *Coisas da Terra*, Av W3 Norte, quadra 703. *Boa Saúde*, Av W3 Norte Quadra 702, Edif Brasília Rádio Center. Open Sunday-Friday 0800-2000, lunch 1100-1400. **Local** *Bom Demais*, Av W3 Norte, Quadra 706. Comfortable, inexpensive, serving fish, beef and rice etc, live music at weekends (cover charge US$0.50).

The Southern Hotel Sector tends to have more restaurants than the north. There are many cheap places on Avenida W3 Sul, eg at Blocos 502 and 506. At weekends, few restaurants in central Brasília are open

Snack bars (ie those serving *prato feito* or *comercial*, cheap set meals) can be found all over the city, especially on Av W3 and in the Setor Comercial Sul. Other good bets are the Conjunto Nacional and the Conjunto Venâncio, 2 shopping/office complexes on either side of the municipal rodoviária, which itself provides the best coffee and *pasteis* in town (bottom departure level). Tropical fruit flavour ice cream can be found in various parlours, eg Av W3 Norte 302. Freshly made fruit juices in all bars.

Bars & nightclubs

There are 2 English-style bars: *Gates Pub*, Av W3 Sul 403; and *London Tavern*, Av W3 Sul 409. The *Grenada* bar near the *Hotel Nacional* has good pavement atmosphere in early evening. Nightclubs in Conjunto Venâncio, Centro Gilberto Salomão and in the main hotels.

Entertainment

Information about entertainment etc is available in 2 daily papers, *Jornal de Brasília* and *Correio Brasiliense*. Any student card (provided it has a photograph) will get you into the cinema/theatre/concert hall for half price. Ask for 'uma meia' at the box office.

Cinema There are 15 cinemas in the Plano Piloto; for programme details, T139, entrance is half price on Wednesday.

Theatre There are 3 auditoria of the *Teatro Nacional*, the Sala Villa-Lobos (1,300 seats), the Sala Martins Pena (450), and the Sala Padre José Maurício (120); the building is in the shape of an Aztec pyramid. The Federal District authorities have 2 theatres, the *Galpão* and *Galpãozinho*, between Quadra 308 Sul and Av W3 Sul. Concerts are given at the *Escola Parque* (Quadras 507-508 Sul), the *Ginásio Presidente Médici* (Eixo Monumental, near TV tower), the *Escola de Música* (Av L2 Sul, Quadra 602) and the outdoor *Concha Acústica* (edge of lake in the Setor Hoteleiro Norte). *Planetarium*, on the Eixo next to the TV tower, gives shows Saturday and Sunday at 1600 and 1700.

Festivals

Ash Wednesday; *Maundy Thursday*, half-day; **8 December** (Immaculate Conception); *Christmas Eve*.

Shopping

Shopping complexes include the vast *Conjunto Nacional* on the north side of the rodoviária, the *Conjunto Venâncio* on the south side, the *Centro Venâncio 2000* at the beginning of Av W3 Sul, the *Centro Venâncio 3000* in the Setor Comercial Norte,

Brasília & the Pantanal

Parkshopping and the *Carrefour* hypermarket just off the exit to Guará, 12 km from the centre. For fine jewellery, *H Stern* has branches in the *Nacional* and *Carlton* Hotels and at the Conjunto Nacional and Parkshopping. The embassy sector is good for low-priced, high quality men's wear. For handicrafts from all the Brazilian states try *Galeria dos Estados* (which runs underneath the *eixo* from Setor Comercial Sul to Setor Bancário Sul, 10 minutes walk from municipal rodoviária, south along Eixo Rodoviário Sul); for Amerindian handicrafts, *Artíndia* in the rodoviária and at the airport. Dried flowers (typical of the region) outside the Cathedral (but not always). There is a *feira hippy* at the base of the TV tower every Saturday, Sunday and holiday: leather goods, wood carvings, jewellery, bronzes. English books (good selection) at *Livraria Sodiler* in Conjunto Nacional and at the airport.

Transport
See also Ins & outs, page 681

Car hire About 9 agencies, including *Budget*, *Hertz*, *Interlocadora* (at airport, T3653694) and *Localiza* (T3651616, also at airport, T0800-992000).

Air Airport, 12 km from centre, T3651224. Flights to Araguaína, Barreiras, Belém, Belo Horizonte, Carajás, Cuiabá, Fortaleza, Goiânia, Ilhéus, Imperatriz, Macapá, Manaus, Marabá, Palmas, Porto Velho, Recife, Rio Branco, Rio de Janeiro, Salvador, São Paulo, Teresina and Uberaba. Airline offices are in the *Hotel Nacional* building. Bus 102 or 118 to airport, regular, US$0.65, 30 minutes. Taxi is US$10 after bargaining, worth it. Left luggage facilities at airport (tokens for lockers, US$0.50).

Buses The bus terminal (rodoferroviária) beside the railway station, from which long-distance buses leave, has post office (0800-1700, Saturday 0800-1200), telephone and telegram facilities and showers (US$0.50). Taxi to Setor Hoteleiro Norte, US$9. Bus 131 between rodoviária, the municipal terminal, and rodoferroviária, US$1.25.

To **Rio**, 17 hours, 6 *comuns* (US$32) and 3 *leitos* (about US$64) daily. To **São Paulo**, 16 hours, 7 *comuns* (about US$30) and 2 *leitos* (about US$60) daily (*Rápido Federal* recommended). To **Belo Horizonte**, 12 hours, 9 *comuns* (US$20) and 2 *leitos* (US$40) daily. To **Belém**, 36 hours, 4 daily (US$55, *Trans Brasília*, T2337589, buses poorly maintained, but no alternative). To **Recife**, 40 hours, US$49-60. To **Salvador**, 24 hours, 3 daily (US$27). To **Campo Grande**, **São Luís**, 15 hours, 1915, US$30, or **Viação Motta** via São Paulo 0930, 1930, or 1820 direct. To **Corumbá**, US$46. To **Cuiabá**, 17½ hours (US$30) daily at 1200 with *São Luis*. **Mato Grosso**, generally Goiânia seems to be the better place for Mato Grosso destinations. **Barra do Garças**, 0830 and 2000, takes 9 hours with *Araguarina*, T2337598, US$13.20 return. All major destinations served. Bus tickets for major companies are sold in a subsidiary office in Taguatinga, Centro Oeste, C8, Lotes 1 and 2, Loja 1; and at the city rodoviária.

Directory

Airline offices *Passaredo*, T3653200. *Rio-Sul/Nordeste*, T2424099. *TAM/BRC*, T3651000. *Transbrasil*, T3651188. *Varig*, T3273455. *Vasp*, T3222020.

Banks *Lloyds Bank*, Av W3 Sul, quadra 506, bloco B. *First National Bank of Boston*, Setor Comercial Sul, quadra 6 bloco A. *Citibank*, SCS Quadra 06, bloco A, lj 186, T2158117. *Banco Francês e Brasileiro*, Av W3 Sul, quadra 506. Foreign currency (but not always Amex cheques) can be exchanged at these banks and at the branches of: *Banco Regional de Brasília* and *Banco do Brasil*, Setor Bancário Sul, latter also at airport, charge US$20 commission for TCs. *Excel*, Setor Comercial Sul, Subterráneo (currency and Amex cheques), 1045-1630. *American Express*, Buriti Turismo, CLS 402 Bloco A, Lojas 27/33, T2252686. *Diners Club*, Av W3 Norte 502. *Mastercard*, for cash against a card, SCRN 502, Bl B, lojas 30 e 31, Asa Norte. Good exchange rates at *Hotel Nacional*. Good exchange rates from hotels with 'exchange-turismo' sign.

Communications **Post Office:** Poste restante, Central Correio, 70001; SBN-Cj 03, BL-A, Edif Sede da ECT, the central office is in the Setor Hoteleiro Sul, between *Hotels Nacional* and *St Paul*. Another post office is in Ed Brasília Rádio, Av 3 Norte. **Internet:** *Liverpool Coffee Shop*, CLS 108, R da Igreijinha.

Cultural centres *British Council*, Setor C Sul, quadra 01, Bloco H, 8th floor, Morro Vermelho Building, T3236080. *Cultura Inglesa*, SEPS 709/908 Conj B, T2433065. *American Library*, Casa Thomas Jefferson, Av W4 Sul, quadra 706, T2436588. *Aliança Francesa*, Sul Entrequadra 707-907, Bloco A, T2427500. *Instituto Cultural Goethe*, Edif Dom Bosco, Setor Garagem Sul 902, lote 73, Bloco C, T2246773. Mon-Fri, 0800-1200, also 1600-2000, Mon, Wed, Thu.

Embassies & consulates *Australia*, Caixa Postal 11-1256, SHIS QI-09, Conj 16, Casa 1, T2485569 (in residential district, south of the lake). *Austria*, SES, Av das Nações 40, T2433111. *Canada*, SES, Av das Nações 16, T2237665. *Denmark*, Av das Nações 26, CP 07-0484, T2428188. Open 0900-1200, 1400-1700. *Finland*, SES, Av das Nações, lote 27, T2428555. *Germany*, SES, Av das Nações 25, T2437466. *Greece*, Shis Q1, 4 Conjunto 1, Casa 18, 704610, T2481127/2480920. *Guyana*, SDS, Edif Venâncio III, 4th floor, sala 410/404, T2249229. *Netherlands*, SES, Av das Nações 5, T3214769. *South Africa*, SES, Av das Nações, lote 06, T3129500. *Sweden*, Av das Nações 29, Caixa Postal 07-0419, T2431444. *Switzerland*, SFS, Av das Nações 41, T2445500. *UK*, SES, Quadra 801, Conjunto K (with British Commonwealth Chamber of Commerce), or Av das Nações, Caixa Postal 070586, T2252710. *USA*, SES, Av das Nações 3, T3217272. *Venezuela*, SES, Av das Nações 13, T2239325.

Security There is a certain amount of gang violence in the city, so caution is advised at night.

Tour companies & travel agents *Buriti Turismo*, Cls 402, Bloco A, lojas 27/33, T2252686, American Express representative. *Stella Barros* (Thomas Cook), SCLS 406, Bloco C, loja 27, T2421121, F2445059. *APS Tur*, Cls 410, Bloco A, loja 29, T2445577. *Jahjah Turismo*, CRS 504, bloco A, loja 11. Friendly. Many tour operators have their offices in the shopping arcade of the *Hotel Nacional*: *Toscana* has been recommended as cheap and good; also *Presmic Turismo*, lojas 33/34, T2255515. Full, half-day and night-time tours (0845, 1400 and 1930 respectively). *Kubitschek Turismo* (Lucas Milhomens speaks English), T3471494. Recommended for city tour and information; 3-4 hr tours with English commentary can also be booked at the airport by arriving air passengers – a convenient way of getting to your hotel if you have heavy baggage. Some tours have been criticized as too short, others that the guides speak poor English, and for night-time tours, the flood lighting is inadequate on many buildings. Teresa Tasso, T2734844, recommended. Also Otoniel, at airport, T3651796, 2½ hrs, US$50.

Tourist offices At the Centro de Convenções, 3rd floor (*Setur*, helpful, good map of Brasília, open to public 1300-1800 – ask for Eliane, who speaks English, T3213318, F2255706); small stand at rodoferroviária, friendly but not very knowledgeable (open 24 hrs, every day). Tourist office at the Air Terminal is on the international arrival side only, will book hotels, no attempt at English, no maps of the city, no helpful suggestions. Setur publishes a book called *Brasília, Coração Brasileiro*, which is full of practical information. *Embratur*, head office, Setor Comercial Norte, Quadra 02, bloco G, CEP 70710-500, T2249100, F3238936, webmaster@embratur.gov.br. *Touring Club do Brasil*, on Eixo, has maps (members only). The information office in the centre of Praça dos Tres Poderes has a colourful map and lots of useful text information. The staff are friendly and have interesting information about Brasília and other places in Goias – only Portuguese spoken. **Maps:** 'Comapa', Venâncio 200 business complex, 2nd floor, have expensive maps.

Voltage 220 volts, 60 cycles.

Around Brasília

From Saída Sul (the southern end of the Eixo), the BR-040/050 goes to **Cristalina** where it divides; the BR-040 continues to Belo Horizonte and Rio de Janeiro, the BR-050 to Uberlândia and São Paulo (both paved).

Also from Saída Sul, the BR-060 to Anápolis, Goiânia and Cuiabá; from Anápolis the BR-153 (Belém-Brasília) heads north to Belém (paved – for a description of this road, see page 695) and from Goiânia the BR-153 goes south through the interior of the states of São Paulo and Paraná (also paved).

From Saída Norte (the northern end of the Eixo), the BR-020 goes north to **Formosa** (1½ hours by frequent buses from Brasília, **D** *Hotel Mineiro* and one other, cheaper, clean and friendly; cheap restaurants), Barreiras, and after

Brasília & the Pantanal

Barreiras on the BR-242 (all paved) to Salvador and Fortaleza. The BR-020 is in good condition for 120 kilometres. At Alvorada do Norte (130 kilometres) there are cheap but very basic hotels. **Posse** (295 kilometres) is picturesque (accommodation on Avenida Padre Trajeiro, including *Hoki Mundial*, friendly). The road is slow with many potholes until Barreiras.

Road distances in kilometres: Belém, 2,120; Campo Grande, 1,134; Cuiabá, 1,133; Foz do Iguaçu, 1,573; Goiânia, 209; Manaus, 3,490; Recife, 2,220; Rio, 1,148; Salvador, 1,531; São Paulo, 1,015.

Of the seven *cidades satélites* that contain between them over half the Federal District's population, five are new and two (Brazlândia and Planaltina) are based on pre-existing settlements.

Planaltina	Forty kilometres northeast of the Plano Piloto via Saída Norte is Planaltina,
Population: 50,000	originally a settlement on the colonial pack route from the mines of Goiás and

Cuiabá to the coast. The old part still contains many colonial buildings. There are two good *churrascarias* on the main street and it is a good place for a rural Sunday lunch. Five kilometres outside Planaltina is the Pedra Fundamental, the foundation stone laid by President Epitácio Pessoa in 1922 to mark the site originally chosen for the new capital.

Also outside Planaltina, at Km 30 on the BR-020, lies **Águas Emendadas**: from the same point spring two streams that flow in opposite directions to form part of the two great river systems, the Amazon and the Plate. Permission from the biological institute in Brasília is required to visit. At Km 70 is Formosa (see above). Some 20 kilometres north of the town is the Itiquira waterfall (158 metres high). From the top are spectacular views and the pools at the bottom offer good bathing. It is crowded at weekends. There are four smaller falls in the area. Camping is possible. To get there from the centre of Formosa, follow the signs or ask. The only bus from Formosa to Itiquira leaves at 0730 and returns at 1700.

Parque
Nacional de
Brasília

Northwest of Brasília, but only 15 minutes by car from the centre, is this park of some 28,000 hectares, founded in 1961 to conserve the flora and fauna of the Federal Capital. Only a portion of the park is open to the public without a permit. There is a swimming pool fed by clear riverwater, a snack bar and a series of trails through gallery forest, which is popular with joggers in the early morning and at weekends. The rest of the park is rolling grassland, gallery forest and *cerrado* vegetation. Large mammals include tapir, maned wolf and pampas deer; birdwatching is good (especially Brasília Tapaculo, Horned Sungem, Yellow-faced parrot, Least Nighthawk). ■ *Contact Ibama, SAIN, Avenida L/4 Lote 04/08, Ed Sede do Ibama, T3161080, or the park's office, Via Epia SMU, T2333251, F2335543.*

Goiás

Goiás is quite a mixture: colonial mining towns, a modern, planned state capital and centres which owe their existence to rapidly expanding agriculture. There is hydrotherapy tourism, fishing in a big way and two fine national parks, Emas and Chapada dos Veadeiros. An interesting festival, with processions on horse-back, is held in Pirenópolis during May.

Colonial mining towns in the state sprang from gold rushes which began in 1722, as Paulistas and Bandeirantes pushed out from Minas Gerais in search of precious stones and new mineral wealth. Development was rapid, including expansion of cattle farming. Goiás was made a captaincy in 1748. By the beginning of the 19th century the mining boom was over, and it was not really until the middle years of the 20th century that the region was given new impetus. This came first from the construction of the new state capital, Goiânia, then from the building of Brasília. The Federal District of Brasília was subtracted from its territory in 1960, which was further split in half in 1990 to form the new state of Tocantins in the north (see page 673).

Today Goiás, with an area of 364,714 square kilometres and some four million inhabitants, is one of Brazil's most rapidly developing frontier agricultural areas, producing coffee, soya and rice, most of Brazil's tin and tungsten, and raising beef on the country's largest cattle ranches.

The eroded Brazilian Plateau, clothed in woodland savannah and varying from 600 metres to 900 metres in height, ripples across the south of the state; most of its rivers flow north to feed the Araguaia and Tocantins rivers. Elsewhere, the climate is subtropical, with distinct wet and dry seasons.

Goiânia

The state capital is famous for its street cafés and is a good place to stop between Brasília and the rest of the Centro-Oeste. Tourism is not as developed as other parts of the country, but the city is pleasant and there are many interesting sights within easy reach.

Population: 958,000
Phone code: 062
Colour map 4, grid A1

Just off the BR-060, 209 kilometres southwest of Brasília, is the second of Brazil's planned state capitals, after Belo Horizonte. Goiânia was founded in 1933 and replaced Goiás Velho as capital four years later. In general, commercial and industrial sectors are to the north, with administration in the centre and residential zones to the south.

Sights

It is a spacious city, with many green spaces and well-lit main avenues, ornamented with plants, radiating out from the central **Praça Cívica**, on which stand the Government Palace and main Post Office.

Brasília & the Pantanal

The unremarkable **Metropolitan Cathedral**, corner Ruas 14 e 19, stands two blocks east of the Praça Cívica. Walk due north of the Praça Cívica on broad Avenida Goiás to see the painted walls of the **Projeto Galeria Aberta**; many city buses are also painted with eye-catching designs.

One and a half kilometres out along the Avenida Araguaia (which runs diagonally northeast from the Praça) is the shady **Parque Mutirama**, with recreational and entertainment facilities and a planetarium. ■ *Sunday sessions at 1530 and 1630.* There is also a pleasant **Parque Zoólogico**, Avenida Anhangüera, some distance west of the main square, with a good zoo, zoological museum, playground, lake and sports fields. ■ *Tuesday-Sunday 0700-1800.*

Museums Just off the Praça Cívica is the **Museu Estadual 'Zoroastro Artiaga'**, Praça Dr PL Teixeira 13, with a collection of local handicrafts, religious objects, animals and Indian artefacts. **Museu Antropológico do UFG** on the Praça Universitária, one kilometre east of Praça Cívica, houses wide-ranging ethnographic displays on the Indians of the Centre West. ■ *Monday-Friday 0900-1700.* **Museu de Ornitologia**, Avenida Pará 395, Sétor Campinas, has more than 8,000 stuffed birds and animals from many countries. ■ *0900-1900, except Monday.*

Brasília & the Pantanal

Goiânia

| 0 metres | 200 |
| 0 yards | 200 |

■ **Sleeping**
1 Augustus   3 Karajás   5 Umuarama
2 Castro's Park   4 Papillon

Excursions

The thermal springs at Cachoeira Dourada, 240 kilometres south on the Rio Paranaíba, are worth a visit, as are the fantastic rock formations of the Serra das Galés at **Paraúna**, 160 kilometres south-south west off BR-060, and a host of delightful, colonial mining villages within two hours' drive on good (often paved) roads. Travel agents in town can arrange day tours, for example *Turisplan Turismo*, Rua 8 No 388, T2241941, which also sells regular bus tickets.

Essentials

L *Castro's Park*, Av República do Líbano 1520, Setor Oeste, T2237766, F2257070. Warmly recommended. **L** *Papillon*, Av República do Líbano 1824, T2238511, F2238381. Good. **AL** *Augustus*, Praça Antônio Lisita 702, T2241022, F2241410. Good. **AL** *Umuarama*, R 4 No 492, T2241555, F2241673. Good.

    A *Cabiúna Palace*, Av Parnaíba 698 (close to Parque Mutirama), T/F2125001. Good value. **A** *Karajás*, Av Goiás and R 3 No 860, T2249666, F2291153, 3 blocks north of Praça. Convenient and comfortable. **A** *Vila Rica*, Av Anhangüera 5308, T2232733, F2232625. Two-star Embratur hotel, convenient.

    Cheaper (**B-C**) are: *Príncipe*, Av Anhangüera 2936 and Av Araguaia, T2240085. Fan, good value. *Paissandú*, Av Goiás 1290 e R 55, T2244925. Fan, 8 long blocks north of Praça. *Hotel del Rey*, R 8 No 321, T2256306. Good location on pedestrian mall, fan, good value. Several cheap hotels (**C-D**) near the rodoviária: eg *Star*, R 68 No 537. Basic, interesting clientele. *Itaipú*, R 29A No 178 at the old rodoviária (Setor Aeroporto), T2124055. *Rodoviária*, opposite bus station. Safe, cheap, good. Northwest of the rodoviária are many cheap *dormitórios*.

    Camping *Itanhangá* municipal site, Av Princesa Carolina, 13 km, T2921145. Attractive wooded location, reasonable facilities.

Sleeping
Av Anhangüera, on which many hotels are located, runs east-west 4 blocks north of the Centro Cívico; it is busy and noisy

Many *churrascarias*, eg *Boi na Brasa*, on Praça Germano Roriz (the first large square due south of Praça Cívica on R 84), open 1100-0100, and the more expensive *Lancaster Grill*, R 89 No 117, T2420311. A/c, live music. *Le Steak*, Av 85 No 352. Excellent, a/c, good atmosphere, expensive by Brazilian standards. *Fim de Tarde*, Av 85 No 301. Good meat dishes (including *picanha* and *kibe*, Arabic appetizer) and beer, open from 1700. *Costeleria do Marcão*, Av 31 de Março, past Praça do Cruzeiro. Best ribs in Goiás. Recommended. Open from 1700. *Bom Gourmet*, Av 85 No 1676. For meat and chicken dishes, very good, seats on street or in a/c room. Varied menu at *Cliff Piano Bar e Restaurante*, R 23 No 72, corner Av República do Líbano. Expensive, nice atmosphere. Highly recommended. *Palatinum*, in *Hotel Augustus*. Italian, very good, elegant, a/c, piano music. Good array of bars and restaurants around the Praça Tamandaré (R 8 and 5, just beyond the Bosque dos Buritis, 1 km west of Praça Cívica), including *Modiglianni* for good pizzas.

    Vegetarian *Arroz Integral*, R 93 No 326 (1100-1400, 1800-2100, self-service), or *Naturalmente Natural*, R 15 No 238, 1 block from the cathedral. Many small eating places near the rodoviária, which also has good food at low prices.

    Regional food *Centro de Tradições Goiánas*, R 4 No 515 (above the Parthenon Centre). Rice and fish cuisine. *Piquiras*, Av Repúlica do Líbano 1758 (near *Castro's Hotel*) and R 139/R 146 No 464, T2814344, Setor Marista, try the appetizer *pastelzinho de piquí* (a regional fruit used in many traditional Goiás dishes). Street stands (*pamonharías*) sell *pamonha* snacks, tasty pastries made with green corn, sweet, savoury, or *picante*/spicy; all are served hot and have cheese in the middle, some include sausage. Recommended are: *Pomonharia 100*, R 101 corner R Dr Olinto Manso Pereira, behind the Forum, Setor Sul. *Frutos da Terra*, Av Perimetral 669, for home delivery T2331507/2814049. *Pura*, Av 83 No 193, Setor Sul. Local meat pies (*empadões de Goiás*) are also delicious.

Eating
Goiânia is much cheaper for eating than Brasília

Brasília & the Pantanal

Bars & nightclubs
Goiânia is famous for its street bars, some with live music

People Club and *Académia da Birita*, R 7 No 1000, Sector Oeste. Dance club, bar and restaurant, very popular, Thursday, Friday, Saturday afternoon. *Cave Bar*, Av 85, Caravelo Center, entrance through back of Center, access by narrow R 85C, on left. Small pub, nice drinks and decor, foreign owner Gisela, good soft music. *Café Madrid*, R 101, No 353, Setor Sul, behind the Forum. A/c, bar and restaurant, best *paella* in Goiânia, famous for *margaritas*, live music (MPB, saxophone groups), open daily from 2100. Av Ricardo Paranhos, Setor Sul, is full of bars and crowds of young people after 2000.

Sports

Many sporting facilities throughout Goiânia, visitors welcome. For sunbathing, swimming and waterskiing go to the *Jaó Club*, T2612122, on reservoir near the city.

Shopping

Ceramic, sisal and wooden handicrafts from *Centro Estadual do Artesanato*, Praça do Trabalhador (0800-1800); Sunday handicrafts markets at the Praça Cívica (morning) and Praça do Sol (afternoon). The latter starts after 1530, until 2100, known as the Honey Fair as all types of honey are sold; also good for a Sunday snack, with many sweets and tarts sold along the street. Two shopping centres: *Flamboyant*, the largest, is some way from the centre (take a bus). *Bougainville*, near R 9, Setor Marista, newer; both have cinemas, snack bars.

Transport

Air Santa Genoveva, 6 km northeast off Rua 57, T2071288. Flights to Brasília, Campinas, São Paulo, Uberaba and Uberlândia. Several car hire firms at the airport. Taxi from centre US$6.

Buses Huge new rodoviária on Rua 44 No 399 in the Norte Ferroviário sector, about a 40-minute walk to downtown (T2248466). Buses 'Rodoviária-Centro' (No 404) and 'Vila União-Centro' (No 163) leave from stop on city side of terminal, US$0.80; No 163 goes on to the Praça Tamandaré.

To **Brasília**, 207 km, part divided freeway, at least 15 departures a day, 2½ hours, US$5, and **São Paulo**, 900 km via Barretos, US$25, 14½ hours, *leito* services at night. To **Goiás Velho**, 136 km, hourly from 0500, 2½ hours, US$5. **Pirenópolis** 0700 and 1700, 2 hours, US$5. **Campo Grande**, 935 km, 4 services daily, 18 hours, US$30. To **Cuiabá** (Mato Grosso), 916 km on BR-158/070 via Barra do Garças, or 928 km on BR-060/364 via Jataí (both routes paved, most buses use the latter route), 4 buses a day, US$25, 15-16 hours, continuing to Porto Velho (Rondônia) and Rio Branco (Acre) – a very trying journey indeed.

Directory

Airline offices *Varig*, Av Goiás 285, T2245059. *Vasp*, R 3 No 569, T2246389. **Banks** National banks. Travel agents will exchange cash, poor rates for TCs. **Tourist information** *Sictur*, Centro Administrativo, Praça Cívica, 7th floor, CEP 74319-000, T2230669, F2233911. *Dirtur*, R 30 corner of R 4, Centro de Convenções, CEP 74025-020, T2171121, F2172256. Extensive information, maps and bus routes in *Novo Guia Turístico de Goiás*, readily available at news stands, US$2.25. **Useful addresses** Immigration office: R 235, Setor Universitário.

Leaving Goiânia

At **Iporá**, 200 kilometres west of Goiânia on BR-158, there is a good hotel. At **Rio Verde** (*population* 100,585), on the BR-060, 241 kilometres west of Goiânia, are several possible hotel stops on the way to Cuiabá; **A** *Rio Verde Palace*, R Nizo Jaime de Gusmão 599, T/F6212527, and **C** *Vitória*, Praça 5 de Agosto, a/c, are the best of a poor lot.

Anápolis
Population: 265,000
Phone code: 062

This busy trading centre, 57 kilometres nearer Brasília, has cheaper accommodation than the capital and is more convenient than Goiânia. The **Centro de Gemologia de Goiás**, Quadra 2, Módulo 13, Daia, about 10 kilometres out on the Brasília highway (near the Embratel tower), has a fine collection of gemstones, library, sales and lapidary courses, and will show visitors how real and synthetic gemstones are distinguished. ■ *Monday-Friday 0730-1630*.

Sleeping and eating AL *Estância Park*, in parkland setting 6 km northeast, T3181200, F3181300. Pool, tennis, minizoo etc, best in town. **A** *Príncipe*, R Eng Portela 165, T3111611, F3240936, and **A** *Itamaraty*, R Manoel d'Abadia 209, T3111444, F3111244, both comfortable. Many cheap ones around the rodoviária (Av Brasil-Norte), eg **D** *Serra Dourada*, Av Brasil 375, T3240051. Restaurant, parking, fans, good value. *Restaurante Caiçara*, 14 de Julho 905, T3243740. Good *churrasco*.

Transport At Anápolis, the BR-153 (Brasília-Belém) turns north and begins the long haul (1964 km) through Tocantins, Maranhão and Pará to Belém, a bumpy, monotonous trip of 35 hours or more, US$55. There are regular bus services to Pirenópolis (66 km north).

This town is famous for its semi-precious stones, which can be bought cheaply in local shops. An interesting excursion is to the panning and mining sites amid magnificent rock formations, about six kilometres away. Take the BR-040 (Brasília-Belo Horizonte road) and at Km 104 take a left turn along a dirt road, just after the highway police post, to the Cristalina waterfall (11 kilometres along this road). There is a small municipal museum at Rua 21 de Abril 156 (daily 0800-1100, 1300-1700, except Tuesday) and a hotel, (**C**) *Hotel Goyás*, at R da Saudade 41, with fan and fridge.

Cristalina
Population: 28,500
Phone code: 062
Altitude: 1,189m

Goiás Velho

The former state capital, 144 kilometres northwest of Goiânia, is a picturesque old gold mining town with narrow streets, seven baroque churches and many well-preserved 18th-century colonial mansions and government buildings. It was founded in 1727 as Vila Boa.

Population: 28,000
Phone code: 062
Colour map 1, grid C5

The oldest church, **São Francisco de Paula** (1761), Praça Alves de Castro, facing the Market, is undergoing restoration. There is a good view of the town from **Santa Bárbara** church (1780), on the Rua Passo da Pátria.

Also worth visiting is the **Museu da Boa Morte**, in the colonial church of the same name (a small, but interesting collection of old images, paintings etc). The **Museu das Bandeiras** is in the Casa da Câmara e Cadeia (old town hall and prison), by the colonial fountain. The old **Government Palace** is next to the red-brick Cathedral in the main praça. The **Palácio Conde dos Arcos**, Praça Castelo Branco (across from the Cathedral), still has its original 1755 furniture on display. ■ *Tuesday-Saturday 0800-1700, Sunday 0800-1200*. The 18th-century **Mercado Municipal** is next to the rodoviária, 500 metres west of the central Praça do Coreto. **NB** Most churches and museums are closed on Monday.

AL *Vila Boa*, Av Dr Deusdete Ferreira de Moura, 1 km southeast on the Morro do Chapéu do Padre, T3711000. Pool, bar, restaurant, good views. Recommended. **C** *Araguaia*, Av Ferreira de Moura (the road into town from the south), T3711462. Best budget place, fan, comfortable. Recommended. Similar is the nearby *Serrano* (no phone), parking, bar. **D** *Pousada do Ipê*, R Boa Vista 32. Breakfast included, friendly, great lunch, garden. **Camping** Attractive, well-run *Cachoeira Grande* campground, 7 km along the BR-070 to Jussara (near the tiny airport), with bathing place and snack bar. More basic site (*Chafariz da Carioca*) in town by the river. *Dona Maninha*, R Dom Cândido, regional food, good value.

Sleeping & eating

Brasília & the Pantanal

Festivals The streets of Goiás Velho blaze with torches during the solemn Fogaréu processions of Holy Week, when hooded figures re-enact Christ's descent from the cross and burial.

Shopping *Centro de Tradições Goianas*, in *Hotel Vila Boa*, and (cheaper) *Associação dos Artesãos de Goiás*, at the Rosário Church and in the Municipal Market, for local crafts; many types of sugary sweets can be purchased direct from the bakeries.

Transport The rodoviária is 2 km out of town. Regular bus services to Goiânia (2½ hours), Aruanã, Barra do Garças and Jussara.

Pirenópolis

Population: 21,000
Phone Code: 062
Altitude: 770m
Colour map 1, grid C5

This lovely colonial silver mining town in the red hills of Goiás, 165 kilometres due west of Brasília, was founded in the same year as Goiás Velho and declared a National Heritage Site in 1989. As the nation's unofficial silver capital, shopping for jewellery and related items here is unsurpassed. *Festa do Divino Espírito Santo*, held 45 days after Easter (Pentecost), is one of Brazil's most famous and extraordinary folkloric/religious celebrations. It lasts three days, with medieval costumes, tournaments, dances and mock battles between Moors and Christians, a tradition held annually since 1819.

The **Igreja Matriz Nossa Senhora do Rosário** is the oldest church in the state (1728), but that of **Nosso Senhor de Bonfim** (1750-54), with three impressive altars and an image of the Virgin brought from Portugal, is the most beautiful. A museum of religious art is housed in the church of **Nossa Senhora do Carmo**. ■ *Daily 1300-1700*. Another displays regional historical items, the **Museu Família Pompeu**, Rua Nova 33. ■ *Tuesday-Friday 1300-1700, Saturday 1300-1500, Sunday 0900-1200*. The **Teatro de Pyrenópolis**, on Rua Com Joaquim Alves, is a testament to turn-of-the-century optimism. Pirenópolis was the birthplace of José Joaquim da Veiga Valle, the 'Aleijadinho of Goiás', many of whose works are in the Boa Morte museum in Goiás Velho. **Fazenda Babilônia**, 25 kilometres southwest by paved road, is a fine example of an 18th-century sugar *fazenda*, now a small museum, original mill, no public transport.

Sleeping

All accommodation is filled during Festa (see above) and even the downtown municipal camp site beside the Rio das Alvas overflows; better to visit from Brasília at this time

AL *Pousada dos Pirineus*, Chácara Mata do Sobrado, Bairro do Carmo, T/F3311345. Restaurant, bar, 2 pools, gym, tennis and other sports, boat hire. **A** *Hotel Fazenda Quinta da Santa Bárbara*, in garden setting at R do Bonfim 1, T/F3311304. All facilities including *Restaurante Brasília*. **B** *Pousada das Cavalhadas*, Praça da Matriz, T3311261. Central, fan, fridge, best of the budget choices. **C** *Rex*, also on the Praça da Matriz, T3311121. Nine sparse rooms, small restaurant. *Pousada Tavares*, *Pensão Central* and *Dormitório da Geny* are all **D** and mostly for the desperate.

Caldas Novas

Population: 40,000
Phone code: 062

This thermal resort, 167 kilometres southeast of Goiânia, has good hotels and campsites with hot swimming pools. There are three groups of springs within this area: Caldas Novas, Fontes de Pirapetinga (seven kilometres from the town) and Rio Quente (29 kilometres from the town, bus from Caldas Novas); water temperatures are 37-51°C. There are many buses from Goiânia; best reached from Morrinhos on BR-153 (Goiânia-São Paulo). The daily bus from Morrinhos costs US$2, 30 minutes.

Sleeping and eating Very fashionable is **L** *Hotel Turismo* (5-star) – **AL** *Pousada do Rio Quente* (4-star) complex at Rio Quente, T4521122, F4521177, São Paulo, T011-8525733, F2825281, Brasília, T061-2247166. Breakfast and lunch, transportation to main pools and recreation facilities included in price, other extras paid for with hotel's own currency, good hotel, accommodation in main buildings or chalets (the *Turismo* has a private airstrip). **AL** *Parque das Primaveras*, R do Balneário 1, T4531355, F4531294. Recommended. **B** *Serra Dourada*, Av Correia Neto 574, T4531300. Recommended. **D** *Imperial*, near rodoviária. Clean, friendly. **Camping** At Esplanada, and *Camping Clube do Brasil* site on the Ipameri Rd, 5 km from the centre. Many other 'Clubes e Campings', all with snack bars, eg *Tropical*, 2 sites in town, and *Berro d'Água*, Bairro do Turista. Recommended. *Caminho do Natural*, R José Borges 550, is a vegetarian restaurant; good, but expensive.

National parks

Goiás has two major national parks. In the elevated region 200 kilometres north of Brasília is the popular Chapada dos Veadeiros. The main attractions are a number of high waterfalls, complete with palm-shaded oases and natural swimming pools, and the varied wildlife: capibara, rhea, tapir, wolf, toucan etc. ■ *US$0.50, contact Ibama Rua 219 No 95, Setor Universitário, 74605-800 Goiânia, T062-2242488/061-6461109.*

Chapada dos Veadeiros

Sleeping There is a small hotel (**D**) by the rodoviária in Alto Paraíso and a very basic *dormitório* in São Jorge (take sleeping bag or hammock), but camping in the park is the most pleasant option, about US$2 per night and busy on weekends in the best visiting season (May-October).

Transport The park is reached by paved state highway 118 to Alto Paraíso de Goiás, then gravel road west towards Colinas for 30 km where a sign marks the turn-off (just before the village of São Jorge). Buses Brasília-Alto Paraíso 1000 and 2200, US$3.60; occasional local buses Alto Paraíso-São Jorge, includes 1600 departure, then 5 km walk to park entrance.

In the far southwest of the state, covering the watershed of the Araguaia, Taquari and Formoso rivers, is the small Emas National Park, 98 kilometres south of Mineiros, just off the main BR-364 route between Brasília and Cuiabá (112 kilometres beyond Jataí).

Emas National Park

Douglas Trent of *Focus Tours* writes: "The near 132,868 hectares of undulating grasslands and 'campo sujo' *cerrado* forests host the world's largest concentration of termite mounds. They provide a surreal setting for large numbers of pampas deer, giant anteater and greater rhea, or *ema* in Portuguese. Maned wolf are frequently seen roaming the grasses in search of tinamou and other prey. The park holds the greatest concentration of blue-and-yellow macaws outside Amazônia, and blue-winged, red-shouldered and red-bellied macaws can also be seen. There are many other animals and birds. A pair of bare-faced currasow, white-woodpeckers, streamer-tailed tyrants and other showy birds visit the park headquarters building daily.

"Along with the grasslands, the park supports a vast marsh on one side and rich gallery forests on the other. The crystal clear waters of the Rio Formosa pass right by the headquarters and wander through the park. Many have compared this park with the African savannas. As many of the interesting mammals are nocturnal, a spotlight is a must."

Sleeping Mineiros: A *Pilões Palace*, Praça Alves de Assis, T6611547. Restaurant, comfortable, and **C** *Boi na Brasa*, R Onze 11, T6611532. Fan, good *churrasco* restaurant attached. Next door **D** *Mineiros Hotel*, with bath and huge breakfast, good lunch. Recommended. Camping within the park costs about US$2 pp and there is simple,

Brasília & the Pantanal

dormitory accommodation at the park headquarters; kitchen and cook available, but bring own food.

Transport The park is most easily reached from Campo Grande (about 6 hours by car, compared with about 20 hours from Goiânia, paved road poor). The road to the park is now paved; there is no regular transport, but tour operators can organize four-wheel drive trips. The São José monastery, Mineiros, can arrange the necessary permission to visit, turn left out of the rodoviária and walk 500m along dirt road (or from Ibama, as above, also from Secretaria de Turismo, Praça Col Carrijo 1, T6611551). A 4-day, 3-night visit to the park can be arranged through agencies (for example, *Focus Tours*, see **Tours and tour operators**, page 30).

Rio Araguaia

Brazilians are firmly convinced that the 2,630-kilometre-long Rio Araguaia is richer in fish than any other in the world; a visit to the 220-kilometre stretch between Aruanã and the Ilha do Bananal during the fishing season is quite an experience. As the receding waters in May reveal sparkling white beaches, thousands of Brazilian and international enthusiasts pour into the area, intent on getting the best camping spots. As many as 400 tent cities spring up, and vast quantities of fish are hauled in before the phenomenon winds down in September, when the rivers begin to rise again and flood the surrounding plains.

Without Brazilian contacts, the traveller's best way of experiencing this annual event is with one of the specialist tour operators; recommended are *Transworld*, Rua 3 No 546, Goiânia, T2244340, F2121047 (one-week group trips in a 'botel' out of Aruanã to Bananal), and *KR International Travel*, Rua Mexico 8th floor, S 801, Rio de Janeiro, T021-2101238, ex-Peace Corps manager, good for info on the Centre-West region. Boats (US$25 an hour) and guides can also be hired in Aruanã, Britânia, Barra do Garças or **Porto Luís Alves** (**AL** *Pousada do Jaburu*, including meals; **A** *Pousada do Pescador*, access to boats and guides), guide Vandeir will arrange boat trips to see wildlife, take food and water. Interesting walks in surrounding jungle with Joel, ask at the hotel.

Health Yellow-fever vaccination is recommended for the region. *Borrachudas*, tiny biting insects, are an unavoidable fact of life in Central Brazil in June and July; repellent helps a little.

Aruanã
Population: 5,500
The Araguaia is most readily accessible from Aruanã, a port 180 kilometres northwest of Goiás Velho by paved highway, which sees little excitement outside the winter fishing season when its comfortable hotels are booked up for months. Boats can be rented to visit some of the beautiful lakes and beaches nearby. Buses from the rodoviária serve Araguapaz, Britânia and Goiânia. Brazilian Canoeing Championships are also held along the river.

Sleeping and eating **A** *Recanto Sonhado*, on the river at the end of Av Altamiro Caio Pacheco (2 km), T3761230, self-service restaurant, boutique, includes lunch (reservations can be made through T062-2417913 in Goiânia). **A** *Araguaia*, Praça Couto Magalhães 53 (opposite the docks), T3761251. Both have pools and meals available. Restaurants in town rather poor, but try *Columbia*, R João Artiaga 221, T3761298 (opposite Municipal Stadium), clean, good menu. The official campground is a 20-minute boat ride away on Ilha Redonda, but open (and full) only in July.

Mato Grosso do Sul

Mato Grosso do Sul is a relatively new state, only being formed in 1977 when it was separated from Mato Grosso. Cattle ranching is very important, with over 21 million head of beef cattle on 16 million hectares of free range pasture.

It is situated to the southwest of Goiás and has a population of about two million. The state is half covered with forest, with the large wetland area (230,000 square kilometres), called the Pantanal (roughly west of a line between Campo Grande and Cuiabá, between which there is a direct road), partly flooded in the rainy season (see page 712). The Noroeste Railway (passenger service indefinitely suspended) and a road run across Mato Grosso do Sul via Campo Grande to Porto Esperança and Corumbá, both on the Rio Paraguai. Much of the road is across the wetland, offering many sights of birds and other wildlife.

Campo Grande

The city was founded in 1899 and became the state capital in 1979. It is a pleasant, modern city. Because of the terra roxa (red earth), it is called the 'Cidade Morena'.

Population: 600,000
Phone code: 067
Colour map 3, grid C3

In the centre is a shady park, the **Praça República**, commonly called the Praça do Rádio after the Rádio Clube on one of its corners. Three blocks west is **Praça Ari Coelho**. Linking the two squares, and running through the city east to west, is Avenida Afonso Pena; much of its central reservation is planted with yellow ypé trees. Their blossom covers the avenue, and much of the city besides, in spring. The city also has a great many mango trees; consequently, it is very leafy.

The **Parque dos Poderes**, a long way from the centre, covers several hectares; as well as the Palácio do Governo and state secretariats, there is a small zoo for the rehabilitating animals from the Pantanal (phone the Secretaria do Meio Ambiente to visit), lovely trees and cycling and jogging tracks.

Museu Dom Bosco (Indian Museum), Rua Barão do Rio Branco 1843, is a **Museums** superb museum with the following collections: exhibits from the five Indian groups with which the Salesian missionaries have had contact in the 20th century: the Bororó, from the region between Bolivia to the border with Goias and between the Rio Garças and Rio das Mortes; the Moro, from Paraguay and Bolivia; the Carajá, from the shores of the Rio Araguaia, including Ilha do Bananal; the Xavante, from central Brazil beyond Rio das Mortes, and tribes of the Rio Uaupés in Amazônia, all with explanatory texts; fossilized shells, malacology (shells), entomology, 2,800 stuffed birds, 7-8,000 butterflies, mammals, minerals and 'monstrous' (two-headed calves etc). Each collection is highly recommended. ■ *Daily 0700-1100, 1300-1700, US$0.50, T3833994.*

Brasília & the Pantanal

Museu do Arte Contemporâneo, Marechal Rondón and Avenida Calógeras, displays modern art from the region. ■ *Monday-Friday 0900-1700, Saturday 0900-1200, free.*

Essentials

Sleeping

The important street in the centre, Rua Marechal Cândido Mariano Rondon, is called either Marechal Rondon, or Cândido Mariano

AL *Exceler Plaza*, Av Afonso Pena 444, T7210102, F7215666. Four-star, very good, luxury, art gallery, pool, tennis, all-you-can-eat business lunches. **A** *Advanced*, Av Calógeras 1909, T7215000, F7257744, **B** with fan, modern. **A** *Buriti*, Av A M Coelho 2301, T/F7212211. Pool, sauna, parking, restaurant. **A** *Campo Grande*, R 13 de Maio 2825, T7216061, F7248349. Central, luxury, cash discounts. **A** *Concord*, Av Calógeras 1624, T3843081, F3824987. Very good, swimming pool, mini bar. **A** *Fenícia*, Av Calógeras 2262, T3832001, F3832862. Mini bar, TV. **A** *Vale Verde*, Av Afonso Pena 106, T7213355. Mini bar, restaurant, pool. Recommended. **B** *Paris*, Av Costa e Silva 4175, T7871795, F7257744. A/c, mini bar, **C** with fan. **B** *Americano*, R 14 de Julho 2311 and Mcal Rondón, T7211454. A/c, fridge, cheaper with fan, a bit run down, friendly. By Praça Ari Coelho are **B** *Pousada LM*, R 15 de Novembro 201, T3833300. Fan, fridge, also rents by the month, and **C** *Central*, R 15 de Novembro 472, T3846442. Fan, basic, cheaper with shared bath.

This area is not safe at night

Near the rodoviária There is a wide variety of hotels in the streets around the rodoviária; leave bags in the *guarda volumes* and shop around. **A** *Internacional*, Allan Kardec 245, T7844677, F7212729, **B** with fan. Modern, pool. On Dom Aquino are **B** *Iguaçu*, No 761, T3844621, F7213215. A/c, fridge, **C** with fan, modern, pleasant. Recommended. **B** *Palace*, No 1501, T3844741. A/c, fridge, **C** with fan, some rooms small.

Campo Grande

B *Nacional*, No 610, T3832461. A/c, cheaper with fan, **C** with shared bath. **B** *Village Palace*, No 802, T7241954. A/c, fridge, **C** with fan. **B** *Saigali*, Barão do Rio Branco 356, T3845775. A/c, mini bar, parking, cheaper with fan, comfortable. Recommended. **C** *Cosmos*, Dom Aquino 771, T3844270. Fan, good value. **C** *Novo*, J Nabuco 185, T7210505. Without breakfast, good value. Recommended. **C** *Turis*, Allan Kardec 200, T3827688. A/c, cheaper with fan, **D** in basement. **C** *Rocha*, Barão do Rio Branco 343, 1 block from rodoviária, T7256874. Without breakfast, fan, parking. **D** *Vânia*, Mcal Rondón 1004, T3842338. Fan, cheaper with shared bath, laundry. Recommended. **D-E** *Santa Inês*, Afonso Pena 1413, T7242621. Fan, comfortable, cheaper with shared bath. **D** *Pamella*, J Nabuco 245, T7243209. Shared bath, fan, buffet restaurant. **D** *Paiva*, R Dom Aquino 523. TV.

Near the railway station B *Gaspar*, Av Mato Grosso 2, opposite station, T/F3835121. A/c, fridge, **C** with fan, ask for quiet room, good breakfast, comfortable. Next door is **C** *União*, Av Calógeras 2828, T3824213. Cheaper with shared bath, good breakfast, ask for quiet room. **D** *Continental*, R Maracaju 229, 2 blocks from railway, 5 from rodoviária. Comfortable, German owner. **D** *Esperança*, R Dr Temistocles 93, 1 block from station. Hot and cold showers, basic, no a/c or fan, restaurant, very helpful. **D** *Caçula*, Calógeras 2704, T7214658. Fan, cheaper with shared bath, basic, hot showers, laundry.

Churrascarias *Vitório*, Av Afonso Pena 1907. Live music evenings. *Terracus Gaúcho*, at rodoviária. Huge meal. *Campo Grande*, Av Calógeras 2199. Good value. *Nossa Querência*, Av Afonso Pena 1267, near rodoviária. *Rodízio*, 2-for-1 special in evenings, good value and quality. Recommended. **Comida caseira** *Carinca*, southeast corner of main square. Modern, clean, good plain food. *Bandeirantes*, Dom Aquino 803. Good and economical. *Papa Gula*, Dom Aquino 1761. Central, good value meals and snacks. *Restaurante da Gaúcha*, Allan Kardek 238, near rodoviária. **Oriental** *Hong Kong*, R Maracaju 131. Centre, good Chinese food, also a legal outlet for *jacaré* meat, closed Monday. **Other** *Cafeteria Lojas Americanas*, Mcal Rondón 1336, in a supermarket, and *Meio Kilo* opposite. Good value buffet. *El Café*, R Dom Aquino 1248. Recommended. *Nutre Bem*, Pedro Celestino 1696. Good vegetarian. Plenty of good, cheap places in R Barão de Rio Branco. *Confidência Mineira*, 14 de Julho 945. Mineiro food and 49 types of *cachaça* on sale, open daily, shows Sunday and Tuesday. *Paulão Pizzeria*, R Candido Mariano 1725. Very clean, also does healthy meals and meat dishes. **Local specialities** *Caldo de piranha* (soup), *chipa* (Paraguayan cheese bread), sold on the streets, delicious when hot, and the local liqueur, *pequi com caju*, which contains *cachaça*. **Eating**

Eme-Ene (see Shopping below) has a *peña* (folk music show) each Wednesday at 2100. Recommended. *Skina*, 13 de Maio and Mcal Rondon. Bar with live music, popular. **Entertainment**

The *Casa do Artesão*, Av Calógeras 2050 and Av Afonso Pena. Open Monday-Friday 0800-1800, Saturday 0800-1200, has a good collection of native crafts, Indian jewellery and arrows on sale. *Eme-Ene*, Av Afonso Pena 2303, T3822373. Regional handicrafts, open 0700-1900, Saturday 0700-1700, Sunday 0800-1200, good. *Arte do Pantanal*, Av Afonso Pena 1743. Regional crafts. A local speciality is Os Bugres da Conceição, squat wooden statues covered in moulded wax. There is a market (Feira Livre) on Wednesday and Saturday. **Shopping**

Car hire On Av Afonso Pena are: *Localiza*, No 318, T7828786, at airport, T0800-992000. *Hertz*, No 2620, T3835331. *Locagrande*, No 466, T7213282, F7213282. *Unidas*, No 829, T7845626, F3846115, at airport, T7632145. **Transport**

Brasília & the Pantanal

A dot served by a lousy railway

"Campo Grande is a small city in the middle of nowhere." Thus Richard Gott opens Land without Evil. Utopian Journeys across the South American Watershed (page 11). It is a dot at the centre of a vast expanse of cattle land, created by the railway from São Paulo to the Rio Paraguai. The area was invaded by Paraguay in 1865, so Brazil made efforts to take a stronger hold. The railway with

which the Brazilians intended to do this was surveyed by the British in 1870 and took 40 years to complete. Colonel Fawcett passed through in 1920 and called it "the worst constructed and least efficiently maintained [railway] in the whole republic..." It's a wonder they managed to keep it going as long as they did. For all that, Campo Grande is a busy, prosperous place and by no means a backwater.

Air Airport, Av Duque de Caxias, 7 km, T7632444. Flights to Cuiabá, Londrina and São Paulo. City bus No 158, 'Popular' stops outside airport. Taxi to airport, US$6. It is safe to spend the night at the airport. *Banco do Brasil* at airport exchanges dollars. Post office, fax and phones in same office.

Buses Rodoviária is in the block bounded by R Barão do Rio Branco, R Vasconcelos Fernandes, R Dom Aquino and R Joaquim Nabuco, T3831678, all offices on second floor. At the R Vasconcelos Fernandes end are town buses, at the R Joaquim Nabuco end state and interstate buses. Eight blocks' walk from Praça República. Taxi to rodoviária, US$3.60. There are shops, *lanchonetes* and a cinema, US$1.25.

Campo Grande has good connections throughout the country: To **São Paulo**, US$23, 14 hours, 9 buses daily, first at 0800, last at 2400, 3 *leito* buses US$33. To **Cuiabá**, US$20, 10 hours, 12 buses daily, *leito* at 2100 and 2200, US$50. To **Brasília**, US$30, 23 hours at 0900 and 1900. To **Goiânia**, *São Luís* company 1100, 1630, 1900, 2300, 15 hours on 1900 service, US$30, others 24 hours, US$1 cheaper. **Rio de Janeiro**, US$40, 21 hours, 4 buses daily, *leito* at 1745, US$84. To **Belo Horizonte**, 22 hours, US$35. To **Corumbá**, with *Andorinha*, 8 daily from 0600, 6 hours, US$15. Campo Grande-Corumbá buses connect with those from Rio and São Paulo, similarly those from Corumbá through to Rio and São Paulo. Good connections to all major cities. **Ponta Porã**, 5 hours, 9 buses daily, US$5. **Dourados**, 4 hours, 14 daily (Queiroz), US$7. Beyond Dourados is Mundo Novo, from where buses go to Ponta Porã (0530) and to Porto Frajelli (very frequent). From Mundo Novo, ferries for cars and passengers go to Guaíra for US$1. Twice daily direct service to **Foz do Iguaçu** (17 hours) with *Integração*, 1200, 1600, US$27; same company goes to Cascavel, US$20. To **Pedro Juan Caballero** (Paraguay), del *Amambay* company, 0600, US$8.50. *Amambay* goes every Sunday morning to **Asunción**.

Directory **Airline offices** *Varig*, R Barão do Rio Branco 1356, Centro, T3834070, at airport, T7631213. **Banks** *Banco do Brasil*, 13 de Maio and Av Afonso Pena, open 1100-1600, commission US$10 for cash, US$20 for TCs, regardless of amount exchanged. *Banco Francês Brasileiro*, Mcal Rondon 1672, open 1000-1200 and 1330-1430, US$ cash, no commission. *Bradesco*, 13 de Maio and Av Afonso Pena, and on Rio Branco between P Celestino and Rui Barbosa, ATM for Visa. *Overcash Câmbio*, R 13 de Maio 2892, open Mon-Fri 1000-1600. *Campo Grande Câmbio*, R 13 de Maio 2484, open Mon-Fri 0930-1630, cash only. **Communications** Post Office: on corner of R Dom Aquino and Av Calógeras 2309, and Barão do Rio Branco on corner of Ernesto Geisel, both locations offer fax service, US$2.10 per page within Brazil. **Telephone:** *Telems*, R 13 de Maio e R 15 de Novembro, open 0600-2200 daily. **Internet:** *Oris Livros y Revistas*, Av Alfonso Pena 1975. **Embassies & consulates** *Bolivia*, R Dom Aquino 1354, T/F3822190. *Paraguay*, R João Crippa 1065, T7214430. **Hospitals & medical services** Yellow and Dengue fevers are both present in Mato Grosso do Sul. There is a clinic at the railway station, but it's not very hygienic, best to get your immunizations at home. **Tour companies & travel agents** Vox Tour, R Cândido Mariano

1777, T3843335, F7258663, English and Spanish spoken, very helpful. *Tainá Turismo*, R Sete de Setembro 1966, T/F3846544. *Impacto*, R Padre João Crippa 1065, sala 101, T3825197, T7243167, F7245124, Pantanal and Bonito tour operators, helpful. *Time Tour*, R Joaquim Murtinho 386, T3842363, F7212879, American Express representative. *Stella Barros* (Thomas Cook), R Euchlides da Cunha 479, T7211040, F7216020. *Gil, Nosso Hotel* opposite rodoviária, T7210505. **Tourist offices** Tourist information from the state run *Casa do Turismo*, R Arthur Jorge 622, by Parque Belmar Fidalgo, T/F7245104, friendly, helpful. Maps and books for sale at the municipal *Centro de Informação Turística e Cultural*, Av Noroeste 5140, corner of Afonso Pena. Housed in Pensão Pimentel, a beautiful mansion built in 1913, also has a database about services in the city and cultural information. Another office on R Barão do Rio Branco between 14 de Junho and 13 de Maio, helpful, Kiosk at airport.

Campo Grande to São Paulo

The Campo Grande-São Paulo journey can be broken at **Três Lagoas** (*population* 70,500), 9½ hours from São Paulo (motorway) and six hours from Campo Grande by paved highway BR-262. Sixteen kilometres east of Três Lagoas is the massive **Jupiá Dam** on the Rio Paraná, which can be visited with prior permission. ■ *Weekends and holidays only, 0800-1800, T5212753.* Further north are other hydroelectric dams, most impressive of which is at **Ilha Solteira** (50 kilometres, several hotels and good fish restaurants on São Paulo state side); guided tours at 1000 and 1500 weekends and holidays. Excellent swimming is to be had at **Praia Catarina**, with bars, playground and kiosks (six kilometres). Overlooking the river 35 kilometres south of Ilha Solteira is restored **Fort Itapura**, built during the War of the Triple Alliance, with beach and restaurants nearby.

Sleeping & eating **A** *Três Lagoas*, Av Rosário Congro 629, T5212500. Best. **B** *Regente Palace*, R Parnaíba 580. A/c, good value. **D** *Novo*, Av Antônio de Souza Queiroz, near rodoviária. *Restaurant Casarão*, R Munir Tomé 30. Good selection. *Boi na Brasa*, Av Antônio Trajano 487. Recommended for *churrascos*.

Transport **Buses** Campo Grande-Três Lagoas 0800, 1200, 2230, US$12.50, an interesting journey, especially for cattle farmers.

Campo Grande to the Paraguayan border

The paved road from Campo Grande to the Paraguayan frontier at Ponta Porã passes through Dourados, the supply centre of a developing agricultural region carved from the red *sertão*, in large part by Japanese immigrants. Apart from a couple of pleasant parks and lakes for swimming, there is little of note for the traveller.

Dourados
Population: 142,000
Phone code: 067

Sleeping and eating **A** *Alphonsus*, Av Pres Vargas 603, T4215211, F4219178. Best. **B** *Figueira Palace*, R Toshinobu Katayama 553, T4215611. A/c, pleasant. **B** *Bahamas*, R Cândido da Câmara 750, T4214714. A/c, simpler but excellent value. *Restaurante Boxexa*, R Munir Araújo 780. Good pizzas. *Churrascaria Guarujá*, No 595 same street, for *churrascos* in enjoyable surroundings.

Transport **Air**: scheduled flights to Marília, Ponta Porã, Presidente Prudente and São Paulo from the small airport (10 km). **Buses**: good bus connections for Campo Grande, Ponta Porã, Mundo Novo, and Presidente Prudente and Maringá to the east of the Rio Paraná.

Ponta Porã
Population: 54,000
Phone code: 067

The highway continues 115 kilometres to Ponta Porã, separated from Pedro Juan Caballero in Paraguay only by a broad avenue. With paved streets, good public transport and smart shops, Ponta Porã is decidedly more prosperous than its neighbour, although Brazilian visitors flock across the border to play the casino and buy cheaper 'foreign' goods. At the **Parque das Exposições**, by the rodoviária, an animal show is held each October.

*Brazilian hotels include
breakfast in tariff;
Paraguayan ones do not*

Sleeping and eating **B** *Porta do Sol Palace*, R Paraguai 2688, T4313341, F4311193. A/c, pool, very nice. **B** *Guarujá*, R Guia Lopes 63, T4311619. Recommended. Opposite is **C** *Barcelona*, maze-like building, a/c, restaurant, pool. **C** *Alvorada*, Av Brasil 2977, T4315866. Good café, close to post office, good value but often full. **C** *Internacional*, R Internacional 1267, T4311243, **D** without a/c. Hot water, good breakfast. Recommended. **E** *Dos Viajantes*, across park opposite railway station. Very basic.

Top Lunches, beside Hotel Barcelona. Cheap and friendly. *Chopão*, R Marechal Floriano 1877. Good food at reasonable prices. *Comabem*, R 7 de Setembro, near Casas Pernambucanas on Av Mcal Floriano. For burgers and pizzas.

Transport **Air**: services to São Paulo, Dourados, Marília and Presidente Prudente. **Buses**: to **Campo Grande**, 9 a day from 0100-2130, 4 hours, US$5. The rodoviária is 3 km out on the Dourados road ('São Domingos' bus, taxi US$3).

Pedro Juan Caballero   # Ponta Porã

Directory Banks: *Banco do Brasil* changes TCs. Many in the centre of town (but on Sun change money in hotels). **Voltage**: 220 volts AC.

There are no border posts between the two towns and people pass freely for local visits. The Brazilian Federal Police office (for entry/exit visas) is on the second floor of the white engineering supply company building at Rua Marechal Floriano 1483. ■ *Weekdays 0730-1130, 1400-1700, T4311428.*

Frontier with Paraguay

The two nations' consulates face each other on Rua Internacional (border street), a block west of Ponta Porã's local bus terminal; some nationalities require a visa from the Paraguayan consul (next to *Hotel Internacional*). ■ *0800-1200 Monday-Friday.* **Check requirements carefully**, and ensure your documents are in order: without the proper stamps you will inevitably be sent back somewhere later on in your travels. Taking a taxi between offices can speed things up if pressed for time, drivers know border crossing requirements, US$4.25.

Into Paraguay There are frequent buses and flights from Pedro Juan Caballero to Asunción. A road also runs to Concepción on the Rio Paraguay, where boat connections can be made. For more details, see the *South American Handbook.*

Bonito

The municipality of Bonito, in the Serra do Bodoquena, yields granite and marble and is clad in forest. The area's main attractions are in its rivers and caves (the formations are comparable to those found in the Lagoa Santa region of Minas Gerais). There are spectacular walks through mountains and forest; wildlife includes birds, rheas, monkeys, alligators and anaconda. Most excursions require authorization; this is not an obstacle to those with their own transport, but as there is no public transport, those without a car will need to use an agency (see below). Bonito has become very popular with Brazilian holidaymakers, especially during December-January, Carnival, Easter, and July (at these times advance booking is essential). Prices are high. The wet season is January-February; December-February is hottest, July-August coolest.

Population: 15,000
Phone code: 067
Colour map 3, grid C2

Caves The first cave to be opened is **Lagoa Azul**, 26 kilometres from Bonito. Lagoa Azul has a lake 50 metres long and 110 metres wide, 75 metres below ground level. The water, 20°C, is a jewel-like blue as light from the opening is refracted through limestone and magnesium. Prehistoric animal bones have been found in the lake. The light is at its best January-February, 0700-0900, but is fine at other times. A 25 hectare park surrounds the cave. You must pay a municipal tax, US$5; if not using your own transport, a car for four costs US$20. Also open is **Nossa Senhora Aparecida cave**, which has superb stalactites and stalagmites; there is no tourism infrastructure.

The **Balneário Municipal** on the Rio Formoso (seven kilometres on road to Jardim) has changing rooms, toilets, camping, swimming in clear water, plenty of fish to see. Strenuous efforts are made to keep the water and shore clean, US$2. **Horminio** waterfalls, 13 kilometres, consist of eight falls on the Rio Formoso, suitable for swimming; bar and camping, entry US$0.20. You can go **rafting** on the Rio Formoso: 12 kilometres, 2½ hours, minimum four people, US$15 per person, a mixture of floating peacefully downriver, swimming and shooting four waterfalls, lifejackets available; arranged by *Hapakany Tour* and many other agencies, see below. The **Aquário Natural** is one of the **springs of the Rio Formoso**; to visit you must have authorization from *Hapakany Tour*; you can swim and snorkel with five types of fish (US$25). Do

River excursions

Brasília & the Pantanal

not swim with suntan oil on. Other tours are: from the springs of the Rio Sucuri to its meeting with the Formoso (permission from *Hapakany* or *TapeTur*), about two kilometres of crystal-clear water, with swimming or snorkelling, birdwatching, very peaceful; **Aquidaban**, a series of limestone/marble waterfalls in dense forest; **Rio da Prata**, a spring with underground snorkelling for two kilometres, very beautiful. The **fishing** season is from 1 March to 31 October. In late October/early November is the *piracema* (fish run), when the fish return to their spawning grounds. Hundreds can be seen jumping the falls.

NB Bonito's attractions are nearly all on private land and must be visited with a guide. Owners also enforce limits on the number of daily visitors so, at busy times, pre-booking is essential.

Sleeping **L** *Zagaia Resort*, Rod Três Morros, 3 km, T2551280, F2551710. Pool, full board and tours available. **A** *Canaã*, R Col Pilad Rebuá 1376, T2551255, F2551282. Parking, restaurant and *churrascaria*. **A-B** *Pousada Olho d'Água*, Rod Três Morros, Km 1, T2551430, F2551470, olhodagua@vip2000.net. 3 km from town, accommodation in cabins, fan, showers with solar-heated water, fruit trees, fresh vegetables, small lake, own water supply, horse riding, bicycles. Recommended. **A** *Tapera*, on hill above Shell station on road to Jardim, T/F2551700. Fine views, cool breezes, comfortable, good. **B** *Bonanza*, R Col Pilad Rebuá (main street) 628, T2551315, F2551235. Suites and family rooms available, a/c. Recommended. Opposite is parking lot, with bar from 1800, darts and *churrascaria* on Friday. **C** *Pousadinha da Praça*, R Col Pilad Rebuá 2097, T2551135. Rooms with 2-4 beds (latter cramped), fan, hot water. **D** pp *Pousada Muito Bonito*, R Col Pilad Rebuá 1448, T/F2551645. With bath, or rooms with bunk beds, nice patio, clean, excellent, helpful owners, including breakfast, also with tour company (Mario Doblack speaks English, French and Spanish). Warmly recommended. Also on Rebuá, at 1800, is a hostal **E**, owned by the Paraíso tour agency, T2551477. Shared bath. Recommended.

Youth hostel **E** pp *Bonito*, R Lúcio Borralho 716, Vila Donária, T/F2551462, www.ajbonito.com.br, IYHA.

Camping *Ilha do Padre*, 12 km north of Bonito. Very pleasant, no regular transport (Hapakany's raft trip ends here), T/F2551430. Four rustic cabins with either 4 bunk beds, or 2 bunks and a double, US$10 pp, youth hostel with 2 sets of 12 beds, US$6 pp, same price for camping, toilets, showers, clothes washing, meals available, bar, electricity, lots of trees, can swim anywhere, to enter the island for a day US$3. Managers are Henrique Ruas and Jane Tatoni. Camping also at *Poliana* on Rio Formosa, 100m past Ilha do Padre, very pleasant.

Eating *Tapera*, Pilad Rebuá 480, T2551110. Good, home-grown vegetables, breakfast, lunch, pizzas, meat and fish dishes, opens 1900 for evening meal. *Comida Caseira*, Luis da Costa Leite and Santana do Paraíso. Good local food, lunch and dinner, not open Sunday afternoon. *Verdo-Frutos e Sucos Naturais*, Pilad Rebuá 1853, next to *Bonanza* car park. Good juices and fruits.

Transport **Buses** Rodoviária is on the edge of town. From **Campo Grande**, US$11, 5½-6 hours, 1500, returns at 0530. Bus uses MS-345, with a stop at Autoposto Santa Cruz, Km 60, all types of fuel, food and drinks available. For **Aquidauana**, take Campo Grande bus. Bus Corumbá-Miranda-Bonito-Jardim-Ponta Porã, Monday-Saturday, leaves either end at 0600, arriving Bonito 1230 for Ponta Porã, 1300 for Miranda; can change in Jardim (1400 for 1700 bus) or Miranda (better connections) for Campo Grande; fare Corumbá-Bonito US$12.50. Also connections on 1230 route in Bela Vista at 2000 for **Asunción** and **Col Oviedo**. Ticket office opens at 1200.

Banks *Banco do Brasil*, for Visa. Some hoteliers may change money. **Communications** Post
Office: R Col Pilad Rebuá. **Telephone:** Santana do Paraíso. **Tour companies & travel
agents** There are 13 agencies and 54 guides in Bonito who accompany visitors to the private
sites. Sérgio Ferreira Gonzales, R Col Pilad Rebuá 628, T2551315 (opposite *Bonanza*), is an
authority on the caves. Recommended. *Hapakany Tour*, Pilad Rebuá 628, T2551315, F2551235.
Jason and Murilo, for all local tours. Recommended. *TapeTur*, next to *Tapera* restaurant. Guides,
information, tours, clothes shop. Also recommended. For information in English and French,
contact Henrique Ruas, T/F2551430, see *Ilha do Padre* or *Pousada Olho d'Água* above. **Tourist
offices** *Setuma*, R Col Pilad Rebuá 1780, T2551351 extension 215.

The road to Jardim is paved. In Jardim, which has a wide, tree-lined main
street, there is a rodoviária for *Cruzeiro do Sul* buses. A few blocks uphill is
Panificadora Massa Pura, clean and bright, and other eating places. From
Bonito there is a road to **Porto Murtinho**, where a boat crosses to Isla
Margarita in Paraguay (entry stamp available on the island).

Sleeping and eating **E** *Eldorado*, friendly, clean, good food. **E** *Beira Rio*, basic.
There are others; 2 *lanchonetes*, *Churrascaria Gaspão*.

Transport **Buses**: to **Campo Grande** 0730, 1300, 1700 and 2 in middle of night,
US$6.50. To **Aquidauana** 0730 and 1700. To **Bonito** (US$3.50), **Miranda** and
Corumbá at 1130. To **Dourados** 0600. **Bela Vista** (Paraguayan border) 0200, 1030,
1500, 1930. To **Porto Murtinho** 0010 and 1530 (bus from Bonito connects). To **Ponta
Porã** 0600, 1500; Sunday only at 1400 to **São Paulo**.

Directory Banks: Elia, a taxi driver, will change money.

Campo Grande to Corumbá

The BR-262 is paved most of the way from Campo Grande to Corumbá and
the Bolivian border; rail service along this route has been suspended indefinitely. It is best to make this journey during the day to take advantage of marvellous scenery.

West of Campo Grande, by 131 kilometres just north of the road, is **Aquidauana**
Aquidauana, with several daily buses from Campo Grande. The BR-412 heads *Population: 41,000*
south from here to Jardim, with connections to Paraguay (see above). Also
turn south here for one route to Bonito. The Ibama-controlled *jacaré* farm,
Olhos d'Água, is not open to visitors. Aquidauana is a gateway to the Pantanal
(see below), excursions in fishing boats negotiable, around US$50 per person
a day, or via *Chalanatur*, T2413396; six-day trips recommended.

Sleeping and eating *Fazenda Toca da Onça*, see page 715; take taxi, owner also
has a campsite. In town, several hotels around the railway station, including
D *Fluminense*, with fan and breakfast, a/c more expensive. **D** *Lord*, R Manoel Paes de
Barros 739, T2411857. Shared bathroom in single room, private bath in double room.
Recommended. *O Casarão (grill)*, R Manoel Paes de Barros 533, T2412219.
Recommended.

Directory Tour companies & travel agents: *Buriti Viagens e Turismo*, R Manoel Paes de Barros
720, 79200, T2412718, F2412719. Recommended. *Lucarelli Turismo*, R Manoel Paes de Barros
552, T2413410. Recommended. *Cordon Turismo*, R Búzios, CEP 79003-101, T3841483. Organizes
fishing trips into the Pantanal. Recommended. *Panbratur*, R Estevão Alves Correa 586,
T/F2413494. Tour operator in southern Pantanal.

Brasília & the Pantanal

Population: 20,800 Seventy seven kilometres further west is **Miranda**, another entrance to the Pantanal (see below). Here too is a *jacaré* farm, *Granja Caimã*, which is open to visitors, US$1 entry. A road heads south to Bodoquena and on to Bonito. Bus Campo Grande-Miranda, seven a day with Expresso Mato Grosso, US$8.50, and others. The Campo Grande-Corumbá road crosses the Rio Miranda bridge (two service stations before it), then carries on, mostly paved, to cross the Rio Paraguai.

Corumbá

Population: 89,000
Phone code: 067
Colour map 3, grid B1

Situated on the south bank by a broad bend in the Rio Paraguai, 15 minutes from the Bolivian border, the city offers beautiful views of the river, great for photography, especially at sunset.

It is hot and humid (70 percent); cooler in June-July, very hot from September-January. It has millions of mosquitoes in December, January and February, but is a pleasant place nevertheless.

Sights

There is a spacious shady **Praça da Independência** and the port area is worth a visit. Avenida General Rondon, between Frei Mariano and 7 de Septembro, has a pleasant palm-lined promenade which comes to life in the evenings. The **Forte Junqueira**, the city's most historic building which may be visited, was built in 1772. In the hills to the south is the world's greatest reserve of manganese, now being worked. Corumbá is the best starting point for the southern part of the Pantanal, with boat and jeep trips and access to the major hotel/farms.

NB The combination of economic hard times since 1994 and drug-running make the city unsafe late at night.

Essentials

Sleeping **B** *Internacional Palace*, R Dom Aquino Corrêa 1457, T2316343, F2316852. Pool, sauna, parking, café. **B** *Nacional Palace*, R América 936, T2316868, F2316202. Good pool, parking. **B** *Santa Mônica*, R Antônio Maria Coelho 345, T2313001, F2317880. Good restaurant, pool. **B** *Carandá*, R Dom Aquino 47, T2312023. Pool, restaurant, good, helpful. **B** *Laura Vicuña*, R Cuiabá 775, T2315874, F2312663. **C** for simpler room, parking, modern. Recommended.

C *Premier*, R Antônio Maria Coelho 389, T2314937. Small rooms, a/c. **C** *Salette*, R Delamaré 893, T2313768, F2314948. A/c, safe, **D** with bath and fan, **E** with shared bath and fan. Recommended. **C** *Santa Rita*, Dom Aquino 860 (unsigned), T2315453. A/c, **D** with fan, noisy, overpriced, good meals in restaurant.

D *Angola*, R Antônio Maria 124, T2317233. A/c, **E** with fan, restaurant. **D** *Beira Rio*, R Manoel Cavassa 109, by the port, T2312554. A/c, cheaper with fan, popular with fishermen. **D** *Copacabana*, R Cuiabá 926, **E** with shared bath, basic. **D** *Lincoln*, R 15 de Novembro 205, T2314483. A/c, parking. **D** *Nelly*, Delamaré 902, T2316001, F2317396. A/c, **E** with shared bath and fan, good breakfast. **D** *Timoneiro*, R Cabral 879, between rodoviária and centre, T2315530. A/c, **E** with fan, cheaper with shared bath. **D** *Pensão do Tato*, R 13 de Junho 720, T2317727. A/c, cheaper with fan, small rooms.

E *Campus*, R Antônio João 1333. Fan, cheaper with shared bath, good value. **E-F** *City*, R Cabral 1031, between rodoviária and centre, T2314187. A/c or fan, private or shared bath, parking. **E** *Roboré*, R Dom Aquino 587. Shared bath, small rooms, basic.

Near the rodoviária **D** *Internacional*, R Porto Carreiro 714, T2314654. Shared bath, fan, basic, simple breakfast, owner organizes fishing trips. **E** *Beatriz*, R Porto Carreiro 896, T2317441. Fan, cheaper with shared bath, small rooms, simple, friendly, clean. **E** *Esplanada*, opposite railway station. Cold shower, basic. **E** *Irure*, R 13 de Junho 776. Small and clean. **E** *Londres*, Joaquim Murtinho 1021, T2316717. Breakfast included until 0800, private bath, fan, poor service, dirty, luggage lockers for those going to the Pantanal.

Outside town **B** *Gold Fish*, Av Rio Branco 2799, on riverfront, 4 km on the road to Ladário, T2315106, F2315433. Pool. **B** pp full board *Porto Vitória Régia*, 12 km from Corumbá past Ladário, on the riverfront. A/c, pool, restaurant, boats, camping area. **B** *Pousada do Cachimbo*, R Allan Kardec 4, on the way to the Bolivian border, T2313910. A/c, fridge, country setting by the river, gardens, pool. **B** *Paraíso do Pantanal*, Cunha Couto 1532, Ladário, T/F2315394. A/c, fridge, pool, restaurant, tours organized.

Youth hostel **E** pp *Pantanal*, R Antônio Maria Coelho 677, T2312305, F2317740, IYHA. Recommended. The owner, Sr Pontis, organizes jungle trips, cheaper for a group, negotiate price.

Several recommended restaurants in R Frei Mariano: *Churrascaria Gauchão*, No 879. **Eating** Good value. *Tarantella*, No 780. Italian. *Barril de Ouro*, No 556. Good. *Drink's*, No 564. Economical set meals. *Peixaria do Lulú*, R Antônio João 410. Good fish. *Churrascaria Rodéio*, 13 de Junho 760. Very good, lunchtime buffet. Recommended. *Churrascaria Paladar*, R Antônio M Coelho 577, *Rodízio*. *Viva Bella*, R Arthur Mangabeira 1, behind Clube Corumbaense, 1 block from Gen Rondon. Fish, meat, pizza, home made pastas, drinks, magnificent views over the river especially at sunset, live music Wednesday-Saturday, opens at 1700, good food and atmosphere. Recommended. *Pastina Nostra*, Av Gen Rondon 1189. Italian and international. *Cacharas's*, Av Gen Rondon 1191. Fish specialities, open evenings and weekends. *Restaurante Peixaria Galpão*, R 13 de Junho 797. Meat and fish. *Soba-Yá*, R Delamaré 1181. Chinese, opens at 1900. *Trivial*, R 15 de Novembro 148, Centro. Good, reasonably-priced buffet. Recommended. *Almanara*, R America 964, next to *Hotel Nacional*. Good Arabic food. On the waterfront you can eat good fish at *Portal do Pantanal*. Lots of open-air bars on the riverfront. Bolivian snacks in *'Sslato*, R Dom Aquino. Lanchonetes tend to overcharge – check prices. Many good ice cream parlours: *Cristal*, R 7 de Setembro and Delamaré. Recommended.

Corumbá

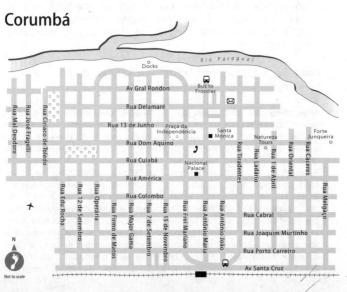

Local specialities These include *peixadas corumbaenses*, a variety of fish dishes prepared with the catch of the day; as well as ice cream, liquor and sweets made of *bocaiúva*, a small yellow palm fruit, in season September-February.

Festivals 2 February, *Festa de Nossa Senhora da Candelária*, Corumbá's patron saint, all offices and shops are closed. 24 June, *Festa do Arraial do Banho de São João*, fireworks, parades, traditional food stands, processions and the main event, the bathing of the image of the saint in the Rio Paraguai. 21 September, Corumbá's anniversary, includes a Pantanal fishing festival held on the eve.

Shopping *Pro-Sol, Casa do Artesão*, R Dom Aquino Correa 405, in a converted prison. Open
Shops tend to open early and close by 1700 Monday-Friday 0800-1200 and 1400-1800, Saturday 0800-1200, good selection of handicrafts and a small bookshop, friendly staff but high prices. *CorumbArte*, Av Gen. Rondon 1011, for good silk-screen T shirts with Pantanal motifs. *Livraria Corumbaense*, R Delamaré 1080, for state maps. **Supermarkets** *Ohara*, Dom Aquino corner Antônio João. *Frutal*, R 13 de Junho 538. Open 0800-2000.

Transport **Car hire** *Localiza*, airport and R Cabral 2064, T2316000, daily rates from US$90 (unlimited km), weekly from US$540. *Unidas*, R Frei Mariano 633, T/F2313124.

Air Airport, R Santos Dumont, 3 km, T2313322. Flights to Campo Grande, Cuiabá, Londrina and São Paulo (via Campo Grande). Check whether flights between Corumbá and Santa Cruz, Bolivia, are still operating. If in doubt, fly from Puerto Suárez in Bolivia. No public transport from airport to town, you have to take a taxi.

Buses The rodoviária is on R Porto Carreiro at the south end of R Tiradentes, next to the railway station. City bus to rodoviária from Praça da República, US$0.80. Taxis are extortionate, but moto-taxis charge only US$0.65.
    Andorinha services to all points east. To **Campo Grande**, 7 hours, US$15, 13 buses daily, between 0630 hours and midnight, interesting journey ('an excursion in itself') – take an early bus to see plentiful wildlife, connections from Campo Grande to all parts of Brazil. To **São Paulo** direct, 22 hours, US$50, 1100 and 1500, confirm bus times in advance as these change (T2312033). To **Rio de Janeiro** direct, 30 hours, US$55, daily 1100. Cruzeiro do Sul operates the route south to the Paraguayan border. To **Ponta Porã**, 12 hours, US$20, via Bonito (6 hours, US$12.50) and Jardim (9 hours, US$15), Monday-Saturday at 0600; ticket office open 0500-0600 only, at other times call T2312383.

Boats The *Acurí*, a luxury vessel, sails between **Cáceres** and Corumbá, once a week, US$600 including return by air. (See page 728, under Cáceres.)

Directory **Airline offices** *TAM*, T2317299. *Visa*, T2311745. **Banks** *Banco do Brasil*, R 13 de Junho 914, Mon-Fri 1100-1600, for cash, US$3 commission per US$100 TCs. *Câmbio Mattos*, R 15 de Novembro 140, Mon-Fri 0800-1700, good rates for US$ cash, 5% commission on TCs. *Câmbio Rau*, R 15 de Novembro 212, Mon-Fri 0800-1700, Sat 0900-1200, cash only, good rates. **Communications** Post Office: main at R Delamaré 708, has fax service. Branch at R 15 de Novembro 229. **Telephone:** R Dom Aquino 951, near Praça da Independência, open 0700-2200 daily. To phone Quijarro/Puerto Suárez, Bolivia, it costs slightly more than a local call, dial 214 + the Bolivian number. **Internet:** *Pantanalnet*, R América 430, Centro, US$2.50 per hr. **Embassies & consulates** *Bolivia*, R Antônio Maria Coelho 881, T2315605, Mon-Fri, 0700-1100, 1500-1730, closed Sat-Sun. A fee is charged to citizens of those countries which require a visa. A yellow fever vaccination certificate is required. **Laundry** *Apae*, R 13 de Junho 1377, same day service. **Tour companies & travel agents** Corumbá has many travel agencies selling tours to the Pantanal, we list some. For more information see page 716: *Mutum Turismo*, R Frei Mariano 17, T2311818, F2313027. For airline tickets, tours, helpful. *Pantanal Tours/Sairú Turismo*, RM Cavassa 61A, T2315410, F2313130, fishing trips, agents for *Cabexy I* and *II*, luxurious floating hotels, day trips on land, US$55 pp, river trips US$15 pp per 3 hrs. Happily recommended. *Pantanal Service*, R Dom Aquino 700, T/F2315998, fishing and photo trips by boat, agents for *Hotel Porto Vitória Régia*. *Corumbatur*, Antônio M Coelho 852, T/F2311532, combined Pantanal/Bonito tours. *JMS Turismo*, RM Cavassa 215, T2315235. Small fishing boats for rent US$60 per day for 3 persons, minivans for trips to Bolivia US$10 pp. *Pérola do Pantanal*, RM Cavassa 255, T2311470, F2316585, river and land tours, good 1-day river tour with *Lancha Pérola*. *Taimã*, R Antônio M Coelho 786, T/F231669, river trips, flights over Pantanal, airline tickets. *Pantur*, R América 969, T2314343, F2316006, tours, agents for *Hotel Fazenda Xaraés* in Nhecolândia. *Receptivo Pantanal*, R Frei Mariano 502, T2315795, helpful (1-day tour US$50, 3-day US$100, 4-day US$130). **Tourist offices** *Emcotur*, R América 969, T2316996, municipal tourist office, for general information and city maps.

Frontier with Bolivia

Immigration and emigration formalities are constantly changing, so check procedures in advance. You need not have your passport stamped to visit Quijarro or Puerto Suárez only for the day. Otherwise, get your passport stamped by Brazilian Polícia Federal at Praça da Republica 51. The visa must be obtained on the day of departure. If exiting Brazil merely to obtain a new visa, remember that exit and entry must not be on the same day. **NB** Money changers at the border and in Quijarro offer the same rates as in Corumbá.

If you arrive in Brazil without a yellow fever vaccination certificate, you may have to go to Rua 7 de Setembro, Corumbá, for an inoculation

Transport Leaving Brazil, take Canarinho city bus marked Fronteira from the port end of Rua Antônio Maria Coelho to the Bolivian border (15 minutes, US$0.35), walk over the bridge to the Bolivian border post (blue building), go through formalities, then take a colectivo to Quijarro or Puerto Suárez.

When travelling from Quijarro, take a taxi or walk to the Bolivian border to go through formalities. Just past the bridge, on a small side street to the right, is the bus stop for Corumbá, take bus marked Fronteira or Tamengo to Praça da República, US$0.80, every 45 minutes between 0630 and 1915, don't believe taxi drivers who say there is no bus. Taxi to centre US$6. Find a hotel then take care of Brazilian formalities at Polícia Federal, address above.

Bolivia-Brazil border - Puerto Suárez, Quijarro & Corumbá

Brasília & the Pantanal

Into Bolivia Over the border from Corumbá are Arroyo Concepción, Puerto Quijarro and Puerto Suárez. From Puerto Quijarro a 650-km railway runs to Santa Cruz de la Sierra. There is a road of sorts. A better road route is from Cáceres to San Matías, thence to San Ignacio (see page 727). There are internal flights from Puerto Suárez. For more details, see the *Bolivia Handbook* or the *South American Handbook*.

Pantanal

This vast wetland, measuring 230,000 square kilometres between Cuiabá, Campo Grande and the Bolivian frontier, is one of the world's great wildlife preserves. Parts spill over into neighbouring Bolivia and Paraguay, and the entire area has been opened up to tourism. The water in the Pantanal is not stagnant, since a gentle gradient ranging for one to three centimetres per kilometre, from north to south, keeps it flowing in that direction; hence, during the wet season, flooding gradually advances southwards. The region is drained by the São Lourenço, Cuiabá, Piquiri, Taquari, Aquidauana, Miranda and Apa rivers, all of which are tributaries of the Rio Paraguai.

Flora and fauna

Similar in many ways to the Amazon basin, though because of the more veldt-like open land, the wildlife can be viewed more easily than in the dense jungle growth. Principal life seen in this area is about 300 species of birds, including the hyacinth macaw, jabiru stork (the *tuiuíu*, almost 1.2 metres tall), plumbeous ibis, both blue-throated and red-throated piping guans and roseate spoonbill. There are some 230 varieties of fish, from the giant *pintado*, weighing up to 80 kilos, to the tiny, voracious *piranha*. Fishing here is exceptionally good (best May-October). Animal life is represented among others by giant and collared anteaters, four species of opossum, five armadillo species, bare-eared marmoset, black-and-gold howler monkey, maned wolf, South American coati, southern and giant river otters, ocelot, margay, jaguarundi, puma, jaguar, three peccary species, marsh deer and two other species, yellow anaconda and the ubiquitous *capivara*, a species of giant aquatic guinea-pig. Probably the most impressive sight is the *jacaré* (Yacare Caiman). The extraordinary thing is that man and his domesticated cattle thrive, together with the wildlife, with seemingly little friction. Local farmers protect the area jealously.

Ecology and conservation

Only one area is officially a national park, the **Parque Nacional do Pantanal Matogrossense** in the municipality of Poconé, 135,000 hectares of land and water, only accessible by air or river. You can obtain permission to visit at Ibama, Rua Rubens de Mendonça, Cuiabá, CEP 78008, T6441511/1581. Hunting in any form is strictly forbidden throughout the Pantanal and is punishable by four years imprisonment. Fishing is allowed with a licence (enquire at travel agents for latest details; see **Fishing**, page 34); it is not permitted in the spawning season or *piracema* (1 October to 1 February in Mato Grosso do Sul, 1 November to 1 March in Mato Grosso). Like other wilderness areas, the Pantanal faces important threats to its integrity. Agro-chemicals and *garimpo* mercury, washed down from the neighbouring *planalto*, are a hazard to wildlife. Visitors must share the responsibility of protecting the Pantanal and you can make an important contribution by acting responsibly and choosing your guides accordingly: take out your rubbish, don't fish out of season, don't let guides kill or disturb fauna, don't buy products made from endangered species, don't buy live birds or monkeys, and report any violation of these norms to the authorities.

The International Union for the Conservation of Nature is concerned at the amount of poaching, particularly of jacaré skins, birds and capivaras. The Forestry Police have built control points on all major access roads to the Pantanal. Biologists interested in research projects in the area should contact the Coordenador de Estudos do Pantanal, Departamento de Biologia, Universidade Federal do Mato Grosso do Sul, Caixa Postal 649, Campo Grande, CEP 79070-900, T067-7873311 ext 2113, F067-7875317.

Climate

There are two distinct seasons. In the rainy season (December-March, wettest in February), most of the area floods, mosquitoes abound and cattle crowd on to the few islands remaining above water. In the southern part, many wild animals leave the area, but in the north, which is slightly higher, the animals do not leave. An ordinary vehicle should be able to manage the Transpantaneira out of Cuiabá throughout most of the year, but in the wet season you should be prepared to get stuck, and muddy, pushing your car from time to time. The dry season (July-October) is the nesting and breeding season. The birds form vast nesting areas, with thousands crowding the trees, creating an almost insupportable cacophony of sounds; the white sand river beaches are exposed, *jacarés* bask in the sun, and *capivaras* frolic amid the grass.

In winter (June-August), temperatures fall to 10°, warm clothing and covers or sleeping bag are needed at night, but it's very hot and humid during summer.

Wear long sleeves and long trousers and spray clothes as well as skin with insect repellent. Insects are less of a problem July-August. Take insect repellent from home as mosquitoes, especially in the North Pantanal, are becoming immune to local brands.

Access

The Pantanal is not easy or cheap to visit. The best starting points are Corumbá, Cuiabá, and to a lesser extent Campo Grande, from where one finds public transport all around the perimeter, but none at all within. Wild camping is possible if you have some experience and your own transport. Remember that the longer you stay and the further you go from the edges (where most of the hotels are located), the more likely you are to see rare wildlife.

From Corumbá there is access to the Pantanal by both road and river, offering a variety of day trips, luxury house boat excursions, and connections to many surrounding *fazendas*. Along the road from Corumbá to Campo Grande (BR-262) are Miranda and Aquidauana, both important gateways to various fishing and tourist lodges. The BR-163, which connects Campo Grande and Cuiabá, skirts the east edge of the Pantanal; Coxim, 242 kilometres north of Campo Grande, offers access via the Rio Taquari but few facilities. From Cuiabá there is year-round road access to Barão de Melgaço and Poconé, both of which can be starting points for excursions. The Transpantaneira Highway runs south from Poconé to Porto Jofre, through the heart of the Pantanal, providing access to many different lodges, but does not have any bus service. Finally Cáceres, 215 kilometres west of Cuiabá at the northwest corner of the Pantanal, offers access along the Rio Paraguai to one of the least developed parts of the region.

Tourist facilities in the Pantanal currently cater to four main categories of visitors. **Sports fishermen** usually stay at one of the numerous speciality lodges scattered throughout the region, which provide guides, boats, bait, ice and other related amenities. Bookings can be made locally or in any of Brazil's major cities. **All-inclusive tours**, combining air and ground transportation, accommodations at the most elaborate *fazendas*, meals, guided river and land tours, can be arranged from abroad or through travel agencies in Brazil's gateway cities. This is the most expensive option. **Moderately priced tours**, using private guides, camping or staying at more modest *fazendas*, can be arranged locally in Cuiabá (where guides await arrivals at the airport) or through the more reputable agencies in Corumbá. **The lowest priced tours** are offered by independent guides in Corumbá, some of whom are unreliable; travellers have reported at times serious problems here (see below). For those with the barest minimum of funds, a glimpse of the Pantanal and its wildlife can be had on the bus ride from Campo Grande to Corumbá, by lodging or camping near the ferry crossing over the Rio Paraguai (Porto Esperança), and by staying in Poconé and day-walking or hitching south along the Transpantaneira. Whatever your budget, take binoculars.

Choosing a guide

A tour of the Pantanal could be the highlight of your travels, so it is best to do some research before contracting a guide

Many budget travellers *en route* to or from Bolivia make Corumbá their base for visiting the Pantanal. Such tourists are often approached, in the streets and at the cheaper hotels, by salesmen who speak foreign languages and promise complete tours for low prices. They then hand their clients over to agencies and/or guides, who often speak only Portuguese, and may deliver something quite different. Some travellers have reported very unpleasant experiences and it is important to select a guide with great care anywhere. By far the best way to do so is to speak with other travellers who have just returned from a Pantanal tour. Most guides also have a book containing comments from their former clients. Do not rush to sign up when first approached, always compare several available alternatives. Discuss the planned itinerary carefully and try to get it in writing (although this is seldom possible – threaten to go to someone else if necessary). Do not pay everything in advance of departure, and try to deal directly with agencies or guides, not salesmen (it can be difficult to tell who is who). Always get an itemized receipt. Bear in mind that a well-organized three-day tour can be more rewarding than four days with an ill-prepared guide. There is fierce competition between guides who provide similar services, but with very different styles. Although we list a few of the most reputable guides below, there are other good ones and most economy travellers enjoy a pleasant if spartan experience. Remember that travellers must shoulder part of the responsibility for the current chaotic guiding situation in Corumbá. Act responsibly and don't expect to get something for nothing. (See also Corumbá guides section.)

It appears to be the case that once guides are recommended by a guidebook, they cease to guide and set up their own businesses working in promoting and public relations, using other guides to work under their names. Guides at the airport give the impression that they will lead the tour, but they won't. Always ask who will lead the party and how big it will be. Less than four is not economic and a guide will make cuts in boats or guides.

Further reading *The Pantanal: Brazil's Forgotten Wilderness*, Vic Banks (Sierra Club Books, 1991, 730 Polk Street, San Francisco, CA 94100). **Websites** For the Pantanal on the net, check out: www.alanet.com.br/ms/pantanal and www. unikey.com.br/pantanal.

Essentials

Camping allows you to see the wildlife at its greatest period of activity at dawn and dusk, but protection against mosquitoes is essential. Care should also be taken to avoid dangerous animals: snakes (especially in the rainy season), piranhas (especially in the dry season), killer bees and the larger *jacarés*. The inexperienced are cautioned not to strike out on their own. There are many lodges with fair to good accommodation, some only approachable by air or river; most are relatively expensive. One option is to hire a car and check accommodation for yourself: in June-September, especially July, it is necessary to book accommodation in advance.

Sleeping

From Campo Grande LL full board *Pousada São Francisco*, 135 km from Aquidauana in the Rio Negro area of Nhecolândia. Accessible only by air during the wet, with bath, fan, screening, horseback riding, price including transport, meals, tours, bookings through *Impacto Turismo*, Campo Grande, T/F067-7243167/7243616. **LL** full board *Refúgio Ecológico Caiman*, 36 km from Miranda, 236 km from Campo Grande. First class, full board, excursions, T0XX67-6872102, F6872103, or São Paulo T0XX11-8836622, member of the *Roteiros de Charme* group (see page 57). **L** full board *Pousada Aguapé*, Fazenda São José, 59 km north of Aquidauana, 202 km from Campo Grande. Farmhouse hotel, screened rooms, some with a/c, pool, horse riding, boat trips, trekking, meals and tours included, bookings through *Impacto Turismo*, as above, or T2412889, F2413494. **L** *Cabana do Pescador*, 65 km from Aquidauana on the Rio Miranda, T067-2413697, F2412406, access by Bonito bus from Campo Grande (see page 704). Fishing lodge, includes breakfast. **AL** *Fazenda Salobra*, T067-2421162, 6 km from Miranda, 209 km from Corumbá, 198 from Campo Grande. Recommended. With bath, including all meals, tours, boat rentals and horses are extra, it is by the Rio Salobra (clear water) and Rio Miranda, with birds and animals easily seen. Take bus from Campo Grande to Miranda, and alight 50m from the bridge over Rio Miranda, turn left for 1,200m to the *Fazenda*. *Fazenda Rio Negro*, 13,000 ha farm on the shores of the Rio Negro, farmhouse dating to 1920, tours, horses, fishing, T7257853, F7249345, or São Paulo T011-2142777. *Pousada Mangabal*, in Nhecolândia, farm setting, horses, tours, walks, bookings through *Panbratur*, Aquidauana, T/F as above, page 707. **A** *Pousada Toca da Onça*, 10 km from Aquidauana on the shores of the Rio Aquidauana, cabins, a/c, restaurant, boats, bookings through *Panbratur*, Aquidauana, T/F as above. **B** *Pousada Águas do Pantanal*, Av Afonso Pena 367, Miranda, T/F067-2421242, contact Fátima or Luis Cordelli, very good, good food, restaurant serves *jacaré* legally. There is a good campsite 30 km past Miranda. Alternatively, hire a car in Corumbá and drive to Miranda, but note that the dirt road is bad after rain (consequently not much traffic and more wildlife can be seen). Car with driver can be hired at Salobra for US$25. There are several camping possibilities along the shores of the Rio Aquidauana, including *Camping Baía*, 50 km from Aquidauana, on a bay on the river, trees for shade, boats; *Pequi Camping*, 48 km from Aquidauana, with toilets, electricity; *Camping Itajú*, sandy beach, cabins, lanchonete, shower, electricity, boat rental.

From Corumbá One day river trips are available on river boats with a capacity of 80 passengers, US$25 half-day; US$50 full day, including transfers and hot fish meal. Smaller boats US$15 pp for 3 hours. Tickets at travel agents and by port. Boats may be hired, with fishing tackle and guide, at the port (US$100 per day, up to 3 people, in season only). Cattle boats will on occasion take passengers on their round trips to farms in the Pantanal, but take your own food – it is not always possible to disembark. Ask at Bacia da Prata, 10 minutes out of Corumbá on the Ladário bus.

Lodges LL full board *Pousada do Pantanal*, T067-7255267/2315212, or T011-2142777, 125 km from Corumbá near the Campo Grande Rd at *Fazenda Santa Clara* (still a working cattle ranch). Very comfortable, easy access by bus, reservations from all agencies in Corumbá; US$190 pp for 3 days/2 nights, minimum 2 persons, good food (but drinks not included), with excursions on horseback (US$8), car (US$20) and boat (US$20), guides included, canoes, simple fishing gear, motor boats for rent (try bargaining in the off-season for reduced rates). **LL** full board *Hotel Fazenda Xaraes*, T067-2316777, T011-8704600, Rio Abobral, 130 km from Corumbá. Luxurious, pool, restaurant, horses, boats. **L** *Pousada Do Castelo*, 3 hours by boat from Corumbá, T067-2313736, F2315040. **A** *Fazenda Santa Blanca*, on the Rio Paraguai, 15 minutes by boat south of Porto Esperança (where the BR-262 crosses the Rio Paraguai). Full board, good kayak excursions, horse riding, information from R 15 de Novembro 659, Corumbá, T2311460, or *Flins Travel* (Walter Zoss), R do Acre 92, 6th floor, 602, CEP 20081, Rio de Janeiro, T021-2538588/0195 or *Safari Fotográfico*, R Frei Mariano 502, Corumbá, T2315797. *Fazenda Leque*, Roberto Kassan (contact through Rua América 262, Corumbá, T2311598). Take mosquito coils, unlimited use of horses and boats, on small lake behind the farm, good food, plenty of wildlife to be seen.

The going rate for a 3-day camping photo safari by jeep is US$100 pp for 4-6 people; US$110-120 pp for 4 days. Fishing trips in luxurious floating hotels for 8 (eg *Tuiuiú* T/F2312052 and *Cabexy II* T2314683, from *Pantanal Tours*, Corumbá – must be booked in advance), US$1,200-2,000 per day, minimum 5 days.

Hotels specializing in fishing, all reached from Corumbá by road: **LL** full board *Pesqueiro da Odila*, on the Rio Paraguai, reservations T067-2315623, from Belo Horizonte T031-2214003. Restaurant. **LL** full board *Porto Morrinho*, on the Rio Paraguai, T2311360. Pool. **LL** full board *Pesqueiro Paraiso dos Dourados*, 72 km from Corumbá, Rios Paraguai and Miranda, Corumbá office at R Antônio João, T/F2313021. Tours. **L** *Pantanal Park*, 20 minutes by boat from Porto Esperança (where the BR-262 crosses the Rio Paraguai), T0182-215332. Restaurant. **L** *Pesqueiro Cabana do Lontra*, including meals, T067-3834532, 180 km from Aquidauana on the Corumbá Rd. **L** full board *Pesqueiro Tarumã*, Rio Paraguai, 65 km from Corumbá, Corumbá office at RM Cavassa 109, T/F2314771.

Directory

Some of Corumbá's many agencies are listed on page 710

Tour companies & travel agents Tours out of Corumbá are of 3-4 days, costing up to US$100 (includes all food, accommodation and transport). Travel is in the back of a pick-up (good for seeing animals), up to a maximum of 6. Accommodation is in a hammock under a palm thatch on a *fazenda*. Food can be good. If you want flushing toilets, showers or luxury cabins, approach an agency. Guides provide bottled mineral water (make sure enough is carried), but you must take a hat, sun screen and mosquito repellent. Some guides go to *fazendas* without permission, have unreliable vehicles, or are inadequately equipped, so try to check their credentials. Agencies sometimes subcontract to guides over whom they have no control. If you are asked to pay half the money directly to the guide, check him out as if he were independent and ask to see his equipment. Guides will generally not make the trip with fewer than 5 people, so if you have not already formed a group, stay in touch with several guides (most important during Mar-Oct, when fewer tourists are around). Decide on your priorities: try to ensure that your guide and other group members share your ideas. We list below those guides who have received positive reports from most travellers: *Green Track*, R Delamaré s/n entre Tiradentes e Antônio João, T2312258, greentk@brasinet.com.br, recommended for those who like excursions that do not involve game fishing. *Katu*, R Dom Aquino 220, T2311987. Recommended. *Tucan Tours*, R Delamaré 576, T2313569, guide William Chaparro speaks English, Hebrew and Spanish, contact him through email at w_chaparro@hotmail.com. *Saldanha Tour*, R Porto Carreiro 896B, T23116891, saldanha_v@hotmail.com or aguia@brasinete.com.br, owner Eliane is very helpful to travellers. *Colibri Pantanal Safari*, in *Hotel City*, R Cabral 1031, T2313934, Swiss owner Claudine. There are many other guides not listed here, some have similar names, lots have received criticisms (some repeatedly) from correspondents. There may be others on whom we have received no feedback.

Another access to the Pantanal from the east is Coxim, 242 kilometres north of Campo Grande on the BR-163 and halfway between Campo Grande and Rondonópolis; it sits in a green bowl, on the shores of the Rio Taquari. The area has great potential for tourism, but there are no official tours to the Pantanal; a great place if you have your own boat.

Coxim
Population: 28,500
Phone code: 067

Sleeping A *Coxim*, 4 km south of town, T/F2911479. Restaurant. **A** *Santa Ana*, R Miranda Reis on the riverbank, T2911602. Cabins for 4, pool. **C** *Santa Teresa*, 5 km south of town, T2912215, F2911289. With bath, fan. *Piracêma*, by the bridge over the Rio Taquari, restaurant. *Sinhazino*, north of the Taquari bridge. There are several simpler hotels in town.

Cuiabá to Pantanal

The Transpantaneira Highway, built in 1976, was originally projected to connect Cuiabá with Corumbá, but currently goes only as far as Porto Jofre on the Rio Cuiabá. Work has been suspended indefinitely because of difficulties, costs and ecological considerations.

A paved road turns south off the main Cuiabá-Cáceres road to Poconé, founded in 1781 and known as the Cidade Rosa. Until 1995 there was much *garimpo* activity north of town and many slag heaps can be seen from the road.

Poconé
Population: 31,500
Phone code: 065

Sleeping and eating E *Hotel Joá*, with bath, basic, acceptable, car parking. Also on the Transpantaneira just south of town are *Aurora do Pantanal*, T7211339, and **A** *Hotel Santa Cruz*, Km 1, T7211439. *Three Poderes Restaurant*, R Beri. Cheap good food. *Doce e Mel*, Praça Matriz. Pleasant café serving good sweets and coffee.

Transport Buses: from **Cuiabá** US$7.50 by *TUT*, T3224985, 6 a day between 0600 and 1900. Poconé has a 24-hour gas station with all types of fuel, but closed on Sunday.

From Poconé the Transpantaneira runs 146 kilometres south to **Porto Jofre**, where there is just a gas station, gasoline and diesel, but no alcohol is available. At the entrance to the Pantanal there is a gate across the road where drivers are given a list of rules of conduct. The road is of earth, in poor condition, with ruts, holes and many bridges that need care in crossing. The easiest access is in the dry season (July-September), which is also the best time for seeing birds, and, in September, the trees are in bloom. In the wet, especially January-February, there is no guarantee that the Transpantaneira will be passable. The wet season, however, is a good time to see many of the more shy animals because more fruit, new growth and other high calorie foods are available, and there are fewer people.

Campos de Jofre, about 20 kilometres north of Porto Jofre, is said to be magnificent between August and October, with very large concentrations of birds and animals. In Poconé one can hitch (not much traffic, bumpy, especially in a truck) to Porto Jofre, or hire a vehicle in Cuiabá. You will get more out of this part of the Pantanal by going with a guide; a lot can be seen from the Transpantaneira in a hired car, but guides can take you into *fazendas* and will point out wildlife. Recommended guides in Cuiabá are listed below. Although there are gas stations in Pixaim and Porto Jofre, they are not always well stocked, best to carry extra fuel.

Brasília & the Pantanal

Pixaim

Colour map 3, grid B2 Pixaim is 63 kilometres south of Poconé, a journey of two hours in the dry season and up to five in the wet. It is the only easily accessible settlement in the Pantanal with any tourist infrastructure. It is located where a bridge crosses the Rio Pixaim and has two hotels, a fuel station (all types available, check that the pump is set to zero) and a tyre-repair shop (*borracheria*). Next to the *Pousada Pantaneira* (see below) is a private Jaguar Ecological Reserve, owned by *pantaneiros*, funded by donation. Further details, donations and reservations can be made through *Focus Tours* (see page 30), who helped to set up the reserve.

Sleeping **In Pixaim and on the Transpantaneira L** *Pantanal Mato Grosso*, T/F065-3219445, modern cabins, 35 rooms for 3-6 people, with full board, fan, clean, hot water (also family-size apartments with a/c), good home-grown food, in radio contact with office on R Barão de Melgaço in Cuiabá, camping possible, boat rental with driver US$30 per hour. On the opposite bank of the Rio Pixaim is **A** *Pousada Pixaim*, T7211899. Full board (meals also available separately), built on stilts, rooms with a/c or fan, mosquito-netted windows, hot water, electricity 24 hours, pleasant setting, boat trips – US$30 per hour with driver, camping possible, US$10 per tent or free if you eat in the restaurant. Recommended. Bookings through *Faunatur* in Cuiabá (reservations through *Focus Tours*, see page 30).

   AL *Hotel-Fazenda Cabanas do Pantanal*, 142 km from Cuiabá, 50 km from Poconé by the Rio Pixaim, on the northern edge of the Pantanal. Ten chalet bedrooms with bath, restaurant, boat trips (few in dry season), horse-riding, fishing, helpful proprietor and staff, everything except boat trips and bar drinks included in price (booking: *Confiança*, Cuiabá). **A** *Pousada Araras*, Km 32 on Transpantaneira. Fourteen rooms with bath. Recommended. Pool, good food, home-made *cachaça*, T6822800, F6821260, or book through *Expeditours* in Cuiabá. **A** *Pousada Pantaneira*, full board, 7 rooms with 2-3 bunk beds each, bath, simple, owned and operated by *pantaneiros* (reservations through *Faunatur* in Cuiabá, or through *Focus Tours*, see page 30), about 45 km from Pixaim.

   L *Sapé Pantanal Lodge*, Caixa Postal 2241 – CEP 78020-970, Cuiabá, T065-3223426, F3614069. Fourteen rooms in basic, self-contained accommodation, meals buffet-style, 4-day, 3-night all-inclusive programme US$500, fishing, wildlife observation and photography excursions, holder of the Embratur 'Ecológico Especial' classification and FEMA (Environmental Bureau) Green Stamp. A complete programme includes road transport from Cuiabá airport to Barão de Melgaço (wet season) or Porto Cercado (dry season), with onward river transportation (1½-2 hours and 1½ hours respectively) and return; outboard powered boats with experienced guides at guests' disposal during entire stay; optional trekking and horse riding in dry season, paddling in wet; English, French, Spanish spoken. *Sapé*, which is highly recommended, is closed 20 December-31 January.

Barão de Melgaço

Colour map 3, grid A2 Situated on Rio Cuiabá, 130 kilometres from Cuiabá (*TUT* bus leaves Cuiabá at 0730 and 1500, US$6.50), Barão de Melgaço is reached by two roads: the shorter, via Santo Antônio de Leverger, unpaved from Santo Antônio to Barão (closed in the wet season), or via São Vicente, longer, but more pavement. The way to see the Pantanal from here is by boat down the Rio Cuiabá. Boat hire, for example from *Restaurant Peixe Vivo* on waterfront, costs up to US$85 for a full day; or enquire with travel agencies in Cuiabá. The best time of day would be sunset, but it would need some organizing to be in the best part at the best time without too much boating in the dark. Remember to protect against the sun when on the water.

Initially farms and small habitations line the river banks, but they become more forested, with lovely combinations of flowering trees (best seen September-October). After a while, a small river to the left leads to the Baia and Lakes Chacororé and Sia Mariana, which join each other. Boats can continue beyond the lakes to the Rio Mutum, but a guide is essential because there are many dead ends. The area is rich in birdlife and the waterscapes are beautiful.

Sleeping

In the town are *Barão Tour Hotel*, apartments with a/c, restaurant, boat trips and excursions (Cuiabá T3221568, or *Melgatur*), and, much humbler, *Nossa Senhora do Carmo Hotel* on the waterfront and *Pousada e Lanchonete Francisco de Asis* on the main road down to the waterfront. *Mercadinho do Povo* minimarket sells provisions, including cheap hats. **Around Barão de Melgaço** On Sia Mariana are *Pousada do Barão*, 6 chalets with bath, swimming pool, first class, boat and trekking expeditions (book through *Melgatur*). *Restaurant Flamingo*, simple food, rooms, camping with permission, popular with fishermen; 1 other restaurant. Barão de Melgaço is also the starting point for the **L** *Pousada Passárgada*, programmes from 3 days up, full board, boat, car and trekking expeditions, transport from Barão de Melgaço, owner speaks English, French and German, food excellent. Highly recommended, closed December to February; reservations T7131128, in Barão de Melgaço on riverside, through *Nature Safaris*, Av Marechal Rondon, Barão de Melgaço, or São Paulo T011-2845434, or Rio de Janeiro T021-2873390. Much cheaper if booked direct with the owner, Maré Sigaud, Mato Grosso, CEP 786807, *Pousada Passárgada*, Barão de Melgaço.

Directory

You should expect to pay US$60-90 pp per day for tours in the Pantanal

Tour companies & travel agents In Cuiabá: *Confiança*, R Cândido Mariano 434, T6234141, very helpful travel agency, tours to Pantanal are expensive. Also recommended **Pantanal Explorers**, Av Gov Ponce de Arruda 670, T3814959/5674, sightseeing, fishing trips for 4-5 days by boat. **Anaconda**, R Comandante Costa 649, T6244142, F6246242, tour operators for Pantanal day tour as far as Pixaim, also 2 and 3 day tours, day tour to Chapada dos Guimarães or Águas Quentes, Amazon trips to Alta Floresta/Rio Cristalino region (price does not include airfare). **Ametur**, R Joaquim Murtinho 242, T/F6241000, very helpful, good for air tickets. Adriana Coningham of *Ararauna Turismo Ecológica*, Av Lavapes 500, loja 07, T/F3216666. Highly recommended. All these agencies arrange trips to the Pantanal, for longer or special programmes, book in advance. *Focus Tours* (see page 30) specializes in tours in this part of the Pantanal and, starting from Cuiabá, to the southern Amazon, with bases at Alta Floresta and on the Rio Cristalino (see page 729).

Recommended guides (in alphabetical order): *Sérgio Alves*, F6235258, speaks English, birdwatching and other tours. *Paulo Boute*, R Getúlio Vargas 64, Várzea Grande, near airport, T6862231, speaks Portuguese, English, French, also sells Pantanal publications. *Marcus W Kramm*, R Franklin Cassiano da Silva 63, Cuiabá, T/F3218982, speaks Portuguese, English, German. *Djalma dos Santos Moraes*, R Arnaldo Addor 15, Coophamil, 78080 Cuiabá, T/F6251457, US$100 pp per day. *Laércio Sá*, *Fauna Tour*, operates from same premises as *Millennium Agência de Viagens*, Av Isaac Póvoas 1008, CEP 78045-640, T/F6233200, millennium@zaz.com.br, www.millenniumtour. com.br, has own car, well-informed, helpful, speaks English, Spanish and Italian, 2 and 3-day Pantanal tours (including transport, accommodation, meals, trekking, horse riding, boat trips, fishing), can arrange longer tours and camping (Aug-Oct) on request, also excursions to Chapada dos Guimarães. *Joel Souza*, can be contacted at the airport, or at Av Getúlio Vargas 155A, next to *Hotel Presidente*, T/F6241456, Mobile 9833552 (24 hrs), speaks English, German and Italian, enthusiastic, knowledgeable, very helpful, checklists for flora and fauna provided, will arrange all transport, farm accommodation, fishing, horse riding, trekking, night excursions. Most guides await incoming flights at the airport; compare prices and services in town if you don't wish to commit yourself at the airport.

Brasília & the Pantanal

Mato Grosso

Although the area that is now Mato Grosso and Mato Grosso do Sul was demarcated as Spanish territory by the Treaty of Tordesillas, it was the Portuguese Aleixo Garcia who was the first to explore it in 1525. Jesuits and then *bandeirantes* entered the Mato Grosso for their different ends during the 17th and early 18th centuries, and when gold was discovered near Cuiabá a new influx of explorers began. Mato Grosso became a captaincy in 1748 and the borders between Portuguese and Spanish territories were resolved in the following years. Throughout the 19th century, after the decline in gold production, the province's economy stagnated and its population dwindled. This trend was reversed when the rubber boom brought immigrants in the early 20th century to the north of the region, while, in the south, there was expansion of cattle farming and mate cultivation. Getúlio Vargas' 'March to the West' in the 1940s brought added development, accompanied first by the splitting off of Rondônia and, some 80 years later, by the formation of Mato Grosso do Sul in 1977. Today, cattle ranching is the principal industry.

The state has a population of about 2,370,000. The topography changes from the marshland of the Pantanal in the south east of the state to hills and low plateaus north of the capital Cuiabá.

Cuiabá

Population: 450,000
Phone code: 065
Colour map 3, grid A2

The state capital on the Rio Cuiabá, an upper tributary of the Rio Paraguai, is in fact two cities: Cuiabá on the east bank of the river and Várzea Grande, where the airport is located, on the west. It is very hot; coolest months for a visit are June, July and August in the dry season. It has a number of praças and is known as the Cidade Verde (green city).

Ins & outs
See also Transport, page 723

Getting there Flights arrive at the airport in Várzea Grande. There are buses and taxis to the centre. Take any white Tuiuiú bus, name written on the side, in front of the airport to Av Tte Col Duarte. Interstate buses arrive at the rodoviária north of the centre. Town buses (see below) stop at the entrance.

Getting around Many bus routes have stops in the vicinity of Praça Ipiranga. Bus 501 or 505 (Universidade) to University museums and zoo (ask for 'Teatro') from Av Tte Col Duarte by Praça Bispo Dom José, a triangular park just east of Praça Ipiranga. To rodoviária, No 202 from R Joaquim Murtinho behind the cathedral, about 20 minutes.

Sights

Cuiabá has an imposing government palace and other fine buildings round the green **Praça da República**. On the square is the **Cathedral**, with a plain, imposing exterior, two clock-towers and, inside, coloured glass mosaic windows and doors. Behind the altar is a huge mosaic of Christ in majesty, with smaller mosaics in side chapels. Beside the Cathedral is another leafy square, **Praça Alencastro**.

On **Praça Ipiranga**, at the junction of Avenidas Isaac Póvoas and Tenente Coronel Duarte, a few blocks west of the central squares, there are market stalls and an iron bandstand from Huddersfield in the UK.

On a hill beyond the square is the church of **Bom Despacho**. In front of the Assembléia Legislativa, Praça Moreira Cabral, is a point marking the **Geogedesic Centre of South America** (see also under Chapada dos Guimarães, below).

Museus de Antropologia, História Natural e Cultura Popular, in the **Museums** Fundação Cultural de Mato Grosso, Praça da República 151, house historical photos, documents, furniture, religious art, a contemporary art gallery, stuffed fauna, stones and woods from the region, Indian items and weapons, archaeological finds and pottery. ■ *Monday-Friday 0800-1730, US$0.50*. **Museu de Arte Sacra** is beside Bom Despacho church. **Museu de Pedras**, Galdino Pimentel 195, exhibits stones from the Chapada dos Guimarães. ■ *Monday-Friday 0800-1100 and 1300-1700, US$2*.

At the entrance to Universidade de Mato Grosso by the swimming pool, 10 minutes by bus from the centre, is the small **Museu do Índio/Museu Rondon** with well-displayed exhibits. Carrying on along the road through the campus, signed on the left before a right turn in the road, is the **Zoológico**. The jacaré, capivara, tortoise and tapir pen can be seen at any time, but are best in the early morning or late afternoon. It also has coatis, otters, emu, monkeys, peccaries, birds etc. ■ *0800-1100, 1330-1700 (closed Monday), free*. Opposite the zoo is the theatre.

Excursions

The **Águas Quentes** hot springs, 86 kilometres (nine kilometres south of the BR-163, 77 kilometres east of Cuiabá), can be visited. **L** *Hotel Águas Quentes* at the springs, all meals included, reservations through *Hotel Mato Grosso Palace*, address below, T6246637. The waters fill pools of 42°C and 36°C; no buses go there, arrange transport through *Hotel Mato Grosso Palace*.

Essentials

L *Eldorado Cuiabá*, Av Isaac Póvoas 1000, T6244000, F6241480. Very smart. **L** *Global* **Sleeping** *Garden*, Av Miguel Sutil 5555, T6241660, F6249966. Pool, bar, restaurant. **L** *Áurea Palace*, Gen Mello 63, T/F3223377. Pleasant rooms, restaurant, swimming pool, good. **L** *Best Western Mato Grosso Palace*, Joaquim Murtinho 170, T6247747, F3212386. Four-star, Central, good. **L** *Paiaguas Palace*, Av Rubens de Mendonça 1718, T6245353, F3222910. Popular with tour groups, rooms OK but no view, pool, sauna, restaurant. **L** *Taiamã Plaza*, Av Rubens de Mendonça 1184, Bosque de Saúde, T6241490, F6243384. Three-star, very good, pool, excellent breakfast. **L** *Veneza Palace*, Av Col Escolástico 738, T3214847, F3225212. Three-star. Recommended. **A** *Diplomata*, Av João Ponce de Arruda 686, by airport, T6822942. Recommended. **A** *Las Velas*, Av Filinto Müller 62, opposite airport, T6823840, F6823734. Pool, good value. **A** *Almanara*, Av Col Escolástico 510, T3231244, F3232049. Opposite but less good is **A** *Bandeirantes*, Av Col Escolástico 425, southeast of centre, T3210920, F6245363. **A** *Abudi Palace*, Av Col Escolástico 259, T3227399. Good. **A** *Skala Palace*, R Jules Rimet 26, T3224347. Restaurant, smart lobby, front rooms noisy. **B** *Brazil*, R Jules Rimet 20, T6212703. A/c, fridge, parking, **D** with fan, cheaper with shared bath, ground floor rooms are best. **B** *Mato Grosso*, R Comandante Costa 2522, T3219121. Two-star, a/c, cheaper with fan. Good restaurant, good value. **B** *Presidente*, Barão de Melgaço and Av G Vargas, T3216162, on a busy central corner. Convenient but lots of traffic outside, a/c, **C** with fan, fridge, cheaper with shared bath. **B** *Real Palace*, 13 de Junho 102, Praça Ipiranga, T3215375, F6111141. Large rooms, some with a/c, good breakfast. **C** *Ipanema*, R Jules Rimet, T6213069. A/c, **D** with fan, cheaper with shared bath, good value, good breakfast. Recommended. **C** *Grande*, R Jules Rimet 30, T6213852. A/c, **D** with fan, cheaper with shared bath, basic. **C** *Samara*, R Joaquim Murtinho 270, T3226001. Central, with bath, hot shower, fan, basic but good, cheaper with shared bath. **D** *Lagunas*, Av Gen Mello 166. Small rooms, basic. **D** *Modelo*, R Jules Rimet 221, by the rodoviária. Fan, basic. **D** *União*, R Poxoréu 13, T6211589. Fan, **E** with shared bath, basic.

Eating *Bierhaus*, Isaac Póvoas 1200. *Tio Ari*, R Comandante Costa 770. Buffet with a wide variety of vegetarian and a few meat dishes, good quality and value. Recommended. *Sachimi*, Av Isaac Póvoas across from *Eldorado Hotel*. Japanese. *O Choppão*, Praça 9 de Abril. Very good, popular. *Cacalo Peixaria*, Av Lavapés 203, Santa Rosa. Traditional fish dishes, popular, good. *Salambô*, Av 31 de Março 720, across from *Shopping Goiabeiras*. Good buffet, not cheap, open evenings. *Getúlio Grill*, Av Getúlio Vargas 1147. Meat specialties. *Cedros*, Praça 8 de Abril 750, Goiabeiras. Arab food. *Casa Suíça*, Av Miguel Sutil 4200. Swiss food, trout. *Na Esquina*, Av Tte Col Duarte 1930. Restaurants in the city centre are closed at night; try Av Getúlio Vargas, between Praças Santos Dumont and 9 de Abril, about 10 minutes' walk from the centre, which has several popular pizza and other restaurants, also along Isaac Póvoas in the same direction (northwest). On Av CPA are many good restaurants and small snack bars. There are several restaurants and lanchonetes on R Jules Rimet across from the rodoviária, *Paladar*, at No 60, good value. Recommended. Good *churrascarias* near the airport on Av da FEB, *rodízio* for about US$10.

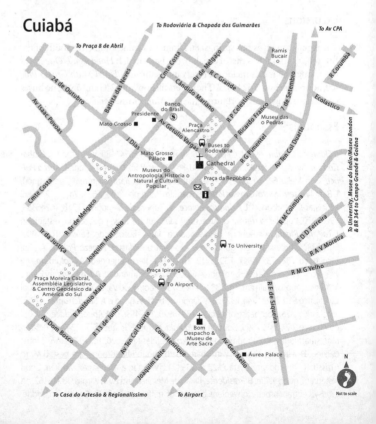

Cuiabá

Monsoons

Although the Brazilian Monsoons (monções) were given their name in association with the weather, they were not, in fact, rainy seasons. They were, like their predecessors, the bandeirantes, another breed of pioneer who expanded Brazil's frontiers. In Portuguese, the monções were winds which determined the seasons which were best for sailing. When the term reached Brazil it was applied to the rainy seasons, rather than the winds, because the rain determined whether journeys into the interior could be made. From about the second decade of the 18th century, the expeditions which penetrated into the far west of Brazil took to the rivers, rather than going on foot. The people who made these trips acquired the name Monsoons.

Taking the Rio Tietê out of São Paulo, the Monsoons sailed to the heart of the continent. Their main destination was the gold mines of Senhor Bom Jesus do Cuiabá and the alluvial deposits on the Rio Coxipó-Mirim. Various routes were tried until the best way was found of getting from the Tietê to Mato Grosso. When this route had been established convoys would set out once a year to trade with the miners and bring the gold back to São Paulo. It was not an easy journey. Everything, including animals, had to be taken to Cuiabá on boats which were modelled on the Indian pirogue, using navigation which was also borrowed from the indigenous people. The remoteness of Cuiabá was only matched by the legends of vast wealth which drew the Monsoons to the area. It took longer to get from São Paulo to Cuiabá than it did from Rio de Janeiro to Lisbon; the journey time was about five months, as long as it took to get from Lisbon to India. Many lives and a great deal of merchandise was lost on the rivers, but this remained the only form of communication between São Paulo and Mato Grosso until the third decade of the 19th century. In the same way that the bandeirantes extended Brazil's boundaries and established Portuguese rule over the south and southwest, so the Monsoons brought the far west into Portuguese possession.

Taken from Sérgio Buarque de Holanda, "The Monsoons", chapter 10 of Richard M Morse (ed), The Bandeirantes (full reference is given in **Further reading**, page 85).

Entertainment Cuiabá is quite lively at night, bars with live music and dance on Av CPA. *Tucano* bar/restaurant, Av CPA. Beautiful view. Recommended. Four cinemas in town.

Shopping Handicrafts in wood, straw, netting, leather, skins, Pequi liquor, crystallized *caju* fruit, compressed *guaraná* fruit (for making the drink, see box on page), Indian objects on sale at the airport, rodoviária, craft shops in centre, and daily market, Praça da República, interesting. The *Casa de Artesão*, Praça do Expedicionário 315, T3210603, sells all types of local crafts in a restored building. Recommended. Fish and vegetable market, picturesque, at the riverside.

Transport
See also Ins & outs, page 720

Car hire *Unidas*, Av Isaac Póvoas 720, T6824062. *JM*, Av Isaac Póvoas 547. *Le Mans*, at airport, T3811651. *Localiza*, Av Dom Bosco 965, T6247979, and at airport, T6827900. *Atlântida*, Av Isaac Póvoas, T6230700. Cheapest at *Vitória*, R Comandante Costa 1350, T3227122.

Air Airport in Várzea Grande, T6822213. Flights to Alta Floresta, Brasília, Campo Grande, Itaituba, Rio Branco, Santarém, São Paulo and Sinop. Taxi from centre US$15, 'Aeroporto' bus from Praça Ipiranga, US$0.50. No bank at the airport; there is a post office and a Sedtur office (not always open).

Guaraná

"In order to obtain guaraná, their favourite stimulant, the inhabitants of Cuiabá organized canoe expeditions lasting more than six months along the Tapajoz. The paste is compressed into a sausage shape and grated on the horny tongue of a pirarucu fish, which is kept in a deerskin pouch. These details are significant, because it is believed that the use of a metal grater or a different kind of leather pouch would cause the precious substance to lose its peculiar properties."

Thus Claude Levi-Strauss described the harvesting of guaraná in the 1930's. Today you can still buy the pirarucu tongues in markets in the Amazon region.

Guaraná is prepared into a paste from the fruit of the creeper Paullinia sorbilis. The Maué Indians of Cuiabá used to be the only ones to appreciate it as a stimulant but it is now world renowned. Guaraná is everywhere, consumed as a soft drink in such quantities that it rivals Coca-Cola in popularity, with massive advertising campaigns and sponsorship deals to boost sales. Taken in its powder form and made into an infusion, it as a natural pick-me-up with similar properties to coffee. It is even available now as a sports drink, consumed by fitness-crazy Brazilians after a long game of futevolei on the beach or a session in the gym. You can also buy it in chewing-gum form in Europe, where it is popular as an energiser after a hard night's clubbing.

Whether or not it really works is another matter; but it remains a popular drink today and some people combine it with alcohol to make cocktails with a distinctly Brazilian flavour. But to enjoy the real effects, perhaps you need to use the same method as the Cuiabans did in the 1930s.

Buses Rodoviária, R Jules Rimet, Bairro Alvorada, north of the centre. Comfortable buses (toilets) to **Campo Grande**, 10 hours, US$20, 12 buses daily, *leito* at 2000 and 2100, US$50. To **Goiânia**, 14 hours, US$25. Direct to **Brasília**, 24 hours, US$30, *leito* US$60. To **Porto Velho**, 6 *União Cascavel* buses a day, US$45, 21 hours. *Andorinha* 1700 bus São Paulo-Cuiabá connects with Porto Velho service. Several to **São Paulo**, eg Motta, US$42. To **Rio de Janeiro**, US$57. To **Barra do Garças**, *Xavante* 0800, 1300 and 2030, US$15, also *Barattur*. Connections to all major cities.

Directory **Airline offices** *Varig*, R 15 de Novembro 230, Bairro Porto, T6246498, at airport T6821140. **Banks** *Banco do Brasil*, Av Getúlio Vargas and R Barão de Melgaço, commission US$10 for cash, US$20 per transaction for TCs, very slow for TCs, but best rates. *Incomep Câmbio*, R Gen Neves 155, good rates. The following travel agents or gold dealers change cash only at poor rates (generally open Mon-Fri): *Mattos-Tur*, R Cândido Mariano 465. *Goldmine*, R Cândido Mariano 400, 0800-1600. *Ourominas*, R Cândido Mariano 401, 0800-1700, may change on Sat 0800-1200 if cash is available, enquire first, T6249400. *Portobello*, R Comandante Costa 555, 0900-1600. It is difficult to get cash advances on credit cards especially Mastercard, for Visa try *Banco do Brasil* or *Bradesco*. **Communications** Post Office: main branch at Praça da República, fax service. **Telephone:** R Barão de Melgaço 3209, 0700-2200, also at rodoviária, 0600-2130, international service. **Internet:** *Copy Grafic*, Praça Alencastro 32, fax and email, English spoken, friendly. **Embassies & consulates** *Bolivia*, Av Isaac Póvoas 117, T6235094, open Mon-Fri. **Security** The port area is best avoided, even in daylight. **Tourist offices** Secretaria de Desenvolvimento do Turismo, *Sedtur*, Praça da República 131, next to the post office building, T/F6249060, Mon-Fri, 0700-1800. Good maps, friendly, helpful regarding general information, hotels and car hire, some English and Spanish spoken. Also very helpful in settling disputes with local tour companies. *Ramis Bucair*, R Pedro Celestino 280, is good for detailed maps of the region. **Voltage** 110 Volts AC, 60 cycles.

Leaving Cuiabá

There is a paved road to Campo Grande (712 kilometres); the 2,400 kilometre BR-364 road from Brasília to Porto Velho and Rio Branco passes through Cuiabá; it is paved all the way between Brasília, Cuiabá (1,133 kilometres) and is in good condition, but between Cuiabá and Porto Velho (1,450 kilometres) there are many pot-holes. Service stations often provide free hot showers and the *prato comercial* is a cheap meal. The more direct road to Brasília through Barra do Garças and Goiás Velho (the BR-070) is paved also. Several paved feeder roads connect the BR-070 and BR-364.

Chapada dos Guimarães

Sixty eight kilometres northeast of Cuiabá lies one of the oldest plateaus on earth. The Chapada dos Guimarães is one of the most scenic areas of Brazil and retains much of the mystery attributed to it for centuries. In the 1920s, Colonel Fawcett was told of many strange things hidden in its depths, and an unusual local magnetic force which reduces the speed of cars has been documented. The birdwatching is very good and mammals, such as puma, giant river otter and black-tailed marmoset, live here.

Population: 13,500
Phone code: 065
Colour map 3, grid A2

The pleasant town of Chapada dos Guimarães, the main population centre, is a base for many beautiful excursions in this area; it has the oldest church in the Mato Grosso, **Nossa Senhora de Santana** (1779), a bizarre blending of Portuguese and French baroque styles, and a huge springwater public swimming pool (on Rua Dr Pem Gomes, behind the town). Formerly the centre of an important diamond prospecting region, today Chapada is a very popular destination for Cuiabanos to escape the heat of the city on weekends and holidays. It is a full day excursion from Cuiabá through lovely scenery, with many birds, butterflies and flora. The *Festival de Inverno* is held in the last week of July, and *Carnaval* is very busy. Accommodation is scarce and expensive at these times.

The Chapada is an immense geological formation rising to 700 metres, with rich forests, curiously eroded rocks and many lovely grottoes, peaks and waterfalls. A **National Park** has been established in the area just west of the town, where the **Salgadeira** tourist centre offers bathing, camping and a restaurant close to the Salgadeira waterfall. The beautiful 85 metres **Véu da Noiva** waterfall (Bridal Veil), 12 kilometres before the town near Buriti (well-signposted, ask bus from Cuiabá to let you off), is reached by a short route, or a long route through forest. Other sights include the **Mutuca** beauty spot, **Rio Claro**, the viewpoint over the breathtaking 80 metres-deep **Portão do Inferno** (Hell's Gate), and the falls of **Cachoeirinha** (small restaurant) and **Andorinhas**.

Eight kilometres east of town is the **Mirante do Ponto Geodésico**, a monument officially marking the Geodesic Centre of South America, which overlooks a great canyon with views of the surrounding plains, the Pantanal and Cuiabá's skyline on the horizon; to reach it take Rua Fernando Corrêa east, drive eight kilometres then turn right (there is no sign anymore).

Continuing east, the road goes through agricultural land and later by interesting rock formations, including a stone bridge and stone cross. Forty five kilometres from Chapada, you reach the access for **Caverna do Francês** or Caverna Aroe Jari ('the dwelling of the souls' in the Bororo language), a sandstone cave over one kilometre long, the second largest in Brazil. It is a two kilometre walk to the cave; in it is Lagoa Azul, a lake with crystalline blue water.

Latest reports say visitors are not allowed to go to the lake. Take your own torch/flashlight (guides' lamps are sometimes weak). A guide is necessary to get through *fazenda* property to the cave, but not really needed thereafter.

Other excursions are to the **Cidade de Pedra** rock formations, 25 kilometres from town along the road to the diamond prospecting town of Água Fria. Nearby is a 300 metre wall formed by the Rio Claro. Sixty kilometres from town are the **Pingador** and **Bom Jardim** archaeological sites, which are caverns with petroglyphs dating back some 4,000 years.

Hiring a car in Cuiabá is the most convenient way to see many of the scattered attractions, although access to several of them is via rough dirt roads which may deteriorate in the rainy season; drive carefully as the area is prone to dense fog. Hitchhiking from Chapada town to the National Park is feasible on weekends and holidays, but expect crowds at the swimming holes.

Tours

Travel agencies in Chapada and Cuiabá offer expensive tours to all the sights. The Secretaria de Turismo e Meio Ambiente office, Rua Quinco Caldas 100 near the praça, provides a useful map of the region and organizes tours. José Paulino dos Santos is a guide working with this office (weekdays 0800-1100, 1300-1800, T7911245). Recommended tours with Jorge Belfort Mattos from *Ecoturismo Cultural*, Praça Dom Wunibaldo 464, T/F7911393; he speaks English and knows the area well; several four to six hour itineraries from US$20-50 per person (minimum four people or prices increase). Cássio Martins of *AC Tour*, Rua Tiradentes 28, T7911122, often waits at the rodoviária. Four hour tours are about US$20 per person, minimum five persons; seven to eight hour tours, US$25 per person, minimum five; horseback day tour, US$25 per person, minimum two; an eight to 10 kilometre hike with a guide, US$20 per person, minimum two; bicycle tour with guide, US$20 per person, minimum two. Tours from Cuiabá cost US$35-40 per person.

Essentials

Sleeping **AL** *Pousada da Chapada*, 2 km out on Cuiabá Rd (MT 251, Km 63), T7911171, F7911299. Cheaper with fan, very comfortable, restaurant, bar, pool, sports facilities, parking. **A** *Estância San Francisco*, at the entrance to town from Cuiabá (MT-251, Km 61), T7911102, F7911537. On 42 ha farm with 2 lakes, said to have the best breakfast in town fresh from the farm. **B** *Rio's Hotel*, R Tiradentes 333, T7911126. A/c, fridge, **C** with fan, cheaper with shared bath, good breakfast. Recommended. **B** *Chapadense*, R Vereador José de Souza 535, T/F7911410. A/c, fridge, **C** with fan, restaurant serves *comida caseira*. **B** *Turismo*, R Fernando Corrêa 1065, a block from rodoviária, T7911176, F7911383. A/c, fridge, cheaper with fan, restaurant, breakfast and lunch excellent, very popular, German-run; Ralf Goebel, the owner, is very helpful in arranging excursions. **C** *Pousada Bom Jardim*, Praça Bispo Dom Wunibaldo, T7911244. Fan, comfortable, parking, good breakfast. Recommended. **D** *São José*, R Vereador José de Souza 50, T7911152. Fan, cheaper with shared bath and no fan, hot showers, basic, good, owner Mário sometimes runs excursions. **D** *Dormitório*, R Tiradentes. Basic, no fan, cheaper with shared bath. **Camping** **E** pp *Aldeia Velha*, in the Aldeia Velha neighbourhood at the entrance to town from Cuiabá, T3227178 (Cuiabá). Fenced area with bath, hot shower, some shade, guard. *Salgadeira*, unorganized camping 16 km from town at the tourist centre, watch your belongings.

Nivios, Praça Dom Wunibaldo 631, for good regional food. *Fogão da Roça*, Praça Dom Wunibaldo 488, *comida mineira*. Generous portions, good quality. Recommended. *O Mestrinho*, R Quinco Caldas 119. Meat, regional dishes, rodízio at weekends. *Choppada* (*O Chopp da Chapada*), R Cipriano Curvo near praça. Drinks and meals, regional dishes, live music at weekends. *Trapiche*, R Cipriano Curvo 580. Pizza, drinks, regional dishes. *O Mestrinho*, *Peixaria Serrano*, R Dr Pem Gomes 505 (near pool). Fish specialities and *comida caseira*, cheaper than those near the praça. *Veu da Noiva*, R Dr Pem Gomes 524. Regional dishes, fish in season (*piracema* fishing ban 1 October-1 March). *Pequi* is a regional palm fruit used to season many foods; *arroz com pequi* is a popular rice and chicken dish.

Eating

Crafts, indigenous artefacts, sweets and locally-made honey from Casa de Artes e Artesanato Mato Grossense (Praça Dom Wunibaldo). Regional sweets from *Docerla Olho de Sogra*, Praça Dom Wunibaldo 21. João Eloy de Souza Neves is a local artist, his paintings, music and history about Chapada (*Chapada dos Guimarães da descoberta aos dias atuais*) are on sale at *Pousada Bom Jardim*.

Shopping

Seven departures daily to and from Cuiabá (Rubi, 0700-1900, last back to Cuiabá 1800), 1½ hours, US$2.75.

Transport

Communications **Post Office:** R Fernando Corrêa 848.

Directory

Cáceres

This city has many well maintained 19th-century buildings painted in pastel colours. It is known for its many bicycles as most people seem to get around on two wheels. Until 1960, Cáceres had regular boat traffic, today it is limited to a few tour boats and pleasure craft. River trips from Cuiabá to Corumbá are very difficult since boats on the Cuiabá river are few and irregular. You can sometimes get to Corumbá by river from Cáceres, a very hot but clean and hospitable town on the banks of the Rio Paraguai, 200 kilometres west of Cuiabá.

Population: 78,000
Phone code: 065
Colour map 3, grid A1

The Municipality runs the **Museu Histórico de Cáceres** on Rua Antônio Maria by Praça Major João Carlos. The main square, **Praça Barão de Rio Branco**, has one of the original border markers from the Treaty of Tordesillas, which divided South America between Spain and Portugal; it is pleasant and shady during the day. In the evenings between November and March the trees are packed with thousands of chirping swallows (*andorinhas*), beware of droppings. The square is surrounded by bars, restaurants and ice cream parlours and comes to life at night.

The beautiful **Serra da Mangabeira** is about 15 kilometres east crossed by the road from Cuiabá; the town is also at the edge of the Pantanal. Vitória Regia lilies can be seen north of town, just across the bridge over the Rio Paraguai along the BR-174. There are archaeological sites on the river's edge north of the city.

Excursions

A *Turbo*, Av São Luiz 1399 by BR 070, T2231984. Luxurious, restaurant, pool. **A** *Ipanema*, R Gen Osório 540, T2231177, F2231743. Garage, good restaurant. **A** *Comodoro*, Praça Duque de Caxias 561, T2232078. **A** *Caiçaras*, R dos Operários 745 corner R Gen Osório, T2233187, F2232692. **B** without fridge and TV, pleasant, modern, parking. **B** *Fênix*, R dos Operários 600, T2231027, F2212243. Fridge, a/c, comfortable. **B** *Rio*, Praça Major João Carlos 61, T2233387, F2233084. A/c, **C** without fridge, TV, **D** with shared bath, fan. **C** *Charm*, Col José Dulce 405, T/F2234949. A/c, **D** with shared bath, friendly. Near the rodoviária are: **C** *Capri*, R Getúlio Vargas 99, T2231711. A/c, comfortable. **C** *13 de Junho*, R 13 de Junho, T2233871. A/c, pleasant. **C** *Gasparin*, Av

Sleeping

Brasília & the Pantanal

Sangradouro 162, T2234579. A/c, fridge, cheaper with fan. **D** *União*, R 7 de Setembro 340. Fan, **E** with shared bath, basic, good value. **D** *Rio Doce*, R 7 de Setembro. A/c, cheaper with shared bath, good value. **D** *Santa Terezinha*, R Tiradentes 485. With fan, breakfast, not clean. Many other cheap hotels.

Eating *Corimbá* on river front. Fish specialities, good, not cheap. *Bistecão*, R Gen Osório 977. Meat, opens erratically. *Kaskata*, floating restaurant at the end of R Col José Dulce, by the port, nice setting, fish and *jacaré* specialities, fanciest in town, expensive. *Gulla's*, R Col José Dulce 215. Buffet by kilo, good quality and variety. Recommended. *Hispano*, Praça Barão de Rio Branco 64. Buffet by kilo. *Kaskata Pizzaria*, R Col José Dulce 250. Expensive. *Panela de Barro*, R Frei Ambrósio 34, near rodoviária, *comida caseira*.

Festivals *Piranha Festival*, mid-March; *International Fishing Festival* in mid-September; annual cattle fair.

Shopping *Náutica Turismo*, R Bom Jardim 119A, by the waterfront, for fishing/camping supplies and boat repairs.

Transport **Car hire** *Localiza*, Padre Cassimiro 630, T2231330, and at airport. **Buses** *Colibrí/União Cascavel* buses Cuiabá-Cáceres, US$9, many daily between 0630-2400 (book in advance, very crowded), 3½ hours. Cáceres-Porto Velho, US$32. **Boats** The *Acurí*, a luxury tourist vessel, sails to Corumbá, 1 week cruise including return by air from Corumbá to Cuiabá, US$600 pp. For information on other boat sailings, ask at the Capitânia dos Portos, on the corner of the main square at the waterfront. If possible phone in advance to Cáceres, Posto Arrunda, T2211707, to find out if any boats are going. Also Portobrás on the outskirts at the waterfront (T2211728). In the dry season there are practically no boats to Corumbá. At the waterfront you can hire a boat for a day trip, US$5 per hour pp, minimum 3 people; on holidays and some weekends there are organized day trips on the river.

Directory **Banks** *Casa de Câmbio Mattos*, Comte Bauduino 180, next to main praça, changes cash and TCs at good rates. **Communications** **Telephone:** Praça Barão de Rio Branco. **Tour companies & travel agents** *Cáceres*, Av Getúlio Vargas 408, T2231428, F2232440, fishing and photo tours to Pantanal, boat rentals, Cláudio Duarte helpful guide. *Pantanal Tour*, R Col Fária 180, T2231200, boat rentals, fishing trips, tickets. *Vereda Turismo*, R Padre Cassemiro 1121, T2234360, tours, boat rentals, fishing.

A journey along the Porto Velho road from Cáceres (BR-174, 364) demonstrates the amount of development and deforestation along Brazil's Far West frontier, see page 662. At **Pontes e Lacerda** (*Verona Palace Hotel* (**A**), T2661507, with restaurant, pool) a side road goes to **Vila Bela** on the Rio Guaporé, which used to be the capital of Mato Grosso. It has a ruined church, cannon balls lying around and is very interesting.

Frontier with Bolivia An unpaved road runs from Cáceres to the Bolivian border at San Matías. Brazilian immigration is at R Col Farías, Cáceres, for exit and entry formalities; when closed (for example Sunday), go to Polícia Federal, Av Rubens de Medarca 909.

Leaving Bolivia, get your passport stamped at Bolivian immigration (1000-1200, 1500-1700), then get your passport stamped at Cáceres, nowhere in between, but there are three luggage checks for drugs.

Transport Buses: the bus fare from Cáceres to **San Matías** is US$9 with *Transical-Velásquez*, Monday-Saturday at 0630 and 1500, Sunday 1500 only (return at same times). *Trans Bolivia* to San Matías, Sunday, Monday, Friday at 1500, Tuesday, Wednesday, Thursday and Saturday at 0700.

Into Bolivia San Matías is a busy little town with hotels, restaurants and a bank. The next major town in Bolivia is San Ignacio de Velasco, which is on the road route to Santa Cruz de la Sierra. There are buses San Matías-San Ignacio and San Ignacio-Santa Cruz; also flights. For more details, see the *Bolivia Handbook* or the *South American Handbook*.

North of Cuiabá

The road due north from Cuiabá to Santarém (1,777 kilometres) has been completed and is all-weather, through **Sinop** (*population* 42,000), with a branch west to **Colíder** (*population* 32,000) and Alta Floresta (daily bus from Cuiabá with *São Luís* at 2000, 12 hours, US$45). Outside Alta Floresta, the *Cristalino Jungle Lodge* on the Cristalino river is a basic lodge, with shared baths, in a very rich and well-preserved section of southern Amazônia. Many rare mammals are found here (including the short-eared dog), as well as five species of macaw, harpy eagle and a few hundred other bird species. *Anaconda Operators* in Cuiabá run tours to *Cristalino Jungle Lodge*, US$100 per person per day plus airfare (US$200 return). *Focus Tours* (see page 30) can also make reservations or arrange guided tours.

Alta Floresta
Population: 68,500
Phone code: 065

   NB When travelling north of Cuiabá, yellow fever vaccination is obligatory; if you do not have a certificate, you will be (re)vaccinated.

Sleeping Sinop: **C** *Italian Palace*, Av das Figueras 493, T5312109. Restaurant, bar, sauna. **Alta Floresta**: **B** *Floresta Amazônica*, Av Perimetral Oeste 2001, T5213601, F5213801. In park, lovely views, pool, sports, all facilities. **C** *Pirâmide Palace*, Av do Aeroporto 445, T5212400. A/c, fridge, restaurant. **D** *Grande Hotel Coroados*, R F 1 118, T5213022. Not too well kept but has a/c, pool and bar.

East of Cuiabá

From Rondonópolis, about 215 kilometres southeast of Cuiabá on the road to Goiânia, a paved road branches southwards to Campo Grande and thence to the western parts of the state of São Paulo. Rondonópolis is one of only three towns of any size on the 934-kilometre Cuiabá-Goiânia road (the others are Jataí and Rio Verde in Goiás). It is a convenient stopping place with many hotels.

Rondonópolis
Population: 143,000
Phone code: 065

Sleeping AL *Novotel*, R Floriano Peixoto 711, T4219355, F4219322. Pool. **A** *Guarujá*, R Fernando Corrêa 624, T/F4218611. **A** *Thaani*, Av Amazonas 472, T4219288, pool. **A** *Nacional*, R Fernando Corrêa 978, T4213245, F4214848. **D** *Dormitório Beija Flor*, near rodoviária.

Transport Air: airport, 6 km, T4213185. **Buses**: to **Brasília**, US$30, 14½ hours. To **Goiânia**, US$20, 11 hours. To **Campo Grande**, US$12.50, 6½ hours. Beware of overbooking on *Viação Motta* buses.

Brasília & the Pantanal

Barra do Garças A direct dirt road (250 kilometres, via Jussara) and a more circuitous paved
Population: 47,500 route through Iporá (340 kilometres) connect Goiás Velho with Aragarças (on
Phone code: 065 the Goiás side) and Barra do Garças (on the Mato Grosso side of the Araguaia).
Barra is the pleasanter of the two and has the better facilities, including several
banks and hotels. A *Festival de Praia* is held locally in July, with fishing tournaments, displays, boat races etc. Five kilometres east of Barra on the road to
Araguaiana is **Parque Balneário das Águas Quentes**, with thermal pools
(42°C), river bathing and recreational opportunities. The abrupt 600 metres
high Morro do Cristo (10 kilometres) gives a wide view over the Araguaia and
surrounding country.

Sleeping and eating A *Esplanada Palace*, R Waldir Rabelo 1009, T8612515,
F8611918. Safe parking. Various **C-D** hotels along Av Ministro João Alberto, eg *Novo
Mundo*, *Presidente* and *Avenida*, all clean and with a/c. *Churrascarias* also on this ave-
nue and near the bridge (eg *Del Fronteyra*, live music, 1100-1400, 1900-2200). Pleas-
ant river beach with bars and snacks. Campsite on an island in the river. Night-time
entertainment by the port. **Aragarças**: A *Hotel Toriuá Park*, BR-158, T/F6381811.
Pool, mini zoo, own launch, lakeside location, 4 km from Barra do Garças.
Recommended.

Transport Buses: to Barra to/from São Paulo direct, 20 hours, US$25. To São Felix
do Araguaia at 2000, US$20, arrives early afternoon, wildlife may be seen in the early
morning. **Roads**: if heading for the Pantanal, note that BR-070 from Barra to Cuiabá is
in poor condition after the turn to Poxoréo; better to go to Rondonópolis, either for
Cuiabá or Campo Grande.

Xavantina The road north to Marabá (BR-158), paralleling the Araguaia on the Mato
Population: 13,000 Grosso and Pará side, leaves Barra do Garças and runs 140 kilometres to
Xavantina on the Rio das Mortes, the famous 'River of Deaths' which once
marked the territorial boundary of the intractable Xavante Indians. The road is
paved for a further 310 kilometres to Alô Brasil, then marginal dirt (465 kilometres) to beyond the Pará state border; it is again paved for the remaining 650
kilometres to Marabá via Redenção and Xinguara (see below). On the other
(east) side of the Araguaia, the Brasília-Belém highway (BR-153) runs north
through the heart of Goiás and Tocantins states.

Sleeping and eating (on BR-158, in Mato Grosso): At **Xavantina**: is **D** *Hotel
Xavantina*, basic but nothing better. *Churrascaria Arca de Noé*. Highly recom-
mended. At **Água Boa** (*population* 15,000), 76 km north of Xavantina, are **B** *Palace*,
Av Gov Júlio Campos 400, T4681930. *Manga Rosa*, good *churrascaria*.

São Félix do This is a large town with some infrastructure for fishing. Many Carajás Indians
Araguaia are found in town; a depot of their handicrafts is between the *Pizzaria* and *Mini
Population: 14,500 Hotel* on Avenida Araguaia. Mosquito nets are highly recommended since
there is a high incidence of malaria.

Many river trips are available for fishing or to see wildlife. Juracy Lopes, a very
experienced guide, can be contacted through *Hotel Xavante*; he has many
friends, including the chief and council, in Santa Isabela (see below). Morning or
afternoon trips to the village or to see wildlife, cost US$15 for two; longer trips
can be made to the meeting of the waters with the Rio das Mortes, or spending a
night in the jungle sleeping in hammocks. *Icuryala* is recommended,
T0XX62-2239518 (Goiâna), excellent food, drink, and service, US$100 per day,
independent visitors also welcomed. Fazenda owners may invite you as their
guest – do not abuse this privilege, and remember to take a gift.

Sleeping and eating A very simple hotel with the best view in town is the **C** *Mini Hotel Araguaia*, Av Araguaia 344, T0XX65-5221154. A/c rooms, not recommended, electricity is turned off at night and the closed-in room gets very hot. Recommended is **C** *Xavante*, Av Severiano Neves 391, T5221305. A/c, frigobar, excellent breakfast, delicious *cajá* juice, Sr e Sra Carvalho are very hospitable. Recommended. A good restaurant is the *Pizzaria Cantinho da Peixada* on Av Araguaia, next to the Texaco station, overlooking the river. The owner, Klaus, rents rooms, **E**, better than hotels, T5221320, he also arranges fishing trips. Recommended. *Bar Paralelos* has live music.

Transport **Air**: access to both São Félix and Santa Teresinha (see below) is by *Brasil Central/TAM* flights, and to São Félix by bus from Barra do Garças, see above. The air service is unreliable and, as the planes hold just 15 passengers, it is common to get delayed up to several days. There is a daily *Votec* flight from São Felix to Belém, stopping at Redenção, Tucumã and many other places.

    Buses: rodoviária is 3 km from the centre and waterfront, taxi US$5. To **Barra do Garças** at 0500, arrive 2300, or 1730, arrive 1100 next day. Also to **Tucumã**, 6-8 hours, and to **São José do Xingu**, 10 hours. No buses to Marabá.

Douglas Trent, of Focus Tours (who arrange tours, see **Specialist Tour Operators**), writes: "Bananal is the world's largest river island, located in the state of Tocantins on the northeastern border of Mato Grosso. The island is formed by a division in the south of the Rio Araguaia and is approximately 320 kilometres long. The entire island was originally a national park (called **Parque Nacional Araguaia**), which was then cut in half and later further reduced to its current size of 562,312 hectares (of an original two million). The island and park are subject to seasonal flooding and contain several permanent lakes. The island, and especially the park, form one of the more spectacular wildlife areas on the continent, in many ways similar to the Pantanal. The vegetation is a transition zone between the *cerrado* (woody savanna) and Amazon forests, with gallery forests along the many waterways. There are several marshlands throughout the island.

    The fauna is also transitional. More than 300 bird species are found here, including the hoatzin, hyacinthine macaw, harpy eagle and black-fronted piping guan. The giant anteater, maned wolf, bush dog, giant otter, jaguar, puma, marsh deer, pampas deer, American tapir, yellow anaconda and South American river turtle also occur here. The island is flooded most of the year, with the prime visiting (dry) season being from June to early October, when the beaches are exposed. Unfortunately, the infrastructure for tourism aside from fishing expeditions (the island is a premier spot for big fish) is very limited."

■ *Permission to visit the park should be obtained in advance from Ibama, Rua 219, No 95, Setor Universitário, 74605-800 Goiânia.*

    Access to the park is through the small but pleasant town of **Santa Teresinha** (*population* 9,000), which is north of São Felix (see above) and is the gateway to the park.

Sleeping A charming hotel is **A** *Bananal*, Praça Tarcila Braga 106, CEP 78395 (Mato Grosso), with full board. There is room only for 10; reserve well in advance, either by mail, allowing several months for the mail to get through, or by phoning the town's telephone operator, asking the hotel to call you back and hoping that you hear from them.

    There is some simple accommodation for scientists at the park, which can sometimes be reserved at the address above or from the national parks department in Brasília. Bring your own food and bedding, and the severely underpaid but dedicated staff would appreciate any extra food or financial help, although it will not be solicited. A boat to the park can be lined up at the *Hotel Bananal*.

Ilha do Bananal

Brasília & the Pantanal

Bananal can be visited from São Félix do Araguaia – see above (with permission from Funai in the town) by crossing the river to the Carajá village of **Santa Isabela de Morra** and asking to see the chief, who can tell you the history of the tribe. The island can be crossed from São Félix to **São Miguel de Araguaia** by taking an eight-hour trip (contact the *Bar Beira*). From São Miguel, a five-hour bus trip brings you to **Porangatu** (**D** *Hotel Mauriti*, shower, restaurant) on the Belém-Brasília highway.

Background

12

Background

History and politics

Indigenous peoples

Some 50,000 years ago the very first peoples crossed the temporary land bridge spanning Asia and America at the Bering Straits, and began a long migration southwards. They were hunters and foragers, following in the path of huge herds of now extinct animals, such as mammoth, giant ground sloth, and antecedents of the camel and horse. The first signs that these people had reached South America date from around 10,000 BC, if not earlier.

Origins

The major handicap to archaeological study of tropical cultures is that most material remains deteriorate rapidly in the warm, humid climate. Since the majority of cultural output from Brazil was in perishable materials such as feathers, wood, baskets, and woven textiles, little has survived for modern analysis. Nevertheless various artefacts have been discovered from all around the country, showing considerable artistic and technical skill. The pottery produced by the early peoples was of a high standard, admired by the European newcomers. Early ceramics have been found on Marajó island at the mouth of the Amazon. The Annatuba culture lived here in small villages by the river. Most of their ceramics found are round bowls and jars, including huge funeral urns, which have been dated with increasing antiquity; the earliest to date from around 980 BC. Textile production was done mainly with hand-twisted fibres, using both cotton and bast. Objects found in Rio Grande do Sul, dating from 550 AD or earlier, included twined bags, nets and ropes. Most of the textiles found throughout Brazil were simple everyday items, such as hammocks and straps, with little decoration.

Archaeological evidence

It was assumed that the first humans in Brazil came down to the lowlands from the Andean chain, following the east-facing river valleys. Some very early human remains have been found in central and northeastern Brazil. In Pedra Furada, in northeast Brazil, a rock-shelter named Toca do Boquirão has yielded evidence of human presence from as early as 47,000 years ago. The cave, in a region well-known for its prehistoric rock paintings, is known to have been occupied by hunters about 8,000 years ago. However, French archaeologist Nièrde Guidon made deeper probings into the ground and claims to have found evidence of much earlier human presence. Guidon's claims sparked hot debate among other experts, many of whom argued that what she described as ash from fireplaces was in fact the remains of naturally caused forest fires. In Monte Alegre, opposite Santarém on the Rio Solimões, recent studies have been made of human remains, dating from around 15,000 BC, also predating previous estimates. These, and other controversial claims from sites in the mid-Amazon region, have led some experts to raise the theory of original human migration from across the Pacific Ocean. In general, however, the most authoritative studies of the first humans in Brazil point to a much later date, between 10,000-5,000 BC.

The earliest people soon learnt to make the most of the rich food sources provided by the rivers of the Amazon basin. They lived on the flood plain and caught fish and manatee (large sea mammals, related to dugongs and sea cows) using spears thrown from the shore, or from dugout canoes. Besides fishing, these people also cultivated manioc and other plants found on the forest floor. They kept turtles in corrals at the river's edge, for eating and also for making tools and other artefacts from their shells.

Their nomadic lifestyle was carefully planned, and they followed planting and harvesting seasons in accordance with the periodic rising and falling river levels. Worship of multiple deities, of the weather and agriculture for instance, was very

Amazon lifestyles

Background

important. The gods had to be appeased to prevent excessive fluctuations in the level of the river. At first, as hunters and gatherers, they built simple, temporary houses out of tree trunks and palm leaves, and slept in hammocks made from plant fibres. Clothing was equally simple; a large, ankle-length tunic called a *kushma* was the main garment worn. Although this may sound impractical wear for people living in a warm, humid climate, the *kushma* provided much-needed protection against biting insects. Compensating for their plain clothing, the people painted their bodies and wore colourful jewellery, such as feather head-dresses. Little has remained of the perishable adornments, but cylindrical and flat ceramic stamps have been found throughout Amazônia, which may have been used to apply ink designs onto the face and other parts of the body, still common today among ethnic groups.

Migration to the coast Around 7000-4000 BC a climatic change increased the temperature throughout the south of Brazil, drawing people down from the inland *planalto* region to the coasts, and leading to an upsurge in population here. These coastal inhabitants lived on shellfish collected from the water's edge, as evidenced by huge shell mounds, *sambaquis*, discovered on the coast here. In rare cases they also fed on whales that had probably been beached, but they did not go far out to sea to fish. Some of the *sambaquis* found measure up to 25 metres high; many of them also served as dwellings, with floors and fireplaces, and as burial sites, with graves often underneath the houses. The dead were buried with personal adornments and some domestic artefacts.

Settlement & political structure By about 100-200 BC, people throughout Brazil were settled in structured, fixed communities by the coasts and rivers, living increasingly by farming instead of nomadic hunting and gathering. The subsequent population growth spread communities further along river courses and into seasonally flooded savanna lands.

Unlike the great empires of the Andes, the lowland peoples did not form political groupings much larger than a few villages. By the 16th century AD, however, there was a very large population of different peoples spread throughout Brazil, some of them settled in chiefdoms. These structured groups contained several hundred individuals. One chieftain led a province composed of several villages, each of which was led by a lower-ranking chieftain. The first European explorers reported that there was at least one case of the title or name of one chief being the same as the local word for god, and as such the chief was revered far from his people's territory. One such chiefdom was at the village of Teso dos Bichos on Marajó island at the mouth of the Amazon. The oval-shaped village was built on a mound some seven metres high and covering 2½ hectares. It is thought that the site was inhabited continuously for about 900 years, by 500-1,000 people living in houses made of earth, wooden poles and thatch. The village appeared to have been kept very clean and tidy and communal life was well organized, with duties divided between men and women.

Linguistic groups The most widespread linguistic grouping in Brazil at the time of the European conquest was the Tupi-Guarani. These people originated from the Atlantic coast and rivers around 500-700 AD. They lived off slash and burn farming, cultivating tropical plants, but when they began moving inland and south they took over from resident hunters and gatherers. By the 16th century AD the Tupi-Guarani, who often moved from place to place, following a prophet, could be found from north of the Amazon south to Rio de la Plata, and west into Paraguay and Bolivia.

Another large, organized group of people were the Tupinambá. They lived on the coast, from the mouth of the Amazon south to São Paulo state. The Tupinambá lived by cultivating crops, such as manioc, sweet potato, yams, as well as cotton, gourds and tobacco. They lived in villages of four to eight large, rectangular, thatched houses, each containing up to 30 families. They usually built their villages on an elevation to catch the breeze, and moved to new sites every five years or so. A chief, the patrilineal head, enforced various social customs, such as marriages and puberty rites. Burial ceremonies were elaborate, with the body wrapped in a hammock and squeezed into a huge ceramic urn. The head of a family was usually buried under his house, others elsewhere within the village. Sometimes a hut was built over the grave, and a fire lit nearby to ward off evil spirits.

Cannibalism was also an important custom for the Tupinambá, as it had been for many other peoples throughout South America for thousands of years. The practice was highly ritualized, using prisoners of war. The victims were kept as slaves, often for long periods, being well fed and looked after; in some cases even marrying the owner's daughter or sister, who had their children. But all such slaves were eventually eaten, after an elaborate ceremony with much singing and dancing. An appointed executioner would kill them with a club and they were then cooked and different parts of the body divided up among various participants in the ritual. There have been many theories as to why people practised cannibalism; since they tended to eat victims of war it was thought that it gave them power over the spirits of their dead enemies. It is most commonly argued that human flesh supplemented the diet for large populations who had scarce resources. But this was not the case for the Tupinambá, who had ample food supplies. When the Tupinambá themselves were asked why they ate human meat they simply said they liked the taste of it.

Ancient South America, by Karen Olsen Bruhns (Cambridge World Archaeology, 1994); *Atlas of Ancient America*, by Michael Coe, Dean Snow, and Elizabeth Hudson (Facts on File, 1993); *Kingdoms of Gold, Kingdoms of Jade, The Americas before Columbus*, by Brian M Fagan (Thames and Hudson, 1991); *Past Worlds – The Times Atlas of Archaeology* (Times Books Ltd, 1988).

Further reading

European colonization

Pedro Álvares Cabral is believed to be the first Portuguese explorer to land on the Brazilian coast, having been blown off his course to India and making landfall on 22 April 1500. He claimed the territory for Portugal as a result of agreements with Spain under the papal bull of 1493 and the Treaty of Tordesillas (1494), but it was some years before the Portuguese realized that this was not just another island as the Spanish had found in the Caribbean, and that in reality they had stumbled across a huge new continent. Further expeditions were sent out in 1501 and 1503-4 and a few trading stations were set up to export the only commodity they felt was of commercial interest: a species of dyewood known as 'pau do brasil'. Little attention was paid to the new colony, as the Portuguese concentrated on the more lucrative trade with Africa, India and the Far East. Some settlers, often banished criminals as well as merchants, gained acceptance with the local Indian tribes and intermarried, fathering the first hybrid cultural Brazilians.

Arrival of the Portuguese

The coastal trading stations at Salvador da Bahia, Pernambuco, São Vicente and Cabo Frio soon attracted the attention of French and British traders, who seized Portuguese ships and started to trade directly with the Indians. The French even proclaimed the right to trade in any part of Brazil not occupied by the Portuguese. This forced the Portuguese Crown to set up a colony and in 1530, Martim Afonso de Sousa was sent out with about 400 men. Faced with the impossibly huge task of colonizing the Brazilian coastline, the Crown turned to private enterprise to stake its claim. In 1534 the coast was divided into 15 captaincies, each of which was donated to an individual captain and governor to develop on behalf of the Crown. Although successful settlements were established in Pernambuco in the north and São Vicente in the south, the problems faced in most captaincies, Indian resistance, lack

Colonization

Background

of capital and the difficulty of attracting settlers, led to the reassertion of Crown control in 1549. The Indians had been happy to barter brazil wood with the Portuguese and had helped in the logging and transporting of timber, but the introduction of sugar plantations was a different matter and the hunter-gatherers had no experience of such exhausting work. When they refused to co-operate in this profitable enterprise, the Portuguese took Indians as slaves on a massive scale, which destroyed the good relations previously enjoyed and led to attacks on Portuguese settlements.

The Jesuits Tomé de Sousa was sent out as Governor-General to the vacant captaincy of Bahia in 1549. He established his seat at Salvador, which became the first capital of Brazil. With him travelled six Jesuit priests, the first of what was to become a hugely powerful missionary and educational order in Brazil. Their role was to smooth the path between Indians and Europeans, convert and educate the Indians in Christian ways and organize them into special villages, or *aldeias* (see box, page 402). This last move brought them into conflict with the settlers, however, for their control over the labour market, and with the clergy, who regarded the Indians as savages who could be enslaved. As a result of disagreements with the first Bishop of Brazil, Fernandes Sardanha, the Jesuits moved in 1554 from Bahia to the captaincy of São Vicente, where they set up an *aldeia* at Piratininga, which later became the city of São Paulo. In 1557 a new governor was appointed, Mem de Sá, who was more sympathetic to the Jesuits and their aims and the *aldeias* began to spread.

Exploration & settlement

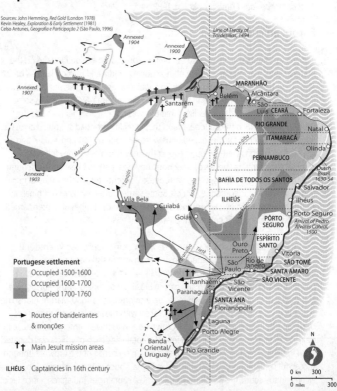

Sources: John Hemming, *Red Gold* (London 1978)
Kevin Healey, *Exploration & Early Settlement* (1981)
Celso Antunes, *Geografia e Participação 2* (São Paulo, 1996)

Portugese settlement
- Occupied 1500-1600
- Occupied 1600-1700
- Occupied 1700-1760

→ Routes of bandeirantes & monções

✝✝ Main Jesuit mission areas

ILHÉUS Captaincies in 16th century

Portrait of a sugar engenho

Sugar cultivation began in Brazil in the 1550s and by early 17th century the colony had become the biggest sugar producer in the world. The fertile soil, warm climate and adequate rainfall of the Northeast meant that the land could produce two crops a year. Since the cane juices went sour within a day of being cut, it was essential that the processing plant was close to the fields; the resulting combination of plantation and factory was known as an engenho. The typical engenho was more than this, however: it also included a chapel, workshops, casa grande (the owner's house), senzala (slave quarters) and fields for growing maize, beans, manioc and rice to feed the slaves. The need for labour was met by importing African slaves but engenhos did not just consist of a white master and black slaves. While the latter did the backbreaking work of planting, weeding and cutting the cane, skilled workers were required to keep the machinery working, repair the buildings and keep the accounts.

One of the most famous of engenhos was Sergipe in Bahia, which was the subject of a long legal dispute over ownership in the 17th century involving the rival claims of two Jesuit colleges. Apart from providing work for lawyers, this dispute created masses of documents which have given historians a vivid picture of life in Sergipe in the late 16th century.

At Sergipe the harvest (safra) continued from the beginning of August to early May, while planting took place between June and August and again in March and April. Because of the daytime heat work began at 1600 and continued to 1000 in the morning, after which the machinery was cleaned. Some of the entries in the Sergipe accounts are particularly intriguing. The biggest expense in 1707 was firewood, used for boiling the cane-juice. Firewood was obviously crucial; lack of it in 1651 led to the loss of 14 days work, while there was no work on another five days owing to repairs. As a Jesuit engenho it is not surprising that there were many religious holidays; 25 to 30 were observed each year, though these differed. Easter, for some reason, was not observed in 1612-13. Over 20 percent of expenses were in salaries, the best paid workers being the sugar master, the banker and the overseers, but there were other costs: in 1707 a slave catcher was paid 9 milreis for catching "the slave Caetano" while another two milreis went to pay for "three shrouds for diseased slaves". Interestingly the accounts indicate that Sergipe made a loss in most years between 1611 and 1754.

The Crown still had difficulties in consolidating its hold on Brazil and other European powers continued to encroach on its territory. A Protestant French expedition found an area which had not been settled by the Portuguese and stayed there from the mid-1550s until they were finally ousted in 1567. Their colony was replaced by a new royal captaincy and a town was founded: Rio de Janeiro (see page 97). São Luis was also occupied by the French in 1612-15, but it was the Dutch who posed the greatest threat on both sides of the Atlantic (see **The Dutch in Brazil**, see page 492). They seized Pernambuco in 1630, Portuguese Angola in 1641 and dominated the Atlantic trading routes until the Portuguese managed to regain Angola in 1648-49 and Pernambuco in 1654.

French & Dutch incursions

Background

Throughout the colonial period Brazil produced raw materials for Portugal. The colonial economy experienced a succession of booms and recessions, the first of these based on sugar: during the 17th century the northeastern provinces of Pernambuco, Bahia and Paraíba were the world's main producers of sugar. As European settlement had led to the death of much of the native population (over a third of the Indians in coastal areas died in epidemics in 1562-63 alone) and Indian slavery was unsuccessful, the Portuguese imported African slaves to meet the demand for labour on the sugar

Sugar & slaves
See also box, above

plantations (*engenhos*). "The most solid properties in Brazil are slaves", wrote the Governor in 1729, "for there are lands enough, but only he who has slaves can be master of them." Over 10 million African slaves survived the dreadful conditions of the Atlantic crossing before the trade was abolished in 1854.

The gold rush
See also box, page 741

As the sugar industry declined in the late 17th century in the face of competition from British, French and Dutch Caribbean colonies, gold was discovered inland in 1695 in Minas Gerais, Mato Grosso and other areas. Despite the lack of communications, prospectors rushed in from all over Europe. Shortly afterwards, diamonds were found in the Serra do Frio. The economy was largely driven by gold until the 1760s and a revival of world demand for sugar in the second half of the 18th century. Thereafter, there was diversification into other crops such as cacao, rice, cotton and coffee, all of which were produced for export by large numbers of slaves.

The gold rush shifted the power centre of Brazil from the northeast to the centre, in recognition of which new captaincies were created in Minas Gerais in 1720, Goiás in 1744 and Mato Grosso in 1748, and the capital was moved from Salvador to Rio de Janeiro in 1763. Legacies of the period can be seen today in the colonial towns of Mariana, Congonhas, São João del Rei, Diamantina and, above all, in the exceptionally beautiful city of Ouro Preto, a national monument full of glorious buildings, paintings and sculpture.

Expansion inland

Although Portuguese settlement was concentrated along the coast, the southern interior was explored by the *bandeirantes* (see box, page 192), groups of adventurers who set out from São Paulo in search of gold and Indian slaves. The other great agents of expansion inland were the Jesuits, who built missions, schools, seminaries and churches throughout the country (except for Minas Gerais from which they were banned). They owned many of the largest sugar plantations and monopolized the Amazon spice trade. Their wealth and power, often in disputed border areas, as well as their opposition to Indian slavery made them enemies of the state and they were expelled in 1759 after being implicated in a plot to assassinate the king.

Marquês de Pombal

The decline of gold in the mid-18th century made economic reform necessary and the Marquês de Pombal was the minister responsible for a new programme for Portugal and her empire. Imbalances had arisen particularly in trade with Britain. Portugal imported manufactured goods and wheat but her exports of oil and wine left her in deficit, which for a while was covered by Brazilian gold. Pombal was a despotic ruler from 1750 to 1777, modernizing and reforming society, education, politics and the economy. In order to revive Portugal he concentrated on expanding the economy of Brazil, increasing and diversifying exports to cover the deficit with Britain. Cacao, cotton and rice were introduced by the new monopoly company of Grão Pará e Maranhão in the north and a similar company for Paraíba and Pernambuco revitalized the sugar industry in the northeast. The monopoly companies led to high prices and were not entirely successful, however, so were closed in 1778-79, but the effects of Pombal's reforms were felt in the latter part of the 18th century and Portugal's trade with Britain turned into a surplus. From 1776 when the American colonies revolted, Britain was constantly at war and Portugal was able to supply rising British demand.

Rebellion

Pombal's influence on society enabled the Portuguese Empire to last much longer than the Spanish Empire. He deliberately offered posts in the militia and the bureaucracy to Brazilians and was careful not to alienate the Brazilian élites. White Brazilians were on the same standing as the Portuguese and identified strongly with the mother country. Rebellion was therefore rare but did occur, influenced partly by the turmoil that was going on in Europe with the French Revolution. In 1788-89 a

The Gold Rush

Although there was no shortage of rumours of gold and silver throughout the 16th and 17th centuries, it was only in the 1690s that large gold strikes were made inland from São Paulo in what became known as the area of the 'general mines' (minas gerais). Later there would be finds further west in Goiás and Mato Grosso, but these would be on a much smaller scale. What all these areas shared was their virtual inaccessibility: In 1755 it took one traveller, Marcos de Noronha, 11 weeks to travel from Goiás to Salvador. Even Minas Gerais, much nearer to the coast than Goiás, could be reached only by a long and dangerous journey across the coastal mountains. There were no roads and the rivers were of little use for transport. Yet early prospectors had to rely almost entirely on equipment and food brought in from the coast.

Despite the problems, reports of gold attracted the usual rush of prospectors and speculators, not only from elsewhere in the colony and from Portugal, but from other European countries. Towns grew up within months; between 1726 and 1729 the population of Cuiabá rose from 7,000 to 40,000. These new settlements were very different, however, from the cities of the coast; largely male, this was a violent, restless society, with little respect for traditional social mores or for the government.

The Portuguese Crown was, not surprisingly, eager to obtain its share, calculated as one fifth (quinto) of the gold produced; it also imposed special taxes and duties such as the special levy charged to help rebuild Lisbon after the earthquake of 1755. Tax collection, was, however, anything but simple. The Crown established royal foundries where the quinto would be subtracted from the gold returned to miners and traders. Faced with widespread evasion, illegal foundries and smuggling, the Crown established controls on the roads and searches in the main ports. The problems involved led to a different approach, with the quinto being collected by a per capita tax on everyone in the gold areas, an unpopular move which was not particularly effective owing to the lack of reliable records. In all 12 different methods were tried by the Crown to get its hands on the quinto; though the level of violent resistance varied, all were unpopular.

Although much of the gold left for Europe, by the late 18th century when production dropped off, the Gold Rush had transformed many aspects of the colony. For the first time large numbers of people settled in the interior. As they spent their newly acquired wealth, skilled building workers were in great demand to work on the beautiful churches and private mansions of Minas Gerais. Fortunes were made elsewhere, particularly in Rio de Janeiro and São Paulo, supplying the mining areas with meat and cereals and other goods. The reliance on African slaves to perform the hardest work in the mining areas pushed up the price of slaves, much to the discontent of the sugar planters of the northeast, and gave increased momentum to the slave trade. These changes were symbolized, perhaps above all, by the decision in 1763 to move the capital from Salvador to Rio de Janeiro, mirroring the decline in the wealth and power of the sugar planter elite and its partial replacement by Rio and São Paulo.

famous plot was uncovered in Minas Gerais called the inconfidência mineira (see page 276), which aimed to establish an independent republic in protest at the decline of the gold industry and high taxes. The rebels, who included many of the local hierarchy, were punished and the most prominent leader, Tiradentes (the teeth-puller), was hanged. Other plots were discovered in Rio de Janeiro in 1794, Pernambuco in 1801 and Bahia in 1807, but they were all repressed.

At the beginning of the 19th century, Napoleon Bonaparte caused a major upheaval in the monarchies of Europe. His expansion into the Iberian peninsula caused panic

The Brazilian Empire

in both Spain and Portugal. In August 1807 he demanded that Portugal close its ports to British ships but the British sent a fleet to Lisbon and threatened to attack Brazil if that happened. In November of the same year the French invaded and occupied Portugal. The Prince Regent decided to evacuate the court to Brazil and under British escort sailed to Rio de Janeiro, which became the capital of the empire in 1808. The court stayed there even after 1814 when Napoleon was defeated and Portugal was ruled by a Regency Council, but King João VI was forced to return to Portugal in 1820 after a series of liberal revolts in the mother country, leaving his son Dom Pedro as Prince Regent in Brazil.

Independence from Portugal

Dom Pedro oversaw a growing rift between Portugal and Brazil as the liberals in Lisbon tried to return Brazil to its former colonial status, cancelling political equality and the freedom of trade granted when the King left Portugal in the hands of the French. In October 1821 the government in Lisbon recalled the Prince Regent but Brazilians urged him not to go. Encouraged by his chief minister, José Bonifácio de Andrada e Silva, a conservative monarchist, Dom Pedro announced on 9 January 1822 that he would stay in Brazil, thereby asserting his autonomy. After another attempt to recall the Prince Regent, Dom Pedro made the final break with Portugal, proclaiming Brazil's independence on 7 September 1822. He was crowned emperor and Brazil became a constitutional monarchy in its own right. There was resistance in the north and northeast, particularly from the militia, but by 1824 violence had subsided. In 1825, under pressure from Britain, Portugal recognized the independent state of Brazil.

The first years of independence were unsettled, partly because of the Emperor's perceived favouritism for the Portuguese faction at court and lack of attendance to the needs of the local oligarchy. De Andrada e Silva resigned as opposition grew. In 1823 Dom Pedro dissolved the constituent assembly amidst fears that he had absolutist designs. However, he set up a royal commission to draft a new constitution which lasted from 1824 until the fall of the monarchy in 1889. This gave the emperor the right to appoint and dismiss cabinet ministers, veto legislation and dissolve parliament and call for elections. The parliamentary government consisted of two houses, a senate appointed by the monarch and a legislature indirectly elected by a limited male suffrage. A Council of State advised the monarch and ensured the separation of the executive, the legislature and the judiciary. Catholicism remained the official religion and the monarchy was supported by the Church.

Abdication   Dom Pedro still failed to gain the trust of all his people. A republican rebellion broke out in Pernambuco in 1824, where the élite were suffering from the declining sugar industry, and there was further resentment from all the planter oligarchy as a result of the Anglo-Brazilian Treaty of 1826. This treaty granted British recognition of the independent Brazil in return for certain trading privileges, but, almost more importantly, stipulated that the Atlantic slave trade should come to an end in three years. There was also a territorial dispute in 1825 with the Argentine provinces over the left bank of the Río de la Plata, called the Banda Oriental, which flared up into war and was only settled in 1828 with the creation of Uruguay as a buffer state. The mistrust between the Portuguese and the Brazilians became even more pronounced. Portuguese merchants were blamed for the rising cost of living and in 1831 rioting broke out in Rio de Janeiro. Dom Pedro shuffled and reshuffled his cabinet to appease different factions but nothing worked and on 7 April he abdicated in favour of his five-year-old son, Dom Pedro II, choosing to leave Brazil a week later on a British warship.

During the 10 years of the young prince's boyhood, there were many separatist movements and uprisings by the oppressed lower classes. In 1832-35 there was the War of the Cabanos, in Pernambuco (see page 489), a guerrilla war against the slave-owning plantocracy of the northeast; in 1835 the Cabanagem rebellion of free Indians and mestizos took place in Pará after a white secessionist revolt and sporadic fighting continued until 1840 (see page 609); in 1837-38 in Bahia there was a federalist rebellion; in 1835 Rio Grande do Sul proclaimed itself a republic, remaining independent for nearly 10 years, with the movement spreading into Santa Catarina, which also declared itself a republic (see page 360). By 1840 there was a general consensus that although he had not come of age, it was imperative that the 14-year old – Pedro should ascend the throne, and he was duly crowned. Administration of the country was centralized again, the powers of provincial assemblies were curtailed, a national police force set up and the Council of State restored.

Regency & rebellion

It took a couple of years for the balance of power to be worked out between the conservative élites of Rio de Janeiro and the liberal élites of São Paulo and Minas Gerais, but once the interests of different groups had been catered for, the constitutional monarchy worked smoothly for 20 years. Coffee was now the major crop in São Paulo and Minas Gerais and it was important that the wealthy oligarchy who produced it shared in the power structure of the nation to prevent secessionist movements.

The second empire

Despite the Anglo-Brazilian Treaty of 1826, the slave trade continued until the British Royal Navy put pressure on Brazilian ships carrying slaves in 1850 and the trade was halted soon afterwards. As slaves in Brazil did not reproduce at a natural rate because of the appalling conditions in which they lived and worked, it was clear that an alternative source of labour would eventually have to be found. Anti-slavery movements gathered strength and in 1871 the first steps towards abolition were taken. A new law gave freedom to all children born to slaves from that date and compensation was offered to masters who freed their slaves. During the 1870s large numbers of European immigrants, mostly from Italy and Portugal, came to work on the coffee plantations, and as technology and transport improved, so the benefits of slavery declined. During the 1880s the abolition movement became unstoppable and, after attempts to introduce compensation for slave owners failed, a law abolishing slavery immediately was passed on 13 May 1888. Some plantation owners went bankrupt, but the large majority survived by paying immigrant workers and newly freed slaves a pittance. Those freed slaves who left the plantations to find employment in the cities were equally exploited and lived in poverty.

Abolition of slavery

Proclamation of the Republic

The monarchy did not long survive the end of slavery. The São Paulo coffee producers resented abolition and resented their under-representation in the structures of power nationwide, while being called upon to provide the lion's share of the Treasury's revenues. The republican movement started in the early 1870s in cities all over Brazil, but grew strongest in São Paulo. It gradually attracted the support of the military, who also felt under-represented in government, and on 15 November 1889 a bloodless military *coup d'état* deposed the monarchy and instituted a federal system. The constitution of the new republic established 20 states with wide powers of self-government, a directly elected president of a national government with a senate and a chamber of deputies. Suffrage was introduced for literate adult males (about three percent of the population) and the Church and state were separated. Although the birth of the Republic was bloodless, there were pockets of resistance in rural areas such as the northeast, where the

The first Republic: 1889-1930

Background

Slavery

For over three centuries African slavery was a central feature of the economy and society of Brazil. Slave labour was a key part of the production of agricultural exports from the mid-16th century through to the abolition of slavery in 1888; slaves also provided much of the labour needed in the Gold Rush of the 18th century. In the 19th century, at a time when slavery was being abolished in the rest of South America, the demand for slaves increased in Brazil as they became the labour force on the new coffee fazendas of the south.

Although the first African slaves arrived in Brazil around 1550, it was only after 1580 with the expansion of sugar engenhos in the northeast that slave labour became common. Faced with a shortage of labour and the resistance of the indigenous population who tended to die of diseases, as well as the attitude of the Church, which opposed indigenous slavery, engenho owners soon resorted to African slave labour. The Church had few moral qualms about African slavery. By the 18th century, when slavery was

introduced on a large scale in the mining areas of Minas Gerais, Goiás and Mato Grosso, slave ownership was common in most strata of white society and had spread north to Amazônia and south to Río Grande do Sul. The importance of slaves in this society was noted by local people and visitors alike: in 1729 Governor Luís Vahia Monteiro commented "the most solid properties in Brazil are slaves and a man's wealth is measured by having more or fewer for there are lands enough, but only he who has slaves can be masters of them".

While no one knows how many Africans survived the terrible 'middle passage' between Africa and the Brazilian ports, let alone how many died, estimates of three to four million are common. Most came from two areas of West Africa, corresponding roughly to the modern states of Ghana and Angola. Slaves were employed in a surprising range of roles: they were often the cowboys who drove herds of cattle to the coastal towns for slaughter, the sailors who navigated the rivers and coast, the stevedores who

---

sugar estates were in recession. In the 1890s O Conselheiro (see box, page 468) led tens of thousands of followers against the secular republic at Canudos, nearly all of whom were eventually killed by government troops. In 1911 there was another rebellion in the southern states of Paraná and Santa Catarina, led by a Catholic visionary in defence of the monarchy. The Contestado movement lasted until 1915, when it too was destroyed by the military.

Brazilian politics were now dominated by an alliance known as *café com leite* (coffee with milk), of the coffee growers of São Paulo and the cattle ranchers of Minas Gerais, occasionally challenged by Rio Grande do Sul, with periodic involvement of the military. The first two presidents of the republic were military: Marshal Deodoro da Fonseca (1889-91) and Marshal Floriano Peixoto (1891-94). In some ways the military took the place of the Crown in mediating between the states' oligarchies, but its interventions were always unconstitutional and therefore gave rise to political instability. By the 1920s tensions between São Paulo and Minas Gerais had come out into the open with the cattle ranchers resenting the way in which the coffee growers used their position to keep the price of coffee artificially high at a time when there was an oversupply. Other social groups also became restive and unsuccessful coup attempts were launched by junior army officers in 1922, 1924 and 1926.

The end of the First World War saw the rise of the USA as an industrial power and the decline of Britain's traditional supremacy in trade with Latin America. Although Brazil was still exporting its raw materials to Europe at ever lower prices, it now imported its manufactured goods from the USA, leading to difficulties with finance

loaded ships bound for Europe and they were frequently domestic workers, midwives and retailers. Despite this, the vast majority were labourers who worked under such poor conditions that there was a continual demand for more imported slaves.

Regardless of the overwhelming odds, slave resistance was continual: whites constantly complained about the reluctance of slaves to work hard and slaves often escaped and formed quilombos or mocambos, communities of escaped slaves. Though these were usually in impenetrable parts of the interior, they were sometimes on the outskirts of town or near plantations, from where they could launch raids for supplies. Though many quilombos were small and short-lived, the most famous, known as Palmares, survived from around 1630 until its final defeat in 1694. Though slave rebellions took place throughout the period of slavery, they were more common in certain parts of the country and occurred with greater frequency in the 19th century. There were over 20 rebellions around

Bahia between 1809 and 1835, some of them led by slaves who were Muslim preachers.

By the late 19th century the days of slavery were clearly numbered; the slave trade to Brazil was finally ended by British pressure 1850. The defeat of the South in the Civil War put a finish to slavery in the USA, leaving Brazil as one of only two states in the Americas where slavery was legal (the other was Cuba). Though there had been an abolitionist movement since the 1830s, it made little headway until the 1860s. In 1871 the children of slaves were freed, a move which, when combined with the abolition of the slave trade, meant slavery would eventually end. Though plantation owners complained of labour shortages and bought slaves from the towns, they were forced to consider new sources of labour and from about 1880 they began to encourage European immigration, especially from Portugal and Italy. Thus, in 1888, when Congress finally debated the issue, there were only nine votes against abolition.

and fluctuating exchange rates. Brazil's terms of trade had therefore deteriorated and the profitability of its export-led economy was declining before the crash of Wall Street in 1929. The cost of stockpiling excess coffee had led to a rise in debt and by 1930 the government was spending a third of its budget on debt servicing. The growth of nationalism was a key feature of this period as well as the emergence of new political factions and parties such as fascists and communists.

The Wall Street crash led to a sudden decline in demand for coffee and the São Paulo élite saw its hegemony wiped out. The elections of 1930 saw another win for the São Paulo candidate but the results were disputed by a coalition of opposition forces. After several months of tension and violence, the army intervened, deposed the outgoing president and installed the alternative candidate of Rio Grande do Sul, Getúlio Vargas, a wealthy rancher, as provisional president. Vargas in fact held office until 1954, with only one break in 1945-50. Vargas' main aim when he took office was to redress the balance of power away from São Paulo and in favour of his own state. However, the effects of his reforms were more far-reaching. He governed by decree, replacing all state governors with 'interventors' who reduced the state militias, and reorganized the system of patronage within the states in favour of Vargas. São Paulo naturally resisted and there was a rebellion in 1932, but it was soon put down by federal troops, effectively wiping out the threat to Vargas' authority. In 1934 a constituent assembly drew up a new constitution which reduced the power of the states and gave more power to the president. The assembly then elected Vargas as president for a four-year term.

Vargas & the Estado Nôvo: 1930-45

Background

With the decline of traditional oligarchic blocs came the rise of political parties. The first to fill the vacuum were the fascists and the communists, which frequently took to street violence against each other. The fascists, called Integralists, were founded by Plínio Salgado in 1932. The Aliança Libertadora Nacional (ALN), a popular front including socialists and radical liberals, was founded by the Brazilian Communist Party in 1935. The ALN attempted to gain power by infiltrating the junior ranks of the army and encouraging rebellions, but Vargas clamped down on the movement, imprisoning its leaders. The fascists aimed to take power in 1938, the year elections were due, at which Vargas was not eligible to stand. However, in October 1937, Vargas declared a state of siege against an alleged communist plot and suspended the constitution which had prevented him being re-elected. Instead, he proclaimed a new constitution and a new state, *Estado Nôvo*. The fascists tried to oust him but failed, leaving Vargas with no effective opposition whatsoever.

The *Estado Nôvo* was also a response to an economic crisis, brought on by a fall in coffee prices, rising imports, a resulting deficit in the balance of payments, a high level of debt and soaring inflation. Vargas assumed dictatorial powers to deal with the economic crisis, censoring the press, banning political parties, emasculating trade unions and allowing the police unfettered powers. There followed a transition from export-led growth to import substitution and industrialization with heavy state intervention. Agricultural resources were channeled into industry and the government became involved in mining, oil, steel, electricity, chemicals, motor vehicles and light aircraft. The military were allowed free rein to develop their own armaments industry. As war approached in Europe, Vargas hedged his bets with both Nazi Germany and the USA, to see who would provide the greatest assistance for Brazil's industrialization. It turned out to be the USA, and in return for allowing US military bases to be built in northern Brazil he secured loans, technical assistance and other investments for a massive steel mill at Volta Redonda and infrastructure projects. Brazil did not declare war on Germany until 1944, but it was the only Latin American country to send troops to join the allies, with a force of 25,000 men going to Italy.

The elections of 1943 had been postponed during the War, but Vargas scheduled a vote for December 1945 in an attempt to dispel his fascist image. He allowed the formation of political parties, which included two formed by himself: the Social Democratic Party (PSD), supported by industrialists and large farmers, and a Labour Party (PTB), supported by pro-Vargas trade unions. There was also the National Democratic Union (UDN), opposed to Vargas, and the newly legalized Communist Party. However, there were growing fears that Vargas would not relinquish power, and when he appointed his brother as chief of police in Rio de Janeiro, the military intervened. Faced with the prospect of being deposed, Vargas chose to resign in October 1945, allowing the elections to take place as planned in the December. They were won by the PSD, led by General Eurico Dutra, a former supporter of the *Estado Nôvo*, who had encouraged Vargas to resign.

The Second Republic: 1946-64 Yet another constitution was drafted by a constituent assembly in 1946, this one based on the liberal principles of the 1891 constitution but including the labour code and the social legislation of the *Estado Nôvo*. Industrialization through state planning was retained, the foreign-owned railways were nationalized, hydroelectric power was developed, but deflation was necessary to bring down spiralling prices. The Communist Party was banned again in 1947. Meanwhile Vargas was elected Senator for Rio Grande do Sul, his home state, and kept active in politics, eventually being elected as candidate for the PSD and PTB alliance in the 1950 presidential elections. Although it was his third presidency, it was only his first by direct elections.

The third Vargas presidency was beset by the problems of fulfilling populist election promises while grappling with debt and inflation. Rapid industrialization required levels of investment which could only be raised abroad, but the nationalists were opposed to foreign investment. He failed to reconcile the demands of the USA and the nationalists, particularly with regards to oil and energy, and he failed to control inflation and stabilize the economy. There were rumours of corruption, and after the president's bodyguard was implicated in a plot to kill a journalist which went wrong and another man was shot, the army issued him with another ultimatum to resign or be ousted. Instead, on 24 August 1954, Vargas shot himself, leaving a suicide note denouncing traitors at home and capitalists abroad.

The next president was Juscelino Kubitschek, who took office in January 1956 with the aim of achieving economic growth at any cost, regardless of inflation and debt. He is best known for building the new capital of Brazil, Brasília, nearly 1,000 kilometres northwest of Rio de Janeiro in the state of Goiás. This massive modernist project served in the short term to expand the debt and in 1961, the next president, Jânio Quadros, inherited huge economic problems which brought his government down after only seven months and Congress unexpectedly accepted his resignation. Power passed to his vice-president, João Goulart, a populist and former labour minister under Vargas, who was mistrusted by the armed forces and the right wing. His powers were curtailed with the appointment of a prime minister and cabinet who would be jointly answerable to Congress. The 1960s were a turbulent time in Brazil as elsewhere, with the universities a hotbed of revolutionary socialism after the Cuban Revolution, Trotskyist and Communist agitators encouraging land occupations, strikes in industry and a move to secure trade union rights for the armed forces. A nationalist Congress passed legislation cutting foreign companies' annual profit remittances to 10 percent of profits, which sparked a massive outflow in foreign capital and a halving of US aid. Goulart was forced to print money to keep the economy going, which naturally put further pressure on an already soaring inflation rate. When Goulart clashed with Congress over approval of an economic adjustment programme and tried to strengthen his position by appealing for popular support outside Congress, he alarmed the middle classes, who unexpectedly supported a military coup in March 1964. Goulart took refuge in Uruguay.

The 1964 coup was a turning point in Brazilian political history. This time the armed forces did not return to barracks as they had before. Opposition leaders were arrested, the press censored, labour unions purged of anyone seen as left wing, and the secret police were given wide powers. The political parties were outlawed and replaced by two officially approved parties: the government Aliança Renovadora Nacional (ARENA) and the opposition Movimento Democrático Brasileiro (MDB). Congress, consisting only of members of these two parties, approved a succession of military presidents nominated by the armed forces. A new constitution, introduced in 1967, gave the president broad powers over the states and over Congress. The worst period of repression occurred between 1968 and 1973 with a wave of urban guerrilla warfare. Around this time, the military government's economic adjustment programme paid dividends and the economy began to grow, making life easier for the middle classes and reducing any potential support for guerrilla groups. In 1968-74 the economy grew at over 10 percent a year, which became known as the Brazilian 'economic miracle'. This spectacular growth, achieved because of the authoritarian nature of the regime, masked a widening gulf between the rich and poor, with the blacks and mulattos, always at the bottom in Brazilian society, suffering the most. Edwin Williamson (*The Penguin History of Latin America*) quotes statistics showing that in 1960 the richest 10 percent of the population received 40 percent of the national income; by 1980 they received 51 percent, while the poorest 50 percent received only 13 percent. In the shanty towns, or *favelas*, which had mushroomed around all the large cities, but especially São Paulo, disease, malnutrition and high mortality rates were prevalent and their citizens battled constantly in appalling housing lacking sewerage, running water and electricity.

Military rule: 1964-85

Background

Political parties in Brazil

*The history of Brazil's modern political parties dates from December 1979 when the law was passed to end the two party system which had been in force since the military government which took power in 1964 outlawed political parties. The military approved two parties, its own supporters in the Aliança Renovadora Nacional (ARENA) and the Movimento Democrático Brasileiro (MDB), the tolerated opposition. (See the **Military rule: 1964-85**, below, for details of this period and the political movements which preceded it.) Between 1982 and 1994, a total of 68 parties put up candidates for some or all the elections held in this period. Only 23 of them obtained final registration, which suggests that the majority were transitory affairs. The fact that a political party can field a candidate while still only provisionally registered explains why there have been so many since the creation of the New Republic, but since 1994 there seems to have been a stabilization within the multiparty system.*

There are two large parties, the PMDB and the PFL. There are also six medium-sized parties: Partido do Movimento Democrático Brasileiro (PMDB – Democratic Movement Party); Partido da Frente Liberal (PFL – Liberal Front Party); Partido da Social Democracia Brasileira (PSDB – Brazilian Social Democracy Party); Partido Progressista Reformador (PPR – Progressive Reform Party); Partido dos Trabalhadores (PT – Workers' Party); Partido do Povo (PP –

Popular Party); Partido Democrático Trabalhista (PDT – Democratic Labour Party); Partido Trabalhista Brasileiro (PTB – Brazilian Labour Party). The PPR was an amalgamation of two earlier parties, the Partido Democrático Social (PDS – Social Democrat Party) and the Partido Democrata Cristão (PDC – Christian Democrat Party), while the PP was formed by former members of the Partido Social Trabalhista (PST – Social Labour Party) and the Partido Trabalhista Renovador (PTR – Labour Party for Renewal). A number of small parties usually hold under 10 seats. Even if the proportion of seats held by different-sized parties is beginning to adhere to a pattern, it does not prevent shifting alliances, the migration of deputies from one party to another or the fusion of parties. The style of government, therefore, is one of concensus, rather than government by majority.

There is no space here to go into all the ramifications of the individual parties' histories, but perhaps a brief overview will help the reader understand some of the names which appear daily in the press. The PMDB was, basically, the successor to the MDB in 1980; at that time, the PDS was the party formed by a large number of ARENA's members. In the former, PMDB camp were such well known names as Itamar Franco, Orestes Quércia, Ulisses Guimarães and Mário Covas, and in the latter (PDS) José Sarney, Paulo Maluf and Antônio Carlos Magalhães. Two politicians, Ivete Vargas and Leonel Brizola,

By 1973 some military officers and their civilian advisors had become alarmed at the rising level of opposition. Arguing that repression alone would merely lead to further opposition and even to attempted revolution, they pressed for 'decompression': policies to relax the repression while remaining in power. The attempt to carry out this policy by legalizing political parties, permitting freer trade unions and strikes and reducing censorship, gave greater space for the opposition to demand an end to military rule. Attempts to introduce elections to Congress which were less controlled faced the same obstacle: they tended to result in victories for candidates who favoured civilian rule.

One of the main reasons for the military deciding to return to their barracks was the dire state of the economy. The armed forces had taken over in 1964 when the economy had hit rock bottom, their authoritarian regime had allowed rapid expansion and change which brought about the 'economic miracle', yet by 1980 the

wished to register the PTB, a labour party that predated the military regime. The electoral tribunal gave the name to Vargas, so Brizola set up the PDT which became the vehicle for Brizola's own brand of left-wing populism (especially during his terms as governor of Rio de Janeiro). After the peaceful transition to the New Republic, the old-style labour movement fragmented into the PTB, PDT and PMDB, while a new party, the PT grew out of the union movement of the São Paulo metal workers in the late 1970s. The urban trades unionists of the PT were joined by members of other urban grass roots movements, rural unions and progressive Catholics. The union movement is represented by two confederations, the Central Única de Trabalhadores (CUT) and the Confederação Geral de Trabalhadores (CGT), which have certain ideological differences. Likewise Brazil's communist parties followed different paths: the Partido Comunista Brasileiro (PCB), founded in 1922 on the principles of the Russian revolution, and the Partido Comunista do Brasil (PC do B), which broke away from the PCB in 1962 to adopt a line in keeping with the Albanian model.

The PFL was founded in 1985 with the full return to democracy. Several of its leaders, among them José Sarney, were formerly in the PDS and they supported Tancredo Neves in the electoral college in his bid for the presidency. Antônio Carlos Magalhães, also of the PDS, joined in

1986. The PSDB was one of the parties formed during the period of the National Constituent Assembly and the 1989 presidential campaign. PSDB was created by parliamentarians unhappy with the position taken by the PMDB on issues such as the length of the presidential term and the system of government to be laid down in the new constitution. Among its founders were the current president, Fernando Henrique Cardoso, and Mário Covas. At this time, Fernando Collor de Mello's election campaign took off and the Partido da Reconstrução Nacional (PRN – National Party of Reconstruction) was created, drawing in several unaffiliated politicians, such as Itamar Franco. Collor's demise led to the collapse of the PRN. One other party that deserves mention is the Partido Verde (PV – Green Party) which was started in 1985 in Rio de Janeiro, first associated with the PT, then becoming a party in its own right in 1988. It was registered in 1993.

Sources: Jairo Marconi Nicolau, Multipartidarismo e Democracia (Rio de Janeiro: Fundação Getúlio Vargas, 1996), pages 9-28; Leôncio Martins Rodrigues, 'As Eleições de 1994: Uma Apreciação Geral,' Dados, 38 (1995), pages 71-92; Michael M Hall and Marco Aurélio Garcia, 'Urban Labour', Modern Brazil, edited by Michael L Conniff and Frank D McCann, pages 161-191 (see **Further reading**, page 85). With thanks to Eduardo Noronha in São Paulo.

economy had gone full circle. Inflation was running at 100 percent a year and was set to go through the roof, foreign debt was the highest in Latin America, estimated at over US$87bn, and unemployment was soaring. When international interest rates rose sharply in 1982, Brazil was no longer able to service its debt and it suspended interest payments. Unwilling to go through another round of authoritarianism and repression, the military decided to let the civilians have a go. Elections in 1982 produced a majority for the pro-government Social Democratic Party (PDS) in the electoral college which was to elect the next president, but splits in the PDS led to the election in January 1985 of the opposition candidate, Tancredo Neves (see under São João del Rei, page 292).

The Landless

The acclaimed Brazilian photographer, Sebastião Salgado, published a book in 1997 entitled Terra – Struggle for the Landless (Phaidon Press) which documents the plight of a portion of Brazilian society which calls itself the Movimento Sem Terra, the Landless Movement. In one of the pictures, the horizon between half-tilled land and the sky is obliterated by an army of people raising flags, hoes and machetes to the clouds. It looks like an unstoppable force and yet conjures up images of the futile peasant revolts of bygone eras. In view of the many unkept promises by successive politicians to speed up the redistribution of unused land, 'unstoppable force' may be wishful thinking. Yet for the thousands who marched on Brasília in 1997, for the squatters who have reclaimed empty property, and for those who have been killed in disputes with landowners, the fight for somewhere to settle and grow crops is a reality. It is one of Brazil's biggest contradictions that so much potentially productive farmland is owned by a tiny proportion of the population and yet 42 percent of privately owned land is unused. For the millions of families who have little or no land to work, such inequality has been the spur for Sem Terra. The demand for land also encompasses the desire no longer to be at the outer margins of the economic and social progress that is taking place elsewhere in the country.

The trek of over 1,000 kilometres that the Movement made from São Paulo to Brasília in 1997 took two months and, as a sign of the popular support for the marchers, they were greeted like heroes by 120,000 people. Top politicians attended, announcements were made of new credit lines for settlements and of land confiscations, even a US$400mn World Bank loan for land reform. But would the landowners who have set up private armies to keep Sem Terra out be convinced? Would the political system be radically altered?

In late 1999 the government said that it had acquired unused farmland for 370,000 families since 1994. Critics claimed, though, that the number of landless was still growing. History has not been on their side and another part of their reality is not to believe in anything until the land rights are in their hands. Even when a landowner is found not to have valid title to a property, the legal process to reallocate the land is lengthy and slows the progress of land reform. Such delays have led to the radicalization of Sem Terra, with some loss of its romantic appeal in Brazil.

The return to democracy

Background

Corruption & impeachment   Tancredo Neves represented a broad opposition to the military regime, but he was unable, because of illness, to take office. The vice-president elect, José Sarney, was sworn in as acting president in March 1985, and in April became president on Neves' death. After complete revision by a Constituent Assembly in 1987-88, Brazil's new constitution of 1988 permitted direct presidential elections in November 1989. The elections, held in two rounds, gave Fernando Collor de Melo, of the small Partido da Reconstrução Nacional, 53 percent of the vote, narrowly defeating his left-wing rival, Luis Inácio da Silva (Lula). Just over half way through his five-year term, Collor was suspended from office after a landslide congressional vote to impeach him over his involvement in corruption. He avoided impeachment by resigning on 29 December 1992. Vice-president Itamar Franco took over, but had scant success in tackling poverty and inflation until the introduction of an anti-inflation package which introduced the *real* as the new currency.

The Plano Real   The success of the *Real* plan was the principal reason for its architect, finance minister Fernando Henrique Cardoso, winning the presidential elections of October 1994. After trailing Lula (see above) of the Workers Party (PT), Cardoso's popularity grew so rapidly between July and October that a second round of voting was not required. Cardoso represented an alliance of the Brazilian Social Democrat Party (PSDB), the Liberal Front (PFL) and the Labour Party (PTB), which failed to gain a majority in either house of congress. This severely hampered the president's plans to reform the tax and social security systems and the civil service. The government was criticized for its slowness in addressing social problems such as land reform and the violence associated with landlessness; the slave-like working conditions in some agricultural areas; human rights; the demarcation of Indian land. A national plan for human rights was announced in May 1996, but swift congressional approval was not expected.

In all areas, the government's lack of a majority in congress prevented rapid progress of any reform. This was best seen in Cardoso's amendment of the constitution to allow the president, state governors and mayors to stand for immediate re-election which was not passed until June 1997. The need for Cardoso's re-election as president was seen by foreign observers as essential to continue his reform programme especially in civil service and social security reforms languishing before congress since 1994. These measures were viewed as essential for reducing the budget deficit and securing economic stability.

In October 1997 the financial crisis in Asia began to threaten Brazil's currency and economic stability. The failure to push through the necessary measures to cut public spending emphasized the scale of the budget deficit and the vulnerability of the *real* to speculation. Cardoso was therefore obliged to introduce swiftly policies, which, at the cost of slowing down economic growth, would prevent an upsurge in inflation and a devaluation of the currency. Either of these eventualities would have severely damaged his re-election chances. At the same time, he was still faced with the social imbalances, which his government had as yet failed to redress. These included rising unemployment, unequal income distribution, crime, the low level of police pay, lamentable prison conditions, poor services in the state-run health and education services, land reform and the violence associated with landlessness.

Despite all these difficulties and probably because of the lack of any other suitable candidates, Cardoso managed to beat Lula again in October 1998 without the need for a second poll.

Cardoso and his allies emerged victorious but seriously weakened from the 1998 elections. Many state governorships had been won by political opponents and the achievement of political progress in Congress was increasingly controlled by its powerful leader, Antônio Carlos Magalhães (popularly known as ACM) of the PFL. Rumours of corruption in Cardoso's government also began to be aired with not even the president himself above implication. A rescue package agreed with the IMF helped Brazil survive a further financial crisis at the end of 1998, but the long delayed social security reforms had still not been passed. Finally when ex-president Itamar Franco, governor of Minas Gerais, refused to pay his state's debts to the Federal Government in January 1999, foreign investors lost confidence and began to withdraw their money from the country. The pressures on the *real* became too great and the central bank was forced to let it float freely against the dollar. It lost 50 percent of its value in the process.

With the failure of his indisputable great achievement, the strong *real*, Cardoso quickly lost most of his remaining credibility. This was further lowered by his failure to act decisively in political problems such as the removal and nomination of a new director of the Polícia Federal. By mid-1999 Cardoso's popularity had fallen to levels as low as Collor's. His complete lack of authority meant that his one-time allies were concentrating on fighting for political advantage rather than governing the country. While the ruling coalition was at such a low ebb, there was no coordinated challenge from the left of centre parties such as the PT and PDT, who were just as divided among themselves. Even a demonstration in August 1999 in Brasília by tens of thousands of

The second term

Background

protesters against the government's austerity plans was not supported by all opposition parties. By October some lost ground began to be made up when Congress approved reform of the private-sector pension system, but not before the Supreme Court had ruled that proposed reform of state pensions was unconstitutional. In this climate of fragmentation and uncertainty, the Brazilian people remained disillusioned with the politicians who were supposed to be serving them.

Land and environment

Geography

Brazil is the largest country in South America and the fifth largest in the world, almost as large as the USA. It is over 4,300 kilometres from north to south and the same from east to west, with land borders of 15,700 kilometres and an Atlantic coastline of 7,400 kilometres. It has a common frontier with all the other South American countries except Chile and Ecuador and occupies almost half the total area of the continent. Its population of 162 million is now, after the recent break-up of the USSR, also the fifth largest in the world, and over half that of South America.

Geology   Although Brazil is dominated by the vast river basins of the Amazon and the Paraná which account for about three-fifths of the country, not much of it is 'lowlands'. Ancient rock structures, some of the oldest in the world, underlie much of the area creating resistant plateaux and a rounded hilly landscape. These ancient Pre-Cambrian rocks culminate in the Guiana highlands to the north and the crystalline ranges which run close to the coastline all the way from near the Amazon to the Uruguayan frontier.

It is believed that South America and Africa were joined in the geologic past, and there is a tolerable fit between the easterly bulge of Brazil and the Gulf of Guinea. Persuasive evidence has been found of identical ostracod fossils (freshwater fish) in corresponding Cretaceous rocks in both Brazil and Gabon, overlain by salt deposits that could have been the first appearance of the South Atlantic Ocean. This suggests that the split began some 125 million years ago. What is now accepted is that the South American Plate continues to move westwards with the consequent elevation of the Andes on the other side of the continent where it meets the Pacific Plates.

The Amazon   The Amazon River is the greatest in the world in area of drainage, about seven million
Basin   square kilometres, and in volume of discharge into the sea averaging 180,000 cubic metres per second (or 170 billion gallons per hour), 10 times that of the Mississippi, and more than all the rivers of Europe put together. Such is the flow that the salinity of the Atlantic Ocean is affected for 250 kilometres out from the river delta. It is 6,400 kilometres long (marginally shorter than the Nile) from its sources in the Andes of Peru, and still has over 3,000 kilometres to go through Brazil when it leaves Leticia on the Colombia/Brazil border, yet with only a fall of 80 metres to sea level. Unlike most major world rivers, the basin is reduced in width near its mouth, indeed hills come down to the river near Monte Alegre only 200 kilometres from the delta. Two hundred kilometres above this at Óbidos, the river is over 75 metres deep, that is the bottom is well below sea level. This reflects the more recent geological history of the basin which until the latter part of the Tertiary Period (say 25 million years ago) was connected to the Pacific and drained through what is now Ecuador. With the uplift of the Andes, this route was closed off, and a huge inland sea was formed, helped by a downward folding of the older rocks (some geologists believe there was also significant rifting of the strata) to create a huge geosyncline. Eventually the water broke through the crystalline rocks to the east and made the new connection to the Atlantic. Deep layers

Cerrado

The cerrado, covering 25 percent of the national territory, is one of Brazil's most common ecosystems. Or perhaps one should say 'was one of the most common'. A study by Ibama suggests that all its cultivable surface will be occupied by the year 2000. Scientists are becoming aware that the cerrado has the richest biodiversity of any savanna on the planet. It has outcrops (chapadas) and valleys, vegetation that ranges from humid grassland to gallery forest to dry forest to scrub. 429 species of tree and bush have been catalogued as endemic. There are many orchids. Several animals that live in the cerrado are threatened with extinction, such as the maned wolf, the great anteater and some bird species. It extends over much of the central plateau and yet, in official documents which stress the importance of protecting various types of forest and coastal vegetation, it is not mentioned at all. It has been seen as a good alternative to the Amazon for the relocation of urban overpopulation. Agricultural development, claims Ibama, has been managed poorly, forcing colonizers to abandon uneconomic farms in favour of new lands in the cerrado. Even the wild plants' adaptation to fire, which occurs naturally every five-seven years, has been misunderstood, leading to intensive burning by cattle ranchers to clear land which never recovers.

The World Wide Fund for Nature is working with Ibama on a project in the Parque Nacional da Chapada dos Veadeiros in Goiás state to try to encourage sustainable development in the cerrado. This is an example of how the consciousness raised by the pressure to conserve Brazil's northern rainforests has prompted conservationists to look more closely at all Brazil's ecosystems.

Source: "Cerrado, o Bioma Esquecido", Ibama On Line.

---

of sediment were laid down and have been added to ever since, with today's heavy tropical rains continuing to erode the surrounding mountains. This gives the largest more or less level area in Brazil, but it is so heavily forested and the soils so continually leached by the climate, with vast expanses frequently under floodwaters, that the potential for agriculture is strictly limited.

A characteristic of virtually all the tributaries which join the Amazon from the south is that upstream navigation ends where the rivers tumble off the plateaux of central Brazil creating dramatic waterfalls and in many cases now providing hydroelectric power.

South of the Amazon basin is a large area of undulating highlands, a dissected plateau mostly between 200 metres and 800 metres. These are ancient rocks, back as far as Pre-Cambrian crystallines. They produce poor soils but sufficient to provide the grasslands or *cerrado* (see box) of the Mato Grosso, Goiás, western Paraná and adjacent areas, widely used for ranching, though now increasingly found suitable for soya bean production, one of Brazil's foremost exports.

The Centre West

From Minas Gerais southwards, the rivers drain into the second largest basin of Brazil, the Paraná, which eventually reaches the Atlantic by way of the River Plate of Argentina/Uruguay. This is another large river system, 4,000 kilometres long, of which about half is in Brazil. A principal tributary of the Paraná is the Rio Paraguay which, in its early stages, flows into a wide depression now filled with many thousands of metres of sediments and known in Brazil as the Pantanal. Further south, the swamps continue into the Chaco of Paraguay and Argentina. To the east of this, again the rivers fall off the old highland strata to form rapids and waterfalls, the largest of which was the former Sete Quedas falls (Salto de Guaíra) on the Paraná, sadly drowned by the Itaipu dam lake in 1982. Nearby however are the Iguaçu falls, the most impressive of South America, created by very resistant layers of basalt.

Background

The Sertão

The sertão (plural sertões) covers almost three-quarters of northeastern Brazil, extending into the north of Minas Gerais. Of the states in the northeast, only Maranhão lacks this geographic zone. It is hot, semi-arid and subject to frequent droughts. The soil is stony and the trees and bushes are twisted, covered in thorns. There is also a great variety of cacti. The vegetation is typical of the caatinga, adapted to land which can be parched, sometimes for years at a time. In the drought, the plants appear to die, the inhabitants and their animals face hunger and misery, and all life awaits the return of the rain.

The caatinga is "not an impenetrable barrier. Its unique vegetation makes it more like a labyrinth, with a multitude of paths and clearings, always alike, and transformed as if by magic, to revive for a day, only when a chance rain fills the merciless sky. If the peril of virgin forest is solitude without trails or egress, the terror of the caatinga is the bewilderment which their multiplicity never fails to cause. The beast, led by instinct, can range to the uttermost parts and reach his destination without straying; but once a man enters the caatinga and his memory falters in choosing a trail, he is a victim whom only a miracle will save." (Quoted from The Bandeirantes, edited by Richard M Morse, page 42.)

To the Portuguese colonists, the sertão was a region of legends. Unlike the routes along the Amazon in the north and the routes taken by the bandeirantes along the Tietê in the south, the trackless northeast was full of mystery because settlers were not tempted into it. The source of the only major river to run through it, the São Francisco, was a cause for speculation; the indigenous people were described as giants, or dwarves, or deformed in a bewildering variety of ways and all were believed to be savage fighters. And, of course, in this dangerous interior there were said to be great riches awaiting the intrepid explorer: silver mines, gold and mountains of emeralds.

In the 20th century the sertão has inspired some of the greatest Brazilian literature, but the geographical and human landscape portrayed is not the mythical sertão of the 16th and 17th centuries. Graciliano Ramos in Vidas secas (Barren Lives, 1938), João Guimarães Rosa in Grande sertão: veredas (The Devil to Pay in the Backlands, 1956) and Antônio Torres in Essa terra (The Land, 1976), among others, have all presented the region in memorable ways (see the **Literature**, page 777, for notes on Ramos and Guimarães Rosa). The direct realism of Ramos' Vidas secas emphasizes the harshness of the sertão, the family driven from their land by drought, by the "enemy vegetation". Yet there is an ambiguity to the flight. They head for the city, where the children will learn "difficult, necessary things", but that too is an alien world, unknown, civilized and it, like the climate they have left, will imprison them.

The coast & escarpment

Highlands follow the coastline, only a short distance inland, for 3,000 kilometres. The ancient crystalline/granite ridges, known as serras, stretch from Porto Alegre in the south to near Belém in the north, just short of the Amazon estuary. Long stretches are in the form of a single or stepped escarpment, abrupt in the east and sloping more gently inland to the west. They are not high in South American terms – the highest point, Pico da Bandeira is only 2,890 metres – but it is no more than 120 kilometres from the ocean near Vitória. The narrowness of the coastal strip has had a profound effect on the history of settlement. Until comparatively recent times, the lack of natural access to the hinterland confined virtually all economic activity to this area, and today most of the major cities of Brazil and 80 percent of the population are on or near the coast.

Because of varying erosion over many millions of years, there are a number of interesting natural features in these highlands. The many granite 'peaks' in and

Other geographical terms

Agreste: a narrow zone inland from the coast in the northeast, with a hot climate the year round. Rainfall is more than in the dry sertão, but less than the abundance on the coast; similarly, there is more rain on the coastal slopes than those facing inland. A wide variety of crops is cultivated, besides cattle raising.

Chapada: a large area of flat land, 600 metres above sea level, usually made up of strata of sedimentary rock; often takes the form of a tableland. The term is used in the northeast and centre west of Brazil.

Mata: woods, forest, jungle; also thicket. Mata galeria (or mata ciliar) gallery forest, in which trees are sustained by the water beside which they grow.

Pampa: extensive areas of grassland in southern Brazil.

Pantanal (see **Flora and fauna**, page 757) and page 712: wetland covering some 160,000 square kilometres, at an altitude of no more than 110 metres, which floods seasonally. It is drained by the Rio Paraguai and its tributaries. It is both a major reserve for birds, animals and fish, and an important region for cattle raising.

Polígono das Secas: the semi-arid part of northeastern Brazil, receiving less than 800 millimetres of rain a year, which is subject to periodic droughts.

Restinga: shrub forest, coastal sand dunes, ponds and wetlands.

Serra: a range of hills or mountains.

Principal source: Celso Antunes, Geografia e participação 2 (São Paulo: Scipione, 1996).

Amazonian terminology

Caaetê: literally 'large trees', the forest which grows on land which is not seasonally flooded.

Furo: natural canals which link rivers or lakes.

Igapó (see **Flora and fauna**, page 759): the river margins, normally of black-water rivers, with little silt deposition, flooded for up to seven months of the year.

Igarapé: narrow rivers which lead off the main rivers into the forest, frequently used as waterways by the inhabitants of Amazonia.

Paraná-mirim: arms of rivers, surrounding islands.

Várzea (see **Flora and fauna**, page 759): seasonally flooded forest, mainly on the banks of white-water rivers. Flooding is normally for short periods only and the soil is very rich.

---

around Rio de Janeiro are the resistant remnants of very hard rocks providing spectacular viewpoints, Pico da Tijuca (the highest, 1,012 metres), Corcovado (710 metres) and Pão de Açúcar (396 metres) the best known. There are others in the neighbouring state of Espírito Santo. Near Curitiba are the eroded sandstones of Vila Velha and the wild scenery through the Serra do Mar towards the coast. In the state of Bahía, there are remarkable caves and waterfalls in the Chapada da Diamantina National Park. In many places, what rivers there are flowing eastwards necessarily have to lose height quickly so that gorges and waterfalls abound. There are also many kilometres of spectacular coastline and fine beaches. South of Porto Alegre, eroded material moved down the coast by the southerly ocean currents added to alluvials brought north from the River Plate by subsidiary currents, have created long sand bars to form several large freshwater lagoons. The longest, Lagoa dos Patos, is over 250 kilometres long.

The escarpment forces most of the rain run-off to flow west into the interior to feed the Amazon and Paraná river systems. However, one major river breaks through the barrier to flow into the Atlantic. The São Francisco rises south of Belo Horizonte – one important tributary starts only 250 kilometres from the sea – but flows, north then east, for 2,900 kilometres before it gets there. Almost 500 kilometres of rapids through the escarpment culminate in the 75 metres Paulo Afonso falls, before completing the final 240 kilometres to the sea. Where it turns east is one of the driest areas of the

The Rio São Francisco

Background

country, known as the *sertão*. The river is therefore of great significance particularly as the rains here are so unreliable. Together with the link it provides to so much of the interior and its course wholly within the country (unlike the Amazon and the Paraná), the São Francisco is revered by the Brazilians as the 'river of national unity'. Its value for irrigation, hydroelectric power, fish and navigation above the rapids is inestimable, but because of sand bars at its mouth and close proximity to the fall line, the river has not proved useful for shipping or access generally to the ocean in spite of being the third largest river system on the continent.

The Northern Highlands
After sinking below the Amazon estuary, the Brazilian Highlands reappear to the north and sweep round to the west to form the border with the Guianas and Venezuela. The highest tabular uplands are near where Guyana, Venezuela and Brazil meet at Monte Roraima (2,810 metres) and further west along the border where a national park has been set up focused on Pico de Neblina, 3,014 metres, the highest point in Brazil.

Climate

The climate of Brazil is a function of latitude and altitude. The average annual temperature exceeds 26°C along the northeast coast and in the central Amazon with little variation throughout the year. The highlands are cooler and further south there are seasonal variations: Brazil extends to 34° south which is equivalent to the latitude of North Carolina. High summer temperatures can occur almost anywhere here, yet frosts are not uncommon in July and August as coffee producers know only too well. Rainfall is more complicated. The northeast Trades bring moist air to the coast north of the Amazon, where there is heavy precipitation all year round.

Rainfall

The same winds push saturated air into the Amazon basin where rainfall is progressively greater from east to west throughout the year and virtually on a daily basis. The abrupt rise of the Andes beyond the borders of Brazil increases the precipitation and so feeds the many tributaries of the river.

During the period December-May, the northeast Trades move north and Brazil between Belém and Recife receives less rain-bearing winds. From Salvador, the southeast Trades bring moisture from the South Atlantic and it is the gap between these two systems, known as the 'doldrums', that explains the dry areas of northeast Brazil. On average there is a significant rainfall here, but sometimes it fails to arrive causing prolonged periods of drought. Precipitation in the southern states of Brazil is concentrated in the escarpment thus feeding the Paraná system and is well distributed throughout the year.

Although there are occasional storms causing local damage, for example in the *favelas* (shanties) of Rio, Brazil is not subject to hurricanes or indeed to other natural disasters common elsewhere in Latin America such as earthquakes, volcanic eruptions or unexpected widespread and catastrophic floods.

Flora and fauna

The neotropical realm is a land of superlatives, it contains the most extensive tropical rainforest in the world; drained by the Amazon which has by far the largest volume of any river. The fauna and flora are to a large extent determined by the influence of the great rivers and mountains – the Andes, which are the longest uninterrupted mountain chain in the world. Although not part of Brazil they dramatically affect the climate and hence the animals and plants that can inhabit the country. There are also huge expanses of open terrain, the Pantanal – a huge wet wilderness, vast mountain grasslands and tree-covered savannahs. It is this wide range of habitats which makes Brazil one of the greatest regions of biological diversity.

This diversity arises not only from the wide range of habitats available, but also from the history of the continent. South America has essentially been an island for some 70 million years joined only by a narrow isthmus to Central and North America. Land passage played a significant role in the gradual colonization of South America by species from the north. When the land-link closed these colonists evolved to a wide variety of forms free from the competitive pressures that prevailed elsewhere. When the land-bridge was re-established some four million years ago a new invasion of species took place from North America, adding to the diversity but also leading to numerous extinctions. Comparative stability has ensued since then and has guaranteed the survival of many primitive groups including a group of pouched mammals, the opossums.

Brazil can be divided into a number of biogeographical zones; two immense river basins comprising the River Amazon and the River Plate, mountains – the Guiana highlands to the north and the Brazilian highlands to the south, and a coastal strip of Atlantic rainforest.

The Atlantic rainforest used to cover 2.6 million square kilometres in a coastal strip 160 kilometres wide and 4,200 kilometres long. The coastal rainforest is bounded inland by a series of mountain ranges which contribute to the varied landscape and hence species diversity. It is one of the Earth's biological hotspots. Now critically fragmented and reduced to less than five percent of its original extent, it remains home to a very high proportion of unique species. For example 17 of the 21 primate species found there are unique to that region, and of those, 13 species, including the golden lion tamarin (see box, page 161), are endangered. Populations of South America's largest primate, the woolly spider monkey, locally known as *muriqui*, were decimated by European colonists who first settled along this coastal zone.

Atlantic rain forest

Background

Along the coast, mangroves provide a breeding ground for numerous species of fish including many that are commercially important. Further inland is the *restinga*, a zone of shrub forest, coastal sand dunes, ponds and wetlands. The lush coastal rainforest itself extends to 800 metres in elevation and grades into cloud forest between 800 metres and 1,700 metres. Drenching by mist, fog and rain leads to a profusion of plant growth, trees and shrubs which are covered with a great variety of epiphytes – orchids, mosses lichens and bromeliads. At the highest elevations, the forest gives way to mountain grasslands or *campos de altitude*. In the southern zone of the Atlantic forest there are large stands of monkey puzzle tree, *araucária*, which is characterized by its own parrot community, many of which are also endemic.

The Amazon River & rainforest   The Amazon basin contains the largest area of tropical rainforest in the world, six million square kilometres, 60 percent of which is located in Brazil. It is home to 20 percent of the world's plant and bird species; perhaps 10 percent of mammal species; an inestimable number of insects and perhaps some 2,000 species of fish inhabiting the 1,000 tributaries of the Amazon. When in flood the great river inundates the forest for a short period in its upper reaches to create a unique habitat called *várzea*; in the lower reaches this flooding may last for four to seven months forming *igapó* swamp forest.

The rivers of the Amazon are either classified as blackwater or whitewater rivers. The former are highly coloured due to the brown humic acids derived from the decomposing materials on the forest floor but contain little suspended material. The whitewaters owe their colour to the suspended soil particles which originate in the run-off from the Andes. Each has its characteristic fish. Within a 30 kilometre radius of Manaus, there are estimated to be over 700 species of fish. The largest of these species is the *arapaima* reaching over three metres and weighing in at over 150 kilos. It gulps air at the surface and is harpooned by fishermen. The *pacu* or silver-dollar fish feeds on fruit falling from trees of the flooded forest. The voracious *piranha* normally feeds on other fishes although they are quite capable of removing the flesh from larger animals. They probably benefit the ecosystem by removing diseased and dying individuals as well as disposing of carrion. A greater risk is posed by the electric eels and sting rays found in turbid waters. An electrical shock of 650 volts has been recorded from a captive electric eel; these electric fields are used to locate and kill prey. The ray does not inject poison but its 10 centimetres long spine can puncture and lacerate flesh.

Climate & vegetation

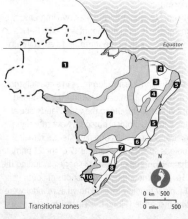

1 Equatorial, hot & humid; dense forest; rivers carrying large volumes of water
2 Tropical, with humid summers; *cerrado*: savanna with isolated bushes or stunted trees, sometimes in clumps; rivers that may dry up in winter
3 Semi-arid; *caatinga*: dry tropical scrub & thorn forest, typical of the so-called Polígono das Secas; intermittent rivers which dry up after the rainy season
4 Tropical; *caatinga*
5 Tropical, humid; forest covering seashore & the banks of the river
6 As 5 but at higher altitudes
7 Subtropical; forest
8 Subtropical with cooler summers & cold winters; tropical forest; rivers with a uniform flow of water the year round
9 Subtropical, as 8; pine forest *(araucárias)*
10 Subtropical with cold winters; *Gaúcho* lowlands, meadows gallery forest; rivers as 8 & 9

Transitional zones

Equator

N

0 km 500
0 miles 500

Várzea is a highly productive seasonally inundated forest found along the banks of the whitewater rivers; it is very rich as a consequence of the huge amount of silt and nutrients washed out of the mountains and trapped by the massive buttress-rooted trees. This lakeland swamp forest is flooded for relatively short periods of time. One of the commonest trees of the *várzea*, the Pará rubber tree, is the source of latex. The Brazilian rubber industry foundered in the 19th century when seeds of this tree were illegally taken to Asia to form the basis of huge rubber plantations and flourished in the absence of pest species (see under **Manaus**, page 631).

In contrast the *igapó* forests are characteristic of the blackwater rivers with little silt deposition leading to sandy beaches fringing the forest. Despite being flooded for up to seven months of the year to a possible depth of 15 metres, palms dominate this swampy habitat, although massive kapok trees are also typical. During the wet season, these flooded forests are inhabited by turtles and small fish, and the predators that feed upon them – otters and caiman.

Flooded meadows are frequently found in the still-flowing reaches of the *várzea*. These vast carpets of floating waterlilies, waterlettuce and waterhyacinth are home to the Amazonian manatee, a large herbivorous aquatic mammal which is the freshwater relative of the dugong of the Caribbean. Vast numbers of spectacled caiman populate the lakes feeding on the highly productive fish community.

The river corridors are often the best places to observe wildlife. Caiman and turtles are commonly seen basking on the riverbanks. Neotropical cormorants, roseate spoonbills and jabiru storks are commonly observed fishing in the shallow waters. The hoatzin is generally found along waterways where it feeds on leaves, and fruit. The newly hatched chicks of this primitive bird have claws at the tip of each wing which enable them to crawl around in the foliage.

In the relatively constant climatic conditions, animal and plantlife has evolved to an amazing diversity over the millennia. It has been estimated that four square kilometres of forest can harbour some 1,200 vascular plants, 600 species of tree, and 120 woody plants. Here in these relatively flat lands a soaring canopy some 45 metres overhead is the power-house of the forest. It is a habitat choked with strangling vines and philodendrons amongst which mixed troupes of squirrel monkeys and capuchins forage. In the high canopy small groups of spider monkeys perform their lazy aerial acrobatics, whilst lower down, clinging to epiphyte-clad trunks and branches, groups of tamarins and marmosets forage for gums, blossom, fruit and the occasional insect prey.

Cross section of Amazonian forest

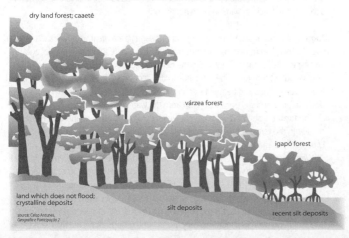

dry land forest; caaetê

várzea forest

igapó forest

land which does not flood; crystalline deposits

silt deposits

recent silt deposits

source: Celso Antunes, *Geografia e Participação 2*

The Macaw

One of Brazil's beautiful birds, "called arat *[macaw], has wing and tail feathers about a foot and a half long, one half of each feather as red as fine scarlet, and the other half a sparkling sky-blue (the colours are divided from each other along the quill), with all the rest of the body the color of lapis lazuli; when this bird is in the sunlight, where it is ordinarily to be seen, no eye can weary of gazing upon it."*

Jean de Léry, History of a Voyage to The Land of Brazil, Otherwise called America, *translated by Janet Whately (Berkeley and Oxford: University of California Press, 1990), page 87. De Léry was a French Protestant cleric who visited Brazil in the mid-16th century.*

Caiman are South American alligators. They are relatively small, usually growing to no more than 2½ metres in length. They are found in areas of relatively still water, ranging form marshland to lakes and slow-flowing rivers. Youngsters feed mainly on aquatic invertebrates while adults also take larger prey, including wild pigs and small travellers. During the dry season when pools dry up caimans can stop feeding altogether and burrow into the mud at the bottom of a pool waiting for the return of the rains.

The **giant otter** is found along the tributaries of the Amazon. It can measure up to two metres in length. They are active by day when they hunt for food, often in small groups. They are not rare but are rarely seen as they are shy and submerge quickly at the slightest hint of danger. They feed on fish, molluscs and crustaceans, also small mammals and birds. They can be tamed easily and are often raised as pets by some tribes.

Pantanal This ecologically diverse zone includes the largest area of wetlands in the world when flooded between December to March. In addition it includes dry savannahs or *cerrado*, chaco scrublands as well as gallery rainforest. The area is very flat and flooded by the rising rivers leaving isolated islands (*cordilheiras*) between vast lakes (*bahias*) which become saline as the waters evaporate. This mixed ecosystem supports a highly diverse fauna characteristic of the constituent habitat types which includes 200 species of mammal. Capybara (see below), tapir and peccaries are common along the waters edge as are marsh deer. Jaguar, more commonly associated with the forest, prey on these herbivores and the cattle and feral pigs which graze here. Spectacular assemblages of wading birds – egrets, jabiru storks, ibises, spoonbills and herons prey on the abundant invertebrate and fish fauna. Anacondas and caiman are still common, although the black caiman has been hunted out.

Jaguars are the largest of the New World cats. Jaguars are great wanderers, roaming even further than pumas. Usually they haunt forests where they hunt for deer, agoutis and especially peccaries. They follow the herds of these South American swine and pounce on the stragglers. They also attack capybara. Unlike most cats, jaguars are often found beside rivers and frequently enter the water. It attacks the tapir as it comes down to drink and will even scoop fish from the water with its paws.

The **tapir** is a shy, nocturnal animal which confines itself to an intricate network of trails in the forests of the marshy lowlands of Bolivia, Brazil, Colombia, Venezuela, Ecuador, Peru and the north of Argentina.

Water is essential for its survival; it drinks a great deal and is an excellent swimmer. It is herbivorous, eating waterplants and the leaves and twigs of trees. Its only enemies are jaguars and alligators against which its only defence is to use its teeth.

The **capybara** is a large aquatic rodent that looks like a cross between a guinea pig and a hippopotamus. It is the largest of all the rodents at over one metre long and weighing over 50 kilograms. They live in large groups along the riverbanks,

The beak of beaks

"The beak of this bird the toucan, which is longer than the whole body and proportionately thick (I will not compare or contrast it with that of the crane, which is nothing by comparison), must be regarded not only as the beak of beaks, but also as the most prodigious and monstrous that can be found among all the birds in the universe."

Jean de Léry, History of a Voyage to The Land of Brazil, Otherwise called America, translated by Janet Whately (Berkeley and Oxford: University of California Press, 1990), page 90.

where they graze on the lush grasses. It comes out onto dry land to rest and bask in the sun, but at the first hint of danger the whole troop dashes into the water. Its greatest enemy is the jaguar. They are rather vocal for rodents often emitting a series of strange clicks, squeaks and grunts.

National parks

Ecotourism is the international passion of this decade, but it is also a question of survival. It is modern and urgent to be a conservationist, to respect flora and fauna, not to pollute the beaches or the forests, to respect local populations, to value our cultural heritage, customs and traditions. Guia do Turismo, 10, 1997, page 25.

Different countries have different approaches to the relationship between national parks and tourism. In Brazil, the system which protects areas of outstanding beauty and unique flora and fauna has the dual role of providing centres of scientific research and places which are open to the public as an alternative form of recreation and education. Ibama (Instituto Brasileiro do Meio Ambiente e dos Recursos Naturais Renováveis – the Brazilian Institute for the Environment and Renewable Natural Resources) has in its care 35 national parks (Parques Nacionais, or PARNA). They are by no means the whole picture, though. They form part of a system of protected areas which go under different titles and which have varying degrees of public access. The network comprises, in addition to the national parks: Estações Ecológicas (ecological stations), Reservas Biológicas (biological reserves), Reservas Ecológicas (ecological reserves), Áreas de Relevante Interesse Ecológico (areas of relevant ecological interest), Reservas Particulares do Patrimônio Nacional (private national heritage reserves) and Áreas sob Proteção Especial (areas of special protection). In all these entities, the exploitation of natural resources is completely forbidden. They are for research, education and recreation only. Three other types of entity are designed to allow the sustainable use of natural resources, while still preserving their biodiversity: Florestas Nacionais (national forests), Áreas de Proteção Ambiental (areas of environmental protection) and Reservas Extrativas (extractive reserves – such as the rubber tapping zones in Acre state). A new initiative is the Projeto Corredores Ecológicos (Ecological Corridors Project), which aims to create avenues of forest between isolated protected areas so that fauna may move over a greater area to breed, thus strengthening the stock of endangered animals which might otherwise suffer the ills of inbreeding. An example of this is project to link the Mata Atlântica of Poço das Antas (see page 160) with other pockets of coastal forest to help the survival of the golden lion tamarin.

Ibama was created in 1989, under Law No 7.735 of the 5 October 1988 Constitution. The Institute was formed by uniting four separate bodies, the environmental secretariat (SEMA), the Brazilian Institute of Forest Development (IBDF), and the superintendencies for the development of fishing and rubber (SUDEPE and SUDHEVEA). Brazil has a long history of passing laws to protect natural resources, such as that of 1808 which excluded from international trade the export of pau-brasil and other woods. At the same time, though, enforcement of such laws has not been easy. Today, the achievement of Ibama's goals is determined by resources, but funds are insufficient to commit either enough money or staff to the job of protecting the areas that have been designated for preservation. Sad though this is, there are still a large number of parks open to the visitor which can give a good idea of the variety of Brazil's natural resources and the value that they hold for the country.

This Handbook does not describe all Brazil's national parks or other conservation entities, only those which have easy access. Nor does the book list all the offices of Ibama or its related departments throughout the country, but those nearest to the parks described are given and it is to these that readers should apply if a permit is needed to visit a specific park.

For more information, contact Ibama at its local addresses, its national headquarters, SAIN, Avenida L-4, bloco "B", Térreo, Edifiço Sede do Ibama, CEP 70.800-200, Brasília DF, T061-2268221/9014, F061-3221058, or at its website, www.ibama.gov.br.

Information can also be obtained from the Ministério do Meio Ambiente (MMA – the environment ministry), Esplanada dos Ministérios, bloco "B", 5-9 andar (5th to 9th floors), CEP 70068-900, Brasília DF, or at its website www.mma.gov.br. See also the book *Parque Nacionais Brasil*, Guias Philips (1999), with a good map, beautiful photographs, sections on history, flora and fauna and tourist services, US$15.

Culture

People

Indigenous peoples How many indigenous Indians were living in Brazil when the Portuguese arrived? The probable figure is somewhere between three and five million. Today there are between 200,000 and 300,000. Whatever the exact numbers, the effects of European colonization have been devastating. Present-day tribal groups number about 220; each has a unique dialect, but most languages belong to four main linguistic families, Tupi-Guarani, Ge, Carib and Arawak. A few tribes remain uncontacted, others are exclusively nomadic, others are semi-nomadic hunter-gatherers and farmers, while some are settled groups in close contact with non-Indian society. There is no agreement on precisely how many tribes are extant, but the Centro Ecumênico da Documentação e Informação (CEDI) of São Paulo said that of the 200 or so groups it documented, 40 percent have populations of less than 200 people and 77 percent have populations of less than 1,000. (See Phillip Wearne, *Return of the Indian*, pages 8-9.) Hemming underlines this depressing statistic when he reports that tribes contacted in recent decades have, as have others in previous centuries, suffered catastrophic reductions in numbers as soon as they encounter diseases which are common to non-indigenous people, but to which their bodies have no immunity (*Red Gold*, page 510).

The struggle of groups such as the Yanomami to have their land demarcated in order to secure title is well-documented. The goal of the Statute of the Indian (Law 6.001/73), for demarcation of all Indian land by 1978, is largely unmet. It was feared that a new law introduced in January 1996 would slow the process even more. Funai, the National Foundation for the Support of the Indian, a part of the Interior Ministry, is charged with representing the Indians' interests, but lacks resources and support. There is no nationwide, representative body for indigenous people. Most of Brazil's indigenous people live in the Amazon region; they are affected by deforestation, encroachment from colonizers, small-and large-scale mining, and the construction of hydroelectric dams. Besides the Yanomami, other groups include the Xavante, Tukano, Kreen-Akrore, Kaiapó, Bororo and Arara.

At first the Portuguese colony grew slowly. From 1580 to 1640 the population was only about 50,000 apart from the million or so indigenous Indians. In 1700 there were some 750,000 non-indigenous people in Brazil. Early in the 19th century Humboldt computed there were about 920,000 whites, 1.96 million Africans, and 1.12 million Indians and people of mixed Portuguese and Indian origin (*mestiços*): after three centuries of occupation a total of only four million, and over twice as many Africans as there were whites.

Mestiços

The arid wastes of the Sertão remain largely uncultivated. Its inhabitants are *mestiço*; most live off a primitive but effective method of cultivation known as 'slash and burn', which involves cutting down and burning the brushwood for a small patch of ground which is cultivated for a few years and then allowed to grow back.

Though there is no legal discrimination against black people, the economic and educational disparity – by default rather than intent of the Government – is such that successful Afro-Brazilians are active almost exclusively in the worlds of sport, entertainment and the arts.

Afro-Brazilians

Brazilian culture is rich in African influences. Those interested in the development of Afro-Brazilian music, dance, religion, arts and cuisine will find the whole country north of São Paulo fascinating, and especially the cities of Bahia and São Luís which retain the greatest African influences. Black Pride movements are particularly strong in Bahia.

Further reading: *Towards the Abolition of Whiteness* by David Roediger (London and New York: Verso), a sociological study of how 'colour' is determined by economic status, mostly in the USA and UK.

Modern immigration did not begin effectively until after 1850. Of the 4.6 million immigrants from Europe between 1884 and 1954, 32 percent were Italians, 30 percent Portuguese, 14 percent Spanish, 4 percent German, and the rest of various nationalities. Since 1954 immigrants have averaged 50,000 a year.

Europeans

Most of the German immigrants settled in Santa Catarina, Rio Grande do Sul, and Paraná. The Germans (and the Italians and Poles and other Slavs who followed them) did not in the main go as wage earners on the big estates, but as cultivators of their own small farms. Here there is a settled agricultural population cultivating the soil intensively.

There are some one million Japanese-descended Brazilians; they grow a fifth of the coffee, 30 percent of the cotton, all the tea, and are very active in market gardening.

Asians

Today the whites and near-whites are about 53 percent of the population, people of mixed race about 34 percent, and Afro Brazilians 11 percent; the rest are either Indians or Asians. There are large regional variations in the distribution of the races: the whites predominate greatly in the south, which received the largest flood of European immigrants, and decrease more or less progressively towards the north.

Religion

In order to discuss religion in Brazil, it is necessary to consider the three main cultures from which the Brazilian people originated, the Indians, the Portuguese and the Blacks. Each has contributed its own religious traditions and in many cases they have intermingled and influenced each other.

Before the arrival of the Portuguese colonizers, Brazil was inhabited by many tribes of Indians. They had their own animist cults and a very rich, poetic mythology. The most important of their divinities was Tupan, the spirit of tempests, fire, lightning and thunder. It was he who had taught their ancestors the secrets of agriculture and hunting. The three other important gods were Jaci, the moon, Guaraci, the sun, and

Brazilian Indians

Background

Rudá, love. There were also minor divinities such as Guirapuru, the lord of the birds, Caapora, the guardian of the animals, and Anhanga, the protector of hunters. There were also devils and one of the most feared was the Jurupari, an evil spirit which came in the night to bring nightmares to men. The designations of Tupan and Jurupari as the most important divinities in relation to Good and Evil were made by the Catholic missionaries in colonial times. The Europeans could not deal with the Indians' polytheistic religion, so they condensed the attributes of these spirits into concepts they could comprehend and educate against.

The priests, or shamans, were called Pagés and they knew the secrets of plants and magic potions. They would cure people in rituals in which they would invoke the spirits of the forest, their ancestors and certain animals. When faced with the diseases brought by the colonizers, however, the Pagés were almost helpless.

The Indians' religious system was based on many aspects of nature and on situations they had to face in their daily life. Today, the traditional cults of the Brazilian Indians have practically disappeared, not only because of the decrease in the numbers of the Indians themselves, but also because of the persistent work of missionaries, Catholic and Protestant, to convert them to Christianity, from the very first moments of European colonization.

Colonizers & the Catholic church A sword in one hand and a cross in the other: one of the principal, official motives for the European colonization of the 'New World' was the necessity to convert the indigenous people to Christianity. Most of the great Catholic religious orders, such as the Benedictines, Carmelites, Franciscans and Jesuits, went to Brazil precisely with this aim. At the beginning of the colonial period, mainly in the 16th and 17th centuries, the religious orders were practically the only institutions providing public education, artistic and academic studies. The Jesuits specifically were dedicated to converting the Indians and they created many missions (*aldeias*).

In the colonial period there was absolutely no tolerance of other religions and many Jewish and Muslim immigrants understood the convenience of converting to the Catholic faith. This practice was also common in Portugal and many of these 'cristãos novos', or newly-converted Christians, acquired Portuguese surnames related to trees and natural elements, such as Pereira (peach tree), Carvalho (oak tree), or Oliveira (olive tree).

At the beginning of the 19th century, when Napoleon invaded Portugal and forced the Portuguese royal family and nobility to move to Brazil, a stronger commercial and diplomatic relationship with the British Empire made the king, Dom João VI, more tolerant of the Protestants. After 1808, many English families and tradesmen emigrated to Rio the Janeiro. Even so, they were only allowed to build a

Indians dancing for the spirit of a Jaguar, Fábio Sombra, 1992

Protestant cemetery in 1811 and their first church in 1819, "as long as it did not have the appearance of a religious temple", according to Dom João VI's decree.

During the Brazilian Empire and up to the creation of the Republic in 1889, Catholicism was the official state religion. After that, as stated in all Brazilian republican constitutions, there is total freedom of religion and no one may suffer any kind of religious persecution, under protection of the law. Nevertheless, the influence of the Catholic church remained very important, both economically and politically. At present, the majority of the Brazilian population is still Roman Catholic, although in the last 10 to 15 years many Brazilians, especially in the very poor areas, have converted to Protestantism. Among the traditional Protestant churches, the most important ones in Brazil are the Baptists, the Presbyterians and the Lutherans, particularly in the south, which was mostly colonized by Germans. In many cases, though, the nonconformists are represented by new evangelical sects, such as the Universal Church of God's Kingdom, directed by its 'bishop', Edir Macedo. These new Christian sects, generally called 'evangélicas', have been very successful in attracting new converts for their flocks. They use modern marketing techniques and electronic media, including their own TV channels, radio stations and newspapers. Their pastors use very dramatic speeches, full of examples of miracles, cures and solutions for all possible material and spiritual problems. In some cases, scandals have been widely reported in the press and the financial operations of certain churches have been subject to investigation.

Afro-Brazilian religions

When the Portuguese colonizers started to plant sugar cane on the northeast coast of Brazil, they soon realized that they would need a large, strong workforce to carry out the labour. The first option was to use the local indigenous population as slaves, but the Indians (those who did not die of European diseases) regarded that kind of work as demeaning, they soon became exhausted, frequently escaped, or simply refused to co-operate. Portugal, therefore, had to bring in black slaves. These people came from different regions of Africa and belonged to many different tribes, such as the Bantu, the Sudanese, the Angolans and the Hotentots. After the rigours of transatlantic shipment, they suffered further trauma on arrival at the Brazilian ports. They were often sold in groups which were segregated to avoid slaves from the same family or speaking the same language being together. By breaking all cultural and sentimental ties, the Portuguese hoped to eradicate ethnic pride and rebellions on the estates. Of course, these people brought their own religions, but the point is that none of their cults remained pure in Brazil. Taking, for example, the region of what is now Nigeria, there were different groups of people, each with its own divinity or Orixá (pronounced 'Orisha'). These Orixás were normally the spirit of a distinguished ancestor or a legendary hero and they were worshipped only in a particular region. As the slaves went to Brazilian estates in groups made up of people from different African regions, they soon started to worship all the Orixás, instead of just one. This was the origin of Candomblé and Umbanda, Afro-Brazilian religions, different from their African antecedents and therefore original.

Background

Religious syncretism

Naturally, the Catholic Portuguese did not allow the slaves to maintain their own beliefs. So the Africans ingeniously began to associate their own gods with the Catholic saints who had more or less the same characteristics. For example, when the masters thought the slaves were praying to Saint George, the warrior saint, they were, in fact, praying to Ogun, the Orixá representing war and battles. This association is called religious syncretism and is one of the defining characteristics of the Afro-Brazilian religions.

The cult of the Orixás

In Candomblé, the figure of God, the Creator is called Olorum. But this figure is almost never mentioned. To some degree, this is because Olorum is too busy to care about mankind's small problems. These are taken care of by the Orixás, the spiritual guides

*Mãe de Santo and
the Buzios Oracle*

responsible for all sorts of matters concerning our lives. According to Candomblé, from the moment of birth, every person has one or two Orixás to act as protector and tutor. The personality and the temperament of everyone is directly influenced by his or her Orixá. For example, a son or daughter of Ogun (the Orixá of war) is likely to be an impulsive and combative person, while the sons and daughters of Oxun (the Orixá of waterfalls and love) tend to be charming and coquettish.

To discover who your protector Orixá is, you must go to a Pai de Santo (male priest) or a Mãe de Santo (woman priest) and ask him or her to use the *Jogo de Buzios*. This is an oracle using 16 sea shells by which the priests can predict the future and answer questions related to material or spiritual matters. It is also very common to make offerings to the Orixás, consisting of special foods (every Orixá has his or her own preferences), alcoholic beverages, cigars, flowers, pop-corn, candles, toys and even ritually sacrificed animals such as cockerels, goats and pigeons. These offerings are delivered in different places, according to the Orixá. For example, offerings to Oxossi, the hunter, are delivered in a forest or a bush, and so on. The offerings are always associated with a wish being made, or by way of thanks to the Orixá for a favour received.

The religious ceremonies take place in *terreiros*, with much singing and drumming. The Pais de Santo and Mães de Santo enter into a trance and each is possessed by his or her protector Orixá, being able to communicate with humans, answer questions, give advice and predict the future.

It is very difficult to estimate the exact number of Brazilians who follow Candomblé and Umbanda. One of the main reasons is that many of their followers also profess themselves to be Catholics, which may be perfectly true. For many years the Afro-Brazilian religions were officially forbidden and only recently are people becoming more open in admitting their beliefs in public. The greatest influence of Candomblé and Umbanda is found in the cities of Salvador da Bahia and Rio de Janeiro. Many writers, academic and otherwise, have written on the subject, notably the novelist Jorge Amado, himself a member of the Candomblé cult (see his book, *The War of the Saints*, 1993).

Some of the most important Orixás

Exu (pronounced Eshoo) is considered the messenger between people and the Orixás. Sometimes associated with the Christian Devil, Exu is always represented with a trident and his colours are black and red. Offerings to this Orixá are always made at crossroads and normally consist of cigars, cachaça and red and black candles. His day is Monday.

An offering to Exu

Ogum the Orixá of war, thunder, lightning and iron. His colour is deep blue and he is always represented with an iron sword. The sons and daughters of Ogum are very combative and impulsive. His day is Tuesday.

Oxossi (pronounced Oshossee) is the hunter and protector of wild animals. This Orixá lives in the forest and is represented with a bow, arrows and a leather hat. His colour is green and sometimes blue. His day is Thursday and all his offerings, including raw tobacco and fruits, must be made in wooded places. People protected by this Orixá are normally very independent and solitary.

Xangô (pronounced Shango) is the Orixá of truth and justice. His colours are red and white and his day is Wednesday. He is represented with a double-headed axe, the African symbol of justice.

Oxum (pronounced Oshoon) is a feminine Orixá, associated with love and the family, found in waterfalls and whitewater. Pretty and extremely coquettish, she is sometimes represented as a siren with a golden mirror. Her colour is yellow and offerings to her should be delivered close to a waterfall. Her sons and daughters are very dedicated to the family. Her day is Saturday.

Yemanjá, the mother of the seas and saltwater. Her principal day is 31 December, New Year's Eve, and on this day people offer her white flowers, champagne and small boats full of candles and gifts placed in the sea. Her colour is light blue.

Iansã (pronounced Iansan) is a female Orixá related to tempests and storms. Very impulsive, Iansã is the only Orixá who can command the **Eguns**, the spirits of the dead. She wears red and her day is Wednesday.

Omolu, a strange Orixá who never shows his face (severely disfigured by smallpox), is always invoked in cases of disease and illness as he has the power to cure. Often referred as the 'doctor of the poor', he is represented as a strong man covered by a straw coat and holding a straw box full of herbs and medicines.

NB Two other terms are sometimes used in relation to Afro-Brazilian religions: Macumba used to be employed, mainly in Rio de Janeiro, as a generic term to describe all Afro-Brazilian cults. It was a popular expression at the beginning of the 20th century, but has become a derogatory term, not very politically correct. To call someone a 'macumbeiro/a' is offensive. The other term is Quimbanda. This is the dark side of Afro-Brazilian religion. It is associated with black magic and sorcery. A 'trabalho de quimbanda' is a ritual designed to hurt someone through offerings or sacrifices. Perhaps performed in cemeteries or at crossroads, these 'trabalhos' may use wax models of the intended victim (like in voodoo), or may involve imaginative and weird practices such as writing the enemy's name on a piece of paper, putting it

Oxum

Omolu

in a frog's mouth, then sewing up the mouth. The victim is supposed to die a death as slow and painful as the frog's. Quimbanda is a taboo subject and no one will profess to being involved with it.

Other important religions in Brazil
Spiritism (*espiritismo*) is a philosophical and religious doctrine founded by the French scientist Allan Kardec (1804-1869), in his famous *The Book of the Spirits*. Spiritists believe in reincarnation and in the possibility of contact between men and spirits. Life is a necessary experience for spiritual progress and death is just the beginning of another stage in the spirit's evolution. Brazil is said to be the country with the greatest number of spiritists in the world and many spiritist mediums have become internationally famous. A good example is Rubens Faria in Rio de Janeiro who performs thousands of mediumistic surgeries every day. Many influential people and artists have been operated on by him. Sadly, his mystique was called into question in 1999 when police investigated him for murder, charlatanism, tax evasion and money laundering.

Although it does not have an impressive number of followers, the sect called Santo Daime deserves mention. It has its origins in the Amazon region and is based in the visions produced by a hallucinogenic beverage called Ayahuasca. This is made from the roots of two plants known to Brazilian Indians for centuries (see Colônia Cinco Mil, page 668).

Arts and crafts

Brazilian arts and crafts spring from a variety of sources which, over the years, have often become intertwined. This section will deal with the main strands only, which will give you a few points of reference as you visit markets and handicraft shops. From here you can make your own discoveries.

Woodcarving
Woodworking has two principal origins, the African and the Jesuit. In northeastern Brazil, many woodcarving and sculpting techniques are inherited from the African slaves who were brought across the Atlantic to work the sugar plantations. One of the most prominent examples is the *carranca*, the grotesque figurehead that was placed on a boat's prow to ward off evil spirits. *Carrancas* are an adaptation of the African mask-making tradition and other carved and sculpted masks can be found in the northeast. The Jesuits passed on skills in the carving and painting of religious figures in wood. Originally they encouraged their Indian converts in the techniques, but today others practice the art. Woodcarving is widespread in Pernambuco and Bahia in the northeast. In Rio de Janeiro many contemporary artists work in wood and Embu, near São Paulo (see page 212), is an important centre for wooden sculptures and furniture making.

Ceramics
In northeastern Brazil, religious figures are also made in clay, for instance the unglazed, lifesized saints made from red clay in Tracunhaém, near Recife (see page 495). Another centre for similar work is Goiana, also in Pernambuco (see page 495). A third place from which the ceramics are even more famous is Alto da Moura, near Caruaru (Pernambuco – see page 510). Here Mestre Vitalino began modelling scraps of clay into little figures depicting everyday life (work, festivals, dancing, political events). He died in 1963, but the tradition that he started has continued and is known throughout Brazil.

The pots that are made in the Amazon region come in various styles, some of them quite strange. Bahian and other northeastern pottery shows African influence.

Ceará, in the north, is famous for its lace-making, and beautiful pieces are sold all over Brazil. In other parts of the north hammocks and other woven items are found. The hammock is, of course, an essential household item and you may well need to buy one if you are travelling up the Amazon on a boat. Other utilitarian articles which have become craft items are the rugs and capes made in the highlands further south, such as Minas Gerais, to keep out the night-time cold.

In the northeast, traditional costumes have their roots in the rituals of the African religions that came to Brazil with the slave trade. In southern areas where European immigration was heaviest, many traditional costumes can be seen, usually at the festivals and dances that have survived. Another type of clothing from the south is that associated with the *gaúchos*, the Brazilian cowboys of Rio Grande do Sul. As well as the clothes, which normally use hide in their manufacture, you may also buy saddlery, stirrups, silverware and the gourds used for drinking mate.

Leatherwork is not confined to the south, but can be found in any region where cattle are raised.

The most popular instruments that tourists like to buy are those connected with African music, espcially the drums, shakers and the *berimbau*, the one-stringed bow that is twanged in accompaniment to Capoeira. Here again, the best places to look are in the northeast where the African heritage is strongest. You can also purchase guitars and other stringed instruments.

In Amazônia, a huge variety of raw materials are available for making baskets, nets, hammocks, slings for carrying babies, masks and body adornments. In the northeast, too, baskets come in all shapes and sizes, especially in Bahia, Pernambuco and Paraíba.

Another northeastern craft, which does not fit into the above categories, is **pictures made in bottles with coloured sands** (Lençóis, Bahia, and Natal, Rio Grande do Norte, are good places to buy them – see pages 445 and 532).

In Minas Gerais, two very common things to see and buy are **soapstone carvings** (for instance birds and animals) and the **cooking pots** used in *mineira* kitchens.

Many people come to Brazil looking for bargains in gemstones. Because so many different types of stone are mined and sold here, it is logical to assume that prices will be better than elsewhere. However if you want good quality, you have to pay for it, especially if you are just looking for a special gift and are not a trained assessor of gemstones. If you decide to buy on the street, you need to beware of imitations, particularly of emeralds, which can easily be manufactured in a laboratory, and of aquamarines. In a shop, you should ask to see the owner's qualification (*título*) as well as the guarantee that the stone is genuine. It is not possible to quantify the cost of a gemstone because, even though its weight, brilliance and cut can be determined, outlets will put their own price on it. You should therefore buy from a reputable retailer, or investigate the market thoroughly. Note that the distinction between 'precious' and 'semi-precious' is no longer used; the demand for rare and interesting stones is such that some types of what used to be called 'semi-precious' are now more valuable than the old 'precious stones'. Similarly, a good quality 'semi-precious stone' will command a higher price than a poor quality 'precious stone'.

There are two high-class stores selling precious stones and jewellery which contains them, H Stern and Amsterdam Sauer. They both have their headquarters in Rio de Janeiro (see page 123) and both provide lots of information in booklets or their museum/displays on the process of turning mined stones into desirable objects. In Rio de Janeiro and São Paulo there are other reputable dealers from whom stones can be bought. In Minas Gerais (Belo Horizonte, Ouro Preto, Teófilo Otôni, Governador Valadares, Itabira) and in other producing areas (Goiás for emeralds, Piauí for opals) the same is true. There are also jewellery stores selling both traditional styles and innovative designs incorporating Brazilian gems. Some of the nicest pieces contain a combination of different stones, selected for their hues to make gradations of colour in a single setting.

Brazilian gems Legends of rich deposits, even mountains of precious stones preceded their discovery in the interior of the country. Prospectors looked for diamonds and emeralds as well as gold and silver to make them wealthy. The existence of gems was known about almost from the earliest days of the Portuguese colony, from the reports given to the new arrivals by the Indians and from scattered discoveries of different stones. But there was nothing to bring riches on the scale of the silver and gold found in the Spanish colonies. Gold was found in Minas Gerais in the 17th century and diamonds in 1725 at Diamantina (Minas Gerais) and thus Brazil's mineral wealth began to appreciate. The search for new deposits has never flagged.

Some of the commercially mined stones are: **diamonds**, found in Minas Gerais, Roraima, Bahia, Tocantins, Mato Grosso and Mato Grosso do Sul. Brazil was the world's largest producer of diamonds until South Africa entered the market in the 19th century. **Emeralds** were not discovered in Brazil until 1963 (many green beryls had been mined before then, but were known not to be true emeralds); they are now mined in Bahia, Minas Gerais and Goiás. **Aquamarine** is a clear blue beryl from Rio Grande do Norte, Paraíba, Bahia, Minas Gerais and Espírito Santo. **Ruby and sapphire** are two shades of the same mineral, corundum, the former rich red, the latter a deep blue. Rubies are found in Santa Catarina, sapphires in Minas Gerais. The two most valued forms of **topaz** found are the rare Imperial Topaz from Ouro Preto (Minas Gerais), which comes in a range of colours from honey-coloured through shades of red to pink, and Blue Topaz from Minas Gerais and Rondônia.

Tourmalines come from Minas Gerais, Ceará and Goiás; they have the widest range of colours of any gemstone, from colourless (white) to red, yellow, greens, blues, lilac and black. They even come in bi- and tricoloured varieties. **Opals**, unique for their rainbow flecks, are mined in Piauí and Rio Grande do Sul. **Amethyst**, a quartz which ranges in colour from pale lilac to deep purple, is mined in Tocantins, Pará, Bahia, Mato Grosso do Sul and Rio Grande do Sul. From the last three states, plus Minas Gerais, comes **citrine**, another quartz which is predominantly yellow. Less well-known, but equally beautiful are **kunzite**, a rare pinkish-violet stone, and **chrysoberyl**, both found in Minas Gerais. Chrysoberyl is found in a variety of forms, a golden-yellow-brown, 'cat's eye' chrysoberyl which has an luminous thread running through it, and the very rare **alexandrite**, which changes colour according to the light. Its most spectacular form changes from green in daylight to red in artificial light.

Sources *Noções de gemologia e roteiro turístico das gemas em Minas Gerais*, by Ruzimar Batista Tavares; *Emeralds and other Gemstones of Brazil*, by Jules Roger Sauer.

The information on arts and crafts in this Handbook has been adapted from Arts and Crafts of South America, by Lucy Davies and Mo Fini, published by Tumi, 1994. Tumi, the Latin American Craft Centre, specializes in Andean and Mexican products and produces cultural and educational videos for schools: at 8/9 New Bond Street Place, Bath BA1 1BH (T01225-462367, F01225-444870), 23/2A Chalk Farm Road, London NW1 8AG (F020-7854152), Little Clarendon St, Oxford OX1 2HJ (T/F01865-512307), 82 Park St, Bristol BS1 5LA (T/F0117-9290391). Tumi (Music) Ltd specializes in different rhythms of Latin America.

Capoeira and berimbau

One of the most exciting sounds to be heard in the streets of Salvador, Bahia, is that of the berimbau, the instrument that accompanies the dance-cum-martial arts form called Capoeira. The berimbau is a vertical wooden bow with a resonator at the lower end and a single steel string played with a thin stick. The player also holds a caxixi, a small rattle, in the stick hand and coin held against the string to modulate the pitch in the other. The berimbau is accompanied by one of a number of 'toques' or chants, such as the São Bento Grande, Angola, Benguela or Cavalaria. Although the objective of the Capoeirista is to knock his opponent off his hands or feet, what the bystander will most appreciate is the wonderful grace with which the two bodies of the opponents whirl and cartwheel around one another, as though participating in some physically powerful ballet, never actually touching until a 'fall' is engineered by one of them. Undeniably of African origin, the Capoeira was practised much more violently in the past and did not acquire respectability until the celebrated Mestre Bimba opened the first Academy in 1932.

Music and dance

Perhaps because of its sheer size, Brazil has a greater musical inventory than any other Latin American country, not only reflected in the immense regional spread of folk music but also in its successive waves of urban popular music. Brazilians express themselves through music and dance to an extraordinary degree and the music covers the whole spectrum from the utmost rural simplicity to the ultimate state-of-the-art commercial sophistication. The far north of the country is virtually in the Caribbean, while the extreme south shares its culture with the Rio de la Plata countries.

The South

In Paraná, Santa Catarina and Rio Grande do Sul, the music is strictly European in origin, rhythm and instrumentation. Rio Grande do Sul shares Gaucho dances such as the Pericom and song styles such as the Milonga, Trova and Pajada with neighbouring Uruguay and Argentina. The Chula is a competitive dance for men to show off with (comparable to the Argentine Malambo), while the Pexinho is for men and women. The guitar and the accordion are the favourite instruments, also true for Santa Catarina and Paraná, where the names of the dances denote their European origins: Mazurkas, Valsas, Chotes, Polquinhas and Rancheiras. The Chimarrita is a song style that came straight from the Azores. If you are feeling sentimental, you sing a Toada, if energetic, you stamp your feet to a Fandango. Except for the Batuque de Rio Grande do Sul in Porto Alegre, closely related to the Candombe of nearby Montevideo, there is no African influence in the music of this region and none of that classic Brazilian syncopation.

São Paulo, Rio de Janeiro & Minas Gerais

Moving north into São Paulo, we enter an area rich in traditional folk dances and music, with the African admixture beginning to show up. At many religious festivals will be found the Congadas (European 'Moors & Christians', but danced by blacks) and Moçambique (a stick dance for men), while the Samba de Lenço, Fandango and Batuque are recreational dances for one or more couples. The instrumental accompaniment branches out into shakers (the *ganzá*), drums (*caixas* and *tambores*) and above all the guitar (*viola*). Try the great pilgrimage church at Aparecida do Norte on a Sunday. You might well see a group of religious dances. In the hinterland of Rio de Janeiro the Folias de Reis are out on the street from Christmas to Epiphany, singing from house to house, accompanying themselves on the *caixa* and *adufe* drums and the guitar, while in the old coastal towns of Paraty and Angra dos Reis are to be found

Dorival Caymmi, Minstrel from Bahia

Dorival Caymmi, born in Salvador in 1914, is not well known outside Brazil, but to most Brazilians he is rated as fine a singer and composer as even this outstandingly musical country has produced. His influence as a precursor of Bossa Nova is acknowledged by such as Tom Jobim, who was at the cutting edge of the movement. The ultimate exponent of what might be termed the 'laid back' as opposed to 'energetic' or even 'frenzied' · style of Brazilian music, Dorival Caymmi arrived in Rio de Janeiro in 1938, aged 24, and has lived there ever since, leaving only his heart in Salvador. Within a year he was singing his own compositions 'O que é que a Bahiana Tem?' and 'A Preta do Acarajé' with Carmen Miranda and over succeeding decades has become both a national icon and a living symbol of his native Bahia. Above all, he is famous for his songs about the fishermen of Salvador, who face the dangers of the ocean in their flimsy jangadas, of which he himself remains by far the best interpreter. Look for a record containing 'O Mar', 'O Vento', 'Promessa de Pescador', 'A Lenda do Abaeté' and the intensely moving 'A Jangada Voltou Só'. You won't be disappointed!

the Dança de Velhos (the old men), performed to the accordion. The Jongo is a dance of African origin for men and women, naturally with a drum accompaniment. And there is hardly need to mention Rio de Janeiro at carnival and its samba schools. Further north again, we come to the states of Espírito Santo, Minas Gerais and Goiás. In colonial Ouro Preto, in Minas, you can hear the old Modinha sung to the Portuguese guitar as a serenade and be transported into the past. Espírito Santo is home to the Ticumbi, a kind of Congada, danced to the guitar and shakers (*chocalhos*). Goiás shares with Minas Gerais a very rich heritage of Portuguese derived religious folk song and dance, centred on Folias, Modas and Calangos.

Bahia Bahia is the heart of African Brazil and a very musical heart it is, born of the Yoruba religion that came with the slaves from what is now Nigeria. The resulting syncretic religion is known as Candomblé in Bahia and the gods or 'Orixás' are worshipped through song, dance and possession in the 'Terreiros', directed by the priests (Pais-de-Santo) and priestesses (Mães-de-Santo). The mainly female adepts, dressed entirely in white, circle gracefully to the background chant of 'Pontos' and the thunderous pounding of the *atabaques*, the tall drums. The two most revered priestesses are Mãe Olga de Alakêto and Mãe Menininha de Gantois. Similar syncretic African religions are found elsewhere in Brazil (see **Religion**, page 763). Another vital African element in Bahian folk music is the spectacular dance-cum-martial arts form of Capoeira (see box page 771). Bodies whirl and cartwheel around each other to the sound of the *berimbau* (a one-stringed bow with resonator) and the accompanying chant. Related to the Capoeira is the stick dance Maculelê. Two of the best *berimbau* groups on record are Camaféu de Oxóssi and the Cordão de Ouro. Bahia has a carnival almost as celebrated as that of Rio and here you can see the Afoxé, a serious religious dance, performed to drums alone.

The Northeast North of Bahia is the Nordeste, with music that runs the whole gamut from black African to mediaeval Portuguese. In colonial times the church directed the peoples' musical energies into religious plays, songs and dances and a large number of these are still performed. The Bumba-Meu-Boi is a folk drama in the course of which a bull is killed and then brought back to life. Particularly popular in Piauí and Maranhão, its variants are found as far afield as Amazônia, where it is called the Boi-Bumbá, and Paraná in the far south, where it is known as Boi-Mamão. Also popular along the coast from Ceará to Paraíba is a nautical drama of Portuguese origin called Marujada

Repentistas and cordel

A fascinating experience in the Nordeste is to come across a pair of 'Violeiros' or 'Repentistas', troubadours who accompany themselves on the melodious Viola Nordestina, developed from the Portuguese seven-string guitar, generally to be found in markets. They will sing, jokingly but flatteringly, about individual members of the audience, expecting a tip in return. They also have a large repertoire of the ballads that deal with regional themes and personalities which are to be found in the 'Folhetos', or pamphlets known under the generic title of 'Literatura de Cordel' (String Literature), because they are traditionally displayed for sale hung from a string. Both the ballads and the pamphlets are of archaic Portuguese origin. The ballads are made up of innumerable verse forms, such as the Mourão, Galope, Martelo, Sextilha and Quadrão. The celebrated bandit, Lampião, is a favourite subject and the compiling of long lists of words or names is popular too.

or Nau Catarineta, a version of Moors and Christians, accompanied by Portuguese guitar (violão), drums and the ganzá scraper. In Alagoas, Sergipe and Pernambuco we find the sword dance called Reisado, danced after Christmas, the Caboclinhos, who are dressed like Indians and dance with bows and arrows, and the Guerreiros Alagoanos, a mixture of both. The last named are accompanied by the classical northeastern musical group called Terno de Pífanos, with the pífano vertical flute, accompanied by maracas and ganzá. The Banda de Pífanos of Caruaru in Pernambuco can be found on record. Recreational dance music in the Nordeste goes under the generic name of 'Forró', said to be derived from the expression 'For All', because the English companies operating at the turn of the century organized weekend dances for their workmen to which all comers were invited. Four very popular recreational folk dances of this region are the Ciranda (a round dance), the Coco, the Bate-Coxa (where the dancers bump bellies) and the Bambelô. Carnival in Recife, the largest city, is when and where to see the energetic and gymnastic Frevo, danced by young men with an umbrella in their hands, and the very stately and superbly costumed Maracatu dancers, with their queen and king. The Nordeste is equally rich in song styles, notably the Desafios, Emboladas, Cocos and Aboios. The Desafios are performed by so-called Repentistas (see box) or Violeiros, who accompany themselves on the Portuguese guitar and whose repertoire includes a large inventory of verse styles. They will sing about individual spectators, who then pay willingly for the compliment. The Emboladas and Cocos are similar, but faster and accompanied solely by tambourines, while the Aboios are haunting songs related to cattle and cattlemen. Repentistas and Emboladores can normally be found at work in markets throughout the region. The premier Repentista is Otacílio Batista do Pajeú, who sang to Pope John Paul II during the latter's first visit to Brazil.

The music of the Nordeste has also been well propagated by more sophisticated groups that have based themselves on folk roots, such as the Quinteto Violado, Ariano Suassuna's Orchestra Armorial and Cussy de Almeida's Quinteto Armorial, not forgetting the veteran accordionist Luiz Gonzaga and the popular Alceu Valença. As a result of the huge migration of nordestinos to the urban south, moreover, it is just as easy to hear this regional music in São Paulo as it is in Recife.

Finally to Pará and the Amazon in the far north, where the music has been heavily influenced from the Caribbean. The most popular musical genre here is the Carimbó, danced to a Merengue-type rhythm and played on drums, wind or brass (usually the clarinet) and strings, particularly the banjo. Notable performers are Pinduca ('O Rei do Carimbó'), Veriquete and Vieira. It is the last-named who thought up the term 'Lambada' for his particular version of the Carimbó and the spectacular,

Pará & the Amazon

Background

thigh-entwining dance form introduced to the world in Paris by Karakos and Lorsac in 1988 had already been popular among young people at 'Forrós' throughout the region for some years. The song 'Bate Forte o Tambor' by the group Carapicho, originally from Parintins, has become an international hit, the English title being 'Tic, Tic, Tac'. The very traditional island of Marajó in the mouth of the Amazon has preserved versions of 18th-century dances, such as the Lundú and Chula.

Urban popular music The vast range of Brazilian regional folk music is only equalled by the chronological depth of its urban popular music, which surges like endless waves on a beach. For the origins we have to go back to Jesuit missions and Portuguese folk music, influenced and blended by African slaves, from which emerged the 19th-century Lundús, Polcas and Maxixes that in turn gave way to the romantic and sentimental Choro song genre (from *chorar*, to weep), accompanied by guitar, flute and *cavaquinho* (small guitar), which became all the rage and indeed still has its adepts in Brazil today.

A key figure in urban music was Ernesto Nazaré, composer and pianist, who occupied a special niche somewhere between popular and light classical, composing between 1880 and 1930 a vast number of Tangos Brasileiros (not to be confused with the Argentine variety), Mazurkas, Polcas, Waltzes and other popular songs.

Around the turn of the century the instrumentation turned to brass and Rio's urban Samba was born, a birth that was announced by the recording in 1917 of Donga's 'Pelo Telefone'. Names from this early period are Pixinguinha, Sinhô, Heitor dos Prazeres, Ary Barroso, Noel Rosa and of course Carmen Miranda, who took the Samba to Hollywood and the rest of the world. It also became intimately connected with the carnival in the form of Marcha Ranchos and Sambas de Enredo as the first samba schools were formed, of which Salgueiro, Mangueira, Partido Alto, Portela, Mocidade Independente and Beija-Flor are some of the most famous. With the Escolas de Samba came the Batucada or percussion groups playing the *pandeiro* (tambourine), *atabaque* and *tamborim* (drum), *agogô* (cowbell), *reco-reco*, *chocalho*, *afoxê* and *cuíca*. This is the real engine room of Samba. Listen to Lúcio Perrone or Mocidade Independente de Padre Miguel. A new phase was ushered in with an invasion from Bahia and the Nordeste in the early 1950s. From Bahia came Dorival Caymmi (see box page 772), who dropped his fishermen's songs in favour of the Samba, and Luiz Gonzaga, who brought his accordion, *zabumba* drum and *triangulo*, with which to play his Baiãos (his 'Asa Branca' is a classic) and almost put the Samba itself into eclipse for several years. Almost, but not quite, for out of the ashes there soon arose Bossa Nova – white, middle class and silky smooth. Vinícius de Moraes and Tom Jobim were its heroes; 1958 to 1964 the years; Copacabana, Ipanema and Leblon the scene; 'Samba de uma Nota Só', 'A Garota de Ipanema' and 'Desafinado' the songs and Nara Leão, Baden Powell, Toquinho, João Gilberto, Luis Bonfá and Astrud Gilberto the main performers. Stan Getz, the American jazz saxophonist, helped export it to the world. What was now being called MPB (Música Popular Brasileira) then took off in several directions. Chico Buarque, Edu Lobo and Milton Nascimento were protest singers. Out of Bahia emerged 'Tropicalismo' in the persons of Gilberto Gil, Caetano Veloso and his sister Maria Bethânia, Gal Costa, João Gilberto and 'Som Livre'. The words were important, but the rhythm was still there. Brazilian rock also now appeared, with such stars as Roberto Carlos, Elis Regina, Rita Lee, and Ney Mattogrosso. Heavy metal is a popular genre that continues to evolve, as exemplified by the band Sepultura. Another band which has achieved cult status is Legião Urbana from Brasília (its vocalist, Renato Russo, died of Aids in 1996). Recently, in turning towards international black consciousness, the Bahianos have mixed Reggae and Samba to produce 'axê'. Still, Samba has survived, either in its more commercialized form 'Pagode', or in the Roda de Samba, an informal meeting of musicians in a 'barzinho'. Amazingly, 40 percent of all Brazilian records sold are of

Brazilian cinema

My first encounter with Brazil came through the medium of its cinema when in the early 1980s I saw Hector Babenco's controversial drama Pixote, a Lei do Mais Fraco. This left a lasting impression and curiosity that I was never to satisfy until my first visit to São Paulo nearly 15 years later. Hopefully the current resurgence of Oscar nominated films such as Walter Salles's Central do Brasil (Central Station) will inspire more people to explore the country where they were filmed rather sooner than I did!

No one knows for sure when the first film was made in Brazil but a travelling Italian showman, Vittorio di Maio, was to claim this when he exhibited four films in Petrópolis in 1897. The industry developed steadily at the beginning of the century with often-repeated adaptations of literary texts such as O Guaraní before later specializing in light entertainment musicals known as chanchadas during the 1930s and 1940s. A national star, Carmen Miranda, grew out of these before moving to Hollywood where she quickly became America's stereotype of the exotic Latin woman.

During the 1950s more serious films such as Nelson Perreira dos Santos's Rio 40 Graus began to appear before Anselmo Duarte's O Pagador de Promessas won best film at Cannes. This golden age continued in the 1960s with the birth of Cinema Novo. Glauber Rocha's Deus e o Diabo no Terra do Sol reinterpreted the popular theme of Lampião and the bandits of the northeast previously used in Lima Barreto's 1953 epic O Cangaçeiro. Other films such as O Barravento also by Glauber Rocha challenged the previously passive role of the viewing public.

In the 1970s and 1980s under the military dictatorship the national film industry led by the state run Embrafilme lost its way as pornochanchadas and comedies like Os Trapalhões dominated the box office. There were however some films such as Bruno Barreto's Dona Flor e Seus Dois Maridos that combined both commercial and critical success and helped to push actress Sonia Braga to international fame. Cult horror film director, José Mojica Marins, better known as Zé do Caixão (Coffin Joe), also flourished during this period and is possibly better know outside his home country than his more artistic colleagues!

The return came in the 1990s with Fabio Barreto's O Quatrilho, showing the life of Brazil's Italian immigrants and Bruno Barreto's O Que é Isso Companheiro based on the 1969 kidnap of the American ambassador. Both were nominated for the Academy Awards best foreign film. Other good recent films, including Anahy de las Missiones based on a Gaúcho legend and Terra Estrangeira exploring the life of a Brazilian immigrant in Portugal, have displayed both excellent photography and innovative plots. Although the hotly-tipped Central do Brasil failed to win the coveted Oscar, it can surely only be a matter of time before Brazilian films gain the international recognition they so richly deserve.

Mick Day

Música Sertaneja, in its more traditional rural style known as Música Caipira, or a newer, highly commercialized pseudo-folk genre which is closer to American Country and Western than to most other Brazilian music. Listen to the 'Duplas' of Tonico & Tinoco, Jacó e Jacozinho, Vieira & Vieirinha or Leonardo & Leandro and you'll see. In the meantime a series of brilliant Brazilian instrumentalists have become international names and often live abroad – Sérgio Mendes, the guitarist Sebastião Tapajós, flautist Hermêto Paschoal, saxophonist Paulo Moura, accordionist Sivuca, percussionists Airto Moreira and Nana Vasconcelos, singer Flora Purim and all-rounder Egberto Gismonti are but a few. On the top of a huge recording industry, we're now a long way from the grassroots and the haunting flute music of the forest Indians.

Background

Brazilian classical composers Ever since the Catholic church and its missionaries arrived in all parts of present-day Latin America, appropriate religious music was being composed locally, particularly by the Jesuits, and this led on to Baroque and other classical music. Brazil was no exception and Carlos Gomes' opera 'Il Guarany' achieved great popularity after its first performance in 1870. During the present century, Brazilian composers (together with those of Mexico and Argentina) are at the forefront of Latin American classical music and have produced many works based on folk and popular themes. The figure of Heitor Villa-Lobos (1857-1959) towers above all others and achieved world renown well within his lifetime. Largely self-taught, his prodigious output included the celebrated nine 'Bachianas Brasileiras' and six 'Choros'. Given to bold experimentation, he composed two pieces of which the melodic line was based on the skyline of New York and that of the Serra da Piedade mountains near Belo Horizonte, respectively. Other major names among the so-called 'nationalist' composers are Francisco Mignone, Camargo Guarnieri, Radames Gnatalli and Cesar Guerra Peixe (who found inspiration in the regional music of the Northeast).

Festivals

Brazilians love a party and the mixing of different ethnic groups has resulted in some particularly colourful and varied celebrations. The difficulties of daily life are often relieved by the fantasy and release of *carnaval* as well as the many other popular festivals held through the year. Wherever you go you will find street vendors selling ice cold beer and the smell of *churrasco* coming from improvised barbecues accompanied by loud vibrant music and dancing in the streets.

Carnaval Almost all Brazilian towns have some form of carnival festivities. Although the most famous is Rio de Janeiro, there are equally spectacular and different traditions in Bahia and Pernambuco as well as a number of other good locations for those who wish only to party. The colonial mining towns of Diamantina and Ouro Preto in the interior of Minas Gerais are good locations to spend carnival in atmospheric surroundings. Florianópolis and Laguna on the coast of Santa Catarina have less traditional but still very popular and lively carnivals.

Carnival dates: 5 March 2000, 25 February 2001, 10 February 2002.

Out of season carnivals Street carnivals with *trios eléctricos* in the style of Bahia are held throughout Brazil at various times of the year. Some of the most popular are *Micareta* in Feira de Santana (April), *Fortal* in Fortaleza (July) and *Carnatal* in Natal (December). Although by no means traditional they are nonetheless exuberant and enjoyable.

Other popular festivities There are several other festivals which are almost as important to Brazilians as Carnaval. *Reveillon* (New Year's Eve) is a significant event and is generally celebrated on beaches. This can be either a hedonistic party as at Copacabana and Arraial D'Ajuda with the revellers dressed in white for luck, or as a respectful Candomblé ceremony in which flowers are launched into the sea at midnight as an offering to Yemanjá.

The Festas Juninhas (*São João*) are extremely popular especially in the northeast and are held around 24 June (St John's day). Fires are built and Forró is the music of choice with the festivities lasting for over a week at times. Fireworks and the co-ordinated dancing of groups called *quadrilhas* are also part of the celebrations.

In the north the African and Indian cultures have mixed to form the *Boi-Bumba* tradition. In Amazonas the Festa do Boi has become more commercialized but is still very impressive and popular. In Maranhão where it is known as *Bumba-meu-boi* the festivities are more traditional but equally as popular.

There are many Catholic saints' days that are sometimes celebrated in conjunction with African deities (especially in Bahia). Every town has a patron saint and his or her day will be an excuse for civic festivities, in addition to those of the foundation day of the town.

Immigrants from Europe to the south of Brazil and elsewhere have brought festivals from their own cultures such as the Oktoberfest held in Blumenau, believed to be second only to Munich.

Literature

Some of the major differences between Brazil and Spanish America spring from the history of colonization in the two areas. There were no great empires with large cities like those of the Incas or the Aztecs, and Portuguese exploitation concentrated first on extractive, then on cultivated export products (brazil-wood, then sugar). Although cities like Recife, Bahia and Rio de Janeiro did finally develop, there was, incredible as it may seem, no printing press in Brazil until the flight of the Regent, later King João VI to Rio in 1808. This is not to say that there was no colonial literature, though scholars can still quarrel about how 'Brazilian' it was. When the Portuguese set foot in Brazil in 1500, the letter sent back to King Manuel by Pero Vaz de Caminha, already wondering at the tropical magnificence of the country and the nakedness of the inhabitants, set themes which would recur in many later works. The first plays to be put on in Brazil were religious dramas, staged in three languages, Portuguese, Spanish, and Tupi, by the Jesuit **José de Anchieta** (1543-97). The most notable 17th-century poet is **Gregório de Matos** (1636-96), famous for his sharp satires on the corrupt life of the city of Salvador, and its tempting black and mulatta women. In the late 18th century, a group of poets from the gold-mining area of Minas, foremost among them **Tomás Antônio Gonzaga** (1744-1810), were at the centre of the early, abortive move for independence, the Inconfidência (1789 – see page 276). Although best known as a lyric poet, Gonzaga has been proved to be the author of the anonymous satirical poem *Cartas chilenas*, which gives a vivid portrait of colonial society.

The colonial period

It is helpful to understand Brazilian literature, even long after political independence, as a gradual and to some extent contradictory process of emancipation from foreign models. Every European literary movement – Romanticism, Realism, Symbolism, etc – had its Brazilian followers, but in each there was an attempt to adjust the model to local reality. A good example is the first of these, Indianism, which flourished in the mid-19th century, and produced two central figures, the poet **Antônio Gonçalves Dias** (1823-64) (himself partly of Indian descent) and the novelist **José de Alencar** (1829-77). It is a form of Romanticism, idealizing the noble savage, and with plots adapted from Walter Scott, and it happily ignored what was happening to real Indians at the time. However, it does express national aspirations and feelings, if in nothing else in the nostalgia for a kind of tropical Eden expressed in perhaps the most famous Brazilian poem, Gonçalves Dias 'Canção do exílio': "My land has palm-trees/ where the sabiá sings./ The birds that sing here/ don't sing like those back home." Alencar's novels, not all of them about Indians, are a systematic attempt to portray Brazil in its various settings, including the city. *O guarani* (1857), turned into a famous opera by Carlos Gomes, and *Iracema* (1865) are his most popular, the latter perhaps the most complete mythical version of the Portuguese conquest, allegorized as a love affair between a native woman and an early colonist, Martim Soares: Iracema, "the virgin with the honeyed lips" dies in childbirth at the end, but the future lies with their mixed-blood son, Moacir.

The 19th century

After his death, Alencar was succeeded as the chief figure in Brazilian letters by **Joaquim Maria Machado de Assis** (1839-1908). Perhaps Brazil's best writer, and certainly the greatest to appear in Latin America until well into the 20th century, he had to fight against formidable obstacles: he was of relatively poor origins, was mulatto, stammered and in later life was subject to epileptic fits. He wrote nine novels

Background

and more than 200 short stories as well as poetry and journalism. He ended his life as an establishment figure, founder of the Brazilian Academy of Letters, but his novels, especially those written after 1880, when he published *Memórias póstumas de Brás Cubas*, and the best of his stories are surprisingly subversive, covert attacks on slavery and on male power, for instance. He avoided detection by not using his own voice, hiding behind quirky, digressive narrators who are not always trustworthy. All the novels and most of the stories are set in Rio, which he hardly left, and give a remarkably varied account of the city and its different social levels. His most famous novel, *Dom Casmurro* (1900) is one of the best-disguised cases of an unreliable narrator in the history of the novel, and still arouses critical polemics.

Machado's atmosphere is predominantly that of the empire, which fell in 1889, a year after the abolition of slavery. In the Republic, a younger generation, more overtly rebellious in their aims, and affected by new scientific ideas from Europe, came to the fore. If Machado is the most famous Brazilian author, perhaps *Os sertões*, by **Euclides da Cunha** (1866-1909) is the most famous book. It is an account of the Canudos campaign in the interior of the state of Bahia in 1896-97 (see page 468). The campaign was a horrific failure, victory being won only at a huge cost in casualties, and Euclides, sent to cover it as a journalist, turned this failure into an indictment of a social system which excluded huge groups of people. Written in a dramatic, somewhat self-indulgent style, with extensive use of scientific words, it has been excellently translated as *Rebellion in the Backlands*.

The other important prose writer of this period, the novelist **Afonso Lima Barreto** (1881-1922), was mulatto like Machado, but there resemblances end. Much more openly rebellious and less of a conscious artist than Machado, his novels, the most notable of which is *Triste fim de Policarpo Quaresma*, are overt attacks on intellectual mediocrity, and the corruption and despotism into which the Republic soon fell. A passing mention ought to be made, too, of one of the 'unclassifiable' books in which Brazilian literature abounds: **Helena Morley's** *Minha vida de menina* (translated by Elizabeth Bishop as *The Diary of Helena Morley*), and only published in 1942, it is the precocious, funny, and remarkably perceptive teenager's diary, written in Diamantina, Minas Gerais, at the end of the 19th century.

The 20th century

In general, the poetry of the turn of the century was imitative and stuffy: renewal did not come until the early 1920s, when a group of intellectuals from São Paulo, led by **Mário de Andrade** (1893-1945) and **Oswald de Andrade** (1890-1954) (unrelated) began the movement known as modernism. This is conveniently supposed to have begun in 1922, the centenary of political independence, with a Week of Modern Art in São Paulo: in fact it began earlier, and took until the mid-1920s to spread to the provinces. In great part, modernism's ideology was nationalist, and though the word spanned the political spectrum, at its best it simply meant the discovery of a real Brazil behind stereotypes: Mário travelled throughout the country, attempting to understand its variety, which he embodied in his major prose-work, the comic 'rhapsody' *Macunaíma* (1928), which in its plot and language attempts to construct a unity out of a complex racial and regional mix. Also in 1928, Oswald launched the 'anthropophagist', or cannibalist programme, which proclaimed that Brazilian writers should imitate their native predecessors, and fully digest European culture: a new kind of Indianism, perhaps ...

The most enduring artistic works to have emerged from modernism, however, are poetic: two of Brazil's major modern poets, **Manuel Bandeira** (1886-1968) and **Carlos Drummond de Andrade** (1902-1987) were early enthusiasts of modernism, and corresponded at length with Mário. Bandeira, the older man, made a slow transition to the new, freer style: his poems, often short and based on everyday events or images, nevertheless have a power and rhythmic accuracy which are deceptively simple. Drummond's poetry is more self-conscious, and went through a complex intellectual development, including a period of political enthusiasm during the Second World War, followed by disillusionment with the beginning of the Cold War. His themes, including some remarkable love-poetry addressed by a 50-year old to a younger woman, and a lifelong attachment to Itabira, the small town in Minas Gerais where he was born, are very varied. Readers without Portuguese can best approach Drummond, widely regarded as Brazil's greatest poet, through an excellent anthology, *Traveling in the Family*.

The 1930s were a crucial decade. With increasing political mobilization, the growth of cities, and of an aspiring middle class, literature began to look to a wider audience: at first, however, it still reflected the dominance of rural life. The realism of this period, which often had a strong regionalist bias, had its *raison d'être* in a society still divided by huge social and/or geographical differences, and indeed played its part in diminishing those differences. Many of the first group came from the economically and socially backward northeast. **José Lins do Rego** (1901-57) is perhaps the most characteristic figure. He was highly influenced by the ideas of **Gilberto Freyre** (1900-1987), whose *Casa grande e senzala* (*The Masters and the Slaves*), published in 1933, one of the most important and readable of Brazilian books. It is a study of the slave-based, sugar-plantation society, and one of the first works to appreciate the contribution made by Blacks to Brazil's culture. It remains, however, very paternalist, and Lins do Rego's fiction, beginning with the semi-autobiographical *Menino de engenho*, reflects that, commenting on the poverty and filth of the (ex-)slave-quarters as if they were totally natural. His 'Sugar-cane cycle' sold in large editions, in part because of its unaffected, simple style.

A greater novelist belonging to the same group is **Graciliano Ramos** (1892-1953). His fiction is much more aggressive, and in later life he became a communist. His masterpiece, turned into an excellent film in the 1960s, is *Vidas secas*, which returns to the impoverished interior of *Os sertões*, but concentrates on an illiterate cowhand and his family, forced from place to place by drought and social injustice: it is a courageous attempt to enter the mental world of such people. *Memórias do cárcere*, published after Ramos's death, is his unflinching account of his imprisonment for a year during the Vargas regime.

The essential novelist to read for anyone visiting the South of Brazil is **Érico Veríssimo** (1905-75), especially his epic trilogy collectively entitled *O tempo e o vento* (*O continente* [1949], *O retrato* [1951], and *O arquipélago* [1961]) spread over two centuries of the turbulent history of Rio Grande do Sul.

Gradually, in the 1940s and 1950s, a subtler and more adventurous fiction began to be published alongside the regionalist realism that was the major heritage of the 1930s. Three writers stand out: **João Guimarães Rosa** (1908-67) published his major novel, *Grande sertão: veredas* in 1956. Almost Joycean in its aspirations and linguistic innovations, it is a kind of mixture of a cowboy story and a modern version of Faustian pact with the devil. For those without stamina (and excellent Portuguese), the translation (*The Devil to Pay in the Backlands*) is unfortunately not an adequate alternative. Rosa is best approached through his stories, those of *Sagarana* (particularly "A hora e vez de Augusto Matraga") being perhaps the best.

The stories and novels of **Clarice Lispector** (1920-77) now have a considerable audience outside Brazil, as well as a huge one inside it. Her stories, especially those of *Laços de família* (1960), are in general set in middle-class Rio, and usually have women as their central characters: the turbulence, family hatreds, and near-madness hidden beneath routine lives are conveyed in unforgettable ways, with a language and symbolism that is poetic and adventurous without being exactly difficult (she said she fought with the Portuguese language daily). Some of her novels have over-ambitious metaphysical superstructures, and may not be to some readers' tastes – *A paixão segundo G H*, for instance, concerns a housewife's confrontation with a dead cockroach in her maid's room, and her final decision to eat it, seen as a kind of "communion". At her best, in some of her journalism, in her late, deliberately semi-pornographic stories, and above all in the posthumous novel, *A hora da estrela*, which approaches the poor in an utterly unsentimental way, Lispector can stimulate and move like no one else.

The greatest poet of this generation is **João Cabral de Melo Neto** (born 1920 in Pernambuco, died 1999), whose best poetry concerns his home state. The drought-ridden interior, the lush but oppressive landscape of the sugar-plantations, and the city slums are all present in the verse-play *Morte e vida severina* (1956), and his tight, spare poetry often returns to the same places, or analogous ones in the several countries (most importantly, in Spain) in which he has resided as a diplomat.

The 1964 military coup, and the increasing use of torture and censorship in the late 1960s and early 1970s, had profound effects on literature, especially as they were accompanied by vast economic changes (industrialization, a building boom, huge internal migration, the opening up of the Amazon). At first, censorship was haphazard, and the 1960s liberation movements had their – increasingly desperate – Brazilian equivalents. Protest theatre had a brief boom, with *Arena conta Zumbi*, about a 17th-century rebel slave leader, produced by **Augusto Boal** (born 1931), being one of the most important. The best fictional account of those years can be find in two novels by **Antônio Callado** (born 1917), *Quarup* (1967), set in the northeast and centred on a left-wing priest, and *Bar Don Juan* (1971), whose focus is on the contradictions of a group of middle-class guerrillas; and in **Ivan Ângelo's** *A festa* (1976), set in Belo Horizonte, a funny and hard-hitting account of a varied set of people, which chronicles the impact of the 'sex and drugs' revolution alongside its political concerns. A remarkable documentary account of the period is ex- guerrilla (now leader of the Green Party) **Fernando Gabeira's** *O que é isso companheiro?* (1982), which chronicles his involvement in the kidnapping of the American ambassador in 1969. Poetry at this time went through a crisis of self-confidence, and it was widely thought that it had emigrated into the (marvellous) lyrics of such popular composers as Chico Buarque de Holanda and Caetano Veloso, who were also the foremost standard-bearers of political protest in the 1970s.

It is impossible in the space available to give more than a few suggestions of some of the best work published in recent decades, concentrating on books which have been translated. A brilliant satirical novel by **Paulo Emílio Salles Gomes** (1916-77) about the São Paulo upper middle class is *Três mulheres e três pppês* (1977); **Darcy Ribeiro** (born 1922), an anthropologist and politician, took time off to write *Maíra* (1978), an updating of Indianism, but with real Indians and a threatened Amazon environment; **Rubem Fonseca** (born 1925), whose story 'Feliz ano novo' (1973) created a scandal because of its brutal treatment of class differences, has dedicated himself to the writing of hardnosed thrillers like *A grande arte* (1983); **Caio Fernando Abreu** (1948-96) is a short-story writer of considerable talent, dealing with the alienated urban young in such books as *Morangos mofados* and *Os dragões não conhecem o paraíso*; finally, **Milton Hatoum's** *Relato de um certo oriente* (1989) is a vivid novel set in Manaus, amongst the Lebanese immigrant community.

Further reading   Essays and books which can be wholeheartedly recommended for those who want more information are: Ray Keenoy, David Treece and Paul Hyland, *The Babel Guide to the Fiction of Portugal, Brazil and Africa in English Translation* (London: Boulevard Books, 1995). Irwin Stern (ed) *Dictionary of Brazilian Literature* (New York: Greenwood Press, 1988). Mike González and David Treece, *The Gathering of Voices* (Verso, 1992) (on 20th-century poetry). Elizabeth Bishop and Emanuel Brasil (eds) *An Anthology of Twentieth-Century Brazilian Poetry* (Wesleyan University Press, 1972). John Gledson, 'Brazilian Fiction: Machado de Assis to the Present', in John King (ed), *Modern Latin American Fiction: A Survey* (Faber, 1987). Many of the essays in Roberto Schwarz, *Misplaced Ideas: Essays on Brazilian Culture* (Verso, 1992), especially those on Machado de Assis, and 'Culture and Politics in Brazil, 1964-69' are very stimulating.

Machado de Assis, Joaquim Maria (1839-1908), the classical satirical novelist of the Brazilian 19th century, is one of the most original writers to have emerged from Latin America. *Epitaph of a Small Winner* (London: Hogarth Press, 1985). *Posthumous Memoirs of Bras Cubas* (New York: Oxford University Press, 1997). (The same novel.) *The Heritage of Quincas Borba* (London: WH Allen, 1954). *Philosopher or Dog?* (New York: Avon Books, 1985, also London: Bloomsbury, 1997). (The same novel.) *Dom Casmurro* (New York: Oxford University Press, 1997, also in Penguin Modern Classics, Harmondsworth, 1994). Abreu, João Capistrano de (1853-1929) A fascinating account of the first three centuries of Brazilian history. *Chapters of Colonia History* (New York: Oxford University Press, 1997). Cunha, Euclides da (1866-1909) The 'epic' story of the military campaign to crush the rebellion centred in Canudos in the interior of the State of Bahia. One of the great books about the Brazilian national make-up. *Rebellion in the Backlands (Os sertões)* (Chicago: University of Chicago Press, 1944-) Often reprinted, including London: Picador, 1995. Lima Barreto, Afonso Henriques de (1881-1922) A sharp attack on some of the failings of the Brazilian political and social system, set in the 1890s. *The Patriot* (London: Rex Collings, 1978). Morley, Helena (1882-1970) The diary of a girl's life in Diamantina, in Minas Gerais: translated by the great American poet Elizabeth Bishop, who lived in Brazil for many years. A delightfully intimate and frank portrait of small-town life. *The Diary of Helena Morley* (London: Bloomsbury, 1997). Bandeira, Manuel (1886-1968) The oldest member of the Modernist movement, and one of Brazil's greatest poets, master of the short, intense lyric. *This Earth, that Sky: Poems by Manuel Bandeira* (Berkeley: University of California Press, 1988). Ramos, Graciliano (1892-1953) The greatest of the novelists of the 1930s and 1940s: a harsh realist. *São Bernardo* (London: Peter Owen, 1975). *Anguish* (New York: Knopf, 1972). *Barren Lives* (Austin: University of Texas Press, 1965). Andrade, Mário de (1893-1945) Written in the 1920s: a comic statement in picaresque form about Brazilian nationality, by the leader of Modernism.

Macunaíma (London: Quartet, 1988). Freyre, Gilberto (1900-1987) A central figure, still controversial: this account of racial mixture, and of sugar-plantation society in the northeast of Brazil in colonial times, is very readable. *The Masters and the Slaves* (Berkeley: University of California Press, 1986). Lins do Rego, José (1909-1957) Highly influenced by Gilberto Freyre, this is an evocative account of childhood on a northeastern sugar plantation. *Plantation Boy* (New York: Knopf, 1966). Drummond de Andrade, Carlos (1902-1987) Perhaps Brazil's greatest poet, with a varied, lyrical, somewhat downbeat style. *Travelling in the Family: Selected Poems* (New York: Random House, 1986). Veríssimo, Érico (1905-) A very popular and important novelist from Rio Grande do Sul, the southernmost State of Brazil. *Time and the Wind* (London: Arco, 1954). Guimareães Rosa, João (1908-1967) The most poetic of modern prose-writers, who sets his work in the rural interior: very difficult to translate. *Sagarana* (Austin: University of Texas Press, 1990). Amado, Jorge (1912-) Over a long career Amado has published many best-sellers: he is often criticized for producing an overly optimistic, sexily tropical view of the country, and of Bahia, his home State. The following is only a selection of his most important and popular novels. *The Violent Land* (London: Collins Harvill, 1989). *Captains of the Sands* (New York: Avon Books, 1988). *Gabriela, Clove and Cinnamon* (London: Abacus, 1984). *Dona Flor and her Two Husbands* (London: Serpent's Tail, 1987; New York: Avon Books, 1988). *Tent of Miracles* (London: Collins, 1989; New York: Avon Books, 1988). Lispector, Clarice (1920-1977) Brazil's greatest woman writer, with a considerable following abroad. *Family Ties* (Manchester: Carcanet, 1986; Austin: University of Texas Press, 1990). *The Foreign Legion* (Manchester: Carcanet, 1986; New York: New Directions, 1992). *The Hour of the Star* (Manchester: Carcanet, 1986; New York: New Directions, 1982). Fonseca, Rubem (1925-) A thriller, set in Rio.

Brazilian Literature in English translation

Background

☞ **Jorge Amado**

Amado is, both among Brazilians and foreigners reading Brazilian fiction, by far the most popular writer of the 20th century. Born in 1912 on a cocoa plantation outside Ilhéus, in the South of the State of Bahia, he had a very adventurous youth, and had direct experience of the endemic violence surrounding land claims that he was later to dramatize in such novels as Terras do sem-fim (The Violent Land) (1943). He was always committed to the left, though his position has softened somewhat in later years, accompanying changes in his fiction. In the early period (1931-1952), it showed first in an interest in the rural and urban poor: in such novels as Jubiabá (1935), about the self-education of a black man, and Capitães da areia (1937), one of his best, centred on a gang of street children, he began to show interest in the power of candomblé (Afro-Brazilian religion) as a political consciousness-raiser. He became, a Federal deputy for the Communist Party in 1946: in 1948, after the party was banned, he went into exile in Europe, and was something of a propagandist for Soviet Communism, receiving the Stalin Peace Prize in 1951. The fiction he wrote at this time (for example Seara vermelha [Red Harvest]) is by common consent his worst.

In 1953 he returned to Brazil, and in 1958 published the novel which gave his career a new lease of life, Gabriela, cravo e canela (Gabriela, Clove and Cinnamon). To achieve this, he abandoned politics for comedy and myth: Ilhéus in the 1920s, its harbour about to be opened so that it can export its cocoa, is presented to us in a colourful array of characters, at the centre of whom are Nacib, an Arab immigrant and shopkeeper, and spicy Gabriela, a girl from the interior whose cooking and sexual prowess keep him in her thrall. It is a modern, optimistic version of Alencar's Iracema (see page 777): immigrant meets native girl, and has to adjust to her culture, while in the background, the (export)

economy is opening up. Gabriela was a phenomenal success, selling 100,000 copies in just over a year. In part, Amado had tuned into the optimism of the years of the Kubitschek presidency which led to the foundation of Brasília.

Sex, comedy and cookery proved a potent combination. Other novels since Gabriela have been equally successful with the public: Dona Flor e seus dois maridos (1966), about a cookery teacher whose respectable second marriage is haunted by the ghost of her bohemian first husband (it actually provides the reader with recipes); Tenda dos milagres (The Tent of Miracles) (1969) about racial discrimination, and others there is no space to deal with here, many of them set in the city of Salvador (Bahia). Amado has been attacked by critics as being unconsciously anti-feminist and even racist (his Blacks do tend to be stereotypically good-hearted, with a perpetual smile on their faces). Perhaps this is to miss the point: essentially, he is a popular novelist in the tradition of Scott, Dumas and hundreds of others, predecessors of television soap operas, and he has often been successfully adapted to that medium.

Jorge Armando

High Art (London: Collins, 1987). *The Lost Manuscript* (London: Bloomsbury, 1997). Ribeiro, João Ubaldo (1940-) A panoramic historical novel, entitled *Long Live the Brazilian People* in the original. *An Invincible Memory* (London: Faber and Faber, 1989; New York: Harper and Row, 1989). Buarque de Holanda, Chico (1944-) Most famous as a pop singer and composer, Chico Buarque has written a short, fast-moving allegory of modern Brazil. *Turbulence* (London: Bloomsbury, 1992). *Benjamin* (London: Bloomsbury, 1997). Ângelo, Ivan (1936-) Much the best novel and about the political, social and economic crisis at the end of the 1960s, the worst period of the military regime. *The Celebration* (New York: Avon Books, 1992). Abreu, Caio Fernando (1948-1996) Short stories: one of the writers most effective in dealing with life in the Latin American megalopolis. *Dragons...* (London: Boulevard Books, 1990). Weishort, Daniel (ed), *Modern Poetry in Translation*, No 6, Brazil (London: King's College, 1994) contains 19 poets, including Mário de Andrade, Oswald de Andrade, Carlos Drummond de Andrade, Manuel Bandeira, João Cabral de Melo Neto.

Fine art and sculpture

No visitor to Brazil should miss visiting a colonial church. During the colonial period in Brazil the Church dominated artistic patronage, with the religious orders vying with each other to produce ever more lavish interiors. In the 17th century the Benedictines included several notable sculptors among their ranks. Much of the magnificent gilded interior of the monastery of São Bento in Rio de Janeiro is by Frei Domingos da Conceição (circa 1643-1718), who worked there during the 1660s. His *Crucifixion* of 1688 in the monastery of São Bento in Olinda sets up a deliberately shocking contrast between the sinuous elegance of Christ's body and the terrible lacerations of his flesh. Frei Agostinho de Piedade (died 1661) of the Benedictine community in Salvador produced some old-fashioned terracotta reliquary busts during the 1630s and 1640s (Museu de Arte Sacra, Salvador) but the powerful *Penitent Peter* in Salvador's Nossa Senhora do Monte (circa 1636), also attributed to him, prefigures the emotional intensity of subsequent generations.

The colonial era: 16th & 17th centuries

A distinctive feature of colonial interiors is the incorporation of decorative scenes in blue and white painted tiles, *azulejos*, around the walls. These were imported from Portugal from the earlier 17th century onwards, with subject matter as often secular as religious. Good examples include the Franciscan foundations in Olinda, Salvador and Recife, and the church of Nossa Senhora da Glória in Rio de Janeiro, which has hunting scenes in the sacristy, Old Testament figures in the choir, and in the nave, astonishingly, scenes of pastoral love loosely based on the Song of Songs.

Although 17th-century church decoration is often lavish there is little warning of the extraordinary theatricality which characterizes the work of the 18th century. Behind their sober façades churches open out like theatres, with the equivalent of balconies and boxes for the privileged, and a stage for the high altar with a proscenium arch and wings of carved and gilded wood. Cherubs whisper to each other or gesticulate from their perches amongst the architectural scrolls; angels, older and more decorous, recline along a cornice or flutter in two dimensions across an illusionistic ceiling. The object of devotion is usually placed high above the altar on a tiered dais, surrounded by a Bernini-esque sunburst of gilded rays. A skilled exponent of this type of design was the sculptor Francisco Xavier de Brito (died 1751), as in Nossa Senhora do Pilar, Ouro Preto and São Francisco de Penitência, Rio.

The 18th century

This theatricality reaches its climax in the work of Aleijadinho, the 'Little Cripple' (1738-1814) a mulatto artist who worked in the province of Minas Gerais (see also page 281). As by far the most famous artist in the colonial period in the whole of Latin America it is perhaps not surprising to find his name attached to an impossible number of projects, but a consideration even of the securely documented reveals a

Background

man of extraordinary passion and energy who worked as a painter, architect and above all sculptor. The church at Congonhas do Campo offers the most dramatic example of Aleijadinho's art. Pilgrims paying homage to the miracle-working Bom Jesus do Matozinhos approach the church along a penitential road winding up the hill between six small chapels, each housing scenes from Christ's Passion represented by lifesize expressive statues of polychrome wood. The final ascent is up an imposing double staircase under the stony gaze of 12 judgmental prophets who variously lament, threaten or cajole, addressing the heavens, the distant horizon, each other, or the faithful on the stone steps below them. In a building beside the church a fascinating display of drawings and photographs of the many accidents and emergencies from which the Good Jesus has saved people testifies to the continuing popularity of this shrine.

The painterly equivalent to Aleijadinho's sculptures can be found in the work of his contemporary, Manuel da Costa Ataíde (1762-1830) from Mariana, whose vividly colourful narrative scenes decorate numerous churches in Minas Gerais. Ataíde's rococo settings are populated with solidly-built saints and angels whose rolling eyes and exaggerated gestures give them an earthy vigour sometimes at odds with the spirituality of the subject matter, as in the illusionistic ceiling of São Francisco de Assis, Ouro Preto, a church whose design is traditionally attributed to Aleijadinho.

In Bahia José Joaquim da Rocha (1737-1807) (see page 417) was one of the most successful artists of his day and his slightly Italianate ceiling paintings survive in many churches in Salvador. The best sculptor of the late colonial period in Bahia was Manuel Inácio da Costa (1763-1857) whose figures, often dramatically gaunt with protruding veins and large eyes, are reminiscent of Aleijadinho's work (see, for example, his *Christ at the Column* in the Museu de Arte Sacra in Salvador). It is in Rio that sculpture first begins to sober up again, as for example in the work of the sculptor Valentim de Fonseca e Silva, known as Mestre Valentim (circa 1750-1813) which can be seen in several churches including São Francisco de Paula and Nossa Senhora da Glória. Valentim also designed the first public gardens in Rio: the Passeio Público was inaugurated in 1783 and included walks, seats decorated with *azulejos* and pavilions. A unique series of six painted views of Rio and Guanabara Bay by Leandro Joaquim (1738?-1798?), originally made for one of the pavilions, are now in the Museu Histórico Nacional in Rio.

French influence in Imperial Brazil After the transfer of the Imperial court to Rio in 1808 João VI made a determined effort to renovate Brazilian culture, and in 1816 the French Artistic Mission – a boatload of painters, sculptors, architects, musicians and craftsmen – arrived from France to found what was to become the Imperial Academy. Two artists were particularly influential: Nicolas-Antoine Taunay (1755-1830) and Jean-Baptiste Debret (1768-1848). Taunay's luminous landscapes of the area around Rio and Debret's lively street scenes helped to open up new areas of secular Brazilian subject matter, and inspired artists throughout the 19th century. The Academy provided scholarships to send promising young artists to Paris, so reinforcing the French influence, and there are echoes of Delacroix in the work of Vítor Meireles (1832-1903) as for example, in his *Battle of the Guararapes* of 1879 in the Museu Nacional de Belas Artes, Rio, and of Ingres in *La Carioca* (1882) of Pedro Américo (1843-1905) in the same museum. The influence of Courbet can be seen in the so-called *belle époque* of the first republican years (1889-1922), in particular in the work of Meireles' pupil, José Ferraz de Almeida Júnior (1850-1899).

The 20th century, towards a Brazilian vision Brazil moved from this essentially academic tradition straight into the radicalism of the early 20th century, and movements such as Cubism, Futurism, Fauvism and Constructivism were quickly translated into distinctively Brazilian idioms. Lasar Segall (1891-1957), Anita Malfatti (1896-1964) and the sculptor Vitor Brecheret

(1894-1955) were pioneers of modernism, working in relative isolation before the Semana da Arte Moderna (Modern Art Week) in São Paulo in 1922 drew together a group of artists and intellectuals whose influence on Brazilian culture can still be felt today. They sought to challenge established bourgeois attitudes, to shake off the traditional cultural subservience to Europe, and to draw attention to the cultural diversity and social inequality of contemporary Brazil. Emilio di Cavalcanti (1897-1976) mocked the artificiality of middle class socialites (examples in the Museu de Arte Contemporânea, São Paulo). Tarsila do Amaral (1886-1973) borrowed her loud colours from popular art while her imagery includes ironic reworkings of European myths about the savage cannabilistic Indians supposed to inhabit the Brazilian jungle. Cândido Portinari (1903-1962) used murals to expose the exploitation and injustice suffered by workers and peasants while Osvaldo Goeldi (1895-1961) explored similar themes in his powerful wood engravings. Portinari, in an interesting revival of the colonial use of *azulejos*, created murals in blue and white painted tiles for modern building such as the MES building by Costa and Niemeyer of Rio, begun in 1937, and Niemeyer's church of São Francisco in Pampulha, Belo Horizonte (1943).

The economic strength of the middle years of the century encouraged state patronage of the arts. President Getúlio Vargas recognized that art and architecture could be used to present an image of Brazil as a modern industrialized nation, with Brasília being the culmination of this vision. Museums of Modern Art were founded in São Paulo and Rio, and in 1951 São Paulo hosted its first Bienal Internacional which attracted abstract artists from Europe and the US and confirmed Abstraction – symbol of progress and technological modernization – as the dominant mode in Brazil during the 1950s. Rivalry between the artistic communities of Rio and São Paulo helped to produce some outstanding avantgarde art. In the 1950s Waldemar Cordeiro (1925-1973), leader of the São Paulo Grupo Ruptura, painted what at first sight appear to be rather simple geometric patterns in bright, contrasting colours, but on closer attention the flat surface seems to break up, suggesting recession, space and restless movement, in some ways prefiguring the British Op Art movement of the 1960s. The Neo-Concrete group of artists of Rio argued for the integration of art into daily life, and experimented with art which makes sensory and emotional demands on the 'spectator' whose participation leads in turn to creation. During the early 1960s Lygia Clark (1920-1988) made *Bichos (Animals)* out of hinged pieces of metal which, as the name implies, are like creatures with a life of their own: they can be rearranged indefinitely but because of their complexity it is impossible to predetermine what shape will result from moving a particular section. Nowadays, unfortunately, they are displayed in museums where touching is not encouraged (as in the Pinacoteca do Estado, São Paulo). Hélio Oiticica (1937-1980) took the idea further, working with people (poor and often black) from the samba schools in the Rio *favelas* to create artistic 'happenings' involving dance, music and flamboyant costumes called *Parangolés (Capes)*. The notion that a key function of art should be to shock the bourgeisie was first voiced by in the 1922 Week of Modern Art. Oiticica often succeeded, and he and other artists of the 1960s also realized another of the aims of the first modernists: to create a Brazilian modern art that was not the poor relation of developments in Europe or the US. A museum of his work has recently opened in Rio. Other important figures of this generation include the neo-concretist painter Ivan Serpa (1923-1973), Sérgio Camargo (1930-1990), who produced textured rhythmic constructions of white on white but because they are made with off-cuts of wood they suggest the tensions between form and material, geometry and nature, and Amílcar de Castro (born 1920) whose deceptively simple sculptures are often cut from one large panel of cast iron.

The military coup of 1964 marked the beginning of a period of political repression and of renewed artistic energy, with figurative tendencies re-emerging. In 1970 Antônio Enrique Amaral (born 1935) took as his theme the banana, so often used in dismissive references to Latin America, and in an extended series of paintings monumentalized it into an extraordinary symbol of power and fruitfulness. In an ironic neo-colonial altarpiece (circa 1966) installed in the Museu de Arte de São Paulo, Nelson Leirner (born 1932) makes the object of devotion the neon-lit head of pop star Robert Carlos. Conceptual art offers different ways of confronting the dominant ideology. Both Cildo Meireles (born 1948) and Jac Lierner (born 1961) have used, misused or forged banknotes, for example, and both they and Waltercio Caldas (born 1946) and Tunga (born 1952) have created installations which draw attention, directly and indirectly to environmental issues. The painter Siron Franco (born 1947) also often addresses the issue of the destruction of the Amazon rainforest, but his disturbing surreal images explore many other areas – industrial pollution, sexual fantasy, political corruption, national identity – making him one of the most exciting artists in Brazil today.

Architecture

Indian architecture
Before the arrival of the Portuguese in 1500, Brazil was inhabited by the Tupi-Guarani Indians, who had developed forms of art and architecture which appeared very primitive in comparison with that of other precolumbian cultures such as the Incas, the Maya and the Aztecs. In fact, the first colonizers were disappointed with what they found. Instead of rich cities, impressive palaces, temples and massive stone walls, they faced relatively small groups of semi-naked Indians living in houses covered mostly with palm leaves.

The tropical climate and their nomadic way of life did not allow these tribes to develop permanent cities or solid, lasting constructions. They lived in *tabas*, temporary sites formed by a group of *ocas* (collective buildings, made of branches, leaves and vegetable fibres), placed around a main square. After a year or two, they would abandon the *taba* and move to another place, in search of better hunting grounds and new fields for their subsistence agriculture. A few examples of these interesting building techniques can be seen in museums, such as the **Museu do Índio** in Rio de Janeiro, or other specific institutions in Brazil.

Brazilian colonial style: houses & civic buildings
The earliest Portuguese colonizers to arrive in Brazil in the 16th century faced many problems in building their houses, forts, churches and other necessary structures. First of all there was a lack of building materials, such as bricks, roof tiles and mortar. Second, there were few trained craftsmen, such as carpenters and bricklayers, in the colony. They therefore had to improvise by developing unusual building techniques and trying different materials. In the hinterland, in places like São Paulo, Goiás and Minas Gerais the majority of the houses were built with *taipa de pilão*. This

A Brazilian colonial house

F.S.

Background

F.S.

A Jesuit-style church

technique consisted in using a wooden form to build thick walls. These forms were filled with a mixture of clay, vegetable fibres, horsehair, ox blood and dung. This paste was then compacted with a pestle and allowed to dry for two to three days before the next layer was added. The roof tiles were often moulded on a female slave's thigh and dried in the sun.

It is quite easy to identify a house in Brazilian colonial style. Their shapes, colours and building techniques remained virtually unchanged for almost three centuries. Firstly, they always had large, visible roofs, made with red clay tiles, finishing in eaves extending beyond the walls. All the buildings were painted in a white wash, with bright colours used only on window and door frames. These were made of wood and had, mostly, elegant arches at the top. In the 19th century, sash windows with squared 10cm by 10cm pieces of glass were added in many houses, as can be seen in cities like Paraty, Ouro Preto and Salvador.

Urban colonial houses had doors and windows opening directly onto the street. Courtyards were never placed in front of the house, but internally, forming airy patios which protected the privacy of the family. The furniture was extremely simple and rough. Often, the only pieces of furniture in a bedroom would be the bed itself and a leather box to store clothes and personal belongings. In the colonial period, the highest status symbol was to live in a *sobrado* (a house with more than one floor, usually two). The ground floor was normally a commercial business and above it the residence of the owner's family.

Houses, public buildings and other colonial civic edifices were generally unelaborate. All the refinement, style and sophistication in art, architecture and decoration was lavished on churches, convents and monasteries. The great religious orders, such as the Jesuits, Franciscans, Carmelites and Benedictines brought to Brazil the latest artistic trends from Europe, mainly the Baroque and Rococo.

Churches, convents & religious buildings: the Baroque in Brazil

Two separate strands in Brazilian religious architecture evolved. In the most important cities, close to the seaboard and more influenced by European culture, the churches and convents were built according to designs brought from Portugal, Italy and Spain. Some were merely copies of Jesuit or Benedictine temples in Europe. Examples of this can be found in Salvador (the main cathedral, the São Francisco church), Rio de Janeiro (the Mosteiro de São Bento, the Convento de Santo Antônio) and Olinda (church and convent of Nossa Senhora das Neves).

At the end of the 17th century gold was found in the region of Minas Gerais (see the Ouro Preto section, page 275). One of the first administrative acts of the Portuguese crown in response to this discovery was to banish the traditional European orders from the mining region. The royal administration wanted to control the mining itself, taxation and traffic in gold and, as the friars were regarded as among the most shameless of smugglers of the metal, the orders in this instance

Brazilian Baroque

Background

Curved church: São Francisco de Assis, Ouro Preto

were denied the support they were given elsewhere in the Portuguese colonies. Therefore the majority of the churches in cities like Ouro Preto, Mariana, Congonhas and Sabará were built by local associations, the so-called 'third orders'. These lay orders had the gold and the will to build magnificent temples but, although they wanted their projects to be as European as possible, the original designs were hard to obtain in such out-of-the-way places. So the local artists had to find their own way. Inspired by descriptions and second-hand information, they created their own interpretation of the Baroque, thoroughly infused with regional influences and culture. This is the reason why the 'Barroco Mineiro' is so original.

Curved churches & the decline of the Gold Era

At the beginning of the 18th century, when gold was easily found in Minas Gerais, the main attraction was the inside of the church, richly and heavily decorated in carved wood and gold. Many of the churches built in this period will be a total surprise for the visitor. Their façades and exteriors are so simple and yet the naves and altars are so highly and artistically decorated. As the mines started to decline, the outside of the buildings became more sophisticated, with curves, round towers and sinuous walls, such as the churches of São Francisco de Assis and Rosário, in Ouro Preto. As the gold for covering walls ran out, it was replaced by paintings and murals.

The 19th century & the Neoclassic style

The beginning of 19th century brought a major change in the history of Brazilian architecture. When Napoleon invaded Portugal in 1808, the Portuguese royal family and some 15,000 nobles and wealthy families fled to Rio de Janeiro, bringing with them their own view of what was sophisticated in the arts. In 1816 the king, Dom João VI, invited a group of French artists (The French Artistic Mission) to Brazil to introduce the most recent European trends in painting, sculpture, decoration and architecture. This was the beginning of the Neoclassic style in Brazil. An Imperial Academy of Fine Arts was created and all the new government buildings were built in Neoclassic style. The great name of this period was the French architect Grandjean de Montigny , who planned and built many houses and public buildings throughout the city of Rio de Janeiro.

The rich and famous also wanted their houses in this newly fashionable style, which revolutionized the Brazilian way of building. The large roofs were now hidden by a small wall, the plat band. Windows and doors acquired round arches and walls

The Neoclassic style

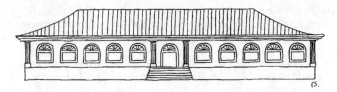

A coffee farmhouse with Neoclassic influences

were painted in ochres and light tones of pink. Public buildings and churches started to look like ancient Greek temples, with triangular pediments and columns. This new style was not best suited Brazil's climate. The earlier, large colonial roofs were much more efficient in dealing with heavy tropical rains and, in consequence, the Neoclassic style never became popular in the countryside.

Even when the coffee planters, in the second half of 19th century, started to become extremely rich and fond of imported fashions, they would build their urban mansions in the Neoclassic style, but still keep their farm houses with large roofs, sometimes adding small Neoclassic details in windows, doors and internal decoration. Good examples of this 19th-century rural architecture can be found very close to Rio de Janeiro, in cities like Vassouras, Valença, Barra do Piraí and Bananal, where some of the old farm houses are open to visitors.

There are many examples of urban Neoclassic building in Rio de Janeiro, such as the Museu Nacional, the Santa Casa da Misericórdia, the Casa de Rui Barbosa and the Instituto Benjamin Constant. Also very close to Rio, in Petrópolis, the Museu Imperial (formerly the Emperor's summer palace) is also a perfect example of the style. This Neoclassic remained popular in Brazil until the end of the 19th century, being also the 'official' style of the First and the Second Brazilian Empires.

The early 20th century & the Eclectic style

After the Republic, in 1889, the Neoclassic style lost favour since it had been serving the king and the emperors for such a long time. A new style, or better, a new harmony of different styles started to gain popularity, also under the influence of Paris and the Belle Époque. There were elements of neoclassic architecture, but also an excess of decoration and adornment on the façades. A broad 'boulevard' was constructed in Rio de Janeiro in 1906, the Avenida Central (today Avenida Rio Branco), with the idea of creating 'a Paris in the Tropics'. There are many examples of buildings in the Eclectic style on this avenue: the Biblioteca Nacional, the Teatro Municipal (Opera House) and the Museu Nacional de Belas Artes, all of them built in the first decade of 20th century. Also in Manaus, during the rubber boom, many buildings adopted this style, such as the Teatro Amazonas (the Opera House). During the first two decades of this century, the Eclectic style remained very popular.

The 'Modern Art Week' of 1922 & national pride

In 1922 a group of artists, painters, poets and architects organized in São Paulo 'A Semana da Arte Moderna' or the Modern Art Week, during which they exhibited their distaste at the extreme influence of foreign standards in Brazilian art. They considered their role

Ecletic style in Rio de Janeiro

Background

to be a continuous quest for a genuine Brazilian form of expression. This search resulted in the rejection of all imported standards and, as far as architecture was concerned, two main currents emerged.

The Neocolonial The first movement sought its true Brazilian style in the past, in the colonial period. Architects like Lúcio Costa, studied the techniques, materials and designs of the 16th, 17th and 18th centuries, soon producing houses with a colonial look, but also combining elements which were only previously found in Baroque churches. These included pediments and decorated door frames. The style was called Neocolonial and remained popular until the 1940s, especially in Rio de Janeiro and São Paulo.

In search of greater authenticity, many architects employed original materials brought from demolished old houses. A good example of this can be found in Rio de Janeiro, in the Largo do Boticário (very close to the train station for Corcovado, in Cosme Velho), a small square surrounded by Neocolonial houses painted in fancy, bright colours.

Modernism The other current generated by the Semana da Arte Moderna looked to the future for its inspiration for Brazilian-ness. Architects such as Oscar Niemeyer, Lúcio Costa, Affonso Eduardo Reidy, the landscape designer Roberto Burle Marx and many others started to design functional and spacious buildings, with large open areas and *pilotis* (pillars carrying a building, leaving the ground floor open). The use of concrete and glass was intense and the masterpiece of the Brazilian architectural Modernism is Brasília, the capital, planned from scratch in the 1950 by Lúcio Costa and Oscar Niemeyer.

Many examples of Modernist building can be found all over Brazil: in Brasília, the Cathedral, the National Congress, the Palácio do Planalto (the presidential palace), in fact the whole city, with its broad freeways and spacious urban blocks, called *quadras*; in Belo Horizonte, the church of São Francisco de Assis, in Pampulha; in São Paulo, the MASP (Museum of Art of São Paulo), the Memorial da América Latina, and many commercial buildings along the Avenida Paulista; in Rio de Janeiro, the Ministério da Educação e Saúde, the Museu de Arte Moderna, the Catedral Metropolitana, the Petrobrás building (Brazilian State Petrol Company), the BNDES building (National Bank of Social and Economic Development), all in the central area of the city.

Brazilian contemporary architecture The most recent trend is the post-modern. Many business centres, shopping malls and residential buildings are being designed in a style which uses coloured mirror glass, granite and stylized structures reminiscent of classical temples.

Brazilian architects are also famous worldwide for their techniques in designing houses for construction on steeply-inclined hills. In Rio de Janeiro, if you are driving along the coastal road in the neighbourhoods of Barra and São Conrado you can see many of these astonishing projects, homes of the very wealthy.

Neocolonial house with a Baroque influence

Background

Economy

Brazil's economy is the largest in Latin America and the 10th in the world, but its gdp per capita has grown little since 1980 and is less than the average for the whole of Latin America and the Caribbean. It has abundant and varied natural resources, not all of which are fully explored or exploited. The 40 years after 1945 were a period of massive state intervention and industrialization with public sector investment in energy, heavy industry, transport equipment and capital goods, but in the 1990s the country has moved towards a market economy with a smaller role for the state.

Agriculture Brazil remains a large farming country; processed and unprocessed agricultural products account for about a third of exports and agriculture, forestry and fishing account for 12 percent of gdp. Brazil is the world's largest producer and exporter of **coffee** and maintains a dominant position in international markets for **soya** and **orange juice**, mostly grown in the state of São Paulo. São Paulo state also produces over half Brazil's harvest of **sugar cane**, most of which is distilled into fuel alcohol for cars or electricity generating power plants. Although Brazil used to be the world's largest **cocoa** grower, with Ilhéus the main area of production, the industry has declined because of underinvestment, fungus and low prices. Most of Brazil's agricultural land is held by large landowners, with 10 percent of the farmers owning 80 percent of the land. Land reform is contentious and has proceeded very slowly with much conflict and violence.

Mining The country is richly endowed with metals and other minerals. Brazil has up to a third of the world's **iron ore** reserves, found mainly in Minas Gerais and certain parts of the Amazon basin, especially the Serra dos Carajás region (Pará). Brazil also exports **manganese** and produces increasing amounts of **tin** and **copper**. In 1996, the state mining company (now 73.5 percent sold to the private sector), Companhia Vale do Rio Doce (CVRD), announced a 150-tonne **gold** find near Carajás, which would make it the largest gold mine in Latin America. It is expected to produce 10 tonnes a year, about 20 percent of Brazil's present output. The mine is also near Serra Pelada, an open mine which in the 1980s attracted a gold rush of 80,000 *garimpeiros*, wildcat goldminers, but the new one is much deeper and not suitable for being dug by hand. CVRD is one of the world's largest natural resources groups and owns mining and exploration rights worth an estimated US$40bn, including Carajás, where reserves of iron ore are sufficient for 500 years.

Manufacturing Industrial production accounts for 22 percent of gdp and sales of mechanical equipment, cars, chemicals, textiles and other manufactures account for the majority of exports. The car industry fluctuates in line with domestic demand but produces on average some two million vehicles a year. The steel and vehicle industries are among the top 10 in the world. The Mercosur free trade area has encouraged exporters to look for markets in neighbouring countries instead of concentrating on the USA and Europe. Privatization, the abolition of price controls and falling tariffs have forced increased efficiency and productivity on to Brazilian companies, which have had to invest in modernization and gear their strategy to coping with competition rather than hyperinflation.

Energy Energy sector development was aimed at substituting local for imported energy. The **oil** industry was nationalized in 1953 and the state monopoly, Petrobrás, controlled exploration, production, refining and distribution of oil and gas. That monopoly was finally ended in 1998, allowing private sector companies to compete, or form joint ventures with Petrobrás. The government planned to privatize almost half of Petrobrás in 1999. Large investments have been made in **hydroelectricity**, **alcohol** and **nuclear power**. The system's total capacity in 1995 was 52,700MW, but investment was not keeping pace with demand of about five percent a year, so shortages and power cuts periodically affect parts of the country. It is estimated that 10 percent of homes are not connected to the electricity grid (47 percent in 1970), and some 16 percent of energy distributed is not paid for because of illegal connections. Privatization in the electricity sector has been taking place piecemeal, with various states selling off utilities. In 1999 the government planned to divide the generating and transmission operations of Eletrobrás, the national company, and sell the former. The proposal was delayed after the currency crisis at the start of the year.

Recent trends High inflation in the 1980s and the early 1990s proved intractable as successive governments introduced stabilization programmes with new currencies but limited success. The principal cause of failure was the lack of political will to tackle the structural causes of inflation, namely the public accounts disequilibrium, supply bottlenecks, inefficiencies and corruption in state governments and enterprises, and widespread indexation of wages, prices and financial instruments. It was not until May 1993, with the appointment of Fernando Henrique Cardoso as Finance Minister that a plan was implemented which contained stringent measures to strengthen the public accounts and thus reduce inflation. However, cooperation from powerful political interests was not forthcoming and inflation soared. On 1 July 1994, a new currency, the real, was introduced at par with the US dollar. Inflation immediately plummeted from over 50 percent a month to less than two percent and while interest rates remained high, the real appreciated. As confidence in the programme grew and price stability led to a rise in real wages, consumer spending also increased. The feelgood factor helped the election of Cardoso to the Presidency. Despite reserves of some US$40bn to support the real, the Mexican financial crisis at the same time brought a bad case of nerves in the financial markets. The Government adjusted the exchange rate regime, introducing a range of floating bands within which the real would trade, raised some tariffs to curb imports and imposed emergency measures to balance the budget.

Turmoil in the Far Eastern markets in late 1997 prompted the Government to speed up its reforms to relieve pressure on interest rates and the currency and cut the fiscal deficit. These pressures became more acute during the Russian financial crisis of August 1998. The IMF and the USA were afraid that a collapse in Brazil would affect the whole of the region, including the United States itself, through 'contagion'. In November, therefore, a US$41.5bn rescue package was agreed through the IMF. An austerity strategy of high interest rates and deep budget cuts was devised to win back international confidence in Brazil.

The process was undermined first by the government's failure to gain congressional support for all its fiscal measures, then by the direct challenge of the state of Minas Gerais declaring a moratorium in January 1999 on interest payments due to central government. Brazil's decision in mid-January to devalue the real by nine percent sent shockwaves through world financial markets as it implied that the IMF plan had failed. The central bank president resigned and his successor was replaced after only 20 days in office. Capital continued to leave the country and the government was forced to let the real float freely. It fell from R$1.20 = US$1 to R$2 = US$1 in a few weeks. In March 1999 the IMF resumed lending to Brazil, with support from the USA, to minimize the inflationary impact of the devaluation and to prevent the ratio of debt to gdp becoming unmanageable. By May 1999 it appeared that Brazil had confounded all the worst expectations, emerging from recession even in the first quarter. Inflation did not soar as predicted and many forecasters revised their figures for the year down to under 10 percent. Interest rates, which climbed to 45 percent at the height of the crisis, had fallen to 19.5 percent by September. The exchange rate was less able to withstand the government's fluctuating fortunes; in mid-year it strengthened to around R$1.65-1.70 = US$1, but by December 1999 it had fallen back to R$1.88. While results overall may have helped to restore Brazil's image abroad, with foreign companies continuing to invest, the domestic picture remained depressed, with unemployment at near-record levels, real wages falling and consumer demand low.

Footnotes

13

Useful words & phrases

Greetings & courtesies

hello	*oi*	How are you?	*Como vai você?/*
good morning	*bom dia*		*tudo bem?/tudo bom?*
good afternoon	*boa tarde*	I am fine	*vou bem/tudo bem*
good evening/	*boa noite*	pleased to meet you	*um prazer*
good night		yes	*sim*
goodbye	*adeus/tchau*	no	*não*
see you later	*até logo*	excuse me/	*com licença*
please	*por favor/faz favor*	I beg your pardon	
thank you	*obrigado (if a man is*	I do not understand	*não entendo*
	speaking)/obrigada	please speak slowly	*fale devagar por favor*
	(if a woman is speaking)	What is your name?	*Qual é seu nome?*
thank you very much	*muito obrigado/*	my name is_	*O meu nome é_*
	muito obrigada	Go away!	*Vai embora!*

In conversation, most people refer to **you** as "você", although in the south and in Pará "tu" is more common. To be more polite, use "O Senhor/A Senhora". For **us**, "a gente" (people, folks) is very common when it includes **you** too.

Basic questions

Where is_?	*Onde está?/onde fica?*	Why?	*Por que?*
How much does it cost?	*Quanto custa?*	What for?	*Para que?*
How much is it?	*Quanto é?*	How do I get to_?	*Para chegar a_?*
When?	*Quando?*	I want to go to_	*Quero ir para_*
When does the bus	*A que hora sai/chega*	Is this the way to the	*Aquí é o caminho para*
leave?/arrive?	*o ônibus?*	church?	*a igreja?*

Basics

bathroom/toilet	*banheiro*	notes/coins	*notas/moedas*
police (policeman)	*a polícia (o polícia)*	travellers' cheques	*os travelers/os cheques*
hotel	*o hotel (a pensão,*		*de viagem*
	a hospedaria)	cash	*dinheiro*
restaurant	*o restaurante*	breakfast	*o café de manh*
	(o lanchonete)	lunch	*o almoço*
post office	*o correio*	dinner/supper	*o jantar*
telephone office	*(central) telefônica*	meal	*a refeição*
supermarket	*o supermercado*	drink	*a bebida*
market	*o mercado*	mineral water	*a água mineral*
green grocery shop	*a sacolão*	soft fizzy drink	*o refrigerante*
bank	*o banco*	beer	*a cerveja*
exchange house	*a casa de câmbio*	without sugar	*sem açúcar*
exchange rate	*a taxa de câmbio*	without meat	*sem carne*

Getting around

on the left/right	*à esquerda/à direita*	bus	*o ônibus*
straight on	*direito*	train	*o trem*
second street on the	*a segunda rua à direita*	airport	*o aeroporto*
right		aeroplane/airplane	*o avião*
to walk	*caminhar*	flight	*o vôo*
bus station	*a rodoviária*	first/second class ticket	*primeira/segunda clase*
train station	*a ferroviária*	ticket	*o passagem/o bilhete*
combined bus &	*a rodoferroviária*	ticket office	*a bilheteria*
train station		bus stop	*a parada*

Accommodation

room	*quarto*	hot/cold water	*água quente/fria*
noisy	*barulhento*	to make up/clean	*limpar*
single/double room	*(quarto de) solteiro/ (quarto para) casal*	sheet(s)	*o lençol (os lençóis)*
room with two beds	*quarto com duas camas*	blankets	*as mantas*
		pillow	*o travesseiro*
with private bathroom	*quarto com banheiro privado*	clean/dirty towels	*as toalhas limpas/ sujas*
		toilet paper	*o papel higiênico*

Health

chemist	*a farmacia*	contraceptive (pill)	*anticoncepcional (a pílula)*
(for) pain	*(para) dor*		
stomach	*o estômago (a barriga)*	period	*a menstruação/ a regra*
head	*a cabeça*	sanitary towels	*toalhas absorventes/ higiênicas*
fever/sweat	*a febre/o suor*		
diarrhoea	*o diarréia*	tampons	*absorventes internos*
blood	*o sangue*	contact lenses	*lentes de contacto*
doctor	*o doutor/a doutora*	aspirin	*a aspirina*
condoms	*as camisinhas/ os preservativos*		

Time

at one o'clock	*a uma hora (da manhã/da tarde)*	it's twenty past six/ six twenty	*são seis e vinte*
at half past two/ two thirty	*as dois e meia*	it's five to nine	*são cinco para as nove*
at a quarter to three	*quinze para as três*	in ten minutes	*em dez minutos*
it's one o'clock	*é uma*	five hours	*cinco horas*
it's seven o'clock	*são sete horas*	Does it take long?	*Dura muito?*

Days

Monday	*segunda feira*	Thurday	*quinta feira*	Sunday	*domingo*
Tueday	*terça feira*	Friday	*sexta feira*		
Wedneday	*quarta feira*	Saturday	*sábado*		

Months

January	*janeiro*	May	*maio*	September	*setembro*
February	*fevereiro*	June	*junho*	October	*outubro*
March	*março*	July	*julho*	November	*novembro*
April	*abril*	August	*agosto*	December	*dezembro*

Numbers

1	*um/uma*	7	*sete*	19	*dezenove*
2	*dois/duas*	8	*oito*	20	*vinte*
3	*três*	9	*nove*	21	*vinte e um*
4	*quatro*	10	*dez*	30	*trinta*
5	*cinco*	11	*onze*	40	*cuarenta*
6	*seis* (note also	12	*doze*	50	*cinqüenta*
	that "*meia*" -	13	*treze*	60	*sessenta*
	half - is	14	*catorze*	70	*setenta*
	frequently	15	*quinze*	80	*oitenta*
	used for	16	*dezesseis*	90	*noventa*
	number 6,	17	dezessete	100	cem, cento
	ie half-dozen).	18	*dezoito*	1000	*mil*

See also Language in Essentials, page 67

Footnotes

Map index

Index

Note: grid references to the colour maps are shown in italics after place names. So Alcântara *M2A2* can be found on Map 2, square A2.

BRAZILIAN MUSIC IS SO BEAUTIFUL BECAUSE COMPOSERS HAVE THE PERFECT SETTING FOR INSPIRATION.

Coming to Brazil, you can easily understand where all the joy and creativity of its music comes from: all you have to do is open any window. The scenery is soothing to the eyes and a treasure to any photo album. The best way to discover all these wonders is by flying VARIG direct from London Heathrow.

Choose one of VARIG s daily overnight flights and enjoy the unequaled service of 72 years experience and the renowned Brazilian warmth and friendliness.

For further information or to make a reservation call your travel agent or VARIG: **0845 603 7601.**
www.varig.co.uk
BRAZIL 500 YEARS OF RHYTHM.

Brasil

✴ VARIG Brasil
✪ A STAR ALLIANCE MEMBER

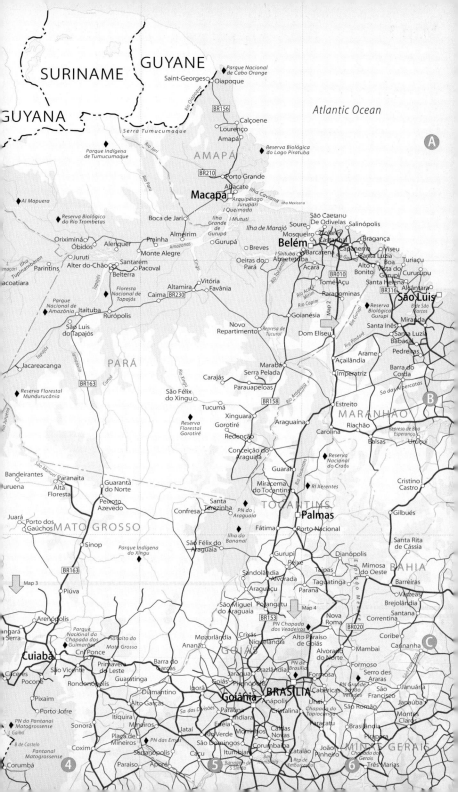

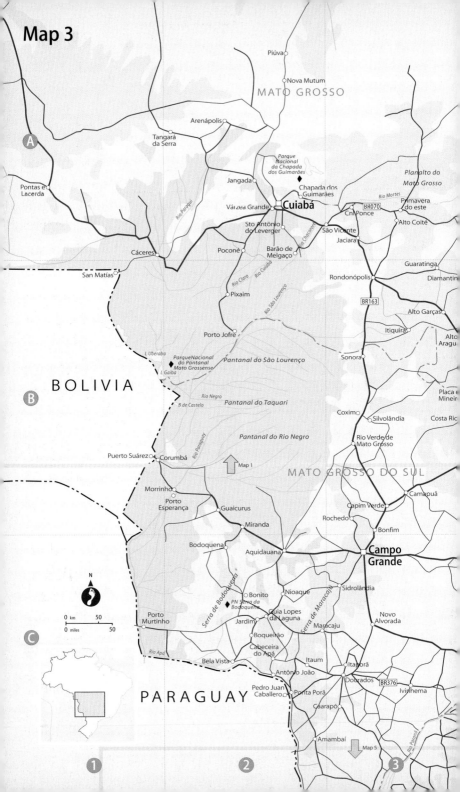

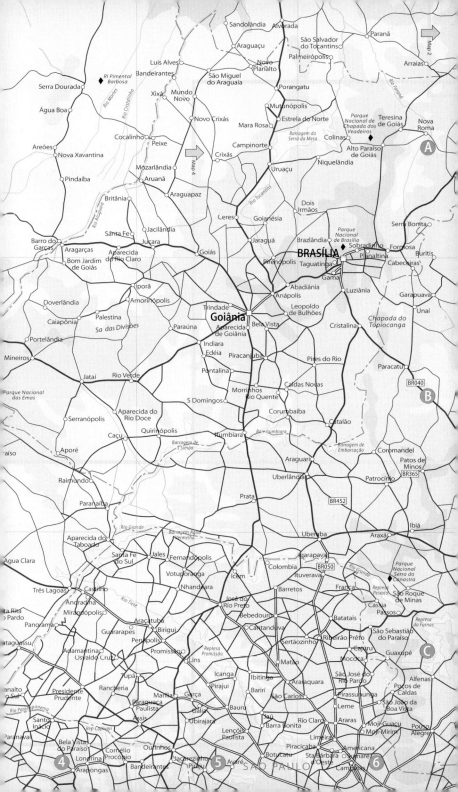

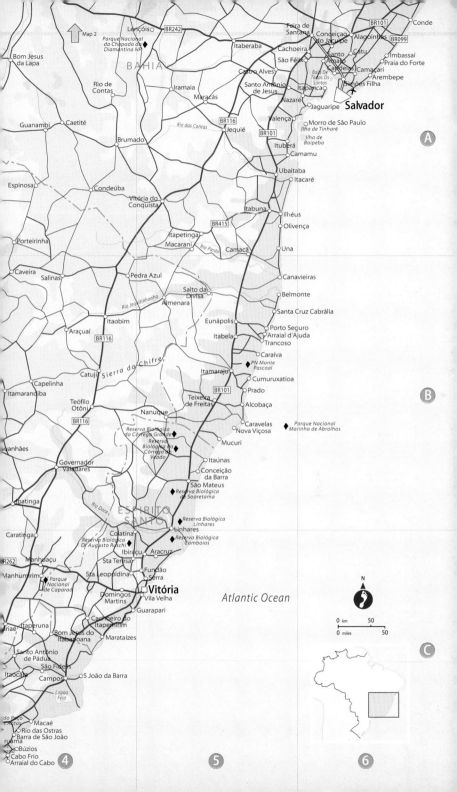

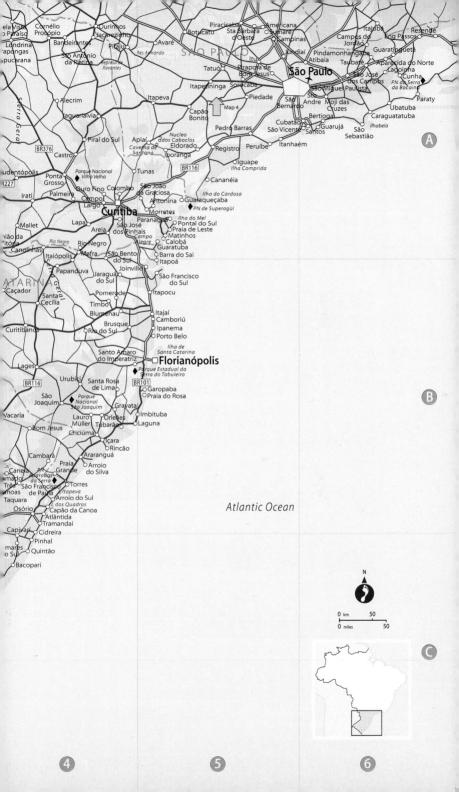

Acknowledgements

Mick Day has great pleasure in thanking the following for their invaluable help and support in the preparation of this Handbook: Ben Box, Marc Starr and all the team at Footprint.

For their help and hospitality in Brazil during 1998 and 1999, Mick would like to thank: in Belém, Patrick Barbier of Amazon Star Turismo, Andréa Ledo of Angel Turismo, Maria Souza of Paratur; in Macapá, Ana Fátima Kohler, Kelly and Creuza Miranda Nascimento, Tony Rocha, Jef and Celia of Pousada Ekinox, Detur; in Manaus, Mark Aitchison of Swallows and Amazons, Carlos Damasceno of Jaguar Tours, Chris Gomes of Jungle Experience, Antônio Moura of Hotel Aquarius, Megumi Sadahiro, Eduardo Urtecho Cury of Green Planet Tours, Fumtur; in Santarém, Steve Alexander of Amazon Tours, Emanuel Júlio Leite of Comtur; in Santos, all the staff of Hotel Natal; in São Luís, Carlos Martins of Maratur, Toquinho of Projeto Reviver, Fumtur, Irlande, Thea; in São Paulo, Lesley Gruit, Natasha Salles. For her subsequent help with the text, Beatrix Boscardin, Rio de Janeiro. Robin Everleigh provided information on Paraná.

Marc Starr would like to thank Vivien, Ian and Ben Starr and all my family and friends in Manchester. My family and friends in Brazil, especially Jorge Lima, Patricia Allen, Jose Allen, Jorge Allen, Malu Allen and Margarida, Neguinha, Brivaldo and everyone in Jardim Atlântico in Olinda for their unswerving friendship and support throughout my time in Pernambuco. John Chesney and all staff at La Tasca, Didsbury, Manchester. Kate, Janet and Miguel of Journey Latin America, London and Manchester. Terry Gallagher in São Paulo, for being there. Eddie Edmundson of the British Council in Recife. Anthony Burnett in Caruaru. Supersoniques and River Raid. Maureliano at Barravento Alves at Musitec and Abílio at Studio Ensaios. All at Varig Air Cargo in Recife. Guti and B-52 in Recife. Nacao Zumbi in Recife. Jorge and Wilson of Cascabulho. Dona Marivalda at Estrela Brilhante. Conor O'Sullivan at Tatur in Salvador. Gustavo and all at Palace Hotel, Salvador. Raimundo Mazzei at Bahiatursa. All at Albergue das Laranjeiras for their hospitality, assistance and all-round good humour. Rubia in Aracaju. Trajano and Helia; Roy Funch in Lençóis. Ivan, Jorge Pitta and Jorge Luiz Alves da Silva of Suingue do Pelo. John Bertholtz of Crossair at Heathrow for bag-rescuing abilities.

Ben Box would like to thank the following for their generosity and assistance in southern Brazil in November 1999: in Rio de Janeiro, Fábio Sombra; in Florianópolis, the Abreu family, Jamir, Coleta, Cláudia and Francisco; in Joinville, Jorge Nicolau Meira (Presidente) and Vilmar Pedro de Souza (Diretor de Marketing e Eventos), Promotur, and Valdir Walendowsky (Diretor Executivo), Joinville Convention and Visitors Bureau; in Foz do Iguaçu: Miguel Angel Allou and Lourdes Campos of Paudimar, and Licério Santos, Diretor do Departamento de Desenvolvimento de Turismo.

We should also like to thank Steve Collins, Robert and Daisy Kunstaetter, Cherry Austin and Sarah Cameron for their contributions to the first edition, as well as Martin Cooper (York, UK) for his researches on Rondônia for the current edition.

Travellers' letters

Edeltrud Kuckenburg, J Makin, Tim McClements, Ann Sleebus, Aubrey Jenkins, Alex Pfeifle, Nigel Shaw, Thomas Ferran Frist, Don Heron, Helmut Zettl, Yvonne Reimann, Eran Fish, Richard Pope, Carlos Roquette, Mark Greenwood, Sven Utcke, Jorn Seemann, Tania and Mark Aitchison, Bonnie Van Caspel, Dieter Bratschi, Stephan Harris, Florian Vogel, Peter Fischer, John Kriste, Sharelle Hart, Amir Matri, Jorge Godoy, Shlomit Sharfman, Helma Hellinga, Fredy Lauener, Ashild Fatland Gregory, Julian Uribe.

Other contributors

Marc Starr

After studying for a year at the University of Paraíba in 1994 during his degree in Hispanic Studies, Marc returned to Brazil in 1999 to research the Northeast and its music. A keen percussionist and fanatical Manchester City supporter he nonetheless feels a certain affection for São Paulo side Corinthians.

Fábio Sombra

Fábio Sombra was born in Rio de Janeiro, Brazil. Besides his work as a painter and illustrator, he teaches and researches History of Art, Brazilian folklore and other subjects related to Brazilian culture. Since 1994 he has been in the tourism business, acting as a consultant and co-ordinating projects on cultural tourism. Fábio has provided many illustrations for this Handbook as well as articles on Búzios, Vassouras, Paraty, religion and architecture and a number of the legends.

Specialist contributors

Peter Pollard, Geography and Climate; Dr Nigel Dunstone (University of Durham), Flora and Fauna; Huw Clough, Archaeology; Charlie Nurse, History; Professor John Gledson (University of Liverpool), Literature; Dr Valerie Fraser (University of Essex), Fine Art and Sculpture; Nigel Gallop, Music and Dance; Dave Willetts, Samba; Dr David Snashall, Health; Piet Hein Snel, Surfing; Mark Eckstein, Responsible Tourism; Richard Robinson, Worldwide Radio; Lucy Davies and Mo Fini (*Tumi*) who allowed us to use material from *Arts and Crafts in Latin America*.

For acknowledgements and travellers' letters, see previous page.

Ben Box & Mick Day

As a freelance writer Ben Box has contributed to
newspapers, magazines and learned tomes, usually
on the subject of travel, and became editor of
Footprint's South American Handbook in 1989. For
Footprint, he has also been involved in the Mexico &
Central America Handbook, Caribbean Islands
Handbook and Brazil handbook since their
inception. Having a doctorate in Spanish and
Portuguese studies from London University, Ben
maintains a strong interest in Latin American
literature. When not travelling, he indulges in the
very un-Brazilian pastime of village cricket.

A regular visitor to Brazil since 1995, Mick Day
graduated from the University of Essex with a BA
(Hons) in Portuguese, Spanish and Linguistics. As a
consultant on Brazil and Latin America he has
travelled and worked extensively in this vast and
varied country. Familiar with the humid Amazon
region, the Afro-Brazilian culture of the
Northeastern coast, the historic mining towns in the
country's rugged interior, the beaches of Rio de
Janeiro as well as the cityscape of São Paulo he feels
that overall the constant friendliness of its people is
what makes the Brazil experience so memorable.